HUMAN
RESOURCE
MANAGEMENT

HUMAN RESOURCE MANAGEMENT

A contemporary perspective

SECOND EDITION

Edited by
Ian Beardwell
and
Len Holden

De Montfort University, Leicester

London · Hong Kong · Johannesburg · Melbourne · Singapore · Washington DC

PITMAN PUBLISHING
128 Long Acre, London WC2E 9AN
Tel: +44 (0)171 447 2000
Fax: +44 (0)171 240 5771

A Division of Pearson Professional Limited

First published in Great Britain in 1994
Second edition published in 1997

Visit the Pitman Publishing Website at:
http://www.pitman.co.uk

© Pearson Professional Limited 1994, 1997

ISBN 0 273 62230 7

British Library Cataloguing in Publication Data
A CIP catalogue record for this book can be obtained
from the British Library.

3 5 7 9 10 8 6 4 2

Typeset by Pantek Arts, Maidstone, Kent
Printed and bound in Great Britain

The Publishers' policy is to use paper manufactured
from sustainable forests

CONTENTS

Part 1
HUMAN RESOURCE MANAGEMENT AND ITS ORGANISATIONAL CONTEXT

Part 2
RESOURCING THE ORGANISATION

Part 3
DEVELOPING THE HUMAN RESOURCE

Part 4
THE EMPLOYMENT RELATIONSHIP

Part 5
INTERNATIONAL HUMAN RESOURCE MANAGEMENT

PREFACE TO THE SECOND EDITION

Human resource management has become one of the most discussed approaches to the practice and analysis of the employment relationship in Western market economies over the past decade. Whether the perspective is supportive or critical, the idea that a reformulated relationship between management and employees is occurring has taken hold to a considerable degree. The purpose of this book is to present an analysis of that relationship in terms of the contemporary HRM debate. Many of the existing texts in the area include HRM as a closing topic at the end of a traditional analysis of Personnel Management or Industrial Relations; this text starts with the nature of the HRM issue and extends that analysis into the key areas of the employment relationship as a means of stimulating critical discussion about the issues affecting the management of employees in contemporary labour markets.

There are few textbooks specifically aimed at the student and practitioner which attempt to cover the debate about human resource management at both the strategic and international level, and which at the same time provide an easy access to these debates both for the non-expert and non-specialist. We hope that this book bridges this important gap. The aim, quite simply, is to provide in a digestible and easily accessible form some of the major developments in the field of HRM, combined with some explanation as to what constitutes its main ingredients. This is by no means an easy feat to accomplish. The difficulty in achieving this balance echoes, to a large degree, the concerns of universities in many disciplines in making their subject relevant, applicable and academically accomplished. We believe this book is unique in the field of HRM studies in providing such a work for students.

A distinguishing feature of the book is the fact that all its contributory chapters have been written by members of the Department of Human Resource Management at De Montfort University. While many textbooks in the field of the employment relationship have been written by one or two authors obliged to cover fields in which they have comparatively limited knowledge, this book is authored by writers who have specialised in their fields and combine a deep academic understanding of their subjects with a wide experience at practitioner level. The questions, exercises and case studies which appear throughout the book are designed to encourage the student to apply the knowledge contained within individual chapters. The recommended reading and references indicate in-depth studies to take the student into deeper areas of interest, and Glossaries listing some of the key terms in the HRM debate appear at the end of certain chapters. There is a long case study at the end of each Part which covers the main concerns of the Part and presents an overview in the form of authentic examples based on companies and organisations. This does not imply that there is a single perspective which dominates either the book or the Department. The focus of the work contained within this text is largely directed towards the critical analysis of HRM as opposed to a belief in its inherent capacities. What does unite its authors is the acceptance of the fact that HRM requires cool analysis rather than simple dismissal; the fact that many of the outward symbols of HRM have been adopted by organisations demands that it is systematically examined from a variety of standpoints.

Since the first successful edition of this book there has been a plethora of literature in the academic and practitioner journals concerning new developments under the increasingly widening umbrella of HRM. A book of this restricted nature cannot possibly hope to do justice to all these trends but we have attempted to incorporate and update sections and chapters where appropriate and feasible, based on the feedback we have received.

A new chapter on the public sector has been added in response to requests of students, readers and reviewers, and there are changes in authorship and approach to the chapters on recruitment and selection. The training and development section has been restructured from three to four chapters with a chapter on the national framework for vocational education and training.

We are indebted to Pitman Publishing for their enthusiasm for this project and their highly professional support. We would like to thank our contributing colleagues for their effort at a time of considerable commitment to other teaching and research obligations. More especially we would like to express our deep gratitude to Margaret Spence, our Departmental Secretary, for all her work on our disks and her life-saving advice on word-processing. In similar vein we would also like to record our thanks, on behalf of all contributors, to our respective spouses, partners and friends for their forbearance as the book progressed. We remain, as Joint Editors, responsible for the final product.

March 1997

Ian Beardwell
Len Holden

PLAN OF THE BOOK

PART 1 – HUMAN RESOURCE MANAGEMENT AND ITS ORGANISATIONAL CONTEXT	
Chapter 1 An Introduction to Human Resource Management	Chapter 2 Human Resource Management in Context

PART 2 – RESOURCING THE ORGANISATION			
Chapter 3 Human Resource Management and the Labour Market	Chapter 4 Human Resource Planning: Control to Seduction?	Chapter 5 Job Design: Signs, Symbols and Re-sign-ations	Chapter 6 Recruitment and Selection

PART 3 – DEVELOPING THE HUMAN RESOURCE			
Chapter 7 Learning and Development	Chapter 8 The National Framework for Vocational Education and Training	Chapter 9 Training	Chapter 10 Management Development

PART 4 – THE EMPLOYMENT RELATIONSHIP		
Chapter 11 The Employment Relationship and Contractual Regulation	Chapter 12 Collective Bargaining	Chapter 13 Remuneration and Reward
Chapter 14 Employee Involvement	Chapter 15 Managing Human Resources in the Public Sector	

PART 5 – INTERNATIONAL HUMAN RESOURCE MANAGEMENT			
Chapter 16 International Human Resource Management	Chapter 17 Human Resource Management and Europe	Chapter 18 Human Resource Management and the USA	Chapter 19 Human Resource Management and Japan

HOW TO USE THIS BOOK

This text is designed to meet the needs of a range of students who are studying HRM either as a core or option subject on undergraduate degrees in Business and Social Science, MBAs, specialised Masters programmes, or for the IPD Professional Education Scheme. The outlines which follow are intended to indicate how the material in this book can be used to cover the requirements of these varying programmes; the one exception to this scheme is an outline for undergraduates, because of the multiplicity of courses at this level which individual tutors will have devised. Nevertheless it is hoped that these suggested 'routes' through the book will be helpful guidelines for tutors who have responsibility for some or all of these courses.

MBA Route
Introduction: Chapters 1 and 2
Core: Chapters 4, 6, 10, 11, 15, 16
Options: Chapters 3, 4, 5, 10, 12, 13, 14, 15, 17, 18, 19

MA/MSc Route
Introduction: Chapters 1 and 2
Core: Chapters 3, 4, 6, 8, 10, 11, 13, 15
Options: Chapters 3, 4, 5, 7, 9, 12, 14, 16, 17, 18, 19

IPD Professional Education Scheme
Introduction: Chapters 1 and 2
Core Personnel and Development: Chapters 3, 4, 6, 7, 8, 11, 12, 13, 15
Employee Resourcing: Chapters 1, 2, 3, 4, 5, 6, 9, 13
Employee Relations: Chapters 1, 2, 3, 11, 12, 14, 15, 16, 17, 18, 19
Employee Development: Chapters 1, 2, 7, 8, 9, 10

The developing range of IPD specialist modules may be supported by the use of the relevant chapter or part, thus Management Development and Vocational Education and Training can be supported by the whole of Part 3.

CONTRIBUTORS

Editors

Ian Beardwell, BSc, MSc, PhD, is Professor of Industrial Relations and Head of Department of Human Resource Management at Leicester Business School. Experienced in industrial relations and manpower policy with the CBI, CIR and NEDO, he has researched and published in the areas of low pay, union recognition, public sector labour relations and the management of industrial relations. He has given formal evidence to both the Megaw Committee of Inquiry into Civil Service Pay (1981) and the Review Body for Nursing Pay (1987). His most recent work includes an ESRC supported study of non-union firms in the UK, and contemporary developments in 'new' industrial relations.

Len Holden, BSC(Econ), MPhil, PhD, Cert of Ed, MIPD, is Principal Lecturer in Human Resource Management at Leicester Business School, De Montfort University. He has lived and worked in Eastern Europe and written on the changes which have taken place there since 1989, particularly in Bulgaria. He has researched, lectured and written extensively on Western Europe, notably on Swedish human resource management, and has co-authored a book comparing British and Swedish management styles. He is also co-editor of a book on European human resource management, and was a founding researcher of the Price Waterhouse Cranfield Project on Strategic Human Resource Management in Europe. His current interests are in comparative employee involvement in Britain and Sweden, and a comparative analysis of middle management functions and HRM in other European countries.

Contributors

Ian Clark is Principal Lecturer in Industrial Relations in the Department of HRM at De Montfort University. His teaching and research interests focus on critical interpretations of HRM and the political economy of industrial relations, in particular the location of industrial relations analysis within macro-economic management and performance. Prior to his current appointment, he was ESRC Research Fellow at De Montfort University, working on the Competitiveness of British Industry Project. Ian is currently researching two projects: patterns of corporate governance and HRM, and the role of the state in industrial relations, particularly during the immediate post-war years.

Tim Claydon, BSocSci, MSc(Econ), PhD, is Principal Lecturer in Industrial Relations at Leicester Business School, De Montfort University. He teaches Industrial Relations and Labour Market Studies to undergraduate and postgraduate students, as well as supervising research degrees. He has written on trade union history, union derecognition, and trade unions and training. He has also undertaken consultancy work in the public sector. Currently he is developing research into 'new' industrial relations in the workplace.

Audrey Collin is Reader in the Department of Human Resource Management, De Montfort University, where she teaches Organisation Theory and Behaviour mainly on postgraduate, post-experience courses. Her early career was in personnel management and she is now a MIPM. She was awarded a PhD for her study of mid-career change; career and lifespan studies, mentoring and older workers are the fields in which she has researched and published. Her 1992 book (co-edited with Richard A. Young), *Interpreting Career: Hermeneutical Studies of Lives in Context*, reflects her commitment to interpretive research approaches.

Trevor Colling is Senior Research Fellow in the Department of Human Resource Management, De Montfort University. He has written and published widely on various aspects of public sector industrial relations, particularly the implications of privatisation and contracting-out. His current research interests include the management of labour in business services companies and the influence of systems of labour market regulation on gender inequality in the workplace.

Mike Doyle is Lecturer in the Department of Human Resource Management at Leicester Business School. He joined the Business School after some 20 years in a line management role, managing in both public and private sector organisations. He holds a Masters degree in Human Resource Management and teaches on post-graduate, post-experience management programmes in the area of management development, organisational development and change management. His current research interests include an exploration into empowerment in the workplace and how to develop managers during a time of radical organisational change.

Susan Marlow is Senior Lecturer in Industrial Relations at De Montfort University, teaching on a range of undergraduate and professional courses. Susan has research interests in labour relations in small firms and the role of female entrepreneurs in modern society. Currently she is co-director of two funded studies in these areas which have resulted in a number of refereed publications and papers at international conferences.

Damian O'Doherty graduated from the University of Newcastle-upon-Tyne where he read for an Honours degree in Economics. In 1991 he completed an MA in Industrial Relations at the University of Warwick. He is now teaching in the Department of Human Resource Management at De Montfort University, Leicester, lecturing on a range of undergraduate degree programmes in Human Resource Management and Industrial Relations. Damian is a doctoral candidate in the School of Management at UMIST where he is studying the processes of construction and deconstruction in the ordering of the organisation in employment relations.

Ian Roberts is Senior Lecturer in Human Resource Management and Organisational Behaviour at De Montfort University. He has a BSc in Management Science and an MA in Industrial Relations which were both awarded by the University of Warwick. He is now involved in setting up an international research project on middle management and the HRM function.

Julie Storey is Senior Lecturer in Human Resource Management at De Montfort University. She joined the University after 10 years' experience in the retail sector. She currently contributes to a range of professional and postgraduate courses, teaching employee resourcing and interpersonal skills. She is also Course Director of the MA in Personnel and Development and an MIPD. Her research interests include HRM in non-union firms and personnel careers.

Mary Wright is Senior Lecturer in Human Resource Management at De Montfort University, lecturing on a variety of undergraduate and professional courses, with specific responsibilities for the part-time IPD programme at the University. She is an active member of the local IPD branch committee. Her current research activity is in international executive search and selection.

HUMAN RESOURCE MANAGEMENT AND ITS ORGANISATIONAL CONTEXT

1

An Introduction to Human Resource Management

2

Human Resource Management in Context

INTRODUCTION

Human Resource Management has become a pervasive and influential approach to the management of employment in a wide range of market economies. The original US prescriptions of the early 1980s have become popularised and absorbed in a wide variety of economic settings: there are very few major economies where the nature of Human Resource Management, to include its sources, operation and philosophy, are not actively discussed. Economies which once seemed to enjoy a distinctive and successful pattern of employee management against a background of economic growth, such as Sweden, have been as attracted to the debate as those economies, Britain for example, which have struggled with a problematic employment relationship and low growth.

Two related themes run through this first part of the book; both are concerned with the nature of HRM. The first chapter looks at the antecedents of HRM in the USA and its translation to other economies, with particular emphasis on Britain – where the HRM debate has been among the most active and has involved practitioner and academic alike. There are many unresolved questions in HRM: What sort of example is it? Can it be transposed from one economy to another? Does it have qualities which make it truly international? Is it a major contribution to strategic management? The type of questions raised by HRM indicates the extent to which it has disturbed many formerly accepted concepts in the employment relationship. For some it has become a model for action and application, for others it is no more than a map that indicates how the management of employees might be worked out in more specific ways than HRM can adequately deal with.

The second chapter looks at the organisational context in which Human Resource Management has emerged and in which it operates. This is important in understanding some of the assumptions and philosophical stances that lie behind it. The purpose of the discussion is to create a critical awareness of the broader context in which HRM operates, not simply as a set of operational matters that describe the functional role of Personnel Management, but as part of a complex and sophisticated process that helps us understand the nature of organisational life.

AN INTRODUCTION
TO HUMAN
RESOURCE MANAGEMENT

Ian Beardwell and Len Holden

OBJECTIVES

To outline the origins and the recent main changes and developments in the employment relationship.

●

To debate the nature of the HRM phenomenon and the different
perspectives from which it is viewed:
– as a restatement of existing personnel practice
– as a new managerial discipline
– as a resource based model
– as a strategic and international function.

●

To review and evaluate the main models, frameworks, maps and
theories of HRM.

●

INTRODUCTION

The debate over human resource management looks set to be as hotly pursued in the last third of the 1990s as it has over the past 15 years of its publicly contested life. Simply in terms of longevity, the term has lasted the course and looks set to continue as a contentious issue into the new millennium. What has prompted this degree of interest? A good starting point might be the fact that working in and for organisations has changed radically over the past 15 years, so that concepts such as skill, career, hierarchy and occupation have changed fundamentally – to be replaced by the prevailing concerns with competence, subcontracting, teams, and core and peripheral workforces. Thus assumptions about occupational choice, career development and employment policy have all been challenged by shifts in the labour market. A clear indication of the depth of change can be seen in the employment profile of managers: a recent study has indicated that the proportion of managers with at least six years' company tenure has dropped from almost 80% in 1955 to an estimated 10% in 1995.

These figures tell a story of delayering and early retirement amongst established managers, as well as the reduced career opportunities and volatility of the managerial labour

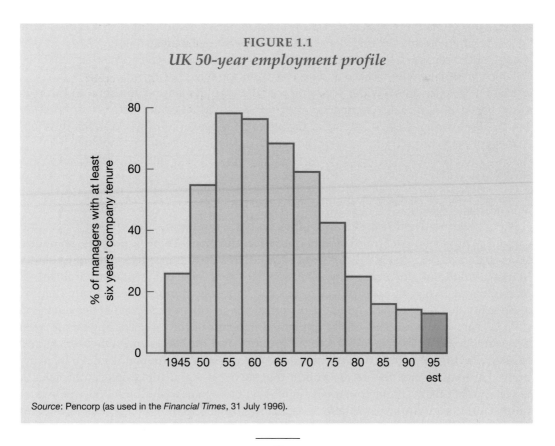

FIGURE 1.1
UK 50-year employment profile

Source: Pencorp (as used in the *Financial Times*, 31 July 1996).

market for new entrants and younger managers from the mid-1970s onwards. The general reshaping of the labour market provides the wider socio-economic background to these changes, but there is a particular significance in these shifts in managerial employment, for they provide further evidence that the former certitudes of the employment relationship have disappeared from almost all levels of organisational life.

These changes provide the background against which human resource management has emerged as the predominant contemporary influence on managing the employment relationships. It is now commonplace to describe HRM as a managerially derived and driven set of precepts with both line and personnel managers actively involved in its operation. What is new and distinctive about the debate, and perhaps explains its capacity to renew itself after each wave of analysis has been assessed and absorbed, is the shift from the broad question of whether HRM exists at all to more focused analyses – for example, whether particular combinations of HRM policies produce better results in output or services so that competitive advantage might accrue to those organisations which adopt them. Thus HRM continues to provide agendas and prescriptions for debate amongst both practitioners and analysts that are contentious, compelling and have no settled orthodoxy.

Why should this be so? Part of the answer lies in the perspective brought to bear upon HRM: there is a diversity in the HRM debate derived from the manner in which particular participants view the essential elements of HRM and what they believe it is representing which colours the discussion. For the purposes of this analysis four broad perspectives are set out here:

- that HRM is no more than a renaming of basic personnel functions which does little that is different from the traditional practice of personnel management;
- that HRM represents a fusion of personnel management and industrial relations which is managerially focused and derives from a managerial agenda;
- that HRM represents a wider conception of the employment relationship, to incorporate an enabling and developmental role for the individual employee;
- that HRM can be viewed as part of the strategic managerial function in the development of business policy in which it plays both a determining and contributory role.

HRM as a restatement of existing personnel practice

It is possible to view this first standpoint as a basic but natural reaction to a new and somewhat threatening reformulation of traditional functions. There is, perhaps, an understandable scepticism that HRM can, or ever could, live up to the wider claims of its ability to transform the employment relationship so totally that some of the inherent problems of managing a volatile set of employee issues can be resolved more satisfactorily than by approaches that have grown out of the historical development of personnel management. In large part such a reaction can be explained in terms of the gulf that appears to exist between personnel management 'on the ground' and the rather more theoretical and 'strategic' nature of a great deal of the discussion surrounding human resource management. For many practitioners the notion that their roles and functions can be seen in anything other than a highly pragmatic light is no more than wishful thinking: there is an important, if straightforward, task of recruiting, selecting, rewarding, managing and developing employees that must be carried out as 'efficiently' as possible. In this sense, HRM might be viewed as no more than another trend in the long line of management prescriptions that have each enjoyed a vogue and then lost favour, while the pragmatic nature of established personnel management has ensured that the operational tasks have been accomplished.

HRM as a new managerial discipline

The second perspective contains more diversity and complexity, and incorporates such issues as the philosophies of personnel and industrial relations, the professional desire to present the management of employees as a holistic discipline (akin to the inclusive approaches of accounting and marketing, for example), and the belief that an integrated management approach can be provided by HRM. This would not only unite the differing perspectives of PM and IR but create a new and broader discipline as a result of the fusion of these traditional elements. An important outcome of this approach is to view some of these traditional components as now irrelevant or outdated and as dealing with problems which typify past, as opposed to current, practice: this is, perhaps, most noticeable in the renaming of functional activities so that industrial relations becomes 'employee relations' and training becomes 'employee development'. This retitling is not solely designed to update an image, although that is important in itself, but is more specifically aimed at expressing the nature of the employment relationship in what are seen as changed circumstances. Thus industrial relations is seen as expressing a relationship based upon a manual, manufacturing (and, often by implication, male) unionised workforce – rather than the supposedly wider concept of 'employee relations' which involves a total workforce which includes white-collar and technical staff of whom many will be female and some or all non-union.

A further significant shift in thinking connected with this second approach is that of the desire by management to extend control over aspects of the collective relationship that were once customarily regarded as jointly agreed between employees (usually via their unions) and management. Treating employees as a primary responsibility of *management* as opposed to the jointly negotiated responsibility of both unions *and* management, suggests an approach which is concerned to stress the primacy of the managerial agenda in the employment relationship and marks a shift away from one of the fundamental assumptions of the postwar approach to managing collective workforces. This shift was underlined in the 1993 employment legislation which removed from ACAS the duty, originally given to it on its inception in 1974, to promote collective bargaining. In reality, this duty was a reflection of a deeply rooted presumption stretching back throughout most of the twentieth century and, in the UK at least, largely shared by employers, unions and the state, that collective bargaining represented a 'politically' acceptable compromise between management and labour.

It might be more honest to describe this approach to the managerial reassertion of control over the total employment relationship as a fundamental element in the 'ideology of HRM' which views human resource management as a transforming agent for established personnel practice. The extent to which such transformations can be achieved is also connected to the third HRM perspective, which is discussed next.

HRM as a resource based model

A further perspective has been brought to bear on HRM from those approaches that stress the role of the individual in organisations, rather than the collective employment models outlined so far. Personnel management, to a large degree at least, has always been concerned with the interface between the organisation and the individual and the necessity of achieving a trade-off between the requirements of the organisation and the needs of individual employees. Traditional personnel management policies which have been developed to cope with this trade-off have often taken a piecemeal approach to certain aspects of this issue: historically, the early twentieth-century personnel function stressed the 'welfare' role that could be afforded employees so that basic working conditions (both physically and contractually) could be established.

Subsequently, other styles of personnel management sought to introduce, administer or rectify particular aspects of jobs and roles that individuals carried out. This tradition fostered a belief in equitable selection and reward systems, efficient procedures for discipline, dismissal and redundancy, and clear and operable rules for administering large numbers of employees to avoid arbitrary judgements over individual cases. The prevailing rationale behind all these activities could be seen as a desire to manage the difficulties of the organisation/individual relationship in as technically neutral a manner as possible. This emphasis has fostered a culture within personnel management which is characterised as 'cost minimisation', with the individual as the cost which has to be controlled and contained. In these circumstances employees become one of the aggregate commodities within the organisation that have to be managed within the organisation's resources, in the same way that, for example, the finance available to the organisation has to be managed within a framework and according to accounting conventions. The logical extent of this model is reached in manpower planning with precise numerical assessments of internal and external demand for and supply of labour.

Any alternative to this formalised approach which treats the individual as a resource rather than an expense and views expenditure on training as an investment rather than a cost poses a profound threat to the conventional wisdom of personnel management.

The conception of personnel as having an enabling capacity for employees has a long tradition, not least in the United States where organisational analysis has often provided prescriptions concerning the role of supervisors, work groups and work organisation. The advent of Japanese management systems has, however, highlighted the impact of this approach on the employment relationship. Whether sustainable or not in the West, the Japanese large-firm emphasis on developing individual employees along particular job paths while undertaking to provide continuous employment throughout the normal working life of the individual has at least provided a model in which the employer seeks to maximise employment opportunities. This approach goes further, however: it regards all employees as potentially able to benefit from further training and development, from which the organisation itself then benefits. So, far from viewing the employee as a cost which has to be borne by the employer, this philosophy sees the employee as an actual and potential return on investment which ultimately strengthens the company. The responsibility of the employer for investment and employment has, at least in the postwar period to date, encouraged large corporate Japanese employers to develop products and markets which have used the invested skills of their workforces.

There has been strong interest in what is termed 'resource based' HRM, in which human resources are viewed as the basis of competitive advantage. This means that advantage is not only derived from the formal reorganisation and reshaping of work, but is also powerfully derived from within the workforce in terms of the training and expertise available to the organisation, the adaptability of employees which permits the organisation strategic flexibility, and the commitment of employees to the organisation's business plans and goals.

HRM as a strategic and international function

The advent of human resource management has also brought forward the issue of the linkages between the employment relationship and wider organisational strategies and corporate policies. Historically, the management of industrial relations and personnel has been concerned either to cope with the 'downstream' consequences of earlier strategic decisions or to 'firefight' short-term problems which threaten the long-run success of a particular strategy. In these instances the role has been at best reactive and supportive to other managerial functions, at worst a hindrance until particular operational problems were overcome.

In the private sector the well-known case of British Leyland in the 1970s demonstrated a situation where considerable amounts of managerial effort (up to 60% of operational managers' time by some estimates) were devoted to 'fixing' shop floor problems. In order to re-establish managerial control the company effectively turned the reshaping of industrial relations into its strategy so that it could refashion its product range and market position. In the public sector throughout the 1980s a series of major disputes affected the operations of schools, hospitals and local authorities (among many such examples); in each of these cases changes to the nature of the employment relationship were the root causes of the dislocation. The Leyland case and the public sector experiences are extreme examples, but each demonstrates the impact that the employment relationship can have on total operations.

Human resource management lays claim to a fundamentally different relationship between the organisation's employment function and its strategic role. The assumption behind HRM is that it is essentially a *strategically* driven activity which is not only a major contributor to that process but is a determining part of it. From this standpoint the contribution which the management of the employment relationship makes to the overall managerial process is as vital and formative as that of finance or marketing, for example. Indeed, the notion that HRM is central to such managerial decision making indicates the extent to which its proponents feel that it has come out of the shadows to claim a rightful place alongside other core management roles. In this respect one of the traditional stances of the personnel practitioner – that of the 'liberal' conception of personnel management as standing *between* employer and employee, moderating and smoothing the interchange between them – is viewed as untenable: HRM is about shaping *and* delivering corporate strategies with commitment and results.

A further element in this construction of HRM points to its *international* potentialities. The employment relationship is materially affected – perhaps even defined – by the national and cultural contexts in which it operates. Thus, variations in national labour markets have given rise to a wide range of employment structures, policies and relationships within the broad definition of market economies. To the extent that employers operate *within* national labour markets, these characteristics do not impinge on neighbouring nationalities; but to the extent that employers operate *across* national boundaries, these different characteristics may become factors that an employer would wish to change or override. Thus international companies which seek to deploy homogeneous employment policies, regardless of national labour markets, have often been cited as seeking and developing broadly based personnel systems which neutralise national differences and which stress, by contrast, organisational cultures that are drawn from the strategic goals of the firm. Among the many examples of firms that have been identified as adopting this approach perhaps the best known and most commonly cited is IBM. An important consequence of this approach is that many of the internal policies of such firms have been used to construct approaches to human resource management which are held to be the role models for other organisations to emulate. From this line of argument one arrives at the proposition that HRM is capable of providing a managerial approach to the employment relationship that is 'culturally neutral', is derived and sustained from within the prescriptions of the organisation, and is capable of being translated across national and organisational boundaries. Indeed one might argue that, in these conditions, HRM is best defined as the product of multinational companies' personnel policies which have the capacity to be translated to other firms regardless of culture. Needless to say, this neutralisation of the strong prescriptive elements of HRM is a highly debatable position, and there are few who would agree that HRM can be so simply defined in terms of its assumptions and values.

SOME ASSUMPTIONS ABOUT HUMAN RESOURCE MANAGEMENT

Figure 1.2 sets out the four perspectives on HRM discussed above and located key aspects of the HRM focus within its framework. It will be seen that such a schematic presentation demonstrates not only the breadth of these operational assumptions, but underlines their ambiguity too. Within many organisations the circumstances in which human resource management is pursued will be critically determined by the state of the labour market at any particular time: it is thus perfectly understandable for an organisation to be moving towards a strategic dimension of HRM in its own terms, but find it necessary to revert or regroup to a modified version of its original policy. A case in point here might be that of British Airways, which deployed both the developmental and strategic/international models of HRM throughout the 1980s in order to support its 'Customer Care' business plan, but has found itself increasingly relying on the restatement and fusion models as it seeks to reorganise its Gatwick operations (including Dan-Air) in the 1990s. This has given rise to industrial relations difficulties, with strong residual problems over wage levels for cabin staff leading to strike threats in 1996.

Although these four interpretations of HRM each contain strong distinguishing characteristics they are by no means mutually exclusive: indeed, it would be surprising if that were so. In this sense they do not constitute a model of HRM but a set of perspectives on HRM which organisations bring to bear on the employment relationship. A more useful

FIGURE 1.2
Four perspectives on human resource management

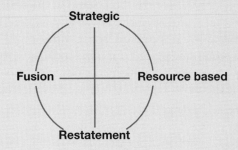

Strategic	Fusion
Employment policy derived from business objectives; HRM major contributor to business policy; translation of HRM policy across cultures	PM and IR no longer seen as operationally distinct; managerially derived agenda; replacement of collectivism with stronger role for individualism

Restatement	Resource based
PM and IR as prevailing model; HRM style outcomes sought within a pluralist framework	Individualistically derived; stress on input provided by organisation on behalf of employee

approach to interpreting these perspectives might be to recognise that many organisations may display at least *one* of these principal perspectives but will also rely on several characteristics drawn from at least one and probably more of the other three constructs. In this sense HRM, as a set of *issues* as well as a set of *practices*, contains ambivalence and contradiction quite as much as clarity and affirmation. In many organisations the tension which arises from this outcome is part of the internal process of the management of uncertainty. With the privatisation of British Rail and the multiplicity of operating companies, there has been a distinct move away from the business-led strategies of the former BR operating divisions to a more traditional pattern of collective agreements involving negotiations between the unions and the individual owners of the new companies. A further example could be drawn from the financial sector, where well-known high street banks have sought to create developmental approaches to their human resource management while at the same time dealing with the staff reductions caused by over-committed expansion of the 1980s on a restatement basis to reduce direct costs. A further discussion of some of these aspects of HRM can be found in Guest (1989a).

THE SEARCH FOR THE DEFINING CHARACTERISTICS OF HRM

An important part of the debate, both in the US and in the UK, has been the search for the defining characteristics that will describe, analyse and explain the HRM phenomenon. To a considerable extent this quest has proved largely unresolved because of the wide range of prescriptions and expectations placed upon the term, and the relative lack of available evidence to determine systematically whether or not HRM has taken root as a sustainable model of employee management. This difficulty is further compounded if one considers a series of critical questions about human resource management:

- Is HRM a practitioner-driven process which has attracted a wider audience and prompted subsequent analytical attention?
- Is HRM an academically derived description of the employment relationship, to which practitioners have subsequently become drawn?
- Is HRM essentially a prescriptive model of how such a relationship 'ought' to be?
- Is it a 'leading edge' approach as to how such a relationship actually 'is' within certain types of organisations?

Each of these questions leads the search for the innate qualities of HRM along different routes and towards different conclusions. If the first approach is adopted, then evidence is required which would identify the location, incidence and adoption of defined HRM practices and suggest factors that caused organisations to develop those approaches. The second approach would have to locate the HRM debate in the academic discussion of the employment relationship and demonstrate why this particular variant of analysis emerged. The third approach would have to explain why, among so many other prescriptions concerning management, the HRM prescription emerged and quite what the distinctive elements were that permitted its prescriptive influence to gain acceptance. The final approach would have to provide satisfactory evidence that, where HRM had developed within certain organisational contexts, the evidence of the particular setting could be applied to the generality of the employment relationship.

However, when these questions have all been taken into account there still remains the residual problem that none of them can conclusively define the nature of HRM in its own terms to the exclusion of each of the others. What are seen as practitioner-derived examples of HRM can be matched by similar policies in non-HRM espousing organisations; what are seen as academically derived models of HRM are each open to large areas of contention and disagreement between analysts; what are seen as prescriptive models of 'what ought to be' might well be just that and no more; and what could be held up as 'leading edge' examples could be wholly determined by the particular circumstances of organisations that are either incapable of translation into other contexts, or may indeed be unsustainable within the original organisations as circumstances change. Storey (1992: 30) outlines this competing set of considerations within the debate very clearly.

These considerations have not prevented the active debate about the *nature* of HRM to proceed with increasing velocity and breadth. A significant division can be noted between those analyses which seek to stress the innovative element of HRM, which is claimed to address the fundamental question of managing employees in new ways and with new perspectives, and those which stress its derivative elements which are claimed to be no more than a reworking of the traditional themes of personnel management. Thus Walton (1985), in attempting definitions of HRM, stresses mutuality between employers and employees:

> Mutual goals, mutual influence, mutual respect, mutual rewards, mutual responsibility. The theory is that policies of mutuality will elicit commitment which in turn will yield both better economic performance and greater human development.

Beer and Spector (1985) emphasised a new set of assumptions in shaping their meaning of HRM:

- proactive system wide interventions, with emphasis on 'fit', linking HRM with strategic planning and cultural change.
- people are social capital capable of development.
- coincidence of interest between stake holders can be developed.
- seeks power equalisation for trust and collaboration.
- open channels of communication to build trust and commitment.
- goal orientation.
- participation and informed choice.

Conversely, some writers, most notably Legge (1989) and Fowler (1987), have commented that personnel management was beginning to emerge as a more strategic function in the late 1970s and early 1980s before the concept was subsumed under the title of HRM, and in this sense there is little new in HRM practice.

However, allowing for problems of definitions and demarcation lines between various conceptions of human resource management, there is little doubt that HRM became a fashionable concept and a controversial subject in the 1980s, with its boundaries very much overlapping the traditional areas of personnel management, industrial relations, organisational behaviour and strategic and operational management. Its emergence created a controversy which extends through most of the issues which touch on the employment relationship. Many proponents of HRM argue that it addresses the centrality of employees in the organisation and that their motivation and commitment to the organisational goals need to be nurtured. While this is by no means a new concept, the HRM perspective would claim at least to present a different perspective on this issue, namely that a range of organisational objectives have been arranged in a strategic way to enhance the performance of employees in achieving these goals. Before examining these arguments in more detail, a brief account of the origins and recent historical development of HRM would be appropriate in order to understand why it emerged when and as it did.

THE ORIGINS OF HUMAN RESOURCE MANAGEMENT

As we saw earlier in this chapter, HRM can be seen as part of the wider and longer debate about the nature of management in general and the management of employees in particular. This means that tracing the definitive origins of HRM is as elusive an exercise as arriving at its defining characteristics. Certainly there are antecedents in organisational theory, and particularly that of the human relations school, but the nature of HRM has involved important elements of strategic management and business policy, coupled with operations management, which make a simple 'family tree' explanation of HRM's derivation highly improbable.

What can be said is that HRM appears to have its origins in the United States in the 1950s, although it did not gain wide recognition until the beginning of the 1980s, and in the UK until the mid to late 1980s. There are a number of reasons for its emergence since then, among the most important of which are the major pressures experienced in product markets during the recession of 1980–82, combined with a growing recognition in the US that trade union influence in collective employment was reaching fewer employees. By the 1980s the US economy was being challenged by overseas competitors, most particularly Japan. Discussion tended to focus on two issues: 'the productivity of the American worker', particularly compared to the Japanese worker, 'and the declining rate of innovation in American industries' (Devanna *et al.*, 1984: 33). From this sprang a desire to create a work situation free from conflict in which both employers and employees worked in unity towards the same goal – the success of the organisation (Fombrun, 1984: 17).

In the UK in the 1980s the business climate also became conducive to changes in the employment relationship. As in the US, this was partly driven by economic pressure in the form of increased product market competition, the recession in the early part of the decade, and the introduction of new technology. However, a very significant factor in the UK, generally absent from the US, was the desire of the government to reform and reshape the conventional model of industrial relations, which provided a rationale for the development of more employer-oriented employment policies on the part of management (Beardwell, 1992). The restructuring of the economy saw a rapid decline in the old industries and a relative rise in the service sector and new industries based on 'high-tech' products and services, many of which were comparatively free from the established patterns of what was sometimes termed the 'old' industrial relations. These changes were overseen by a muscular entrepreneurialism promoted by the Thatcher government in the form of privatisation and anti-union legislation 'which encouraged firms to introduce new labour practices and to re-order their collective bargaining arrangements' (Hendry and Pettigrew, 1990: 19).

A further important theme in the development of HRM in the UK was some recognition of the fact that the poor performance of British management was partly responsible for the weakened state of the economy. Taking their cue from overseas experience (particularly Japanese, German and American), critics accused employers of poor training and management development which shifted the whole debate on these and related human resource issues 'straight into the board room' (Coopers Lybrand, 1985; Constable and McCormick, 1987; Handy, 1987).

The influence of the US 'excellence' literature (for example Peters and Waterman, 1982; Kanter, 1984) also associated the success of 'leading edge' companies with the motivation of employees by involved management styles which also responded to market changes. As a consequence, the concepts of employee commitment and 'empowerment' became another strand in the ongoing debate about management practice and HRM.

A review of these issues suggests that any discussion of HRM has to come to terms with at least three fundamental problems:

● first, that HRM is derivative of a range of antecedents, the ultimate mix of which is wholly dependent upon the stance of the analyst and which may be drawn from an eclectic range of sources;

- that HRM is itself a contributory factor in the analysis of the employment relationship, and sets part of the context in which that debate takes place;
- that it is difficult to distinguish where the *significance* of HRM lies: whether it is in its supposed transformation of styles of employee management in a specific sense, or whether in a broader sense it is in its capacity to sponsor a wholly redefined relationship between management and employees which overcomes the traditional issues of control and consent at work.

This ambivalence over the definition, components and scope of HRM can be seen when examining some of the main US and UK analyses. An early model of HRM, developed by Fombrun, Tichy and Devanna (1984), introduced the concept of strategic human resource management by which HRM policies are· inextricably linked to the 'formulation and implementation of strategic corporate and/or business objectives' (Devanna *et al.*, 1984: 34). The model is illustrated in Figure 1.3.

The matching model emphasises the necessity of 'tight fit' between HR strategy and business strategy. This in turn has led to a plethora of interpretations by practitioners of

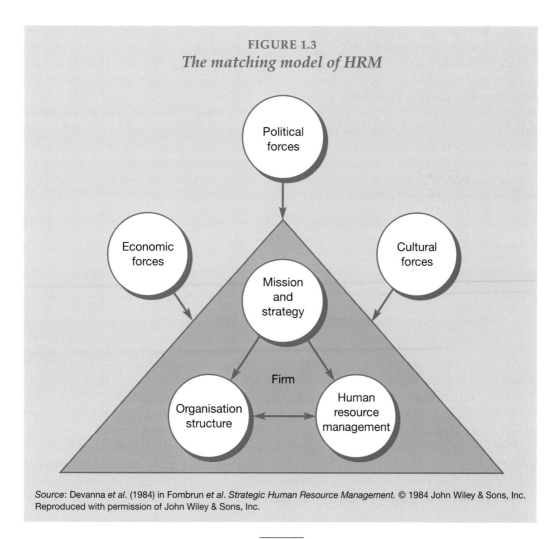

FIGURE 1.3
The matching model of HRM

Source: Devanna *et al.* (1984) in Fombrun *et al. Strategic Human Resource Management.* © 1984 John Wiley & Sons, Inc. Reproduced with permission of John Wiley & Sons, Inc.

how these two strategies are linked. Some offer synergies between human resource planning (manpower planning) and business strategies, with the driving force rooted in the 'product market logic' (Evans and Lorange, 1989). Whatever the process, the result is very much an emphasis on the 'unitarist' view of HRM: 'unitarism' assumes that conflict or at least differing views cannot exist within the organisation because the actors – management and employees – are working to the same goal of the organisation's success. What makes the model particularly attractive for many personnel practitioners is that HRM assumes a more important position in the formulation of organisational policies.

The personnel department has often been perceived as an administrative support function with a lowly status. Personnel was now to become very much part of the human resource management of the organisation and HRM was conceived to be more than personnel and to have peripheries wider than the normal personnel function. In order for HRM to be strategic it had to encompass all the human resource areas of the organisation and be practised by all employees. In addition, decentralisation and devolvement of responsibility are also seen as very much part of the HRM strategy as it facilitates communication, involvement and commitment of middle management and other employees deeper within the organisation. The effectiveness of organisations thus rested on how the strategy and the structure of the organisation interrelated, a concept rooted in the view of the organisation developed by Alfred Chandler (1962) and evolved in the matching model.

A more flexible model, illustrated in Figure 1.4, was developed by Beer and his associates (1984) at Harvard University. 'The map of HRM territory', as the authors titled their model, recognised that there were a variety of 'stakeholders' in the corporation, which included shareholders, various groups of employees, the government and the community. At once the model recognises the legitimate interests of various groups and that the creation of HRM strategies would have to recognise these interests and fuse them as much as possible into the human resource strategy and ultimately the business strategy.

This recognition of stakeholders' interests raises a number of important questions for policy-makers in the organisation.

> How much responsibility, authority and power should the organisation voluntarily delegate and to whom? If required by government legislation to bargain with the unions or consult with workers' councils, how should management enter into these institutional arrangements? Will they seek to minimize the power and influence of these legislated mechanisms? Or will they share influence and work to create greater congruence of interests between management and the employee groups represented through these mechanisms?
> (Beer *et al.*, 1984: 8)

The acknowledgment of these various interest groups has made the model much more amenable to 'export' as the recognition of different legal employment structures, managerial styles and cultural differences can be more easily accommodated within it. This 'neopluralist' model has also been recognised as being useful in the study of comparative HRM (Poole, 1990: 3-5). It is not surprising therefore that the Harvard model has found greater favour among academics and commentators in the UK, which has relatively strong union structures and different labour traditions from the United States. Nevertheless, some academics have still criticised the model as being too unitarist while accepting its basic premise (Hendry and Pettigrew, 1990).

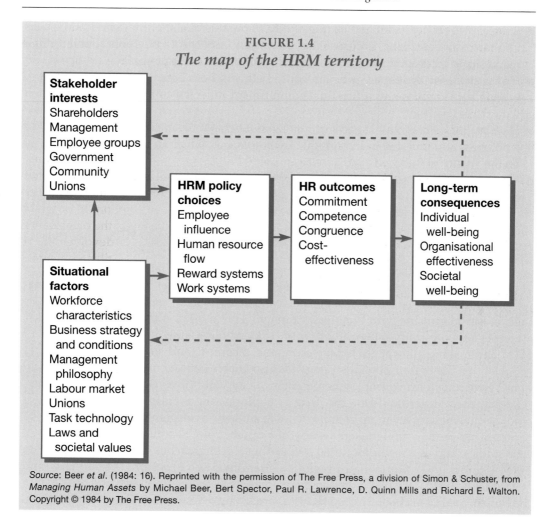

FIGURE 1.4
The map of the HRM territory

Stakeholder interests
Shareholders
Management
Employee groups
Government
Community
Unions

Situational factors
Workforce
  characteristics
Business strategy
  and conditions
Management
  philosophy
Labour market
Unions
Task technology
Laws and
  societal values

HRM policy choices
Employee
  influence
Human resource
  flow
Reward systems
Work systems

HR outcomes
Commitment
Competence
Congruence
Cost-
  effectiveness

Long-term consequences
Individual
  well-being
Organisational
  effectiveness
Societal
  well-being

Source: Beer *et al.* (1984: 16). Reprinted with the permission of The Free Press, a division of Simon & Schuster, from *Managing Human Assets* by Michael Beer, Bert Spector, Paul R. Lawrence, D. Quinn Mills and Richard E. Walton. Copyright © 1984 by The Free Press.

The first two main approaches to HRM which have emerged in the UK are based on the Harvard model which is made up of both prescriptive and analytical elements. Among the most perceptive analysts of HRM, Guest has tended to concentrate on the prescriptive components while Pettigrew and Hendry rest on the analytical aspect (Boxall, 1992). Although using the Harvard model as a basis, both Guest and Pettigrew and Hendry have some criticisms of the model and derive from it only that which they consider useful (Guest, 1987, 1989a and b, 1990; Hendry and Pettigrew, 1986, 1990).

As we have seen, there are difficulties of definition and model building in HRM and this has led British interpreters to take alternative elements in building their own models. Guest is conscious that if a model is to be useful to researchers it must be useful 'in the field' of research and this means that elements of HRM have to be pinned down for comparative measurement. He has therefore developed a set of propositions which he believes are amenable to testing. He also asserts that the combination of these propositions, which include 'strategic integration', high commitment', 'high quality' and 'flexibility', creates more effective organisations (Guest, 1987).

- *Strategic integration* is defined as 'the ability of organisations to integrate HRM issues into their strategic plans, to ensure that the various aspects of HRM cohere and for line managers to incorporate an HRM perspective into their decision making'.
- *High commitment* is defined as being 'concerned with both behavioural commitment to pursue agreed goals and attitudinal commitment reflected in a strong identification with the enterprise'.
- *High quality* 'refers to all aspects of managerial behaviour, including management of employees and investment in high-quality employees, which in turn will bear directly on the quality of the goods and services provided'.
- Finally *flexibility* is seen as being 'primarily concerned with what is sometimes called functional flexibility but also with an adaptable organisational structure with the capacity to manage innovation' (Guest, 1989b: 42).

The combination of these propositions leads to a linkage between HRM aims, policies and outcomes as shown in Table 1.1. Whether there is enough evidence to assess the relevance and efficacy of these HRM relationships will be examined later.

Hendry and Pettigrew (1990) have adapted the Harvard model by drawing on its analytical aspects. They see HRM 'as a perspective on employment systems, characterised by their closer alignment with business strategy'. This model, illustrated in Figure 1.5, attempts a theoretically integrative framework encompassing all styles and modes of HRM and making allowances for the economic, technical, and sociopolitical influences in society on the organisational strategy. 'It also enables one to describe the "preconditions" governing a firm's employment system, along with the consequences of the latter' (Hendry and Pettigrew, 1990: 25). It thus explores 'more fully the implications for employee relations of a variety of approaches to strategic management' (Boxall, 1992).

Storey has recently undertaken a study of a number of UK organisations in a series of case studies, and as a result modified still further the approaches of previous writers on HRM (Storey, 1992). Storey had previously identified two types of HRM – 'hard' and 'soft' (Storey, 1989) – the one rooted in the manpower planning approach and the other in the human relations school. He begins his approach by defining four elements which distinguish HRM:

- First, that 'it is human capability and commitment which, in the final analysis, distinguishes successful organisations from the rest'.
- Second, because HRM is of strategic importance, it needs to be considered by top management in the formulation of the corporate plan.

TABLE 1.1
A human resource management framework

HRM aims	HRM policies	HRM outcomes
For example:	For example:	For example:
● high commitment	● selection based on specific	● low labour turnover
● quality	criteria using sophisticated	● allegiance to company
● flexible working	tests	

Source: Storey (1989: 11).

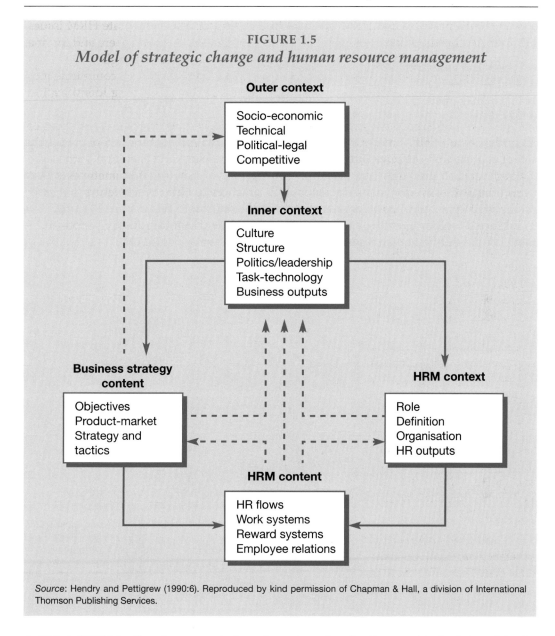

FIGURE 1.5
Model of strategic change and human resource management

Source: Hendry and Pettigrew (1990:6). Reproduced by kind permission of Chapman & Hall, a division of International Thomson Publishing Services.

- Third, 'HRM is, therefore, seen to have long-term implications and to be integral to the core performance of the business or public sector organisation. In other words it must be the intimate concern of line managers.'
- Fourth, the key levers (the deployment of human resources, evaluation of performance and the rewarding of it, etc.) 'are to be used to seek not merely compliance but commitment'.

Storey approaches an analysis of HRM by creating an 'ideal type', the purpose of which 'is to simplify by highlighting the essential features in an exaggerated way' (1992: 34). This he does by making a classificatory matrix of 27 points of difference between personnel and IR practices and HRM practices (see Table 1.2). The elements are categorised in a four-part basic outline:

- beliefs and assumptions
- strategic concepts
- line management
- key levers.

This 'ideal type' of HRM model is not essentially an aim in itself but more a tool in enabling sets of approaches to be pinpointed in organisations for research and analytical purposes.

His *theoretical* model is thus based on conceptions of how organisations have been transformed from predominantly personnel/IR practices to HRM practices. As it is based on the ideal type there are no organisations which conform to this picture in reality. It is in essence a tool for enabling comparative analysis. He illustrates this by proposing 'A model of the shift to human resource management', shown in Figure 1.6.

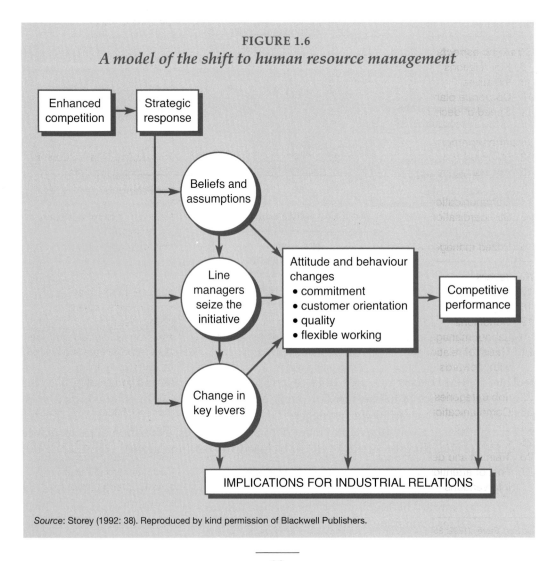

FIGURE 1.6
A model of the shift to human resource management

Source: Storey (1992: 38). Reproduced by kind permission of Blackwell Publishers.

TABLE 1.2
Twenty-seven points of difference

Dimension	Personnel and IR	HRM
Beliefs and assumptions		
1 Contract	Careful delineation of written contracts	Aim to go 'beyond contract'
2 Rules	Importance of devising clear rules/mutuality	'Can-do' outlook; impatience with 'rule'
3 Guide to management action	Procedures	'Business-need'
4 Behaviour referent	Norms/custom and practice	Values/mission
5 Managerial task *vis-à-vis* labour	Monitoring	Nurturing
6 Nature of relations	Pluralist	Unitarist
7 Conflict	Institutionalised	De-emphasised
Strategic aspects		
8 Key relations	Labour management	Customer
9 Initiatives	Piecemeal	Integrated
10 Corporate plan	Marginal to	Central to
11 Speed of decision	Slow	Fast
Line management		
12 Management role	Transactional	Transformational leadership
13 Key managers	Personnel/IR specialists	General/business/line managers
14 Communication	Indirect	Direct
15 Standardisation	High (e.g. 'parity' an issue)	Low (e.g. 'parity' not seen as relevant)
16 Prized management skills	Negotiation	Facilitation
Key levers		
17 Selection	Separate, marginal task	Integrated, key task
18 Pay	Job evaluation (fixed grades)	Performance-related
19 Conditions	Separately negotiated	Harmonisation
20 Labour management	Collective bargaining contracts	Towards individual contracts
21 Thrust of relations with stewards	Regularised through facilities and training	Marginalised (with exception of some bargaining for change models)
22 Job categories and grades	Many	Few
23 Communication	Restricted flow	Increased flow
24 Job design	Division of labour	Teamwork
25 Conflict handling	Reach temporary truces	Manage climate and culture
26 Training and development	Controlled access to courses	Learning companies
27 Foci of attention for interventions	Personnel procedures	Wide ranging cultural, structural and personnel strategies

Source: Storey (1992: 35). Reproduced by kind permission of Blackwell Publishers.

HUMAN RESOURCE MANAGEMENT:
THE STATE OF THE DEBATE

The question of whether human resource management has the capacity to transform or replace deeply rooted models of personnel management and industrial relations, or could become a fully worked-through theory of management, is one that cannot be answered in a simple manner. Human resource management has many cogent critics and many sceptical supporters. Initial criticism which claimed that it was 'old wine in new bottles', the restatement perspective outlined earlier in this chapter, still has strong adherents (Keenoy and Anthony, 1993). Others see it as a version of 'the emperor's new clothes' (Legge, 1989) or a 'wolf in sheep's clothing' (Armstrong, 1987; Fowler, 1987; Keenoy, 1990a).

Tom Keenoy is one of the most eloquent and persuasive of critics and his examination of HRM has exposed many of the *a priori* assumptions and *non sequiturs* which abound in the reasoning of its supporters. He claims that HRM is more rhetoric than reality and has been 'talked up' by its advocates. It has little support in terms of evidence and has been a convenient dustbin of rationalisation to support ideological shifts in the employment relationship brought about by market pressures. It is also full of contradictions, not only in its meanings but also in its practice.

In examining the meanings of HRM Keenoy notes that a 'remarkable feature of the HRM phenomenon is the brilliant ambiguity of the term itself'. He later continues: 'On the "Alice principle" that a term means whatever one chooses it to mean, each of these interpretations may be valid but, in Britain, the absence of any intellectual touchstones has resulted in the term being subject to the process of almost continuous and contested conceptual elision' (Keenoy, 1990b).

Legge (1989) has shown that a close examination of the normative models of HRM and personnel management reveals little difference between the two, and that HRM contains a number of internal contradictions. Legge points out that there is a problem with integration in the sense that HRM policies have to integrate with business policy. She asks: 'Is it possible to have a corporation-wide mutually reinforcing set of HRM policies, if the organisation operates in highly diverse product markets, and, if not, does it matter, in terms of organisational effectiveness?' (Legge, 1989: 30). She also asks: 'If the business strategy should dictate the choice of HRM policies, will some strategies dictate policies that . . . fail to emphasise commitment, flexibility and quality?' (Legge, 1989: 30). Legge also comments on the probable incompatibility of creating an organisational culture which attempts to pursue both individualistic and teamwork policies at the same time.

Other critics have indicated that many organisations are driven by stronger objectives than HRM. Armstrong (1989) has pointed to the financial orientations of most companies which are incompatible with those prescriptions described as imperative in the practice of HRM. Furthermore, the belief that human resource management can transcend national cultures has attracted considerable critical comment (Pieper, 1990).

The 1990s have seen a growing sophistication in the nature of the debate involving HRM. One very strong characteristic is the desire on the part of a number of commentators to explore the consequences of implementing HRM techniques for organisations. Thus the nature of the argument now strongly incorporates the concept of HRM outcomes rather than relying largely on descriptions of styles or types of HRM philosophies. Part of this development has been promoted by the realisation that traditional sources of competitive advantage, such as technological supremacy, patents, capital and so forth, are very much less important than they were in a world in which many countries can display equal advantage in at least some of these critical aspects (Pfeffer, 1994). Thus the extent to which an organisation can mobilise its internal human resources may hold the key to achievable advantage in the future (Prahalad and Hamel, 1990). The general managerial epithet that 'people are our greatest asset' is a tired cliché; what distinguishes the most recent work is its focus on the resource based model of HRM and the particular mix of skills and attributes that can be developed and applied to economic performance. Thus Huselid (1995) has argued that high performance work practices have an economically and statistically significant impact on such employee outcomes as turnover and productivity and both short- and long-term measures of corporate financial performance. Wood (1995) has examined high commitment management in terms of what he calls the 'four pillars of HRM' and their ability to deliver significant HRM performance; Guest and Hoque (1996) have examined the concept of 'fit' in the specific circumstances of HRM techniques in greenfield sites and the 'bundles' of practice that might affect performance; Purcell (1996) has critically examined the notion of 'bundles' but has provided a thoughtful analysis of resource based HRM in the context of corporate strategy (1995); while Boxall has sought to relate resource based analysis to the strategic HRM debate (1996).

A further element in the contemporary discussion is the question of whether HRM is now affording line management more control of the personnel function than personnel specialists themselves have. If one of the attributes of HRM is its devolution to the line, then perhaps a logical consequence is the relative loss of influence and control by the erstwhile keepers of the corporate personnel conscience. Does this matter? In the words of Fernie *et al.* (1994), is HRM all 'Big Hat, No Cattle'? The extent to which HRM activity has shifted to the line, and the associated question of whether personnel managers are any more strategic in their role than in the past, is difficult to determine conclusively. The Second Company Level Industrial Relations Survey (Marginson *et al.*, 1993) found no evidence to support general strategic involvement and some evidence that, without a personnel director on the board, involvement in the formulation of human resource policy was weakened, findings largely supported by Purcell and Ahlstrand's (1994) study of multi-divisional organisations. Perhaps the clearest evidence to suggest that personnel management was losing out to the line is provided by Storey's (1992) study of 'mainstream' companies and the introduction of HRM, although a study of 28 organisations by Kelly and Gennard (1994) presented a different picture based on interviews with personnel directors.

In an important sense, therefore, one answer to Storey's (1995) rhetorical question 'HRM: still marching on or marching out?' is that the debate is still progressing, with very little sign that it will abate in the short term. There are many aspects of HRM approaches to managing the employment relationship which contain notes of contradiction, not the least of which are the implications of the restructuring of managerial careers noted at the beginning of this chapter. If it is accepted that HRM assumes a managerial frame of reference and requires managers to conduct it, then any impact on managerial career structure could be expected to have a potential bearing on the extent to which managers themselves are committed to high commitment management and work practices. The ambivalence of running these management processes in circumstances where managers, as individuals, are themselves vulnerable and under constant review of their competencies and commitment simply highlights the dilemmas bound up with HRM.

Nevertheless, HRM continues to stake its place in the analysis of the employment relationship and it is not possible to dismiss it out of hand, for as Legge (1995) points out:

> The importance of HRM as a rhetoric that speaks to the concerns of a wide range of stakeholder groups – personnel and line managers, government and academics – should not be underestimated.

SUMMARY

● Human Resource Management presents significant issues for the analysis and operation of the employment relationship. The management of employees is one of the key elements in the coordination and general management of work organisations. Considerable controversy exists as to the origins, characteristics and philosophy of HRM, and its capacity to influence the nature of that relationship. The debate surrounding HRM can be characterised by these four predominant approaches:

- HRM as a contemporary 'restatement' of industrial relations and personnel management policies;
- HRM as a 'fusion' of industrial relations and personnel management to create a 'new' management discipline and function;
- HRM as a 'resource based' approach, stressing the potential of the individual employee in terms of an investment rather than a cost;
- HRM as a 'strategic/international' phenomenon, making a determining contribution to corporate strategy and capable of being translated across cultures.

● The origins of HRM are indistinct but may be traced back to the 1950s in the United States. By the early 1980s a number of US analysts were writing about HRM and devising models and explanations for its emergence. Among the most significant of these commentators are Devanna (the matching model), Beer (the Harvard model), and Walton. In the UK significant commentary on HRM has been provided by Guest, Pettigrew and Hendry, Storey and Poole.

● For Guest the test of HRM is its applicability 'in the field' and its capacity to satisfy some key propositions such as 'strategic integration', 'high commitment', 'high quality' and 'flexibility'. Pettigrew and Hendry stress the analytical elements of the Harvard model and argue that HRM is characterised by its close alignment with business strategy. Storey defines the 'schools' of HRM – 'hard' (rooted in the manpower planning tradition) and 'soft' (rooted in the human relations approach to organisational analysis), and has developed a model which sets out four areas for analysis: beliefs and assumptions; strategic aspects; line management; key levers as major determinants of HRM practice. Poole has suggested that the Harvard model of HRM is useful in the study of comparative HRM.

● Particularly critical perspectives on HRM in the UK have been provided by Legge, Armstrong and Keenoy. Legge argues that the underlying values of Personnel Management and HRM differ little, and that organisational constraints may well make a truly integrated HRM approach highly impractical, while Armstrong has noted that financial orientations may well clash with HRM prescriptions. Keenoy sees HRM as being constructed around the highly ambiguous nature of the term, which can come to mean anything to anyone.

● Whatever the perspective taken on HRM, two important points cannot be overlooked: the first is that it has raised questions about the nature of the employment relationship that have stimulated one of the most intense and active debates to have occurred in the subject over the past forty years; the second is that the management of employment relations and the question of employee commitment to the employment relationship remain at the heart of the debate.

ACTIVITY

Personnel values

Does the human resource department have a future?
Richard Donkin reports

If the late spaghetti western producer Sergio Leone had made a feature film about personnel management – and the likelihood of that was about as remote as the planet Pluto – he would probably have billed it *The Job With No Name*. Its sheer fuzziness and lack of hard performance measures are a constant source of frustration in management circles, as well as provoking suspicions among employees and scepticism among academics. The Trades Union Congress, for instance, recently wrestled with the meaning of human resource management – as personnel is sometimes called – describing it as a "slippery concept" and questioning the motive behind some HRM practices.

The formation earlier this year of the Institute of Personnel and Development – the professional body combining the old Institute of Personnel Management and the Institute of Training and Development – came at a time when some companies were dispensing with their personnel departments completely, choosing to assign the responsibility to line managers. Indeed at this week's annual conference of the

IPD in Harrogate, which finishes today, Sir Brian Pitman, the chief executive of Lloyds Bank, told delegates that removing the central personnel department at Lloyds was one of the most effective changes the bank had made.

He said: "Line managers now understand the pains of some of the decisions that personnel has to take."

However, in spite of this, there seems a sense among delegates that their time has finally come.

Mike Bett, the IPD president, summed it up by pointing to a growing recognition that the survival and success of organisations will increasingly depend on their ability to build highly skilled workforces and to release the full potential of employees. "There should be a professional personnel and development specialist on all top management teams: in the boardroom and on the executive committees," he suggested, adding that personnel should be involved in developing front-line boardroom strategy.

Bett's confidence in a rosy future, however, is not universally shared. Earlier in the year a team headed by David Metcalf at the London School of Economics described personnel specialists as "big hat, no cattle" with lots of pretentions and few results. Its research suggested that the presence of a personnel manager was associated with poorer employee relations.

Drawing from the same body of research as that used by the LSE team – the third Workplace Industrial Relations Survey – but taking a different definition of personnel, David Guest, of Birkbeck College in London, and Kim Hoque, a researcher at the LSE, presented a more positive picture. Their study concluded that HRM was producing superior performances in the workplace. The contribution of personnel specialists, said Guest and Hoque, had been difficult to identify because they often worked by exercising influence in partnership with line managers. This sometimes created ambiguity about personnel responsibilities so that when things went wrong it proved expedient to blame the personnel specialist.

Personnel's influence on strategy is equally a subject of debate and contradictory research. Guest and Hoque quote earlier research which suggests that personnel departments often have insufficient responsibility to influence human resource strategy. They noted another study, however, by Cranfield School of Management and Price Waterhouse International, which found that 43 per cent of personnel directors claim to be involved in the formulation of corporate strategy from the outset.

The IPD's response to personnel's uncertain role has been to place a strong emphasis on sifting good practice from bad in an effort to position itself in Bett's words, as "the pre-eminent professional body influencing and improving the quality, thinking and practice of people management and development".

On the one hand the IPD is promising to extend training and support for often hard-pressed personnel professionals, on the other it is wedging open the door, making itself accessible as a consultancy service and provider of books, reports, seminars and conferences.

Conscious of the jargon, Geoff Armstrong, the IPD's director general, has also committed the institute to encouraging greater clarity of the personnel role. "By removing jargon and barriers to understanding, we must spread the message that the development and management of people is much more than a series of fashionable programmes," he said shortly after the formation of the institute. He believes personnel is "a systematically learnable discipline, with a wide range of explicit competencies which need to be applied appropriately by everyone who has responsibility for other people".

The IPD has warned against what Armstrong calls the promotion by gurus of "the wonders of human resource management" at the expense of collectivism, industrial relations and some personnel procedures. "Performance management, single status and individually tailored payment packages are presented as the new snake oil which can achieve miracles anywhere", he says. "Such dogma is misleading and dangerous.

"Useful tools have been packaged up under the banner of human resource management and sold as panaceas, to be applied at any time and place. Without proper regard for the organisation's established culture and particular needs, most such flavours of the month prove deeply disappointing."

The role of the personnel officer or manager, argues Armstrong, is to apply new practices where they are helpful and

▶

26

where they can be adapted to the specific needs of organisations. "We have seen recently the immense problems which arise when performance-related pay, decentralised bargaining and commercial imperatives are imposed as though they, in isolation, can provide all the answers in our schools and hospitals," he said.

He is distancing the IPD from the concept that HRM should be used as an exploitative tool of management. What lessons can be drawn from human resource management? Will it be a distinct learnable discipline at the cutting edge of organisational and employee development in the 21st century or will it fade away, remembered only as a brave attempt to bag up an elusive set of ideas? The challenge for personnel is to maintain its separate identity in the shifting emphasis within rapidly changing organisations. Leading that shift could ensure that it has a bright future.

Source: The *Financial Times*, 28 October 1994.

EXERCISES

Read the above article and discuss the questions that relate to it. Consider how far the questions raised by the article touch on themes in this chapter.

1 How far is HRM a systematic approach to managing people?

2 What obligations do managers have to ensure equity in an HRM culture?

3 How far does HRM affect managers as well as employers?

REFERENCES AND FURTHER READING

Those texts marked with an asterisk are recommended for further reading.

Adler, N.J. and Ghadar, F. (1989) 'International business research for the twenty first century: Canada's new research agenda', in Rugman, A. (ed.) *Research in Global Strategic Management: A Canadian Perspective*, Vol. 1. Greenwich, Conn.: JAI Press.

Armstrong, M. (1987) 'Human resource management: A case of the emperor's new clothes?', *Personnel Management*, Vol. 19, No. 8.

Armstrong, P. (1989) 'Limits and possibilities for HRM in an age of management accountancy', in Storey, J. (ed.) *New Perspectives on Human Resource Management*. London: Routledge.

Beardwell, I.J. (1992) 'The new industrial relations – a review of the debate', *Human Resource Management Journal*, Vol. 2, No. 2.

*Beer, M., Spector, B., Lawrence P.R., Quinn Mills, D. and Walton, R.E. (1984) *Managing Human Assets*. New York: Free Press.

Beer, M. and Spector, B. (1985) 'Corporate wide transformations in human resource management', in Walton, R.E. and Lawrence, E.R. (eds) *Human Resource Management Trends and Challenges*. Boston, Mass.: Harvard Business School Press.

Boxall, P.F. (1992) 'Strategic human resource management: Beginnings of a new theoretical sophistication?', *Human Resource Management Journal*, Vol. 2, No. 3, Spring.

*Boxall, P. (1996) 'The strategic HRM debate and the resource-based view of the firm', *Human Resource Management Journal*, Vol. 6, No. 3, pp. 59–75.

*Brewster, C. and Bournois, F. (1991) 'Human resource management: A European perspective', *Personnel Review*, Vol. 20, No. 6, pp. 4–13.

Chandler, A. (1962) *Strategy and Structure*. Cambridge, Mass.: Harvard University Press.

Constable, J. and McCormick, R. (1987) *The Manning of British Managers*. London: British Institute of Management.

Coopers & Lybrand (1985) *A Challenge of Complacency: Changing Attitudes to Training*. London: MSC/NEDO.

*Devanna, M.A., Fombrun, C.J. and Tichy, N.M. (1984) 'A framework for a strategic human resource management', in Fombrun *et al.* (eds) *Strategic Human Resource Management*. New York: John Wiley

Evans, P.A.L. and Lorange, P. (1989) 'Two logics behind human resource management', in Evans, P., Doz, Y. and Laurent, A. (eds) *Human Resource Management in International Firms*. Basingstoke: Macmillan.

Fernie, S., Metcalf, D. and Woodland, S. (1994) *Does HRM Boost Employee Management Relations?* London: LSE CEP Working Paper No. 546.

*Fombrun, C.J., Tichy, N.M. and Devanna, M.A. (1984) *Strategic Human Resource Management*. New York: John Wiley.

Fombrun, C.J. (1984) 'The external context of human resource management', in Fombrun, C.J., Tichy, N.M. and Devanna, M.A. (eds) *Strategic Human Resource Management*. New York: John Wiley.

Fowler, A. (1987) 'When the chief executive discovers HRM', *Personnel Management*, Vol. 19, No. 3.

*Gaugler, E. (1988) 'HR management: an international comparison', *Personnel*, August, pp. 24–30.

Guest, D. (1987) 'Human resource management and industrial relations', *Journal of Management Studies*, Vol. 24, No. 5, pp. 503–521.

*Guest, D. (1989a) 'Personnel and human resource management: can you tell the difference?', *Personnel Management*, January.

Guest, D. (1989b) 'Human resource management: its implications for industrial relations and trade unions', in Storey, J. (ed.) *New Perspectives on Human Resource Management*. London: Routledge.

*Guest, D. (1990) 'Human resource management and the American dream', *Journal of Management Studies*, Vol. 27, No. 4, pp. 377–397.

*Guest, D. and Hoque, K. (1996) 'Human resource management and the new industrial relations', in Beardwell, I. (ed.) *Contemporary Industrial Relations*. Oxford: Oxford University Press.

Handy, C. (1987) 'The making of managers', *Report on Management Education, Training and Development in the United States, West Germany, France, Japan and the UK*. London: NEDO.

Hendry, C. and Pettigrew, A. (1986) 'The practice of strategic human resource management', *Personnel Review*, Vol. 15, No. 5, pp. 3–8.

Hendry, C. and Pettigrew, A. (1990) 'Human resource management: an agenda for the 1990s', *International Journal of Human Resource Management*, Vol. 1, No. 1.

*Huselid, M. (1995) 'The impact of HRM practices on turnover, productivity and corporate financial performance', *Academy of Management Journal*, Vol. 38, No. 3, pp. 635–672.

Kanter, R. (1984) *The Change Masters*. London: Allen & Unwin.

Keenoy, T. (1990a) 'HRM: a case of the wolf in sheep's clothing?', *Personnel Review*, Vol. 19, No. 2, pp. 3–9.

*Keenoy, T. (1990b) 'Human resource management: rhetoric, reality and contradiction', *The International Journal of Human Resource Management*, Vol. 1, No. 3, December, pp. 363–384.

Keenoy, T. and Anthony P. (1992) 'Human resource management: metaphor, meaning and morality', in Blyton, P. and Turnbull, P. (eds) *Reassessing Human Resource Management*. London: Sage.

Kelly, J. and Gennard, J. (1994) 'HRM: The views of personnel directors', *Human Resource Management Journal*, Vol. 5, No. 1, pp. 15–30.

*Kochan, T.A., Katz, H.C. and McKersie, R.B. (1986) *The Transformation of American Industrial Relations*. New York: Basic Books.

*Legge, K. (1989) 'Human resource management: a critical analysis', in Storey, J. (ed.) *New Perspectives on Human Resource Management*. London: Routledge.

*Legge, K. (1995) *HRM: Rhetorics and Realities*. Basingstoke: Macmillan Business.

Marginson, P., Armstrong, P., Edwards, P., Purcell, J. and Hubbard, N. (1993) *The Control of Industrial Relations in Large Companies*. Warwick Papers in Industrial Relations No. 45, IRRV School of Industrial and Business Studies, University of Warwick.

*Millar, P. (1991) 'Strategic human resource management: an assessment of progress', *Human Resource Management Journal*, Vol. 1, No. 4, Summer.

*Niven, M.M. (1967) *Personnel Management 1913-1963*. London: IPM.

Peters, T. and Waterman, R. (1982) *In Search of Excellence*. New York: Harper & Row.

Pfeffer, J. (1994) *Competitive Advantage Through People*. Boston, MA: Havard Business School Press.

Pieper, R. (ed.) (1990) *Human Resource Management: An International Comparison*. New York: Walter de Gruyter.

Poole, M. (1990) 'Editorial: Human resource management in an international perspective', *The International Journal of Human Resource Management*, Vol. 1, No. 1, June.

*Poole, M. (1986) *Industrial Relations: Origins and Patterns of National Diversity*. London: Routledge & Kegan Paul.

*Prahalad, G. and Hamel, C.K. (1990) 'The core competencies of the corporation', *Harvard Business Review*, May–June, pp. 79–91.

*Pucik, V. (1984) 'The international management of human resources', in Fombrun, C.J., Tichy, N.M. and Devanna, M.A. (eds) *Strategic Human Resource Management*. New York: John Wiley.

*Purcell, J. (1995) 'Corporate strategy and its link with human resource management strategy', in Storey, J. (ed.) *Human Resource Management: A Critical Text*. London: Routledge.

Purcell, J. (1996) *Human Resource Bundles of Best Practice: A Utopia Cul-de-sac?* Paper presented to ESRC Seminar on *Contribution of HR Strategy to Business Performance*, Cranfield.

Purcell, J. and Ahlstrand, B. (1994) *Human Resource Management in the Multi-Divisional Company*. Oxford: Oxford University Press.

Storey, J. (ed.) (1989) *New Perspectives on Human Resource Management*. London: Routledge.

Storey, J. (1992) *Developments in the Management of Human Resources: An Analytical Review.* London: Blackwell.

*Storey, J. (1995) *Human Resource Management: A Critical Text.* London: Routledge.

Walton, R.E. (1985) 'From control to commitment in the workplace', *Harvard Business Review*, Vol. 63, No. 2, March–April.

Wood, S. (1995) 'The four pillars of HRM: are they connected?', *Human Resource Management Journal*, Vol. 5, No. 5, pp. 49–59.

HUMAN RESOURCE
MANAGEMENT IN CONTEXT

Audrey Collin

OBJECTIVES

To indicate the significance of context for the understanding
of HRM.

●

To discuss ways of conceptualising and representing the nature of
context generally and this context in particular.

●

To analyse the nature of the immediate context of HRM: the problematical nature of organisations and the need for management.

●

To indicate the nature of the wider context of HRM and illustrate
this through selected examples.

●

To examine how our ways of interpreting and defining reality for
ourselves and others construct and influence how we understand
and practise HRM: perception, epistemology and ideology.

●

To suggest the implications for the readers of this book.

●

To present a number of activities that will facilitate readers'
understanding of the context of HRM.

●

INTRODUCTION

The significance and nature of context

An event seen from one point-of-view gives one impression. Seen from another point-of-view it gives quite a different impression. But it's only when you get the whole picture you fully understand what's going on.

Source: Copyright © *The Guardian.*

This advertisement for *The Guardian* newspaper a few years ago made its point by showing how we need to be aware of the context of human affairs in order to understand them. We can easily misinterpret facts, events and people when we examine them out of context, for it is their context that provides us with the clues necessary to enable us to understand them. Context locates them in space and time and gives them a past and a future, as well as the present that we see. It gives us the language to understand them, the codes to decode them, the keys to their meaning.

This chapter will carry forward your thinking about the issues raised in Chapter 1 by exploring the various strands within the context of HRM that are woven together to form the patterns of meanings that constitute it. As the last chapter explained, and the rest of the book will amplify, HRM is far more than a portfolio of policies, practices, procedures and prescriptions concerned with the management of the employment relationship. It is this, but more. And because it is more, it is loosely defined and difficult to pin down precisely, a basket of multiple, overlapping and shifting meanings, which users of the term do not always specify. Its 'brilliant ambiguity' (Keenoy, 1990) derives from the context in which it is embedded, a context within which there are multiple and often competing perspectives upon the employment relationship, some ideological, others theoretical, some conceptual. HRM is inevitably a contested terrain, and the various definitions of it reflect this.

You will recognise in the various models of HRM presented in Chapter 1 that this context is a highly complex one, not just because of its increasing diversity and dynamism, but also because it is multi-layered, each of these layers affecting the others. The organisation constitutes the immediate context of the employment relationship, and the debate over how this relationship should be managed begins here. The nature of organisation and the tensions between the stakeholders in it give rise to issues that have to be addressed by managers, for example, choices about how to orchestrate the activities of organisational members and whose interests to serve. These issues of managerial control are of considerable significance for HRM, as subsequent chapters indicate.

Beyond the organisation itself lie the economic, social, political and cultural layers and beyond them again the historical, national and global layers of the context. Considerable change is taking place within those layers, making the whole field dynamic. It is not the purpose of this chapter to register these many changes; you will become aware of some of them as you read the remainder of this book, particularly Chapters 1 and 3. However, we need to note here that the events and changes in the wider context have repercussions for organisations and present further issues to be managed and choices to be made.

The various layers and the elements within them, however, exist in more than one conceptual plane. One has a concrete nature, like a local pool of labour, and the other is abstract, like the values and stereotypes that prejudice employers for or against a particular class of person in the labour market. The abstract world of ideas and values overlays the various layers of the context of HRM: the ways of organising society, of acquiring and using power, and of distributing resources; the ways of relating to, understanding and valuing human beings and their activities; the ways of studying and understanding reality and of acquiring knowledge; the stocks of accumulated knowledge in theories and concepts.

It is the argument of this chapter that to understand HRM we need to be aware not just of the multiple layers of its context – rather like the skins of an onion – but also of these conceptual planes and the way they intersect. We are, therefore, using 'context' to mean more than the surrounding circumstances that exert 'external influences' on a given topic: context gives them a third dimension. We are arguing, further, that events and experiences, ideas and ideologies are not discrete and able to be isolated, but are interwoven and interconnected. Moreover, HRM itself is embedded in its context: it is part of that web and cannot, therefore, be meaningfully examined separately from it. Context is highly significant yet, as we shall see, very difficult to study.

Conceptualising and representing context

How can we begin to understand any subject that is embedded in a complex context? We seem to have awareness at an intuitive level, perceiving and acting upon the clues that context gives to arrive at the 'tacit knowledge' discussed later in Chapter 7. However, context challenges our formal thinking. In order to be able to see a subject in its context, we need to be able to stand back to take in the wider picture (and to reflect upon it, as Chapter 7 suggests). It is not easy for HRM practitioners and theorists to obtain this perspective when they are also part of that picture. The context of HRM is theirs too. They are like the fish in water that 'can have no understanding of the concept of "wetness" since it has no idea of what it means to be dry' (Southgate and Randall, 1981: 54). We have, therefore, to stand back as far as we can to take their interpretations of HRM into consideration, although we, too, are bounded by context.

Second, we need the conceptual tools to grasp the whole (and dynamic) picture. To understand a social phenomenon such as HRM, we cannot just wrench it from its context and examine it microscopically in isolation. To do this is to be like the child who digs up the newly planted and now germinating seed to see 'whether it is growing'. In the same way, if we analyse context into its various elements and layers, then we are already distorting our understanding of it, because it is an indivisible whole. Rather, we have to find ways to examine its interconnectedness and interdependence with other phenomena.

The study of context, therefore, is no easy task, and poses a major challenge to our established formal, analytical and detached ways of thinking. Nevertheless, as we shall discuss later in this chapter, there are ways forward that will enable us to conceptualise formally the many loops and circularities of these complex interrelationships in an often dynamic context.

FIGURE 2.1
HRM: the warp and weft of a tapestry

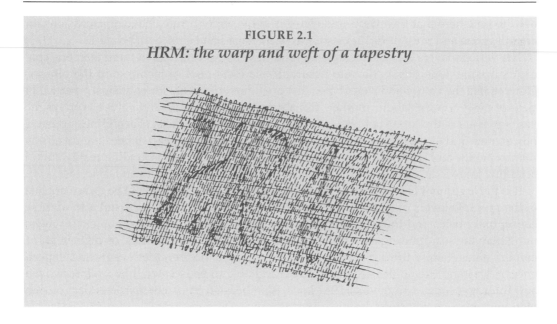

Meanwhile, we shall try to conceptualise it through metaphor; that is, envisage it in terms of something concrete that we already understand. We shall use the metaphor of a tapestry, for this conveys interconnectedness and texture: tapestry is a 'thick hand-woven textile fabric in which design is formed by weft stitches across parts of warp' (*Concise OED*, 1982). This allows us to become aware of the different dimensions of context: the warp threads that run the length of the tapestry, the weft as the lateral threads that weave through the warp to give colour, pattern and texture. In terms of this metaphor, our ways of seeing and thinking about our world are the warp, the threads that run the length of the tapestry contributing to its basic form and texture. They, therefore, play their part throughout the context of HRM. Ideologies and the rhetoric through which they are expressed are the weft threads that weave through the warp threads to give the tapestry pattern and texture. Events, people, ephemeral issues are the stitches that form the surface patterns and texture of HRM. We see this in Figure 2.1. In the case of the context of HRM, this tapestry is being woven continuously from threads of different colours and textures. At times one colour predominates, but then peters out. In parts of the tapestry patterns are intentionally fashioned; while observers (such as the authors of this book) believe they can discern a recognisable pattern in other parts.

This metaphor again reminds us that an analytical approach to the study of context, by taking it apart to examine it closely, would be like taking a tapestry to bits: we would be left with threads. The tapestry itself inheres in the whole, not its parts. How, then, can the chapter begin to communicate the nature of this tapestry without destroying its very essence through analysis? The very representation of our thinking in written language is linear, and this incapacitates our ability to communicate a dynamic, interrelated complexity clearly and succinctly. We need to think in terms of the 'mind-maps' or 'rich pictures' (Checkland, 1981; Cameron, 1991) devised to express systems thinking, to which we shall later return, or we can follow the key contextual trends in Morgan (1988), as illustrated in Figure 2.2.

It is not feasible nor, indeed, necessary to attempt to portray the whole tapestry in detail; we shall focus instead upon a number of strands that run through it. You will be able to identify and follow them through the remainder of the book, and observe how their interweaving gives us changes in pattern and colour, some distinct, others subtle. Before beginning to read our exposition of the context of HRM, you will find it helpful to return to the various models that were presented in Chapter 1 in order to identify some of the elements of context and the relationships between them that we shall be describing. This will help you keep the total picture in mind as we discuss parts of it. In this way you will develop some more appropriate mental 'hooks' upon which to hang your new understanding.

We shall begin with the immediate context of HRM and note how the nature of organisations presents their managers with choices over how to manage people. We shall then examine a number of the choices that managers make and some of the interpretations that theorists make of them. We shall then look briefly at the wider context of HRM, picking out a few elements to examine. It is when we turn to the outer layers of the world of ideas, philosophies and ideologies that we become fully aware of the need to represent context as a tapestry rather than a many-skinned onion, for we find there various strands of meaning that managers and academics are drawing upon to make sense of HRM.

The concepts and language needed to understand context

To understand context, we have suggested, we need to stand back as far as we can from it. We, therefore, need to move beyond description of the concrete world to the abstract world of ideas. Although the appropriate language to enable us to do this may be largely unfamiliar to you, you will find that you already have considerable understanding of the concepts it expresses. Your own experience in thinking about and responding to the wider environment will have given you the basic concepts we are using and a useful set of 'hooks' upon which to hang the new knowledge this chapter will give you. We, therefore, suggest that you examine some of the 'hooks' you are already using to think about the environment, and perhaps clarify and refine them, so that they can be helpful to your understanding of this chapter. (In this way, as Chapter 7 explains, the new material can be more effectively transferred into and retrieved from your long-term memory.)

The Activity at the end of the chapter proposes an exercise that will focus your thinking and enable you to recognise that you already have the 'hooks' you will need to classify the material of this chapter in a meaningful way and increase your understanding of the nature of the context of HRM. For example, you recognise the following:

● the multi-layered, multi-dimensional, interwoven nature of the environment in which concrete events and abstract ideas intertwine to create issues, and thinking, feeling, interpreting and behaving are all involved: it is like the *tapestry* described earlier in the section;
● our understanding depends upon our *perspective;*
● it also depends upon our *ideology;*
● there are, therefore, *competing or contested interpretations* of events;

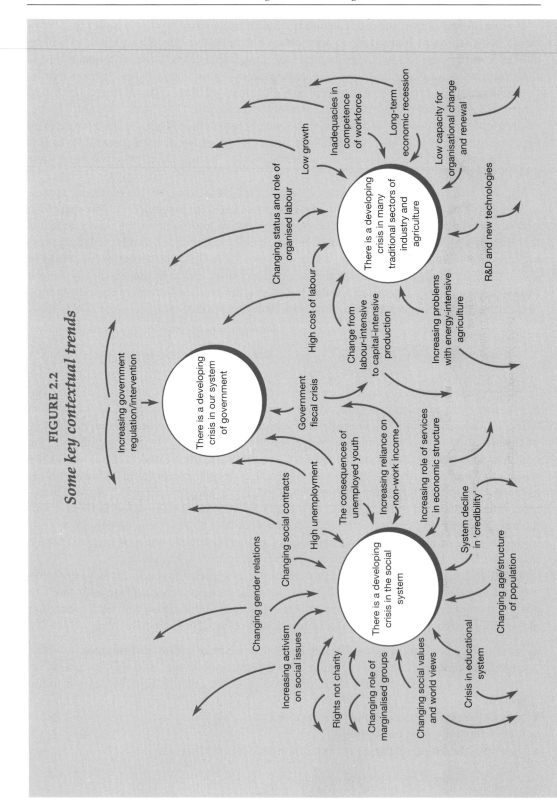

FIGURE 2.2
Some key contextual trends

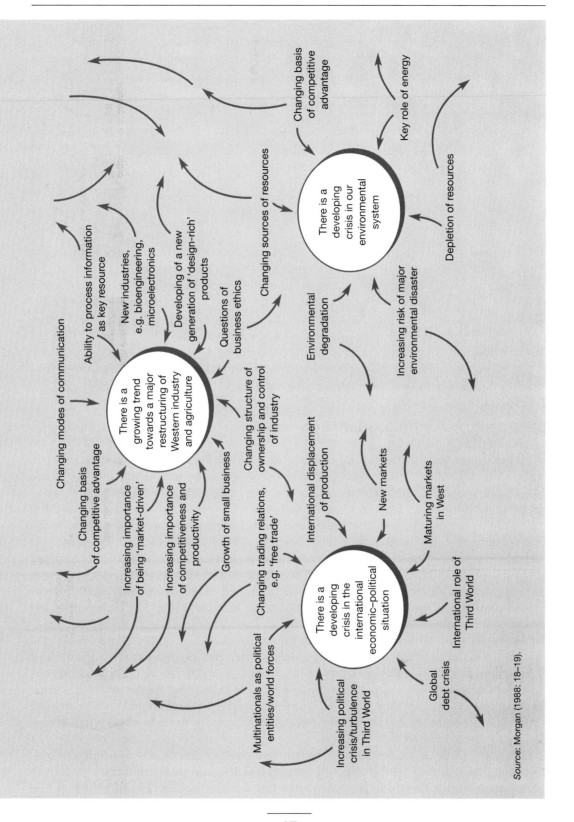

Source: Morgan (1988: 18–19).

- different groups in society have their own interpretations of events, stemming from their *ideology*, which incorporate an explanation for competing interpretations. They use the *rhetoric* of their own interpretations to express competing interpretations, thus suppressing the expression of competing views;
- there are powerful others who try to impose their interpretations of events, their version of reality, upon the less powerful majority: this is *hegemony*.

This subsection has perhaps given you a new language to describe what you already understand well. Later sections of this chapter will amplify the definitions of these concepts and use them in its exploration of the context of HRM.

THE IMMEDIATE CONTEXT OF HRM

Human resource management, however defined, concerns the management of the employment relationship: it is practised in organisations by managers. The nature of the organisation and the way it is managed, therefore, constitute the immediate context within which HRM is embedded, and generate the tensions that HRM policies and practices attempt to resolve. In this section we shall be introducing the theme of managerial control that recurs throughout this book, noting the ways in which it is exercised through the management of performance and the devolving of decision making or empowerment. This section will also note the deeper questions about managing people that such issues imply, which we shall later trace through the outer layers of the context of HRM.

The nature of organisations and the need for management

At its simplest, an organisation comes into existence when the efforts of two or more people are pooled to achieve an objective that one would be unable to complete alone. The achievement of this objective calls for the completion of a number of tasks. Depending upon their complexity, the availability of appropriate technology and the skills of the people involved, these tasks may be subdivided into a number of sub-tasks and other people employed to help carry them out. This division of labour constitutes the lateral dimension of the structure of the organisation. Its vertical dimension is constructed from the generally hierarchical relationships of power and authority between the owner or owners, those employed to complete these tasks, and the managers employed to coordinate and control the workers and their working activities. Working on behalf of the organisation's owners or shareholders and with the authority derived from them, managers draw upon a number of resources to enable them to complete their task: raw materials; finance; technology; appropriately skilled people; legitimacy, support and goodwill from the organisation's environment. They manage the organisation by ensuring that there are sufficient people with appropriate skills, that they work to the same ends and timetable, that they have the authority, information and other resources needed to complete their tasks, that their tasks dovetail and are performed to an acceptable standard and at the required pace.

The very nature of organisation, therefore, generates a number of significant tensions: between people with different stakes in the organisation, and therefore different perspectives upon and interests in it; between what owners and other members of the organisation may desire and what they can feasibly achieve; between the needs, capabilities and potentials of organisational members and what the environment demands of and permits them. Management is the process that keeps the organisation from flying apart because of these tensions, that makes it work, secures its survival and, according to the type of organisation, its profitability or effectiveness. Inevitably, however, as Chapter 11 discusses, managerial control is a significant and often contentious issue.

The need to manage people and relationships is inherent in the managing of an organisation, but the very nature of people and the way they constitute an organisation makes management complex. Although the organisation of tasks packages people into organisational roles, individuals are larger and more organic than those roles tend to be. The organisation, writes Barnard (1938, in Schein, 1978: 17) *'pays* people only for certain of their *activities* . . . but it is *whole persons* who come to work'. Unlike other resources, people interact with those who manage them and among themselves, they have needs for autonomy and agency, they think and are creative, they have feelings, they need consideration for their emotional and their physical needs and protection. Their characteristics as human beings greatly complicate the tasks of managers who can only work with and through people to ensure that the organisation survives and thrives in the face of increasing pressures from the environment.

The management of people is, therefore, not only a more diffuse and complex task than the management of other resources, but also an essentially moral one. Owners and managers are confronted with choices about how to manage people and resolve organisational tensions. The next subsection examines some of these choices and the strategies adopted to handle them. We must first, however, note that as organisations become larger and more complex, the division of managerial labour often leads to a specialist 'people' function to advise and support line managers in the complex and demanding tasks of managing their staff. This is the personnel function, which has developed a professional and highly skilled expertise into certain aspects of managing people, such as selection, training and industrial relations, which it offers in an advisory capacity to line managers who nevertheless remain the prime managers of people. However, this division of labour has fragmented the management of people: human resource management can be seen as a strategy to re-integrate it into the management of the organisation as a whole.

The approaches adopted by managers to resolve the tensions in organisations

The previous subsection suggested that there are inherent tensions in organisations. In brief, these are generated by:

- the existence of several stakeholders in the employment relationship;
- their differing perspectives upon events, experiences and relationships;
- their differing aims, interests and needs;
- the interplay between formal organisation and individual potential.

These tensions have to be resolved through the process of management, or rather, continuously resolved, for these tensions are inherent in organisations. A continuing issue, therefore, is that of managerial control: how to orchestrate organisational activities in a way that meets the needs of the various stakeholders. The owners of organisations or those who manage them on their behalf have explored many ways to resolve these tensions: the emergence of HRM to develop alongside, subsume or replace personnel management is witness to this. The strategies they adopt are embodied in their employment policies and practices and the organisational systems they choose to put in place (see also Chapters 5 and 11). They are also manifested in the psychological contract they have with their employees, the often unstated set of expectations between organisation and individual that embroiders the legal employment contract. In this subsection we shall briefly outline some of the strategies they have adopted, while in the next subsection we shall discuss the interpretations of theorists and other commentators of the choices managers make. However, we must keep in mind that managers are to some extent influenced by the concepts and language, if not the arguments, of these theorists.

In very crude terms, we can identify four strategies that managers have adopted to deal with these tensions. The first is represented by what is called scientific management, or the classical school of management theory. The second is the human relations approach, and the third could be labelled a contingency (or even a human resource management) approach. The fourth approach is perhaps more an ideal than a common reality. It must be emphasised that these brief pen-pictures cannot do justice to the rich variety of approaches that can be found in organisations. You can elaborate upon the material here by reading the different views and models of Drucker (1954, 1980), Braverman (1974), Rose (1978) and Quinn *et al.* (1990).

The first approach addressed the tensions in the organisation by striving to control people and keep down their costs: the scientific management approach. It emphasised the need for rationality, clear objectives, the managerial prerogative, the right of managers to manage and adopted work study and similar methods. These led to the reduction of tasks to their basic elements and the grouping of similar elements together to produce low-skilled, low-paid jobs, epitomised by assembly-line working, with a large measure of interchangeability between workers. Workers tended to be treated relatively impersonally and collectively ('management and labour') and the nature of the psychological contract with them was calculative, with a focus on extrinsic rewards and incentives. Such a strategy encouraged a collective response from workers, and hence the development of trade unions.

These views of management evolved in North America. In Britain they overlaid the norms of a complex, though changing, social class system that frames the relationships between managers and other employees (Child, 1969; Mant, 1979). This facilitated the acceptance of the outcomes of the X-theory management (McGregor, 1960): hierarchy; paternalism; the attribution to workers of childlike qualities, laziness, limited aspirations and time horizons. Its limitations are identified by Argyris (1960). While this strategy epitomised particularly the management approach of the first half of the century, it has not been completely abandoned (see Clegg, 1990) and, moreover, has left its legacy in many areas such as organisation and method study, job analysis and description, selection methods, an overriding concern for efficiency and the 'bottom line', appraisal and performance management.

The human relations approach to the tensions in organisations emerged during the middle years of the century and developed in parallel with an increasingly prosperous society in which there were strong trade unions and (later) a growing acceptance of the right of individuals to achieve self-fulfilment. Child (1969) identifies its emergence in British management thinking as a response to growing labour tensions. It tempered scientific management by its recognition that people differed from other resources, that – if they were treated as clock numbers rather than as human beings – they would not be fully effective at work and could even fight back to the point of subverting management intentions. It also recognised the significance of social relationships at work, the informal organisation (Argyris, 1960). Managers, therefore, had to pay attention to the nature of supervision and the working of groups and teams, and to find ways of involving employees through job design (see Chapter 5), motivation, and a democratic, consultative or participative style of management. The nature of the psychological contract was cooperative.

The third and most recent approach adopted by managers to address the tensions within the organisation has developed as major changes and threats have been experienced in the context of organisations (recession, international competition, Japan's business success). It is a response to the need to achieve flexibility in the organisation and workforce (see Chapters 3 and 5) and improved performance through devolving decision making and empowerment (see Chapter 14) and, as Chapter 7 indicates, requiring that employees become multi-skilled and work across traditional boundaries. This approach, therefore, attempts to integrate the needs of employees with those of the organisation in an explicit manner. The psychological contract embodies mutuality. It recognises that people should be invested in as assets so that they achieve their potential for the benefit of the organisation. As such, employees are approached individually rather than collectively.

Unlike the other two strategies for dealing with tensions in the organisation, the third approaches the organisation holistically and often with greater attention to its culture, leadership and 'vision', the 'soft' Ss of McKinsey's 'Seven S' framework (Pascale and Athos, 1982: 202–206). It also pays greater attention to the individual rather than the collective, so that these notions of developing the individual's potential have been accompanied by individual contracts of employment (see Chapter 11), performance appraisal and performance-related pay (Chapter 13).

The very title of 'HRM' suggests that this third approach to the management of organisational tensions is also an instrumental one. Although it differs greatly from the approaches that see labour as a 'cost', to be reduced or kept in check, it construes individuals as a resource for the organisation to use. The fourth, idealistic, humanistic approach aims to construct the organisation as an appropriate environment for autonomous individuals to work together collaboratively for their common good. This is the approach of many cooperatives. It also informed the early philosophy of organisation development (see Huse, 1980), although the practice of this is now largely instrumental, and it underpins the notion of the learning organisation (Senge, 1990).

When we look more deeply into the various strategies, we can recognise that they implicate some much deeper questions. Underlying the management of people in organisations are some fundamental assumptions about the nature of people and reality itself, and hence about organising and managing. For example, managers make assumptions about the nature of the organisation, many interpreting it as having an objective reality that exists separately from themselves and other organisational members – they reify it. They make assumptions about the nature of their goals, which they identify as the goals of the organisation. They make assumptions about the appropriate distribution of limited power throughout the organisation.

These assumptions are rarely made explicit and they are, therefore, rarely challenged. Moreover, many other members of the organisation appear to accept these premises on which they are managed, even though such assumptions virtually disempower or disenfranchise them. For example, many may assert the need for equal opportunities to jobs, training and promotion, but do not necessarily challenge the process of managing itself despite its gender-blind nature (Hearn *et al.*, 1989).

Nevertheless, these assumptions inform the practices and policies of management, and hence define the organisational and conceptual space that HRM fills and generate the multiple meanings of which HRM is constructed. We shall examine some of them in greater detail shortly.

Competing interpretations of organisations and management

When we stand back from the concrete world of managing to that of theories about organisations and management, we find that not only have very different interpretations been made over time, but there exist simultaneously several strongly competing interpretations. Again, we can only skim over this material, but you can pursue the issues by reading, for example, Child (1969), who traces the development of management thought in Britain, or Morgan (1986), who examines in a very accessible way eight different metaphors or ways that theorists as well as others have construed organisations. Clegg (1990) follows the development of organisation theory into the 'postmodern' world, which we shall return to in the next main section, while Reed and Hughes (1992: 10–11) identify the changing focus of this theory over the last thirty years from a concern with organisational stability, order and disorder, then with organisational power and politics, to the contemporary concern with the construction of organisational reality. Some of these changing concerns are seen below.

The reification of the organisation by managers and others, and the general acceptance of the need for it to have rational goals to drive it forward in an effective manner, has long been challenged. Simon (1947, in Morgan, 1986) recognised that rationality is 'bounded', that managers have to make decisions on the basis of limited and imperfect knowledge. Cyert and March (1963) adopt a similar viewpoint: the many stakeholders in an organisation make it a 'shifting multigoal coalition' (Pugh, Hickson and Hinings, 1983: 108) that has to be managed in a pragmatic manner. Others (see Pfeffer, 1981; Morgan, 1986) recognise the essentially conflictual and political nature of organisations: goals, structures and processes are defined, manipulated and managed in the interests of those holding the power in the organisation. Yet others have pointed us in new directions: the systems approach (Checkland, 1981), the learning organisation (Morgan, 1986; Senge, 1990), transformational leadership and 'excellence' (Peters and Waterman, 1982; Kanter, 1983), the significance of rhetoric (Eccles and Nohria, 1992), among many others.

The established views of managers are subject to further interpretations. Weick (1979) argues the need to focus upon the process of organising rather than its reified outcome, an organisation. Organising is a continuous process of meaning-making: 'organizations keep falling apart . . . require chronic rebuilding. Processes continually need to be re-accomplished' (Weick, 1979: 44). Cooper and Fox (1990) and Hosking and Fineman (1990) adopt a similar interpretation in their discussion of the 'texture of organizing'.

Brunsson (1989) throws a different light on the nature and goals of organising, based on his research in Scandinavian municipal administrations. He suggests that the outputs of these kinds of organisations are 'talk, decisions and physical products'. He proposes two 'ideal types' of organisation: the 'action' organisation that depends on action for its legitimacy (and hence essential resources) in the eyes of its environment, and the 'political' organisation that depends on its reflection of environmental inconsistencies for its legitimacy. Talk and decisions in the 'action' organisation (or an organisation in its action phase) lead to actions, whereas the outputs of the political organisation (or the organisation in its political phase) are talk and decisions that may or may not lead to action.

> . . . hypocrisy is a fundamental type of behaviour in the political organization: to talk in a way that satisfies one demand, to decide in a way that satisfies another, and to supply products in a way that satisfies a third.
>
> (Brunsson, 1989: 27)

There are similarly competing views upon organisational culture, as we see in Frost *et al.* (1991). The established view interprets it as a subsystem of the organisation that managers need to create and maintain through the promulgation and manipulation of values, norms, rites and symbols. The alternative view argues that culture is not something that an organisation *has*, but that it *is*.

Just as many managers leave their assumptions unaddressed and unstated, taken for granted, so that their actions appear to themselves and others based upon reason and organisational necessity, so also do many theorists. Many traditional theorists leave unstated that the organisations of which they write exist within a capitalist economic system and have to meet the needs of capital. They ignore the material and status needs of owners and managers, and their emotional (Fineman, 1993) and moral selves (Watson, 1994). Many also are gender-blind and take for granted a male world view of organisations. These issues tend to be identified and discussed only by those writers who wish to persuade their readers to a different interpretation of organisations (for example, Braverman, 1974; Hearn *et al.*, 1989).

Having now examined some of the choices managers make to deal with the tensions within organisations and some of the competing interpretations offered by theorists of those tensions and choices, we need to step back even further to become aware of the ways of thinking and of seeing that inform their assumptions. First, however, we shall examine the next layer of the context of HRM.

ECHOES FROM THE WIDER CONTEXT OF HRM

Defining the wider context

The definition of the wider context of HRM could embrace innumerable topics (for example, from the Industrial Revolution to globalisation) and a long time perspective (from the organisation of labour in such constructions as Stonehenge onwards, perhaps). Some of these contextual elements are represented in Morgan's (1988) 'key contextual trends', reproduced in Figure 2.2. Such a vast range, however, could only be covered in a perfunctory manner in a book of this kind, which would, therefore, render the exercise relatively valueless. It is more appropriate, first, to suggest that you identify for yourself what you consider to be the most important sources of influence upon HRM; and, second, to explore a few of these influences in a little detail. This is how we shall proceed.

EXERCISES

Go back to the models of HRM presented in Chapter 1 and start to elaborate upon the various contextual elements that they include. Look, for example, at the 'outer context' of Hendry and Pettigrew's (1990) model illustrated in Figure 1.5.

1 What in detail constitutes the elements of the socio-economic, technical, political-legal and competitive context?

2 What other influences would you add to these?

3 What are the relationships between them?

4 And what, in your view, have been their influence upon HRM?

Examples of influences upon HRM from the wider context

We shall now take just two elements from this context to note their impact on the field we are examining. The first example is of influence upon the management of the employment relationship from the sociopolitical sphere: the two world wars. This influence has already been exerted and, indirectly, is still being felt. The second example comes from the cultural sphere: the influence of modernism and the emergence of postmodernism.

Although what follows is not a complete analysis of these influences, it illustrates how the field of HRM resonates with events and ideas from its wider context.

The First World War and the Second World War

The two world wars, though distant in time and removed from the area of activity of HRM, have nevertheless influenced it in clearly identifiable and very important ways, some direct and some indirect. These effects can be classified in terms of changed attitudes of managers to labour, changed labour management practices, the development of personnel techniques, and the development of the personnel profession. We shall examine these and then note how the outcomes of the Second World War continue, indirectly, to influence HRM.

Changed attitudes of managers to labour

According to Child (1969: 44), the impact of the First World War upon industry hastened changes in attitudes to the control of the workplace that had begun before 1914. The development of the shop stewards' movement during the war increased demand for workers' control; there was growing 'censure of older and harsher methods of managing labour'. The recognition of the need for improved working conditions in munitions factories was continued in the postwar reconstruction debates: Child (1969: 49) quotes a Ministry of Reconstruction pamphlet that advised that 'the good employer profits by his "goodness".' The outcome of these various changes was a greater democratisation of the workplace (seen, for example, in works councils) and, for 'a number of prominent employers', a willingness 'to renounce autocratic methods of managing employees' and 'to treat labour on the basis of human rather than commodity market criteria' (Child, 1969: 45–46). These new values became incorporated in the newly emerging distinctive body of management thought, practice and ideology (see later section on ways of seeing and thinking), upon which later theory and practice are founded.

Changed labour management practices

The need to employ and deploy labour effectively led to increased attention to working conditions and practices during both wars; the changes that were introduced then continued and interacted with other social changes that ensued after the wars (Child, 1969). For example, the Health of Munitions Workers Committee, which encouraged the systematic study of human factors in stress and fatigue in the munitions factories during the First World War, was succeeded in 1918 by the Industrial Fatigue Research Board (DSIR, 1961; Child, 1969; Rose, 1978). During the postwar reconstruction period progressive employers advocated minimum wage levels, shorter working hours, and improved security of tenure (Child, 1969).

'The proper use of manpower whether in mobilizing the nation or sustaining the war economy once reserves of strength were fully deployed' was national policy during the Second World War (Moxon, 1951). As examples of this policy, Moxon cites the part-time employment of married women, the growth of factory medical services, canteens, day nurseries, and special leave of absence.

The development of personnel techniques

Both wars encouraged the application of psychological techniques to selection and training, and stimulated the development of new approaches. Rose (1978: 92) suggests that in 1917, the American army tested 2 million men to identify 'subnormals and officer material'. Seymour (1959: 7–8) writes of the Second World War:

> . . . the need to train millions of men and women for the fighting services led to a more detailed study of the skills required for handling modern weapons, and our understanding of human skill benefited greatly . . . Likewise, the shortage of labour in industry led . . . to experiments aimed at training munition workers to higher levels of output more quickly.

The wars further influenced the development of the ergonomic design of equipment, and encouraged the collaboration of engineers, psychologists and other social scientists (DSIR, 1961).

The exigencies of war ensured that attention and resources were focused upon activities that are of enormous significance to the field of employment, while the scale of operations guaranteed the availability for testing of numbers of candidates far in excess of those usually available to psychologists.

The development of the personnel profession

Very significantly, the Second World War had a major influence on the development of the personnel profession. According to Moxon (1951: 7), the aims of national wartime policy were:

> . . . (i) to see that the maximum use was made of each citizen, (ii) to see that working and living conditions were as satisfactory as possible, (iii) to see that individual rights were reasonably safeguarded and the democratic spirit preserved. The growth of personnel management was the direct result of the translation of this national policy by each industry and by each factory within an industry.

Child (1969: 111) reports how government concern in 1940 about appropriate working practices and conditions:

> . . . led to direct governmental action enforcing the appointment of personnel officers in all but small factories and the compulsory provision of minimum welfare amenities.

Moxon (1951: 7) comments on the 'four-fold increase in the number of practising personnel managers' at this time. Child (1969: 113) records the membership of what was to become the Institute of Personnel Management (and much more recently the Institute of Personnel and Development) as 760 in 1939, and 2993 in 1960. He also notes a similar increase in other management bodies.

The postwar reconstruction of Japan

We have so far noted some of the direct influences the two world wars had upon the field of HRM. We come now to an indirect and still continuing influence. The foundation of the philosophy and practice of total quality management, which is of considerable current significance in HRM, was laid during the Second World War. Edwards Deming and Joseph Juran were consultants to the US Defense Department and during the Second World War ran courses on their new approaches to quality control for firms supplying army ordnance (Pickard, 1992). Hodgson (1987: 40) reports on the outcomes:

> Vast quantities of innovative and effective armaments were produced by a labour force starved of skill or manufacturing experience in the depression.

After the war, America 'could sell everything it could produce' and, with the belief that 'improving quality adds to costs', the work of Deming and Juran was ignored in the West. However, Deming became an adviser to the Allied Powers Supreme Command and a member of the team advising the Japanese upon postwar reconstruction (Hodgson, 1987: 40–41). He told them that 'their war-ravaged country would become a major force in international trade' if they followed his approach to quality. They did.

Western organisations now attempt to emulate the philosophy and practices of quality that have proved so successful in Japan and, as you will read in this book, so influential in the preoccupations of human resource managers.

Modernism and postmodernism

It was in the fields of art and architecture, in which there had been early twentieth-century schools of thought identified as modernism, that new approaches became labelled 'postmodern'. Commentators upon culture recognised the relevance of the emerging concept of postmodernism to other fields. There followed in the 1980s a debate, which you can read about in Turner (1990), on the provenance, nature and direction of postmodernism; whether it is a continuation of or a disjunction with the past; whether it is the phenomena we experience or a critical approach to these phenomena.

The concept and ongoing debate have widened into the social sciences generally and are now permeating the HRM field. For example, Connock (1992) included post-modernist thinking among the contemporary 'big ideas' of significance to human resource managers. However, because these are current experiences upon which we cannot yet have a clear perspective, the terms of the debate are still far from clear. Connock's description is, necessarily, superficial; other commentators are suggesting that these developments are as significant in HRM as in other fields (Fox and Moult, 1990). We shall, therefore, briefly outline some of the characteristics of modernism and postmodernism, which we can now recognise as further sources of influence upon HRM.

In the field in which we are interested here, the questions about postmodernism merge with others on the topics of postindustrialism, post-Fordism, and the present stage of capitalism (see Reed and Hughes, 1992 and other chapters in this book). We can identify three strands of influence. The first is upon the nature of organisations and HRM; we shall note this below. The second is upon the nature of the individual. Although this, too, is relevant to the management of people in organisations, we shall not explore it further here, but you can read of it further in Collin (1996) and Reed and Hughes (1992: 214). The third influence is upon our way of looking at and understanding organisations.

Clegg (1990: 180–181) discusses the possible existence of a 'postmodern organisation' and, by contrasting it with a 'modernist organisation', identifies its characteristics. For example, he suggests that modernist organisations (that is, the organisations that we have been familiar with until the last decade or so) were rigid, addressed mass markets and were premised on technological determinism; their jobs were 'highly differentiated, demarcated and de-skilled'. Postmodernist organisations, however, are flexible, address niche markets and are premised on technological choices; their jobs are 'highly de-differentiated, de-demarcated and multiskilled'.

The recognition of a postmodern critique of organisations has greater potential value than this classification of organisations. (We are unable to do justice to Clegg's wider argument here.) You will find that the differences between the postmodern way of thinking about organisations and what preceded it echo some of the issues discussed in the following main sections of this chapter. Here you will find Reed and Hughes (1992) helpful.

Whereas the modernist discourse was premised on belief in a universal objective truth, knowable by means of rational, scientific approaches, postmodernism assumes that knowledge of reality is constructed and perspectival. Whereas modernism was premised on a belief in the possibility of social progress, for postmodernism everything is open to question and there are always alternative interpretations; it is eclectic in its recognition and acceptance of diversity. Whereas modernism often ignored or, indeed, disguised ideologies (see the section on ways of seeing and thinking), postmodernism is aware of the significance of such perspectives and so undermines the 'meta-narratives' that have constructed twentieth-century understanding, such as 'progress' and 'the value of science' or 'Marxism'. Whereas modernism treated language as a tool to reflect essential reality, postmodernism sees language as the means by which reality is constructed. Postmodernism encourages self-reflexivity and, therefore, a critical suspicion towards one's own interpretations, and an ironic and playful treatment of one's subject.

The postmodern critique of organisations leads to the recognition of multiple and competing views of organisations that are legitimate; that the significance of theory lies not in its 'truth' but in its usefulness for practice. (This, perhaps, is a significant issue for the learning organisation we discuss in Chapter 7.) The influences of modernism and postmodernism upon the field of HRM are identified in Fox and Moult (1990), and Fox (1990) interprets strategic HRM as a self-reflective cultural intervention responding to postmodern conditions.

We are all currently experiencing these phenomena and cannot, therefore, fully grasp their nature yet. However, we can now perhaps recognise from today's vantage point that the way in which we once conceptualised and managed the employment relationship was influenced by modernism. Moreover, it could now be argued that the emergence of HRM with its ambiguous, or debatable, nature, discussed in Chapter 1, is consistent with the spread of postmodern phenomena and postmodern critiques. The recognition of multiple, coexisting yet competing realities and interpretations, the constant re-interpretation, the eclecticism, the concern for presentation and re-presentation – all of which you will recognise in this book – can be interpreted as a postmodern rendering of the debate about the postmodern employment relationship. But, with a true postmodern irony and playfulness, there are also other interpretations . . .

WAYS OF SEEING AND THINKING

We shall now step right back from HRM and its immediate context to give our attention to our ways of seeing and thinking about our world; ways that generate the language, the code, the keys we use in conceptualising and practising HRM. To continue the metaphor of the tapestry, these ways of seeing are the warp, the threads that, running the length of the tapestry, give it its basic form and texture, but are generally not visible on its surface. They are more apparent, however, when we turn the tapestry over, as we are doing now. It can present a very different appearance then, the pattern and colour may seem very different. This section can only provide a brief introduction to some of these very profound subjects that make up the warp, but if you return to the organisational and management contexts of HRM you will see how their interweaving gives us changes in pattern and colour, some distinct, others subtle.

We have noted how the very term 'human resource management' confronts us with an assumption. This should cause us to recognise that the theory and practice of the employment relationship rest upon assumptions. The assumptions we shall examine in this section are even more fundamental than these for they shape the very way we think. Some are so deeply engrained that they are difficult to identify and express but they nevertheless become embodied in the way we approach life, including the way we conceptualise, theorise about and manage the employment relationship. They, therefore, have important implications for our interpretation of HRM.

We shall first note that perception, defence mechanisms and epistemological assumptions colour or, rather, construct our initial approach to reality. After that, we shall examine the social science philosophies and their impact on the ways we think; and lastly we shall consider some of the different ideologies and rhetoric that come into play in the field of HRM.

Perceiving reality

Perception

Before discussing the ways in which people approach reality, we must note that human beings do not necessarily do so – perhaps cannot do so – in a completely detached and clinical manner. The barriers between ourselves and the world outside us operate at very basic levels:

> Despite the impression that we are in direct and immediate contact with the world, our perception is, in fact, separated from reality by a long chain of processing.
> (Medcof and Roth, 1979: 4)

Psychologists have identified that perception is a complex process involving the selection of stimuli to which to respond and the organisation and interpretation of them according to patterns we already recognise. In other words, we develop a set of filters through which we come to make sense of our world. Kelly (1955) calls these our 'personal constructs', which channel the ways we conceptualise and anticipate events (see Ribeaux and Poppleton, 1978).

Defence mechanisms

Our approach to reality, however, is not just through cognitive processes. There is too much at stake for us, for our definition of reality has implications for our definitions of ourselves and for how we would wish others to see us. We, therefore, defend our sense of self – from what we interpret as threatening from our environment or from our own inner urges – by means of what Freud called our 'ego defence mechanisms'. In his study of how such adaptive behaviour changes over time, Vaillant (1977: 7) wrote:

> Often such mechanisms are analogous to the means by which an oyster, confronted with a grain of sand, creates a pearl. Humans, too, when confronted with conflict, engage in unconscious but often creative behaviour.

Freudians and non-Freudians (see Peck and Whitlow, 1975: 39–40) have identified many forms of such unconscious adaptive behaviour, some accepted as healthy, others as unhealthy and distorting. Without going to the lengths of the mechanisms of 'intellectualisation' and 'dissociation', which Vaillant (1977: 384–385) describes as 'neurotic' defences, a very common approach to the threats of the complexity of intimacy or the responsibility for others is to separate our feelings from our thinking, to treat people and indeed parts of ourselves as objects rather than subjects. The scene is set for the objective and 'scientific' approach to reality and, further, to the management of people.

Making assumptions about reality

Writing about personal construct theory, Bannister and Fransella (1971: 18) argue:

> . . . we cannot contact an interpretation-free reality directly. We can only make assumptions about what reality is and then proceed to find out how useful or useless those assumptions are.

However, we have developed our assumptions from birth, and they have been refined and reinforced by socialisation and experience so that, generally, we are not even aware of them. We do not, therefore, generally concern ourselves with epistemology, the theory of knowledge, and we find the discussion of metaphysical issues difficult to follow. Nevertheless, we are undoubtedly making significant assumptions about 'what it is possible to know, how may we be certain that we know something' (Heather, 1976: 12–13). These assumptions underpin thinking and contribute to the filters of perception; they, therefore, frame any understanding of the world including the ways in which researchers, theorists and practitioners construe HRM. To understand something of HRM and its context we need at least to recognise some of the implications of these epistemological and philosophical issues.

In crude terms, we can distinguish some fundamentally different approaches, Pepper's (1942) 'world hypotheses' constructed from two pairs of polarised assumptions. The first set makes assumptions about the universe. One of the pairs expects to find an ordered and systematic universe, 'where facts occur in a determinate order, and where, if enough were known, they could be predicted, or at least described' (Pepper, 1942: 143). The other sees the universe as a 'flowing and unbroken wholeness' (Morgan, 1986: 233) and accept 'real indeterminateness in the world' (Harré, 1981: 3) in which there are 'multitudes of facts rather loosely scattered and not necessarily determining one another to any considerable degree' (Pepper, 1942: 142–143). Pepper's second polarity is between approaching the universe through analysis or synthesis: fragmenting a whole into its parts in order to examine it more closely or examining it as a whole within its context.

Differences as basic as these inevitably lead to very different ways of seeing and thinking about reality and, indeed, of understanding our own role in the universe. The processes of socialisation and education in any given society nudge its members in a particular direction, although some may wander off the highway into the byways or, like the author of *Zen and the Art of Motorcycle Maintenance* (Pirsig, 1976), into what are assumed to be badlands. Much Western thinking appears to derive from an analytical approach to what is assumed to be an ordered universe. Hence, 'we are taught to break apart problems, to fragment the world' (Senge, 1990: 3); we examine the parts separately from their context and from one another, 'wrenching units of behaviour, action or experience from one another' (Parker, 1990: 100). These approaches, which shade into the positivism discussed in the next subsection, lead us in our research to examine a world that we interpret as

> . . . abstract, fragmented, precategorized, standardized, divorced from personal and local contexts or relevance, and with its meanings defined and controlled by researchers.
>
> (Mishler, 1986: 120)

Our orthodox approach itself impedes our recognition of these epistemological issues. It can be easier to discern them in the contrast offered by the epistemological positions adopted in other societies. We can, for example, recognise more of our own deeply embedded assumptions when we encounter a very different world view in an anthropologist's account (Castaneda, 1970) of his apprenticeship to a Yaqui sorceror. Of this, Goldschmidt (in Castaneda, 1970: 9–10) writes:

> Anthropology has taught us that the world is differently defined in different places. It is not only that people have different customs; it is not only that people believe in different gods and expect different post-mortem fates. It is, rather, that the worlds of different peoples have different shapes. The very metaphysical presuppositions differ: space does not conform to Euclidean geometry, time does not form a continuous unidirectional flow, causation does not conform to Aristotelian logic, man [*sic*] is not differentiated from non-man or life from death, as in our world . . . The central importance of entering worlds other than our own – and hence of anthropology itself – lies in the fact that the experience leads us to understand that our own world is also a cultural construct. By experiencing other worlds, then, we see our own for what it is . . .

Most of the epistemological threads in the tapestry that we are examining in this chapter reflect Western orthodoxy, but not all. And this orthodoxy itself may be gradually changing; some commentators have argued that it has reached a 'turning point' (Capra, 1983), that they can detect signs of a 'paradigm shift'. Indeed, over the last decade or so there have emerged new developments in the natural sciences (for example, the theory of chaos: the Gaia hypothesis: Lovelock, 1979; Prigogine and Stengers, 1985; Gleick, 1987), and elsewhere (feminist thinking: Gilligan, 1982) that offer challenges to orthodoxy.

We shall now turn to a more accessible level of our thinking, easier to identify and understand, although again we do not customarily pay it much attention. The contrast between the several modes of thinking outlined in the following subsections draws attention to the significant way in which our thinking influences our everyday operations.

Defining reality for ourselves

The distinctions between the epistemological positions in the last section and the philosophical stances examined here appear very blurred (Heather, 1976; Checkland, 1981). There is certainly considerable affinity between some of Pepper's (1942) 'world hypotheses' and the approaches noted below. Our discussion will be restricted to aspects of these approaches relevant to our understanding of concepts and practices like HRM.

Orthodox thinking

By orthodoxy we mean 'correct' or currently accepted opinions inculcated in the majority of members in any given society through the processes of socialisation and education and sustained through sanctions against deviation. In our society, for example, most people trust in rationality or 'orthodox medicine' and have doubts about the paranormal or 'alternative medicine'. We do not generally question our orthodox beliefs: they 'stand to reason', they work, everyone else thinks in the same way. By definition, therefore, we do not pay much attention to them, nor consider how they frame the interpretations we make of our world, nor what other alternatives there may be. Here we shall identify some characteristics of Western orthodoxy and, in the subsequent subsection, some alternatives to them.

The orthodox approach in Western thinking is based on positivism which, very importantly, has informed most social science research (and hence the study of HRM) which in turn reproduced, through the kind of new knowledge generated, this orthodoxy. It has also been the basic stance of many managers.

The positivist approach is characterised by 'a readiness to concede primacy to the given world as known through experimental evidence' (Checkland, 1981: 316). It forms the basis of scientific method, and applies the rational and ordered principles of the natural sciences to human affairs generally. It manifests itself (see Heather, 1976; Rose, 1978: 26) in a concern for objectivity, in the construction of testable hypotheses, in the collection of empirical data, in the search for causal relationships and in quantification. It is, at the same time, uneasy with subjective experience, and attempts to maintain distance between the researcher and those studied (called 'subjects' but regarded more as objects). For example, the Western view is that the individual has (rather than is) a self, 'the bounded, reified, highly individualized, autonomous self . . . self as a natural object' (Collin and Young, 1992: 4). It is also based upon a male world view, as we are increasingly recognising (Gilligan, 1982; Spender, 1985). We shall note the feminist challenge to this shortly.

We can perceive positivism's orthodox role in the contrast to which Kelly (1970: 1–2, quoted in Bannister and Fransella, 1971: 17–18) draws attention between the assumptions that underpin his personal construct theory to which we have already referred and those of orthodox science:

> A scientist . . . depends upon his [*sic*] facts to furnish the ultimate proof of his propositions . . . these shining nuggets of truth . . . To suggest [as Kelly does] . . . that further human reconstruction can completely alter the appearance of the precious fragments he has accumulated, as well as the direction of their arguments, is to threaten his scientific conclusions, his philosophical position, and even his moral security . . . our assumption that all facts are subject . . . to alternative constructions looms up as culpably subjective and dangerously subversive to the scientific establishment.

It will be clear from our discussion earlier of the immediate context of HRM that many managers and theorists of management espouse this orthodox approach. It underpins many organisational activities such as psychometric testing for selection and human resource planning models, as well as much of the research into this field.

Challenging alternatives

This subsection will outline four alternative ways of thinking that challenge orthodoxy: the phenomenological approach, social constructionism, feminist thinking, and systems and ecological thinking. It is important to note that the forms of the latter two that we have chosen to include here are those that espouse the constructionist or phenomenological approaches: in other words, there are positivist versions. While these are four distinctive approaches, having different origins and, to some extent, values and constituencies, they also, as we shall note, share some similarity apart from their express opposition to positivism.

The phenomenological and social constructionist approaches

The phenomenological approach stands in marked contrast to the positivist; it is characterised by 'a readiness to concede primacy to the mental processes of observers rather than to the external world' (Checkland, 1981: 315). It is concerned not with reality itself, but with how we experience reality, our lived experience. Whereas positivism subordinates subjectivity to objectivity, those who espouse a phenomenological approach acknowledge its significance (Heather, 1976: 34) and try to make explicit the conscious phenomena of experience. They access these experiences empathetically, through shared meanings, intersubjectivity, approaching them holistically without attempting to fragment them.

This approach in its purest form is infrequently found in the field of HRM and management (Sanders, 1982), although it is sometimes invoked as a rationale or discussion point in qualitative studies. However, social constructionism seems to be gaining a stronger footing in these areas and has considerable relevance to subjects such as HRM. (You will become aware that this approach is colouring the message of this particular chapter.)

Social constructionism holds that reality is socially constructed through language and social interaction, developed through 'shared, accumulated experiences' that give rise to 'assumptions, ideas, values, and norms' (Rosen, 1991: 273).

> . . . human beings in the social process are constantly creating the social world in interaction with others. They are negotiating their interpretations of reality, those multiple interpretations at the same time constituting the reality itself.
>
> (Checkland, 1981: 277)

Knowledge is, therefore, a social phenomenon (Hoffman, 1990), and meaning is 'produced rather than is expressed' (Murray, 1992: 32).

> That which appears to be objective – the naturalness of formal organization, the structuring of hierarchies, the immutability of economic laws, nine innings to a baseball game, the stability of order – is only illusorily so, where fronts are actively maintained through management of common backstages of meaning.
>
> (Rosen, 1991: 273)

According to this approach, there is no objective social reality to be experienced or researched. Rather, we create that reality together and have to study it through interpretation and the negotiation of meaning with others. There is, therefore, no single definitive meaning but, Hoffman (1990: 3) suggests:

> . . . an evolving set of meanings that emerge unendingly from the interactions between people. These meanings are not skull-bound and may not exist inside what we think of as an individual 'mind'. They are part of a general flow of constantly changing narratives.

This further means that we cannot separate ourselves from our created reality: 'man [*sic*] is an animal suspended in webs of significance he himself has spun' (Geertz, 1973: 5).

Importantly, this approach draws attention to perspective, the position from which an interpretation is made; to the way in which some people contrive to impose their interpretations and so define the reality of others; and the possibility, therefore, that less powerful people are disempowered, overlooked, remain silent, are left without a 'voice' (Mishler, 1986; Bhavnani, 1990).

Some of the competing interpretations we noted in an earlier section – those of Brunsson (1989) and Weick (1979), for example – are compatible with this approach and, indeed, there are a growing number of research studies that are underpinned by it (see Frost *et al.*, 1991).

Feminist thinking

Feminist thinking challenges what is increasingly becoming acknowledged as the male world view of the positivist approach. This challenge stems from the recognition of differences between the world views of women and men. Gilligan's (1982) study concluded that women value relationship and connection, whereas men value independence, autonomy and control. Some of these differences are visible, for example, in the careers of women entrepreneurs studied in Young and Richards (1992). Marshall (1989: 279) explores this further by means of Bakan's (1966) distinction between 'agency' and 'communion'. Agency is 'an expression of independence through self-protection, self-assertion and control of the environment'; Bakan associates it with maleness. The basis of communion, which Bakan associates with femaleness, is integration with others.

> The agentic strategy reduces tension by changing the world about it; communion seeks union and cooperation as its way of coming to terms with uncertainty. While agency manifests itself in focus, closedness and separation, communion is characterized by contact, openness and fusion.
>
> (Marshall, 1989: 289)

Therefore, Marshall (1982: 281) argues, feminist thinking 'represents a fundamental critique of knowledge as it is traditionally constructed'. With echoes of soft systems thinking, which we shall examine shortly, it challenges traditional knowledge, which 'has largely been constructed by and about men' and either ignores or devalues the experience of women.

> . . . its preoccupation with seeking universal, immutable truth, failing to accept diversity and change; its categorization of the world into opposites, valuing one pole and devaluing the other; its claims of detachment and objectivity; and the predominance of linear cause-and-effect thinking. These forms reflect male, agentic experiences and strategies for coping with uncertainty. By shaping academic theorizing and research activities, they build male power and domination into the structures of knowledge . . .
>
> (Marshall, 1989: 281)

Calas and Smircich (1992: 227) discuss how gender has been 'mis- or under-represented' in organisation theory and explore the effects of re-writing it in. These would include the correction or completion of the organisational record from which women have been absent or excluded, the assessment of gender bias in current knowledge, and the making of a new, more diverse organisation theory that covers topics of concern to women.

Hearn *et al.* (1989) identify similar shortcomings in organisation theory in their discussion of the sexuality of organisations. For example, Tancred-Sheriff (1989: 55) argues that women are located in organisational roles in which their sexuality can be utilised in the interface with workers and customers to effect 'adjunct control' in the difficult-to-manage space between employer and worker, producer and consumer, while management can remain in control of them through sexual domination.

Systems and ecological thinking

We devote more attention here to systems thinking than to the other alternatives to orthodoxy because it offers particularly useful insights into the subject of this chapter, the nature of context.

There are both orthodox and alternative views of systems: here we are examining the kind of systems thinking that concerns social phenomena and challenges Western orthodoxy. Checkland (1981), for example, adopts a phenomenological approach in his 'soft systems methodology', employing systems not as 'descriptions of actual real-world activity' (1981: 314), but as 'tools of an epistemological kind which can be used in a process of exploration within social reality' (1981: 249). Systems thinking, moreover, shifts our attention from what orthodox thinking allows us to see. It allows us to see the whole rather than just its parts, interconnectivity rather than isolated elements, and to recognise that we are a part of that whole. It registers patterns of change, relationships rather than just objects, a web of interrelationships and reciprocal flows of influence rather than linear chains of cause and effect.

The similarities here with Marshall's (1989) view of feminist thinking noted above raise some interesting questions about how systems thinking could gain greater acceptance. However, it is Senge's (1990) 'fifth discipline' and in his view it is essential for the development of the learning organisation that we shall discuss in Chapter 7:

> At the heart of a learning organization is a shift of mind – from seeing ourselves as separate from the world to connected to the world, from seeing problems as caused by someone or something 'out there' to seeing how our own actions create the problems we experience. A learning organization is a place where people are continually discovering how they create their reality. And how they can change it.
> (Senge, 1990: 12–13)

The concept of system denotes a whole and coherent entity that can be distinguished from its environment and may comprise a hierarchy of subsystems, where the whole is greater than the sum of its parts. Much of what has been written about systems draws upon General Systems Theory, a meta-theory that offered a way to conceptualise phenomena in any disciplinary area. Very importantly, the systems approach does not argue that social phenomena are systems, but rather that they can be modelled (conceptualised, thought about) as though they had systemic properties. The concept of system used in the social sciences is, therefore, a very abstract kind of metaphor. However, we can only give a brief outline of systems concepts here: you will find further detail in Checkland (1981), Morgan (1986) and Senge (1990).

Systems may be 'open' (like biological or social systems) or 'closed' to their environment, like many physical and mechanical systems. As shown in Figure 2.3, the open system imports from, exchanges with, its environment what it needs to meet its goals and to survive, and converts or transforms these inputs into a form that sustains its existence and generates outputs that are returned to the environment and can be used to exchange for further inputs, along with waste products. The environment itself comprises other systems that are also drawing in inputs and discharging outputs. Changes in remote parts of any given system's environment can, therefore, ripple through its environment to affect it eventually. There is a feedback loop that enables the system to make appropriate modi-fications to its subsystems in the light of the changing environment. Thus the system constantly adjusts to achieve equilibrium internally and with its environment.

Reflecting upon the management approaches identified earlier, we can now recognise that the scientific management, human relations and perhaps also the humanistic approaches treated the organisation as a closed system, whereas the human resource approach recognises it as open to its environment. Brunsson's identification of the 'action' and 'political' organisations could also be seen as an open system approach.

The significance of systems thinking, then, lies in its ability to conceptualise complex, dynamic realities – the system and its internal and external relationships – and model them in a simple, coherent way that is yet pregnant with meaning and capable of being elaborated further when necessary. This means that we can use it to hold in our minds such complex ideas as those discussed in this chapter, without diminishing our awareness of their complexity and interrelationships. If we construe the contextually-embedded body of HRM thinking to be a system, then the ways of seeing and thinking

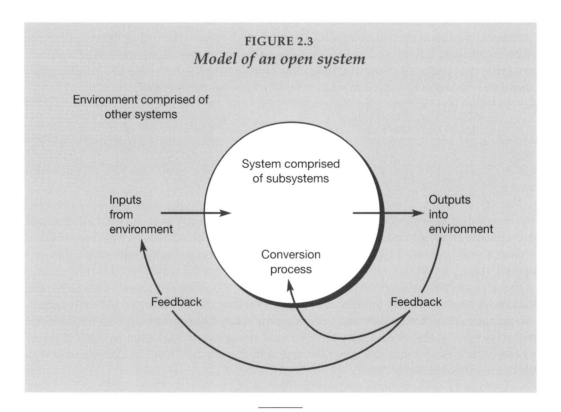

FIGURE 2.3
Model of an open system

being discussed in this section, the sociohistorical issues and the nature of organisations and management discussed in the earlier sections, are all inputs into it from its wider environment. It 'converts' them to produce the HRM philosophies, policies and practices that are discussed throughout this book, and these outputs themselves influence, indeed change, the wider environment by their effects upon, for example, the labour market, management–union relationships, or changing values about employment.

We can also model the HRM of an organisation in a similar manner. In this case, its inputs would include the outputs of the labour market, the policy outputs of the organisation's business strategy, values about people and employment, the existence of specialist HRM personnel. The conversion process transforms these inputs through many of the processes discussed in this book, such as recruitment and selection processes, training and development processes, disciplinary and performance appraisal processes. The outputs of this organisational HRM system are the kinds of personnel and skills, attitudes and conditions of employment required to service the organisation. The 'waste' by-products may be ineffectual personnel systems, highly-trained staff who decide to leave the organisation, or poorly-motivated, exhausted or stressed staff.

We could also conceptualise an organisation as a system in a complex and dynamic relationship with its complex and dynamic environment. Changes in one part of the environment – the collapse of a supplier, for example, or the reduction of energy sources – will change the nature of the inputs and lead to the need for adjustments in and between the subsystems, either to ensure the same output or to modify the output. The environment consists of other organisations, the outputs of which – whether intentionally or as by-products – constitute the inputs of others. A change in output, such as a new or improved product or service, however, will constitute a change in another organisation's input, leading to a further ripple of adjustments.

Defining reality for others

The weft interweaves through the warp to produce the basic pattern of the tapestry. This chapter identifies the ways in which others define our reality (or we define reality for others) as the weft threads. They have differing colours and textures, and also differing lengths (durations), so that they do not necessarily appear throughout the tapestry. They run across the warp: there are versions of some that adopt a positivist approach, whereas others are constructionist.

The definitions of reality to be examined here are ideology, language and rhetoric, hegemony and discourse. It may be inferred that they are important contextual influences upon HRM and in part account for the competing definitions of it.

Ideology

Gowler and Legge (1989: 438) define ideology as 'sets of ideas involved in the framing of our experience, of making sense of the world, expressed through language'. It has a narrower focus than the 'ways of thinking' we have been discussing above, and could be seen as a localised orthodoxy, a reasonably coherent set of ideas and beliefs that often goes unchallenged:

> . . . ideology operates as a reifying, congealing mechanism that imposes
> pseudoresolutions and compromises in the space where fluid, contradic-
> tory, and multivalent subjectivity could gain ground. (Sloan, 1992: 174)

Ideology purports to explain reality objectively, but within a pluralist society it actually represents and legitimates the interests of members of a subgroup. It is a 'subtle combination of facts and values' (Child, 1969: 224). What we hear and what we read will be conveying someone else's interpretations. The way they express them may obscure their ideology and vested interest in those interpretations. We shall first briefly examine how ideology serves the purpose of a powerful minority in society and, second, how it is expressed.

As you will recognise from earlier in the chapter, the organisation is an arena in which ideologies of many kinds are in contest: capitalism and Marxism, humanism and scientific approaches to the individual, feminism and a gender-biased view. For example, in contrast to the orthodox view of culture, Jermier (Frost *et al.*, 1991: 231) argues that culture is:

> . . . the objectified product of the labor of human subjects . . . there is a pro-
> found forgetting of the fact that the world is socially constructed and can be
> remade . . . Exploitative practices are mystified and concealed.

Child (1969) discusses the ideology embodied in the development of management thinking, identifying how the human relations approach chose to ignore the divergence of interests between managers and employees and how this dismissal of potential conflict influenced theory and practice. Commentators such as Braverman (1974), Frost *et al.* (1991) and Rose (1975) will help you recognise some of the ideologies at work in this field; you will also find them discussed in subsequent chapters in this book.

Hegemony

Hegemony is the imposition of the reality favoured by a powerful subgroup in society upon less powerful others. Such a group exerts its authority over subordinate groups by imposing its definition of reality over other competing definitions. This does not have to be achieved through direct coercion, but by 'winning the consent of the dominated majority so that the power of the dominant classes appears both legitimate and natural'. In this way, subordinate groups are 'contained within an ideological space which does not seem at all "ideological": which appears instead to be permanent and "natural", to lie outside history, to be beyond particular interests' (Hebdige, 1979: 15–16).

Hegemony can clearly be identified in the way in which gender issues are generally completely submerged in organisations and theories of them (Hearn *et al.*, 1989). Although the feminist voice is now frequently heard, it appears to be unnatural and shrill, so 'natural' do the male-defined realities of organisations appear.

Language and rhetoric

Ideology achieves its ends through language and rhetoric. Whereas we would customarily assume that language is neutral, Gowler and Legge (1992: 438) and others (for example, Fowler and Kress, 1979; Spender, 1980) challenge those assumptions by asserting that it is 'ideological': both the means through which ideologies are expressed and the embodiment of ideology (they point to sexist and racist language).

Rhetoric is 'the art of using language to persuade, influence or manipulate' (Gowler and Legge, 1989: 438–439). The high symbolic content of rhetoric 'allows it to reveal and conceal but above all develop and transform meaning'. It 'heightens and transforms meaning by processes of association, involving both evocation and juxtaposition'. In other words, its artfulness lies in playing with meanings.

It can be argued that rhetoric is audible in organisations in, for example, the way in which changes to structure and jobs are described as 'flexibility' rather than as the casual-isation of work (see, for example, Chapter 4) and in this description of increased pressures upon employees as 'empowerment' (see Chapter 14).

Discourse

Discourse is an interrelated 'system of statements which cohere around common mean-ings and values' particular to a specific group (Hollway, 1983, in Gavey, 1989: 463–464). The concept bridges and extends those of rhetoric and hegemony as defined above, but is generally used to denote the ways in which academic writers exercise power over the production of knowledge and seek to influence their readers. By providing the language and meanings whereby its members and others can interpret reality, this group estab-lishes, exercises and perpetuates its power. Discourse interprets competing positions in its own terms and thereby shuts down all other possible interpretations but its own. It offers individuals an identifiable position to adopt upon a given subject, thereby constituting their own identity, behaviour and reality (Gavey, 1989).

In acknowledging discourse, we become aware of how the various ways of thinking described earlier become shared and accepted. Turner (1987: 61), drawing upon the ideas of Foucault, asserts:

> . . . scientific concepts are not neutral descriptions of patterns of behaviour, but on the contrary they produce through discursive activity the behaviour they seek to describe.

Similarly, Parker and Shotter (1990: 9) draw our attention to the way in which acade-mics have to learn:

> . . . a vocabulary and a set of analytic procedures for 'seeing' what is going on . . . in the appropriate professional terms. For we must see only the partially ordered affairs of everyday life, which are open to many interpre-tations . . . *as if* they are events of a certain well-defined kind.

Of relevance to the argument of this chapter, Parker and Shotter (1990: 2–3), in con-trasting 'everyday talk' and academic writing, indicate that academic text standardises the interpretations possible by being divorced from any context:

> The strange and special thing about an academic text . . . is that by the use of certain strategies and devices, as well as already predetermined mean-ings, one is able to construct a text which can be understood (by those who are a party to such 'moves') in a way divorced from any reference to any local or immediate contexts. Textual communication can be (relatively)

decontextualised. Everyday talk, on the other hand, is marked by its vagueness and openness, by the fact that only those taking part in it can understand its drift; the meanings concerned are not wholly predetermined, they are negotiated by those involved, on the spot, in relation to the circumstances in which they are involved . . . Everyday talk is situated or contextualised, and relies upon its situation (its circumstances) for its sense.

We can identify various discourses in the field of organisation and management studies. There are those that emanate from a humanist ideology: Argyris (1960), for example, or many of the views expressed in Chapter 7. Others stem from an industrial relations perspective, which you see later in this book.

CONCLUSION . . . AND A NEW BEGINNING?

We have examined something of the warp and weft that give the tapestry its basic form, pattern, colour and texture. To complete our understanding of the context of HRM we need to recognise that events, issues and people constitute the surface stitching that is drawn through the warp and weft to add further pattern and colour. You will be aware of examples from your own experience and the reading of this and other books, but we can instance the influences of recession, equal opportunities legislation, the European Social Chapter, management gurus, Margaret Thatcher, Arthur Scargill that resonate with the warp and weft to produce the patterns that have come to be known as HRM.

The tapestry of which HRM forms a part is continuously being woven, but we can now become aware of the sources of the differing approaches to organisation and management and of the contesting voices about the management of people. We can now recognise that their contest creates an organisational and conceptual space which is being filled by an HRM constructed of multiple meanings. However, this awareness allows us to recognise further that yet other meanings, and hence potentials for the management of the employment relationship, remain to be constructed.

By pointing to the need to recognise the significance of the context of HRM, we are also acknowledging that you will find therein more interpretations than this book of 'academic text' (Parker and Shotter, 1990: see the previous section), shaped by our own agendas and values and the practicalities of commercial publication, can offer you. The process both of writing and publication is that of decontextualisation, fragmentation, standardisation, and presentation of knowledge as 'entertaining education', in bite-sized chunks of knowledge or sound bites. But by urging you to become aware of the context of HRM we are at the same time inviting you to look beyond what we have to say, to recognise the nature of our discourse or, rather, discourses, to challenge our assumptions (and, indeed, your own) and to use your own critical judgements informed by your wider reading and personal experience.

This, then, is why we have begun our exploration of HRM by examining its context. This chapter had a further aim (and this betrays this writer's 'agenda and values'). This is to orientate your thinking generally towards an awareness of context, to think contextually, for ultimately awareness of context is empowering. One of the outcomes may well be greater knowledge but less certainty, the recognition that there may be competing interpretations of the subject being considered, that the several perspectives upon the area may yield different conclusions. Attention to context, therefore, encourages us not to be taken in by our initial interpretations, nor to accept unquestioningly the definitions of reality others would have us adopt (the 'hegemony' of the previous section). There are, however, no easy answers, and we have to make the choice between alternatives. Reality is much messier and tentative than theory and, like 'everyday talk', it is 'marked by its vagueness and openness', its meaning open to interpretation through negotiation with others. The acceptance of this, however, as we shall later see in Chapter 7, is one of the marks of the mature learner: the ability to recognise alternative viewpoints but, nevertheless, to take responsibility for committing oneself to one of them.

By definition, one chapter cannot begin to portray the complexity and diversity of the context of HRM, but nor does it have a need to. It will have achieved its purpose if it causes you to recognise the significance of context and the need to adopt ways of thinking that enable you to conceptualise it. It can point you in some directions, and you will find many others in the chapters that follow, but there are no logical starting points, because context is indivisible; and you will never reach the end of the story for, from the perspective of context, the story is never ending.

SUMMARY

● The chapter argues that the keys to the understanding of human affairs, such as HRM, lie within their context. Although context as construed here is difficult to conceptualise and represent, readers can draw on their existing understanding of environmental issues to help them comprehend it. Awareness and comprehension of context are ultimately empowering because they sharpen critical thinking by challenging our own and others' assumptions.

● Multiple interests, conflict, and stressful and moral issues are inherent in the immediate context of HRM, which is comprised of the organisation (the nature of which generates a number of lateral and vertical tensions) and management (defined as the continuous process of resolving those tensions). Over time, managers have adopted a range of approaches to their task: scientific management; the human relations school; humanistic organisation development; and now HRM. Understanding of even this layer of HRM's context calls for the recognition of the existence of some significant assumptions that inform both managers' differing practices and the competing interpretations that theorists make of them.

● The wider social, economic, political and cultural context of HRM is diverse, complex and dynamic, but two very different and unconnected strands of it are pulled out for examination. The identification of some of the legacies of the two world wars for the management of the employment relationship acknowledges the historical antecedents of HRM, while the recognition of emerging 'postmodern' experiences and critiques locates it within a contemporary framework of ideas that could eventually challenge some assumptions about the management of the employment relationship.

● The chapter, however, finds it insufficient to conceptualise context as layered, like an onion. Rather, HRM is embedded in its context. The metaphor of a tapestry is therefore used to express the way in which its meaning is constructed from the interweaving and mutual influences of the assumptions deriving from basic perceptual, epistemological, philosophical and ideological positions. The notions of 'warp' and 'weft' are used to discuss such key contextual elements as positivism, phenomenology, social construction-ism, feminist thinking, systems thinking, ideology, hegemony, language, rhetoric and discourse. People, events and issues are the surface stitching.

● The nature of this tapestry, with its multiple and often competing perspectives, ensures that HRM, as a concept, theory and practice, is a contested terrain. However, the chapter leaves readers to identify the implications of this through their critical reading of the book.

ACTIVITY

Drawing on your understanding of the environment

The nature of our environment concerns us all. As 'environment' and 'green issues' have crossed the threshold of public awareness to become big business, we have become concerned about our natural environment as no previous generation has been. We are now aware of the increasing complexity in the web of human affairs. We recognise the interrelationships within our 'global village', between the world's 'rich' North and the 'poor' South (1980s Brandt Report) and between politics, economies and the environment (Rio Summit 1992), and at home between, for example, unemployment, deprivation and crime. Another feature of our environment which we cannot ignore is its increasingly dynamic nature. Our world is changing before our very eyes. Comparing it with the world we knew even five years ago, and certainly with that known by our parents when they were the age we are now, it has changed dramatically and in ways that could never have been anticipated.

EXERCISES

1 You will have considerable knowledge, and perhaps personal experience, of many environmental issues such as the problems of waste disposal and pollution, food and health scares, the impact on the countryside of the construction of new roads, or the threats to the survival of many species of animals and plants.

Working individually or in groups, choose two or three such issues for discussion.

a Identify those who are playing a part in them (the actors) and those directly or indirectly affected by them (the stakeholders). How did the event or situation that has become an issue come about? Who started it? How do they explain it? Will the situation change over time, and how long will it last? Who benefits in this situation? How do they justify this? Who loses in it? What do – or can – they do about it? Why? Who is paying the cost? How and why?

b Look for concrete examples of the following statements:

● *We have an impact upon the environment and cause it to change, both positively and negatively.*
● *The environment and changes within it have an impact upon us and affect the quality of human life, both positively and negatively.*
● *The environment has a differential influence upon each of us, these differences being partly attributable to differences between us: each of us could, therefore, be said to have a different environment.*

- *There are different levels of events and elements of the environment: some are local, others national or international.*
- *They include both concrete events and abstract ideas.*
- *The interrelationships between events and elements in the environment are so complex that they are often difficult to untangle.*
- *It may not be possible or even meaningful to identify the cause of events and their effects; the cause or causes may have to be inferred, the effects projected.*
- *Sometimes these effects are manifested far into the future, and so are not easily identifiable now, though they may affect future generations.*
- *Our relationship with our environment, therefore, has a moral dimension to it.*
- *Many significant environmental changes have not been accurately predicted – or predicted at all – or recognised for what they are.*
- *To deal with some of the negative causes may be gravely damaging to some other groups of people.*
- *The understanding of these events will differ according to the particular perspective of the observer, and will arise from interpretation rather than ultimately verifiable 'facts'.*
- *These issues often involve powerful power bases in society, each of which has its own interpretation of events, and wishes others to accept its definition of them.*
- *The actors involved in the events may have yet a different perspective, and so may other stakeholders.*
- *The nature of our relationship with our environment challenges our traditional scientific ways of thinking, in which we value objectivity, analyse by breaking down a whole into its parts, and seek to identify cause and effect in a linear model.*
- *It also, therefore, challenges our traditional methods of research and investigation, deduction and inference.*

2 The opening section of the chapter suggested such an examination of environmental issues would allow us to recognise that:

- the nature of the environment is multi-layered, multi-dimensional and interwoven, in which concrete events and abstract ideas intertwine to create issues, and thinking, feeling, interpreting and behaving are all involved: it is like the *tapestry* described in the section;
- our understanding depends upon our *perspective*;
- it also depends upon our *ideology*;
- there are, therefore, *competing or contested interpretations* of events;
- different groups in society have their own interpretations of events, stemming from their *ideology*, which incorporate an explanation for competing interpretations. They use the *rhetoric* of their own interpretations to express competing interpretations, thus suppressing the authentic expression of competing views;
- there are powerful others who try to impose their interpretations of events, their version of reality, upon the less powerful majority: this is *hegemony*.

Can you give concrete examples of these?

QUESTIONS

1 In what ways does the conceptualisation of context adopted by this chapter differ from more commonly used approaches (for example, in the models of HRM in Chapter 1)? Does it add to the understanding they give of HRM and, if so, in what way?

2 What assumptions and 'world hypotheses' underpin those models, and what are the implications for your use of them?

3 What assumptions and 'world hypotheses' underpin this chapter, and what are the implications for your use of it?

4 Identify some recent events that are likely to play a significant part in the context of HRM.

5 This chapter has been written from a British perspective. If you were working from a different perspective – South African, perhaps, or Scandinavian – what elements of the context of HRM would you include?

6 The chapter has been written for students of HRM. Is it also relevant to the practitioners of HRM and, if so, in what way?

EXERCISE

Having started to think in terms of context and to recognise the significance of our ways of thinking, you should be reading the rest of this book in this same critical manner. As you go through it try to identify the following:

- the assumptions (at various levels) underlying the research and theory reported in the chapters that follow;
- the implications of these assumptions for the interpretations that the researchers and theorists are placing upon their material;
- the possibility of other interpretations deriving from other assumptions;
- the assumptions (at various levels) that the writers of the following chapters appear to hold;
- the implications of these assumptions for the interpretations that these writers are placing upon their material;
- the possibility of other interpretations deriving from other assumptions;
- the implications of the various alternatives for the practice of HRM.

REFERENCES AND FURTHER READING

Those texts marked with an asterisk are particularly recommended for further reading.

Argyris, C. (1957) *Personality and Organization*. New York: Harper & Row.

Bakan, D. (1966) *The Duality of Human Existence*. Boston: Beacon.

Bannister, D. and Fransella, F. (1971) *Inquiring Man: The Theory of Personal Constructs*. Harmondsworth: Penguin.

Bhavnani, K.-K. (1990) 'What's power got to do with it? Empowerment and social research', in Parker, I. and Shotter, J. (eds) *Deconstructing Social Psychology*. London: Routledge, pp. 141–152.

Braverman, H. (1974) *Labor and Monopoly Capital: The Degradation of Work in the Twentieth Century.* New York: Monthly Review Press.

*Brunsson, N. (1989) *The Organization of Hypocrisy: Talk, Decisions and Actions in Organizations.* Chichester: Wiley.

Calas, M.B. and Smircich, L. (1992) 'Re-writing gender into organizational theorizing: Directions from feminist perspectives', in Reed, M. and Hughes, M. (eds) *Rethinking Organization: New Directions in Organization Theory and Analysis.* London: Sage, pp. 227–253.

Cameron, S. (1991) *The MBA Handbook: An Essential Guide to Effective Study.* London: Pitman.

Capra, F. (1983) *The Turning Point: Science, Society and the Rising Cultures.* London: Fontana.

Castaneda, C. (1970) *The Teachings of Don Juan: A Yaqui Way of Knowledge.* Harmondsworth: Penguin.

*Checkland, P. (1981) *Systems Thinking, Systems Practice.* Chichester: Wiley.

Child, J. (1969) *British Management Thought: A Critical Analysis.* London: George Allen & Unwin.

Clegg, S.R. (1990) *Modern Organizations: Organization Studies in the Postmodern World.* London: Sage.

Collin, A. (1996) 'Organizations and the end of the individual?', *Journal of Managerial Psychology,* Vol. 11, No. 7, pp. 9–17.

Collin, A. and Young, R.A. (1992) 'Constructing career through narrative and context', in Young, R.A. and Collin, A. (eds) *Interpreting Career: Hermeneutical Studies of Lives in Context.* Westport, Conn.: Praeger, pp. 1–12.

Concise Oxford Dictionary (1982) 7th edn. Oxford: Clarendon Press.

Connock, S. (1992) 'The importance of "big ideas" to HR managers', *Personnel Management,* June, pp. 24–27.

Cooper, R. and Fox, S. (1990) 'The "texture" of organizing', *Journal of Management Studies,* Vol. 27, No. 6, pp. 575–582.

Cyert, R.M. and March, J.G. (1963) *A Behavioral Theory of the Firm.* Englewood Cliffs, NJ: Prentice Hall.

Department of Scientific and Industrial Research (1961) *Human Sciences: Aid to Industry.* London: HMSO.

Drucker, P.F. (1954) *The Practice of Management.* New York: Harper & Row.

Drucker, P.F. (1980) *Managing in Turbulent Times.* London: Heinemann.

*Eccles, R.G. and Nohria, N. (1992) *Beyond the Hype: Rediscovering the Essence of Management.* Boston, MA: Harvard Business School Press.

Fineman, S. (ed.) (1993) *Emotion in Organizations.* London: Sage.

Fowler, R. and Kress, G. (1979) 'Rules and regulations', in Fowler, R., Hodge, R., Kress, G. and Trew, T. (eds) *Language and Control.* London: Routledge & Kegan Paul, pp. 26–45.

Fox, S. (1990) 'Strategic HRM: postmodern conditioning for the corporate culture', in Fox, S. and Moult, G. (eds) *Postmodern Culture and Management Development,* Special Edition: *Management Education and Development,* Vol. 21, Pt 3, pp. 192–206.

Fox, S. and Moult, G. (eds) (1990) *Postmodern Culture and Management Development,* Special Edition: *Management Education and Development,* Vol. 21, Pt 3 (whole issue).

*Frost, P.J., Moore, L.F., Louis, M.R., Lundberg, C.C. and Martin, J. (1991) *Reframing Organizational Culture.* Newbury Park, Calif.: Sage.

Gavey, N. (1989) 'Feminist poststructuralism and discourse analysis: Contributions to feminist psychology', *Psychology of Women Quarterly,* Vol. 13, pp. 459–475.

Geertz, C. (1973) *The Interpretation of Cultures.* New York: Basic Books.

Gilligan, C. (1982) *In a Different Voice: Psychological Theory and Women's Development.* Cambridge, Mass.: Harvard University Press.

Gleick, J. (1987) *Chaos.* New York: Viking Press.

Goldschmidt, W. (1970) 'Foreword', in Castaneda, C., *The Teachings of Don Juan: A Yaqui Way of Knowledge.* Harmondsworth: Penguin, pp. 9–10.

Gowler, D. and Legge, K. (1989) 'Rhetoric in bureaucratic careers: managing the meaning of management success', in Arthur, M.B., Hall, D.T. and Lawrence, B.S. (eds) *Handbook of Career Theory.* Cambridge: Cambridge University Press, pp. 437–453.

Harré, R. (1981) 'The positivist-empiricist approach and its alternative', in Reason, P. and Rowan, J. (eds) *Human Inquiry: A Sourcebook of New Paradigm Research.* Chichester: Wiley, pp. 3–17.

*Hearn, J., Sheppard, D.L., Tancred-Sheriff, P. and Burrell, G. (1989) *The Sexuality of Organization.* London: Sage.

Heather, N. (1976) *Radical Perspectives in Psychology.* London: Methuen.

Hebdige, D. (1979) *Subculture: The Meaning of Style.* London: Methuen.

Hendry, C. and Pettigrew, A. (1990) 'Human resource management: an agenda for the 1990s', *International Journal of Human Resource Management*, Vol. 1, No. 1.

Hodgson, A. (1987) 'Deming's never-ending road to quality', *Personnel Management*, July, pp. 40–44.

Hoffman, L. (1990) 'Constructing realities: an art of lenses', *Family Process*, Vol. 29, No. 1, pp. 1–12.

Hollway, W. (1983) 'Heterosexual sex: Power and desire for the other', in Cartledge, S. and Ryan, J. (eds) *Sex and Love: New Thoughts on Old Contradictions.* London: Women's Press, pp. 124–140.

Hosking, D. and Fineman, S. (1990) 'Organizing processes', *Journal of Management Studies*, Vol. 27, No. 6, pp. 583–604.

Huse, E.F. (1980) *Organization Development and Change*, 2nd edn. St. Paul, Minn.: West Publishing.

Kanter, R.M. (1983) *The Change Masters.* New York: Simon & Schuster.

Kelly, G.A. (1955) *The Psychology of Personal Constructs*, Vols 1 and 2. New York: W.W. Norton.

Keenoy, T. (1990) 'Human resource management: rhetoric, reality and contradiction', *The International Journal of Human Resource Management*, Vol. 1, No. 3, pp. 363–384.

Lovelock, J.E. (1979) *Gaia.* Oxford: Oxford University Press.

McGregor, D. (1960) *The Human Side of Enterprise.* New York: McGraw-Hill.

Mant, A. (1979) *The Rise and Fall of the British Manager.* London: Pan.

Marshall, J. (1989) 'Re-visioning career concepts: A feminist invitation', in Arthur, M.B., Hall, D.T. and Lawrence, B.S. (eds) *Handbook of Career Theory.* Cambridge: Cambridge University Press, pp. 275–291.

Medcof, J. and Roth, J. (eds) (1979) *Approaches to Psychology.* Milton Keynes: Open University Press.

Mishler, E.G. (1986) *Research Interviewing: Context and Narrative.* Cambridge, Mass.: Harvard University Press.

*Morgan, G. (1986) *Images of Organization.* Beverly Hills, Calif.: Sage.

Morgan, G. (1988) *Riding the Waves of Change: Developing Managerial Competencies for a Turbulent World.* San Francisco: Jossey-Bass.

Moxon, G.R. (1958) *Functions of a Personnel Department.* London: Institute of Personnel Management.

Murray, K.D. (1992) 'The construction of a moral career in medicine', in Young, R.A. and Collin, A. (eds) *Interpreting Career: Hermeneutical Studies of Lives in Context.* Westport, Conn.: Praeger, pp. 31–47.

Parker, I. (1990) 'The abstraction and representation of social psychology', in Parker, I. and Shotter, J. (eds) *Deconstructing Social Psychology*. London: Routledge, pp. 91–102.

Parker, I. and Shotter, J. (eds) (1990) 'Introduction', in *Deconstructing Social Psychology*. London: Routledge, pp. 1–14.

*Pascale, R.T. and Athos, A.G. (1982) *The Art of Japanese Management*. Harmondsworth: Penguin.

Peck, D. and Whitlow, D. (1975) *Approaches to Personality Theory*. London: Methuen.

Pepper, S.C. (1942) *World Hypotheses*. Berkeley, Calif.: University of California Press.

Peters, T.J. and Waterman, R.H. Jr (1982) *In Search of Excellence*. New York: Harper & Row.

Pfeffer, J. (1981) *Power in Organizations*. London: Pitman.

Pickard, J. (1992) 'Profile: W. Edward Deming', *Personnel Management*, June, p. 23.

Pirsig, R.M. (1976) *Zen and the Art of Motorcycle Maintenance*. London: Corgi.

Prigognine, I. and Stengers, I. (1985) *Order Out of Chaos*. London: Fontana.

Pugh, D.S., Hickson, D.J. and Hinings, C.R. (eds) (1983) *Writers on Organizations*. Harmondsworth: Penguin.

Quinn, R.E., Faerman, S.R., Thompson, M.P. and McGrath, M.R. (1990) *Becoming A Master Manager: A Competency Framework*. New York: Wiley.

*Reed, M. and Hughes, M. (eds) (1992) *Rethinking Organization: New Directions in Organization Theory and Analysis*. London: Sage.

Ribeaux, P. and Poppleton, S.E. (1978) *Psychology and Work: An Introduction*. London: Macmillan.

Rose, M. (1978) *Industrial Behaviour: Theoretical Development Since Taylor*. Harmondsworth: Penguin.

Rosen, M. (1991) 'Scholars, travelers, thieves: on concept, method, and cunning in organizational ethnography', in Frost, P.J., Moore, L.F., Louis, M.R., Lundberg, C.C. and Martin, J. (eds) *Reframing Organizational Culture*. Newbury Park: Sage, pp. 271–284.

Sanders, P. (1982) 'Phenomenology: a new way of viewing organizational research', *Academy of Management Review*, Vol. 7, No. 3, pp. 353–360.

Schein, E.H. (1978) *Career Dynamics: Matching Individual and Organizational Needs*. Reading, Mass.: Addison-Wesley.

*Senge, P. (1990) *The Fifth Discipline: The Art and Practice of the Learning Organization*. London: Century.

Seymour, W.D. (1959) *Operator Training in Industry*. London: Institute of Personnel Management.

Simon, H.A. (1947) *Administrative Behavior*. New York: Macmillan.

Sloan, T. (1992) 'Career decisions: A critical psychology', in Young, R.A. and Collin, A. (eds) *Interpreting Career: Hermeneutical Studies of Lives in Context*. Westport, Conn.: Praeger, pp. 168–176.

Southgate, J. and Randall, R. (1981) 'The troubled fish: barriers to dialogue', in Reason, P. and Rowan, J. (eds) *Human Inquiry: A Sourcebook of New Paradigm Research*. Chichester: Wiley, pp. 53–61.

Spender, D. (1980) *Man Made Language*. London: Routledge & Kegan Paul.

Spender, D. (1985) *For the Record: The Making and Meaning of Feminist Knowledge*. London: Women's Press.

Tancred-Sheriff, P. (1989) 'Gender, sexuality and the labour process', in Hearn, J., Sheppard, D.L., Tancred-Sheriff, P. and Burrell, G. (eds) *The Sexuality of Organization*. London: Sage, pp. 45–55.

Turner, B.S. (1987) *Medical Power and Social Knowledge*. London: Sage.

Turner, B.S. (ed.) (1990) *Theories of Modernity and Postmodernity*. London: Sage.

Vaillant, G.E. (1977) *Adaptation to Life: How the Brightest and Best Came of Age*. Boston: Little, Brown.

Watson, T.J. (1994) *In Search of Management: Culture, Chaos and Control in Managerial Work*. London: Routledge.

*Weick, K.E. (1979) *The Social Psychology of Organizing*. New York: Random House.

Young, R.A. and Richards, R. (1992) 'Entrepreneurial women and the relational component of identity: a hermeneutical study of career', in Young, R.A. and Collin, A. (eds) *Interpreting Career: Hermeneutical Studies of Lives in Context*. Westport, Conn.: Praeger, pp. 117–133.

PART 1 CASE STUDY

HUMAN RESOURCES MANAGER – EUROPE

The position will support a sales, marketing and support organisation in several European countries and will be based in the Thames Valley area.

Key responsibilities include salary and benefit surveys; recommendations; administration; recruiting and staffing; employee relations; performance improvement planning; training needs analyses and employee communications. The candidate will be responsible for ensuring consistent human resource policies and procedures and translating corporate programmes to meet local needs.

To fill this challenging position we are looking for a high profile candidate with the following qualifications:

- University degree preferably in psychology or business or related, with postgraduate courses in human resources.

- Ten years' experience in progressive personnel functions with positions in US-based companies; experience in field generalist roles.

- High-tech background.

- Expertise in compensation, benefits, recruiting, staffing, employee relations, training and organisation development.

- Fluency in English, French and German. Spanish and Italian an asset.

The company offers excellent social benefits and pleasant working conditions in an international environment.

If you fulfil these requirements do not hesitate to send your résumé to Bob Smith who will treat your file confidentially.

PERSONNEL OFFICER

UK Head Office and a number of Sales Divisions are moving to new headquarters in Thames Valley in September this year. In anticipation of this move we need a Personnel Officer to join us now.

Located at our new Head Office you will be responsible initially for recruiting local staff. During the period between appointment and September it will be necessary to spend some time in existing company locations. After the move the position will involve providing support to several Divisions. Reporting to the Personnel Manager, the areas of responsibility will include: recruitment; advice on procedures and conditions of employment; personnel administration and training.

Applicants should be graduates with a minimum of three years' experience in a general Personnel Department. Preference will be given to someone studying for, or having completed, a recognised course in Personnel Management.

Excellent salary is provided, together with good Company benefits including pension scheme, BUPA, and free life assurance.

1 The two advertisements reproduced here are separated by ten years and have been selected from commonly available advertising sources for personnel posts. One post was advertised in 1983 and one in 1993. Analyse (a) the respective employment philosophies behind the two adverts and (b) decide which advert appeared first. What are the significant factors that you would point to in comparing and contrasting these adverts?

2 If you have organisational experience (either in your current or previous occupation, or as a result of work placement in your course) draw up an advertisement for your job in that organisation to reflect that organisation's current needs and employment philosophy. Would your advert differ from one that might have been drawn up in the 1980s? Indicate the major differences that might be made.

3 If you *do not* yet have organisational experience, select a job known to you, of a relative or a friend, and draw up an advert for it based on the issues that this chapter discusses. What issues would you emphasise in setting out the requirements for employees?

PART

2

RESOURCING THE

ORGANISATION

3

Human Resource Management and the Labour Market

4

Human Resource Planning: Control to Seduction?

5

Job Design: Signs, Symbols and Re-sign-ations

6

Recruitment and Selection

INTRODUCTION

This part deals with the internal and external human resourcing of organisations. The four chapters within it examine the operation of labour markets, manpower and human resource planning, job design, and recruitment and selection. Although each chapter deals with specific aspects of the processes of acquiring, deploying and extracting performance from employees, four main themes provide a common thread which links them to each other.

Our first theme is the relationship of HRM to the search for flexibility, the related development of new production concepts such as just-in-time production and total quality management, and new concepts of organisations and how they should be managed, e.g. business process re-engineering. Chapter 3 outlines the various forces that have encouraged organisations to pay increased attention to cost reduction, productivity improvement and quality, and how this 'holy trinity' has been encapsulated, in theory at least, in the 'flexible firm'. Chapters 4 and 5 examine the implications of just-in-time, total quality management and business process re-engineering for human resource planning and job design. Likewise, Chapter 6 reflects on their implications for the recruitment and selection process. Chapters 4 and 5 also draw on recent theoretical and empirical literature which suggests that the concept of organisations as 'things', having permanence and stability and identifiable boundaries between the 'inside' and 'outside', is not only problematic in theoretical terms, but may also be beginning to be undermined empirically. This may have profound consequences for the nature of work and the employment relationship.

Following on from this, our second theme concerns how far and in what ways human resource management challenges older-established practices within organisations. Thus in Chapter 3 an economics perspective on HRM is developed which argues that HRM can be understood as an attempt to modify the operation of internal organisational arrangements for acquiring, deploying, rewarding and managing the performance of employees. Chapter 4 examines the basis for distinguishing between traditional 'manpower' planning and human resource planning, with the latter claiming to pay more attention to qualitative aspects of human capital such as commitment and flexibility than traditional manpower planning, with its emphasis on measuring and forecasting quantitative flows of labour through the organisation. Chapter 5 explores innovations in work organisation and job design which have been claimed for and by HRM and which are often represented as being a rejection of the previously dominant Taylorist approach. Chapter 6 discusses how far HRM has led to a questioning of the procedures for recruitment and selection that are associated with traditional personnel management, as recruitment and selection come to be viewed as strategic rather than merely operational activities.

The third theme is the way in which organisations' policies for human resources are influenced by wider contextual influences. Organisations may be seen in general as pursuing the goals of cost reduction, productivity improvement and quality, but the relative emphasis attached to these goals, the ways in which they are defined, and the specific actions taken to attain them vary widely across organisations and even more widely across countries. These strategic choices are influenced profoundly by the product market strategy of the firm, the supply of skills available in the labour market, and the extent to which financial structures and public policy encourage or discourage long-term investment, not only in physical capital but also human capital. These issues are discussed in each of the chapters, with reference to international comparisons.

Our final theme is the problematic nature of HRM, both in theory and in practice. In its insistence on strategic integration, HRM remains within the dominant approach to management, that of rational functionalism. That is, management is seen as an activity involving rational choices and planned actions aimed at achieving defined goals in the most efficient manner. However, this tends to imbue HRM with a unitarist perspective which pays insufficient attention to the contested nature of organisational relationships, the inevitability of conflict, the legitimacy of conflict, and the likelihood that all strategy is doomed to at least partial failure. This undermines HRM's claim to the status of theory. It also generates practical tensions, as evidenced by the concept of 'tough love' wherein employees are valued only as long as they are seen to be 'adding value' to the business. This may mean that employees experience HRM not so much as a humanising influence at work, but as a more onerous source of material and moral pressure to increase effort levels.

HUMAN RESOURCE MANAGEMENT AND THE LABOUR MARKET

Tim Claydon

OBJECTIVES

This chapter develops three economic perspectives on the labour market and how they can be used to analyse HRM. In developing and presenting the theoretical arguments contained here, no prior knowledge of economics has been assumed. We have tried to present theory in a way which is understandable on an intuitive rather than a formal level. Those of you who have some prior knowledge of economics and would like a more formal treatment of some of the arguments presented here are referred to the additional reading at the end of the chapter. King (1990) provides a useful treatment of labour economics.

•

To introduce competing theories of the labour market.

•

To examine how labour markets operate in practice, introducing the concepts of unemployment and wage rigidity.

•

To introduce the institutional and radical theories of the labour market.

•

To analyse labour market theories in relation to human resource management.

•

To make a critical analysis of the debates surrounding 'flexibility'.

•

INTRODUCTION

Human resource management has emerged as a set of prescriptions for managing people at work. Its central claim is that by matching the size and skills of the work-force to the productive requirements of the organisation, and by raising the quality of individual employees' contributions to production, organisations can make significant improvements to their performance. While the specific tools to achieve this may vary from organisation to organisation, human resource management seems to be charac-terised by the following principle:

- Human resources are key organisational assets since organisational performance depends on the quality of employee effort and, hence, on their ability and motivation.

From this there follows a set of prescriptions which have become commonplace in the human resource management literature:

- Human resource decisions should be integrated with other key business decisions at a strategic level within the organisation in order that the size, structure and deployment of the workforce are matched to market-led production requirements.
- Human resource policies, e.g recruitment, selection, remuneration, are integrated with each other so that they cohere.
- A crucial aspect of HRM is managerial action aimed at ensuring that employees have high levels of organisational commitment and motivation.
- Line managers rather than personnel managers play the main role in developing and implementing human resource strategy and policy.

There is little doubt that considerable tensions exist between the different elements of this prescription, as indicated by Storey's (1987) distinction between 'hard' and 'soft' human resource management. HRM is almost certainly less unified and coherent in prac-tice than in the prescriptive models which have sought to define it. Contingent factors exert a powerful influence on the way employment is managed in the real world.

This chapter is concerned with those contingencies which arise through the operation of the labour market. The policies associated with HRM can be seen as a particular set of responses to the way labour markets work and how this affects the employment relation-ship within organisations. As yet, however, little has been done to examine the economics of human resource management. While there is a burgeoning debate over how the labour market works, little attempt has been made to relate it to the HRM debate. This chapter aims to go some way towards filling that gap. The task is complicated by the fact that there is no single theory of labour markets, rather a number of differentiated and often competing approaches. Nevertheless, as the debate has evolved more attention has been paid to the internal relationships and managerial processes of organisations. By tracing this evolution it is possible to develop a labour market perspective on HRM.

THEORIES OF THE LABOUR MARKET

The debate over how labour markets work has led to a proliferation of theoretical insights and approaches. However, a basic division exists between those approaches which see the labour market as an arena of competition between individuals and those which see it as shaped and controlled by collective institutions, pressures and custom. As we shall see, the pure competitive theory of labour markets has nothing to say about HRM, since it is not concerned with what goes on inside organisations. However, the concepts which underlie the theory also underpin the refinements of and amendments to it, so it is necessary first to set out its main features in order that the subsequent evolution of the labour economics debate and its relevance to HRM can be properly understood.

The theory of competitive markets

The competitive theory of the labour market derives from *neoclassical economics*. The starting point is that our resources are scarce in relation to our wants so that we have to make choices as to how to allocate them. In making these choices it is asserted that we act individually as *rational economic maximisers*. In other words, in making our choices we seek to maximise the economic satisfaction that we can obtain from our resources. The process of rational individual maximisation can be outlined as follows:

- We have an ordered set of preferences such that if we prefer A to B and B to C then we must also prefer A to C.
- We act so as to maximise our economic well-being in the light of our preference schedule.
- Our preference schedules are independent of those of other individuals, i.e. we are not influenced by the preference schedules of others when we order our own preferences.

The condition for maximising the satisfaction that we can obtain from our scarce resources is that we will allocate them in such a way that no further reallocation can yield a higher level of satisfaction. Thus as consumers we will spend relatively more on satisfying our preference for A over C, but we will also allocate that expenditure so that the satisfaction we gain from our last penny spent on A is equal to that obtained from our last penny of expenditure on C. If this were not the case, and we were able to gain greater satisfaction by spending relatively more on A and less on C or vice versa, then as rational economic maximisers we would do so.

As workers our chief aim in work is to earn income to finance our consumption of goods and services. But that income itself carries a cost in the form of the leisure that we have to give up in order to earn it. As rational economic maximisers we will allocate our time between work and leisure in such a way as to maximise the amount of satisfaction we can obtain given our preferences as consumers. This combination will be different for different individuals, since some of us may be money-driven, with a relatively high preference for income relative to leisure; others of us may have a high leisure preference which makes us willing to forgo income in favour of free time.

Employing organisations are also assumed to operate as maximising individuals. This means identifying a level of output and a combination of inputs to produce that which results in the maximisation of total revenues relative to total costs. For non-profit organisations such as charities or public sector services, maximising behaviour will aim to maximise the benefits to recipients of services generated from a given set of inputs. In either case, rational maximisers will seek out the least-cost combination of inputs to produce the desired level of output.

Private sector firms operate in two sets of markets: markets for inputs or factors of production, the chief ones being labour and capital, and product markets in which outputs are sold. The theory of competitive markets argues that the greater the degree of competition in both sets of markets, the greater the pressures for cost minimisation. Competition between firms in product markets encourages them to seek ways of reducing costs and forces them to pass cost reductions on to consumers. Competition in factor markets prevents owners of factors of production from raising their own incomes at the expense of others by artificially raising the price of their inputs.

Market competition is therefore seen as producing *efficient outcomes* in two senses:

● it results in production being organised on the basis of least-cost combinations of inputs;
● it results in an efficient distribution of income in that each factor of production's share of total income equals its relative contribution to output. None can be made better off without making others worse off.

The desire to maximise economic well-being on an individual basis is often presented as a basic aspect of human nature, therefore the search for better economic efficiency is seen as a powerful inherent force among humans. From this it follows that market competition is a natural state since it is most consistent with individual maximising behaviour. While particular groups may have an interest in increasing their share of income above what is warranted by their contribution to output, competitive forces will prevent them from being effective except in the short run. However, government policy can encourage or inhibit market competition. Within the neoclassical approach there is a preference for policies which support and encourage competition. In effect this means a preference for government non-intervention unless it is to remove obstacles to the efficient working of the market. These arguments have been used to justify changes in government policy towards the public sector, e.g eliminating subsidies, privatising certain areas and introducing elements of market competition into those remaining in public ownership.

The basic competitive model of the labour market

In analysing the real world, economics, like other sciences, makes use of models. These are simplified versions of the real world. They are not meant to be realistic descriptions of it, rather they identify its key aspects in such a way as to enable us to make statements about how the real world works which can be tested against evidence. The starting point for the competitive analysis of the labour market is to build a model in which labour markets are *perfectly competitive*.

The characteristics of a perfectly competitive, and by definition, a perfectly efficient labour market are as follows.

● There is a large number of small, independent employers competing for labour in the market and also a large number of workers competing for jobs.

- New firms and new workers can enter the labour market at any time.
- All jobs within the same labour market require the same skills and all workers are equally productive in that they possess the same skills and ability. Any worker can do any job within that labour market. Furthermore, the only benefit to the worker from the job is the wage. There are non-wage benefits which attach to specific jobs which might lead workers to prefer them to other jobs available in the market.
- As well as being able to move freely between jobs workers are also perfectly mobile geographically; there is no advantage in working in one place as opposed to any other and there are no obstacles to movement from one place to another.
- The only cost to the employer of hiring labour is the wage. There are no 'fixed' costs of employment that may lead employers to prefer to retain existing workers rather than replace them with new ones.
- There is perfect information. All workers and all firms know the state of the market and are instantly aware of any changes in the market.

It follows from these conditions that there will be a single, uniform wage in the labour market. Wage differences between firms cannot exist because if they did, workers would know about them and move instantly from lower-paying to higher-paying firms. If the low payers wished to remain in business they would have to raise wages in order to retain workers, while high payers would reduce wages when faced with a queue of workers competing for jobs. The result is a single, uniform wage across all firms. It is therefore clear that individual employers and workers have no power to influence the market wage. They are all price-takers in the labour market. The only decision the firm has to take is how many workers to employ at the given wage. Two factors will determine this decision in the short run, the short run being defined as that period of time in which the firm is unable to alter the amount and/or type of physical plant used in production. These factors are:

- the law of diminishing marginal returns, and
- the conditions for profit-maximisation under perfect competition.

The law of diminishing marginal returns states that as successive units of one factor of production are added to a fixed amount of another, the amount which each successive unit will add to total output (i.e. its *marginal product*) will, at some stage, diminish. In the short run firms are unable to increase their equipment or buildings or introduce new technologies; capital is therefore fixed in the short run. Any increase in demand for a firm's output will be met in the short run by increasing labour inputs. Labour is the variable factor in the short run. However, adding more and more units of labour to a fixed amount of capital yields diminishing returns after a time. Adding one further worker to the labour force may raise output and revenue significantly. By the time the fiftieth additional worker has been hired, the value of the resultant addition to output may only just cover that worker's wage. Any further workers hired would add less to the value of production than the cost of their wage.

The condition for profit-maximisation in the short run in conditions of perfect competition is that the marginal product of the last unit of the variable factor equals the price (*marginal cost*) of that factor. In the labour market this means that employers will hire successive hours of labour up to the point at which the addition to revenue generated by the last hour of labour hired equals the hourly wage.

In the long run organisations can vary the amount of capital equipment they employ and adopt new technologies. This means that in the long run organisations can replace labour with capital or vice versa. Such substitutions will occur in response to changes in the relative price of labour and capital. Should capital become cheaper relative to labour, there will be a long-run shift to more capital-intensive methods of production since costs are reduced by employing relatively more of the cheaper factor of production. The optimum (least-cost) combination will be that where the ratio of marginal product to marginal cost for each factor is the same, or to put it another way, where the ratio of their prices is equal to that of their marginal products.[1]

Predictions of the competitive model

This model generates a number of statements or predictions about how real-world labour markets operate. The most important of these are as follows.

- The wage is determined by the marginal product of labour.
- The number of workers employed will vary inversely with the wage, i.e. as wages rise the quantity of labour employed will fall and vice versa.

This follows from the points made in the previous two paragraphs. Since the marginal product of labour diminishes and at the same time firms seek to equate the marginal product of labour with the wage, employers will only hire extra units of labour at progressively lower wage rates, assuming that other key variables such as the demand for output remain constant.

- The amount of labour offered in the market will vary positively with the wage. This is because an increase in the wage effectively raises the benefits that can be obtained from work relative to leisure. This leads to a rational decision to substitute extra hours of work for leisure.
- Since firms and workers adjust their demand and supply of labour in response to wage changes, it follows that the wage rate acts as the mechanism which 'clears' the market, i.e. brings the quantity of labour employed into equality with the quantity offered. A consequence of this is that the labour market operates like an auction with firms bidding for labour in the market. Should firms as a whole face a decline in demand for their output, fewer workers will be required in production. This means that at the current wage more labour is being offered than is needed. In this situation employers will reduce their wage offers until the amount of labour offered is once more equal to that demanded. If, on the other hand, product demand rises, in the short run at least so will employers' demand for labour. Firms will compete with each other for the available pool of labour, bidding up the wage. This will encourage existing workers to offer more hours of labour and encourage new workers to enter the market. Once again this process continues until the quantity of labour supplied is equal to that demanded.
- There will be no unemployment at the market clearing wage. While there may be some who are unwilling to work at that wage because of the nature of their leisure/income

---

[1] A formal demonstration of the conditions for profit maximisation in the short and long runs can be found in King, J.E. (1990) *Labour Economics*, 2nd edn, Macmillan, pp. 12–27.

preference, by definition they will not be seeking work and therefore cannot be said to be unemployed except in the sense that they are voluntarily so. All those wishing to work at the market clearing wage will be employed.

It should be clear that this model is a heroic simplification of the real world. It has nothing to say about the internal processes of managing people at work. Workers are hired up to the point at which marginal product equals the marginal cost of hiring them, i.e. the wage. Workers come equipped with necessary skills and their productivity is not affected by anything other than the technology of production. There is no need for firms to train workers, there is no need for policies designed to motivate them. Labour is a simple commodity, like fish. The marble slabs are missing in the labour market, but it is less than a century ago that dockers stood 'on the stones' outside dock gates waiting to be hired for a few hours' work. The model has nothing to say about HRM since it does not recognise the key problems with which HRM is concerned. There is, however, a clear view that the ideal employment relationship is an individual rather than a collective one.

The controversy that exists among labour economists centres largely on how far this model can cope with the complexities of the real world. As we shall see, it is necessary to relax some of the assumptions of the basic model and add a number of refinements to it in order to explain the operation of labour markets in reality. Even then, a growing number of economists, as well as sociologists and students of industrial relations, have questioned the adequacy of the competitive approach to analysing labour markets. Two key criticisms are that even its most refined versions cannot explain the things that we actually observe satisfactorily, and that by adding refinements to the model in order to take them into account, the competitive market approach is actually changing into something else. The following section identifies some of the main ways in which real labour markets do not seem to conform to the predictions of our initial model. We will then go on to examine the different attempts that have been made to explain these features and the light that they shed on the HRM phenomenon.

LABOUR MARKETS IN PRACTICE

Unemployment and wage rigidity

One of the first things that we observe in the real world is that unemployment exists. Contrary to the prediction of our initial model, not all of those seeking work can find a job at the prevailing wage rate. Moreover, we observe that unemployment can coexist with unfilled vacancies and rising wages for those in work. The wage adjustment mechanism does not seem to work, or if it does, only imperfectly. Table 3.1 presents statistical information about how unemployment and wage rates have moved in recent years.

One reason for unemployment is that the wage adjustment process does not operate in the way described in the basic competitive model. Employers do not immediately reduce wages as their demand for labour falls. Rather than adjusting the wage, employers will first cut back on recruitment, leave vacancies unfilled, cut overtime working, introduce short-time working and, ultimately, lay off workers. When their demand for labour rises the initial response is not to raise the wage but to demand increased overtime working and intensify recruitment. Employers initially go for quantity adjustments to changes in

TABLE 3.1
Unemployment rates and earnings movements, 1976–1996

Year	Seasonally adjusted unemployment, annual average in 000s	Average earnings index (1985 = 100)	Average weekly earnings, adult male workers (£)
1976	1298.9	37.9	67.0
1977	1413.6	41.3	72.9
1978	1410.5	46.6	83.5
1979	1312.1	53.8	96.9
1980	1611.2	65.0	111.7
1981	2481.8	73.3	121.9
1982	2904.1	80.2	133.8
1983	3127.4	87.0	143.6
1984	3158.3	92.2	152.7
1985	3281.4	100.0	163.6
1986	3312.4	107.9	174.4
1987	2993.0	116.3	185.5
1988	2425.7	126.4	200.6
1989	1841.3	137.9	217.8
1990	1664.5	151.3	237.2
1991	2291.9	163.4	253.1
1992	2778.6	173.3	268.3
1993	2919.2	179.2	274.3
1994	2636.5	185.5	– [1]
1995	2325.6	192.5	–
1996[2]	2158.1	200.7	–

[1] This series ceased to be published in 1994
[2] July figures only

Source: Employment Department/Department for Education and Employment, *Employment Gazette*, December 1980, 1984, 1986, 1991, 1993; *Labour Market Trends*, October 1996.

demand rather than wage adjustments. In severe recessions, when the demand for labour collapses, examples can be found of wage freezes and wage reductions. However, this is unusual, even in recessions as severe as those of the early 1980s and 1990s, as can be seen from Table 3.1 above. It is apparent that wages do not move flexibly in response to shifts in the demand for and supply of labour.

Not only do wages not instantly adjust in the face of changing demand and supply conditions, when they do move they do so asymmetrically, i.e. wages move up more readily than they move down. *Downward wage rigidity* has been offered as a major explanation for the large increases in unemployment that occur during recessions since, when the demand for labour falls, it prevents wages moving so as to simultaneously lead workers to reduce the quantity of labour they supply to the market and encourage employers to hire more hours of labour as wage rates fall. This suggests that competitive labour market forces are circumscribed, since the competition between workers for the reduced number of available jobs, which should bring about the wage reduction, does not appear to occur.

Inter-industry and inter-firm wage differences

The impression that competitive forces in the labour market are attenuated is reinforced by the existence of large wage variations across industries and even between firms in the same industry. From our model of perfect competition we predict that workers of the same ability doing the same job will be paid the same wage regardless of for whom they work. What we actually observe is very different. A study of a local labour market for engineering workers undertaken by Nolan and Brown (1983) found that there was a wage differential of more than 50% between the highest and lowest paying firms, with the remaining firms paying a variety of rates in between. Nor did these differences even out over time as we might have expected if competitive forces were in operation. The range of pay and the relative position of individual firms in the pay dispersion remained much the same over a period of ten years. It seems that who you work for does make a difference to your pay. This impression is reinforced by research conducted by Routh (1989), who found that the dispersion of rates of pay *within* occupations was greater than that *between* them. Not only does it seem to be the case that who you work for affects your pay; it could be that who you work for is the *most important* influence on your pay!

Internal labour markets

Our simple model of perfect competition pictured a world in which labour was casually hired and fired as necessary. Workers acquired their skills outside the firm and the wage rate was determined externally to the firm. We call this type of labour market an *external labour market*. In practice, however, many organisations operate differently, at least for certain sections of their labour force. Rather than relying on the external labour market to supply skills at an externally determined market rate of pay, many employers develop their own *structured internal labour markets*. Doeringer and Piore (1971) defined the main features of structured internal labour markets as follows:

- External recruitment is confined to junior and trainee positions which constitute limited 'ports of entry' into the organisation. Most other vacancies are filled by internal promotion and transfer. In this way current jobholders are shielded from direct competition from workers in the external labour market.
- Jobs are designed and arranged so as to provide career progression paths. Workers can move up job ladders by acquiring experience in lower level jobs and undertaking appropriate firm-specific training.
- Rates of pay attach to jobs rather than to individual workers, contrary to the competitive model.
- Pay structures are rigid and unresponsive to pressures from the external labour market. A study of firms employing professional engineers (Mace, 1979) found that they were unwilling to alter the salary structure even when faced with shortages of particular skills.

In summary, pay and the allocation of workers to jobs are determined by administrative rules rather than the market process. Thus in many organisations in the USA and Japan length of service (seniority) in one job is the most important criterion for promotion to a higher position. Pay progression is also often organised on the basis of seniority. Alternatively pay structures are defined through job evaluation procedures which reflect the relative status of jobs within the organisational hierarchy as much as competitive forces in the external labour market.

It should not be surprising that workers tend to remain with such organisations for a long time. Research into job tenure and worker mobility in the early 1980s found that adult males who were in full-time employment would, on average, remain in their jobs for twenty years. For women the figure was twelve years (Main, 1982). Most job-changing was concentrated among young workers. This is consistent with the idea that young workers move between firms seeking out the most advantageous job ladder within different internal labour markets. Older workers, having already progressed some way along job ladders, will be reluctant to move owing to the limited opportunities for entering other firms at a comparable point in their job hierarchies.

Internal labour markets are most highly developed in large Japanese corporations (see Chapter 19). Internal labour markets are also common in the USA where length of service rules often govern who is to be promoted or laid off. Within the UK internal labour markets probably grew in importance with the growth in the size of businesses during the 1960s and 1970s. Studies of firms employing professional engineers and professional chemists found evidence of internal promotion, rigid wage structures and low labour turnover (Mace, 1979; Creedy and Whitfield, 1986). Stable wage structures were also found among manual workers in engineering (George and Shorey, 1985). However, job ladders and internal promotion opportunities for manual workers were very limited, suggesting that internal labour market arrangements are more highly developed for non-manual than manual workers.

Summary: limits to competition in the labour market

We have seen that actual labour market behaviour often deviates from the predictions of the competitive model. There is persistent unemployment, even when wages are rising. Wages are rigid downwards and therefore do not act as the main means of adjustment to reductions in labour demand. Persistent wage differentials exist for similar types of labour. Structured internal labour markets are a feature of many organisations, especially for professional, technical and managerial personnel.

The features of labour markets outlined above suggest that organisations' decisions on wages and employment are not simply driven by the forces of labour market competition. Rather, organisations may be able to exercise considerable discretion in their employment policies. This raises some important questions. Is there more than one way to minimise costs? If so, why should this be the case rather than competition between firms defining the most economically efficient combination of inputs into the production process? Or does it mean that organisations do not maximise profits, that their goals, in so far as they can be identified, are more varied and complex? In the next section we look at different explanations for the features of real-life labour markets that we have identified here.

EXPLAINING THE REAL WORLD

Neoclassical economics: refining the competitive model

Neoclassical economists have responded to the apparent limitations of the basic competitive model by arguing that they can be explained by the fact that the labour market is not perfectly competitive and by special features of the effort-reward exchange. What we observe as deviations from or contradictions of the model's predictions are in fact examples of individual maximising behaviour within the constraints imposed by market imperfections. Once we recognise the existence of market imperfections it becomes possible to explain unemployment and wage differentials within the competitive framework.

Heterogeneous jobs and workers

Our initial model assumed that all jobs and all workers were the same. Clearly this is not the case. In reality there is not one homogeneous labour market but a number of sub-markets for different jobs and occupations. Worker mobility between sub-markets is restricted by the different skills and abilities required in them and the time and other costs involved in developing new skills. In other words, perfect general mobility of labour does not exist. Jobs and workers require and possess different skills. It is therefore possible for unemployment to occur as some occupations decline and others expand because of the time taken to rematch skills across sub-markets. This is compounded by obstacles to geographical mobility of labour, e.g. costs of moving house. It also follows that wage rates will differ between occupations.

The explanation for wage differentials advanced by Adam Smith as long ago as 1776 recognised the existence of differences between occupations and argued that wage differentials compensated workers for the relative disadvantages attached to jobs. Some jobs involve more physical danger than others. Some involve unpleasant tasks or anti-social hours. Others carry a high degree of earnings insecurity. There are jobs which are seen to involve heavy responsibility and a high degree of accountability. Some require lengthy periods of training during which earnings are low or non-existent. Such jobs will have to offer higher pay compared with jobs which do not carry these disadvantages in order to attract sufficient workers to them. Pay differences between occupations or jobs therefore equalise their net advantages in relation to each other. Thus someone doing a safe, secure job with easy hours in a pleasant environment will not feel badly off compared with a higher paid worker undertaking dirty, dangerous work involving weekend and night shifts.

Competitive labour market theory suggests that wage differentials are the outcome of competitive market forces given the heterogeneous nature of jobs. They represent an efficient mechanism for allocating labour between occupations of varying disagreeableness.

Smith also identified other, non-competitive sources of differences in pay such as nepotism, i.e. rewarding friends and relatives, and the use of rules limiting entry to occupations to create artificial shortages of labour within them and so increase the relative wage. These market imperfections distort the process of allocation, resulting in too many workers seeking jobs in occupations where the wage is artificially high and thereby giving rise to unemployment in the form of a queue of workers waiting for entry to the occupation.

This does not only mean that there is imperfect competition within the labour market as a whole. It also follows that we do not have perfect competition within sub-markets since workers cannot enter them entirely freely, at least in the short run, i.e. the time taken to acquire new skills. It is still possible, however, to assume that jobs and workers' skills and abilities are identical within each sub-market. But if this is so, how do we explain the kind of wage variations reported by Nolan and Brown (1983) and by Routh (1989)?

In order to explain *intra*-occupational wage differentials, that is different wage rates for the same or very similar work, in a way that is consistent with the basic competitive model two arguments are advanced. The first is an extension of the above argument with reference to differences in the size of employing organisations. It has been observed that wage rates tend to be higher in large organisations than in small ones. It is suggested that working in a large establishment is less pleasant than doing the same type of job in a smaller workplace. This is because large workplaces are alleged to be more impersonal and bureaucratic and more productive of stress. Workers in large establishments are therefore paid more than comparable workers in small establishments.

The second argument allows for differences in worker quality within occupations. Rather than assuming all workers within the occupational sub-market are of equal ability, differences in ability are assumed. These differences may be due to variations in natural ability or they may be the fruits of experience in the job. Since more able workers will have a higher marginal productivity than less able workers they will also be paid more. Intra-occupational differentials are therefore consistent with the competitive model. The question that arises, however, is whether differentials of the size observed in the labour market are readily explicable in these terms.

Imperfect information and labour market search

We saw above that perfect information was one of the assumptions underlying the perfectly competitive model of the labour market. Once we relax this assumption to allow for imperfect information, it is possible to add to our explanations of unemployment and persistent wage differentials while remaining within the basic framework of the competitive approach.

When information concerning wage offers and job content is incomplete it is rational for workers not to accept the first job they are offered. Instead they engage in *job search* with a view to maximising their future income stream. In practice workers will have a minimum acceptable wage (*reservation wage*) in mind. Any job offering a wage below the reservation wage will be rejected by the worker. However, job search is costly. It involves direct costs such as stationery, postage, travel and also *opportunity costs*, the most important of which is the income forgone by engaging in search rather than taking a job offer (it is assumed that job search is a full-time activity). Workers engaged in job search have to trade off the possible income gains from continuing their search against the income forgone by not accepting the latest job offer. As the period of search lengthens diminishing marginal returns to further search set in. This is because workers are likely to approach first those employers who are most likely to meet or exceed the worker's reservation wage. Subsequent search will be among employers less likely to do so. Consequently workers may be forced to adjust their reservation wage downwards. At the same time the additional costs arising from further periods of search will rise. The worker will stop searching and accept the next job offer when the expected additional benefits of further search are equalled by the expected additional costs.

Two things follow from this: first, job search can explain why unemployment can co-exist with unfilled vacancies. Because search is costly workers may not undertake sufficient search to enable all vacancies to be filled. Second, with imperfect information it is likely that some job-seekers will be luckier than others, i.e. some workers will find relatively well-paid jobs while others of equal productive ability will find less well-paid jobs. Imperfect information and costly job search mean that inter-firm wage variations need not even out.

The problem with this is that workers do not usually accept or reject jobs, although this is by no means unknown. More usually it is employers who select among workers in order to fill a vacancy. Employers' search behaviour can be analysed in a similar way to that of workers in that rational employers will seek to equate the marginal costs and benefits of labour market search.

Imagine an employer operating in a labour market where there are no variations in the quality of workers but where workers each have different reservation wages. In this situation a high wage offer by the employer will increase the likelihood of getting vacancies filled and necessitate less search for suitable workers. Alternatively the employer can offer a lower wage and take longer to fill the vacancy, the cost of this choice being the resultant loss of output until the post is filled.

A different case arises if we assume that the quality of workers is variable. Here organisations may employ various costly selection and screening procedures to identify workers of suitable quality. Organisations employing the most rigorous selection procedures will be those where an applicant's chances of being appointed are least – only the very best will be appointed. Therefore a relatively high wage will have to be offered to attract applicants. Organisations using less rigorous selection methods will be able to offer a lower wage. In this case wage differences reflect differences in the quality, i.e. marginal productivity, of workers.

Special features of the effort–reward bargain

So far we have explained deviations from the predictions of the basic competitive model of the labour market in terms of market imperfections. It is often argued that since perfect competition is simply a model of the real world rather than a description of it, we can make it more complex by allowing for these imperfections without losing the essential features of the model itself.

Employers and workers are constrained in their ability to maximise their well-being because of market imperfections, so labour markets will not function perfectly efficiently. There will be unemployment and persistent wage differentials which do not simply reflect differences in the nature of jobs or the quality of workers. Nevertheless, competition between rational maximising individuals is seen as the main influence in labour markets and outcomes are consistent with this. Wages are still determined by the worker's marginal product and wage differentials are mainly due to different job features and to variations in worker quality. This is particularly true in the long run, since this allows for technological change and the substitution of less expensive for more expensive factors of production, for the acquisition of new or additional skills, and the entry of new competitors into markets.

Labour market imperfections are, however, compounded by government policies where these reduce the force of labour market competition, and by the exercise of monopoly power by groups of employers or workers. Trade unions in particular are often singled out as sources of labour market imperfection in that they seek to raise wages above the market clearing wage, thereby creating unemployment. However, the labour market is still an external labour market; the question of structured internal labour markets has not yet been addressed. In this section we look at some particular features of the effort–reward bargain and how these influence organisations' employment policies. This in turn will raise further questions about the adequacy of the competitive theory of labour markets.

Labour as a quasi-fixed factor of production

In the simple competitive model of the labour market the only cost to the employer of hiring workers is the wage that has to be paid. Labour costs vary directly with production levels in both the short and long run. This distinguishes it from capital, the amount of which cannot be varied in the short run as production levels vary. This also means that labour turnover imposes no cost on the employer. In practice, however, there are certain fixed costs associated with employment. We have already noted the existence of costs involved in organisations searching for workers, the costs of recruitment and selection. There are also costs involved in training workers, particularly in skills which are specific to the organisation. The existence of these fixed costs means that labour turnover is costly to the employer. These costs include:

- losses of output due to unplanned reductions in the workforce resulting from workers quitting;
- financial costs of recruitment and selection;
- costs of training new recruits – these costs consist of direct costs of training provision and the cost in terms of reduced output while the worker is being trained.

The existence of fixed employment costs has important consequences for the management of labour and the operation of the labour market:

- The value of a worker's output has to cover the fixed costs of employment as well as the wage cost. Therefore workers will be paid less than the value of their marginal product.
- Employers will try to retain workers for at least as long as it takes the value of their output to cover the fixed costs of their employment. This is particularly the case where workers receive large amounts of employer-financed training. From this it follows that employers are not indifferent as between 'insiders' – those currently employed – and 'outsiders' – their possible replacements. They prefer to retain 'insiders'.

To avoid the costs of high rates of labour turnover employers adopt a variety of employment policies:

- Deferred benefits, i.e. benefits which are contingent on the worker remaining with the organisation. Examples include pension and holiday entitlements which only become available after a minimum period of service.
- Seniority wages, whereby pay rises with length of service.
- Avoidance of layoffs during temporary downturns in production. Organisations will look first to non-replacement of workers who leave the organisation, reducing hours worked, e.g. by cutting back on overtime, before laying workers off.
- During upturns in production, employers will first look for ways of increasing the output of the current workforce, e.g. through overtime working, before hiring additional workers. This is because the higher costs of overtime premia may still be less than the additional fixed costs of recruiting, selecting and training new workers.

Organisations will therefore seek to foster long-term employment relationships. This reduces inter-organisational mobility of labour and hence the degree of competition among workers in the labour market. It becomes harder for unemployed workers to compete for jobs with those already in work because of the fixed costs the employer would incur in replacing current workers with outsiders. This in turn means that there is less pressure on workers to accept wage reductions when the demand for labour falls. On the other hand, when the demand for labour rises, employed workers are able to raise wages because fixed employment costs initially deter employers from additional hiring. Persistent unemployment, asymmetry of wage movements and downward wage rigidity are further explained by the existence of fixed costs of employment.

Organisation-specific human capital

An extension of the above argument is the concept of organisation-specific human capital. 'Human capital' refers to the investment in education and training which is embodied in the worker. Some types of training develop 'general' or 'transferable' skills which can be used equally productively across different organisations. Others provide 'organisation-specific' skills which enhance the worker's productivity within the training organisation only. These latter skills tend to be those which are best learned or can only be learned on the job. Workers having organisation-specific skills will only be able to obtain a wage premium in respect of that skill within the organisation where they were trained. To leave would be to have to take jobs in which they were less productive and therefore less well paid.

Two things follow from this. First there is an incentive for such workers to remain with the organisation in which they acquired their skills. This gives the employer a measure of monopoly power over those workers. Second, however, the loss of organisation-specific skills would involve the employer in costly training of new workers. This means that workers with organisation-specific skills are in the short run monopoly providers of those skills. There is thus a situation of *bilateral monopoly*. In such a situation, competitive forces exert little direct influence on wage rates, at least in the short run. Instead the wage is the outcome of the relative bargaining power of the two sides.

Indeterminacy of the effort–reward bargain

In our initial model of the labour market output varied directly with the quantity of labour inputs, the precise relationship being determined by the technology of production. The level of effort supplied by workers is taken as given and assumed to be non-problematic. In the real world workers can exercise considerable control over their effort. When they hire workers employers are paying for productive potential rather than delivered output. Productive potential is converted into output in the production process. The extent to which productive potential is utilised, i.e. the actual effort level supplied, cannot be specified in advance and is dependent on a number of factors, one of which is the worker's own motivation. This distinction between productive potential and actual effort provides the basis for the neoclassical analysis of the role of management in the employment relationship.

Alchian and Demsetz (1972) argued that in any kind of team production, in which individual rewards depend on team performance, there is a possibility that individuals will shirk, supplying less effort than their fellows in relation to the rewards obtained. This will be most likely in large teams where it is difficult to measure individual contributions to team performance. Management therefore performs a necessary role of supervision. This is in the workers' own interest as well as that of the employer since shirking either reduces output and hence profits and employment, or else leads to inequities in the effort–reward bargain as between individual workers. From this viewpoint workers *want* to be managed; it is as likely that workers will hire managers as that managers will hire workers.

Supervision, however, is itself costly. Costs of effective supervision will be greatest in large organisations and where measurement of effort levels is difficult, or where it is difficult for management to define appropriate effort levels. The implications of this have been analysed by Williamson (1975, 1985). Where workers possess knowledge of the production process which can only be acquired on the job, management is prevented from sharing this knowledge and outsiders are no longer efficient substitutes for currently employed workers. In these circumstances Williamson describes the effort–reward bargain as being characterised by *idiosyncratic exchange*, i.e. the terms of the exchange are influenced by the idiosyncrasies, or special features, of jobs and the knowledge which attaches to them.

Idiosyncratic exchange means that there are limits to the extent of supervision that can be exercised without incurring disproportionate costs. In this situation it is possible for workers to behave *opportunistically*, that is to mislead managers about what are appropriate effort levels or about what actual level of effort is being supplied. Also, labour market discipline on existing workers will be weak since they cannot easily be replaced. This provides currently employed workers with what Williamson refers to as 'first mover advantages', i.e. bargaining power deriving from their position as 'insiders'. Once again we have a situation of bilateral monopoly.

Because of the limits to effective supervision it may be profitable for employers to offer incentives to workers in order to obtain their cooperation in delivering effort levels desired by management. Such incentives might include agreements on employment security, wage progression and promotion ladders. Another variant of this approach is the *efficiency wage hypothesis*. Given the costs of monitoring workers' effort it may be more profitable to pay a wage higher than can be earned in other employments as an inducement to supply high levels of effort. Thus management tries to minimise *unit labour costs*, i.e. total labour costs per unit of output (including costs of turnover and potential shirking) rather than simply minimising wage costs per unit of output.

Once we acknowledge the possibility that workers may withhold effort from the employer we add to our explanation of observed labour market behaviour. First, the effect of paying a wage higher than the market rate is to generate unemployment as workers are attracted into the labour market. This queue of potential applicants acts as a disciplinary force on those already employed since, while employed workers may not be easily replaceable, failure to meet management standards may ultimately result in dismissal. The efficiency wage also helps to explain inter-firm wage differentials since the costs of supervision vary among firms. The efficiency wage hypothesis can therefore be seen as an alternative to the theory of compensating differentials in explaining why wages in large establishments tend to be higher than in small ones. Efficiency wages also explain downward wage rigidity because a reduction in wage rates in response to a downturn in labour demand would reduce employee morale and weaken the basis for worker–management cooperation.

Taken together, quasi-fixity of labour and the indeterminacy of the wage–effort bargain provide a basis for explaining internal labour markets, although they have been put forward as competing explanations. Doeringer and Piore's (1971) approach to internal labour markets sees them as originating in the need for organisation-specific skills and training and the consequent attempt by employers to protect their training investment. Williamson (1985) emphasises instead the role of internal labour markets in reducing the *transactions costs* that would be involved in drawing up and enforcing highly detailed and specific contracts of employment. Nevertheless, there is a lot of common ground between them as the ability of workers to behave opportunistically stems from the specific nature of their skills, which in turn may be related to the technologies employed by organisations.

We may argue, therefore, that organisations seek to protect their training investments by deploying policies to retain trained workers. The same policies, e.g. promotion ladders, pay increments based on length of service, together with efficiency wages may also serve to elicit desired effort levels from workers, thereby reducing transactions costs.

Rent-seeking by workers

Another way of looking at policies aimed at securing worker cooperation with management is to see them as the result of rent-seeking behaviour by workers. Given the imperfect nature of competition in both product and labour markets, it is possible for organisations to generate 'surplus' profits (*rents*). This ability stems from the market power which organisations can exert when shielded from the full force of competition in the product market. In essence, output can be priced at a level higher than that which would obtain in a competitive market, generating profits over and above the minimum necessary to keep the organisation in business. Where workers possess a measure of bargaining power, they can use it to gain a share of the rents of the organisation. Rent-seeking can also be seen as a source of inefficiency in labour and capital utilisation since it may manifest itself in limits on effort levels imposed unilaterally by workers or agreed, informally or even formally, with management. Opportunistic behaviour can therefore be seen as a form of rent-seeking behaviour as workers use idiosyncratic job knowledge and first mover advantages to obtain a share of the rents of the organisation. It follows that such behaviour will be most noticeable in sectors of the economy where competition between organisations is weakest.

Implications for the competitive theory of labour markets

In developing theories of idiosyncratic exchange, bilateral monopoly and efficiency wages, how far have we moved away from a conception of the labour market based on competition between maximising individuals? On the one hand internal labour markets and efficiency wages can be presented as being consistent with profit-maximising or cost-minimising behaviour by employers. Their aim is to minimise unit labour costs rather than unit wage costs. It might be suggested that internal labour markets are in fact proxies for competitive external labour markets. In setting wages organisations undertake wage surveys in the relevant section of the labour market. These surveys provide information about the market wage to which the internal wage structure can conform. Internal wage differentials represent rewards for different productivities as between grades of worker. By using wage surveys and job evaluation organisations seek to ensure equitable wages which reflect performance. In this way it could be argued that internal labour markets are simply an institutional expression of competitive market forces.

However, for this to be so it has to be shown that external influences on wage levels and wage structures within organisations are stronger than internal ones. Evidence of large, persistent inter-firm wage differentials suggests that internal factors may often predominate and that it is not obvious that internal labour markets simply replicate competitive forces.

The efficiency wage hypothesis also challenges the competitive model. While it may be argued that efficiency wages are consistent with cost-minimisation, the main assumption underlying efficiency wages contradicts one of the main assumptions of the competitive model. Rather than the wage being determined by the productivity of the worker, the productivity of the worker is now determined by the wage. Firms may therefore be able to choose between alternative strategies regarding labour: a high wage, high productivity strategy, or a low wage, low productivity strategy.

Once we admit that employers may prefer to retain existing workers rather than seeing them as interchangeable in the labour market, that workers may value current employment more highly than alternatives, that workers can to some extent control their own effort levels, and that terms and conditions of the effort–reward bargain may be influenced by bargaining power, we move considerably away from our initial model of competition. The employment relationship ceases to be simply an act of economic exchange and takes on social and political dimensions. It becomes necessary to examine how employment relationships are structured and perceived, and how they relate to outcomes such as pay and productivity.

INSTITUTIONAL THEORIES OF THE
LABOUR MARKET

The refinements which have been incorporated into neoclassical theory in order to explain institutional arrangements such as rigid pay structures and internal labour markets mean that there is considerable overlap with institutional theories of labour markets. The main point of difference lies in institutionalism's rejection of the individual maximising postulate on which competitive theory rests.

Institutionalists argue that our preferences are not independent of those of others, but are interdependent. In other words we formulate our own preferences in the light of those of others. This idea has strong intuitive appeal; 'keeping up with the Joneses' is an everyday way of saying that the satisfaction that we get from our income depends not only on its absolute value, but also on its relative value compared with others. The importance which workers and their unions or professional associations attach to pay differentials suggests that the force of inter-group comparisons is strong. Institutionalists argue that notions of fairness and custom are important factors in establishing and maintaining pay differentials, which appear to remain stable over time.

Organisations' decisions are also seen to be interdependent. This is because in many product markets competition is not between a large number of small producers, but between a relatively small number of large ones. This means that, contrary to the assumption of the competitive model, an individual producer can, by its pricing and output policies and non-price strategies of competition such as marketing and advertising, influence the market conditions facing its rivals. Competition between producers then becomes like a game in which each player has to take into account the actions of others when deciding what strategy or tactic to adopt. They also have to consider how others will respond to the strategy or tactic adopted. In such a situation simple profit-maximisation is impossible. This is because the market situation facing each producer is indeterminate, since the outcome of any decision will depend also on the decisions made by others. Therefore other goals may be pursued rather than profit-maximisation, for example market share, organisational growth or a target rate of return on capital employed. The inability to maximise profits means that a certain amount of inefficiency is present within organisations. This is manifested in the under-utilisation of capital and labour, referred to as X-*inefficiency* (Leibenstein, 1987). X-inefficiency also results from the limits to competition which are the result of the ability of large producers to exercise a degree of power in the market.

While institutionalists accept that employers' needs to retain skills and obtain desired levels of cooperation may play a part in explaining efficiency wages, rigid pay structures and internal labour markets, they place more emphasis on the role of group norms, custom and collective power. These may be present among employers as well as workers but most attention has focused on the role of collective labour in influencing the labour market.

The starting point is the long-term nature of the employment relationship, which allows social bonds and a sense of collective interest and identity to develop among groups of workers. The emergence of group norms concerning 'fairness' in the effort–reward bargain is part of this process. Such norms include what is seen as an appropriate level of effort given the wage, how much any one group's wage rate should be relative to other groups, and what the limits are to the reasonable exercise of managerial authority. The development of such norms or standards is an attempt by workers to gain some control over the employment relationship in order to advance and defend their interests. There is no reason why these group interests should coincide with those of other groups, such as managers or shareholders. For example, workers' desire to maintain a given wage structure on grounds of 'fairness' may conflict with management's desire for change in the interests of 'flexibility'. The establishment and maintenance of norms may therefore require the exercise of power, and this encourages the development of collective organisation by workers. Therefore the terms of the effort–reward bargain are not simply the outcome of cost-minimising decisions by managers; rather they are negotiated outcomes which reflect the relative bargaining power of different collective interests.

LABOUR MARKET THEORIES AND
THE ANALYSIS OF HRM

It is evident that there is some overlap between the perspectives reviewed in the previous sections. Crucially, the refined competitive theory and both of the institutionalist approaches accept that there are special features of the employment relationship which make the conversion of productive potential of workers into actual effort problematic. This leads each of the perspectives to recognise that bargaining power plays a role in influencing labour market structures and the terms of the effort–reward bargain. However, the neoclassical view emphasises individual maximising behaviour as the main force underlying labour market behaviour, while institutionalist-structural approaches stress the role of collective forces. The competitive analysis of structural features of the labour market such as rigid wage structures and internal labour markets sees them as rooted in cost-minimising behaviour, i.e. efficiency-driven. Institutionalists argue that efficiency may not be the sole or even the main basis for such structures and radical institutionalists argue that profit, not efficiency, drives employers' policies in the labour market. We now go on to ask what these different perspectives tell us about HRM, focusing on the following questions:

- What is the rationale for HRM?
- Is this rationale equally compelling for all organisations?
- What are the implied outcomes of HRM in terms of its effects on established labour market structures and the distribution of rewards, in the labour market and as between wages and profits?

The rationale for HRM

Whether we take the competitive approach or adopt the institutionalist or radical perspectives outlined above, HRM can be seen as a management-led challenge to existing institutional arrangements within the labour market, particularly the internal labour market arrangements of employing organisations. The competitive and institutionalist approaches identify the sources of this challenge as lying in changing conditions in product markets and changes in technology. These changes can be summarised as follows.

- intensification of international competition;
- an acceleration in the pace of both process and product innovation, with a consequent shortening of product lifecycles;
- the re-emergence of major recessions as part of the dynamic of capitalist development;
- as a consequence of the above, product markets have become more volatile as well as more competitive, with sharper and more frequent changes in the level and pattern of demand;
- within the public sector, pressure to contain the level of public expenditure has led to increased attention being paid to cost control and resource allocation.

These changes have put organisations under pressure to reduce unit costs of production and/or raise product quality. They have also led to a search for ways of increasing the flexibility of organisations, i.e. their ability to respond to and indeed anticipate them. In terms of the management of labour this has meant reducing 'rigidities' and 'inefficiencies' in the allocation of labour and its utilisation which are seen to be associated with current features of the employment relationship.

As we have seen, many of the observed aspects of labour market operation have been explained in terms of the substitution of bureaucratic methods of allocating workers to jobs and determining the level and distribution of rewards in place of the competitive market mechanism. However, these methods, aimed at obtaining workers' cooperation in supplying effort and at generating and retaining skills within the organisation, are themselves costly.

- The need to provide promotion ladders as part of the internal labour market structure may create rigid job specifications which run counter to employers' needs for flexibility in the deployment of labour.
- Rigid wage structures run counter to employers' needs for wage flexibility, i.e. the need to link pay to aspects of performance and to vary pay structures in line with changes in the pattern of demand for different levels and types of skill.
- The provision of incentives to effort through job security arrangements, promotion ladders based on seniority, and/or efficiency wages may not succeed in eliminating opportunism by workers so long as idiosyncratic exchange remains a feature of the effort–reward bargain.

The competitive labour market perspective

From the perspective of the competitive theory of labour markets we expect rational maximising organisations to look for ways of reducing these costs when faced with increased competition in their product markets. Moreover, if it is the case that these arrangements are the outcome of rent-seeking behaviour rather than being efficiency-oriented, then the pressure for their modification will be all the stronger. This is because any intensification of competition will reduce the size of the rent which can be shared with the workforce.

In the light of this we can make some observations on the purpose of recent innovations in the management of labour which have been tagged with the HRM label.

- The decentralisation of pay bargaining within multi-establishment organisations and the vogue for individual performance-related pay are attempts to reduce rigidities in pay structures. Individual performance-related pay linked to appraisal can also be seen as an attempt to overcome problems of asymmetric information stemming from idiosyncratic job knowledge. By agreeing or setting performance targets for individual employees through appraisal, and linking pay reviews to performance outcomes, managers are seeking to gain greater control over the terms of the effort–reward bargain.
- The removal or relaxation of strict demarcations between jobs and the associated interest among managers in developing teamworking may represent a modification of the structure of the internal labour market which aims to make it compatible with the flexible deployment of labour. Job progression may continue to characterise the internal labour market; in fact opportunities for progression may be enhanced, but the criterion for progression is changed from length of service to the acquisition of bundles of skills through training.

- The reorganisation of work around quality control circles and work teams, and the replacement of supervisors with team leaders who are members of the work group, are consistent with management's interest in reducing information asymmetries and the scope for opportunism by workers. Quality control circles encourage workers to share their job knowledge with management and direct that knowledge towards improving productive efficiency. Team-based production with team leaders working as members of the group can be seen as providing management with access to detailed job knowledge, reducing information asymmetries in production.
- Selection procedures which emphasise a job applicant's personal values and attitudes as much as technical skills seek to ensure that selected employees are amenable and responsive to the systems of incentives and control, such as those outlined above, which are employed by the organisation.

An institutionalist perspective

The points above can be admitted within the institutionalist perspective, but its main emphasis is on how HRM policies alter the nature of power within organisations and the distribution of power between different interests. Thus an institutionalist view of labour markets leads us to view HRM as a means of coopting workers into the managerial vision of the organisation by establishing new norms of attitude and behaviour. 'Soft' HRM policies such as employee involvement seek to generate a 'commitment culture', sometimes centred round concepts of 'customer care' or 'total quality management'. Cooption may be extended to trade unions. This is most clearly exemplified by some recent agreements in which companies have recognised a single union as representative of the workforce in return for a commitment by the union to cooperate with management in programmes aimed at enhancing labour flexibility, increasing productivity and improving quality. Alternatively, where cooption of unions is seen to be impracticable or undesirable HRM policies may be used to marginalise the union role and individualise the employment relationship.

Radical perspectives

Taking a radical labour market perspective we might argue that policies such as those above stem from capital's need to raise the rate of profit by increasing the surplus value extracted from workers. However, institutional features of labour markets, as we have seen, are not just the product of capitalists' efforts to control and exploit labour. They have also been shaped by workers' resistance to exploitation. HRM represents an effort by capitalists to reshape labour markets and so create the basis for the more effective exploitation of workers. While this may involve policies designed to coopt certain sections of the workforce, others will be subject to work intensification, more direct control by management, diminished employment security and possibly lower pay.

From a radical perspective we would therefore extend the institutional approach to include the following aspects of HRM:

- Policies aimed at individualising the employment relationship seek to divide workers internally and weaken the basis for collective resistance to management. This may be particularly the case when technology or the need for flexibility requires teamworking and with it the possibility that workers might develop solidaristic attitudes and behaviour.

- Policies aimed at restructuring the workforce by reducing the proportion of 'core' or primary sector workers and expanding the 'periphery' or secondary sector of the labour market. Such policies are an intensification of divide and rule strategies across the labour market as a whole.

Radical theory also emphasises the role of state policy in the labour market and its relationship to patterns of exploitation at the organisation level. Examples are:

- policies of labour market deregulation as practised in the USA and the UK during the 1980s and 1990s, e.g. withdrawal or curtailment of legal protections for workers in respect of minimum wages, employment protection and social security, and anti-union legislation;
- the use of unemployment as a policy weapon to weaken further the bargaining power of labour. This is diametrically opposed to the view of unemployment taken by proponents of the competitive view of labour markets, namely that unemployment *is caused by* the bargaining power of trade unions.

The incidence of HRM

The competitive viewpoint

Depending on which view of the labour market that we adopt, is the rationale for HRM equally compelling for all organisations? From a competitive labour market perspective we would argue that cost-minimising organisations face a number of labour market decisions, among which the following are probably the most important:

- the amount of search to be undertaken in the labour market;
- how to acquire and retain skills in the workforce;
- how to obtain and maintain desired effort levels.

We have also seen that there may be trade-offs in each of these areas:

- increasing search against raising the wage or trading off worker quality against the wage rate;
- accepting costs of labour turnover as against offering (costly) incentives to retain workers;
- the degree of (costly) managerial supervision against the provision of (costly) incentives to workers to supply desired effort.

We have also seen that HRM is rationalised within the competitive model as a means of reducing unit labour costs, particularly those costs associated with the operation of internal labour market structures. However, we must remember that HRM policies are also costly. HRM will only be adopted by rational organisations where the ratio of benefits to costs exceeds that of other approaches to the management of labour. This implies considerable variety in organisations' labour market policies, since the costs and benefits associated with different policies will be contingent on numerous factors relating to the organisation and the labour market or markets within which it operates.

The classic external labour market policy is a casual 'hire and fire' regime. Labour turnover is high and wages tend towards the market rate. In the light of the modified competitive theory of labour markets such a policy is most likely where the employer operates in the market for unskilled labour. This is because search costs are low since the supply of unskilled labour is plentiful relative to that of skilled workers and there is a minimal requirement for the firm to invest in training. Employers will therefore accept labour turnover in preference to relatively more costly employee retention policies.

Unskilled workers will also have little scope for opportunistic behaviour since they possess little idiosyncratic job knowledge. This makes it relatively easy for management to monitor effort rather than having to provide incentives through internal labour market arrangements or efficiency wages. This is even more likely to be the case where the size of the workforce is small. Therefore there is no need for HRM policies aimed at protecting training investments or reducing information asymmetries and opportunistic behaviour within the internal labour market. The prescriptions of 'soft' HRM are therefore unlikely to be put into practice in such organisations.

In contrast, structured internal labour markets are predicted where organisations operate in skilled labour markets. Employers often contribute to the costs of training of skilled workers so they have an interest in retaining them. It is also the case that skilled workers have the ability to behave opportunistically by virtue of possessing idiosyncratic job knowledge. Therefore managers are to some extent reliant on the willing cooperation of these workers. Employment security, seniority wage progression and opportunities for internal promotion as well as efficiency wages are therefore more likely where skilled workers are employed. Indeed, the more discretion and individual responsibility workers are required to exercise in their jobs, and the greater the difficulty of exercising effective supervision, the greater will be the reliance upon incentives to effort. Therefore HRM policies that are designed to reduce the information asymmetries and reduce incentives to behave opportunistically within the internal labour market will be concentrated on skilled workers and workers required to exercise a high degree of discretion in their work roles. However, there is an additional condition which must be met for HRM to be introduced: that HRM policies result in net cost reductions. Given that introducing HRM may involve significant costs, we would predict its implementation only where perceived inefficiencies resulting from existing internal labour market arrangements are considerable.

Institutionalist and radical views

Here we would argue that HRM policies are most likely to be developed in organisations where

- employee pressure has generated significant rigidities within the organisation's internal labour market, and
- there is a strong need for organisational and behavioural commitment from workers which makes cooption strategies necessary.

Again this is most likely in organisations employing skilled workers exercising significant discretion in their jobs. The first of the above conditions on its own is probably insufficient to encourage HRM policies. This is because the success of workers in establishing gains at the expense of organisational rigidity could simply reflect the insulation of the organisation from competition in its product market. Once exposed to these forces organisations could opt to reduce labour costs and increase flexibility by exposing workers to competition in the labour market, as the following example shows.

Historically unskilled workers in the public sector have enjoyed terms and conditions superior to those of workers in comparable jobs in the private sector. However, since 1980 government has introduced competition into large areas of the public sector by means of compulsory competitive tendering for a range of services, e.g. rubbish collection, hospital cleaning. Public sector organisations can no longer simply employ their own workers to perform these tasks but must offer contracts which private firms can bid for against the public sector organisation. The lowest tender has to be accepted, subject in some cases to quality thresholds being met. This has meant that competition from cheaper labour employed by private sector firms has forced managers in the public sector to insist that their employees raise effort levels and productivity and/or accept pay reductions if work is to be kept in-house.

In this example the low skill content of jobs and the ready alternative supply of labour has meant that policies to elicit worker cooperation have been unnecessary and the discipline of the market has been used to reduce labour costs.

HRM outcomes

From the competitive perspective HRM outcomes must be viewed as positive since they are the product of efficiency-seeking behaviour. Unit costs will be lowered where HRM is adopted and pay will reflect worker productivity more accurately.

Institutionalist analysis might suggest that HRM is an efficiency-oriented response to the emergence of conflict between the external demands on organisations for flexibility and competitiveness on the one hand, and the 'rigidities' and 'inefficiencies' accumulated within their internal labour market structures on the other. While the successful implementation of HRM should therefore reduce inefficiencies in the allocation of labour and in the utilisation of both labour and capital, successful implementation cannot in itself be assumed. This is because institutionalist analysis stresses the role of different interests in the development and implementation of policies and their consequent impact on outcomes.

A perspective based on radical labour market theory sees HRM as being geared to profits rather than efficiency. HRM is depicted as extending managerial control over labour, even if in an indirect rather than a direct form, permitting the extraction of increased surplus value. However, the need to divide workers in order for this to happen means that some may gain in absolute and relative terms while others lose. Those most likely to gain are primary sector core workers occupying high-discretion roles. This may explain why HRM has been directed disproportionately towards management grades rather than lower grade clerical and manual workers. However, these gains could be transitory. We might argue that the cooption of high-discretion workers as part of a process of divide and rule based on segmentation of the labour market into primary and secondary sectors is a precursor to the redesign and downgrading of high-discretion jobs. This is because labour market segmentation weakens the ability of both primary and secondary workers to resist attempts to redesign and restructure work in order to increase the rate of exploitation of labour.

Meanwhile the main losers will be workers who are displaced from the primary to the secondary sector as a result of work restructuring and the redivision of labour. Other losers may be workers who remain in the primary sector but who have nevertheless been exposed to increased competition from the external labour market. These workers may well experience work intensification and declining relative earnings. Some recent commentators have suggested that this is actually happening as employers are withdrawing from previous commitments to long-term employment security, even for 'core' workers, and the concept of employment security is being replaced by that of 'employability'. In other words, employees can no longer expect a secure job, but the employer will help to maintain the employee's value in the labour market by providing opportunities for training and updating of knowledge and skills. Thus:

> Security no longer depends on a job or an organisation, but on the employee's competences and willingness to learn and adapt to changes in the organisation about the labour market. Core employes, incidentally, pay a heavy price for their position within the organisation; in the present circumstances of persistent high unemployment, they are under constant pressure to improve their performance. (Van Ruysseveldt *et al.*, 1995: 3–4)

Essentially, this means a transfer of risk and responsibility from employer to employee, coupled with more intense exploitation.

The limits to HRM

On the basis of the foregoing discussion it may be possible to offer some reasons for the rarity of HRM in practice (see Guest, 1989):

- Many organisations require low levels of skill and discretion from employees. Therefore conventional methods of controlling the effort–reward bargain are more cost-effective than HRM.
- Reductions in the size of employing establishments may have eased some of the problems of monitoring and control from management's point of view.
- Workers' ability to put pressure on the effort–reward bargain has been eroded by the rapid growth of unemployment during the early 1980s and 1990s, by legal restrictions on trade unions and the curtailment of legal protection of individual employees at work. These factors have had a disproportionate effect on the bargaining power of less skilled workers, but it may also be the case that managers can obtain compliance from skilled workers without having to pursue HRM policies aimed at securing willing cooperation. As one writer observed:

> Why should managers persist with complex, often delicate, schemes to involve workers in production systems, when the grim state of the market required swift and abrasive action. Far quicker and cheaper to play on employees' fears and kick a few arses, while trusting that the law has taken care of the unions. (Dunn, 1993)

Summary

So far we have viewed HRM from three different labour market perspectives. In each case, however, we have defined HRM as an attempt by employers to modify the operation of internal labour markets in response to changing external pressures. HRM has been presented as a means by which managers seek to reduce perceived costs, inefficiencies or obstacles to the exploitation of labour which are embedded in existing internal labour market structures.

This enables us to say something about the incidence of HRM and why it is so rare that it appears in the fully developed form laid out in so many textbooks. Briefly, we have argued that HRM is most likely to be attempted in organisations where bureaucratic mechanisms for the management of labour have replaced direct labour market competition. At the same time HRM initiatives will be more likely to occur when the workforce is predominantly comprised of skilled, high-discretion workers. Interestingly, these predictions remain broadly the same whichever theoretical perspective on the labour market we use as the basis for our analysis.

Regarding outcomes, the competitive approach suggests that HRM will result in efficiency gains. However, given the recognition of the relevance of bargaining power which is implicit in some versions of this approach, e.g. asymmetric information and insider–outsider models, group processes and collective pressures may influence outcomes in ways not necessarily consistent with cost-minimisation.

Institutionalist and radical approaches pay more attention to the processes by which the employment relationship is regulated. Indeed, an understanding of the various influences on processes is seen as essential to a proper explanation of outcomes. The subjects of HRM, the employees themselves as well as their managers, will influence HRM processes and outcomes in central rather than merely marginal ways. The force of this argument is illustrated in the following section.

CONTROVERSIES: THE FLEXIBILITY DEBATE

The central argument of this chapter has been that HRM involves the reshaping of organisations' labour markets so as to facilitate the more efficient use of labour or, alternatively, its more effective exploitation. This involves two categories of managerial initiatives. The first aims at increasing management's ability to structure the workforce and deploy and redeploy workers in line with changes in production requirements. The second is concerned with raising the quality and/or level of individual workers' efforts in production. There are clear links between the concept of HRM and that of *flexibility*. Flexibility has come to be seen as a goal of 'strategic' HRM with its 'hard' emphasis on the planned use of labour aimed at reducing unit costs of production. While labour is a valued resource it has to be deployed as efficiently as possible. This approach has found popular expression in the term 'lean production', used to label production systems which minimise overhead labour costs by stripping out jobs which do not contribute directly to production and by looking for ways to economise on the use of directly productive labour. Flexibility means the ability to adjust the size and mix of labour inputs in response to changes in product demand so that 'excess' labour is not carried by the organisation.

At the same time 'soft' HRM techniques, e.g. employee involvement and employee development programmes, can be seen as ways of achieving certain forms of flexibility at work. By involving workers in managerial decisions and plans for organisational change and by broadening workers' skills through training, HRM claims to create workforces which are flexible. This means being willing and able to acquire new or additional skills as production requirements change, and accepting of the need for the periodic redeployment of workers within the organisation.

An important element of tension within the concept of HRM is how far the 'hard' emphasis on managing the size of the workforce and utilising labour more fully is consistent with the 'soft' emphasis on obtaining worker cooperation with management and raising performance through improved motivation. This tension is clearly illustrated through the flexibility debate.

Origins of the flexibility debate

The flexibility debate emerged as a result of the changes which were experienced by Western European economies during the 1970s and 1980s. These changes undermined what had come to be seen as a stable pattern of economic growth and rising living standards in the 1950s and 1960s. The concept of flexibility emerged as a key element in debates over how Western Europe should respond to change. The main elements of change have been as follows:

- a long-term rise in unemployment throughout most of Western Europe – at the same time, the rate at which new jobs have been created has slowed down;
- product markets have become much more volatile and uncertain;
- the pace of technological change has accelerated;
- there has been a sharp increase in competition from newly industrialised countries such as Japan, Taiwan and Korea.

Labour market flexibility

At one level the flexibility debate has been about the reasons for unemployment and low rates of job creation. Advocates of the free market have blamed rigidities within labour markets in Western Europe. Legally enforceable employment rights for workers and trade union bargaining power have been presented as obstacles which prevent the labour market from adjusting to the changes that have taken place in product markets and technology. For example, restrictions on employers' rights to dismiss workers have been seen as preventing labour from being released from stagnant or declining sectors for employment in more dynamic areas of the economy. It has also been argued that by making it more difficult for employers to dismiss workers, employment protection legislation has discouraged employers from creating new jobs and led them in the long run to substitute capital for labour in production (Giersch, 1986). Trade unions have also been seen as preventing the necessary wage adjustments to encourage the reallocation of labour in the economy and permit fuller employment (Hayek, 1984).

Labour market flexibility is achieved by removing these rigidities so as to allow the labour market to approximate more closely to the competitive model. This implies a particular role for government policy;

- reduce legal restrictions on the hiring and dismissal of workers;
- remove state intervention in pay-setting, e.g. abolish minimum wage legislation;
- use the law and government policy to curb trade union influence over pay and employment.

Clearly, this view sees the labour market as being similar to other markets, and is one which has guided British government policy on employment issues throughout the 1980s and 1990s. Critics of this view argue that lowering labour costs by cutting back on workers' employment rights and making wages more flexible downwards is a 'cheap labour' policy. It is undesirable because it will result in low-paid, low-skilled jobs for the majority while at the same time being insufficient to give Western countries a competitive advantage against lower-wage countries in the Far East (Nolan, 1989).

The alternative vision is to develop a high-skills, high-wage response to changes in the world economy. This means developing production of products with high value-added where competition is on the basis of quality rather than simply on price. This requires high levels of skill and adaptability on the part of workers and high levels of management–worker cooperation within organisations. For the reasons outlined earlier in this chapter, it is argued that these conditions are unlikely to be realised within a framework of hire and fire and pressure on pay and working conditions.

This dimension of the flexibility debate relates to the question of HRM since government policy decisions influence the environment within which organisations make their labour market decisions. It may be that while society as a whole might benefit from a high-skills, high-wage path of economic development, individual firms may decide that it is more profitable to minimise investment in equipment and training, reduce labour costs and intensify work. It may be that government policies are needed to make such a route less attractive to employers. Recent European Union social legislation, in particular the social chapter of the Maastricht Treaty and the hostile response from some employers and especially the British government, can be seen as reflecting this aspect of the debate.

Organisational flexibility

One of the intentions behind government attempts to increase external labour market flexibility in the UK has been to provide employers with greater freedom to determine terms and conditions of employment in line with their own specific requirements. There is a strong conceptual link between the debate over labour market flexibility and the discussion of labour flexibility within organisations.

The need for labour flexibility within organisations stems from the following factors:

- Increased market volatility and uncertainty require that organisations should improve their ability to adapt to changes in markets. The implications for the management of labour are that organisations should be freer to vary the size and composition of their workforces in line with changes in demand.

- The acceleration of technological change, and the pervasiveness of applications of microprocessor technologies in particular, have eroded traditional job definitions and divisions between jobs. There is a need to reorganise work and redesign jobs in ways best suited to the efficient use of the new technology.
- The intensification of international competition has increased the importance of reducing unit costs of production and raising product quality. This in turn demands work reorganisation and job redesign to raise labour productivity and build quality into the production process.

Discussion has focused around how far and in what ways organisations are reshaping their labour market policies in the light of these factors. The key issues that have emerged in this discussion are:

- What forms does labour flexibility take at the level of the organisation?
- Have organisations introduced new, more flexible patterns of employment on a significant scale?
- What are the reasons for such changes? Is flexibility being developed as a strategic response to changes in market conditions? Might it therefore be seen as an aspect of strategic HRM?

The 'flexible firm' model

The idea of the flexible firm was developed during the mid-1980s at the Institute for Employment Studies at the University of Sussex (Atkinson, 1984, 1985). It starts by identifying the different forms of labour flexibility that might be sought by organisations and how they might be achieved. These elements are then brought together in the model of the 'flexible firm'. Four types of flexibility are identified:

- *Numerical flexibility*, defined as the 'ability to adjust the level of labour inputs to meet fluctuations in output' (Atkinson and Meager, 1986: 3–4). This is achieved by altering working hours or by altering the number of workers employed.
- *Functional flexibility*, defined as 'the firm's ability to adjust and deploy the skills of its employees to match the tasks required by its changing workload, production methods and/or technology' (Atkinson and Meager, 1986: 4). Functional flexibility is obtained by training workers to perform a wider variety of tasks and breaking down barriers to the deployment of workers across tasks.
- *Distancing*, in other words replacing employees with subcontractors. Contracts of service, i.e. employment contracts, are replaced by contracts for services, i.e. commercial contracts. Distancing enhances numerical flexibility of the organisation.
- *Pay flexibility* 'is concerned with the extent to which a company's pay and reward structure supports and reinforces the various types of numerical and/or functional flexibility which are being sought' (Atkinson and Meager, 1986: 4).

Taken together these elements amount to 'a reorganisation of firms' internal labour markets and their division into separate components, in which the worker's experience and the employer's expectations of him/her are increasingly differentiated' (Atkinson and Gregory, 1986: 13). The form of this reorganisation is illustrated in Figure 3.1. As we can see the segmentation of the employed workforce is into 'core' and 'peripheral' workers.

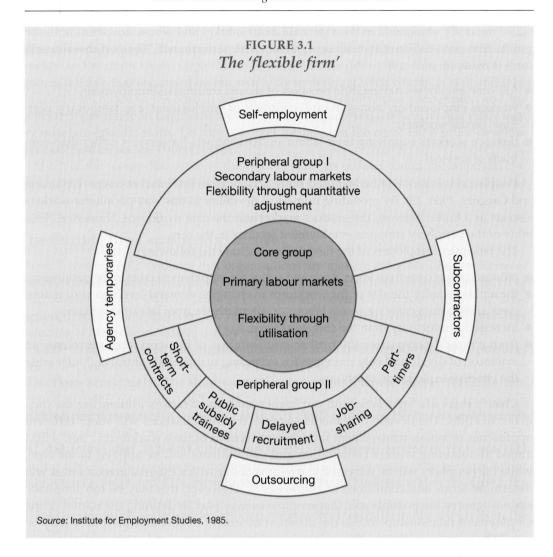

FIGURE 3.1

The 'flexible firm'

Self-employment

Peripheral group I
Secondary labour markets
Flexibility through quantitative
adjustment

Core group

Primary labour markets

Flexibility through
utilisation

Agency temporaries

Subcontractors

Short-term contracts

Public subsidy trainees

Peripheral group II

Delayed recruitment

Job-sharing

Part-timers

Outsourcing

Source: Institute for Employment Studies, 1985.

The *core workers* deliver functional flexibility by virtue of training, retraining and redeployment across tasks. The size and composition of the core will depend on organisational decisions on work organisation and the design of jobs, since core worker status applies mainly to those supplying firm-specific skills. Because organisations will have to invest in training core workers they will try to provide long-term employment security in order to protect their training investment. Moreover, continuity of employment is necessary for the build-up of skills and experience which form the basis of functional flexibility. Additionally, management is reliant on the cooperation of core workers in implementing and adapting to change. Therefore policies of cooption, i.e. 'soft' HRM, will be directed at the core workforce.

Peripheral workers supply numerical flexibility. That is, they are subject to variations in hours and to layoff and rehiring as required. Again, the size of the periphery will reflect the nature of skills sought by the organisation. Peripheral workers will be those whose

Ferodo deal on changes in working practices

Management and unions at Ferodo, the brake lining maker, have reached agreement in principle on widespread changes in working practices at the company's Derbyshire plant.

The changes are likely to include multi-skilling, the elimination of demarcation between grades, a job evaluation system, and site performance related pay.

A series of joint working parties, with representatives from management and the trade unions, have been set up to make specific proposals for change at the Chapel-en-le-Frith plant. They are expected to take some months to prepare their proposals, and the changes will come into effect gradually.

The negotiations have been going on since last November and have encountered stumbling blocks. In December, shop stewards representing the 1,600 workers were told that the company would consider closing the plant and moving operations to a greenfield site in the north-east if they did not accept more flexible practices.

Ferodo said yesterday the objective of the plan was to optimise the use of expensive capital intensive equipment by learning new skills and becoming more flexible.

At the moment, the company has many types of machines and numerous job levels for each machine. The company wants to both reduce the number of operating levels and eliminate the present system whereby a man operating a grinding machine, for example, would never operate a drilling machine.

There will be a review of working practices in all departments. Present job definitions, grading, pay structures and pro-

EXERCISES

Read the passages on the Burton Group and Ferodo and consider the following:

1 What are the main forms of labour flexibility?

2 What different forms of flexibility are illustrated in each case?

3 How might you explain the differences in the approach of the two companies to the question of flexibility?

How far organisations are consciously restructuring their workforces on a core–periphery basis in order to combine numerical and functional flexibility is, however, doubtful. There is nothing inherently new about employing part-time and temporary workers. Much of the growth of part-time employment, for example, has occurred as a result of the relative growth of the service sector of the economy which includes industries such as retailing where part-timers have always been widely employed. This is important because the flexible firm model was originally developed to be applied to changes in manufacturing. Yet it is in manufacturing that the moves to employ peripheral labour have been slowest.

The extent to which functional flexibility has been developed is also subject to doubt. The ideal depicted by the proponents of the flexible firm was the 'multi-skilled craft worker' able to straddle hitherto discrete areas of work such as mechanical and electrical engineering operations. Generally, progress in this direction has been slow. Where craft workers have developed some functional flexibility it has usually been limited to carrying out relatively minor additional tasks which are ancillary to their main skill. The expansion of the work of machine and process plant operators has generally been restricted to very minor maintenance work only (Cross, 1988). This has been confirmed in a more recent study by Incomes Data Services which found that employers have not aimed to create 'all-round craftsmen' but, rather, to 'equip them with the skills necessary to progress specific tasks more quickly, by avoiding the need to call on other craftsmen'. Moreover, multi-skilling was found to require employees' consent and cooperation, and this was often only gained following 'protracted negotiations between management and unions' (Incomes Data Services, 1994: 1). Neither is it clear what proportion of workers are affected by such changes. WIRS3 found that changes in working practices affecting 'all non-managerial employees' had taken place in only 8% of establishments (Millward *et al.*, 1992).

Empirical evidence also suggests that moves to increase the number of non-standard workers and/or to improve the flexibility of working practices owe little to the flexible firm concept. A survey of employers who had made use of one or more types of non-standard labour found that the reasons for employing such workers were much the same as they have always been. Tasks requiring limited time to complete and the need to match staffing levels to demand were the main reasons for hiring part-time workers. Temporary workers were hired mainly to meet fluctuations in demand, deal with one-off tasks and provide cover for absent permanent workers. There was no evidence that firms as a rule were using non-standard workers to provide employment security for a core of functionally flexible workers. Neither was there strong evidence to suggest that employers saw non-standard labour as a way of reducing wage costs by paying lower rates compared with full-time, permanent workers. In most cases hourly rates of pay were the same for all workers. It is possible, however, that this may be changing. The survey also found that organisations *increasing* their use of non-standard workers were much more likely to give reasons for doing so which were more in line with the flexibility thesis, i.e. reduced wage and non-wage costs and lower unionisation (McGregor and Sproull, 1992).

The limits to flexibility

There has been a tendency for the proponents of the flexibility thesis to see flexibility as something that is non-problematic. Moreover, anything which impedes the development of functional or numerical flexibility becomes a 'rigidity' which is by implication a 'bad thing'. However, the nature of the employment relationship, in particular the unspecified nature of the effort–reward bargain and the need for worker cooperation, means that in practice employers find that there are limits to flexibility. Greater labour flexibility may in some cases only be achieved at the expense of other aspects of employment relations which are valued by employers.

Organisations often perceive that there are significant costs attached to the use of non-standard labour. Temporary workers are seen to be less committed and reliable than permanent staff. Part-time workers employed on a permanent basis are seen as reliable but more difficult to manage than full-time workers because they spend less time at work. There seems to be a paradox here – the inflexibility of the flexible workforce! This not only restricts the uses to which non-standard workers are put; it has also meant that some organisations have moved away from non-standard contracts. This is because initial cost savings were seen to be outweighed by additional costs arising from lower commitment (Hunter and MacInnes, 1991, 1992).

The extensive use of non-standard labour can also pose other problems for organisations. A study of US-owned electronics plants in Ireland (Geary, 1992) found that local managers were keen to minimise their use of temporary workers despite certain advantages they provided in terms of the exercise of managerial control. This was because of the following:

- problems in providing necessary training for temporary workers within the period of their employment;
- widespread use of temporary workers was seen to lead to reduced commitment from permanent staff;
- conflicts between permanent and temporary staff which impeded the development of good working relationships;
- difficulty of terminating temporary workers once they had become integrated within the workforce and the organisation;
- a fear that being seen to operate different standards of treatment for temporary and permanent staff, e.g. in terms of non-wage benefits such as sick pay, might undermine management's claim to be following enlightened HRM policies for the workforce as a whole. This in turn could threaten the basis of trust and cooperation between managers and permanent staff.

The study concluded that 'management would have preferred to attain a requisite level of control over their labour force by engendering their cooperation and commitment to the organisation' (Geary, 1992: 267).

In other cases management's efforts to increase labour flexibility may conflict with other work arrangements and with existing agreements between management and unions. This is illustrated by a study of British Rail's introduction of 'flexible rostering' during 1982–3 (Pendleton, 1991). Flexible rostering was an attempt to increase the proportion of the time on their shift that train drivers actually spent driving trains. While management succeeded in moving from fixed eight-hour shifts to a work rota which provided for shifts varying from seven to nine hours, this increase in labour flexibility actually 'obstructed flexibility in both work scheduling and in day-to-day labour deployment' (Pendleton, 1991: 249). This was because of the need to reconcile management's aim of flexibility with existing agreements with trade unions regarding working hours and arrangements. The nature of the compromise was such that while flexibility of hours worked was increased, this detracted from, rather than improved, operational flexibility.

There are also limits to how far employers may wish to extend functional flexibility. Where highly specialist skills involving considerable training are required, it makes sense for the workers possessing those skills to be specialists.

ACTIVITY

The Coryton refinery

The Coryton refinery of the Mobil Oil Company concluded a flexibility agreement with unions in 1984 which provided for eventual total inter-craft flexibility. However, since then changes in working practices have led to a move back to craft specialism, albeit within new job definitions, and away from multi-skilling. This is due to changes in technology such as the increased use of computer technologies which require highly specialist training. Management feels that it would be uneconomic to use such employees to perform other work.

Source: Industrial Relations Review and Report 512, May 1992: 8–15.

EXERCISES

1 Draft your own version of the report to senior management which results in this partial return to craft specialisms. You should focus on the economic arguments for doing so.

2 Discuss how elements of functional flexibility might be retained within the new craft specialisms.

3 In discussion, identify two or three other industries where 'total' functional flexibility might not be cost effective and explain why this might be the case.

Summary: flexibility in perspective

The balance of research evidence relating to the flexibility debate suggests that while organisations have made efforts to increase flexibility in numerical and/or functional respects, these efforts do not conform very closely to the model of the flexible firm. In particular there is little evidence of core–periphery strategies being employed by organisations. More broadly, this may reflect the relative absence of any form of strategic thinking on labour matters among organisational managers.

The prevalence of short-term pragmatism in labour matters also suggests that organisations' labour policies may be influenced by the general labour market environment. Government policies aimed at increasing general labour market flexibility coupled with recession may encourage some organisations to cut costs by reducing standards of employment and taking advantage of workers' vulnerability to intensify work as suggested above on pp.101–2. While this may be presented in terms of the flexibility thesis, it is debatable whether such actions contribute to the long-term health of organisations or that of the economy. Some managers appear to recognise this, as shown in some of the case studies above. In particular, there may be significant costs attached to both numerical and functional flexibility initiatives if they weaken the basis for worker cooperation in production and discourage training and the development of improved skills.

CONCLUSION: HRM, FLEXIBILITY AND THE LABOUR MARKET

We can see that there are close links between HRM and notions of flexible labour strategies within organisations. On the one hand, flexibility, with its emphasis on the efficient deployment of labour, is an expression of the 'hard' strategic thrust within HRM. On the other, 'soft' HRM can be seen as a way of gaining the commitment of the 'core' section of the workforce. This implies that different HRM policies will be applied, not only as between organisations but also as between different groups of workers within the same organisation. This appears to be consistent with the perspectives on the labour market outlined earlier in this chapter.

There is, however, a tension within both HRM and the flexible firm thesis. Can organisations operate different approaches to the management of workers without detracting from the very outcomes that the policies are designed to achieve? Are 'hard' and 'soft' HRM compatible with each other? Is the existence of a peripheral workforce exposed to market forces consistent with a cooperative core? Radical theory might suggest that these compatibilities do exist since the aim is to divide workers and limit their ability to resist exploitation.

Refined competitive theory might reach a similar conclusion by a different route, arguing that rational policies aim to improve the efficiency with which the labour market works. Since one criterion of efficiency is that the market should meet the *various* needs of both buyers and sellers of labour, there is no reason why the efficient operation of one set of policies should interfere with that of the other.

These arguments both underplay the significance of workers' interest in influencing the terms of the employment relationship and their ability to do so. This is particularly ironic in the case of radical theory since, although it starts from the position that workers' resistance to exploitation is an important factor influencing the strategies and policies adopted towards labour by capital, it also tends to assume that the actual operation and outcomes of these strategies and policies are in line with capitalists' intentions. Somewhere along the line worker resistance drops out of the picture! The examples of electronics workers in Ireland and train drivers at British Rail suggest that to exclude workers' actions from the picture produces an incomplete view of the landscape of the employment relationship.

It may therefore be necessary to pay more attention to the role of workers and their organisations in shaping the content and outcomes of policies for the management of labour. If HRM is a response to the limitations of earlier attempts at resolving management's problem of converting labour power into actual productive effort, why should we expect HRM to succeed unequivocally when earlier, equally 'rational' policies have not?

Although HRM has as its text the cliché that people are an organisation's most valued asset, much HRM prescription has assumed that workers are in fact passive. In other words, given the right style of leadership, the appropriately packaged message delivered through properly designed channels of communication, workers will align their interests with those of management. Performance is non-problematic as long as reward structures, both intrinsic as well as extrinsic, are consistent with performance aims. While all this implies a lot of effort from managers, it continues to regard employees as a commodity rather than an active agent shaping the employment relationship. While it emphasises the need for consent in the employment relationship, the basis for consent is managerially determined. For all its attention to the question of how to manage people at work, HRM provides hardly any more insight into the nature of the employment relationship than the model of perfect labour market competition. HRM is therefore a set of prescriptions for labour market policy which requires rather than provides analysis and explanation.

SUMMARY

- This chapter has developed three economic perspectives on the labour market and the analysis of HRM: the competitive market, institutional and radical perspectives.

- The competitive market approach sees the labour market as an arena in which competing individuals – workers and employers – seek to maximise the benefits they can each obtain from the effort–reward exchange. The starting point is the model of perfect competition, but this is refined to allow for market imperfections which constrain maximising behaviour and lead to less than 'ideal' outcomes.

- Institutionalist approaches reject the concept of individual maximising behaviour, arguing that individuals' preferences and decisions are not independent of those of others. They focus on the interdependence of choices made by individuals, and the role of collective influences on them. This approach emphasises the role played by group norms, custom and collective pressure in shaping labour markets and labour market outcomes.

- The radical perspective takes the class nature of capitalist society as its starting point and argues that the condition for the accumulation of capital and the survival of the capitalist class is the exploitation of labour. Capitalist employers therefore seek to structure labour markets so as to weaken the ability of workers to resist exploitation.

- Each of these perspectives provides a particular focus on the HRM debate. The competitive market approach identifies HRM policies such as individual performance pay, relaxation of job demarcations and 'participative' approaches to work reorganisation as examples of flexibility which reduce inefficiencies in the employment relationship and lead to a closer approximation to competitive labour market outcomes.

- The institutionalist approach leads to an emphasis on the role of HRM in altering perceptions of power and conflict within organisations. HRM initiatives seek to promote acceptance of managerially-defined goals and priorities throughout the organisation, either by incorporating potential sources of organised dissent into management, or, if this is seen to be unnecessary or undesirable, by marginalising their influence.

- The radical critique of HRM sees it as an attempt to reshape labour markets so as to further divide workers among themselves and create a more effective basis for the exploitation of labour.

- HRM seems most likely to be attempted where bureaucratic forms of labour management have replaced direct labour market competition. In addition, however, HRM will be more likely to occur where workers have a high degree of discretion in their jobs, or where this is desired by management. These outcomes appear to follow from whichever theoretical perspective is used to analyse the labour market. It is in the evaluation of HRM in terms of the distribution of benefits between employers and employees and between different groups of workers, that the three perspectives differ significantly.

- It has been argued here that a weakness of HRM theory lies in its lack of attention to the active role that workers may play in shaping the employment relationship and the outcomes of the effort–reward exchange. A key question is how far HRM's emphasis on active worker cooperation with management is compatible with its other concern to maximise the efficient utilisation of labour as a *resource*. This issue is illustrated in the discussion of the debate over labour market flexibility and the flexible firm.

ACTIVITY

1 Analyse the approach to the management of workers in your own employing organisation or one with which you are familiar. It might even be your own college! See how far it can be explained in terms of any of the perspectives outlined in the sections 'Explaining the real world' and 'Labour market theories and the analysis of HRM' in this chapter.

2 Imagine you are in a management team setting up a factory or office for the first time in your area of the UK. You are aware that a range of wages and salaries is paid in the local labour market. Decide whether you should pitch your pay levels at the higher or lower end of the range.

QUESTIONS

1 What are the grounds for arguing that the labour market is different from the markets for capital and goods and services?

2 What are the main labour market issues that HRM seeks to address?

3 What features of their labour markets might lead many organisations to decide *not* to adopt an HRM approach to the management of their workers?

4 Identify the tensions and possible contradictions contained within the concept of flexibility.

5 Explain how (a) labour flexibility is an aim of HRM, and (b) labour flexibility might conflict with HRM.

REFERENCES AND FURTHER READING

Those texts marked with an asterisk are particularly recommended for further reading.

Advisory, Conciliation and Arbitration Service (1988) *Labour Flexibility in Britain: the 1987 ACAS Survey*, Occasional paper 41. ACAS.

Alchian, A.A. and Demsetz, H. (1972) 'Production, information costs, and economic organization', *American Economic Review*, Vol. 62 (Papers and Proceedings), pp. 44–49.

Atkinson, J. (1984) 'Manpower strategies for flexible organizations', *Personnel Management*, August, pp. 28–31.

Atkinson, J. (1985) 'Flexibility: planning for the uncertain future', *Manpower Policy and Practice*, Vol. 1, pp. 26–29.

Atkinson, J. and Gregory, D. (1986) 'A flexible future. Britain's dual labour market', *Marxism Today*, Vol. 30, No. 4, pp. 12–17.

Atkinson, J. and Meager, N. (1986) *Changing Working Patterns: How Companies Achieve Flexibility to Meet their Needs*. National Economic Development Office.

Braverman, H. (1974) *Labor and Monopoly Capital*. New York: Monthly Review Press.

Casey, B. (1991) 'Survey evidence on trends in non-standard employment', in Pollert, A. (ed.) *Farewell to Flexibility?* Oxford: Blackwell, pp. 179–199.

Creedy, J. and Whitfield, K. (1986) 'Earnings and job mobility. Professional chemists in Britain', *Journal of Economic Studies*, Vol. 13, pp. 23–37.

Cross, M. (1988) 'Changes in working practices in UK manufacturing, 1981–1988', *Industrial Relations Review and Report*, No. 415, pp. 2–10.

Doeringer, P.B. and Piore, M.J. (1971) *Internal Labor Markets and Manpower Analysis.* Lexington, Mass.: Heath.

Dunn, S. (1993) 'Hard times for workers' rights', *The Guardian*, 19 May, p. 18.

Edwards, R. (1975) 'The social relations of production in the firm and labor market structure', *Politics and Society*, Vol. 5, pp. 83–108.

Geary, J.F. (1992) 'Employment flexibility and human resource management: the case of three American electronics plants', *Work, Employment and Society*, Vol. 6, pp. 251–270.

George, K. and Shorey, J. (1985) 'Manual workers, good jobs and structured internal labour markets', *British Journal of Industrial Relations*, Vol. 23, pp. 424–447.

Giersch, J. (1986) *Liberalisation for Faster Economic Growth.* London: Institute of Economic Affairs.

Guest, D. (1989) 'Human resource management: its implications for industrial relations and trade unions', in Storey, J. (ed.) *New Perspectives in Human Resource Management.* London: Routledge, pp. 41–55.

Hayek, F.A. (1984) *1980s Unemployment and the Unions.* London: Institute of Economic Affairs.

Hunter, L.C. and MacInnes, J. (1991) *Employers' Labour Use Strategies – Case Studies*, Employment Department Group Research Paper 87. London: Employment Department.

Hunter, L.C. and MacInnes, J. (1992) 'Employers and labour flexibility: the evidence from case studies', *Employment Gazette*, June, pp. 307–315.

Income Data Services (1994) 'Multiskilling', *IDS Study* 538, July.

Kerr, C. (1954) 'The balkanisation of labour markets', in Bakke, F.W. (ed.) *Labour Mobility and Economic Opportunity.* Cambridge, Mass.: MIT Press.

*King, J.E. (1990) *Labour Economics*, 2nd edn. London: Macmillan.

Leibenstein, H. (1987) *Inside the Firm: the Inefficiencies of Hierarchy.* Cambridge, Mass.: Harvard University Press.

*Lindbeck, A. and Snower, D.J. (1988) *The Insider–Outsider Theory of Employment and Unemployment.* Cambridge, Mass.: MIT Press.

Mace, J. (1979) 'Internal labour markets for engineers in British industry', *British Journal of Industrial Relations*, Vol. 17, pp. 50–63.

McGregor, A. and Sproull, A. (1992) 'Employers and the flexible workforce', *Employment Gazette*, May, pp. 225–234.

Main, B. (1982) 'The length of a job in GB', *Economica*, Vol. 49, pp. 325–333.

*Marginson, P. (1991) 'Change and continuity in the employment structure of large companies', in Pollert, A. (ed.) *Farewell to Flexibility?* Oxford: Blackwell, pp. 32–45.

*Marsden, D. (1986) *The End of Economic Man?* Brighton: Wheatsheaf.

Millward, N. *et al.* (1992) *Workplace Industrial Relations in Transition. The ED/ESRC/PSI/ACAS Surveys.* Aldershot: Dartmouth.

Nolan, P. (1989) 'Walking on water? Performance and industrial relations under Thatcher', *Industrial Relations Journal*, Vol. 20, pp. 81–92.

Nolan, P. and Brown, W. (1983) 'Competition and workplace wage determination', *Oxford Bulletin of Economics and Statistics*, Vol. 45, pp. 269–287.

Osterman, P. (ed.) (1984) *Internal Labor Markets*. Cambridge, Mass.: MIT Press.

Pendleton, A. (1991) 'The barriers to flexibility: flexible rostering on the railways', *Work, Employment and Society*, Vol. 5, pp. 241–257.

Pollert, A. (1988a) 'The flexible firm: fixation or fact', *Work, Employment and Society*, Vol. 2, pp. 281–316.

Pollert, A. (1988b) 'Dismantling flexibility', *Capital and Class*, Vol. 34, pp. 42–75.

*Pollert, A. (1991) 'The orthodoxy of flexibility', in Pollert, A. (ed.) *Farewell to Flexibility?* Oxford: Blackwell, pp. 3–31.

Routh, G. (1989) 'Order and chaos, turbulence and strange attractors in labour markets'. Paper presented at the British Universities Industrial research Association Annual Conference, Cardiff.

Storey, J. (1987) 'Developments in the management of human resources: an interim report', *Warwick Papers in Industrial Relations,* Vol. 17.

*Thomason, G.F. (1991) 'The management of personnel', *Personnel Review*, Vol. 20, pp. 3–10.

Van Ruysseveldt, J., Huiskamp, R. and van Hoof, J. (1995) *Comparative Industrial and Employment Relations*. London: Sage.

Watson, G. (1994) 'The flexible workforce and patterns of working hours in the UK', *Employment Gazette*, July, pp. 239–247.

Williamson, O. *et al.* (1975) 'Understanding the employment relation: the analysis of idiosyncratic exchange', *Bell Journal of Economics*, Vol. 6, pp. 250–280.

Williamson, O. (1985) *Markets and Hierarchies: Analysis and Antitrust Implications*. Glencoe: Free Press.

HUMAN RESOURCE PLANNING: CONTROL TO SEDUCTION?

Damian O'Doherty

OBJECTIVES

To examine critically the discursive and metaphorical figures which underpin and support the traditional vision and interpretation of manpower planning.

●

To assess the extent to which the responsibility for manpower planning has shifted in response to strategic managerial initiatives designed to appropriate aspects of human resource management.

●

To locate areas of dissension within organisations over the objectives and practice of manpower planning and to evaluate the extent to which a more 'unitarist' human resource planning transcends divergent 'stakeholder' interests.

●

To outline and elaborate the methods and techniques typically associated with manpower planning and contrast this with the supposed distinctiveness of human resource planning.

●

To identify internal and external political (economic and labour) and market factors which both complicate and distort 'pure' manpower/human resource planning.

●

To consider the organisation and discipline associated with new forms of manpower planning such as team working and self development.

●

To consider the 'ideals' of human resource planning in the context of differing European labour market structures and regulation. Is human resource planning compatible therefore with the political management and regulation of the UK labour market?

●

MANPOWER PLANNING: DEFINITIONS

Traditional definitions and approaches to 'manpower planning' have tended to delimit and define it as a central personnel activity which attempts to reconcile an organisation's need for labour with available supply in local and national labour markets. In essence, manpower planners initially seek to estimate their current and future employment needs and, like the analogy sometimes made with the practice of navigation, 'uses scientific method in applying his knowledge and skills, within the limits of the equipment available, in order to establish first his position and then his best possible course and speed, with a view to arriving at a chosen destination by the most suitable route' (Smith, 1976: 16).

For many years large organisations would vest considerable faith and trust in the techniques and science of specialism and expertise. Specialist departments or groups within personnel would typically concentrate exclusively on manpower planning. Typical issues which these departments address would include the following:

- How many employees does the organisation currently employ?
- What is the age profile, by department, of our employees?
- Where in the organisation are these employees to be found?
- Which are the biggest departments in the organisation?
- What skills do our employees possess?
- How many employees, on average, leave the organisation every year?
- In which areas of our business do we tend to 'lose' more employees?

These questions are fundamental to the day-to-day activities of manpower planners and are crucial for the future success of the business. Human resources are considered the most valuable, yet the most volatile and potentially unpredictable, resource which an organisation utilises. If an organisation fails to place and direct human resources in the right areas of the business, at the right time, and at the right cost (Smith, 1971; Bramham, 1990), serious inefficiencies are likely to arise creating considerable operational difficulties and likely business failure. Consider the rather unlikely, but illustrative, example of a business which one day finds that all its employees in the accounts department suddenly retire! This ridiculous situation is an extreme example of poor manpower planning. Most organisations would keep records on the age profile of their departments so that such events can be catered for with specific development, progression, recruitment and training plans. Forecasting, record keeping and statistical projection have traditionally been the staple diet of manpower planners as they seek to ensure that human resources are channelled through organisations in an orderly and disciplined fashion.

The simple example of a football team manager may well illustrate the importance of monitoring the age, skill and cost of human resources. A good football team requires a balance of maturity and experience together with youthful skill and dynamism. Football managers need to reconcile a number of competing demands in order to maintain a settled and competitive side. They face choices between recruiting through the 'ranks', developing their own home-grown talent and buying in outside players who have developed elsewhere. Of course all successful teams manage to blend and balance these sources of supply. Buying in skill in reaction to poor performances may cost a lot of money and unsettle the side and prove no guarantee of success, as Manchester United, for many years, were wont to demonstrate!

Sophisticated statistical and computer technology is often used in large organisations in an attempt to plot accurately where current resources are in the business, where they are going and with what speed, and the likely need and timing of 'stock replacement'. For example, if an organisation is aware that historically it has always lost 25% of its graduate intake within the first 18 months of employment, it can make contingency plans to recruit and train resources to 'replace' those that leave. In this way the manpower planner is not 'shocked' by manpower needs as accurate forecasting has allowed the planner to develop contingency plans.

In the current pursuit of Human Resource Management many organisations appear to be practising Human Resource Planning as opposed to Manpower Planning. How are we to understand this change? Is it one which is best described as 'old wine in new bottles', and hence simply a matter of semantic change, or is something more fundamental happening in the process, techniques, ambitions and outcomes of resource planning? This is part of a far greater theoretical and practical reorientation in the way in which employees are thought to be best managed and regulated. At this stage it is probably easier to recognise that empirically it is a mixed picture with some organisations claiming to be fundamentally changing the way they plan, develop and regulate human resources, while for others it appears that a simple name change has taken place. At its most radical human resource planning claims to abandon the '"them and us" attitudes of the past, based on control systems and discipline, budgets and bureaucracy. Today, the emphasis is all on fairness and flexibility, integrity and development, creativity and commitment' (Bramham, 1989). The role of personnel departments, it is argued, is being devalued as organisations seek to vest far more flexibility and responsibility in the role of the production line managers. The administration associated with 'form filling' and 'pen pushing' is now seen as tiresome and time-consuming leading to sclerosis and the bureaucracy associated with the inefficiencies of cumbersome large institutions. Whether UK organisations have the entrepreneurial ability to reorientate and replace the values and practices of traditional manpower planning towards conflict-free creativity and development in teamworking, cellular manufacturing process teams, or multi-functional project groups is a central concern of this chapter. We show how manpower planning confronts a series of constraints and pressures in the context of institutional and legislative structures in the UK labour market. Together with the tensions and vicissitudes characteristic of organisational morphology and the divisions and persistent inequalities in the employment relation, we question the extent to which manpower planning can be a discrete, strategic or well-defined activity which remains the exclusive preserve of 'management'.

In sum, advocates and prescriptions for a more strategic human resource planning, which adopts multiple and flexible patterns of employment, need to be examined within the context of an organisational politics that recruits, retains and disciplines to effect an efficient movement and distribution of employees. By maintaining control over the quantitative and qualitative 'flows and stocks' of manpower, the organisation should function smoothly by having the right labour, in the right place, at the right time and cost. This requires the coordination of what is called demand and supply forecasting, together with the monitoring and assessment of productivity and technological changes (Armstrong, 1979; Timperley and Sisson, 1989). Hence there is both a quantifiable and qualitative dimension in the successful planning and management of human resources requiring careful coordination between the 'external' product and labour markets and the 'internal' organisation of resources.

In the following section we outline a theoretical critique within which we can begin to approach and understand manpower and human resource planning. Following this we explore the traditional schematic prescription of manpower planning by identifying those who 'do' manpower planning, the rationale and need for such planning, and the components and stages which form the creation of a manpower plan. Developments in contemporary organisation, teamworking and self development are then explored and in the final sections we locate manpower planning in the changing context of the UK and European labour market regulatory systems. Students may wish to follow through these sections *before* they consider the section on assumptions and the field of vision in manpower planning, especially those who are studying this subject for the first time. This theoretical critique is intended to be challenging and provocative and may appear rather 'difficult' and 'novel' on first reading. Yet we believe it is essential for deepening our appreciation of the complexity of manpower and human resource planning to frame contextually the rather abstract statistical and modelling techniques – which for far too long remained institutionalised as the orthodox. It would be naive if manpower planning was simply introduced as a set of techniques and procedures, whose failure and increasing contemporary irrelevance can perhaps be understood through a study of this kind.

ASSUMPTIONS AND THE FIELD OF VISION IN MANPOWER PLANNING

The discourse of manpower planning has traditionally appropriated metaphors of 'stocks', 'flows', 'systems', 'state' and 'equilibrium' (see Smith, 1976; McBeath, 1978) often directly from meta-sociological and economic theory. Such meta-theoretical work remains at best contested and partial, if not discredited by developments and revisions in the understanding of the limitations not just of the theory from which this borrows but all grand narrative 'catch-all' theoretical explanations. Second-order business administration techniques and methodologies typically borrow indiscriminately from versions of Talcott Parsons' sociological model of structural functionalism (see Cole, 1991). This was contested within its own field in the 1950s and subsequently subject to such revision and critique that contemporary students of social theory and the philosophy of social science may only come across Parsons in footnotes to textbooks. However, the situation remains in the field of business administration, personnel management and the 'sciences' of marketing and accounting that this appropriation is forgotten, its contested nature suppressed, and its metaphors and methodology reified to an extent whereby it comes to take on the status of *science* and *truth*. The political and economic pressures which encourage this remain too complex to engage with in this introduction, but students should remain vigilant about the language, metaphors and world view which are perpetuated in personnel management. In George Cole's orthodox account of personnel management, this bias remains an integral, and even celebrated feature of his text in his claim that 'the approaches described throughout this book are firmly part of the functionalist approach, complete with managerial bias!' (Cole, 1991: 32).

In terms of manpower planning, the assumptions of human behaviour and the human subject, the 'purposes' and values presumed to hold in something called organisation, and the nature of the employment relation, remain hidden if not actively suppressed. If we consult the *Oxford English Dictionary* we appreciate the sense of divorce and detachment (Cooper, 1993) involved in many of the assumptions and practices of manpower planning. By divorce and detachment we mean the abstraction involved in the assumptions which enable orthodox manpower planning to proceed. To plan implies to *derive* or *contrive* by means and media to control and attempt to 'tame' the active forces, energy and agency which remain only loosely under the classificatory and designative capacity of 'planners'. To plan is to construct an 'imaginary' flat surface or plane, as in a perspective drawing where 'several imaginary planes perpendicular to the line of vision form a grid within which the objects represented appear to *diminish in size* according to the distance between the viewer and the planes' (*Oxford English Dictionary*, emphasis added). Here one can see the abstraction and detachment involved in the planning process.

Planning derives from the root *plano-* which is from the Greek *planos* which captures a richer and more ambiguous sense – of wandering, of 'free living' and 'mobility', as in planetary movement. Over time this conceptual ambiguity of planning has been lost as it becomes increasingly equated with the rational, interventionist construction of active self-centred human subjects in ordering, classifying and organising the world around them. Robert Cooper (1993) explores a similar conceptual emaciation which takes place in contemporary orthodox accounts of 'technology' and 'representation'. Technology is seen to derive from the Greek *techne* which meant the art of bringing something forward or present to the senses of the human body, as in making something available for use and understanding. However, the root of *techne*, namely *tech*, derives from the Greek *tuche* which named that which was not under the control of the human being – in particular, accidents, chance and fate. Therefore *techne* was that which controlled and ordered the vagaries of chance and accident, hence that which conquers chance for the advantage of the human subject. Furthermore, *techne* was considered to be more *detached* from the interference of chance and accident:

> Human action expresses itself in relation to *tuche* in terms of attachment (at-tach-ment) and detachment (de-tach-ment). The more attached action is to *tuche*, the more it is influenced by chance and vagary; the more detached it is, the more able it is to exert mastery and control.   (Cooper, 1993: 279–280)

In modern uses of the word technology we tend to lose sight of this ontological relation as conceptually technology is confidently reduced and equated solely with that which masters and controls.

This narrow rationalist frame of reference governs much of the manpower planning tradition and remains explicit in the work of those concerned with the planning of manpower resources in the civil service (see Smith, 1976). The tone of the contributors to this text is that of an unquestioned faith in the rational and abstract principles of statistical forecasting. It is assumed that if these techniques are adopted rigorously and exercised within sufficient domains which impinge on the planning of resources, regularity and control can be achieved in the movement and distribution of labour. In reducing what is a complex and contradictory play of political, economic and social-psychological relations to one of quantified abstraction, where individuals appear simply as 'data' to be manipulated in a multi-variable regression equation (Rowntree and Stewart, 1976), an injustice is done to the difficulty and practice of management. That such statistical techniques are assumed to remain neutral and without value bias appears naïve in the extreme.

Following the logic of Rowntree and Stewart (1976) we are informed that staff numbers can only be correctly calculated and projected if the manpower planner is able to

de-correlate the *factors* which are causally related to workload levels. If, in calculating differing workload levels, for example L1, L2, L3 and L4, we fail to account for 'inter-related'
forces which affect staffing requirements (p. 41), we fail to capture the underlying and
essential factors which affect the workload level and hence staff numbers. Manpower
planning has a tendency incorrectly to isolate the contribution of forces $x1$, $x2$ . . . etc. by
coefficients $b1$, $b2$ . . . etc., which results in a situation where the coefficient $b1$ for example
is not simply a measure of $x1$ but picks up the influence of cross-correlated forces.

Here the adoption of multi-variate regression in orthodox manpower planning takes
account of a complex number of factors which are positively or negatively related to staff
requirements and which require both correct identification and measurement. So, for
example, in a tax office processing tax claims staffing levels will depend not only on the
number of tax claims made ($x1$) but on the complexity of the claims, which can be
assessed, forecast and quantified by a variable $x2$ and the size of the claim $x3$. One
member of staff may be required therefore for each 100 tax claims made of type i, and in a
simplified regression analysis the bi coefficient would equate to 0.01. Staff numbers (y)
would equal $biXi$ where bi represents the coefficient of x which translates Xi into staff
numbers. In the example here, where t=time period 1:

$$y^t = biXi$$

therefore:

$$y^t = 0.01(100)$$

and hence the calculation reveals we need 1 member of staff for each 100 tax claims made of
type i. Cross-correlation would disturb our result if we calculated a figure for the numbers of
individuals falling into a particular tax bracket and calculated this as a variable having an
independent effect on staffing levels. There is likely to be a cross-correlation because an
increasing number of individuals falling within a relevant tax bracket will affect the number
of tax claims of Xi and therefore the coefficient bi will not be measuring an independent variable. By measuring one variable, one X, and assuming its independence, we may wrongly
calculate the number of staff required to service this demand. Our calculation would be
wrong because there is a strong cross-correlation between the variables. Hence, according to
this analysis, we may overestimate or perhaps underestimate our calculation of staff levels.
What is required is a de-correlation of the factors in order to arrive at the underlying funda-
mentals which can be measured directly in terms of their impact on staff levels:

> In theory staff numbers can be expressed in terms of these underlying factors,
> which may be projected into the future and used to derive forecasts of staff.
>
> (Rowntree and Stewart, 1976: 43)

On the basis of such rigorous statistical techniques in developing forecasts and trend
analysis, we are led to believe that staffing levels appear as some *fait accompli* of the neutral
tools of science. But it is the very abstraction and detachment of these techniques from power
relations and contestation within social relations which belie its neutrality. Consequently, no
matter what effort we effect to de-correlate and measure underlying factors, if these underlying factors are not predictable, but irrational and subject to the caprice of accident, chance or
contingency, our statistics necessarily *border* the *tuche* as identified by Cooper (1993) above.

Although most orthodox approaches to manpower planning pay tacit recognition to
the contribution of trade unions, in the negotiation over issues such as productivity,

expectations, norms, standards, work organisation and acceptable staffing levels, the acknowledgement tends to be couched in terms of order and predictability. Trade unions are seen simply to add legitimacy to the neutral techniques of statistical forecasting. This extends the managerial prerogative by drawing unions into the logic of the neutrality of these techniques and the procedures which support a normative commitment to the values of agreement, resolution and regulation (see Clegg, 1975, 1979; Hyman, 1978).

Staffing levels may reflect the consolidation over time of contested, variable and negotiable relations in the organisation, allocation and distribution of work. Thus, the assumption of some neutrality in the measurement of variables and forecasts of staffing levels is simply a projection from an assumed 'state of nature', a 'state' which may reflect simply a temporary consolidation or alliance in the struggles and caprices of social relations. At any moment one could interpret this arrangement of relations and norms as only a temporary and partial *solidification* of what remains in tension, fractious, perhaps even chaotic. In the violent abstraction of planning, which detaches from these social relations and power inequalities which organise and construct a 'balance of forces' in the employment relation, we see how complexity is *diminished* in size. The tradition of manpower planning is one which tends to construct analysis as if looking through an inverted telescope. As Foucault (1971) observes in his critique of the faith in the purity and singularity of origins in linguistic, conceptual and categorical thought, this represents almost a timeless-ness, a faith in the stable continuity of history. For Foucault this commitment:

> is an attempt to capture the exact essence of things, their purest possibilities, and their carefully protected identities because this search assumes the existence of immobile forms that precede the external world of accident and succession. (1971: 78)

The persistence of manpower planning techniques which maintain a commitment to utilitarian and unitarist rationality colours and blinkers to such an extent that those factors which cannot be subsumed within its logic are relegated to a distant dustbin of error, deviance and irrationality. Consider the work of McBeath (1978), who in discussing the necessity of control over recalcitrant subordinate managers urges the importance of vigilance in audit control (pp. 188ff). The rationality of the techniques of manpower planning are not called into question and thus any deviance from the manning norms established by these methods must be the result of irrationality, a lack of understanding or the irrational grandiose ambitions of empire builders. The chance that capitalist organisations are precisely about aggrandisement, growth, power and empire building does not enter into consideration. Deviance from prescribed standards must be punished and the managers 'red circled' (p. 189) for the convenience of the corporate gaze so as to enable it quickly to identify likely future sources of transgression:

> Unfortunately, a few managers and supervisors are exceptionally able at maintaining their over strength establishments, somehow managing to get replacements even when someone does transfer or leave. It is these areas that the audit seeks to identify. (McBeath, 1978: 189)

Such a perspective remains consistent with the command-and-control discipline of authority, hierarchy and tradition, which perhaps until recently governed the perspective and management of organisation. The manner in which discipline and authority are understood and constructed in contemporary organisations may of course differ, but it is arguable, as we shall see, that the one-dimensional rationality (Marcuse, 1964) of techni-cal utilitarianism persists in the context of traditional and emergent corrosive forces and lines of division.

The language of manpower planning, in addition, continues to remain masculine – the discourse of 'power', 'efficiency', 'control' and 'manpower'. Fundamentally organisations reflect sobriety, control and exactitude in geometry and essence, although one which can be disturbed and polluted, led astray, by the as yet unconquered irrationality of conflict, deviance and stupidity. The exhaustive procedures and information-gathering techniques of manpower planning will eventually tend to order. A steady-state equilibrium is the natural state of affairs which can be maintained in vitality and health, unified and coher-ent in order to allow further conquest and expansion. The language of 'conquest' pervades texts on manpower planning – the conquest and control of nature and the assumption that precautionary contraceptive safeguards will guarantee 2.2 offspring together with the optimal allocation and distribution of resources. This desire for comple-tion and wholeness involves the repression and suppression of 'otherness' – whether competing frameworks, alternative rationalities, or novel epistemology and ontology (see Inayatullah, 1990). The conquest and control which support the metaphors and perspec-tives of manpower planning suggest and reflect the military and imperial history from which they derive. In fact, in many places in the manpower planning library, unashamed explicit reference is made to the roots of planning, recruitment, selection, training and regimen. According to Bartholemew and Forbes (1979), 'The statistical techniques of man-power systems must be as old as the planning of the military and building exploits of the ancient world' (p. 8). Acceptable statistical risks in trench warfare have been translated into the language of redundancy and wastage, and where muscle, power, force and pro-ductivity remain the common currency in mapping and constituting those variables which form the essential characteristics of employees and their social relations. The cen-tral planner at the apex of the organisation carefully calculates and calibrates, classifying and arranging, mapping movements and change, resolving the complexity of human relations by the slide rule and calculation. As McBeath (1978) argues, manning systems require the constant attention and supervision of an elite of 'management':

> The regular attention of a systems man is essential, as much to ensure that
> some activities are discontinued or reduced in frequency, as to enable fresh
> demands to be made. (pp. 189–190)

This image of the white-coated male technician, omnipotent in virility, rendering the world calculable for order (see Kallinikos, 1995), not only seems dangerous but in some ways rather sad. The discussion which follows attempts a modest introduction to man-power planning which recontextualises these heroic assumptions. The analysis attempts a novel introduction and critique by developing the often obscured and hidden context, referred to above as 'traditional and emergent corrosive forces and lines of division', which limits the coherence and utility of the abstractions and techniques typically thought to accompany planning and to be available for use in our heroes' 'toolbox'. As we will seek to show, manpower planning remains an idealised abstraction from the struggle and contesta-tion which characterise the day-to-day interaction of social and non-material relations. What Law (1991) calls the heterogeneous network can be seen continually to compose, decompose and recompose under and within the ordering imperative of the calculated plan.

———

WHO DOES MANPOWER PLANNING?

Traditionally in large organisations the function of manpower planning was carried out by either the personnel department or a specialist manpower planner within the personnel department. In many smaller organisations, often in the absence of any well-defined separate personnel department, the process of manpower planning would have been conducted by the manager of the organisation. In small family-owned firms, for example, it may well be that the manpower planner would also be the wages clerk, the financial manager, the marketing and distribution manager. It is really only in large-scale and often bureaucratic businesses that specialised personnel departments and manpower planners exist. Large-scale organisations like the Civil Service, the National Health Service, the Royal Air Force and the large high street retail banks have traditionally been the focus of study for manpower planning. In the 1950s and 1960s, with full employment and an expanding dynamic international economy, the emphasis within manpower planning was one of recruitment and retention and as such manpower planning came to be seen as providing a critical contribution to profitability. In times of labour scarcity manpower planning expanded as a credible managerial practice seeking to provide and maintain sufficiently skilled resources within organisations. If organisations suffered from a high turnover of staff in the 1960s it would have created considerable operational difficulties as with full employment staff would have been difficult and costly to replace. Consequently these large organisations sought to invest considerable resources into the management of manpower planning at a time when 'organisation structures were highly centralised and relatively stable, with the emphasis on promotion and upward mobility; and the main concerns were recruitment and retention' (Timperley and Sisson, 1989: 103). The scale at which such organisations were operating, both geographically and hierarchically, clearly necessitated some planning and coordination of where human resources were, and where they were needed, through identifying shortages and surpluses. Keeping a tight control on the cost of maintaining such a large and diversified workforce required considerable time and effort in manpower planning and control. Centralised within specialised head office departments incumbent with their hierarchical vantage point, manpower planners could literally provide an overview of manpower flows throughout the entire organisation.

In the context of the 1980s traditional manpower planning has fallen somewhat out of favour as organisations have sought to reduce their staffing levels in response to product market crisis and international economic competition. With its associated bureaucracy and red tape manpower planning has been forced to reorientate its contribution to organisational success in an era which has seen large-scale rationalisations, redundancies and restructuring. In the 1987 report of the Manpower Services Commission 'competence, commitment and the capacity to change' were deemed to challenge the quantitative traditions of manpower planning. However, this might strike one as odd on reflection, as the number of redundancies, early retirements, plant closures and reorganisations have multiplied, often entailing the use of novel forms of labour and labour contracts. In addition, during the late 1980s personnel managers were increasingly expressing concern over UK demographic changes with all the attendant fears over supply shortages and recruitment difficulties. For many there was the very real fear that there would be an insufficient number of young and qualified individuals, prompting management to seek new, and often controversial, forms of employment. What might be a more realistic interpretation, therefore, of the state of contemporary manpower planning may be an appreciation of the restructuring of manpower planning itself as it is forced to reorientate its own values and approach to the regulation of employment. In a recent study it has been reported that organisations 'prefer neither to use the term "manpower" nor to return to the large and elaborate planning documents produced by head offices a decade ago' (Cowling and Walters, 1990: 3). This is taken up in greater detail in the section on the management of change later in the chapter. For the moment it is necessary to stress that many organisations are seeking to redirect the responsibility for manpower planning from centralised specialised departments towards production line managers while maintaining strategic hold and direction at corporate level (see Storey, 1991, 1992; Salaman, 1992). This might be consistent with some of the supposed moves towards human resource management in general.

With the current emphasis on flexible manpower use, novel forms and contracts of employment, together with innovative approaches to career and succession planning, one might be tempted to suggest that the nomenclature Human Resource Planning does capture the essence of contemporary personnel and human resource management. As Bennison and Casson (1984: ix) suggest, in a somewhat cavalier fashion, manpower planning 'belongs to the world of calculation, computers and big bureaucracies'. In its place it would appear that many theorists are recommending, and, although far from typical, many organisations are seeking to develop, strategies and policies which address 'labour skill shortages and cultural change rather than hierarchical structures, succession plans, and mathematical modelling' (Cowling and Walters, 1990: 3).

THE NEED FOR MANPOWER PLANNING

The importance of manpower planning was seen for many years to lie with the contribution it could make to reducing shocks and disturbances within the employment patterns of large organisations.

In large organisations the simple numerical flow of individuals is a task which requires careful and detailed monitoring. Over a number of years patterns may be expected to emerge and in many cases the role of manpower planning was to build up a picture of such resource flows. In a stable environment, where the features and characteristics of product and labour markets could be expected to continue and persist in a predictable and orderly fashion, a model of long-term patterns of employment within the organisation would emerge. This would show the expected number of retirements, the expected turnover of staff within departments and the average number of staff which leave for 'involuntary reasons'. This would give a broad and rather crude picture of numerical turnover, and hence could be used to provide valuable information on replacement times and rates. In other words, in order to maintain numerically stable employment over time management requires data on when, where, and how many employees need to be recruited.

The precise statistical and qualitative complexities and details which contribute to a manpower plan will be considered in more detail later in the chapter. At this stage it is important to appreciate that manpower planning is a critical managerial function because it provides management with information on resource flows which is used to calculate, amongst other things, recruitment needs and succession and development plans. This has been described above as an attempt to reduce shocks and disturbances. With detailed study of past and projected trends in 'employment loss' management can seek to minimise the shock of unexpected shortages of labour, inefficient and costly surpluses, and needless redundancies.

For example, if historically you have always recruited two junior members in the marketing department leading you once again to seek to recruit two employees, management would be 'shocked' if they found the marketing department understaffed and unable to complete work on time. Upon further enquiry it might transpire that in that particular year there were more retirements, an 'unusual' amount of sabbaticals, a large amount of maternity leave, an unexpected high degree of sickness leave, or indeed a higher than expected amount of deaths! On closer analysis of relevant variables one might find that the marketing department was increasingly becoming a top heavy and mature department. Furthermore, British Airways were offering free around-the-world tickets for that year, child allowances had trebled due to a rather generous restructuring of the Treasury under a Labour administration and an epidemic of typhoid flu had been sweeping across Western Europe! Although a rather humorous example, it highlights the importance of manpower planning and the endless possibility of variables that one could possibly consider. This is partly why the task of manpower planning is such a difficult and time-consuming process involving a considerable amount of research and knowledge of current events which may shape and affect the availability of internal resources and indeed the current stocks of human resources available for recruitment in the local and national labour market.

How many variables is it sensible therefore to consider in a detailed manpower plan? If all variables are not considered then it may well be the case that at some stage management will be 'shocked' by 'disturbances' in organisational employment patterns in response to both internal and external environmental changes. It was well known, for example, that in certain British car factories in the 1960s and 1970s there would be a heavier than normal rate of sickness and absence on Fridays! Being aware of the variables which affect manpower supply is a crucial area of concern for professional manpower planners and as the examples above show it can be critical for the success of the organisation. If management remained ignorant of the ebb and flow in the organisation's employment patterns and the variables which led to changes, then severe operational difficulties would emerge as management found itself with some departments over-staffed, other departments suffering from a chronic shortage of employees, and possibly some departments which could not function on Fridays because of the absence of staff. The need for manpower planning arises therefore from the operational needs of an organisation and its importance lies in maintaining a sufficient supply of employees, in the right place and time, and at the right cost. Only through detailed observation and planning of many variables, both internal to the organisation and external in the wider political socio-economic environment, can management ensure a reconciliation of labour supply and demand such that shocks and disturbances are avoided.

It should be sufficiently obvious at this stage that manpower planning involves both a quantifiable and quantitative dimension leading to:

- recruitment plans: to avoid unexpected shortages etc.;
- the identification of training needs: to avoid skill shortages;
- management development: in order to avoid bottlenecks of trained but disgruntled management who see no future position in the hierarchy but also to avoid managerial shortages – this often requires careful planning;
- industrial relations plans: often seeking to change the quantity and quality of employees will require careful IR planning if an organisation is to avoid industrial unrest.

In practice, 'manpower planning is concerned with the demand and supply of labour and problems arising from the process of reconciling these factors' (Tyson and York, 1989: 76). In summary, the need for manpower planning lies with the long-term and short-term operational needs of the organisation but also, critically, with the needs and aspirations of individuals within the business.

THE CREATION OF A MANPOWER PLAN

In this section we will look more closely at those traditional techniques which contribute to the planning of manpower resources both in terms of internal considerations and external factors which influence the final outcome of the manpower plan.

Internal considerations

Wastage analysis

Initially the manpower planner will be concerned with the average number of employees that leave and therefore need replacing just in order to maintain a constant number of employee resources in the organisation. In large organisations with many departments and demarcated lines of responsibility this can become quite a difficult statistical task requiring considerable time and effort in the collection, synthesis and analysis of data. In smaller organisations it can often be calculated very simply because the informality and personal nature of the organisation create a climate where everybody knows everyone else and when someone leaves it is quite an important and visible event. In large organisations it is far more likely that an employee is simply seen as a payroll number, or a job code. The constant ebb and flow of 'numbers' within the organisation requires a far more rigorous calculation of 'wastage' than the rule of thumb and management–owner discretion in smaller firms.

The simplest way of calculating wastage is through a turnover analysis:

$$\frac{\text{Number leaving in one year}}{\text{Average number of employees}} \times 100 = x\%$$

However, this gives a somewhat crude and unrealistic picture of wastage because it fails to locate where these people are leaving from. In general, though, it gives a broad picture of the current state of employees in total and it is usual to consider a 25% turnover rate as perfectly respectable in modern large-scale organisations. Anything approaching 30–35% may well start alarm bells ringing because it suggests that a large amount of money is being directed into advertising and recruiting employees who are more likely to leave than in an average 25% turnover organisation. However, as we suggested above, when the manpower planner comes to formulate plans and policies to address this turnover this figure does not provide much useful and practical information. For example, where are these people leaving from? What is the average age of the person who is leaving? For example, it could be that your turnover figure has become distorted over the recent past because of the age profile of the organisation and in any one year it may be that there are far more employees than on average reaching retirement age. Consequently it would be more useful to decompose this figure into those that are retirements from those which are 'voluntary'. Furthermore, turnover might be limited to one particular category of employment, one department, a certain grade or one geographical area. The variety of influences which affect employee turnover are far too numerous to be captured by one calculation such as the labour turnover ratio. Thus for practical reasons we need a more subtle index of turnover which is more closely identifiable with factoral influences.

An alternative to the labour turnover ratio is the Labour Stability Index (Bowey, 1974) which is calculated from the following formula:

$$\frac{\text{Number of employees exceeding one year's service}}{\text{Number of employees employed one year ago}} \times 100 = x\%$$

This calculation, by contrast, calculates and emphasises those that stay and hence is known as a stability index. Its importance can be demonstrated through a calculation and comparison with the turnover ratio. Consider two companies:

- Company X which in January 1990 employs 2000 assistants, but by January 1991 800 have 'voluntarily' left. This gives a turnover of $800/2000 \times 100 = 40\%$.
- Company Y which in January 1990 employs 2000 assistants, but by January 1991 only 100 have actually 'voluntarily' left the company, although they have been replaced eight times during the year. This would again give a turnover of 40%.

The labour stability index by contrast would show that Company X has a stability rate of only 60% whereas company Y has a far more impressive stability rate of 95%.

Far more sophisticated techniques have evolved in order to more accurately plot and account for employee wastage. In recent years many companies have become interested in the length of service of employees and it is possible to develop a frequency distribution of leavers by length of service. Figure 4.1 illustrates this technique.

From Figure 4.1 it is possible to identify three distinct phases in the analysis of turnover. Following the work of the Tavistock Institute, in particular by Hill and Trist (1953, 1955) in two notable papers of study at the Park Gate Iron and Steel Company, a relationship was established between an initial 'induction crisis', a period of 'differential transit', and a concluding 'settled connection'. During the induction crisis it can be seen that the relationship between the individual and the organisation is unsettled and a little insecure as the frequency of leavers was far greater in the first eighteen months of service than during subsequent periods of employment. This can be seen as a 'trial period' in which employees are not sure if they are going to stay. Furthermore, the 'shock' of employment and the concomitant attention to discipline, hard work and regular time-keeping takes some time to adjust to. In the crisis period therefore there are likely to be a far greater incidence of inductees leaving than in subsequent periods. Hill and Trist also found that other problems associated with manpower planning could be discerned during this period as the rates of 'unsanctioned' absence and industrial accidents were far greater during the induction crisis than during the period of settled connection. In attempting to explain and analyse this relationship they found considerable evidence to suggest 'that accidents are in part used, however unconsciously, as a means of withdrawal from the work situation' (Hill and Trist, 1955: 121). Over time the incidence of accidents would fall and relatively 'sanctioned absences' would rise. This was explained as a result of the quality of the relationship established between the individual and the organisation. After the induction crisis a more stable and secure relationship was established such that a more positive relationship between the individual and the organisation reduced accidents and unauthorised absences so that:

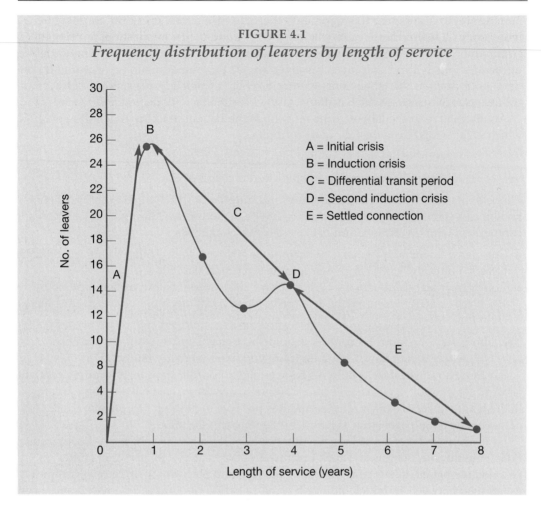

FIGURE 4.1

Frequency distribution of leavers by length of service

A = Initial crisis
B = Induction crisis
C = Differential transit period
D = Second induction crisis
E = Settled connection

No. of leavers (y-axis)

Length of service (years) (x-axis)

> Only sickness, therefore, remains; and the suggestion is that recourse is had
> to some kind of sickness when the individual, no longer able, in virtue of
> his improved relationship, to project his . . . bad feelings on to the firm as
> freely as he once did.   (Hill and Trist, 1955: 136)

Thus the authors conclude that employees internalise stress and dissatisfaction and do not 'blame' the organisation after the induction crisis. The word 'blame' is used by the authors to denote a psychological reaction to the organisation such that the individuals are looking to punish or hit back at the organisation for the stress of employment. Accidents are likely to be higher because of the lack of commitment and dedication to the organisation, and thus absences are more likely to be a result of the organisation's fault rather than the individual employee. Therefore an overall fall in the level of absence after the induction crisis suggests 'a dynamic connectedness between sanctioned absence (in the form of sickness) and the phase of settled connection' (Hill and Trist, 1955: 136). Consequently the employee moves from being a victim at the psychological level to one who increasingly looks to him- or herself for the cause of sickness or the need for absence.

Such internal considerations as absence, accidents and sickness ratios provide, as Timperley and Sisson (1989) state, manpower planning policy implications in that 'there are inherent predictabilities in the process, allowing wastage to be expected and therefore, forecast' (p. 109).

Not only do manpower planners need accurate information on absence and turnover rates but also statistical records and forecasts of retirements by department, sabbaticals, and the average number of employees engaged in training and retraining.

Business objectives

It may be of course that stability in employee numbers is not what is required as the business may well be expanding or contracting in response to product market pressures. If an organisation is experiencing rapid product market growth as it launches a new innovative product the requirements for staff may well increase to cover the extra workload. In the short term organisations can adjust to unpredicted 'shocks' in the product market through making short-term adjustments to the supply of employees within the organisation. The most obvious ways in which an organisation adjusts its manpower in response to growing demand are to increase the use of overtime, temporarily to extend the hours of those employed, to draw on subcontract labour, and to recruit short-term labour from temporary employment agencies. Of course if manpower planning was integrated with business strategy and planning in a more human resource planning mould the launch of a new product and the projections for sales would have allowed manpower planners more time to make resourcing adjustments. The launch of a new product belies the detailed planning and preparation that goes into this event, and in more strategically integrated organisations professing to practise human resource management, the detailed planning of resources would reduce the need to make 'shock' adjustments to the supply of labour.

Equally in an organisation which is contracting or restructuring into new business areas there may be a need temporarily to reduce the numbers of staff in old business areas. It may be that retraining and relocation packages are insufficient to resource the new plant or project and consequently there will be a need to 'downsize' in one area of the business while expanding in other areas. This was the case for many UK organisations during the 1980s as they responded to market and political pressures by restructuring their businesses. In the UK banking industry, for example, many of the old routine clerical and book-keeping functions are being removed through the introduction of new technology while at the same time employment opportunities are increasing in the sales and insurance functions (Cressey and Scott, 1992; O'Doherty, 1993).

This shows the importance of considering business objectives during the process of manpower planning and the creation of a manpower plan.

Markov models

These models are often used by manpower planners in the consideration of internal factors which need to be considered in the development of a manpower plan. The Markov model and variants of it attempt to model the flow of individuals within the organisation. It states that organisations have predictable wastage patterns according to length of service, and that this pattern can be discerned early on in an individual's career. Once 'survival' rates have been calculated and barring no future shocks, a fairly stable pattern of progression and replacement needs over time can be calculated. Furthermore, adaptations of the basic Markov model are used to project recruitment on the basis of stable patterns of both wastage and promotion. From this a planner can predict the probability and the likely time span of an individual progressing from one grade to another further up the hierarchy. From a consideration of these factors important planning information can be used in the recruitment and selection process, but also importantly in the training needs of individuals such that the organisation does not suffer from supply shortages. If a planner knows with some certainty that an individual tends to spend only two years in a particular managerial grade before being promoted to some other department, contingent training and recruitment plans can be made so that shortages in that area can be eliminated. Thus if 'recruitment, promotion and wastage patterns of staff are stable over reasonable periods of time, . . . the probability that someone in a particular grade at any time will be in some other grade at a later time can be established from the detailed recent career histories of staff' (Timperley and Sisson, 1989: 111).

External considerations

State legislation

One extremely important area that needs to be considered while formulating a manpower plan is the restrictions which are imposed on organisations by the government in the areas of individual and collective labour law (see Torrington and Hall, 1989). The evolution of the industrial system in the UK has been characterised by successive governmental interference in the way in which labour is recruited, deployed, trained, promoted and made redundant. It is a long time since managers and employers could simply 'hire and fire' according to their own whims and in response to market changes. Far more responsibility for the welfare of employees is enshrined in state legislation to the extent that many organisations and manpower planners may develop specialist legal advisory departments to assist them in the development and management of manpower planning.

Increasingly this legislation is of a European-wide nature enacted and passed by the European Parliament in Brussels and Strasbourg. Of course this is causing some friction between the directives and legislation of the European Parliament and the traditions of economic and industrial regulation in the member states. In the UK much of the legislative initiatives, including those within the social chapter of the Maastricht Treaty, are seen to be overly onerous and restrictive. However, it seems almost inevitable that the role of European legislation is to become far more important in the day-to-day activities of UK organisations and in particular the management of manpower planning.

Of most significance recently have been the Sex Discrimination Acts and the Race Relations Act. This legislation imposes a responsibility on manpower planners to recruit, train and promote employees on an indiscriminate basis such that religion, race and gender cannot by law be considered as a basis for employing, promoting, training or redundancy. Of course manpower planners can discriminate on the basis of being ablebodied! This rather bizarre practice is rare but in recent press advertisements some councils have advertised to recruit handicapped people only. At first sight this might appear somewhat discriminatory but in fact there is no legislation proscribing discrimination on the basis of being able-bodied. Thus for manpower planners seeking to maintain the recommended 3% of handicapped employees within the organisation, they are quite within their rights to insist that only those deemed handicapped may apply for the advertised post.

Legislation on the hours that people can be expected to work, the time that can be spent working in front of a VDU, rest periods, the provision of basic medical facilities and recently the necessity to provide facilities for pregnant employees, all impose some restriction on the practice of manpower planning. Organisations cannot simply consider their own operational and internal organisational needs. They are restricted within certain guidelines on what they can and cannot do in the management and employment of individuals. This has important considerations for those that are responsible for manpower planning as there are a number of legal considerations to bear in mind when developing and conducting manpower planning.

Regional development schemes

Successive UK governments have attempted to influence the direction and level of investment through offering tax and other financial incentives for companies to establish new plants and outlets in particular regions of the economy. This is an economic and often a politically motivated policy initiative to boost employment in recession hit areas. The North-West and the North-East for example have suffered in the post-1945 economy due to industrial restructuring and the decline of the heavy coal, steel and shipbuilding industries. In an attempt to boost employment in these areas companies have been offered a package of financial incentives to move and locate new departments, factories and retail outlets in these areas.

The importance for manpower planners is that in the development of manpower plans the organisation needs to know where it is likely to trade more profitably. So, for example, if the development of a new product is going to necessitate the construction of a new site and the creation of 2000 new jobs, it will be the responsibility of the manpower planner to provide information on the most profitable location for this plant. It may well be that as a result of regional development schemes the company would be far better locating its new plant in the North-East where cheap local reserves of labour are available together with tax privileges which reduce the costs of production relative to constructing the new plant more locally. In the creation of a manpower plan it is important that such 'external considerations' are evaluated such that the organisation's manpower plan provides the most profitable resourcing alternatives (see Clark, 1993).

Micro-level factors

Finally in the development of a credible manpower plan attention needs to be focused on the nature of the local labour markets. Successful manpower planning not only provides information on the immediate local labour market, but needs to compare and contrast the age, skill and cost profiles of each local labour market. In this way the organisation plans the resource implications of organisational expansion, contraction and structural change in terms of quantity, quality and price. It may be the case, for example, that different local labour markets offer different average age profiles which could be important for organisations seeking to recruit young employees. Alternatively, organisations might seek to locate new plants in areas where unemployment is high in order to guarantee the availability of sufficient employees and also to benefit from the likely wage cost advantages. If supply exceeds demand, as characterises depressed regional economies, economic theory would predict a tendency for wages to fall. Thus in comparing the South-East to the North-West in terms of wage costs it has been a well observed phenomena for a number of years that cheaper labour is to be found in the North-West.

ANALYSING DEMAND AND SUPPLY

Once the external and internal considerations have been brought together in the development of the manpower plan the planning department is in a position to analyse the net demand and net supply of new and current employees. This has been captured in Figure 4.2 which synthesises the major components of the human resource planning process.

From this diagram it can be seen that there are two distinct stages in the planning process, namely an analysis of the current state of play in the organisation's human resources and an analysis of the future plans and requirements of the business.

It should be clear from the preceding section that manpower planning adopts a number of techniques which seek to predict and project the availability of current staff. Predictability arises because manpower flows tend typically to follow a fairly orderly pattern when analysed and measured quantitatively. Thus a good manpower plan is able to locate which employees are likely to leave, where they are likely to leave from, the rate at which they leave, and the training implications arising from the need to keep a constant flow of suitably qualified employees to fill vacant positions. Any change in this pattern should also be able to be predicted by the manpower planner because at this stage they should have a fairly comprehensive understanding of the variables which impact on these patterns of employment. By carefully monitoring these variables shocks should be avoided and adjustments made relatively slowly and smoothly in order to avoid difficulties in the conduct of the business.

From the objectives of the business, the developmental and the relocation plans, the manpower planner is able to project the number of future staff that will be required by the organisation. At this stage the manpower planner is also in a position to advise on the strategic direction of the business in terms of what is possible strategically given the constraints and opportunities in the internal and external labour market. For example, it is pointless to plan for organisational growth within a region that will be unable to supply the required number and skills of employees. In the absence of alternatives, organisational growth may be impossible given the future projection of labour supply availability. Good manpower planning can show how an organisation is best advised to develop and grow – where supply is available, the recruitment and training needs arising from growth, and the most profitable location for new plant and capital.

The third stage in Figure 4.2 shows the process of reconciliation. This arises because there is undoubtedly a mismatch between the quantitative and, importantly, *qualitative* demand for employees based on future plans and projections and what the current projections of employee availability are able to deliver. Initially organisations would be interested in the numerical surpluses or shortfalls in staff that are likely to emerge in the future. A shortfall of staff will result if business growth and increasing product market success has not resulted in compensatory plans to resource the organisation. This would

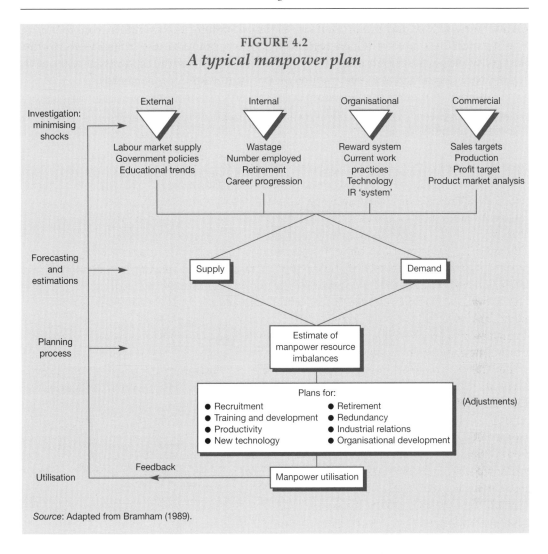

FIGURE 4.2
A typical manpower plan

Source: Adapted from Bramham (1989).

result in the all too familiar scenario of departments being run at over-capacity, such that the increasing use of overtime, subcontract and temporary agency staff lead to long-term operational difficulties. Orders may start to be processed late and consequently deliveries to customers become erratic. If this persists customers will begin to search for alternative sources of supply and the organisation may well find itself losing market share. This highlights the critical role which manpower planning plays and if it is able to project future shortfalls and surpluses, adjustments and contingency plans can be developed to reconcile the mismatch between net demand and net supply.

The fourth stage in Figure 4.2 demonstrates the function of manpower planning which is concerned with presenting and evaluating alternative policies to manage and reconcile shortfalls and surpluses. The final stage of the manpower planning process is those changes that are made in the areas of recruitment and selection, training and development, redundancies and early retirements, in order to plug the gap between projected availability of staff and projected need. Figure 4.3 attempts to synthesise all the movements and flows of staff which typically exist in organisations. It clearly shows that simply tracking and monitoring these movements is a difficult task in itself without the complexity of qualitative factors and the projection of resource mismatches.

A number of factors further complicate the process of manpower plan projections, however, and these need to be addressed before recruitment and selection plans are actually implemented.

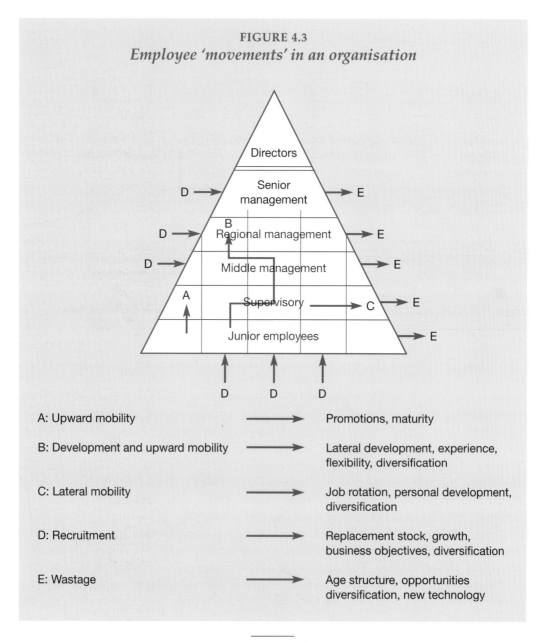

FIGURE 4.3

Employee 'movements' in an organisation

A: Upward mobility ⟶ Promotions, maturity

B: Development and upward mobility ⟶ Lateral development, experience, flexibility, diversification

C: Lateral mobility ⟶ Job rotation, personal development, diversification

D: Recruitment ⟶ Replacement stock, growth, business objectives, diversification

E: Wastage ⟶ Age structure, opportunities diversification, new technology

COMPLICATIONS – DYNAMICS AND CHANGE

Until now we have presented what we define as a rather static and decontextualised view of the procedures and practices involved in manpower planning – calculating the flows and patterns of employees through an organisation, reconciling the surpluses and deficits of employee stock levels, and the means by which manpower planning can maintain the qualitative and quantitative supply of labour. The only dynamism which has been allowed has been the recognition that some companies project growth, others plan for decline, while others seek simply to maintain current quantitative and qualitative supply. Of course there are a number of dynamic qualifications which can be added to this basic model which attempt more realistically to capture the actual practices of manpower planning.

Productivity

Since the findings of the Donovan Commission in 1968, considerable public policy concern has been expressed over the comparative productivity levels of British industry. In the final report of the Royal Commission on Trade Unions and Employers Associations it was suggested that the inefficient use of manpower both in terms of 'restrictive practices' and the training provisions of British industry explained a considerable amount of the productivity gap between British industry and its competitors (Donovan, 1968: 74). Restrictive practices were defined as 'rules or customs which unduly hinder the efficient use of labour' (Donovan, 1968: 77), and the Donovan report outlined a number of areas of manpower planning where, to quote Bramham (1989: 49), 'the standards of the job may be based more on tradition and expectation rather than on a logical assessment of what is possible. This may be especially true where standards are negotiated and therefore become politically charged.' Of course, we might argue that all standards, workloads and expectations are 'negotiated' – in the sense that there can be no *a priori* foundations to effort levels which remain outside the purview of political struggle and contestation. These practices had developed historically over a long period of time, and were seen by Donovan as a conservative anachronism by work groups seeking to maintain 'traditional' rights and prerogatives in the context of changed circumstances and technological advance. The kinds of restrictive practices which Donovan was drawing attention to can be seen in a review of the work practices, work group norms, values and attitudes which persisted in the British docks and shipping industry. In a series of articles Peter Turnbull and his colleagues have documented and historically analysed the changing work practices in the British docks (Turnbull and Sapsford, 1991, 1992; Turnbull *et al.*, 1992; Turnbull, 1992). The practice of 'welting', for example, allowed workers on the docks to secure time and leisure during the actual practice of work:

> . . . dock workers were able to indulge in the practice of 'welting', where only half the gang works the cargo at any one time. The other half might be playing cards, drinking tea or coffee, or in extreme (well organised) cases working at the local market or driving a taxi.   (Turnbull and Sapsford, 1992: 306)

It is these kinds of practices, which arguably were considerable and widespread throughout British industry during the 1950s and 1960s, that acted as serious manpower

> Modern style human resource planning, as outlined in the IPM guide, places considerable emphasis on a proactive strategy which anticipates and responds to changes in the environment, linked to a corporate strategy designed to enhance competitive advantage or quality of service.
>
> (Cowling and Walters, 1990: 7)

Far more emphasis was placed by personnel departments on the extent to which personnel and line management worked together in an integrated manner, whereby both jointly determined the role, function and implications for HRP, emerging from strategically defined organisational goals. This seems consistent with our earlier definition of human resource planning, which sees more operational responsibility given down to line managers, whereby line managers 'own' human resource planning but are constrained within strategically defined boundaries, in contrast to the rules and procedural bias of old-style personnel management and manpower planning. Commitment and integration of all organisational departments and resources is pursued far more through attempts to develop cultural awareness and homogeneity, rather than the imposition and control of rules and procedures. The advantages of this form of management are assumed to lie with creativity, commitment and flexibility, all those characteristics of employees which are deemed to be of crucial importance to competitive success in the 1990s (Peters, 1993). In this way human resource planning has a far more developmental role to play, both in terms of planning for flexibility (Atkinson, 1985), and developing quality, skill and 'excellence' within employees. It is becoming a consensus amongst many management 'gurus', consultants and academics (Peters and Waterman, 1982; Kanter, 1983) 'that markets, machinery and the money are available to everyone: success goes to those organisations which are able to recruit and develop the right people and not just at the top' (Timperley and Sisson, 1989: 120).

The two major issues which have concerned human resource planners over the past decade have been concerned with the implications of demographic changes and the need for flexibility.

Demographic changes

Towards the end of the 1980s many personnel departments began to express concern over the demographic changes in the British economy, which projected that the number of young people coming on to the labour market was going to decline significantly. It is clear that in a mature industrialised economy like the UK the average age of the working population is likely to increase as the number of births and deaths decreases. Eurostat figures forecast a decline of 1.7% per annum in the supply of labour in the age group 20–30 throughout Western Europe. The median age of the UK population was 34.6 in 1980 compared with 35.9 in 1990 and a projected 37.7 for the year 2000. In the old Federal Republic of Germany the figures are even more striking, rising from an average of 36.7 in 1980 to 41.1 in the year 2000 (IRDAC, 1990). These projections are largely explained by the increasing proportion of retirements which is not compensated for by an equivalent number of young people coming on to the labour market such that:

> Even if the forecasts mentioned should be used with caution, they indicate that the starting base for the next decade is far from excellent. If no corrective action is taken, there is a major risk that Europe will lose some of its competitive strength because of a lack of sufficiently qualified manpower.
>
> (IRDAC, 1990: 8)

This so-called demographic time bomb has forced employers increasingly to look to their manpower planners to seek new and innovative forms of labour so that the projected difference between labour demand and traditional labour supply may be breached. These observations help explain the increasing proportion of part-time labour use strategies, which in the main are composed of married female returners to the labour market. A simple cursory glance through the pages of recent editions of *Personnel Review, Personnel Management* and the *International Journal of Manpower Planning* emphasises the current interest expressed in the areas of innovative labour contracts, part-time labour use strategies, job-sharing, temporary employment contracts and the potential of mature returners to the labour market. These observations and analyses accompany prescriptions and advice for manpower planners and human resource managers on the best ways to plan, manage, motivate, remunerate and regulate these novel forms of employment use.

In addition, it is generally argued that industry and business are increasingly demanding more skilled labour and that relatively unskilled manual blue-collar jobs are in terminal decline, to be replaced by more highly skilled computer programmers, professional technically qualified managers and other service sector functions.

The 1993 Institute for Employment Research review of employment and the economy predicts on the basis of trends established over the past two decades that occupational change will continue to favour the growth of corporate management and professional services in health, education, science and engineering. Craft and Skilled Manual Occupations and Plant and Machine Operatives, by contrast, declined on average 1.3% and 1.9% each year between 1971 and 1991. High-level professional and managerial occupations constituted 35% of total employment in 1991 and this is expected to rise to 41% by the year 2000 (IER, 1993). The Institute for Employment Research at the University of Warwick projects similar labour market changes in the demand for highly qualified people with social science degrees and graduates of science and vocational subjects. An increase of some 1.5 million jobs are expected for the highly qualified by the year 2001 in comparison to 1991 (IER, 1995/6). Employment in primary industries will continue to decline throughout the 1990s. Current projections anticipate a decline of some 14% between 1991 and 2000, a loss of 520 000 jobs. Figure 4.4 attempts to represent those jobs affected by changes in numbers and skill levels.

Based upon the research of Rajan (1993) and the Centre for Research in Employment and Technology in Europe (CREATE) this diagram suggests the emergence of the so-called new 'knowledge worker'. In addition to this increasing demand for high-skilled occupational employees organisations are seeking to develop and expect more flexibility and adaptability from their employees. Technological, organisational and broader macro-economic changes are creating a situation where employees need to have a heightened awareness of their own skills profile and status. Increased 'reflexivity' and attention to personal economic and social development remains a controversial but arguably predictable outcome as organisations expect employees to exercise and demonstrate their own 'entrepreneurial' worth. It is also interesting to note that Rajan projects an increased demand for deskilled jobs in secretarial, junior clerical and recreational occupations. Such jobs will increasingly be filled by part-time employees, or, indeed, even more insecure and casualised forms of employment. This may suggest a contradictory series of outcomes in the labour market – highly trained and skilled professional employees, together

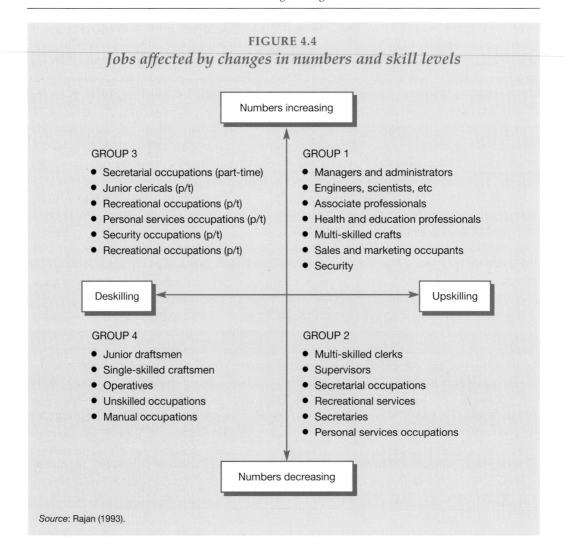

FIGURE 4.4

Jobs affected by changes in numbers and skill levels

Numbers increasing

GROUP 3
- Secretarial occupations (part-time)
- Junior clericals (p/t)
- Recreational occupations (p/t)
- Personal services occupations (p/t)
- Security occupations (p/t)
- Recreational occupations (p/t)

GROUP 1
- Managers and administrators
- Engineers, scientists, etc
- Associate professionals
- Health and education professionals
- Multi-skilled crafts
- Sales and marketing occupants
- Security

Deskilling ←——————————→ Upskilling

GROUP 4
- Junior draftsmen
- Single-skilled craftsmen
- Operatives
- Unskilled occupations
- Manual occupations

GROUP 2
- Multi-skilled clerks
- Supervisors
- Secretarial occupations
- Recreational services
- Secretaries
- Personal services occupations

Numbers decreasing

Source: Rajan (1993).

with pockets of low-paid 'ghettoised', deskilled employment which offers few prospects for career progression or personal development. The complex relationship and causality between these contradictory labour market outcomes and the emergence of 'hard' and 'soft' variants of human resource management is one which needs to be carefully considered and researched. What contribution, therefore, does human resource planning make to the creation of low-paid and insecure temporary or part-time employment which, we may note, tends to be filled by women workers? This remains an ethical and political question, but a question which nonetheless tends to be ignored by the majority of enthusiastic practitioner based articles and writing which tends to celebrate the newsworthy and novel at the expense of careful scholarly research and erudition.

Nevertheless, even accepting an increased demand for professional and skilled employees there remains the problem of supply (Keep, 1994; Keep and Rainbird, 1995). As economists have known for a long time, free markets have a tendency to fail in the provision of what are known as 'public goods'. A major problem facing UK organisations is that the free market dynamic has a tendency to discourage investment in training by businesses operating in isolation. As one company unilaterally decides to invest in training another company will seek to reduce the costs of its training by buying in pre-trained employees. This cost competitive dynamic operates to dampen down training investment as companies seek to pay slightly more for individuals who have been training elsewhere and thus avoid the costs of training themselves. The market therefore fails and in recognising this dynamic governments often step in to support and counteract the deficiencies of pure market-based solutions to training and investment. Training and labour supply is therefore a macro-economic and political problem which is generated above and beyond the capacity of organisation based managers and decision makers.

Unless educational opportunities are expanded in the UK, and the needs of training are seriously addressed at national level, it is argued that Britain will not only face a shortage of traditional sources of labour supply, but also a skills shortage will develop, creating a serious obstacle to future organisational growth and economic development.

In response to these supply developments, and to cater for the increased demands placed on organisations to develop less bureaucratic and more responsible creative employees, manpower planners have sought to develop flexible manpower plans.

Flexibility

There is some debate within academic journals over the precise nature of flexibility within the UK labour market and with organisations' use of flexible labour. One central debate focuses on the novelty and progressiveness of using part-time labour, female returners, casual labour and temporary employees (Pollert, 1988, 1992; Hakim, 1990).

Of less contention is the observation that during the 1980s most of the employment growth was in the area of part-time employment, and specifically female part-time employment. John Atkinson and his colleagues at the IMS have suggested in a series of papers (1984, 1985) that one of the responses to the demographic and competitive changes in the British economy has been a notable increase in the use of more flexible forms of labour. Atkinson not only suggests that this is becoming an increasingly popular form of manpower planning and practice but one that needs to be seriously considered by other companies seeking to remain competitive in the market.

Essentially, flexible manpower plans have sought to introduce three forms of flexibility.

Numerical

Here, organisations in response to fluctuations in the business cycle have begun seeking a more numerically flexible labour force. For example, in organisations such as banks and retail stores there is a predictable and stable pattern in the fluctuation of business activity. In banks the lunchtime period is particularly busy, and therefore a more flexible and cost-efficient manpower plan would seek more accurately to accommodate the peaks and troughs of business activity with available labour supply. By having pools of labour resources which can be called in at short notice, often called 'keytime labour' by banks, manpower planning can cut waste and efficiency by only having labour in the organisation when it is needed. Thus manpower planning uses its employees like a tap which can be turned on and off at will in response to demand cycles, customer arrival patterns, servicing peaks and troughs, etc.

Numerical flexibility is also achieved through the use of annualised hours contracts which allows management to alter the number of employees at very short notice in response to operational and business needs.

Financial

Rather than paying individuals the 'going rate', or a collectively negotiated wage, companies are seeking to pay employees and their labour a more flexible wage, which, it is claimed, more accurately relates to their performance and productivity. In this way manpower planning keeps costs far more under control by using and deploying labour according to business needs and its contribution to output. This avoids the rigidity in manpower plans which arises because of a fixed wage dictating that the employee resource is either used or is not used. Financial flexibility allows manpower planners to vary employment levels and departmental employee numbers.

Functional

This form of flexibility is heralded as one of the most important developments in manpower planning and provides a lot of the justification for the title human resource planning. Functional flexibility attempts to remove rigidities and demarcations in the organisation which prevent employees from performing a range of tasks and exercising a polyvalence of skills. It is here that we encounter the developmental potential of human resource planning in that increasingly employees are required, because of operational needs, to be moved through the shop floor, or into other departments. This is often seen as part of the multi-skilling initiatives of many organisations whereby employees are encouraged to develop a multiple range of skills and aptitudes so that:

> Employees can be redeployed quickly and smoothly between activities and tasks. Functional flexibility may require multi-skilling – craft workers who possess and can apply a number of skills covering, for example, both mechanical and electrical engineering, or manufacturing and maintenance activities.
> (Armstrong, 1992: 106)

Whether these manpower, or rather, human resource plans, amount simply to an extension of managerial prerogative, intensification and increased employee stress levels is a moot point (Wood, 1989; Elger, 1990). It is clear, however, that human resource planners are emphasising the developmental potential and flexibility which these initiatives encourage.

One consequence of flexibility and flexible manpower planning is that with the attendant delayering of managerial hierarchies and the attempted breakdown of the typical pyramid structure of organisations, promotions and traditional hierarchical development may not be possible in the future. Increasingly human resource planners are having to develop alternatives to hierarchical succession planning in response to a rapidly changing business context which requires fluid and rapid change and adaptability at the operational level. Therefore hierarchies and functionally rigid structures of responsibility, seniority and status can no longer develop because of the rapid change and flux in consumer demand, market fashion and international product markets.

In order to resource this external volatility human resource planners are being forced to seek corresponding flexibilities and 'turnover' so that: 'Workers, instead of acquiring a skill for life, can now look forward to at least one if not multiple bouts of deskilling and reskilling in a lifetime' (Harvey, 1989: 230). In the banking industry, for example, many of the traditional style accountancy biased branch managers are increasingly finding their skills redundant as banks seek to promote sales as the central focus of their business activities. The old-style paternalism in manpower planning in which employees, especially in the old large bureaucracies such as banks, were guaranteed 'cradle to grave' employment security is being replaced by far more uncertainty and turnover. In terms of development banks are now emphasising lateral development, or 'progression' across an organisation, rather than hierarchical promotion (Cressey and Scott, 1992; O'Doherty, 1993).

NEW ORGANISATION, TEAMWORKING AND SELF-DEVELOPMENT

The fracturing and disintegration of formerly unified bureaucracies and hierarchies has attempted to reconstitute the organisation, discipline and planning of resources at a devolved level. Subject to the financial control of senior corporate management (Marginson *et al.*, 1988; Sisson and Marginson, 1995) these devolved 'business units' exercise far less autonomy than some of the more enthusiastic management consultants and celebrants are likely to recognise. However, there has been a discernible shift in many sectors of the economy to shift the burden of day-to-day planning and management to 'empowered' team leaders and 'coaches' of small, team-based work groups (Storey, 1992; IRS, 1995, 1996). According to Storey (1992, 1995) there has been a welter of HRM initiatives and restructuring programmes in an effort to reconstruct the balance of individual and collective forms of employment regulation, not simply in the new service sectors of the 1980s, but in the heartland of British industry. In an effort to encourage commitment and performance, much organisational restructuring has focused on the attitudes and expectations of the first-line supervisor–employee relation. From this point in the production process organisational change has sought to remove the detailed layers of bureaucracy and management which service, monitor, discipline and plan from above. These layers of middle management which hold in place the traditional command-and-control model of organisation have been eroded to refocus those activities in small 'gangs' or 'teams'. The importance of the coach or first-line supervisor has been enhanced with added responsibilities which allow for a degree of delayering of middle-management grades. In the place of these massed ranks of middle management a more streamlined and flatter structure of assistant managerial, first-line managers or heads of shifts takes on responsibilities for budgeting, planning and resourcing. The expanded supervisory role that Storey (1992) uncovers in his research 'embraced aspects of planning, scheduling, agreeing budgets, being responsible for a cost centre, ensuring quality and being the main managerial representatives in human resource management' (Storey, 1992: 239). Research has discovered the importance attached to loyalty and commitment fostered within these teams, in which performance appraisals focus the gaze of the disciplinary imperative on the individual employee.

More extreme forms of devolution and empowerment have attempted to constitute the individual employee as a manager of themselves (Townley, 1994) in what Tom Peters has defined as the 'entrepreneurializing of every job' (Peters, 1994: 67). Ideally, those responsible for their own businesses will go anywhere, do everything, find anyone and break every barrier, procedure and 'tradition' to get the job done and done well. Some have seen the kind of organisational 'structure' which this kind of construction and management encourages as resembling the Jackson Pollock composition *Autumn Rhythm*. Here, flexible lines of responsibility and authority continually shift and redefine, only temporarily resting to take form and shape, before moving on. It remains difficult to identify a 'source' of manpower planning in these admittedly extreme, avant-garde and probably idealistic, if not terroristic, postmodern organisations (Clegg, 1991; Hassard and Parker, 1994).

In the film and television industry, Starkey and Barratt (1994; see also Lash and Urry, 1994) have identified the emergence of similar 'vertically disaggregated' forms of organisation and planning. Planning takes place within a diffuse heterogeneous network, assembled by reputation and personal contact. To produce a new drama series, for example, involving the employment and cooperation of thousands of employees, or rather a temporary network of labour brought together under multiple and myriad forms of contract association, the form in which manpower planning is exercised changes and shifts. Manpower planning 'takes place' at multiple points of intersection where budgets and 'financial constraints' are subject to negotiation and movement, albeit at the margins and within some acceptable 'tolerance' level to the investors and financiers of the project. Lash and Urry (1994) discuss the growth in these forms of 'structure' in the broadcasting media – film, television and music – and in publishing and tourism. The key feature of this form of organisation is the temporary coalescence in organisational form and the temporary and shifting draft of labour. Figure 4.5 attempts to represent the nature and form of 'manpower planning' within this kind of organisation. In this example we represent the design, production and broadcast of a new television drama series.

The 'Producer Choice' strategy embarked on by the BBC over the past few years has further encouraged this form of planning and organisation. Instead of using in-house production, editing, and BBC-employed actors and actresses, all paid under terms and conditions negotiated by the structures of union–management collective bargaining, producers can now recruit from outside the walls of the BBC. They may presage the future possibilities for the 'empowered' first-line managers identified in the study by Storey (1992), increasingly responsible for planning, management and the allocation of financial and human resources. With the freedom to manage their own budgets they do not remain constrained in the same way as traditional BBC producers who were obliged to draw on resources and facilities pre-funded and provided by their own organisation.

Within these disaggregated and delayered, some would say 'disordered', organisations, teams of flexible and multi-functional alliances of labour, infrequently employees in the traditional sense, come to take on an increased prominence and importance. This might seem superficially as some utopian-empowered challenge to traditional power, authority and hierarchy, in which planning and the management of resources seems to lie closer to the actual labour and point of production. On further enquiry, however, somewhat transformed, but in many ways traditional conflicts and breakdown associated with the employment relation emerge. Kondo (1990) and the work of Sewell and Wilkinson (1992) have documented the tremendous symbolic, discursive and material pressure,

FIGURE 4.5

The new diffused network of HRM

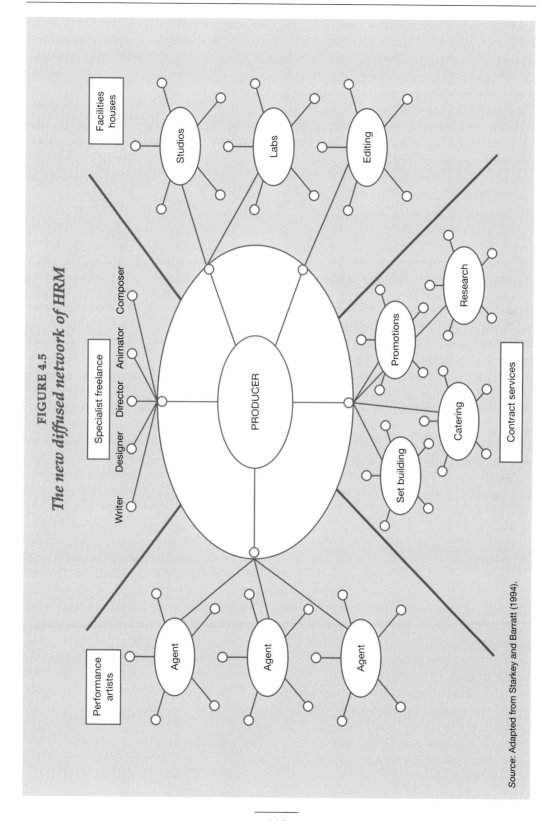

Source: Adapted from Starkey and Barratt (1994).

often operating subliminally, associated with the construction and constitution of team-based working. Individuals become objects of a power–knowledge incursion and subjects of their own discipline and self-management as performance appraisals and devolved schemes of career management increasingly turn work into a reflexive project of self. Employees are encouraged to reflect on their own performance, conduct, action and habits, to consider the ways in which they may benefit or hinder the performance of work. Increasingly, responsibility to one's self and one's team is reflected in attitudes of guilt and shame and, conversely, attitudes of a pious and sanctimonious kind. Self-surveillance, vigilance and group surveillance become institutionalised as the responsibility for the successful completion of work is devolved to self and team. According to Barker and Tompkins (1994):

> Team members expect each other to identify with the team and to behave according to the team's norms and rules. By violating team norms or exhibiting elements of 'dis-identification', a team member risks punishment by the team. The offending teammate may be accused of not being a team player or of not being faithful to the 'team's personality'. (pp. 225-226)

Many recent commentators have turned to the work of Foucault as a means of understanding the process and mechanisms of such discipline. As Foucault has argued, the beauty of this form of discipline is its subtlety and invisibility (Foucault, 1977, 1980, 1984), which serves to obscure the operation of power. Foucault suggests that 'power is tolerable only on condition that it masks a substantial part of itself. Its success is proportional to its ability to hide its own mechanisms' (Foucault, 1980: 86). Quality circles, employee assistance programmes and so-called 'employee wellness' initiatives (Townley, 1994) can all be seen as new powerful forms of self-surveillance in the planning and management of one's own 'manpower'. They represent a significant deepening of disciplinary mechanics over the humanism of old paternal, welfare-style personnel institutions and schemes. Self-management and career development are increasingly the responsibility of individuals engaged in projects of the self, rather than the structured guidance and certainty offered by the detailed linear 'onwards and upwards' cultures of hierarchy and status.

The 'directors' programme' at Royal Mail (IRS, 1995b) and the 'Development Partnership' scheme at the Trustee Savings Bank emphasise the importance of a shift in the conception of manpower and career planning. As one regional personnel manager at a large high street retail bank reported, 'We are moving away from a culture of "Do it to me" or "Do it for me" to one which emphasises self-development, empowerment, initiative and responsibility' (see O'Doherty, 1994, 1996). In addition, the conception of a career as some progressive and linear development through the ranks of middle management is seen as anachronistic and redundant. In the fluid, delayed networks and alliances characteristic of contemporary organisational arrangements the old hierarchies are often no longer in place to the same extent or degree. Employees are being encouraged to broaden their understanding of career, to see a career as one which emphasises 'lateral development' which may be harnessed with the adoption of multiple and flexible forms of contract, exchange and relationship with the organisation. Temporary project work, part-time employment, job-sharing and service contracts across a range of business units and even organisations are seen by some to be the future of career planning, development and management (Handy, 1989, 1994).

The entrepreneurial and Thatcherite rhetoric is barely disguised in the discourse of these new-style career-management strategies. In many ways this mirrors the withdrawal of institutional support and paternal welfare structures, the withdrawal of the 'nanny state' and the liberation of what is assumed to be a state of nature – competitiveness, entrepreneurialism, self-help and the ideals of neoclassical economic liberalism. The Royal Mail 'directors' programme' is explicit in its efforts to encourage employees to view themselves as a project to be worked on and a self to be managed:

> The first aim of the directors' programme is to increase your awareness of who you are. What are your skills, strengths and abilities? What are your interests, weaknesses and values? One way of discovering where you want to go in the future is to look back at where you have been.
>
> (quoted in IRS, 1995b)

Most of the career planning initiatives of contemporary organisations remind employees, or contracted self-employed staff, that there are no guarantees, 'the only person that can make this work is you', and the only chance of success is a constant awareness and attentiveness to self and performance. Manpower planning becomes individualised and empowered, but exposed far more immediately and directly to the vagaries and contradictory dynamics of market forces. Rather than eliminating the conflict and tensions associated with the traditional power structures, hierarchy and inequalities of the employment relation, these new forms of manpower planning and organisation simply shift the 'space' within which discontent is constituted and expressed. From stress to anxiety to disorientation (see O'Doherty, 1994), these forms of organisation and employment relations are subject to a range of interruptions, breakdowns and conflicts. This is perhaps different in form to the traditional organisation and expression of conflict and tension, but arguably no less debilitating in terms of the efficient functioning and reproduction of organisation, profit and capital.

Research finds considerable evidence to support the claim that power and authority continue to function within these contemporary forms of work relations. Barker (1993) details how in small, self-managing teams new rules, regulations and normative expectations of attendance, performance and commitment rapidly emerge to replace traditional and formal management 'command-and-control' directives. Prominent team members soon arise from within this self-governing democracy, which soon reproduces power, hierarchy and seniority. Team leaders are only able to maintain their position with the support of a majority of the team, support which remains tenuous and fragile. These 'elected' team leaders seek to manage, guide and steer the rest of the group into conformity with the rules and norms but their status remains insecure, partial and contingent on the day-to-day alliances of political traffic. What Tomkins and Cheney (1985) define as 'concertive control' operates to regulate and manage work teams far more perniciously through informal hierarchies and seniority. Paradoxically this form of control can be seen to be both tighter and more powerful, but also more fragile in terms of the work and effort which employees must routinely invest to maintain discipline and order. Barker's ethnography of ISE (1993) reveals how this discipline operates with the example of 'Stephi', a short-term worker seeking to gain full-time employment status with the team. She was considered by the team to have a bad attitude and failed to identify sufficiently with the team. In Stephi's words:

> When I first started I really didn't start off on the right foot, so I've been working to re-prove myself as far as a team player. My attitude gets in the way. I let it get in the way too many times and now I've been watching it and hoping they [her team] will see the change in me and I can prove to them that I will make a good ISE employee.　　(quoted in Barker, 1993: 425)

Of course, this may simply represent self-interested guile and instrumentalism on Stephi's behalf in an effort to secure a full-time position. Indeed, Barker details the expression of tension and conflict in the arguments which regularly attend team meetings. Rivalries, personalities and what we may speculate to be nascent political cliques and alliances emerge as the social relations within the team attempt to tackle the exigencies of performance and market competition in their efforts to plan, organise and discipline human resources. In the work of Catherine Casey (1995) these contradictions – loyalty to one's team, one's identity as a worthy and productive employee, and the pressures of effort and performance requirements – are explored. In rich ethnographic detail Casey begins to expose the weaknesses and lines of division that accompany such initiatives in restructuring the form and locus of manpower planning.

QUESTIONS

1 How does HRP attempt to 'smooth out' the complications associated with economic and political dynamics?

2 How convinced would you be as a Human Resources Manager that effective HRP eliminates conflicting objectives?

TOWARDS HUMAN RESOURCE PLANNING – DEVELOPMENTS IN THE UK AND EUROPE

We now turn to examine more macro-structure labour market conditions and exigencies which shape and direct organisational change and restructuring. We seek to locate human resource planning through an analysis of the legislative developments and the economic and social initiatives undertaken under the auspices of the European Union. In drawing comparisons with the management and structure of the French and German labour markets, we seek to elucidate the pressures and constraints which encourage or discourage the adoption of HRM-style initiatives in human resource planning.

The onset of the much-publicised internal European economic market has created a number of competing pressures for organisations seeking to plan and regulate their human resources. Efforts by member states to establish the right of labour to freedom of movement within the borders of the European Union to seek employment within any European economy will clearly have considerable future impact.

This has been a fundamental feature and one of the basic principles of the common market based on the equal treatment of 'European' labour with the nationals of the host country (article 3(c) of the EC treaty). Directives (a legal instrument which requires member states to bring their national laws into line with Union law within a specified time period) based on article 57 of the EC treaty have sought to encourage the mutual recognition of diplomas so that mobility is not restricted on the basis that an individual's qualifications and training have been obtained in one member state. Increasingly universities and institutions of higher education are seeking to integrate degrees and qualifications so that students obtain cross-national training and qualification. A series of supportive European Council directives have attempted to facilitate an integrated internal labour market. National governments have been committed to abolish restrictions on the movement and residence within the Union for workers of member states and their families. This has necessitated social security and pension coordination so that individuals do not lose pension and social welfare rights as a result of working in a country other than their own.

The European Commission has also invested in training programmes for staff of public employment services of the EC member states so that a network of European employment advisers based nationally within domestic state employment services are in a better position to advise individuals on mobility and employment throughout Europe. Such training involves an appreciation of the cultural and employment conditions current in member states, an understanding of the legal and social framework pertaining in EC economies, and a working knowledge of job opportunities and sources of information for individuals seeking work within the Union. Such training seeks to educate the staff of public employment services from all EC member states and to provide an opportunity for advisers to broaden their basic knowledge of the working and living conditions in the various countries of the Union. In this way advisers will be in a far better position in the counselling of employers and employees on European employment opportunities.

Directives have sought to overcome and remove legislation, regulations, circulars and administrative practices adopted by member states which appear to work against the rules of freedom of movement. For example, in the UK standard local authority administrative practice with respect to state-subsidised housing discriminated against Union workers (*Social Europe*, special edition, 1988). However, in Italy the law itself explicitly excluded EC workers from access to and ownership of state-subsidised housing. More specifically the French Maritime Code which regulates employment in the shipping industry categorically excludes EC workers from access to employment as seamen. Member states had adopted these practices and legislation since 1968, and they have only been resolved as a result of directives and coordination at a supra-national level within the European Union.

The increased possibilities for cross-national and occupational mobility within an internal European labour market are rapidly changing the framework within which manpower planning and control operate. It should now be possible for organisations to recruit and select individuals from a far larger labour market. This could lead to a number of possibilities, such as the reduction in supply bottlenecks, as logically it could be thought that with a larger labour market more people are potentially available for recruitment. However, a cursory look at unemployment figures throughout Europe (Eurostat, 1990) suggests that supply bottlenecks arise because of skill and qualitative shortage rather than simply a quantitative insufficiency of labour. As unemployment increases we appear to observe a simultaneous complaint by companies that they cannot obtain employees with the requisite skills and knowledge (see Streek, 1989). In this case what might be expected is that the internal labour market becomes highly competitive and fluid for high-skilled employees while unemployment and recession become more typical in non- and low-skilled sectors. The real risk for the UK economy is that with the weak institutional support for skills and training development the British economy will become a location for low-skilled, low value-added employment (see Lane, 1989; Nolan, 1989; Nolan *et al.*, 1992). This has recently been exemplified with the movement of the Lyon Hoover plant to Scotland where wages and the 'costs of employment', i.e. state pension and social security payments, are lower. This raises the second major implication for domestic organisational manpower planning. As a result of the single European labour market, organisations face contradictory pressures which simultaneously encourage convergence and divergence in manpower planning and practice. With a fully integrated and 'harmonised' single European market we should not observe what has been called 'social dumping' because there could be no competitive advantage for Hoover to relocate to Scotland. Harmonisation of statutory legal frameworks should ensure a convergence, or to use political rhetoric a 'level playing-field', within which manpower planning operates. Thus competitive advantage could not be sought by locating in areas of low-cost wage labour.

It has long been understood that one of the fundamental problems facing harmonisation and the single European market is the challenge of radically different traditions of state employment regulatory frameworks. Regini (1986) has sought to characterise these differences in Europe on the basis of three styles of settlement or relationship between the three main parties – the government or the state, representatives of employers and the organised interests of employees:

- 'concertation' – the active and proceduralised involvement of unions in state policy;
- 'isolation' – the rejection of a legitimate and active role for unions at the level of the state;
- 'pluralistic separation' – 'free collective bargaining' between employers and employees and the separation of politics from industrial relations.

In attempting to integrate and harmonise these very different systems of national industrial relations regulation the European Commission has been confronted with considerable, what we might call 'technical' problems, but also a significant amount of political and ideological opposition. The European-wide employment legislation enacted by the European Commission has been based far more on the social democratic legislative framework of the German system of industrial relations and employment. The UK in particular has voiced considerable opposition to what it perceives as onerous and bureaucratic regulation of labour markets. The UK government believes that social and welfare legislation as favoured by Brussels and the European Commission will place too great a burden on manpower planning and control in UK firms. In order to understand this hostility we need to examine some of the key differences in approach to labour market regulation in European member states (see Chapter 3).

State involvement in the German and French industrial relations systems is currently far greater than that of the UK in terms of direct and positive legislation which proceduralises and more specifically defines the roles and legitimate action of management and worker representatives. In Germany centralised bargaining between employers and unions has remained very strong and disciplined, stabilising wages and bargaining agreements throughout each industry in the economy. By representing all workers in a given industry workers in weaker firms are 'protected' in the sense that the system prevents weak firms from pursuing competitiveness through cutting wages. As Lane (1989) argues, such centralised bargaining 'need not make allowance for economically weak employers and thus helps to ease out inefficient enterprises within an industry' (p. 210).

In Germany the law supports this coverage by giving representation rights to unions for all employees within an industry and not just its own members. Free collective bargaining is guaranteed by the 1949 Collective Agreement Act and German legislation provides considerable support for collective representation. This stands in stark contrast to the UK's current industrial relations initiatives which have sought to limit and in many cases remove statutory supports to collective bargaining. The 1980 Employment Act, for example, repeals the previous right of trade unions to use a legal process to obtain recognition from employers.

The 1949 German Works Constitution Act legally requires the workforce to elect a 'works council' which is legally guaranteed rights to information, consultation and co-determination. These councils negotiate, consult and bargain over a range of workplace issues and the law guarantees co-determination rights on 'social matters' covering issues concerning pay, bonus rates, performance-related pay, and daily and weekly work schedules. According to Streeck (1984) works councils do not operate independently of trade union influence but are in the main composed of trade union members. In this way the 'regulation' of employment and manpower planning is bargained between 'social partners' in what is considered a highly efficient social democratic system where 'the strong involvement of works councils in manpower regulation have compelled employers to engage in more careful and long-term manpower planning' (Lane, 1989: 176).

In addition the state-directed formal national system of vocational training in Germany compels all school leavers to attend vocational schools until the age of 18 where they acquire standardised and intensive qualifications of both a practical and theoretical nature. This system bolsters and supports the regulatory force of works councils in companies in the sense that it once again discourages employers from manpower planning which seeks deskilling and peripheralisation. It creates 'opportunities for internal mobility and functional flexibility, reduces the significance of job demarcations, and avoids over specialisation' (Jacobi *et al.*, 1992: 229). This system has been shown to be particularly influential in the manpower planning style of the German financial services sector. A rigorous three-year apprenticeship imparts craft rather than technical skills to German lower white-collar workers which gives far more occupational power in the sense that they are not tied to one individual employer through firm-specific skills. This training encourages a career-minded approach to clerical work through raising the expectations, aspirations and attitudes of employees. As a consequence employers are encouraged to seek restructuring and competitiveness through manpower planning which develops high-skilled functionally flexible workers.

> The clear labelling of skills makes selection of workers more reliable and efficient, renders utilisation of labour more flexible and provides employers with a better disciplined and more motivated staff. (Lane, 1987: 76–77)

This combination of strong institutional bargaining and representation directed by positive state involvement and legislation on employment matters encourages German employers to seek manpower planning which upgrades and reskills.

The Auroux reforms in France during the early 1980s have similarly sought to institutionalise collective bargaining at workplace level by giving the rights of 'expression' to employees. This is attempting to create greater 'citizenship' within French firms and to establish employees as agents of restructuring and change. In addition the *salaire minimum interprofessionnel de croissance* which is linked to the national consumer price index prevents employers from seeking to compete on the basis of low wages. The 'erga omnes' provisions have also sought to extend collective bargaining agreements in non-signatory firms, a further move by the French government in the 1980s to adopt many of the institutional and state supports to bargained manpower regulation that exist in Germany. Legal intervention in France seeks to compensate unions' organisational weakness and hence regulate employment conditions and shape the eventual outcome of restructuring and the modernisation of French industry (see Goetschy and Rozenblatt, 1992).

In France and Germany employers are seemingly encouraged to compete on the basis of high skill and a functionally flexible workforce. In the UK the government has sought to deregulate the labour market, removing statutory supports to collective bargaining and abolishing wages councils, encouraging manpower planning to take the easier competitive option of low wages, low skill and numerically flexible work practices. This is in contrast to French and German industrial relations where the regulation of employment matters, over issues such as working time, rest periods, the working week and holiday periods, reflect considerable state commitment to ordering competition within 'socially acceptable' limits. In Britain deregulation is likely to encourage employers to maintain and seek competitiveness which cuts costs through the employment of cheap and disposable labour. In the German system by contrast employers are prevented and directed away from this tendency by strong entrenched institutional bargaining and regulation which encourages employers to see employees as a resource to be invested in rather than as a cost to be minimised.

In terms of the transition from personnel to human resource management and the professed need for organisations to move towards high-skilled multi-functional workers and away from traditional bureaucratic and sclerotic manpower planning, it might seem odd that 1992 and the emergence of regulated European-wide social democracy might actually provide a better support and impulse for such changes.

SUMMARY

● This chapter has attempted to introduce students to the discursive, linguistic and theoretical suppositions which structure and inform traditional understandings in manpower planning. It was argued that a degree of suppression is evident in the myopic focus and reification of order. It was suggested that a process of undoing was simultaneously in play with the process of ordering through the practice of organisation and control.

● In seeking to reduce shocks and disturbances in the distribution and movement of human resources, planners traditionally seek to calculate manpower needs in the short-, medium- and long-term. The devolution of aspects of manpower planning to the line manager, and indeed to the individual employee, associated with the practice of HRM, may lead to a situation where more diffuse lines of division undermine coherence and the strategic management of human resources.

● The traditional emphasis and faith in forecasting meant a considerable reliance on statistical methodologies. Only large organisations, such as the Civil Service and banks, seemed to pursue intricate statistical manpower planning. Perhaps this reflects the resources and expertise which they were able to invest in because of their insulation from the pressures and immediacy of market competition.

● The purported use of less mechanistic approaches to manpower planning, under the influence of human resource management, was seen to contain new lines of tension and division which undermined a rational and coherent approach to the planning, organisation and distribution of resources.

● In the rhetoric of HRM we find a considerable emphasis on the 'needs' and aspirations of employees. However, there appears to be a serious potential conflict between the promise and expectations associated with HRM and the 'delivery' of responsibility, empowerment and career development.

● In the normative models of HRM (see Legge, 1995) we find a considerable emphasis on strategic management and the importance of integrating human resource issues with business strategy. This chapter has argued for a contextual approach to human resource planning which recognises the interactions and contradictions associated with the play of economic and social relations.

● The chapter ends with an analysis of the possible effects of the internal European economic market on human resource flows within the EU. An examination is undertaken of the relative effects of various national European systems of collective bargaining, training and employee resourcing in relation to skill shortage. The conclusion is reached that regulation, such as is practised in Germany, will have considerable positive effects in providing a skilled workforce to meet company needs and provide protection for workers, while at the same time enabling organisations to carry out planning in the knowledge that there is a greater supply of skilled labour available to facilitate change and enhance the efficiency of the organisation. By contrast, the deregulated market of Britain will result in a low-skilled and lowly paid workforce which ultimately has the effect of restricting planning of the human resource to a short-term reactive role.

ACTIVITY

Imagine that you are a regional personnel manager responsible for food retail stores in a growing regional economy. You have 36 stores in your area, ranging in size from small local grocery-style stores in which there are typically only about seven people employed, to large city centre superstores usually employing a store manager, two assistant managers, twelve line supervisors, 24 full-time employees working as check-out specialists, 45 full-time warehouse and stores staff, and 35 shop floor assistants.

Over the last six months you have noticed a steadily increasing demand for your products within the region as a whole. Your chain is not renowned for paying particularly high wages relative to other employers in the area.

EXERCISES

1 Carefully draw up an initial manpower plan for the organisation, indicating when and where staff are currently employed within the organisation, how long they are likely to stay in that position, and the future projections for staffing requirements. You can assume that within your region there are seven city centres in which you have two stores each. The remaining 22 stores are located in small to medium-sized peripheral towns.

▶

2 Imagine now that you have been given the responsibility for designing an alternative method of planning and utilising labour. In your efforts to construct a new manpower plan and utilisation process you recognise that there are a number of aspiring career-minded individuals within the organisation. How are you going to reconcile the organisation's desire to maintain high productivity and low cost together with individual employee requirements for progression and change?

3 How might the existence of a trade union affect the design and final outcome of a manpower plan?

QUESTIONS

1 What is the point in preparing detailed manpower plans when there is so much economic and business uncertainty?

2 In what ways are manpower planners responsible for maintaining staffing levels?

3 What are the advantages and disadvantages of constructing a labour turnover index?

4 Is it fair to suggest that employees experience an induction crisis when first joining an organisation?
Which type of people do you feel this is likely to affect more and are there organisations where this phenomenon is potentially more damaging for the operational needs of the business?

5 In what ways does human resource planning differ operationally from manpower planning? Is there a significant philosophical and strategic difference between human resource planning and manpower planning?

6 How and why is manpower planning increasingly seeking to construct flexible organisations?

7 In what ways could it be suggested that manpower planning in the UK political and economic context is at a significant disadvantage from its European competitors?

EXERCISES

1 Consider the reasons why the *responsibility* for manpower planning may have shifted away from head office personnel management. What is meant by organisational de-bureaucratisation and in what ways may this interact with the supposed change from MP to HRP?

2 As a manpower planner in a large manufacturing firm producing components for television sets, prepare a report to senior management outlining the reasons for high turnover amongst recent inductees. Suggest methods and policies with which senior and line management may tackle this issue.

3 List those advantages and disadvantages which you associate with HRP in relation to MP.

REFERENCES AND FURTHER READING

Those texts marked with an asterisk are particularly recommended for further reading.

Armstrong, M. (1979) *Case Studies in Personnel Management*. London: Kogan Page.

Armstrong, M. (1992) *Human Resource Management: Strategy and Action*. London: Kogan Page.

*Atkinson, J. (1984) 'Manpower strategies for flexible organisations', *Personnel Management*, August.

Atkinson J. (1985) 'Flexibility: planning for an uncertain future', *Manpower Policy and Practice*, Vol. 1, Summer. IMS.

Atkinson, J. (1989) 'Four stages of adjustment to the demographic downturn', *Personnel Management*, August, pp. 20–24.

Barker, J. (1993) 'Tightening the iron cage: concertive control in self managing teams', *Administrative Science Quarterly*, 38, pp. 408–437.

Barker, J. and Tompkins, P. (1994) 'Identification in the self-managing organisation: characteristics of target and tenure', *Human Communications Research*, Vol. 21, No. 2, December.

Bartholomew, D. and Forbes, A. (1979) *Statistical Techniques for Manpower Planning*. Chichester: John Wiley.

*Bennison, M. and Casson, J. (1984) *Manpower Planning*. Maidenhead: McGraw-Hill.

Bowey, A. (1974) *A Guide to Manpower Planning*. London: Macmillan.

*Bramham, J. (1989) *Human Resource Planning*. London: IPM.

*Bramham, J. (1990) *Practical Manpower Planning*. London: IPM.

Casey, C. (1995) *Work, Self and Society: After Industrialism*. London: Routledge.

Clark, J. (ed.) (1993) *Human Resource Management and Technical Change*. London: Sage.

Clegg, H. (1975) 'Pluralism in industrial relations', *British Journal of Industrial Relations*, Vol. 13.

Clegg, H. (1979) *The Changing System of Industrial Relations in Great Britain*. Oxford: Blackwell.

Clegg, S. (1991) *Modern Organizations: Organization Studies in the Postmodern World*. London: Sage.

Cole, R. (1991) *Personnel Management: Theory and Practice*. London: DP Publications.

Cooper, R. (1993) 'Technologies of representation', in Ahonen, P. (ed.) *Tracing the Semiotic Boundaries of Politics*, Berlin/New York: Mouton de Gruyter.

Cowling, A. and Walters, M. (1990) 'Manpower planning – where are we today?', *Personnel Review*, Vol. 19, No. 3.

Cressey, P. and Scott, P. (1992) 'Employment, technology and industrial relations in the UK clearing banks: is the honeymoon over?', *New Technology, Work and Employment*, Vol. 7, No. 2.

Donovan, Lord (1968) *Report of the Royal Commission on Trade Unions and Employers Associations*. London: HMSO.

Edwards, P. (1990) *Conflict at Work: A Materialist Analysis of Workplace Relations*. Oxford: Blackwell.

Elger, T. (1990) 'Technical innovation and work reorganisation in British manufacturing in the 1980s: continuity, intensification or transformation?', *Work, Employment and society*, special issue, pp. 67–101.

Eurostat (1990) *Basic Statistics of the Community*. Luxembourg: Office for Official Publications of the EC.

Foucault, M. (1971) 'Nietzsche, genealogy, history', in Rainbow, P. (ed.) (1984) *The Foucault Reader*. Harmondsworth: Penguin.

Foucault, M. (1977) *Discipline and Punish*. Harmondsworth: Penguin.

Foucault, M. (1980) *Power/Knowledge*. Ed. Colin Gordon, Hemel Hempstead: Harvester Wheatsheaf.

Foucault, M. (1984) *The History of Sexuality Volume One*. Harmondsworth: Penguin.

Goetschy, J. and Rozenblatt, P. (1992) 'France: the industrial relations system at a turning point?', in Hyman, R. and Ferner, A. (eds) *Industrial Relations in the New Europe*. Oxford: Blackwell.

Guest, D. (1989) 'Personnel and HRM: can you tell the difference?', *Personnel Management*, January.

Guest, D. (1990) 'Human resource management and the American dream', *Journal of American Studies*, Vol. 27.

Guest, D. (1991) 'Personnel management: the end of orthodoxy?', *British Journal of Industrial Relations*, June.

Hakim, C. (1990) 'Core and periphery in employers' workforce strategies: evidence form the 1987 ELUS survey', *Work Employment and Society*, Vol. 4, No. 2.

Handy, C. (1989) *The Age of Unreason*. London: Business Books.

Handy, C. (1994) *The Empty Raincoat*. London: Hutchinson.

Harvey, D. (1989) *The Condition of Postmodernity*. Oxford: Blackwell.

Hassard, J. and Parker, M. (eds) *Postmodernism and Organisations*. London: Sage.

Hill, J.M.M. and Trist, E.L. (1953) 'A consideration of industrial accidents as a means of withdrawal from the work situation, *Human Relations*, 6 November.

Hill, J.M.M. and Trist, E.L. (1955) 'Changes in accidents and other absences with length of service', *Human Relations*, 8 May.

Hyman, R. (1975) *Industrial Relations: A Marxist introduction*. London: Macmillan.

Hyman, R. (1978) 'Pluralism, procedural consensus and collective bargaining', *British Journal of Industrial Relations*, Vol. 16, No. 1, March.

Inayatullah, S. (1990) 'Deconstructing and reconstructing the future: predictive, cultural and critical epistemologies', *Futures*, Vol. 22, No. 2.

Industrial Relations Services (IRS) (1995a) 'Customer service drive at BT', *Employment Trends*, 579, March.

Industrial Relations Services (1995b) 'New directions at Royal Mail', *Employee Development Bulletin*, 67, July.

Industrial Relations Services (1996), *Employment Trends*, 604, March.

Institute for Employment Research (1995/6) *Review of the Economy and Employment: Occupational Studies*. University of Warwick.

Institute of Personnel Management (1975) *Manpower Planning in Practice*. London: IPM.

IRDAC (1990) [Industrial Research and Development Advisory Committee of the Commission of the European Communities] 'Skill Shortages in Europe'.

Jacobi, O., Keller, B. and Müller-Jentsch, W. (1992) 'Germany: Codetermining the future', in Hyman, R. and Ferner, A. (eds) *Industrial Relations in the New Europe*. Oxford: Blackwell.

Kallinikos, J. (1995) 'Mapping the intellectual terrain of management education', in French, R. and Grey, C. (eds) *Rethinking Management Education*. London: Sage.

Kanter, R.M. (1984) *The Change Masters*. London: Allen & Unwin.

Keep, E. (1989) 'Corporate training strategies: the vital component?', in Storey, J. (ed.) *New Perspectives on Human Resource Management*. London: Routledge.

Keep, E. (1994) 'The transition from school to work', in Sisson, K. (ed.) *Personnel Management in Britain*, 2nd edn. Oxford: Blackwell.

Keep, E. and Rainbird, H. (1995) 'Training', in Edwards, P. (ed.) *Industrial Relations: Theory and Practice*. Oxford: Blackwell.

Kondo, D. (1990) *Crafting Selves: Power, Gender and Discourses of Identity in a Japanese Workplace*. London: University of Chicago Press.

Lane, C. (1987) 'Capitalism or culture: a comparative analysis . . .', *Work, Employment and Society*, Vol. 1, No. 2.

Lane, C. (1989) *Management and Labour in Europe*. Aldershot: Edward Elgar.

Lash, S. and Urry, J. (1994) *Economies of Signs and Space*. London: Sage.

Law, J. (ed.) (1991) *A Sociology of Monsters: Essays on Power, Technology and Domination*. London: Routledge.

Legge, K. (1995) *Human Resource Management: Rhetorics and Realities*. Basingstoke: Macmillian.

Mackay, L. and Torrington, D. (1986) *The Changing Nature of Personnel Management*. London: IPM.

Manpower Services Commission (1987) *People: The Key to Success*. London: NEDO.

Marcuse, H. (1964) *One Dimensional Man*. London: Routledge & Kegan Paul.

Marginson, P., Edwards, P.K., Martin, R., Purcell, J. and Sisson, K. (1988) *Beyond the Workplace: The Management of Industrial Relations in Large Enterprises*. Oxford: Blackwell.

McBeath, G. (1978) *Manpower Planning and Control*. London: Business Books.

Nolan, P. (1989) 'Walking on water? Industrial performance and industrial relations under Thatcher', *Industrial Relations Journal*, Vol. 20, No. 2.

Nolan, P., Evans, S. and Ewing, K. (1992) 'Industrial relations and the British economy in the 1990s: Mrs Thatcher's legacy', *Journal of Management Studies*, Special Issue, September.

O'Doherty, D. (1992) *Banking on Part-time Labour*. Occasional Paper, Leicester Business School, De Montfort University.

O'Doherty, D. (1993) *'Strategic conceptions, consent and contradictions: Banking on part time labour?'*. Paper presented to the Organisation and Control of the Labour Process, 11th Annual Conference, Blackpool.

O'Doherty, D. (1994) 'Institutional withdrawal? Anxiety and conflict in the emerging banking labour process, or "How to get out of it".' Paper presented to 12th Annual International Labour Process Conference, Aston University, Birmingham.

O'Doherty, D. (1996) 'Deflation and disappointment: The collapse of self and the failure of HRM in the banking industry.' Mimeo, Department of HRM, De Montfort University.

Peters, T. (1993) *Necessary Disorganisation in the Nano-second nineties*. London: Macmillan.

Peters, T. (1994) *The Tom Peters Seminar: Crazy Times Call for Crazy Organizations*. London: Macmillan.

Peters, T. and Waterman, R. (1982) *In Search of Excellence*. New York: Harper & Row.

Pollert, A. (1988) 'The flexible firm: fact or fiction?', *Work Employment and Society*, Vol. 2, No. 3.

Pollert, A. (ed.) (1992) *Farewell to Flexibility*? Oxford: Blackwell.

Quinn-Mills, D. (1985) 'Planning with people in mind', *Harvard Business Review*, July–August.

Rajan, A. (1993) *1990s: Where the New Jobs Will Be*. Centre for Research in Employment and Technology in Europe (CREATE).

Regini, M. (1986) 'Political bargaining in Western Europe during the economic crisis of the 1980s', in Jacobi, O., Jessop, B., Kastendiek, H. and Regini, M. (eds) *Economic Crisis, Trade Unions and the State*. London: Croom Helm.

Rowntree, J.A. and Stewart, P.A. (1976) 'Estimating manpower needs II: statistical methods', in Smith, A.R. (ed.) *Manpower Planning in the Civil Service*, HMSO.

Salaman, G. (1992) *Human Resource Strategies*. London: Sage.

Sewell, G. and Wilkinson, B. (1992) '"Someone to watch over me": surveillance, discipline and the just-in-time labour process', *Sociology*, Vol. 26, No. 2, pp. 271–289.

Sisson, K. and Marginson, P. (1994) 'Management: systems, structures and strategy', in Edwards, P. (ed.) *Industrial Relations: Theory and Practice in Britain*. Oxford: Blackwell.

Smith, A.R. (1971) 'The nature of corporate manpower planning', *Personnel Review*, Vol. 1.

Smith, A.R. (ed.) (1976) *Manpower Planning in the Civil Service*. London: HMSO.

Starkey, K. and Barratt, C. (1994) 'The emergence of flexible networks in the UK television industry', *British Journal of Management*, Vol. 5, No. 4.

Storey, J. (ed.) (1991) *New Perspectives on HRM*. London: Routledge.

Storey, J. (ed.) (1992) *Developments in the Management of HRM*. Oxford: Blackwell.

Storey, J. (ed.) (1995) *Human Resource Management: A Critical Text*. London: Routledge.

Storey, J. and Bacon, N. (1993) 'Individualism and collectivism: into the 1990s'. Paper presented to the East Midlands Work, Employment and Society Seminar, Leicester.

Streeck, W. (1984) *Industrial Relations in West Germany: A Case Study of the Car Industry*. London: Heinemann.

Streeck, W. (1989) 'Skills and the limits of neo-liberalism: the enterprise of the future as a place of learning', *Work, Employment and Society*, March.

*Timperley, S. and Sisson, K. (1989) 'From manpower planning to human resource planning', in Sisson, K. (ed.) *Personnel Management in Britain*. Oxford: Blackwell.

Tomkins, P.K. and Cheney, G. (1985) 'Communication and unobstrusive control in contemporary organization', in McPhee, R.D. and Tompkins, P.K. (eds) *Organizational Communication: Traditional Themes and New Directions*. Beverley Hills, California: Sage.

Torrington, D. and Hall, L. (1989) *Personnel Management: A New Approach*. Hemel Hempstead: Prentice Hall.

Townley, B. (1994) *Reframing Human Resource Management: Power, Ethics and the Subject at Work*. London: Sage.

Turnbull, P. (1992) 'Dock strikes and the demise of the "occupational culture"', *Sociological Review*, Vol. 40, No. 2, May.

Turnbull, P. and Sapsford, D. (1991) 'Why did Devlin fail? Casualism and conflict on the docks', *British Journal of Industrial Relations*, Vol. 29.

Turnbull, P. and Sapsford, D. (1992) 'A sea of discontent: the tides of organised and "unorganised" conflict on the docks', *Sociology*, Vol. 26, No. 2, May.

Turnbull, P., Woolfson, C. and Kelly, J. (1992) *Dock Strike: Conflict and Restructuring in Britain's Ports.* Aldershot: Avebury/Gower.

Tyson, S. and Fell, A. (1986) *Evaluating the Personnel Function.* London: Hutchinson.

Weber, M. (1964) *The Theory of Social and Economic Organisation.* Edited with and introduction by Talcott Parsons. New York: Free Press.

Wood, S. (ed.) (1989) *The Transformation of Work? Skill, Flexibility and the Labour Process.* London: Allen & Unwin.

JOB DESIGN:
SIGNS, SYMBOLS AND
RE-SIGN-ATIONS

Damian O'Doherty

OBJECTIVES

To consider and explore the contemporary applications of new technology in job design and its interaction with emerging forms of organisation.

●

To critically evaluate the meaning and scope of the concept 'job design' and the tensions which exist between 'sign' and 'de-sign' in applications of traditional and novel contemporary job design initiatives.

●

To analyse HRM-styled job design and the challenge which this poses to our usual categories of understanding – management, labour and machine.

●

To outline and detail the proto-typical Taylorist form of job design and work organisation; the demands this made of management; the impact on the psychological relationship between the individual and the organisation; and the problems encountered by firms practising this method of management and job design.

●

To analyse the extent to which the ideals and theory of Taylor
were typical of job design and work organisation.

•

To detail the motivation and contribution of the human relations
of work approach to the design of jobs and the organisation
of work.

•

To uncover and debate the validity and legitimacy of the
theoretical presuppositions made by those working within the
human relations approach to job design.

•

To analyse the importance of culture and flexibility in the new
human resource management approach to job design and work
organisation.

•

To undertake a theoretical and empirical consideration of
teamworking, business process re-engineering and the
implications which may affect the management and organisation
of employment relations.

•

To carry out European comparisons of the interaction between
national labour market and legislative frameworks and consider
whether and ideals and claims made of human resource
management job design are realistic in the context of the
UK economy.

•

INTRODUCTION

The deconstructive impulse of contemporary innovations and applications of information and communication technology, artificial intelligence and de-territorialising trans-architecture, is threatening to collapse spatial and temporal boundaries, borders and coordinates. In work environments which are fluid and without geography, subject to perpetual construction and reconstruction, strange new evanescent forms, part workhouse, part shopping mall, part home, part slaughterhouse, may emerge to form the 'virtual organisation'. Hybrid man/machine, cyborgs (Haraway, 1985) and perhaps even the 'replicants' anticipated by science fiction writer Philip K. Dick may replace the awkward and historically inefficient and recalcitrant bone, muscle, tissue and spirit which have evolved to take the shape of the human body. Nexus 5 replicants, which for the moment remain inhabitants only of the fictitious world of science fiction and the films of Ridley Scott, may perhaps portent the future outcome of contemporary movements in 'job design'. These replicants are designed to work 'offworld' in basic engineering, maintenance and transportation employment in alien hostile conditions impossible for human subjects. Replicants are designed to perform with all the 'best' features of a human – intelligence, self-reflection, the capacity to learn from mistakes – but without the fallibilities and weaknesses of the human body. Whereas the human body 'naturally' gets tired and requires rest, occasionally questions the meaning and value of the work it is performing, gets hung up on the existential absurdity of it all and is subject to the inconvenience of emotional complexity and irrational interference, replicants are designed to work assiduously, efficiently and without question. Does the future of job design entail the mass redundancy of traditional labouring subjects and their replacement with replicants and cyborgs, or indeed perhaps spell the end of the human subject as we know it?

Strange questions to be asking in the context of a chapter on job design but applications of new technology and organisational restructuring in manufacturing and engineering, and the emergence of the communications and education services, have led to job designs which not only disturb patterns of employment but threaten the meaning of our categories 'job', 'technology' and 'human'. Contemporary education is not the exclusive preserve of lecturers and tutors who ply their trade in preparing weekly lecture and collective seminar material. Increasingly education takes the form of distant and isolated students surfing and interacting with other students on the Internet, attending cyberspace courses and lectures from around the 'world'. The future student of job design theory and practice may attend a series of Internet workshops at the 'virtual university' rather than sit in front of the ancient media of a heavy 500-page textbook. A morning lecture at the University of California, lunch of *Wienerschnitzel* at a Viennese *Heurigen* and an afternoon seminar organised by the Moscow Institute of Business Process Re-engineering. This would clearly have job design implications for the job of tutors and lecturers, but does it replace them? One can imagine self-selecting, structure and filtering software which designs courses of study for the student. Software programs may be designed to reflect and respond to academic text and articles, integrating and synthesising work in a field, summarising and even offering logical and 'intellectual' critique and which begins to produce text of its own (see Woolgar, 1991). This may result in a situation where job design theory is split by the Warwick IBM 600 software dispute with the IBM 900 LSE program. One can imagine ideological hardware battles which may ultimately threaten Internet peace!

Applications of new computer and information technology are fundamentally redesigning jobs, in many cases blurring the distinction between organisational change and job design. In most academic texts on job design there is a signal lack of critical attention and detail on the interaction between capital, technology and the complexity of social relations, composed of centrifugal and centripetal collective and individual forces. Rather, job design is seen to be a discrete and linear top-down intervention by representatives of some personnel department which aims to restructure or transform the boundaries, allocation and distribution of job tasks. This chapter attempts a modest introduction to understanding and locating job design in the rational and what is being increasingly recognised as the emotive and irrational context (Jackall, 1988; Fineman, 1993) of organisation and social relations. Deliberate and purposeful activity remains folded and shadowed by the accidental and contingent, the proximal forces of organising (Cooper and Law, 1995) where management intention 'means "in tension", a pattern of actions that is distributed throughout such a field and which serves to *maintain* it or hold it together' (p. 246). Of course, this maintenance does not reproduce unproblematically but remains a contingent and oxymoronic outcome of a multiple and heterogeneous process. In a remarkable and illuminating study, Yiannis Gabriel (1995) has illustrated one aspect of these processes, namely the marginal terrain he calls the 'unmanaged organization'. In this 'dreamworld', emotions, anxieties and desires find expression in stories, myths and fantasies which refashion formal or official discourse and rhetoric for pleasure and perhaps simply for the 'kick'. As Dostoyevsky (1864) argues,

> even if man really were nothing but a piano key, even if this were proved to him by natural science and mathematics, even then he would not become reasonable, but would purposely do something perverse out of simple ingratitude, simply to gain his point. (p. 21)

A more disturbing question, which we address in the following chapter, is the extent to which we can maintain such hope in organisations which incorporate vast computer and information technology in their job design initiatives.

CONTEMPORARY JOB DESIGN

Design is derived etymologically from the Latin *designare* and the French *designer*, which on reflection opens up a rather richer understanding of the complexity of the concept design than that typically employed by personnel and human resource managers. In exploring this complexity we actually capture a better sense of the subtle and contradictory nature of contemporary job design in which order and disorder emerge as mutually overlapping forces present in employment relations. Design encapsulates a range of understanding, one which implies a 'marking out', to trace and denote. The *Oxford English Dictionary* suggests the sense of design giving 'something form, an outline and definition' whereby ideas and material are fashioned and 'de-sign-nated' by a title, a profession or trade. It also implies a deliberate calculation 'a purpose, an intention, plot, ambition . . . an end in view, a goal'. A rather circumscribed sense of design has typically been understood and appropriated in the field of personnel management, reducing it to one simply of purposeful change and reconstruction in the content of jobs, which has cost us flexibility and subtlety in our understanding.

The word design also captures the sense of contemplation – to contemplate or project a plan, to lay a plot; as the Renaissance architect Moxon claimed, 'Tis usual . . . for any person before he begins to erect a building, to have Designs or Draughts drawn upon paper' so that each floor of the building is 'de-lineated' in a flat, geometric, two-dimensional projection. The material outcome of the intention (in-tension) is marked by its 'limit' in multi-flexible dimensions subject to the pressures of composition and decomposition which 'work on' the abstract geometric projection. These multi-dimensional forces are captured by the concept of 'sign' which design attempts to rationalise and limit, to prescribe and contain. Signs are less conclusive, open to interpretation; they merely suggest, perceive or indicate in some representative form or medium something often beyond rational cognition and the intellect. Signs have to wait to be coded and are subject to recoding and reinterpretation; as the *Concise Oxford Dictionary* defines it, signs are 'actions or gestures to convey information'. As we shall see, job design never manages to circle and enclose with definitional precision, and in fact in many contemporary organisations and workplaces the boundaries and content of 'jobs' remain ambiguous and subject to various pressures of de-stabilisation.

In addition, design evokes notions of 'crafty contrivance' in which people have cunning designs on others, a plot or intrigue in medieval court society in which political forces are realigned by the ambitions and designs of cliques, cabals and gangs. As the well-worn adage of B. Harris states, 'They who ask relief have one design; and he who gives it another'. Those organisations studied by Robert Jackall (1988) reflect this understanding of design as management coteries plot and design the downfall of other management groups which has repercussions in coups and counter-plots, all of which add contingency and ambiguity in the evolution of roles and responsibilities:

> Because of the interlocking ties between people, they know that a shake-up at or near the top of a hierarchy can trigger a widespread upheaval, bringing in its wake startling reversals of fortune, good and bad, throughout the structure.
>
> (p. 33)

Finally, design contains within it an important aesthetic dimension. One fashions or designs with artistic skill or decorative device. In contemporary job design this aesthetic dimension comes to play a fundamental role in which the 'dressage' of costume, language, posture, customer interaction rituals, and the furniture and stage props of employment take on a significant element in the efforts to structure and organise efficient work (Hochschild, 1983; Austrin, 1991). As Featherstone's studies in contemporary culture (1988, 1991) have shown, there has been a process of 'aestheticization' where design proliferates in signs, symbols, myths and images which saturate the fabric of everyday life. Lash and Urry (1994) argue that objects in contemporary political economies lose their spatial and temporal referents and are progressively emptied of content:

> objects in contemporary political economies are not just emptied out of symbolic content. They are progressively emptied out of material content. What is increasingly being produced are not material objects, but signs.
>
> (pp. 14–15)

In contemporary work organisations the content of many people's jobs is arguably becoming more cognitive in nature and 'emptied out' as companies increasingly compete in the fields of information and ideas. Organisations often exist on the basis of networks of computer terminals which transcend the limitations of time, space and geography. The Californian advertising agency Chiat/Day offers its employees the option of working from home, and in any one day there are only 60% of staff on the premises. In addition, there are no private offices for employees of any status but rather collective 'living rooms' and for meetings staff must book multi-purpose 'project rooms'. The accounting firm Ernst & Young has completely abandoned the traditional design and structure of jobs and offices, replacing its Chicago head office with a 'hotel'. A hotel coordinator books rooms and arranges for special files or software to be available. Employees' jobs are designed to be mobile and flexible, 'out in the field', or in the relative peace of their home where they can study, reflect and complete reports in an environment they can better control. In giving employees more control and autonomy in the design of their own work routines the quality of work, which in these sectors is increasingly of a cognitive nature, is likely to improve. Oticon, the Danish hearing aid company, has abandoned offices and desks, taken out walls and barriers, erased job descriptions and auctioned off all its office furniture to employees (Peters, 1994). Employees stow their effects in caddies or personal carts and physically arrange themselves as they see fit and as the project or task demands. The plant is a completely open space and employees have no fixed place but move around the interior of the plant as the job, which they are responsible themselves for organising and coordinating, changes and evolves. From a situation in which their market share had fallen 50% in 1991, Oticon recovered and began to make record profits (Peters, 1994: 29). A similar idea of 'hot desking' has been introduced in many professional management service organisations. This removes all fixed furniture in a 'cordless office' designed with ponds and plants and infused by the Chinese philosophy of *feng shui* (Farmbrough, 1996). Workers become nomadic, equipped with their 'office in a briefcase', wired into the centre-less organisation through mobile phones, car phones, paging systems, radio networks, portable fax machines, laptop and other portable technologies.

Organisational and job design initiatives in many sectors of the economy do not depend exclusively on centralised personnel management departments. In efforts to tap into the intangibles of ideas and imagination which now arguably fuel the competition in education, tourism, entertainment, management consultancies and services, job design becomes a less easily identifiable centre and source in organisations but is diffused and decentralised to encourage networking, mobility and flexibility. Many contemporary social and economic theorists argue that even in traditional 'hard' material products, such as cars, what consumers purchase is the life-style image, the seduction of narrative, symbols and myths which promise fabulous identity management and development (see Armstrong and Tomes, 1996; of course Baudrillard is essential here, especially 1983, 1990).

We can begin to see the relevance of this when we look at the case of the Philip Morris company. When Philip Morris bought Kraft for $12.9 billion the accountants were able to identify $1.3 billion of tangible assets. The remaining $11.6 billion dollars was defined as 'other', those intangibles including good will, brand equity and ideas in the heads of the employees. Tom Peters (1994) calls this the 116/129 principle. Most management remains concerned with the 13/129 fraction and the rest is left without concern, guidance or management. Peters also notes that only 6% of IBM staff actually work in the factory producing 'things'; the rest remain in design, servicing, product development, logistics and finance in which the premium is on ideas and imagination. Even those in the factory mostly perform service tasks:

> Factory 'hands' (ah, words!) now spend much of their time working with outsiders in multifunctional teams that streamline processes, improve quality, or customize products.
>
> (Peters, 1994: 14)

HRM AND JOB DESIGN

The enthusiasm with which HRM has been embraced by many working within the theory and practice of job (re)design is founded on its prediction and promise that individuals need to be provided with stimulating and 'enriched' jobs which tap those intellectual and cognitive domains left dormant by the traditions of organisation and management. Not only will individual employees perform far more varied and skilled jobs, but through the resulting quantitative and qualitative performance improvements organisations will become far more competitive. Hence one of the most important components of organisational effectiveness and economic prosperity is the attention and detail paid to the design of work tasks. It is held that 'multi-skilled' highly discretionary jobs will influence the critical psychological state of an employee promoting a sense of meaningfulness, responsibility and value. Once an employee begins to experience a more positive psychological relationship with their job, manager, employer and organisation, it is expected that improved performance will follow (Hackman and Lawler, 1971; Hackman and Oldham, 1976).

In contrast to the rather jaded and in many ways discredited quality of working life movement in the 1960s and 1970s, it is argued that job design is back on the agenda as a critical component of organisational performance. This has emerged as a result of qualitative changes in product markets, manufacturing and information technology, and trading conditions (Reich, 1983; Hirschorn, 1984). For many this promises to end the degradation and dehumanisation associated with the repetitive assembly line of mass production industries. A new utopia of management–worker consensus based on single-status empowered craft-style working practices is predicted within flatter, less hierarchical and autocratic organisational structures (Peters and Waterman, 1982; Deming, 1986). As Buchanan (1992) has claimed, acceptable worker control and autonomy have increased as a result of new environmental pressures giving 'employees considerably more control over work activities, personal skills and development and career opportunities, and also offer[ing] significant opportunities for improved organisational performance' (Buchanan, 1992: 138). In contrast to the prescription and 'detailed' control of work tasks in the typical Western car factory the modern worker is not only granted increased discretion and 'high trust' (Fox, 1974), but is actually a functional prerequisite of successful economic performance (Piore and Sabel, 1984; Kern and Schumann, 1987).

Increased discretion and high-trust employment relations are often used as a justification for job redesign, which is today a prerequisite of competitiveness and market sustainability. However, the assumption remains that redesign initiatives remain the preserve of interventionary personnel management. An assumption of linearity, even in those writers purporting to make a critical and interrogative examination (Buchanan, 1989, 1994) of job design, reduces change to something which personnel order and channel into predictable and stable outcomes.

'Management' is seen in a relatively unproblematic manner, as a category which locates and identifies those agents of change that purposefully design, allocate, distribute and organise work. The outcome of this top-down job redesign within the discourse of HRM is one which then leaves high-powered and discretionary, autonomous, high-skilled labour to tinker with aspects of their work organisation and therefore 'impinge' *subsequently* on traditional managerial domains. The assumption remains, however, that the high trust granted to employees will be reciprocated by employees who reflect on their organisation of work and seek to continuously improve 'high performance work systems' (Buchanan, 1994). The agency status of employees is reduced to one which can only *respond* to higher managerial initiatives. Management is the primary change agent: only it has the capacity effectively to intervene to restructure and redesign. If it does this correctly, new structures and order in the organisation of employment can be established, which can then be sustained and reproduced more efficiently by the autonomy vested in high-performance work teams.

In addition, these approaches maintain faith in the progressive evolution of managerial thinking. History is examined from the standpoint of today which confines managerial practice such as Taylorism essentially to one of an unenlightened past which is overcome by the undisputed progress assumed in management development. Such liberal Whig interpretations see history as a movement from ignorance to enlightenment, whereby managers learn from the mistakes of the past, enabling them to develop and introduce improved remedies and methods in the contemporary organisation and design of work. From the rather crude Taylorism of mass production, management thinking has progressed through the humanisation initiatives of Elton Mayo, the work of the Hawthorne studies and the Tavistock Institute, to contemporary 'radical' and enlightened job design. Contemporary job redesign, it is claimed, seeks a systemic or organisation-wide orientation through just-in-time, cellular organisation forms, and systematic and coherent business process re-engineering (Buchanan, 1994) which corrects for the deficiencies of earlier approaches.

Conflict and tension in job-redesign initiatives are seen to stem simply from contingency and irrationality which can be eliminated and restructured by enlightened management. The usual recipe for eliminating such contingency is careful strategic planning, projection and negotiation among all relevant parties. This builds coherence initially through a process of political lobbying by attempting to mobilise sufficient political interest among organisational cliques (see Storey, 1992: 118–161). In addition, technology remains a benign but essentially good force. It can only be successfully utilised, though, by management in job design programmes with due consideration given to the concerns and needs of employees for discretion, interest and involvement. However, no consideration is given to the more broad processes of instrumentalism and abstraction involved in this technical control which fundamentally reduces and confines rationality to one of perpetuating mastery and objectification (Marcuse, 1964; Habermas, 1971; Heidegger, 1977; Brennan, 1993). As a recent commentary in the tradition of such critical theory argues, the epistemological strait-jacket of contemporary management can:

> mark and reproduce an attitude whereby society and nature are looked on as if they were things to be made and remade, changed and transformed, corrected, amplified, destroyed, reconstructed, etc.   (Kallinikos, 1994: 37–38)

A corollary of this is a certain subjectification and closure in the constitution of the human subject which dim down critical reflection on the purposes and values of the human being. A narrow instrumental orientation to control which subjugates nature requires an ontology in human beings which represents humans as the centre and measure of all things. A technological order which subjugates, aligns and coordinates individual and collective subjects restricts critical enquiry to an inexorable egotistical drive for instrumental rationality (Weber, 1964). Human relationships are reduced to impersonal exchanges as technology and organisation concentrate on the means to ends rather than on the ends themselves. In the summary of Marcuse (1964), technology reifies whereby 'The world tends to become the stuff of total administration, which absorbs even the administrators' (p. 169) and thus it is only:

> in the medium of technology [that] man and nature become fungible objects of organization. The universal effectiveness and productivity of the apparatus under which they are subsumed veil the particular interests that organize the apparatus.   (p. 168)

The technology of job design

In the following sections we attempt to trace the development of job design techniques against the background of these theoretical concerns. In particular we focus on the *sustainability*, consistency and order of design and its relation to breakdowns, accidents, contingencies and incoherence. In maintaining a critical study of technology and its border with capitalist forces of production and social relations in production, we can draw out the *tension* in design/sign. In contemporary efforts to structure and form work organisations this tension may be reaching a new crisis in which ontological categories – man/technology-machine – and the horizontal and vertical boundaries and definition of 'jobs' are subject to decomposition. Whether a new composition or coalescence is emerging is a question that can only be raised at this stage.

In the next section we look at the classic Taylorist approach to job design and the interpretation of this offered in Baverman's (1974) work. Following this we examine the so-called human relations school of job design which sought to overcome the fragmentation and 'anomic' consequences (Mayo, 1949; Durkheim, 1984) associated with Taylorism. We then go on to look at the prior orientation and socialisation process inherent in employment relations to assess the validity of some of the assumptions made by the human relations school. The following section seeks an understanding of the change process itself and how HRM attempts to overcome the inertia and impotency found in typical bureaucratic organisations. We then critically evaluate the future or 'trajectory' of job design initiatives and reflect on the possibility that the determinism of Braverman and deskilling has been replaced by the reskilling determinism of the 'second industrial divide' (Piore and Sabel, 1984). Following this we take a look at recent initiatives in organisation/job redesign, drawing on recent empirical research to illustrate potential new pressures and areas of breakdown and tension. This pursues the question raised above as to whether 'design' and even 'job' are not now redundant as analytical categories (see Watson, 1994; Iles and Salaman, 1995). As organised work relations mutate and disintegrate (Lash and Urry, 1994: 116ff) what we may be increasingly left with are simulated mosaics and bricolage. Perhaps we are left simply with signs, impossible to designate, identify and locate with referents.

The concluding section comes back down to earth and analyses current European initiatives in job design and examines the extent to which the institutions and programmes of the EU can effectively encourage sustainable high-skilled competitiveness.

TAYLORISM AND THE DEGRADATION OF LABOUR

Frederick Winslow Taylor (1856–1917) was in many ways the founder of modern rationalised management methods of organising and disciplining work and employees. It was Taylor who systemised the use of work study, piece-rate schemes, and time and motion studies in his drive towards designing jobs in their most basic and simple manner.

Taylor's life and early ideas

Taylor dropped out of his study of law and against the wishes of his affluent Philadelphia family took up a job as a manual craft apprentice in a firm whose owners were close friends of his parents. Later, Taylor became a gang boss in a lathe department at the Midvale steel works, one of the most technologically advanced companies in the steel industry. In his youth Taylor apparently displayed odd behavioural characteristics, counting his steps, calculating his time in performing various duties and tasks, and studying his bodily motions while doing basic domestic chores (Kakar, 1970). This obsessive and compulsive type of behaviour was explained by his desire to cut down to a minimum waste and inefficiency. Even at this early stage in his life he seemed to be searching for the one best way to carry out tasks which would minimise bodily movements and reduce mental and physical effort.

While employed at the Midvale steel works he became obsessed by what he called 'natural' and 'systematic' soldiering. This emerged as a result of what he assumed to be the natural tendency and desire of workers to take it easy, to control the speed and effort with which they exercised their jobs, and to work no harder than was absolutely necessary. 'Systematic' soldiering was for Taylor far more inefficient and pernicious because this type of soldiering was controlled, regulated and supported by informal social groups of employees. A body of 'rules' and norms supported by the close social networks and relationships on the shop floor regulated the speed and output with which employees were 'allowed' to perform their jobs. As a worker Taylor claimed he never once broke the agreed norms on work restrictions, but once he became responsible for output and productivity as a gang boss he was determined to reorganise and maximise production. In his own words Taylor claims:

> As soon as I became gang boss the men who were working under me and who, of course, knew that I was onto the whole game of soldiering or deliberately restricting output, came to me at once and said, 'Now Fred, you are not going to be a damn piecework hog, are you?' I said, 'If you fellows mean you are afraid I am going to try to get a larger output from these lathes,' I said, 'Yes; I do propose to get a larger output from these lathes'.
>
> (Taylor, 1912; quoted in Clawson, 1980: 212)

For Taylor the importance and strength of the workers lay in the fact that it was they who had far more knowledge and understanding of jobs. How tasks were performed, the tools that were used and the precise way and speed with which jobs were done lay primarily in the experience and 'craft' of the employees. The legacy of craft control had been 'imported' into the early factories whereby the workers themselves organised the way in which work was to be done and hence controlled the actual process of labour. Workers would deliberately keep management ignorant of the speeds that could potentially be achieved in the machine rooms and, as Taylor insisted, this was perfectly rational because of course as soon as management discover the maximum potential speed of work tasks they would naturally insist on speed-ups and more 'efficiency'. Systematic and natural soldiering were therefore rational attempts by workers to control the labour process, to control the speed and effort that they had to put into their jobs.

The management prerogative and the breaking down of work tasks

Taylor emphasised the importance of acquiring and monopolising the knowledge of work tasks so that management could better control and discipline employees. It was management's duty to impose themselves in the shop floor, to actually get down into the work process and observe, measure and calculate how tasks were done and how jobs could actually and potentially be performed. Taylor embarked on a series of systematic studies of shop floor practice with the intention of redesigning jobs so that all knowledge, expertise and hence control of work rested with management. Jobs were broken down and fragmented to their most basic components in an extreme division of labour. It was held, following Adam Smith and Charles Babbage, that by breaking down tasks into their most elemental structures workers would become more efficient and productive in performing one routinised and repetitive task. If discretion and decisions could be entirely eliminated from workers so that all they had to concentrate on was the maximisation of output through the maximum exertion of physical effort, then productivity and efficiency in the factory would increase. Adam Smith had claimed that as a result of familiarity and dexterity workers would become progressively quicker and more efficient in the practice of work tasks. If jobs could be made far more simple and broken further down through the detailed division of labour, then workers could more easily master the movements and motions necessary to perform the job and consequently became far quicker in a far shorter period of time. According to Charles Babbage this had the additional advantage that it would reduce costs so that previously skilled labour could be replaced with unskilled labour. As jobs became fragmented there would be no need to employ and pay skilled workers as the newly designed jobs could be performed by unskilled labour.

This extreme fragmentation and division of tasks created a series of mundane and repetitive jobs whereby instead of employing one person to do the whole job a number of employees would be required to work on highly specialised and routinised simplified jobs. Furthermore the design and knowledge of tasks were appropriated by management so that they could far better control the labour process. As Clawson (1980) observes, 'As long as workers knew more than managers about how to do the work, management would have to find a way to get workers' voluntary cooperation' (p. 214).

This led Taylor to revise entirely the design of machine and hand tools and in his book, *On the Art of Cutting Metals*, he devised an entirely new set of standard tool sizes and shapes which he insisted all tools should comply to. Taylor gave them obscure titles, symbols and names so that only he and his management colleagues would understand which tools were going to be used and allocated to specific jobs. In the Taylor system, of course, far more detailed instruction cards and job details needed to be written and transferred from management to the shop floor. In designing new symbols and titles it would be far quicker for management to write down and record which tools were to be used on which jobs. Equally it meant that workers were unable to challenge the instructions on the job card until the very last moment, by which time it would be too late to resist or organise protest about the way that management wanted the job to be done. For example what had previously been known as a horizontal miller No. 7 would have been retitled as a 7MH. Far more obscure symbols were used in an attempt by Taylor to appropriate and control the knowledge of how tasks were to be performed. This effectively meant replacing the knowledge which workers had over the labour process with managerial knowledge, hence management was trying to learn what the workers themselves already knew: how precisely work was done.

A major consequence of this system which Taylor introduced, and later lectured on, was a concomitant increase in the number of managerial and administrative staff. Taylor insisted that the conception of work and the way work was to be organised and performed, should be placed in the hands of a planning department. It was the responsibility of the planning department to devise the 'one best way' of carrying out jobs. This divorce in the conception and execution of tasks left the 'science of work' in the hands and minds of management leaving only the physical execution of work as the responsibility of the manual labourer. This led Taylor to claim that workers were not supposed to challenge managerial instructions on how tasks were to be performed nor indeed the speed insisted upon. In Taylor's scientific management workers were not 'paid to think' but simply to perform their tasks as prescribed in their instruction cards, written, devised and planned by management. It was management's 'right' to correct or modify the way work was to be done through the careful calculation and analysis of job record cards, instruction cards, etc., and through shop floor time and motion studies.

The role of reward under the Taylor system

In order to prove that jobs could be done far quicker Taylor would often make use of what were known as 'rate-busters' during his time and motion studies. Taylor was also able to increase the productivity of tasks through the use of differential piece-rate payment systems. Essentially this offered one rate for the first, for example, one hundred units of output and then a higher rate for any output in excess of this amount. This rested upon the assumption of course that employees are purely financially motivated, but it was one way that Taylor attempted to break down what he saw as an institutionalised pattern of natural and systematic soldiering. By offering a worker called Schmidt a higher rate to shift what would have been considered an impossible amount of pig iron Taylor was able to show that effort and productivity could be improved through the combination of financial inducement and the detailed organisation of work by management. Schmidt was basic-ally offered more money to shift more pig iron in a given period of time. Of course Taylor extracted more effort and output for what he paid for – this is what made the system more 'efficient' – but more importantly, by using Schmidt as an example he was able to demonstrate that there was nothing natural, inevitable or sacrosanct in the work speeds which had been established by employee norms on the shop floor. In this example of Schmidt, financial incentives were shown to complement and secure the control and monopoly of information and knowledge which management sought to gather and use in its control of the labour process. In Taylor's own words to Schmidt one can see the commitment and importance which Taylor attached to the managerial design of jobs and the divorce in the conception and execution of work:

> 'Well, if you are a high-priced man, you will do exactly as this man tells you to-morrow, from morning till night. When he tells you to pick up a pig and walk, you pick it up and you walk, and when he tells you to sit down and rest, you sit down . . . And what's more, no back talk.'
>
> (Taylor, quoted in Braverman, 1974: 105)

Taylor's view of employees was that they did not have the ability or intellect to be able to design and organise jobs effectively and efficiently and, therefore, it needed to be left to a specialist élite of 'industrial engineers' in managerial planning departments. In his discussion of the incident with Schmidt, Taylor reveals his inherent elitism in his acknowledgement that he had been aggressive and harsh in his manner:

> 'This seems to be rather rough talk. And indeed it would be if applied to an educated mechanic, or even an intelligent laborer. With a man of the mentally sluggish type of Schmidt it is appropriate and not unkind, since it is effective in fixing his attention on the high wages.'
>
> (Taylor, quoted in Braverman, 1974: 105–106)

For a man who was engaged in building his own house it is questionable whether this view of Schmidt, or indeed any manual employee, is justified.

In Taylor's ideal, therefore, workers should be left to perform those simple and routinised jobs for which they were inherently far better suited, leaving all 'possible brain work' in the hands of management. Taylor argued that efficiency and productivity could only be guaranteed if management took control over the design and responsibility for the performance of jobs. This necessitated collecting all relevant information and knowledge over how traditionally jobs were to be done and classifying, tabulating and restructuring work to prescribed rules, laws and formulae. Second, all possible brain work should be removed from the workers and the shop floor and be placed in the responsibility of the planning department. Finally, this knowledge and conception of work should be monopolised by management so that each stage of the production process is designed and controlled exclusively by management who then simply give detailed instructions to workers. All pre-planning and pre-calculation is done by management at least one day in advance of its execution so that all conception is removed from the imagination of the employee. In this way, according to Braverman (1974):

> Dehumanisation of the labour process, in which workers are reduced almost to the level of labour in its animal form, while purposeless and unthinkable in the case of the self-organised and self-motivated social labour of a community of producers, becomes critical for the management of purchased labour.
>
> (p. 113)

BRAVERMAN AND THE LABOUR PROCESS

For Braverman the scientific management principles of Frederick Taylor and the extreme simplification and fragmentation of jobs expressed the essence of capitalist management and rationality. Braverman argues that Taylorism was the dominant form of management and job design to which all industries and indeed all forms of extraction, production and distribution in the economic system would eventually conform. In a manner reminiscent of Weber's ideal type concept and his conception of the inevitability of bureaucratisation, Braverman posited a similar 'trend' towards deskilling and degradation in the design and control of jobs. The central concern for management was the necessity to maintain control and discipline in the labour process and Taylor theoretically and practically showed how he thought this could be achieved. In this assumption Braverman has been criticised and amended, both for his mechanical-like determinism, and his over-structuralist reading of Marx from which he draws his inspiration and main theoretical assumptions (Storey, 1983; Thompson, 1989; Knights and Willmott, 1990).

It is not necessary in this chapter to rehearse the entire theoretical and empirical amendments, corrections and modifications which have been made to Braverman, primarily in the UK through the annual Aston–UMIST labour process conference and attendant series of papers, articles and books. However, the influence and take-up of Taylor's ideas are important in order to assess the impact and consequence management science of this kind has had on job design. According to the work of Craig Littler (1982) and Littler and Salaman (1984), however, Taylorism was never as popular as Braverman has suggested. In its purest form it is difficult to find examples of the practice and successful application of concerted Taylorist deskilling and 'dehumanisation' of work tasks. In contrast to the USA, for example, Taylorism was far less popular in the UK and Japan. The existence of a stronger and more entrenched craft tradition in the UK and the paternalistic approach of many large-scale capital owners in the early twentieth century goes some way to explaining the slow spread and unpopularity of Taylorism. In Japan the cultural traditions of teamwork and group fraternalism have acted both to resist Taylorist style job design and promote more participative and multi-skilled job design.

> Japanese factories depended on a tradition of work teams incorporating managerial functions and maintenance functions, with few staff specialists. There was a lack of job boundaries and continued job flexibility, unlike the prescriptions of Taylorism.
> (Littler and Salaman, 1984)

This debate has been stimulated in part by the work of Andrew Friedman (1977, 1990) who has constructed an alternative approach to Braverman by questioning the importance and centrality of control. As Friedman argues, management itself is not concerned primarily with control *per se* but with the profitability of business. If profit can be maintained or even enhanced through the continuation of skilled discretionary work then there will be little necessity or compulsion for management to seek to enhance control through deskilling and routinisation. Friedman goes on to construct a continuum of job design and control structures. At one end of the pole we have direct control, deskilling and low trust employee relations, while at the other we have high-skilled jobs based on flexibility and high trust relations. Management is therefore assumed to have a choice rather than the assumption made by Braverman which sees management as inert pawns in an inevitable and predictable model of deskilling. The only historical role for management in the Braverman schema is to interpret correctly their role, which would anyway be difficult to interpret *incorrectly* because their job would ultimately depend on their ability to deskill and manage routinisation.

Friedman's work is important because it demonstrates both the strategic choice which management has and the constraints which partially 'guide' managerial practice. Direct control of the Taylorist type would be difficult to introduce in a situation where workers were currently highly skilled and discretionary. In these situations it would be better for management to seek a strategy of 'responsible autonomy' as the 'more complex and sophisticated the worker's knowledge and experience, the more difficult normally for management to prescribe tasks in detail and to monitor closely their performance'

(Hyman, 1987: 39). Management in these situations would be better advised to seek to manage and maintain a working relationship based on trust whereby workers are not subject to intense direct control through detailed instructions, simplification and routinisation. Resistance is clearly going to be a problem if management looks to deskill workers who have previously been used to and socialised into high-discretion employment. Direct control is possible on work groups that are less central to the production process, those workers which Friedman and others have called 'peripheral workers'. This form of labour can be more ruthlessly managed because they can be more easily replaced and the insecurity associated with this form of employment does not bode well for collective organisation and resistance. Where this is the case management is likely to face less resistance in its attempts to impose deskilled low trust work relationships. In the peripheral labour force management may be able to pursue output maximisation and high volume intensity through repetitive and deskilled work tasks associated with the assembly line of car production (see also Fox, 1974).

QUESTIONS

1 How might the job of an academic be 'Taylorised'?

2 Is this a realistic form of job design?

3 Would Braverman have argued that academic Taylorisation was inevitable?

4 Why is it 'inevitable'?

The influence of Taylor

Despite a considerable amount of evidence which suggests that Taylorism was not adopted, or where it was adopted it was re-negotiated, contested and modified by craft and work group resistance, considerable concern over its consequential impact on jobs and individuals has continued to promote academic and managerial interest in alternative forms of job design. Some have gone beyond simply seeking alternatives and possibilities to deskilling to develop broader critiques of the assumed rationality of Taylorism as a system of management control and utilisation of labour. For example, if all work is inevitably deskilled then everyone becomes a routinised and dehumanised worker simply acting as an adjunct to a vast technological automaton. In this situation workers are homogenised and accordingly there arises the risk that a collective consciousness will emerge whereby workers realise their common interest in the resistance of forces which seek to reduce them to non-thinking degraded functionaries. Although Braverman assumes an immense amount of knowledge, foresight and cunning in those he assumes are able to design and implement such production systems, he does not recognise the possibility, and indeed arguably the logical conclusion, of resistance and conflict.

THE HUMAN RELATIONS OF WORK

One of the central criticisms often made in response to Taylorism and its inherent deskilling is that it is inhumane because it provides work which is not stimulating or challenging. It may be argued that this is a feature more of a capitalist system than one of 'management science', but as we noted above in the work of Braverman, Taylorism and capitalism are often seen as coterminous.

Alienation and work – Blauner's thesis

The concept of alienation is often drawn upon in any discussion of Taylor. To suffer from alienation is to experience an estrangement from what is assumed to be one's own natural physical, mental and intellectual essence. It is argued that human beings have an inherent need to express and control their surroundings so that they may experience fulfilment and development. Where this 'need' is suppressed or prevented from being expressed it is suggested that individuals will suffer from alienation. Robert Blauner (1964) studied the impact of Taylorist style technology and work organisation on the attitudes and orientation of employees. Blauner sought to analyse the worker's 'relationship' to the technological organisation of work in order to determine 'whether or not he characteristically experiences in that work, a sense of control rather than domination, a sense of meaningful purpose rather than futility, a sense of social connection rather than isolation, and a sense of spontaneous involvement and self expression rather than detachment and discontent' (Blauner, 1964: vii).

To suffer from a sense of powerlessness according to Blauner is when an individual experiences a lack of control over the pace and method of work. For example, assembly line work in which the machine sets the pace of work allows for little control and involvement of the employee. There is very little autonomy granted to the individual employee in this work situation as generally the quality of work, the techniques of work and the time allowed to perform it are dictated by the machine. Hence, there is a sense of powerlessness because there is no subjective input by the employee, who simply becomes an object itself controlled and manipulated by what seems to be an impersonal and alien system. In performing highly specialised and simplified tasks the employee may also experience a sense of meaninglessness because they have no conception of the end product. In situations where there is an extreme division of labour with employees performing repetitive work cycles, the scope and size of the individual's contribution to the end product is small. It may not be a car that the individual is producing even though they may be considered a car worker. For the individual concerned it may simply be screwing and tightening three bolts to a gear box in an engine. Such fractionalised jobs may entail that the individual achieves no sense of purpose or satisfaction from their contribution:

> Tendencies towards meaninglessness therefore stem from the nature of modern manufacturing, which is based on standardised production and a division of labour that reduces the size of the worker's contribution to the final product.
>
> (Blauner, 1964: 22)

Blauner also suggested that self-estrangement arises because the worker is likely to become 'removed from themselves'. By this Blauner means that the extreme division of labour in which tasks are broken down into their most simplified components provides work which is somehow *unnatural* for human beings. Whereas independent craftworkers would actually manufacture and produce an entire product, a table or a chair for example, in modern industry a worker may continually and repeatedly put headlights on the front of a car. This provides work which is repetitive and incessant in its regularity, allowing no variety in pace, method, location or discretion. Hence, to quote Marx, the employee: 'In his work, therefore, [the worker] does not affirm himself, does not feel content but unhappy, does not develop freely his physical and mental energy but mortifies his body and ruins his mind' (Marx, quoted in Blauner, 1964: 27).

Although this concept of alienation has its roots in a Marxist critique of capitalism, it can be seen to enter the work of the human relations school of job design. It does this through the slightly different but related concept of *anomie* as first developed and applied by Emile Durkheim (1984) at the end of the nineteenth century. *Anomie* is that state of moral confusion and purposelessness consequent upon the extreme fragmentation of roles and tasks in contemporary society. An exclusive emphasis on individualism, encouraged by the routinisation and fragmentation of tasks in Taylor's system, would in the absence of strong guiding principles, norms and values associated with social regulation, inevitably lead to breakdown in the social fabric. This arises because as more and more individuals begin performing highly individuated tasks, in isolation and distance from other individuals, problems of social solidarity will emerge. Individuals no longer feel a part of societal community. Cut off from interaction and social relationships, there is the risk that community values and social order will become meaningless for the individual. Blauner drew on both *anomie* and alienation in his critique of monotony and the assembly line production system and, despite the weaknesses in his approach, his technological determinism and over-optimistic projection of the possibilities of future technology, his work provides an interesting and stimulating account of the problems and 'injustices' associated with Taylorism and the one best way of production of scientific management.

Elton Mayo's thesis

The human relations school of management, of which Elton Mayo is probably the most well-known exponent and theorist, attempted to attend to these alienative and anomic consequences of large-scale production and organisation. Mayo drew attention to the social needs of individuals. It is argued in this tradition that individual employees need a sense of social worth and satisfaction which could only be developed if work was provided which allowed for social interaction and communication. Furthermore, managers needed to express a concern and interest in employees' personal problems and to emphasise the importance of each individual in the organisation. Management needed to integrate the various elements of the organisation almost through the recreation of the lost values and norms consequent upon Taylorism. A sense of community and 'belongingness' needed to be created and fostered by active managerial intervention, through communication, participation and more attention to behavioural variables than simply the cash nexus and economic incentives of Taylor. Hence, Mayo emphasised the need for Durkheimian style 'moral communities', whereby 'only by the integration of the individual into the [management-led] plant community could systemic integration be maintained and the potential pathologies of the industrial society avoided' (Watson, 1987: 40). Within the field of the human relations approach to job design many attempts have been made to recreate the 'social man' (Schein, 1965). The idea that man was a social being as much as an economic actor was uncovered through a series of studies of the human relations in work organisations.

Hawthorne studies

The Hawthorne studies in the mid-1920s appeared to show that informal work groups and associations were significant variables in explaining productivity and output performance. The Hawthorne studies were conducted in the Hawthorne plant of the United States Western Electrical Company where 29 000 employees were engaged to produce telephone equipment for the Bell system. Changing environmental variables such as the amount of lighting did not seem to have any consistent effects on the productivity of the work groups. Indeed, productivity would increase despite the contradictory changes in the degree of lighting and the number of rest pauses. This led the study to conclude that the work group was responding to the very act of being studied and analysed. Hence the result that paying attention and showing interest in work groups would itself lead to productivity increases – the Hawthorne effect.

In the later studies of the 'bank wiring room' the consultants and academics discovered, like Taylor, that work groups would systematically control and restrict output in order to maintain what they considered to be a fair day's work for a fair day's pay. Workers appeared to be responding to what in management's eyes were irrational sentiments such as 'fairness' and the 'right to work'. The recognition that informal groups, norms and attitudes could inhibit the efficient production and output of the enterprise led the leading authors of the study, Roethlisberger and Dickson (1939), to conclude that the best approach for management should not be to try and undermine and force the informal organisation to conform to the formal organisation. Rather, it was patently obvious that informal organisations would be likely to re-emerge and appear as a natural consequence of employees' needs for social solidarity, community and group association. The informal work groups in effect were substituting for the lack of social interaction and communication experienced in highly fragmented, individuated and specialised work tasks. Management were advised to attempt to engineer and channel sentiments and attitudes that prevailed in the informal work organisation. Through controlled participation, effective means and channels of communication, and socially skilled enlightened supervision, management could harness the strength and solidarity of the informal work groups to the productive needs of the 'formal organisation'.

QUESTIONS

1 How might an individual be alienated in their workplace yet not suffer from the condition of *anomie?*

2 How far did the Hawthorne studies demonstrate that management could 'condition' the work experience of employees rather than 'condition' the employee?

The work of the Tavistock Institute

These studies led to a number of further programmes and initiatives designed to release and tap into the individual's inherent need for creativity and social interaction. In Britain the Tavistock Institute for Human Relations made a number of important studies into the productivity of work organisations. They found that in the coal-mining industry, for example, productivity fell after the introduction of mechanised technology. The formal and elaborate division of labour that this entailed reduced the amount of social interaction, teamwork, discretion and 'responsible autonomy' that miners had become used to (Trist and Bamforth, 1951). The researchers within the Tavistock Institute were firmly committed to an approach which emphasised the need and desirability of providing individuals with the satisfaction of completing a whole task, of being able to control their own activities, and of organising work tasks so that individuals can develop satisfactory social relationships (Trist *et al.*, 1963). Their conclusion in their study of the coal-mining industry during the late 1940s and early 1950s was that technical work organisation needed to pay careful attention to the social needs and social organisation that existed within work groups. Hence there was a tendency for managers and industrial engineers to introduce the most technically efficient system of production which would result in a low productive response from employees because it was the only:

> . . . adaptive method of handling, in the contingencies of the underground situation, a complicated, rigid and large-scale work system, borrowed with too little modification from an engineering culture.
>
> (Trist and Bamforth, 1951: 23)

These studies have been influential in the development of ideas in job design such as job enlargement, job enrichment, teamworking and semi-autonomous work groups. Job enlargement basically means that more tasks are added to the one that an individual employee is currently doing to add a variety in task, pace and location. Job enrichment, by contrast, attempts to add responsibility and discretion to an individual's job so that not only do they experience a variety of tasks but are also provided with an opportunity for development and realisation of 'self-actualising needs' (Maslow, 1954). Teamworking and semi-autonomous work groups (SAWGs) attempt to restore the opportunity for social interaction and communication. These schemes usually include measures which allow teams to establish their own patterns and routines of working, electing their own leaders, organising their own rest periods, and scheduling their own workloads. The recent collapse of the SAWGs at the Volvo plant in Kalmar highlights a significant problem with these schemes, notably productivity. Indeed criticism has been made of the tokenistic nature of many of these schemes and in one famous quote an employee claims that this simply means that:

'You move from one boring, dirty, monotonous job to another boring, dirty, monotonous job, and somehow you're supposed to come out of it all "enriched". But I never feel "enriched" – I just feel knackered.'

(quoted in Nichols, 1980: 279)

SOCIALISATION AND ORIENTATIONS TO WORK

A common assumption made by theorists and consultants working in the field of job redesign, and especially the quality of working life movement, is the inherent or essential needs which individuals possess for creative employment. Buchanan (1989) in his work on job design has stressed the debilitating effects of Taylorist style work regimes and the stultifying impact on the physical, emotional, and psychological well-being of individuals:

> . . . people have higher levels of ability and higher expectations of working life . . . they have a physiological need for sensory stimulation, for changes in the patterns of information that feed to the senses to sustain arousal.

(Buchanan, 1989: 80)

Similarly Michael Cross (1990) in his uncritical and prescriptive 'advice' to management suggests that because of an inherent need for creativity and self-fulfilment jobs need to be designed which test the initiative and ability of individuals so that they 'seek to provide meaningful jobs which build upon and stretch people's abilities so that they can realise their potential' (p. 29).

This *essentialism* has been the subject of a sustained critique by radical social psychologists (Knights and Willmott, 1989; Knights, 1990; Willmott, 1990), and indeed we can look back to studies of plant sociology for examples where frustration and dissatisfaction have not arisen from the experience interpreted by some as the hallmark of conditions fostering the alienation of human nature.

Car workers

In their influential study of the Vauxhall car workers in Luton, Goldthorpe, Lockwood *et al.* (1968) discovered that despite the machine-like Taylorist monotony of the work process employees were neither militant nor sought to resist or seek to renegotiate the content of jobs. The jobs themselves were the very ones which many in the school of human relations were arguing would lead to dissatisfaction and unrest because they denied the essential creativity and the self-actualising needs of human beings. Goldthorpe, Lockwood *et al.* found that certain groups of workers were not getting any intrinsic satisfaction from their work but equally were not prepared or inclined to do anything about it. This paradox was partly explained by what was identified as the employees' instrumental attitudes to work. This new class of affluent manual worker was prepared to labour on monotonous and intrinsically unrewarding work because they viewed employment as simply a means to pay for private housing, cars and other new consumer items proliferating during the 1960s. As the authors conclude, 'It is by no means those groups whose work-tasks and roles appeared least rewarding whose members had thought most often or most seriously about leaving' (p. 25). Furthermore, consumption and not production appeared as an equally important variable in employees' *orientation* to work:

> Workers within all groups in our sample tend to be particularly motivated to increase their power as consumers and their domestic standard of living, rather than their satisfaction as producers and the degree of their self-fulfilment in work.
> <div align="right">(Goldthorpe, Lockwood <i>et al.</i>, 1968: 38)</div>

The work of Burawoy

Theoretical and empirical studies have shown that a deskilling-resistance/frustration model is far too simple and does not explain adaptation and habituation to routine and monotony. Michael Burawoy (1979, 1985), drawing on the pioneering work of Donald Roy (1952, 1953) and Tom Lupton (1963), has developed empirical work which demonstrates that workers *adapt* to what may be perceived as intolerable low discretion roles through the ritualised engagement in game playing. The resistance which many theorists had predicted would emerge from a Taylorist style work regime needs to be countered, according to Burawoy, by an equal tendency by management and worker relations to generate or 'manufacture consent'. In the study of the Allied Corporation, Burawoy (1979) describes how workers would both ease the routinised nature of Taylorist style job design and actively create time and space for themselves within the working day. Through a game of 'making out', workers would gain a relative amount of satisfaction from low discretion deskilled work by manipulating output levels so that quotas could be achieved by workers. In essence there were two types of job on the shop floor, jobs on which it was difficult to achieve quota levels, and 'gravy jobs' where it was relatively easy to reach the quota level of output. In order to 'make out' workers needed to manipulate work schedules, and cajole and 'bargain' with workers whose cooperation was essential for success in the game of making out. Close working and social relations needed to be fostered with the scheduling man, the crib attendant, the truck driver bringing stock to the work station, and the set-up man. Informally the work groups studied by Burawoy maintained a restriction on output of 140%. It was believed that if you were able to produce in excess of this then management would reduce the rate for the job as it would become apparent to management that the job was a 'gravy job'. Workers would therefore hoard work in excess of 140% in a 'kitty' and keep the work for a 'rainy day' or to create time and space for themselves in the future. Also workers would 'chisel', which meant that time would be redistributed so that workers could maximise the time they spent on the gravy jobs where they could turn out work in excess of 100%.

As Burawoy comments, on first entering the shop individual employees may have perceived the game as being banal and 'mindless' but after a while this aloofness would recede as employees actively became caught up in the game of 'making out'. Individuals would be evaluated by their peers and work group colleagues on their ability to make out and hence, 'Each worker sooner or later is sucked into this distinctive set of activities' (Burawoy, 1979: 64).

This study of informal work groups and the restrictions and games which they engage in has long fascinated sociologists because at first sight it appears paradoxical in that it relieves the boredom of work, neutralises any discontent felt towards the job or management that were 'responsible' for its design, and hence perpetuates the conditions for its ultimate survival. Employees appear to generate consent to the work process through this game of making out, ensuring profitability and the competitiveness of the organisation. For the employee:

> The rewards of making out are defined in terms of factors *immediately* [author's italics] related to the labour process – reduction of fatigue, passing time, relieving boredom, and so on – and factors that emerge from the labour process – the social and psychological rewards of making out on a tough job.
>
> (Burawoy, 1979: 64)

For the employer, production and output targets are maintained, and even, according to Burawoy, guaranteed, while *diverting* concern from potential management – employee conflict over job content and work design. Conflict is actually *dispersed laterally* to colleagues on whom individual employees are dependent in order to make out. Obstructive behaviour by other workers is likely to frustrate the ability to make out and so potential conflictual relations emerge *between* employees. The role of the foreman is seen as crucial in this respect as it is they who 'referee' the game by either facilitating the game of making out through relaxing formal rules on health and safety, i.e. running on the shop floor may be overlooked, or obstructing the game through the enforcement of formal rules and procedures. Hence conflict is dispersed down the organisation and laterally across the organisation so that when 'the labour process is organised into some form of game involving the active participation of both management and worker, the interests of both are concretely co-ordinated' (Burawoy, 1979: 85).

Some conclusions

The work of Burawoy has been outlined in some detail because it has re-worked many classic assumptions in labour process and industrial sociology theory. From Braverman's work on deskilling it is easy to assume that workers would have no interest in the perpetuation of deskilled Taylorist style jobs. The conditions are restrictive, the discipline harsh, and the jobs are of little interest and variety. However, from the work of Goldthorpe, Lockwood *et al.* we can see that workers may adapt and habituate to deskilled work for a variety of seemingly rational reasons. Second, it challenges the school of human relations in their assumptions that jobs need to be provided which offer a variety of pace, skill and initiative so that workers do not become alienated from themselves. What is the essential self of human beings? According to some readings of Marx it may be assumed that the self-actualising and developmental needs of individuals cannot be met in a production system continually forced to seek cheaper and more productive ways of carrying out labour. This implies that individuals will feel estranged from themselves and hence are likely to resist. However, the adaptive and acquiescent behaviour of employees which Burawoy and others have charted can be explained by reference to the dynamic nature of individuals (Fromm, 1991). Individuals adapt themselves to external circumstances and hence create something new in their 'nature':

THE POST-FORDIST WORKER AND HRM CONTROVERSY

An influential current body of theory and writing has sought to demonstrate the breakdown of production systems based on Fordist assembly line methods (Aglietta, 1979; Piore and Sabel, 1984; Boyer, 1988). Each writer shades a nuanced approach to what is causing the breakdown, ranging from the inherent productivity limitations of Taylorism to theories which emphasise the collapse and saturation of mass markets, i.e., where consumers are now demanding individualised 'niche' products which require and necessitate a more flexible approach to production. Here workers are required who have the initiative, ability and skill to develop and continually retrain to acquire new skills in response to rapidly changing tastes and styles in the product market. Aglietta (1979), probably the most influential contribution to this debate, suggests three reasons internal to the labour process of Fordism which places constraints on its development as a system (pp. 119–121):

- there exist technical limits to the further fragmentation of assembly line tasks;
- simply intensifying this process of production will lead to concomitant increases in absenteeism, and the deterioration in the quality of the product – for example, in 1913 Henry Ford was to experience a turnover rate of 380%;
- it becomes increasingly difficult and more 'expensive' to motivate employees – the five dollar day which Ford introduced in response to the above failed to significantly counter labour problems.

The so-called Fordist system of manufacture was premised upon the systemic consistency between the existence of a mass of consumers demanding mass produced invariant products. The standard cliché offered during Ford's early car factories was that consumers could have any colour of Model T car they wanted so long as it was black.

This theoretical analysis has been taken up in many accounts within the critical theory of job redesign (Kelly, 1985; Littler, 1985). Kelly (1985), for example, suggests that a breakdown between product markets, labour markets and the organisation of the labour process expressed itself through a *disarticulation* in these various spheres of capital accumulation. The restructuring of organisations in response to global product market reorganisation and the domestic Thatcher-driven recession provided both a need and the incentive to restructure production systems.

This level of analysis is far more subtle and satisfactory than some overly deterministic accounts of movements towards high multi-skilled flexible working groups (Piore and Sabel, 1984; Atkinson and Meager, 1986). These analyses focus on some assumed direct link between consumer demands for uniqueness and product variability, the prevailing level of technology and the internal labour market of economic organisations. Piore and Sabel (1984) argue that a new system of flexible specialisation is emerging demanding the return to craft-style multi-skilled work. Flexible specialisation is seen as 'a new form of skilled craft production made easily adaptable by programmable technology to provide specialised goods which can supply an increasingly fragmented and volatile market' (Gilbert *et al.*, 1992). In Robin Murray's work (1985) we are presented with a future called 'Benetton Britain', which according to Murray is an ideal-typical representation of flexible specialisation. Products have a short life span and the relationship between the product market and the internal labour process of Benetton is almost fully integrated and symbiotic. Sophisticated 'early warning' information technology provides almost instantaneous feedback from current tastes and fashions in the retail outlets to the internal labour process of Benetton. Within less than three days Benetton claim their production can respond to changing tastes and fashions.

From this we can see how one might be led to suggest that the future for job design is based on flexibility and multi-skilling driven by a market imperative, fostered by intensive marketing and advertising. Walton (1985), in an influential account of the restructuring of organisations consistent with an overall HRM philosophy, suggested that it was both a market necessity to restructure and an opportunity to unleash the infinite potential of human labour. Walton argues that workers respond best and most productively when they are not tightly controlled by hierarchical layers of management and are provided with opportunities to move beyond narrowly defined and prescribed jobs. The influence of the early human relations philosophy and studies are clearly apparent here when Walton argues that workers should be given broader responsibilities harnessing commitment to the organisation rather than expensive and conflictual coercion through direct control and discipline:

> Jobs are designed to be broader than before, to combine planning and implementation, and to include efforts to upgrade operations, not just to maintain them. Individual responsibilities are expected to change as conditions change, and teams, not individuals, often are the organisational units accountable for performance. With management hierarchies relatively flat and differences in status minimised, control and lateral coordination depend on shared goals.
> (Walton, 1985; quoted in Armstrong, 1992: 98)

In a series of articles on flexibility Atkinson and his colleagues at the Institute for Manpower Studies have argued that firms are responding to changing external market circumstances by restructuring their internal labour markets. Flexibility is achieved primarily through functional, numerical and financial flexibility. Functional flexibility represents attempts by management to develop broad ranged polyvalent skills amongst their workforce. This provides organisations with the requisite flexibility to adapt to changing technology and product market fashions and tastes. In the 1980s companies have sought to remove internal rigidities between craft union lines of demarcation so that workers can combine production and maintenance work. Within this group of employees skills and training are extremely important in ensuring the adaptability of the organisation. Atkinson describes these employees as the core group or primary labour market for organisations. Promotion, skill development and favourable terms and conditions of employment are the rewards offered to highly valued employees in this category. In contrast the secondary labour market, or the peripheral group of employees and quasi-employees consisting of part-time labour, short-term contracts, public subsidy trainees, job-sharing and 'delayed' recruitment, provides the organisation with numerical flexibility. This peripheral group of employees can be quickly called in and disposed of in response to fluctuations in the product market. They can be seen as labour on call, providing a buffer stock of resources enabling the organisation to 'organically' expand and contract (see Chapter 4).

The concept and existence of flexibility have generated much academic and business interest, both favourable and critical. Some have questioned the empirical validity of the studies conducted by the IMS (Pollert, 1988; Marginson, 1989) drawing attention to figures which suggest that there has been minimal growth in the number of peripheral and core employees. In fact many studies have shown that it may actually be in the public sector that the changes outlined by Atkinson and Meager have occurred. This is an unusual finding in that Atkinson and Meager have stressed that flexibility is primarily a radical private sector strategy designed to meet the requirements of changing manufacturing technology and shifting product market patterns.

However, the conclusion that these production systems are based on job design emphasising multi-skilling and functional flexibility alone is clearly inadequate in its empirical and explanatory utility. The so-called leading-edge examples of these new production systems, Benetton and the Emilia-Romagna region in northern Italy, appear to resort to exploitative subcontract relationships using familiar methods of low discretion and intensive labour input (see Pollert, 1988, 1991; Elger, 1990). Furthermore from the discussion above we can question the determinism of some of these accounts in a similar way to the criticisms which have emerged of Braverman. Braverman, as was shown, posited only one future and direction for production which was based on deskilling and intensification. In the accounts of flexible specialisation and multi-skilled craft working as proposed by Piore and Sabel and Robin Murray, we are equally presented with an account which posits unilinearity. Generally these accounts assume a considerable amount of consensus and managerial foresight and ability in restructuring organisations. However, as Kelly (1985) suggests, the recession has probably provided management with the incentive and means to drive through change in a situation in which individuals are glad just to have a job.

Many writers have attempted to account for the apparent contradiction in recent restructuring initiatives which appear to be based simultaneously on reskilling and functional flexibility together with peripheralisation, intensification and deskilling (see Shaiken *et al.*, 1986; Smith, 1989). This has been coined neo-Fordism in contrast to post-Fordism, and reflects a significant theoretical advance in moving away from overly deterministic 'unilinear' accounts which either stress deskilling or reskilling (see Badham and Mathews, 1989; Lovering, 1990). As Batstone has argued the development and form of labour relations outcomes must always be seen as provisional and contested, not simply between management and worker but within political struggles within management itself:

> Strategic change in organisations is accompanied by intra-management bargaining and micro-political struggles that make the outcome of the process of change uncertain and at the very least 'negotiable'. The ambiguities of the strategic process mean that the implications of strategy for labour relations are likewise uncertain, provisional and complex.
>
> (Batstone, 1984; quoted in Hyman, 1987: 49)

Attempts by management to develop strategically such production systems are based on the simultaneous desire for commitment and consent from labour to work and the maintenance of sufficient power within management to adjust numerically the workforce in response to market and technological developments. This contradiction has been usefully explored by Michael Burawoy (1979, 1985) who argues that management seeks simultaneously to secure and obscure the power relations in production. Ultimately management is responsible to the interests of capital and if profitability is threatened management will need the power to preserve capital. The burden of adjustment to external market and technological shocks must fall asymmetrically on the quantitative and qualitative nature of labour. In our discussion of the flexible firm it can be seen that this contradiction has been partially 'managed' by organisations by obtaining their numerical flexibility through peripheral labour and their commitment and consent from a privileged core of employees.

Teamworking, business process re-engineering and aesthetics: disorientation, simulation and re-sign?

A relatively recent response to this so-called crisis of Fordism has been the fervour surrounding the concept of business process re-engineering (BPR), sometimes peddled under the title business process transformation or business process redesign. The two key seminal articles propounding the miracle of BPR were published by Hammer in the July–August 1990 *Harvard Business Review* and by Davenport and Short in the summer 1990 *Sloan Management Review*. Hammer and Champy's *Reengineering the Corporation: A Manifesto for Business Revolution* was published in the UK in 1993 and rapidly became a best-selling management text. The principles of BPR in themselves may not seem particularly revolutionary in the light of the above discussions, but the novelty seems to lie in the manner in which they are introduced, the holistic nature of the package, the synergy and coherence which the key principles are said collectively to deliver, and the inspirational and aggressive aesthetic of the texts. Tied in with these principles is the concomitant importance attached to human resource job design change in empowerment, devolution and autonomy. Managers are continually reminded of the market imperative to take a hammer, or an axe, to the structures and principles governing their organisation. Organisations require personality transplants, nothing less than a lobotomy will suffice and employees who cannot and will not change need to be 'shot'.

Hammer and Champy perceive the problem to originate in the manner in which capitalist organisations have developed large and unwieldy bureaucracies based on division, specialisation, hierarchy, long lines of authority relations, complicated functional structures of status and layers of career divisions and deskilling. Furthermore, the production, manufacture or service products which organisations generate stay divorced from the customer, who remains a forgotten and distant element in this traditional supply-led and production-dominant system. According to Hammer and Champy (1993), employees need to 'deeply believe' that they are working not for bosses or to keep pace with targets, but simply for the customers (p. 14). Authority needs to be vested in small, multi-functional teams who can respond rapidly and competently to the vagaries and whim of customer requirements. Grint (1995) offers an example of an organisation selling books:

> if the business is concerned with selling books by post then a customer wanting to buy books from different departments, pay for them by credit card, and have them delivered by special delivery, should not have to be switched through departments that deal with different categories of books, then be switched to a new section that deals with accounts, and then find themselves trailing through the telephone network in an attempt to have the books sent out.
>
> (pp. 92–93)

Organisational barriers need to be smashed to create self-guiding, team-based process units. Although sceptical of much of BPR, Tom Peters recommends a similar reorganisation in job design which enables employees to get closer to the customer. Union Pacific Railroad was in many ways a classic example of the ordered and structured bureaucratic, functional organisation. If a customer or a track inspector reported a problem it would be passed on to the manager of that yard where the problem was discovered. The manager would report this to his or her boss who would subsequently pass the problem on to the divisional superintendent for transportation. Then it would go to the general divisional superintendent to be passed on to the region and finally to the apex of the management structure. From there it would make a horizontal shift to sales and marketing and *pass back down this convoluted hierarchy* to the district sales representative who would liaise with the customer (as Tom Peters adds, if the customer is still alive!):

> Today, if a track inspector discovers a problem at a customer-owned rail siding, he informs the customer directly. If the customer disagrees with the track inspector . . . then the customer can call the track inspector's boss, the Superintendent for Transportation Services. But the super will say in effect, 'Look, I don't know anything about track. I'm just a boss. Keep talking to the track inspector.'
>
> (Peters, 1994: 31–32)

BPR integrates a whole set of practices (Hammer and Champy, 1993) from flattening hierarchies, to shifting from 'training' to 'education', incorporating pay systems which calculate added value rather than rewarding attendance, and where managers become coaches rather than supervisors. Perhaps its singular most innovatory component, however, is the evangelism combined with aggression in the accompanying aesthetic. Managers are exhorted to see the world in a new way, as dangerous, unstable and subject to rapid shifts. The vagaries and fashion in style and customer demand will not tolerate organisations that do not have the capacity for rapid and immediate, rather than incremental, change. One of the interesting features of BPR gurus is their emphasis on those organisations which have failed. The figure of 80% is widely documented as the number of organisations that have not been sufficiently radical in adopting the BPR package (see Willmott, 1995), leaving room therefore for continued pressure and cajoling. It seems managers need to be continually pressured to attend the weekly ecclesiastical sermon – to strengthen their commitment and moral fibre so as to remain faithful to the cause in the face of pressures to deviate and temptations to seek an easy answer.

The recent customer service drive at British Telecom (IRS, 1995: 579) seeks to develop team-based working which resonates with many of the job redesign implications of BPR. With market changes – a product of political engineering, intervention and management – customers now have an increasing choice of suppliers for telephone equipment and maintenance. A BT marketing department survey found that 80% of customers wanted engineers to be available on Saturdays and 25% of its customers wanted service availability on Sundays. Following a complicated and lengthy 18-month negotiation with the union, which ended in September 1994 with an 85% ballot rejection, BT sought volunteers directly for their new attendance schedule package. Engineers were offered the option of three different attendance patterns ranging from intensive 12-hour, 3-day working between Friday and Tuesday to conventional 5-day working Monday to Friday but with evening work obligatory and remunerated at standard rates. Management wanted to loosen up the rigid start and stop times which governed the traditional rostering system. In addition to the change in attendance patterns, a vital component of the Customer Service Improvement Programme (CSIP) was the demand for flexibility, whereby engineers could be called up an hour before their scheduled shift start and requested to work an additional hour after the formal termination of their shift. This could be 'averaged out' and balanced over time by letting engineers go home early or start later as and when customer demand patterns dictate. As part of the CSIP BT introduced a new Resource Administrative Management System (RAMS) which was able to store and load every individual engineer's roster and, by drawing on customer order data from the Customer Service System RAMS, could automatically build work schedule rosters.

As part of this strategic programme BT sought to introduce small teams of field engineers which, instead of the traditional supervisory–management authority relations, would take on increased responsibility and initiative themselves. A major problem with the traditional structure was found to be the role of the first-line managers who had increasingly become 'deskbound', tied up with administration and paperwork. BT wanted to get these managers back into the field, closer to the customer, and therefore created a new role of 'field manager'. This entailed a considerable effort in delayering in which the old supervisory grade had become surplus to requirements. These new field managers were being trained to take on the role of 'coach' – managing, building and developing teams through an attention to quality, workmanship and customer satisfaction. Field managers were provided with no dedicated office space but were linked into a field support office by mobile phones and home-based faxes.

WH Smith has embarked on a similar restructuring exercise following increased competition from supermarkets and petrol stations selling stationery, magazines and newspapers (IRS, 1995: 596). A retail branch restructuring exercise sought a shift from a process- to customer-driven orientation, reducing unnecessary hierarchy, redefining job roles, rewriting job descriptions and reducing the number of grades. The old paternal 'command-and-control' model which held the boundaries and structures of job design in place was deemed to be anachronistic given the present competitive climate. Departmental and assistant departmental managers were replaced with more flexibly defined customer service and support managers, with a team of customer support leaders responsible for coaching and developing their customer service teams. The guiding principles governing this change programme emphasised the importance of empowerment and flexibility:

> Managers and staff should feel a sense of personal ownership and accountability, making them quicker to respond to selling opportunities . . . We want to give people power to use their own initiative, make decisions and take responsibility. (IRS, 1995: p. 6)

Similar to the changes taking place in the customer–employee interface in the high street retail banks (see O'Doherty, 1994), employees are being refocused and reconstituted (Du Gay and Salaman, 1994) to service, satisfy and even 'excite' the customer, as Peters and Waterman (1982) have urged throughout the 1980s and 1990s.

These accounts, however, present the formal, or official, version of events. Typically, empirical research which has examined new innovations in teamworking and BPR has tended to rely on surveys of management or on interview-based case-study material which again relies wholly or primarily on the accounts of those who have formally 'designed' the change programmes. Detailed longitudinal and ethnographic research is far more rare. That research which has adopted a rich ethnographic tradition (including Jackall, 1988; Kondo, 1991; Collinson, 1992; Casey, 1994 and Watson, 1994) has tended to emphasise the precarious and partial nature of these 'deliberate' interventions and design programmes which seek to re-engineer the organisation of employment relations. In the work of Tony Watson, the uncertainty and anxiety which attend managerial work, especially that which accompanies organisation change, tend to destabilise the dispassionate rational–technical functionality in which employees are meant to carry out their duties. Recent efforts to tap into the hearts and souls of employees attempt to constitute and appropriate irrational and emotional aspects of employee behaviour (Hochschild, 1983; Burrell, 1992) in an instrumental and purposive manner designed to secure the efficient and profitable exercise of one's economic commodity status.

However, the same instability, if not heightened instability, often accompanies these efforts as employees attempt to make sense of the ambiguity of devolved responsibility. Managers are seen to be preoccupied with a search for themselves; in effect they are concerned with the management of themselves. Managers are seen to confront ambiguity and dilemmas in situations where they have to negotiate some compromise or trade-off between their own sense of identity and the demands of work. This often challenges and impinges on assumptions of self and identity. Steve Loscoe, a technical manager at ZTC Ryland, the pseudonym which Watson (1994) adopts for his case-study organisation, reflects on this ambiguity and complexity in defining both himself and his role in the corporation:

> I really do wonder what my bloody job is sometimes. I say to myself 'I'm in charge of this office and this office and the office in Birmingham' but then I ask whether I'm really in charge of even myself when it comes down to it. I get told to jump here, jump there, sort this, sort that, more than I ever did before I was a section leader.
>
> (Watson, 1994: 29)

Catherine Casey (1995) reports similar findings in her book examining the 'Hephaestus' Corporation, where the interrelation between work, self and identity continually disrupts the smooth functioning and reproduction of technical relations in production. An employee she calls Hal reflects on the turbulence of change and the attendant uncertainty of role, position and status as occupational boundaries are destructured to make way for multi-functional organic 'product teams' (p. 106). Knowledge and skill which were previously valued under the former locus of occupational identity are becoming redundant, as fluidity and change disrupt former certainties demanding a continual investment and reinvestment in skill acquisition. Employees are left to search for the 'signs' of what is required as they are brought nearer to what Karen Legge has called the 'indiscriminate deconstructive impact of "free" market forces' (Legge, 1995: 244). One manager in the Watson (1994) study had to reprimand Watson for using the redundant language of 'jobs': 'To use the term "job" was to be slapped down by, for example, the injuction to "wash your mouth out"'(p. 115). On asking about job design the researcher was told 'For God's sake don't use that term; "job" is a dirty word here' (p. 115). Conventional job analysis assumes that there exists something stable called a 'job' which can be traced, marked and identified in terms of a stable set of tasks, responsibilities and knowledge. As one manager in the Jackall (1988) study comments, there are no rules, requirements, responsibilities which can be categorically defined as the boundaries of one's 'job'. Rather extreme, but perhaps reflecting the sentiments of those ambitious and desirous of success, is the following comment quoted in Jackall:

> The code is this: you milk the plants; rape the business; use other people and discard them; fuck any woman that is available, in sight and under your control; and exercise authoritative prerogatives at will with subordinates and other lesser mortals who are completely out of your league in money and status.
>
> (p. 97)

Perhaps the only unrealistic assumption in contemporary organisations is the comfortable assertion of 'subordinate'! Employees are 'positioned' in open and fluid skill grades, or in 'job clusters' in which the content and boundaries remain negotiable and subject to change. Bouts of reskilling and deskilling are commonplace as the life expectancy of skills is reduced to one in which last week's knowledge and skill are today redundant. Hal comments on the nature of his job:

> My job? Well, it just changed. Yesterday, I think. Principal Information Systems Consultant is what it changed to. And I used to be Manager Assistant Projects, I think it was called.

Specialisation and demarcation are rapidly dissolving, leading to a synthetic post-occupational culture of flexibility and generalisation, precariously held together by the glue of corporate culture. Corporate culture attempts to engineer and foster team-based harmony through the manipulation of myths, symbols and stories with which employees can identify and cohere around common purpose and identity. Class-based and occupational affiliations are giving way to simulated families which tap into individuals' needs for direction and purpose (see also Willmott, 1993). However, this remains a precarious and unstable form of design as the existential concerns and questions of individuals and collectives can never be indefinitely cocooned in the artificial warmth of corporate culture and charismatic leadership (see Hopfl and Linstead, 1993). As Bauman (1995) argues, passion, emotion and what he calls 'new forms of togetherness' in a mode of 'Being-for' – that is concern, empathy and emotional commitment – always threaten the 'courthouse' of instrumental reason:

> In the garden of Reason, sentiments are weeds – plants that seed themselves in unexpected and inconvenient spots. The spots are inconvenient because they have not been allocated in advance – they are random from the point of view of the master plan, and hence undermine the design because the design is, first and foremost, about the impossibility of randomness.
>
> (Bauman, 1995: 54)

A major problem with this critical existential humanism is its foundational reliance on the ontological features of the human being. Much radical literature has explored the historical and cultural contingency of what it is to be human. The critical work of the University of Keele's Social Theory and Technology group (see Law, 1991; and Latour 1987, in the first instance) has done much to examine the relationship between power, self and technology. This work seeks to incorporate post-structuralist advances in social theory into contemporary technological and organisational design. One of its main concerns is the boundary or difference between humans and technology. As our introduction suggests, hybrid forms of man/machine cyborgs may portend the future of job design. As Law (1991) suggests, 'the very dividing line between those objects that we choose to call people and those that we call machines is variable, negotiable' (p.17). To capture a sense of this complex literature, consider your own helplessness once your Internet port breaks down, the next time your car won't start, or the sense of a limb missing when your word-processor won't work. In fact, if you walk to work instead of driving you may experience a whole new sense of self as the route and surroundings take on new dimensions of sensuous, topographical and temporal meaning. Perhaps you may reflect on the extent to which the body has become composed, constituted and assembled by material computer and information technology. Corbett (1995) examines contemporary fears and possibilities as the advance of computer and information technology creates simulated environments of artifical intelligence and virtual reality which break down comfortable definitions of the real and the unreal. Machines which develop human characteristics and humans which increasingly resemble robots, as portrayed in the film *Bladerunner*, challenge the categorical divisions human/technology, reason/feeling and culture/nature. Is the future of job design one which undoes its own conceptual and practical foundations when the notion of 'job' and 'design' as top-down managerial delimitation and structure gives way to self-reflexive, quasi-organic cybernetic systems? Who (or what) remains in control? Are we left with the rapid circulation of information bits, symbols and part-composed narratives which float as 'signs' in an uncontrollable and unstable cyberspace (see Gibson, 1984)?

MULTI-SKILLING AND EUROPEAN DEVELOPMENTS

At the outset of this chapter it was suggested that organisations seeking to introduce HRM strategies and policies would begin placing considerable emphasis on the development of, and investment in, employees' skills. It has become somewhat of a cliché to suggest that HRM organisations see employees as resources to be developed rather than as costs to be minimised. As our discussion has demonstrated, however, the process of changing to or introducing HRM is not as simple as some of the prescriptive literature on job design and total quality management would have us believe. Although this literature suggests that there are 'internal obstacles', i.e. the possibility of recalcitrant trade unions, the need for 'enlightened management', the development of new methods of communication and the urgency of an 'attitudinal' revision amongst management and shop floor workers (see Cross, 1990; James, 1992), it is still largely voluntarist in its broad assumptions. By this we mean that management and the organisation are extracted from deeper and more profound 'structures of constraint' which they may have little influence on individually but which has a considerable influence on their activities and practices. This we might call 'external obstacles' and can be thought of as 'determinators' which impress upon management a prescribed direction in policy and outcome. We have seen how Braverman, for example, stressed the inevitability of deskilling as a structural necessity of capitalism driven by the need continually to increase productivity and output. Braverman saw the system of scientific management as developed by F.W. Taylor as the apogee and perfection of management rationality. This sought a progressive deskilling of labour so that control and direction of the labour process could be effectively monopolised by management and used more accurately to determine and operationalise desired levels of output and efficiency. However, from the discussion in this chapter we have seen how this somewhat crude and mechanical view of management and job design was far too determinist in its assumptions. This can be seen as an approach which sits at the opposite end of the pole to the overly voluntarist position of job design. As Harvie Ramsay (1985) has cogently concluded:

> No analysis of any social process under capitalism can proceed by a priori, determinist fatalism, for this ignores the possibility of contradictions and so unintended outcomes. Nor, incidentally, can it employ the equally abstracted, a priori reasoning that characterise many of the voluntarist counterparts of this view. (p. 74)

Braverman ignores the central dynamic of struggle and resistance as workers seek to reject and renegotiate the impact of deskilling and degradation. Similarly consensus within management is often more a strategic, or in Braverman's view conspiratorial, ideal of management. There is considerable 'space' and negotiation within and between management groups such that the process from strategic design to implementation and operationalisation does not proceed smoothly. In the work of Wood and Kelly (1982) it is argued that it would be naïve to believe that policy statements of managerial strategy add up to their successful implementation. In the influential work of Mintzberg (1978) it has been argued that managerial processes are best thought of as an uneasy combination of intended, deliberate and realised strategy together with unrealised strategy such that the emergent strategy is part intention, accident and 're-negotiation'. Hyman (1987) has summarised this confusion over the voluntarist–determinist axis of management strategy in terms of the perspective one adopts on management:

> Viewed from without, corporate management may appear as an integrated totality. From beneath, the image may be similar . . . But seen from within, organisational stability and integrity may be far more problematic. (p. 30)

In the more recent literature on post-Fordism and the return of the multi-skilled craft worker we see an equally suspect determinism between the demands of a qualitatively different labour market and the assumed unilinear impact on the management of labour and the design of jobs.

When we examine economies within an international perspective it becomes clear that the crude determinism of Braverman and Piore and Sabel does not hold up. Economies are structured by different legislation and institutions of economic regulation and exist within a unique historically developed culture. The organisation, design and control of internal labour markets are situated within a broader framework of policies and rules as defined by the respective national governments which places an element of constraint on the shape and outcome of management policy and change. We have already noted how the diffusion of Taylorism was tempered by the culture and politics of individual economies. In France, despite the enthusiasm for Taylorism amongst the technical elites, the predominance of small owner-managed firms together with the resistance of the working class constrained the take-up of rationalisation and deskilling. The autocratic control of the 'patronet' in French firms proved a considerable obstacle to the introduction of Taylorism as this would have meant 'the entry into these enterprises of an intermediate stratum of technical specialists whose appeal to knowledge as a basis of authority would have undermined owners' "divine rights" to rule' (Lane, 1989: 146).

Germany

Germany was less penetrated by Taylorism than either France or the UK because of the persistence of a craft orientation to work bolstered by managerial support for responsible autonomy. This was based on the high skill level of the manual working class in Germany (Maurice *et al.*, 1986) who were able to exercise a range of skills in the production process based on polyvalency. The strong representational and co-determination rights of works councils in Germany has provided a further obstacle to management unilateralism and the imposition of Taylorism. The result in Germany has been the persistence of a strong and competitive high-skilled and craft production sector. The machine tool industry and the car production sector has continually sought to compete on the basis of high skill, high technology and high wages, rather than direct cost economies based on deskilling and low-cost products. Production sectors based on a low skill and low value-added labour input have conversely been exported from Germany. This has stimulated within German academic studies a concern with the new international division of labour based on the retention of high-skilled sectors in the developed industrial world and the export of older, less technologically and skills advanced sectors to the Third World (Fröbel, Heinrich and Kreye, 1980).

The strong legislative and institutional regulation of German enterprise has resulted in constraints on what management can do while simultaneously encouraging the development of competitiveness based on high skill and high wages. In effect the route towards competition based on low skill and low-wage cost economies has been cut off for German employers based on the 1949 Works Constitution Act requiring the appointment of a works council. These councils have co-determination rights on social matters defined as payment methods, work schedules, rest periods and holiday arrangements. In addition they have information and consultation rights on personnel planning and changes in the work process. This juridified and regulated system of industrial relations has sought to steer the development of the German economy towards an acceptable social democratic consensus based on high-wage rewarding jobs, profitability and competitiveness. German governments have by and large continually maintained and actively intervened and supported organisational democracy and social democratic planning. The approach of the government was reaffirmed amidst the restructuring crisis of Western economies in 1981 when the Council of Economic Advisers stated:

> Competitiveness is the ability to develop new speciality products and new technical solutions to an extent that permits rising incomes under conditions of high employment even though competitors *gradually acquire the necessary technical knowledge and organising abilities to manufacture those products as well.* A high wage country cannot afford to fall back on second-hand innovation.
>
> (Emphasis added, quoted in Jacobi *et al.*, 1992; see also Kern and Schumann, 1987: 162–165)

In addition, as many commentators have stressed, the training system in Germany provides a further stimulus to seek competition through high-skill, high-wage production. The commitment of the government to vocational and academic training and education has been witnessed in major pieces of legislation, in particular the Vocational Education Act of 1969 and the Federal Training Promotion Acts of 1969 and 1976. The common efforts of government, employers and unions has guaranteed a firm financial commitment to education and training. German apprenticeships have been underwritten by the state to guarantee their continuation as industrial training is seen as far too important to be left to individual and isolated firms. In Britain by contrast training and investment has been traditionally given a low priority (see Chapter 9), reflected in a number of recent reports emphasising the increasing lack of skills in the UK (IMS, 1984; IT Skills Shortage Committee, 1985) hampering the development of industry and more recently preventing the economy from moving out of recession. In contrast to Germany the UK government, especially since 1979, has been ideologically committed to the role of the market. In this view individual companies do not need state interference in the provision of training, rather it should be left to the market to decide which skills and training need to be provided.

In contrast to Germany, individual employees in Britain have tended to receive restricted and firm-specific training which not only makes them extremely vulnerable to organisational restructuring and unemployment but encourages firms to seek short-term and quick-fix solutions to competitiveness. The fundamental weakness of a market approach to training is that by and large skills and skill development are public goods in the jargon of the economist. This means in effect that we get a free-rider problem: instead of companies seeking to invest their own resources in training they seek to poach skilled labour that has been trained elsewhere. The common complaint that audio-visual and production technicians obtain their training at the BBC only to go and 'earn their money' at an ITV company reflects this free-rider problem. Therefore there is an inbuilt tendency in situations where labour is free to go and search for work where it pleases that companies will be reluctant to invest in training and future resources only to see labour depart at a later date. As Streeck has pointed out,

> Unlike in Japanese firms, training investment in Western firms can never be safely internalised as the skills imparted on a worker cannot be appropriated by the employer: to the contrary they become the property of the worker which he may take with him when he leaves. (Streeck, 1989: 93)

Streeck goes on to highlight some of the major problems with leaving skills and training to the free market. He argues that individuals need to acquire their work skills at a young age but it is at this age that young individuals are least likely to want or to see the benefit of deferring financial reward until the future. Furthermore, the inherent uncertainty attached to personal investment is based on the information and understanding one has of what skills will be required and valued in the future. Myopia and 'information constraints' as economic concepts have a long history in explaining 'market failures' and used in this way they highlight the extent to which they can tend to retard the development of high skill based economies. The fundamental uncertainty both within firms and individuals of recovering their costs in training tends to suggest that where such market failures exist there is a role for the government to intervene and support the market where the market left to its own mechanics is likely to fail.

CONCLUSIONS

This chapter has attempted to explore the techniques of job design in terms of a theoretical analysis which remains sensitive to the 'contextual exchanges' between internal organisational forces, macro-external legislative and labour market structures, and the process of job design. Job design does not take place as some neat, well-defined managerial activity in an autonomous vacuum within discrete and coherent functional organisations. We have seen that the application and practice of job design do not respond mechanically to society-wide economic pressures either demanding deskilling or reskilling as some prerequisite of economic success. A degree of choice clearly exists within job design, but one restricted by rational and what we might call irrational forces. In addition, the economics of market competition and the imperatives of the capitalist 'system', tempered within a framework of national rules, regulations and culture, sets limits and constraints on management strategy, process and outcome.

In this chapter we have made a tentative effort to introduce ideas which suggest that contemporary technological advances and their application in increasingly 'hollowed out' and 'virtual' evanescent organisations may even begin to challenge and perhaps erode conventional categories and ontological boundaries in employment relations. If organisations are going to seek the high-skilled HRM route there must be recognition of this and we must be attentive to what has been called 'market failures'. As Hendry (1990) suggests in his account of the internal organisational construction of new technology and careers, 'management cannot construct, "de novo", the conditions under which labour is to function' (p. 37). In addition it needs to be emphasised that managements cannot construct the external conditions 'de novo' for the successful introduction and application of HRM and HRM-inspired job design.

The UK experience

The UK government's persistent reluctance to commit itself to the European Union, especially with respect to the UK's protocol on social policy in the Maastricht Treaty on political union, will likely result in a labour market which increasingly tends towards a low-wage, low-skill form of 'development'. In opting out of the social policy dimension to Europe Britain is now excluded from provisions arising under articles 117, 118, 118a, 118b, 118c, 119 and 122. These conditions under the 1989 Social Charter seek to pursue the regulation and the promotion of strong employee representation in the Union's overall aim of promoting 'employment, improved living and working conditions, proper social protection, dialogue between management and labour, the development of human resources with a view to lasting high employment and the combatting of exclusion'. Furthermore, article 118 seeks the 'protection of workers where their employment contract is terminated' and 'representation and collective defence of the interests of workers and employers, including co-determination'.

Based more on the social democratic structures of the German model of industrial relations, the European Union's initiatives in the labour market and the social field have raised considerable political and business opposition within the UK. Many employers view EC legislation and directives on employment to be onerous, overly regulative and unworkable. However, with the expressed fear of social dumping, that is the transfer of economic organisation and operations to areas within the Union which offer low costs through low social and employee welfare provision, it might seem odd that the UK may attract such activity at a time when HRM as a developmental and 'progressive' dynamic within managerial circles is apparently so dominant. Hence, job design consistent with HRM, which seeks a reconciliation of the interests of employers and employees, may well be better served under a regulative framework which corrects for 'market failures' in training and skills provision.

SUMMARY

● This chapter started with an exploration of recent ideas and applications in computer and information technology which exercise a profound challenge to both our understanding and the shape and content of people's jobs.

● We explored the conceptual relation between 'sign' and 'de-sign' through an etymological analysis to enrich our understanding of the process and dynamics of job design. It was argued that this complexity is often obscured by the conceptual poverty of orthodox job design analysis. Perhaps we can speculate that this is in the interests of selling cheap, quick-fix solutions to managerial and organisation problems.

● The relation between HRM and job design was discussed drawing a critique of analysis which sees HRM as a novel and progressive approach by analysing the assumptions and conceptions which shape commentators' historical and interpretative analysis (this links with Chapter 2 in this volume).

● 'Fordist' and 'Taylorist' approaches to work design were critically examined in the light of Braverman and the nascent labour process debate. We read that Braverman argues that these types of job design and work structure deskilled employees through an often violent appropriation of craft-based knowledge, leaving little control in the hands of the workers. Following the adoption of Taylorism most control rested in the ranks of specialist, élite managerial planners and organisers whose expertise in scientific management sought to design work for optimum productive efficiency. Detailed studies by later critics such as Friedman, Littler and Salaman revealed that these extreme forms of control were not as widespread in Europe and Japan as Braverman had suggested in his work on American organisations.

● In contrast, the Human Relations school stresses the necessity of recognising the intrinsic value of the workforce and criticises the dehumanising effects of Taylorist approaches to work design. The work of Blauner, Mayo, Schein, the Tavistock Institute and the Hawthorne Studies revealed the complicated relationship which humans have with work, particularly in being able to exercise some degree of control over the work process within socially constituted work groups. Such analyses led to the emergence of job enrichment, job rotation, job enlargement, teamworking and semi-autonomous groups in the 1960s and 1970s, particularly exemplified in Volvo's Kalmar plant in Sweden. According to some critics, however, the claims made that these techniques make work more 'interesting' have been much exaggerated.

● Other investigators, most notably Burawoy, have observed the ability of workers involved in 'boring' job operations to exercise limited influence over the work process through initiating games which exercise a subtle degree of control via an existential dynamic whereby individuals subsequently become trapped by identity. These games involve the active participation of both management and workers and help to disperse conflict in the organisation.

● A critical view was also undertaken of various post-Fordist forms of work design, particularly flexible specialisation in relation to the views of Walton and Atkinson. These views have been challenged, by Pollert and others, as being exaggerated, particularly relating to the existence of strategically organised core and periphery workers.

● Recent approaches to job design such as business process re-engineering and teamworking were theoretically and empirically examined. We questioned the extent of novelty while recognising the importance of aesthetic symbolic and discursive resources in constituting new practices and conceptions of work.

● Finally, job design was viewed in a European context, where it was noted that because of a range of regulatory, institutional and cultural factors, which shape and inform management practice, Taylorist work design had much less impact than elsewhere. The development of a skilled workforce ultimately allows workers to exercise a degree of control over the work process, not only through their expertise, but also via co-determination mechanisms such as works councils which are supported by a strong legislative structure. This is in marked contrast to Britain where forms of labour market deregulation operate, leaving the development of workplace skills to the whims of the free market, underscored by the rejection of EC legislation, particularly the Social Charter.

ACTIVITY

Imagine that your group represents the large personnel department of a car manufacturing company. The research department has recently passed on the research and results of the 'Affluent Workers' study by John Goldthorpe and his colleagues. Senior management within the company feel that this research largely debunks the notion and validity of job redesign which, as a department, you have been actively sponsoring as part of your overall philosophy that good job design is fundamental to the success of the company. For many years you have been encouraging senior management to consider the possibilities of restructuring jobs as a means of reducing turnover, increasing commitment and morale, and generally improving the climate of employee relations.

EXERCISE

Divide the group into three specialist working parties. Group A is required to prepare and present a short summary of the research and results of the Affluent Workers study, paying particular attention to its strengths and merits as a piece of academic research with important practical implications for companies such as yours. Group B is to critically evaluate the Goldthorpe study drawing attention to its defects, oversights and methodological weaknesses. Group C is requested to adjudicate between Group A and B by presenting a short summary of the strengths and weaknesses of the Affluent Workers study, concluding by drawing together what appears to be the long-term impact of this study for the approach taken to job design by your department.

QUESTIONS

1 Outline and define what is meant by a structuralist approach to job design and theory in contrast to an agency approach.

2 In what ways did Taylorism seek to 'degrade' workers?

3 In what ways may employees resist and/or consent to the deskilled nature of many of the jobs designed by Taylor and his methods of scientific management?

4 Do you think 'Taylorism' is justified in its claim to be a science? What is scientific about scientific management?

5 How might an 'essentialist' view of human nature lead one to the conclusion that job redesign is necessary?

6 What is meant by alienation and how does it differ from *anomie*?

7 Define what is meant by determinism in respect to job design. In what ways could it be suggested that theories of the post-Fordist worker are deterministic?

8 How may developments in the European Union actually promote UK companies to seek the redesign of their jobs?

9 How far are the claimed moves away from Fordism to do with technology and product markets in comparison to enlightened managerialism?

EXERCISES

1 Consider any recent employment you may have had and list all the positive sides of the job which you particularly enjoyed and found rewarding. Then, list all the negative aspects of the job and the reasons for which you find them tedious, repetitive or monotonous.

2 What would you like in an ideal job in the situation you have outlined above? Consider how realistic your ambitions for this job may be. For example, it may well be that what seems rational and ideal to you may seem impossible operationally for production and line managers.

3 Then prepare a report for personnel outlining the assumed benefits of job redesign and the importance both for employees and the organisation of restructuring jobs and responsibilities more in tune with the philosophy of human resource management.

4 Consider the validity of the reasons which are suggested for the assertion that workers 'learn to enjoy' monotony in their jobs.

5 Outline the future economic structure of the UK and Germany and what this might mean for job design.

6 As a member of a head office personnel department in a large British bank you have been asked to consider the recent work of David Collinson and David Knights. Prepare a brief report with the help of three of your colleagues outlining the theoretical approach adopted by Collinson and Knights, and the results they obtained. Present this report with the help of visual aids so that as a group your personnel department can quickly digest the information

so that they can consider and reflect on the impact the work of Collinson and Knights is likely to have in your approach to job design. The rest of the personnel department is largely suspicious of the approach taken in the work of Collinson and Knights and have come prepared to give the group a hard time in what is hoped will be a lively and stimulating debate.

7 Imagine that your group represents a highly successful firm of management consultants. Divide the group into three working parties. Group A has recently been sent on a fact-finding mission to Germany where they have discovered that the approach taken to job design in medium-size engineering firms is far more progressive and advanced than typically found in similar-size UK firms. On your return you are asked to present a summary of your findings. Critically reflect on the reasons why management appears to be more proactive in job design initiatives and more successful in the outcomes they achieve.

Group B has been sent on a similar tour of French banks where, amongst other things, it has been discovered that individual employees do not appear to spend the vast majority of their time specialised in the dedication to one task. Present your findings to the group outlining the distinctiveness of French job design programmes.

Group C has been requested to reflect on the lessons for British management that the work of groups A and B seem to suggest. In your terms of reference you have been asked to delineate between what British management can do within British organisations and the limitations they face within the context of a different political and economic structure. Consider the role that governments play in facilitating job design initiatives.

REFERENCES AND FURTHER READING

Those texts marked with an asterisk are particularly recommended for further reading.

Aglietta, M. (1976) *A Theory of Capitalist Regulation: The US Experience*. London: Verso (English trans. 1979).

Armstrong, M. (1992) *Human Resource Management: Strategy and Action*. London: Kogan Page.

Armstrong, P. and Tomes, A. (1996) 'Art and accountability: languages of design and managerial control'. Paper presented to the 14th Annual International Labour Process Conference, Aston, Birmingham.

Atkinson, J. and Meager, N. (1986) 'Is flexibility just a flash in the pan?', *Personnel Management*, September.

Austrin, T. (1991) 'Flexibility, surveillence and hype in New Zealand financial retailing', *Work, Employment and Society*, Vol. 5, No. 2, pp. 201–221.

Badham, R. and Mathews, J. (1989) 'The new production systems debate', *Labour and Industry*, Vol. 2, No. 2, pp. 194–246.

Batstone, E. (1984) *Working Order*. Oxford: Blackwell.

Baudrillard, J. (1983) *Simulations*. New York: Semiotext.

Baudrillard, J. (1990) *Fatal Strategies*. New York: Semiotext/Pluto.

Bauman, Z. (1995) *Life in Fragments*. Oxford: Blackwell.

Blauner, R. (1964) *Alienation and Freedom*. Chicago: University of Chicago Press.

Boyer, R. (ed.) (1988) *The Search for Labour Market Flexibility: The European Economies in Transition*. Oxford: Clarendon Press.

*Braverman, H. (1974) *Labour and Monopoly Capital*. New York: Monthly Review Press.

Brennan, T. (1993) *History after Lacan*. New York and London: Routledge.

*Buchanan, D. (1989) 'Principles and practice in work design', in Sisson, K. (ed.) *Personnel Management in Britain*. Oxford: Blackwell.

Buchanan, D. (1992) 'High performance: new boundaries of acceptability in worker control', in Salaman, G. (ed.) *Human Resource Strategies*. London: Sage.

Buchanan, D. (1994) 'Principles and practices in work design', in Sisson, K. (ed.) *Personnel Management: A Comprehensive Guide to Theory and Practice in Britain*. Oxford: Blackwell.

Burawoy, M. (1979) *Manufacturing Consent*. Chicago: University of Chicago Press.

Burawoy, M. (1985) *The Politics of Production*. London: Verso.

Burrell, G. (1992) 'The organisation of pleasure', in Alveson, M. and Willmott, H. (eds) *Critical Management Studies*. London: Sage.

Camus, A. (1961) *The Outsider*. London: Penguin.

Casey, C. (1995) *Work, Self and Society: After Industrialism*. London: Routledge.

Clawson, D. (1980) *Bureaucracy and the Labour Process: The Transformation of US Industry, 1860–1920*. New York and London: Monthly Review Press.

Collinson, D. (1992) *Managing the Shopfloor: Subjectivity, Masculinity and Workplace Culture*. Berlin: Walter de Gruyter.

Collinson, D. and Knights, D. (1986) 'Men only: theories and practices of job segregation in insurance', in Knights, D. and Willmott, H. (eds) *Gender and the Labour Process*. Aldershot: Gower.

Cohen, S. and Taylor, L. (1992) *Escape Attempts: The Theory and Practice of Resistance to Everyday Life*. London: Routledge.

Cooper, R. and Law, J. (1995) 'Organization: distal and proximal views', *Research in the Sociology of Organizations*, Vol. 13, pp. 237–274.

Corbett, M. (1995) 'Celluloid projections: images of technology and organizational futures in contemporary science fiction film', *Organization*, Vol. 2, No. 3/4.

Cross, M. (1990) *Changing Job Structures: Techniques for the Design of New Jobs and Organisations*. Oxford: Heinemann Newnes.

Davenport, T.H. and Short, J.E. (1990) 'The new industrial engineering: information technology and business process redesign', *Sloan Management Review*, Summer, pp. 11–27.

Deming, W. (1986) *Out of Crisis*. Cambridge: Cambridge University Press.

Dostoyevsky, F. (1864) *Notes from the Underground*. New York: 1992 Dover Thrift Edition.

Du Gay, P. and Salaman, G. (1994) 'The conduct of management and the management of conduct: contemporary managerial disclosure and the constitution of the "competent" manager', *Making up Managers Working Papers Series*, No. 1, The Open University.

Durkheim, E. (1984) *The Division of Labour in Society*. London: Macmillan.

Elger, T. (1990) 'Technical innovation and work reorganisation in British manufacturing in the 1980s: continuity, intensification or transformation?', *Work, Employment and Society*, Special Issue, pp. 67–101.

Farmbrough, H. (1996) 'Man's journey desk into space', *Voyager*, March/April, pp. 30–36.

Featherstone, M. (ed.) (1988) *Postmodernism*. London: Sage.

Featherstone, M. (1991) *Consumer Culture and Postmodernism*. London: Sage.

Fineman, S. (ed.) (1993) *Emotion in Organizations*. London: Sage.

Fox, A. (1974) *Beyond Contract*. London: Faber.

Fröbel, F., Heinrichs, J. and Kreye, O. *et al.* (1980) *The New International Division of Labour*. Cambridge: Cambridge University Press.

Friedman, A. (1977) *Industry and Labour*. London: Macmillan.

Friedman, A. (1990) 'Managerial strategies, activities, techniques and technology: towards a complex theory of the labour process', in Knights, D. and Willmott, H. (eds) *Labour Process Theory*. London: Macmillan.

Fromm, E. (1991) *The Fear of Freedom*. London: Routledge & Kegan Paul.

Gabriel, Y. (1995) 'The unmanaged organization: stories, fantasies and subjectivity', *Organization Studies*, 16/3, pp. 477–501.

Gibson, W. (1984) *Neuromancer*. London: Victor Gollancz.

Giddens, A. (1991) *Modernity and Self Identity*. Cambridge: Polity Press.

Gilbert, N., Burrows, R. and Pollert, A. (1992) *Fordism and Flexibility: Divisions and Change*. London: Macmillan.

Goldthorpe, J.H., Lockwood, D., Bechhofer, F. and Platt, J. (1968) *The Affluent Worker: Industrial Attitudes and Behaviour*. Cambridge: Cambridge University Press.

Grint, K. (1995) *Management: A Sociological Introduction*. Cambridge: Polity Press.

Habermas, J. (1971) *Towards a Rational Society*. London: Heinemann.

Hackman, J.R. and Lawler, E.E. (1971) 'Employee reactions to job characteristics', *Journal of Applied Psychology*, Vol. 55, pp. 259–286.

Hackman, J.R. and Oldhan, G.R. (1976) 'Motivation through the design of work: test of a theory', *Organisational Behaviour and Human Performance*, Vol. 16, pp. 250–279.

Hammer, M. (1990) 'Reengineering work: don't automate, obliterate', *Harvard Business Review*, July–August, pp. 104–112.

Hammer, M. and Champy, J. (1993) *Reengineering the Corporation: A Manifesto for Business Revolution*. London: Nicholas Brealey.

Haraway, D. (1985) 'A manifesto for cyborgs: science, technology and socialist feminism in the 1980s', *Socialist Review*, No. 80, pp. 65–107.

Heidegger, M. (1977) *The Question Concerning Technology and Other Essays*. New York: Harper & Row.

Hendry, C. (1990) 'New technology, new careers: the impact of company employment policy', *New Technology, Work and Employment*, Vol. 5, No. 1, Spring.

Hirschorn, L. (1984) *Beyond Mechanisation*. Cambridge, Mass.: MIT Press.

Hochschild, A. (1983) *The Managed Heart: Commercialization of Human Feeling*. Berkeley, California: University of California Press.

Hopfl, H. and Linstead, S. (1993) 'Passion and performance: suffering and the carrying of organizational roles', in Fineman, S. (ed.) *Emotion Organizations*. London: Sage.

Hyman, R. (1987) 'Strategy of structure: capital, labour and control', *Work, Employment and Society*, Vol. 1, No. 1, pp. 25–55.

Iles, P. and Salaman, G. (1995) 'Recruitment, selection and assessment', in Storey, J. (ed.) *Human Resource Management: A Critical Text*. London: Routledge.

Industrial Relations Services (1995) 'Customer service drive at BT', *Employment Trends*, 579.

Industrial Relations Services (1995) 'Putting the customer first: organisational change at WH Smith', *Employment Trends*, 596.

Information Technology Skills Shortage Committee (1985) *Second Report: Changing Technology, Changing Skills*. London: Department of Trade and Industry.

Institute of Manpower Studies (1984) 'Competence and Competition – Training and Education in the FRG', *Report for NEDO and the MSC*. London: IMS.

Jackall, R. (1988) *Moral Mazes: The World of Corporate Managers*. New York: Oxford University Press.

Jacobi, O., Keller, B. and Müller-Jentsch, W. (1992) 'Germany: co-determining the future', in Ferner, A. and Hyman, R. (eds) *Industrial Relations in the New Europe*. Oxford: Blackwell.

James, G. (1992) 'Quality of working life and total quality management', *International Journal of Manpower*, Vol. 13, No. 1, pp. 41–58.

Kakar, S. (1970) *Frederick Taylor: A Study in Personality and Innovation*. Cambridge, Mass.: MIT Press.

Kallinikos, J. (1996) 'Mapping the intellectual terrain of management education', in French, R. and Grey, C. (eds) *Rethinking Management Education*. London: Sage.

Kelly, J. (1985) 'Management's redesign of work: labour process, labour markets and products markets', in Knights, D. *et al.* (eds) *Job Redesign: Critical Perspectives on the Labour Process*. Aldershot: Gower.

Kern, H. and Schumann, M. (1987) 'Limits of the division of labour: new production and employment concepts in West German industry', *Economic and Industrial Democracy*, No. 8, pp. 51–71.

Knights, D. (1990) 'Subjectivity, power and the labour process', in Knights, D. and Willmott, H. (eds) *Labour Process Theory*. London: Macmillan.

*Knights, D., Willmott, H. and Collinson, D. (eds) (1985) *Job Redesign: Critical Perspectives on the Labour Process*. Aldershot: Gower.

Knights, D. and Willmott, H. (1989) 'Power and subjectivity at work: from degradation to subjugation in social relations', *Sociology*, Vol. 23, No. 4.

Knights, D. and Willmott, H. (eds) (1990) *Labour Process Theory*. London: Macmillan.

Kondo, D. (1991) *Crafting Selves: Power, Gender, and Discourses of Identity in a Japanese Workplace*. London: University of Chicago Press.

Lane, C. (1989) *Management and Labour in Europe*. Aldershot: Edward Elgar.

Lash, S. and Urry, J. (1994) *Economics of Signs and Space*. London: Sage.

Latour, B. (1987) *Science in Action*. Milton Keynes: Open University Press.

Law, J. (ed.) (1991) *A Sociology of Monsters? Essays on Power, Technology and Domination*, Sociological Review Monograph 38. London: Routledge.

Legge, K. (1995) *Human Resource Management: Rhetorics and Realities*. Basingstoke: Macmillan.

Lipietz, A. (1987) *Mirages and Miracles: The Crisis of Global Fordism*. London: Verso.

Littler, C. (1982) *The Development of the Labour Process in Capitalist Society*. London: Heinemann.

Littler, C. and Salaman, G. (1984) *Class at Work: The Design, Allocation and Control of Jobs*. London: Batsford.

Littler, C. (1985) 'Taylorism, Fordism and job design', in Knights, D. *et al.* (eds) *Job Redesign: Critical Perspectives on the Labour Process*. Aldershot: Gower.

Lovering, J. (1990) 'A perfunctory sort of post-Fordism: economic restructuring and the labour market segmentation in Britain in the 1980s', *Work, Employment and Society*, May.

Lupton, T. (1963) *On the Shopfloor*. Oxford: Pergamon.

Lynn-Meek, V. (1992) 'Organisational culture', in Salaman, G. *et al.* (eds) *Human Resource Strategies*. London: Sage.

Marcuse, H. (1964) *One-Dimensional Man*. London: Routledge & Kegan Paul.

Marginson, P. (1989) 'Employment flexibility in large companies: change and continuity', *Industrial Relations Journal*, Summer, No. 20.

Maslow, A.H. (1943) 'A theory of human motivation', *Psychological Review*, No. 50, pp. 370–396.

Maslow, A.H. (1954) *Motivation and Human Personality*. New York: Harper & Row.

Maurice, M., Sellier, F. and Silvestre, J-J. (1986) *The Social Foundations of Industrial Power*. London: MIT Press.

Mayo, E. (1949) *The Social Problems of an Industrial Civilisation*. London: Routledge & Kegan Paul.

Mintzberg, H. (1978) 'Patterns in strategy formation', *Management Science*, Vol. 24, No. 9, pp. 934–948.

Murray, R. (1985) 'Benetton Britain', *Marxism Today*, September.

Nichols, T. (ed.) (1980) *Capital and Labour*. Glasgow: Fontana.

O'Doherty, D. (1994) 'Institutional withdrawal? Anxiety and conflict in the emerging banking labour process or "How to get out of it"', *Paper to the 12th Annual International Labour Process Conference*, Aston University.

Peters, T. (1994) *The Tom Peters Seminar: Crazy Times Call for Crazy Organizations*. London: Macmillan.

*Peters, T. and Waterman, R. (1982) *In Search of Excellence*. New York: Harper & Row.

Piore, M. and Sabel, C. (1984) *The Second Industrial Divide: Possibilities for Prosperity*. New York: Basic Books.

Pollert, A. (1988) 'Dismantling flexibility', *Capital and Class*, No. 34, pp. 42–75.

Pollert, A. (ed.) (1991) *Farewell to Flexibility?* Oxford: Blackwell.

Ramsay, H. (1985) 'What is participation for? A critical evaluation of "labour process" analyses of job reform', in Knights, D. *et al.* (eds) *Job Redesign: Critical Perspectives on the Labour Process*. Aldershot: Gower.

Reich, R.B. (1983) 'A structuralist account of political culture', *Administrative Science Quarterly*, No. 28, pp. 414–437.

Roethlisberger, F.G. and Dickson, W.J. (1939) *Management and the Worker*. Cambridge, Mass.: Harvard University Press.

Roy, D. (1952) 'Quota restriction and goldbricking in a machine shop', *American Journal of Sociology*, No. 57.

Roy, D. (1953) 'Work satisfaction and the reward in quota achievement', *American Sociological Review*, No. 18.

Schein, E.L. (1965) *Organisational Psychology*. Englewood Cliffs, NJ: Prentice Hall.

Schein, E.H. (1985) *Organisational Culture and Leadership*. San Francisco: Jossey-Bass.

Shaiken, H., Herzenberg, S. and Kahn, S. (1986) 'The work process under flexible production', *Industrial Relations*, Vol. 25.

Smith, C. (1989) 'Flexible specialisation, automation and mass production', *Work, Employment and Society*, Vol. 3, No. 2, pp. 203–220.

Storey, J. (1983) *Managerial Prerogative and the Question of Control*. London: Routledge & Kegan Paul.

Storey, J. (1992) *Developments in the Management of Human Resources*. Oxford: Blackwell.

Streeck, W. (1989) 'Skills and the limits of neo-liberalism: the enterprise of the future as a place of learning', *Work, Employment and Society*, March.

Thompson, P. (1989) *The Nature of Work*. London: Macmillan.

*Trist, E.L. and Bamforth, K.W. (1951) 'Some social and psychological consequences of the Longwall method of coal-getting', *Human Relations*, Vol. 4, No. 1, pp. 3–38.

Trist, E.L., Higgin, G.W., Murray, H. and Pollock, A.B. (1963) *Organisational Choice*. London: Tavistock.

Walton, R.E. (1985) 'From control to commitment in the workplace', *Harvard Business Review*, No. 63, March/April, pp. 76–84.

Watson, T. (1987) *Sociology, Work and Industry*. London: Routledge & Kegan Paul.

Watson, T. (1994) *In Search of Management: Culture, Chaos and Control in Managerial Work*. London: Routledge.

Weber, M. (1964) *The Theory of Social and Economic Organisation*. New York: Free Press.

Willmott, H. (1990) 'Subjectivity and the dialectics of praxis: opening up the core of labour process analysis', in Knights, D. and Willmott, H. (eds) *Labour Process Theory*. London: Macmillan.

Willmott, H. (1993) 'Strength is ignorance; slavery is freedom: managing culture in modern organisations', *Journal of Management Studies*, Vol. 30, No. 5, pp. 515–552.

Willmott, H. (1995) 'The odd couple? Reengineering business process, managing human resources'. Mimeo, Manchester School of Management, UMIST.

Wood, S. (ed.) (1982) *The Degradation of Work: Skill, Deskilling and the Labour Process*. London: Hutchinson.

Wood, S. and Kelly J. (1982) 'Taylorism, responsible autonomy and management strategy', in Wood, S. (ed.) *The Degradation of Work: Skill, Deskilling and the Labour Process*. London: Hutchinson.

Woolgar, S. (1991) 'Configuring the user: the case of usability trials', in Law, J. (ed.) *A Sociology of Monsters: Essays on Power, Technology and Domination*. London: Routledge.

RECRUITMENT AND SELECTION

Mary Wright and Julie Storey

OBJECTIVES

To examine recruitment and selection from an HRM perspective.

●

To examine the external and internal factors affecting the recruitment and selection process.

●

To consider the effectiveness of recruitment and selection practices.

●

To consider recruitment and selection from an international perspective.

●

To highlight contemporary issues and controversies in the field of recruitment and selection.

●

INTRODUCTION

Finding the right person for the job has always been important and 'the decision to appoint an individual is one of the most crucial an employer will ever take' (IRS, 1991a). This is particularly true in the light of the HRM notion of 'people as competitive advantage'; indeed, Beaumont (1993) identifies three themes in the HRM literature which 'appear to have enhanced the potential importance of the selection decision in individual organisations in the current operating environment' (p. 56). First, demographic trends and changes in the labour market have led to a 'less homogenous workforce' which has placed increasing pressure on the notion of fairness in selection. Second, the desire for a multi-skilled, flexible workforce and an increased emphasis on teamworking has meant that selection decisions are more concerned with behaviour and attitudes than with matching individuals to immediate job requirements. And third, the link between corporate strategy and HRM has led to the notion of strategic selection, i.e. a system that links selection to the overall organisational strategy and that aims to match the flow of personnel to emerging business strategies.

The importance of recruitment and selection in an HRM environment is further supported by empirical evidence. A study of HRM in 15 organisations (Storey, 1992) found that a number of the case companies had introduced initiatives promising more systematic selection and some were trying to test for 'appropriate' attitudinal and behavioural characteristics. Even the companies that had not introduced new initiatives claimed to be addressing selection with a 'new seriousness' (p. 100). Thus the practice of recruitment and selection is increasingly important from an HRM perspective.

At the same time, the contemporary context in which organisations operate is challenging the accepted assumptions in recruitment and selection:

> These assumptions tend to have emerged from experiences based on organisation structures that have now passed. The future will involve far more complexity, greater ambiguity, more rapid change and a challenge to the methods that made sense to those managers who constructed the old organisations. This challenge will reduce the meaning and usefulness of traditional methods of recruitment and selection.
>
> (Sparrow and Hiltrop, 1994: 316)

The focus of this chapter is the extent to which HRM and the current climate challenge the traditional approach to recruitment and selection. We begin by clarifying what we mean by recruitment and selection, outline the traditional, systematic approach and introduce key differences associated with HRM. We then describe the context in which recruitment and selection is practised and examine the external and internal factors which might influence the process. From there we explore recruitment and selection from an HRM perspective in more detail, focusing specifically on four critical decisions:

- What/who do we want?
- Where do we find them?
- How do we attract them?
- How do we identify them?

We then revisit these critical decisions from an international perspective with particular emphasis on multinational corporations. In the final section we highlight particular issues relevant to recruitment and selection, including strategic issues, in particular the need for the integration of recruitment and selection initiatives with corporate objectives and with other HR initiatives; the impact of business initiatives, e.g. TQM and BPR, on recruitment and selection practices; and ethical issues surrounding recruitment and selection. The chapter concludes with a summary and a number of self-test exercises.

Definitions

The recruitment and selection process is concerned with identifying, attracting and choosing suitable people to meet an organisation's human resource requirements. They are integrated activities and 'where recruitment stops and selection begins is a moot point' (Anderson, 1994). Nevertheless, it is useful to try to differentiate between the two areas; Whitehill (1991) describes the recruitment process as a positive one, 'building a roster of potentially qualified applicants', as opposed to the 'negative' process of selection. So a useful definition of recruitment is 'searching for and obtaining potential job candidates in sufficient numbers and quality so that the organisation can select the most appropriate people to fill its job needs' (Dowling and Schuler, 1990); whereas selection is more concerned with 'predicting which candidates will make the most appropriate contribution to the organisation – now and in the future' (Hackett, 1991).

THE SYSTEMATIC APPROACH TO RECRUITMENT AND SELECTION

Several personnel texts discuss an approach to recruitment and selection based on a systematic analysis of the requirements of an individual job (see, for example, Armstrong, 1991; Torrington and Hall, 1995). The key stages of a systematic approach can be summarised as: defining the vacancy, attracting applicants, assessing candidates and making the final decision. Here we describe the main components of each stage and indicate ways in which recruitment and selection activities may differ depending on whether an organisation adopts an HRM or a more traditional approach.

Defining the vacancy

Authorisation

Securing authorisation ensures that the need to start the recruitment process is agreed by management as being compatible with the organisational/departmental objectives, i.e. necessary, timely and cost-effective. At the same time, it provides an opportunity to consider options other than recruitment and selection, e.g.:

- to debate the potential for restructuring workloads/departments and redeploying existing staff
- to delay or eliminate expenditure on staffing and recruitment budgets.

Both opportunities are not without risk: redeployment of surplus staff may mean the incoming jobholder is not necessarily the 'best person for the job' and result in management resentment against the system; inadequately thought-through restructuring or short-term cost-saving measures may damage the department and organisation in the long term, as opportunities fail to be exploited for lack of suitable human resources.

HRM approaches emphasise the links to wider organisational strategy and effective human resource planning. Debates at this stage may consider long-term human resource development (HRD) objectives and succession planning alongside the immediate requirement to fill an operational post.

Define the job

The traditional approach involves writing a comprehensive *job description* of the job to be filled. This enables the recruiter to know exactly what the purpose, duties and responsibilities of the vacant position will be and its location within the organisation structure. Figure 6.1 gives an example of a job description for the post of personnel assistant at a hypothetical university.

The need for greater flexibility has led a number of organisations to replace the traditional job description with a concise list of 'bullet points' or accountability statements, often limited to one sheet of paper. Greater ambiguity and fluidity of job content are compatible with a shift from the 'careful delineation of written contracts' associated with a personnel and IR environment towards a 'beyond contract' approach associated with HRM (Storey, 1992).

Define the person

The traditional approach involves drawing up a *personnel specification* based on the job description which identifies the personal characteristics required to perform the job adequately. The two examples most commonly referred to are the seven-point plan (Rodger, 1952) and the five-fold grading system (Munro Fraser, 1954). Figures 6.2 and 6.3 illustrate both in relation to the job of the personnel assistant described in Figure 6.1.

It is common to differentiate between requirements which are essential to the job and those which are merely desirable. The personnel specification is a necessary part of the recruitment and selection process; it can form the basis of the recruitment advertisement and help determine the most effective selection methods. The IPD Code on Recruitment states that 'all recruitment must begin with a job specification and/or person specification' (IPD, 1995).

Under the HRM banner there is greater emphasis on securing people with the 'right' behaviour and attitudes rather than focusing on immediate job requirements. This may lead to a reversal of the job first – person later approach, and is discussed in more detail later in the chapter.

FIGURE 6.1

Example of a job description

SOARBRIDGE UNIVERSITY

Job description

Job title: Personnel assistant
Location: City campus
Responsible to: Personnel officer (staffing)
Responsible for: 2 clerical officers

Purpose of post

To assist the Personnel officer (staffing) with the recruitment and selection programme.

Key duties

1. To assume special responsibility for the recruitment and selection of all non-academic staff including:

    1.1 writing of job descriptions and person specifications;

    1.2 writing and placing of appropriate advertisements and monitoring their effectiveness;

    1.3 making arrangements for selection interviews;

    1.4 representing the Personnel Department on selection interview panels;

    1.5 taking up references and despatching offer letters.

2. To be responsible for the collation and maintenance of staffing records and monitoring applications by race, sex and disability. This work will also involve working on the Department's computer.

3. To prepare and issue contracts of employment, open a personal file for each staff member and inform Payroll of all necessary details.

4. To arrange initial induction training for all non-academic staff.

5. To supervise two clerical officers in the staffing section.

6. Special projects and other duties as required.

FIGURE 6.2

Personnel specification for personnel assistant
(following Rodger's seven-point plan)

Feature sought	Essential	Desirable
1. Physical makeup	Able to communicate orally with confidence and sensitivity	None
2. Attainments	At least one year's previous experience of recruitment/general personnel administration	Previous experience of project work Previous experience of supervising staff Knowledge of current employment law, good practice in R & S, EO CPP/IPD qualification
3. Intelligence		Able to pick up organisation's culture/systems quickly
4. Aptitudes		Able to: Carry out job analysis, especially drawing up JD & PS Design of advertisements, induction training Organise programmes and records systems Compile statistical returns Demonstrate computer literacy and with experience of computers in work environment
5. Interests	None	None
6. Disposition	Able to relate well to all categories of employee within the organisation Conscientious, thorough in task completion	Enhances professional image of Personnel Department Can cope with mundane as well as high profile activities
7. Circumstances	None	None

FIGURE 6.3

*Personnel specification for personnel assistant
(following Munro Fraser's five-point grading)*

Aspects of individual to consider	Essential	Desirable
1. Impact on others	Able to communicate orally with confidence and sensitivity, and relate well to all categories of employee within the organisation Conscientious	Enhances professional image of Personnel Department
2. Acquired knowledge or qualifications	At least one year's previous experience of recruitment/general personnel administration	Previous experience of project work Previous experience of supervising staff Knowledge of current employment law, good practice in R & S, EO CPP/IPD qualification Computer literate Experience of computers in work environment
3. Innate abilities	To learn job requirements and perform effectively in short time scale	Potential to pick up organisation's culture/systems quickly Writing job descriptions, person specifications, design of advertisements and induction training programmes, maintain accurate records and produce statistical returns
4. Motivation	Can cope with mundane aspects of job as well as high profile activities	Wishes to develop career in personnel management
5. Adjustment	Achieves and reacts calmly to time pressure deadlines Conscientious and thorough in task completion	

Agree terms and conditions

Decisions on terms and conditions are made at various points in the process. Some of these are often not negotiated (e.g. hours, reward) until the final selection stages. There is a case for deciding the salary band (if not the specific amount) and other elements of the reward package before attracting candidates. This can take time (for example, if the position has to be processed through a job evaluation exercise), but potential candidates may fail to apply without some indication of the reward offered as this often gives an indication of the level and status of the position. An independent survey carried out by Price Waterhouse in 1988 reported that 64% of respondents (typically middle and senior managers) would probably not apply to an advertisement that did not state a salary, although a similar figure would continue to read it if the salary was not attractive, as they regarded the stated figure as negotiable (Golzen, 1988).

The alternative is to wait and see who applies and then negotiate terms and conditions with the favoured candidate. This is a less restrictive approach and may provide a better chance of employing high-calibre people who match the long-term aims of the organisation. On the other hand, the organisation may project a poor image by appearing to be disorganised and unsure of what is on offer. Additionally, the perception that the company is trying to take advantage of a weak labour market and pay 'what they can get away with' may damage its reputation in the long term.

The most appropriate approach is, at least partially, determined by the organisation's reward strategy, including the relative importance of internal pay equity and external competitiveness and the emphasis on individual and collective pay-setting.

Attracting applicants

Recruitment methods

A wide variety of recruitment methods are available and the advantages and disadvantages of each are described in Table 6.1. The most appropriate method for any particular vacancy will be influenced by the resources available, the level of the post and its importance within the organisation, the perceived target group and the organisation's stance on internal versus external recruitment. The human resource management literature emphasises the need to have well-developed internal labour market arrangements for promotion, training and career development, which would suggest that many openings can and should be filled internally (Beaumont, 1993).

Design of advertisements

The most popular formal recruitment method is press advertising. Effective communication from the employer to potential applicants requires thought and skill and many organisations use the services of a recruitment agency for the design of the advertisement and advice on the most effective media. The aim of the advertisement is to attract only suitable applicants and therefore it should discourage those who do not possess the necessary attributes while, at the same time, retaining and encouraging the interest of those with potential to be suitable. Although there is evidence that selection is taken more seriously by organisations practising HRM (Storey, 1992), there is little indication of any fundamental challenge to common forms of recruitment advertising.

Recruitment documentation

The response to applicants should be indicative of the overall image the organisation wishes to project. Some organisations prepare a package of documents which may include the job description, the person specification, information about the organisation, the equal opportunities policy, the rewards package available and possible future prospects. Some

TABLE 6.1
Recruitment methods

Method	Comments	Advantages	Disadvantages
1. Internal existing employees	Internal advertising may be requirement for some organisations under union negotiated agreements.		
1.1 Self-applicants		Inexpensive, quick. Motivational factor.	Can be indirectly discriminatory. No new 'talent' into organisation.
1.2 Supervisor/manager recommendations		Know applicant's strengths/ weaknesses/ behaviour well.	Records of existing/ acquired skills and experiences need constant updating.
1.3 Succession planning		Training and development already in place therefore succession smoother.	Information may be subject to bias.
NB: May well be overlap between categories.			
2. Using existing contacts			
2.1 Unsolicited enquiries	Write-ins, personal enquiries 'on spec'. NB: Should be handled courteously or may affect success of other external methods.	Less expensive. Know applicants are already interested.	Needs system implementation to cope. Need to review 'hold' file after time period (? six months). May be indirectly discriminative.
2.2 Previous applicants	Maintain forms of unsuccessful applicants for given time period and assess against new vacancies as they arise.	Can enhance organisation image if handled well. May speed process considerably.	As 2.1.

TABLE 6.1 contd

	Method	Comments	Advantages	Disadvantages
2.3	Previous employees	Particularly retirees, or others leaving to 'no paid job' (e.g. new mothers, or carers of elderly/sick dependants) in the 'would re-employ' category.	By changing terms of employment (especially by increasing flexibility/ reducing hours). Could re-attract to part-time, flexible or temporary working to meet peak organisational demands. Known work behaviour.	Inbuilt flexibility requirement for employee not always feasible in given situations. Requirements for peaks of job may be outside remit of individual.
2.4	Existing employee contacts	Existing employees encourage family, friends, contacts to apply for vacancies.	Employee may well know others with similar skills, knowledge, attitudes. May have passed on knowledge of culture and job requirements.	May well be indirectly discriminative if not combined with other methods. May be 'weaker' employees who recommend, whose attitudes etc. organisation 'does not wish to have reinforced through peer recruitment'

3. External contacts

	Method	Comments	Advantages	Disadvantages
3.1	Union referrals	Register kept by union of members seeking employment. Usual in some sectors (e.g. printing) where 'closed-shop' and/or custom and practice arrangements traditional.	Confidence in skills. Cost.	Indirectly discriminative. Overlooks those in work.
3.2	Professional referrals	Registers as above, particularly for professions, e.g. lawyers, doctors, accountants, engineers, linguists.	As 3.1.	As 3.1.

TABLE 6.1 contd

Method	Comments	Advantages	Disadvantages
3.3 Jobcentres	Central government provision via Department of Employment. Network covering most towns/cities acting as agents for potential employers/employees. Particularly concerned with manual and junior positions in administration, clerical and retail areas.	Variety of free services, which can be provided at local or national level. Speed. Perceived as providing socially responsible service within a secure, non-profit making framework. Extremely valuable if effort made to cultivate Jobcentre contact.	Unemployed, rather than employed register, reinforcing the old labour exchange image. As with all agencies, results reflect quality of job description and person specification supplied.
3.4 Outplacement consultants	Providing practical help to redundant employees, enforced early retirees, etc. Registers, Job Shops and retraining.	Actively seeking to place and may provide training required.	Available when recruitment needs reduce and vice versa, reflecting economic situation.
3.5 Private selection consultants – local	Deal mainly with clerical typing, junior admin, shop staff, etc. Recruit and select for positions.	Reduces administration for employer. 'Normal' method in many cities.	Employers pay for recruits. No guarantee against recruit leaving quickly. Some poor practice has led to employer distrust on occasions.
3.6 Management selection	Usually recruitment plus initial stages of selection of managerial, professional and specialist staff.	Specialist knowledge, objectivity, selection skills (especially when unusual recruitment need for organisation).	Payment by employer. May lack cultural awareness of organisation. Internal applicant exclusion.
3.7 Search consultants – 'head-hunters'	Informal network of contacts keeping track of those likely to be in constant demand, especially senior management. Promising candidates sought out and approached directly.	Possibility of joining can be discussed without commitment. Concentrates on those in employment.	Potential candidates outside head-hunter's network excluded. Recruit may be head-hunted again, by same consultant! Cost (because labour intensive).

TABLE 6.1 contd

Method	Comments	Advantages	Disadvantages
3.8 Schools and the Careers Service	Guidance and some testing of young people under 18. In-depth knowledge of potential 'applicants'.	Useful source of raw recruits to be developed by the organisation. Can assist in image enhancement. Cost.	Some 'guidance' of higher quality than other methods. Possibility of indirect discrimination if recruitment concentrated on one or two institutions.
3.9 Colleges	Recruitment of college leavers after conclusion of variety of courses. Tendency to recruit in local colleges in catchment area.	Work experience placements offer opportunity to preview. Increased employer impact on training provided, which can be very work specific.	Tends to be once-yearly process. Recruits lack experience. Possible indirect discrimination.
3.10 Universities	Traditional 'milk round' by large national/ international employers. *Ad hoc* enquiries by leavers. Frequently appointment boards provide full-time careers advisory service.	Can build strong relationship with those offering specialisms, prestige, etc. Sandwich and other work placements offer opportunity to preview potential.	Travel/accommodation costs can be high. Takes recruiters away from organisation for long periods.
3.11 Resettlement services	Armed Forces personnel at end of contracts, provided with practical help on obtaining work in civilian life.	High quality of training in a variety of trades, including management.	Possible (preconceived?) cultural differences between civilian/service life.
3.12 Government training schemes e.g. YT, Apex	Central government funded initiatives targeted at specific skills shortages and/or disadvantaged groups.	Many skills provided at government cost, can be integrated with on-the-job experience. Opportunity to preview before offering permanent employment. Financial incentives.	Perception of 'cheap labour' can reduce organisational image unless well managed. Administration heavy. Training commitment required.

TABLE 6.1 contd

Method	Comments	Advantages	Disadvantages
3.13 Temporary agencies	Provision of short or longer term cover (an alternative to recruitment of permanent employees).	Provide cover to cope with the unexpected absence (e.g. sickness), peaks in workloads, one-off or temporary requirement for skills (installation of new specialist machinery) or transitional developments in work organisation.	Time scale often makes integration into organisational culture difficult. Quality can vary. Cost.
4. Advertising/media	An overlap between advertising and previous methods discussed frequently exists. Recruitment agencies can provide external expertise.		Essential to monitor cost effectiveness.
4.1 Press	Local and national papers, trade and professional journals.		Only reach those using that media. Expensive, especially TV, national press. Must be targeted to identified groups.
4.2 TV	Local and national channels, Oracle, Prestel.	Can provide non-recruitment advantages through increased customer awareness. Sound and sight used.	
4.3 Radio	Local, occasional national broadcasts.	Cheaper than TV.	
4.4 Cinema		May be useful for 16–25 year old groups where several recruits needed; targets likely to have some prior knowledge of organisation.	

TABLE 6.1 contd

Method	Comments	Advantages	Disadvantages
4.5 Posters		Cost.	More difficult to target readers.
4.6 Careers exhibitions		Target groups likely to be present in large numbers.	Cost of organising. Dependency on others and their organisational skills if not.
4.7 Conferences		Target groups likely to be present in large numbers.	Cost of organising if self-managed. Dependency on others and their organisational skills if not.
4.8 Cassettes, videos, brochures		Useful for large-scale recruitment.	Cost. Longer time scale because of preparation.
4.9 Open days	Allowing potential recruits (and sometimes their families and friends) access to site, working methods, facilities, products.	Opportunity for 'no commitment' dialogue while giving favourable impression of the organisation at work. Allows self-selection. Useful for large-scale or specific skills campaigns.	Organisation, as opposed to personnel department involvement. Message can go 'wrong'.

give candidates the opportunity to discuss the position with an organisational representative on an informal basis. This provides an opportunity for withdrawal from the process with the minimum activity and cost to the organisation. Other organisations provide little apart from a request for a letter, CV or completion of an application form.

The design of application forms can vary considerably, but the traditional approach tends to concentrate on finding out about qualifications and work history and usually includes a section in which candidates are encouraged to 'sell' their potential contribution to the organisation. Take-up of HRM may lead to a more behavioural focus, requiring candidates to answer a series of questions in which they describe how they have dealt with specific incidents such as solving a difficult problem, demonstrating leadership skills, etc. The management application form used by Pizza Hut is nine pages long and includes a personality questionnaire in addition to questions about qualifications and work experience (IDS, 1995).

A variant on the traditional application form, 'biodata' (short for biographical data), may also be used. Forms usually consist of a series of multiple-choice questions which are partly factual (e.g. number of brothers and sisters, position in the family) and partly about attitudes, values and preferences (Sadler and Milmer, 1993). The results are then compared against an 'ideal' profile which has been compiled by identifying the competencies which differentiate between effective and non-effective job performance. For example, a study of executives sent to foreign countries found that the more successful were more likely to have travelled voluntarily when young and to have learned a foreign language (Mitrani *et al.*, 1992).

Assessing candidates

The stages described above constitute recruitment and are primarily concerned with generating a sufficient pool of applicants. The focus now shifts to selection and the next stages concentrate on assessing the suitability or otherwise of candidates.

Shortlisting

As economic conditions and technological developments are likely to lead to more people chasing fewer jobs across the employment spectrum (Lewis, 1985), it is increasingly the norm for organisations to receive more applicants than they can reasonably interview. Thus, the initial step in selection is to categorise candidates as probable, possible or unsuitable. This is done by comparing the information provided on the application form or c.v. against pre-determined selection criteria. The criteria may either be explicit, i.e. detailed on the personnel specification, or implicit, i.e. only in the mind of the person doing the shortlisting. However, this latter approach is potentially discriminatory and would provide no defence if an organisation was challenged on the grounds of unlawful discrimination (see discussion on legislative requirements later in this chapter). Potentially suitable candidates will proceed with the selection process. Best practice recommends that unsuccessful candidates should be informed as soon as possible; in practice, written notification of rejection is less common and several application forms warn candidates that if they have not had a response by a set date they can assume they have been unsuccessful.

The take-up of HRM may lead to sifting on the basis of relevant personal characteristics rather than qualifications and work experience. The use of biodata can also provide a clear focus, as 'selectors can concentrate solely on those areas of the form found in the biodata validation exercise to be particularly relevant to the prediction of effective performance in the job concerned' (IRS, 1994). Some organisations have adopted random selection as a way to reduce large numbers of applications to a manageable quantity. Although there is concern that it may operate against equal opportunities, it can be argued that 'randomised selection may produce a better short-list than one based on human intervention where the wrong selection criteria are used consistently or where the correct selection criteria are applied inconsistently' (IRS, 1994: 15).

Selection methods

A number of selection methods are available and a selection procedure will frequently involve the use of more than one method. The most popular methods are outlined here and their validity and effectiveness are discussed later in the chapter.

Interview

This is by far the most popular selection method and is described as 'a controlled conversation with a purpose' (Torrington and Hall, 1995). Interviews are usually conducted face to face, although some organisations are now using telephone interviews as part of their selection procedure. The number of interviews involved in the selection process is frequently determined by the status of the vacancy. Survey data has found that the majority of organisations used two or more interviews for managerial and graduate posts, but used single interviews for clerical and manual appointments (IRS, 1991c). The number of interviewers can also vary from one to panels of four or more, although the IRS survey found two interviewers to be the most common format. The take-up of HRM has done little to affect the popularity of the interview as a selection technique; the last 15 years have witnessed an increasing use of more sophisticated methods such as psychometric tests and assessment centre techniques, but these have been in addition to, rather than instead of, interviews.

Tests

'Testing is essentially an attempt to achieve objectivity, or, to put it more accurately, to reduce subjectivity in selection decision-making' (Lewis, 1985: 157). The main types of tests used for selection are attainment tests, aptitude tests, intelligence tests and personality questionnaires. Attainment tests (e.g. typing tests) are concerned with skills and abilities already acquired by an individual, whereas aptitude tests (e.g. verbal reasoning tests, numerical aptitude) focus on an individual's potential to undertake specific tasks. Intelligence tests can give an indication of overall mental capacity and have been used for selection purposes for most of the twentieth century. Personality questionnaires allow quantification of characteristics which are important to job performance and difficult to measure by other methods (Lewis, 1985). There exists a fairly vociferous debate about the value of personality tests and whether or not personality can be measured (see, for example, Blinkhorn *et al.*, 1991).

Armstrong (1991) lists four characteristics of a good test:

1 It is a sensitive measuring instrument which discriminates well between subjects.

2 It has been standardised on a representative and sizeable sample of the population for which it is intended so that any individual's score can be interpreted in relation to others.

3 It is reliable in the sense that it always measures the same thing. A test aimed at measuring a particular characteristic should measure the same characteristic when applied to different people at the same time, or to the same person at different times.

4 It is valid in the sense that it measures the characteristic which the test is intended to measure. Thus, an intelligence test should measure intelligence and not simply verbal facility. (Armstrong, 1991: 370)

The use of tests has increased significantly over recent years; an IRS survey (1991a) found that 58% of employers used personality tests for at least some types of vacancy and 48% used ability and aptitude tests. Their use is frequently associated with HRM practices, particularly the focus on potential rather than past performance:

The topic of selection and assessment has shifted from one based historically on matching past performance to a defined job which was held for life to the need to estimate a person's probable adaptability to learn new skills and tasks. (Sparrow and Hiltrop, 1994: 358)

This focus on potential has also led to an increased use of assessment centre techniques.

Assessment centres

An assessment centre is not a place but rather a process which 'consists of a small group of participants who undertake a series of tests and exercises under observation, with a view to the assessment of their skills and competencies, their suitability for particular roles and their potential for development' (Fowler, 1992). The Task Force on Development of Assessment Centre Standards (quoted in Blanksby and Iles, 1990) specified a number of conditions which must be met in order for an assessment technique to be classified as an assessment centre:

1 Multiple assessment techniques must be used; at least one of these techniques must be a simulation.
2 Multiple assessors must be used and they must receive training prior to participating in the centre.
3 Judgements resulting in outcome (i.e. recommendation for selection, promotion, specific training or development) must be based on pooled information from assessors and techniques.
4 An overall assessment of behaviour must be made by the assessors at a separate time from the observation of behaviour.
5 Simulation exercises are used. These exercises are developed to tap a variety of predetermined behaviours and have been pre-tested prior to use to ensure that they provide reliable, objective and relevant behavioural information for the organisation.
6 The dimensions, attributes, characteristics or qualities evaluated by the assessment centre are determined by an analysis of relevant job behaviours.
7 The techniques used in the assessment centre are designed to provide information which is used in evaluating the dimensions, attributes or qualities previously determined.

Assessment centres techniques are most often used for the selection of managers and graduate trainees. Their use is increasing; survey data suggests that they are now in use in 30% of organisations (IRS, 1991a). How far this increase can be attributed solely to the emergence of HRM is unclear as other factors, such as size of the workforce and industrial sector, may also influence the adoption of these techniques. The IRS survey (1991a) found that assessment centre techniques were most likely to be used by larger employers (over 5000 employees) and in financial services and distribution and leisure industrial sectors.

Job simulation/work sampling

A key component of an assessment centre is the job simulation exercise, which is designed to be an accurate representation of performance in the job itself. The candidate is placed in a situation which they are likely to face if they are selected; examples include in-tray exercises and role-play interviews.

An extension of job simulation is work sampling, i.e. giving the candidate the opportunity to perform in the role for a specified length of time. An article in *People Management* describes how work sampling helped make a successful senior appointment:

> We invited each short-listed candidate to spend two full days at the factory, in a task-force comprising them, the managing director and the research director. The candidates had access to anyone they wanted to talk to in the company to create the specification for the new range. The exercise took eight days in all, but a very important decision was to be made upon which the future of the firm depended.
>
> (Harrison, 1995)

The successful candidate had not shone during his first interview but was the most effective performer during the work-sampling exercise.

References

These are used to obtain additional information about candidates from previous employers, academic tutors or just someone who knows them. The accuracy of the information is variable; Armstrong (1991) suggests that factual information (e.g. nature of previous job, time in employment, reason for leaving, salary, academic achievement, etc.) is essential but opinions about character and suitability are less reliable. He goes on to say that 'personal referees are, of course, entirely useless. All they prove is that the applicant has at least one or two friends' (p. 375).

References can be used at different stages in the selection process: some organisations only use them to confirm details of the chosen candidate after the position has been offered, whereas others will request references for all short-listed candidates prior to interview. The format may also vary, with some organisations using standardised report forms and others not. Whatever the format and timing, there is little doubt that references are a popular component of the selection process; an IRS survey (1991b) found that they were used by 97% of organisations. Perhaps surprisingly, the same survey also found that the use of references was increasing; 6% of current users had introduced the use of references over the last two years and 21% had increased their use in this period. The survey authors suggest that this is possibly due to the formalising or tightening of selection procedures.

Other methods

Some of the more unconventional methods of selection can include physiognomy (the idea that personal characteristics are reflected in facial features or body shape), phrenology ('reading' bumps on the head), astrology and graphology (for more detail see Mackenzie Davey, 1982). Their use in the UK is limited and there is no evidence of a link to HRM-style initiatives.

Making the decision

The aim of the overall recruitment and selection process is to provide enough information to enable recruiters to differentiate between those who can do the job and those who can't. The prescriptive approach stresses that the final decision should involve measuring each candidate against the selection criteria defined in the person specification and not against each other (Torrington and Hall, 1995). The combination of a number of different selection methods can enhance the quantity and quality of information about each candidate, although Anderson and Shackleton (1993) warn of the dangers of information overload in selection.

Even the decision-making process might be affected by the contemporary situation and employers' increased desire for flexibility. Sparrow and Hiltrop (1994) suggest that the combination of technological change, low economic growth, low voluntary turnover rates and an increasingly legislated environment may lead to new employees having to perform a series of jobs over time with changes not necessarily linked to promotion, which may lead to a different approach to selection:

> Traditional 'go/no go' decisions, based on information and data relating to a specific job, will be replaced by decisions to manage a gradual entry of people into the organisation (via probationary periods, fixed term contracts, part time work and so forth).
>
> (Sparrow and Hiltrop, 1994: 316)

Evaluation

The final stage of the recruitment and selection process concerns measurement of its success, both qualitatively and quantitatively. ACAS guidelines suggest that any recruitment and selection system should be based on three fundamental principles: effectiveness, efficiency and fairness (ACAS, 1983). *Effectiveness* is concerned with distinguishing accurately between suitable and unsuitable candidates; Mayo (1995) suggests a number of ways in which this can be measured for young entrant recruits, including retention rates, promotion rates and percentage of recruits perceived as having high potential after three to five years. *Efficiency* is more concerned with the costs of the exercise, and measures here may include average cost per recruit, average time lapsed between various stages, percentage of offers made and offer-acceptance rate (Mayo, 1995). *Fairness* is concerned with dealing with all applicants fairly and honestly, but has often been taken to refer to equal opportunity monitoring and has been limited to record keeping on the gender, ethnic origin and disability of successful and unsuccessful candidates.

In theory, the integration of recruitment and selection activity with other HR initiatives and business objectives should lead to more extensive evaluation. In practice there is little to indicate that this is happening:

> The ripple effects of recruitment practices on other HRM areas, such as . . . the effects of salary incentives offered to one group of recruits having a knock-on effect on salary claims of existing staff, or the effects of going outside to recruit staff on the aspirations and commitment of existing staff, are . . . often not considered.
>
> (Iles and Salaman, 1995: 214)

RECRUITMENT AND SELECTION IN CONTEXT

The processes of recruitment and selection take place within a framework of influential external and internal factors. On the one hand these influences may impose standardised approaches to recruitment and selection (for example the need to comply with specific aspects of legislation). On the other, critical influences may prevent or constrain those involved in the process from acting strictly in accordance with the codes of 'best practice' suggested, for example, by the Institute of Personnel and Development (IPD, 1995) and ensure that recruitment and selection activities vary from organisation to organisation.

In looking at recruitment and selection it is useful to consider both external and internal influences. A model to assist in this is shown in Figure 6.4.

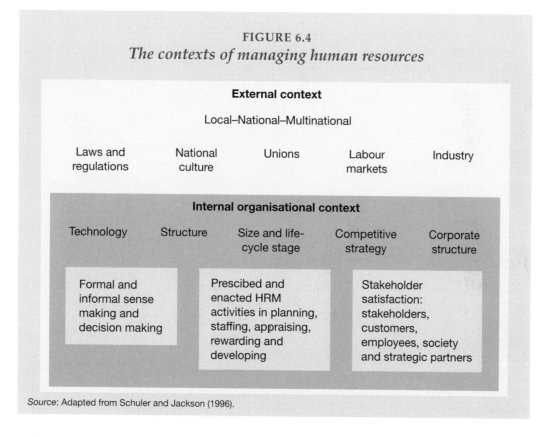

FIGURE 6.4

The contexts of managing human resources

External context

Local–National–Multinational

| Laws and regulations | National culture | Unions | Labour markets | Industry |

Internal organisational context

| Technology | Structure | Size and life-cycle stage | Competitive strategy | Corporate structure |

| Formal and informal sense making and decision making | Prescibed and enacted HRM activities in planning, staffing, appraising, rewarding and developing | Stakeholder satisfaction: stakeholders, customers, employees, society and strategic partners |

Source: Adapted from Schuler and Jackson (1996).

Concentrating on those issues which particularly affect recruitment and selection, the following appear relevant.

External context

Government policy and legislation

The processes of recruitment and selection are designed to discriminate between people, but in the UK legislation has been introduced to prevent *unfair* discrimination. The UK, however, remains less regulated than some other countries.

> As a general principle, employers are free to pick and choose to whom they offer employment and can reject an applicant for all manner of reasons including qualifications, attitude, references or suitability.   (Harrison, 1995: 91)

More recently decisions within the European legal framework have affected UK organisations. The concept of the 'working environment' was introduced with the addition of Article 118A to the Treaty of Rome in 1986. Consequently with qualified majority procedures (rather than previous unanimity requirements), the adoption of various health and safety provisions affects all members of the European Union. Most of these provisions are narrow health and safety measures, but directives on limiting working hours (to 48 in the working week), extending rights for part-time and temporary workers, national minimum wages and protection of young people are likely significantly to affect the areas of recruitment and selection because of their impact on the availability and rights of those in the external and internal labour markets and the definition of the jobs themselves.

Government policy in the UK has particularly heavy impact on the public sector. The privatisation of many nationalised industries (gas, telephone, steel, water, electricity, transport, communications, etc.), various pieces of legislation to devolve activities away from authorities to contractors or providers (e.g. compulsory competitive tendering, devolved school budgets, Care in the Community, the establishment of hospital trusts) and strict limits on public sector funding have changed the nature of many of the jobs in the sector. The result has been an increasing emphasis on recruiting those who possess business skills, particularly in finance, information technology and strategic decision making. A reduction in the strict adherence to nationally negotiated terms and conditions has meant that the recruitment of such individuals has been increasingly accompanied by an individual negotiation of terms and conditions.

National approach to education and training

The quality of potential recruits available in external and internal labour markets will be influenced by the quantity and quality of learning opportunities experienced by the individuals concerned. The education and training scene within the UK generally underpins those experiences, and has been the subject of much debate (Keep, 1989; Twigg and Albon, 1992; Harrison, 1993; Ashton and Felstead, 1995; Hendry, 1995; Dearing, 1996).

Within the UK in 1992, 66% of 16-year-olds remained in full-time post-compulsory education, compared with figures of between 80 and 95% in most other industrialised societies. This is coupled with a heavy reliance on voluntarist approaches to training, relying on employers to achieve an adequate level of skill for the nation as a whole, the market supposedly ensuring that such provision is made.

Recruitment can be influenced by government initiatives to increase skills training or provide schemes for the unemployed. One strand to current government policy is the introduction of Training and Enterprise Councils (TECs), locally generating training effort to meet skills shortages. A complementary strand consists of creating a training market through initiatives such as career development loans and training credits. A recent example is 'Workfare', where, in pilot schemes, long-term unemployed people 'earn' their benefits through 13 weeks of help looking for work followed by 13 weeks of work experience.

National culture

Various elements of the national culture of a country affect recruitment and selection: the perception of the role of men and women in that society, whether different groups are considered worthy of equality of opportunity, whether the link between an organisation and its employees is expected to remain intact for the whole of that individual's working life (and the extent to which the individual subsumes their personality to the demands of the organisation), where power is located, the perceived value of education and training to society as a whole, and opinions as to where responsibility and cost for such investments should be vested, etc. Several of these issues are examined more deeply in later sections of this chapter.

External labour markets

A detailed analysis of key labour market issues is found in Chapter 3.

Goss (1994) sees labour markets in terms of territories in which job-seekers and organisations operate, the territories being related not only to geography but also to economic and social factors such as actual/potential occupation, gender, ethnicity, age, education, physical health, etc. Newspaper and journal advertising illustrates that senior executives seek work in a national, perhaps international, market, whereas the local market may serve the interests of the less skilled or those tied by other constraints (many part-timers, individuals whose partners have local careers, parents not wishing to relocate). Goss also introduces the concept of institutionalised prejudice against certain social groups (part-time positions for men, engineering for women, concerns about employing young married women, managerial positions for those from ethnic minorities).

The latest edition of *Social Trends* (1996) highlights changes in the external labour market which may affect recruitment and selection activity in the UK (Whitfield, 1996):

- Nearly half of the 16.4 million women in work are employed in part-time jobs; women comprise a larger proportion of the labour force than men, and nearly half of British women are at work.
- There is a bulge in the working population of those aged between 25 and 44, while the number of economically active people in the age group 16–24 fell by 1.6 million (about a quarter) between 1986 and 1994, with the trend expected to continue until 2006 because of demographic factors and a tendency for school leavers to stay on into higher education.
- More than 1.5 million workers are in temporary employment (53.5% of whom are women).
- Full-time British workers average a 45.4-hour working week, the highest in Europe, with a third of male workers working in excess of 48 hours.
- Greater use is being made of flexible hours contracts (11.3% full-timers, with a further 6% working annualised hours).
- Traditional apprenticeships have fallen by a half since 1989, with less than 200 000 young people covered by schemes.

Developments in the UK market

The UK economy is dominated by large, diversified, multi-product, multi-site organisations. Well over a third of Europe's multinationals are based in the UK. These large organisations are often organised into strategic units for 'business' rather than geographical or territorial reasons (Purcell, 1995). A 1993 survey suggested that large companies in particular have had extensive recent history of merger/acquisition, new location investment, expansion on existing site, closed or run-down existing sites, and/or divestment out of existing businesses, often with the objective of achieving some form of synergy. In turn these major changes have brought about internal re-structuring in all but 6% of those organisations sampled (Purcell, 1995). This includes decentralisation and the growing importance of management accounting techniques (Armstrong, 1995), driven in turn by a demand from many shareholders for excellence in short-term results:

> the trend then has been to push down management policy-making on the substantive conditions of employment to the establishment level, and within that, towards a dominance of line management over the personnel/industrial relations function. (Armstrong, 1995: 146)

Increasingly this has been coupled with a devolvement of traditional activities, including recruitment and selection, to line management.

Recession, restructuring and growth

Recruitment and selection are processes which can demand very differing skills in times of general economic growth and in recession. The UK has experienced two major recessions in the last 20 years. It is easy to assume that minimal recruitment is required in times of recession, if the organisation concerned is one that is suffering economically in line with the economy as a whole. However, some industries may buck the recessionary trend and in these recruitment for general positions may be easier than in times of overall economic growth.

Because of the external labour market situation, advertised jobs may attract large numbers of applicants. Often such recruitment is taking place at the same time as headcount elsewhere in the organisation is being reduced. Both situations require sensitive handling if the organisation is to maintain public respect and approval.

Similarly, restructuring may be taking place within organisations with a requirement for organisations to take from the internal 'at risk' market before looking outside. There is the potential for conflict here if those 'at risk' are perceived not to possess the key competencies required in the changing situation. Recessionary situations may influence the qualities and experiences sought by organisations in the people to be recruited. Senior management in particular may need to demonstrate skills and abilities in restructuring, reducing headcount and managing change.

Despite the national recessionary picture and surplus of labour in the market, difficulties may remain for the recruiter as particular skills are in short supply. As the economic cycle evolves and the national recession passes, many organisations may experience increased difficulties in attracting candidates on the external market, especially in particular geographical locations or for state-of-the-art skills/knowledge. For example, an acute shortage of secretarial staff was reported by one agency in July 1995, with only one applicant per vacancy, rather than six during the depths of the recession (*People Management*, 1995b).

Strategies to overcome difficulties include attracting applicants through upper-quartile salaries and reward packages, joining bonuses, training and development opportunities, the use of external contractors or temporary employees, and responsive and user-friendly recruitment systems. Sound human resource planning allows proactive rather than reactive policies to address shortfalls and mismatches, but there is little evidence in the UK of strategic planning in this area.

Issues around flexibility

More challenging still are the situations where recruitment is undertaken to remove full-time jobs in the name of flexibility or rationality. The recruitment of part-time staff to replace those on full-time contracts in retailing, the recruitment of schoolchildren to work on temporary part-time contracts in banking when employers have shed thousands of full-time permanent jobs in the preceding four years, or recruiting for new skills in the hospitality industry while current incumbents are still in place illustrate the changing scenario.

Internal organisational context

Organisational culture

> It is obvious that, faced with similar environments, organisations will respond differently . . . the response is likely to be influenced by the past experience of managers and by the wider social and political processes in the organisation . . . an essentially cultural process.
>
> (Johnson and Scholes, 1989: 37–38)

Decisions in recruitment and selection are likely to be as subject to an organisation's cultural influences as any other business decision. Johnson and Scholes' cultural recipe, illustrated in Figure 6.5, suggests where influences may be based.

For example, those in power may have strong preferences for one particular recruitment method, or a dislike of any selection method apart from one-to-one interviewing. The structure of the organisation may be multi-layered, requiring several layers of decision making to be passed before agreement to recruit is obtained. Custom and practice in the approach to recruitment and selection often have a strong impact. A well-established routine may exist, perhaps backed by written policies and procedures and strong monitoring systems, and deviation from this would not normally be countenanced. Alternatively, recruitment may be perceived as a marginal activity, undertaken, as needed, in an *ad hoc* manner by a delegated employee.

Ownership, size and structure

The recruitment and selection practices of an organisation will be affected by issues of size. Small organisations may not have access to well-developed personnel functions or

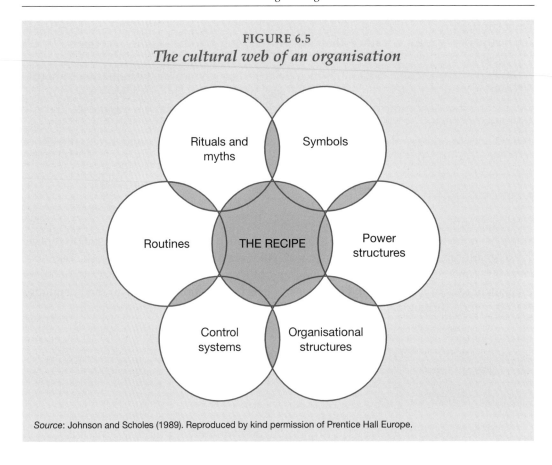

FIGURE 6.5

The cultural web of an organisation

Source: Johnson and Scholes (1989). Reproduced by kind permission of Prentice Hall Europe.

recruitment and selection systems and may recruit irregularly, with heavy reliance on informal methods and/or those that worked well previously. Responsibility for the recruitment activity in particular may be passed to third parties, or enthusiastic individuals within the organisation.

Larger organisations may be more likely to have established and regularly used procedures for recruitment and selection, though the responsibility may be vested differently depending on the organisation's general approach to the management of human resources. There appears to be greater devolvement of at least some of the activity to line managers than was previously the case in organisations where the personnel function was well established.

The largest organisations may find that HR policies are decided by a powerful central function, with strict adherence to written policy and procedure expected in the business units. Increasingly, however, policy determination and delivery are seen as the remit of the unit rather than the centre, and diversity of practice can ensue within the one organisation. Organisations which were/are perceived as part of the public sector can be seen to illustrate this latter point, with large centralised personnel functions being downsized and the decision making formerly associated with them being devolved to individual departments, sections or functions.

Organisational lifecycle

Products, industries and markets are deemed in marketing terms to have 'lifecycles': periods of development, growth, shakeout, maturity and decline (Johnson and Scholes, 1989). Adapted from this concept is the idea that organisations too have similar lifecycles and that changing managerial priorities are associated with each period, which in turn has implications for HR management generally and recruitment and selection specifically (Schuler and Jackson, 1996).

Storey and Sisson (1993) discuss the expected HR strategies in relation to the business lifecycle and consider that the following are likely for recruitment, selection, and staffing:

- **Start-up**   Attract the best technical and professional talent.
- **Growth**   Recruit an adequate number and mix of qualified workers. Management succession planning. Manage rapid internal labour market movements.
- **Maturity**   Encourage sufficient turnover to minimise layoffs and provide new openings. Encourage mobility as reorganisations shift jobs around.
- **Decline**   Plan and implement workforce reductions and reallocations. Transfers to different businesses. Early retirement.

Each of these stages will require different characteristics and competencies from the people recruited/employed, especially in managerial terms. Even in the final stage where concentration is focused on downsizing, there may be a need to recruit people with specific skills in handling the reduction in activity.

Technology of organisation

Certain industries, notably finance, banking, travel, information technology and retailing, are experiencing major changes due to technological advances. In many cases the result is a requirement for fewer people employed than before and for different skills and competencies within those who remain to ensure that the technology is appropriately harnessed to meet organisational objectives.

Financial situation

The financial position of an organisation can have a great impact on the recruitment and selection practices found. Financial constraints can prevent investment to improve the quality of the internal labour market, or the availability of cash to fund higher reward packages which would attract the highest-quality applicants in the external labour market. It may be difficult to argue for the budget to carry out sophisticated selection procedures, or use of a variety of recruitment methods.

Soft versus hard HRM approaches

The above discussion of external and internal variations inevitably leads to the conclusions that organisational differences should be expected and that the resulting HR and particularly recruitment and selection policies will vary considerably between organisations. Organisations on the whole adopt their own management philosophies and policies, which are not static but change according to circumstances.

One of the critical decisions from the point of view of HRM and recruitment and selection is the stance taken by the organisation on whether a soft or harder approach to the management of people is to be adopted:

> Soft contracting implies an elaborate internal labour market, managed by a sophisticated HR function, with strong HR policies to govern relationships, pay, promotions, appraisal and development. Hard contracting implies a link back into the wider labour markets with a more legalistic and instrumental attachment to work as the norm for the effort reward bargain.
>
> (Storey and Sisson, 1993)

An organisation's perception of the appropriate stance along the hard/soft axis will have considerable implications for the choice of labour market in which to recruit, the emphasis of present job requirements as opposed to potential for development, and the selection techniques used.

CRITICAL DECISIONS IN RECRUITMENT AND SELECTION

Recruitment and selection from an HRM perspective can be summarised as four critical decisions:

- What/who do we want?
- Where do we find the people we want?
- How do we attract them?
- How can we identify them?

In this section we shall deal with potential responses to each of these questions.

What/who do we want?

Which comes first – the job or the person?

As discussed earlier in the chapter, the usual response to the 'What do we want?' question is to start by defining the requirements of the job in a job description and then use this information to identify the necessary personal characteristics in a person specification. This method has been described as 'job first – person later' (van Zwanenberg and Wilkinson, 1993) or 'task-oriented' (Iles and Salaman, 1995). However, several problems are associated with this approach. The first is that the writing of the job description is time-consuming, especially if a system for job analysis is not already in place. There is a need to gain information from a variety of parties (e.g. boss, current jobholder, colleagues, observer) as to the nature, actual duties and responsibilities involved. And it is not a one-off exercise; regular updating of the job description is necessary, especially in fast-changing environments.

The second, and perhaps the greater, problem lies with the lack of attention paid to the changing requirements of the jobholder and whether the list of duties and responsibilities is too constraining, especially where teamworking is introduced. This concentration on 'the job' and its place in a bureaucratic structure may be detrimental to the development of the skills and aptitudes needed for the long-term benefit of the organisation.

Problems also exist with the compilation of the person specification, not least because techniques for translating information about jobs or organisations into person specifications remain mysterious and ill defined (van Zwanenberg and Wilkinson, 1993). A common assumption is that the existence of such a document can avoid unfair discrimination during the selection process. However, pre-determined criteria can contribute to effective recruitment and selection only if careful consideration has been given to the necessity and fairness of all the requirements. Preconceived or entrenched attitudes, prejudices and assumptions can lead, consciously or unconsciously, to requirements which may not be job related at all but aimed at meeting the assumed needs of customers, colleagues and the established culture of the organisation. Examples of this might include insistence on a British education, possession of a driving licence, unnecessary height restriction, sex role stereotyping and setting age bands.

These issues have led to a discrepancy between prescription and practice in the field of recruitment. The IPD's Recruitment Code of Practice states that 'all recruitment *must* begin with a job specification and/or person specification' (IPD, 1995: 18, emphasis added), yet Torrington and Hall (1995) have found that 'less than half of personnel departments use job analysis and its products for recruitment and selection, usually because they wish to avoid the close definition and inflexibility that careful specification often implies' (pp. 215–216).

A potentially more flexible alternative is to replace the more traditional approach with a 'person-oriented' approach (Iles and Salaman, 1995) which focuses on the generic qualities and behaviour required by the organisation rather than those determined by a specific job. These 'behavioural dimensions affecting job performance' can be defined as competences (Armstrong, 1992) or competencies, to use American terminology. Pizza Hut identified nine competencies required for trainee managers as adaptability, quality customer service, interpersonal communications, team motivation, team leadership, business administration, emotional resilience, tenacity/commitment, and planning and organising. The process they use to test for these competencies is rather elaborate and involves a nine-page application form, a competency-based interview, a one-day assessment centre and four to five hours on-the-job experience in one of their restaurants (IDS, 1995).

This competency-based approach is frequently seen as being compatible with HRM initiatives such as flexibility, teamworking and multi-skilling; for example, Armstrong (1992) suggests that organisational requirements will include commitment and the ability to work effectively in a team. However, there is also a rather sinister side to this development: the increased focus on behavioural and attitudinal characteristics may imply the expectation that 'a workforce could gradually be constructed which would be more receptive to the broad span of HR philosophy than is the case with existing manpower stocks' (Storey, 1992: 100).

In practice, a combination of the task-oriented and people-oriented approaches may be adopted in order to recruit people who not only can do the job but will fit well into the organisation. The increased popularity of assessment centres (AC) provides an example of this:

> AC techniques, such as job samples, in-tray exercises and the like, are usually derived from a 'job first – person later' approach, whereas the specification of broad requirements in terms of, say, personality variables, and the use of personality tests to measure these implies a 'person first – job later' approach.   (van Zwanenberg and Wilkinson, 1993)

The type of approach adopted may also be determined by the type of job and the nature of the employment relationship. The concept of the flexible firm (see Chapter 3) could reasonably include investment in sophisticated recruitment and selection techniques, emphasis on behaviour and potential for core positions, and a more 'downbeat' approach focusing on current ability, or possibly even just availability, for peripheral positions.

External influences

While organisations have considerable freedom of choice in the type of people they want to recruit, legislation plays a significant role in the recruitment and selection process, particularly in attempts to prevent discrimination on the grounds of sex, race and disability.

Sex and race discrimination

Key legislation

Two acts are specifically designed to prevent discrimination in employment on the basis of sex or race. The *Sex Discrimination Act 1975* makes it unlawful to discriminate against a person directly or indirectly in the field of employment on the grounds of their sex or marital status. The *Race Relations Act 1976* makes it unlawful to discriminate against a person in the field of employment on the grounds of their race, colour and nationality, including ethnic or national origin.

Both Acts prohibit direct and indirect discrimination. Direct discrimination occurs when an individual is treated less favourably than another because of their sex, marital status or race. Indirect discrimination occurs when requirements are imposed which are not necessary for the job and which may disadvantage a significantly larger proportion of one sex or racial group than another.

Although concerned with discrimination in a number of areas of employment, both Acts specifically prohibit discrimination during recruitment and selection. This includes advertisements, selection arrangements, interviews and terms offered as well as the actual offer or refusal of a job. Only the Equal Opportunities Commission or the Commission for Racial Equality can initiate proceedings relating to discrimination in advertisements, but individuals can complain of discrimination in all other aspects of the process.

Both Acts make it lawful for employers to take positive action to encourage applications from members of one sex or of racial groups who have been under-represented in particular work over the previous 12 months. However, positive discrimination is unlawful, which means that, although advertisements can explicitly encourage applications from one sex or particular racial groups, no applicant can be denied information or be discriminated against in selection because they do not fit the 'preferred' category. Sex or race discrimination is only permitted where sex or race is a defined 'genuine occupational qualification' (GOQ). Examples of GOQs include models, actors and some personal welfare counsellors.

Effectiveness of the legislation

These Acts have had only limited success in achieving sexual and racial equality. The size of the task was recognised from the outset:

> Nobody believes that legislation by itself can eradicate overnight a whole range of attitudes which are rooted in custom and are, for that very reason, often unchallenged because unrecognised. But if the law cannot change attitudes overnight, it can, and does effect change slowly.
>
> (House of Lords, 1972/3)

One could reasonably question whether changes are occurring too slowly. Twenty years on there has been a removal of overt discrimination, particularly in recruitment advertising, but less evidence of eradication of discrimination in employment practices generally. *Social Trends* (1995) statistics indicate that, at a macro level, very little has changed in the distribution of employment on the grounds of gender or race. Women's participation in the workforce is steadily increasing and women are expected to make up 46% of the workforce by 2006, but there are more than five times as many women as men working part-time and men are twice as likely to be in managerial or administrative positions. Sex role stereotyping still seems prevalent; women comprised three-quarters of people in clerical and secretarial jobs. The *Social Trends* (1995) statistics also show that unemployment rates vary markedly between different ethnic groups: overall unemployment rates were highest for Pakistanis and Bangladeshis at 27.9% compared with 9.1% for whites; while long-term unemployment (over one year) was 15.8% for those from the Black ethnic group compared with 4.0% for whites.

Part of the problem is that the legislation requires an end to discrimination but 'does not actually require that employers do anything to promote equality' (Dickens, 1994: 275). Equalising opportunity in employment is therefore largely dependent on initiatives undertaken voluntarily by organisations such as targeted recruitment, pre-recruitment training or participation in national initiatives.

In order to attract more women and members of ethnic minorities, a number of organisations have adopted targeted recruitment through the design of adverts and the media in which they are featured. Paddison (1990) suggests that job-seekers form a generalised perception of individual organisations and the people they employ, and so the gender and ethnic mix of applicants will tend to reflect the composition of the existing workforce, despite the ubiquitous slogan 'we are an equal opportunities employer'. A number of employers have recognised that this slogan has become less significant with over-use and can seem particularly meaningless when attached to advertisements which give a different message through the use of male-dominated job titles, e.g. salesmen, or pictures of a predominantly white, able-bodied, male workforce. As a result an increasing number of advertisements feature pictures showing a racial and ethnic mix (Paddison, 1990) or state that applicants from certain groups are particularly encouraged.

An extension of this is pre-employment training which seeks to increase the number of employees from previously under-represented groups. For example, the Metropolitan Police has recently agreed to pilot a pre-recruitment course designed to increase the number of officers from ethnic minority communities. The course focuses on literacy, numeracy, current affairs, physical fitness and interpersonal skills, and is aimed at helping participants to 'compete on an equal basis with other applicants for places at the Met's training school at Hendon, north-west London' (Arkin, 1996: 10). A similar scheme on Merseyside resulted in 10 participants becoming officers, out of the 15 who started the programme (Arkin, 1996).

In addition to initiatives on the part of individual employers, there are also national initiatives in the UK aimed at improving employment prospects for women and members of ethnic minority groups. Opportunity 2000 was launched with government backing in 1991 in order to improve the position of women in the labour market. Initiatives introduced by organisations participating in the scheme include the provision of training to increase women's opportunities at work, flexible working arrangements, childcare and career breaks. Results to date seem encouraging, if relatively limited: a survey of the 293 member organisations of Opportunity 2000, reported in *People Management* (1995d), found that women in middle and senior management positions had increased to 28% and 17% respectively (from 24% and 12% the year before); and the percentage of women directors had doubled from the previous year to 16%. They also found that women tended to do better in smaller organisations: women account for 28% of senior managers in companies employing less than 500 people compared with 12% in organisations with more than 2 000 employees.

A similar initiative aimed at improving employment opportunities for members of ethnic minority groups was launched in October 1995. Race for Opportunity aims 'to make racial equality more than just an employment issue' and recommends that managers are trained on equality issues, publicity material is reviewed and suppliers are encouraged to develop equal opportunity policies. Companies who have expressed support for the scheme include British Gas, the BBC, Littlewoods, TSB, WH Smith and Northern Foods (*Personnel Today*, 1995) but it is too early to make an assessment of the likely impact of the scheme.

These forms of positive action may be aimed at improving opportunities for previously disadvantaged groups, but they are not without their critics. Kandola (1995) suggests that such measures can be counter-productive because people who are perceived to have gained advantage through positive action are likely to be viewed negatively by others. Further, he states that women and ethnic minorities do not want extra training and help because this 'implies that they are deficient in some way and that consequently they are the problem . . . [when] invariably the problem lies not with the targeted group itself but elsewhere in an organisation's own processes or culture' (p. 20). He advocates a more strategic approach to managing diversity rather than the traditional equal opportunities emphasis.

Disability discrimination

Key legislation

Prior to 1996, although legislation concerned with the employment of people with disabilities existed, it was not designed to prevent discrimination. Rather, the aim of the *Disabled*

Persons (Employment) Acts of 1944 was to 'secure for the disabled their full share, within their capacity, of such employment as is ordinarily available' by introducing a register for people with disabilities and establishing a quota of 3% registered disabled workers for all employers with more than 20 workers. It was not an offence to be below this quota, but employers who failed to achieve it had to apply to the then Department of Employment for a permit to recruit non-disabled employees. In addition, the Act designated two occupations as reserved only for registered disabled workers: car park attendant and passenger lift attendant. Employers were required to keep detailed records to show their compliance with the legislation. Further information regarding the employment of people with disabilities resulted from the *Companies (Directors' Report) (Employment of Disabled Persons) Regulations* which require organisations with more than 250 employees to include a policy statement in their annual report about the employment of people with disabilities.

The situation regarding employment of people with disabilities changed at the end of 1996 when the *Disability Discrimination Act* (1995) came into force. The Act defines disability as a physical or mental impairment which has a substantial and long-term adverse effect on a person's ability to carry out normal day-to-day duties and includes progressive conditions, such as HIV infection, cancer and multiple sclerosis (Arkin, 1995). The legislation makes it unlawful for companies with 20 or more employees to treat people with disabilities less favourably than they do others unless they can justify their actions. In addition, employers are required to make 'reasonable adjustment' to the workplace or to working arrangements where this would help to overcome the practical effects of a disability.

Effectiveness of the legislation

To date it has been widely recognised that the legislation has not been effective. The quota scheme was recognised by the Department of Employment as 'ineffectual, outdated and unenforceable' (IDS, 1992) and the stigma attached to being 'registered disabled' meant that many disabled people chose not to register. In April 1989 the number registered was 366 768, whereas Labour Force Survey data for 1987 identified 3 987 000 people who categorised themselves as having a disability limiting the kind of work they could do (Hall, 1989). It is too early to say what the impact of the 1995 Act will be. However, there appears to be some confusion over what constitutes reasonable adjustment, and employers, charities and trade unions have complained that the draft code of practice is too vague to provide clarification (Overell, 1996).

Other groups

Key legislation

Discrimination on other grounds, such as sexual orientation and age, is not currently covered by legislation although these issues are widely discussed. One minority group which has some protection from legislation for recruitment purposes consists of certain categories of ex-offenders. The *Rehabilitation of Offenders Act 1974* enables offenders who have received sentences of 30 months or less to have their convictions 'spent'. This means that, after a specified period, they can reply 'no' when asked if they have a criminal record. Although it is unlawful for an employer to discriminate on the grounds of a 'spent' conviction, the candidate who is discriminated against has no individual remedy (IDS, 1992). In addition, a wide range of jobs and professions are exempt from the provisions of this Act, including teachers, social workers, doctors, lawyers and accountants.

Effectiveness of the legislation

Ex-offenders account for over 20% of the UK workforce (IDS, 1992). However, whether their ability to secure employment is based on the effectiveness of the Act or ignorance on the part of employers remains unclear. More than half the respondents in a survey carried out on behalf of the Birmingham Chamber of Commerce believed that they had never employed anyone with a criminal record (Falconer, 1990) and a survey conducted by Apex Scotland found that only 4% of employers had knowingly taken on someone with a criminal record (North, 1992).

Where do we find the people we want?

Organisations have choices when recruiting. One critical decision is whether to recruit from within the organisation, having acted as 'game keeper' and reared suitable employees for the positions concerned, or whether to look in external labour markets, either poaching employees from other organisations or recruiting from those who are unemployed.

Tyson and Fell (1991) list three different types of recruitment policy practised by organisations:

1 One-tier recruitment, where recruitment takes place at the lowest level in organisation and higher positions are filled by promotion through the ranks, typified by the police force and (at least in 1991) large retail banks.
2 Two-tier recruitment, where one entry point exists for graduate/management trainees and a second for routine administrative and operative entrants, typified by many large businesses including Shell and ICI and to some extent the Armed Forces.
3 Multi-point recruitment, concerned with filling jobs rather than careers and which carries no promise or expectation of promotion. Tyson and Fell consider that most small businesses, including small engineering, retail and computing organisations, fall into this category.

Internally focused recruitment

These decisions have strategic implications. To opt for the 'gamekeeper' approach reduces the need to recruit externally, provides possibilities for career advancement which may well add to job satisfaction, and gives the organisation considerable control and payback over the developmental experiences of its employees. The strategy is a long-term one and fits within a long-term planning approach to the management of the human resource. It is the approach one would expect to find in an organisation that wished to promote human resource management, particularly the softer variety, heavily dependent on training and development initiatives.

A typical example of an organisation that prefers to use the internal labour market is WH Smith:

> Like most other companies, our strategy is, wherever possible, to promote from within and 'grow our own'.
> (Rubin, 1993: 103)

Some commentators are firmly in favour of such an approach:

> The first port of call should be internal to the organisation. This may result in a form of 'internal labour market' forming and we see examples of this in large firms and in particular in local authorities and health boards, who seem to recruit from within their own sector at the expense of candidates from other industrial and commercial sectors.
> (Anderson, 1994: 48)

The Chubb Corporation in the US adopts elements of the two-tier approach, combined with an emphasis on its internal market. It:

> makes a substantial investment in its employees and that investment begins with recruiting. Historically it has gone to the most prestigious undergraduate schools and hired graduates, who, regardless of major, have good interpersonal and communication skills upon which insurance-specific skills could be built . . . Second, Chubb fills vacancies internally, moving people frequently and retraining them for new jobs.
> (Schuler and Jackson, 1996: 218)

An approach which concentrates on the internal labour market is not without potential difficulties:

- It requires high-level commitment to the provision of developmental opportunities, at least part of the cost of which will need to be borne by the organisation.
- Existing inequalities in employment opportunities may be reinforced, e.g. a lack of women in senior positions, lack of employment opportunities for disadvantaged groups.
- Larger organisations may have well-developed systems for the identification of high fliers; for example, the National Westminster Bank uses assessment centre techniques at three separate stages over a period of years (Sadler and Milmer, 1993). However, problems may still exist when those identified are promoted too quickly, or held back by senior managers reluctant to lose their expertise. Motivation of those not identified may decline and expectations of those identified may not always be met. Perhaps such identification has elements of a self-fulfilling prophecy if the best developmental opportunities are restricted to those who have been identified?
- A potentially critical problem in times of increasing competitiveness and change is that an approach with a long-term focus may be inappropriate for rapidly changing markets where new and urgently required skills are not available within the existing workforce. Major financial institutions in the City of London had to change recruitment policy rapidly and recruit externally in order to attract the skills required after deregulation of the industry.

With large-scale restructuring of organisations over the last decade, there has been increasing emphasis on using internal recruitment where a positive result for the recruit does not carry the promise or expectation of promotion, but merely of job retention. Against a perception that the overall headcount of the organisation will fall (and that

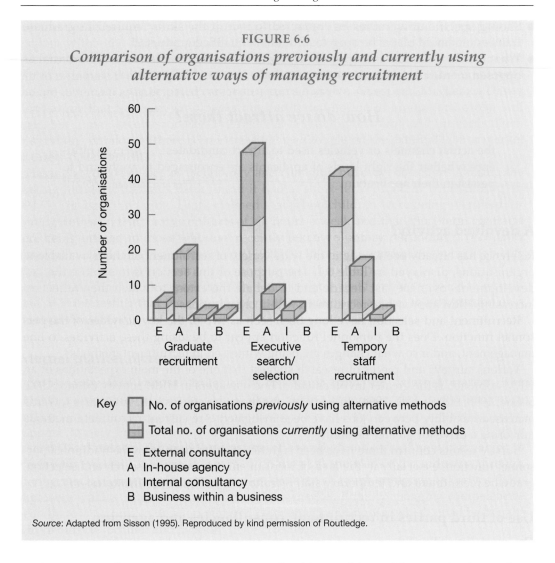

FIGURE 6.6
Comparison of organisations previously and currently using alternative ways of managing recruitment

Key
☐ No. of organisations *previously* using alternative methods

▦ Total no. of organisations *currently* using alternative methods

E External consultancy
A In-house agency
I Internal consultancy
B Business within a business

Source: Adapted from Sisson (1995). Reproduced by kind permission of Routledge.

Agencies are becoming increasingly involved in working with organisations where strategic decisions to resource via a third party have been taken. For example, Reed Employment has recently won a contract to provide a temporary workforce of thousands to retune the videos in millions of UK homes for the new Channel 5, taking on the responsibility for training, selection and employment (Overell, 1996).

At the senior executive end of the market, the use of executive search and selection consultants continues, both in the UK and internationally. Research in the area (Britton *et al.*, 1992; Anderson, 1994; Ball *et al.*, 1996) suggests that further subcontracting of activity, particularly of psychometric testing, may take place. Executive search (finding candidates through direct personal contact) and executive selection (identifying candidates through advertising and short-listing) tend to be used where there is a need for an intermediary because of the need for confidentiality, a lack of in-house recruitment knowledge and skills, for senior and/or specialist positions or simply where senior management lack the time to devote to the activity. Recent research suggests that a key requirement in the process is more effective communication, particularly with potential candidates (Ball *et al.*, 1996).

Certain developments are also occurring regarding the traditional networking or word-of-mouth methods of recruiting for senior positions. From April 1995, vacancies for posts as non-executive trust directors in NHS trusts, traditionally awarded via government patronage, have to be advertised and open to all and candidates are sifted by independent selection panels (*People Management,* 1995a).

How can we identify them?

Selection techniques in practice

Earlier in the chapter we outlined the various techniques and methods available to help organisations differentiate between suitable and unsuitable candidates. In this section we look at the popularity of the different techniques in practice and try to determine the factors which may influence this popularity.

Popularity

Figure 6.7 shows selection methods in current use in the UK, including those introduced in the two years prior to 1991 (IRS, 1991a). The data is taken from a survey of 173 organisations of different sizes in both public and private sectors. Despite the frequent criticism levelled at the interview as a selection process and predictions that its days were numbered (e.g. Herriot, 1989), the findings demonstrate that the interview remains the most

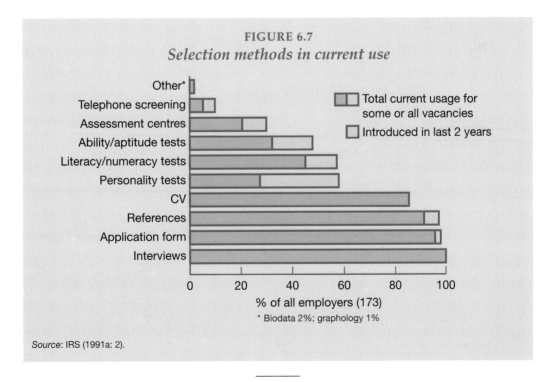

FIGURE 6.7
Selection methods in current use

% of all employers (173)
* Biodata 2%; graphology 1%

Source: IRS (1991a: 2).

popular method of selection. There has been considerable growth in the use of tests, particularly personality tests, as part of the selection process, but 'alternative' methods of selection such as graphology and biodata remain relatively rare.

What determines the popularity of different techniques? One could reasonably assume that a key factor in determining the type of method would be its accuracy at predicting who is suitable and unsuitable for the position. Whatever technique is used, people who do well should be capable of doing the job and people who do badly should not.

Accuracy

Figure 6.8 shows the accuracy of selection methods measured on the correlation coefficient between predicted and actual job performance, with zero for chance prediction and 1.0 for perfect prediction.

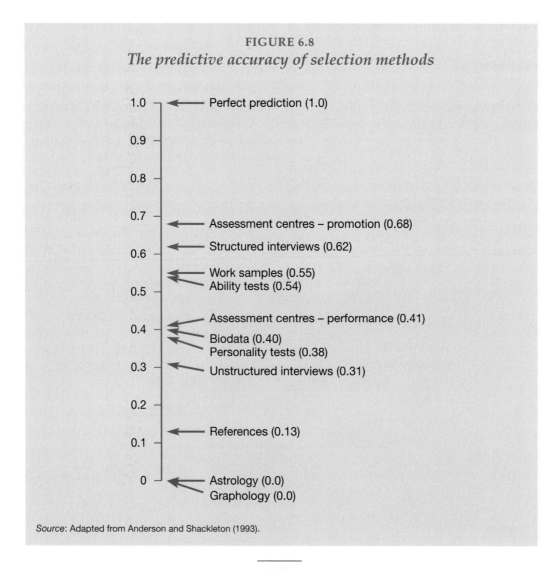

FIGURE 6.8
The predictive accuracy of selection methods

Source: Adapted from Anderson and Shackleton (1993).

248

If one compares Figures 6.7 and 6.8, it appears that accuracy cannot be the key determinant as the most popular methods (interviewing and references) are not the most accurate. Further comparison of the two charts may suggest that the situation is changing, as the increased use of assessment centres and selection testing may help improve the accuracy of the selection process. However, the use of these techniques has tended to be in addition to rather than instead of interviews and, while this has the potential advantage of providing more information on which to base the selection decision and might therefore improve the accuracy of the total process, there is evidence to suggest that this advantage is less frequently exploited than it might be. Findings from the IRS survey (1991b: 2) show that 'the interview completely overshadows any other selection method as the *most* important method in helping employers to reach a final decision to appoint'. Interviews were the key determinant in 85% of organisations, whereas assessment centres only accounted for 6%. Tests are designed as a supplementary method and this role is perhaps confirmed by the fact that 34% of survey respondents (IRS, 1991b) considered tests as their second most important selection method. It is rather alarming that 3% of organisations considered tests to be their most important method and this is discussed in more detail later in this section. Biodata is a relatively accurate predictor of job performance but is only used by a very small minority of companies in the survey and was not considered as key selection method by any of the respondents. But if accuracy is not the main factor to influence the type of selection method used, then what is? Other possible factors are the level of the vacancy, the costs incurred by the various techniques and custom and practice.

Level of vacancy

By and large organisations tend to use cheaper and more straightforward techniques for selecting personnel for junior or manual jobs and to reserve more elaborate or sophisticated methods for managerial posts. Survey data (IRS, 1991b) found that three-quarters of manual vacancies were filled by a single-stage interview (often with only one interviewer), whereas less than one in twenty managerial vacancies were filled in this way. The survey also reported differences between selection procedures for manual and non-manual workers: only a fifth of manual vacancies involved two interview stages, compared with one-third of clerical vacancies.

The use of sophisticated selection techniques is often reserved for managerial or graduate positions. The IRS survey (1991b) found that assessment centre techniques were used more for managerial positions than for any other group, including even graduate vacancies. In part, this may be due to the willingness of organisations to invest more heavily in the selection of some parts of the workforce than others, particularly where the posts warrant higher salaries and the repercussions of a wrong decision can be severe. It may also be due to expectations on the part of the candidates themselves and the organisation's need to present itself in such a way as to attract the highest-quality applicants:

> Historically, it used to be employers who chose the successful few recruits from the many candidates who presented themselves. Now, increasingly, the tables are turned: those same employers are now brushing up their own international curriculum vitae for the recruitment beauty contest in which candidates at all levels choose for whom they wish to work.
>
> (Curnow, 1989: 40)

The restriction of sophisticated selection methods to managerial posts may be less apparent in companies adopting an HRM approach, although Storey (1992) found that sector circumstances and wider employment-management policies being pursued also influenced the selection techniques being used. Storey's (1992) survey found that some motor companies were using tests for hourly paid workers as well as supervisors: the tests at Jaguar 'were designed around dimensions such as "independence of thought", "team working" and "cooperativeness" and Peugeot-Talbot tested operatives for reasoning ability and mechanical aptitude (Storey, 1992: 99). Other companies use assessment centres for the appointment of non-managerial staff; Häagen-Dazs uses them to assess customer service skills of front-line restaurant staff but the assessment centres are 'noticeably shorter and cheaper than the one- or two-day models used by other employers' (IDS, 1995: 1).

Cost of selection techniques

There is no doubt that recruitment and selection can be costly activities and the costs incurred by some selection techniques can make them prohibitive for all but a few 'key' vacancies in an organisation. For example, Barclays Bank estimates that its assessment centres usually cost about £15 000, including necessary materials (IDS, 1995: 5). However, in deciding on the most cost-effective methods, the 'up-front' costs need to be balanced against the costs of wrong decisions, which may include costs associated with labour turnover due to lack of ability. Jaffee and Cohen (cited in Appelbaum *et al.*, 1989: 60) suggest that consideration should include some or all of the following: the start-up time required by a replacement for the jobholder; the down-time associated with the jobholder changing jobs internally or externally; training and/or retraining for the replacement and the jobholder; relocation expenses; the shortfall in productivity between an effective and ineffective jobholder; and the psychological impact on the 'failed' jobholder and the morale of others in the department.

Custom and practice

A possible explanation for the continued popularity of interviews is the simple fact that people are familiar with them. Although, at an academic level, the general consensus is that interviews are unreliable, invalid and provide ample opportunity for personal prejudice (Herriot, 1989), at a practical level many interviewers feel that they are good judges of people and can make effective selection decisions, and most of us would probably feel unhappy in starting a job without undergoing some form of face-to-face meeting with our prospective employer. It seems, then, that the appeal of interviews is universal and they are 'both *favoured* and *expected* as an indisposable [*sic*] part of the selection process by organisations and applicants alike' (Anderson and Shackleton, 1993: 1). The notion that individual interviewers feel they are better than is indicated by the general statistics raises another issue pertinent to the selection debate, in that the statistics on the accuracy of different types of selection techniques mask wide variations within each technique.

Variations in effectiveness

The effectiveness of interviews can be influenced by a number of factors including the number of interviewers; their proficiency in interview techniques; the time of day or day of the week when the interview is conducted; and whether or not the interview follows a structured format. Structured interviews have a higher predictive validity than unstructured ones. Anderson and Shackleton (1993) describe two recent advances in structured interview techniques which they claim to improve the interview as a method of predicting job performance: patterned behaviour description interviews (PBDI) and situational interviews. The PBDI is based on job analysis to identify the behaviours which distinguish between effective and ineffective job performance; these 'critical incidents' are then grouped into between five and ten 'performance dimensions' which are subsequently checked with the jobholder's supervisor. Once agreed, they are used as the basis for questions which follow a structured format and the interviewer rates the candidates' replies on a pre-determined rating scale. The situational interview also uses job analysis to determine critical incidents, but these are then translated into a series of 'What would you do in this situation?' questions. Once again, the replies are noted on a pre-determined rating scale (for further detail on these techniques see Anderson and Shackleton, 1993: 85–89). The results of both these approaches are claimed to be comparable with more sophisticated selection techniques, but they are not necessarily suitable for everyone:

> Their accuracy depends entirely on setting up the structured interview properly . . . to construct these interview techniques properly one needs the support of specialist expertise.　　　　　　　(Anderson and Shackleton, 1993: 89)

Perhaps because of the need for specialist expertise, these two methods are still comparatively rare in practice. However, the IRS survey (1991c) found that 81% of respondents included situational-type questions in their interviewing, although some only used them for graduate and managerial posts. The extent to which such questions have been based on thorough job analysis remains unclear.

Job analysis is also an important factor influencing the effectiveness of other selection methods such as assessment centres and psychometric tests. In assessment centres, the effectiveness of the exercises in predicting job performance is limited by the extent to which they represent the performance content and behavioural requirements of the job they are designed to sample. In practice, the standard of assessment centre can vary from organisation to organisation:

> Because properly designed and applied ACs work well, it does not mean that anything set up and run with the same name is equally good. A lot of so-called ACs in the UK use badly thought-out exercises and inadequately trained assessors; they probably achieve little other than to alienate candidates, who are usually quick to spot their shortcomings.　　　(Fletcher, 1993: 46)

The same can be said of tests which are only relevant if the behaviours and attitudes they measure are those necessary for effective job performance. Additional problems are also associated with the use of tests. Both the British Psychological Society (BPS) and the Institute of Personnel and Development (IPD) have issued codes of practice on the use of tests which stress that the tests should only be used by people who are properly trained in their administration and assessment and that feedback should be given to candidates 'by people who are not only qualified in the use of tests but also skilled in the feedback process' (IPD, 1995: 29). The guidelines also make it clear that 'test results alone should not be used as the sole basis for decision-making' (IPD, 1995: 28) as tests are designed to provide the basis for in-depth discussion during the interview process. However, a survey conducted by Newell and Shackleton (1993) found that, although companies used trained personnel to administer tests, the majority did not always give feedback of results to candidates and some were using the tests to make definitive judgements about people. This latter point is also supported by the findings from the IRS survey (1991b), referred to earlier in this section, which reported that 3% of respondents considered test results as the main selection method.

Parties involved in selection

A number of different people may be involved in the recruitment and selection process: internally, they could include personnel specialists, line managers, supervisors and team members; externally, they could include agencies, consultants and even customers. Personnel specialists have traditionally held a key role in the process but, as human resource issues are increasingly being devolved to line managers, this role is changing from 'direct involvement in shortlisting, interviewing and control and administrative procedures . . . towards provision of specialist advice, guidance and training and evaluation of selection effectiveness' (Torrington and Hall, 1995: 229). This shift in responsibility is frequently supported by the personnel function; at Heinz, personnel officers provide training and support materials to help line managers undertake recruitment activities (Torrington and Hall, 1995: 191).

Consultants may be used to provide specialist knowledge and expertise which is lacking in an organisation. This is particularly relevant in the use of psychometric tests; Newell and Shackleton (1993) found that organisations with no internally trained staff used consultants for the administration and interpretation of tests. However, it is also applicable to more traditional approaches to selection; Storey (1992) reported an increased use of consultant-provided packages which 'offer a method, and the training support, to improve the selection process without abandoning the interview – indeed these programmes retain the interview at centre stage' (p. 99).

Employment agencies have traditionally been used in the recruitment and selection of both temporary and permanent workers, but changing circumstances, especially the growth in fixed-term and temporary contracts, may lead to a greater reliance on them in the future.

Third-party selection is not necessarily confined to consultants or employment agencies; some organisations involve their customers in the process. For example, Southwest Airlines 'flies some of its best customers to Dallas and involves them in the flight attendant hiring process, believing those who are in contact with front line employees probably know best what makes a good employee' (Pfeffer, 1995: 34). Although this is not yet common practice in the UK, it may be the next logical step from the use of 'mystery customer' reports for assessment of employee performance.

INTERNATIONAL PERSPECTIVES ON RECRUITMENT AND SELECTION

Labour markets

The size of national and regional labour markets varies considerably in the major countries of the world (see Table 6.2).

The composition of the labour force, particularly the skills and experiences available, is as important as its size. The number of skilled managers available is particularly crucial. As Sterling Health discovered when recruiting in Central and Eastern Europe, even when technical and educational bases were sound, it was difficult to obtain the desired business skills, particularly in marketing, sales, finance and administration (Smith, 1995).

Throughout the European Union, free movement of labour means that recruiters can search beyond their national borders for the best candidates in what many see as a single labour market. However, mobility is not yet high between member countries and practices are still constrained by variations in direct state involvement in recruitment and the need for worker involvement. In France and Portugal, for example, workplace collective agreements can regulate the recruitment procedure by insisting on internal advertising of vacancies.

In Japan, regular 'core' employees have traditionally been viewed as the most valuable asset. Lifetime employment has been a shared aim of both employer and employee, and organisations depend heavily on the internal labour market to fill promotion opportunities. The initial choice of recruit, particularly graduates, is therefore critical. Rather than relying on an open labour market, Japanese graduate recruiters, reluctant to deal with strangers and preferring to build up contacts over time, have traditionally recruited once a year from universities and colleges, with professors playing a dominant role. Social science, law and humanities graduates will be expected to enter administrative roles and

TABLE 6.2
National labour markets by size

Country	Millions of employees
China	400
United States	120
Japan	60
Mexico	60
Germany	56
France	25
Great Britain	25
South Korea	16
Canada	12
Australia	7
Sweden	4

Source: Adapted from Schuler and Jackson (1996: 68).

are asked to apply directly to employers. A set of interviews (seeking potential, ability, balanced personality and moderate views), background checks from private investigators and the company entrance examination are the selection techniques. Technical appointments from technical disciplines rely far more heavily on the recommendations of the professor, with whom good relations have been cultivated. Little emphasis is placed on final grades; employers prefer to recruit from a chosen (usually prestigious) university and gaining a place through entrance examination to the university plus professor recommendation is deemed a sufficiently rigorous test of suitability (Schuler and Jackson, 1996).

'Special workers' represent the second tier of employment status found in Japanese society and include full- and part-time women, mid-career recruits (often possessing highly specialised skills), temporary workers and foreigners. Discriminated against in terms of job security, reward, training opportunities, etc., these 'special workers' provide the flexibility required in the employment system where one group has near lifetime security of employment. The open labour market is more apparent for these workers, though again organisations develop links with schools, subcontractors, subsidiaries and retrenching firms. There is little tradition of 'poaching' from competitors, even in the market for 'special workers', but the women within this group are particularly vulnerable to economic recession and there are far fewer recruitment opportunities for them (Hollingshead and Leat, 1995).

Infrastructure and government support

The national level of education (and its infrastructure), emphasis on vocational and professional training, the cultural values and status attached to acquiring work-related skills and knowledge, and the degree of economic and other support given by national and regional authorities to the establishment of work opportunities can vary from country to country. The attraction of the UK to Asian, particularly Japanese, companies is partially based on the support given by national and regional government and assistance with costs. Fujitsu, for example, was one of several multinationals attracted to County Durham in the early 1990s as part of a development programme funded jointly by the EU and local public interest groups.

Government regulations and legislation

In addition, there may be government requirements regarding the employment of foreigners and immigration. Under current Mexican law, for example, no more than 10% of a foreign company's employees may be non-Mexican (Schuler and Jackson, 1996).

Other legislation may affect recruitment practice. US organisations have to comply with equal employment laws, especially in respect of affirmative action plans which are designed to ensure proportional and fair representation of qualified employees on the basis of race, colour, ethnic origin, sex and disability, and which are necessary to be considered for the majority of federal contracts and where past discrimination has been judged to have occurred. In addition, many organisations voluntarily establish such plans.

Culture of the individual country

Recruitment and selection at an international level have to take account of a variety of cultural differences which are based on national identities, conditioning, political and legal systems, extent of individualism, power distance, uncertainty avoidance and division of roles based on gender. A more thorough discussion of these is found in Chapter 16.

The culture of an individual country has a strong influence and its perceived 'toughness' leads Tirbiorn (quoted in Dowling and Schuler, 1990) to suggest that India/ Pakistan, South-East Asia, the Middle East, North Africa, East Africa and Liberia pose particular difficulties for the Western expatriate. One problem is a lack of realisation that there is no universal organisation model:

> Much of the world still runs its organisations on a model of human relationships that is more akin to the traditional family than the functionally organised, formal, vision led type of organisation prevalent in the US and North West Europe.
>
> (Hall, 1995: 22)

Additional problems may exist in recruiting particular groups of workers. For example:

> While there are many successful female expatriates working in the region, several organisations would not consider choosing a woman for an assignment where they may have to deal directly with government officials or negotiate with existing or potential joint-venture partners.   (Edkins, 1995: 34)

Foreign ownership of large organisations

The practices of recruitment and selection in individual countries may be influenced by foreign ownership of larger organisations. In Australia there is a relatively high incidence of foreign multinational ownership, coupled with a relatively small number of large organisations which account for the employment of nearly a quarter of the workforce (Hollingshead and Leat, 1995). A similar situation is increasingly to be found in Spain where foreign ownership of large organisations is now common. The probability of recruitment and selection practices reflecting organisational rather than national values increases if the culture of the organisation is stronger than that of the host country, or if host nationals are less involved in the recruitment and selection activity.

Recruitment methods

Within Europe the methods most frequently used to attract suitable candidates are newspaper advertising, the state employment service (especially for non-managerial positions), employment agencies and more informal methods such as word of mouth and speculative applications. While the state employment service has a monopoly on placement of all labour in Germany and in public services in Belgium, the use of private recruitment agencies (though not in Germany and Spain) and executive search and selection consultants is becoming increasingly popular. However, the extent of differences in the use of recruitment methods within European countries is sufficiently great to suggest that no single best way of recruiting in Europe exists.

Within the USA the methods of recruitment are very similar to those established in the UK, although the 'blind' advertisement where organisation name and/or salary offered are omitted is more popular and there appears to be an increased likelihood of employees becoming liable to fees on placement by private agencies.

By contrast, in some countries one of the main sources of recruits is through relatives, friends or acquaintances of existing employees. This nepotistic approach is found in varying degrees throughout the world, the key consideration being the extent to which this may affect employee relations, equal opportunities, etc.

> In . . . certain parts of Africa, *where* you studied is not as important as *who you know*, and the people you know may be more important than *what you know*.
>
> (Langtry, 1994)

Selection process and techniques

International similarities in selection methods are discussed in Robertson and Makin (1993), who present a summary of results from studies of selection practice in six (mainly European) countries (see Table 6.3).

The data illustrates that the use of interviews is widespread in all countries covered by the results, the use of references and recommendations is high in the UK (and to some extent the Netherlands), and that graphology is used by over 50% of the French sample and by less than 5% of other countries represented.

TABLE 6.3

Percentage use of selection methods in six different countries

Method of selection	UK	France	Germany	Israel	Norway	Netherlands	All
Interviews	92	97	95	84	93	93	93
References/recommendations	74	39	23	30	–	49	43
Cognitive tests	11	33	21	–	25	21	22
Personality tests	13	38	6	–	16	–	18
Graphology	3	52	–	2	2	24	13
Work sample	18	16	13	–	13	5	13
Assessment centres	14	8	10	3	10	–	8
Biodata	4	1	8	1	8	–	4
Astrology	–	6	–	1	–	–	2

Source: Robertson and Makin (1993).

Recruitment in multinational organisations and international joint ventures

It is becoming increasingly important to understand international differences in recruitment and selection.

> Almost without exception, faced with mature 'developed' markets, major companies are turning to Eastern Europe and Asia as the source of their future growth. If they fail to find ways to work in these very different cultures, the most significant opportunities of the next 20 years will be lost to them.
>
> (Hall, 1995: 25)

How do international differences affect organisations wishing to recruit and select people to work in a variety of international contexts? Hendry (1995) lists five general issues brought about by the increasing internationalisation of business which are relevant for the consideration of recruitment and selection:

- an increasing number of managers and professionals are affected by internationalisation
- certain competencies and skills are at a premium
- managerial teamwork and learning is a critical process
- the management of international careers has increased in importance
- organisational culture is a key issue (as it is in UK recruitment and selection).

What are the competencies and skills that are in demand?

Apart from possessing the technical competence to carry out the requirements of the position effectively, language competence is deemed to be one of the key requirements in international recruitment, although many organisations will provide training and development opportunities rather than insist on potential recruits possessing this at the start of the selection process. General international awareness has been found to be useful in successful placements, as has an individual's ability to amend his or her personal behaviour to fit with cultural requirements.

> It is critical that expatriates selected to work in Russia have the right personal profile. Cultural sensitivity is always important, but never more so than in a country where there is such immense pride.
>
> (Pottinger, 1995: 35)

Approaches to recruitment

Four distinct approaches can be identified for recruitment in multinational companies. Each implies different patterns of control over the 'overseas activities' which in turn have varying impacts on the probable career development of those affected:

- *Ethnocentric*, where all key positions are filled by nationals of the parent company. This is a typical strategy employed in the early days of the new subsidiary, and suggests that power, decision making and control are maintained at parent headquarters.
- *Polycentric*, where host country nationals fill all key positions in the subsidiary. Each subsidiary is treated as a distinct national entity, though key financial targets and investment decisions are controlled by parent headquarters, where key positions remain with parent country nationals.
- *Regiocentric*, where decisions will be made on a regional basis (the new subsidiary will be based in one country of the region), with due regard to the key factor for success of the product/service. For example, if local knowledge is paramount, host country nationals will be recruited; if knowledge of established product is the key factor, parent

country nationals are likely to be targeted, though anyone from the geographic region would be considered.

● *Geocentric*, where the 'best people' are recruited regardless of nationality for all parent and subsidiary positions, e.g. a national of a country in which neither the parent nor subsidiary is based could be considered. This results in a thoroughly international board and senior management and is uncommon.

Organisational considerations

Without international experience opportunities for individuals to develop career paths appear increasingly limited. However, problems arise with high levels of expatriate failure rates, which Tung (in Dowling and Schuler, 1990) discovered to be between 25 and 40%, rising to 70% in developing countries and also higher with US nationals than those from Europe or Japan. To some extent these failures can be seen to emphasise the difficulties in moving from working in one culture to another. In addition, the costs of internationally relocating an individual and his or her family are considerable and Harvey (in Dowling and Schuler, 1990) estimates them to approach three times the base salary plus relocation expenses in some cases.

Specific training and preparation become vitally important to ensure that such relocation is effective, with likely interventions being individual manager visits to the proposed host country (plus family on occasions); language and cross-cultural training for manager and family; and briefing by both host country and in-house representatives.

The relative imbalance of salary costs between parent country nationals and other recruits (especially when the subsidiary is based in a less developed country) and the problems of perception that this can cause are other issues which have to be addressed.

ISSUES IN RECRUITMENT AND SELECTION

Strategic fit

> All definitions of human resource management agree on one point: that there must be a link between a firm's strategy and the deployment and utilization of the human resource. Quite what that link is, where it is realized and how it is developed, are separate matters. (Purcell, 1995: 63)

Corporate strategy can be defined from a classical perspective, implying 'a senior management activity, involving directing the organisation towards some goal or goals' (Legge, 1995). Much of the literature in the 1980s focused on business lifecycles, competitive advantage and strategic management styles (see Legge, 1995 for a comprehensive review), with a strategic HRM framework, including strategies for recruitment and selection, reflecting the proposed corporate strategic approach.

More recently, however, a wider perspective has emerged which recognises diversity in terms not only of whether strategy is planned or emerges, but also of differing preferred outcomes and the fact that profit maximisation may not be the overriding concern of all organisations (Whittington, 1993).

> Clearly the feasibility and even what is meant by integrating HRM policies with business strategy will very much depend on which perspective on strategy and strategy-making one adopts.
>
> (Legge, 1995: 103)

Purcell (1989) perceived three levels of strategic decision making:

- First order, comprising the long-term direction of the firm and the scope of its activities, markets and locations.
- Second order, the internal operating procedure and the relationship between parts of the firm.
- Third order, including the strategic choice in human resource management.

Strategic choice in human resource management was decided after first- and second-order strategic decisions had been made. Operational issues and the conduct of HRM, including recruitment and selection, were even further downstream.

As highlighted in the introduction to this chapter, the notion of strategic recruitment and selection, i.e., of a system linking recruitment and selection to the overall organisational strategy and aiming to match the flow of personnel to emerging business strategies, is suggested in the HRM literature. Instead of being seen as a separate, marginal task, recruitment and selection would become a key, integrated task (Storey, 1992). In organisations practising 'hard' HRM, recruitment and selection would involve the widescale use of external labour markets, with non-employment options being openly canvassed and emphasis placed on people employed in jobs, rather than careers. In those adopting a 'soft' approach, external recruitment would be focused on those whom the organisation thought suitable for career development and around whom the internal labour market would evolve. Selection from this internal market would be accomplished through rigorous appraisal and development systems.

Evidence to date on the take-up of these two distinctly different positions is limited. Storey (1992) found that in 12 of 15 surveyed organisations selection was seen as an integrated key task, and that in all 15 general managers were coming to the fore in terms of the management of HRM. Only 3, however, had initiatives which Storey felt could be labelled 'integrated'. Tyson (1995) found evidence in his survey of hard and soft strategies. However:

> Although all the companies in our sample subscribed to the idea that HR policies should be coherent and be totally integrated with business strategy there were few who could claim to have achieved such a state of perfection.
>
> (Tyson, 1995: 108)

Problems with strategic fit

Problems with the perceived need to investigate the integration of corporate, human resource and recruitment strategies include:

- the difficulties in agreeing what corporate strategy is and the extent to which it is perceived as planned rather than emergent;
- the chosen corporate strategy may be in conflict with the traditional culture and custom of the organisation and in particular of its existing policies. If one accepts Purcell's suggestion that HR policies are third level, a time lag is implied between the strategic decision making and implementation of policies deemed necessary to achieve corporate objectives;

- a financial investment in training and development may also be required to bring about the required changes in practice (towards the increasing use of either form of labour market) and this may sit uncomfortably with some organisations' objectives of cost-minimisation;
- pressures to recruit and select in the short term to meet urgent needs via the external labour market may conflict with the chosen longer-term strategy to develop and utilise internal labour markets.

Fit with other HR strategies and policies

For an effective contribution to the achievement of corporate objectives, it is argued that HR policies need to 'fit together'. In particular, recruitment and selection strategies can be seen to have strategic links with human resource planning, conditions of employment, reward management and training and development. Lack of fit, such as internally focused recruitment and selection strategies being coupled to non-existent training and development opportunities for the individuals likely to be active in that market, or strategies designed to resource the organisation with strong team players coupled with individual incentive schemes, can be avoided through careful planning. However, this planning may be complicated as many of the techniques in these areas (psychometric tests, individual and group performance reward mechanisms, interactive training interventions) are still being developed and are dependent on the commitment of all those involved with them to be effective.

Recruitment with selection

In a similar way, there is a need to ensure recruitment and selection policies fit together cohesively. Advertisements that sell a dynamic, state-of-the-art organisation can lead to disappointment if they are followed by lacklustre administration, poor selection practice and lengthy delays. Recruits attracted to organisations 'selling' care, commitment and partnership will be disappointed by selection procedures which fail to sell the same message.

Comment

Those who make critical decisions about recruitment and selection strategy would do well to bear in mind that decision making about employment at this stage is a two-way process. Potential employees in both external and internal labour markets will, like the organisations who seek to recruit them (or their like), be looking for something better – better job security, better promotional opportunities, better terms and conditions of employment, a more interesting job, a better boss – and only the individual can define 'better'. Certainly the economic environment and the individual's perception of his or her value in the labour market affect which of these are paramount at any point, but organisations seeking increased motivation and commitment from their employees might also ask what they are offering in return. The use of the external labour market for recruitment can suggest to employees that their best opportunities for advancement lie with using that market. They may not always become active within it at a time convenient to the employer.

New organisational initiatives

There are a number of recent developments in organisational structure and practice which could influence recruitment and selection. This section concentrates on three particular initiatives: total quality management (TQM), business process re-engineering (BPR) and the flexible firm.

Total quality management

A standard definition of TQM is provided by Oakland (cited in Egan, 1995):

> Total Quality Management is an approach to improving the effectiveness and flexibility of businesses as a whole. It is essentially a way of organising and involving the whole organisation; every department, every activity, every single person at every level. For an organisation to be truly effective, each part of it must work properly together, recognising that every person and every activity affects, and in turn is affected by, others   (Egan, 1995: 98)

This approach is founded on three basic principles:

- *customer orientation*, i.e. the belief that customer satisfaction is the primary goal for all organisational activities and the recognition of both internal and external customers;
- *process orientation*, i.e. that activities performed in an organisation can be broken down into processes (each of which has a customer), which are linked together to form 'quality chains';
- *continuous improvement* of products and processes to satisfy customer requirements (Hill and Wilkinson, 1995).

Common features of TQM are quality teams, autonomous work units and individual responsibility for quality control.

Several HR processes are critical to the success of TQM, including extensive training, advanced career development systems, reward based on quality measures, 360-degree feedback, flattened management hierarchies and selection systems which are not only geared towards the skills and behaviours that support TQM but also involve all the relevant stakeholders in decision making (Flood *et al.*, 1996). Different skills may be required for the effective implementation of a total quality programme: 'for instance, if TQ ultimately depends on the self responsibility for quality it may require a different type of employee with different educational and training levels to meet these skills' (Collard, 1992). Recruitment methods may be designed to ensure that people understand the true nature of the job for which they are applying; for example, Diamond Star Motors (a Chrysler Mitsubishi company) uses 'a realistic preview video that warns applicants that they must learn several jobs, change shifts, work overtime, make and take constructive criticisms and submit a constant stream of suggestions in improving efficiency' (Flood *et al.*, 1996: 20). Selection processes may also differ in a TQM environment in that teams may play a significant role in the selection of new team members or, more radically, family members of applicants may be evaluated as part of the selection process to ensure total commitment to the organisation (Flood *et al.*, 1996). These examples are from the US and it may be that the impact of quality initiatives is less in the UK, where evidence suggests that quality management is more 'partial' than 'total' (Hill and Wilkinson, 1995).

Business process re-engineering

BPR was embraced with considerable enthusiasm in the early 1990s as many companies believed that it 'was the route to future commercial success in a highly competitive market environment' (Mumford and Hendricks, 1996: 23). As a technique, it has some similarities with TQM in so far as it focuses on organisational processes and customer satisfaction, but the key difference is that it is 'aimed at radical rather than continuous improvement' (Egan, 1995). BPR consists of:

> a radical scrutiny, questioning, redefinition and redesign of businesses processes with the aim of eliminating all activities not central to the process goals . . . and automating all activities not requiring human judgmental input, or facilitating that judgement at reduced cost.   (Thomas, 1994: 29)

The case is often made for the close links between BPR and job design. For example, before re-engineering Mutual Benefit Life's handling of policy applications was a multi-step clerical process which involved twenty people in five departments and had a turnaround time of between five and ten days. After re-engineering, applications were handled by single 'case managers' supported by workstations running expert systems linked to databases, and turnaround time averaged two to five days and capacity doubled (Thomas, 1994). This type of job enrichment through up-skilling and the broadening of job definitions is not an automatic result from BPR; Thomas (1994) also cites the example of Argos where re-engineering has been accompanied by deskilling of staff. In either case one could reasonably assume that the reorganisation of work will be supported by an assessment of new skills and behaviours required and the design of appropriate recruitment and selection methods to assess these.

Unfortunately, the biggest impact which BPR appears to have had on recruitment and selection in practice is to reduce the need for it. The re-engineering at Mutual Benefit Life described above involved the elimination of 100 positions, BPR at Ford allowed the company to reduce headcount by 75% (Thomas, 1994) and the story is similar elsewhere. BPR's critics claim that this focus on reduced costs through staff cuts rather than improvement through reorganisation is partly to blame for its lack of success to deliver the competitive advantage it promised (Mumford and Hendricks, 1996).

The flexible firm

Flexibility is a key component of HRM and much has been made of the emergence of the flexible firm (described in Chapter 3). As with the other initiatives described here, one could assume that the emphasis on flexibility would alter the skills and behaviours required and therefore influence the recruitment and selection techniques in use. For example, if core workers are the ones undertaking the functional flexibility, then one could expect that more sophisticated selection methods would be applied to assess attributes such as potential, trainability and propensity to teamwork, whereas less time and resources may be allocated to the selection of periphery workers who are to be perceived as dispensable and interchangeable. However, the lack of empirical evidence to support the existence of the flexible firm makes this a largely academic proposition.

While there has been steady growth in the use of non-standard forms of work (part-time, temporary, self-employment) there is little indication that this reflects significant change in the utilisation of labour other than in the public sector. The Employers' Labour

Use Strategy Survey (ELUS) found that the main reasons employers gave for using non-standard forms of work were traditional ones such as catering for tasks requiring limited time inputs, matching staffing levels to fluctuations in demands for products and services (e.g. seasonal workers) and meeting the preference of some groups in the labour force for non-standard work (McGregor and Sproull, 1992). This latter point is supported by Labour Force Survey data which found that the majority of part-time workers did not want full-time work and less than half of employees in temporary jobs had taken them because they could not find full-time work (Beatson, 1995). This suggestion of 'business as usual' could imply that, at a practical level, there has been very little change in the approach to recruitment and selection.

There is still little evidence to support the existence of widespread functional flexibility; survey data suggests that the movement towards flexibility is gradual and tends to be concentrated in quite narrow sectors (IDS, 1990). However, where it does exist it does seem to have an impact on recruitment and selection practices; the same survey noted that 'full flexibility remains almost entirely confined to greenfield sites where companies are extremely choosy about whom they recruit' (IDS, 1990: 1). The emphasis on work reorganisation, multi-skilling and teamworking is frequently supported by increased investment in training and selection. For example, the selection methods used by Nissan to appoint 22 supervisors 'who would be capable of meeting performance requirements in terms of flexibility, teamworking and quality consciousness' involved the investment of over 100 manager-days (Goss, 1994: 43).

Ethical issues in recruitment and selection

Ethical issues arise in both recruitment and selection. To a large extent these reflect the prevailing attitudes *within the society/societies* in which an organisation operates, but differences in ethical stance also reflect the judgement and positioning chosen by major stakeholders and determined by traditional values inherent *within the organisation itself.*

Recruitment

Providing equality of opportunity for a diverse number of groups is considered important by certain organisations. However, opportunity to apply for positions can be restricted through the (sometimes unnecessary) insistence on previous experience, prior development of skills and competencies. 'Glass ceilings' exist in internal labour markets for women and minority groups. In addition, in the case of third-party recruitment, particularly executive search, opportunities to widen the net of opportunity can be forestalled, with organisations frequently relying on the knowledge and networking of one consultant to deliver the chosen recruit, often to a specification that ensures that the status quo is maintained. The existence of such practices suggests a society in which those in power tolerate them as rational and sound and there is insufficient groundswell of opinion from society at large to insist on change. As Goss remarks:

> if HRM is to be serious in its commitment to the development of all human resources, it may need to face the challenge of wider patterns of social inequality. This means looking not only at disadvantage, but also addressing the issue of who benefits from the status quo. (Goss, 1994: 173)

In a similar vein, multinational and other organisations which have overseas supplier links have to consider their ethical position in relation to both employment conditions and more particularly targeted recruits. (To some extent a similar discussion can be held concerning UK organisations where work is subcontracted to UK agencies and suppliers, on relatively poor conditions of employment, or where schoolchildren (already 'fully employed') are recruited in lieu of those already available in the external labour market.)

The business decision may be difficult and involve weighing up important economic, financial, marketing and public relations considerations. While component costs may fall dramatically through the use of overseas subsidiaries and suppliers, bad publicity and loss of sales can ensue through dealing with an organisation where, for example, child labour is found to be extensively used, employment conditions unsafe or recruits paid less than a living wage. Model codes of practice are being promoted by organisations (e.g. Levi Strauss), industry associations (e.g. British Toy and Hobby Association), worker federations (e.g. International Textile, Garment and Leather Workers) and charities (e.g. Oxfam), but for many organisations this will continue to prove an ethical dilemma (Littlefield, 1996).

Selection

Issues in selection revolve around areas of individual rights, the potential for abuse of power, issues of control and social engineering, use of certain assessment techniques and the issues of equality of opportunity implied in the above.

Ownership of information and the individual's right to privacy

The ownership of information about an individual passes in the recruitment and selection process from the individual to the organisation. While some protection is afforded by data protection legislation, the organisation is perceived to increase its power over the individual by holding such information and by accumulating more through the use of various selection techniques, the findings of which are not always made known to the candidate.

An individual's right to privacy is further challenged by the impact of scientific developments assisting the prediction of future employment scenarios. For example, tests now exist to enable organisations to conduct pre-employment medicals which predict the future health of candidates. In the USA, where most health costs are met by the employer, discrimination against apparently healthy people who have, or may have, a genetic defect is common and health insurance has been found to be refused to one in five of this group (Thatcher, 1996). With genetic tests becoming increasingly available, will UK employers use them to screen out anyone who they see as potentially expensive to employ? As certain genes occur more frequently in particular ethnic groups, the issues become even more complex.

Issues of conformance and control

Apart from questions about the technical effectiveness of various selection techniques, ethical questions remain about their use at all:

> there are questions of a more ethical nature surrounding personality tests. It has been suggested that organisations have no right to seek to control access to jobs on the grounds of individual personality. (Goss, 1994: 47)

Professional guidance in the area of occupation testing exists, both in specific codes of practice (IPD, 1995) and as part of ethical codes of practice within large organisations in particular. However, recent research has shown that, while selectors claim to recognise the rights of those being tested (for example to be fairly treated, to expect counselling where needed, to confidentiality of data, to know the tests used are valid, etc.), these rights are not upheld in practice (Baker and Cooper, 1996). In addition, questions remain to be asked as to whether:

- the selection of one personality type leads to a weakened 'inbred' profile of employees in organisations, incapable of thinking or acting in original ways when the situation demands;
- an organisation has the right to enforce a unitarist perspective on employees – some selection tests, for example, are designed to filter out those who are 'prone to unionise' (Flood *et al.*, 1996), others to ensure potential employees' values are in line with the organisation's thinking:

> At the heart of these concerns seems to be a fear about the totalitarian possibilities of work organisations and the role of personality profiling as a form of 'social engineering' for corporate conformity.   (Goss, 1994: 47)

Against the spirit of equality of opportunity?

The use of interviews as a selection method has long been open to criticism on the grounds of subjectivity and stereotyping. Using biodata as a basis of selection has potential for misuse, discriminating against individuals and groups on factors which are beyond their control (education, social class, gender, for example). Graphology attracts criticism for similar reasons of social stereotyping and superficial judgements.

Concerns exist too about competency-based recruitment and selection systems, where there is often a need to screen a large number of applicants quickly through the identification of a few core competencies, which either have already developed (e.g. initiative), indicate long-term prospects for success (achievement motivation) or can be assessed using behavioural interviewing, based on past events (Hooghiemstra, 1992). Designed to eliminate those with little work experience on which judgement could be made (recent college graduates etc.) such selection places those without work experience in the typical 'catch 22' situation and aims to reduce rather than increase the labour market pool.

In conclusion, the use of both external and internal labour markets and associated selection techniques can raise ethical issues. Poaching experienced people from the external labour market implies an approach that only 'takes' from society, in terms of the costs of education and previous training and development, and the higher wages needed to attract applicants can be perceived as inflationary.

Alternatively one can view the use of the internal labour market through in-house development around organisation-based objectives as somewhat menacing, tying the individual closely to the organisation from which escape is perceived as increasingly difficult and from which the measurement of individual freedom, and the quality of the conditions of employment enjoyed, become more difficult to judge.

CONCLUSIONS

The focus of this chapter has been the extent to which HRM and the current climate challenge the traditional approach to recruitment and selection, so to conclude we have to address the question 'have there been significant changes in recruitment and selection?'. The answer is yes – and no. In support, there is undoubtedly evidence to suggest that some organisations have taken a greater interest in selecting the 'right' people in terms of behaviour and attitudes and have adopted more sophisticated techniques in order to do so. Likewise, a number of organisations have adopted radically new approaches in line with organisational initiatives such as total quality management and business process re-engineering. Against this, one can balance evidence that traditional forms of recruitment and selection, e.g. press advertising, interviews and references, continue to dominate current practice, suggesting that little has changed.

The current state of recruitment and selection is complex because of the number of external and internal factors which can influence the process. As discussed, external factors include legislative requirements, labour market conditions, the national approach to training and education and the state of the economy; internal factors include the size and structure of the organisation, the type of work undertaken, the use of technology and management philosophy. Further complexity is added by international differences and the growth of multinational enterprises. These factors are constantly changing and the environment in which the recruitment and selection process operates is uncertain and increasingly ambiguous. What is certain, however, is that there is no universal solution to this complexity – no 'one size that fits all' – and this is how one can account for the co-existence of both new and traditional approaches to the recruitment and selection of employees. Organisations tend to adopt a pragmatic approach to the attraction and selection of employees based on their assessment of current and future conditions and their response to the four critical questions outlined in this chapter. Thus, not only will one find differences in approaches between organisations but also within organisations depending on the level of vacancies and organisational requirements.

Although the focus of this chapter has been on recruitment and selection from an HRM perspective, readers should not infer that the traditional approach is seen as a 'poor relation'. The chapter has explored the extent to which the current climate has challenged the assumptions underpinning the systematic approach, but this does not mean that all the developments can be endorsed wholeheartedly. On the positive side, the use of more sophisticated techniques can be seen as an attempt to improve the quality of the selection decision, through increasing objectivity and reducing the scope for bias and prejudice. On the other hand, the emphasis on personality and behavioural characteristics can be used to create and manipulate a workforce that is more amenable to management initiatives. Ethical considerations continue to be important and care must be taken in the use of these techniques, particularly in the handling of the increasingly large amount of information that can be gained about prospective workers.

The most appropriate recruitment and selection techniques will continue to be those which balance the requirements of organisations with those of current and prospective employees, and the approach adopted is likely to be determined, at least in part, by external circumstances. If predictions about the demise of 'jobs for life' and the growth of 'portfolio careers' are true, then the experience of recruitment and selection may become an increasing feature in all our lives regardless of the techniques involved.

SUMMARY

The chapter began with five key objectives. Here we revisit those objectives and outline our key responses:

● The role of recruitment and selection has become increasingly important in an HRM environment. A key development is the increased emphasis on attracting and selecting people with the personal characteristics and attitudes believed necessary for effective organisational performance, rather than a requirement for particular work experience and acquired skills. Organisations which claim to practise HRM have tended to adopt more elaborate methods of selection, including the use of psychometric tests and assessment centre techniques. In spite of this, there has been little decline in the importance of traditional methods such as interviews and references in the selection decision.

● A number of external and internal factors affect the recruitment and selection process and influence the type of techniques adopted. External factors can be located at local, national and international level and may include legislation and government policy, training and education, labour markets and the state of the economy. Internal factors may include the size, structure, culture, ownership and history of organisations and their financial situation. The complexity of these factors and the range of their influences suggests that there is unlikely to be one best approach to recruitment and selection, but rather a number of options from which appropriate choices can be made.

● There is wide variety in the effectiveness of various recruitment and selection techniques. Although the use of selection methods with higher predictive validity is increasing, the most popular methods are not necessarily the most effective in terms of differentiating between people who can do the job and people who cannot. Effectiveness can also be considered in the light of equal opportunity issues, such as the extent to which applications from previously under-represented groups are encouraged and the existence of checks that selection methods are 'fair', i.e. only discriminate on job ability. In measuring effectiveness organisations need to balance the costs involved in the actual process against the costs of choosing the wrong person.

● Although countries cannot be viewed as homogenous units, variations in recruitment and selection practices can be partially determined by international differences. Influences can include the national infrastructure and level of state involvement, custom and practice, key competencies and skills required and cultural characteristics.

● A number of contemporary issues are pertinent to recruitment and selection policy and practice. The first is the concept of business strategy and the need for recruitment and selection policies to be compatible with corporate goals and with other HR initiatives, implying that recruitment and selection needs to be considered as an integrated process rather than a marginal, *ad hoc* activity. The second issue concerns the varying impact of different organisational initiatives such as TQM and BPR on recruitment and selection activity, in particular the resultant changes in the quality and quantity of human resources required in contemporary organisations. Finally, consideration is given to ethical issues in recruitment and selection, in particular issues surrounding equality of opportunity, ownership of information and questions of conformance and control.

ACTIVITY

ShopCo is a nationwide high street retailer which recruits 100 graduates each year into trainee management positions. A recent decision has been taken to adopt a competency-based approach to recruitment of this group and the following 11 competencies have been identified as key indicators:

- analytical ability
- achievement motivation
- business awareness
- competitiveness
- effective decision making
- drive and enthusiasm
- leadership
- oral communication
- written communication
- planning and organising
- interpersonal sensitivity.

EXERCISES

1 Design an assessment centre which will provide at least two pieces of evidence for each competency outlined, detailing the exercises, timing and potential costs involved.

2 In addition, outline the training requirements for assessors.

QUESTIONS

1 To what extent is equality of opportunity in recruitment and selection ever possible?

2 What are the advantages and disadvantages of devolving the recruitment and selection process to line managers?

3 'An organisation's desire to discover as much information as possible about prospective candidates in order to make sound selection decisions outweighs an individual's right to privacy.' Discuss.

EXERCISES

1 Multinational recruitment and selection

'During the start-up phase McDonald's drew upon the expertise of their employees from around the world. Initially there were 45 Western managers from various countries. This number was gradually reduced, so that by March 1991 only seven remained. All these managers were replaced by Soviets . . .

[For crew members] Moscow McDonald's placed a single advertisement in Moscow newspapers soliciting applications. By the fall of 1989, when they started to hire workers they had received approximately 27 000 applications. This created a base for selecting the most energetic, motivated, intelligent and outgoing young men and women . . . following its practice widely used in its US restaurants, McDonald's decided to hire Moscow teenagers as crew members . . . people with no prior work experience. The idea was that it would be easier to instil McDonald's work habits and standards in people who knew no other way to work than to disabuse people of unacceptable work habits they had acquired in previous jobs.' (Vikhanski and Puffer, 1993: 104)

'All the Directors at Nissan UK are British, except the finance director and deputy managing director. None of the managers are Japanese. Only a handful of Japanese are to be seen in the factory, mostly specialist engineers on temporary assignment to help iron out problems in the early stages of production of the new car.' (Popham, 1992)

Discuss the extent to which these examples correspond to the patterns of recruitment and selection associated with multinational corporations, i.e. ethnocentric, polycentric, regiocentric and geocentric.

2 TQM

You are part of the HR team in a medium-sized manufacturing organisation which is currently introducing TQM. As part of this each manager is required to demonstrate how his or her function can contribute to quality improvements and you have been asked to focus on recruitment and selection.

a Outline the recruitment and selection strategy you feel is most likely to lead to quality improvements.

b Consider how this might affect recruitment and selection methods for the following job categories:

- middle managers
- team leaders
- skilled production workers
- unskilled packers
- administrative support staff.

REFERENCES AND FURTHER READING

ACAS (1983) *Recruitment and Selection*, Advisory Booklet No. 6. London: Advisory, Conciliation & Arbitration Service.

Anderson, A. H. (1994) *Effective Personnel Management: A Skills and Activity-based Approach*. Oxford: Blackwell Business.

Anderson, N. and Shackleton, V. (1993) *Successful Selection Interviewing*. Oxford: Blackwell.

Appelbaum, S., Kay, F. and Shapiro, B. (1989) 'The assessment centre is not dead! How to keep it alive and well', *Journal of Management Development*, Vol. 8, No. 5, pp. 51–65.

Arkin, A. (1995) 'Improving access to the workplace', *People Management*, 16 Nov, pp. 18–23.

Arkin, A. (1996) 'Haringey gives green light to police project', *People Management*, 7 Mar, pp. 10–11.

Armstrong, M. (1991) *A Handbook of Personnel Management Practice*, 4th edition. London: Kogan Page.

Armstrong, M. (1992) *Human Resource Management: Strategy and Action.* London: Kogan Page.

Armstrong, P. (1995) 'Accountancy and HRM', in Storey, J. (ed.) *Human Resource Management: A Critical Text.* London: Routledge.

Ashton, D. and Felstead, A. (1995) 'Training and development', in Storey, J. (ed.) *Human Resource Management: A Critical Text.* London: Routledge.

Baker, B. and Cooper, J.N. (1996) 'Beyond the rhetoric of good practice in psychological testing', paper presented to conference on Ethical Issues in Contemporary Human Resource Management at Imperial College London.

Ball, D.F., Britton, L.C. and Wright, M. (1996) 'Using co-ordination theory to improve service quality in the executive recruitment consultancy industry', paper presented to workshop on Quality Management in Services V1 at Universidad Carlos III in Madrid, April 16 1996.

Beatson, M. (1995) 'Progress towards a flexible labour market', *Employment Gazette*, Feb, pp. 55–66.

Beaumont, P. (1993) *Human Resource Management: Key Concepts and Skills.* London: Sage.

Blanksby, M. and Iles, P .(1990) 'Recent developments in assessment centre, theory, practice and operation', *Personnel Review*, Vol. 19, No. 6, pp. 33–44.

Blinkhorn, S., Johnson, C., Fletcher, C., Mackenzie Davey, D., Dulewicz, V., Smith, M., Lewis, C. and Handyside, J. (1991) 'Personality tests: the great debate', *Personnel Management*, Sept, pp. 38–42.

Britton, L.C., Clark, T.A.R. and Ball, D.F. (1992) 'Executive search and selection: imperfect theory or intractable industry?', *The Service Industries Journal*, Vol. 12, No. 2, pp. 238–250.

Collard. R. (1992) 'Total quality: the role of human resources', in Armstrong, M. (ed.) *Strategies for Human Resource Management: A Total Business Approach.* London: Kogan Page.

Curnow, B. (1989) 'Recruit, retrain, retain; personnel management and the 3 Rs', *Personnel Management*, November, pp. 40–47.

Dearing, R. (1996) *Review of Qualifications for 16 to 19-year-olds.* Hayes: School Curriculum and Assessment Authority Publications.

Dickens, L. (1994) 'Wasted resources? equal opportunities in employment', in Sisson, K. (ed.) *Personnel Management: A Comprehensive Guide to Theory and Practice in Britain.* Oxford: Blackwell.

Dowling, P.J. and Schuler, R.S. (1990) *International Dimensions of HRM.* Boston: PWS-Kent.

Edkins, M. (1995) 'Making the move from West to East', *People Management,* 29 June, pp. 34–37.

Egan, C. (1995) *Creating Organizational Advantage.* Oxford: Butterworth-Heinemann.

Falconer, J. (1990) 'Courage of convictions', *Personnel Today*, 24 July, pp. 22–23.

Fletcher, C. (1993) 'Testing times for the world of psychometrics', *People Management*, Dec, pp. 46–50.

Flood, P.C., Gannon, M.J. and Paauwe, J. (1996) *Managing Without Traditional Methods: International Innovations in Human Resource Management.* Wokingham: Addison-Wesley.

Fowler, A. (1992) 'How to plan an assessment centre', *PM Plus*, Dec, pp. 21–23.

Golzen, G. (1988) 'Job ads that do their job', *Sunday Times Appointments*, 9 October.

Goss, D. (1994) *Principles of Human Resource Management.* London: Routledge.

Guest, D. and Mackenzie Davey, K. (1996) 'Don't write off the traditional career', *People Management,* 22 February, pp. 22–25.

Hackett, P. (1991) *Personnel: The Department at Work.* London: IPM.

Hall, K. (1995) 'Worldwide vision in the workplace', *People Management*, May, pp. 20–25.

Hall, L. (1989) 'On the register', *Personnel Today*, 10 October, pp. 29–31.

Harrison, K. (1995) 'Actions do speak louder than words', *People Management*, 13 July, pp. 34–35.

Harrison, R. (1993) 'Developing people for whose bottom line?', in Harrison, R. (ed.) *Human Resource Management: Issues and Strategies*. Wokingham: Addison-Wesley.

Harrison, T. (1995) *Employment Law*, 2nd edition. Sunderland: Business Education Publishers.

Hendry, C. (1995) *Human Resource Management: A Strategic Approach to Employment*. Oxford: Butterworth-Heinemann.

Herriot, P. (1989) *Recruitment in the 1990s*. London: IPM.

Hill, S. and Wilkinson, A. (1995) 'In search of TQM', *Employee Relations*, Vol. 17, p. 4.

Hollingshead, G. and Leat, M. (1995) *Human Resource Management: An International and Comparative Perspective on the Employment Relationship*. London: Pitman Publishing.

Hooghiemstra, T. (1992) 'Integrated management of human resources', in Mitrani, A., Dalziel, M. and Fitt, D. *Competency Based Human Resource Management: Value-driven Strategies for Recruitment, Development and Reward*. Paris: Les Editions d'Organisation.

IDS (1990) *Flexibility at Work*, Study No. 454, March.

IDS (1992) *Employment Law Supplement: Recruitment*, IDS Brief No. 64, April.

IDS (1995) *Assessment Centres*, Study No. 569, January.

Iles, P. and Salaman, G. (1995) 'Recruitment, selection and assessment', in Storey, J. (ed.) *Human Resource Management: A Critical Text*. London: Routledge.

IPD (1995) 'The IPM Code on Recruitment', in *The IPD, IPM and ITD Codes of Practice*. London: IPD, pp. 17–24.

IRS (1991a) 'The state of selection 1', *Recruitment and Development Report 16*, April.

IRS (1991b) 'The state of selection 2', *Recruitment and Development Report 17*, May.

IRS (1991c) 'The state of selection 3', *Recruitment and Development Report 19*, July.

IRS (1994) 'Ensuring effective recruitment' and 'Random selection', *Employee Development Bulletin 51*, March.

Johnson, G. and Scholes, K. (1989) *Exploring Corporate Strategy: Text and Cases*. Hemel Hemstead: Prentice Hall International.

Kandola, B. (1995) 'Firms must rework race bias policies', *Personnel Today*, 25 Oct, p. 20.

Keep, E. (1989) 'Corporate training strategies: the vital component?', in Storey, J. (ed.) *New Perspectives on Human Resource Management*. London: Routledge.

Langtry, R. (1994) 'Selection', in Beardwell, I. and Holden, L. (eds) *Human Resource Management: A Contemporary Perspective*. London: Pitman Publishing.

Legge, K. (1995) *Human Resource Management: Rhetorics and Realities*. Basingstoke: Macmillan Business.

Lewis, C. (1985) *Employee Selection*. London: Hutchinson.

Littlefield, D. (1996) 'Danger at work in the supply chain', *People Management*, 4 April, pp. 22–27.

Mackenzie Davey, D. (1982) 'Arts and crafts of the selection process', *Personnel Management*, August, pp. 24–27.

McGregor, A. and Sproull, A. (1992) 'Employers and the flexible workforce', *Employment Gazette*, May, pp. 225–234.

Mayo, A. (1995) 'Economic indicators of HRM', in Tyson, S. (ed.) *Strategic Prospects for HRM.* London: IPD.

Mitrani, A., Dalziel, M. and Fitt, D. (1992) *Competency Based Human Resource Management: Value Driven Strategies for Recruitment, Development and Reward.* Paris: Les Editions d'Organisation.

Mumford, E. and Hendricks, R. (1996) 'Business process re-engineering RIP', *People Management,* 2 May, pp. 22–29.

Munro Fraser, J. (1954) *A Handbook of Employment Interviewing.* London: Macdonald & Evans.

Newell, S. and Shackleton, V. (1993) 'The use and abuse of psychometric tests in British industry and commerce', *Human Resource Management Journal,* Vol. 4, No. 1, pp. 14–23.

North, S.-J. (1992) 'Ex-offenders silent', *Personnel Today,* 10 November, p. 6.

Overell, S. (1996) 'Reed wins Channel 5 retuning assignment', *People Management,* 21 March, p. 15.

Overell, S. (1996) 'Disability code takes a beating', *People Management,* 21 March, p. 7.

Paddison, L. (1990) 'The targeted approach to recruitment', *Personnel Management,* November, pp. 54–58.

People Management (1995a) 'NHS trust reform plans criticised', 23 Feb, p. 11.

People Management (1995b) 'Secretarial staff in short supply', 13 July, p. 11.

People Management (1995c) 'Barclays denies child labour plan', 24 Aug, p. 9.

People Management (1995d) 'Women rise to the top', 30 Nov, p. 5.

People Management (1996) 'Temp managers slot in', 18 April, p. 10.

Personnel Management (1994) 'Barclays considers redundant workers to solve staffing problem', Sept, p. 21.

Personnel Today (1995) 'Race plan targets managers', 25 October, p. 1.

Pfeffer, J. (1995) *Competitive Advantage Through People.* Boston: Harvard Business School Press.

Popham, P. (1992) 'Turning Japanese', *The Independent Magazine,* 12 September, pp. 25–29.

Pottinger, J. (1995) 'Expats steer joint venture', *People Management,* 29 June, p. 35.

Purcell, J. (1989) 'The impact of corporate strategy on human resource management', in Storey, J. (ed.) *New Perspectives on HRM.* London: Routledge.

Purcell, P. (1995) 'Corporate strategy and its link with human resource management strategy', in Storey, J. (ed.) *Human Resource Management: A Critical Text.* London: Routledge.

Robertson, T.R. and Makin, P.J. (1993) 'Selection methods and their usage', *Recruitment, Selection and Retention,* Vol. 2, p. 1.

Rodger, A. (1952) *The Seven Point Plan.* London: National Institute of Industrial Psychology.

Rubin, J. (1993) 'Don't forget the Engine Room', in Armstrong, G. (ed.) *View from the Bridge.* London: IPD.

Sadler, P. and Milmer, K. (1993) *The Talent-Intensive Organisation: Optimising your Company's Human Resource Strategies.* Special Report No. P659. London: The Economist Intelligence Unit.

Schuler, R.S. and Jackson, S.E. (1996) *Human Resource Management: Positioning for the 21st Century,* 6th edition. St Paul: West Publishing Company.

Select Committee on the Anti-discrimination Bill (House of Lords) (1972/3) *Second Special Report from the Select Committee.* London: HMSO.

Sisson, K. (1993) 'In search of HRM', *British Journal of Industrial Relations,* Vol. 31, No. 2, pp. 201–210.

Sisson, K. (1995) 'Human resource management and the personnel function', in Storey, J. (ed.) *Human Resource Management: A Critical Text.* London: Routledge.

Smith, L. (1995) 'Good business skills scarce', *People Management*, 15 June, p. 27.

Social Trends (1995) London: HMSO.

Social Trends (1996) London: HMSO.

Sparrow, P. and Hiltrop, J-M. (1994) *European Human Resource Management in Transition.* New York: Prentice Hall.

Storey, J. (1992) *Developments in the Management of Human Resources.* Oxford: Blackwell.

Storey, J. and Sisson, K. (1993) *Managing Human Resources and Industrial Relations.* Buckingham: Open University Press.

Storey, J., Ackers, P., Bacon, N., Buchanan, D., Coates, D. and Preston, D. (1994) *Human Resource Management Practices in Leicestershire: A Trends Monitor.* Loughborough: Training and Enterprise Council in Association with Loughborough University Business School.

Thatcher, M. (1996) 'Contending with a genetic time bomb', *People Management*, 7 March, pp. 30–33.

Thomas, M. (1994) 'What you need to know about business process re-engineering', *Personnel Management*, Jan, pp. 28–31.

Torrington, D. and Hall, L. (1995) *Personnel Management: HRM in Action.* London: Prentice Hall.

Twigg, G. and Albon, P. (1992) 'Human resource development and business strategy', in Armstrong, M. (ed.) *Strategies for Human Resource Management: A Total Business Approach.* London: Kogan Page.

Tyson, S. (1995) *Human Resource Strategy: Towards a General Theory of Human Resource Management.* London: Pitman Publishing.

Tyson, S. and Fell, A. (1991) *Evaluating the Personnel Function*, 2nd edition. Cheltenham: Stanley Thornes.

van Zwanenberg, N. and Wilkinson, L. (1993) 'The person specification – a problem masquerading as a solution?', *Personnel Review*, Vol. 22, No. 7, pp. 54–65.

Vikhanski, O. and Puffer, S. (1993) 'Management education and employee training at Moscow McDonald's', *European Management Journal*, Vol. 11, No. 1, pp. 102–106.

Walker, L. (1996) 'Instant staff for a temporary future', *People Management*, 25 January, pp. 34–35.

Whitehill, A.M. (1991) *Japanese Management: Tradition and Transition.* London: Routledge.

Whitfield, M. (1996) 'Britain grapples with changing job market', *People Management*, 8 February, pp. 10–11.

Whittington, R. (1993) *What is Strategy and Does it Matter?* London: Routledge.

PART 2 CASE STUDY

French promise to make Hoover pay dear

David Buchan in Dijon discovers why the switching of
jobs to Scotland touched such a raw nerve

"IT IS social dumping, and it's shameful," says a striker, stamping his foot yesterday outside Hoover's Longvic plant which is to lose most of its jobs to a more compliant Scottish workforce.

"We've nothing against the Scottish workers, just against Maytag (Hoover's owner) and the British government for not signing the European Social Charter," adds another worker. "The big lesson of the Hoover affair," says Mr Jean-Claude Quentin, secretary general of the local Force Ouvrière trade union, "is that social dumping does not necessarily come from south-east Asia, but from among us Europeans."

What is social dumping? Mr Richard Rankin, marketing director of Hoover Europe, says he is not sure. For him, Hoover has simply made a business decision to stem the red ink on its European operations by shifting all its vacuum cleaner production to its Cambuslang plant near Glasgow. This will entail the loss of 650 jobs at Longvic on Dijon's outskirts, but Hoover says it will save 25 per cent on its costs by having all vacuum cleaners made in one place.

What is clear to everyone in France, as Mr Rankin ruefully acknowledges, is that "we have upset – and provoked a powerful reaction from – the French government, and we will have to deal with it."

That is an understatement. Egged on by all political and union leaders, the French government has asked the European Commission to investigate whether Hoover was unfairly or illegally bribed with social and financial concessions, into shifting production to Cambuslang, and made clear that it will make Hoover pay dear for its decision.

It is not clear whether Hoover will be able to carry out its decision. The government, for example, says the Hoover redundancies will be among the first to be affected by the new law sponsored by Mrs Martine Aubry, the labour minister who is also the daughter of Mr Jaques Delors, the European Commission president. This law requires employers to produce alternative employment plans for redundant workers, and that without the approval of the government, and effectively of the unions, redundancies will be legally invalid.

Why has the Hoover affair struck such a raw French nerve? It is not just that unemployment is bumping up against the 3m threshold less than two months before a general election, or that it is another sign that high interest rates and a strong exchange rate are killing the French economy. Other foreign companies are quitting France for lower cost venues, including the UK, with far less fuss.

What has aroused French fury is the public concessions made by Scottish workers to win 400 extra jobs at Cambuslang. These include limited period contracts for new workers, constraints on their right to strike, a freeze on regular pay this year and cuts in overtime pay rates, flexible working time and practices and the introduction of video cameras on the factory floor.

To the French, this is a clear case of the competitive undercutting of worker pay and standards to attract investment, or social dumping as it is catchily known on the continent.

Not surprisingly, the Hoover management contests this. Mr Rankin says the company's decision to shift to Scotland was made on its calculation that it would cut costs by a quarter and that this calculation does not include the Cambuslang workers' concessions.

The other key factor, says Mr Rankin, was the fact that social charges amount to 40 per cent of the payroll in France and only 15 per cent in the UK. Actual pay rates in the two countries are similar, as was the government aid offered.

Why then did Hoover press its Cambuslang workers so hard? "We have responsibilities to our customers to produce as efficiently as possible, to our shareholders to save their money, and to our workforce," Mr Rankin says. "You may not think we have exercised this last responsibility in regard to the Dijon workforce, but we have in regard to Cambuslang and our total 3,600 workforce in Europe."

But Hoover never sought similar concessions from its French workforce. Why not? "The savings were so great in shifting to Cambuslang that the Dijon workforce would have to have made enormous concession to offset these," Mr Rankin says. Hoover would not, in any case, have found the Longvic workers pliable. Mr Jean-Marie Groscolas, distribution manager at Longvic and leader of the protesting workforce, says they offered to freeze their pay this year, but would have flatly refused any other concessions.

Alternative job prospects for the Hoover workers are not promising. The Burgundy region jobless rate has risen sharply in the last year.

None the less, its prosperity remains well above that of the Glasgow region. That economic gap explains much of the different attitude of the workers of Scotland and Burgundy.

Source: Financial Times, 4 February 1993.

The Hoover 'job poaching' case has infuriated France.
FT writers examine the implications

Social dumping: hardly an open and shut case

The arguments about switching jobs between countries are not so simple,
writes **David Goodhart, Labour Editor**

THOMSON Consumer Electronics, the state-owned French group, last year rationalised its European operations by closing its Ferguson television plant in Gosport, southern England, with the loss of more than 3,000 jobs.

The event scarcely merited a mention at the time on either side of the Channel. But some British trade unionists are now recalling it, as the acrimonious dispute over the transfer of work from Hoover's plant in eastern France to Scotland rumbles on.

This sort of cross-channel sniping reflects how completely relations between British and French unions have broken down.

But it also illustrates the difficulty facing unions in dealing with the ebb and flow of jobs across the European Community as a wave of recession-induced restructuring begins.

Following the British opt-out from the Maastricht social chapter, and the subsequent devaluation of sterling, many continental European workers and politicians fear that capital will be sucked into the "Hong Kong of Europe" at their expense.

The propaganda material of Britain's inward investment agencies certainly stresses the relative freedom of Britain's "hire and fire" workplace culture and the relatively low labour costs.

But the reality is that neither the opt-out nor the devaluation were factors in Hoover's decision to shift some jobs to Scotland.

Britain has always had a rela-

tively unregulated labour market which used to be qualified by strong trade unions, now considerably weakened. British wages are also low by EC standards, but the real advantage enjoyed by the UK is low non-wage labour costs.

These are usually about 15 per cent of wage costs compared with more than 50 per cent in many other EC countries. That is partly because the UK pays for health care through general taxation while employers have to bear a large part of health care costs in several continental countries.

This clearly was just one factor in Hoover's decision but it is not something that the social chapter directly affects.

Mr William Foust, president of Hoover Europe, said yesterday that non-wage labour costs of only 10 per cent in Scotland, compared with 45 per cent in France, was a factor in the company's decision. But the decision was also influenced by the fact that the Scottish plant had spare capacity.

Hoover's decision is unlikely to herald any significant increase in Britain's comparative advantage. It is based on long-established factors which Hoover, a particularly footloose US investor in Europe, has often found attractive in the past.

Britain has always been the most popular destination for new international investment within the EC (see chart) and that has not changed markedly in recent years.

Until German car workers started to worry about the Japanese car industry investing in Britain, new

international investment has not been the source of much tension, and is unlikely to be much of an issue over coming years as that new investment will not be plentiful.

On beggar-my-neighbour" industrial restructuring within the EC, where one country loses jobs and another gains them, things are more complex.

But as the Thomson Electronics case illustrates, Britain has often lost out in such restructuring precisely because it is easier and cheaper to close plants in Britain than in most EC countries.

In the Thomson case at Gosport the average redundancy payment was £7,000 compared with £47,000 in Spain. In Holland, Spain and Germany agreement on a redundancy package has to be reached with workplace representatives before closure is allowed.

If, for example, British Leyland Daf decides to keep open its Belgian and Dutch plants and close only its British plant, as seemed possible yesterday, that differential cost of redundancy is likely to be a factor.

Britain also loses out from its relatively low skill base and poor educational standards, one reason behind Ford's decision to switch more of its R&D work to Germany.

The "social dumping" theory that capital will flow to areas where labour is cheapest and least protected, dragging down labour standards elsewhere, has scarcely materialised in the EC because low wages are usually cancelled out by low productivity.

Source: Financial Times, 4 February 1993.

1 Analyse the Hoover decision from a competitive labour-market perspective and a radical perspective.

2 To what extent is the Hoover decision a vindication of British government policies to deregulate the labour market?

3 What do you consider to be the implications of the Hoover case for the practice of HRM?

INTRODUCTION

One of the main outcomes of the spread of human resource management (HRM) over the past decade has been increasing attention to what has become labelled 'human resource development' (HRD). However, like HRM, this is a term which is often used loosely and, indeed, poses problems of definition. Stewart and McGoldrick (1996: 1), who write authoritatively in the HRD area, suggest that the question of what it is 'is not yet amenable to a definitive answer', but offer the following 'tentative' definition:

> Human resource development encompasses activities and processes which are *intended* to have impact on organisational and individual learning. The term assumes that organisations can be constructively conceived of as learning entities, and that the learning processes of both organisations and individuals are capable of influence and direction through deliberate and planned interventions. Thus, HRD is constituted by planned interventions in organisational and individual processes.
>
> (Stewart and McGoldrick, 1996: 1)

HRD is seen as having a significant part to play in achieving and maintaining the survival and success of an organisation. Managers have not only to acquire appropriate people to resource it, as discussed in Part 2, they also need to train and develop them, for the following reasons:

- New employees are, in some respects, like the organisation's raw materials. They have to be 'processed' to enable them to perform the tasks of their job adequately, to fit into their work group and into the organisation as a whole, but in a manner that respects their human qualities.
- Jobs and tasks may change over time, both quantitatively and qualitatively, and employees have to be updated to maintain adequate performance.
- New jobs and tasks may be introduced into the organisation, and be filled by existing employees, who need redirection.
- People need training to perform better in their existing jobs.
- People themselves change their interests, their skills, their confidence and aspirations, their circumstances.
- Some employees may move jobs within the organisation, on promotion or to widen their experience, and so need further training.
- The organisation itself, or its context, may change or be changed over time, so that employees have to be updated in their ways of working together.
- The organisation may wish to be ready for some future change, and require (some) employees to develop transferable skills.
- The organisation may wish to respond flexibly to its environment and so require (some) employees to develop flexibility and transferable skills.

● Management requires training and development. This will involve training for new managers, further development and training for managers, management succession and the development of potential managers.

As the chapters that follow show, changes in the context of the organisation increase the need to train and develop its members to ensure effectiveness, quality and responsiveness. Because these changes are not being made once and for all, employees are having to adjust to continuous change and their managers are having to pay greater attention to HRD than ever before. However, HRD does not take place in an organisational vacuum. To be effective, it presupposes effective selection, effective supervision and an appropriate management style, the opportunity to transfer learning to the workplace, career paths and promotion possibilities, appropriate incentives and rewards. It also presupposes some degree of planning and linkage to the strategy of the organisation, and is, therefore, implicit within organisation development. Indeed, for the organisation that espouses 'human resource management' and addresses the human resource implications of its strategic positioning, training and development become investment decisions and operations that are as important as investments in new technology, relocation or entry into new markets.

This, however, is solely an organisational view of HRD; it can be viewed much more broadly than this. In Asian and African countries, for example, HRD encompasses government initiatives and policies to improve knowledge and skills to enhance economic growth. As Rao (1995: 15) states:

> at the national level HRD aims at ensuring that people in the country live longer; live happily; free of disease and hunger; have sufficient skill base to earn their livelihood and well being; have a sense of belongingness and pride through participation in determining their own destinies. The promotion of the well being of individuals, families and societies provides a human resource agenda for all countries the world over.

We therefore need to recognise the role that the HRD that takes place in organisations plays in the overall economy and hence in the well-being of society. At the same time, it can have considerable significance in the lives of individuals and, indeed, can only be effective when the individual is actively engaged in it. It is for this reason that Part 3 looks beyond and beneath organisational HRD, examines both its national context and the basic processes that constitute it and, where appropriate, invites readers to reflect on their own learning and development.

Chapter 7 identifies the need for HRD in the organisation, and considers the basic processes of learning and development involved and the ways in which they can be facilitated in the organisation. This chapter underpins the subsequent chapters of Part 3 and introduces some of the concepts they use. Chapter 8, new to this second edition, sets out the national framework for vocational education and training, with some international comparisons, which is the context within which organisational HRD operates. Chapter 9 focuses on training, the processes and activities intentionally undertaken within organisations to enable employees to acquire, improve or update their skills. Chapter 10 examines the development, of managers, noting both their formal and informal modes of development, and relates management to organisation development.

As these chapters show, HRD takes several forms: the development of the employee both as an individual and as an employee; development of the employee by the employer or by self; training; education; career development; group development; staff development; professional development, management development and, even more widely, organisation development. These differ not only in terms of the hierarchical levels of the organisation but also in purpose and form. While recognising these different kinds of training and development in organisations, we have to understand that they are not necessarily easily distinguishable in practice, and that some activities contribute to more than one form of development. There is necessarily some overlap between the chapters of Part 3. Thus specific training to enable an employee to perform more effectively now can also contribute to that person's overall career development. What is intended as instrumental by the employer may be construed as empowering by the individual. This raises the question about who owns the individual's development, one of the controversial issues addressed in Chapter 7.

The basic terms used in these chapters are common enough, but often used without great thought and sometimes interchangeably, although they are, indeed, closely interrelated. Harrison (1992: 4) provides us with a helpful starting point by making the following connections:

> Development is the all-important primary process, through which individual and organisational growth can through time achieve its fullest potential. Education is the major contributor to that process, because it directly and continuously affects the formation not only of knowledge and abilities, but also of character and of culture, aspirations and achievements. Training is the shorter-term, systematic process through which an individual is helped to master defined tasks or areas of skill and knowledge to pre-determined standards. There needs to be a coherent and well-planned integration of training, education and continuous development in the organisation if real growth at individual and organisational levels is to be achieved and sustained.*

REFERENCES

Harrison, R. (1992) *Employee Development*. London: IPD.

Rao, T.V. (1995) *Human Resource Development*. New Delhi: Sage.

Stewart, J. and McGoldrick, J. (eds) (1996) *Human Resource Development: Perspectives, Strategies and Practice*. London: Pitman Publishing.

*This extract is taken from *Employee Development* by Rosemary Harrison and is reproduced with permission of the publishers, The Institute of Personnel and Development, IPD House, 35 Camp Road, London SW19 4UX.

LEARNING AND
DEVELOPMENT

Audrey Collin

OBJECTIVES

To examine the reasons why human resource managers need to
understand the processes of learning and development.

●

To identify the characteristics of the learner.

●

To indicate the outcomes of learning.

●

To outline the process of learning.

●

To discuss the concept and process of development.

●

To outline the processes of lifespan, career and continuing
professional development.

●

To examine the organisation as a context for learning and
development.

●

To identify how the organisation can facilitate learning
and development through action learning, mentoring, and the
development of the learning organisation.

●

To pose some controversial issues for reflection and discussion.

●

To offer some activities which encourage readers to review their
own learning and development.

●

INTRODUCTION

Why do human resource managers need to understand learning and development? A brief examination of what organisations are now looking for in their members will help you recognise the need to understand these basic processes in order to harness them effectively for the organisation.

In today's 'information society', according to Morgan (1988: 7), managers will have to:

> . . . find ways of developing and mobilizing the intelligence, knowledge, and creative potential of human beings at every level of organization . . . become increasingly skilled in placing quality people in key places and developing their full potential. It will become increasingly important to recruit people who enjoy learning and relish change and to motivate employees to be intelligent, flexible, and adaptive.

Kanter (1992: 39) expresses this as the need to develop people as a key lever in 'human resource management', and makes the connection between the learning of organisational members and the survival and effectiveness of the organisation. Her 'model company statement' is a response to this need:

> Our company faces competitive world markets and rapidly changing technology. We need the flexibility to add or delete products, open or close facilities, and redeploy the workforce. Although we cannot guarantee tenure in any particular job or even future employment, we will work to ensure that all our people are fully employable – sought out for new jobs here and elsewhere. We promise to:
>
> - Recruit for the potential to increase in competence, not simply for narrow skills to fill today's slots.
> - Offer ample learning opportunities, from formal training to lunchtime seminars – the equivalent of a month a year.
> - Provide challenging jobs and rotating assignments that allow growth in skills even without promotion to 'higher' jobs.
> - Measure performance beyond accounting numbers and share the data to allow learning by doing and continuous improvement.
> - Retrain employees as soon as jobs become obsolete.
> - Recognise individual and team achievements, thereby building external reputations and offering tangible indicators of value.
> - Provide three-month educational sabbaticals or external internships every five years.
> - Find job opportunities in our network of suppliers, customers, and venture partners.
> - Tap our people's ideas to develop innovations that lower costs, serve customers, and create markets – the best foundation for business growth and continuing employment.

According to Barrow and Loughlin (1993: 198), abilities that organisations will be expecting of their employees are:

- a high level of education, possibly up to degree level, so that employees can operate new technology, understand the contribution of their role to the company and take decisions appropriate to their jobs;
- the ability to learn new skills and adapt to changing circumstances – by taking responsibility for their own learning, keeping their skills up to date, learning new processes;
- the ability to work in organisations with flatter structures and fewer layers of management – to work without supervision, set own objectives, monitor own performance, correct failures;
- the ability to manage the interface with customers and between departments, requiring a good level of interpersonal skills;
- the ability for problem solving, creative thinking about future possibilities, and contributing their own unique ideas.

Barrow and Loughlin (1993: 198) describe how one organisation, Grand Metropolitan Foods Europe, is confronting the challenges of the 1990s with a training strategy that will give employees of all levels access to qualifications in business and management; the programmes focus on learning, self-development and developing others.

In those organisations that adopt a 'human resource management' perspective, development and training are not the Cinderellas they have typically been in the majority of British organisations. Rather, their budgets, their mode of operation, the attention paid to their quality and effectiveness are treated as areas of considerable organisational significance.

> Toyota [Derbyshire] has put the same thoroughness into training as it has into recruitment. It spent £7.2 million and 100 'man-years' on off-the-job training before production started.
>
> It uses a cascade approach. The company took 350 group and team leaders on a five-week round trip to Japan, Kentucky and a third plant in Canada to absorb the Toyota philosophy and production techniques and learn the firm's approach to training. It then trained team members.
>
> Maintenance workers were sent on specially commissioned courses at local colleges and an Astra training centre. They then trained on computer-controlled rigs specially commissioned by Toyota UK, which simulated production machinery. This was rounded off by on-the-job training.
>
> . . . their efforts were vindicated when a Toyota quality engineer from group headquarters approved the first cars off the line as being up to Japanese standards. (Pickard, 1993: 19)

The regular employee development section of the news round-up in *People Management*, the magazine for human resource professionals, provides many illustrations of the way in which organisations are developing their human resources (see also Littlefield and Welch, 1996). They are also extending their activities to developing the skills of both suppliers and customers in order to improve the quality of their 'supply chain' (Rothwell, 1992). In order to be effective, therefore, human resource managers need to understand the processes of learning and development, what influences them and how they may be facilitated. This is the purpose of this chapter, which thus forms a foundation for Chapters 8, 9 and 10.

Defining learning and development

To understand the processes of learning and development and use this understanding to good effect in developing people and their organisations, you have to be able to think clearly about the concepts you are using. The concepts 'learning' and 'development' are frequently used loosely and even interchangeably. The following definitions will enable you to distinguish them and understand the relationship between them.

Learning is:

> . . . a process within the organism which results in the capacity for changed performance which can be related to experience rather than maturation.
>
> (Ribeaux and Poppleton, 1978: 38)

It is not just a cognitive process that involves the assimilation of information in symbolic form (as in book learning), but also an affective and physical process (Binsted, 1980). Our emotions, nerves and muscles are involved in the process, too. Learning leads to change, whether positive or negative for the learner. It is an experience after which an individual 'qualitatively changed the way he or she conceived something' (Burgoyne and Hodgson, 1983: 393) or experienced 'personal transformation' (Mezirow, 1977). Learning can be more or less effectively undertaken, and it can be more effective when we pay it conscious attention.

Development, however, is the process of becoming increasingly complex, more elaborate and differentiated, by virtue of learning and maturation. In an organism, greater complexity, differentiation among the parts, leads to changes in the structure of the whole and to the way in which the whole functions (Reese and Overton, 1970: 126). In the individual, this greater complexity opens up the potential for new ways of acting and responding to the environment. This leads to the opportunity for even further learning, and so on. Learning, therefore, contributes to development. It is not synonymous with it but development cannot take place without learning.

The outcomes of a person's learning and development are the way they think, feel and interpret their world (their cognition, affect, attitudes, overall philosophy of life); the way they see themselves, their self-concept and self-esteem; and their ability to respond to and make their way in their particular environment (their perceptual-motor, intellectual, social, interpersonal skills). In the section on the nature of the learner you will find the description that Daloz (1986: 24–26) gives of development. He likens it to a journey that starts from the familiar world and moves through 'confusion, adventure, great highs and lows, struggle, uncertainty . . . toward a new world' in which 'nothing is different, yet all is transformed'; 'its meaning has profoundly changed'. Learning and development, therefore, are significant experiences for individuals and for organisations.

Learning and development are processes that we all experience, active processes in which we all engage: we do not have learning and development done to us. However, we rarely pay conscious attention to them and so may not fully understand them. This chapter, therefore, addresses you, the reader, directly and in this section and elsewhere invites you to draw upon your own experience in order to understand and make use of the issues that it will discuss.

The pursuit of quality and flexibility

Quality

Quality is achieved through continuous improvement in the processes, products and services of the organisation: Deming's 'journey of never-ending improvement' (Hodgson, 1987: 41). It calls for the transformation of the management of people 'so that employees become involved in quality as the central part of their job' (Sheard, 1992: 33). Indeed, the drive for quality (closely followed by organisational restructuring) was given as the most common motive for the increased investment in training reported in a *Personnel Management Plus* survey (Saggers, 1994).

The main features of total quality management (TQM) are giving satisfaction to customers, both internal and external; continuous improvement in process and product; employee involvement, usually through teamwork; management by data and facts (Brown, 1992; see also Chapter 14). It, therefore, demands an organisation-wide culture that emphasises the importance of attitudes and the generation of enthusiasm and commitment to quality from top to bottom of the organisation (Fowler, 1992). An example of this is given by Wibberley (1992), writing of the introduction of TQM at the German multinational Bosch's UK greenfield site at Cardiff, where the statement of corporate values is intended 'to motivate new employees, guide our actions in putting in place policies and procedures and develop a unique Bosch, Cardiff culture' (Wibberley, 1992: 32). The statement includes a commitment to 'training and development to achieve continuous improvement in quality, productivity and individual skills'; 'being a responsive organisation, which not only encourages flexibility, teamworking and team development but which also focuses on the individual in terms of accountability, recognition and reward.'

The striving for quality, therefore, makes great demands for extensive learning and development in organisations, and not just at the level of training employees in task skills and in the operation of quality procedures. This can be seen in Wibberley's description (1992: 32) of how Bosch approaches TQM:

> This is the restless searching for continuous improvement, the 'little steps' forward every day, that the Japanese call *kaizen*. This incorporates the notion that total quality is a 'race without a finish' and harnesses the innate desire to make progress that we believe is in all our employees. We have spent much time explaining to employees that everyone has a responsibility to participate in continuous improvement, and people respond enthusiastically to this approach.

Morgan's (1988: 21–22) description of the method of operations called just-in-time (JIT) working also intimates the deep-seated nature of the learning and development required by this element of the quality approach. It transforms the 'patterns of management and control':

> Four-hour margins [in supply of stock] allow little room for error or prolonged decision-making, and spread responsibility and control throughout the system . . . These systems call for a new type of involvement in the work process and dissolve the traditional relations between workers and managers. Every person in the system becomes a kind of manager and quality controller.

Flexibility

In a complex, changing environment and with increasing global competition, organisations need to be flexible: 'the business outlook is uncertain and the response must be flexibility. The prerequisite for flexibility is a highly-skilled body of staff', states a human resource director (in Crofts, 1990: 16). Moreover, in today's information society, they must employ people with the appropriate new skills to be knowledge workers. Organisations are, therefore, seeking competitive advantage through the use and development of their human resources (who at the same time have increased expectations about their job content and quality of life). As Syrett and Lammiman (1994) argue, this means that they need to invest in their peripheral as well as their core workers (Atkinson and Meager, 1986; see also Chapter 3), especially since these 'flexible workers' are growing in number (White, 1996).

The widened repertoire of skills that employees use is frequently referred to as multi-skilling. There are many examples of this. Barry (1988) reports how one company used multi-skilling to rectify the skills imbalance that resulted from restructuring and redundancy. It initiated a major programme of training and development for its fitters and electricians (Barry, 1988: 46) to 'introduce cross-trade competency, increasing core trade skills, significantly increasing flexibility and developing a team approach in the engineering department'. The programme called for attitude change, improved communication and team-building; it also involved the supervisors. It was carried out through college and in-house training, including residential weekends and work-based projects; it led to City and Guilds accreditation of this multi-skilling. Crofts (1990: 17) reports on another multi-skilling programme that followed on company restructuring and rationalisation after a merger:

> The aim was to end up with core employees fully trained to carry out all aspects of production, changeovers and maintenance. Quality would be improved through their own corrective action rather than by inspection.

Arkin (1995a) outlines another scheme which led to accreditation by S/NVQs (see Chapter 8).

The introduction of multi-skilling has implications for more than just narrow task skills training or, indeed, the industrial relations and reward scheme issues considered by the two companies above. It creates the need for an even more fundamental flexibility and hence for even greater attention to the learning and development needs of employees:

> One of the first hurdles facing the organisation before any multi-skilled training could take place was to achieve a major shift in management style. A new breed of participative manager was needed who was prepared to involve employees and foster their creativity. It required greater delegation, a lot of information-giving and building up levels of trust.   (Crofts, 1990: 16)

> . . . when multiskilling is introduced, new technology has an impact not only on the skills of those directly affected by it, but also on the skills of others, and on the culture and structure of the organisation; it may even require the rethinking of concepts like motivation and careers.
>
> (Hendry and Pettigrew, 1988: 36)

The need to understand learning and development in the organisation

It will be clear from the above that organisations seeking excellence and quality, flexibility and adaptability are clustering tasks in new and flexible ways. Indeed, it is being suggested that 'jobs are disappearing' (Bridges, 1995). Whereas work had previously been packaged into jobs, Martin (1995: 20) argues, it now needs to be reconstructed into the 'competencies' needed to achieve customer satisfaction. 'The future will see a world based more on skills than on organisations' (Tyson and Fell, 1995: 45). These changes are demanding new ways of thinking and working from employees. These include the ability to:

- break down traditional barriers and work outside the definition and security of traditional job descriptions;
- develop new working relationships that modify the organisation's hierarchical structure;
- deploy and develop these personal skills to the benefit of the working group and the organisation as a whole.

According to Wisher (1994: 37), among the 'competencies that occur frequently in the most successful clusters of different organisations' are conceptual, 'helicopter' and analytical thinking. Organisations are, thus, demanding more of their employees than new or enhanced task skills. They are requiring higher order thinking skills that are not easily picked up within the constraints of existing jobs, nor even in everyday life. Moreover, it is being increasingly argued that human resource development will only become truly effective when it achieves, and is carried out within, a learning organisation (Wills, 1993):

> . . . where people continually expand their capacities to create the results they truly desire, where new and expansive patterns of thinking are nurtured, where collective aspiration is set free, and where people are continually learning how to learn together.   (Senge, 1990: 3)

> The organizations that will truly excel in the future will be the organizations that discover how to tap people's commitment and capacity to learn at *all* levels in an organization.   (Senge, 1990: 4)

However, there is a long way to go for many organisations. According to Myers and Davids (1992: 47):

> . . . workers are a resource which has not been well understood by management in the past. Blue-collar workers in particular have been regarded as a static commodity incapable of innovation and self-development. Consequently reservoirs of skill and ability remain untapped.

The subject of this chapter, therefore, is of enormous significance: not only for human resource managers and organisational members, but also for their organisations and the societies of which they are a part. And this is not solely the humanistic idealism of the middle-class academic or the so-called 'chattering class'; though, as the section on controversial issues reminds us, we need to be aware of the implications of a humanistic orientation. Cooley (1987: 139) reports on how the Lucas Aerospace Combine Shop

Stewards' Committee as long ago as 1975 challenged their organisation to retain its highly skilled workforce by moving into markets for 'socially useful' products:

> What the Lucas workers did was to embark on an exemplary project which would inflame the imagination of others. To do so, they realised that it was necessary to demonstrate in a very practical and direct way the creative power of 'ordinary people'. Further, their manner of doing it had to confirm for 'ordinary people' that they too had the capacity to change their situation, that they are not the objects of history but rather the subjects, capable of building their own futures.

Human resource managers, therefore, need to understand the processes and nature of the learning of the higher order and other task skills in order to be able to facilitate the learning and development of individual employees and, ultimately, the organisation itself. It is the purpose of this chapter to explain these.

THE NATURE OF THE LEARNER

> Learning organizations are possible because, deep down, we are all learners. No one has to teach an infant to learn. In fact, no one has to teach infants anything. They are intrinsically inquisitive, masterful learners who learn to walk, speak . . . Learning organizations are possible because not only is it our nature to learn but we love to learn.
>
> (Senge, 1990: 4)

Learning is a natural process in which we all engage. It is not just a cognitive activity and it affects the person as a whole. This section will first note these points and identify some barriers to learning and development. It will then reflect on the fact that the learners in whom we are interested in this chapter are adults. It will continue by identifying some characteristics of different classes of learners within the organisation: older workers, whose learning capacities are frequently discussed, and women, disabled people and people from ethnic minorities.

Learning and development throughout life

From birth, humans, like all animals, learn and develop, and this learning and development leads to skilful and effective adaptation to and manipulation of the environment, which is one element in a much-quoted definition of intelligence (Wechsler, 1958, in Ribeaux and Poppleton, 1978: 189). Society fosters and facilitates these activities of its members, but also channels and controls them through socialisation and education so that they yield outcomes that contribute to and are acceptable to it.

People continue learning throughout life, whether encouraged or not, whether formally taught or not, whether the outcomes are valued or not. They learn at work and at home, in their hobbies and their social lives.

> Most of us have learned a good deal more out of school than in it. We have
> learned from our families, our work, our friends. We have learned from
> problems resolved and tasks achieved but also from mistakes confronted
> and illusions unmasked. Intentionally or not, we have learned from the
> dilemmas our lives hand us daily.   (Daloz, 1986: 1)

However, although individuals have a lifetime's experience of being learners, some of
their experiences (especially those in formal educational settings) may not have been
happy ones. Although they are experienced learners, they may not necessarily be competent or confident learners.

Lifelong learning means continuous adaptation. Increased knowledge and improved
skills enlarge the individual's capacities to adapt to the environment and to change that
environment. As the systems model in Chapter 2 implies, such external changes will lead
on to further internal changes, and hence new possibilities for the individual emerge.
Moreover, these changes feed the individual's self-esteem and confidence and enhance
social status. It is the conscious promotion of this that is a major characteristic of the
learning organisation, as we can see in the various organisations referred to in the introduction to this chapter.

Learning generates far-reaching changes in the individual: learning promotes development. In his very warm-hearted and insightful book on 'the transformational power of
adult learning experiences', Daloz (1986: 24–26) draws on mythology to convey the
nature of this development:

> The journey tale begins with an old world, generally simple and uncompli-
> cated, more often than not, home . . . The middle portion, beginning with
> departure from home, is characterized by confusion, adventure, great highs
> and lows, struggle, uncertainty. The ways of the old world no longer hold,
> and the hero's task is to find a way through this strange middle land, gen-
> erally in search of something lying at its heart. At the deepest point, the
> nadir of the descent, a transformation occurs, and the traveler moves out of
> the darkness toward a new world that often bears an ironic resemblance to
> the old.
>   . . . Nothing is different, yet all is transformed. It is seen differently. . . .
> Our old life is still there, but its meaning has profoundly changed because
> we have left home, seen it from afar, and been transformed by that vision.
> You can't go home again.

We shall return to the nature of development in a later section, but meanwhile we need
to comment that the facilitation of another's learning is a moral project: it has the potential to promote changes that may have a profound effect in the other's life. This, too, has
implications for the debate about the ownership of learning, as we shall see later.

Barriers to learning and development

Mumford (1988), writing primarily about managers, identifies significant blocks to learning. They are also relevant to other learners in the organisation, as the remainder of this
chapter will demonstrate. They are given in Table 7.1.

TABLE 7.1
Blocks to learning

Perceptual	Not seeing that there is a problem
Cultural	The way things are here . . . .
Emotional	Fear or insecurity
Motivational	Unwillingness to take risks
Cognitive	Previous learning experience
Intellectual	Limited learning styles
	Poor learning skills
Expressive	Poor communication skills
Situational	Lack of opportunities
Physical	Place, time
Specific environment	Boss/colleagues unsupportive

Source: Mumford (1988: 26).

Anxiety and lack of confidence are frequently emphasised as significant impediments to learning. Barry (1988: 47), for example, notes that the considerable apprehension felt by the fitters and electricians who were returning to college after 20 years was an obstacle in the introduction of a multi-skilling programme (see p. 289). Their anxieties were dissipated once they learned that some of the tutors belonged to the same union and had the same craft background as themselves. Personality characteristics, such as an external rather than an internal locus of control (Rotter, 1966), may also make the individual less open to new learning.

The significance of other people and of the organisation as a learning environment is noted in the section on the organisation as a context for learning, together with the implications for the effective facilitation of learning and development in organisations.

Adult learners

What we know about learning and teaching derives mainly from the study of children and young people: pedagogy. The needs and experiences of adults are different: we need an androgogical model of learning (Knowles, 1984: 10–12). Knowles suggests that:

- The adult learner is self-directing.
- Adult learners have experience on which to draw and learning events need to take this into consideration. They may have developed poor learning habits, and be defensive about their habitual ways of thinking. However, their former experience is a source of self-identity, so it must be approached sensitively and with respect.
- Adults are ready to learn when they become aware that they need to know or do something to make themselves more effective: they 'do not learn for the sake of learning' (Knowles, 1984: 12). Learning experiences, therefore, have to be related to their needs and situation.

- What motivates them most are their needs for 'self-esteem, recognition, better quality of life, greater self-confidence, self-actualization' (Knowles, 1984: 12).

Human resource development has to address these needs appropriately. We shall return to them in the section on the organisation as a context for learning.

Learners in the organisation

Older workers

Older people have been widely discriminated against when seeking employment and when employed (Naylor, 1987; Dennis, 1988; Laslett, 1989; Waskel, 1991). They are commonly stereotyped as having failing cognitive and physical abilities, as being inflexible, unwilling and unable to learn new ways. However, the Carnegie Inquiry into the Third Age (Trinder, Hulme and McCarthy, 1992: 20) reports:

> . . . there does seem to be a decline in performance with age . . . but such deterioration as there is, is less than the popular stereotype . . . Except where such abilities as muscular strength are of predominant importance, age is not a good discriminator of ability to work; nor of the ability to learn.

Trinder, Hulme and McCarthy (1992) also note that performance is influenced as much by experience and skill as by age: skill development in earlier years will encourage adaptability in later life.

Although older people are 'at a disadvantage with speedy and novel (unexpected) forms of presentation', Coleman (1990: 70–71) reports little or no decline with age in memory and learning, particularly 'if the material is fully learned initially'. (We shall examine the role of rehearsal and revision in memory later in this chapter.) He goes on to cite a study in which the majority of the 80 volunteers aged 63 to 91 years learned German from scratch and in six months reached the level of skill in reading German normally achieved by schoolchildren in five years.

The experience of the do-it-yourself retail chain B & Q provides a telling example of older workers' skills, flexibility and ability to learn.

> Typically . . . the trainees B & Q are looking for are 'young people [aged 16–17], who are self-motivated, eager to learn, communicate well, are presentable and enthusiastic, and who show commitment and flexibility'.
>
> (Evans, 1992: 48)

Nevertheless, the company departed from its customary practice and staffed one store solely by people over the age of 50. It was 'an overwhelming success . . . In commercial terms the store has surpassed its trading targets' (Hogarth and Barth, 1991: 15). This trial, which B & Q intended to repeat in other stores, found these older workers willing to train, although initially reluctant to use new technology, and not requiring longer or different training from others.

These older workers demonstrate the ability to continue to learn through life; their learning will be facilitated if employers adopt appropriate approaches, which we shall examine in the section on the organisation as a context for learning.

Other classes of employees

The three classes of employees, women, disabled people, cultural and ethnic minorities, are often socialised and educated in ways that do not advantage them in labour markets or organisations; they may develop correspondingly low expectations and aspirations. Negative stereotyping of them in employment is frequently discussed (see Gallos, 1989; Thomas and Alderfer, 1989). (Little appears to have been written about disabled people in organisations, Moreton (1992) identifies the role of the Training and Enterprise Councils in providing training programmes for them, and Arkin (1995b) summarises the implications for employers of the 1995 Disability Discrimination Act.) Here we shall briefly note some aspects of their experience that will influence them as learners in the organisation: these need to be viewed in terms of the barriers to learning identified earlier.

As we identified in Chapter 2, there is now a considerable body of theory, including feminist critiques, that addresses the nature of women and their experiences in their own right, rather than as a subset of a supposed 'universal' (but often Eurocentric, middle-class male) nature. For example, Gilligan (1977: see Daloz, 1986: 134–135) argues that unlike men, who see their world as 'a hierarchy of power', women see theirs as 'a web of relationships'. The connected self interprets the environment differently, and so responds to it differently, from the separate self. These and other ways in which women may differ from men (Bartol, 1978) will influence their approach to, experience of and outcomes from learning. They may, indeed, advantage women in the development of some of the higher order skills needed in organisations.

Different cultures imbue their members with different basic assumptions about the nature of reality and the values and the roles in social life. Cultural experiences differ, and hence the accumulated experience of the members will also differ. The concept of intelligence is not culture-free. Gardner (1985: 240), who expounds a theory of multiple intelligences which include interpersonal and intrapersonal intelligence, recognises that:

> . . . because each culture has its own symbol systems, its own means for interpreting experiences, the 'raw materials' of the personal intelligences quickly get marshaled by systems of meaning that may be quite distinct from one another . . . the varieties of personal intelligence prove much more distinctive, less comparable, perhaps even unknowable to someone from an alien society.

Hence as women differ from men, so also may members of cultural and ethnic minorities have ways of learning which are dissimilar to those of the dominant culture, and also different outcomes from their learning. It is, therefore, important to assess such constructs as intelligence in as culture-fair manner as possible (Sternberg, 1985: 77 and 309), and to seek appropriate means to facilitate learning of the skills required in organisations. Learning through action may be particularly appropriate.

Understanding of and fluency with English are not the only language issues in organisations. As discussed in Chapter 2, language is ideological and can embody racism and sexism. Similarly, the construction of knowledge is a social and ideological process. Through the very nature of language and knowledge, these learners may be internalising constructions of themselves which ultimately undermine their self-esteem, alienate them from self-fulfilment, and erect barriers to their effective learning.

THE OUTCOMES AND PROCESS OF LEARNING

We have concluded above that human resource managers need to understand the nature of learning and development. This section will, therefore, examine the following:

- the outcomes of learning:
  - skill
  - competence
  - 'know-how' and tacit knowledge
  - employability
  - hierarchies of cognitive and other skills;
- the process of learning:
  - theories of the process of learning
  - elements in the process of learning
  - learning stages
  - cyclical models of learning and learning styles.

The outcomes of learning

This subsection will examine skill, competence, 'know-how' and tacit knowledge, hierarchies of cognitive and other skills, all direct outcomes of learning and development, and employability, an indirect outcome. These are all of concern to human resource managers.

Skill

> . . . the performance of any task which, for its successful and rapid completion, requires an improved organisation of responses making use of only those aspects of the stimulus which are essential to satisfactory performance.
>
> (Ribeaux and Poppleton, 1978: 53–54)

> . . . an appearance of ease, of smoothness of movement, of confidence and the comparative absence of hesitation; it frequently gives the impression of being unhurried, while the actual pace of activity may of course be quite high . . . increasing skill involves a widening of the range of possible disturbances that can be coped with without disrupting the performance.
>
> (Borger and Seaborne, 1966: 128–129)

These definitions are particularly appropriate to perceptual-motor skills, which involve physical, motor responses to perceived stimuli in the external world. Such skills are needed at every level of an organisation, from the senior manager's ability to operate a desktop computer to the cleaner's operation of a floor-scrubbing machine. High levels of such skills are particularly needed to operate complex and expensive technology. There are many other kinds of skills needed in organisations, such as cognitive, linguistic, social and interpersonal skills, that could also be defined in these terms. However, their complexity suggests that we need to recognise various levels of skill, and this we shall do in the subsection below which presents some hierarchies of skills.

Competence

Competence may be defined as:

> . . . an underlying characteristic of a person which results in effective and/or superior performance in a job.
>
> (Boyatzis, 1982)

> . . . the ability to perform the activities within an occupational area to the levels of performance expected in employment.
>
> (Training Commission, 1988)

The core of the definition is an ability to apply knowledge and skills with understanding to a work activity. While the concept of skill has long been an intrinsic part of theories of selection and training, the notion of competence is a much more recent arrival. It is, however, now becoming a major element in the design of training and development in Britain, and Chapter 8 suggests some reasons for this. Martin (1995: 20) proposes that it is a means of 'aligning what people can offer – their competencies – against the demands of customers rather than against the ill-fitting and ill-designed demands of jobs'.

The differences between the definitions above indicate some of the confusion that is discussed by Woodruffe (1991) and outlined in the section on controversial issues in Chapter 8. These are important discussions, for they concern not only how we conceptualise and hence facilitate the learning and development of organisational members, but also the practicalities of doing so. We shall, however, leave those discussions until later. What we need to note at this point is that the concept of competence integrates knowledge and skill which are assessed via performance. This brings us to the distinction between 'know-how' and formal knowledge, in which tacit knowledge has a significant part to play.

'Know-how' and tacit knowledge

'Knowing how to do something' is a very different matter from *knowing about* 'knowing how to do something'. This truism is captured in the everyday suspicion and disparagement of 'the ivory tower': 'those who can, do; those who can't, teach'. It is also apparent in the reluctance of British employers to value higher education, evidenced in the small proportion of managers with degrees, documented in the Handy (1987) and Constable and McCormick (1987) reports (see Chapters 9 and 11). By contrast, 'can do' became a buzzword for pragmatic effectiveness in the 1980s.

Gardner (1985: 68) makes the distinction between 'know-how' and 'know-that'. For him, 'know-how' is the tacit knowledge of how to execute something, whereas 'know-that' is the statement of formal thinking (propositional knowledge) about the actual set of procedures involved in the execution:

> Thus, many of us know how to ride a bicycle but lack the propositional knowledge of how that behaviour is carried out. In contrast, many of us have propositional knowledge about how to make a soufflé without knowing how to carry this task through to successful completion.

Tacit knowledge is an essential ingredient of 'know-how'. Sternberg (1985: 269) recognises this in his definition of practical intelligence:

> Underlying successful performance in many real-world tasks is tacit knowledge of a kind that is never explicitly taught and in many instances never even verbalized.

The example that he gives, of the tacit knowledge relevant to the management of one's career, is outlined in the section on the organisation as a context for learning. The individual also draws upon tacit knowledge in the fluent performance of perceptual-motor skills, as seen in the definition of skill above; indeed, Myers and Davids (1992) write of 'tacit skills'.

This tacit knowledge would appear to be acquired through experience rather than through instruction, and is embedded in the context in which this experience is taking place. This can be seen in Stage 2 of the model of Dreyfus *et al.* (see below), in which the learner becomes independent of instruction through the recognition of the contextual elements of the task, and thereafter develops the ability to register and 'read' contextual cues. However, unlike the formal knowledge that it accompanies, this tacit knowledge never becomes explicit, although it remains very significant. Myers and Davids (1992: 47) question whether 'tacit skills' can be taught, and identify that they are often transmitted in 'an environment of intensive practical experience' and in task performance: 'We may yet be able to learn much from "sitting next to Nellie"!' They also note the need to take account of both formal and tacit knowledge in selection. Later we shall examine the concept of action learning, which contextualises learning and hence draws upon tacit knowledge, and is needed for the development of all levels of skills.

Traditionally, practical knowledge tends to feature at a lower level in any representation of the social hierarchy of skills and thereby institutionalised in occupations. In discussing the public's understanding of science, Collins (1993: 17) writes about:

> . . . the all too invisible laboratory technician . . . Look into a laboratory and you will see it filled with fallible machines and the manifest recalcitrance of nature . . . Technicians make things work in the face of this . . . Notoriously, techniques that can be made to work by one technician in one place will not work elsewhere. The technician has a practical understanding of aspects of the craft of science beyond that of many scientists. But does the technician 'understand science'?

Cooley (1987: 10–13) draws attention to the way in which practical knowledge, craft skill, is devalued in the face of technological progress. This is the starting point for his reflections upon the way 'ordinary people' could achieve something extraordinary. He believes that technological systems:

> . . . tend to absorb the knowledge from them ['ordinary people'], deny them the right to use their skill and judgement, and render them abject appendages to the machines and systems being developed.

Myers and Davids (1992: 47) come to a similar conclusion after their discussion of the significance of 'tacit skills'.

It is clear, however, that organisations need both 'know-how' and 'know-that': the concept of competence, therefore, as defined above is potentially a significant one for them. However, as the section in Chapter 8 dealing with controversial issues indicates, it is argued that the institutionalised, transorganisational process of identifying and defining competencies has wrenched them from their context and hence from the tacit knowledge that contributes so significantly to them.

Hierarchies of cognitive and other skills

We concluded earlier that today's organisations need their employees generally, and their managers in particular, to practise higher order thinking skills. We also pointed above to the need to recognise not only a variety of but different levels of skills. We, therefore, need to consider a hierarchy of skills. This subsection presents several hierarchies, each with a somewhat different focus. They imply not just different levels but different stages: the individual can progress from the lower to the higher stages, but does not necessarily do so. The lower levels are prerequisites for, and subsumed by, the higher. We shall return to the notion of the stages of learning in the subsection on the process of learning, which outlines what it calls the micro levels of the acquisition of learning, each of which *could be interpreted* as needing to take place within each of the macro levels of the hierarchies here.

These hierarchies give insights into the higher level thinking skills, which are clearly identifiable in higher levels of the hierarchies below: in Argyris and Schon's double loop learning; in the analysis, synthesis and evaluation levels of Bloom's taxonomy; in the characteristics of proficiency and expertise as defined by Dreyfus *et al.*; and in Perry's continuum. The human resource manager can, therefore, use these hierarchies, first to identify the prior learning that needs to take place before the higher order skills can be attained and, then, to plan ways of facilitating their learning.

Single and double loop learning

The concepts of single and double loop learning do not actually constitute a hierarchy or stages of learning. They are rather two different approaches, and individuals do not necessarily progress from single to double loop learning, nor is the former an essential prerequisite for the latter. They are, however, important elements in learning and it is convenient to present them here.

Whereas single loop learning refers to the detection and correction of deviances in performance from established (organisational or other) norms, double loop learning refers to the questioning of those very norms which define effective performance. Learning how to learn calls for what Argyris and Schon (1978) call double loop learning.

Bloom et al.'s taxonomy of cognitive skills

Bloom *et al.* (1956) identify the various levels of thinking skills at which learning can take place:

- knowledge (i.e. simple knowledge of facts, of terms, of theories, etc.)
- comprehension (i.e. an understanding of the meaning of this knowledge)
- application (i.e. the ability to apply this knowledge and comprehension in new concrete situations)

- analysis (i.e. the ability to break the material down into its constituent parts and to see the relationship between them)
- synthesis (i.e. the ability to re-assemble these parts into a new and meaningful relationship, thus forming a new whole)
- evaluation (i.e. the ability to judge the value of material using explicit and coherent criteria, either of one's own devising or derived from the work of others). (Fontana, 1981: 71)

Dreyfus, Dreyfus and Athanasion's stage model of skills acquisition

Dreyfus, Dreyfus and Athanasion (1986, in Cooley, 1987: 13–15, and Quinn *et al.*, 1990: 314–315) set out a five-stage model of the process of acquisition of skill that moves from the effective performance of lower to higher order thinking skills.

- *Stage 1: the novice.* Novices follow context-free rules, with relevant components of the situation defined for them; hence they lack any coherent sense of the overall task.
- *Stage 2: the advanced beginner.* Through their practical experience in concrete situations learners begin to recognise the contextual elements of their task. They begin to perceive similarities between new and previous experiences.
- *Stage 3: competent.* They begin to recognise a wider range of cues, and become able to select and focus upon the most important of them. Their reliance upon rules lessens; they experiment and go beyond the rules, using trial-and-error.
- *Stage 4: proficient.* Those who arrive at this stage achieve the unconscious, fluid, effortless performance referred to in the definitions of skill given at the start of this subsection. They still think analytically, but can now 'read' the evolving situation, picking up new cues and becoming aware of emerging patterns; they have an involved, intuitive and holistic grasp of the situation.
- *Stage 5: expert.* At this stage, according to Cooley (1987: 15), 'Highly experienced people seem to be able to recognise whole scenarios without decomposing them into elements or separate features.' They have 'multidimensional maps of the territory'; they 'frame and reframe strategies as they read changing cues' (Quinn *et al.*, 1990: 315). With this intuitive understanding of the implications of a situation, they can cope with uncertainty and unforeseen situations.

Managers' levels of learning (Burgoyne and Hodgson)

A similar hierarchy has been proposed specifically for the learning of managers. Burgoyne and Hodgson (1983) suggest that managers have a gradual build-up of experience created out of specific learning incidents, internalise this experience, and use it, both consciously and unconsciously, to guide their future action and decision making. They identify three levels of this learning process:

- *Level 1 learning*, which occurs when managers simply take in some factual information or data which is immediately relevant but does not change their views of the world.
- *Level 2 learning*, which occurs at an unconscious or tacit level. Managers gradually build up a body of personal 'case law' which enables them to deal with future events.
- *Level 3 learning*, when managers consciously reflect on their conception of the world, how it is formed, and how they might change it.

Perry's continuum of intellectual and ethical development

Perry's (1968) schema (see Daloz, 1986) emerged from his research into his students' experiences. He interpreted their intellectual and ethical development as a continuum, and he mapped out how individuals develop multiple perspectives while at the same time becoming able to commit themselves to their own personal interpretation. At one extreme is basic dualism, where everything is seen as good or bad. This moves through the perception of the diversity of opinion; of extensive legitimate uncertainty; through perception that all knowledge and values are contextual and relativistic; to the recognition of the need to make a commitment to a viewpoint; the making of the commitment; experiencing its implications; and, finally, to the affirmation of identity as this commitment is expressed through lifestyle.

Employability

An indirect outcome of learning and development is 'employability', a notion that has recently become current because of the proliferation of flexible contracts of employment and insecurity in employment during the 1990s. According to Kanter (1989a), employability is the 'new security': if individuals have acquired and maintained their employability then, should their job come to an end, they would be able to find employment elsewhere.

Employability results from investment in the human capital of skills and reputation. This means that individuals must engage in continuous learning and development so that they update their skills and acquire others that will be needed in the future. It is also argued that, as part of the 'new deal' in employment, good employers will ensure that their employees remain employable (Herriot and Pemberton, 1995) by keeping them up to date through training and development.

The process of learning

We have identified what learning has to be achieved; we now need to examine the process by which it will be achieved. The following section will, therefore, now examine theories of the process of learning and elements within it. This is a very rich and complex field to which we cannot do justice here and you are recommended to read a text such as Atkinson *et al.* (1993) or Ribeaux and Poppleton (1978).

Theories of the process of learning

Behaviourist approach to learning

The behaviourist approach has been one of the most influential in the field of psychology. It proposes that learning is the process by which a particular stimulus (S), repeatedly associated with, or conditioned by, desirable or undesirable experiences, comes to evoke a particular response (R). This conditioning can be of two kinds. Classical conditioning occurs when a stimulus leads automatically to a response. Dogs, for example, salivate at the presentation of food; Pavlov demonstrated that they could also be conditioned to salivate at the sound of a bell rung before food is presented. Operant conditioning (Skinner) takes place after a desired response, which is then reinforced, or rewarded, to increase the probability of the repetition of the same response when the stimulus recurs.

There has been much experimental research (including many animal studies) into such issues as the nature of the reinforcement (negative reinforcement, or punishment, is not as effective for learning as positive reward); the schedule of reinforcement (whether fixed or variable intervals: intermittent reinforcement is more effective than continuous reinforcement). This form of conditioning is also used to shape behaviour, that is to continue to reinforce responses that approximate to the desired behaviour until that behaviour is finally achieved. We are familiar with this kind of approach to the encouragement of fairly simple forms of learning: we use it with small children, with animals, and in basic forms of training.

The S–R approach pays no attention to the cognitive processes whereby the stimulus comes to be associated with a particular response. Cognitive learning theory, however, offers a more complex understanding of learning, proposing, again on the basis originally of animal studies, that what is learned is not an association of stimulus with response (S–R), but of stimulus with stimulus (S–S). The learner develops expectations that stimuli are linked; the result is a cognitive 'map' or latent learning. Hence insightful behaviour appropriate to a situation takes place without the strengthening association of S–R bonds. Social learning theory also addresses what is in the 'black box'. It recognises the role in learning of the observation and imitation of the behaviour of others, but as seen in the debates over the influence of the media upon, say, young people's behaviour, there are clearly many moderating variables.

Information-processing approach to learning

This approach regards learning as an information-processing system in which a signal, containing information, is transmitted along a communication channel of limited capacity and subject to interference and 'noise' (Stammers and Patrick, 1975). The signal has to be decoded before it can be received, and then encoded to pass it on. In learning, data received through the senses are filtered, recognised and decoded through the interpretive process of perception; this information is then translated into action through the selection of appropriate responses. The effectiveness of learning depends on attention being paid only to the relevant parts of the stimuli, the rapid selection of appropriate responses, the efficient performance of them, and the feeding back of information about their effects into the system. Overload or breakdown of the system can occur at any of these stages.

Gagné (1974, in Fontana, 1981: 73) expresses this as a chain of events, some internal and others external to the learner. It begins with the learner's readiness to receive information (motivation or expectancy), and continues as the learner perceives it, distinguishes it from other stimuli, makes sense of it and relates it to what is already known. The information is then stored in short- or long-term memory. Thereafter it can be retrieved from memory, generalised to and put into practice in new situations. Its final phase is feedback from knowledge of the results obtained from this practice. Those concerned to facilitate learning in others can use their understanding of this chain to prevent failure to learn, which can take place at any one of these levels.

Elements in the process of learning

This subsection will deal briefly with other important elements in the process of learning that need to be taken into account when designing or facilitating learning. These are the need for feedback, the choice of whole or part learning, and the role of memory.

Feedback (or knowledge of results)

The feedback to learners of the results of their performance is recognised as essential to their effective learning. This is discussed in Ribeaux and Poppleton (1978) and Stammers and Patrick (1975). Feedback will be either intrinsic or extrinsic (or augmented). Learners receive visual or kinaesthetic feedback (intrinsic) from their responses to stimuli in the learning situation; they need to be encouraged to 'listen' to such bodily cues in order to improve performance. They may also receive feedback (extrinsic, augmented) from an external source while they are performing (concurrent feedback) or after it (terminal). Learners may also benefit from guidance given before their performance about what to look out for during it. The sources cited above set out the characteristics, advantages and disadvantages of these different kinds of feedback.

The notion of feedback is frequently discussed in terms of learning perceptual-motor or similar skills. It is also of considerable importance in the learning of the higher order skills discussed in this chapter, but here it is very complex in nature and difficult for the learner to be aware and make sense of it. However, by reflecting and engaging in the whole loop learning discussed below, the learner will have opportunity to pay attention to both intrinsic and extrinsic feedback.

The choice of whole or part learning

Psychologists continue to debate the appropriateness of whole or part learning in learning to perform various tasks, that is, whether the task is learned as a whole, or in parts. Ribeaux and Poppleton (1978: 61) report on one approach that classifies tasks according to their 'complexity' (the difficulty of the component sub-tasks) and 'organisation' (the degree to which they are interrelated). Where complexity and organisation are both high, whole methods appear superior; where either is low, part methods are superior in most cases; while when both are low, part and whole methods are equally successful. Stammers and Patrick (1975: 85–88), however, report on research that draws opposite conclusions: where the elements of a task are highly independent the task is best learned as a whole, but where they are interdependent, they should be learned in parts.

It tends to be the whole method in operation when learning takes place during the performance of a job, through action learning, or through observing others.

The role of memory in learning

Memory plays a significant role in learning, and some understanding of it can, therefore, be used to make learning more effective. Once again, it is not possible to do more than present an outline here, but texts such as Stammers and Patrick (1975), Ribeaux and Poppleton (1978), Fontana (1981) and Atkinson *et al.* (1993), give further information.

Memory involves three kinds of information storage: the storage of sensory memories, short-term or primary memory, and long-term or secondary memory. Unless transferred to short-term memory, the sensory memory retains sense data for probably less than two seconds. Unless incoming information is paid particular attention or rehearsed, short-term memory holds it for up to 30 seconds and appears to have limited capacity, whereas long-term memory appears to have unlimited capacity and to hold information for years. What is, therefore, of concern for effective learning is the ability to transfer information to the long-term memory.

There are two aspects to such transfer. The first is 'rehearsal', that is paying attention to and repeating the information until it is coded and enters the long-term store; it is otherwise displaced by new incoming information. The second aspect of the transfer of information to long-term memory is coding: the translation of information into the codes that enable it to be 'filed' into the memory's 'filing system'. Information is largely coded according to meaning (a semantic code) or through visual images, but sometimes (where the meaning itself is unclear) according to sound.

The ability to retrieve information from long-term memory depends in part upon how effectively it has been organised ('filed') in storage (for example, words may be stored according to sound and meaning), but also upon having the most appropriate retrieval cue. We experience this when we are searching for something that we have lost: we think systematically through what we were doing when we believe we last used the lost object. Recognition is easier than recall from memory because it follows the presentation of clear retrieval cues.

Difficulty in retrieving information, or forgetting, occurs for several reasons apart from those concerning the degree of organisation in storage. Interference from other information can disrupt long-term as well as short-term memory (where new items displace existing items in the limited capacity). Interference may be retroactive, when new information interferes with the recall of older material, or proactive, when earlier learning seems to inhibit the recall of later information. Forgetting also takes place through anxiety or unhappy associations with the material to be learned, which may become repressed. Unhappy childhood experiences, for example, may be repressed for many years.

Finally, memory does not just operate as a camera recording what is experienced: it is an active and a constructive process, particularly when learning the kind of complex material that constitutes the world of organisations and human resource management. As well as recording its data inputs, the process of memory draws inferences from the data and so elaborates upon them, filtering them through the individual's stereotypes, mind-set and world view. What is then stored is this enhanced and repackaged material.

An understanding of the nature of memory suggests various ways in which it might be improved to make learning more effective. The transfer of new information to long-term memory is clearly crucial: attention, recitation, repetition and constant revision (known as 'overlearning') are needed. The coding and organisation of material to be stored is also important: this is helped by associating the new information with what is already familiar, especially using visual imagery, by attending to the context giving rise to the information to be learned, and by making the effort to understand the information so that it can be stored in the appropriate 'files'. Facilitators of learning need to ensure that the learning context or event does not provoke anxiety.

Learning stages

The previous subsection identified higher order thinking skills within various hierarchies of skills. Here we shall note some of the micro stages through which, it may be inferred, the learner has to pass within each of the levels of those hierarchies. (See the next section on development for a further reference to stages.)

Fitts's stages of skills acquisition

Fitts (1962, in Stammers and Patrick, 1975) distinguished three stages of learning, in particular of perceptual-motor skills acquisition. It is recognised that they may overlap.

- *Cognitive stage.* The learner has to understand what is required, its rules and concepts, and how to achieve it.
- *Associative stage.* The learner has to establish through practice the stimulus–response links, the correct patterns of behaviour, gradually eliminating errors.
- *Autonomous stage.* The learner refines the motor patterns of behaviour until external sources of information become redundant and the capacity simultaneously to perform secondary tasks increases.

Gagné's classification of learning

Gagné (1970, in Stammers and Patrick, 1975) studied both the process of learning and the most effective modes of instruction, and has made several classifications of types of learning. For example, he identified the ability to make a general response to a signal; to develop a chain of two or more stimulus–response links, including verbal chains and associations; to make different responses to similar though different stimuli; to achieve concept learning and identify a class of objects or events; to learn rules through the acquisition of a chain of two or more concepts; and, finally, to combine rules and so achieve problem solving.

Gagné's classification allows us to identify the processes whereby skills of all levels are acquired, and hence suggests how to facilitate learning and prevent failure to learn at the various levels.

The learning curve

It is recognised that there is a relationship between the rate of learning and the passage of time: managers working on the introduction of a new system, for example, may say 'we are on a learning curve'. According to Hodgetts (1991: 99), many psychologists 'feel that the S-shaped curve represents the most accurate description of learning'. This is shown in Figure 7.1. However, since the shape of the curve must clearly depend on the nature and circumstances of the learning, this notion of a learning curve perhaps adds little of value to the understanding of learning.

Cyclical models of learning and learning styles

Here we examine a related, but more dynamic, notion of the process of learning; that of a cycle of learning. The recognition that learning is a process that may have different identi-

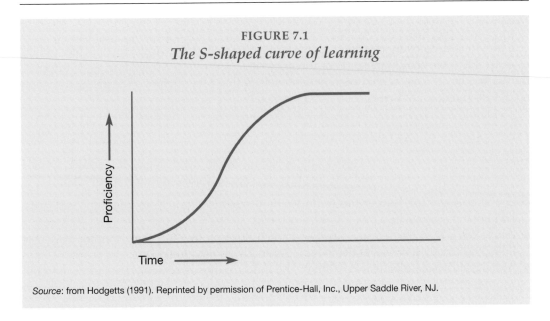

FIGURE 7.1
The S-shaped curve of learning

Proficiency

Time

Source: from Hodgetts (1991). Reprinted by permission of Prentice-Hall, Inc., Upper Saddle River, NJ.

fiable phases, and that more effective learning may be facilitated if methods appropriate to the various phases are used, has led to the development of models of learning as a cycle. (The assumptions here echo those underlying the concept of development, which is to be discussed in the next section.) As you will see, they offer a number of important insights to the human resource manager concerned to facilitate higher order skills in the organisation. They draw attention to the significance of learning through action and reflection, as well as through the traditional channels of teaching/learning. They recognise that individuals may prefer different phases of the cycle and have different styles: they offer means to identify those preferences; to engage in dialogue about them with individuals; and to identify means of helping individuals complete the whole cycle.

Kolb's learning cycle

The best known learning cycle in the field in which we are interested is that of Kolb. There are two dimensions to learning (Kolb *et al.*, 1984): concrete/abstract (involvement/detachment) and active/reflective (actor/observer). Learning is an integrated cognitive and affective process moving in a cyclical manner through concrete experience (CE) to reflective observation (RO) to abstract conceptualisation (AC) to active experimentation (AE) and so on (Kolb, 1983).

Effective learning calls for learners:

● to become fully involved in concrete, new experiences (CE);
● to observe and reflect on these experiences from many perspectives (RO);
● to use concepts and theories to integrate their observations (AC);
● to use these theories for decision making and problem solving (AE).

However, many people have a preference for a particular phase and so do not complete the cycle; thus they do not learn as effectively or as comprehensively as they could. Kolb's Learning Styles Inventory identifies these preferences (Mumford, 1988: 27). The 'converger' (AC and AE) prefers the practical and specific; the 'diverger' (CE and RO) looks from different points of view and observes rather than acts; the 'assimilator' (AC and RO) is comfortable with concepts and abstract ideas; and the 'accommodator' (CE and AE) prefers to learn primarily from doing.

Honey and Mumford's learning styles

Honey and Mumford (1992) identify four learning styles similar to those of Kolb, and develop norms based on the results of those who have completed their Learning Styles Questionnaire. Their 'activists' learn best when they are actively involved in concrete tasks; 'reflectors' learn best through reviewing and reflecting upon what has happened and what they have done; 'theorists' learn best when they can relate new information to concepts or theory; 'pragmatists' learn best when they see relevance between new information and real-life issues or problems (Mumford, 1988: 28). They discuss how this information can be used to design effective learning events. Individuals, too, can use it to build on their strengths and reduce their weaknesses in learning.

The Lancaster cycle of learning

A cyclical model said to represent 'all forms of learning including cognitive, skill development and affective, by any process' (Binsted, 1980: 22) is the Lancaster model. This identifies three different forms of learning: receipt of input/generation of output, discovery and reflection. As Figure 7.2 shows, they take place in both the inner and outer world of the individual. The receipt of input results from being taught or told information, or reading it in books. Learners follow the discovery loop (action and feedback) through action and experimentation, opening themselves to the new experiences generated, and becoming aware of the consequences of their actions. They follow the reflection loop (conceptualising and hypothesising) when making sense of the information they receive and the actions they undertake, and when, on the basis of this, theorising about past or future situations.

Each form of learning is cyclical, and the cycles can be linked in various ways (for example, learning in formal classroom settings links receipt of input with reflection), but in effective learning the learner will complete the overall cycle.

DEVELOPMENT

This section discusses the process whereby, over time, learning brings about significant changes in the individual.

The concept of development

We can conclude from earlier sections that what organisations need of their members is development, for this is the process whereby a person (or any organism) through learning and maturation becomes increasingly complex, more elaborate and differentiated, and

FIGURE 7.2

The Lancaster model of the learning cycle

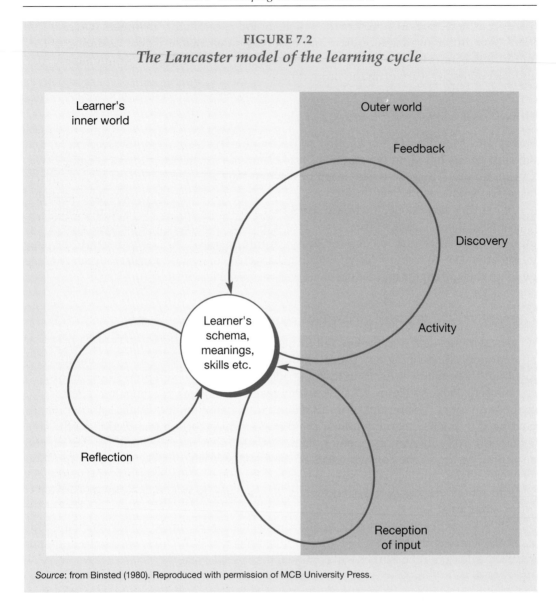

Source: from Binsted (1980). Reproduced with permission of MCB University Press.

thereby better able to adapt to the changing environment. In an organism, greater complexity and differentiation among its parts lead to changes in the structure of the whole and in the way in which the whole functions (Reese and Overton, 1970: 126). In the individual, this greater complexity opens up the potential for new ways of acting and responding to the environment. This leads to the opportunity for even further learning, and so on.

Development, whether of an organism, individual or organisation, is a process of both continuity and discontinuity. Quantitative changes lead to qualitative changes or transformations; development is irreversible, although regression to earlier phases can occur.

> ... the disintegration of the old phase of functioning ... creates the condi-
> tions for the discontinuous 'step-jump' to a new phase. This succeeding
> phase incorporates yet transforms the repertoire of principles, values, etc.,
> of earlier phases and adds to them. The new phase is therefore not entirely
> new – it is a transformation. Each succeeding phase is more complex, inte-
> grating what has gone before. (Pedler, 1988: 7–8)

Development is a significant topic, for it contributes to the understanding of how
people change through life, an understanding needed in many areas of policy and practice. Social and psychological development is studied by developmental psychologists
(see Baltes, Reese and Lipsitt, 1980) and sociologists interested in the 'life course' and the
interaction between individual lives and the social structures of which they are a part (see
Hareven and Adams, 1982). However, development is a difficult area to study, embracing
as it does both the individual's inner life and the changing nature of a complex world,
with the lifespan as the time dimension. Researchers and theorists have, therefore, often
focused upon segments of the lifespan and drawn implications for the remainder, or
upon aspects, rather than the whole range, of development.

Assumptions underlying the theories and models of development

The theories and models of development have to be considered carefully, because they
can have an impact on individuals' lives, either through the frameworks used in guidance and counselling or through their influence on writers in other fields. For example,
Daloz (1986), whose work is discussed earlier in the chapter, draws on these developmental theories to help him understand the needs of adult learners, and Waskel (1991)
examines their implications for human resource management. In this chapter we, too, are
drawing on this literature to establish what we need to know about learning and development as an underpinning of effective human resource development. It is, therefore,
important to recognise that researchers and theorists make assumptions about the nature
of the individual's experience and these assumptions influence what they tell us about
development. We shall first outline these assumptions and then introduce some alternative views. They apply to all forms of development, as you will see from the subsection
below on career development. (You will find examples of these various assumptions and
of the ongoing debate between their proponents in Arthur, Hall and Lawrence (1989) and
Smelser and Erikson (1980).)

Chapter 2 discussed the nature of various assumptions about social and personal reality, and you should return to that to understand the argument of this subsection.
Positivist assumptions about individuals and the social and economic environment
within which their lives are led (construed as an objective, orderly, stable framework)
give rise to the definition of development in terms of sequential phases or stages, often
with their own developmental tasks. Some theorists argue that their models represent
universal, normative patterns of experience, that all individuals follow similar patterns of
experiences, and that their models, therefore, allow some degree of prediction to be made
about the basic outline of individual lives (for example, Levinson *et al.* (1978)). However,

these models frequently interpret the experiences of women and black people in terms of those of white males.

Those working with these assumptions may also recognise that individuals have subjective experiences that cannot be studied in this scientific manner. They may, therefore, disregard them, although individuals base decisions about their life on their subjective experiences. However, as Chapter 2 outlined, there are alternative approaches. The phenomenological approach acknowledges the significance of a person's subjective experiences, and the social constructionist approach recognises that, because individual experiences are socially constructed, the context of the individual has to be taken into account. These alternative assumptions lead to a focus upon individual cases and the search for insights rather than generalisable conclusions. They also emphasise the significance of context, and the dynamic, intersubjective processes through which individuals interpret and make decisions about their lives and careers.

The subsections that follow will illustrate views about development that are based on both orthodox and alternative assumptions.

Lifespan development

Lifespan development embraces the total development of the individual over time, and results from the interweaving of the biological, social, economic and psychological strands of the individual's life. It is the framework within which individuals learn and hence constitutes an important background to the development of the employee, of which the employer needs to be aware. We shall briefly outline some approaches to lifespan development, and then note some implications for human resource development.

The influence of the sociocultural context

There are two perspectives in the literature upon the influence of the sociocultural context on the individual's lifespan experiences. The first interprets that there are tendencies towards common patterns in individual experiences resulting from socialisation. In any given social setting, whether culture, class or organisation, the members of that social group experience pressures to conform to certain patterns of behaviour or norms. Sometimes these pressures are expressed as legal constraints: the age of consent, marriage, attaining one's majority (becoming an adult); or as quasi-legal constraints such as the age at which the state pension is paid and hence at which most people retire from the labour force; or as social and peer group expectations. For example, Neugarten (1968: 146) recognises how family, work and social statuses provide the 'major punctuation marks in the adult life', and the:

> . . . way of structuring the passage of time in the lifespan of the individual, providing a time clock that can be super-imposed over the biological clock . . .

Organisations also have their own 'clocks'. Sofer (1970: 239) writes of his respondents' 'sensitive awareness' of the relation between age and organisational grade for they were:

> . . . constantly mulling over this and asking themselves whether they were on schedule, in front of schedule or behind schedule, showing quite clearly that they had a set of norms in mind as to where one should be by a given age.

The other perspective, however, emphasises that the environment offers different opportunities and threats for individual lives. The process of development or elaboration takes place as the individual's innate capacity to grow and mature unfolds within a particular context, which in turn facilitates or stunts growth, or prompts variations upon it. For example, it is argued that there are significant differences in physical, intellectual and socio-economic attainments between children from different social classes (Keil, 1981). The interaction and accommodation between individuals and their environment, therefore, cannot be meaningfully expressed in a model that is cross-cultural or universal. Hence, Gallos (1989) questions the relevance of many of the accepted views of development to women's lives and careers, while Thomas and Aldefer (1989) note that 'the influence of race on the developmental process' is commonly ignored in the literature.

Musgrove's (1977) study of adult change as socialisation rather than maturation, undertaken from a non-positivist approach, illustrates some of the issues made above. He interprets the changes through life as 'a moral quest for one's real and authentic self' (1977: 224) and concludes that although people are 'capable of fundamental change' (1977: 220), they are not 'chameleons' (1977: 13):

> . . . 'real selves' often remained latent though undimmed and available for recall . . . saved up and carefully maintained . . . [until] 'real selves' are disinterred after . . . years of camouflage.
> (1977: 14)

This reminds us that the changes an individual experiences, at work as well as elsewhere in their lives, may have significant effects for them. Managers planning developmental activities for others need to remain aware of this and consider development holistically.

Models of lifespan development

We present three very different models of the lifespan, each of which has been influential in lifespan psychology. It is important to be aware of the assumptions underlying these models, as the subsection above discussed. Their implications for human resource development will be noted below.

Erikson's psychosocial model

Erikson (1950) conceives of development in terms of stages of ego development and the effects of maturation, experience and socialisation (see Levinson *et al.*, 1978; Wrightsman, 1988). Each stage builds on the ones before, and presents the expanding ego with a choice or 'crisis'. The successful resolution of this 'crisis' achieves a higher level of elaboration in individuality and adaptation to the demands of both inner and outer world, and hence the capacity to deal with the next stage. An unsuccessful or inadequate resolution hinders or distorts this process of effective adaptation in the subsequent stages.

For example, the adolescent strives for a coherent sense of self, or identity, perhaps experimenting with several different identities and as yet uncommitted to one; entry to work and choice of work role play a part here. The choice, however, has to be made and responsibility assumed for its consequences: unless this occurs, there is identity confusion. Young adults have to resolve the choice between achieving closeness and intimate relationships, fusing identity with another without the fear of losing something themselves, *or* the readiness to isolate themselves from others.

Erikson paid less attention to the remainder of the lifespan, but indicated that the choice for those aged 25 to 65 is between the stagnation that would result from concern only for self, indulging themselves as though they were 'their own only child' (Wrightsman, 1988: 66) *or* generativity. This is the reaching out beyond the need to satisfy self in order to take responsibility in the adult world, and show care for others, the next generation or the planet itself. The choice of the final stage is between construing life as having been well *or* ill spent.

The model of Levinson et al.

The research of Levinson *et al.* (1978) was into the experiences of men. They model men's lifespan in terms of alternating, age-related periods of stability and instability, as shown in Figure 7.3. In the stable periods, lasting six to eight years, a man builds and enriches the structure of his life: work, personal relationships and community involvement. The structure, however, cannot last and during the transitional periods, of four to five years, the individual reappraises that structure, explores new possibilities and sets the scene for adapting or changing it, which can be a painful experience. (You can read more about this model in Daloz, 1986, and Wrightsman, 1988.)

Kegan's model

Kegan (1982) examines individual growth in terms of the balance between self-centredness and other-centredness: he sees the 'evolving self' as a helix spiralling upwards (see Daloz, 1986). Each transformation within this development involves risk, a move away from familiarity towards uncertainty. In the early 'impulsive' phase, young children cannot distinguish their impulses from those of others, but as they get older they can get outside themselves and understand the value of reciprocity: their 'imperial' phase. Teenagers move into an 'interpersonal' balance as they redefine themselves through others. The 'institutional' balance is achieved as individuals draw the boundaries around themselves more clearly, and define themselves in their own terms. The final stage sees individuals dissolving the boundaries of self again and reaching out to others in a new 'interindividual' balance.

Implications for human resource development

People develop through their lifespan, achieving greater degrees of complexity, even transformation. They are, therefore, continuously engaging in learning processes as they seek balance between changing self and changing environment. The theories and models of lifespan development have several implications for human resource development, for the organisation is one of the major arenas in which this adult development is taking place.

Those concerned with human resource development need to recognise that these developmental pressures may be exacerbated or compounded by work pressures. Managers need to be aware of the possible effects of developmental changes upon performance at work, some positive, others not. Young people entering adulthood, for example, may lack enthusiasm for or commitment to their job as they juggle with their potential various identities. Later the needs of their developing intimacy with another person may lead to conflicts with educational or organisational demands.

FIGURE 7.3

FIGURE 7.3

The model of Levinson et al. of the developmental periods in early and middle adulthood

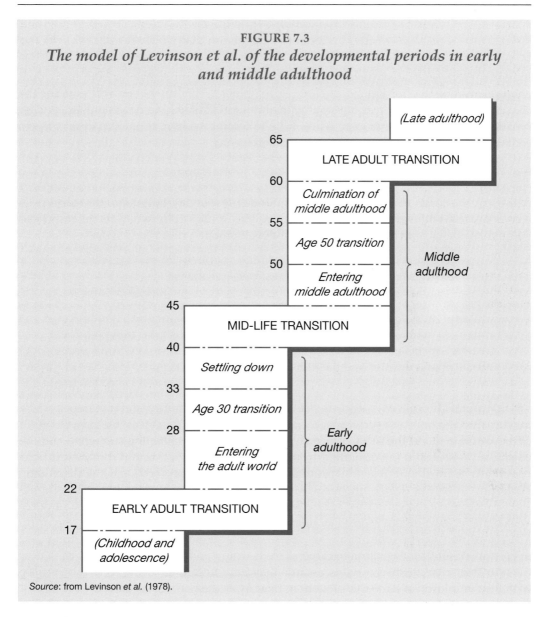

Source: from Levinson *et al.* (1978).

Opportunities for promotion, the mid-career plateau, training to ensure continuous improvement or cutbacks in training: these may influence the choice between generativity and stagnation. The outcome may influence the way in which supervisors and managers relate with their subordinates. Human resource development needs to harness the generativity and combat the potential stagnation of organisational members, by perhaps giving them the role of mentor (see the section on the organisation as a context for learning). Managers also need to be aware of the age clock (Neugarten, 1968), of individuals' vulnerability and the possibility that they suffer when their roles in different social subsystems do not synchronise.

Overall, human resource managers need to provide an environment in which the capacity to learn and adapt can be harnessed to benefit the organisation.

Career development

Individual development interacts with the organisation and its development through the individual's career. Career development, therefore, is of significance for both individual and organisation and for human resource development. This subsection will examine the concept and theories of career development, although, like lifespan development , it is far broader than organisational experience. (The following section on the organisation as a context for learning will deal with career management.)

The concept of career

Although the term 'career' is well understood in everyday language, the concept is a complex one with several levels of meaning. This is shown in two of its much-quoted definitions, which both imply the concept of development:

> . . . a succession of related jobs, arranged in a hierarchy of prestige, through which persons move in an ordered, predictable sequence.
>
> (Wilensky, 1960: 554)

> . . . a career consists, objectively, of a series of status and clearly defined offices . . . subjectively, a career is the moving perspective in which the person sees his [*sic*] life as a whole and interprets the meaning of his various attributes, actions and the things which happen to him.
>
> (Hughes, 1937: 409–410)

The core of the concept suggests the experience of continuity and coherence while moving through time and social space. Career, therefore, has two faces, the private world of the individual and the social structure (Collin and Watts, 1996), the subjective and the objective career (as in the quotation from Hughes, above). Because of the assumptions commonly made about objectivity and subjectivity (see Chapter 2, and the discussion about the concept of development earlier in this section), much of the literature emphasises the objective career, but the subjective is clearly also of relevance to human resource development. As individuals become more skilled and flexible, they gain more opportunties for promotion or other intra- or inter-organisational moves: their learning and development affect their objective career. This learning and development also influences the way they view themselves, the rewards they gain from their work, their relationship with their employer, and the role of work in their lives: their subjective career.

The theories of career development

The theories (see Watts *et al.*, 1996) which have attempted to explain this rich concept of career can be classified into several families as follows:

- Theories concerned with external influences upon the individual's career:
  - economic and labour market theories
  - social structure and social mobility
  - organisational and occupational structure and mobility.
- Theories concerned with factors internal to the individual:
  - factors such as age, gender
  - psychoanalytical explanations

- lifespan development
- implementation of self-concept
- matching personality and occupation.
- Theories concerned with the interaction of internal and external factors:
  - decision making
  - social learning.
- Theories concerned with the interpretation of the individual's subjective experiences.

It is clear from works that draw together much recent thinking about career (Arthur, Hall and Lawrence, 1989; Brown and Brooks, 1996) that, despite the recognition of their limitations and the emergence of new ideas, many of the early theories (from the 1950s) continue to have currency. We shall, therefore, first note some of the common characteristics of these traditional approaches to career, and then outline two examples of them: the lifespan view of career, and the organisational career. Next we shall note some other forms of career to which the career literature has so far paid less attention, but which are of interest to those concerned with human resource development in today's organisations.

Characteristics of the traditional theories of career

We have already outlined in an earlier subsection the assumptions underlying the concept of development. The theories of career development have similar characteristics to those of lifespan development.
Career development theories:

- are more frequently formulated from a positivist than a phenomenological or constructionist approach;
- focus upon objective rather than subjective experience;
- emphasise intra-individual rather than contextual factors;
- largely disregard the significance of gender, race and social class.

These traditional theories are now starting to show their age. The kinds of organisations, their environments, and individual needs, expectations and values to which they once referred are disappearing. These theories will perhaps continue to linger still, but their limitations have to be noted.

Examples of mainstream theories

Career and lifespan development
The concept of lifespan development has been an important influence on career theories. For example, Cytrynbaum and Crites (1989) and Dalton (1989) relate career development to adult development, as does Evans (1986) writing about career management in organisations. His model of the stages of career development is very similar to those they cite, and is illustrated in Figure 7.4.

Career 'anchors' in organisations
Another influential, but very different, approach is that of Schein (1978) (see also Dalton, 1989). Schein identifies a number of 'career anchors' (self-perceived talents and abilities, motives and needs, and attitudes and values) that guide, constrain, stabilise and integrate individuals' careers. These are:

315

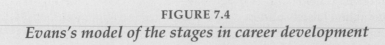

FIGURE 7.4

Evans's model of the stages in career development

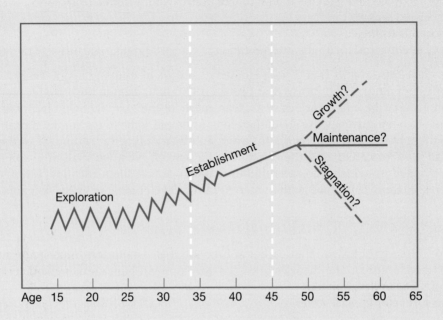

Source: Reproduced with permission of *Personnel Management* (now *People Management*), the official journal of the Institute of Personnel and Development.

- technical-functional competence;
- managerial competence (analytical, interpersonal, emotional);
- security and stability;
- creativity;
- autonomy and independence.

He concludes that there is a need to examine the 'dynamics of careers' in order to achieve both organisational and individual effectiveness, and argues for a 'human resource planning and development system' (Schein, 1978: 243–256).

Other forms of career

Bureaucratic, professional and entrepreneurial forms of career

Kanter (1989b: 508) draws our attention to these different forms of 'organizing principle around which a career logic unfolds'. The 'bureaucratic' career, defined by a 'logic of advancement', is only one form of career but, she points out, it is the form that has come to colour our view of organisational careers generally. Indeed, theorists have, as we shall see, tended to neglect the career experiences of certain classes of people. Those concerned with human resource development, however, will need to pay them attention.

Kanter (1989b: 510) indicates that there are other forms of career. The 'professional' form is wider than the career pursued by members of professional bodies. It is defined by craft or skill; occupational status is achieved through the 'monopolization of socially valued knowledge' and 'reputation' is a key resource for the individual. Career opportunities are not dependent in the same way as the 'bureaucratic' career upon the development of the organisation, nor is satisfaction as dependent upon the availability of extrinsic rewards.

Kanter notes how some professional careers may be only weakly connected to employing organisations. This is a similar point to that made about administrators by Gouldner (1957; see Pugh, Hickson and Hinings, 1983). Writing about the conflicts between expert and hierarchical systems of authority in organisations employing a large number of professionals, he distinguished between two categories of administrators. 'Cosmopolitans' are committed to their specialist skills rather than to the organisation, and construe themselves as professionals with a reference group outside the organisation. 'Locals' are very loyal to the organisation, and construe themselves in its terms, rather than those of their specialist area.

Kanter defines (1989b: 516) as 'entrepreneurial' the career that develops 'through the creation of new value or new organisational capacity'. Its key resource is the capacity to create valued outputs, and it offers freedom, independence and control over tasks and surroundings. However, while those with a 'bureaucratic' career have (relative) security, and 'professionals' can command a price in the market-place, 'entrepreneurs' 'have only what they grow'. The affinity between the notions of the 'enterpreneurial' career, employability and self-development (see a later section of this chapter) can be recognised.

Kanter concludes that we need to know more about these different forms of career, the relationships between them, and the differing contributions they make to organisations and society itself. These issues are certainly of significance for human resource development.

Careers in flexible organisations

The nature of career in increasingly flexible organisations is increasingly demanding the attention of theorists. Weick and Berlinger (1989) argue that the subjective career will be the appropriate form in 'self-designing organizations' (the learning organisation of the next section). In the absence of the typical attributes of career such as advancement and stable pathways, 'the objective career dissolves' and the subjective career 'becomes externalized and treated as a framework for career growth' (Weick and Berlinger, 1989: 321), and a resource for the further organisational self-design.

They liken career development in such organisations to what Hall (1976) described as the 'Protean career' in which people engage in 'interminable series of experiments and explorations'. Such a career calls for the acceptance of frequent substantial career moves in order to incorporate a changing, complex and multi-layered sense of self; the 'decoupling' of identity from jobs; the preservation of the ability to make choices within the organisation; the identification of distinctive competence; and the synthesis of complex information (Weick and Berlinger, 1989: 323–326).

These are very different requirements from those in traditional organisations, calling for different approaches to careers and to human resource development. However, they may reflect many of the changes in today's organisations, and highlight the significance of employability, discussed in the last section, and the need for lifelong learning. The future of careers, however, is still uncertain, and will be looked at as a controversial issue at the end of this chapter.

Blue-collar careers

The concept of career (Kanter, 1989), we noted above, has generally meant the 'bureaucratic' career) which does not usually embrace the notion of a blue-collar career. Thomas (1989: 355), however, recognising that 'blue-collar workers do indeed accumulate skills . . . over time and are concerned about the meaning of their work experiences', analyses the processes that shape their experiences. He discusses how social class, the organisational arrangement of occupations and labour market segmentation structure career opportunities. Opportunities for upward movement, he suggests, are more likely to occur in organisations with an internal labour market (ILM), and identifies three types of career based on opportunities for advancement to blue-collar positions of greater skill or reward or to lower levels of management:

- dead-end or little opportunity for advancement: unskilled workers in ILM, unskilled and semi-skilled in non-ILM;
- moderate opportunity for advancement: semi-skilled in ILM, skilled in non-ILM;
- high opportunity for advancement: skilled in ILM.

Thomas also discusses how individuals respond to these opportunities: through instrumentality, 'touring' between jobs at the same level, creating meaning in otherwise routine activities, and creating status hierarchies in the workplace. It should be remembered, however, that Thomas's research was undertaken within a North American setting, and that British experiences could be different.

Women's careers

We shall restrict ourselves here to some of the issues raised about the careers of women by two contributors to Arthur, Hall and Lawrence (1989), Gallos and Marshall. Among them are the following, some of which have been alluded to in an earlier section and Chapter 2:

- the construction of identity and the role of relationships;
- autonomy and control;
- partnership, pregnancy and children;
- social stereotypes, roles and socialisation;
- the relationship between work and home life (see also Statham, Miller and Mauksh, 1987).

Gallos and Marshall both recognise the need for 'revision' (Marshall, 1989: 282) of career theory, currently 'rooted in male values and based on disguised male psychology', in order to have approaches that take the needs of both women and men into account. According to Marshall (1989: 285), career theory could then have a more cyclical interpretation of phases, 'based in notions of ebb and flow, of shedding and renewal'. Further, it would allow the recognition of 'giving something up, letting achievements go, in order to create anew and differently'.

Such 'revisioning' would appear to echo some of the components of the subjective career in the self-designing organisations to which Weick and Berlinger (1989) refer (see above) and which appear to reflect the characteristics of many of today's organisations. It challenges some of the thinking behind the stage models of career, but offers a way of conceptualising change as renewal rather than destruction of the old.

Consequences for human resource development

The career development of employees is one manifestation of human resource development, and those responsible for it will benefit from a knowledge of the theories of it and of lifespan development. Indeed, unless they construe the work of blue-collar workers and of women in terms of career, the development of these classes of employees may continue to be neglected (see the subsection on the need to understand learning and development in the organisation, pp. 286–291).

Managers will understand career development better with an awareness of, for example, the nature and effects of career anchors, and of the differences between 'cosmopolitans' and 'locals'. There are implications for other aspects of human resource management: attention must be paid to the nature of changes in blue-collar jobs incurred by quality management and similar initiatives if the organisation is to benefit from them.

The ideas raised here about 'entrepreneurial' careers, careers in self-designing organisations and women's 'cyclic' careers offer starting points for effective human resource development in flexible and learning organisations.

Continuing professional development

We shall not discuss the making of the members of professional and quasi-professional bodies here, except to note the useful term 'formation' to embrace the (engineering) professional's education, training and professional development, 'the progressive process through which a young engineer develops his or her technical and personal capabilities. This process starts while he or she is still at school . . . thereafter is one which will continue throughout each engineer's working life . . .' (Committee of Inquiry into the Engineering Profession, 1980: 77). We shall, however, now briefly examine continuing professional development (CPD) because some of its principles and practices are relevant to human resource development in changing organisations.

Many professional institutions (see Arkin, 1992) are now requiring their members to undertake CPD because the changing environment is rendering obsolete some of their original skills and knowledge and demanding the development of others. For example, the Project on Post Registration Education and Practice (PREPP) proposes that all nurses, midwives and health visitors will have to demonstrate that they have maintained and developed their professional knowledge and competence (UKCC, 1990). However, CPD is more than updating: it calls for a continuous process of learning and of learning to learn, and so is likely to have considerable benefits for organisations employing professionals, especially when part of the overall corporate strategy (Young, 1996).

Likely to be of particular relevance to readers of this book are the requirements for CPD that the Institute of Personnel and Development (IPD) has introduced. Whittaker (1992) states that CPD is needed to ensure that professionals remain up to date in a changing world and that the reputation of the profession is enhanced, and to encourage professionals to aspire to improved performance and ensure that they are committed to learning as an integral part of their work. She identifies the following principles underlying CPD:

● development should always be continuous, the professional always actively seeking improved performance;

- development should be owned and managed by the learner;
- development should begin from the learner's current learning state – learning needs are individual;
- learning objectives should be clear, and where possible serve organisational as well as individual goals;
- investment in the time required for CPD should be regarded as being as important as investment in other activities.

CPD for the IPD is undertaken through engagement in professional activities, formal learning, and self-directed and informal learning (see also Haistead, 1995).

The previous subsection referred briefly to the 'professional' form of career, and suggested that it might be more widely adopted in future. Continuing development, even where not required or monitored by a professional body, would be an important element of it. It should also be noted that the framework of vocational qualifications outlined in Chapter 8 is expected to accommodate the work of professionals at its level 5 (see Welch, 1996 and Whittaker, 1995 on the routes to the personnel and development profession). Professional formation, therefore, may have to be articulated with this framework.

Other forms of development within organisations

We shall now briefly note some other forms of development within organisations.

Self-development

Self-development is the term used to denote both 'of self' and 'by self' types of learning (Pedler, 1988). People developing themselves take responsibility for their own learning, identify their own learning needs and how to meet them, often through the performance of everyday work, monitor their own progress, assess the outcomes and reassess their goals. The role of others in self-development is not to teach or to train, but perhaps to counsel or act as a resource.

In the absence (or paucity) of the training and development of employees (especially managers) by their employers, the need for self-development has long been recognised. It has also been regarded positively as proactive and entrepreneurial, but for it to receive some form of accreditation, it has often involved arduous part-time study, which can increase the pressures on and conflict between the individuals's work and home roles. Such programmes of study have in the past been largely dictated by the traditions and values of the educational providers, rather than the specific needs of the learner. This is now changing with the establishment of the Credit Accumulation and Transfer Scheme, the Accreditation of Prior Learning and of Experiential Learning (see Chapter 8). Moreover, the approach and framework of S/NVQs (see Chapter 8) is now allowing individuals to gain recognition for aspects of their work performance. The existence of employee development schemes (see below) should also help individuals in their self-development, whether systematic or sporadic.

What is now becoming widely recognised is that, with the increasing flexibility of organisations and their contracts of employment, individuals need to engage in lifelong learning – and many will find that they will not receive from their employers the continuous development they will need. The need for self-development, associated with the need for employability, is likely to be seen in the future as greater than ever.

Employee development

One definition of employee development is:

> . . . the skilful provision and organization of learning experiences in the workplace . . . [so that] performance can be improved . . . work goals can be achieved and that, through enhancing the skills, knowledge, learning ability and enthusiasm at every level, there can be continuous organizational as well as individual growth. Employee development must, therefore, be part of a wider strategy for the business, aligned with the organization's corporate mission and goals.*
>
> (Harrison, 1992: 4)

The section earlier on the need for learning and development made clear the importance for the organisation of developing, or 'investing in', employees generally. However, many British employers have continued to ignore this need. This is seen in the quotations from Cooley (1987) we have used throughout this chapter and in points made in Chapters 9 and 10. Nevertheless, as Chapter 8 shows, the establishment of the Investors in People award may be beginning to raise the awareness of employers of the value of employee development. Furthermore, those employers who have already recognised their own self-interest in their employees' continuous learning and employability are encouraging their employees to engage in learning activities for such self-development. In employee development schemes, sometimes established by a consortium of TECs (see Chapter 8) and local employers, the employer provides some degree of financial or other activities that are not necessarily related to the needs of their jobs. A much-quoted example of this is Ford Motor Company's Employee Development and Training Programme (Corney, 1995).

Although these are still exceptions, people still continue to learn even though their employers may not formally 'develop' them or encourage them to develop themselves, as we shall note in the following section.

Staff development

This is similar to employee and professional development, but generally refers to the development of administrative, technical and professional staff in organisations, such as local authorities, in which such staff form a large proportion of those employed. Its aim is to enable such employees to perform their current and future roles effectively, but does not generally include their systematic development as managers.

Management and organisational development

Management development forms the subject of Chapter 10.

It is not within the remit of this book to examine how organisations develop, but we note here that organisations, like people, need to develop to become more flexible, differentiated and adaptable to their environment. Indeed, the very development of organisational members will contribute to the development of the organisation itself. For example, as Chapter 10 recognises, management development is both needed by the developing organisation and sets in train further organisation development.

*This extract is taken from *Employee Development* by Rosemary Harrison and is reproduced with permission of the publishers, The Institute of Personnel and Development, IPD House, 35 Camp Road, London SW19 4UX.

THE ORGANISATION AS A CONTEXT FOR LEARNING

This chapter has examined how people learn and develop. This section now examines how individuals can learn and develop within organisations.

Learning and development sans frontières

The process of learning knows no boundaries; learning in one domain, such as employment, hobbies or maintenance of home and car, cross-fertilises that in another and thereby achieves a wider understanding and more finely honed skills. People bring the fruits of this naturally occurring and continuous process into their place of work and so, as Cooley (1987: 169) shows, 'ordinary people' have the potential to contribute the knowledge, skills, attitudes and creative thinking that organisations need for survival, flexibility and development. Moreover, their learning and development continues within the organisation. Employers benefit from – indeed, depend on – this. Some recognise this and encourage, facilitate and extend those aspects of their employees' learning that are essential for the organisation and support them informally or undertake formal employee development activities (see, for example, Corney, 1995).

However, organisations themselves can sometimes make inhospitable environments for the learning and development individuals bring to them. As we saw in the section on the nature of the learner, learning involves the whole person, but as Chapter 2 identified, organisations are systems of roles and these roles can distort or strait-jacket individuals, as Argyris (1957) and McGregor (1960) argue. While they were both writing in a very different organisational era, and much has already moved in the directions they were advocating, nevertheless, the urgent calls for human resource development and for the development of the learning organisation hint that there still remain vestiges of those traditional assumptions and practices.

Some employers ignore the significance for the organisation of this learning, and do little either to overcome the way in which their organisation may thwart the development of their employees, or to foster that learning and development. In these cases, employee development is not a planned nor a systematic process. It takes place nevertheless: employees learn for themselves how to carry out their jobs, or improve their performance; how to make job changes or achieve promotions; how to become managers and develop others.

We must, therefore, recognise in our overview of human resource development that much employee development may not be intended, planned or systematic: Chapter 9 indicates that this may be the case in the majority of organisations. Nevertheless, individuals may:

- learn how to carry out their initial and subsequent jobs through doing and observing, through trial and error, through the influence of and feedback from their peers and supervisors, through modelling themselves on others, and through informal mentors;
- develop themselves through their own more or less systematic analysis of their learning needs;
- take the initiative to acquire additional knowledge or understanding by attending educational and other courses.

Because of this, employee development is problematical. Employers will receive many of its benefits without effort on their part while at the same time, unlike recruitment and selection, they cannot fully control or contain it. Some employers may feel threatened by the potential of their employees' learning and development, and not welcome significant changes in the people they had been at pains to select as employees. Through their work, employees may acquire knowledge and skills that make them marketable to other employers, and perhaps less than fully committed to their present employer. Equally, not exposed to best practice, they may learn poor lessons; they may also learn ineffectively and in an unnecessarily uncomfortable, effortful or wasteful manner. Thus they may not necessarily benefit from the learning and development they contribute to their organisation, although they will not be able to withhold some of its benefits from their employers.

To manage people effectively and fairly, and in a way that benefits the organisation, therefore, it is important, first, to be aware of these thorny and, at times, moral, issues. (You will have the opportunity to consider them in greater depth in the next section on controversial issues.) Then, it is necessary to understand how the processes of learning and development can be facilitated in the organisation and, indeed, how the organisation can itself learn. This is the subject of this section.

Influences upon learning and development in the organisation

The organisation and its management

Employees learn and develop through carrying out their jobs: this chapter has already noted the significance of action for learning. For example, the design of those jobs and the organisation structure, the degree to which it is centralised and bureaucratised, influence employees' learning opportunities. People may outgrow their jobs as they learn, and need to be able to grow in their jobs, or to move into new jobs that will allow them to continue the process of their development. An organisation that is growing or changing is more likely to offer these opportunities than one that is static or declining.

Earlier sections have identified the need for learners to have self-confidence, and to receive feedback on their performance. Effective learning and development in the organisation, therefore, call for a managerial style that is compatible with this need. The higher order skills needed in organisations require the opportunity to take risks and hence to make mistakes. This presupposes not only a risk-taking and supportive management style, but also a risk-taking and confident approach on the part of employees. The existence and nature of an appraisal scheme (see Chapter 13) could have positive or negative effects upon employees' learning (Thatcher, 1996). Essentially, organisations that want to develop these characteristics need also themselves to learn to learn, to become learning organisations.

The people of the organisation

Other people are significant for learning and development, to provide instruction and feedback (see previous section), support and encouragement, confidence-building, perhaps even inspiration. They are also major actors in the context of the individual's learning. They may be, perhaps unknown to themselves, mentors, models or points of comparison for learners who learn not just from their formal instructors or supervisors, but also from peers and subordinates. This informal method of learning, 'sitting next to Nellie', may have its weaknesses, but it also has strengths. It offers (see previous section) whole rather than part learning, and the opportunity to apprehend tacit knowledge.

Some organisations attempt to capture and use formally some of these informal ways of learning through people. Mentoring, to be discussed below, is an example of this. Shadowing is a method that gives the opportunity for a learner to observe the actions of a senior manager systematically and over a period of time. From this observation the learner can infer certain general principles, grounded in everyday organisational realities. However, as the novel *Nice Work* (Lodge, 1988) suggests, without feedback from the manager, the 'shadow' may misinterpret some of the situations witnessed.

Career management in the organisation

Herriot (1992) argues the importance of career management which, according to Mayo (1992: 37), is 'making sure that the organisation will have the right people with the right skills at the right time'. Organisations that promote the careers of their employees are likely to provide learning and development opportunities for them. One step in Mayo's framework for career management is the review and revision of opportunities for learning through experience.

A somewhat different approach is career path appreciation (Stamp, 1989) which is a structured interview procedure designed to focus 'on the relationship between [decision making] capabilities and the challenges that exist for both the individual and the organisation' (Stamp, 1989: 29). It involves 'career path planning', the identification of the individual's various career 'curves': the potential growth curve, the historic curve, the opportunity curve, the effective level of work curve, and the development curve. Both individual and organisation are responsible for the development path, ensuring that learning and development will benefit both.

Sternberg (1985: 278; see p. 286) indicates that tacit knowledge is important in achieving successful organisational careers:

> Tacit knowledge relevant to managing one's career appears to be more important to career success than does tacit knowledge relevant to managing people, tasks, or self.

By 'managing career' he means 'knowing what activities lead to the enhancement of one's reputation and success in one's field of endeavor' (Sternberg, 1985: 270).

Influences outside the organisation

Many significant influences upon learning and development emanate from outside the organisation. Government-driven education and training initiatives and changes have contributed to the institutionalisation of competency-based education and training. The history, purpose and nature of these developments are discussed by Harrison (1992: 17–77) and more fully in Chapter 8. Within a comprehensive and continually updating national framework agreed across all sectors and occupations, elements in an individual's learning and development, whether achieved through formal education, training or experiential learning across the lifespan, are identified and assessed against nationally agreed standards. The language, philosophy and procedures of this framework are likely to shape individuals' perceptions of their learning and learning needs, and to influence how employers articulate the learning needs of their employees. As Chapter 8 suggests, the Investors in People initiative will also affect human resource development practices.

The facilitation of learning and development in organisations

This subsection will now examine how organisations can facilitate the learning and development of their members through the design of learning, mentoring, action learning and becoming a learning organisation.

The design of learning

The messages about how to design effective learning are very consistent. For example, the advice that Sternberg (1985: 338–341), a theorist of intelligence, gives on how intelligent performance can be trained includes the following: make links with 'real-world' behaviour; deal explicitly with strategies and tactics for coping with novel tasks and situations; be sensitive to individual differences and help individuals capitalise on their strengths and compensate for their weaknesses; be concerned with motivation. The implications of the androgogical model of learning introduced in an earlier section (Knowles, 1984: 14–18) are that the facilitator of adult learning needs to:

1 set a climate conducive to learning, both physical and psychological (one of mutual respect, collaborativeness, mutual trust, supportiveness, openness and authenticity, pleasure, 'humanness');
2 involve learners in mutual planning of their learning;
3 involve them in diagnosing their own learning needs;
4 involve them in formulating their learning objectives;
5 involve them in designing learning plans;
6 help them carry out their learning plans – use learning contracts;
7 involve them in evaluating their learning.

Belbin and Belbin (1972) draw upon their experience of studying training in industry for this advice on training 40 to 55 year old adults:

1 Reduce anxiety and tension in the adult learner:
   - provide social support and allow social groups to form;
   - use acceptable instructors;
   - offer a secure future.

2 Create an adult atmosphere.

3 Arrange the schedule:
   - appropriate length of sessions;
   - preference for whole rather than part method;
   - start slowly.

4 Correct errors:
  - at the appropriate time.

5 Address individual differences:
  - different instructional approaches;
  - effects of previous education and work;
  - spare-time interests.

6 Follow-up after training.

The value of these approaches is illustrated in the lessons drawn from the adoption in Britain of the Deming-inspired quality and continuous improvement programmes (Hodgson, 1987: 43):

> Train with extreme sensitivity – pick trainers who have operators' confidence, are alert to remedial training needs and people's fears about going back to class; minimise the gap between awareness, training and use; gear course contents to people's learning needs – don't impose blanket programmes.

Action learning

> . . . there can be no action without learning, and no learning without action.
>
> (Revans, 1983: 16)

The role of action in learning, and the role of tacit knowledge in action, noted earlier, is now examined more closely here.

The competence movement's focus upon outcomes rather than inputs into learning, and the integration of knowledge and skill assessed via performance, could have offered a route towards the development of learning through action; but, as suggested in Chapter 8, the way it is being approached may be undermining its potential. However, there is an established approach that has been shown (Pedler, 1983) to achieve the kind of learning that organisations, and particularly managers, are seeking, action learning, and this is discussed more fully in Chapter 10.

Action learning offers a philosophy and a practice that human resource managers can adopt to help bring about the higher order skills needed in an organisation. It is a greatly demanding process, one that will change the organisation and its members, but nevertheless one that could be carried out at all levels of the organisation, perhaps as a continuation of 'the restless searching for continuous improvement' and total quality management (see the earlier section on the need for learning and development). However, it demands commitment and support from the top, and would need to be cascaded down from higher learning sets.

Mentoring

The nature and purpose of mentoring

During the last 15 years or so many organisations have introduced mentoring programmes. Their experience suggests that mentoring facilitates the learning to learn of their employees, contributes to the process of meaning-making in the organisation (see Chapter 2) and hence to its responsiveness to its environment, while meeting the developmental needs of employees.

Mentor was the friend to whom Ulysses entrusted the care of his young son before embarking on his epic voyages. In organisations mentors are more experienced employees (and often managers) who guide, encourage and support younger or less experienced employees, or 'protégés' (Hunt and Michael, 1983; Kram, 1985; Collin, 1988; Megginson, 1988; Clutterbuck, 1991). Their relationship is a developmental one that serves career-enhancing and psychosocial functions for the protégé while also benefiting the mentor.

Organisations set up formal mentoring programmes for various reasons (Kanter, 1977; Missirian, 1982; Thomas and Aldefer, 1989; Clutterbuck, 1991). These include supporting a graduate intake or training scheme and developing 'high fliers' or senior managers; encouraging career advancement of women or those from minority groups (see Crofts, 1995); nurturing employees with skills in short supply; stimulating and fostering innovation in the organisation; supporting managers in training or other learners in the organisation. Examples are to be found in a wide range of private and public sector organisations in Britain, Europe, North America and elsewhere (PA Report, 1986; Clutterbuck, 1991).

Protégés are not the only beneficiaries of mentoring: mentors also gain greatly from being challenged to understand their jobs and the organisation, and to find ways of helping their protégés share this understanding and work effectively. Mentors may also find that they, too, need mentoring. Mentors draw upon their own networks to give experience and support to their protégés, and encourage them to develop networks of their own. In this way, the practice and benefits cascade through the organisation.

The requirements for effective mentoring

This literature generally agrees on the following requirements for effective mentoring.

- *The status and characteristics of the mentor.* Mentors will generally be senior to protégés in status, experience and probably age. They should not have a line relationship with their protégé because the element of control inherent in it would conflict with the developmental nature of the mentoring relationship. It is highly desirable that senior managers act as mentors, and that top management be involved with the programme. Mentors should have the skills and qualities that protégés respect, good empathic and people-developing skills, good organisational knowledge and personal networks, and patience and humility to be able to learn from the protégé. Not all managers, therefore, would make appropriate mentors.
- *The protégé.* Protégés should have potential and be hungry to learn and develop in order to realise it. There will be many more potential protégés in the organisation than can be mentored; it is, therefore, commonly noted that mentoring is elitist.
- *The relationship.* The relationship should be one of mutual trust, and will develop over time. Unless limits are set by the programme, it will continue until the protégé no longer needs its support. Sometimes it develops into a full friendship.
- *The activities.* Mentors encourage their protégés to analyse their task performance and to identify weaknesses and strengths. They give feedback and guidance on how weaknesses can be eliminated or neutralised. They help them recognise the tacit dimensions

of the task skills, an important element in the development of competence and 'know-how'. Mentors act as a sounding board for their protégés' ideas, and support them as they try out new behaviours and take risks. They give honest, realistic but supportive feedback, an important element in learning generally and learning to learn in particular. They encourage their protégés to observe and analyse the organisation at work through their own and others' actions. Through this process the protégé begins to identify and then practise tacit knowledge and political skills. Mentors help protégés to identify and develop potentials, question and reflect on experiences and prospects within the organisation, apply formal learning to practice, learn more widely about the organisation and develop networks. Overall, the mentor stimulates, encourages, guides, supports and cautions, acts as a role model, nurtures learning to learn, and encourages the adoption of a future orientation.

The development of higher order skills through mentoring

These activities contribute to the development of the higher order skills needed in the organisation. Daloz (1986: 209–235), for example, suggests that mentors offer their protégés support, challenge and vision. They support their protégés through listening, providing structure, expressing positive expectations, serving as advocate, sharing themselves with their protégés, and 'making it special'. They offer challenge by setting tasks, engaging in discussion, drawing attention to ('heating up') dichotomies, constructing hypotheses, and setting high standards. They offer vision by modelling, keeping tradition, offering a map, suggesting new language, and providing a mirror.

The learning organisation

The notion of the learning organisation has achieved currency during the 1990s, although Garratt (1995: 25) sees it as 'an old idea that has come of age'. Its advocates emphasise that it rarely describes on-the-ground reality but it is, rather, a vision of what might be, 'an aspirational concept' (Burgone, 1995: 24). Burgoyne (1995: 24) interprets it as a 'transitional myth' – the ideas that make sense both in the world that is passing and the one that replaces it and hence enable people to bridge the gap – in this case as 'more emotionally involving, inclusive forms of organisation' emerge from the information-based organisation. We have already quoted Senge's vision of it (towards the end of the section on the need for learning and development in the organisation), while Pedler *et al.* (1991: 1) see it as 'an organization that facilitates the learning of all its members *and* continuously transforms itself'. These are powerful ideas, and this chapter has, therefore, suggested that human resource development will become truly effective when it achieves, and is carried out within, a learning organisation. This subsection will draw on Morgan (1986) to indicate some of the characteristics of a learning organisation.

Following through his metaphor of the organisation as a brain, Morgan (1986) discusses how an organisation can become more intelligent, transcend the 'bounded rationality' of bureaucracy, learn to learn and challenge assumptions. The way to do this, he argues (Morgan, 1986: 91–95), is to: encourage openness and acceptance of error and uncertainty; recognise the need to explore different viewpoints; offer guidelines on the limits to action rather than specific targets, and let the goals emerge from these processes; create the kinds of structures and processes that will allow the above to take place. One such way is to adopt the 'holographic approach' to organisation, which we shall now examine.

Morgan (1986: 80) compares both brain and organisation with a holographic system, 'where the whole can be encoded in all the parts, so that each and every part represents the whole', so allowing the system 'to learn and self-organise' (p. 95). Such a system has 'a pattern of rich connectivity' between the nerve cells so that the system functions in a way that is both generalised and specialised. This degree of connectivity creates more capacity than may be needed at a given time and allows new activities to develop. He next considers how to introduce these holographic features into the organisation, reminding us that they already exist in the brains of employees and the brain-like capacities of computers. He identifies four interacting principles: redundant functions, requisite variety, learning to learn, and minimum critical specification.

Redundancy

The self-organising, learning organisation needs redundancy of functions rather than redundancy of parts (Morgan, 1986: 98–99). The latter exists when each part has a specific function, with additional parts for back-up or replacement; this allows a degree of 'passivity and neglect' in the system (it's 'someone else's problem'). The capacity for redesigning the system is, therefore, delegated to specialised parts, and the capacity to self-organise is not generalised throughout the system. Where, instead, each part has redundant functions and so can do more than it currently does, and the capacities for the functioning of whole are built into the parts, the system as a whole has flexibility, the capacity to reflect on and question how it is operating and hence be able to change its mode of operating.

Requisite variety

The internal diversity of a self-regulating system must match the variety and complexity of its environment in order to deal with the challenges. All elements of the organisation should, therefore, 'embody critical dimensions' of the environment with which they have to deal; this variety can be achieved, where appropriate, through 'multifunctioned teams' (Morgan, 1986: 100–101).

Minimum critical specification

Because specification, as in a bureaucracy, erodes flexibility, then no more than is necessary should be adopted, and the manager should have a facilitating role to create enabling conditions. Morgan (1986: 102) proposes that roles should be left 'deliberately ambiguous and overlapping'. This runs counter to the accepted personnel practice of job descriptions (see Chapter 6), but will achieve a flexible organisation still capable of evolving an appropriate and sufficient structure to deal with problems as they arise.

Learning to learn

Finally, the organisation needs double loop learning (see earlier) so that it guides itself 'with reference to a set of coherent values or norms, while questioning whether these norms provide an appropriate basis for guiding behaviour' (Morgan, 1986: 102).

The notion of the learning organisation, as expressed in Morgan, enables us to see how the needed higher order skills can be generated and nurtured not only among managers but also among all organisational members. However, to translate the vision into everyday reality, the learning culture has to be championed by a senior manager and embedded in

○ the organisation's strategy, structure, systems and norms (Mayo and Lank, 1995).

Membership of a learning organisation will itself provide the stimulus, prompts and cues for individuals to learn and develop, and thereby also achieve the excellence and quality, flexibility and adaptability needed by organisations in a changing world.

CONTROVERSIAL ISSUES

This section presents a number of problematical or controversial issues for you to reflect upon and discuss:

- Who owns the individual's learning and development?
- Differing interpretations of human resource development.
- The future of career.

Who owns the individual's learning and development?

There are two routes to finding the answers to this question:

- reflecting on your own experience;
- identifying the stakeholders in the individual's learning and development.

You can then identify the implications for human resource development.

Reflections on your own experience

In order to recognise the significance of this question, complete the following exercise.

EXERCISES

1 What is it costing you to learn?
   For example, take your reading of this book. What does this activity cost you?

2 Who pays the costs of your learning and development?

3 Who benefits from your learning and development?
   List the beneficiaries of your reading of this book.

The stakeholders in the individual's learning and development

When you examine the potential benefits of your learning, you can see that there are several beneficiaries, or 'stakeholders', in it. In the case of reading this book, you may have purchased it yourself and be reading this late at night in order to succeed in examinations for a qualification that will advantage you in getting a job, or a better job, or in order to do your present job better. Because this learning is likely to enhance your job satisfaction and career, you may have initiated the process of development or, if it was initiated by your employer, have been prepared to bear much of its costs (financial, opportunity cost, time, energy). Your employers, however, present or future, also benefit from your learning and development and are, therefore, also stakeholders in it, and may or may not initiate the process and bear the cost (or part) of it.

There are, moreover, other stakeholders in your learning. Your family and dependants benefit from the increased income or status that this development may bring, but have to forgo time and money to achieve it. Society benefits from a skilled and satisfied work-force, and pays for it through the educational system and government benefits from potential employees in training rather than unemployment, and pays for this through various state-sponsored training programmes.

The learner benefits in ways that spill over from the work situation. Much learning enlarges the individual, who gains not only knowledge and skills but a breadth and depth of understanding, and from this increased self-confidence and esteem. Learning, in other words, fosters development, so that through their learning people change: they are no longer the people they once were. As employees, they may become more demanding and less compliant. This enlargement of self may also be accompanied by an enhance-ment of status as learning enables individuals to move into more prestigious social roles or better-rewarded jobs.

The implications for human resource development

By reflecting upon your own motivation and experiences, you will already have an insight into some of the thorny issues inherent in human resource development (others are dis-cussed by Rainbird and Maguire, 1993). These issues can be summarised as follows:

- Learning and development take place throughout life, and in every aspect of life, as well as through performance of the job.
- Employer-initiated and sponsored and delivered learning can only constitute a small part of an individual's total learning.
- Some of such activities are undertaken as part of planned development; some are random or opportunistic.
- The employer cannot ring-fence such employer-provided learning.
- Employer-provided learning will be infiltrated by learning from other arenas – from home or social life, but also from undertaking the daily job, or observing boss or colleagues. Such learning may influence, strengthen, challenge or undermine employer-provided learning.
- The processes of learning and development may work counter to the processes of matching and control in which some employers invest heavily in the selection process.
- Learning and development are difficult to evaluate, because they often need an in-terval of time for their outcomes to be manifested.
- It is not easy to apportion their benefits to either employer or employee.
- It is not easy to calculate their costs, nor apportion them between employer and employee.
- Some of the costs are not borne by either of these; partners, families and the state through the educational and vocational training systems also pay some of the price of employee development.
- Individuals expect reward for their training or development – they have put effort in, become more skilled – expect greater reward. This reward may be either extrinsic (pro-motion, increase in pay) or intrinsic (greater fulfilment through a more demanding or higher status job).

- As employees learn and develop, they may become less compliant to their employer and more demanding of changes at work and further development.
- It may result in the employee's dissatisfaction with his/her present job or employer.
- Because of all the above, employers may be reluctant to pay to develop their employees.
- It is difficult formally to provide effective learning – it often seems false in comparison with the ongoing spontaneous learning from life in general, and there are often difficulties in transferring from formal learning situations to everyday work.
- Some of the processes, activities, benefits depend upon the individual's context (including the presence of significant others), age and stage of development in life.

The issue of the ownership of the learning and development of individuals, as employees, reminds us that managing people has a moral dimension – human resource management juggles with empowering and controlling. This is the unanswered (and unanswerable?) question at the heart of human resource development and poses dilemmas to both employer and employee.

Differing interpretations of human resource development

The philosophy underpinning this chapter's presentation of its material is humanistic – learning and development have largely been interpreted as empowering of the individual. The chapter has not questioned whether the harnessing of individual learning and development by the organisation could not be interpreted in a very different way. The awareness that the ownership of individual learning is a matter of debate, however, presents the opportunity to look for other interpretations.

Consider this for yourself. What interpretations might the other chapters of this book have of human resource development? How idealistic or cynical are calls for activities such as mentoring and the learning organisation in today's flexible organisations? Is mentoring elitist or empowering? Is the learning organisation rhetoric or reality? Are there other possible interpretations?

The future of career

This chapter has outlined some aspects of career as it has traditionally been understood. However, the flatter and more flexible forms of today's organisations, the emergence of 'a workplace without jobs' (according to Bridges, 1995), and the changing relationship between employees and employers ('the new deal', according to Herriot and Pemberton, 1995) could well change the nature of career dramatically. There are also some slow, deep-seated changes taking place in the context (see Chapter 2) of career. Demographic changes and shifts in public and private values, for example, may over time have significant impacts upon individuals' opportunities, attitudes and aspirations. It is for this reason that it is being questioned whether the future of career is 'death' or 'transfiguration' (Collin and Watts, 1996).

Meanwhile, the possibilities, potentials and implications of some of these changes – for individuals, employers, educationalists, careers guidance practitioners and policy-makers of various kinds – are being discussed widely (see Jackson *et al.*, 1996). It is suggested that the traditional 'onward and upward' form of career – Kanter's 'bureaucratic' form' – may be under threat and that the 'professional' and 'entrepreneurial' careers may become the predominant forms (see Kanter, 1989b, and Collin and Watts, in press). However, 'don't write off the traditional career', advise Guest and Davey (1996: 22), who have found little evidence of major organisational transformations in their own research.

Many have seen the traditional career as elitist, available only to a few, characterised largely by social background and education. The future career may also be elitist, available to a few, but perhaps a different few. At this point it is possible to identify some of the winners and losers from the changes that are taking place. So far the losers have included both workers in manufacturing, unskilled workers of many kinds, clerical workers of many kinds, middle managers of many kinds, full-time workers of many kinds (see also Chapters 3 and 4); many of these have been men. The winners have been the knowledge workers, those with the skills required by the new technologies, those with the attitudes and skills needed in service jobs, those who are able (or want) to work only part-time; women seem to be benefiting from some of the changes. To be employable, employed and to have a career in the future, individuals will have to have, as this chapter has reiterated, the ability to learn new knowledge and skills, and above all to learn how to learn.

The changing nature of career is also of considerable significance for society as a whole, as well as for individuals and for the economy. For example, the future orientation that a career gives an individual is essential when making decisions about such key issues as starting a family, taking out a mortgage, changing one's occupation, re-entering education, or retiring from employment. Uncertainty about career could, therefore, over time affect the structure of the population or the housing market, while the effects of unemployment may be damaging the social fabric severely. (Hutton, 1995: 105–110, writes that today's Britain has a 'thirty, thirty, forty society': 30% are 'disadvantaged' – unemployed or economically inactive; 30% are 'marginalised' and 'insecure, – in poorly paid or poorly protected employment; while 40% are 'privileged' – in relatively secure full-time or self-employment.) The future of career, therefore, is of concern to us all.

EXERCISES

1 Assess your present employability.

2 What do you need to do to achieve, maintain or improve this?

3 What would be the implications for the nature and quality of your life overall if your career proved to be flexible and/or fragmented?

SUMMARY

● This chapter addressed the issue of why individuals generally and human resource managers in particular need to understand learning and development.

● It began with a series of definitions of learning which essentially rested on the view that the acquisition of knowledge and understanding facilitates change in perceptions and practice. These attributes are increasingly essential in the modern world of work in which employees are expected to cope with change and new technology, take more responsibility, become more skilled and knowledgeable and develop the ability for problem solving and creative thinking.

● The characteristics which today's organisations need for their survival were examined, in particular, the need for quality and continuous improvement, flexibility and adaptability. In attempting to meet modern challenges, organisations are becoming more flexible and flatter with a greater degree of responsibility devolved to the workforce in decentralised functions. Individual employees, therefore, must engage in a continuous process of learning how to learn.

● The nature of the learner in relation to work and career was examined; but it was also emphasised that learning is a lifelong process which means making continuous adaptations. In many senses it is a journey. In the process of learning many barriers are thrown up including anxiety and lack of confidence on behalf of the learner. Discrimination also exists and often creates barriers for certain groups such as older workers, women, disabled people and cultural and ethnic minorities. This may impair their ability to learn by undermining their confidence and/or preventing them from taking courses and training programmes which will lead to greater opportunities. Many in these groups belong to the most disadvantaged in our society.

● The outcomes of learning – the acquisition of new skills, competence, 'know-how', tacit knowledge and employability – were highlighted. It is equally important for managers to have an awareness of the hierarchies of learning, the various levels of learning through which learners proceed in the pursuit of knowledge and understanding. Each level adds a further layer of sophistication to this process, from the simple acquisition of knowledge of facts through to the ability to understand complicated analyses involving complex abstract processes. Such understanding will take the learner through the various stages of learning: novice, advanced beginner, competent, proficient and finally, expert. Various theories and models of learning and learning styles were also examined in relation to these developments.

● The concept of development was explored as a process which is being demanded more and more of employees in the modern organisation. It is a process in which the learner 'becomes increasingly complex, more elaborate and differentiated, and thereby able to adapt to the changing environment'. A number of theories and models of lifespan, career and other forms of development were then examined and their implications for human resource development noted.

● Much learning and development takes place within the organisational context, and is influenced by the nature of the organisation. Although learning knows no frontiers, organisations can often make inhospitable environments for the learning and development of individuals, and with this in mind it must be recognised that organisations are learning instruments as well. This has considerable implications for training and development within the organisation, which is also influenced from outside by national training initiatives.

● The final part of the chapter examined three controversies for the reader to reflect on. These were who owns the individual's learning and development, the differing interpretations of human resource development, and the future of career. Rather than giving 'answers' the author posed a number of probing questions for the reader to develop their thoughts in pondering issues – a form of self development in itself.

ACTIVITY

ABC & Sons is a third generation family business, producing components for manufacturers of luxury consumer goods. It has established a reputation for quality and service and exports a quarter of its output overseas.

Family members have generally entered the business as new graduates and, starting on the shop floor, have spent several years working in every department of the company. They have later broadened their knowledge by attending courses on new developments and technology, and on various aspects of management. As a result, the company has kept up to date in its production and administrative techniques and is making use of sophisticated levels of information technology in several areas. However, it has paid little attention to the development of its other managers beyond essential updating in, for example, health and safety regulations.

Until recently, ABC & Sons had a relatively stable workforce of 500 employees, was seen as a good employer, and viewed with pride by its many long-serving employees who encouraged their own children to work there. The skilled workers have traditionally been men and the assembly, packing and clerical workers have been women, many from ethnic minorities.

More recently, however, there have been some significant changes. The introduction of the new technology has necessitated the recruitment of new technical managers and some graduate management trainees. Some of the older craft skills have become redundant, while new technical skills are now needed in many areas. Moreover, although the new technology has given the company a competitive edge, the market world-wide for its customers' products has dwindled and, indeed, some of its major customers and key suppliers are in difficulties. While so far avoiding redundancy, the company has responded to natural wastage by taking on most newcomers on part-time contracts and has increased the proportion of women and young people employed.

The senior management of ABC & Sons is beginning to recognise that the company is facing more than recession and that the industrial sector as a whole is in decline: the company needs to plan its future strategically. It is also becoming aware that the changes introduced over the last few years have radically altered the nature of the company. Senior managers have recently been dismayed by incidents that suggest a growing cynicism among the longer serving employees and desire for early retirement, and among the young a lack of commitment and a disappointingly narrow range of skills. To deal with all these issues, a new post of human resource manager has been created, reporting to the managing director's daughter who is the board member responsible for staff and administration. The existing personnel and welfare officer will now assist the new manager.

EXERCISES

Working on your own or in a group, carry out the following exercises:

You are the newly-appointed human resource manager.

1 What human resource development issues confront you in this situation? What are your priorities for dealing with them?

▶

2 What opportunities and threats is the company facing? What are the strengths and weaknesses of the workforce in the present situation? Who needs development? Of what kind? How will it be undertaken? Who will be responsible for it? Who else would play a part in it? What are the barriers to or constraints upon their development likely to be?

3 What overall growth points or potential for learning and development do you see in the company? How may they be stimulated and nurtured?

4 What further learning and development will you need yourself?

QUESTIONS

1 Why do human resource managers need to understand the processes of learning and development?

2 What are the higher order skills needed in organisations and how may they be developed?

3 How may practical knowledge be developed in an organisation?

4 How may learning transform an individual? What are the implications of such transformation for an organisation?

5 What are the implications for an individual's career of new flexible forms of organisation?

EXERCISES

1 Keep a learning diary

Reflection is essential for effective learning. Systematically reflect upon what and how you learn by keeping a learning diary. It will also help you remember issues to discuss with your tutor, and may also contribute to your continuing professional development portfolio.

Spend half-an-hour every week recording the following:

- the most meaningful or stressful events of the week
- how they came about and who was involved
- your interpretation of them
- the emotions evoked by them
- how you dealt with them
- the outcomes of your actions
- your evaluation of your actions
- what you would do or avoid doing in future
- what further skills, knowledge and understanding you need to perform more effectively
- how you could acquire these
- your action plan.

Kolb, D.A., Rubin, I.M. and MacIntyre, J.M. (1984) *Organizational Psychology: An Experiential Approach*, 4th edn. New York: Prentice Hall.

Kram, K.E. (1985) *Mentoring At Work: Developmental Relationships in Organizational Life*. Illinois: Scott, Foresman.

Laslett, P. (1989) *A Fresh Map of Life: The Emergence of the Third Age*. London: Weidenfeld & Nicolson.

Levinson, D.J., Darrow, C.M., Klein, E.B., Levinson, M.H. and McKee, B. (1978) *The Seasons of a Man's Life*. New York: Alfred A. Knopf.

Littlefield, D. and Welch, J. (1996) 'Trainers focus on a more strategic role', *People Management*, 4 April, pp. 11–14.

Lodge, D. (1988) *Nice Work: A Novel*. London: Secker & Warburg.

McGregor, D. (1960) *The Human Side of Enterprise*. New York: McGraw-Hill.

Mangham, I.L. and Silver, M.S. (1986) *Management Training: Context and Practice*. Bath: University of Bath, School of Management.

Martin, S. (1995) 'A futures market for competencies', *People Management*, 23 March, pp. 20–24.

Marshall, J. (1989) 'Re-visioning career concepts: A feminist invitation', in Arthur, M.B., Hall, D.T. and Lawrence, B.S. (eds) *Handbook of Career Theory*. Cambridge: Cambridge University Press, pp. 275–291.

Mayo, A. (1992) 'A framework for career management', *Personnel Management*, February, pp. 36–39.

Mayo, A. and Lank, E. (1995) 'Changing the soil spurs new growth', *People Management*, 16 November, pp. 26–28.

Megginson, D. (1988) 'Instructor, coach, mentor: three ways of helping for managers', *Management Education and Development*, Vol. 19, Pt 1, pp. 33–46.

Mezirow, J. (1977) 'Personal transformation', *Studies in Adult Education* (Leicester: National Institute of Adult Education), Vol. 9, No. 2, pp. 153–64.

Missirian, A.K. (1982) *The Corporate Connection*. Englewood Cliffs, NJ: Prentice Hall.

Moreton, T. (ed.) (1992) 'The education, training and employment of disabled people', *Personnel Review*, Vol. 21, No. 6.

*Morgan, G. (1986) *Images of Organization*. Beverly Hills, Calif.: Sage.

Morgan, G. (1988) *Riding the Waves of Change: Developing Managerial Competencies for a Turbulent World*. San Francisco: Jossey-Bass.

Mumford, A. (1988) 'Learning to learn and management self-development', in Pedler, M., Burgoyne, J. and Boydell, T. (eds) *Applying Self-Development in Organizations*. New York: Prentice Hall, pp. 23–27.

Musgrove, F. (1977) *Margins of the Mind*. London: Methuen.

Myers, C. and Davids, K. (1992) 'Knowing and doing: tacit skills at work', *Personnel Management*, February, pp. 45–47.

Naylor, P. (1987) 'In praise of older workers', *Personnel Management*, November, pp. 44–48.

Neugarten, B.L. (1968) 'Adult personality: toward a psychology of the life cycle', in Neugarten, B.L. (ed.) *Middle Age and Aging: A Reader in Social Psychology*. Chicago: University of Chicago Press, pp. 137–147.

PA Personnel Services (1986) *Management Development and Mentoring: An International Study*. London: PA.

Pedler, M. (ed.) (1983) *Action Learning in Practice*. Aldershot: Gower.

Pedler, M. (1988) 'Self-development and work organizations', in Pedler, M., Burgoyne, J. and Boydell, T. (eds) *Applying Self-Development in Organizations*. New York: Prentice Hall, pp. 1–19.

Pedler, M., Burgoyne, J. and Boydell, T. (eds) (1988) *Applying Self-Development in Organizations*. New York: Prentice Hall.

Pedler, M., Burgoyne, J. and Boydell, T. (1991) *The Learning Company: A Strategy for Sustainable Development*. London: McGraw-Hill.

Perry, W.G. (1968) *Forms of Intellectual and Ethical Development in the College Years; A Scheme*. New York: Holt, Rinehart & Winston.

Phillips-Jones, L. (1982) *Mentors and Protégés: How to Establish, Strengthen and Get the Most from a Mentor/Protégé Relationship*. New York: Arbor House.

Pickard, J. (1993) 'Toyota's Derby novices on the Kentucky track', *Personnel Management Plus*, Vol. 4, No. 3, pp. 18–19.

Pugh, D.S., Hickson, D.J. and Hinings, C.R. (eds) (1983) *Writers on Organizations*. Harmondsworth: Penguin.

Quinn, R.E., Faerman, S.R., Thompson, M.P. and McGrath, M.R. (1990) *Becoming a Master Manager*. New York: Wiley.

Rainbird, H. and Maguire, M. (1993) 'When corporate need supersedes employee development', *Personnel Management*, February, pp. 34–37.

Reese, H.W. and Overton, W.F. (1970) 'Models of development and theories of development', in Goulet, L.R. and Baltes, P.B. (eds) *Life-Span Developmental Psychology: Theory and Research*. New York: Academic Press, pp. 115–145.

*Revans, R. (1983) *ABC of Action Learning*. Bromley: Chartwell-Bratt (Publishing and Training).

*Ribeaux, P. and Poppleton, S.E. (1978) *Psychology and Work: An Introduction*. London: Macmillan.

Rothwell, S. (1992) 'Polishing up the supply chain', *Personnel Management*, September, pp. 28–32.

Rotter, J. (1966) 'Generalized expectancies for internal versus external control of reinforcement', *Psychological Monographs*, Vol. 80, No. 1, pp. 1–28.

Saggers, R. (1994) 'Training climbs the corporate agenda', *Personnel Management*, July, pp. 40–45.

Schein, E.H. (1978) *Career Dynamics: Matching Individual and Organizational Needs*. Reading, Mass.: Addison-Wesley.

*Senge, P. (1990) *The Fifth Discipline: The Art and Practice of the Learning Organization*. London: Century.

Sheard, A. (1992) 'Learning to improve performance', *Personnel Management*, November, pp. 40–45.

Sheard, M. (1992) 'Why Dow went for BS5750', *Personnel Management*, November, pp. 33–34.

Smelser, N. and Erikson, E. (eds) (1980) *Themes of Work and Love in Adulthood*. London: Grant McIntyre.

Sofer, C. (1970) *Men in Mid-Career*. Cambridge: Cambridge University Press.

Stammers, R. and Patrick, J. (1975) *The Psychology of Training*. London: Methuen.

Stamp, G. (1989) 'The individual, the organisation, and the path to mutual appreciation', *Personnel Management*, July, pp. 28–31.

Statham, A., Miller, E.M. and Mauksch, O. (eds) (1988) *The Worth of Women's Work*. Albany: State University of New York Press.

Sternberg, R.J. (1985) *Beyond IQ: A Triarchic Theory of Human Intelligence*. Cambridge: Cambridge University Press.

Syrett, M. and Lammiman, J. (1994) 'Developing the "peripheral" worker', *Personnel Management*, July, pp. 28–31.

Thatcher, M. (1996) 'Allowing everyone to have their say', *People Management*, 21 March, pp. 28–30.

Thomas, D.A. and Alderfer, C.P. (1989) 'The influence of race on career dynamics: theory and research on minority career experiences', in Arthur, M.B., Hall, D.T. and Lawrence, B.S. (eds) *Handbook of Career Theory*. Cambridge: Cambridge University Press, pp. 133–158.

Thomas, R.J. (1989) 'Blue-collar careers: meaning and choice in a world of constraints', in Arthur, M.B., Hall, D.T. and Lawrence, B.S. (eds) *Handbook of Career Theory*. Cambridge: Cambridge University Press, pp. 354–379.

Townsend, T. (1992) 'How the lead body sees it', *Personnel Management*, November, p. 39.

Training Commission (1988) *Classifying the Components of Management Competences*. Sheffield: Training Commission.

Trinder, C., Hulme, G. and McCarthy, U. (1992) *Employment: the Role of Work in the Third Age*, The Carnegie Inquiry into the Third Age, Research Paper Number 1. Dumfermline: The Carnegie United Kingdom Trust.

Tyson, S. and Fell, A. (1995) 'A focus on skills, not organisations', *People Management*, 19 October, pp. 42–45.

UKCC (1986) *Project 2000: A New Preparation for Practice*. London: UK Central Council for Nursing, Midwifery and Health Visiting.

UKCC (1990) *The Report of the Post-Registration Education and Practice Project*. London: UK Central Council for Nursing, Midwifery and Health Visiting.

Waskel, S. A. (1991) *Mid-Life Issues and the Workplace of the 90s: A Guide for Human Resource Specialists*. New York: Quorum.

Watts, A.G., Law, B., Killeen, J., Kidd, J. M. and Hawthorn, R. (1996) *Rethinking Careers Education and Guidance: Theory, Policy and Practice*. London: Routledge.

Wechsler, D. (1958) *The Measurement and Appraisal of Adult Intelligence*, 4th edn. London: Baillière, Tindall & Cox.

Weick, K.E. and Berlinger, L.R. (1989) 'Career improvisation in self-designing organizations', in Arthur, M.B., Hall, D.T. and Lawrence, B.S. (eds) *Handbook of Career Theory*. Cambridge: Cambridge University Press, pp. 313–328.

Welch, J. (1996) 'HR qualifications get the go-ahead at last', *People Management*, 30 May, p. 11.

White, M. (1996) 'Flexible response', *People Management*, 21 March, p. 33.

Whitaker, A. (1992) 'The transformation in work: post-Fordism revisited', in Reed, M. and Hughes, M. (eds) *Rethinking Organization: New Directions in Organization Theory*, pp. 184–206.

Whittaker, J. (1992) 'Making a policy of keeping up to date', *Personnel Management*, March, pp. 28–31.

Whittaker, J. (1995) 'Three challenges for IPD standards', *People Management*, 16 November, pp. 30–4.

Wibberley, M. (1992) 'Why Bosch went for total quality', *Personnel Management*, November, pp. 31–32.

Wilensky, H. (1960) 'Work, careers and social integration', *International Social Science Journal*, Vol. 12, No. 4, pp. 543–574.

Wills, G. (ed.) (1993) *Your Enterprise School of Management*. Bradford: MCB University Press.

Wisher, V. (1994) 'Competencies: the precious seeds of growth', *Personnel Management*, July, pp. 36–39.

Woodruffe, C. (1991) 'Competent by any other name', *Personnel Management*, September, pp. 30–33.

Wrightsman, L.S. (1988) *Personality Development in Adulthood*. Newbury Park, Calif.: Sage.

Young, C. (1996) 'How CPD can further organisational aims', *People Management*, 30 May, p. 67.

THE NATIONAL FRAMEWORK FOR VOCATIONAL EDUCATION AND TRAINING

Audrey Collin and Len Holden

OBJECTIVES

To identify the stakeholders in the individual's learning and development.

●

To examine vocational education and training in the leading industrial nations with an in-depth investigation of the training systems of Germany, Japan and France.

●

To examine the implications of these international comparisons for the UK.

●

To examine the national framework for vocational education and training in the UK.

●

To outline possible future policy developments in vocational education and training into and beyond the millennium.

●

To identify some controversial issues in the field of vocational education and training.

●

INTRODUCTION

Learning and development are not solely matters of concern for individuals and their employers. An educated and skilled workforce is essential for the effective functioning of the economy, the competitiveness and wealth of the nation, as well as for the overall well-being of society. Indeed, Tyson and Fell (1995: 45) suggest that 'the future will see a world of work based more on skills than organisations'. To ensure that a nation achieves the level of skills it needs, its government, therefore, puts in place the vocational education and training (VET) policies and systems that will facilitate their development. Such national strategies, therefore, form an important part of the context (see Chapter 2) of individual learning and organisational human resource development (HRD).

As new technology progresses, replacing jobs and changing skill requirements, there is an increasing need for a skilled and highly trained workforce able to meet these changing situations. Traditional skills, for example in the engineering and construction industries, are rapidly changing, and the type of economy in which a young person can receive an apprenticeship which would stand them in good stead for a lifetime career is dwindling.

This trend is an international one and poses problems for the USA, Japan, Germany, France, Sweden and other industrialised nations. However, comparisons with competitor nations indicate that Britain is suffering from a severe skills shortage. Its 'first ever national audit of job skills' (Welch, 1996b: 11), which the government published in 1996 to accompany its third 'competitiveness' White Paper, compares Britain with France, Germany, Singapore and the USA.

> Its findings confirm fears that Britain's skills are lagging behind those of Germany, which has had a policy of investment in vocational training for years. More worrying is the rapidly shrinking gap between the UK and Singapore in the league tables. (Welch, 1996c: 11)

Britain's greatest deficiency is in basic and level two skills, though 'Britain is ahead of its competitors both on quality and the quantity of its population' possessing degrees and vocational qualifications of a comparable level.

Many see the solution as investing more capital in education and training and the creation of an ever more skilled and knowledgeable workforce, partly because the industrialised countries can never compete with developing world economies in terms of cheap labour. The developments in VET in Britain, as elsewhere, have to be seen within this context. However, the efficacy of VET to achieve such national needs is not fully demonstrated. For example, the relative economic decline in Britain has led to much debate as to the adequacy of training in helping to arrest this trend. (This is a controversial issue that will be discussed in a later section.)

There has been considerable criticism of the training policy in the UK both at national and organisational level (though other views are also now being expressed: see Harrison, 1995 and Merrick, 1995). As a later section will show, Britain has not compared favourably with Germany, Japan, Sweden or France in VET terms. Many surveys throughout the 1980s and 1990s have shown that employers regard training as being important, but the problem seems to be that, despite this recognition, not enough has taken place to meet the changing needs of the economy. What we have therefore seen is the British government tackling the training needs for the economy in an energetic way, and introducing many new policies and systems. These are having a major impact upon how learning individually and in organisations takes place by providing a framework of philosophies (e.g. competencies), structures (e.g. the National Council for Vocational Qualifications), resources (e.g. the Training and Enterprise Councils), and incentives (e.g. the Investors in People award).

The purpose of this chapter is to outline some of the VET policies and systems currently in place in Britain, and to indicate some possible future developments in order to provide an informative backcloth for Chapters 9 and 10. It opens, however, by first recognising the key stakeholders in VET, and then setting British provision in the context of that of some of its major competitors.

STAKEHOLDERS IN VOCATIONAL EDUCATION AND TRAINING

Chapter 7 identified several stakeholders in the individual's learning and development, and it examined the needs and responses of the individual and the employer in particular. There are several stakeholders in VET, too, and their values and actions constitute the framework within which individual learning and development and organisational HRD have to take place. This chapter focuses particularly on the part the government plays in this field, which will be examined in some detail later in this chapter. It should be noted that in Britain the departments concerned with education and employment have both been involved, and that they were eventually merged to form the Department of Education and Employment.

Employers themselves are also significant stakeholders in VET. This is apparent in the international comparisons in the following section. During the 1990s, the British employers' body, the Confederation of British Industry (CBI), played an influential role. For example, recognising the need for a 'skills revolution' (Confederation of British Industry, 1989), it proposed training targets (later adopted by the government) for the minimum standards needed to increase Britain's competitiveness.

The trade unions are further stakeholders in VET. At present the role of British unions in this regard is somewhat limited compared with their German and French counterparts, 'where unions are involved widely at national, regional, sectoral and company levels in promoting and regulating the training process. This role is supported in France by law. In Germany it constitutes one part of the corporatist system of compromise and consensus between the "social partners"' (Claydon and Green, 1992).

However, British trade unions have recently been examining their role in the economic system, particularly in the light of their decline over the past decade. One strategy they have begun to adopt is to advocate training as a collective bargaining issue other than in the narrow context of setting wages and conditions for apprentices (Kenney and Reid, 1988). Some unions, for example the EEPTU, have advocated a policy of training their members to update their skills and improve their employability, in order to demonstrate to employers that the presence of unions can be beneficial (Lloyd, 1990). The TUC discussed training initiatives in *Skills 2000* (TUC, 1989) and *TUC: Joint Action over Training*

(TUC, 1990), and have advocated greater 'involvement in the planning and provision of training and educational opportunities through participation at European, national and firm levels' (TUC, 1991, quoted in Claydon and Green, 1992).

Nevertheless, while British unions may have a small direct influence on training provision, Claydon and Green (1992) suggest that 'participation in training is about a third greater for union members than for non-union members which suggests that there is a substantial positive impact of unions on the training of workers in small establishments particularly for non-manual workers'. They explain this correlation by the 'otherwise absent pressure for training' and support the TUC proposals for workplace training committees, which would have trade union representation. Such committees would raise the consciousness for training and should have a considerable impact on training provision. The present Conservative government would oppose such regulatory measures and emphasise that employers should choose whether they think training is necessary; in this way, it argues, training responds to market trends and needs. Given the present government attitudes to trade unions, it is highly unlikely that the TUC's proposals will gain backing in law. Only a change of government may effect that.

This chapter sets out the values and activities of some of these various stakeholders because they constitute a significant context (see Chapter 2) for individual learning and development and organisational HRD.

VET IN THE LEADING INDUSTRIALISED NATIONS

This section compares and contrasts VET in six leading industrialised nations: Britain and five competitor countries. It can be seen that there are a number of similarities. All six countries have compulsory education of similar ages (Table 8.1) and therefore recognise the importance of at least a basic education in a modern industrialised society. All six countries will experience decline in the number of children of school-leaving age in the 1990s (Table 8.2), and Germany will experience the most severe decline.

An examination of the statistics of 16 to 18-year-olds shows that the majority continue with some form of education or training, either full or part time (Table 8.2). Britain, however, has the least number involved, being 10% below the French comparable figure.

TABLE 8.1
Compulsory school education ages

Britain	5–16 yrs
Germany	6–15 yrs
France	6–16 yrs
Sweden	7–16 yrs
Japan	6–15 yrs
USA	6–16 yrs*

* Varies from state to state.

TABLE 8.2

Indices of the 16 to 18-year-old population and participation in eduction rates

	16 to 18-year-olds population indices (year)			16 to 18-year-olds participation in education and training%		
	1980	1990	2000	Full	Part	All
Britain	121	106	94	33	31	64
Germany	125	83	72	47	43	90
France	100	103	90	66	8	74
Sweden	99	102	86	76	2	78
Japan	91	114	92*	77	3	79
USA	102	83	85*	79	1	80

100 = 1970
* = 1996
Source: DES (1990). Reproduced by permission of the Controller of Her Majesty's Stationery Office.

There are also significant differences between these countries in the amount of financial investment which their organisations make in training. This is demonstrated in Tables 8.3 and 8.4.

TABLE 8.3

Proportion of salaries and wages spent on training 1990–91

	UK	France	Spain	Sweden	Germany
0.01–1.0%	21	4	33	9	20
4% and above	11	27	13	16	11
Don't know	41	2	25	48	47

Source: Price Waterhouse Cranfield Survey (Holden, 1991: 120).

TABLE 8.4

Proportion of salaries and wages spent on training 1991–92

	Switzerland	Germany	Denmark	Spain	France	Italy	Norway	Netherlands	Sweden	UK
0.01–2.0%	64	61	66	76	25	76	63	65	57	62
4% and above	11	16	13	10	32	9	19	16	25	18
Don't know	25	42	33	18	2	24	30	23	44	38

Source: Price Waterhouse Cranfield Survey (Holden and Livian, 1992: 15). Reproduced with permission of MCB University Press.

As we shall see shortly, Germany has a thoroughgoing VET infrastructure and Sweden also has a well-established vocational system which begins when children are 14 years old. These countries, therefore, while having a large proportion of organisations ignorant of their training expenditure, have tried and tested systems of VET. The large UK 'Don't know' figures are therefore all the more ominous given the unclear and contradictory approaches to VET.

VET policies and practices

An examination of the VET systems beyond compulsory school age for the same six countries reveals a varying, and sometimes widely varying, set of practices (see Table 8.5). They can be roughly divided into 'voluntarist' and 'directed'. By 'voluntarist' is meant a system which has little or no government interference and to all intents and purposes leaves training to the choice of the individual or the organisation. By 'directed' is meant the existence of state legislation or regulation which has an element of compulsion for employers to train their staff.

Britain and the United States clearly have voluntarist systems and Germany, France and Sweden have directed systems, whereas Japan, while not having legislation which makes VET compulsory, has strong directives set by local and central government which enforce high-quality training standards (Dore and Sako, 1989). The Japanese also have a 'culture' which highly values training and education and such policies have a collectivist rather than an individualist imperative (Hofstede, 1984).

What can also be discerned is that in each country there are a considerable number of routes through vocational education and training which vary from relatively low grade schemes such as Training for Work in Britain to university graduate and postgraduate degrees. However, it is apparent that the British system lacks homogeneity and consistency in courses and standards of occupational qualifications compared with those of Japan, Sweden and Germany. These various systems will be examined in greater detail shortly.

In Europe there are two main types of vocational training: the sequential and the dual systems. The sequential system is practised in France, Italy, Belgium, the Netherlands and Sweden, and is conducted in specialist vocational training colleges which school leavers attend full time. The German *Berufsbildungssystem* is the main exemplar of the dual system and is described below.

TABLE 8.5
VET policies and practices

Britain

- Training for Work (includes old Youth Training for 16 to 18-year-olds, and Employment Training for adult unemployed (Action Programme))
- Training and Enterprise Councils (TECs) (England and Wales); Local Enterprise Companies (LECs) (Scotland) – to encourage companies to train their employees
- National Vocational Qualifications (NVQs) Levels 1 to 5
- Competency movement, e.g. Management Charter Initiative (MCI)
- Investors in People (IIP) – to encourage companies to attain a recognised level of strategic training
- Apprenticeships – declining, about 13 000 places
- Colleges of higher and further education
- Universities (including the 'old polytechnics')
- Business schools, usually part of universities

Training culture – voluntarist: finance rather than industry oriented; class based; public/private education.

Germany

- Dual system: in-company training (practical); vocational school (theoretical)
- Apprenticeships – 319 000 places, though demand is decreasing
- Technical colleges
- Universities

Training culture – directed: functionalist; industry oriented, particularly engineering.

France

- Much VET in school system
- Apprenticeship places 300 000
- University institutes of technology
- Universities
- Grandes écoles
- Law requiring employers to spend 1.2% of total gross salaries on training employees

Training culture – directed: mathematical/engineering orientation; centralised; elitist, e.g. grandes écoles; the educational establishment attended often decides career prospects.

Sweden

- Upper secondary school – large vocational content
- Technical and specialist universities
- Universities
- VET in most organisations is strong; heavy emphasis on HRD
- Retraining for unemployed
- Labour Market Training Board (AMU) is very influential
- Considerable free adult education
- Emphasis on 'self-development' and open learning systems

Training culture – directed: state will use training to affect labour market policy. Companies are strongly encouraged to train.

TABLE 8.5 contd

Japan

- High schools take up to 90% of pupils up to 18 years
- Two-year college – vocationally specific training
- Four-year university courses
- Five-year college of technology courses
- Considerable continuous in-company training

Training culture – directed/voluntarist: central and local government set and enforce training standards; meritocratic – top companies will take from top universities etc.; lifetime employment and training in large companies; self-development emphasised.

United States

- Junior or community college two-year associate degree course
- Technical institutes
- Vocational, trade and business schools
- 'GI Bill' federal loans/grants for four years' higher education after completion of four years' military service
- Private schools and colleges
- University courses
- Apprenticeships are increasingly less common and of low status
- Excellent training by leading companies but this is not universal

Training culture – voluntarist: anti-federalist in nature with wide variation; uncoordinated with emphasis on individual effort and individual payment.

Sources: Dore and Sako (1989); Carnevale, Gainer and Schulz (1990); Brewster *et al.* (1992).

The German system of VET

The German 'directed' and dual system of vocational training has frequently been referred to as an example of excellent practice. A common misunderstanding is that the VET is funded and run by the state. In reality employers fund two-thirds of VET, and employers and trade unions have a considerable influence on the control of the system, together with central and local government. Laws and guidelines of VET regulate the system so that employers are duty bound to provide funding and resources for training. The institutions and procedures which operate the system are, however, administered jointly between employers, unions and the state.

There are three stages in the dual system (see Figure 8.1), the first of which begins in the latter years of school, where emphasis is placed on a high level of education for all. A good general education, it is recognised, provides the solid basis for later learning. Nearly all young school leavers enter apprenticeships, as do a quarter of youths with

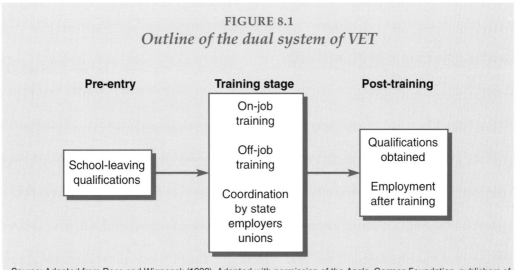

FIGURE 8.1

Outline of the dual system of VET

Source: Adapted from Rose and Wignanek (1990). Adapted with permission of the Anglo–German Foundation, publishers of Rose and Wignanek.

qualifications similar to A levels, the rest entering the college and university system (Rose and Wignanek, 1990).

The dual system stresses the strong relationship between theoretical and practical training; part of the apprentice's time is taken up in attending vocational college, and part in receiving structured training from a meister worker (skilled craftsman) in the workplace. The meister worker, it must be stressed, is also trained in instruction techniques (Thorn, 1988). On-the-job and off-the-job instruction is carefully coordinated to produce a vocational course which gives a thorough grounding in the skills of the apprentice's trade, which, once acquired, is acceptable in all parts of the German labour market.

The costs of the dual system are shared by firms, government and youths. Firms pay for on-the-job training, youths accept relatively low wages and the vocational colleges are paid for by public funds (Rose and Wignanek, 1990). There are approximately 319 000 apprenticeship places available in Germany compared with approximately 13 000 in Britain. However, since 1986 young people in Germany have only taken up about 172 000 apprentice places, but that trend may have reversed with the advent of more difficult times (Gaugler and Wiltz, 1992).

Germany has three times more skilled workers than Britain, even though the labour force of each country is of similar size (Rose and Wignanek, 1990). Nevertheless, as will be noted in the section on controversial issues, Germany's much admired VET policies and practices are apparently no longer effective in reducing the number of the unemployed.

The Japanese system of VET

While the German system illustrates the comparative efficiency of its youth training programmes, an examination of the Japanese 'directed' and 'voluntarist' system of VET reveals the advantages of continuous development of employees throughout their careers. 'Lifetime employment' is a much referred to Japanese employment practice, although in reality '40% of new recruits leave within three years of entering their first job'

(Dore and Sako, 1989). However, there is still a considerable proportion of lifetime employment in large-scale companies among the managerial and professional workforce in particular, who tend to form the 'core' (those with relatively permanent positions and career structures) of company employees.

Lifetime employment allows for the long-term development of employees and enables the creation of a structured succession programme mutually beneficial to both the organisation and the individual employee. Decision making is shared at all levels and there is a strong sense of collective responsibility for the success of the organisation, and cooperative rather than individual effort is emphasised, although achievement is encouraged. Training and development is part and parcel of company policy in helping to reinforce these working practices, and improving skills in technology and other related working practices. Training and development is thus 'embedded' in Japanese companies, rather than extraneous as in British organisations. A study of eight comparable British and Japanese companies recently revealed the inherent weaknesses of the British system (Storey, 1991). While the study concentrated on management development, the fact that the Japanese have no term for this was significant. They believe all workers should be developed and this should be an ongoing part of systematic employee development. Line managers in Japanese organisations are expected to spend time developing their subordinates and this is deeply imbued in their expectations.

> In the main, the Japanese treated training and development more seriously. In Britain, despite many good intentions and recent advances, there was a level of ambiguity about the real value of training and development that was not found in Japan.
>
> (Storey, 1991).

The French system of VET

In the 1970s training initiatives and expenditure were similar in Britain and France. In the 1970s and 1980s, however, successive French governments initiated a number of training laws which compelled organisations to train, making this a 'directed' system. The *taxe d'apprentissage* (apprenticeship tax) required employers engaged in commercial, industrial and handicraft activities to be subject to a tax of 0.6% which was to be used to finance technical and apprenticeship training. An employee training tax was also introduced which compelled employers of nine people or more to allocate a minimum amount equal to 1.2% of total annual wages and salaries to staff training (Price Waterhouse, 1989). The effects on training were quite dramatic. At first a considerable number of training consultancies came into existence to cater for the expected demand (Barsoux and Lawrence, 1990). Another longer-term factor was that, as companies were forced to train, many found that it brought benefits and they began to spend above the 1.2% requirement, as Tables 8.3 and 8.4 indicate.

French organisations, in conforming to French law, have a much greater knowledge of their training expenditure compared to other European countries, as the Price Waterhouse data consistently shows in both years of the survey, even when extended from five to ten countries (see Tables 8.3 and 8.4). Only 2% of French organisations did not know how much they spent on training, but well over 40% did not know this in the UK, Sweden and Germany. Similar figures can be found in the 1991–92 survey.

Overall, French organisations:

> have been forced to pay more attention to training since under law they also have to draw up a training plan to be submitted and discussed with the *comité d'entreprise* [works council] [and]. . .gradually firms have begun to look on it [training tax] as an investment that can be integrated into the firm's strategy.
>
> (Barsoux and Lawrence, 1990)

The implications of these international comparisons for Britain

Statistics reveal that Britain has one of the lowest percentages of young people between the ages of 16 and 18 years of age staying on at school or undertaking vocational education schemes (see Table 8.2), compared with other industrialised countries of the European Union and the world (DES, 1990). Concerns have been raised at the relative decline of literacy and numeracy among school leavers and the relevance of the school curriculum to the world of work, for example the narrow and restrictive role of A levels. Moreover, there is also considerable concern about a rising tide of long-term unemployed people condemned to a life of inactivity because they have not been able to receive adequate training to create a suitable career. The experience of relative economic decline in Britain has raised a number of questions regarding the role of training and education policy in helping to halt or reverse that trend. Yet despite severe recession and high unemployment there are organisations experiencing recruiting difficulties for certain highly skilled positions. The comparisons made above between the British system of VET and that of some of its major competitors do little to allay such concerns. A recent report (*The Skills Audit*) shows that Britain's workforce has slipped further behind its main economic rivals in training and education. In comparing Britain with France, Germany, Singapore and the United States, the report indicated that, while the number of young people staying on in full-time education in Britain had improved, it was still behind the other four nations. It was in VET, particularly in craft and technical skills, that the report stated that Britain still had much to do to equal its rivals (Targett, 1996: 3; Macleod and Beavis, 1996: 6).

Some critics claim that Britain is becoming a 'low tech' (untrained and unskilled), cheap labour economy with an increasing proportion of the potential labour force condemned to a lifetime of economic inactivity. Professor Layard of the London School of Economics states: 'Two-thirds of British workers had no vocational or professional qualification, compared with only a quarter in Germany.' As a result, he continues, 'Britain has a lumpenproletariat unlike any other advanced nation, and this shows not only in British factories but on football terraces around the world' (*Financial Times*, 1992).

These issues raise many questions as to the scope and type of training that are needed. The following subsections outline some of the recent VET initiatives designed to improve Britain's competitiveness. It is too soon to judge their effects, but the conclusion that Britain lags behind its competitors is now being questioned: 'the UK system may eventually be seen as an example of how to create a more flexible workforce' (Merrick, 1995: 8).

VOCATIONAL EDUCATION AND TRAINING IN BRITAIN

The involvement of government in VET in the UK

With its 'voluntarist' system of VET, Britain has traditionally left the provision of training and employee development to employers, and has largely had an educational system that was geared to preparing young people as members of society rather than as workers. However, the experience of relative economic decline in Britain has raised a number of questions regarding the role of education and training policy in helping to halt or reverse that trend. It has become clear that employers by themselves would not achieve the major investment needed by the nation in training and development. This is not only because they serve their own self-interest rather than that of the economy at large, but also because they have had to operate within a patchwork of complex and poorly integrated VET courses, standards and qualifications. The only way to deal strategically with the nation's shortfall in skills has been for the government to modify its 'voluntarist' approach and develop an overall framework for VET. However, whether 'voluntarism' should be abandoned entirely is being currently debated (see Harrison, 1995; and the sub-section on Labour Party policies later in this chapter).

A further impetus for the government's increasing involvement in VET during the 1980s and 1990s was the dramatic rise in unemployment, among young people and adults, with a high incidence of long-term unemployment. Consequently, over the last decade there has been a plethora of initiatives in the fields of education and training that now constitute the context for both individual learning and organisational HRD. These include schemes of training for the unemployed, the establishment of bodies to initiate, foster and undertake training of direct relevance to employers (the Training and Enterprise Councils), the development of a comprehensive national framework of vocational qualifications, and national targets for training. The following subsections will outline the major elements of this context.

The recent history of government involvement

The history of government initiatives in training is a relatively short one. Not until 1964 when Industrial Training Boards (ITBs) were set up was there an attempt by government to influence employer training behaviour. Subsidies were given to companies which were able to show that they were carrying out training programmes of a type approved by the Training Boards, and Boards were set up to oversee most sectors of the economy.

The ITBs did have some impact on popularising training by pointing to its benefits which also helped influence companies to set up training departments and improve their training methods (Manpower Services Commission, 1981). One major criticism, however, was that ITBs were heavily wedded to the apprenticeship system and its outmoded practices, and control of entry into training was considerably influenced by craft unions with vested interests in keeping entry exclusive.

With the advent of a Conservative government under Margaret Thatcher in 1979, a very different set of policies was to be set in train. These were based very much on the belief that market forces should shape economic events. Thus the 'voluntarist' tradition was re-emphasised and bolstered by this neo-liberalist philosophy. It is surprising, therefore, that the last 17 years have seen more government initiatives than at any other period. The Employment and Training Act 1981 abolished most of the ITBs and the government stressed that 'it is for employers to make the necessary investment in training for the work that they require' (IMS, 1984).

During this same period the government introduced initiatives in education that were intended to generate an enterprise culture. Moreover, the new national curriculum for schools was designed expressly to meet the needs of employers. The merging of the Department for Education and Department of Employment into one ministry expressed how close the relationship between education and employment was deemed to be.

Schemes to deal with unemployment

The dramatic rise of unemployment in the recession of the early 1980s forced the government to take action. In particular, youth unemployment, combined with the impact of the inner-city riots in 1981, led to the creation of youth schemes, and the Youth Opportunities Programme (YOP), introduced by the previous Labour government in 1978, was revived. However, there was considerable criticism levelled against YOPs for being ineffective and a way of relieving unemployment statistics by involving unemployed school leavers in poor quality and, in some cases, exploitative work experience programmes. Under the Manpower Services Commission (MSC), therefore, the Youth Training Scheme (YTS) was introduced in 1983. The government claimed that it would not suffer the same faults as YOPs. Its aims were:

> to equip unemployed young people to adapt successfully to the demands of employment; to have a fuller appreciation of the world of industry, business and technology in which they will work; and to develop basic and recognised skills which employers will require in the future.
>
> (Department of Employment, 1981; quoted in Keep, 1989a)

The scheme soon covered a large proportion of unemployed youth and this was an achievement in itself; but critics continually pointed out that the haste with which these programmes were created also left the quality much to be desired, and they were often regarded as a political measure to disguise youth unemployment (Sako and Dore, 1986). In 1986 the government extended the scheme from one to two years and it can be argued that, despite its faults, it extended training to this section of the population often where none had previously existed, and it raised awareness of the need for training (Bevan and Hutt, 1985). In 1990 it changed its title to simply Youth Training (YT) with some minor extensions to its powers.

The equally pressing need to help the adult unemployed back into the job market, particularly those who had been without work for a considerable time and those made redundant as a result of changing technology, led the government to set up Employment Training (ET) in 1988. ET was considered by critics as an even worse failure than YTS and was 'often pilloried by trade unions as providing opportunities for unscrupulous employers to obtain cheap labour' (Reid, Barrington and Kenney, 1992). By the end of 1992 ET 'had petered out through lack of cash and commitment' (Lowe, 1992). Since then it has been merged with the Employment Action programme and retitled Training for Work, with many alterations to the original aims and approaches. Both schemes were originally strongly geared towards NVQs, but since 1993 and due to the effects of the recession the emphasis has been getting the unemployed into jobs with the subsequent neglect of high-level education and training (Felstead, 1994). As one review body has stated:

> The concern is that both YT and ET (now Training for Work) are headed for low skill, low quality, low expectation, low takeup, and low prestige 'aid of last resort' position.
>
> (G10 Group of Training and Enterprise Council Chairmen, House of Commons, 1993: 4, quoted in Felstead, 1994: 1)

Training and Enterprise Councils

Another major government initiative was to set up Training and Enterprise Councils (TECs) in England and Wales, and Local Enterprise Companies (LECs) in Scotland. Between 1991 and 1992, 82 TECs and 22 LECs were set up. Local business people were to be encouraged to sit on the TEC and LEC boards, as it was felt they would be in tune with local business needs and thus able to direct training schemes which would have relevance to local employers. The emphasis was put on closing the 'skills gap', i.e. training people, such as the unemployed, to be able to fill jobs where there were shortages, which were often in skilled areas such as computer skills and electrical engineering skills. Training providers were not allowed to join the main board.

Since their inception they have come in for a barrage of criticism, not only from political opponents but from the world of industry and commerce and those administering the TECs and LECs themselves (Milne, 1991; *Personnel Management*, 1992; Felstead, 1994). Many argue that leaving training to the voluntary decisions and exigencies of the business community cannot succeed because it has been shown time and again that many business organisations will not train enough to suit the needs of the economy, but only their own needs. Critics further claim that voluntary systems have not worked and either a form of compulsion to force employers to train and/or an increase in direct government involvement is needed.

In addition, TEC board members have reproached the government for not providing enough funding to make the scheme viable and for leaving resources far too stretched to fulfil the aims for which they were originally intended (Graham, 1992; Wood, 1992). Moreover, the recession in the early 1990s also severely affected the scheme as companies went out of business and a number of those remaining have cut their training budgets and commitment to training. TECs are now also responsible for administering YT, and the cutbacks in funding have found them unable to fulfil the guarantee that all youngsters under 18 years old are to have training places. This has often had the consequence of creating severe hardship as income support is bound up with having a YT training place (Brindle and Mihill, 1992).

There has also been devastating criticism of the nature of funding from central government, not only in terms of slashes in budgets over a number of years but the way funding is geared to outcomes, that is to reported numbers trained and gaining jobs, rather than to the training needs of individuals (Felstead, 1994). The emphasis on placing people in jobs and not retraining for new skills has skewed the way the system operates, leading to accusations of corruption and abuse of government funds (Panorama, 1994). Irregular practices by private training companies in collusion with TECs have led to accusations of funding for jobs and training being given to people already about to be employed or even in employment. There have also been accusations of the presentation of training certificates to people who have not finished or even attended training courses. However, the nature of the funding mechanism ensures that emphasis will be placed on outcomes rather than long-term quality training and education better suited for a changing economy (Panorama, 1994).

As Felstead (1994: 21) claims:

> the prospect of TECs/LECs curing Britain's well known deficiencies in intermediate skills therefore looks bleak, the more likely outcome is the production of more and more workers with low level skills in business administration, community care and retailing. The 'skills revolution' that TECs/LECs were meant to prompt looks a long way off.

Competencies

Chapter 7 has identified competence as one of the outcomes of learning and development. Of itself, therefore, it is not a new concept. Defined as the ability to apply knowledge and skills with understanding to a work activity and, importantly, assessed via performance, the notion has resonated with the values that have come to pervade the recent thinking of government policy-makers on VET, with their increasing emphasis upon outcomes rather than inputs into education and training. During the later 1980s, therefore, competence and competency (see section on controversial issues) was adopted as a major building block in the new thinking about VET and has now achieved wide currency in this field.

> [Competencies] provide a common language for the organisation and its members to specify what is needed. They help to drive changes that are required for future success and they lend coherence to the entire performance management system.
> (Woodruffe, 1996: 19)

They 'are now firmly established as the basis of a strategic approach to human resources' (Kandola, 1996: 21).

However, these notions are not universally accepted, and there has been considerable debate about the way they have been conceptualised and used in practice (Kandola, 1996). A key issue for those critical of this approach is the status given to the knowledge underpinning the performance of skills. The issue rumbles on in the various debates (see, for example, the subsection on the Dearing Report later in this chapter; Armstrong, 1996; and the controversial issues section).

Nevertheless, the competency approach has been a major innovation in the field of HRD, and has permeated it widely during the 1990s. Although it may be applied in different ways (see Kandola, 1996), there is no sense yet that it is fragmenting or fading. Buttressed by its adoption in various government-led VET initiatives (see below), it is likely that it will withstand its critics for some time yet and will, therefore, continue to influence the format of and philosophy underpinning much individual and organisational training and development activity.

A national framework of vocational qualifications

The establishment in 1986 of the National Council for Vocational Qualifications (NCVQ) and the Scottish Vocational Educational Council (SCOTVEC) institutionalised the competency approach. These bodies provide a framework of National Vocational Qualifications (S/NVQs, or VQs) which accredit competencies across organisations so that an individual's performance at work can now be taken into account in an educational qualification. In addition, GNVQs are an alternative to academic A levels for those preparing for the world of work.

> There will be for the first time in the UK agreed national standards of competence in every recognised occupational area. (Harrison, 1992: 28)

S/NVQs are statements 'confirming that the individual can perform to a specified standard' and that he or she 'possesses the skills, knowledge and understanding which makes possible such performance in the workplace' (Harrison, 1992: 28). There are five levels of S/NVQ: from the most basic level through craft, technician and lower level professional skills to the higher professional levels. The standards of competence for particular occupations and professions are, after a lengthy analytical and consultative process, set by industry lead bodies that include representatives of employers and trade unions, as Townsend (1992) illustrates in the work of the Personnel Standards Lead Body, to ensure that the standards are relevant to work and are valued by employers.

There is a wide range of lead bodies, such as the Small Firms Lead Body and the Guidance and Counselling Lead Body. The comparable body in the field of management is the Management Charter Initiative (MCI), the work of which is described in Chapter 10. Many occupational areas are, therefore, embraced in the new qualifications framework: bouncers, caterers, translators, teachers are just a few referred to in *Personnel Management* and *People Management*. Awarding bodies such as City and Guilds, RSA and BTEC are changing their awards to meet S/NVQ criteria. The nature of the lead bodies has evolved, and some have formed themselves into occupational standards councils (OSCs) for particular sectors of employment. For example, the Personnel Standards Lead Body, the Training and Development Lead Body and the Trade Union Sector Development Body merged in 1994 to become the Employment OSC. This has not always been a smooth process, as Welch (1996a) indicates when reporting the eventual accreditation by NCVQ of the IPD's new qualifications in personnel, training and development.

The developments so far, however, may not be an unqualified success. There have been a number of criticisms of definitions, purposes and methodology. For example, see Holmes (1992), and Smithers in Littlefield (1994b) and in Pickard (1996); and a response from NCVQ's chief executive (Hillier, 1995). Although according to the 1995 government-commissioned Beaumont report (see Merrick, 1996) most employers saw the value of VQs, there was considerable frustration with their excessive bureaucracy and the 'jargon-ridden language' of the standards, and the recognition of the need for the lead bodies or OSCs to provide external quality checks on the standard of assessment. Moreover, the take-up by employers has not always been enthusiastic. A CBI survey (CBI, 1994; see also Littlefield, 1994a) showed that employers believed VQs to be 'irrelevant'. For example, in the retail sector Pickard (1996: 23) reports that it is 44% of firms employing more than 500 and 6% of those employing fewer than 50 which are using the 'purpose-built' VQ, and that many colleges of further education 'still run their old BTEC and City and Guilds courses alongside programmes leading to an NVQ'. Pickard (1996: 23) further notes the 'tensions' between 'the desire for a national standard and the reality of local delivery', and between the work-based nature of VQs and hence their availability for those without work. She concludes (Pickard, 1996: 27) that 'the progress of the NVQ system is likely to be slower than its advocates would like'.

This is further backed by evidence given in a recent report conducted by the London School of Economics, which accuses the National Council for Vocational Qualifications of giving misleading information concerning the number of NVQs being taken which the report claims is far less (Robinson, 1996). The controversy and debate surrounding this issue will undoubtedly be exercising the minds of interested parties for some time to come.

Nevertheless, like the competency approach, the language and framework of VQs are influencing how individuals construct their own development, and how organisations approach and deliver HRD, and hence the nature of the learning environment they offer their employees.

Investors in People

The Investors in People (IIP) initiative was a response to the UK's need 'to maintain and increase its competitive position in world markets' by increasing 'its commitment to developing a more highly skilled and flexible workforce' (IIP UK, 1995: 1). It is another element in the 'standards movement' which grew from 'the need to establish nationally-recognised criteria to underpin quality of work at every level' (IIP UK, 1995: 3), and which includes national targets for education and training (see below), S/NVQs (see above), and the various quality awards such as BS 5752 and ISO 9000.

The initiative was launched in 1991, created out of the collaborative work of the National Training Task Force, CBI, Department of Employment, TUC and IPD; since 1993 it has been a private company limited by guarantee – Investors in People UK (see IIP UK, 1995; Taylor and Thackwray, 1995). Based on 'the practical experience of businesses that have improved their performance through investing in people' (Employment Department Group, 1990), IIP gives a national framework which specifies 'the principles which tie training and development activity directly to business objectives', ensures that the 'resources committed to training and development are put to the most effective use', and provides 'a clear benchmark of good practice. . .against which any organisation, large or small, can measure progress towards improved business performance' (IIP UK, 1995: 1). The management, delivery and task of assessing whether an organisation has achieved the standard lie with the TECs (there are different models in Scotland and Northern Ireland; see Taylor and Thackwray, 1995).

The Employment Department Group's (1990) brochure *What is an Investor in People?* states:

An Investor in People makes a public commitment from the top to develop all employees to achieve its business objectives.

- Every employer should have a written but flexible plan which sets out business goals and targets, considers how employees will contribute to achieving the plan and specifies how development needs in particular will be assessed and met.
- Management should develop and communicate to all employees a vision of where the organisation is going and the contribution employees will make to its success, involving employee representatives as appropriate.

An Investor in People regularly reviews the training and development needs of all employees.

- The resources for training and developing employees should be clearly identified in the business plan.
- Managers should be responsible for regularly agreeing training and development needs with each employee in the context of business objectives, setting targets and standards linked, where appropriate, to the achievement of National Vocational Qualifications (or relevant units) and, in Scotland, Scottish Vocational Qualifications.

An Investor in People takes action to train and develop individuals on recruitment and throughout their employment.

- Action should focus on the training needs of all new recruits and continually developing and improving the skills of existing employees.
- All employees should be encouraged to contribute to identifying and meeting their own job-related development needs.

An Investor in People evaluates the investment in training and development to assess achievement and improve future effectiveness.

- The investment, the competence and commitment of employees, and the use made of skills learned should be reviewed at all levels against business goals and targets.
- The effectiveness of training and development should be reviewed at the top level and lead to renewed commitment and target setting.

Taylor and Thackwray (1995) report that to that date almost 2000 organisations (or units within them) had achieved the national standard as Investors in People, and that almost 17 000 had made a commitment to it. However, they draw attention to the preponderance of organisations employing fewer than 200 in the figures from these early years of the initiative, in the ratio of 2:1, and relay concern that 'blue chip companies' may be holding back.

Nevertheless, although *People Management* (27 June 1996: 6) reports 'sharp criticism' of IIP from the Association of Metropolitan Authorities because of its costs and lack of understanding of local government, Taylor and Thackwray (1995) report that organisations find considerable benefit in working for and achieving the standard. They quote a survey and case studies that suggest that the benefits derive from ensuring that training is strategic and relates to the organisation's business needs. In particular, organisations cite that working towards IIP helps clarify and communicate business objectives, stimulates continuous improvement initiatives (see Chapter 7), increases the involvement of managers in individuals' development, brings together some seemingly unrelated activities, and gives attention to administrative staff who are often otherwise overlooked. Taylor and Thackwray (1995: 30) also note that some organisations believe that through IIP they have increased profitability, efficiency, sales and income, and reduced costs.

The achievement of this standard calls for considerable effort, but it is becoming clear that its benefits lie in the diagnostic and reflective process that it sets in train rather than, perhaps, in the award itself.

New developments in education to increase flexibility

During the 1980s there were a number of developments which have made educational provision more flexible and the qualifications system more responsive to the needs of individuals. These are:

- the Credit Accumulation and Transfer Scheme (CATS) to help non-traditional entrants and eliminate unnecessary repetition of learning, by giving credit for learning achievements, the transfer of credits from one educational institution or programme to another, and so the possibility of exemption from relevant parts of a course;
- Accreditation of Prior Learning (APL) to give credit for previous learning, whether certificated or uncertificated;
- Accreditation of Experiential Learning (AEL) to give credit for learning from life and work experiences;
- modularisation.

National training targets

These various VET initiatives are pulled together by the setting of national training targets, first proposed by the CBI in 1989 to benchmark the UK's skills base against that of other nations, and launched in 1991. The National Advisory Council for Education and Training Targets (NACETT) came into being in 1993 to monitor and report on progress towards achievement of the targets. It was a successor to the National Training Task Force (the body charged by a 1988 White Paper with setting up the TECs/LECs). The targets appear to have been well received, though Armstrong (1996: 23) pleads that the 'qualification cuckoo should not be allowed to push competence-based learning out of the nest'. This is an issue for many commentators on the British VET policy. Welch (1996c) reports that 'a quarter of large British firms' do not see higher academic qualifications 'as reliable indicators of skills'; and 40% do not consider that they indicate 'basic skills' (see also the subsection on the Dearing Report below).

The targets are ambitious, but following wide consultation were updated and the revised targets for the year 2000 launched in 1995. It is, however, already recognised that they will not be met (see Welch, 1996c).

The aim of the training targets (NACETT, 1996: inside front cover) is:

> To improve the UK's international competitiveness by raising standards and attainment levels in education and training to world class levels through ensuring that:
>
> 1 All employers invest in employee development to achieve business success
>
> 2 All individuals have access to education and training opportunities, leading to recognised qualifications, which meet their needs and aspirations
>
> 3 All education and training develops self-reliance, flexibility and breadth, in particular through fostering competence in core skills.

The targets for the year 2000 are as follows:

Foundation learning

1 By age 19, 85% of young people to achieve 5 GCSEs at grade C or above, an Intermediate GNVQ or an NVQ level 2.

2 75% of young people to achieve level 2 competence in communication, numeracy and IT by age 19; and 35% to achieve level 3 competence in these core skills by age 21.

3 By age 21, 60% of young people to achieve 2 GCE A levels, an Advanced GNVQ or an NVQ level 3.

Lifetime learning

1 60% of the workforce to be qualified to NVQ level 3, Advanced GNVQ or 2 GCE A level standard.

2 30% of the workforce to have a vocational, professional, management or academic qualification at NVQ level 4 or above.

3 70% of all organisations employing 200 or more employees, and 35% of those employing 50 or more, to be recognised as Investors in People.

Source: NACETT (1996: inside front cover).

NACETT (1996) charts the progress achieved so far – see Figures 8.2 to 8.5.

These targets are used to direct, motivate and reinforce the various other VET initiatives already referred to in this chapter, so that what is emerging in the UK is a systematic, self-reinforcing framework for VET rather than, as hitherto, a patchwork of piecemeal initiatives. A common characteristic of the elements of this framework is the emphasis upon observable, tightly defined and often measurable outcomes. This, in some respects, contrasts with other contemporary developments. For example, as noted in Chapter 2, in the fields of philosophy and the social sciences those (positivist) approaches which favour measurement are being increasingly challenged by those favouring interpretation; in organisations, multi-skilling and flexible working are to some extent eroding the traditional boundaries and definitions of jobs; while notions of total quality management and of the learning organisation (see Chapter 7) are breaking down traditional internal and external organisational boundaries. This contrast prompts the question whether the underpinning philosophy of today's VET will remain unchallenged for long, and what would become of the VET framework if its philosophy were undermined.

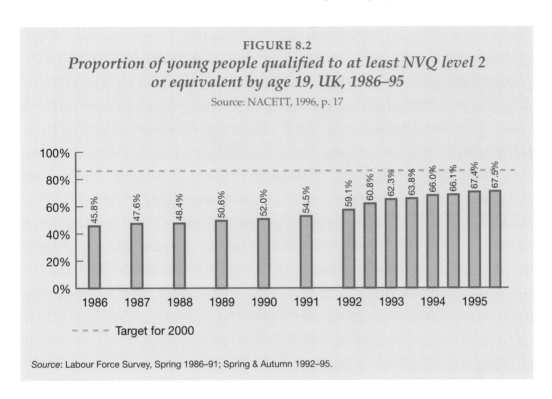

FIGURE 8.2

Proportion of young people qualified to at least NVQ level 2 or equivalent by age 19, UK, 1986–95

Source: NACETT, 1996, p. 17

- - - - Target for 2000

Source: Labour Force Survey, Spring 1986–91; Spring & Autumn 1992–95.

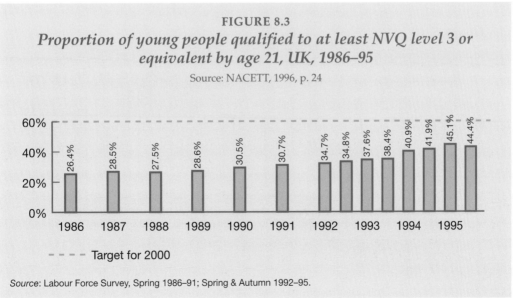

FIGURE 8.3

Proportion of young people qualified to at least NVQ level 3 or equivalent by age 21, UK, 1986–95

Source: NACETT, 1996, p. 24

- - - - Target for 2000

Source: Labour Force Survey, Spring 1986–91; Spring & Autumn 1992–95.

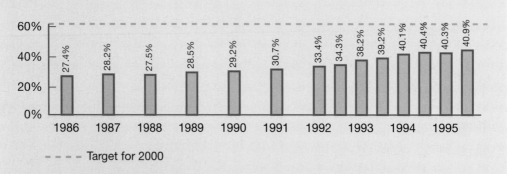

FIGURE 8.4

Proportion of the employed workforce qualified to at least NVQ level 3 or equivalent UK, 1986–95

Source: NACETT, 1996, p. 27

- - - - Target for 2000

Source: Labour Force Survey, Spring 1986–91; Spring & Autumn 1992–95.

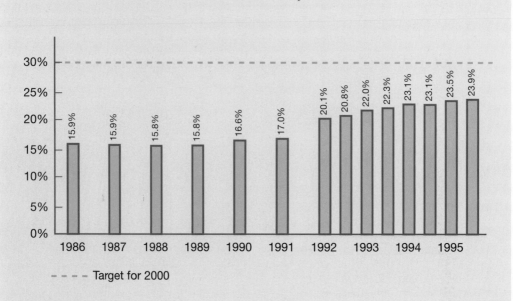

FIGURE 8.5

Proportion of the employed workforce qualified to at least NVQ level 4 or equivalent, UK, 1986–95

Source: NACETT, 1996, p. 31

- - - - Target for 2000

Source: Labour Force Survey, Spring 1986–91; Spring & Autumn 1992–95.

VET DEVELOPMENTS ON THE HORIZON

> Industry is no longer drawn to the comparative advantage of abundant natural resources, but instead to pools of human skills. American – and British – governments neither provide the education nor the training in depth, nor the infrastructural foundations necessary for the post-electro-mechanical society. (Ford, 1993, in Thurow, 1992)

Advanced economies of the future will not be based on a cheap and unskilled workforce. As we have noted, Britain and similar economies can never compete with Third World countries on these terms. If economies are to remain relatively prosperous, one of the policy imperatives for the future must be a considerable investment in education and training by both organisations (public and private sector) and governments.

There will have to be greater accessibility to universities for more of the population, a coherent system of VET in which harmonised qualifications are accredited and appreciated by all employees, and a commitment to lifelong learning. This implies an increase in funding for education. As noted in Chapter 7, the future organisation is a learning organisation and future employees are those who are continually seeking to develop themselves.

Further developments in VET are, therefore, inevitable in the UK. The final shape that they will take will to some extent be determined by the result of the next General Election, in which education and training are likely to provide key issues which put 'clear blue water' between the two major parties. The Dearing Report and Labour Party policies, both of which are outlined below, already give an indication of what some of these issues might be. It is clear that further attention will be paid to VET in the UK for some time to come.

One major issue will be whether training should be voluntary or compulsory. Observers and interested bodies are divided on the issue. The Liberal Democrats, the TUC, the Commission for Social Justice and, previously, the Labour Party have argued 'that the problem must be tackled with legislation. Employers should be compelled to provide training' (Harrison, 1995: 38). On the other hand, a strong case can be made for 'voluntarism' (Harrison, 1995). The Labour Party has now moved its position from one where organisations should be compelled to provide training (the levy system) to the most recent proposal, 'learning accounts', which backs away from elements of compulsion and retains the elements of persuasion (Littlefield and Welch, 1996). The CBI, the Institute of Directors and the IPD have argued for 'carrot' rather than 'stick' measures, as levies or compulsory learning accounts could act as a tax on jobs. In the face of the failure of the Australian levy system and the fact that proposals for levy systems in New Zealand, Ireland and Sweden have not been taken up, it would appear that the Labour Party has seen these as precautionary tales (Beresford and Gaite, 1994; Harrison, 1995).

The Dearing Report

As part of its revision of the educational system, the British government commissioned an examination of the range of qualifications for 16–19-year-olds. The resulting Dearing Report proposes a framework that brings both academic and vocational qualifications into line under the NVQ system. The main recommendations are:

- Equally weighted academic (A level), applied (GNVQ) and vocational (NVQ) pathways through further education.
- New advanced national diploma for those with vocational and academic qualifications.
- Achievement across all pathways to be pegged to four national levels: entry, foundation, intermediate and advanced.
- AS level to credit one year of A level study, allowing greater breadth of study.
- 'Key skills' – communication, applied numeracy, and information technology – added to the curriculum.
- Relaunch of YT as national traineeships.
- Revision and relaunch of National Record of Achievement to promote lifelong learning.
- Encouragement for accreditation and awarding bodies to 'join forces' to provide a more coherent provision of awards.

While (at the time of writing) this is still only a discussion document, these proposals have met with a mixed response, some very critical. Armstrong (1996: 23) fears that, while attempting to achieve parity of esteem between academic and vocational qualifications, Dearing may have given greater weight to the academic, proposing that GNVQs be renamed 'applied A levels' and assessed as such.

> We mustn't swamp the UK's innovative approach to competence-based learning, or indeed the NVQ system itself, by burdening it with excessive paraphernalia driven by the needs of awarding bodies rather than those of employers.
> (Armstrong, 1996: 23)

Moreover, he regrets that Dearing does not emphasise some of the other skills that employers regard as important – 'personal and interpersonal skills, the ability to learn continuously, to work in teams and to solve problems'. Like Armstrong, Harrison, also of the Institute for Personnel and Development (IPD), claims that the report 'does not dispel the concern over the continuing divide between academic and vocational pathways'. He continues by warning 'that we must be aware of cultural attitudes hidden deep within people – and in this report itself ' (Littlefield and Welch, 1996: 6). This was a veiled reference to the predominant culture of academic elitism still endemic in many educational institutions and among leaders in many national spheres, which in Harrison's opinion the Dearing proposals do not adequately address.

Labour Party policies

As the next UK General Election approaches, the Labour Party is starting to translate some of its policy objectives for VET into statements of policy, though there is still a long way to go to make them operational. Much of the discussion focuses on how they will be funded, and the implications for smaller businesses.

As reported by Welch (1996b), the Labour Party is committed to help the 'lost generation' of 16–25-year-olds by changing from the 'unsupportive and demotivating' programmes currently provided to offering 'opportunities for continuing learning'. Its Target 2000 scheme would replace the present 'much maligned' Youth Training programme (see section on schemes to deal with unemployment above). All 16–18-year-olds without a level 2 qualification would spend a day a week studying for an NVQ. The core skills of teamworking and information technology would be included in all training.

As noted above, the Labour Party now espouses the use of 'learning accounts' rather than training levies. These will be 'targeted at employees in most need of basic training. One million people will each be given £150 if they contribute £25 from their own pocket. This would allow individuals to take the first step up the learning ladder by enrolling on, say, an IT course for beginners or taking basic literacy skills' (Littlefield and Welch, 1996: 5). This 'Learn as You Earn' proposal 'is designed to give people the freedom to choose the training courses and skills which fit with their aspirations' (Butters, 1996: 2).

Further plans are to expand the Investors in People scheme (see above), giving organisations that have achieved the award preferential treatment when bidding for government contracts, to set up a technology-based 'University of Industry', and to require employers to set out their training policies in their annual reports.

CONTROVERSIAL ISSUES

Two controversial issues will be noted here: the debate about competence, and the contribution of training to national competitiveness.

The debate about competence and competencies

Despite the widespread establishment of the competency approach (discussed earlier), the concept of competence is by no means clearly defined and there are variations in the term used. For example, Morgan (1988) and the Training Commission (1988) use 'competence'. Boyatzis (1982) and Mangham and Silver (1986) use 'competency'. Woodruffe (1991) regards 'competency' as the ability to perform something or as the behaviour that allows someone to perform, and Investors in People UK (1995: 41) define 'competence' as 'the ability to perform in the workplace to the standards required in employment', and 'competency' as 'the proven ability to perform to the standards required in employment'.

It has already been noted that the competency approach is compatible with the values and assumptions underpinning recent VET developments, such as:

- government policies and provisions for training for the unemployed, particularly the young unemployed, and for the development of skills needed for Britain to compete effectively in the 1990s (see above);
- the government's intention to have national standards for all occupations by 1991 (see Training Commission, 1988);
- the establishment of the National Council for Vocational Qualifications and the Scottish Vocational Educational Council, and the development of a framework of vocational qualifications (S/NVQs) (see above);
- the recognition of the need for increased and more effective management education, expressed in the Handy (1987) and Constable and McCormick (1987) reports, and the establishment of the Management Charter Initiative (see Chapter 10 and above);
- the disenchantment of employers with the outputs of the educational system, the view that young people were not being prepared appropriately for the world of work, and the development of the national curriculum for schools;
- an anti-academic ideology that rates 'know-how' more highly than 'know-that' (see Chapter 7 and above).

Indeed, the notions of competence and competency have provided the basic skeleton of the VET initiatives outlined in earlier sections.

However, when you read more widely about this you will find that there is considerable debate about competence and competency. Whereas human resource professionals and VET policy-makers have in large measure found this approach acceptable and useful, other commentators raise questions about the concepts and how they are operationalised:

- What is the role of knowledge in competence? This reflects the wider questions of the relationships between theory and practice, and between education and employment.
- How can competence or discrete competencies be identified? Can they be identified separately from their contexts and interrelationships, and from the tacit knowledge therein (see Chapter 7)?
- Is it meaningful to seek to identify competencies common to a range of jobs?
- If competencies can be identified in this way, are they the most significant competencies in a given job?
- How meaningful, and therefore valuable and practical, are the frameworks of competence used by, for example, MCI (see Chapter 10)?
- Can competence be measured? If so how, and against what criteria? How are the criteria established?
- In these approaches to competence, what assumptions are being made about the nature of reality and the appropriate ways to study it (the epistemological and philosophical considerations noted in Chapter 2)?
- Given the need for both 'know-how' and 'know-that' and for tacit as well as formal knowledge, how relevant to these needs are the concept of competence and the way in which it is being operationalised?

These and similar questions are still being debated. In 1992 Bolton Business School, for example, ran a conference on 'Reframing Competencies: The Debate in Business and Management Education'. You can pick up this debate in its early stages in the literature (for example Burgoyne, 1989; Collin, 1989).

The contribution of training to national competitiveness

In the past economic growth has been seen to have been bound up as much with the wealth of a nation's 'human capital' as with its material resources. Japan and Germany are two oft-cited cases. Both countries have relatively few natural resources and both have relied heavily on the development of the skills, aptitudes and efforts of their people. Both had suffered considerable war-time destruction by 1945, but had largely rebuilt their economies by the 1960s as a launch pad from which to challenge world markets.

The problem with training and education is that, although most observers acknowledge their importance, it is very difficult, if not impossible, to correlate directly their contribution to economic growth. Attempts have been made by some researchers to do this, albeit with questionable results (Prais and Steedman, 1986; Steedman, 1988; Prais and Wagner, 1988; Prais *et al.,* 1989). Recent comparative economic research by Freeman (*Analysis,* 1996) finds that although the Philippines has increased and improved education, it is not doing as well economically as China, which has not significantly increased its education and training but is experiencing high economic growth. He warns that education and training alone are not a prescription for getting a country out of low economic growth, and other writers from developing nations have also attested that the hopes invested in education in the 1960s and 1970s have not been realised in economic terms for many Asian and African countries (Halls, 1990).

However, Ashton and Sung (1994) cite the impressive economic growth of the Singaporean economy in recent years and claim that much of this growth can be related to a comprehensive state-directed VET programme integrated into the Singaporean government's long-term economic aims. They claim that 'the relative autonomy of the state apparatus is the ability of the political elite to define long term goals for political and economic action' (Ashton and Sung, 1994: 5). From these examples we can at best conclude that the experience of developing economies is varied and the way VET policy is conceived and implemented is of utmost importance, and is an area of research which is receiving increasing attention.

It should also be noted that in recent years the much-vaunted German VET system has come under criticism, mainly because training for the unemployed is not affecting the labour market in the way it had done previously, and levels of unemployment are now equivalent to those of Britain. It would seem that in certain areas of the economy training and retraining in practical skills are proving less effective, largely because of the changing nature of the economy which is requiring fewer and fewer engineering, construction and other manual skills. As world competition increases and new technology replaces many occupations which would have once absorbed the unemployed, retraining schemes appear increasingly out of date and ill equipped to help the 'new' unemployed (*Analysis*, 1996). Unification has also had a negative economic impact on the new German state. The changing labour requirements of the economy in terms of numbers of employees and skills needed will be an increasingly pressing problem for the major economies, having ramifications for social as well economic policy making.

Similarly, while in-firm training has considerably increased in France, there remains the problem of what to do with the unemployed, particularly unemployed youth in which there has been a considerable increase. Long-term unemployment in France has also risen over the past decade and labour-market policies have not been particularly effective in providing the skills-based training to help these people find jobs. France, like Britain, has not succeeded in bridging the skills gap and this may be partly due to the low esteem in which vocational training initiatives are held (Bournois, 1992).

Training is also regarded as an instrument for solving specific economic problems such as unemployment and breaching the skills gap. Many advanced economies have pursued such training policies with, at best, mixed results and usually little long-term effect on the unemployment register. Social arguments seem to fare better and according to Lord Young it is preferable to have unemployed youngsters on training schemes than out 'ram-raiding' (*Analysis*, 1996). In addition, as we shall see in Chapter 16 on international HRM, such factors as social attitudes and culture are also bound up with explanations of the economic success of these nations and their education and training systems. Nevertheless, comparative study can highlight weaknesses and strengths in national systems of training and education from which we may learn some vital lessons.

SUMMARY

● The chapter began by examining the stakeholders in the individual's learning and development, concentrating on the role of the employer, the state and the trade union movement.

● An examination was undertaken of training in a comparative international context which made an in-depth exploration of vocational training policies and practices in Germany, Japan and France and outlined some of the lessons they might afford for the British experience.

● This was followed by an in-depth critical examination of the recent history of training in the UK context. Public policy initiatives such as ITBs, YOPs, YTS, ET, TECs, the competency approach, vocational qualifications, Investors in People, new developments in education, national training targets and more recently proposals emanating from the Dearing Report and the Labour Party were evaluated.

● The chapter ended by examining two controversial issues: the debate on competence and competencies, and the contribution of training to national competitiveness.

ACTIVITY

A debate on national vocational education and training

Assume you are the Minister for Employment and, by referring to the references and further reading and other sources, put the case for the government's previous initiatives. Then assume that you are a member of the opposition.

EXERCISES

1 What criticisms would you make in reply to the minister's speech?

2 Take a vote among your group on the motion that: 'Successive Tory governments have done more than any other government to improve the state of training in Britain.'

3 Divide the class into groups, and each group into two groups of two or four. One group should marshall arguments *for* present government policies on training. The other group should marshall arguments *against* present government policies on training.

This exercise can either be carried out as a one-off during one lecture period or students can be sent away to carry out research and give formal presentations of their arguments in a study period sometime in the future, e.g. a week later.

QUESTIONS

1 What weaknesses exist in present systems of training in the UK?
What suggestions would you make to both government and employers to rectify this?

2 In your view, have there been any other developments that have influenced the emergence of this current preoccupation with competence?

3 What policies ought future governments to pursue in creating a better trained workforce?

4 Examine the experience of those countries mentioned in the international section and comment on whether Britain can learn from their policies and approaches.

5 What are the potential effects of government initiatives such as National Training Targets, Vocational Qualifications (S/NVQs) or the Investors in People award upon the human resource development of an organisation?

EXERCISE

Divide into three groups. One group should identify the particular strengths of the French VET as compared with the British; the second should do the same for the German; and the third for the Japanese. Report back to the whole class.

GLOSSARY OF TERMS AND ABBREVIATIONS

BTEC   Business and Technology Education Council.

CBI   Confederation of British Industry.

Competence   The ability to apply knowledge and skills with understanding to a work activity and assessed via performance.

Competencies   Behavioural repertoires which people input to a job, role or organisation context, and which employees need to bring to a role to perform to the required level.

DES   Department of Education and Science, now renamed the Department for Education and Employment.

Dual system   German system of vocational training for apprentices, which combines off-the-job training at vocational colleges with on-the-job training under the tutelage of meister (skilled craft) workers.

ET   Employment Training.

Firm-specific skills   Skills which can only be used in one or a few particular organisations.

GNVQs   General National Vocational Qualifications.

HRD   Human resource development.

IIP   Investors in People (see main text for in-depth information).

IPD   Institute of Personnel and Development.

ITBs   Industrial Training Boards. Set up in 1964 to monitor training in various sectors of the economy. Most were abolished in 1981 but a few still survive.

LECs   Local Enterprise Companies. Scottish equivalent of TECs. There are 22 in existence. (See TECs.)

MCI   Management Charter Initiative.

MSC   Manpower Services Commission. Previously had responsibility for training but was abolished in 1988.

NACETT   National Advisory Council for Education and Training Targets.

National curriculum   Obligatory subjects of the UK's school system introduced via the Education Reform Act 1989.

NCVQ   National Council for Vocational Qualifications.

NVQs   National Vocational Qualifications. An attempt to harmonise all VET qualifications within the UK by attributing five levels to all qualifications, from Level 1, the lowest, to Level 5, the highest.

OSC   Occupational Standards Council.

SCOTVEC   Sottish Vocational Education Council.

SVQs   Scottish Vocational Qualifications.

TECs   Training and Enterprise Councils. These operate in England and Wales and there are 82 at present. They are made up of local employers and elected local people, to create local training initiatives in response to local skill needs.

Transferable skills   Skills which can be used anywhere in the economy.

VET   Vocational education and training.

VQs   Vocational qualifications.

YOPs   Youth Opportunities Programme. A programme initially set up in 1978 and revived in 1983 to help unemployed youth to gain employment skills.

YT   Youth Training (formerly Youth Training Service – YTS).

REFERENCES AND FURTHER READING

Those texts marked with an asterisk are particularly recommended for further reading.

Analysis (1996) 'Train and prosper', BBC Radio 4, broadcast 11 April.

Armstrong, G. (1996) 'A qualifications cuckoo in the competency nest?' *People Management*, 16 May, p. 23.

Ashton, D. and Sung, J. (1994) *The State, Economic Development and Skill Formation: A New Asian Model?*, Working Paper No. 3, Centre for Labour Market Studies. Leicester: University of Leicester.

Barsoux, J.-L. and Lawrence, P. (1990) *Management in France*. London: Cassell.

Beresford, K. and Gaite, J. (1994) *Personnel Management*, April, pp. 38–41.

Bevan, S. and Hutt, R. (1985) *Company Perspectives on the Youth Training Scheme*, Report No. 104. Falmer: University of Sussex, Institute of Manpower Studies.

Bournois, F. (1992) 'France', in Brewster, C., Hegewisch, A., Holden, L. and Lockhart, T. (eds) *The European Human Resource Management Guide*. London: Academic Press.

Boyatzis, R.E. (1982) *The Competent Manager: A Model for Effective Performance*. New York: Wiley.

Brewster, C., Hegewisch, A., Holden, L. and Lockhart, T. (eds) (1992) *The European Human Resource Management Guide*. London: Academic Press.

Brindle, D. and Mihill, C. (1992) 'Training flop creates crisis', *Guardian*, 29 April.

Burgoyne, J. (1989) 'Creating the managerial portfolio: building on competency approaches to management development', *Management Development and Education*, Vol. 20, Pt 1, pp. 56–61.

Butters, T. (1996) 'Labour's plans for a skills revolution', *Guardian*, Careers Supplement, Saturday 27 April, pp. 2, 3.

Carnevale, A., Gainer, L. and Schulz, E. (1990) *Training the Technical Workforce*. San Francisco: Jossey-Bass.

Claydon, T. and Green, F. (1992) *The Effect of Unions on Training Provision*. Discussion Papers in Economics, No. 92/3, January. Leicester: University of Leicester.

Collin, A. (1989) 'Managers' competence: rhetoric, reality and research', *Personnel Review*, Vol. 18, No. 6, pp. 20–25.

Confederation of British Industry (1989) *Towards a Skills Revolution*. London: CBI.

Confederation of British Industry (1994) *Quality Assessed: the CBI Review of NVQs and SVQs*. London: CBI.

Constable, J. and McCormick, R. (1987) *The Making of British Managers*. London: BIM/CBI.

Crabb, S. (1991) 'Certified competent', *Personnel Management*, May, pp. 57, 58.

Department of Education and Science (1990) 'International statistical comparisons of the education and training of 16 to 18 year olds', *Statistical Bulletin*, 1/90, January. London: DES.

Department of Employment (1981) *A New Training Initiative: A Programme for Action*, Cmnd. 8455. London: HMSO.

*Dore, R. and Sako, M. (1989) *How the Japanese Learn to Work*. London: Routledge.

Employment Department Group (1990) *What is an Investor in People?*, IIP 17, September. London: Employment Department Group.

Employment Department Group (1991) *A Strategy for Skills: Guidance from the Secretary of State for Employment on Training, Vocational Education and Enterprise*. London: Department of Employment.

Felstead, A. (1994) *Funding Government Training Schemes: Mechanisms and Consequences*. Working Paper No. 3, Centre for Labour Market Studies. Leicester: University of Leicester.

Financial Times (1992) 'Call for training system reform', 11 December.

Ford, G. (1993) 'Losing ground', *New Statesman*, 19 March, p. 41.

Gaugler, E. and Wiltz, S. (1992) 'Federal Republic of Germany', in Brewster, C., Hegewisch, A., Holden, L. and Lockhart, J. (eds) *The European Human Resource Management Guide*. London: Academic Press.

Graham, A. (1992) 'YT funding and the TECs: a tragedy in the making', *Personnel Management*, February, p. 4.

Halls, W.D. (1990) *Comparative Education: Contemporary Issues and Trends*. London: Jessica Kingsley Publishers for UNESCO.

Handy, C. (1987) *The Making of Managers*. London: MSC/NEDO/BIM.

*Harrison, R. (1992) *Training and Development*. London: Institute of Personnel Management.

Harrison, R. (1995) 'Carrots are better levers than sticks', *People Management*, 19 October, pp. 38–40.

Hillier J. (1995) 'Questioning the value of NVQs', *People Management*, 9 February, pp. 26–28.

Hofstede, G. (1984) *Culture's Consequences*. Newbury Park, Calif.: Sage.

Holden, L. (1991) 'European trends in training and development', *International Journal of Human Resource Management*, Vol. 2, No. 2, pp. 113–131.

Holden, L. and Livian, Y. (1992) 'Does strategic training policy exist? Some evidence from ten European countries', *Personnel Review*, Vol. 21, No. 1, pp. 12–23.

Holmes, L. (1992) 'Taking the lead on professional standards', *Personnel Management*, November, pp. 36–39.

House of Commons (1993) *The Work of the Training and Enterprise Councils, Minutes of Evidence*, House of Commons Session 1992–93 (cited in Felstead, 1994).

Institute of Manpower Studies (IMS) (1984) *Competence and Competition: Training and Education in the Federal Republic of Germany, The United States and Japan.* London: MSC/NEDO.

Investors in People (IIP) UK (1995) *The Investors in People Standard.* London: Investors in People UK.

Kandola, B. (1996) 'Are competencies too much of a good thing?', *People Management*, 2 May, p. 21.

*Keep, E. (1989a) 'A training scandal?', in Sisson, K. (ed.) *Personnel Management in Britain.* Oxford: Blackwell.

Kenney, J. and Reid, M. (1988) *Training Interventions*, 2nd edn. London: IPM.

Littlefield, D. (1994a) 'The trouble with NVQs. . .', *Personnel Management*, July, pp. 47–48.

Littlefield, D. (1994b) 'Getting to grips with the GNVQ', *Personnel Management*, October, pp. 89–90.

Littlefield, D. and Welch, J. (1996) 'Training policy steals the political limelight,' *People Management*, 4 April, pp. 5, 6.

Lloyd, J. (1990) *Light and Liberty: The History of the EEPTU.* London: Weidenfeld & Nicolson.

Lowe, K. (1992) 'End of the line for ET', *Personnel Today*, 8 December, p. 14.

Macleod, D. and Beavis, S. (1996) 'Britain trails rivals for want of skills', *Guardian*, 14 June, p. 6.

Mangham, I.L. and Silver, M.S. (1986) *Management Training: Context and Practice.* Bath: University of Bath, School of Management.

Manpower Services Commission (1981) *A Framework for the Future: A Sector by Sector Review of Industrial and Commercial Training.* London: MSC.

Merrick, N. (1995) 'Moving up the class?', *People Management*, 30 November, pp. 8–9.

Merrick, N. (1996) '"Jargon-ridden" NVQs back on the defensive', *People Management*, 25 January, pp. 14–15.

*Miller, L. (1991) 'Managerial competences', *Industrial and Commercial Training*, Vol. 23, No. 6, pp. 11–15.

Milne, S. (1991) 'TECs failing to back training guarantees', *Guardian*, 4 November, p. 6.

Morgan, G. (1988) *Riding the Waves of Change: Developing Managerial Competencies for a Turbulent World.* San Francisco: Jossey-Bass.

National Advisory Council for Education and Training Targets (1996) *Skills for 2000: Report on Progress Towards the National Training Targets for Education and Training.* London: NACETT.

Panorama (1994) 'Gravy training', Tartan Television for BBC News and Current Affairs.

Personnel Management (1992) 'TECs must get the resources to do the job, CBI director warns', May, p. 6.

Pickard, J. (1996) 'Barriers ahead to a single currency', *People Management*, 21 March, pp. 22–27.

Prais, S. and Steedman, H. (1986) 'Vocational training in France and Britain', *National Institute Economic Review*, No. 116, May, pp. 45–56.

Prais, S. and Wagner, K. (1988) 'Productivity and management: the training of foremen in Britain and Germany', *National Institute Economic Review*, No. 123, pp. 34–37.

Prais, S., Jarvis, V. and Wagner, K. (1989) 'Productivity and vocational skills in services in Britain and Germany', *National Institute Economic Review*, No. 130, November, pp. 52–74.

Price Waterhouse (1989) *Doing Business in France.* Paris and London: Price Waterhouse.

Price Waterhouse Cranfield Project (1991) *Report on International Strategic Human Resource Management.* Cranfield: Cranfield School of Management.

*Reid, M.A., Barrington, H. and Kenney, J. (1992) *Training Interventions: Managing Employee Development*, 3rd edn. London: IPM.

Robinson, P. (1996) *Rhetoric and Reality: Britain's New Vocational Qualifications*. London: London School of Economics.

*Rose, R. and Wignanek, G. (1991) *Training Without Trainers? How Germany Avoids Britain's Supply-side Bottleneck*. London: Anglo-German Foundation.

Sako, M and Dore, R. (1986) 'How the Youth Training Scheme helps employers', *Employment Gazette*, June, pp. 195–204.

Steedman, H. (1988) 'Vocational training in France and Britain: mechanical and electrical craftsmen', *National Institute Economic Review*, No. 126, November, pp. 57–71.

*Storey, J. (1991) 'Do the Japanese make better managers?', *Personnel Management*, August, pp. 24–28.

Targett, S. (1996) 'Shepherd admits skills shortage', *Times Higher Education Supplement*, 14 June, p. 3.

Taylor, P and Thackwray, B (1995) *Investors in People Explained*. London: Kogan Page.

Thorn, J. (1988) 'Making of a Meister', *Industrial Society Magazine*, June, pp. 19–21.

Thurow, L. (1992) *Head to Head: The Coming Economic Battle Among Japan, Europe and America*. London: Nicholas Brealey.

Townsend, T. (1992) 'How the lead body sees it', *Personnel Management*, November, p. 39.

Trades Union Congress (1989) *Skills 2000*. London: TUC (quoted in Claydon and Green, 1992).

Trades Union Congress (1990) *TUC: Joint Action over Training*. London: TUC (quoted in Claydon and Green, 1992).

Trades Union Congress (1991) *Collective Bargaining Strategy for the 1990s*. London: TUC (quoted in Claydon and Green, 1992).

Training Commission (1988) *Classifying the Components of Management Competences*. Sheffield: Training Commission.

Tyson, S. and Fell, A. (1995) 'A focus on skills, not organisations', *People Management*, pp. 42–45.

Welch, J. (1996a) 'HR qualifications get the go-ahead at last', *People Management*, 30 May, p. 11.

Welch, J. (1996b) 'YT alternative comes out of the shadows', *People Management*, 30 May, p. 12.

Welch, J. (1996c) 'Britain slipping behind in the race for skills', *People Management*, 27 June, p. 11.

Williams, M. (1993) 'Spectre of skills levies is raised', *Personnel Today*, 12 January, p. 19.

Wood, L. (1992) '"Urgent need" found for government to examine TECs funding', *Financial Times*, 25 March.

Woodruffe, C. (1991) 'Competent by any other name', *Personnel Management*, September, pp. 30–33.

Woodruffe, C. (1996) 'Competencies are not the problem', *People Management*, 30 May, p. 19.

TRAINING

Len Holden

TRAINING: A DEFINITION

As we have seen from the previous chapter on employee development, arriving at a consensus definition of terms such as development, education and training is difficult because of the varied ways in which they are translated into work and life situations.

The Manpower Services Commission, which was set up by the 1973 Employment and Training Act until it was replaced in 1988, defined training as:

> A planned process to modify attitude, knowledge or skill behaviour through learning experience to achieve effective performance in an activity or range of activities. Its purpose, in the work situation, is to develop the abilities of the individual and to satisfy the current and future needs of the organisation. (Manpower Services Commission, 1981)

The emphasis on developing the skills of employees and the future needs of the organisation may be in conflict. For example, many organisations prefer to train employees in firm-specific skills rather than transferable skills, and thus these two objectives may prove mutually exclusive, or, at best, only partly achievable. In a recent survey the authors conclude:

> . . . much of the training reported was for organisational rather than individual development, suggesting that many employees would not regard the training they receive as training at all, since it neither imparts transferable skills nor contributes to personal and educational development. (Rainbird and Maguire, 1993)

The loss of employees in whom considerable sums have been invested in training and development influences some employers to concentrate on training in areas which are specific to their organisation, while the 'poacher' organisations use money as an attractor and invest little or nothing in training their employees.

Other commentators believe that the idea of transferable skills is used far too widely and that many processes are particular to organisations and their products and services. Even in a country such as Japan, whose training systems are much admired, the programmes involve a considerable proportion of training for firm-specific skills (Dore and Sako, 1989).

This in essence is one of the major problems facing British organisations – a situation upon which we shall expand in a section in the chapter.

THE NEED FOR TRAINING

Up until a decade ago there had been evidence to suggest that little training took place in British organisations, in comparison to some other industrialised countries. This was confirmed by a number of surveys (Coopers and Lybrand, 1985; Industrial Society, 1985; Mangham and Silver, 1986; Constable and McCormick, 1987; Handy, 1987) which collectively had a considerable impact on the consciousness of the nation. This added to an increasing awareness of the importance of change and the key role which training had played in helping that process.

Encouragingly, recent surveys in the early 1990s reveal that British companies seem to be taking training more seriously (Saggers, 1994). The Price Waterhouse Cranfield Project Survey indicates that training and staff development is the leading issue for most personnel departments across Europe, including the UK (Brewster and Hegewisch, 1993).

This growing awareness of the importance of training over the past decade is also supported by reports that employers are spending more in aggregate terms on training activities (Training Agency, 1989). However, the measurement of training expenditure is still very much a controversial issue, and those figures which do exist are very much open to question, interpretation and political manipulation (Finegold, 1991; Ryan, 1991). Other commentators share the view of Layard who states that:

> The tragic reality is despite all the rhetoric about new initiatives, real expenditure in off-the-job vocational education and training has if anything fallen over the past five years.   (Williams, 1993)

No doubt such views are heavily influenced by the effects of the recent deep recession (*Personnel Management*, April 1992: 12).

There thus seems to be some gap between the perceived importance of training and the willingness to do something about it. The view strongly persists in the commercial and industrial culture of the UK that training is a 'cost' and not an 'investment'. This is a theme which we have discussed in Chapter 8.

Training and HRM

Recognition of the importance of training in recent years has been heavily influenced by the intensification of overseas competition and the relative success of economies such as Japan, Germany and Sweden where investment in employee development is considerably emphasised. Technological developments and organisational change have gradually led some employers to the realisation that success relies on the skills and abilities of their employees, and this means considerable and continuous investment in training and development.

This has also been underscored by the rise in human resource management with its emphasis on the importance of people and the skills they possess in enhancing organisational efficiency. Such HRM concepts as 'commitment' to the company and the growth in the 'quality' movement have led senior management teams to realise the increased importance of training, employee development and long-term education. There has also been more recognition of the need to complement the qualities of employees with the needs of the organisation. Such concepts require not only careful planning but a greater emphasis on employee development. Indeed, some commentators have seen this aspect of HRM as so important that they see human resource development (HRD) as being a discipline in its own right and as important as HRM (Hall, 1984; Nadler, 1984).

In HRM companies, such as Hewlett-Packard, Xerox, IBM and Marks & Spencer, HRD is seen as a major key to the success of the organisation and is heavily emphasised at all levels.

HRD programmes are continuous and shaped to fit the culture changes in the organisation in relation to the needs of the individual. In this way training and HRD become tools for effecting change and the policy ramifications can be wide ranging and strategic. As a result, training takes on a variety of forms and covers a multitude of subjects.

Training is just one of the instruments at the disposal of the HR department and the organisation in creating HR strategy, and as Keep (1989) reminds us:

> The inter-relationship between training and recruitment strategies is usually a very close one, not the least because if an organisation wishes to improve the skills of its workforce, it has the choice of either training its existing employees or recruiting pre-skilled labour that has been trained elsewhere.

Training and individual needs

So far we have looked at the training issues at national and organisational level, but also of significance to employees is the training which can fulfil their own needs. One problem is that individuals are often unaware of their own needs. Helping them towards some awareness is becoming an important issue, especially in terms of the emphasis on 'self-development', an issue raised in the previous chapter.

A sad fact is that the further down the organisational ladder one descends the less money is spent on training (see Table 9.1). Thus managers and professionals generally receive more financial support for training than do clerical and manual workers. Given the need to encourage individuals to recognise their training needs and, more importantly, to seek ways to improve their knowledge and skills which would advance their career prospects, advantage seems to lie with individuals further up the organisational hierarchy. In many organisations the level at which one is recruited often determines one's career opportunities. For example, a typist or wordprocessor operator has few prospects of rising to the level of a PA (personal assistant) or to a management position. Programmes to enable secretaries to take a new career path have been initiated by British Airways, Reed Employment and WH Smith, but such schemes are rare (Cole and Povall, 1991).

TABLE 9.1

Increased investment in training for occupational
groups in UK organisations 1987–90

Managers	71%
Professional/technical	65%
Clerical	47%
Manual (skilled/semi-skilled/unskilled)	32%

Source: Price Waterhouse Cranfield Project Report (1990).

The divide between professional and non-professional workers is increasing with the growing use of flexible work patterns which emphasise core and periphery workers (see Chapter 3 and elsewhere) engaged on part-time or restricted contracts. As a result of these changes, management is less likely to be committed to training periphery workers, which is reflected in the time and money devoted to training and developing these groups (Syrett and Lammiman, 1994).

Another issue which further emphasises the status divide is that non-professional and non-managerial employees have less awareness of the need for training, and, more importantly, less ability to do something about it, which places considerable barriers in the way of improving their working life prospects. Professionals are imbued with the value of education and self-development which is often acquired in the routes to, and in, higher education. This need for continual self-development is becoming increasingly important throughout the working life of most professionals who continue to embark on courses of varying kinds into their 40s and 50s.

Importantly, this process also helps them cope with change. Awareness of the power of education and training leads to self-activation in meeting career changes and organisational change. By contrast, non-professional workers often rely heavily on the exigencies of external agencies to help them cope with redundancy through skills obsolescence. In the UK in the past such agencies as ET have been less than adequate in dealing with the needs of the long-term unemployed and those wishing to retrain to employment needing new skills, such as a redundant coal-miner seeking to learn computer skills. Of most importance is that once new skills are acquired there need to be opportunities available to practise them! This situation is most difficult in areas undergoing structural change or even industrial decay, such as mining and shipbuilding areas.

THE CREATION OF A HUMAN RESOURCE DEVELOPMENT PLAN

While there are no set procedures which organisations should strictly follow in creating a human resource development (HRD) plan, the eight basic points listed in Table 9.2 should act as guidance. This can also be summed up diagrammatically as in Figure 9.1.

TABLE 9.2
A human resource development plan

1 Discern the training and development requirements from the organisational strategy and business objectives.

2 Analyse the training requirements for effective work performance in organisational functions and jobs.

3 Analyse the existing qualities and training needs of current employees.

4 Devise an HRD plan which fills the gap between organisational requirements and the present skills and knowledge of employees.

5 Decide on the appropriate training and development methods to be used for individuals and groups.

6 Decide who is to have responsibility for the plan and its various parts.

7 Implement the plan and monitor and evaluate its progress.

8 Amend the HRD plan in the light of monitoring/evaluation and changes in business strategy.

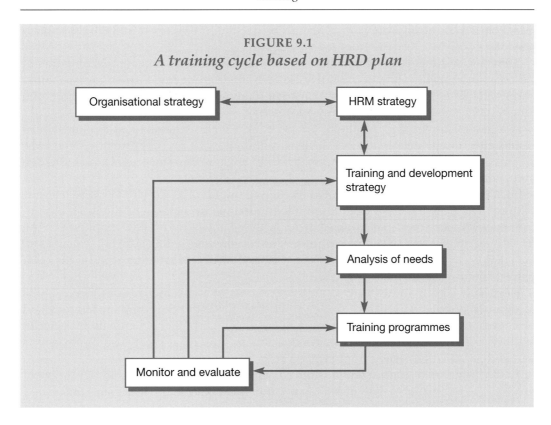

FIGURE 9.1
A training cycle based on HRD plan

This has strong elements of the systems approach to training (SAT), but the mechanistic overtones of a SAT approach should be qualified by one which recognises the human needs of employees and the changes (sometimes rapid) which can affect organisations. Therefore a more organic approach is recommended in the sense that strict adherence to training schemes which are patently not working due to changes in personnel, occupations, job specifications, personal relationships, business plans, economic performance and other factors should be abandoned or adapted to accommodate the change.

Analysing training needs

The first step of vital importance in human resource development (HRD) is 'the identification of needed skills and active management of employee learning for their long-range future in relation to explicit corporate and business strategies' (Hall, 1984).

For training to be effective it is therefore necessary not only to discern the training needs of the individual and the group, but also how their needs fit the overall organisational objectives. As we have suggested already, achieving this may be more difficult than it appears.

Researchers and commentators are very dubious about whether managerial hierarchies recognise the importance of these relationships in training initiatives or, if they do, doubt whether they have the will or the ability to carry them out. As Hall (1984) comments, 'many organisations invest considerable resources in training and development but never really examine how training and development can most effectively promote organisational objectives, or how developmental activities should be altered in the light of business plans'.

Bernhard and Ingolis (1988), in studying training and its strategic implementation in US companies, believe that a considerable amount of money is 'thrown away' mainly because fundamental issues such as analysis of training needs in relation to the short- and long-term business plans had not been addressed.

A recent example, in a prominent French bank which witnessed less than beneficial results after a huge investment in an extensive training scheme, was primarily seen to be a consequence of the failure to analyse training needs within the organisation (Holden and Livian, 1992).

Such criticisms are clearly illustrated by the sad but familiar story of Del the Delegate, who returns from a course full of new ideas, anxious to implement them. He is confronted with scepticism and cynicism from both his bosses and fellow employees. 'The friction set up between Del and his company undermines his enthusiasm and exhausts all his energy. Del's behaviour reverts to what is (and always was) reinforced by the company' (Fairbairns, 1991).

Fairbairns rightly indicates that an integral part of analysing training needs is the recognition of what will 'fit' the company culture, as well as the company strategy and objectives. In other words, the training scheme which may fit one company may not fit another, and these company differences can only be ignored at great cost. Again, this is part and parcel of the organic approach to HRD.

Another important consideration is the reconciliation of the training and development needs of the individual to that of the organisation (see Figure 9.2). These may conflict and reconciling these conflicts needs to be resolved for the benefit of both. Unfortunately, this may be easier to accommodate for professional and managerial employees than for the workforce lower down the organisation. Many companies, for example, recognise the advantages of having managers with an MBA degree or a Diploma in Management Studies, a situation mutually beneficial to both the individual and the organisation. A shop floor worker in a production company is much more likely to be trained in firm-specific skills which cannot be easily transferred to other organisational contexts. Professionals such as accountants and lawyers have the advantage of transferable knowledge and expertise.

The relationship between individual and organisational training needs can be shown by means of a matrix, as in Figure 9.3.

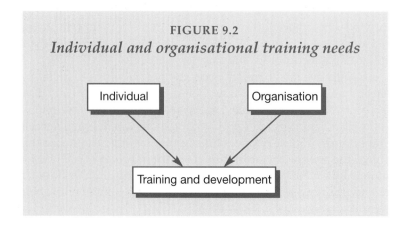

FIGURE 9.2
Individual and organisational training needs

Individual

Organisation

Training and development

FIGURE 9.3

Relationship between individual and organisational training needs

High individual/ Low organisational 1	2 High individual/ High organisational
3 Low individual/ Low organisational	4 Low individual/ High organisational

The ideal situation is shown in quadrant 2, i.e. high individual/high organisational training and development needs being met. High for the individual only (quadrant 1) is relatively rare, although high for the organisation (quadrant 4) is much more common. Both have a distorting effect for HRD strategy. Low for the individual and low for the organisation (quadrant 3) is, unfortunately, all too common, but the least desirable situation.

Methods of training needs analysis

Two elements need consideration in carrying out a training needs analysis – the job requirements and the person requirements.

For the job

Job description

Given the recent popularity of flexible work practices in many organisations, there has been criticism levelled at job descriptions which are too highly structured. Critics claim that this narrows too strictly the perceived responsibilities of the employee, and can be counter-productive, by creating a protectionist attitude on the part of employees to a job which could lead to demarcation disputes and other work-role related problems.

Nevertheless, there must also be a recognition that employees are usually hired to take a specific responsibility within the organisation (e.g. accountant, receptionist, cleaner, etc.) and that other responsibilities may have to be taken on in times of emergency in order to enhance organisational efficiency. Therefore job descriptions are necessary in order to give the employee a sense of purpose and to enable his or her immediate superiors to appraise performance, but a culture must prevail which enables employees to deal with problems which may be outside their immediate work domain. A good example of these flexible work practices can be seen in the Scandinavian Airline SAS (Carlzon, 1987).

Job analysis

Job analysis is a more sophisticated method of evaluating job functions and is often used to discern the levels of skill necessary to do a job primarily for the purpose of creating pay structures. Many modern organisations have rejected such techniques, as one executive of IKEA states: 'We reward individuals and not the job' (Pickard, 1992). However, the information gleaned from such procedures can be useful in analysing the skill needs and requirement of jobs.

Interview with jobholders

This is one of the most commonly used methods, whereby a manager, supervisor or member of the personnel department interviews the current jobholder about the duties and functions of the job. The interview can be structured in the sense of having a series of questions framed to cover all aspects of the job.

Interview with managers and supervisors

Alternatively, a personnel manager or senior manager can interview the immediate supervisors of the job. Often descriptions arising are compared with the interview responses of the jobholder to act as a double check for discrepancies or elements missed by either party.

Performance objectives

The aim of increased quality, for example, will require performance objectives to be laid down. In doing so, assessment must take place as to whether current employees need training to reach these objectives.

Analysis of competencies

An analysis of competency requirements could be useful to match 'NVQ (National Vocational Qualification) or MCI (Management Charter Initiative) standards which are considered relevant to the various jobs involved. These can be compared with assessments of the current general levels of employee skills and abilities' (Fowler, 1991).

Characteristics of people required (Person Specification)

In the effort to identify skills and competency requirements, often forgotten are the characteristics of the people required for the job. This will to some extent emerge in the competencies analysis. For example, sales personnel would need an ability to deal with people and this would undoubtedly be identified as an essential part of the job; but in other occupations and jobs, personal characteristics are often forgotten in the desire to isolate purely functional job requirements.

For the individual

Concomitant with an analysis of organisational needs is the analysis of the training needs of current employees. Much information about employees can be gleaned from organisational records, including original application forms and other biodata bases.

Personal profiles

Increasingly used in organisations and useful for training needs analysis are personal profile records, which also include information concerning career aspirations of employees which may well be of significance in creating training initiatives.

Performance appraisal

Although appraisal has come in for much criticism recently, a good appraisal can reveal much about the strengths and weaknesses of individuals in terms of their performance. Indications of areas where training and development programmes could improve performance are vital to both the individual and the organisation.

Assessment centre techniques

Though rather elaborate and expensive, assessment centres are the most thorough way of analysing individual strengths and weaknesses. Using a variety of methods including in-depth interviews and re-interviews, psychometric tests, team performance simulation exercises and other techniques, a detailed profile of employees can be constructed useful for analysing training needs. Caution must be counselled, however, in terms of cost effectiveness and an expectation that infallible results are produced (Dulewicz, 1991).

'Global review' and training audits

The most wide-ranging method of training needs analysis is to undertake a 'global review', or more modestly a training audit. These are usually undertaken when far-reaching changes are planned within an organisation. The use of survey questionnaires and in-depth interviews are often used, together with all, or combinations of, the approaches previously mentioned.

Relating resources to the training objective

An across-the-board use of all these methods should be cautioned against, as they could be too expensive in terms of time and money. Reid, Barrington and Kenney (1992) correctly point out that the 'global review' could end up producing large amounts of paperwork unjustified by the returns gained. It is essential therefore to assess the cost effectiveness of training needs analysis in relation to the outcomes and returns expected.

Training methods

A careful use of training methods can be a very cost-effective investment in the sense of using the appropriate method for the needs of a person or group. However, many commentators have frequently mentioned that organisations often use inappropriate methods which can be both costly and time wasting and bring very little improvement in the performance of the employee. Storey, in a comparative analysis of training in British and Japanese organisations, found that some British training is wasted as it is not embedded in the organisation as is the Japanese. British organisations also suffered from the 'band wagon effect' and what she calls 'programmitis', i.e. a constant series of newly launched programmes and initiatives which led to chopping and changing rather than consistently coherent long-term training initiatives (Storey, 1991).

Generally, training methods can be divided into 'on-the-job' and 'off-the-job' training. There is a place for both types of training and each can be effective at meeting certain training requirements.

On-the-job training

On-the-job training is probably the most common approach to training, and can range from relatively unsophisticated 'observe and copy' methods to highly structured courses built into workshop or office practice.

Evidence suggests that in most organisations in Western and European countries training is still carried out in traditional ways. This is not to condemn traditional methods, for there is much to admire, for example, in the German 'dual' apprenticeship system which is based on a thoroughgoing traditional scheme composed of a combination of 'on-the-job' and 'off-the-job' training (Rose and Wignanek, 1991).

'Sitting by Nellie' and 'learning by doing'

These are still very popular methods of teaching new skills and methods to employees. While they have been frowned on by recent commentators, particularly those involved with training consultancies, these old traditional methods can still be very effective.

The advantages are that they are tried and tested and that they fit the requirements of the organisation.

The disadvantages are that 'Nellie' is not usually trained herself in the skills and methods of training and therefore it can be a process that may be time-consuming as a newcomer struggles to cope with Nellie's explanations. In some organisations this approach to training is used in all areas when other methods might prove to be more effective.

Far more successful is to use a senior or experienced worker who has been trained in instruction or training methods and whose teaching skills are coordinated with a developed programme linked to off-the-job courses. Such a system is clearly exemplified by the apprenticeship system in Germany.

Mentoring

This is another version of the system whereby a senior or experienced employee takes charge of the training and development of a new employee. This suggests a much closer association than master/apprentice and elements of a father/son mother/daughter relationship can exist, whereby the mentor acts as an adviser and protector to the trainee.

Shadowing and job rotation

Shadowing is another oft-practised on-the-job training method. This method usually aims to give trainee managers a 'feel' for the organisation by giving them experience of working in different departments. This is an old technique and has been criticised less for the concept itself, but for the way it is often implemented. Trainees may feel it is time wasting and people in the various departments in which they are temporarily working must also feel a commitment and involvement in the training if it is to work. Trainees are often not warmly welcomed and are seen by supervisors and workers in the department as obstacles to the daily routines. If well structured and planned with the cooperation of all departmental supervisors, this method can be a worthwhile learning experience.

Another version of training by switching roles is job rotation, which became popular in the 1970s to help relieve boredom and thereby raise the productivity of shop floor workers. If appropriately implemented, this can be an excellent learning experience for workers and suitably fits with HRM concepts of teamworking and empowerment, whereby people are encouraged to take greater responsibility for their work and that of the team. On the negative side there have been criticisms that not enough structured training is given to enable workers to do these jobs well, and that it is also bound up with functional flexibility initiatives, often criticised for their deskilling and exploitative propensities.

Off-the-job training

Courses and other types of 'off-the-job' training have come in for much criticism recently. As we have seen from the experience of Del the Delegate, it can be viewed by both recipients and fellow employees as a waste of time and money. Yet rejecting off-the-job training in this way would be 'throwing out the baby with the bath water'.

Off-the-job training is sometimes necessary to get people away from the work environment to a place where the frustrations and bustle of work are eliminated. This enables the trainee to study theoretical information or be exposed to new and innovative ideas. The problem arises when those ideas or learning experiences do not appear to relate to the work situation. As we have seen from the research of Storey (1991), the predilection for sending employees on courses which do not appear to have much relevance to the employee or the job ('programmitis') only enhances the negative view of this type of training.

Perceptions of courses

Another factor is the perceived status attached to courses by employees. Being sent on a course can be interpreted by the trainee as a sign of approval or disapproval from above. For example, an approval sign would be that you are considered suitable for promotion, and the course is part of the training required for that position. A negative perception could be that the employees feel that they are being sent on a course because they are not very efficient in their jobs. Sending the correct messages to the trainees is also an important aspect of training initiatives.

Variety of methods

In a book of this nature it would be impossible to cover in depth all the rich variety of approaches to training. Many of these the reader will have experienced before – sometimes with negative consequences. It is best to bear in mind that there may be nothing wrong with the methods, but they may be utilised ineffectively by the trainer and the learner. In other words, making the appropriate match between the training requirements of the employee and the training methods available is the key.

Active and passive learning

Much traditional training is a one-way learning process whereby the student is normally a passive learner receiving information from a lecturer, tutor or instructor. While this can be an efficient way of imparting information, all education theorists agree that the best form of learning is where the student is actively involved in the learning process.

Interactive learning methods

There are a wide variety of interactive learning techniques, some of them adaptations of one-way approaches:

- workshops
- case studies
- role play
- simulations
- interactive computer learning packages, video and audio tapes
- problem solving.

For a fuller explanation of these techniques and others see Harrison (1988) and Reid, Barrington and Kenney (1992).

Induction training

One of the most important initial steps in the training process is the induction course. It has long been recognised that new employees often experience an induction crisis. The new work environment is often perceived by the new recruit as perplexing and even frightening. An unwelcoming or indifferent reception can ferment the view that it was a mistake to begin work there. Not surprisingly, there is a high turnover rate in the first few weeks in many jobs, which gradually trails off with increased service with the organisation (see Figure 9.4).

Much can be done to allay the fears of the inductee. Many organisations try to reduce uncertainty in the new employee by presenting them with lots of information concerning:

- the history of the organisation
- the mission statement and organisational objectives
- company ethics
- the structure of the organisation
- personnel policies
- terms of employment
- payment systems and benefits
- holidays and sickness arrangements
- rules and regulations of the organisation

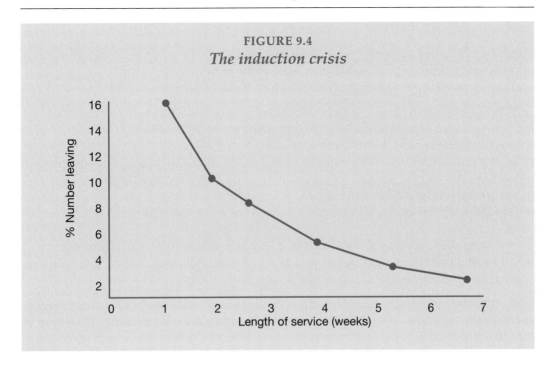

FIGURE 9.4
The induction crisis

- discipline and grievance procedures
- trade unions and/or staff associations
- welfare and social facilities
- health and safety measures
- job description
- introduction to immediate supervisor
- introduction to fellow workers.

This is by no means a fully comprehensive list. While it is necessary for the new employee to know all this information, to be given everything on the first day, or even within the first week, would be overwhelming. Sometimes well-meaning initiatives can have the opposite effect to the one intended. Therefore the induction programme should be planned around the needs of the new employee and the imparting of information should be given at appropriate moments, e.g. explanation of pay and related issues on pay day. The information is more likely to be remembered by the inductee. Too much lecturing can also have a negative effect. Inductees want to have a go at the job to see if they can do it. Therefore the programme needs to be spread over time to give variety. A break from the job to give further information could be a welcome change of activity (Reid, Barrington and Kenney, 1992).

Responsibility for and delivery of training

An important consideration is who is to be responsible for training and who will deliver training.

Training departments

From the 1950s, and particularly the 1960s, the responsibility for and delivery of training in many large organisations rested very much with specialist departments. By the 1980s and 1990s, however, training departments had come in for considerable criticism and were accused of:

- being too rigid to respond to the changing needs of the organisation;
- being too much of an administrative expense;
- having lost contact with the changing skills needed on the shop floor or at the place of work;
- being self-serving and bureaucratic;
- providing 'off-the-job' training at their various centres which did not match up to 'on-the-job' needs;
- providing training that was too theoretical and not sufficiently practically based;
- not providing training and development which met individual needs. Courses were too class/group based.

Despite these criticisms, there are signs in some organisations that the 'bandwagon' effect is moving in the opposite direction with a return to in-house training. This is partly due to the poor quality of some bought-in training consultancies, which often make claims beyond their capacity to deliver, and partly due to the necessity to make economies in time of recession. There has also been growing awareness that, once the razzmatazz of some new ideas has died down and the results are seen to be not as spectacular as envisaged, there has been a recognition that some older methods and delivery systems have merit as well. In addition, the view is beginning to prevail that consistency in approach is more likely to produce desired outcomes, and a training function in tune with organisational needs can more than adequately meet these needs.

Consistency is important so that everyone knows where they are aiming and how to get there. 'Programmitis' and chopping and changing do not allow such clarity.

Training consultancies

Over the last decade the number of consultancies, many of them specialising in training, has burgeoned into an 'industry'. While there are many excellent consultancies, there are also the inevitable 'cowboy operations' which sometimes have unqualified, inexperienced and untrained staff, and at present there is no regulation to stop such operations being set up. Some companies and organisations have spent considerable sums on ineffective programmes or to be told things they already knew. Of course, it is in the interest of the consultancy to push sometimes costly and unwarranted programmes onto unsuspecting clients, in order to drum up business.

It would be naïve, however, to believe that consultants are brought into organisations only to provide training programmes. They are also used to resolve political conflicts, to add kudos and status, to justify having larger budgets, to support political manoeuvring and for other questionable reasons.

Used carefully, reputable consultancies can provide invaluable specialist services and expertise which are often not available within organisations, particularly small and medium-sized ones.

Training and the line manager

In order to counteract the perceived inflexibilities of training and personnel departments, there has been a notable trend to devolve many functions to line managers, including training policy. The justification is usually couched in terms of meeting the needs of people where it matters – at workplace level. Part and parcel of the line manager's brief is to discern the training needs of individuals in their department and to suggest training scenarios suitable for them, usually in consultation with the personnel or training department. Training budgets have also been devolved to the line manager in the belief that funding can be spent most effectively at the point where needs have been identified.

This can be very effective because the assessment and delivery of training are more closely attuned to people in their working environment, but of course its efficacy depends very much on how it is carried out.

Research by the Price Waterhouse Cranfield Project team shows that there are many problems in splitting responsibilities between line managers and the personnel department.

> First there is often a dichotomy between the decentralised role and increasing responsibility of line managers, and the centralised role of the personnel/human resource function which must act as an interpreter of organisation-wide information and as a creator of human resource strategies. Secondly, the desire to empower the line manager may lead to sacrifices by the central personnel function in ensuring the relevant information is being relayed back. (Holden and Livian, 1992)

For example, as discussed in Chapter 8, 41% of personnel departments in the UK survey did not know how much money was spent on training and 38% did not know the average number of training days allocated per person in the organisation (Holden, 1991; Holden and Livian, 1992). Further investigations and explanations of this are mentioned in a later section of the chapter.

Evaluation and monitoring of training

The penultimate stage in the training strategy is the evaluation and monitoring of training. It is one of the most important but often the most neglected or least adequately carried out parts of the training process.

In many respects this stage can be viewed as both simplistic and complicated. It can be seen as simplistic in that monitoring is a process whereby information is gleaned from the trainees and then the courses and programmes are amended in the light of these comments. It is in fact far more complex because there are other 'stakeholders' in the process besides the trainees, i.e. the designers of the courses, the trainers and the sponsors. Each has their own purposes, aims and objectives and these must be clearly identified before evaluation can proceed (Easterby-Smith and Mackness, 1992).

Another problem is that, while it is relatively easy to evaluate a formal off-the-job course, much on-the-job training often takes place in an informal way, which is usually subjective and open to wide interpretation (Holden, 1991).

Methods of evaluation

- *Questionnaires* (feedback forms) or 'happiness sheets' are a common way of eliciting trainees' responses to courses and programmes.
- *Tests or examinations* are common on formal courses which provide a certificate, e.g. diploma in wordprocessing skills, although end-of-course tests can be provided after short courses to check the progress of trainees.
- *Projects* are initially seen as learning methods but they can also provide valuable information to instructors.
- *Structured exercises and case studies* are opportunities to apply learned skills and techniques under the observation of tutors and evaluators.
- *Tutor reports.* It is important to have the opinions of those who deliver the training. This gives a valuable assessment from a different perspective.
- *Interviews of trainees* after the course or instruction period. These can be informal or formal, individual or group or by telephone.
- *Observation* of courses and training by those devising training strategies in the training department is very useful and information from these observations can be compared with trainee responses.
- *Participation and discussion* during training must be facilitated by people who are adept at interpreting responses, as this can be highly subjective.
- *Appraisal.* Over the past decade this has become an increasingly important method of evaluation and has the advantage that the line manager and trainee can mutually assess the training undergone in terms of performance and employee development.

For complicated training evaluations it is recommended that a combination of these approaches be used. It is necessary to elicit the responses from the trainees and the tutors or trainers, and others involved in the assessment process, and then compare and contrast the responses for correlations.

Amending the HRD plan

While many organisations carry out excellent training programmes, the final and perhaps most vital stage is often ignored. As Easterby-Smith and Mackness (1992) wryly state:

> Training evaluation is commonly seen as a feedback loop, starting with course objectives and ending by collecting end-of-course reactions which are then generally filed away and not acted on.

Adjustments can be carried out after a small course to tighten up its effective operation, or when a training strategy cycle has been completed after six months or a year. At the end of such a phase it is essential to see whether training has effectively met the business objectives. Usually adaptations and changes are necessary and the evaluation and monitoring process is invaluable in ensuring that these are appropriate.

COMMENT

In reading this section on training strategy two points need to be borne in mind:

- These training prescriptions can appear too simplistic, particularly in a textbook which has limited space to give to this complicated subject. The reality of creating training strategies is much more complex, and frustration and failure to achieve objectives are common, even in organisations that take such approaches seriously.

● There is limited evidence connecting training to organisational efficiency and profitability, although there is a widespread belief that this is the case.

SUMMARY

● This chapter examined the practicalities of training, offering a definition and highlighting the problem of transferable and non-transferable skills. Although there has been a growing recognition of the need for training in organisations, controversy still exists as to the extent and quality of training required.

● Training is seen as a key instrument in the implementation of HRM policies and practices, particularly those involving cultural change and the necessity of introducing new working practices. Of equal importance in the training process is the recognition of individual needs. These may, however, clash with organisational needs, and the harmonising of these demands to the mutual benefit of both parties is crucial.

● The major part of the chapter dealt with the practicalities of creating a human resource development plan. The first and most vital step in an HRD plan is to analyse the training needs of the organisation in relation to its strategy and equate it with the needs of the individuals within it. Proposals were then made as to how this might be effected, including the use of various forms of analysis of job requirements and personnel performance. A choice of methods was then outlined which fell into the basic categories of 'on-the-job' and 'off-the-job' training, followed by the equally important consideration of who was to deliver the training. The last and perhaps least well-performed part of the HRD plan is evaluating and monitoring the training. This section reviewed various methods by which this can be carried out, the results of which should be fed back into the HRD process to improve the effectiveness and increase the relevance of future programmes.

ACTIVITY

Shield Insurance initiated a two-day training course in wordprocessing skills. The training objectives were:

> To enhance the skills of wordprocessor operators and secretarial staff in the wordprocessing package used by the organisation.

An evaluation was made of the course with the following results gleaned from feedback forms, interviews and discussion with the participants.

What was liked about the course:

● A lot of useful information and skills were gained.
● The course content was relevant to the needs of the trainees.
● The instructors responded to requests to change approaches.
● The instructors were friendly.
● It was nice to get a break from normal office routines.

What was disliked about the course:

- Instructions by tutors were too quick and complicated.
- Not enough time was given by tutors for trainees to absorb new instructions.
- There was not enough time to practise the new skills learnt.
- Many new skills were forgotten by the time trainees had returned to the office.
- The wordprocessing handbooks provided were not easy to understand.

EXERCISES

1 How would you amend the original training objectives in the light of this evaluation information?

2 Provide a short- and long-term training strategy to accommodate these criticisms.

3 Devise a feedback form for evaluating a course on communication skills. Bear in mind the aims of the course and the types of communication skills to which the course is directed.

QUESTIONS

1 Why is it essential to build training into overall organisational and HRM strategy? What evidence exists to show that organisations are achieving this?

2 How could training and development aims differ between the organisation and the individual employee? How could this be resolved?

3 What advantages and pitfalls could there be in designing and implementing an 'Investors in People' programme for your organisation?

EXERCISES

1 Prepare a plan to evaluate the training needs of an organisation.

2 Prepare a human resource development (HRD) plan for two organisations which are to amalgamate.

3 Devise an HRD personal strategy for:

- An administrative assistant at a university
- A middle-grade engineer in a production factory
- A junior manager in a banking organisation
- Yourself.

Draw up the strategy assuming that you and they have ambitions to move into more senior positions and/or have ambitions to change their careers.

REFERENCES AND FURTHER READING

Those texts marked with an asterisk are particularly recommended for further reading.

Bernhard, H.B. and Ingolis, C.A. (1988) 'Six lessons for the corporate classroom', *Harvard Business Review*, Vol. 66, No. 5, pp. 40–48.

Brewster, C. and Hegewisch, A. (1993) 'A continent of diversity', *Personnel Management*, January, pp. 36–40.

Carlzon, J. (1987) *Moments of Truth*. New York: Harper & Row.

Cole, P. and Povall, M. (1991) 'Take a new career path, Ms Jones', *Personnel Management*, May, pp. 44–47.

Constable, J. and McCormick, R. (1987) *The Making of British Managers*. London: British Institute of Management.

Coopers & Lybrand Associates (1985) *A Challenge to Complacency: Changing attitudes to training*. London: MSC/NEDO.

*Dore, R. and Sako, M. (1989) *How the Japanese Learn to Work*. London: Routledge.

Dulewicz, V. (1991) 'Improving assessment centres', *Personnel Management*, June, pp. 50–55.

*Easterby-Smith, M. and Mackness, J. (1992) 'Completing the cycle of evaluation', *Personnel Management*, May, pp. 42–45.

*Fairbairns, J. (1991) 'Plugging the gap in training needs analysis', *Personnel Management*, February, pp. 43–45.

Finegold, D. (1991) 'The implications of "Training in Britain" for the analysis of Britain's skills problem: a comment on Paul Ryan's "How Much Do Employers Spend on Training?"', *Human Resource Management Journal*, Vol. 2, No. 1, Autumn, pp. 110–115.

Fowler, A. (1991) 'How to identify training needs', *Personnel Management Plus*, Vol. 2, No. 11, November, pp. 36–37.

Hall, D.T. (1984) 'Human resource development and organisational effectiveness', in Fombrun, C., Tichy, N. and Devanna, M. (eds) *Strategic Human Resource Management*. New York: John Wiley.

Handy, C. (1987) *The Making of Managers: A Report on Management Education, Training and Development in the United States, West Germany, France, Japan and the UK*. London: National Economic Development Office.

*Harrison, R. (1988) *Training and Development*. London: IPM.

Holden, L. (1991) 'European trends in training and development', *International Journal of Human Resource Management*, Vol. 2, No. 2, pp. 113–131.

Holden, L. and Livian, Y. (1992) 'Does strategic training policy exist? Some evidence from ten European countries', *Personnel Review*, Vol. 21, No. 1, pp. 12–23.

Industrial Society (1985) *Survey of Training Costs: New Series No. 1*. London: Industrial Society.

*Keep, E. (1989) 'Corporate training strategies: the vital component?', in Storey, J. (ed.) *New Perspectives on Human Resource Management*. London: Routledge.

Mangham, I.L. and Silver, M.S. (1986) *Management Training Context and Practice*. School of Management, University of Bath: ESRC/DTI Report.

Manpower Services Commission (1981) *Glossary of Training Terms*. London: HMSO.

*Nadler, L. (1984) *The Handbook of Human Resource Development*. New York: John Wiley.

Personnel Management (1992) 'TECs must get the resources to do the job, CBI director warns', May, p. 6.

Pickard, J. (1992) 'Job evaluation and total management come under fire', *Personnel Management*, May, p. 17.

Price Waterhouse Cranfield Project (1990) *Report on International Strategic Human Resource Management*. London: Price Waterhouse.

Rainbird, H. and Maguire, M. (1993) 'When corporate need supersedes employee development', *Personnel Management*, February, pp. 34–37.

*Reid, M.A., Barrington, H. and Kenney, J. (1992) *Training Interventions: Managing Employee Development*, 3rd edn. London: IPM.

*Rose, R. and Wignanek, G. (1991) *Training Without Trainers? How Germany Avoids Britain's Supply-side Bottleneck*. London: Anglo-German Foundation.

Ryan, P. (1991) 'How much do employers spend on training? An assessment of "Training in Britain" estimates', *Human Resource Management Journal*, Vol. 1, No. 4, Summer, pp. 55–57.

Saggers, R. (1994) 'Training climbs the corporate agenda', *Personnel Management*, July, pp. 40–45.

*Storey, J. (1991) 'Do the Japanese make better managers?', *Personnel Management*, August, pp. 24–28.

Syrett, M. and Lammiman, S. (1994) 'Developing the peripheral worker', *Personnel Management*, July, pp. 28–31.

Training Agency (1989) *Training in Britain*. Norwich: HMSO.

Williams, M. (1993) 'Spectre of skills levies is raised', *Personnel Today*, 12 January, p. 19.

MANAGEMENT
DEVELOPMENT

Mike Doyle

OBJECTIVES

To explain the meaning and nature of management development
in organisations.

●

To examine aspects of the relationship between management
development and human resource management.

●

To recognise the significance of management development to
organisational success.

●

To contrast 'piecemeal' and unified approaches to management
development.

●

To examine the methods, techniques and processes used to
develop UK and international managers.

●

To draw attention to some of the contemporary issues and
controversies in management development.

●

INTRODUCTION

Within organisations there is now a growing awareness that the managerial role has become a 'critical' component in business strategies designed to deliver competitiveness, change and renewal (Kanter, 1982; Jackson and Humble, 1994; McClelland, 1994; Salaman, 1995). This has led many organisations to review the nature of their managerial assumptions, attitudes and behaviours to determine the degree of 'fit' with strategic goals and desired levels of business performance (Fulop, 1991). As a consequence, what we now appear to be seeing is the emergence of a new 'agenda' of organisational demands and expectations in respect of the manager's role and its contribution to organisational success. In effect, managers are now being told they must manage 'differently'. Some management commentators are predicting that this will have 'complex implications' for managers (Dopson and Stewart, 1993). In some cases, 'management itself has to be reinvented' (Salaman, 1995).

You might consider it to be somewhat self-evident to state that organisational expectations in respect of managerial roles and levels of performance will be largely unmet if managers are not provided with the necessary level of training, commitment, resources, support, encouragement, etc. But it is only since a series of highly critical reports on the development of British managers were published in the late 1980s – *The Making of British Managers*, Constable and McCormick (1987); *The Making of Managers*, Handy (1987); and a more recent publication, *Management Development to the Millennium*, Cannon and Taylor (1994) – that we now see UK organisations beginning to discover and appreciate the significance of management development as a key process in delivering organisational transformation and renewal. This has led to the emergence of a range of organisational and national initiatives, all of them designed to raise the overall standards of management training and education (see Chapter 8 for a more detailed description of national frameworks and initiatives).

However, despite this growing awareness of management development as a strategic 'tool' (McClelland, 1994) all too often there has been a tendency by organisations to view management development as a discrete and isolated process within the wider organisational 'system'. This has given rise to 'piecemeal' and fragmented approaches in which management development makes little or no contribution to organisational development and ends up wasting organisational investment, time and effort (Burgoyne, 1988; Mumford, 1993). Management development therefore 'fails' managers in the sense that it is unable to deliver the skills and knowledge they require to meet the requirements of the new agenda. Often this is because management development strategies and practices cannot deal with or come to terms with wider organisational influences such as organisational culture and politics (McClelland, 1994; Molander and Winterton, 1994). The outcome, therefore, is often ineffective management development and considerable frustration and demotivation among managers (Doyle, 1995).

And so, as we approach the millennium, the key issue for those who have responsibilities for, are involved in or affected by management development is how to integrate management development with other organisational systems and processes to ensure their effectiveness in delivering business goals (Cannon and Taylor, 1994). This is not just about reconciling and handling the complexity and diversity introduced by factors such as changing goals and priorities, new cultures and structures, new technology and new working practices. It also must involve consideration of the different rationales that justify the development of managers within a wider environmental, social, ethical and political context (Lees, 1992).

The main aim of this chapter is to assist you in exploring management development from within what is often constituted as an ambiguous, rhetorical and sometimes conflictual organisational context. In the first section of the chapter you will be presented with a brief summary of 'management': what it is or purports to be and how it is changing under the influence of a host of internal and external contextual factors, not least the influence of HRM philosophies and practices. This will 'set the scene', so to speak, for a more detailed exploration of management development embedded within the wider organisational system. This exploration will begin with a discussion of management development: how it is defined and how it might be differentiated from management training and education.

Consideration will then be given to the role and objectives of management development within the overall formulation of organisational policy and strategy. The aim here is to demonstrate how different conceptions of the role and significance of management development in relation to business strategy can give rise to contrasting approaches to developing managers within varying organisational contexts. This in turn raises a number of important issues for developers and the organisation as a whole which have to be addressed if implementation is to be considered effective.

We then move on to the functional aspects of organising and implementing management development programmes. These are examined in some detail, beginning with a critical look at those who have responsibility for development, how that responsibility is shared, and the need for contingent and diverse approaches to meet varying contextual needs. We then examine the broader range of methods and techniques employed in the development of managers.

The chapter then adopts an international perspective. British and US models of management development are compared and contrasted with those from European and other countries, and the skills required to be an 'international manager' are examined.

Management development, like management itself, is now in a state of considerable flux. As you would expect, this is giving rise to considerable controversy and tension and a number of these issues are discussed in the closing section of the chapter. It concludes with questions, activities and case studies which help you to review and consolidate what you have learned. There is also a list of recommended and further reading included for guidance and reference purposes.

DEFINING MANAGEMENT DEVELOPMENT

What is management?

Before we explore the way in which managers are developed, it is useful to have an understanding about 'management' and what managers do. Since the nineteenth century, rapid industrialisation and the growth of capitalism have given rise to organisational bureaucracies and functional divisions which, in turn, have led to the 'separation, extension and dispersion of the management process' (Hales, 1993: 4). The outcome has been the emergence of 'management' as a discrete set of activities and responsibilities (Keeble, 1992; Reed and Anthony, 1992).

However, the concept of 'management' has evoked varying interpretations and contributions to the what-is-management debate. In the early part of the century, it was the rational, functional perspectives of the classical, scientific schools that dominated, only to be challenged later by social and behavioural scientists from the human relations school who provided alternative perspectives rooted in a different set of assumptions about people at work (Thomas, 1993).

Child (1969) provides one of the most enduring contributions to the what-is-management debate. He views it from three perspectives:

- an economic resource performing a set of technical functions associated with the administration of other resources, e.g. the organisation of work
- a system of authority through which policies and strategies are translated into the execution of tasks, e.g. defining roles and responsibilities
- an elite social group which acts as an economic resource and maintains an associated system of authority, e.g. status, power and control over others.

Smith *et al.* (1980) describe management as 'making organisations perform' and claim it is concerned with:

- individuals who are delegated authority to manage others
- activities for achieving goals
- a body of knowledge represented by theories and frameworks about people and organisations.

More contemporary studies of management have been less concerned with theories or principles of management and more with the practice (some would say the art) of management itself. As Lupton (in Thomas, 1993) declares, 'management is what managers do during their working hours'. This concern about what managers *actually* do rather than what theorists *think* they do has formed the basis of studies such as Mintzberg's (1973) *The Nature of Managerial Work*, Kotter's (1982) *The General Managers* and, more recently, ethnographic studies such as Watson's (1994) *In Search of Management*. Watson argues that:

> The image which has taken shape is one of management as essentially and inherently a social and moral activity; one whose greatest successes in efficiently and effectively producing goods and services is likely to come through building organisational patterns, culture and understandings based on relationships of mutual trust and shared obligation among people involved with the organisation.
>
> (Watson, 1994: 223)

As well as pointing up the social, behavioural nature of management, these and other studies have revealed the complex, fragmented, dynamic nature of management which is influenced by a whole host of contextual variables. In the past 'management' has too often been defined in functional, 'closed system' terms that revolve around tasks such as:

- forecasting
- planning
- organising

- monitoring
- motivating
- controlling.

Such relatively narrow conceptions of the managers' job are now giving way to a more 'open systems' orientation in which 'management' itself is seen as being socially constructed, given meaning and practised within the framework of interactions and relationships that exist between individuals, organisations and their environment (Whitely, 1989).

This more systemic orientation has begun to reveal a 'hidden' side to management which to date has received little attention and in some organisational contexts has remained 'undiscussable'. Although modern theories and frameworks of management have highlighted the contextual complexity of the role, they have yet to provide adequate guidance and information to practitioners in areas such as:

- organisational politics
- effective change management
- ethical issues and dilemmas
- developing women managers
- personal survival and stress in rapidly changing organisations
- the changing nature of the relationship between managers and their organisations.

Understanding and appreciating the complexity of management is a vital prerequisite for understanding management development, for three reasons. First, different people, at different times, have different conceptions of what 'management' is about and this will shape their view about the way managers ought to be developed, often giving rise to a number of tensions and contradictions. Second, development itself has to be pragmatic, located, embedded and practised within what managers themselves consider to be *their* unique organisational context. If it isn't, it becomes a largely meaningless exercise. Third, and linked to the second point, any development investment or action has to keep pace with and match the 'reality' of what managers do and not (however well intentioned) be rooted in abstract or rapidly redundant models of what others might think they should do or used to do. We are in an era of rapid and far-reaching change. The use of rigid and inflexible approaches to management development can no longer be tolerated when they create frustration and disillusionment amongst managers which leads to lower levels of morale and motivation and ultimately wastes resources and threatens future organisational success (Doyle, 1995). These are important issues to bear in mind as you read the rest of this chapter.

The need to develop effective managers

In earlier chapters, the philosophical debate surrounding the management of the human resource was discussed. Implicit in the discussion was the growing recognition by many organisations 'that the quality of an organisation's human resources represents a critical success factor (Coulson-Thomas, 1989).

But it was also pointed out that if the human resource is to become a 'critical success factor', organisations must be prepared to develop individual managers and management teams that are not only flexible, adaptable and innovative in technical, financial and business issues, but skilled in human resource management as well. To achieve this, organisations must be prepared to establish, as a strategic imperative, 'greater investment in continuous management eduction and development' (Coulson-Thomas, 1989: 14).

Organisations that fail to make this type of investment are unlikely to:

- exploit future opportunities and potential;
- adapt successfully in the face of major change;
- develop new markets and products;
- retain and motivate employees;
- create and sustain an effective management team;
- survive and prosper.

Management development has therefore become a strategic goal for organisations in the 1990s. (Cannon and Taylor, 1994). But success depends upon the way organisations *choose to approach* development. All too often, programmes are failing to deliver effective managers because the approach selected was uncoordinated, fragmented and with little linkage to strategic goals or the 'reality' of managerial work (Mumford, 1987). Effective and ineffective approaches to development will be discussed later in the chapter.

Developing managers

Having briefly discussed management and the job of a manager, we can now begin to look at the way managers are developed. Before doing this, we need to take a closer look at some of the terminology that is used. It is not uncommon to find some degree of misunderstanding and confusion surrounding the terms *management education, management training* and *management development*, largely because they are seen as synonymous.

In Chapter 7, the concepts of education, training and development were discussed. In practice, these terms are often seen as overlapping and interchangeable and, to some extent, they are. Problems arise, however, when the development of managers is narrowly defined around some notion of 'sending managers on a course'. As we will see later, this is one of the significant factors leading to uncoordinated, fragmented, 'piecemeal' approaches and ineffective development.

Management education and training are <u>not</u> development

Management education and training are important components in a development programme but they do not, by themselves, constitute management development. When we educate managers, we seek to introduce, extend or improve their learning and understanding about the managerial world they occupy. For example, managers on a postgraduate Diploma in Management Studies will study and learn about the psychology of individuals and organisations. This will begin to raise their awareness and understanding about human behaviour and how to manage people more effectively in the 'reality' of the workplace.

Management training tends to be more specific and short term. It is primarily concerned with teaching managers the skills to perform their jobs more effectively. For example, managers will attend short courses during their careers on a whole range of business topics such as financial planning, improving communication skills, etc.

Defining management development

Management development is defined in the texts as:

> A conscious and systematic process to control the development of managerial resources in the organisation for the achievement of goals and strategies.
> (Molander, 1986)

> An attempt to improve managerial effectiveness through a planned and deliberate learning process.
> (Mumford, 1987)

> That function which from deep understanding of business goals and organisational requirements, undertakes (a) to forecast need, skill mixes and profiles for many positions and levels; (b) to design and recommend the professional, career and personal development programmes necessary to ensure competence; (c) to move from the concept of 'management' to the concept of 'managing'.
> (Beckhard, quoted in Storey, 1989)

Although such definitions represent useful starting points for discussion and debate, they tend to constrain the notion of development to processes that are seen as being formalised, planned and deliberate. It is true that many aspects of development are like that, but as you will see later, development is also a continuous, ever-changing process where managers often learn through informal, unplanned experience (Mumford, 1993).

To achieve a more comprehensive view of development, we need to incorporate additional aspects such as:

- frameworks for setting, linking and balancing individual and organisational objectives;
- systems for identifying and selecting managers;
- structures to support, motivate and reward;
- plans to enable career progression;
- mechanisms to measure and evaluate performance.

There is therefore a need to create a more holistic, integrated framework for development (Ready, Vicere and White, 1994). This wider perspective of management development will be a theme running throughout the rest of the chapter.

HRM AND MANAGEMENT DEVELOPMENT

HRM and the role of management

In earlier chapters, the concept of HRM was discussed at some length and you were introduced to some of the relevant debates and issues. For example,

- the different models and characteristics of HRM;
- its aims, goals, philosophies, strategies, policies;
- some of the issues and controversies associated with it.

In this section we will examine HRM from a particular perspective, namely the inter-relationship that exists between HRM and 'management'. We will explore the ways in which HRM may be seen to have shaped and influenced the managerial role in recent years and identify some of the ways in which managers have responded. To introduce you to the main theme of this chapter, we will also begin to analyse some of the implications that HRM is likely to have for the development of managers.

Human resource management, as the name implies, is somehow linked to the effective management of people in organisations. But people have been 'managed' in one form or another for well over a hundred years. What is it about HRM that makes it distinctive from what has gone before? There is much debate about the nature, meaning and sub-stance of HRM from both a normative and critical-evaluative perspective (for a comprehensive account see, for example, Legge, 1995). For the purposes of this chapter we will be concerned with two features of HRM:

- The notion that HRM involves the integration of people with business goals and strate-gies. People are to be viewed as 'strategic' capital or resources which can be used for the purposes of attaining competitive advantage (Hendry and Pettigrew, 1986; Kerfoot and Knights, 1992: 654).
- That people are considered to be 'assets' to be developed and utilised in productive ways rather than costs to be minimised or eliminated. It is therefore essential that the organisation achieves and maintains an effective 'fit' between its human resource strat-egy and its business or corporate strategy (Hendry, 1995; Mabey and Salaman, 1995).

Within these elements of HRM, managers are primarily concerned with the practical issues associated with the formulation and implementation of an effective human resource strategy (Salaman, 1995). Senior managers provide the required vision and transformational leadership, setting the mission, values and goals of the organisation, establishing HR strategies and policies. Those at middle and junior levels are tasked with operationalising HR strategies and policies through a range of practices, behaviours and attitudes which are designed to gain employee commitment and cooperation (Sissons in Legge, 1995: 92). But as they manage the practical aspects of HRM, managers are begin-ning to discover that the impact on their managerial role is likely to be a profound one. Not only are they now expected by their organisations to change behaviours, manage-ment styles, review long-held assumptions and entrenched values; they must acquire new knowledge, skills and competences while at the same time adapting to the implica-tions that the new order will have for their personal careers and lifestyles (Stewart, 1994).

As Salaman (1995: 15) observes: 'the role, practice and skills of the managers are first redefined, and second given enormous emphasis. Management itself is reinvented.'

But there exists within the philosophy and practice of HRM considerable scope to reinterpret and redefine the managerial role. How managers and other interpret their role is mainly a function of the organisational context in which managers themselves operate and in which people are to be managed, e.g. the nature of an organisation's markets, products, technology, the size, structure of the organisation, its culture and political systems, etc. Context will also shape the attitudes and assumptions that managers hold about the employment relationship and the behaviour patterns and management styles they adopt. Attitudes and behaviours may also be shaped by personal factors such as age, experience, background, aspirations, beliefs, etc. Interpretations of the role are also linked to the way managers see themselves, how they construct their managerial identity and how they give meaning to that identity for both themselves and others through the use of rhetoric and politically focused techniques such as 'impression management' (Marchington, 1995; Gowler and Legge, 1996).

A clear example of the different ways in which managers redefine their role can be found in the 'harder' and 'softer' variants of HRM (Legge, 1995: 66). A 'harder' approach to human resource management emphasises a rational-economic perspective where people, although acknowledged as vital to an organisation's success, are viewed as a resource to be used alongside and in conjunction with capital and plant. They are deployed in a seemingly calculative, instrumental way for economic gain, with people being viewed as a means to an economic end. In a 'softer' form of human resource management, a more humanistic perspective is adopted where organisational goals are achieved with and through people. People are seen as a valued resource to be nurtured and developed. The emphasis here is on generating mutuality, commitment, improved cooperation, communication, job satisfaction and an improved quality of working life.

In both variants, there are contrasting management styles and behaviours. In a 'harder' regime, behaviour is characterised by a rational-economic, scientific management orientation with tight control and monitoring of employees. In a 'softer' regime, the manager's role shifts to one of gaining commitment, facilitating and encouraging participation and involvement, training and developing people to their full potential, motivating through techniques such as empowerment, appraisal and job enrichment.

There is no doubt that both variants of HRM are fairly extreme, stereotypical representations of the way people are managed in organisations, and it is unlikely that, in practice, managers would redefine their role exclusively in this way. You should also grasp that neither approach should be seen as being somehow right or wrong. In one set of circumstances it may be that the degree of 'fit' required between people and business goals demands a 'harder' approach by managers. In other cases, it may be that a 'softer' approach is more appropriate and organisationally effective.

But it is also important to note that, despite efforts to develop and transmit clear and coherent visions by senior managers of HRM in the workplace, those below them will often place different and sometimes complex interpretations on their role. This, in turn, can give rise to considerable ambiguity and contradiction, which can lead to tension and conflict in the workplace. For example, a key tenet within HRM discourse is the notion of flexibility (see Chapter 3) about the way labour is to be managed and deployed (Legge, 1995). Within the 'softer', mutuality variants of HRM we might find personnel and line managers relating flexibility to notions of *responsible autonomy* or *empowerment*. This requires managers to provide the opportunities for employees (or, indeed, employees themselves being encouraged to create the opportunities) to undertake more responsibility with greater autonomy for decision making, problem solving and task performance (Ripley and Ripley, 1992). The aim is to increase levels of personal motivation, satisfaction and self-fulfilment.

However, organisations may find some of their managers adhering to a 'harder' perspective in which the employment relationship is more functionally and instrumentally defined. For personal and organisational expediency, managers may create an impression that they are willing to operate within a softer frame of reference but in practice interpret flexibility as a way of increasing employee workloads to achieve higher levels of productivity, quality, etc., often in response to urgent and immediate organisational pressures to reduce operational costs and headcounts. They may also view empowerment as a way of 'dumping' onto employees the risk and stress that accompany structural changes such as flattening or downsizing and alleviating themselves of the more routine and mundane aspects of management (Claydon and Doyle, 1996).

The outcome for both organisation and individual can often be a confused and contradictory set of meanings and motives in relation to the way HRM is deployed in the workplace. This undermines the employment relationship to the extent that any anticipated organisational benefits that such initiatives claim to deliver may disappear as perceived dysfunctional management practices undermine trust and damage the psychological contract between employees and their organisation. It is important to note that this effect is not confined to employees but affects managers too (Scase and Goffe, 1989; Watson, 1994).

Curiously, these and other tensions and ambiguities surrounding the management role and its interrelationship within a HRM philosophy, although clearly identified in much of the mainstream management literature, are seldom explicitly addressed within the management development literature. There is an apparent recognition that managers must change their attitudes and behaviours, but little debate about how, in practice this is to be achieved within existing managerial frameworks. Does it follow, therefore, that if 'management' is to contribute positively to organisational effectiveness, then the development of managers must be extended well beyond the immediate concerns of education and training in requisite theoretical and practical knowledge and skills, to encompass deeply entrenched managerial cultures and behaviour patterns which often militate against such fundamental changes?

This is likely to become a matter of growing concern for many organisations as responsibility for managing the HR aspects of the employment relationship shift away from personnel specialists and towards line managers (Storey, 1992a; Legge, 1995). As Legge (1995: 134) points out, 'this brings human resource issues higher up the line manager's agenda' with 'implications for a whole host of HRM issues such as recruitment, selection, training, and achieving attitudes and behaviours that deliver the required quality and flexibility'. However, as a recent survey indicated, when transferring personnel responsibilities to line managers 'the underlying concern of most [personnel] managers is that line managers are not sufficiently competent to carry out their new roles' (Hutchison and Wood, 1995: 6).

In summary, we have gone some way in considering the relationship between the managerial role and HRM. We have seen that the way HRM is experienced and practised is in many respects a function of the managerial role: the attitudes and behaviours that managers adopt in respect of the employment relationship. And so, by operating from within existing frameworks of management orthodoxy, tensions emerge to draw managers towards behaviours and attitudes that are rooted in the 'harder' variants of HRM, even when these may be at odds with organisational goals and strategies that seek mutuality, commitment and cooperation. This poses the question of how far is it legitimate to consider managers as 'villains' when they may well be 'victims' of the apparent inability of conventional frameworks and models of management development to adapt and respond to the demands and challenges that HRM presents. This raises a number of important issues for those who are interested and involved in the development of managers. Some of these issues will be addressed later in this chapter, not least the argument that the time may have come to reconsider and reframe the practice of management development.

MANAGEMENT DEVELOPMENT AND ORGANISATIONAL STRATEGY

Formulating a strategy

Major environmental shifts are now demanding a more strategic perspective from those who manage and lead in organisations. Organisations are 'globalising' in their quest for markets that will bring new opportunities for growth and prosperity. Developments in technology, especially in computing and communications, are leading to greater efficiencies, reduced costs and opportunities to launch new products and services. The nature of organisation life itself is changing. Organisations are now more complex and sophisticated than ever before. Change is becoming a dominant feature of organisational life. Adaptability and flexibility are the essential characteristics for survival and success. As a consequence, organisations are now espousing values that regard people, not as costs to be minimised but as assets to be maintained and developed.

Such changes are setting new challenges for managers and employees alike. Managers must respond by providing *strategic leadership*. Their task is to establish a clear mission, linked to a set of strategic business objectives that enable organisations to acquire, control and allocate resources to maximise the opportunities available and to minimise any threats to its survival and success.

In this respect, management development is attaining strategic significance because it not only:

> ensures the right mix of management competences to secure current competitive position . . . it is a means to develop management competences to enable the organisation to maintain or shift its competitive position in the future.
>
> (Buckley and Kemp, 1989: 158)

The goals and objectives of management development

Storey (1989: 5) points out that 'conceptualisations about what management development is are obviously closely wrapped up with what it is for because clearly it is not an end in itself'. Increasingly, the objective of management development is becoming indistinguishable from the need to respond effectively to pressures and challenges of organisational change and renewal. There are now many examples and case studies where management development has been used as a vehicle to facilitate and 'engineer' different forms of culture change in both the public and private sector (Hofl and Dawes, 1995). It has also become a 'tool' in the pursuit of quality, cost reduction and 'profitability through excellence' and the introduction of new roles and responsibilities for managers (Storey, 1989).

Although the key objective has been to use management development as a way of engineering change, there is a concern that a reliance on traditional, conventional approaches may be failing to deliver the anticipated outcomes.

> The firm had sent many managers to a variety of training and development programmes over the years with little direct pay off to the firm in terms of improved performance.   (Pate and Nielson, 1987: 17)

In a recent study, a research-focused organisation sought to develop its managers to meet the challenge of moving from a bureaucratic structure with a perceived autocratic management style to one that was much more participative, customer focused and entrepreneurial in orientation. A food-processing industry had a strong techno-culture where human, commercial aspects of managing were subordinated to technical considerations. As it began to face rising costs, lost market share and operational inefficiencies, it sought to use traditional development approaches to imbue its managers with a greater level of commercial awareness to reverse the decline.

In both cases it was concluded that management development had been relatively ineffective in bringing about the desired changes (Doyle, 1995). This was attributed not only to traditional development approaches but to structural, political and cultural barriers which 'interfered' with the organisations' objectives of changing managerial attitudes and behaviours (McClelland, 1994; Molander and Winterton, 1994). Some measure of success was only achieved when a more holistic and systemic approach was adopted, one that linked management development firmly to a wider consideration of contextual influences (Doyle, 1995). As Pate and Nielson (1987: 28) conclude, there 'must be a system wide strategy'. Management development must go hand in hand with organisational development.

Some propositions

Based on the preceding discussion we can make the following propositions:

- Management development can be viewed as a source of competitive advantage and a strategic tool for developing organisational effectiveness.
- Management development is seen as a function of business strategy, and achieving congruence between strategic goals and management development is vital.

These propositions represent a useful basis on which to formulate an effective management development policy but there are a number of points to consider:

- Strategic missions, goals and objectives are dynamic and evolutionary. As they evolve and change in response to organisational and environmental pressures, so development processes will have to be adapted.
- As managers are developed, new skills, attitudes and behaviours produce new outlooks, perspectives and orientations. These 'act back' on strategic goals and objectives to further change and develop the organisation.
- Integrating management development processes with strategic business objectives has proved problematical in the past, in part because organisations have not been able to develop and articulate a coherent business strategy, but also because the strategic significance of people has not been fully appreciated.
- Identifying, measuring and evaluating management development as a source of competitive advantage is a difficult task and few organisations really attempt it, preferring instead to rely upon an ideological commitment to development.

These, and other considerations, highlight the need to adopt a more *contingent* view of management development that leads to policies, approaches and practices that are *organisation focused* and contextual. Management development objectives and activities must be firmly grounded in organisational strategy. They must 'fit' with the organisational situation at any given moment and yet be flexible and adaptable enough to change and evolve as the organisation and manager develops.

One organisation has produced a three-tier framework to link its management development and business strategy.

Strategic Management Development at Thorn EMI Home Electronics

Corporate level

Psychological environment for management development explicitly linked to key business characteristics:

- Sector businesses strategically led
- Competitively focused
- Marketing oriented
- People driven.

Business performance measured and reviewed against management capabilities.

Strategic business unit (SBU) level

Management development tailored to suit the specific business needs of SBUs.

Strategy-manager matching model employed to identify and match available manager competences with job requirements.

Development centre resource available to support SBUs.

Functional level

Focused on bridging the gap between individual manager competences and business requirements.

Linked to comprehensive appraisal system.

Extensive use of short-term, individual specific programmes (self-awareness, planning, finance, problem solving, etc.).

(*Source*: Buckley and Kemp, 1989)

Devising a management development policy

Management development will fail if there is no clear policy.

(Margerison, 1991)

Developing effective managers begins with the formulation of a detailed management development policy. It is vital that when drafting a policy there is full consultation and involvement with all managers to achieve ownership and commitment to the subsequent development process.

Guidelines for preparing a management development policy

- Link development plans and activities to business strategies, human resource planning and employment policies.
- Determine responsibilities for developing managers.
- Decide the characteristics for an effective manager within the organisation context.
- Identify the managerial competences required to implement strategy.
- 'Map out' the organisation's cultural philosophy with regard to management.
- Communicate the organisation's strategic goals and objectives to managers and those involved in manager development.
- Ensure development links to the reality of what managers do, not what the organisation thinks they do.
- Develop a flexible approach to management development that can accommodate both organisational and individual needs.

Policy statements are useful because they express an organisation's commitment to development and clearly set out a framework within which it can take place. What is sometimes less clear is the extent to which organisations are prepared to implement them and how effective they are. Like other areas of management development, this is difficult to evaluate. Some of the reasons for these difficulties will be explored later in the chapter.

Extracts from a management development policy

- We accept that it is the Group's responsibility to provide every manager with the opportunity to develop his/her ability and potential so that he/she does their existing job effectively.

- We believe that people derive more satisfaction from working when they themselves have helped to establish and are committed to the objective of their job.
- The policy requires that through the Divisions we create an environment in which all managers contribute to the objectives of the business to their maximum ability.
- We have undertaken to support this policy by providing an organisational structure within which the responsibilities of each manager are clearly defined.
- We expect that increasing the influence and scope for initiative and self-motivation of managers and their subordinates will lead to increasing job satisfaction and to direct improvement in the Group's commercial performance.

(*Source*: Mumford, 1993: 10. This extract is taken from *Management Development* (1993) by Alan Mumford and is reproduced by permission of the publishers, The Institute of Personnel and Development.)

Having determined its policy guidelines, the next step for the organisation is to consider how it should *approach* the development of its managers.

ORGANISATIONAL APPROACHES TO MANAGEMENT DEVELOPMENT

Why develop this manager?

In designing a management development programme, those responsible need to think through and be able to justify why they are developing an individual manager (or group of managers). Above all, they must ensure that development is linked to the philosophies and strategic objectives of the organisation, while at the same time taking account of individual needs, expectations and aspirations. This can often be a difficult balance to achieve and frequently becomes a source of tension.

ACTIVITY

'The bottom line'

Managers who are seeking to buy a new piece of plant or equipment, develop a new product, explore a new market, build a new warehouse, will have to produce a well researched, carefully drafted investment plan. Knowing that the plan will be submitted to rigorous examination by senior managers and financial experts, managers will carefully prepare their justification and response to the predictable question 'Why do you want to purchase/invest in . . .?'

EXERCISE

Suppose you were responsible for initiating a management development programme. What difficulties might you encounter in trying to prepare a supporting investment plan?

413

Another problem is justifying an investment in management development. Making the causal connections between (sometimes considerable) investment in management education, training and development, and evaluating future managerial performance and organisational success, is extremely difficult (see Easterby-Smith, 1994). Some of the issues connected with evaluation will be discussed later.

Because it is difficult to justify, management development has often to rest on some notion of it being 'the right thing to do'. Senior managers seeking a quick-fix solution to a deep-rooted managerial problem will often consult with development 'experts' who are only too pleased to solve the problem by introducing them to the latest development fad. When the 'quick-fix' solution fails to produce the anticipated results, or worse, it exacerbates an existing problem, management development is undermined and discredited. It is therefore vital that organisations view management development as a long-term investment in a key part of their human resource and select an approach that is suited to their specific needs and requirements.

Selecting the right approach

Management development can be approached in a number of different ways. Mumford (1993) describes three types of approach which are broadly representative of UK management development at the present time.

Type 1: 'Informal managerial' – accidental processes
Characteristics:

- occurs within manager's activities
- explicit intention is task performance
- no clear development objectives
- unstructured in development terms
- not planned in advance
- owned by managers.

Development consequences:

- learning real, direct, unconscious, insufficient.

Type 2: 'Integrated managerial' – opportunistic processes
Characteristics:

- occurs within managerial activities
- explicit intention is both task performance and development
- clear development objectives
- structured for development by boss and subordinate
- planned beforehand and/or reviewed subsequently as learning experiences
- owned by managers.

Development consequences:

- learning is real, direct, conscious, more substantial.

Type 3: 'Formalised development' – planned processes

Characteristics:

- often away from normal managerial activities
- explicit intention is development
- clear development objectives
- structured for development by developers
- planned beforehand or reviewed subsequently as learning experiences
- owned more by developers than managers.

Development consequences:

- learning may be real (through a job) or detached (through a course)
- is more likely to be conscious, relatively infrequent.

(*Source*: Mumford, 1987. This article first appeared in *Management Education and Development*, Vol. 18, Part 3 (1987). We are grateful to the editor for permission to reproduce it here.)

Burgoyne (1988) argues that management development may be considered as progressing through different levels of maturity (see Table 10.1). At Level 1 there is no systematic approach to management development, and at Level 6 management development not only shapes and informs corporate strategy, it actually enhances the process of strategy formation. In practice, management development approaches for most organisations rarely extend beyond Levels 1 and 2. Those who reach Levels 5 and 6 find it is 'often precariously achieved and lost' (p. 44). Burgoyne argues that to progress through the levels of maturity to the point where management development is making the fullest contribution to organisation development demands a much more holistic approach to development in which both 'hard' (roles, duties, technical competence, etc.) and 'soft' (career, quality of life, ethos, values, etc.) managerial issues are considered in framing the right approach.

TABLE 10.1
Levels of maturity of organisational management development

1	2	3	4	5	6
No systematic management development	Isolated tactical management development	Integrated and coordinated structural and development tactics	A management development strategy to implement corporate policy	Management development strategy input to corporate policy formation	Strategic development of the management of corporate policy
No systematic or deliberate management development in structural or developmental sense, total reliance on *laissez-faire* uncontrived processes of management development	There are isolated and *ad hoc* tactical management development activities, of either structural or develop-mental kinds, or both, in response to local, problems, crises, or sporadically identified general problems	The specific management development tactics which impinge directly on the individual manager, of career structure management, and of assisting learning, are integrated and coordinated	A management development strategy plays its part in implementing corporate policies through managerial human resource planning, and providing a strategic frame-work and direction for the tactics of career structure management and of learning, education and training	Management development processes feed inform-ation into corporate policy decision-making processes on the organisation's managerial assets, strengths, weaknesses and potential and contribute to the forecasting and analysis of the manage-ability of proposed projects, ventures, changes	Management development processes enhance the nature and quality of corporate policy-forming processes, which they also inform and help implement

Source: Burgoyne (1988).

A 'piecemeal' approach

Programmes that have characteristics similar to Mumford's Type 1 and Type 3 develop-ment and Burgoyne's Levels 1 and 2 tend to lead to *piecemeal* approaches, which in turn lead to inefficient and ineffective development.

'Piecemeal' approaches to development are characterised by the following:

- There is no management development infrastructure. Development is not linked to business strategy. Activities are unrelated and lack overall direction or philosophy. They fail to reinforce each other and reduce the potential for organisational effectiveness.
- Development often focuses on the needs of the organisation and fails to meet the learning needs and aspirations of individuals and groups.
- Development is largely defined in terms of a range of universal, off-the-shelf internal or external courses.
- There is tacit support for management education and training because it is seen as a 'good thing to be doing' irrespective of organisational needs.
- There is a lack of common vision among those responsible for management development. For instance, some managers see development as a central part of their job, others see it as peripheral and a nuisance.
- Management development effort can be wasted because it is used as a solution to the wrong problem. Rather than developing managers, the correct solution may be to change aspects of organisation structure or systems.
- It is difficult to evaluate the effectiveness of a piecemeal approach that lacks clear direction and established objectives.

But, there are a number of reasons why organisations might choose or be forced to adopt these approaches:

- resource constraints (in the case of smaller organisations);
- a lack of awareness about linking management development to business strategy on the part of those responsible for initiating or delivering development;
- groups who seek to exert control over development (personnel departments);
- a focus on formalised , intensive management training courses.

Sadly, piecemeal, fragmented and discrete approaches to management development are commonplace (Hitt, 1987). Such approaches are a significant contributor to the failure of management development to fulfil personal and organisational expectations (Temporal, 1990; Mumford, 1993). Not only do they waste investment, time and effort, there is a risk of damage to existing levels of morale and commitment among managers as efforts to develop them founder on organisational barriers to change. As Molander and Winterton (1994: 89) argue:

> Where such conditions exist, what is required is an organisation-wide assessment of the elements in the culture which require changing, followed by an effective change programme. Focusing attention on individual managers . . . will not bring about required change. In this case the organisation itself should be the focus of change.

Evidence of piecemeal approach?

An organisation spent a considerable amount of money running a series of in-house management training courses. It became concerned when the training produced no tangible results. The root cause of the problem became evident during a time management module. The external consultant running the module realised from the the reaction of the delegates that the structure and culture of the organisation would act as barriers to the implementation of time-management techniques, e.g. managers had little flexibility to

▶

change existing rules and procedures to enable them to manage their time more effectively. The message was fed back by the consultant to the organisation that their management training would not produce desired changes until issues connected with existing culture, structures, rules, procedures, etc. were addressed.

After discussions with senior managers, the consultant was asked to design a long-term organisational development programmed designed to tackle cultural and structural issues which were acting as barriers to management development. Measures were initiated to change the management style and promote a more participative, supportive culture. A more focused management development programme was established linked to 'live' issues in the workplace and the organisation's business goals.

An open systems approach

In Chapter 2, the *open systems model* was introduced as a way of conceptualising and making sense of the complexity of organisational life (Kast and Rosenweig, 1985). If organisations can be persuaded to adopt an open systems perspective on management development they are likely to overcome many of the problems created by the piecemeal approach. Instead of looking at management development in isolation, it becomes an integral part of a wider organisational system, and, more importantly, is linked to the context and 'reality' of managerial work (see, for example, Mumford's Type 2 development).

Viewing management development in open systems terms recognises and focuses attention on the following:

- Management development is at one and the same time *a system and a process* (see Figure 10.1). It is composed of identifiable parts or components which act together in an organised way. A range of inputs are transformed in the management development process to produce a range of outputs. In some cases, the primary output will be increased organisational effectiveness. But in piecemeal approaches, we may find that reduced effectiveness is an output.
- Figure 10.1 also shows that in an open system, the management development process *interacts, influences and is influenced by* variables from other environmental and organisational subsystems (social, technological, cultural). For example, prevailing ideologies, values and beliefs exist within the organisation as a *cultural subsystem*. This subsystem shapes managers' attitudes and values and exerts pressure upon them to conform and display 'acceptable' behaviour patterns. The *technological subsystem* can have a profound effect upon managers. For example, information technology has transformed managerial work by removing layers of middle managers whose primary task was to receive and process information for management control and decision making (*Management Today*, May 1991).
- The relationship between these different subsystems is dynamic and constantly changing as internal and external *influencers* operate upon them. Some of the main internal and external influencers are listed in Table 10.2.

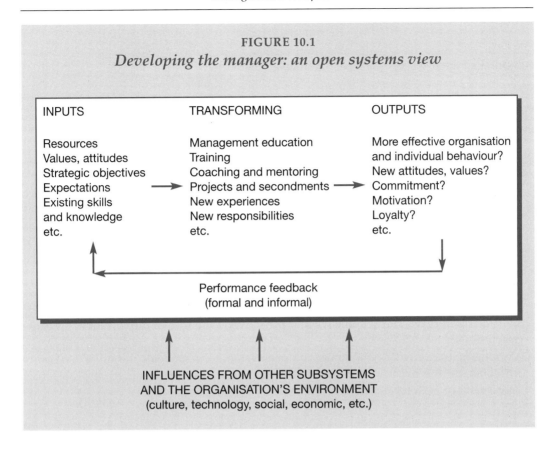

FIGURE 10.1
Developing the manager: an open systems view

INPUTS	TRANSFORMING	OUTPUTS
Resources	Management education	More effective organisation
Values, attitudes	Training	and individual behaviour?
Strategic objectives	Coaching and mentoring	New attitudes, values?
Expectations	Projects and secondments	Commitment?
Existing skills	New experiences	Motivation?
and knowledge	New responsibilities	Loyalty?
etc.	etc.	etc.

Performance feedback
(formal and informal)

INFLUENCES FROM OTHER SUBSYSTEMS
AND THE ORGANISATION'S ENVIRONMENT
(culture, technology, social, economic, etc.)

TABLE 10.2
Internal and external influencers

Internal influencers	External influencers
● Culture	● Technology
● Structure	● Government/politics
● Strategic goals	● Macro-economic factors
● Organisation size	● Social change
● Organisation growth	● Market forces
● Ownership	● Demographic change
● Power distribution and politics	● Professional groups
● Individual goals	● Education system

● Management development is *integrated* with, and *mutually dependent* upon, other organisational subsystems, activities and processes. For example, the system for strategic planning and the setting of organisational goals must interact with a management development system that seeks to develop the managerial skills and knowledge to organise and implement the business strategy (Ready, Vicere and White, 1994).

The benefits of an open systems approach

Adopting an open systems approach to management development offers the organisation a number of benefits:

- A broader set of strategies, policies and plans are developed that take fuller account of the organisation's unique situation and its specific requirements in respect of managerial skills and knowledge.
- The notion that *if you develop the manager, you develop the organisation*, and vice versa, becomes apparent (see Figure 10.2). An open systems view identifies the way management development contributes to overall organisational effectiveness. As the organisation changes and develops, so positive influencing 'loops' are created that lead to the further development of managers. Similarly, as managers are developed, positive influencing 'loops' lead to changes in the organisation which produce greater effectiveness. It can, of course, work the other way. Poor or ineffective development can create negative influencing 'loops' that undermine organisational or managerial effectiveness.
- By identifying, analysing and monitoring the complex network of influences and patterns of relationships in managerial work, development programmes can become more adaptable, flexible, responsive and proactive in the face of organisational change and turbulence.
- Viewing management development in open system terms reveals the full extent of its influence on the organisation and is likely to lead to more detailed and objective assessment of performance and overall effectiveness.

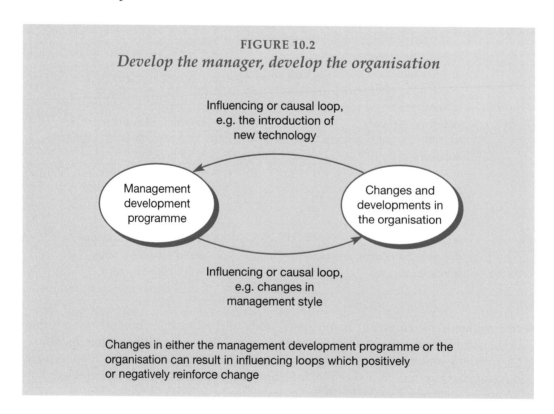

FIGURE 10.2

Develop the manager, develop the organisation

Influencing or causal loop,
e.g. the introduction of
new technology

Management
development
programme

Changes and
developments in
the organisation

Influencing or causal loop,
e.g. changes in
management style

Changes in either the management development programme or the
organisation can result in influencing loops which positively
or negatively reinforce change

A unified approach to management development

We saw in the previous section that an open systems approach can offer real benefits. But how can an open systems approach be translated into an effective management development programme? Figure 10.3 shows the example of a *unified management development programme* built on open systems principles.

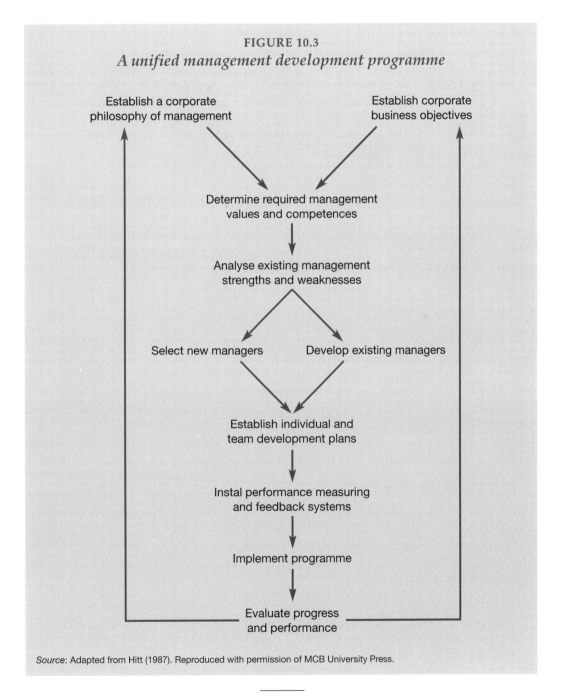

FIGURE 10.3
A unified management development programme

Establish a corporate philosophy of management

Establish corporate business objectives

Determine required management values and competences

Analyse existing management strengths and weaknesses

Select new managers

Develop existing managers

Establish individual and team development plans

Instal performance measuring and feedback systems

Implement programme

Evaluate progress and performance

Source: Adapted from Hitt (1987). Reproduced with permission of MCB University Press.

In a unified programme, management development is located at the very heart of the organisation's philosophy, mission, business goals and human resource strategy. The process is integrated and coherent across all functions and hierarchies. Manager performance is measured and development activity can be linked clearly to the organisational values and the achievement of strategic goals. As Hitt (1987: 53) makes clear, 'effective management of the enterprise and development of managerial talent are a single integrated activity'. Others reinforce this point. By adopting a unified, integrated approach to management development, 'all elements of the executive process are linked together to focus on the most essential outcome of the process – the development of a sustainable focus on organisational learning and ultimately competitiveness' (Ready, Vicere and White, 1994: 66). But an open systems approach to management development will have implications for the role of management development professionals who have to move away from the role of 'needs assessor', 'programme coordinator' and 'administrator' to a role that is much more results and change oriented (Temporal, 1990). As Temporal rather pointedly remarks, 'get into the business of results or get out of the business of development' (p. 13).

Some considerations for effective management development

In the previous section, it was stressed that a unified, integrated approach based on an open systems model can overcome many of the problems associated with a fragmented, piecemeal approach. But there are a number of important considerations.

Management development as a rational process?

So far in this chapter, the rationale for developing managers has been very much bound up in a functional framework where the aim is 'to directly improve managerial functioning and thereby corporate performance' (Lees, 1992). A range of interventions are employed by management development professionals in a systematic and logical fashion. Techniques are devised to select managers, e.g. assessment centres. They are then formally educated, trained and assessed against using a range of standardised academic and vocational criteria often linked to a qualification. Performance management systems are used to provide feedback and to reward what are deemed the 'right' attitudes and behaviour patterns.

Developing managers in this formalised, functional fashion offers a number of benefits, such as a focus on business objectives, coherent framework of agreed standards and consistency of approach. However, what it fails to acknowledge is that management development can be driven by other rationales, which may be social, political, emotional, legitimatory, psychic or symbolic. As Lees (1992: 104) points out, these and other rationales:

> are often given insufficient attention in management development being ignored or dismissed as insignificant. Yet their importance in making managers feel whole, rather than simply corporate functionaries with enhanced competencies, is immense.

Lees points out that any combination of rationales may operate at any given moment, which suggests that management development will mean different things to different managers at different times in different contexts. This is clearly demonstrated in Salaman and Butler (1990), where managers were adopting seemingly irrational attitudes to their learning and development. For example, management learning was only legitimate if it enhanced their power, status and reward within a particular structure and culture. The existence of different, often competing rationales reinforces the need for managers and management development professionals to take a much more holistic, contextual approach in planning and implementing their programmes.

Managers' attitudes and awareness

Different attitudes and degrees of awareness with regard to management development will exist at different levels within the organisation and influence the approach that is adopted. For instance, there might be a lack of knowledge, awareness, vision, even fear on the part of senior managers about considering development as an integral part of long-term business strategy. Development may be constrained and attract little enthusiasm from middle managers because they cannot find the time or view the development of their junior managers as posing a threat to their own position. Junior managers may have a very positive attitude, with a consequent demand for training in areas such as supervisory skills, but development is undermined by a lack of awareness on the part of their boss about the need to create opportunities for them to transfer knowledge into the workplace to gain practical experience.

In some cases, managers may fail to recognise the need for learning or see development as unnecessary for them. Such views often arise because of a lack of management education or the fear of implied incompetence if they seek development, especially with senior managers. Resistance to development then builds up and it is seen as a waste of time or not treated seriously (Tovey, 1991: 69).

The context of management development

Criticism has been levelled at the management development literature for its tendency to propound 'universalistic nostrums' without 'due regard for context' (Storey, 1990). Context can be thought of as a complex network of variables with which managers interact, and out of which they are able to construct a social reality (their perceived managerial 'world') with sense and meaning. It is context which shapes and influences the way development is formulated and enacted. Some of the more important contextual variables are shown in Figure 10.4. Boyden and Leary (1994) argue that increasingly the role of management development professionals will focus on 'managing management development'. An understanding of context is a vital consideration.

Evaluating management development

If management development is to be effective in meeting individual needs and delivering organisation goals, the process must be evaluated to make judgements about its cost effectiveness and to aid organisational learning and improvement (Easterby-Smith, 1994). The literature on evaluation tends to focus heavily on the training and education 'components' of development (Rae, 1986; Warr *et al.*, 1970). Evaluation is concerned with the

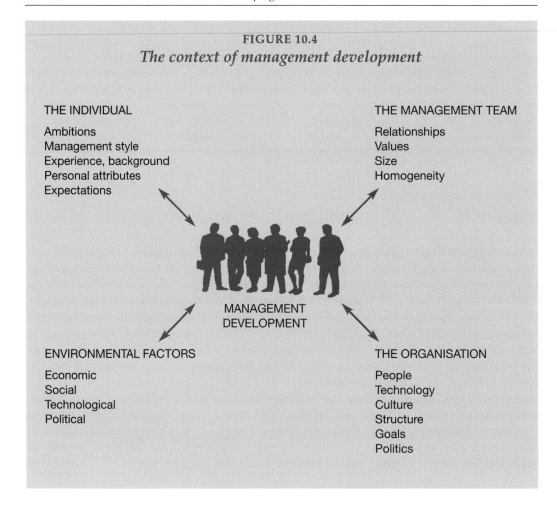

FIGURE 10.4
The context of management development

THE INDIVIDUAL

Ambitions
Management style
Experience, background
Personal attributes
Expectations

THE MANAGEMENT TEAM

Relationships
Values
Size
Homogeneity

MANAGEMENT
DEVELOPMENT

ENVIRONMENTAL FACTORS

Economic
Social
Technological
Political

THE ORGANISATION

People
Technology
Culture
Structure
Goals
Politics

immediate training or educational 'event': measuring the inputs to the event, the process itself and immediate outcomes (see Figure 10.5). Measurement is against identified development needs and training objectives within the framework of a systematic training cycle (Harrison, 1992). There is often less concern with the longer-term impact and effects of the event or activity (Rae, 1986).

There are different approaches to evaluation. Some may be regarded as being objective, rigorous and scientific, while others are much more pragmatic, subjective and interpretive in orientation (Easterby-Smith, 1994). In collecting data, a range of quantitative and qualitative methods are normally employed (see Smith and Porter, 1990; and Easterby-Smith, 1994).

Methods include:

- in-course and post-course questionnaires;
- attitude surveys and psychological tests before and after the event;
- appraisal systems;
- observations by trainers and others;
- self-reports and critical incident analysis.

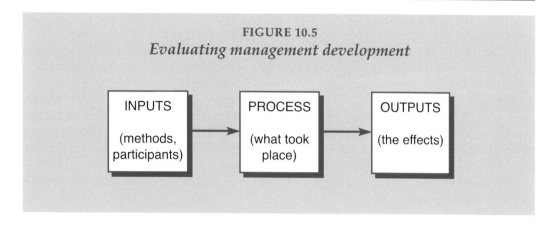

FIGURE 10.5
Evaluating management development

Whichever method or combination of methods is chosen, it is important to realise that evaluation does not take place in a vacuum. Judgements about the outcomes of management development programmes must be viewed within the context in which they are embedded. This immediately raises a number of political, cultural and social issues, which in turn generate considerable controversy for those involved in developing managers. These controversies will be discussed in more detail later in the chapter.

Ownership by the personnel function

Many development programmes are designed, administered and operated by personnel and training specialists, but this can create problems.

Personnel practitioners view management development as an important part of their role. It is a highly visible activity that offers them a source of political leverage and an opportunity to demonstrate their professional skills. However, some writers have pointed to the weak position of the personnel function in attaining and holding organisational power and the marginalisation of personnel in a number of organisations (see Davis, 1987; Guest, 1989). If this is occurring, it may be preventing management development finding a place on the strategic agenda (Molander and Walton, 1984).

Towards a more successful approach?

The theme running through this section has been that management development cannot be viewed as a closed system. If it is, there is the likelihood of piecemeal and fragmented approaches with adverse consequences for organisational development and renewal. As Mumford (1987: 230) states:

> any management development process which emphasise discrete activities, organised thinking processes, neatness and freedom of choice, is likely to be out of synchronisation with the *reality of management* that managers engage in.

But piecemeal approaches may also contribute to organisation dysfunction and become what Varney (1977) terms a 'counterproductive process'. As managers encounter structural, cultural and political barriers to their development they rapidly become disillusioned and frustrated, which may lead to a worsening of an already problematical situation in respect of organisational effectiveness (Hopfl and Dawes, 1995).

What is therefore required is a more holistic, integrated perspective in which development is both *contingent* upon the interplay of contextual variables and embraces formal and informal learning opportunities and processes. However, such an approach will demand a radically different outlook and role from those with responsibilities for making sure that managers deliver business goals (Doyle, 1995).

In the next section we explore the way in which management development is organised and implemented.

ORGANISING AND IMPLEMENTING MANAGEMENT DEVELOPMENT PROGRAMMES

Organising management development programmes

With a clear set of policies, objectives and approaches established, the organisation is now in a position to consider the best way to organise and implement the development programme.

To organise an effective management development programme, even a modest one, requires considerable effort. This may partially explain why programmes have a tendency to become piecemeal and fragmented, and why line managers often leave them to personnel and training specialists to organise. Certain decisions will have to be made within the context of the organisation's strategic plans and environmental influences.

Determining who is responsible for management development

If a development programme is to be successfully planned and implemented, there has to be clear and unambiguous allocation of responsibility and a willingness to accept that responsibility.

Traditionally, responsibility for development has rested with the personnel function with some input from the manager's boss. The individual manager was essentially passive in the process: they were only required to 'turn up and be developed'.

More recently, organisations are adopting and promoting a stakeholder view (see Figure 10.6) where the main responsibility is shared between the personnel specialist, the boss and the individual (Davis, 1990). But other 'stakeholders' have an interest in the process and outcomes.

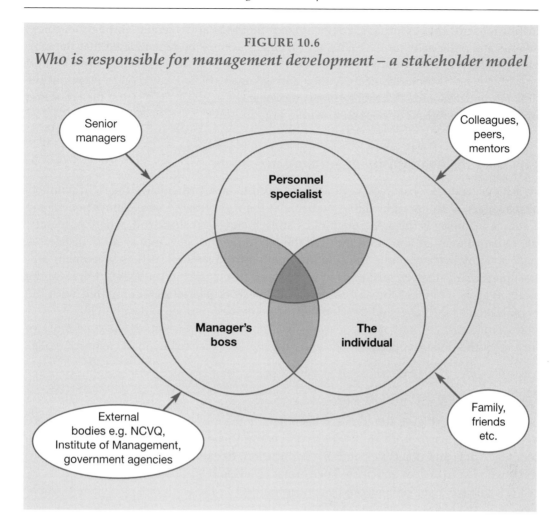

FIGURE 10.6
Who is responsible for management development – a stakeholder model

The effective development of managers requires the full involvement and participation of all of these parties. An active process of discussion and negotiation usually results in all parties accepting and owning a share of responsibility for development objectives, planning and implementation. However, although these three parties are central to the development process, other 'stakeholders' will also have an input (Mabey and Salaman, 1995). For example, within the organisation the role of senior management is vital in terms of resourcing, commitment and establishing a supportive culture. Colleagues and mentors will advise and assist in overcoming particular problems and issues (Mumford, 1993).

Beyond the organisational boundary, national bodies such as the Institute of Management, lead bodies, NCVQ, TECs, etc. are all influential in shaping management development policies and direction through mechanisms such as funding, reports, lobbying, contact with industry representatives, etc. Similarly, academic and vocational institutions are able to influence development methods and agendas through teaching, awards and other activities (see Chapter 8). Finally it must be remembered that the individual's friends and family have a crucial role to play in providing support and encouragement (Mumford, 1993). Mabey and Salaman (1995: 176) go on to point out the linkages between each stakeholder are complex and each will 'help shape the ethos and practice of training and development within organisations'.

Ensuring the availability of suitable managers

To achieve strategic objectives, organisations need to ensure they have the right numbers of managers, with the right skills, available at the right time. A core element of human resource planning is the assessment of existing managerial stock and, where necessary, the replenishment of that stock through the recruitment of new managers. A *managerial audit* is normally carried out, utilising information from sources such as assessment centres, performance appraisals, personnel files and discussions with bosses, to reveal the skills available to meet forecasted demand. These skills are then compared with the organisation's HRM plan and development objectives established (Vineall, 1994).

In certain cases, it may not be feasible or appropriate to develop the existing stock of managers and organisations will then enter the market-place to buy in the required skills.

Designing reward and appraisal systems

Since the 1980s, growing attention has been paid to the introduction of performance management systems to both motivate and reward those managers who contribute to strategic goals and objectives and, by implication, to exert sanctions on or to 'punish' those who fail to deliver anticipated performance levels.

Performance management can be conceptualised in the form of a cycle consisting of five elements (Mabey and Salaman, 1995):

- setting of performance objectives;
- measuring outcomes;
- feedback of results;
- rewards linked to outcomes;
- amendments to objectives and activities.

Within the cycle, performance-related pay (PRP) and performance appraisal are key components: the former to produce the extrinsic financial rewards in the form of shares, income differentials, profit sharing schemes, bonuses, etc., and the latter to provide the essential mechanism for setting objectives and feeding back performance criteria (Hendry, 1995).

In terms of management development, there is a close interaction with performance management systems. First and foremost, performance management systems must be seen to reward personal development and achievement. This is leading a number of organisations to link their systems of reward more closely to the attainment of higher levels of competence, which is one way of overcoming 'the subjectivity and arbitrariness of assessment' (Hendry, 1995: 309). The achievement of objectives is also closely linked to management training and education which provide the skills and knowledge required to meet objectives. Performance appraisal provides the forum for identifying development needs. It also serves as the mechanism for feeding back information to the manager about current levels of performance, enabling him or her to identify and negotiate adjustments or further development needs.

Although the focus of performance management is on extrinsic rewards , intrinsic rewards through praise, encouragement and reassurance are vital components in management development, particularly in the area of coaching and mentoring. For younger managers who may be on fast-track graduate programmes, continuous positive feedback during the early stages of the programme is vital to sustain motivation and commitment. Older, experienced managers also need regular praise, encouragement and above all reassurance that their skills and experience are still valued and appreciated, and that any investment in personal development is seen as being positive from the organisation's viewpoint (Mumford, 1993).

Provision of resourcing and support

To be successful, development requires adequate planning, resourcing and support (Vineall, 1994). Integrating management development with strategic planning clearly identifies the financial commitments which the organisation will undertake. Budgets can then be prepared in conjunction with those responsible for development. In smaller organisations, the physical resources to carry out development (trained personnel, training space and materials) are rarely available and external resources in the form of consultants, academics and professional institutions are utilised.

In larger organisations, skilled training personnel are normally available, together with dedicated training and residential facilities, etc. External resources may also be used if it is cost-effective to do so or specialist skills are required.

Whatever the resources available, no development programme will succeed if it is not supported by senior and middle management (Margerison, 1991). One of the main strengths of the unified approach discussed earlier is in building that support from the outset. Development is integrated with strategic objectives and senior managers can clearly see how development will benefit the organisation (Ready, Vicere and White, 1994). The main issue then becomes one of sustaining support for the duration of the programme, especially during a time of major change.

Promotion and succession planning

In conjunction with considerations regarding performance management systems and adequate resourcing and support, it is argued that management development can only be effective if careful consideration is given to career paths and opportunities for promotion and progression (Mumford, 1993; Margerison, 1994a). This requires a well-prepared human resource plan that is future oriented (see Chapter 4).

As well as developing managers to step into the positions vacated by leavers and retirees, succession planning needs to consider the growth and future direction of the organisation. Plans should include the older, experienced, so-called 'plateaued' managers as well as your high fliers. As organisations downsize and restructure, vertical opportunities are fast disappearing and innovative ways need to be found to set new challenges and provide opportunities to motivate managers through horizontal progressing, e.g. in the form of projects, secondments, etc.

Despite the opportunities offered by horizontally focused initiatives, some would argue that the picture for managers is becoming increasingly bleak. While there are winners, there are also losers in career terms (Caulkin, 1994). The lack of managerial career opportunities is increasingly becoming a factor influencing the changing nature of the 'psychological contract' between the individual and their organisation (Herriot and Pemberton, 1996). As these authors remark, 'careers are becoming more complex sequences of actions based on choices and constraints which can take the individual from the core to the periphery and back again' (p. 338). This is leading some managers towards a much more instrumental interpretation of their relationship with the organisation, captured in the notion of a 'new deal' (Herriot and Pemberton, 1995).

The predictions therefore are that some managers, if they are to survive, will have to take more and more responsibility for their careers. With a more developed, professional and mobile management workforce there is every opportunity for them to do so (Stewart, 1994). For those involved in developing managers, there is a new role emerging where the emphasis will switch towards development for employability rather than career progression, and their role will increasingly become one of enabling and facilitating rather than controlling development (Cannon and Taylor, 1994).

Suitable structures and systems

Implementing management development successfully is dependent upon an effective, integrated management development infrastructure that:

- identifies and allocates responsibility;
- provides and disseminates information efficiently;
- provides administrative support;
- increases awareness and 'visibility'.

Acknowledging the diversity of management

We saw earlier that development has to be linked to the reality of managerial work. When organising development programmes, it is important to cater for the diversity of management skills, attitudes and experience that reside within the organisation. One example is given by Odiorne (1984) who advocates a *portfolio* approach. A 'mix' of objectives and techniques might be arranged to match the profile of the management team in the organisation.

> **A Portfolio Approach to Development**
> **'Stars'**: high performing, high potential managers
>
> *Aim:*
> - create challenge
> - provide incentives and reward
> - allocate adequate resources and effort.
>
> **'Workhorses'**: high performing, limited potential managers
>
> *Aim:*
> - emphasise value and worth of experience
> - motivate and reassure
> - utilise experience on assignments, projects, coaching.
>
> **'Problem employees'**: high potential, underperforming
>
> *Aim:*
> - identify weaknesses
> - channel resources to address weaknesses
> - regular performance monitoring and feedback.
>
> **'Deadwood'**: low performing, low potential managers
>
> *Aim:*
> - identify weaknesses, resolvable?
> - if not, consider release, early retirement, demotion.
>
> (Adapted from Odiorne, 1984)

The diverse nature of management means that key questions need to be answered before development commences:

- *Who is being developed?*

- Is it older managers seeking new challenges or younger 'high fliers' on a fast-track development programme?
- Is it senior managers seeking to enhance their strategic skills, middle managers seeking to update and broaden existing skills or junior level managers looking to acquire additional managerial skills?
- Is it technical specialists seeking to expand their cross-functional capabilities or supervisors receiving training for the first time?

● *What is being developed?*

- Does the programme seek to develop new attitudes and values as in the case of a recently privatised public utility or a private sector company that has just undergone a take-over?
- Does the programme aim to develop technical, financial, business or interpersonal skills? What are the priorities?
- Does the programme seek to change existing managerial behaviours and styles to reflect an internal organisational restructuring, i.e. the introduction of new technology?

● *Where will the development take place?*

- Should development be on-the-job in the office, factory or sales territory, or off-the-job in a residential hall, academic institution or individual's home, or a combination of both?

● *What are the most appropriate techniques to achieve the best fit between individual and organisational requirements?*

- What are the most cost-effective/appropriate techniques available?
- How much scope is there to accommodate individual learning needs and preferences?
- How much choice is delegated to the individual over the choice of development techniques?
- How is conflict resolved between individual and organisational needs?

It is only when these questions have been considered, is the organisation in a position to construct a framework of development techniques that best fits its needs. The next section discusses some of the more commonly used techniques. It is important to reiterate the point made earlier in this chapter that a great deal of development takes place in unstructured and informal ways (Mumford, 1993).

Implementing management development programmes

Earlier on the question 'Why are we developing this manager?' was explored. In this section attention will focus on the techniques and choices available to organisations when they implement development programmes. But before that there needs to be a careful identification of development needs.

Development needs analysis

If managers are to be developed effectively, their individual development needs must be assessed in a careful and systematic fashion. There are several ways to do this. Traditionally, the diagnosis of development needs for managers has relied upon an often *ad hoc* and piecemeal process of observation and the 'constructive' input of others in the organisation.

Increasingly, organisations are turning to performance appraisal as an effective way of identifying the skills and behaviours required to meet business objectives (Mumford, 1993). During the appraisal process both the individual and their boss review performance against departmental/organisational objectives and other performance criteria to determine development needs. Once analysed, the development needs form the basis of a negotiated and agreed personal development plan, which is regularly reviewed and modified in the light of changing organisational and individual circumstances.

With a greater emphasis on performance management in which individual reward is more closely aligned with and directed towards the attainment of business objectives, there has been a trend towards the greater use of assessment/development centres. Development centres are 'workshops which measure the abilities of participants against the agreed success criteria for a job or role' (Lee and Beard, 1994). It should also be borne in mind that the term development centre relates to the process of identifying needs, not to a specific place (Munchus and McArthur, 1991).

The main aim of a development centre is to 'obtain the best possible indication of people's actual or potential competence to perform at the target job or job level' (Woodruffe, 1993: 2). Most development centres operate in the following way:

- There is careful selection of job-related criteria which may be in the form of competencies, dimensions, attributes, critical success factors, etc.
- A group of managers is identified and brought together in the form of a workshop of around 6 people and lasting 1–2 days. In the workshops a series of diagnostic instruments and/or multiple assessment techniques are administered which aim to measure an individual's ability to perform against the job-related criteria. These can take the form of psychometric tests, planning exercises, in-tray exercises, interviews, games, simulations.
- A team of trained assessors observe and measure performance, evaluate and provide structured feedback and guidance to individuals.
- After the workshop, line managers and/or trainers utilise the feedback to help the individual construct a personal development plan.

Although the use of development centres is growing, there have been a number of criticisms which tend to revolve around assessment techniques that do not relate to the task or job, poor organisation, poorly trained assessors, ineffective feedback and no follow-up action (Dulewicz, 1991; Whiddett and Branch, 1993).

Whichever method or combination of methods is selected, it is vital that each manager's needs are carefully assessed before implementing a development programme and that an effective system of providing feedback is established.

Competency-based development programmes

Recent years have seen something of a 'mini-revolution' in UK management education and development, one of the catalysts for which was the publication in the late 1980s of two searching reports into the development of UK managers (*The Making of British Managers*, Constable and McCormick, 1987; *The Making of Managers*, Handy, 1987). These reports examined the education and development needs of UK managers and concluded that current provision and standards were wholly inadequate and that development had a low priority in many organisations. They identified an urgent need to develop managers more effectively which, it was predicted, would raise standards and levels of performance, thereby ensuring that the UK economy was able to compete more successfully in an increasingly global market.

In response to these findings, there were a number of initiatives, beginning with the establishment of the National Forum for Management Education and Development and culminating in the Management Charter Initiative (MCI). Since its inception in the early 1990s, MCI has commissioned extensive research into UK management development needs and approaches. The aim has been to focus on the development of managers through workplace activities. What matters is the manager's ability to perform and deliver pre-determined outcomes rather than development being concerned with the acquisition of specific knowledge or academic qualifications.

MCI is now the Management Lead Body within the NVQ system (see Chapter 8). As lead body, its primary aim has been to establish a *generic set of standards and qualifications* based upon 'the areas of activity which the majority of managers would be expected to perform competently' (Miller, 1991). These areas of activity are identified as the ability to:

- manage operations;
- manage finance;
- manage people;
- manage information.

Within each area of activity or role, there are associated *units of competence* derived from a functional analysis of what constitutes 'the manager's job'. For example, in the role of Managing People, one unit of competence is to 'contribute to the recruitment and selection of personnel'. Having identified units of competence, there is a further subdivision into a series of *elements* against which there are established *performance criteria* and *range statements*. A standard is therefore established by which managerial performance can be assessed. Evidence can then be gathered and presented by the manager to a trained assessor who will judge if their performance is deemed to be 'competent' in their current position.

Currently, there are national standards of competence for supervisory and middle manager which equate to NVQ Levels 3 and 4. New standards are being introduced for those at senior manager level.

Competency-based development programmes such as those set up by MCI have attracted considerable criticism, both in philosophical and practical terms. At the heart of the criticism is the belief that competence approaches such as that used by MCI are fundamentally flawed because they are too functional and behavioural in orientation (Stewart and Hamlin, 1992a). Some see them as bureaucratic and overly simplistic, unable to take account of the complex, contextual, contingent and ever-changing nature of the managerial role (Canning, 1990). Because of the growing significance of competency-based management development programmes, these and other criticisms will be explored more fully in the controversial issues section of this chapter.

Despite these criticisms, it would appear that the notion of competency-based development has now established itself within the framework of UK management development. However, there have been some interesting changes and adaptations. For example, in an MCI sponsored survey, 20% of those surveyed reported that they were using the MCI framework but within that figure 45% said they had customised the standards to suit their own purposes (MCI, 1993). More recent evidence supports this and shows that many organisations are beginning to move away from the original model developed by MCI to a more contextually based approach. Rather than adhere to what they judge to be a somewhat costly, bureaucratic, prescriptive and rigid framework of national standards, organisations appear to be 'doing their own thing'. They are retaining the competency philosophy and principle, but devising their own competence framework for managers within the unique context of their organisational situation. They feel this is necessary if they are to respond to the complexity induced by rapid environmental change (Cockerill, 1994; Roberts, 1995). Evidence would also suggest that competency frameworks for managers are now becoming more fragmented and differentiated to suit changing circumstances, e.g. organisational lifecycles (Sparrow and Bognanno, 1994; Roberts, 1995).

Other adaptations of the original model include the growing use of competencies to assess management behaviour and performance: 'the majority of organisations favour frameworks based on the development of behaviour rather than prescribed national standards' (Mathewman, 1995: 1). Management competencies now form the basis for HR systems in areas such as development centres and performance management, and appear to be underpinning the drive towards more unitarist, behaviourist organisational cultures. More controversially, there is now a growing quest to identify higher order, supra or meta competencies which can be used to inform personality testing for selection and other 'judgements' about managerial behaviour and performance (Sparrow and Bognanno, 1994).

What appears to be happening, therefore, is a process of adjustment whereby NVQ/MCI frameworks of competencies are being utilised for basic skills provision in a bottom-up approach, while new behavioural competencies are being cascaded down to set behavioural patterns and cultural imperatives (Mathewman, 1995). This adjustment may be seen as an inevitable consequence of what some would judge to be inherent flaws in the national framework. But although this more pragmatic, flexible response is likely to be welcomed by many, it does raise a number of issues, not least how to maintain and guarantee a system of assessment and national accreditation for management qualifications with any measure of confidence.

Mainstream management education and training methods

While competency-based programmes continue to grow, they are still only part of the wider portfolio of frameworks and methods used in manager development. A great deal of management development is formalised, planned and structured. It can take place 'on-the-job' (in the workplace environment) or 'off-the-job' (away from the workplace) (Mumford, 1993). For example, a business studies graduate might leave university after four years of study and join a 'fast-track' development programme in a medium to large national or multinational organisation. The programme would typically last some 12–18 months, during which time the graduate moves through the different functional areas of the organisation. During their time in each functional department, they would undertake carefully planned and supervised project-based tasks designed to stimulate and challenge their business and interpersonal skills. Performance would be carefully monitored at each stage. Towards the end of the programme, those graduates who are successful will select a particular career path and begin to climb the 'managerial ladder', usually beginning with the acceptance of a junior managerial position.

Older, more experienced managers might attend short courses, either internally or externally, which are designed to 'top up' their managerial skills base. A number of them will embark on longer-term programmes of full- or part-time study at higher education institutions. For those managers who find it difficult to fit such programmes into their daily routines, distance learning schemes operated by institutions such as the Open University Business School and independent management colleges are available and are increasingly being seen as a flexible, cost-effective approach to education.

Within these and other programmes, we find a diverse range of formalised learning methods. These methods have tended to evolve through a pragmatic process of trial and error. Research by Burgoyne and Stuart (1991) reveals that the following methods are likely to be used (in order of predominance of use):

Learning methods:

1. Lectures
2. Games and simulations
3. Projects
4. Case studies
5. Experiential (analysis of experience)
6. Guided reading
7. Role playing
8. Seminars
9. Programmed instruction (computerised/packaged).

Although these methods are widely used in education and training, their abstract, detached and artificial nature can never compensate for the reality of dealing with everyday managerial problems and issues (Burgoyne and Stuart, 1991). A summary of the other weaknesses that have been identified in formalised management education and training are:

● a clash between academic culture/expectations and managerial culture/expectations (Cunnington, 1985);
● difficulty in transferring and applying knowledge to the 'reality' of the workplace (Newstrom, 1986);
● the relevance of course material to the needs and wants of individual managers and organisations.

Increasingly organisations are turning to experientially based techniques.

Action learning

In chapter 7, the significance of experiential learning processes to the development of managers was identified. Much of the theory relating to experiential learning is drawn from the theoretical work of Kolb (1984) and Honey and Mumford (1986), who introduced the concept of a learning cycle where managers learn through a process of:

● implementation
● reflection
● making changes
● initiating further action.

Burgoyne and Stuart (1991) point out that a greater focus on experiential learning in the workplace, coupled to a reaction against the 'remoteness', complication and institutionalisation of management development, has encouraged organisations to adopt new methods of learning. Many of these new approaches are built around the principles of *action learning* pioneered by writers such as Reg Revans.

Revans' key principles of action learning

1. Management development must be based on real work projects.
2. Those projects must be owned and defined by senior managers as having a significant impact on the future success of the enterprise.
3. Managers must aim to make a real return on the cost of the investment.
4. Managers must work together and learn from each other.
5. Managers must achieve real action and change.
6. Managers must study the content and process of change.
7. Managers must publicly commit themselves to action.

(Margerison, 1991: 38)

Revans saw learning (L) as a combination of what he terms 'programmed knowledge' (P) and 'questioning insight' (Q), thus L = P + Q. When facing unprecedented changes, managers cannot know what programmed knowledge they will need. Instead, they need to 'understand the subjective aspects of searching the unfamiliar, or learning to pose useful and discriminating questions'. Therefore action learning becomes a 'simple device of setting them to tackle real problems that have so far defied solution' (Revans, 1983: 11).

Revans argues that managerial learning has to embrace both 'know-how' and 'know-that', and be rooted in real problem solving where 'lasting behavioural change is more likely to follow to reinterpretation of past experiences than the acquisition of fresh knowledge' (p. 14). Managers will be more able to make their interpretations, which are 'necessarily subjective, complex and ill-structured' (p. 14), and reorder their perceptions by working with colleagues who are engaged in the same process, rather than with non-managers such as management teachers who are 'not exposed to real risk in responsible action'. In other words, managers form 'learning sets' (groups of 4–6 people) who, with the aid of a facilitator, work together and learn to give and accept criticism, advice and support. Margerison (1994b: 109), citing Revans, likens this approach to 'comrades in adversity'. Managers will only 'learn effectively when they are confronted with difficulties and have the opportunity to share constructively their concerns and experiences with others'.

Margerison (1991), drawing on case studies and personal experience of supervising action learning programmes, points out that managers learn a considerable amount

- about themselves
- about their job
- about team members, and most of all
- about how to improve things and make changes.

Experientially based development has led to new innovations in development such as 'learning contracts', 'learning communities' and the 'learning organisation'.

In a *learning contract*, there is a formal agreement between the participant (the manager being developed), the boss and the trainer. Not only does it reinforce responsibility for development, it brings a number of benefits (Boak and Joy, 1990):

Participants:
- contracts are of their own choosing
- relevant to their needs
- improves their learning abilities.

Managers:
- become involved in training and development
- can influence the activities of trainer and participant.

Trainers:
- tackle a wide variety of real problems
- see real developments in skills and attitudes.

In *learning communities* managers are seen as self-developers who come together to share skills, resources and experiences, in much the same fashion as therapeutic self-help groups operate in the fields of social and psychiatric work.

In a *learning organisation* structures and processes are adapted to encourage managers to take responsibility for their own development. As they learn and improve, so the organisation is learning and improving with them (Pedler *et al.*, 1990).

Experiential learning methods such as action learning are gaining prominence in the field of management development. As organisations confront the growing uncertainty and instability brought about a far-reaching and radical change, they are discovering that management development is likely to be more effective when it is rooted in the everyday reality of what managers do and how they behave.

Coaching and mentoring

Coaching

To many managers, coaching and mentoring represent the most tangible, practical and, if done effectively, most useful forms of on-the-job development.

Coaching is defined by Torrington *et al.* (1994: 432) as 'improving the performance of somebody who is already competent rather than establishing competence in the first place'. It is analogous to the sports coach who is seeking to improve performance by continually analysing and offering constructive criticism and guidance to an athlete or player. The coach (boss) must be willing to share tasks and assignments with the individual. Each task must have scope, responsibility and authority to challenge and test the individual. Coaching usually begins with a period of instruction and 'shadowing' to grasp the essential aspects of the task. There is then a transfer of responsibility for the task to the individual. Throughout the process there is a dialogue with regular feedback on performance in the form of constructive criticism and comments. The effectiveness of this feedback is dependent upon a sound working relationship.

In most organisations, coaching is done on an informal basis and is dependent on the boss having the inclination, time and motivation to do it, as well as possessing the necessary expertise and judgement for it to succeed.

Mentoring

Mentoring was described more fully in Chapter 7. It differs from coaching in two ways:

- The relationship is not usually between the individual and their immediate boss. An older manager unconnected with the workplace is normally selected to act as mentor.
- Mentoring is about relationships rather than activities.

Mentoring represents a powerful form of management development for both the parties involved. For the individual, it allows them to discuss confusing, perplexing or ambiguous situations, and their innermost feelings and emotions, with somebody they can trust and respect. They gain the benefit of accumulated wisdom and experience from somebody who is knowledgeable and 'street-wise' in the ways of the organisation, especially its political workings. For older managers looking for new challenges and stimulation in their managerial role, mentoring represents an ideal development opportunity. It gives them an opportunity to achieve satisfaction and personal reward by sharing in the growth and maturity of another individual.

Projects and secondments

Task-based projects have always been used for the development of individual skills, knowledge and awareness in junior or inexperienced managers. Typically, they would work independently, or as part of a team, on a problem or issue, gathering and analysing information, drawing conclusions and making recommendations for action.

Project management is also increasing in prominence as the role and function of a manager is changing within an increasingly turbulent, uncertain and often ambiguous world (Coulson-Thomas, 1989; Dopson and Stewart, 1990). Managers are having to develop new skills and take on board new values. Research by Ashridge Management College (see Buchanan and Boddy, 1992) highlights the need to develop the notion of the 'flexible manager' who has the ability to:

- understand and relate to the wider environment;
- manage in that environment;
- manage complex, changing structures;
- innovate and initiate change;
- manage and utilise sophisticated information systems;
- manage people with different values and expectations.

To develop such competences, organisations are increasingly turning to project management as a development technique. Line managers are given responsibility for managing cross-functional teams of people who are tasked with achieving a specific organisational goal within a fixed time scale and to a set budget.

Organisations are discovering that cross-functional project management not only improves core management skills such as communication and motivation but is proving effective at developing 'higher order' diagnostic, judgemental, evaluative and political skills (Buchanan and Boddy, 1992).

Secondments are also increasingly being used for manager development. Multinational companies have highly sophisticated management exchange programmes that are used, not only to develop important language and cultural skills in managers, but to reinforce the organisation's central belief and value systems. Exchange programmes also exist between public and private sector organisations to transfer knowledge and broaden understanding. Some larger organisations are seconding their managers to various initiatives designed to assist small business ventures and community programmes.

Outdoor management development

In a climate and environment of greater risk, challenge, change and ambiguity for managers, increasing attention is focusing on the benefits of outdoor management development (OMD) as a development tool. OMD has its roots in the outward bound movement founded by Kurt Hahn (Burnett and James, 1994). The aim is to provide opportunities for personal growth and for managers to realise the potential of their 'inner resources' (Irvine and Wilson, 1994). In OMD, managers are exposed to emotional, physical and mental risks and challenges in which skills such as leadership and teamwork become *real* to the individuals and groups concerned (Burnett and James, 1994) and where 'the penalties for wrong decisions are painful; the consequence of bad judgements can be as real as being lost in a cold rainstorm at the edge of a dark forest' (Banks, 1994: 11). Others have likened OMD to 'outdoor action learning' in which 'the physical tasks at the core of outdoor development courses, whether they be abseiling a rockface, climbing a mountain peak or navigating rapids in canoes are real tasks which present real problems to real people in real time with real constraints' (Banks, 1994: 9).

However, OMD has received considerable criticism in recent years, a great deal of it stemming from a controversial 1993 TV documentary from the Channel 4 *Cutting Edge* series which featured a group of managers being 'damaged in body and mind' while on such a course (Banks, 1994). Others are critical of the degree of risk and adventure that managers *actually* experience and argue that many of the claimed 'benefits' of OMD can be attained within existing development frameworks (Irvine and Wilson, 1994). Jones and Oswick (1993) identify a plethora of claimed benefits for OMD, many of which are anecdotal and unsubstantiated and, where they are evaluated, there is evidence of bias when the evaluation is carried out by those who provide the training.

Management team development

With growing complexity and interdependence between functions and departments, many organisations wish to see their managers working together as a management team. This has led a range of techniques to instil a sense of team spirit or *esprit de corps* among managers. Activities range from outdoor training to intensive workshops and game playing at informal residential venues. This enables them to get to know their management colleagues as 'people rather than in their formal roles' (Margerison, 1991: 88). The aim is to build up a climate of trust and a feeling of togetherness and cooperation in achieving organisational goals.

However, the rhetoric of management teamwork may be some distance from the reality (Critchley and Casey, 1994). The assumption that organisations are more effective when managers work as a team may be questionable if managers are more concerned with achieving their own personal and departmental goals. Seeking cooperation from their colleagues does not necessarily mean cultivating a sense of openness, trust and common purpose. Indeed, such a team-based philosophy flies in the face of the political culture that often permeates management teams.

On some occasions teamworking can be beneficial and productive, e.g. during a time of maximum uncertainty where there has to be a pooling of ideas and resources to arrive at common perceptions and possibilities and enable the organisation to make strategic decisions. But on other occasions, pushing managers into a sharing, open, team-based culture can be counter-productive and a source of disillusionment for managers (Critchley and Casey, 1994).

Management team-building

The management team in a medium-sized manufacturing company was not performing effectively. There was evidence of a lack of trust and confidence in the team and relationships between individuals were poor. The managers were brought together in a series of workshops and asked to examine their managerial role and how it related to other managers and staff. They explored key issues and 'blockages'. After a short time it was realised that there were a number of misperceptions and misunderstandings. The workshops also revealed confusion over roles and responsibilities. An action plan was implemented to tackle these problems.

EXERCISES

1 As management development manager, what steps will you take to ensure that the action plan is successfully implemented?

2 How would you measure the effectiveness of the action plan?

Self-development

Organisations which invest in effective management development programmes are encouraging their managers to take more responsibility and control of their own development. As Boydell and Pedler (1981: 3) remark:

> Any effective system for management development must increase the manager's capacity and willingness to take control over and responsibility for events, and participating for themselves in their own learning.

If managers take responsibility for their own development they are likely to:

● improve career prospects;
● improve performance;
● develop certain skills;
● achieve full potential/self-actualisation.

Organisations also benefit if they are willing to support their managers in self-development (Temporal, 1984).

Benefits include:

● increased individual participation and commitment;
● greater flexibility in the face of change;
● greater visibility of individual strengths/weaknesses;
● cost-effectiveness – 'the DIY approach'.

A range of techniques exist for self-development. Some involve managers helping each other by sharing experiences in self-managed learning groups. Other approaches are more personally focused, using techniques such as distance learning materials, computer-based training and interactive videos. (For a fuller discussion of the methods used, see Pedler *et al.*, 1990).

INTERNATIONAL MANAGEMENT DEVELOPMENT

Starting in the 1980s and continuing through the 1990s, many organisations have sought to 'globalise' in their quest for greater market and product opportunities. A number of factors were responsible for this trend:

- favourable changes and improvements in the world political and social situation (EC, Eastern Europe);
- advances in technology and transport (communication, computing, air travel);
- greater cooperation between countries (joint ventures, i.e. in aerospace);
- a range of incentives to encourage inward investment to create job opportunities (Japanese car and electronics production in the UK).

These, and other changes, have encouraged organisations to expand into areas previously not considered. As a result, a number have become truly multinational organisations. For example, 39% of Ford Motor Company's employees now work outside of the USA and 43% of ICI's employees work outside the UK (Phillips, 1992).

For managers working in these organisations, there has been a major transformation in managerial work and managerial careers. This gives rise to a number of questions:

- To what extent does the concept of management move easily across international boundaries?
- Are we seeing the appearance of the 'truly' international manager?
- What skills and knowledge do managers need to develop to enable them to work and survive in a global market-place?
- How do you develop international managers?

Management as an international concept

In this section we will examine the development of international managers. You should read and study this section in conjunction with Chapters 16–19 which deal with the topic of international HRM.

To reiterate a key point made elsewhere on page 707, there are methodological and conceptual issues and controversies connected with studying HRM from an international perspective. Of particular relevance to this section are issues connected with the lack of accurate and longitudinally focused data; diversity in language and culture leading to variations in meaning and interpretation; and a tendency to generalise from specific data sources which makes any comparison between countries difficult. For example, you might ask yourself how far it is feasible or sensible to consider management as a concept that can move freely across international boundaries. There is some evidence to suggest that certain aspects of management are starting to converge, e.g. a shared technical language, and certain HR practices such as job evaluation and staff appraisal (Brewster and Tyson, 1992). Phillips (1992: 40) describes the success of global teams using concepts derived from the USA.

However, others argue that it is *divergence* not *convergence* that is taking place. National cultural diversity (residual effects of history, beliefs, values, attitudes, religion, language, etc.) is a key determinant in influencing management behaviour and 'these differences may become one of the most crucial problems for management – in particular, for the management of multinational, multicultural organisations whether public or private' (Hofstede, 1990: 392). This view is supported by others such as Hansen and Brooks (1994: 70) who observe that, while structures and technologies may converge, 'cultural factors influence management models, thinking styles, career expectations, organisational culture, change efforts and instructional needs and development'.

> A French manager working in a subsidiary of an American corporation that insisted upon an open-door policy may well leave his office door open – thus adjusting to the behavioural requirements of the corporate culture – without any modification whatsoever to his basic concept of managerial authority.   (Laurent, cited in Hansen and Brooks, 1994: 57)

The issue of cultural diversity is an important one because management development itself must be considered to be 'embedded' in national cultural forms which, together with other social, economic and political factors, determine the nature, philosophy, practice, priorities and focus of management development in different national contexts. Some of these contexts will be explored shortly.

In a sense, it might be argued that diversity poses a challenge to some of the rhetoric that surrounds notions of 'global villages' and 'global market-places'. For instance, in countries such as China, South Africa and those in Eastern Europe which have undergone major economic and social disruption and upheaval, the quest for growth and stability has seen the importation of Western concepts of business and management, especially those associated with management development. But as you will see shortly, although the demand for management development in these regions is becoming very strong, 'implanting' these Western concepts is often problematical for the host country. As the quality circles example below suggests, the problem of transfer is just as likely to be felt by Western countries. For example, in the UK there is evidence of problems in importing ideas and concepts such as total quality management (TQM) and quality circles from other countries, notably Japan.

Quality circles – a case of convergence or divergence?

A number of UK organisations have 'imported' and adapted the concept of *quality circles* from Japanese organisations during the 1980s and used it as an HRM technique. (It is interesting to note that the Japanese developed quality circles from 'imported' American ideas about quality during the 1950s!)

What is a Quality Circle?

A group of four to twelve people coming from the same work area, performing similar work who voluntarily meet on a regular basis to identify, investigate, analyse and solve their own work-related problems. The circles present solutions to management and are usually involved in implementing and later monitoring them.   (Russell and Dale, 1989)

Proponents of quality circles claim that, although the idea was imported, it is not 'culture bound'. The Work Research Unit, which is part of ACAS, seeks to promote quality of working life through techniques such as greater employee participation, and views quality circles as an important element in achieving that goal.

Russell (1983: 3) quotes Dr Ishikawa, a Japanese authority on QCs:

. . . I am convinced that quality circle activities have no socioeconomic or cultural limitations. Human beings are human beings wherever they live, and quality circle activities can be disseminated and implemented anywhere in the world for human benefit.

There is a case history of success with quality circles in the UK and other countries, especially amongst Japanese companies who have located in the UK and those who are competing with them, i.e. the UK car industry. However, there is also evidence of resistance and failure (Russell and Dale, 1989; Brennan, 1991; Miller and Cangemi, 1993; Redman *et al.*, 1995). One of the main factors seems to be 'cultural dissonance' where the underlying philosophy of quality circles (greater employee involvement, more responsibility and a reduction of managerial control) 'clashes' with countervailing UK managerial philosophies. The UK is not alone in experiencing difficulties; similar problems with quality circles have occurred in France (Barsoux, 1990).

How far such clashes are a result of a failure to adapt organisational cultures (i.e. to develop management styles that are supportive to quality circles) and how far they stem from a more fundamental, deep-rooted rejection by managers on the grounds that such ideas are at odds with wider sociocultural values and belief systems is not clear. It may be that some UK managers are adhering to an 'elitist' view of management and a 'manager's right to manage' derived from their education and life experiences in a *national* rather than organisational culture.

Some different perspectives on management development

In viewing international management development there are a number of possible perspectives that might be taken:

- global
- international
- Euro
- Western imported.

Global

Some have argued that managers can be developed to overcome and transcend the barriers of national culture and identity through the creation of 'microworlds' (McBride, 1992). Here, the focus is on creating a strong and influential organisational culture which can be transported across the world to operate within any national cultures and into which managers of all nationalities can be developed. As Stumpf, Watson and Rustogi (1994: 16) observe, 'they must manage diversity *less* by appreciating and utilising national and cultural differences and more by establishing an organisational culture which *transcends* those differences'. A good example of such organisations might be the McDonald's and Pizza Hut food chains. The development of truly global managers involves careful attention to behavioural simulations in which there is an effort to replicate real-life situations through the extensive use of analytical exercises, business games and discussions which enable managers to develop 'shared visions and mental models' and equip them with appropriate 'culture shaping skills' (McBride, 1992; Stumpf, Watson and Rostogi, 1994). However, such global approaches may run into problems when they fail to address the tensions that are created by corporate politics and the clashes between corporate and national cultures that emerge after take-overs or acquisitions (Ferner, 1994).

International

Much of the international management development literature is dominated by a Western international perspective. Here, the strategic goal of transnational/multinational organisations such as Philips and Unilever is to develop elite 'cadres' of international managers who are tasked with building efficient networks of organisations operating across national boundaries (Barlett and Ghoshal, 1989; Handy and Barham, 1990; Barham and Oates, 1991).

Most organisations aim to develop one or more of the following types:

- local nationals to manage locally (host);
- managers who live abroad and run overseas divisions or companies (expatriates);
- managers or short missions or projects (sales teams, plant installation);
- managers who work across national boundaries (Euro-manager, Middle East).

Research has shown that, in the past, UK companies have tended to use expatriate managers to retain control and safeguard their investment (Wilson and Rosenfeld, 1990). However, more recent research suggests that many managers in the USA and UK are 'simply not global animals' and this may mean that a multinational's ability to disseminate its corporate strategy overseas is contingent upon its individual managers' propensity to adapt (Ferner, 1994: 91).

What, then, are the skills and knowledge required to operate as an international manager and how might these be developed? Phillips (1992) argues that international managers must demonstrate skills in the following areas:

- technical skills and experience often beyond those normally required at home, e.g. the engineer who needs sound financial management skills;
- people skills, e.g. cultural empathy, team-building and interpersonal;
- intellectual skills, e.g. seeing the big picture, thinking in a macro not micro way;
- emotional maturity, e.g. being adaptable, independent, sensitive, self-aware;
- motivation, e.g. drive, enthusiasm, stamina, persistence.

Successful development of the international manager is often predicated on the establishment of clear international management development policies supported by and integrated with an appropriate international manager selection, recruitment, appraisal, career and reward infrastructure (Harzing and Van Ruysseveldt, 1995). Development activities themselves are primarily based on education, language skills, secondments, exchanges, projects and action learning programmes, with a heavy emphasis on cross-cultural training which is designed to 'get beyond the home country mentality' (Handy and Barham, 1990) and engender a new level of cultural awareness: 'management development must contribute to the creation of a new corporate culture and a new managerial mind-set' (Barham and Oates, 1991). Increasingly, the evidence suggests that the failure of foreign assignments may be rooted in emotional and family circumstances rather than personal capabilities and there is now growing attention being paid to including partners and families in the preparation and training process to prepare them for life overseas (Harzing and Van Ruysseveldt, 1995: 221).

> GrandMet's approach to management development is founded on an active interventionist approach to careers in which the individual must agree to 'mortgage' any short-term career considerations. Started in 1988, the 'cadre' programme aims to send young managers of high potential on international assignments before ultimately placing them in senior management positions in their home countries. At any one time there are 12–15 managers of 25–30 years of age sent on a maximum of four assignments each lasting 18–24 months. Selection is via a rigorous assessment process designed to detect 'international traits'. The process is designed to flush out any prejudices that might hinder a manager from adjusting to an unfamiliar culture.
>
> (Burnham and Oates, 1991)

Euro

As monetary, economic and social convergence and cooperation across Europe are seen to be growing, attention is now being focused on the 'Europeanisation' of management and, more recently, on how to develop what might be termed a 'Euro-manager'. This is seen as an essential requirement if Europe is to be properly equipped to fend off the competitive challenges posed by US and Japan, and more recently by the 'Tiger' economies of Taiwan, Singapore and Malaysia (Tijmstra and Casler, 1992).

However, any notion of a Euro-manager has to be located within Europe's rich and diverse set of social and cultural contexts. For the proponents of the Euro-manager concept, any lack of homogeneity created by such diversity need not necessarily represent a barrier. Indeed, it is argued that any barriers may be overcome through effective management development programmes which focus on and emphasise an understanding of the European business environment and European management dynamics (Tijmstra and Casler, 1992). Barriers may also be overcome through greater cooperation, sharing and integration in the field of management education and research (Easterby-Smith, 1992). And Fox (1992) argues that in the long term such a lack of homogeneity may be an advantage to European managers because it will develop cultural tolerance and understanding.

Others take a more cautious view. Hilb (1992) argues that there are major disparities in selection, appraisal and reward systems across Europe and that management development is neither strategically oriented nor properly evaluated. Additionally, HRD practices in general are too heavily influenced by variations in national labour markets, cultures and legislative frameworks. Kakabadse and Myers (1995), studying 959 chief executives in Europe, found wide variations in terms of management orientation across a number of criteria which are predicted to have implications for management development. For Thornhill (1993) any move towards Europeanisation raises significant issues for management trainers who have to contend with variations over job content, context, expectations, experiences and work-related values. (Hilb (1992) reports the following statistics:

- Job rotation is used in 32% of Italian firms but only 8% of French.
- Career high fliers are identified in 44% of French firms but only 22% of German.
- Assessment centres are used in 22% of UK firms but only 3% of Norwegian.
- In Swiss organisations 66% of promotions are internal but only 31% in Danish.

Thurley and Wirdenhuis (1991) also point up these cultural and other national variations, arguing that the concept of the Euro-manager will only be relevant in certain industrial contexts. Storey (1992b) identifies managerial parochialism and the lack of a European 'mindset' as a barrier, concluding that:

> The notion of the Euro-manager may not quite be a myth but the extent to which there is a clear conceptual and practical difference between this species and the international manager is open to question. (Storey, 1992b: 2)

Western imported

This final perspective might be generically termed 'Western imported' and refers to those countries who have sought to import Western and Japanese ideas and approaches to management development. There are a number of reasons for this. Management development may be seen as a vehicle for speeding up industrial development (China). It may be used to aid recovery after major social and political upheaval (Eastern Europe, South Africa) or in the case of Third World countries (Latin America, Africa, India) it may be linked to geo-political and economic efforts to survive in what for them is an increasingly competitive, even hostile world.

In summary, it is clear there are different perspectives on the way in which international management development is viewed. Thus, for those involved in the development of international managers, the issue remains a fundamental one: how to develop managers in a context where 'cultural factors influence management models, thinking styles, career expectations, organisational culture, change efforts, and international needs and development' (Hansen and Brooks, 1994: 70). Such considerations will become apparent in the next section when we review the development approaches in different countries.

Management development: A Cook's Tour?

In the next section you will embark on a brief tour of management development in different countries. You will recall the point made earlier, that any 'universal' comparison between the ways in which each country develops its managers is difficult, mainly because they cannot be separated from the cultural, social and economic context in which they are located. This will become even clearer as the tour progresses.

United States/United Kingdom

In respect of management development, both the US and the UK are very similar in their approach. Development is viewed as a separate, discrete and heavily individualised activity, aimed at correcting identified 'weaknesses' in skills and knowledge or 'deviances' in individual attitudes and behaviour. A rational-functional philosophy dominates which views the main justification of any development programme as being its contribution to business strategy and performance (Lees, 1992). Increasingly, the aim is to develop generalist managerial rather than narrow specialist skills to improve mobility and the ability to take on new assignments and challenges (Heisler and Benham, 1992). Development in the past has often been synonymous with management education and/or short, intensive training courses. In both countries attention is now focused on competency-based approaches. In the UK such approaches are institutionalised and championed through initiatives such as the Management Charter Initiative (see Chapter 8 for more details). However, as we have seen in this chapter, there is now an increasing emphasis on more holistic, contextual forms of development that are experientially based, e.g. action learning projects, coaching, mentoring.

Europe

In contrast to the Anglo-Saxon model above, many European approaches have in the past been less concerned with management development as a discrete activity. In France, for example, the development of managers is more closely linked to its social and historical context. Rather than management being something that can be explicitly developed in individuals, it is perceived as 'more a state of being' (Lawrence, 1992). Those who become managers form part of a social elite (*cadre*) and much of their development begins within the higher education institutions (*grandes écoles*) where the study of natural sciences and mathematics predominates.

In Germany, the approach is much more functional, with specialist expertise, especially in engineering and science, being closely linked to the vocational system of education. Again, there is a weaker concept of management which is less likely to be considered as something separate and instead is seen as part of the overall functional system. Managers have less mobility than in the US/UK, tending to stay in their functional role much longer. There is therefore less need for generalist skills development. Discrete management development activity is seen as less salient and does not flourish to the same extent (Lawrence, 1992). Where there is management teaching, Germans tend to favour 'structured learning situations with precise objectives, detailed assignments and strict timetables' (Hill, 1994).

Despite their relatively weak tradition in explicitly focused forms of management development, both France and Germany are beginning to establish institutions specifically aimed at developing managers. For example, there has been an apparent explosion of MBA activity in Germany and France (Easterby-Smith, 1992) and in France there is a belated emergence of US-style business schools (Hill, 1994). Additionally there are European initiatives such as ERASMUS designed to promote the exchange of European business and management students between educational institutions.

Japan

A great deal of attention has been focused on the prowess of Japanese management practice on the world stage. This success may have as much to do with social and cultural factors as it does with the way Japanese managers are developed, since the two are inextricably linked. For Japanese managers, the experience of development is much more likely to be a long-term affair rather than the short-term, 'sink-or-swim' approach which characterises the Anglo-Saxon countries. In Japan there is a strong foundation of individual loyalty to the organisation and an emphasis on providing job security for employees. The approach to development is likely to be much more systematic, structured and carefully planned (Neelankavil, 1992). Whereas Anglo-Saxon models stress individualism and development through short, intensive bursts of training to prepare managers for assignments characterised by challenge and risk, Japanese development programmes are longer and more culturally reflective in focusing on collectivism and group/team effort. The influence of role models is also strong. Unlike the US/UK where management development is in the hands of specialists, the Japanese view the relationship between the individual and the boss as a significant factor in developing the manager. The aim is to nurture growth, loyalty, commitment and retention (Storey *et al.*, 1991).

Central Europe

The main force driving the development of managers in countries such as Russia, Poland, Hungary and Romania is the rapid transition from a centrally planned to a market-based economy. As Vecsenyi (1992) observes, there are no 'road maps' in respect of management development and it is often carried out in an atmosphere of crisis. The aim has been to import ready-made Western models to provide know-how and practical skills. In Russia, for example, management education is booming and demand massively outstrips supply as the country struggles to adapt to major economic, social and political upheavals. However, in a number of cases Western models have been found wanting as they have failed to adapt to local conditions and there is a lack of infrastructure to support managers who wish to implement their newly acquired skills. Similarly, there is a lack of congruence between what is being taught and the state of the economy (Kwiatkowski and Kozminshi, 1992). Recent evidence suggests that, in general, Western 'recipes for success' fail because they do not take into account the context confronting them, they lack strategic credibility and have not responded to the variations in learning styles of Eastern European managers (Lee, 1995; Redman, Keithley and Szalkowski, 1995). Interestingly, it has been suggested that Western-style management development may be at a crossroads. Taking a pessimistic outlook, Western-oriented business schools may be accused of contributing to rampant capitalism engendering resentment, but if they can adapt they may contribute positively to a more sophisticated economic infrastructure, changing social attitudes and new forms of political decision making (Puffer, 1993).

Hong Kong and People's Republic of China (PRC)

In both countries, there are two concerns: the economic expansion of the PRC and the impending return of Hong Kong to Chinese rule in 1997. Strategically, management development has been concerned with meeting both concerns.

In China, there is a massive shortage of managers and management training has become a national imperative as the country opens itself up to global markets and Western capitalism. Like other countries, China has experienced the problems of discrepancies between the models of Western management development and Chinese culture and society. For example, many imported Western models of management development are based on techniques such as group discussion and classroom participation, with an emphasis on reflection and abstract reasoning and a free and open critique and challenge of ideas and assumptions. However, in Chinese culture there is a strong emphasis on collective ideals, conformity, social status, the need to preserve 'face' and self-esteem, the unchallenged position of the 'expert' and associative rather than abstract reasoning, all of which militate against the adoption of Western models (Bu and Mitchell, 1992). The preference is for more didactic development methods such as formal management courses. Experiential methods are almost unheard of (Kirkbridge and Tang, 1992).

In Hong Kong, the approach to management development is similar in many respects to that found in the PRC. However, in recent years, Western management education and know-how have been sought by managers in Hong Kong to provide them with the adaptive, flexible skills and knowledge they will require to handle the transition to Chinese rule and the challenges of the Confucian, bureaucratic, centralising society that will shortly confront them (Chong, Kassener and Ta-Lang Shih, 1993).

South Africa

In broad terms, the challenges facing those involved in management development in South Africa are not dissimilar to those found elsewhere. The country has undergone massive social and political upheaval in recent years. However, the issue confronting the country is how to use management development as a tool to overcome major societal gulfs in respect of the disadvantaged black majority and the well-educated white minority, e.g. 50% of the black population is illiterate and only 2–3% of middle managers and 1% of senior managers are black (Templer, Beatty and Hofmeyer, 1992).

The need therefore is to 'South Africanise' development through a more holistic, integrative approach that unifies the country by providing and sharing opportunities. One way to achieve this goal is to educate black managers and then coach them and allow them to practise their management skills. However, just as in organisational cultures, the problem of transfer to the workplace emerges when black managers are denied access to experiential learning opportunities. The situation is forecast to remain largely unchanged until there is a 'critical mass' of black managers who can take on the coaching role (Templer, Beatty and Hofmeyer, 1992).

Third World

For those countries in the Third World (Latin America, India, Africa) management development faces yet another set of challenges as it is used as a stimulus to growth and survival in a more competitive global market-place. However, the barriers are invariably rooted in the multicultural, multi-racial and multi-religious context which characterises many Third World countries. Again, the individualised Western model of management development may not be appropriate in those societies seeking greater synergy and cohesion and where culturally attuned models are preferred, e.g. in Africa where the need is for approaches that stress group solidarity rather than self-development (Srinivas, 1995). Although much use is made of Western ideas, their use requires sensitivity. There is also the issue of dependency, where decisions have to be made about when to cut the umbilical cord and allow managers in these countries to face the realities of global competition (Srinivas, 1995).

To conclude this section, you have seen that there is a considerable and growing interest in developing the skills and mindsets of the 'global' or 'international' manager. There is also a desire by many countries across the world to import Western (mainly Anglo-Saxon) conceptions and models of management development and utilise them as powerful tools in their quest for social and economic transformation and renewal. However, you will have noted that, although Western models are considered by many to be dominant across the world, efforts to import them by different countries have not been entirely successful. This reinforces a point made earlier, namely that there is growing evidence to suggest that management development cannot easily be removed or separated from the wider cultural, social, political and economic context in which it is embedded and which it shapes and is shaped by (Hansen and Brooks, 1994). It therefore becomes clear that any development policy, activity or programme is likely to be more effective if it is made *contingent* upon the unique set of circumstances that confronts it.

CONTROVERSIAL ISSUES IN MANAGEMENT DEVELOPMENT

The development of managers, like so many aspects of organisational life, is surrounded by debate and controversy. If we accept the notion that managers play a pivotal role in human resource management in the sense that they contribute to the creation of its 'reality' and are a means through which it is shaped and enacted, then such debates and controversies cannot be ignored.

In this section, a number of the more significant contemporary issues and controversies will be reviewed. It is not intended to discuss them at great length, merely to illuminate important aspects of the debate. Further reading is indicated at the end of the chapter.

Developing political skills

Managers are employed by organisations to 'get things done through people' (Torrington *et al.*, 1994). Managers 'make things happen' (Lee, 1987). However, getting things done and making things happen within an organisation are rarely simple or straightforward tasks. As well as technical, human and administrative problems, managers are confronted by 'political' factors. They have to contend with 'obstacles' such as:

- competition for scarce resources;
- conflicting viewpoints and priorities;
- confrontation with coalitions of vested interests;
- managing ambitious and self-interested individuals.

To cope, and more importantly to survive, in an organisation, there is a growing view that managers have to become 'politically competent'. As Baddeley and James (1987: 4) point out, 'political and survival skills are likely to become increasingly prized amongst managers'. Buchanan and Boddy (1992: 29) argue that managers can only be effective if they engage in 'backstage' activities such as 'politicking and wheeler dealing'.

To achieve political competence, managers must first understand the nature of power in organisations: *the ability to make things happen* (Lee, 1987). They must be aware of how power manifests itself, its sources and how it is used. They need to understand the way political strategies and tactics are formulated and how they are used by various 'actors' (Ryan, 1989). They must develop an awareness of political context: the rules of the game, individual actors' power bases, relationships and coalitions, political agendas, etc. (Lee, 1987).

But if political competence is required to get things done, why does the teaching of political skills not appear on the majority of mainstream management development programmes? There are a number of possible explanations.

Lee (1987) suggests it may be because political behaviour carries connotations of being 'bad', 'dishonest', 'subversive', 'dysfunctional'. Baddeley and James (1987) point to different viewpoints about the need or practicality of developing political skills or a link with the (sometimes distasteful) activities and behaviours of local and national politicians. Baddeley and James (1990) suggest that teaching organisational politics to managers is an admission that the 'rational' system of resolving problems and making decisions has failed.

Whatever the reason, there is now a growing realisation that managers require some measure of political competence and awareness. The absence of politics on development programmes, which tend to be politically neutral, is generating frustration and confusion in managers who find difficulty in relating or applying what they learn to the 'reality' of managing back in the workplace (Baddeley and James, 1990). Political behaviour has implications for organisational effectiveness. However, there is often incongruity between 'acceptable' political behaviour and the nature and reality of political processes (Ryan, 1989).

In other words, a politically competent manager can contribute to organisational effectiveness. Equally, a politically incompetent manager can hamper and 'damage' organisations as well as themselves.

ACTIVITY

A case of political incompetence?

An experienced middle manager was seconded to manage a major project. The project team was effectively managed and a feasibility study carried out on time and within budget. The manager circulated copies of the team's report to the board of directors and arranged a presentation. During the presentation it became obvious that the feasibility study was being seen as a threat by certain directors who criticised it heavily and successfully blocked its recommendations. Amid much recrimination and argument, it was decided to shelve the report and disband the project team.

EXERCISE

Where do you think this manager went wrong politically?

ACTIVITY

A case of political competence?

A new finance director joined a large manufacturing company and brought with him an experienced credit control manager with whom he had worked closely at his previous organisation. The close relationship continued in the new organisation and together they put together a detailed proposal for sweeping changes in the finance function which were designed to improve its overall efficiency.

After a number of months, it became apparent that the finance director was having problems persuading his senior management colleagues to accept the fundamental changes contained in the proposal and it was rumoured that his position in the organisation was under threat.

The credit control manager heard the rumours and decided to distance herself from the proposal by letting it be known that she disagreed with many of the changes. She also took steps to reduce the number of informal meetings held with the finance director and to communicate through formal memos.

EXERCISE

Do you think this manager was being politically astute?

To what extent can political skills be taught? A number of commentators suggest they can. Lee (1987) argues that managers can improve their political skills by analysing the process, tactics and the context of political activity. Kakabadse and Parker suggest a psychological approach that focuses on the differences in people and the way people interact. Baddeley and James (1987) identify key models of political behaviour around which role play and discussion can centre. Ryan (1989) and Lees (1992) suggest that conventional management development programmes are already 'political' in promoting certain ideologies and practices. Indeed, there should be a closer scrutiny of the values underpinning practices such as coaching, mentoring, etc.

The ethics of management development

Like power and politics, the ethical conduct of management and the ethical frameworks used by developers have only recently attracted attention. Examples of ethically questionable behaviour by certain managers have attracted widespread publicity, e.g. that of senior managers in large corporations and privatised utilities. There is now growing pressure and a rhetoric urging managers to behave 'ethically'; to manage their responsibilities in what is deemed an ethical fashion; to build trust; to be fair and equitable in their treatment of employees and to respect their rights as individuals. This is prompting various governing institutions to issues guidelines and codes of conduct to managers designed to control their behaviour.

ACTIVITY

Quality of Working Life (QWL)

'As a philosophy, QWL views people as "assets" capable of contributing skills, knowledge, experience and commitment, rather than as "costs" that are merely extensions of the production process. It argues that encouraging involvement and providing the environment in which it can flourish, produces tangible rewards for both individuals and organisations'.

(*Source*: ACAS advisory booklet No. 16, p. 7)

EXERCISE

What ethical dilemmas might confront a manager adhering to a QWL philosophy?

The Institute of Management, in its Code of Conduct and Guides to Professional Management Practice, states:

> The discharge of one's duties as a professional manager also involves the acceptance and habitual exercise of ethical values, among which a high place should be accorded to integrity, honesty, loyalty and fairness. But the Institute recognises that . . . it is usual for managers to encounter circumstances or situations in which various values, principles, rules and interests appear to conflict . . . no ready answer can be given for such conflicts.

We may ask ourselves: 'Is ethical conduct rarely taught on development programmes because there is actually nothing to teach?' In other words, managerial work is so complex, ambiguous, and at times confusing, that it is not possible to legislate or create an all embracing framework of moral competencies (Snell, 1990). Reed and Anthony (1992: 606) point to the dilemmas facing managers who subordinate their moral values to the notion of 'corporate good', and claim that, in such instances, 'simplistic' ethical rules and codes of practice may not be helpful to managers and serve only to create 'managerial cynicism'.

Indeed, they raise the question of whether management education can improve management behaviour. They argue that it can, but it will require a more critically reflexive stance on the part of managers and those who teach them. Can we conclude, therefore, that it is up to individual managers to define and review their own ethical code of conduct and behaviour within the context of a given situation?

Whether or not a manager defines his or her own ethical conduct according to their personal values, or adheres to some external code of business ethics linked to their profession or organisation, it cannot be ignored that ethical conduct is an output of, amongst other things, the ideology of management developers. So should there be an ethical code to cover the behaviour of developers? Snell (1986) argues against such a code because of the disagreements, contradictions and dilemmas that arise in trying to define what is 'good' or 'bad' ethical conduct for developers. He argues that managers and developers should 'catch' and confront each other's conduct as it occurs and discuss its legitimacy. But such a course is likely to be uncomfortable and will rely upon a close relationship between developer and manager.

Managerial competencies

In Chapters 7 and 8 you were introduced to the concept of competency-based forms of training and development within the framework of National Vocational Qualifications (NVQs). You were also introduced to some of the controversies that surround the notion of competence in the workplace.

Earlier in this chapter we examined competency-based approaches as they apply in the field of management development and focused on the Management Charter Initiative (MCI) and its framework of national standards. We now turn to explore some of the controversial issues that surround the notion of management competency and, as you will discover, it is here that the whole debate about competence probably generates the most passion and controversy.

Since competencies were introduced, they have attracted considerable criticism, both at a philosophical and practical level. Philosophically, there has been a long-standing, fundamental disagreement about the whole basis on which competencies were conceived and the way in which they are enacted. Some have drawn attention to the rational, functional, behaviourist orthodoxy that underpins competency-based training and development which, ideologically, grew from the 'social efficiency' movement in the USA, and represents a form of 'social engineering' in which habitual behaviour is a key principle (Hyland, 1994). In the case of management development, this objection is particularly relevant as such a philosophical stance seemingly precludes a consideration of the more complex, innovative, creative elements that underpin managerial work, especially in a time of radical change (Jacobs, 1989). As Jacobs observes, although competency-based forms of management training and development can introduce more structure and discipline, they can only ever be a partial solution because they fail to deal with the softer, qualitative aspects of managing. This is even more acute in the case of managers who have to rely heavily upon others to achieve their goals. However, the whole basis of developing competence as a manager is currently focused on the individual and the clear understanding of the manager as leader rather than any notion of developing 'collective competence' (Kilcourse, 1994).

This seems somewhat paradoxical given the massive surge in team-based working arrangements and empowerment, but perhaps it accounts for some of the problems encountered in these areas and discussed earlier in this chapter.

Others have challenged the functional, reductionist, mechanistic approach and the extent that it leads to an 'abstraction of reality', and questioned how far competencies can be generalised from a particular context (Collin, 1989; Stewart and Hamlin, 1992a). For example, can you provide managers with a set of generic competencies which they 'carry around like a tool kit' as in the case of MCI's national standards, or should competencies be more contextually based, reflecting the changing needs of the organisation and the individual (Canning, 1990; Donnelly, 1991)? As Kilcourse (1994: 14) remarks: 'competencies thought to have general application will fit where they touch when it comes to specific organisations'. Managers may be competent in one contextual setting, but will they be judged competent when faced with new challenges if and when they leave to take up a post in another organisation?

In a related area, another issue emerges. Buchanan and Boddy, with reference to managers in the role of change agents, have argued that if you develop a 'toolkit' of competencies you must develop the diagnostic, judgmental capabilities to use the 'tools' in different contexts, what they term 'expertise' (Buchanan and Boddy, 1992). Linked to this last point a further question emerges: how far can a competence approach be 'taught' to managers (Donnelly, 1991)? How far, for example, can you derive, develop and measure competencies in areas such as interpersonal skills; creativity and innovation; strategic thinking and the cognitive processes linked to decision making and problem solving (Donnelly, 1991). Kilcourse (1994) goes so far as to argue that during a time of radical change, when innovation and creativity are at a premium, competency-based forms of development may be the 'antithesis of what is required'. However, others would appear to disagree. Cockerill (1994) argues that, on the basis of work done at NatWest Bank, it is possible to identify 'high performance managerial competences, relevant to rapidly changing environments and flexible forms of organisation' (p. 74).

Some have argued that there is too much emphasis on assessment and not enough on learning (CNAA, 1992). This might be interpreted as a way of saying that the focus on practical, workplace outcomes is subordinating learning and understanding to the extent that the competency approach might be seen as almost anti-theory/anti-academic. There may therefore be a case of reasserting the role of established methodologies within the existing and expanding educational and vocational framework (Stewart and Hamlin, 1992b). However, many managers might argue (and regularly do) that the gulf between learning and knowledge and its application in the workplace still remain. Theory, it would seem, does not travel easily into the workplace.

Could it therefore be that the issue is not one of competence (however defined) but in finding a way of bridging the theory/practice 'gap'? Should there be a review of the whole basis of development itself, e.g. should institutions such as business schools be teaching management theory at all? It could be claimed that much of it is too generic, difficult to transfer to unique contexts and rendered virtually meaningless in a time of radical change. Perhaps the focus should shift to managers becoming their own 'practical theorists' (Thomas, 1993). Managers would be encouraged to develop the higher order, reflective competencies to analyse, synthesise, judge and reflect, not in some narrow rational-functional way, but one that takes account of the wider social, moral, cultural and political relationships and interdependencies which have consequences for their actions (Reed and Anthony, 1992; Roberts, 1996).

At an operational, practical level, there are major concerns in respect of the way competency-based approaches are seen to operate and many of these concerns carry over into management development (Stewart and Hamlin, 1992a). A recent piece of empirical research, examining the effects of NVQ Levels 3 and 4 programmes in a recently privatised organisation, seemed to confirm a great deal of this anecdotal evidence and echoes many of the earlier concerns (Currie and Darby, 1995). The main issues can be summarised as:

- the way management competencies were defined;
- their generic nature;
- a lack of attention to softer qualities;
- bureaucracy and cost;
- not being future oriented;
- the approach was not seen by managers to be developmental.

This last point is of some concern when the managers concerned viewed the approach as formalising and confirming *current* levels of competency and not developing new skills. After two years, the organisation concerned reintroduced traditional methods to supplement its competency-based approaches. The authors concluded that 'competence based development is not a panacea for all management development ills but is one approach which may be taken with others' (p. 17).

In summary, despite the criticisms, it would appear that competency-based approaches have raised the profile of management development and are proving to be a useful input to the portfolio of methods available to developers. Earlier efforts to introduce (some would say impose) a national framework appear to be giving way to a much more pragmatic and flexible stance as more and more organisations develop their own models of management competencies tailored to suit their specific needs and now shorn of the unacceptable bureaucracy and cost (Mathewman, 1995). But this raises a new set of issues, not least how to maintain the integrity of the national standards and present a coherent national approach to management development, if that is what is required.

Problems in evaluating management development

Although the proper evaluation of management development is a difficult task, it is rarely seen as a problem because so few organisations bother to carry it out often! Instead, it often becomes an act of faith for those involved. However, this appears somewhat paradoxical when organisations that are increasingly concerned about their cost base and overheads fail properly to consider a significant bottom-line expenditure such as management development. It is even more paradoxical given that a failure to evaluate and justify such expenditure renders those who operate as development specialists vulnerable to cut-backs and job insecurity.

In attempting evaluation, a number of problems emerge. The first arises when the management development process itself becomes 'decoupled' from the individual manager's unique context. This is often because providers are keen to find greater homogeneity and conformity in the way programmes and activities are designed and delivered (Mole, 1996). For the sake of efficiency and expediency, many providers are in the business of delivering programmes designed to provide off-the-shelf 'solutions' to organisational problems. It therefore becomes the organisation's responsibility to select and utilise those programmes in ways which meet both individual and organisational needs. In practice, a great deal of development activity then becomes 'commodified and standardised', with an almost mechanical reproduction of ideas and methods usually based upon the latest fad or flavour-of-the-month. This gives rise to evaluation methodologies that are left striving to display some form of pseudo-scientific objectivity in an environment that is often highly complex and subjective (Smith, 1993; Mole, 1996). In other words, 'the complexity of management training and development demonstrates the point that measuring its effectiveness cannot be adequately accomplished by using a single, generic formula' (Endres and Kleiner, 1990).

A second set of problems emerges when the question is posed of what is being measured and how. In the case of management development, it is crucial that measurement incorporates emotional, attitudinal and behavioural changes alongside the measurement of harder aspects such as financial performance and technical competence. This necessitates the use of carefully constructed and focused methodologies incorporating ethnographic, interpretive techniques (Fox, 1989; Currie, 1994). But this presupposes that those tasked with evaluation have the time, commitment and skills to conduct research in these areas.

A third set of issues emerges to reflect the way in which management development is approached in organisations. Earlier in this chapter it was shown that a great deal of development is often isolated, fragmented, piecemeal and mechanistic, removed from the everyday reality of managing complex, rapidly changing organisations. It was argued that developers should adopt a more holistic, contextual approach where internal and external influences such as structure, culture, politics, technology, etc. are considered to be integral features in the evaluation process and, in effect, evaluation is seen to 'travel with the organisation' as it learns, adapts and renews itself (Smith, 1993). As Smith (1993: 23) observes, 'management development programmes are not context free but dependent on the cultural baggage of the participants and the organisation'.

This point is reinforced in the fourth set of issues which revolves around the political dimension of evaluation. It is an inescapable fact of organisational life that, given its subjective and interpretive nature, evaluation will be rendered prone to bias and manipulation and become an arena for political 'games'. As Fox (1989: 192) explains, 'because a pseudo-scientific approach does not deal with human issues and value judgements, it is not surprising that they fall into disuse or are simply done by token [then] politics takes over'. Both Fox (1989) and Currie (1994) have examined the evaluation of management development programmes in the National Health Service and concluded that political and cultural factors were influential, e.g. there was a low value attached to management development, and responses were biased by people's fear for their positions. In the author's own experience of management development in the private sector, politics and culture do play a key role in evaluation, e.g. efforts at 'impression management', 'eyewash' and 'whitewash' by external providers keen to secure future business; unsubstantiated and unsupportable claims for the 'success' of programmes; evaluation findings that are 'doctored' to ensure that they meet with senior management's expectations.

It therefore has to be assumed that the evaluation of management development will always be a difficult process so long as it involves human behaviour. In many organisations it is rarely carried out with any degree of enthusiasm or effectiveness and so evaluation is often tagged onto development programmes, treated in a piecemeal fashion and concerned with immediate outcomes rather than examining wider systemic issues. A more systemic, holistic perspective of evaluation would examine the extent to which development activity fits with individual needs and organisational context; how far new behaviours can be applied in the workplace; whether new behaviour corresponds with espoused organisational culture and values (Easterby-Smith, 1994; Mole, 1996). Questions must also be raised over the level of commitment to the evaluation processes shown by developers and sponsors alike, and to what extent they are perceived as capable or credible to conduct evaluation exercises. But in a sense, are we asking too much? Is evaluation a chimera? As Easterby-Smith (1994: 143) states:

> Thus attempts to evaluate development methods may fail to satisfy the purist, and much of this stems from the diffuseness of the target that is being examined and the difficulty of isolating procedures from the real constraints and politics of the organisations in which they are taking place.

Perhaps it is only if and when organisations wake up to the real and hidden costs of management development and its possible consequences for organisational learning and development that we will see progress. Until then it is likely to remain an act of faith and a fertile playground for political games.

ACTIVITY

Problems evaluating management development

You are the personnel director of a medium-sized manufacturing company. You have had a hard task persuading your board colleagues that they should invest a considerable sum of money in a management development programme for middle managers to ensure succession and the continuing success of the business. However, they finally agreed to your request and the funds were made available a year ago.

The programme is now underway and you have just reported progress to your colleagues. The operations manager, who fought against the programme a year ago because he wanted the money to install a new piece of plant, turns to you somewhat aggressively in a board meeting and says: 'This programme of yours has been running for a year now. In that time I could have saved this company considerable sums of money and increased both quality and revenue. What will you produce and when will we see some pay-back on our investment?' The rest of the board look expectantly in your direction.

EXERCISE

How might you respond?

The development of women managers

There is no doubt that women are grossly under-represented in UK management generally. In 1989, 44% of the UK labour force were women (this proportion is forecast to rise to some 50% by the year 2000) and yet only 11% of UK general management are women (Davidson, 1991). At chief executive level, the picture is even grimmer with only 1% of women reaching the top (Davidson and Cooper, 1992).

Not only are women poorly represented, there has also been a certain degree of 'ghetto-ing' where women managers tend to be concentrated in the banking, retail and catering industries, at the lower managerial levels, and in the 'softer' areas such as personnel and customer service.

What factors are inhibiting the development of women managers?

A study by Ashridge Management College (1980) has highlighted a number of key inhibitors:

- *Career factors and personnel systems:*
- Career paths to management that are designed to fit the working life patterns of men, i.e. job mobility in early years, commitment to study and learning for advancement.
- Many women were disqualified because of family commitments, i.e. career breaks to raise children.
- Current selection, appraisal and training systems also inhibit women, i.e. asking for qualifications rarely held by women, no formal re-entry process after career breaks.
- *Women's attitudes and behaviour*: Women's lack of confidence in their perceived ability, and a belief that competence in their current job and technical ability were the sole criteria for advancement, were cited as significant inhibiting factors.
- *The attitudes of senior executives*: A 'kindly, protective' attitude by senior managers tending to concentrate women in jobs that were felt to be suitable for them (specialist roles and client contact roles).
- *Individual and organisational factors*: Prejudice, men seeing women as a threat, assumptions about women's capabilities, and organisations with poor management development systems.

More recent studies confirm these factors and add to the list. Wentling (1992) highlights a lack of political 'savvy' and bosses who don't encourage development, while Grondin (1990) cites high expectations and misperceptions about career opportunities as barriers to women advancing in management. Davidson (1984) provides an extensive list of factors which she argues generate stress in women managers. Flanders (1994) points to factors such as traditional work patterns, attitudes and prejudice, lack of role models and exclusion from the 'old boy network' as inhibiting women's progress.

What can be done to develop women managers?

Davidson (1991) makes the point that those organisations which fail to utilise the potential of women managers will be committing 'economic suicide'.

Apart from demographic and economic reasons, there are many potential benefits that women managers can bring to organisations, i.e. participative, caring management styles (for an extensive list of costs/benefits see Fritchie and Pedler, 1984: 178).

Davidson (1991) argues that the first and perhaps the most important step that organisations can take is to encourage their managers (both male and female) to recognise and acknowledge masculine/feminine strengths and weaknesses and build these into development programmes. They should also realise that 'when comparing male and female managers in terms of managerial efficiency and performance, numerous cross-cultural studies and reviews have concluded that there are far more similarities than differences' (Davidson, 1991: 8).

Other writers argue that organisations should aim for an increased cross-cultural perspective where male and female managers learn to value each other's differences and to cooperate in their own development to increase organisational effectiveness (see Fischer and Gleijm, 1992; Whitaker and Megginson, 1992).

So what practical measures can be taken?

If we acknowledge that the tasks facing men and women managers are similar but that women managers do face particular difficulties, what practical help can be given? The literature contains many ideas and suggestions. The following list is by no means exhaustive:

- integrating women's development into mainstream HRD
- mentoring/providing role models
- reviewing childcare provisions
- reviewing equal opportunities policies
- auditing attitudes towards women
- providing women-only training
- encouraging women into management education
- putting equality on the organisational agenda
- reviewing selection/promotion/appraisal processes
- promoting the networking of women
- assertiveness training
- moving women out of the 'ghetto' into front-line positions
- career planning strategies for women
- training before promotion.

Demographic, economic and social changes in the 1990s should place the development of women managers firmly on the agenda of an increasing number of board meetings. However, the structural and cultural barriers confronting women managers are formidable. The initiatives outlined above seem to be leading to some improvement, but in many cases the effects are at best marginal. How will further progress be made? Stead concludes by calling for a:

> . . . new and more comprehensive understanding [about development] . . .
> which can benefit both men and women. Business is finally realising that
> some areas of concern for women are also areas in which men have needed
> consideration all along.
>
> (Stead, 1985: 1)

SUMMARY

● The terms 'management' and 'manager' have different meanings within different contexts. The role and 'reality' of managing in organisations is often more complex, confusing and chaotic than many management texts would suggest.

● Management development is more than just management education and training. It involves the holistic development of the manager taking account of factors such as: the needs, goals and expectations of both the organisation and the individual; the political, cultural and economic context; structures, systems for selection, reward and monitoring performance.

● Human resource management is essentially a philosophy of management control over employees depicted in management strategies, polices and behaviour. Management acts as a conduit through which human resource management is enacted. The prevailing values and ideologies of senior managers create and influence human resource strategies and policies. Middle and junior managers translate and 'operationalise' these strategies and policies and it is their preferred management style and actual behaviour that give meaning to what people experience as human resource management. Management development therefore has important implications and consequences for human resource management enactment within organisations.

● As part of an overall human resource strategy, management development is now identified by many organisations as a source of competitive advantage and one of the key ingredients for success. However, if management development is to be effective it must link to, and support, the organisation's business strategy. This enables those responsible for development to respond to the question, 'why are you developing this manager?'.

● Development programmes cannot be isolated from other organisational systems and processes in a series of 'piecemeal' approaches. An open systems perspective takes account of the interactions and dependencies that exist between the organisation's context and management development programmes. An open systems approach offers a way of constructing a unified, integrated framework within which the organisation can organise and implement development programmes.

● Development is more effective when a stakeholder partnership exists between the individual, their boss and the organisation. A wide range of development techniques are available. The selection of the most appropriate techniques will depend upon the learning preferences and needs of managers. To be effective, development must reflect organisational context and the 'reality' of managerial work. An increasing reliance is being placed on the use of experiential techniques.

● Like many aspects of organisational life, management development cannot be isolated from controversy and debate. Areas of challenge, conflict, tension, and ambiguity remain to be resolved.

ACTIVITY

The right approach?

As part of its strategic planning, an organisation decided to introduce a system of budgetary control to improve financial planning and control. A two-day course titled 'Finance for the Non-Financial Manager' was arranged.

The course, although highly intensive, was delivered competently by an external consultant. However, a number of managers felt that the universal nature of the course meant that a lot of the content was not relevant to them. They were especially concerned because the course made only a passing reference to budgets. What they wanted was a course that would take them through, step-by-step, the process of preparing and administering a departmental budget. Some managers pointed out that it would have made sense to consult them first and then develop a tailored course to suit both their and the organisation's needs. The course was therefore viewed as a waste of their time and the organisation's money.

EXERCISES

1 What type of management development approach is indicated in this scenario?

2 Why might the organisation have approached management development in this way?

3 Imagine you are responsible for management development in the organisation. How would you respond to avoid the criticisms voiced by the line managers being repeated in the future?

QUESTIONS

1 What do you understand by the term 'management development'? Distinguish between management development, management education and management training.

2 To what extent does management development influence the human resource strategy in an organisation?

3 Who is responsible for management development? What are their roles and responsibilities?

4 What management skills and knowledge do international managers require? In what way do they differ from those required by UK managers?

5 'To survive in an organisation today, a manager must become a "political animal".' What are your views with regard to this statement?

EXERCISES

1 List the different methods and techniques used to develop managers. How would you judge and evaluate their effectiveness?

2 Examine the internal and external influencers identified in Table 10.2 on page 419. Working in groups, discuss each influence in turn. In what ways do you think each factor influences the development of managers in the UK?

3 Organisations are increasingly turning to self-development as a management technique. Imagine you are the manager responsible for a group of young graduates about to embark upon your organisation's graduate development programme. Working in groups, discuss ways in which you might encourage them to adopt a self-learning culture.

CASE STUDY

Chris Evans joined Midcounty Hospital as a management trainee after completing a four-year Business Studies degree at Midshires University. When he was interviewed for the position, he was told by the interviewing panel that the hospital was still coming to terms with its successful application for Trust status and things were going to be a bit chaotic for a time. They then asked him how he would cope. Chris responded by telling the panel that he saw this as a development opportunity and went on to explain in detail how he intended to put into practice many of the skills he had learnt at university and during his industrial placement year.

Chris's response impressed the panel and he was offered a place on the graduate management training programme. The programme is administered by the Personnel Department. Trainees on the programme are rotated at six-monthly intervals through the main administration departments where they gain knowledge and experience of the complex systems and processes required to run the business side of the hospital. At the end of the training programme, trainees are assessed by their supervising managers, and those who are successful are appointed to permanent positions as junior managers within the hospital.

Chris began his training in the Finance Department, working as a deputy for Jeff Thomas, the Director of Finance. Jeff is a recent appointment to the hospital. He was headhunted from a major firm of City accountants three months ago. Although an experienced accountant, Jeff has had little management experience, apart from super-vising a small office of secretaries and filing clerks in his old company. In fact he never really liked that side of the job and was lucky to have an experienced supervi-sor who dealt with 'the people problems'.

At the beginning things went well. After a brief welcome, Jeff introduced Chris to Sarah, the supervisor in the Finance Office and told her to 'show Chris how things operate in the office'. Sarah was a bit taken aback. Jeff had not discussed this with her and she wasn't really prepared for Chris's arrival. However, as the department was putting together its first budget, an extra pair of hands was very welcome. After a bit of rearranging, she was able to spend a couple of hours with Chris explaining how the office worked and then gave him a job checking invoices. Chris set about the task with enthusiasm and two days later reported to Sarah that the job was complete. When Sarah checked the work, she found Chris had done a first class job and he had discovered a number of errors for correction. Pleased with his initial performance, Sarah gave Chris another job working on the office computer inputting data onto the sales ledger file.

A couple of weeks later, Sarah noticed that Chris was becoming withdrawn and spending frequent periods looking out of the window. His work was becoming care-less and when he completed a task he would not come and report to her. Instead, he would wander away from the office to see another trainee working on the other side of the hospital.

Sarah decided to speak to Jeff because Chris's behaviour was disrupting the work in the office. Although always busy, Jeff promised to speak to Chris and, after frequent reminders and eventually protests from Sarah, he called Chris into his office. Jeff explained what Sarah had told him and asked him what the problem was. Chris began by explaining that the work he was doing was routine and boring and not really making full use of his skills. At this point, Jeff interrupted him and pointed out rather frostily 'that in the financial world, everybody has to cope with routine, boring work'.

Chris left the office dejected and worried. He knew that he had to obtain a favourable report from Jeff and he hadn't got off to a very good start. When he arrived back at his desk Sarah presented him with a six inch thick computer printout for checking.

1 What do you see as the main issues or problem areas?

2 What actions would you suggest might be taken to overcome the current difficulties and avoid problems in the future?

GLOSSARY OF TERMS AND ABBREVIATIONS

Closed system A system which does not interact with other subsystems or its environment.

Culture The prevailing pattern of values, attitudes, beliefs, assumptions, norms and sentiments.

Developmnet centres Normally used for the selection of managers. They utilise a range of intensive psychological tests and simulations to assess management potential.

Holistic Treating organisations, situations, problems as totalities or wholes as opposed to a specific, reductionist approach.

MCI (Management Charter Initiative) An employer-led initiative with the aim of developing recognised standards in management practice.

NCVQ (National Council for Vocational Qualifications) A government-backed initiative to establish a national system for the recognition of vocational qualifications.

Networking Interacting, usually on an informal basis, with individuals and groups internal and external to the organisation for mutual benefit.

Psychological contract The notion that an individual has a range of expectations about their employing organisation and the organisation has expectations of them.

Psychological (psychometric) testing Specialised tests used for selection or assessing potential. Usually in the form of questionnaires. They construct a personality profile of the candidate.

Open system A system that is connected to and interacts with other subsystems and its environment.

Sociotechnical The structuring or integration of human activities and subsystems with technological subsystems.

System An assembly of parts, objects or attributes interrelating and interacting in an organised way.

Systemic Thinking about and perceiving situations, problems, difficulties as systems.

REFERENCES AND FURTHER READING

Those texts marked with an asterisk are particularly recommended for further reading.

ACAS (1991) *Effective Organisations: The People Factor*. London: ACAS.

Ashridge Management College (1980) *Employee Potential: Issues in the Development of Women*. London: Institute of Personnel.

Baddeley, S. and James, K. (1987) 'Owl, fox, donkey or sheep: political skills for managers', *Management Education and Development*, Vol. 8, Pt 1, pp. 3–19.

Baddeley, S. and James, K. (1990) 'Political management: developing the management portfolio', *Journal of Management Development*, Vol. 9, No. 3, pp. 42–59.

Banks, J. (1994) *Outdoor Development for Managers*, 2nd edn. Aldershot: Gower.

Barham, K. and Oates, D. (1991) *The International Manager*. London: Business Books.

Barsoux, J.-L. (1990) 'Group behaviour in French business: quality circles à la française', in Wilson, D. and Rosenfeld, R. *Managing in Organisations*. London: McGraw-Hill.

Bartlett, C. and Ghoshal, S. (1989) *Managing across Borders: The Transnational Solution*. London: Hutchinson.

Boak, G. and Joy, P. (1990) 'Management learning contracts: the training triangle', in Pedler, M., Burgoyne, J., Boydell, T. and Welshman, G. (eds) *Self-Development in Organisations*. Maidenhead: McGraw-Hill.

Boydell, T. and Pedler, M. (1994) 'From management development to managing development: the changing role of the manager in the learning organisation', *Transitions*, Vol. 94, No. 9, November, pp. 8–9.

*Boydell, T. and Pedler, M. (1981) *Management Self-Development*. Westmead: Gower.

Brennan, M. (1991) 'Mismanagement and quality circles: how middle managers influence direct participation', *Employee Relations*, Vol. 13, No. 5, pp. 22–32.

Brewster, C. and Tyson, S. (1992) *International Comparisons in Human Resource Management*. London: Pitman.

Bu, N. and Mitchell, V. (1992) 'Developing the PRC's managers: how can Western Europe become more helpful?', *Journal of Management Development*, Vol. 11, No. 2, pp. 42–53.

*Buchanan, D. and Boddy, D. (1992) *The Expertise of the Change Agent*. Hemel Hempstead: Prentice Hall.

Buckley, J. and Kemp, N. (1989) 'The strategic role of management development', *Management Education and Development*, Vol. 20, No. 1, pp. 157–174.

Burgoyne, J. (1988) 'Management development for the individual and the organisation', *Personnel Management*, June, pp. 40–44.

Burgoyne, J. and Stuart, R. (1991) 'Teaching and learning methods in management development', *Personnel Review*, Vol. 20, No. 3, pp. 27–33.

Burnett, D. and James, K. (1994) 'Using the outdoors to facilitate personal change in managers', *Journal of Management Development*, Vol. 13, No. 9, pp. 14–24.

Canning, R. (1990) 'The quest for competence', *Industrial and Commercial Training*, Vol. 22, No. 5, pp. 12–16.

Cannon, T. and Taylor, J. (1994) *Management Development to the Millennium*. Corby: Institute of Management.

Caulkin, S. (1994) 'Rewriting the rules', *Observer*, Sunday 25 September.

Child, J. (1969) *British Management Thought*. London: Allen & Unwin.

Chong, J., Kassener, M.W. and Ta-Lang Shih (1993) 'Management development of Hong Kong managers for 1997', *Journal of Management Development*, Vol. 12, No. 8, pp. 18–26.

Claydon, T. and Doyle, M. (1996) 'Trusting me, trusting you: the ethics of employee empowerment', *Personnel Review*, forthcoming.

Cockerill, T. (1994) 'The kind of competence for rapid change', in Mabey, C. and Iles, P. (eds) *Managing Learning*. London: Routledge.

Collin, A. (1989) 'Managers' competence: rhetoric, reality and research', *Personnel Review*, Vol. 18, No. 6, pp. 20–25.

Constable, J. and McCormick, R. (1987) *The Making of British Managers*. London: BIM/CBI.

Coulson-Thomas, C. (1989) 'Human resource: the critical success factor, *Leadership and Organisation Development Journal*, Vol. 10, No. 4, pp. 13–16.

Council for National Academic Awards (CNAA) (1992) *Review of Management Education*. London: CNAA.

Critchley, B. and Casey, D. (1994) 'Team-building', in Mumford, A. (ed.) *Gower Handbook of Management Development*, 4th edn. Aldershot: Gower Publishing.

Cunnington, B. (1985) 'The process of educating and developing managers for the year 2000'. *Journal of Management Development*, Vol. 4, No. 5, pp. 66–79.

Currie, G. (1994) 'Evaluation of management development: a case study', *Journal of Management Development*, Vol. 13, No. 3, pp. 22–26.

Currie, G. and Darby, R. (1995) 'Competence-based management development: rhetoric and reality', *Journal of European Industrial Training*, Vol. 19, No. 5, pp. 11–18.

Davidson, M. (1984) 'Women in management in Europe', in Hammond, V. (ed.) *Practical Approaches to Women's Management Development*. Brussels: European Foundation for Management Development.

Davidson, M. (1991) 'Women managers in Britain: issues for the 1990s', *Women in Management Review*, Vol. 6, No. 1, pp. 5–10.

*Davidson, M. and Cooper, C. (1992) *Shattering the Glass Ceiling: The Women Manager*. London: Paul Chapman Publishing.

Davis, T. (1987) 'How personnel can lose its Cinderella image', *Personnel Management*, December, pp. 34–36.

Davis, T. (1990) 'Whose job is management development – comparing the choices', *Journal of Management Development*, Vol. 9, No. 1, pp. 58–70.

Donnelly, E. (1991) 'Management Charter Initiative: a critique', *Training and Development*, April, pp. 43–45.

Dopson, S. and Stewart, R. (1990) 'What is happening to middle managers?, *British Journal of Management*, Vol. 1, No. 1, pp. 3–16.

Dopson, S. and Stewart, R. (1993) 'Information technology, organisational restructuring and the future of middle management', *New Technology, Work and Employment*, Vol. 8, No. 1, pp. 10–20.

Doyle, M. (1995) 'Organisational transformation and renewal: a case for reframing management development?, *Personnel Review*, Vol. 24, No. 6, pp. 6–18.

Dulewicz, V. (1991) 'Improving assessment centres', *Personnel Management*, June, pp. 50–55.

Easterby-Smith, M. (1992) 'European management education: the prospects for unification', *Human Resource Management Journal*, Vol. 3, No. 1, pp. 23–36.

Easterby-Smith, M. (1994) *Evaluation of Management Education, Training and Development*. Aldershot: Gower.

Endres, G. and Kleiner, B. (1990) 'How to measure management training and effectiveness', *Journal of European Industrial Training*, Vol. 14, No. 9, pp. 3–7.

Ferner, A. (1994) 'Multi-national comparisons and HRM: an overview of research issues', *Human Resource Management Journal*, Vol. 4, No. 3, pp. 79–102.

Fischer, M. and Gleijm, H. (1992) 'The gender gap in management', *Industrial and Commercial Training*, Vol. 24, No. 4, pp. 5–11.

Flanders, M. (1994) *Breakthrough: The Career Women's Guide to Shattering the Glass Ceiling*. London: Paul Chapman Publishing.

*Fox, S. (1989) 'The politics of evaluating management development', *Management Education and Development*, Vol. 20, Pt 3, pp. 191–207.

Fox, S. (1992) 'The European learning community: towards a political economy of management learning', *Human Resource Management Journal*, Vol. 3, No. 1, pp. 70–91.

Fritchie, R. and Pedler, M. (1984) 'Training men to work with women', in Hammond, V. (ed.) *Practical Approaches to Women's Management Development*. Brussels: European Foundation for Management Development.

Fulop, L. (1991) 'Middle managers: victims or vanguards of the entrepreneurial movement?', *Journal of Management Studies*, Vol. 28, No. 1, pp. 25–43.

*Gowler, D. and Legge, K. (1996) 'The meaning of management and the management of meaning', in Linstead, S., Grafton-Small, R. and Jeffcutt, P. (eds) *Understanding Management*. London: Sage.

Grondin, D. (1990) 'Developing women in management programmes: two steps forward and one step back', *Women in Management Review*, Vol. 5, No. 3, pp. 15–19.

Guest, D. (1989) 'Personnel and HRM: can you tell the difference?', *Personnel Management*, January, pp. 48–51.

Hales, C. (1993) *Managing Through Organisation*. London: Routledge.

Handy, C. (1987) *The Making of Managers*. London: MSC/NEDO/BIM.

Handy, L. and Barham, K. (1990) 'International management development in the 1990s', *Journal of European Industrial Training*, Vol. 14, No. 6, pp. 28–31.

Hansen, C.D. and Brooks, A.K. (1994) 'A review of cross-cultural research on human resource development', *Human Resource Development Quarterly*, Vol. 5, No. 1, pp. 55–74.

Harrison, R. (1992) *Employee Development*. London: IPM.

Harzing, A.-M. and Van Ruysseveldt, J. (1995) *International Human Resource Management*. London: Sage.

Heisler, W.J. and Benham, P. (1992) 'The challenge of management development in North America in the 1990s', *Journal of Management Development*, Vol. 11, No. 2, pp. 16–31.

Hendry, C. (1995) *Human Resource Management: A Strategic Approach to Employment*. Oxford: Butterworth-Heinemann.

Hendry, C. and Pettigrew, A. (1986) 'The practice of strategic human resource management', *Personnel Review*, Vol. 15, No. 5, pp. 3–8.

Herriot, P. and Pemberton, C. (1995) *New Deals: The Revolution in Managerial Careers*. Chichester: John Wiley.

*Herriot, P. and Pemberton, C. (1996) 'A new deal for middle managers', in Billsberry, J. (ed.) *The Effective Manager: Perspectives and Illustrations*. London: Sage.

Hilb, P. (1992) 'The challenge of management development in Western Europe in the 1990s', *International Journal of Human Resource Management*, Vol. 3, No. 3, pp. 575–584.

Hill, R. (1994) *Euro-Managers and Martians*. Brussels: Euro Publications.

Hitt, W. (1987) 'A unified manager development programme', *Journal of Management Development*, Vol. 6, No. 1, pp. 43–53.

Hofstede, G. (1990) 'The cultural relativity of organisational practices and theories', in Wilson, D. and Rosenfeld, R. *Managing Organisations*. London: McGraw-Hill.

*Honey, P. and Mumford, A. (1986) *Manual of Learning Styles*, 2nd edn. Maidenhead: Peter Honey.

Hofl, H. and Dawes, F. (1995) 'A whole can of worms! The contested frontiers of management development and learning', *Personnel Review*, Vol. 24, No. 6, pp. 19–28.

Hutchinson, S. and Wood, S. (1995) *Personnel and the Line: Developing the New Relationship*. London: IPD.

*Hyland, T. (1994) *Competences, Education and NVQs: Dissenting Perspectives*. London: Cassell Education.

Irvine, D. and Wilson, J.P. (1994) 'Outdoor management development: reality or illusion?', *Journal of Management Development*, Vol. 13, No. 5, pp. 25–37.

Jackson, D. and Humble, J. (1994) 'Middle managers: new purpose, new direction', *Journal of Management Development*, Vol. 13, No. 3, pp. 15–21.

Jacobs, R. (1989) 'Getting the measure of management competence', *Personnel Management*, June, pp. 32–37.

Jones, P. and Oswick, C. (1993) 'Outcomes of outdoor management development: articles of faith?', *Journal of European Industrial Training*, Vol. 17, No. 3, pp. 10–18.

Kakabadse, A. and Myers, A. (1995) 'Qualities of top management: comparisons of European manufacturers', *Journal of Management Development*, Vol. 14, No. 1, pp. 5–15.

Kakabadse, A. and Parker, C. (1984) 'The undiscovered dimension of management education: politics in organisations', in Cox, C. and Beck, J. (eds) *Management Development: Advances in Practice and Theory*. Chichester: John Wiley.

Kanter, R. (1982) 'The middle manager as innovator', *Harvard Business Review*, Vol. 60, No. 4, pp. 95–105.

*Kast, F.S. and Rosenweig, J.E. (1985) *Organisation and Management: A Systems Approach*, 4th edn. New York: McGraw-Hill.

Keeble, S.P. (1992) *The Ability to Manage: A Study of British Management, 1890–1990*. Manchester: Manchester University Press.

Kerfoot, D. and Knights, D. (1992) 'Planning for personnel? – Human resource management reconsidered', *Journal of Management Studies*, Vol. 29, No. 5, pp. 652–668.

Kilcourse, T. (1994) 'Developing competent managers', *Journal of European Industrial Training*, Vol. 18, No. 2, pp. 12–16.

Kirkbride, P. and Tang, S. (1992) 'Management development in the Nanyang Chinese societies of S.E. Asia', *Journal of Management Development*, Vol. 11, No. 2, pp. 54–66.

Kolb, D. (1984) *Experiential Learning*. New York: Prentice Hall.

*Kotter, J.P. (1982) *The General Managers*. Glencoe: Free Press.

Kwiatkowski, S. and Kozminski, A. (1992) 'Paradoxical country: management education in Poland', *Journal of Management Development*, Vol. 11, No. 5, pp. 28–33.

Lawrence, P. (1992) 'Management development in Europe: a study in cultural contrast', *Human Resource Management Journal*, Vol. 3, No. 1, pp. 11–23.

Lee G. and Beard, D. (1994) *Development Centres: Realising the Potential of Your Employees through Assessment and Development*. Maidenhead: McGraw-Hill.

Lee, M. (1995) 'Working with choice in Central Europe', *Management Learning*, Vol. 26, No. 2, pp. 215–30.

Lee. R. (1987) 'Towards an "appropriate theory" of organisational politics', *Management Education and Development*, Vol. 18, Pt 4, pp. 315–329.

Lees, S. (1992) 'Ten faces of management development', *Management Education and Development*, Vol. 23, Pt 2, pp. 89–105.

*Legge, K. (1995) *Human Resource Management: Rhetorics and Realities*. Basingstoke: Macmillan.

*Mabey, C. and Salaman, G. (1995) *Strategic Human Resource Management*. Oxford: Blackwell.

Management Charter Initiative (MCI) (1993) *Management Development in the UK*. London: MCI.

Marchington, M. (1995) 'Fairy tales and magic wands: new employment practices in perspective', *Employee Relations*, Vol. 17, No. 1, pp. 51–66.

Margerison, C. (1991) *Making Management Development Work*. Maidenhead: McGraw-Hill.

Margerison, C. (1994a) 'Managing career choices', in Mumford, A. (ed.) *Gower Handbook of Management Development*. Aldershot: Gower.

Margerison, C. (1994b) 'Action learning and excellence in management development', in Mabey, C. and Iles, P. (eds) *Managing Learning*. London: Routledge.

Mathewman, J. (1995) 'Trends and developments in the use of competency frameworks', *Competency*, Vol. 1, No. 4, whole issue supplement.

McBride, M. (1992) 'Management development in the global village: beyond culture, a micro world approach', *Journal of Management Development*, Vol. 11, No. 7, pp. 48–57.

*McClelland, S. (1994) 'Gaining competitive advantage through strategic management development', *Journal of Management Development*, Vol. 13, No. 5, pp. 4–13.

Miller, L. (1991) 'Managerial competences', *Industrial and Commercial Training*, Vol. 23, No. 6, pp. 11–15.

Miller, R and Cangemi J. (1993) 'Why TQM fails: perspectives of top management', *Journal of Management Development*, Vol. 12, No. 7, pp. 40–50.

*Mintzberg, H. (1980) *The Nature of Managerial Work*. Englewood Cliffs: Prentice Hall.

Molander, C. (1986) *Management Development*. Bromley: Chartwell-Bratt.

Molander, C. and Walton, D. (1984) 'Getting management development started: the manager as trainer', in Cox, C. and Beck, J. (eds) *Management Development: Advances in Practice and Theory*. Chichester: John Wiley.

Molander, C. and Winterton, J. (1994) *Managing Human Resources*. London: Routledge.

Mole, G. (1996) 'The management training industry in the UK: an HRD director's critique', *Human Resource Management Journal*, Vol. 6, No. 1, pp. 19–26.

Mumford, A. (1987) 'Using reality in management development', *Management Education and Development*, Vol. 18, Pt 3, pp. 223–243.

Mumford, A. (1993) *Management Development: Strategies for Action*. London: IPD.

Munchus, G. and McArthur, B. (1991) 'Revisiting the historical use of assessment centres in management selection and development', *Journal of Management Development*, Vol. 10, No. 1, pp. 5–13.

Neelankavil, J. (1992) 'Management development and training programmes in Japanese firms', *Journal of Management Development*, Vol. 11, No. 3, pp. 12–17.

Newstrom, J. (1986) 'Leveraging management development through the management of transfer', *Journal of Management Development*, Vol. 5, No. 5, pp. 33–45.

Odiorne, G.S. (1984) *Strategic Management of Human Resources: A Portfolio Approach*. San Francisco: Jossey-Bass.

Pate, L. and Nielson, W. (1987) 'Integrating management development into a large-scale, system-wide change programme', *Journal of Management Development*, Vol. 6, No. 5, pp. 16–30.

Pedler, M. (1990) 'A biography of self-development', in Pedler, M., Burgoyne, J., Boydell, T. and Welshman, G. (eds) *Self-Development in Organisations*. Maidenhead: McGraw-Hill.

Pedler, M., Burgoyne, J., Boydell, T. and Welshman, G. (1990) *Self-Development in Organisations*. Maidenhead: McGraw-Hill.

Phillips, N. (1992) *Managing International Teams*. London: Pitman Publishing.

Puffer, S. (1993) 'The booming business of management education in Russia', *Journal of Management Development*, Vol. 12, No. 5, pp. 46–59.

Rae, L. (1986) *How to Measure Training Effectiveness*. Aldershot: Gower.

Ready, D., Vicere, A. and White, A. (1994) 'Towards a systems approach to executive development', *Journal of Management Development*, Vol. 13, No. 5, pp. 3–11.

Redman, T., Keithley, D. and Szalkowski, A. (1995) 'Management development under adversity: case studies from Poland', *Journal of Management Development*, Vol. 14, No. 10, pp. 4–13.

Redman, T., Snape, E. and Wilkinson, A. (1995) 'Is quality management working in the UK?', *Journal of General Management*, Vol. 20, No. 3, pp. 44–59.

*Reed, M. and Anthony, P. (1992) 'Professionalising management and managing professionalisation: British management in the 1980s', *Journal of Management Studies*, Vol. 29, No. 5, September, pp. 591–613.

*Revans, R. (1983) *ABC of Action Learning*. Bromley: Chartwell-Bratt.

Ripley, R.E. and Ripley, M.J. (1992) 'Empowerment, the cornerstone of quality: empowering management in innovative organisations in the 1990s', *Management Decisions*, Vol. 30, No. 4, pp. 20–43.

Roberts, G. (1995) 'Competency management systems: the need for a practical framework', *Competency*, Vol. 3, No. 2, pp. 27–30.

Roberts, J. (1996) 'Management education and the limits of technical rationality: the condition and consequences of management practice', in French, R. and Grey, C. (eds) *Rethinking Management Education*. London: Sage.

Russell, S. (1983) 'Quality circles in perspective', *WRU Occasional Paper No. 24*. London: ACAS.

Russell, S. and Dale, B. (1989) 'Quality circles: a broader perspective', *WRU Occasional Paper No. 43*. London: ACAS.

Ryan, M. (1989) 'Political behaviour and management development', *Management Education and Development*, Vol. 20, Pt 3, pp. 238–253.

*Salaman, G. (1995) *Managing*. Buckingham: Open University Press.

Salaman, G. and Butler, J. (1990) 'Why managers won't learn', *Management Education and Development*, Vol. 21, Pt 3, pp. 183–191.

*Scase, R. and Goffe, R. (1989) *Reluctant Managers: Their Work and Lifestyles*. London: Routledge.

Smith, A. (1993) 'Management development evaluation and effectiveness', *Journal of Management Development*, Vol. 12, No. 1, pp. 20–32.

Smith, A. and Porter, J. (1990) 'The tailor-made training maze: a practitioner's guide to evaluation', *Journal of European Industrial Training*, Vol. 14, No. 8, complete issue.

Smith, H., Carroll, A., Kefalas, A. and Watson, H. (1980) *Making Organisations Perform*. New York: Macmillan.

Snell, R. (1986) 'Questioning the ethics of management development: a critical review', *Management Education and Development*, Vol. 17, Pt 1, pp. 43–64.

Snell, R. (1990) 'Managers' development of ethical awareness and personal morality', *Personnel Review*, Vol. 19, No. 1, pp. 13–20.

Sparrow, P. and Bognanno, M. (1994) 'Competency forecasting: issues for international selection and assessment', in Mabey, C. and Iles, P. (eds) *Managing Learning*. London: Routledge.

Srinivas, K. (1995) 'Globalisation of business and the Third World: the challenge of expanding the mind-set', *Journal of Management Development*, Vol. 14, No. 3, pp. 26–49.

Stead, B. (1985) *Women in Management*, 2nd edn. Englewood Cliffs: Prentice Hall.

*Stewart, J. and Hamlin, B. (1992a) 'Competence based qualifications: the case against change', *Journal of European Industrial Training*, Vol. 16, No. 7, pp. 21–32.

*Stewart, J. and Hamlin, B. (1992b) 'Competence-based qualifications: a case for established methodologies', *Journal of European Industrial Training*, Vol. 16, No. 10, pp. 9–16.

Stewart, R. (1994) *Managing Today and Tomorrow*. Basingstoke: Macmillan.

*Storey, J. (1989) 'Management development: a literature review and implications for future research, Part 1: conceptualisations and practice', *Personnel Review*, Vol. 18, No. 6, pp. 3–19.

Storey, J. (1990) 'Management development: a literature review and implications for future research – Part II: profiles and contexts', *Personnel Review*, Vol. 19, No. 1, pp. 3–11.

Storey, J. (1992a) *Management of Human Resources*. Oxford: Blackwell.

Storey, J. (1992b) 'Making European managers: an overview', *Human Resource Management Journal*, Vol. 3, No. 1, pp. 1–10.

Storey, J., Okazaki-Ward, L., Gow, I., Edwards, P.K. and Sisson, K. (1991) 'Managerial careers and management development: a comparative analysis of Britain and Japan', *Human Resource Management Journal*, Vol. 1, No. 3, Spring, pp. 33–57.

Stumpf, S., Watson, M-A. and Rustogi, H. (1994) 'Leadership in a global village: creating practice fields to develop learning organisations', *Journal of Management Development*, Vol. 13, No. 8, pp. 16–25.

Templer, A., Beatty, D. and Hofmeyer, K. (1992) 'The challenge of management development in South Africa: so little time, so much to do', *Journal of Management Development*, Vol. 11, No. 2, pp. 32–41.

Temporal, P. (1984) 'Helping self-development to happen', in Cox, C. and Beck, J. (eds) *Management Development: Advances in Practice and Theory*. Chichester: John Wiley.

Temporal, P. (1990) 'Linking management development to the corporate future – the role of the professional', *Journal of Management Development*, Vol. 9, No. 5, pp. 7–15.

*Thomas, A. (1993) *Controversies in Management*. London: Routledge.

Thornhill, A. (1993) 'Management training across cultures: the challenge for trainers', *Journal of European Industrial Training*, Vol. 17, No. 10, pp. 43–51.

Thurley, K. and Wirdenhuis, H. (1991) 'Will management become European? Strategic choice for organisations', *European Management Journal*, Vol. 9, No. 2, pp. 127–135.

Tijmstra, S. and Casler, K. (1992) 'Management learning for Europe', *European Management Journal*, Vol. 10. No. 1, pp. 30–38.

Torrington, D., Weightman, J. and Johns, K. *Effective Management: People and Organisations*, 2nd edn. Hemel Hempstead: Prentice Hall.

Tovey, L. (1991) *Management Training and Development in Large UK Business Organisations*. London: Harbridge House.

Varney, G. (1977) *An Organisation Development Approach to Management Development*. Reading, MA: Addiston-Wesley.

Vecsenyi, J. (1992) 'Management education for the Hungarian transition', *Journal of Management Development*, Vol. 11, No. 3, pp. 39–47.

Vineall, T. (1994) 'Planning management development', in Mumford, A. (ed.) *Gower Handbook of Management Development*, 4th edn. Aldershot: Gower.

*Watson,T. (1994) *In Search of Management*. London: Routledge.

Warr, P., Bird, M. and Rackham, N. (1970) *Evaluation of Management Training*. London: Gower.

Wentling, R.M. (1992) 'Women in middle management: their career development and aspirations', *Business Horizons*, Vol. 35, No. 1, pp. 47–54.

Whiddett, S. and Branch, J. (1993) 'Development centres in Volvo', *Training and Development UK*, Vol. 11, No. 11, pp. 16–18.

Whitaker, V. and Megginson, D. (1992) 'Women and men working together effectively', *Industrial and Commercial Training*, Vol. 24, No. 4, pp. 16–19.

*Whitely, R. (1989) 'On the nature of managerial tasks and skills: their distinguishing characteristics and organisation', *Journal of Management Studies*, Vol. 26, No. 3, May, pp. 209–224.

*Wilson, D. and Rosenfeld, R. (1990) *Managing Organisations*. London: McGraw-Hill.

Woodruffe, C. (1993) *Assessment Centres: Identifying and Developing Competence*. London: IPM.

PART 3 CASE STUDY

ACT Ltd

ACT Ltd is a thriving electronics manufacturing and distribution company. Set up ten years ago, the company produces components for the PC assembly market. Growth has been rapid, with a lot of new business won on a reputation for product innovation and high quality. The company currently employs 150 people at a greenfield site in the South of England. It is now planning a further expansion of its facility to take advantage of the new markets which are opening up in Europe and beyond.

Although the company is a success, the managing director is feeling uneasy about the way the company is managing its human resources. There are two areas that give him cause for concern. The first involves the way non-technical training is organised.

Training organisation

The company has always invested heavily in training its workforce. Indeed, the managing director is convinced that ACT's reputation is mainly attributable to its highly trained workforce. In the past, training was confined to technical areas. However, with the expansion of the company, it has been necessary to develop the training organisation to provide additional skills in areas such as administration, finance, marketing, team-building and communication.

There is no Personnel Department. Training has always been left to the line managers to organise. With technical training, this was never a problem. It was always well organised, consisting of mainly on-the-job training and day release courses provided by the local college. However, now that training is extending into non-technical areas, the managing director is having increasing doubts about the effectiveness of the training organisation within his company. A recent incident serves to highlight this.

Walking through the production department a few weeks ago, the managing director spotted a memo and a list on the notice board. It was written by the department manager and alongside the memo was a 'glossy' brochure from an external training consultancy advertising a wide range of administration and supervisory courses. The memo invited staff to study the brochure, select a course they felt would benefit them and add their name to the list.

The managing director studied the list. Many of the courses that people were applying for appeared to be peripheral to the needs of their job. Then he realised that if everybody who was applying actually went on the courses, a serious hole would appear in the company's training budget! He removed the memo and brochure and made a mental note to have a word with the manager concerned.

As he walked back to his office, he reflected upon the incident. There was no doubt in his mind that something would have to be done to ensure that training was organised in a more structured and professional way. The company had to ensure that it obtained a return on its training investment.

The managing director's second concern is with the capabilities of his management team.

The calibre of the management team

The management team consists of three board directors, four departmental managers, and four supervisory staff (see organisation chart below).

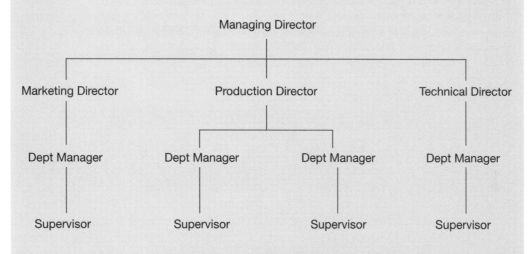

ACT Ltd organisation chart

With the company's rapid expansion, emphasis has always been on product design, quality, achieving high levels of output and maximising sales. What has now become obvious, is that in the rush to achieve business growth, the development of core management skills has been neglected. Without these skills, the managing director fears there will be a real threat to the future survival and success of the company. A number of examples highlight the managing director's concern.

In the boardroom, none of the directors seems capable of discussing and dealing with strategic issues. The other day the managing director wanted to discuss the exploration of new markets in Europe and the sourcing of components from the Far East to reduce production costs. But the meeting was taken up with a discussion about the technical details of the latest semi-conductor design!

The departmental managers are all good engineers and are respected by the workforce for their technical capabilities. All of them have grown with the company and promotion has largely rested on the possession of sound technical skills. But the department managers seem unwilling to delegate and 'step back' from the day-to-day running of the company. The other day, the managing director heard one of the supervisors complaining about the level of interference she was experiencing from her department manager. 'He won't keep his nose out. He takes all the decisions so I just let him get on with it.' He has also noticed that some of the supervisors are too 'laid back' with the workforce while others seem to be managing through a culture of fear and intimidation.

The managing director has tried to communicate his concerns at management team meetings but his managers keep avoiding the issue. When he presses them, they become defensive and withdrawn. The managing director is approaching retirement age and wants to resolve these issues before he retires.

Imagine you are a firm of management consultants that has been approached by the managing director for advice and guidance. You have been asked to review and make recommendations that will improve the way training is organised and develop managers to achieve organisational goals.

INTRODUCTION

The employment relationship is a key feature in the nature of managing employment. It brings together the sources of power and legitimacy, rights and obligations, that management and employees seek for themselves and apply to others. This Part is concerned with explaining this relationship and examining how it works out through a variety of applications such as the law, collective bargaining, performance and reward, and employee involvement.

Chapter 11 deals with the role and influence of the law in determining the nature of contract. The contract of employment is not simply a document which is presented to employees on appointment, but is a complex set of formal and informal rules which govern the whole basis of the employment relationship. Thus, the way employees and managers conform with, or break, those rules determines how that relationship works out in practice. Moreover, the nature of contract can have an important bearing on whether such newer concepts as Human Resource Management can fundamentally change the nature of such a relationship which is so dependent upon the interaction of formal and informal legal regulation.

Chapter 12 introduces the concept and practice of collective bargaining. In recent years the collective determination of pay has reduced in scope and breadth in many market economies, but it still remains the most important single method of arriving at broad pay settlement for many employees and its impact and effect is often felt throughout economies. For these reasons its nature, structure and outcomes form the basis of analysis. Chapter 13 discusses the processes which go towards settling pay for individuals when criteria which test their own performance are introduced. In recent years there has been an increasing use made of individualised pay, and this chapter examines some of the problems and issues in operating and evaluating such processes. Chapter 14 is concerned with the development of employee involvement. This is a topic which has seen great interest recently, but there are contradictory elements within it which this chapter explores, among them whether involvement can genuinely bring employee and managerial interests together and whether involvement is a vehicle for 'empowerment' or simply a further way in which the managerial prerogative is asserted in the employment relationship.

Finally, Chapter 15 considers the particular issues involved in managing human resources in the public sector.

THE EMPLOYMENT RELATIONSHIP AND CONTRACTUAL REGULATION

Ian Clark

OBJECTIVES

To introduce the reader to the central significance of the basis of contract in the employment relationship.

•

To introduce the reader to the contract of employment in terms of the legal regulation of economic activity within the labour market.

•

To introduce the reader to the wider employment relationship as a process of socio-economic exchange through a discussion of the management function and its prescription, the role of management in the UK's industrial capitalism and the role of management in the realisation of legal authority in the employment relationship.

•

INTRODUCTION

This chapter examines the employment relationship and its contractual regulation. In particular, the chapter looks at the central significance of contract in terms of how it regulates the employment relationship and legitimises the managerial prerogative. The employment relationship is visualised as a process of socio-economic exchange. That is, unlike other contractual relationships, for example something as mundane as the purchase of a railway ticket, the employment relationship is an open-ended contractual relationship, thus it is not an immediately closed relationship of exchange. The employment relationship contains an economic component, the exchange of work for payment, but also includes a sociological dimension centred around power and authority. The economic and sociological components are both structured by the contract of employment, but in the wider employment relationship they are subject to a range of issues, for example management competence and efficiency, work group control, management and worker motivation and the potential for workplace conflict and disagreement. All of these factors make the apparently rational economic exchange much more complicated and to some extent indeterminate.

The social component looks at the issue of power within the employment relationship and its central focus is on the management process. The economic side of the exchange looks at the need to manage employees in their work in order that the efficiency criteria of market economies are met. This chapter deals with this issue in two ways: first, it seeks to locate the function of management within the context of market economies. Thus, we examine the role of management as an adjunct to contract and, with it, the managerial prerogative within the employment relationship. Second, we detail the limitations of contractual regulation in relation to operational control within organisations in market economies. In relation to this limitation we examine how management seeks to control and structure the labour process, that is, how individuals who perform work interact with the means of production. In the UK the majority of the working population work within an employment relationship, thus for individuals who work for somebody else – an employer – they interact with the means of production through the employment relationship. A contrast is drawn between whether management autonomy and discretion are free-standing in the organisation of work or if they are derived from the managerial prerogative and expressed in its contractual base; that is, whether the contractual nature of employment informs the managerial prerogative and provides a structure for the labour process.

These two approaches of contractually determined employment and management control seek to provide a socio-economic context within which the prescription, rhetoric and reality of HRM operate. This approach seeks to illustrate the contextual and operational difficulties which HRM faces in the effort to stimulate employees to go beyond contract in the performance of their work. Equally, because much of the discussion is determined by the context of market economies, we ask the question 'what does management do?' Thus, the function and role of management are examined through the context and dictates of a market economy.

The chapter is divided into three sections:

1. We examine the central significance of contract to the employment relationship by discussing four issues: the concept of contract; the philosophical basis of contract; the need for the contractual regulation of employment within the market economy; and lastly, we discuss in more detail the employment relationship as a socio-economic exchange within the market economy.
2. We discuss the contract of employment in terms of the legal regulation of economic activity within the labour market by examining four issues: the regulation of employment through the legal process; the 'common law' duties of the employer and employee; the effects of 'statute' law on the contractual regulation of employment; and finally we briefly discuss HRM in terms of some of its practical effects on the nature and form of the contractual regulation of employment.
3. We look at the employment relationship more conceptually and historically by discussing three issues: the process of management functions and their prescription; the role of the management function within the development of the UK's industrial capitalism; and finally we examine the management process as the realisation of legal authority in the employment relationship.

The issues under discussion are general to industrial economies, but specific examples are drawn from British experience to explain particular points.

THE CENTRAL SIGNIFICANCE OF THE EMPLOYMENT CONTRACT

This section is divided into four parts. First, the concept of contract is examined. Second, the philosophical bases of contract are briefly introduced. Third, the need for the contract of employment is examined within the context of the market economy. Lastly, the emergent nature of the wider employment relationship is introduced as the socio-economic exchange within which the contract of employment operates.

The concept of contract

In order to explain the concept of contract, it is useful to distinguish between commercial contracts and employment contracts, the area of our particular focus. Commercial contracts, for example something as simple as buying a bus ticket or something as complex as a house purchase, contain four elements:

● offer
● acceptance
● consideration
● an intention to create legal relations.

To illustrate these four elements we can draw on the example of a house purchase. An individual may visit a particular house and decide they would like to buy it. As a result of this they decide to make an offer. The current property owner may decide to accept this offer – subject to contract. 'Subject to contract' will necessarily involve the person who wishes to buy the house, the offeror receiving a satisfactory structural survey and acquiring the necessary purchase price either in cash or more likely through a mortgage. If these requirements are satisfactorily fulfilled, a contract can be drawn up. In consideration for the agreed purchase price the existing property owner, the offeree, agrees to give up their property rights to the house and exchange them through contract to the offeror. Thus consideration is the mechanism which validates the contract, that is each party gives something to the contract, in this case a house for money by the offeror and money for a house by the offeree. If a contract contains offer, acceptance and consideration it is taken as indicative that the parties to the contract wish to create a legally binding relationship.

In order to be valid a contract must also satisfy the following factors. First, the contents of the contract, to which the parties have agreed, must be reasonable. Second, the contract in itself must be legal, in terms of the prevailing law: for example, a contract to assassinate a person may contain offer, acceptance and consideration and an intention to create a legally binding relationship between the parties; however, conspiracy to murder is illegal, that is a criminal offence, thus any contractual relationship is void. Third, there must be genuine consent between the parties and the parties themselves must have the capacity to consent to the agreement. For example, minors and bankrupts have only limited capacities in contract.

From this brief introduction we can now proceed to look at employment contracts which are a very specialised form of contract.

A contract of employment is a contract of service, that is where an employee, the subject of the contract, is in the personal service of their employer. It is necessary to distinguish an employment contract of personal service from a commercial contract for services. As Wedderburn (1986: 106) makes clear, the law marks off the employee under a contract of service from independent contractors, the self-employed, who may provide services to an organisation under a commercial contract. For example, a commercial contract whereby catering or cleaning services are provided to one firm by a second firm is a contract for services, not an employment contract, even though the work is performed by labour. Catering staff may be employees in the offeror firm but the offeree firm has bought their services under a commercial contract for catering services.

A contract of employment differs from a commercial contract for services in the sense that an employment contract of personal service to an employer is intended to be an open-ended relationship, that is one which continues until either party decides to end it through due notice, whereas a commercial contract is more likely to be a precise exchange of services over a clearly defined period of time. Some employment contracts today are of a temporary or fixed-term nature, but nonetheless an employment relationship is created, whereas in commercial contracts of a long-term duration, for example computer or photocopier servicing, an employment relationship is not created. Equally, such commercial contracts are likely to contain clear and precise contractual duties for each party. Thus commercial contracts are a purely contractual relationship which, unlike employment contracts, are not subject to the 'common law duties' of an employer and employee. The common law refers to areas of law which are not covered by Parliamentary or European Union legislation. The common law has been developed by the judiciary, that is the common law is judge-made law. In the following section we detail the common law duties of both parties, which are incorporated into contracts of employment. At this stage we need go no further into this issue, other than to make it clear that under an employment contract of personal service both employer and employee are subject to particular duties, whereas in commercial contracts these duties are not present.

Now that we have defined contract and distinguished between commercial and employment contracts, it is possible to proceed with a discussion of the underlying assumptions behind contract theory.

Equality and freedom of entry: market individualism

The philosophical basis of contract is derived from the principle of market individualism. Market individualism suggests that the individual is the best judge of their own interests. From this suggestion the notion of 'freedom of contract' is introduced, which assumes that individuals are self-determining agents who are primarily self-interested. Thus, individuals are able to fulfil their own self-interest most effectively if they are free to enter into contracts between themselves within the market mechanism.

All the above suggests that individuals both freely enter into contractual arrangements and jointly determine the terms and conditions of the contract with equal status in terms of the law. In other words, the component parts of a contract – offer, acceptance and the consideration between the parties – are arrived at through a process of negotiation and then agreement. This may be the situation in the case of a house purchase but in relation to employment the situation is somewhat different. As Fox (1985: 6) points out, contract theory alone, with all that it entails in terms of equality and references to adjudication by an outside body, cannot be an effective mode of regulation in the case of employment if the parties to the contract are in dispute. In the UK this has been the case because the employment relationship has always been one of status. The notion of status is derived from the paternal master and servant relationship inherent to 'employment' before the rise of industrial economies. Examples of this relationship can be easily seen in the cases of domestic service, tied cottages and general agricultural labourers. In the nineteenth century domestic servants and agricultural labourers were not employees in the modern sense of the word, rather they were subject to a crude form of commercial contract whereby they provided their labour services to a master in return for board and lodgings. Servants and agricultural labourers were not the subjects of employment contracts. Once employment became contractually determined in a formal legal sense its basis was not free standing. By this we mean that the legal process incorporated characteristics of the previous form of employment, that is the status bias of the master and servant relationship. Fox (1985: 3–5) identifies paternalism as the basis of status within employment. That is, although employment contracts provide employees with a degree of independence from their employer, for example in the sense that employees can terminate their employment through due notice, employees are still the subject of the employment contract and subject to the reasonable and legitimate authority of their employer to whom they provide personal service.

Paternalism refers to a situation of subordination to legitimate authority. Prior to the contractual determination of employment the process of subordination to legitimate authority was entirely within the master–servant relationship. Within contractually determined employment, the employee subordinates him or herself to the greater legal authority of the employer, the superiority of which is derived from the status-based relationship of master and servant.

In order that our understanding of the fusion of contract and status is clear in relation to employment, two points have to be made. First, the notion of freedom of contract between two consenting parties is present in relation to employment contracts, but only in terms of individual equality before the law. Second, and relatedly, equity before the law in employment contracts is not autonomous because it is underpinned by authority on the part of the employer which is derived from their paternal status. That is often referred to as the managerial prerogative. Thus, in short, although in the general case of contract the agreeing parties are thought to be the best judge of their own interests, in the case of employment the status bias of the employer gives them the privilege of being able to determine their own self-interest and have a partial say in the determination of the interests of the employee. This is derived from the concept of subordination which implies that the junior partner to the employment contract cannot perceive all their real interests. Kahn-Freund (1984) described the individually based contract of employment as an act of submission on the part of the employee:

> In its operation it is a condition of subordination, however much the submission and the subordination may be concealed by that indispensable figment of the legal mind known as the contract of employment.

Thus, the employer is able to determine the organisation of work, levels of payment and duration of working time. The employee is bound by such impositions if they are reasonable. Thus, as Hyman (1975: 23) argues, the notion of free employment contracts bears little resemblance to the real world. Relatedly, although most employees have an individual contract of employment, the terms and conditions of an individual's contract of employment are likely to be determined and regulated by means of a collective agreement, the details of which are normally incorporated in an individual's contract of employment. This point again illustrates that the notion of individual negotiation and freedom of contract may only exist at the surface level of relations between employer and employee. These points are clarified further in the next section of this chapter which details the common law and statute law requirements in relation to the make-up and terms and conditions of a contract of employment.

Having noted the philosophical underpinning of the concept of contract we can proceed to examine the emergence of the need for employment and therefore its regulation within the UK's market economy.

The need for employment and its regulation: the emergence of the firm

In market economies commercial relations between individuals are governed by contract. Contracts are of two types: those where services are bought and sold (a commercial contract); and those where the services of individuals are the subject of the contract (an employment contract). In the second instance a contract of employment creates the employee who is in the service of the employer, whereas if a firm uses an independent subcontractor to perform work on their behalf a commercial contract exists between two independent firms. Thus, the crucial difference between a contract of employment and a commercial contract is constituted by their respective legal obligations and expectations. In the case of employment it is a contract of subordination based on the service of the employee. In contrast, a commercial contract exchanges commercial services between independent individuals. It is important for us to consider this distinction because one feature of contemporary HRM is the strategic use of indirect labour sourced through commercial contracts. This use of subcontractors and independent traders/consultants is part of the drive for greater flexibility in the management and deployment of human resources.

Institutional economists, for example Coase (1937) and in more contemporary vein Williamson (1975), suggest that the market determines which type of contract will predominate in particular situations. Take the example of a house purchase by an individual. In this situation the individual is likely to require the personal services of a solicitor to convey the property. Thus, the individual enters into a contract for the personal services of a solicitor to undertake this task. In a different situation where a property company is continually buying property, the market is likely to dictate that it is more efficient for the company to employ a solicitor to be responsible for the large number of property purchases and sales in which it is involved. Thus an employment contract is created.

The central question at issue here is why are there not millions of independent contractors who sell their personal services to one another? Coase (1937) argues that this situation does not occur because in many situations the details of what the supplier is expected to do are defined in very general terms, with the specific details being determined at a later date. For Coase, market transactions which buy in materials and services can be eliminated and the complicated market structure can be replaced with an entrepreneurial coordinator who directs production, that is an employer.

Where direction of labour resources is dependent on the buyer, a relationship, which Coase terms the firm, will be created. A firm is likely to emerge when the use of short-term contracts would prove unsatisfactory, as is often the case with labour. Instead of a series of commercial contracts for the personal services of independent contractors, one contract, the employment contract, is substituted. This places the employee in the service of the employer. As we have already established, in the case of employment contracts the employee agrees to obey the directions of the employer within the reasonable limits of the contract. The decision to use a commercial contract or an employment contract is balanced in terms of the costs of using the market price mechanism to create a commercial contract against the costs of organising an extra transaction – the creation of an employee, subject to an employment contract within the firm. Extreme product market competition together with favourable government policies appear to be shifting this balance today in favour of the market mechanism. See, for example, Atkinson (1984), where the notion of the flexible firm is presented in rational economic terms; equally see Hutton (1995) and Clark (1996) for more polemic and critical evaluations of a return to market principles over employment creation.

Thus, the economic and legal rationale for the firm creates an employment relationship of employer and employee. This occurs when the use of one contract is more efficient than the use of many commercial contracts through the market mechanism.

The employment relationship, although it is contractually based and freely entered into, removes the freedom of action that an individual would have if they operated as an independent contractor. This is the case because, as the above discussion on the philosophical base of contract indicates, the theory of contract is fused with status in the specific case of employment. Hence, the employment relationship within the firm is one of subordination to a market authority relation, which is subject to the reasonableness of the contract of employment. The contract of employment defines the relationship of subordination between employee and employer which creates the legal requirement to obey. It is important to emphasise that it is the reasonableness of the legally vested requirement to obey which can be challenged, not the overall requirement to obey. Over the past 30 years there has been a growing body of statute law which has had the effect of reducing the imbalance in the employment contract referred to by Kahn-Freund. Much of this employment protection legislation is discussed in the next section of this chapter. At this stage we can summarise its aim by saying that it is designed to recognise that the employee has some property rights in their employment. The majority of such protections are built into the contract of employment. Therefore, any property right or contractual protection against unreasonable treatment is not an absolute. This is the case because the protection operates in the contract of employment and therefore recognises the employee as subordinate. Therefore the protection is not a constitutional right but a contractually defined right, that is an individual right subject to the details of a specific case.

Now that we have examined the emergence of employment within the firm it is clear that its contractual nature and regulation are derived in part from the concept of contract and in part from the status bias of traditional paternal employment in the UK. The wider employment relationship which has grown out of the emergence of contractual employment within the firm is discussed in further detail in the next two sections of this chapter. However, we now briefly introduce and examine the employment relationship as a socio-economic exchange.

The employment relationship: a socio-economic exchange

The term 'socio-economic' exchange suggests that the employment relationship has two dimensions. First, it is an economic exchange where an employee, under an employment contract, receives monetary reward for the work they perform. Second, the employment relationship has a sociological dimension in that under a contract of employment a power relationship exists. While they are at work, employees are providing their labour service to their employer and are therefore under a legal direction as defined in their contract of employment. In strictly economic terms the employee sells their labour power to the employer which the employer has to transform into labour that produces value (in the form of goods and services) which the employer can then sell. The purchase of labour power is the subject of the employment contract and the economic dimension of the employment relationship.

By labour power we refer to the capacity of an employee to perform work as detailed in the requirements of a job description and any person specification. The processes of recruitment and selection are carried out in order that a particular organisation can make an informed judgement on the basis of references, previous work experience as detailed in a CV, and the overall selection criteria as to which candidate is best suited to the employment vacancy, that is which candidate from a given shortlist of interviewees appears most qualified in terms of labour capacity to perform the requirements of the employment vacancy.

Through the employment contract the employing organisation buys the labour capacity of an employee. However, the organisation will, once employment is created, be necessarily concerned with the employee's performance. It is this latter requirement of performance which necessitates the employing firm structuring an employee's labour process in order for labour capacity to be effectively transformed into labour performance.

If labour power was transformed into labour in a deterministic fashion as suggested by neoclassical economics, there would be no need for real management. Neoclassical economics, as developed between the seventeenth and nineteenth centuries, seeks to conceptualise the structure of civil society on the basis of society's economic foundation. Such theories abstract the individual and private property through the exchange mechanism of the market as regulated by contract. That is, civil society and the labour market in particular are visualised in terms of the rational actor model, whereby individuals enter into contracts determined on a free and individual basis on equal terms. Essentially labour is visualised like any other inanimate factor of production such as land or capital. In this visualisation management is merely an integrative process which coordinates the factors of production as described in the neoclassical theory of the firm. However, this is not the case in operational conditions and illustrates the failure of purely economic conceptions of the employment relationship. Within market economies, where the majority of people work within an employment relationship, the control, deployment and regulation of human resources is a major management function.

The central issue for the employer is how to manage employees in order to get the maximum economic benefit from their economic control as vested in the contract of employment. In other words, systems of management within the organisation must be designed and implemented to assist management in the process of transforming raw labour power into efficient labour performance in the form of goods and services which the employer can then sell through the market mechanism. This area is central to the evaluation of industrial relations and management strategies such as HRM, because labour is animate and subject to irrationality. This is equally the case for that labour which is deployed in management functions.

It is important to emphasise that the sociological dimension to the employment relationship is the main area of our concern here. There are two aspects to the sociological dimension of the employment relationship which are of particular interest in the study of the management of human resources. First, the way in which the employer organises work so as to enable labour power to be transformed into effective employee performance in the most efficient and productive manner. The starting point of analysis here is to examine the notion of 'scientific management' as developed by Frederick Taylor. The second area of interest centres on the systems of job regulation which an organisation uses to manage and regulate labour at the workplace. Human resource management techniques are the latest prescription for efficient and productive job regulation at the workplace.

The legal control which an employer is entitled to via the contract of employment does not lead to full operational control in practice because of the socio-economic dimension of the exchange of labour. For this reason effective operational performance is a central management concern, which is examined in the third section of this chapter.

Summary

This section has examined the central significance of the contract of employment in the management and regulation of human resources in four ways. First, the concept of contract has been detailed in order to provide a distinction between commercial contracts and employment contracts. Second, the underlying philosophical assumptions behind the notion of a voluntary bargain have been discussed in order to show that, while contracts are freely entered into in the case of employment, freedom of action within a contract is relative in the sense that an employee is subordinate to their employer. Third, the emergent character of the firm has been examined in order to position the contract of employment within the wider employment relationship. Lastly, the employment relationship has been discussed as a socio-economic exchange. This discussion illustrates that, while the contract of employment is central to the employment relationship, the legal control over employees which it gives to an employer does not automatically translate into operational control over the organisation and regulation of work. Thus, the employment relationship has to be actively managed in order that the benefits of legal control derived from the contract of employment can be made effective in terms of orderly and efficient employee performance.

In order to amplify on our discussion of employment as a socio-economic exchange, the following section details the common law and statutory components to the contract of employment.

THE CONTRACT OF EMPLOYMENT

Now we turn to what could be described as a functional or legal explanation of the contract of employment.

This section is divided into four parts. First, the regulation of employment through the law is outlined. Here we distinguish between the common law and statute law. Second, we examine the common law duties of employer and employee in further detail. Third, we identify the effects of statute law on the contractual regulation of employment. Lastly, HRM is discussed in relation to some of its practical effects on the regulation of employment at the workplace.

The contract of employment: common law and statutory regulation

There are two features of the English legal system which have to be highlighted as the contexts within which all aspects of the law must be examined. First, the English legal system, unlike most other legal systems (for example those of other European Union states), does not operate in conjunction with a written constitution or a Bill of Rights. In the specific area of employment the lack of a written constitution and a Bill of Rights means that British subjects do not possess any specific inalienable rights as employees; for example, the right to strike, the right to collective consultation and participation or the right to union membership. Second, and relatedly, the system is very conservative, some would say obsessed with the past. This explains why the role of precedent within the common law is so prominent. Advocates of Britain's unwritten constitution argue that one of its major benefits is adaptability over time, as opposed to being a rigid mechanism around which new developments have to be moulded. As a consequence of these two settings English citizens have no absolute rights. In relation to employment any rights which British subjects hold have been developed through a process of case law and precedent, which is referred to as the common law.

Common law rights have, in the employment field, been supplemented through the introduction of various statutory rights, by which the contractual regulation of work is bound. For example, under the common law a contract of employment can be verbal, implied by the conduct of the parties or written. However, the 1978 Employment Protection (Consolidation) Act (EPCA) as amended imposes certain statutory obligations on the employer and introduces certain statutory rights for employees. For example, the employer must give employees itemised wage statements. Second, the ECPA gives a full-time employee the statutory right not to be unfairly dismissed and in the case of job redundancy through no fault of their own to be compensated by their employer. Both of these statutory rights are subject to a two-year qualification period. This period of qualification illustrates the partial nature of an employee's statutory rights within the employment relationship. That is, protection against unfair dismissal and access to redundancy payment are not inalienable rights, they are acquired by continuity of employment in a particular organisation for a defined period of service. Hence, employees with periods of employment service of less than two years can be fairly 'unfairly dismissed' and/or have no statutory redress to redundancy payment.

A third statutory requirement is covered by the 1993 Trade Union Reform and Employment Rights Act (TURER). TURER requires that all employees who work more than eight hours per week must be given a written statement of the particulars of their employment in one principal document within two months of the commencement of employment. These written particulars of an individual's contract of employment are referred to as the express terms of the contract.

The regulation of employment through the common law operates on the basis of decisions previously arrived at in a higher court. In effect it is judge-made law which creates a precedent for lower courts and/or subsequent future cases of a similar nature. Thus, a precedent creates an example for subsequent cases or acts as a justification for subsequent decisions.

Common law precedent acts in two ways. First, it regulates in disputes where there is no relevant Act of Parliament and thus has the status of an Act of Parliament. Second, common law precedent is independent of Parliament in the sense that rulings which judges arrive at are a creation of their own interpretation of common law principles or their interpretation of how particular statutory rulings should be interpreted by the judiciary in future cases. The common law duties of employer and employee are detailed in the next part of this section; however, before going on to that part we can make some brief reference to the effects of statute law.

Statute law comes from two sources: first, Parliament, and second, the European Union. In the majority of cases domestic legislation rules supreme; however, if domestic law clashes with European Union law the situation is more complex.

A central theme within the English legal system which runs through both the common law and statute law is that of reasonableness. In relation to the contract of employment, the common law terms and conditions and the statutory interventions both have to be reasonable in their effects on the employer and employee. Thus in many cases judgements on disputes between employer and employee often turn on the question of reasonableness. The notions of reasonable and unreasonable are therefore both questions of interpretation in the circumstances of particular cases.

In relation to the contract of employment statutes have the effect of incorporating express or implied terms into an employee's contract. Statutory express or implied terms can have a significant effect on the ordering and regulation of employees at the workplace and therefore are of central significance to human resource practitioners and researchers. The details of express, implied and incorporated terms of employment contracts are considered in further detail in the third part of this section. We now move on to discuss the common law duties of employer and employee.

Common law duties of employer and employee

The first section of this chapter introduced the concept of freedom of contract. This concept assumes that individuals are self-determining agents who are primarily self-interested. On this basis it is presumed that individuals both freely enter into contractual arrangements and jointly determine the terms and conditions of, say, an employment contract. It is important to point out that in the case of employment, this notion of freedom of contract operates in conjunction with the common law duties of employer and employee. That is, although contracts of employment are assumed to be freely entered into, the contract of employment itself incorporates the common law duties of employee and employer.

The common law duties of the employer can be summarised in the following manner. First, the employer must provide a reasonable opportunity for the employee to work and be paid the agreed wages as consideration for work performed. It is a matter of some debate as to whether the employer has a common law duty actually to provide work; the issue appears to turn on the notion of reasonableness, which will depend on the details of any particular case. Building and construction work is a particular case in point. Here employees may be able to claim job redundancy, if they qualify in terms of length of service, if they are maintained on short-time working or laid off for 6 weeks out of the last 13 weeks of employment or for 4 consecutive weeks. In such a case the employees are required to notify their employer within 4 weeks of the end of the lay-off or short-time working that they intend to claim job redundancy. The employer has the opportunity to contest such a claim. Second, an employer must take reasonable care to ensure that all employees are safe at the workplace and must indemnify any employee for injury incurred during employment. That is, employers have a vicarious common law duty to provide a safe working environment for their employees. Some of this liability has been codified in statute under the 1974 Health and Safety at Work Act. Lastly, the employer has the duty of treating all employees in a courteous and polite manner. That is, employers should not 'bully', abuse or subject their employees to racist or sexist remarks. Some of this liability has been codified in the Sex Discrimination Act of 1975 and the Race Relations Act of 1976. We can contrast the common law duties of the employer with those of the employee.

An employee is obliged to undertake the following common law duties: be ready and willing to work for their employer, offer personal service to the employer, that is not hold a second job without agreement, and take reasonable care in the conduct of their personal service. Second, the employee must work in the employer's time, obey reasonable orders during that time and undertake not to disrupt the employer's business on purpose. Lastly, the employee is required not to disclose any trade secret to their employer's competitors.

The common law duties of the employee and employer are not always detailed in the written particulars of a contract of employment and may be implied terms in the contract derived from custom and practice or statutes.

In market economies the contract of employment is freely entered into; however, the terms and conditions, whether they are express or implied, are not jointly determined and in terms of employee and employer obligations they are not equal in terms of their scope and coverage. In the vast majority of cases the employer is in the dominant bargaining position because they are offering employment. Hence the employer is able unilaterally to determine how the common law duties of the employee are to be fulfilled. The common law duties of the employee, as listed above, are clear and precise but open to considerable interpretation. In contrast, the common law obligations of the employer are imbued with the tenet of limited reasonableness, that is the obligations imposed on the employer should not be unreasonable. Thus, the general concept of reasonableness can only be tested in individual cases. As Hyman (1975: 24) argues, the symmetrical equality within the concept of self-determining individuals freely entering into contracts of employment is really asymmetrical because of the form which the notion of equality and freedom of entry actually take. By this we mean to suggest that equality before the law belies the market power which any potential employer has, that is individual equality before the law visualises firms who have access to necessarily expensive legal advice on the formulation of employment contracts and individuals bereft of such a capability on the same plane. As we pointed out in the first section of this chapter, within the contract of employment freedom and equality are fused with the traditional status bias of employment, and it is this which appears to reduce the equality of the employee and raise the equality of the employer. This de-alignment of equality creates the asymmetrical situation described by Hyman.

Statute law and the employment contract

There are two sources of statute law in the UK: Parliament and the European Union. One of the most significant pieces of domestic legislation is the 1978 Employment Protection (Consolidation) Act (EPCA). The EPCA defines a contract of employment as a contract of service between an employer and an employee. As we have already made clear, a contract of employment can come into being in three ways. It can be written or oral, in which case it is termed express, or a contract can be deduced through the conduct of the parties, in which case it is termed implied. Thus, the express terms of a contract of employment (that is, those which are stated to form part of the contract) do not have to be written down; however, under the TURER 1993 an employee must be given a written statement of the key terms within their contract of employment within eight weeks of employment commencing. The written statement must include information on the following items: the names of the employer and employee, that is the parties to the contract; the date on which the contract began; the methods by which pay is calculated, including any overtime or bonus payments; and the intervals of payment. The statement must also contain information on required working time. Lastly, items such as holiday entitlement, holiday pay, sickness arrangements, pension provisions and periods of notice must be clearly specified. In addition to these specified details the employee must also be made aware of procedures over discipline and grievance handling. The details of the discipline procedure must be specified or the employee must be directed to a document where they can find such details, for example, a collective bargaining agreement or company handbook.

The statement of express terms is not in itself a contract but merely a statement of the express terms within the contract which can itself be written, oral or implied. The express terms of the contract, as long as they are reasonable and legal, take precedence over all other implied terms such as those derived through custom and practice, but they cannot undermine implied terms incorporated by statute.

Statutory incorporated terms applicable to a contract of employment are designed to give an employee some 'property right' to their job. That is, 'rights' to be treated fairly and reasonably beyond the parameters of the employee's common law duties. Some of these property rights are technical in nature, for example the right to receive itemised pay slips, whereas others are concerned with the treatment of the employee as an individual within the wider employment relationship, for example, the right of complaint to an industrial tribunal and redress against racial and sexual discrimination in employment. We discuss the most significant statutory incorporated terms below.

The employment contract is assumed to be freely entered into. It is further assumed that employees are treated reasonably and equitably within the employment relationship. Notwithstanding these assumptions, discrimination within the employment relationship is widespread. Discrimination occurs where an employer treats one person less favourably than another in the same or similar circumstances, whether by intention or unintentionally, in respect of an employee's age, sex, colour, marital status, discrimination resulting from pregnancy or ethnic origin or religion.

Discrimination can occur in terms of remuneration and entry into the employment relationship or in terms of the working of an organisation's internal labour market, that is over issues of career progression and promotion. The most far-reaching statutory incorporated terms are those which relate to these areas.

The Equal Pay Act of 1970, as amended by the Equal Pay (Amendment) Regulations of 1983, inserts, that is incorporates, an equality clause into an employee's contract of employment where they are employed to perform 'like work', work rated as equivalent or work of equal value to that of another employee of the opposite sex in the same employment.

Thus, men and women must be treated the same where they are employed in the same employment organisation or at workplaces in the UK which follow common terms and conditions of employment. The object of the equality clause is to remove any terms within the contract over pay or other issues which are less favourable than those for other employees performing like work, equivalent work or work of equal value. Thus it is against the statutory incorporated terms of the 1970 Equal Pay Act to pay employees differently who perform the same work. For example, men and women performing like work, equivalent work or work of equal value cannot be given different hourly pay rates, other than in the case of genuine material or occupational differences which are not related to their sex. In the case of like work the situation is straightforward; however, in the case of work rated as equivalent under a job evaluation scheme or work not covered by job evaluation schemes which might be of equal value to the employer, the situation is more complex. Several organisations have had to redress their job evaluation schemes as a result of pressure from the Equal Opportunities Commission, who have argued that the basis of the job evaluation scheme within the organisation is sexist in that the hierarchy of jobs, and hence their evaluation, is more significantly related to the sex of the job occupant than the job itself.

The 1983 Equal Pay (Amendment) Regulations were significant in that they followed a long dispute between the UK and the EU. The dispute centred around whether or not the 1970 Act infringed the EU directive on equal pay and equality of treatment at work as defined in article 119. The issue turned on the voluntary nature of job evaluation schemes as defined within the 1970 Act. In the case of like work any discrimination is clear and easily remedied; job evaluation schemes were designed with the purpose in mind of work and its remuneration where the work could be rated as equivalent. On this basis the EU argued that work of 'equal value' to an employer (predominantly performed by one sex) could not be compared to other work, perhaps rated differently under a job evaluation scheme, even though it might be of equal value to the employer.

The effect of the Equal Value (Amendment) Regulations has been to widen the scope of the 1970 Equal Pay Act so that claims for equal pay can be heard by tribunals and courts on the basis of equal value to the employer of work performed by distinct jobs within one organisation. Thus, the regulations move beyond the limited nature of voluntary job evaluation schemes. As a result of several test cases it has been possible for check-out workers employed in supermarkets, who are predominantly women, to compare themselves to warehousemen in terms of their value to the organisation. This has resulted in all the major supermarket chains giving substantial pay increases to check-out workers in recent years.

In summary, the statutory incorporated terms covered by the Equal Pay Act, as amended, are now substantial and far reaching in their implications for many organisations. The amendment regulations have required aspects of human resource activity, such as job design, job evaluation and remuneration systems, to be re-evaluated in many organisations. We can now turn to the statutory incorporated terms within the sex discrimination legislation of 1975 and the Race Relations Act of 1976. The 1975 Sex Discrimination Act (SDA), as amended, covers discrimination in employment and other areas, for example training provision. Discrimination occurs where an employer or potential employer treats one sex, usually a woman, less favourably than another employee or potential employee, usually a man. In the field of employment sex discrimination is of three types: direct, indirect and discrimination through victimisation.

Direct discrimination occurs where an employer or potential employer makes it clear that applicants of one sex will not be considered for a post. The removal of direct intentional discrimination is the principal aim of the SDA. Direct discrimination can be against all women or married women, that is treating female married employees or potential female employees who are married less favourably than single men and women (discrimination on grounds of marital status).

Indirect discrimination occurs when apparently neutral conditions for employment or promotion are in effect, but which because of their make-up and nature affect one sex more than the other so as to be discriminatory. For example, apparently sex-neutral height and weight requirements, which in themselves are unrelated to the performance of a job, would fall into the category of indirect discrimination if they affected women more than men. The same situations hold in terms of promotion criteria which stipulate required periods of continuous service. These may have a discriminatory impact on married women who have taken career breaks to have a child.

Victimisation occurs in situations where an employee is treated less favourably because they have instituted proceedings against their employer under the Equal Pay Act or the SDA, that is as a result of seeking to enact statutory rights.

The Race Relations Act (RRA) of 1976 covers discrimination against an employee on account of colour, race, ethnic origin or national origin. The provisions of the RRA mirror those of the SDA in that discrimination can be direct, indirect or via victimisation. Thus a requirement that applicants must have lived in the UK for a defined period of time or hold certain qualifications which do not materially affect the performance of the job will generally be discriminatory. Recently several hundred West Indian London Transport workers were awarded retrospective damages for discrimination over the past twenty years because of the imposition of such unreasonable requirements.

Most employers have now instituted their own equal opportunities policies which are designed to combat race and sex discrimination at the workplace; however, we must point out that these alone may not debar a firm from liability in terms of sex and race discrimination. The statutory provisions in the Equal Pay Act, the SDA and the RRA are incorporated terms of employment designed to provide a right of access to an industrial tribunal where an employee has a complaint of discrimination in the terms and conditions of men and women by deeming every contract of employment to contain an equality clause which automatically modifies any term or condition of employment which is less favourable to one sex in comparison to another. There is no period of service necessary for an employee to acquire this statutory protection.

Other implied terms within a contract of employment arise through custom and practice or the relations between the parties. To be effective, custom and practice arrangements as incorporated terms of a contract of employment must be clear, precise and certain; however, they cannot undermine statutory provisions.

In summary, statutory incorporated terms within the provisions of the EPCA, the Equal Pay Act, the SDA and the RRA do go some way in reducing the asymmetrical nature of employer and employee common law obligations. However, some provisions, for example protection against unfair dismissal and redundancy, are subject to a qualification period of two years.

We can now relate the common law and statute law provisions of the contract of employment to the practice of HRM in the organisation in order to comment on how HRM initiatives might influence or be influenced by legal provisions relating to employment.

HRM and the contract of employment

We take as our starting point some of the issues and themes raised in Chapter 1. It is possible to argue that the overriding message within HRM centres on the premise that a greater appreciation of how human resources are deployed and organised within an organisation can have a direct influence on its level of competitive performance. This is certainly the prescriptive message in Guest (1989, 1991). If we look at this assumption in another way it is possible to argue that HRM is concerned with (re-)asserting the managerial prerogative over industrial relations within the workplace, and as Beardwell (1992) suggests, HRM appears to be a prescription for the management of industrial relations at the workplace. Two questions of particular relevance to our discussion of the contract of employment and the employment relationship come out of this series of assumptions and presumptions. First, which elements of industrial relations are specifically and generally most accessible to HRM at the workplace? Second, what effects might this more managerially determined approach to job regulation have on the contract of employment? We can proceed to discuss both questions in relation to two models of HRM developed in the UK, those of Guest (1987) and Storey (1992), both of which seek to delineate HRM from traditional personnel management and its contribution to the management of industrial relations at the workplace.

Both of these models share common elements in terms of their central beliefs and assumptions and preferred systems of management structure. Both models of HRM stereotype personnel management by suggesting that it centres on a highly bureaucratic system of defined work roles where job design is based on the division of labour which in consequence creates many separate job roles with many separately defined pay systems and conditions of work organisation. Hence, contracts and work rules are clearly delineated, with management initiative bound by the institutional procedures this delineation creates.

We can now relate this situation to the questions posed above. The HRM prescription suggests that a different consideration of management roles and work rules can transform this situation into something better in terms of organisational outputs. As a consequence, either improved internal efficiency in the allocation of human resources or the creation of an environment within the organisation where employees are not merely compliant but committed to the goals of the organisation will both have the effect of improving organisational performance.

It appears that the position of contract is central to the compliance-based system of personnel management, whereas within the HRM models its central significance is downplayed. In order to break the institutional bureaucracy of personnel management it would appear that management have to be able to exert their prerogative over work organisation rather than over pay and conditions. This is the case because if aspects of work organisation are removed from the plurality of existing employee relations other essential elements of job regulation will flow from it, for example strategic integration, fewer job categories, increased teamwork and harmonised employment conditions.

On the first question, the organisation of work is of prime concern if an organisation wishes to go down the HRM road. Kessler and Bayliss (1995: 264–266) suggest that changes in working methods and the pursuit of flexibility in the use of human resources were the main components of the managerial agenda during the 1980s. In terms of the argument presented here this is one of the main stimuli for a movement towards a so-called take-up of an HRM style in the management of workplace industrial relations; see Storey (1992; 1995). However, there is considerable debate on the coherence and extent of HRM take-up; equally, the potential for HRM-style initiatives to transform the workplace and push employees beyond contract is open to debate, see Marginson *et al.* (1993) for survey evidence and Purcell and Ahlstrand (1994) for case study data. In the latter it is argued that wider patterns of corporate governance associated with the multi-divisional firm are likely to dissipate and fragment the transformational potential of HRM via its decentralisation to separate business units and cost centres; that is decentralisation of the human resource function to disparate and financially separate business units debilitates the potential of any central coherence. Lastly, we can cite anecdotal evidence from the Railtrack RMT signal workers' dispute of 1995. Railtrack wished to wind up the signal workers' specific collective bargaining arrangements and create the potential for efficiency savings, raise productivity and secure signal workers' employment. Signal workers represented by the RMT would not accept new contracts of employment and pursued industrial action in support of their position. The failure of Railtrack to deliver new contractual arrangements illustrates the difficulty which managers encounter if they attempt to transform existing patterns of workplace relations in the face of a well-motivated and collectively coherent work group.

On the second question concerning the position of contract, both Guest (1987) and Storey (1992) suggest that HRM seeks to make work less contractually determined and less perfunctory in its performance. Guest concentrates on the psychological environment in his suggestion that the formality of personnel management and its associated bureaucracy create an air of compliance, whereas HRM seeks to generate an air of compliance which is in Storey's work termed 'beyond contract'. In many ways Guest (1987 and 1989) and Storey (1992) are looking at the same issues as Fox (1974). Fox examined the notion of 'high trust/low trust' and discretion as a critique of traditional Taylorist control systems based on low trust and low discretion. Fox was primarily concerned to show the limitations of low trust work environments because of the effects of alienation, distrust and the reinforcement of (contractual) regulation. The delineating factor between Fox on the one hand and Guest and Storey on the other is to be found in the effects of the form of management and regulation. Fox illustrates its limitations, whereas Guest and Storey are concerned to illustrate how management might minimise these limitations via re-orientation of work so as to downplay the regulatory effects of contract.

The central question for the reader to consider is what does this tell us about HRM? Is it about replacing existing forms of managerial regulation? Or is it a reconstitution of existing modes in an effort to raise worker performance and therefore improve organisational performance in terms of greater flexibility and higher productivity?

We might conclude that within HRM-style organisations contracts of employment are generally written and not carefully delineated. For example, job descriptions are more likely to be general in their make-up than highly specific. This is likely to be facilitated if work organisation is more unilaterally determined. There are likely to be fewer job grades, fewer demarcated areas of responsibility and therefore a greater use of teamwork. It is presumed that such innovations will encourage employees to improve their commitment to the organisation and go beyond contractual obligations. However, it must be emphasised that other components of the HRM philosophy must be set in place in tandem with these types of innovations if competitive performance is to improve. For example, the dissemination of and general pick-up of ideas and aims by general or line managers which is inherent to the Harvard model must take place. Similarly, employees must have some effective voice mechanism within the organisation, whether through briefing groups, appraisals, better training and development and other 'softer' aspects of HRM, in order that their willingness to be compliant and stay beyond contract is maintained.

Thus in summary the contract of employment enables the employer to exercise their managerial prerogative in alignment with the common law duties which employees have to them. It would appear that the prescription behind HRM is ideally suited to this end. The job of HRM practitioners is to do this in such a manner that they do not infringe employees' common law and statutory protections, while at the same time generating an air of collective consent to the intensification of the employment relationship through increased commitment and a willingness to go beyond what is necessary. This is clearly a fine line and any failure here can frustrate wider managerial objectives. For example, consider the long-running teachers' dispute in 1991–93 over national curriculum testing and individual student assessment in GCSE examinations. John Patten, the then Secretary of State for Education, argued that industrial action undertaken by teacher unions in support of their grievance over workloads was not a trade dispute but a politically motivated dispute inspired by opposition to the new national curriculum. Successive courts held that the teachers' grievance was a trade dispute and reasonable. Thus, the efforts of the then Department for Education and Science to instil an air of flexibility and improved pupil, school and teacher performance was held to be an unreasonable intensification of teacher workloads beyond their contractual commitments, which also had the effect of inhibiting effective classroom delivery of syllabus material.

The result of the teachers' industrial action and their legal victory was the non-completion of many national curriculum tests, the recruitment of part-time test markers and a change of minister at the Department for Education and Science.

OPERATIONAL CONTROL IN THE EMPLOYMENT RELATIONSHIP

In this section we consolidate our arguments, detailed in the previous sections, that the employment relationship is a process of socio-economic exchange. This section is divided into three parts; first we look at the issue of management and the management process. This discussion is pursued on two dimensions. Initially management functions and their prescription are examined, leading to a brief discussion of scientific management techniques. Beyond this initial introduction the process of management as a function within the UK's industrial capitalism is examined. This discussion leads us into an examination of the effects of scientific management on the labour process. Additionally we pose the question, 'What do managers do?' This issue is further detailed in the second part of this section, which is an issue of debate on the management process and the emergence of centralised workplaces. The final part of this section looks at management as the realisation of legal authority and control within the employment relationship. This discussion takes into consideration issues such as moral involvement, collective consent and participation. Additionally this discussion looks at the emergence of organisation-specific employee relations policies which are in part designed to assist the employer to realise their legal control over employees as vested in the contract of employment. In this respect we pay particular reference to the use of HRM techniques.

Management and management functions

Management and the functions of management both appear to be so obvious that they do not need prescriptive or critical evaluation. People who work within the employment relationship are subject to management and may on occasions operate in managerial mode themselves. Thus the process of management is something which surrounds us all. As a consequence of this presence we all think we have a good idea of what it's all about and who is a good manager. Asking people what a manager does is rather like asking new appointees in their induction programme what a grievance procedure represents. The same might be the case in relation to the issue of management. Thus, the process of management contains many elements with which managers may not in fact be familiar.

Management can be defined as the administration of business concerns and covers the persons engaged in this process, whereas a manager can be defined as someone who controls the activities of a person (OED, 1982). In order to fulfil the role of management or manager a person must perform several functions.

The functions of management can be summarised under three main headings. First, as already alluded to in the above definition of a manager, management is concerned with control. In the first two sections of this chapter we quite clearly stated that, once a worker enters the employment relationship and offers their personal service to an employer, they are under the control and direction of that employer. Thus in order to work effectively an employee has to be directed and controlled in the delivery and performance of their work.

Direction and control can be undertaken in a variety of ways. One is direct supervision, for example the use of supervisors and inspectors in textile factories. Technical supervision exists through the use of methods of work organisation, job design, job descriptions and the use of technology to regulate and oversee the performance of work – an example of the latter might be the use of scanners at supermarket check-outs. Lastly, control can be implemented through the use of bureaucratic controls such as the completion of time sheets, the use of appraisal schemes, quality circles, team briefings, TQM and follow-up meetings. Essentially a controlled performance is required in order for an organisation, whether in the private or public sector, to be efficient and competitive within the wider framework of industrial capitalism.

The second function of management can be described as coordination. A central feature of the employment relationship in centralised workplaces is the division of labour. The idea behind the division of labour centres on the productive benefits which are derived from the process of employee specialisation. Specialised employees are assumed to be more productive in their work and at the same time have the opportunity to earn higher levels of wages, if their wage is related to the quantity of production. It is important to point out that Adam Smith, who conceptualised the division of labour, stated that its internal benefits were potential in their advantages – in other words, for the potential benefits to be realised, the division of labour requires management and supervision.

The division of labour has to be managed. Managers have to coordinate the number of workers required in order that the potential benefits of the division of labour can be realised. Thus the second function of management is to coordinate human and capital resources in an efficient and productive manner. The third function of management can be summarised under the heading of motivation and compliance.

In the first section of this chapter we identified the difference between labour power and labour. To recap, we argued that an employer via the contract of employment buys an employee's labour power. The employer then has to transform this into effective performance by creating either goods or services which can be sold at a profit. This issue is central to the sociological dimension of the employment relationship. This is the case because the employer has to realise legally vested superiority, that is power within the employment relationship, by controlling and coordinating employees. In addition, and more crucially, management must acquire the collective consent of employees to their subordinate position within the employment relationship whereby they are controlled and coordinated. Employees can be motivated to accept directed control through various remuneration and participation schemes. These issues are discussed below in relation to the codification of management functions in management science. Additionally this issue is further detailed in the third part of this section on the realisation of managerial authority.

Although we have discussed the functions of management under several headings, at this stage we are still lacking a framework within which to locate and visualise the application of these functions. This is where we need to examine the prescription behind management science.

Management science

Management science seeks to codify and rationalise a framework within which the functions of management can operate. Additionally, management science is a quantitative academic discipline. In the functional sense management science is a prescription which seeks to legitimise the superior position of management within the employment relationship. It therefore emphasises the importance of the managerial prerogative. Thus, property ownership in the form of a business gives the employer and their management agents the authority to direct factors of production. In respect of human resources this authority is clearly derived from the authority relation vested in the employer by the contract of employment.

The most well-known theory of management science is that of Frederick Taylor (1911). Taylor argued correctly, if somewhat egotistically, that prior to his work no one had studied and visualised work in a scientific manner, thus he described all previous forms of management as 'ordinary' and distinguished them from his principles of scientific management.

We have defined a manager as someone who controls the work of others. This definition appears to be very similar to that of scientific management: 'The science of the management of others' work under capitalist employment relations.' In order to be able to do this an employee who operates in managerial mode must be able to fulfil the functions of management in three ways.

First, management must dissociate the labour process from skilled workers, in short management needs to gather all necessary knowledge on the organisation and deployment of work. This will enable those who operate in managerial mode to reduce work to a series of laws, procedures and rules which are arrived at and varied by systematic study. The objective behind the dissociation is to make the labour process dependent on management, that is to reinforce their prerogative and superior position as vested in the contract of employment. The first principle directly leads to the second one.

If management is able to dissociate the labour process from labour it succeeds in separating the conception of work from its execution. In other words, those who operate in managerial mode conceptualise work whereas other employees execute it. By effectively separating the conception and execution of work, Taylor argued that the methods of work and their pace could be dictated by management. In both the first and second principles of scientific management Taylor implicitly follows the division of labour as formulated by Smith. Perhaps the most well-known advocate of Taylor's ideas was Henry Ford. The car assembly line was created from a fusion of Smith's division of labour and Taylor's scientific management.

The third principle in Taylor's prescription was the monopoly of knowledge by management in order to control each step in the labour process. Taylor followed the arguments put forward by Smith, in particular the assertion that the division of labour would improve productivity via specialisation. Specialisation and improved productivity also give the employee the opportunity to earn high wages. Therefore the prescription of scientific management is in the interests of the employer in that it facilitates effective work by employees leading to maximum profits, as well as being in the employees' interest in the sense of improved earning potential.

The idea of scientific management as formulated by Taylor has been criticised on many levels. First, it treats labour as purely economic in the sense that all employees want from employment is an effective wage. Other management theorists, in particular the human relations school, have heavily criticised this assumption and argued that a preoccupation with economic return is short-sighted in terms of the effective realisation of all management functions. Braverman (1974) has also been a notable critic of Taylor.

Braverman has argued that the prescription behind Taylor, while it might have an overall efficiency motive, has many degrading effects on labour. In summary, he argues that the primary motive behind Taylor's prescription is the need to deskill skilled labour. Another general criticism of Taylor centres on the overt rationality and simplicity of his prescription. In particular he fails to consider the likelihood of effective individual or collective worker resistance through trade unions or established spheres of worker control in the labour process. This point has been made with particular vigour in the case of the UK, where trade union power was in part created by skilled unions wresting some control over their labour process from the employer. It has been argued (Clarke, 1991) that we need to examine the principles of scientific management in terms of the bigger picture of capitalist production relations.

In summary, Clarke argues that the process of management only becomes necessary once capitalist production relations, that is centralised workplaces, the employment relationship and the use of the division of labour, become naturalised as the only way to organise work. Thus, Clarke (1991) derives the need for prescriptive management science from the omnipresence of industrial capitalism and its production relations. These points are all covered in more detail below where we ask the question 'what do managers do?' and discuss the labour process.

To summarise, this section has examined the notion of management as a set of functional skills which are necessary to legitimise and reinforce the authority of the employer. This authority is legally ordained in the contract of employment. In essence the functions of management are codified within theories of management science such as that of Taylor. The techniques of scientific management are designed to give employees who operate in management roles control over all aspects of the production process. In tandem the functions of management and theories of management science assist management in turning labour power purchased through the contract of employment into useful and productive labour performance in terms of goods and services which can then be sold in the market.

The management of industrial relations at the workplace, and as such the prescription of HRM, is seen as the most effective way in which management can turn contracted labour power into productive labour. In the 1990s new managerial strategies and HRM in particular are visualised as new methods by which management can transform performance. However, data material in WIRS3 and the second company level industrial relations survey (Marginson *et al.*, 1993; 1995) and anecdotal reporting of individual industrial disputes suggest two caveats. First, the prescription behind HRM is not necessarily being taken up and where it is, the take-up is disparate and not integrated (see also Sisson, 1993 and Purcell and Alhstrand, 1994). Second, traditional patterns of corporate governance, such as the central power of the accounts function and the M–form structure of corporate organisation, suggest that in the UK HRM is becoming an adjunct to performance management and has only a qualitative effect on economic performance as distinct from any quantitative effects. That is, a concentration on the reconfiguration of labour cannot necessarily improve quantitative economic performance and competitive advantage, which are in the main derived from improved capital investment and the upskilling of labour. For a sector-wide case study in support of this see Guest and Peccei (1994), Purcell and Alhstrand (1994) for further case studies, and Armstrong (1995) and Purcell (1995) for general arguments.

We now expand our discussion of management by locating the function of management within the UK's industrial capitalism, which is followed by a discussion of management in relation to the labour process.

Management and the UK's industrial capitalism

In the first section of this chapter it was argued that contractual employment and its regulation occurred because of two factors: first, the formalisation of employment which downgraded the strictly paternal master and servant relationship; second, and relatedly, the emergence of the firm or centralised workplace necessitated the active management of work performed by employees. In this section we have expanded on this point to illustrate how the management process is designed to regulate employment by turning labour power into productive labour. If we accept the arguments of Coase (1937) that the market process determines which form of contractual regulation governs the relations between individuals, that is commercial or employment relations, we have also to accept that the requirement for the employment of labour and its regulation is derived from the market mechanism.

The arguments put forward by Coase are correct at the level of general economic analysis; however, because economic theory is concerned with rationally defined efficiency, it fails to consider the social side of the employment relationship. In short, the pre-occupation with efficiency overlooks or belies any consideration of power within the employment relationship. This leads us to consider two questions of controversy and debate: why did the centralised workplace emerge? And what is the relation of management to this emergence?

Controversies and debates: The centralised workplace and management

We can discuss the first question by reviewing the contrasting arguments of Landes (1986) and Marglin (1974). This discussion will enable the relationship of management to the centralised workplace to be visualised in two ways.

Marglin argues that the movement from pre-capitalist (and therefore pre-capitalist production relations) to centralised workplaces was largely inspired by a need on the part of capitalists to acquire greater control over the production process by using the division of labour centrally as distinct from de-centrally via cottage industry and the putting-out system. This argument contrasted strongly with the orthodox account of the movement to centralised workplaces as formulated by Landes (1969 and 1986). Essentially Landes (1986) argues that the movement to the centralised workplace was inspired by the needs of the market and its scale of operation. To put it crudely, Landes argues that the dynamic of the UK's industrialisation process became too big for existing forms of production relations such as cottage industry and putting out. Thus, the movement to centralised workplaces was motivated by the logic of economic efficiency in the sense described by Coase. This movement to the factory resulted in the extended use of the division of labour and eventually the deployment of scientific management techniques. Out of these two developments came the emergence of management and hierarchy within the employment relationship.

Landes and Marglin agree that the movement to the factory resulted in the use of the division of labour in an extended fashion; however, they disagree on the basis of the movement and its effects. Marglin argues that the use of the division of labour was not motivated by efficiency considerations in the Coasian sense, but by a desire on the part of capitalists to gain greater control over the production process than would have been possible under existing production relations. Thus, in terms of our perspective that the employment relationship is a socio-economic exchange, Marglin concentrates on the social side. In summary, Marglin emphasises the division of labour as a form of control and power. Neither of these was motivated by a concern for economic efficiency.

Landes (1986) accepts some of Marglin's arguments but counter-argues that the extended use of the division of labour led to hierarchy and was itself inspired by efficiency criteria because that was the way it happened! Thus, Landes concentrates on the economic side of the socio-economic exchange and downplays considerations of power and control as initiators, but accepts that a power relation does exist.

A second theme particular to Marglin (1974) centres on the lack of a technical role for management at the workplace within the division of labour. Marglin (1974) argues that the role of management within the division of labour is not derived from the pursuit of economic efficiency but from a desire to control the work process of employees, which could not be satisfactorily undertaken through traditional work systems such as cottage industries, putting out and subcontracting. This latter point is significant because during the 1980s and 1990s we have seen the widespread use of putting out and subcontracting in a more modern form of competitive tendering and self-employment. One reason to explain this process is the more developed protection a large firm is able to obtain through improvements in contractual regulation of personal services. The prescription behind the notion of the flexible firm as popularised by Atkinson (1984) cites this development as one method by which firms can acquire greater flexibility. (See Chapter 3 for further discussion of flexibility.)

If we ally the arguments of Marglin to those of Clarke (1991) we can add further substance to the view that management is only necessary once capitalist production relations become the norm. Clarke argues that this point is overlooked by economists because of their primary concern with efficiency within market economies. Hence, micro-economics naturalises the market process and the division of labour in an effort to illustrate its omnipresent prescription. We can also derive management and the functions of management science as essential for efficiency within market economies. The pursuit of efficiency and the concentration on the economic side of the wider socio-economic exchange within the employment relationship have caused economists to underplay the effects of the drive for efficiency on those who are employed and subject to management direction under a contract of employment. That is, the rational actor model views enterprise and labour as inanimate factors of production and therefore ignores the reality of workplace relationships where management and employees act in less than a rational manner. We recall that management direction is concerned to actualise the legal control vested in the contract of employment and therefore centres on transforming labour power into productive labour performance. We can further this discussion by briefly examining the labour process, an area which is more comprehensively covered in Chapter 3.

The labour process and management

When we refer to the 'labour process' we are seeking to describe the process of work and how it seeks to satisfy the social needs of humans in their societal form. This process has three elements: first, how the activities of individual humans are directed to work; second, how work is performed – here the focus is on how natural objects or raw materials are transformed into a more useful state; third, how technology is allied to the direction of work. Thus, essentially the labour process describes how individuals who perform work interact with the means of production within which their work or labour process operates.

Work occurs in all societal forms whether they are tribal or industrial. The discussion and debate which surround the labour process centre on how the means of production are controlled and organised. It is likely that the ordering of economic activity is particular to specific societal forms. In terms of market economies the arguments of Marx (1958) are of particular relevance.

In terms of the control and organisation of the means of production, Marx distinguishes between cooperative production and manufacturing production where the division of labour becomes effective. The delineating factor between the two centres on the directed activity of workers. In cooperative production labour may be involved in holistic production, whereas in industrial economies individual labour units concentrate on the production of one component or element of a good. This delineation between the two production modes tells us something about the social relations of production. The social relations of production are derived from the ownership and control of the means of production. In cooperative production directed work activity, the raw materials on which the work is directed and the instruments of work may all be owned by one group. On the other hand, within manufactured production the materials and the means of production are likely to be owned by a second group, the capitalist entrepreneur who may be the manager or who in larger work organisations employs managers to realise the productive labour performance of employees in the form of profit. Marx made a valuable contribution to the evaluation of work by locating work and its management in the context of market economies. In market economies a specific form of the social relations of production operates. This specific form is centred on the contractually determined employment relationship described in the previous two sections.

Marx made two points of profound significance in this regard. First, the market mechanism within which work is constituted operates as a competitive anarchy. Second, in order for capital to reproduce itself it has to reproduce labour. In combination these two points suggest that work can never be free-standing in market economies. Because the market mechanism is competitively based, it puts all employers on a competitive basis within their defined market. This is one reason why productivity improvements and management control and motivation strategies are all central to work within market economies.

Marx therefore evaluated work as a socio-economic exchange. In terms of economic analysis Marx illustrates how the apparently docile market mechanism dictates the need for continual improvements in productivity in order that profits can be earned to enable capital to reproduce itself. In terms of the sociological side of work Marx illustrated the contradictory nature of its economic requirements. First, capital has to employ labour, pay it and therefore reproduce it. In the context of the UK and most other capitalist economies this requirement has always been problematic and is indeed the basis of industrial relations as a subject. Second, as detailed above Marx identified that the anarchy of the market mechanism would force employers to intensify work through improvements in productivity and better management control. In addition Marx argued that these economic requirements would actually undermine capitalism. In particular the need to reduce wages, the introduction of new technology and the growth of urban unemployment are all visualised as inhibiting the reproduction of capital because they inhibit the reproduction of labour. This situation would either lead to the overthrow of capitalism through a workers' revolution or see market economies in periodic crisis. Once in a crisis market economies have to restructure themselves. HRM can be visualised as one method by which management is seeking to restructure employment in market economies during the 1990s.

Within the confines of industrial capitalism the entrepreneur has to be concerned with efficiency and control as dictated by the market mechanism. As we have seen in our discussion of Landes (1986) and Marglin (1974), this is one reason why the centralised workplace emerged. Landes saw this movement as an opportunity to improve efficiency within the market, whereas Marglin concentrated on the opportunities for greater entrepreneurial control over the labour process. Sisson (1989: 7) suggests that from the labour process perspective the management of people is essentially concerned with the instruments of management control. Thus, from the labour process perspective management is a prerequisite function of industrial capitalism which is concerned to deliver economic efficiency on the controlled terms of the social relations of production found in market economies.

In summary, work is a universal activity which can take place in a variety of societal settings, each of which has its own social relations of production. These relations are derived from the ownership of the materials and means of production, which in tribal and other non-industrial societies can be inclusive but which in industrial society are likely to be exclusive. This is not to say that all societal types prior to industrial capitalism were without exploitation. The distinction between pre-industrial and industrial society centres on the mode of exploitation. In this chapter we are primarily concerned to illustrate the role of contract and management within the process of efficient and controlled production, which from the labour process perspective are mechanisms of exploitation.

Classical political economists such as Smith, Ricardo, Mill and Malthus were essentially concerned with the regulation of the employed class so as to create efficient market conditions. Marx, too, was a political economist, but his point of departure was his, perhaps, undeveloped argument that employment was a socio-economic exchange. As a consequence of this Marx looked not at the technical efficiency to be derived from the use of the division of labour, but at its effects on labour who operate within the social relations of industrial capitalism. To this end the differentiating concept of labour power and labour performance is essential.

The market mechanism dictates that goods must be exchanged at a market value, that is at a price greater than their use value. This difference is created by the surplus value of labour. The level of surplus value depends not on the functional input of labour but the intensity of its labour power, that is the pace at which work, whether manual or non-manual, is performed. This issue is significant and is often termed productivity or output per person per hour of employment. This concern is inherent to the market mechanism; in consequence, systems of management control to ensure productive delivery become essential.

Taylor (1911) argued that the use of what he described as scientific management techniques would best ensure an effective, productive delivery of goods within market economies. As we have already suggested, Braverman (1974) provided a powerful critique of Taylorism in an effort to illustrate that his central theme was the predominant need to deskill work via the separation of the conception and execution of work. Simultaneously this process reduces or removes the control which skilled workers have over their labour process. Thus, for Braverman, the essential concern of management as a function within industrial capitalism is to get a controlled work performance which stimulates economic efficiency within the market process. Edwards (1979) amplified on the issue of control by discussing different types of control, ranging from simple supervisory controls, technical controls which affect the pace and direction of work and bureaucratic controls which are likely to be organised via the personnel or HRM department. These controls are designed to proceduralise and codify work functions.

The principal questions for our discussion centre on the issue of to what degree the contract of employment facilitates management control over the labour process, and to what degree the management process is autonomous or pre-determined in its effort to realise labour power bought through the contract of employment. This is really a question of interpretation and perspective. However, the central issue revolves around the degree to which one accepts or denies that employees operating in management functions have autonomy and discretion on how they fulfil their roles. That is, to what extent management and the deployment of management strategies and structures can enact strategic choice. The notion of strategic choice is central to all models of HRM and suggests that managers are capable of responses to their competitive environment which are independent of historically and institutionally formed patterns of corporate governance, broader public policy enacted by the state and entrenched patterns of industrial relations management. In support of strategic choice, 'exemplar firms' are often generalised as the norm, for example British Airways under Lord King, British Leyland under Michael Edwardes, British Coal and British Steel under Ian McGregor, Asda under Archie Norman and Burtons under Ralph Halpern. Notwithstanding these exemplar firms, a key issue is the degree to which market opportunities and relations dictate choices made by firms as distinct from individual strategic choices. We expand on this point in our discussion of the direct control versus responsible autonomy debate within the study of the labour process.

We can examine the first question by arguing that labour is animate and therefore cannot be considered in the same way as other factors of production. Therefore labour has to be managed, even though legally it is in a subordinate position within the contractually defined employment relationship. Notwithstanding this point, the management of employees operates within a variety of perspectives, for example plural and unitary. The former recognises that employees have an interest in their labour process and its management; thus employers may recognise unions and in effect share the management process. Therefore the types of rules discussed by Edwards (1979) may in part be jointly determined. Within the unitary perspective the managerial prerogative is emphasised, whereby to varying degrees employees are excluded from the management function and may only be consulted in management decisions. What Braverman (1974) overlooked was the need to contextualise his arguments by examining the specific development of industrial capitalism within particular market economies. In the UK, for example, skilled craftsmen developed considerable control over their labour processes, which in some cases management had great difficulty in breaking.

In the postwar period the central significance of the frontier of control at the individual workplace frustrated the systematic introduction and use of scientific management techniques without an employee input. Thus, in relation to the first point, we have to make it clear that the contract of employment only facilitates management control over the labour process in the legal sense. To summarise, management failure and effective worker resistance, however sectional, cannot be overlooked as factors of frustration to the goal of management control. See Tomlinson and Tiratsoo (1993) where the effects of management reticence and failure as well as labour resistance are surveyed in relation to postwar reconstruction of British industry and its management.

The second question turns on the issue of how control in the employment relationship can be derived. In some respects the arguments of Braverman are reductionist and omnipresent in their view on the management process. The arguments may be correct at the general level of aims but in terms of processes there may be other ways. Friedman (1977) has argued that employers may derive operational control within the employment relationship through a process of stimulating 'responsible autonomy', which is likely to play down some of the 'direct control' aspects of Braverman. This is precisely what HRM attempts to do. In many respects the arguments of Guest and Storey detailed above are, in the context of HRM, making the same argument as Friedman. In the argument of Guest and Storey the focus is on how HRM can improve operational control by stimulating motivation, identification and organisational culture. These processes seek to align the goals of the employee with those of the organisation, whereas Friedman is more concerned with the specific organisation of work rather than its organisational context. Similarly, Fox (1974 and 1985) has discussed the issues of high trust work atmospheres, collective consent and participation. In summary, the conclusion we draw is two-fold. First, at the level of generality, managers within market economies are concerned with ensuring a controlled and efficient performance of the labour process within the wider social relations of production. Second, and significantly, there may be a variety of ways in which this can be achieved, ranging from deskilling as emphasised by Braverman and utilised by organisations such as McDonald's and the food retailing industry, to the more sophisticated HRM approaches employed by organisations such as Gent, IBM, Pedigree Pet Foods and Bechtel. We can now move on to discuss the notion of collective consent within the employment relationship and the contribution of HRM in this process.

Management and the realisation of legal authority and control

We have established that the legal authority to control the employment relationship which is vested in the employer via the contract of employment does not equate to operational control over the employment relationship. Management has to transform the labour power it purchases into productive labour performance which produce goods and services that can be sold through the market mechanism. Here we make some brief comments on the realisation of control within the employment relationship in order to produce a regulated and disciplined human resource performance.

As Fox (1985) points out, management strategy is a blend of coercion and consent. Both these issues relate to the social side of the socio-economic exchange which is the employment relationship. This blend occurs because both consent and control relate to power.

Coercion represents the naked use of power to determine a situation. In the context of the employment relationship it may take the form of a highly controlled work environment or the use of high profile direct control by the employer or their agents, for example supervisors. In highly controlled work environments the social technology of the work, that is management structures which seek to order workplace behaviour and workplace relationships, combines with material technology to create a disciplined regime of work, for example the use of bar coding in virtually all types of retailing, the use of information technology and automation within banks and the deskilled working environment of fast-food restaurants. In these cases and many others the combination of material and social technology creates a highly disciplined work environment and is in some respects an expression of power in the management process. This does not mean to say that coercion is highly visible in these types of working situation. As stated above, management strategy is a fusion of coercion and consent.

By consent we mean voluntary agreement and compliance. Within the context of the employment relationship we are referring to agreement and consent to management authority. Thus, collective consent to the exercise of management authority and control is our essential concern. Management has to legitimise its decisions to the employed labour force. At one extreme this can be done through total coercion, while at the other it can be derived through total consent; however, it is likely to be realised within a continuum.

If we move outside the framework of Braverman (1974), we accept that management can be in control of the employment relationship without placing a total emphasis on the issue of control via deskilling and degrading labour. It is possible, therefore, to visualise a situation where management can legitimise its authority and get the workforce to consent to changes in the management of job regulation which may have the benefits described by Braverman without all the attendant negatives. This is partly the line developed by Friedman (1977) in his critique of Braverman, which highlights the notion of responsible autonomy. The degree and level of responsible autonomy given to workers may depend on the type of work they perform. 'High discretion' workers who have a professional standing or status may be subject to less overt control within the employment relationship. In these types of employment control may be self-imposed or imposed by professional discipline or by vocational ethics. These forms of control are less related to the contract of employment and direct managerial supervision, but nonetheless are powerful controlling agents. Labour process theorists can counter-argue that the control and organisation of the white-collar or professionalised labour process is only different to that of the blue-collar or manual employees in its form, not in its objective. For further elaboration of this position see Hyman and Price (1983) and Smith, Knights and Wilmott (1991).

In order successfully to downplay the coercive side of job regulation some form of participation within the employment relationship is necessary. By participation we mean the participation of non-managerial employees within the decision-making process of an organisation. Thus, participation can represent a situation which accepts the presence of conflicting and differing views within an organisation; alternatively it can express the notion of a community of interests and common goals. In the postwar period the preferred form of participation within the majority of employment relationships in the UK and most other Western European states was some nationally determined combination of proceduralised personnel management and collective bargaining. Thus, participation tended to operate on a collective basis through the employee voice mechanism of trade unions. The issue of collective bargaining is discussed in further detail in Chapter 12.

Two points need to be made in connection with participation in the employment relationship and its contractual regulation. First, the existence of participation in whatever form, be it collective bargaining, profit sharing or quality circles, represents attempts to realise managerial control and stimulate an effective work performance without a complete reliance on direct control mechanisms. Second, more individualised forms of participation may only be partial in the generation of consent. For example, they may not be subject to the process of negotiation but merely part of what the organisation 'gives' in terms of 'soft' HRM for the benefits of 'hard' HRM.

As part of the process of changing or supplementing the traditional form of employee participation in the UK and other European countries, we have seen the emergence of employee relations as an adjunct to the management of job regulation operating at the level of the organisation. We can define employee relations by following the position of Marchington and Parker (1990: 7–8).

Marchington and Parker define the emergence of employee relations in three ways. First, it has arrived through slippage, that is it may be the politically correct term to use when describing industrial relations. This position bears some similarity to that of Guest (1989) on the correctness of the term HRM *vis-à-vis* personnel management. Second, employee relations covers that part of the personnel function, as described by practition-ers, which is concerned with the regulation of employees at organisation level. Such policies can be collective or individual in nature. Third, although employee relations is concerned with job regulation, that is the substance of industrial relations, its focus is less on the process but more concerned with the management of employees or the managerial perspective on the employment relationship.

In consequence, the rise in the significance of employee relations as an active manager-ial concern has stimulated an alteration in the form of employee participation within many organisations.

The aim of organisation-specific employee relations policies is to generate active employee involvement and consent in the process of change at the workplace as well as its general management. Within the HRM rubric this may take the form of seeking to create a high trust working atmosphere and/or giving employees greater responsibility, or what Friedman refers to as responsible autonomy. These movements have two effects on the realisation of management control. Both are significant to our discussion of con-tract and the employment relationship.

First, the new forms of participation tend to be based around small work teams if not individuals. These modes of participation have decollectivised the work process at the workplace; in consequence they have reduced the central significance of any trade union presence.

Second, any moves to individualise employee participation have an effect on the organisation of work. In this respect we could argue that individualised employee partici-pation is part of what the organisation gives in terms of 'soft' HRM for the benefits of 'hard' HRM. One such benefit is greater flexibility in the use and deployment of labour. The terms 'use and deployment' represent work organisation which, as Kessler and Bayliss (1995) argue, were major areas of the management agenda for change during the 1980s. This process of change often involved removing elements of work organisation from the collective bargaining process, thereby making employee participation on this subject more individually based or less collective, whichever you prefer!

Our discussion of the management process and the realisation of controlled work per-formances has illustrated that work has to be managed, monitored and regulated. By examining the issues of coercion, consent and participation in either collective or individ-ual mode, it becomes clear that management can seek to realise operational efficiency and control over the employed workforce in a variety of ways. The choice of methods may in part depend on the type of employee under consideration and the type of change being sought. HRM techniques are the latest or current vogue prescription to assist manage-ment in this process. The central message which comes out of this brief examination of the realisation of efficiency and control within the employment relationship centres on the primary significance of these concerns within the employment relationship as it oper-ates within market economies. Much of this chapter has focused on the UK, but the aim of the management process within market economies in other European states is much the same; however, the processes of realisation may differ in form.

Summary

In this section we have consolidated our argument, developed in the first two sections, on the employment relationship as a process of socio-economic exchange. Our argument centres on the complex nature of the employment relationship in terms of its management. Thus we argue that the management process within the efficiency criteria as determined by the economics of the market mechanism is not the mere amalgamation of inanimate factors of production, but is a real process within the overall efficiency criteria of market-oriented industrial capitalism.

We developed this argument by examining the role and nature of the management function and process. This discussion was gauged in terms of the prescription behind management science. We then subjected the prescription of management science to some critical evaluation and came to the conclusion that, while it was basically correct in terms of economic analysis, its operation could not be simple and deterministic.

We furthered these arguments by looking at the emergence of the centralised workplace and the technical role of management or otherwise in this process. Finally, we briefly commented on how the management process within the production relations of market economies seeks to realise economic efficiency and control in a less deterministic fashion than the way described by Taylor and criticised by Braverman.

CONCLUSION

This chapter has done three things. First, it has established the central significance of contract within the management and regulation of the employment relationship. Within contract the employment relationship is visualised as an essentially private exchange between employer and employees. In the second section of this chapter we explained how the form of contractual regulation through the common law and associated statute law confirms this visualisation. In the third section we broadened our discussion of the employment relationship into a process of a socio-economic exchange. The purpose of this section was to illustrate the weakness of a purely economic and contractual visualisation of employment. We detailed the emergent nature of the employment relationship in the UK's market economy to illustrate how the management of employees has become essential if employers are to realise their contractually vested authority.

Human resource management appears to be central to all three areas. As this chapter has illustrated, contractual regulation and the wider employment relationship are derived in specific states over a long period of time. This derivation and its institutionalisation form the context within which HRM has to operate. Thus, although the prescription of HRM appears to be universal, its application and effectiveness must be conditioned by the context within which it seeks to operate. Therefore, in the UK, the prescription of HRM cannot be free-standing; it is conditioned by the specific forms of employment regulation inherent to particular economies. Hence we can only fully appreciate the notion of HRM and the new industrial relations by examining what came before them.

SUMMARY

● The contractual relationship between the organisation and its employees regulates the socio-economic exchange of the wider employment relation. The concept of contract can be visualised as an agreement between two or more parties which is enforceable by means of three elements: offer, acceptance and consideration. In the case of the contract of employment this is expressed in terms of an offer of engagement, an agreement to sign the terms of the offer, and the subsequent exchange of labour for wages as consideration. To be valid a contract must be reasonable, legal and between consenting parties.

● The philosophy of contract is based on market individualism, expressed as each individual's own best judgement of their own interests. Thus freedom of contract assumes that individuals are self-determining who are primarily self-interested. Employment contracts differ from other contractual forms in that they are based on notions of authority, legitimacy and managerial prerogative. Thus, the individual employee is not simply agreeing to a contract as a free agent but also accepts that managerial authority will be part of the contract. This acceptance by an employee of a relationship as a subordinate to a superior marks the contract of employment as different from other contracts for services where equality between the supplier and the purchaser is assumed. Further, employment is typified by one dominant mode of contract – the employment contract – rather than millions of independent contracts between firms and employees, because employers tend to buy 'labour' as a generic commodity from individuals.

● Both the common law and statutory regulation underpin this socio-economic exchange. The former provides the interpretive element that derives from judge-made rulings; the latter provides the regulative framework provided by Parliament. Both types of law are concerned with the concept of 'reasonableness'. European Union law now provides a further context in which UK law must operate.

● How far does HRM, as a managerially derived agenda, change the nature of the contract? If it is accepted that HRM has been concerned with the managerial prerogative and the reorganisation of work, then it clearly has a large impact. This is emphasised where employers seek to use HRM to go 'beyond contract' and pursue flexibility and compliance which are over and above what the contract requires. Thus HRM-style organisations may well have less specifically defined contracts in order to achieve greater fluidity and commitment in the way that tasks are performed. This becomes even more important in the context of debate over the labour process, where the role of management is viewed as not simply a partner in a contractual relationship, but as the prime mover in the control and organisation of work. The employment contract has, in these circumstances, to be evaluated against a background of the wider issues in managerial control and the employment relationship more broadly defined.

ACTIVITY

Buxford University has instituted the following 'contractual' agreement between staff and students governing the substantive and procedural organisation of tutorials:

Each week two of the fifteen students in any tutorial group are required to present a paper on the topic for discussion that particular week. Students who are not presenting the paper are expected to read material appropriate to the discussion as directed in the course document and the prescribed course textbook. Lastly, all 15 students in a particular group are required to attend and positively contribute to the learning process in the one-hour class.

Each tutorial group has one student convenor who is responsible for liaising with staff on student concerns. The sanctions available to staff in the case of this contract being breached are rebuke which can be followed by exclusion.

EXERCISES

1 Assume you are the group representative. A student comes to you after having been excluded by the tutor. The particular student claims that they did not breach the collective agreement but merely chose not to contribute to the group discussion on subjects they found less interesting.

   How would you go about representing this student? What measures would you need to take in order to clarify the situation and determine if the contractual nature of the tutorial system had been breached?

2 In what ways do you think that the tutorial agreement described above gives the tutor operational control over the tutorial process? In what ways might it replicate the division between legal control and operational control over the employment relationship discussed in this chapter?

3 In what sense is the tutorial contract valid? In what way does its formulation 'shadow' the establishment of the terms and conditions within an employment contract?

QUESTIONS

1 How is a contract formed in the following situations:
   (a) Buying a magazine in a newsagents?
   (b) An offer of full-time permanent employment?
   (c) The hiring of a subcontractor to perform maintenance work on a firm's computers?

2 How does employment protection legislation actually protect full-time and part-time employees?

3 Do you think that the employment protection legislation provides for effective and reasonable protection of employees?

4 How does contract assist management in the control of the labour process?

5 How would you interpret the Marglin/Landes debate in terms of:
   (a) the managerial prerogative;
   (b) the emergence of centralised workplaces?

6 Is Braverman correct, or are his views too general to be applied with any consistency to particular economies?

7 Is employment protection legislation necessary in an era of HRM?

EXERCISES

1 Outline what you think the central significance of contract is in relation to the management of human resources.

2 Discuss with your friends or work group colleagues the following proposition: 'The common law and statute law ensure the equality before the law of employers and employees'.

3 Outline how the emergence of an HRM-style culture within a firm may alter the way employees might be treated at work. Consider whether the emergence of an HRM culture and its attendant changes in the work organisation have to be contractually determined.

4 Coase (1937) suggested that economic efficiency criteria determine what type of contract a firm will use in any particular situation. If we accept the premise that HRM is all about making organisations more efficient, consider what factors will influence the decision to employ or not to employ labour.

REFERENCES AND FURTHER READING

Those texts marked with an asterisk are particularly recommended for further reading.

Armstrong, P. (1995) 'Accountancy and HRM', in Storey, J. (ed.) *HRM: A Critical Text*. London: Routledge.

Atkinson, J. (1984) 'Manpower strategies for flexible organisations', *Personnel Management*, August, pp. 28–31.

Beardwell, I. (1992) 'The new industrial relations: a review of the debate', *Human Resource Management Journal*, Vol. 2, No. 2, pp. 1–8.

Braverman, H. (1974) *Labour and Monopoly Capitalism*. New York: Monthly Review Press.

Clark, I. (1996) 'The state and new industrial relations', in Beardwell, I. (ed.) *Contemporary Industrial Relations*. Oxford: Oxford University Press.

Clarke, S. (1991) *Marx, Marginalism and Modern Sociology*, 2nd edn. London: Macmillan.

Coase, R. (1937) 'The nature of the firm', *Economica*, No. 4, pp. 386–405.

Edwards, R. (1979) *Contested Terrain*. London: Heinemann.

Farnham, D. and Pimlott, J. (1990) *Understanding Industrial Relations*. London: Cassell.

Fox, A. (1974) *Beyond Contract*. London: Faber.

Fox, A. (1985) *History and Heritage*. London: Allen & Unwin.

Fox, A. (1991) *Man Mismanagement*. Warwick: IRRU.

Friedman, A. (1977) *Capital and Labour*. London: Macmillan.

Guest, D. (1987) 'Personnel management and industrial relations', *Journal of Management Studies*, Vol. 24, No. 5, pp. 503–521.

Guest, D. (1989) 'Personnel management and HRM: can you tell the difference?', *Personnel Management*, January, pp. 48–51.

Guest, D. (1991) 'Personnel management: the end of orthodoxy', *British Journal of Industrial Relations*, Vol. 29, No. 5, pp. 149–177.

Guest, D. and Peccei, R. (1994) 'The nature and causes of effective human resource management', *The British Journal of Industrial Relations*, Vol. 32, No. 2, pp. 219–241.

Hutton, W. (1995) *The State We're In*. London: Jonathan Cape.

Hyman, R. (1975) *Marxist Introduction to Industrial Relations*. London: Macmillan.

Hyman, R. and Price, R. (1983) *The New Working Class? White Collar Workers and their Organizations*. London: Macmillan.

Kahn-Freund, O. (1984) 'Labour and the Law', 2nd edn. London: Stevens.

Kessler, S. and Bayliss, F. (1992) *Contemporary British Industrial Relations*. London: Macmillan.

Kessler, S. and Bayliss, F. (1995) *Contemporary British Industrial Relations*, 2nd edn. London: Macmillan.

Landes, D. (1969) *The Unbound Prometheus*. Cambridge: Cambridge University Press.

Landes, D. (1986) 'What do bosses really do?', *Journal of Economic History*, Vol. XLVI, No. 3, pp. 585–623.

*Lewis, D. (1991) *Essentials of Employment Law*. London: IPM.

*Lewis, R. (ed.) (1986) *Labour Law in Britain*. Oxford: Blackwell.

Marchington, M. and Parker, P. (1990) *Changing Patterns of Employee Relations*. Hemel Hempstead: Harvester Wheatsheaf.

Marginson, P., Armstrong, P., Edwards, P., Purcell, J. and Hubbard, N. (1993) 'The control of industrial relations in large companies: initial analysis of the second company level industrial relations survey', *Warwick Papers in Industrial Relations*, No. 45. University of Warwick Industrial Relations Research Unit.

Marginson, P., Edwards, P., Armstrong, P. and Purcell, J. (1995) 'Strategy, structure and control in the changing corporation: a survey-based investigation', *Human Resource Management Journal*, Vol. 5, No. 2, pp. 3–27.

Marglin, S. (1974) 'What do bosses do?: the origins and functions of hierarchy in capitalist production', *Review of Radical Political Economics*, No. 6, pp. 33–60.

Marx, K. (1954) *Capital*. London: Lawrence & Wishart.

Oxford Economic Dictionary (1992) 7th edn. Oxford: Oxford University Press, p. 614.

Purcell, J. (1995) 'Corporate strategy and its link with human resource management strategy', in Storey, J. (ed.) *HRM: A Critical Text*. London: Routledge.

Purcell, J. and Ahlstrand, B. (1994) *Human Resource Management in the Multi-Divisional Company*. Oxford: Oxford University Press.

*Putterman, L. (ed.) (1991) *The Nature of the Firm: A Reader*. Cambridge: CUP.

Sisson, K. (ed.) (1989) *Personnel Management in Britain*. Oxford: Blackwell.

Sisson, K. (1993) 'In search of HRM', *British Journal of Industrial Relations*, Vol. 31, No. 2, pp. 201–211.

Smith, A. (1904) *The Wealth of Nations*, Vols. 1 and 2. London: Methuen.

Smith, C., Knights, D. and Wilmott, H. (1991) *White Collar Work – The Non-Manual Labour Process*. London: Macmillan.

Storey, J. (1992) *New Developments in the Management of Human Resources*. Oxford: Blackwell.

Storey, J. (ed.) (1995) *Human Resource Management: A Critical Text*. London: Routledge.

Taylor, F. (1911) *The Principles of Scientific Management*. New York: Harper & Row.

Tomlinson, J. and Tiratsoo, N. (1993) *State Intervention and Industrial Efficiency 1939–1945*. London: Routledge.

Wedderburn, W. (1986) *The Worker and the Law*. London: Penguin.

Williamson, O. (1975) *Markets and Hierarchies*. New York: Macmillan Free Press.

COLLECTIVE

BARGAINING

Sue Marlow

INTRODUCTION

Collective bargaining is a joint process of job regulation undertaken by management and trade unions who negotiate to establish pay and conditions of employment. Until recently there was little debate that the collective bargaining process was a key area in the study of the employment relationship, given that a majority of labour in most industrialised nations were covered by collective agreements. However, a relatively recent survey of British industrial relations has indicated that this is no longer the case in the UK:

> Over the whole sample, 54 per cent of employees were covered by collective bargaining in 1990. When grossed up to the population of employees covered by the sample this amounted to some 8.4 million out of a total of 15.3 million. As the 6.6 million employees excluded from our survey population – essentially those in small workplaces – are generally much less likely to be covered, it is clear that collective bargaining directly affected only a minority of employees in Britain.   (WIRS 3, p. 92)

Given the political, economic and social pressures prevailing since this survey was undertaken in 1990, it is most likely that the percentage of the workforce covered by collective bargaining has further decreased. Consequently, there may be some debate about the relevance of discussing collective bargaining if it is experiencing a marked decline and influence. However, collective bargaining remains significant as a substantial minority of the workforce as a whole are still covered by such agreements, with the majority of the public sector still subject to collective agreements. There is no certainty that the current decline in collective bargaining is terminal; indeed, a future Labour government may facilitate the work of trade unions in recruiting 'atypical' groups of labour and encourage collective agreements in areas not currently covered. To further contradict the notion of terminal decline, in 1994 it was found that 47 of Britain's most profitable 50 companies recognise trade unions (*Daily Telegraph*, 2 March 1994). Moreover, there is little evidence for a credible 'alternative model' of employee relations emerging to replace the collective bargaining approach, leaving what Beaumont (1995) describes as an 'institutional vacuum'. Successive Conservative governments have made clear their dislike of trade unions and collective bargaining, but have failed to promote or support an appropriate system of regulation relating to the contemporary employment relationship. Clearly, there is a role for HRM to fill this vacuum, but there is little indication that there is a wholesale, coherent and strategic adoption of HRM practices and policies by British management; indeed, rather the opposite would appear to be evident (Mabey and Salamon, 1995).

Consequently, if there are a number of parallel systems aimed at regulating the employment relationship, it is essential to explore all of these systems. Most commentators now explore the extent of HRM initiatives and practices in the established pluralist organisations with trade union representation, as well as investigating the non-union sector (Beaumont, 1995), and there are many examples of corporate enterprises maintaining a role for collective bargaining while introducing HRM initiatives (Rover, British Airways,

Cadbury's). Thus, to understand fully the role of HRM in the contemporary organisation, it is essential to understand existing practices which shape the employment relationship.

Collective bargaining – definitions, analyses and criticisms

The term 'collective bargaining' was first utilised by Sidney and Beatrice Webb writing at the beginning of this century (Webb and Webb, 1902). They believed that collective bargaining was the collective equivalent to individual bargaining, where the prime aim was to achieve economic advantage. This has become known as the 'classical viewpoint' upon collective bargaining. Thus, collective bargaining had primarily an *economic* function and was undertaken between trade unions and employers or employers' organisations.

The 'classical' definition of collective bargaining has been subject to a number of critical analyses. In the late 1960s, Flanders (1968) argued that this view of collective bargaining was erroneous; rather, collective bargaining should be understood as a *rule-making process* which established the rules under which the economic purchase of labour could initially take place. Further to establishing rules, collective bargaining outlines a framework for future negotiations regarding the buying and selling of labour. Thus, collective bargaining is not a collective equivalent of individual bargaining, as nothing is actually bought or sold; only the conditions under which the commodity of labour can be bought or sold are established. It is in fact 'a body of rules intended to regulate . . . the terms of employment contracts . . . collective bargaining is itself essentially a rule making process' (Flanders, 1968: 6).

Flanders goes on to argue that collective bargaining also entails a power relationship; the imbalance of economic power, status and security between the single employee and that of the management can, to some degree, be addressed by collective pressure such that agreements are compromise settlements of power conflicts. In consequence, collective bargaining is a political activity undertaken by professional negotiators and this clearly differentiates it from individual negotiation.

Fox (1975), however, disputes Flanders' argument, that an individual bargain is an economic exchange which always concludes with an agreement, whereas collective bargaining is essentially a process to establish rules for exchange. In fact, there is no assurance that either process will achieve agreement on terms acceptable to the parties involved in negotiation. Moreover, Fox strongly argues that Flanders' view of collective bargaining as primarily political ignores the fact that 'the intensity of conviction, effort and feeling which many trade unionists appear to invest in pay claims hardly seems to be given sufficient recognition and weight in the Flanders analysis' (Fox, 1975: 170). Thus Fox believes that the economic function of collective bargaining has not been afforded sufficient attention in the Flanders analysis.

Rather than isolating one major function of collective bargaining, Chamberlain and Kuhn (1965) offer an analysis which outlines three distinct activities which interact to form the bargaining process:

- *Market or economic function.* This determines the price of labour to the employer, thus the collective agreement forms the 'contract' for the terms under which employees will work for the employer. The collective agreement also forms a non-legal grievance procedure which obliges employers to abide by the terms of the agreement. The market or economic function establishes the *substantive terms* (see below) of the employment relationship.

- *Decision-making function*. In this role, collective bargaining offers employees the opportunity, if they wish, to 'participate in the determination of the policies which guide and rule their working lives' (Chamberlain and Kuhn, 1965: 130). Through union representatives, labour can influence management strategy on matters considered to be of joint concern, covered by the collective bargaining process. However, this depends upon a mutual understanding and consent regarding which areas are to be jointly controlled through collective bargaining and the existence of the following conditions:
  - management must accept that some strategies and actions will be subject to labour scrutiny and approval before they can be implemented.
  - the employees and their unions must be willing to contribute to, and become involved in, decision-making processes.
  - employees and their unions must have sufficient power to enforce their wish to be involved in the decision-making processes of the employer.
- *Governmental function*. This is similar to the Flanders (1968) analysis where collective bargaining establishes rules by which the employment relationship is governed. Thus bargaining is a political process as it establishes a 'constitution' (Salamon, 1992) by which both interest groups abide as they each have power to 'veto' the actions of each other.

From the above points it is clear that collective bargaining is concerned with the establishment of:

- *Substantive rules*. These regulate all aspects of pay agreements including overtime rates, productivity bonuses, minimum payments, sick pay, shift pay, etc. Substantive rules also deal with hours of work, holiday arrangements, shift rotas, etc. These are all aspects of the market or economic function of the collective bargaining process. Clearly, substantive rules will be subject to frequent review as conditions of employment are renegotiated.
- *Procedural rules*. These establish the rules under which negotiation over the terms and conditions of employment can take place and establish grievance and dispute procedures. Procedures for recruitment, training, dismissals and redundancies are also established by procedural agreements. As such they define managerial authority and trade union power, establishing a regulatory framework for the bargaining relationship.

Bargaining principles

The aim of collective bargaining is to reach negotiated agreements upon a range of issues pertaining to the employment relationship. From this range of issues, some will hold the potential for a conflict situation where the distribution and division of scarce resources are under negotiation (for example, division of profit as dividends or wage increase). Others, however, will have mutual benefit for employees and management with the major debate focusing upon the most beneficial manner in which to implement change (for example, introduction of health and safety procedures). These differences were noted by Walton and McKersie (1965) who outlined two approaches to collective bargaining:

- *Distributive bargaining*. One party will seek to achieve gains at the expense of the other; the aim is the division of a limited resource between groups both of whom wish to maximise their share. Thus, pay bargaining is distributive bargaining as one party's gain is the other's loss. The important factor in distributive bargaining is the extent to which each side has power to damage their opponent if they do not comply with their demands. Thus the threatened use of sanctions, for example strike action or lock-outs, becomes of primary importance. Although distributive bargaining is focused on the use of power by opposing groups to achieve their aim, within collective bargaining it is recognised that each side will have to make concessions to reach a mutually acceptable compromise; the threat or use of sanctions only becomes necessary when one side refuses to compromise or is perceived to be acting provocatively.
- *Integrative bargaining*. This approach seeks mutual gains in areas of common interest with a problem-solving approach from the parties involved. Successful integrative bargaining depends upon a relatively high level of trust between parties and a willingness to share information.

These models of bargaining outlined by Walton and McKersie (1965) are reflected in the work of Chamberlain and Kuhn (1965) who use the terms 'conjunctive' and 'cooperative' bargaining.

From these views of collective bargaining it is apparent that it is subject to many interpretations. In reality, however, the bargaining activity is likely to encompass aspects of the analyses outlined above. Before leaving the question of interpretation of collective bargaining processes and functions, we will review it from differing theoretical perspectives remembering that this can only be an overview given the constantly changing nature of the collective bargaining process.

Theoretical approaches

- *Unitary perspective*. For those who view the firm as an essentially cooperative system where management and labour share a 'unitary' outlook a union presence and collective bargaining procedures are unnecessary. If management are working efficiently and remain sensitive to the individual's employment conditions, any collective voice attempting to influence the working environment is superfluous. Moreover, the introduction of a collective and potentially critical force into the employment relationship will lead to conflict and questioning of the legitimacy of managerial prerogative.
- *Pluralist perspective*. Pluralists largely support the collective bargaining process as a channel to institutionalise conflict situations. Where management and labour have some common and some conflicting aims within the employment relationship, collective bargaining processes offer the opportunity to establish areas of commonality, negotiate around issues of disparity and inevitably, upon some occasions, take industrial action to re-establish power relations and reach new consensus. (For a more in-depth analysis of the pluralist approach, see Beaumont (1990: 107–109).)
- *Radical perspective*. The major critique of the collective bargaining process is that it focuses very narrowly on terms and conditions of employment without challenging the structure of the capitalist market economy. There is no recognition of the essentially

exploitative nature of the labour/capital (employee/employer) relationship and so is no effective challenge to the power of capital. As such the processes of collective bargaining constrain any real political threat to the power of management. Furthermore, when conflict does arise, the institutionalisation of channels of protest into acceptable sanctions effectively constrains possibilities for any real change in the power balance between labour and capital. Thus collective bargaining obscures the exploitative nature of the employment relationship and prevents any effective political, social or economic challenge to capital. (For a more extensive discussion, see Hyman (1975).)

Summary

Collective bargaining remains an important part of the contemporary employment relationship, although in recent years has become subject to decline. However, in terms of numbers of employees covered and the scope of agreements concluded, it remains an important channel for establishing terms and conditions of employment. There has been considerable debate regarding the fundamental nature and purpose of the bargaining process, but any definition of collective bargaining must take account of historical and contemporary influences which will impinge upon those involved in bargaining practices. Furthermore, collective bargaining must be analysed critically, from differing theoretical perspectives.

Having outlined critical approaches to collective bargaining, we now turn to the collective agreements and the bargaining functions.

THE COLLECTIVE AGREEMENT

At the end of the negotiating and bargaining process, collective agreements are reached. Traditionally, British collective bargaining has been notable for the informality with which agreements are recorded and, as has been noted above, in the UK collective agreements are voluntary, as they are not legally enforceable on a collective basis. From the early 1970s, however, there has been a growing trend to establish formal written contracts to avoid any potential problems given the possibility of differing interpretations of negotiation outcome. The written agreement also contributes to a rationalisation and codification of industrial relations procedures. Clearly, the existence of formal written agreements will not prevent informal bargaining at local level. The extent to which this occurs will depend upon the nature of the existing power relationship between management and trade unions. There are several levels outlined below at which collective agreements can be reached.

Multi-employer agreements

Such agreements cover specific groups of employees (described within the contract) from a particular industry and are negotiated by employers' associations or federations and full-time national trade union officials. These agreements are complex as they have to recognise numerous occupational groupings, and the many different sectors which will fall under the general umbrella of the industry heading itself, for example the printing, textile and engineering industries. Multi-employer agreements also form guidelines for employers who are not members of the industry association, and for non-union firms, particularly those in the small firm sector where trade union representation and collective bargaining procedures are rare (Marlow and Patton, 1992).

Industry-wide agreements may take the following forms:

- *comprehensive* – leaving little or no scope for further bargaining at company or plant level;
- *partial* – leaving scope for enhancement of national agreement through further negotiation at plant or company level and/or covering only some elements of the employment relationship, again leaving the remainder to be negotiated at company/plant level;
- *minimum* – setting a safety net of minimum conditions which apply to the lowest paid workers in the industry. Other employers use this as a floor to bargain their terms and conditions at company/plant level.

Single-employer bargaining (organisational bargaining)

Organisational bargaining may occur at a number of levels:

- *corporate* – all those employed by the organisation are covered by agreements bargained by the company and relevant trade union officials;
- *plant* – the collective agreement is negotiated for a specific site or plant within the corporate structure affecting only the employees of that location. These agreements may be totally independent of national terms or constructed upon an industry agreement.

Determinants of bargaining level within organisations

Research (CBI, 1988) indicates that company-level bargaining is associated with large organisations and the presence of professional industrial relations specialists in corporate level management. Site bargaining is associated with firms where labour costs are a high percentage of total costs and there are substantial numbers of workers on each site. At present, the choice of bargaining level falls within managerial prerogative influenced by a number of variables; for example, corporate-level bargaining may be favoured as one channel to neutralise potentially powerful plant-based union pressure and avoid inter-plant comparisons. Plant-based bargaining, however, will tie down labour costs to local conditions, bargained by negotiators who have a shared awareness of regional conditions which may not always be to management's advantage.

DEVELOPMENT OF COLLECTIVE BARGAINING IN BRITAIN

Early development of collective bargaining

There is some evidence (Littler, 1980) that simple forms of collective bargaining were in existence in the eighteenth century amongst skilled weavers and London shipbuilders and, by the beginning of the nineteenth century, collective agreements were in existence for work groups based on subcontracting or family labour contracts, but that such agreements were limited to pay issues and hours of work. By the end of the nineteenth century, however, locally bargained collective agreements were established in areas where previously family labour and subcontracting had predominated. These methods of working were being replaced by piecework thus, prices were bargained and agreed between employers and labour in textiles, coal-mining and shipbuilding. Collective bargaining had also become established for skilled workers; the Webbs commented:

> In all skilled trades, where men work in concert, on the employers' premises, ninety per cent of the workmen find, either their rate of wages or their hours of work, and often many other details, predetermined by collective bargaining.
> (Flanders, 1968: 261)

As collective bargaining became established at local level in these two areas at the end of the nineteenth century, this development prompted demands for collective agreements from other groups of employees in semi- and unskilled trades. Despite considerable employer opposition, these groups formed trade unions and won recognition for collective bargaining in the early years of the twentieth century. Thus the two important factors pertaining to the development of collective bargaining at the turn of the century were:

- the relatively rapid spread of collective bargaining procedures from skilled trades to semi- and unskilled trades by the outbreak of the First World War;
- although collective bargaining processes were becoming more prevalent, they remained locally based and unenforceable.

The system of local bargaining changed during the early years of the twentieth century with the First World War acting as a stimulus to promote national procedure agreements. Employers supported national agreements to reduce local wage competition as pressure mounted upon the labour market after 1914, when there was a sharp rise in the cost of living resulting in constant local wage adjustments. Trade unions also endorsed national bargaining as it ensured recognition for union officials whose impact would be enhanced in a national arena of negotiation and bargaining. However, the greatest influence upon the move to industry-wide settlements was the government. The decision to take control of vital industries such as munitions factories, the rail system and coal mines favoured the development of national bargaining. Moreover, the government banned strikes and lock-outs (although this did not prevent strike activity, particularly in the engineering industry) through the 1915 Munitions of War Act, so without recourse to strike action a system of compulsory arbitration became necessary where decisions were focused upon national terms and conditions, further encouraging the growth of industry-level action.

The greatest influence upon the growth of a national system of bargaining, however, came from the reports of the Whitley Committee in 1917 and 1918. The Whitley Committee was formed in response to major industrial unrest in the early years of the First World War and the growth of radical trade union action at local level (the 'first shop stewards movement' – see Hyman (1975) for an in-depth discussion). The mandate for Whitley was to offer suggestions upon improving contemporary industrial relations and to establish a system whereby future employment issues could be evaluated and controlled effectively. The Committee produced a number of reports which were acceptable to both employers and trade unions. Essentially, they suggested major changes to existing bargaining arrangements: first to further develop the system of statutory wage regulation in poorly organised areas; second to extend the powers already held by the government to conciliate and arbitrate during disputes; and third to establish joint employer/trade union councils known as Joint Industrial Councils (JICs) which would meet at regular intervals for national bargaining purposes but also to discuss wider issues such as labour efficiency. Between the beginning of 1918, and the end of 1921, 73 Joint Industrial Councils were established and, through the extension of the Boards of Trade Act in 1918, the statutory regulation of wages for vulnerable labour groups was established (Gospel and Palmer, 1993: 201–204).

The aim of the Whitley Committees was to regulate industrial relations in general, and collective bargaining in particular, but, although initially the proposals generated support and were termed innovative, in reality they made little difference to industries where national bargaining was established. By the early 1920s, the Joint Industrial Committees were in fact being used to negotiate wage cuts as the inter-war recession developed and by 1938 there were only 45 JICs still operating (Jackson, 1991: 144). The advent of Whitley Committees did, however, make a significant difference to public sector workers where, for the first time, collective bargaining spread to white-collar staff. The system prevailed even during the inter-war depression years, being subject to considerable revision by the 1979 Thatcher government.

Thus, collective bargaining was initially confined to labour whose skills gave them leverage to force employers to enter into a bargaining relationship, rather than being able to impose their own conditions and terms of employment. A bargaining system also emerged for group and subcontract labour where it was essential to set the price of the job before the onset of work. The social, political and economic pressures which emerged immediately before and during the years of the First World War ensured that by 1918 the majority of private sector manufacturing labour was covered by some form of national agreement concerning terms and conditions of employment. The postwar Liberal government formalised national bargaining, extending the process to some public employees by the endorsement of the Whitley Committee system.

Developments in collective bargaining from the Second World War to the 1980s

During the Second World War there was a revival of national bargaining machinery; 56 Joint Industrial Committees were in existence by 1945, and 15.5 million employees from a working population of 17.5 million (Palmer, 1983: 157) were covered by some type of national agreement. The influence of corporatism, where joint negotiations between employers and trade unions are encouraged by the state, ensured that industry-level collective bargaining became firmly established. The nationalisation programme and the advent of the welfare system ensured that the state became a major employer and, indeed, the postwar Labour government enacted legislation which obliged management in the newly nationalised industries to establish negotiating procedures for all employees. Although the majority of manual and skilled employees in these industries were already covered by national agreements, for the first time non-manual and professional groups were included in national bargaining agreements further extending the scope of centralised, industry-level agreements.

It is incorrect, however, to presume that local or domestic bargaining ceased to be of relevance because of the formal establishment of national bargaining machinery for the majority of British labour by the early 1950s. Indeed, the conditions of full employment coupled with high demand offered considerable leverage for local bargaining by shop stewards, in the less bureaucratic, private manufacturing sector. Table 12.1 outlines issues upon which shop stewards were actively engaged in domestic negotiation in the 1960s.

Negotiation issues

The result of this shop floor bargaining was increased wage drift, growth of short informal disputes and a growing tendency for national agreements to be utilised as a bargaining floor upon which local agreements were based leading to inflationary pressures. This latter point generated concern from the Labour government, given the problems of introducing and operating incomes policies in the face of informal, unregulated local bargaining and growing inflation. Thus the growth and economic effect of domestic bargaining was deemed an 'industrial relations problem'.

Batstone *et al.* (1977), however, found that local shop stewards in the car industry were not, in fact, independently bargaining but remained in close contact with full-time officials, while the Commission on Industrial Relations established at the end of the 1960s found many managers reluctant to move away from the intimate channels of negotiation and personal style of bargaining they had established. Given that domestic bargaining was a problem for employers who faced increasing international competition and found

TABLE 12.1

Respondents who negotiated (%)

Issues	Works manager	Personnel	Foreman	Steward
Wages	82	80	72	83
Working conditions	88	89	79	89
Hours of work	78	73	62	75
Discipline	76	76	61	67
Employment issues	71	76	43	67

Source: McCarthy and Parker (1968).

wage costs difficult to control, and was also a potential threat to government economic policy, a Royal Commission was established to examine industrial relations practices and procedures in both the public and private sector. The Donovan Commission reported in 1968, arguing that Britain had two systems of industrial relations, the formal and informal (Donovan Commission, 1968: 12). In private sector manufacturing, the formal system was based upon national bargaining between employers' organisations and full-time trade union officials. Through these channels, basic levels of pay and conditions of employment procedures for negotiations were agreed. The informal system was based upon local bargaining between management and shop stewards under the influence of full employment and buoyant demand for goods. Wage issues were of central importance focusing upon overtime and piecework rates, but shop floor bargaining was already extending to cover aspects such as redundancy payments, sick pay and working arrangements, including manning levels. Overall, the Donovan Commission argued that workplace bargaining had become of greater importance than national bargaining in the private manufacturing sector. This local level of bargaining, it was suggested, was 'largely informal, largely fragmented, and largely autonomous' (Flanders, 1970: 169) as it was based upon verbal agreements backed by custom and practice. Fragmented bargaining was undertaken by individual or small groups of stewards negotiating with individual or small groups of managers who did not consult with employers' organisations or full-time trade union officials, and did not respect national agreements. The Commission members concluded:

> The extent to which at the moment industry-wide agreements both on pay and other issues are effective in the workplace cannot exactly be determined. What is of critical importance is that the practices of the formal system have become increasingly empty, while the practices of the informal system have come to exert an ever greater influence on the conduct of industrial relations throughout the country; that the two systems conflict and that the informal system cannot be forced to comply with the formal system.
> (Donovan Commission, 1968: 37)

The Commission argued that multi-employer bargaining on a national industry level could no longer effectively accommodate differentiated working practices throughout the private sector. The responsibility for introducing reform lay with management. The Commission did not denounce local informal agreements but insisted that local agreements should achieve a level of formality such that they did not totally ignore and undermine national agreements. Moreover, the system of local informal bargaining effectively hampered the development of effective and orderly workplace bargaining: '. . . the objection to the state of plant bargaining at that time, therefore was its doubtful legitimacy and furtive character' (Clegg, 1979: 237). What was required was a rationalisation of the existing system which would effectively combine the two systems of industrial relations into one coherent, ordered process which did not then undermine the formal rules in multi-employer agreements.

This reform of the content and structure of existing bargaining should be undertaken by senior management within their own companies, argued Donovan. It was necessary to develop a framework of bargaining issues with extensive procedural agreements where management and trade unions could formally negotiate terms and conditions of employment. Changes in pay should be linked to changes in productivity thus establishing a clear connection between formal domestic bargaining and enhanced profitability with this tactic verified by the National Board for Prices and Incomes. Moreover, a Commission on Industrial Relations was established in 1969 to encourage and advise upon the formalisation of domestic bargaining in both corporate, nationalised and public industries.

The reform of local-level bargaining

One of the earliest and best documented cases of reform of domestic bargaining occurred at the Esso Oil Refinery at Fawley. Management negotiated agreement which explicitly involved shop stewards in the centralisation of domestic bargaining into a single, plant-level agreement. Productivity bargaining, as it was known, offered employees pay increases, extension of fringe benefits and improved job security. In return management obtained a reduction in the workforce and considerable changes in working practices, for example the deployment of employees, craft demarcation, manning arrangements, use of supervisors and a wide range of other issues, most of which were subject to detailed, formal written agreements. The Fawley agreement was received enthusiastically as an innovative agreement which, while including shop stewards in the bargaining process, also introduced formal, precise descriptions of working practices at local level (Flanders, 1964).

Other large employers, particularly in the chemical industry, began to introduce similar agreements to establish plant- or company-level negotiations around domestic work arrangements. However, productivity bargaining was not widely effective due largely to pressure from incomes policies imposed by the Labour government and, moreover, consequent agreements were not as detailed or precise as the exemplary case of the Fawley plant.

In consequence, most companies, encouraged by the Conservative government (1970–74) and the Labour government (1974–79) undertook voluntary reform of collective bargaining procedures. Using survey evidence from Brown (1981), it was apparent that by the late 1970s, single employer bargaining at establishment or corporate level had become the most prevalent level of bargaining for both manual and non-manual employees (see Table 12.2).

Brown (1981) argued that on the basis of their survey evidence, significant changes had occurred in collective bargaining processes since the recommendations of Donovan. It was found that management had facilitated the formalisation of domestic bargaining by recognising shop stewards, providing paid time-off to conduct union business and supporting union organisation through closed shop agreements and check-off procedures (whereby union subscriptions are deducted by the company from wages and then paid to the trade union account).

However, the survey also found that industrial sector and size of establishment affected bargaining level where, according to Deaton and Beaumont (1980: 201), single-employer bargaining was associated with larger firms, foreign ownership, multi-site operations and the existence of a professional tier of senior industrial relations management.

The reform of collective bargaining during the 1970s was largely initiated by management with government support. Although there were clear benefits to trade unions from increased recognition and better facilities (for a critique of the incorporation of shop stew-

TABLE 12.2
Bargaining level at which the most recent pay increase had been negotiated

| | Manufacturing 1977/1978 | |
| | Manual | Non-manual |
	%	%
Industry	33	17
Regional	3	1
Corporate	11	15
Establishment	42	40
Other	1	2
No bargaining	10	25

Source: Brown (1981; 8, Table 2.1, and 12, Table 2.3).

ards into formal management/trade union bargaining hierarchy – 'the bureaucratisation thesis' – see Hyman, 1975), it is apparent that rapidly rising inflation, growing international competition and greater foreign ownership combined with state intervention in industrial relations issues created a climate favourable for management to press for reform.

Thus, although there was a trend towards decentralisation of bargaining and a growth in formal recognition of domestic bargainers there remained considerable variation in collective bargaining processes within British industry during the 1970s.

Summary

In the postwar period there was a rapid expansion in domestic bargaining at local level in private sector manufacturing industry despite the existence of national agreements negotiated by multi-employer organisations and full-time trade union officials. The Labour government of 1964–70 was concerned that local bargaining was compromising its incomes policy programme, adding to inflationary pressure and adversely affecting Britain's competitive performance. The Donovan Commission was charged with investigating contemporary industrial relations and concluded that Britain had two systems of industrial relations, informal and formal. The informal was conducted at plant level between shop stewards and management, the formal at industry level. The solution was to incorporate the two, establishing formal bargaining processes and procedures at the domestic level with an emphasis upon productivity bargaining. Reforms were evident throughout the 1970s with workplace surveys indicating that for large companies in private sector manufacturing there was a significant trend towards formal, professional single-employer bargaining.

CHANGES IN COLLECTIVE BARGAINING
SINCE THE 1980s

Since the late 1970s, the British economy has suffered severe economic depression and growing levels of unemployment. Such structural changes, combined with the election of successive Conservative governments since 1979, hostile to the ethos of collective action by trade unions, has prompted substantial change in the nature of collective bargaining in both the public and private sector. It is important to note that such changes have resulted from joint pressures experienced by industry attempting to maintain profitability, by trade unions attempting to attract new membership, and from government influence encouraging a move away from collective representation. It is a combination of such factors which has prompted change.

Recent workplace studies (Daniel and Millward, 1983; Millward and Stevens, 1986; Gregg and Yates, 1991), however, while agreeing that the nature, scope and processes of collective bargaining are changing, find that collective bargaining remains the most important vehicle for fixing pay and conditions of employment in the public sector and private sector manufacturing, although the following trends are emerging.

Decentralisation of bargaining

As argued above, there has been a growing trend towards the decentralisation of collective bargaining away from multi-employer/industry level, to organisation or plant level. This trend has continued during the 1980s and 1990s. This pattern has been encouraged by the current Conservative government who, in the 1990 White Paper *Employment for the 1990s*, state that plant- or company-level negotiations result in more 'realistic pay settlements' and thus avoid wage inflation. Support from government legislation constraining industrial action has also acted to dissipate further any union resistance to plant bargaining.

From the corporate stance, decentralised bargaining offers the opportunity to link pay and productivity together at local level where regional variations and conditions can be accounted for accurately by local management and trade union officials. Decentralised bargaining also complements contemporary corporate strategic trends to downsize to core business units and local profit centres. For these smaller-scale initiatives to operate effectively, local management require autonomy to manage collective bargaining in order to control labour costs. Moreover, the weakened state of contemporary trade unions ensure they are less able to resist managerial strategy to utilise local bargaining to review labour costs and reform working practices, for example the introduction of new technology, flexible working practices, etc.

There is little doubt that regional variations in the labour market and the growing preference for local profit centres suggest that local bargaining is an appropriate step for many large companies. Survey evidence from Marginson *et al.* (1988) supports this argument, highlighting a number of cases where major corporate firms have withdrawn from national-level bargaining, including Sealink, Tesco and Midland Bank. Privatisation of public sector industries (water, electricity, British Telecom) has also offered management the opportunity to decentralise bargaining structures.

There is, however, a need for a note of caution regarding whether decentralised bargaining is a useful strategy for all corporate structures and also regarding the true extent of the 'decentralisation' process. Purcell (1988) argues that large firms should consider a 'checklist of conditions' before committing themselves to a policy of decentralisation, stating that the decision to change the level of bargaining can have destabilising effects on existing industrial relation systems and personnel management. This effect is particularly intrusive in areas such as job evaluation, where the comparative framework becomes narrowed, and disputes procedures, where final appeal to the highest level of corporate management is denied. For full-time, national trade union officials, there is concern that their influence in the negotiation process is declining if bargaining falls to local level. Considering the issue of decentralisation in more detail, Kinnie (1990) finds a false image of local autonomy in bargaining, suggesting that local management are subject to head office directive even when there is an appearance of local autonomy. Three specific dimensions of corporate control are illustrated, the degree to which local decisions are directed in head office, the degree to which policy is constructed by head office before being 'passed down' to plant level, and finally the manner in which management accounting and budget setting at central level are utilised as measures of local management performance. Thus there may be a perceived autonomy for local management, but this could be a false premise.

Consequently, while there is evidence for changes in bargaining level, large-scale survey evidence indicates a move to enterprise bargaining but little support for the emergence of local plant-level bargaining (WIRS3).

> the clearest indication of a move towards local decision making in the unionised sector would have been an increase in the extent of plant bargaining. In fact, there was no increase of this kind in the unionised sector; nor was there any reduction in the extent to which managers involved in plant-level negotiations consulted their colleagues or superiors at head office or other higher levels in the enterprise. Rather than lead to more plant-level negotiations, the move away from multi-employer negotiations was accompanied by an increase in negotiating structures at enterprise or company level.
>
> (Millward *et al*.: 355)

There is some suggestion that corporate and local-level bargaining may be interacting in larger firms, so, for example, British Telecom is adopting a two-tier approach, establishing basic conditions at national level with local bargaining offering scope to relate pay and terms to domestic conditions. Marginson (1988) found support for this system, with data indicating that in 90% of companies who appeared to have adopted a decentralised bargaining structure, corporate management were still influencing local decisions through directives regarding what would constitute an 'acceptable settlement'. This clouding of autonomy between levels of management also raises more complex issues of employee access to decision-making processes. When local trade union officials enter into negotiation concerning pay and conditions at the domestic level, they are in fact entering a constrained process where there is an illusion of autonomy for the bargaining team, whereas management are operating under restraint regarding their limits of concession. This has other implications in that local trade union negotiators are denied access to corporate decision makers when in fact they are highly influential upon local management actions.

There is also evidence that where established industrial relations processes have favoured the development of professional negotiating teams at corporate level, decentralisation can lead to considerable disorientation when plant- or site-level management and trade union officials are required to undertake formal bargaining activities. Indeed, Ahlstrand and Purcell (1988) found resistance to decentralisation policies in several companies they studied and identified one case in particular where corporate personnel influence prevented the move to decentralised bargaining. There is also employee resistance to this approach. In 1995 this approach was tried in the health service with reference to nursing staff, but was greeted with such hostility and a real threat of industrial action that the strategy had to be significantly modified. While there can be little doubt that there has been a shift in bargaining levels which has complemented contemporary corporate strategies to downsize and focus upon local profit centres, the extent to which local management achieve independence and autonomy in the bargaining arena is questionable.

ACTIVITY

A corporate enterprise has always undertaken multi-employer, national-level bargaining, developing a specialised team of negotiators bargaining annually with full-time trade union officials. However, the corporation is considering a complete restructuring whereby local 'profit centres' would be developed as single business units. As part of this restructuring it has been suggested that collective bargaining should be devolved to local level, with outline directives issued from head office regarding acceptable bargaining agendas and final settlements.

EXERCISE

As HRM consultants, outline the presentation you would make to the board to include the following issues:
(a) the origins and extent of local bargaining;
(b) the advantages and potential problems of local bargaining to both management and trade unions;
(c) possible solutions to such problems;
(d) recommendations concerning the move to local bargaining.

Flexibility issues

The notion of flexible working encompasses a considerable range of practices and has been the subject of academic study since the late 1960s (Piore, 1971). However, since the early 1980s flexible working has become a central issue and refers to a wide range of new working practices, many of which have been introduced through collective bargaining processes. A conceptual analysis of the flexible workforce has been put forward by Atkinson (1984) who argues that a multi-skilled 'core' workforce offers 'functional flexibility' trained to undertake a range of tasks within the labour process as required by management. The periphery workforce offers 'numerical' flexibility, that is temporary, part-time or casual employees who can be utilised as and when demanded by production schedules; subcontracted and self-employed labour also offer numerical flexibility as again they can be offered fixed-price, short-term contracts.

If a company introduces flexible working, such changes usually form an overlapping agreement to become part of a complete package which constitutes a flexibility agreement. The terms and conditions of flexibility agreements evident in the 1980s and 1990s will depend on such factors as the state of union–management relations, the bargaining environment and the nature of technology employed. The interaction of vertical and horizontal flexibility agreements leads to teamworking, semi-skilled employees undertaking some craftwork and vice versa, changes in supervisory roles, geographical mobility between and within plants, changes in manning levels and flexibility amongst staff grades. None of these activities are mutually exclusive (IR Review and Report, 1984).

An ACAS survey of 584 companies reported that between 1985 and 1988:

● 33% had introduced horizontal flexibility between skilled employees, thus craft workers were undertaking other tasks outside their central skill area;
● 25% reported vertical flexibility where divisions between manual, non-manual and technical staff were blurred (ACAS, 1988).

Focusing upon the detail of such agreements, Cadburys at Bournville has introduced flexible working between sheet metal workers and all AEEU mechanical grades, and has established integrated work groups where craft and process workers form multi-skilled teams, where each individual will have a core skill but can undertake a range of other maintenance skills when and where necessary. A further development at Cadburys is the introduction of an area of overlap between craft and non-craft workers at the lowest level of craft competence, where skilled production workers are practising some maintenance work and maintenance workers are undertaking some basic production tasks. This type of flexibility agreement negotiated early in the 1980s (1983) specified in detail the changed tasks of employees. In recent years there has been a move towards more open agreements to facilitate complete flexibility at managerial discretion; for example the Nissan agreement which allows for 'complete flexibility and mobility of employees', where there are only two job titles for employees and a teamwork approach (Marchington and Parker, 1990: 33). The agreement at Shell Carrington specifies only one grade of employee with a training programme which aims to equip all workers to undertake any task on site.

The implications for collective bargaining of flexibility agreements are as follows:

● Trade unions are no longer bargaining terms and conditions for a specific craft or activity. Flexibility between tasks blurs lines of demarcation such that the possession of a specific skill or talent is no longer exclusive as tasks are spread throughout the workforce. Thus bargaining leverage is reduced.
● As employees undertake a wider range of tasks throughout the labour process, fewer 'core' workers are required with an increasing dependence upon numerically flexible labour, thus leading to redundancies and a consequent fall in trade union membership and growth in unemployment.
● The growing links between flexibility bargaining and pay increases means that there is a growing trend to bargain around issues of exchange, for example for wage increases in exchange for changes in work organisation, manning levels and redundancies.

This latter point is of some importance. This notion of exchange between improved pay and acceptance of changes in working methods, it is argued (Jackson, 1991), is reminiscent of productivity bargaining during the 1960s. In return for accepting flexibility agreements, employees have been offered a range of benefits including pay increases, enhanced status and greater job security. Thus, trade unions have been forced to bargain for better conditions on the basis of making concessions allowing significant changes in the labour process. Where trade unions have resisted a bargaining nexus focused upon change in employment practices in exchange for improvements in terms and conditions, the social, economic and political environment of the 1980s has offered employers the power to impose change in the face of union resistance. Using British Leyland in the early 1980s and the News International dispute as examples from the public and private sector, it is clearly evident that where the employer is determined to effect radical change in work organisation, and is prepared to endure a prolonged and bitter dispute, the resistance of labour will be overcome. However, such instances of 'macho management' have remained rare in the UK.

As with many other issues discussed, there is a robust critique of the ideas surrounding the flexible workforce idea. Regarding the conceptual divisions of the workforce described by Atkinson (1984), it is argued that there is little empirical evidence to support a fundamental restructuring of the labour force (Marsh, 1992). While there certainly has been a growth in part-time work, temporary work and self-employment, it is argued that much of this change is focused within the public sector rather than private corporate enterprise, which Atkinson believed would be the model of flexible firm. In a succinct, critical review of the flexibility debate, Pollert (1988) argues that flexibility is not a new strategic attempt by employers to establish a labour force suitable for changing markets in a recessionary environment. Rather, employers have always made *ad hoc* attempts to make labour more flexible, but have been hampered by state and union regulation of terms and conditions of employment. Successive Conservative governments enacting legislation to deregulate the labour market, combined with mass unemployment and a weak trade union movement, have made flexibility more accessible to employers, but she argues:

> after a review of the changes in the workforce and in employment prac-
> tices, the flexible firm model is left standing with few clothes. Where there
> has been most major restructuring this has been led by the state as
> employer. But in the private sector, sectoral continuity is far more in evi-
> dence than change, with little evidence of polarisation between an (ill
> defined) 'periphery' and a 'privileged core'. (Pollert, 1988, p. 56)

A series of case studies by the Department of the Employment examining the incidence of employment of 'flexible' workers found evidence for an increase in the use of non-standard labour but, on the whole, management found few advantages in using this type of labour, with the researchers commenting upon the 'little sign of strategic thinking about labour utilisation in British industry – employers typically improvise' (Hunter and MacInnes, 1992, pp. 314–315).

So, while there is some evidence concerning the development of flexible working and the inclusion of flexibility agreements in the bargaining forum, there is only a limited indication of a link between improved productivity and flexibility initiatives (Edwards, 1987). This, together with the critique of flexibility, suggests that, while flexibility issues are undoubtedly an important HRM initiative to effect change in the labour process with implications for collective bargaining, caution is required in interpreting the extent of such change, particularly to what degree it represents a strategic approach to the employment relationship.

Bargaining initiatives of the 1980s and 1990s

Single union deals, single table bargaining, no-strike clauses and pendulum arbitration are largely associated with Japanese management strategies given their initiation within Japanese subsidiaries locating on greenfield sites in the UK. The earliest examples of such practices are cited in Toshiba (1981) with subsequent examples at Nissan and Komatsu. However, from the 21 agreements (single union, no strike, pendulum arbitration) existing in the late 1980s only seven were Japanese subsidiaries, with the remainder being North American (where the strategy originally emerged) or local firms (Beaumont, 1990).

Single union deals have posed difficult questions for the existing form and structure of the British trade union movement, having a number of implications for the collective bargaining process. The single union agreement occurs where management grants recognition to only one trade union to represent employees in the bargaining process. This process has been strongly opposed over the 1980s, with the main protagonist of such agreements the (then) EETPU being suspended from the TUC in 1988 for refusing to withdraw from such an agreement with Christian Salvesen and Orion Electric.

The major objection to single union deals is the promotion of what Salamon (1992) describes as a 'beauty contest approach' between trade unions. Thus management outline the envisaged approach to industrial relations and a personnel strategy, inviting trade unions to state how they might measure up to the managerial view of employee relations – with the reward being a new pool of members during a time when trade unions are experiencing decline. As such the relationship between management and union becomes one in which unions must offer to fulfil the behavioural expectations of management in order to be granted recognition, rather than prioritising the needs of the membership. The single union deal has other implications for traditional union organisation as it raises the issue of 'poaching' members, i.e. where other unions would have a more legitimate right to represent specific employee skills within the organisation. Furthermore, employees have no choice concerning who represents their interests and indeed, for reasons stated above, may not have access to trade union representation versed in knowledge of their specific trade or skill. This has clear implications for the efficacy of bargaining processes. Finally, single union deals raise the unedifying spectacle of trade unions squabbling amongst themselves to achieve recognition as the pressure mounts to gain new members.

Having opposed the concept of single union deals initially, the TUC adopted a 'code of practice' in 1988 establishing a number of practices which a trade union considering a single union deal should adopt. For the trade union organisation and established bargaining processes, however, the real threat from single union deals is their representation of a different approach to industrial relations based on greater flexibility, consultation and managerial prerogative.

Regarding the collective bargaining process, as argued above, there will be some employees whose interests will not be best served by a union which has no history of representing them and with which they feel no basis of affiliation. However, it could be argued that, given the labour process of organisations who adopt single union deals (single status working, flexibility, fewer separate job titles), the scope for a differentiated approach to bargaining is significantly constrained. A further constraint upon the bargaining process in single union firms is the association between single union deals, no-strike deals and pendulum arbitration.

Obviously, a no-strike clause, once accepted by a trade union on behalf of the membership, effectively deprives union negotiators of the threat of strike action should bargaining break down and, moreover, denies employees the option of withdrawing their labour unilaterally. The attachment of no-strike clauses to single union agreements is further indication of the growth of managerial prerogative concerning the ability to dictate terms of the employment relationship. The controversial element relating to no-strike clauses is employees forgoing the right to strike, where this is seen as the only positive right enjoyed by labour in the employment relationship; moreover, during the bargaining process it is the ultimate sanction. For trade union negotiators the threat of labour withdrawal offers significant advantage in periods of high demand when a loss of productivity would be damaging to management. Changing patterns of demand also infringe upon managerial approaches to bargaining where, for example, anticipation of low product demand would encourage an adversarial approach to negotiations as a loss of production would not be damaging to the firm's market position; at one point this was a common bargaining tactic in the car assembly industry when stocks of cars were high.

No-strike clauses are usually (but not always) accompanied by pendulum arbitration facilities where a third party will arbitrate on behalf of the two principals should they fail to reach agreement. There is some debate concerning the extent and novelty of pendulum arbitration strategy (Salamon, 1992), but the practice undoubtedly originated in North America where it was felt that employees denied the fundamental right to strike should have recourse to some form of arbitration. However, traditional arbitration, which draws from both sides of the negotiation stand-off, may encourage principals to hold back on their final stance as they believe the arbitrator will find middle ground between the two parties. Consequently, where both sides are aware that an arbitrator will adopt one side or the other's position and this will represent a cost to the other party, they are more likely to bargain in good faith, making every effort to settle (Singh, 1986).

While pendulum arbitration offers scope for redress for one interest group in the bargaining relationship, the practice is not without difficulty. The arbitrators may find themselves faced with multiple issue disputes, which cannot be judged as a 'whole'. Thus, the arbitration service may become involved in highly complex analysis of a series of issues, each of which may require a separate decision. The other difficulty with this particular practice is defining the final position of each side within the negotiation process. Such difficulties were encountered during the recourse to pendulum arbitration by Sanyo and the EETPU in the mid-1980s. Indeed, the arbitrators undertook the role of mediator between the two parties to achieve consensus which, in reality, contravened the theory of pendulum arbitration. The limited use of this practice in Britain makes it difficult to assess the impact upon the bargaining process. More evidence has emerged from the United States where the practice is associated with public sector employees. It is argued (Salamon, 1992) that it avoids a 'chilling' effect, where each side holds back from their final position during negotiation, keeping arguments in reserve in case of resort to conventional conciliation/arbitration, or to draw upon in case of dispute. Thus the nego-tiation process is not so drawn out and each side is encouraged to outline their final arguments clearly and convincingly.

Pendulum arbitration has, therefore, the potential significantly to manipulate the nego-tiation process of collective bargaining as either of the final arguments from each side may act as the basis of a compulsory settlement.

The trade union movement has recognised that practices such as single union deals and pendulum arbitration offer employers competitive advantage. Single table bargain-ing is one alternative which offers employers similar benefits to single union deals while maintaining a multi-union site. Bargaining takes place between unions to establish a negotiation proposal, which is articulated by one bargaining unit which negotiates for both manual and non-manual employees. However, for single table bargaining to operate it is essential for all employees to share similar conditions of employment in respect of hours, holidays, pension and sick pay entitlements. A number of companies within the private manufacturing and service sector have adopted a single bargaining table although the process is not widespread. Marginson and Sisson (1990) identify three incen-tives for favouring single table bargaining:

- Multi-unit bargaining does not utilise management resources efficiently and offers potential sources of inter-union conflict.
- The introduction of new working methods, for example flexible working, is most effec-tively achieved through single table bargaining, bypassing the complexity of fragmented bargaining.
- It facilitates the introduction of single status or harmonises working conditions.

To achieve single table bargaining, it is argued that there must be management com-mitment to the process indicated by a willingness to discuss a wide range of issues:

> The key significance of single table bargaining is not that it replaces exist-ing arrangements, but that it adds a top tier where matters affecting all employees, such as training, development, working time and fringe bene-fits can be discussed. So too can the overall direction of the business.
>
> (Marginson and Sisson, 1990)

Thus, managerial perception of single table bargaining must extend beyond that of the negotiation forum to encompass information sharing. Marginson and Sisson (1990) argue that single table bargaining will become more widespread as the impact of European Union directives and legislation regarding information sharing, communication and col-lective bargaining encourage management to review bargaining processes. Moreover, they foresee the single table forum as offering management opportunities to introduce issues beyond the conventional bargaining agenda, with the aim of engaging trade union support for HRM issues relating to employee commitment and cooperation for change.

However, there are some potential problems with single table bargaining as unions must reconcile their bargaining priorities in order to agree upon a united negotiation agenda, rather than being able to prioritise issues of particular importance to individual memberships. Careful consideration must be given by participating unions to establish how bargaining priorities are to be decided upon – whether this is based upon size of membership sector or each union given equal representation, regardless of size. The major effect of this process, however, is that management is presented with an agreed bargaining agenda representing the majority of employees (the exception being higher levels of management) and no longer engage in inter-union disputes concerning bargaining priorities.

Summary

A number of bargaining initiatives have emerged during the 1980s which have changed the level and structure of the collective bargaining process. These initiatives have facilitated the exercise of managerial prerogative in the bargaining relationship and further narrowed the scope of bargaining channels. Overall, however, the collective bargaining function has remained intact but constrained in scope.

PUBLIC SECTOR BARGAINING

Public sector industrial relations can be differentiated from the private sector on a number of points:

- the persistence of historically established processes of national level collective bargaining;
- the role of the government as employer seeking to promote a specific model of industrial relations to the private sector, reflecting a political ethos;
- the problem of responding to market forces where the market is remote or a monopoly of service exists;
- the complex structure of bargaining arrangements consisting of local management and central government personnel.

Although public sector bargaining recognises a different set of variables from that of the private sector, until the mid-1970s, the stability of public sector industrial relations largely excluded it as an area of study. The origins of public sector collective bargaining are to be found in the reports of the Whitley Committee (1917–18) which established national negotiating machinery and local consultative committees (see above). Despite some resistance to the system from successive inter-war governments, by the end of the Second World War the Whitley system covered most public sector employees. With the advent of the National Health Service and an extensive nationalisation programme, the system of national-level, bureaucratic collective bargaining machinery was firmly established.

Nationally negotiated terms and conditions of employment persisted as the focal point of collective bargaining throughout the 1950s and 1960s. Agreements pertaining to public sector employees were notable for their detailed and extensive coverage of procedural and substantive systems which offered little scope for managers and trade unionists to negotiate enhanced conditions reflecting local circumstances. Thus, in the 1950s and 1960s, the public sector did not reflect the pattern of fragmented, domestic bargaining synonymous with the private sector during these years.

A further feature of public sector collective bargaining is that of comparability. Due to the difficulty of establishing performance indicators based on market conditions, the Priestly Commission (1955) recommended that the terms and conditions of employment for the Civil Service should be established through comparison with similar work groups in the private sector. Comparability agreements were then adopted as the most efficient manner in which to agree terms and conditions throughout the public sector, and indeed proved highly beneficial to employees, particularly in the mid-1970s. Between 1973 and 1975, the average increase in the growth of earnings touched nearly 30% due to a combination of incomes policy influences and comparability claims.

However, this formula for conducting collective bargaining – highly centralised, bureaucratic and detailed, comparability based – led to a number of difficulties. Linking pay to productivity or establishing local agreements became a major problem due to the hurdles presented by national bargaining. Other difficulties arose in the late 1970s when, in response to growing inflation and falling competitiveness, the government introduced a series of incomes policies which no longer acted to enhance public sector pay. However, while the government was able to utilise incomes policies through highly centralised bargaining processes to control public sector pay settlements, this restraint was not reflected in the private sector. The growing differentials between private and public sector pay led to a series of major industrial disputes by public employees in the late 1970s which the Labour government failed effectively to manage or resolve. Consequently, after the General Election of 1979, the Thatcher government focused upon industrial relations problems as a major source of economic disruption. It was determined to effect change in managing the employment relationship in the public sector, and this example, combined with a series of legislative acts to constrain trade union activities, would act to prompt similar change in the private sector.

In reviewing collective bargaining practices the government has encouraged a number of changes. Independent pay review bodies have been established for doctors, dentists, nurses, teachers and civil servants which bypass the collective bargaining process with pay being index linked. Index linking has also been applied to the police and firefighters, although the present government is reviewing this practice due to the level of pay increases. This has prompted threats of industrial action from both of these groups.

Another noticeable trend during the 1980s has been an identifiable shift in public sector bargaining away from national-level to local-level collective bargaining. This has been facilitated by successive Conservative government attempts to slim down the public sector through initiatives such as privatisation and opt-outs, while introducing market economy discipline to other areas through contracting out and competitive tendering.

The 1983 Water Act encouraged management to decentralise collective bargaining to local areas, and while national bargaining has not been completely abolished, there has been a trend towards each water authority negotiating separate terms and conditions. This policy of decentralisation has met with considerable resistance in other parts of the public sector, particularly the Department of Social Security.

The government's commitment to privatisation has resulted in 16 separate enterprises being sold since 1979, while there are many examples of services within the remainder of the public sector being contracted out or subject to competitive tendering. This is particularly evident in the health service where local health authorities will encourage cost-cutting by offering non-core services to the private sector, where evidence suggests that employees are unlikely to have access to trade union representation.

Along with attempts to reform established forms of collective bargaining the government has encouraged the introduction of performance pay indicators. Initially this was largely focused upon senior management, particularly in the NHS, local authorities and the Civil Service, although in the late 1980s, forms of merit pay were introduced for lower grade civil servants, London Transport and the Civil Aviation Authority (Gospel and Palmer, 1993).

There has been a clearly identifiable shift away from national-level bargaining towards local initiatives within the public sector. Successive Conservative governments have argued that pay should be linked to local performance and away from comparability agreements, with the aim of taking advantage of local conditions and controlling inflationary pressures. Initiatives such as privatisation, contracting out, opting out and competitive tendering have supported the move to local-level bargaining, although there has been opposition from public sector trade unions to decentralisation policies. The unions argue that the most vulnerable sections of the workforce will be adversely affected by moves to local-level bargaining, while contracting services out to non-union, private sector service firms represents a loss of members for public sector unions. It is likely, however, that decentralisation will continue to be encouraged, while other initiatives such as flexibility and performance-related pay will become more common in the collective bargaining agenda of the public sector.

Summary

Traditionally, the public sector has enjoyed stable industrial relations with a formally established system of national-level collective bargaining with a comparative ethos. Due to intolerable pressure upon this formula during the 1970s, largely as a result of economic crises and the attempted use of incomes policies as a wage restraint, there was a series of wide-ranging bitter industrial disputes. Successive Conservative governments since 1979 have attempted to reform industrial relations in the public sector with the dual aims of offering the example of the private sector as what they believe to be 'good practice' in industrial relations conduct, while also contributing to the control of public sector spending. There has been an identifiable trend towards decentralisation facilitated by the sale of publicly owned enterprises and other privatisation-type initiatives. There has been some resistance to these practices from unions, with a recent increase in the level of industrial action within the public sector. However, in the future there will undoubtedly be further progress in establishing local bargaining with flexibility and performance-related pay appearing on the collective bargaining agenda.

EUROPEAN TRENDS IN COLLECTIVE BARGAINING

The decentralisation of collective bargaining is a trend which is discernible across Europe and is most pronounced in Britain and Italy. However, initiatives to promote decentralisation are evident in the Netherlands, France and Germany. Although there is a common theme of localised bargaining, we can discern significant differences between the approach to reforming collective bargaining. Thus in the UK where, since the early 1980s, there has been a move away from the corporatist approach to managing industrial relations, there has been a more adversarial approach to the introduction of change –

particularly in the public sector. Successive British Conservative governments have attempted to reform and regulate industrial relations through legislation and confrontation. While there is little indication that the private sector has adopted a significantly more aggressive stance towards industrial relations in general, and collective bargaining in particular, the economic and political environment has acted to constrain the opportunities for resistance from the trade union movement, such that the scope of bargaining has been narrowed and the introduction of local bargaining initiatives has been facilitated.

Where the corporatist approach has not been abandoned, for example in Scandinavia and Germany, it has been weakened by contemporary economic pressures and this is reflected in the move away from national bargaining. Furthermore, throughout Europe decentralisation has been accompanied by a range of plant-level initiatives such as new technology agreements, productivity deals and performance-related pay developments which are compromising the scope and effectiveness of collective bargaining procedures. The greatest issue dominating the contemporary European bargaining agenda, however, is that of labour flexibility where every country is employing multi-skilling of core groups and tackling the problem by introducing external flexibility at the periphery.

Thus throughout Europe the common themes in the development of collective bargaining are decentralisation and flexibility. The manner in which such initiatives are introduced and established, however, is highly dependent upon the prevailing approach to industrial relations. Where corporatism survives, the state will encourage the use of trade union channels and bargaining processes to facilitate the introduction of workplace change, but resistance will be constrained by external economic pressures weakening the corporatist bonds. Where corporatism has been virtually abandoned as, for example in Britain, the state has encouraged a less discursive, bargained approach to workplace change, instead using the public sector as an example to bypass collective bargaining channels where possible, and enacting a legislative framework to constrain trade union resistance to change.

CONTROVERSIES IN HRM AND COLLECTIVE BARGAINING

The early conceptual notion of HRM being focused and only possible in the unitary firm, where collective action or resistance is not considered a legitimate form of employee response to managerial authority, is no longer considered as a useful framework. This view of HRM as a complete package only possible within the unitary structure is too restrictive; it virtually narrows HRM to a theoretical construct existing only as an 'ideal type'. In contemporary usage, HRM is employed as a set of strategic initiatives focused upon the employee with the aim of improving competitiveness, where any firm, depending on product and market demands, may utilise any number from a range of initiatives included under the HRM umbrella (although there remains considerable debate concerning the strategic element, given the argument that the majority of British management is not able to employ strategic tactics (Mabey and Salamon, 1995)). Yet introducing and managing HRM practices in a collective bargaining environment does raise a number of contentious issues, primarily whether a series of initiatives aimed at the individual employee can be compatible with the collective approach.

It appears that HRM initiatives are more evident in unionised firms and this can be taken as evidence that the two practices, HRM and collective bargaining, are not mutually exclusive (Mishel and Voos, 1992). Guest (1989) argues that the values underpinning HRM – strategic integration and the pursuit of quality – are not incompatible with collective representation where bargaining channels can be effectively utilised to introduce change. There is some evidence that collective bargaining procedures are being utilised to introduce flexibility and technology agreements linked to pay bargaining (Lindopp and Haslett, 1988). Moreover, Storey (1989) argues that the two systems can coexist in harmony where HRM initiatives are focused upon areas which do not pose a threat to the scope of collective bargaining, or where they do not attempt to bypass established bargaining channels. It appears that companies may also operate a dual system of collective bargaining and HRM where there is the clear ambition of bypassing bargaining channels in favour of consultation and communication schemes associated with a HRM approach; Beaumont (1995) refers to Cadburys as one such example.

Consequently, it is not axiomatic that if HRM is to be introduced, collective bargaining must be derecognised; the critical issue here is the motivation for the introduction of HRM. If, as appears to be the case in Cadburys, individualised HRM practices are aimed at undermining union effectiveness, there is a real threat to existing procedures. However, if change is deployed after discussion and/or negotiation with existing unions, there is an opportunity for joint regulation of new working practices. This is not to argue that collective bargaining will be unaffected by the adoption of HRM; from research undertaken in 1992, Storey found that, while collective bargaining had become less of a management priority, new HRM practices and collective bargaining tended to exist as parallel arrangements. The emphasis was upon reducing the union role rather than replacing it.

Collectivism versus individualism?

The essence of collective bargaining is the utilisation of collective power to achieve and maintain acceptable conditions of employment for the labour force. As such agreements reached arise from, and pertain to, the collective, this contradicts the individualistic philosophy of HRM, thus we find a major area of dissent between the two practices. This represents an incompatibility which is only reconciled by a dual system where HRM initiatives aimed at the collective, for example flexible working, can be channelled through bargaining procedures, but other issues such as performance-related pay can be policed through bargaining but not collectively applied. Thus, while we would argue that collective bargaining procedures can be operated in firms employing HRM initiatives, there will inevitably be areas of tension in the full adoption of a strategic HRM policy.

Collective bargaining and equal opportunities

While there have been a number of legislative initiatives to outlaw discrimination on the grounds of sex, race, age and disability, statistical data describing the contemporary workforce indicate that such groups still experience discrimination in the employment market. So we find that in crude terms women, for example, earn approximately 77% of the wages of their male counterparts (Rubery, 1992), which leads us to question whether legislation can adequately address the sources of discrimination and prejudice in the workplace. To examine this issue further, we can consider the role of collective bargaining in challenging existing sex discrimination in the labour market. Collective bargaining does not create discrimination but may perpetuate it by reflecting stereotypical assumptions concerning the appropriate roles and rewards of men and women at work.

Colling and Dickens (1989) argue that collective bargaining is conservative in outlook with, for example, a focus upon pay increases rather than pay structures and grading systems, with women crowded into the lowest categories. Among negotiators there was an unquestioning acceptance of this skewed distribution of reward, this lack of recognition of discrimination in fact contributes to stereotypical assumptions regarding women's role in waged labour. Moreover, the structure of trade unions, the manner in which officials are elected and the negotiating arena are highly discriminatory against women which means that issues of specific relevance to female labour are rarely taken into account (Purcell, 1988).

An empirical study of collective bargaining and equality issues in three industrial sectors explored the extent to which there was 'equality awareness' in commonplace bargaining agenda issues, for example pay, as well as considering an 'equality dimension' in negotiation of 'change', for example performance-related pay. The authors, Colling and Dickens (1989), concluded that there was little evidence that collective bargaining and collective agreements were addressing issues of discrimination and subordination. While there are many equality issues which remain outside the mandate of collective bargaining, such as recruitment, selection, training and promotion, here is scope for 'equality bargaining' which incorporate issues into collective agreements which are likely to be of particular importance to women in facilitating an equitable participation in the workforce. Colling and Dickens (p. 48) argue that:

> for equality bargaining to occur requires pressure on collective bargaining and bargainers. The pressure needs to be both informed and appropriately channelled; there needs to be receptiveness to it and an ability and preparedness to act. Pressures may be generated internally (from within the union or the workplace, from above or below) or externally. The ideal situation would seem to be where various influencing factors are operating simultaneously on employer and trade union negotiators, pushing in the same direction.

Thus there is a requirement for both unions and employers to recognise the need for the 'equality agenda', which will entail a review of presumptions concerning the construction of pay structures, career progressions, bonus/productivity schemes as well as the introduction of issues such as childcare facilities, paternity leave and job-sharing which must be afforded serious attention. From a pragmatic stance, employers cannot afford to dismiss issues of discrimination and subordination because of the risk of legal action; but, with the changing demographic profile of the workforce, if employers are to attract and utilise the human resource most efficiently, equality bargaining needs to be perceived as a priority. Likewise, if trade unions are to attract new members from the feminised workforce, they must demonstrate understanding of discrimination and a determination to address these issues. There is some evidence that there is a growing awareness of this from trade unions, with the GMB in particular displaying a commitment to improving the position of women at work through the bargaining channel.

Given that a main aim of the HRM approach is to maximise utilisation of individuals in the workplace, it is immediately evident that a discriminatory approach will hamper performance as well as devalue individuals in the organisation. Clearly, evidence indicates that there is a potential and actual discriminatory element within the collective bargaining format. Thus the adoption of an HRM environment, aiming – even if for pragmatic performance reasons – to maximise individual performance in a collective bargaining forum has the potential to initiate positive changes in the negotiation agenda. However, this is only likely where management and trade unions can fully recognise the value, need and possibility for addressing equality through the collective bargaining channel.

Summary

It is argued that collective bargaining processes can coexist with HRM initiatives and indeed may be introduced through such channels. Evidence suggests that in new plants, single union or non-union structures will prevail which will offer management greater freedom in achieving strategic HRM integration. In established plants, while HRM initiatives are evident, they have not seriously challenged the main focus of collective bargaining upon pay issues, but the scope of bargaining has been narrowed, with consultation being employed as a preferred channel of communication. There is opportunity for a consensual approach to inequality in the workplace where the priorities of individual development may be addressed through the collective bargaining agenda, if the commitment is present from all concerned.

SUMMARY

● Collective bargaining has customarily been defined in Britain as the process of joint regulation of job control, undertaken by management and trade unions who negotiate to establish the terms and conditions which govern the employment relationship. Human resource management might be viewed as posing a threat to this joint process by its emphasis on the managerial dominance of the relationship which requires that employees accept a managerially derived employment agenda.

● The classical definitions of collective bargaining stress a variety of characteristics that are associated with the process, such as the acceptance of a collectively organised expression of interests on the part of employees (rather than a variety of individualised responses), and an acceptance of the collective employee interest by management (usually by their recognition of trade unions). The consequence of this mutual recognition of interests is the development of both *substantive* and *procedural* rules to govern, respectively, the pay and conditions of employees and the regulatory framework in which they are negotiated.

● Theoretical approaches to the analysis of collective bargaining may be grouped around three dominant perspectives: the *unitary*, the *pluralist*, and the *radical*. The unitary perspective views the organisation as a cooperative system with no perceived difference in interest between management and employees. Collective bargaining is seen as unnecessary and intrusive and likely to engender a conflictual relationship; the pluralist perspective views the organisation as the venue for conflicting interests between management and labour which collective bargaining moderates by providing a means to arrive at mutual agreements, thus reducing inherent conflict; the radical perspective views collective bargaining as a limitation on wider employee aspirations in a capitalist society because of its focus on the narrow set of issues connected with job regulation and the channelling of conflict into acceptable formats – such as strikes – which can be regulated.

● Contemporary developments in collective bargaining in the private sector have seen a narrowing of its coverage as a result of the decline in unionisation and managerial pressure to limit its scope amongst employees; in the public sector the government has limited collective bargaining by introducing pay review bodies for many classes of public employee, where pay is set without using bargaining processes at all. On a more general level, human resource management approaches are held to be inimical to collective bargaining, but it is still the case that many major organisations use a mix of both processes, and that there is some evidence from the Workplace Industrial Relations Survey that mature collective bargaining environments are often the location of the very HRM policies that are held to be incompatible with traditional collective bargaining.

ACTIVITY

Malone Engineering is a medium-sized manufacturing firm employing approximately 450 people, having been established for nearly 50 years. The majority of the workforce are skilled males represented by the AEEU; however, there are a number of other unions on site representing service employees and semi/unskilled workers. Trade unions have, in the past, had a good relationship with management, but over recent years this has deteriorated somewhat as management have tried to introduce change through collective bargaining, to cope with a declining market and recessionary pressures. The unions have resisted change in both working methods and payment systems thus far, settling instead for some redundancies and only small increases in annual pay. The firm has managed to maintain profitability, largely through its reputation for quality in a specialised market, but there has been a notable downturn in recent years.

This situation is in the process of change as Malone Engineering has been acquired by the Parks Corporation, a large modern company which believes it can turn Malone Engineering into a highly profitable subsidiary by developing the specialist nature of production. As part of this process of change, management have stated their aim to reform working methods but to introduce change through the collective bargaining arena. This will inevitably lead to some redundancies and substantial changes in the labour process; however, the trade unions recognise that Parks Corporation will need the specialist skills of the membership which they intend to use as bargaining leverage.

EXERCISES

1 Outline the major issues to be introduced through the collective bargaining agenda.

2 Outline the major changes which Parks Corporation management might introduce to the collective bargaining format.

3 How will these possible changes affect the trade union bargaining process?

4 What tactics might trade union negotiators use to resist change?

QUESTIONS

1 What have been the major developments in British collective bargaining since 1979?

2 Examine the argument that HRM initiatives can be successfully integrated into established unionised plants.

3 'Collective bargaining processes contradict the basic assumptions of the HRM approach'. Discuss.

EXERCISES

1 Prepare a report in which you define and outline the advantages and problems of:
- single table bargaining;
- single union deals.

2 Write a short explanation of the following terms:
- bargaining level;
- scope of bargaining;
- integrative bargaining;
- distributive bargaining.

3 Debate the proposition that 'collective bargaining has the potential to redress the power imbalance within the employment relationship'.

4 Identify and explore the major differences between public and private sector collective bargaining processes, levels and structures.

REFERENCES AND FURTHER READING

Those texts marked with an asterisk are particularly recommended for further reading.

Advisory, Conciliation and Arbitration Service (1988) *Labour Flexibility in Britain*, Occasional Paper No. 41. London: HMSO.

Ahlstrand, B. and Purcell, J. (1988) 'Employee relations strategy in the multi-divisional company', *Personnel Review*, Vol. 17, No. 2, pp. 3–11.

Atkinson, J. (1984) 'Manpower strategies for flexible organisations', *Personnel Management*, August.

Atkinson, J. and Meager, N. (1986) *Changing Patterns of Work – How Companies Introduce Flexibility to Meet New Needs*. London: IMS/OECD.

Bain, G.S. (ed.) (1983) *Industrial Relations in Britain*. Oxford: Blackwell.

Batstone, E., Boraston, I. and Frenkel, S. (1977) *Shop Stewards in Action*. Oxford: Blackwell.

Beaumont, P.B. (1990) *Change in Industrial Relations*. London: Routledge.

Beaumont, P.B. (1995) *The Future of Employment Relations*. London: Sage.

Brown, W. (ed.) (1981) *The Changing Contours of British Industrial Relations*. Oxford: Blackwell.

CBI (1988) *The Structure and Processes of Pay Determination in the Private Sector: 1979–1986*. London: CBI.

Chamberlain, N.W. and Kuhn, J.W. (1965) *Collective Bargaining*. New York: McGraw-Hill.

Clegg, H. (1979) *The Changing Systems of Industrial Relations in Great Britain*. Oxford: Blackwell.

Colling, T. and Dickens, L. (1989) *Equality Bargaining, Why Not?* Equal Opportunities Commission, London: HMSO.

Daniel, W. and Millward, N. (1983) *Workplace Industrial Relations in Britain*. London: Heinemann.

Deaton, D.R. and Beaumont, P.B. (1980) 'The determinants of bargaining structure: some large-scale survey evidence for Britain', *British Journal of Industrial Relations*, Vol. 18, p. 201.

Donovan Commission (1968) *Report of the Royal Commission on Trade Unions and Employers' Associations, 1965–68*, Cmnd. 3623. London: HMSO.

Edwards, P. (1987) *Managing the Factory: A Survey of General Managers*. Oxford: Blackwell.

Flanders, A. (1964) *The Fawley Productivity Agreement*. London: Faber.

Flanders, A. (1968) 'Collective bargaining: a theoretical analysis', *British Journal of Industrial Relations*, Vol. 6, No. 1, pp. 1–26.

Flanders, A. (1970) 'Collective bargaining: prescription for change', *Management and Unions: The Theory and Reform of Industrial Relations*. London: Faber.

Fox, A. (1975) 'Collective bargaining, Flanders and the Webbs', *British Journal of Industrial Relations*, Vol. 13, No. 2, pp. 151–174.

Gospel, H. and Palmer, G. (1993) *British Industrial Relations*. London: Routledge.

Gregg, P. and Yates, A. (1991) 'Changes in wage-setting arrangements and trade union presence in the 1980s', *British Journal of Industrial Relations*, Vol. 29, No. 3.

Guest, D.E. (1989) 'Human resource management: its implications for industrial relations and trade unions', in Storey, J. (ed.) *New Perspectives on Human Resource Management*. London: Routledge.

*Guest, D. (1987) 'Human resource management and industrial relations', *Journal of Management Studies*, Vol. 24, No. 5, September.

Hunter, L. and MacInnes, J. (1992) 'Employment and labour flexibilty', *Employment Gazette*, June, pp. 314–315.

Hyman, R. (1975) *Industrial Relations, A Marxist Introduction*. London: Macmillan.

Industrial Relations Review and Report 316, March 1984. London: Industrial Relations Services.

Jackson, M. (1991) *An Introduction to Industrial Relations*. London: Routledge.

Kinnie, N. (1990) 'The decentralisation of industrial relations? Recent research considered', *Personnel Review*, Vol. 19, No. 3, pp. 28–34.

Lindopp, E. and Haslett, P. (1988) 'Long term pay deals: an interim verdict', *Personnel Management*, April.

Littler, C.R. (1980) 'Internal contract and the transition to modern work systems: Britain and Japan', in Dunkerley, D. and Salamon, G. (eds) *International Yearbook of Organisation Studies*. London: Routledge & Kegan Paul.

Mabey, C. and Salamon, G. (1995) *Strategic Human Resource Management*. Oxford: Blackwell.

McCarthy, W.J. and Parker, S.R. (1968) *Shop Stewards and Workshop Relations*. London: HMSO.

Marlow, S. and Patton, D. (1992) 'Managing the employment relationship in smaller firms: possibilities for HRM', in Welford, R. (ed.) *Businesses and Small Business Development – A Practical Approach*. Bradford: European Research Press.

Marchington, M. and Parker, P. (1990) *Changing Patterns of Employee Relations*. Hemel Hempstead: Harvester Wheatsheaf.

Marginson, P., Edwards, P., Martin, R., Purcell, J. and Sisson, K. (1988) *Beyond the Workplace*. Oxford: Blackwell.

Marginson, P. and Sisson, K. (1990) 'Single table talk', *Personnel Management*, May, pp. 46–48.

Marsh, D. (1992) *The New Politics of British Trade Unionism*. London: Macmillan.

Millward, N. and Stevens, M. (1986) *British Workplace Industrial Relations 1980–1984*. London: Gower.

Millward, N., Steven, M., Smart, D. and Hawes, W.R. (1992) *Workplace Industrial Relations in Transition*. Aldershot: Dartmouth.

Mishel, L. and Voos, P.B. (eds) (1992) *Unions and Economic Competitiveness*. New York: Sharpe.

Palmer, G. (1983) *British Industrial Relations*. London: Unwin & Hyman.

Piore, M.J. (1971) 'The dual labour market: theory and implications', in Gordon, D.M. (ed.) *Problems in Political Economy: An Urban Perspective*. Lexington Heath.

Pollert, A. (1988) 'Dismantling flexibility', *Capital and Class*, Vol. 34, Spring, pp. 42–75.

Purcell, K. (1988) 'Gender and the experience of employment', in Gallie, D. (ed.) *Employment in Britain*. Oxford: Blackwell.

Rubery, J. (1992) 'Pay, gender and the social dimension of Europe', *British Journal of Industrial Relations*, Vol. 30, No. 4, pp. 605–621.

Salamon, M. (1992) *Industrial Relations, Theory and Practice*. Englewood Cliffs, NJ: Prentice Hall.

Singh, R. (1986) 'Final offer: arbitration in theory and practice', *Industrial Relations Journal*, Winter, pp. 329–330.

Storey, J. (ed.) (1989) *New Perspectives on Human Resource Management*. London: Routledge.

Storey, J. (1992) *Developments in the Management of Human Resources*. Oxford: Blackwell.

Walton, R.E. and McKersie, R.B (1965) *A Behavioural Theory of Labor Negotiations*. New York: McGraw-Hill.

Webb, S. and Webb, B. (1902) *Industrial Democracy*. London: Longman.

REMUNERATION

AND REWARD

Ian Roberts

To explain the theoretical foundations of reward and remuneration strategies in organisations.

●

To examine the issues in designing a reward system.

●

To examine the methods and aims of different forms of payment systems.

●

To critically examine contemporary issues and trends in remuneration and reward strategies, techniques and philosophies.

●

To analyse remuneration and reward in an international context.

●

To highlight the relationship between remuneration and reward and human resource management.

●

INTRODUCTION

The introductory chapter illustrated the extent to which human resource management seeks to achieve an integrated philosophy. This chapter explores the role played by remuneration and reward management and policy in achieving human resource management outcomes and objectives (for example, see Beer *et al.*, 1984; Hendry and Pettigrew, 1990; Poole, 1992; Storey, 1992).

As one writer states:

> . . . the pay package is one of the most obvious and visible expressions of the employment relationship; it is the main issue in the exchange between employer and employee, expressing the connection between the labour market, the individual's work and the performance of the employing organisation itself.
> (Hegewisch, 1991a: 28)

The design and operation of payment systems in many organisations have often been institutionalised by custom and practice, tradition and collective bargaining mechanisms, and as Smith (1992: 75–76) indicates, frequently as a result of simply 'muddling through'. Nevertheless trends show that the movement towards human resource management has corresponded with the introduction of supposedly 'new' forms and strategies of reward management, particularly concentrating on performance–reward contingencies in an individual and unitarist framework. However, literature on this subject seems riddled with imprecise clichés, generalisations, confusing terminology, byzantine methodological accounts and evangelical reports using the latest buzzwords. A balance needs to be found between the academic and the practitioner and a sense of the historic development of payment systems needs to be provided in order to paint a more realistic picture of the dissemination and failings of the methods currently in use.

THEORETICAL FOUNDATIONS OF REMUNERATION STRATEGIES

Due to competitive pressures organisations are continually looking to increase the 'added value' of their employees by encouraging them to increase their effort and performance beyond that which is at a minimally acceptable standard, or by reducing labour costs to a minimum. Thus the study of employee motivation has remained a constant managerial concern.

This section considers three of the main theories of motivation which provide the theoretical foundations for remuneration and reward strategies. We then look briefly at the theory of behaviour modification which attempts to explain how desirable employee behaviour can be encouraged.

The first set of theories considers the proposition that workers are motivated to satisfy their personal needs at their place of work.

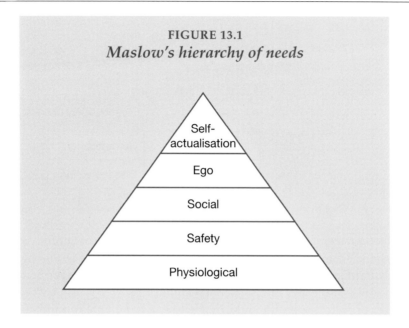

FIGURE 13.1
Maslow's hierarchy of needs

Maslow's hierarchy of needs

Abraham Maslow devised a theory of human nature which proposed that everyone is motivated to satisfy a series of instinctual needs. Everyone's needs, Maslow believed, were arranged in a hierarchy as illustrated in Figure 13.1.

● *Physiological needs* are basic biological needs essential for survival. They include food, drink, shelter, rest, sleep, sex, oxygen.
● *Safety and security needs* include protection from physical and psychological threats in the environment such as freedom from fear, and a wish for certainty.
● *Social and belonging needs* include a need for love, affection, friendship, social interaction and acceptance of others.
● *Ego and esteem needs* include a need for self-respect, confidence, recognition, respect from others, status, power and competence.
● *Self-actualisation* includes self-fulfilment, achievement, individual growth, and the realisation of potential.

Maslow believed that once one level of needs had been satisfied they no longer motivated the individual and other needs would become prominent. Individuals would be motivated to progressively work their way up the hierarchy, satisfying each level until they reached the final level of 'self-actualisation'. Thus in order to increase employees' motivation managers have to consider the higher levels of needs as well as physiological and safety needs.

Herzberg's two-factor theory of motivation

Another contributor to motivation theory, Frederick Herzberg, made the distinction between hygiene factors and motivators in the work environment.

FIGURE 13.2
Herzberg's two-factor theory of motivation

Level of provision

	Adequate	Inadequate
Motivators	Motivation	No motivation
Hygiene factors	No dissatisfaction	Dissatisfaction

Hygiene factors were thought to be environmental and prevented workers from becoming dissatisfied and demotivated. Herzberg believed, however, that hygiene factors did not motivate. Examples include pay, working conditions, supervision, company policy and administration, and interpersonal relationships.

A second set of factors were thought by Herzberg to be able to motivate individual employees. These 'motivators' included such factors as: interesting and meaningful work, achievement, recognition, responsibility, personal growth and advancement. The lack of these factors at work would simply mean employees were not motivated. Thus an organisation must be concerned with ensuring that both the hygiene factors and motivators are to an adequate standard.

Figure 13.2 summarises Herzberg's propositions.

Porter and Lawler's model of motivation (1968)

Porter and Lawler modified and built upon Vroom's (1964) expectancy and Adams' (1963) equity theories of motivation. These theories can be termed process theories of motivation as they consider the relationship between effort–performance–reward for each individual and thus provide a more dynamic theoretical reasoning for most reward strategies.

Figure 13.3 illustrates the main variables in the Porter and Lawler model of motivation.

Intrinsic and extrinsic rewards (Factor 1)

Intrinsic rewards are less tangible, originate from the person or job itself and reflect Herzberg's motivators. Examples of such factors include:

- variety in job content;
- sense of being part of the whole 'value adding' process;
- belief that they are a valuable member of a team;
- increased responsibility and autonomy;
- sense of accomplishment;
- participation in setting targets and opportunities to achieve them;
- feedback of information;

FIGURE 13.3
Porter and Lawler's model of motivation

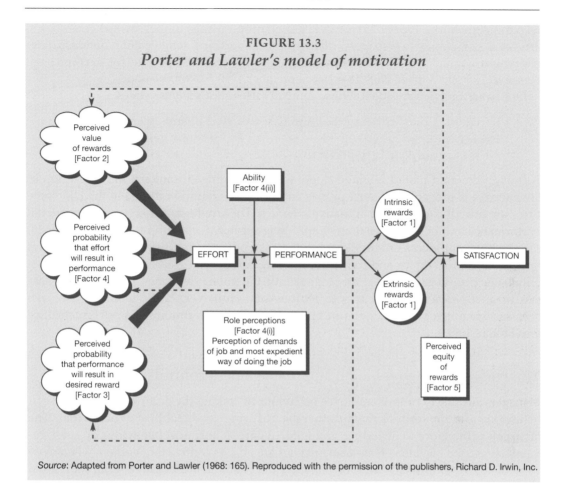

Source: Adapted from Porter and Lawler (1968: 165). Reproduced with the permission of the publishers, Richard D. Irwin, Inc.

- recognition;
- opportunities to learn and grow.

(See also Hackman and Oldman, 1976 and 1980.)

Extrinsic rewards result from the actions of others such as supervisors and are more easily controlled by managers. Examples include pay, fringe benefits, praise and promotion.

Pay is frequently used as a motivator and reinforcer as it can easily be differentiated and computed, linked clearly and visibly to desired performance and is generally a valued reward (Child, 1984: 189). White (1982: 272) outlined the major components in the meaning of money to people:

- short-term material enjoyment;
- long-term security;
- social status;
- recognition of personal achievement.

The importance of recognition for employee motivation is well documented. For several years companies in the US have realised the strength of this motivational factor and have attempted to provide mechanisms to address this need by installing employee recognition awards. Types of award vary, including medals, dinner, award ceremonies, articles in companies' newspapers, photographs advertising achievement, holidays, jewellery, gift vouchers, business accessories, clothing and cash prizes (for example, see *Personnel Journal*, October 1988: 144–156; September 1990: 92–93).

One American vice-president whose company uses such schemes states:

> Recognition must speak to the employee receiving it, and awards are only
> one aspect of this. The symbolism, meaning and intrinsic value attached to
> the reward are equally important.   (Cited in Rawlinson, 1988: 141)

Although the gold plated carriage clock, watch or engraved tankard in recognition of long service is probably the most prominent form of recognition award in the UK, some firms are introducing more imaginative schemes. The emphasis is to reward exceptional performance and effort rather than simply long service. For example, Simons (1992: 25) reports how employees at HMV can receive cash bonuses and prizes for meeting sales targets, customer service and the cleanest store. For 'special' yearly competitions when only a few people gain, prizes can range from a £20 holiday voucher to a set of two tickets for an all-expenses-paid trip to Hollywood. However, HMV tends to use cash bonuses when it is a more regular incentive, for example for monthly sales targets. (See also Hilton, 1992.)

The Porter and Lawler model and management control

Managers are able to control employee behaviour by linking the occurrence of the desired behaviour to some form of reward, thereby ensuring predictability of behaviour. The intention is therefore to introduce and enforce agreed norms of behaviour on management's prescribed agenda. Thus management are able to control the workers when close supervision is not possible and/or worker's discretion is not possible. If an individual manager therefore has discretion as to which behaviour to reward and who to reward then he or she has power. (See also Baldamus 1961: 91; Behrend, 1961: 103–104; Etzioni 1961, 1964; Flanders, 1970: 73.)

The Porter and Lawler model – summary of principles

By utilising this model the following principles can be stated:

- Employees must value the rewards (intrinsic or extrinsic) offered by the organisation (Factor 2).
- Employees must believe that good performance will be linked to the achievement of the desired rewards. Thus employees should perceive that higher performance will result in greater rewards (Factor 3).

  However, many managers reward behaviour which they do not wish to encourage and conversely do not reward behaviour which they do. Some examples of this type of behaviour include:
  - often staff suggestions on improving work procedures etc. may mean their jobs are threatened or in some cases they are given the extra workload in implementing the suggestion;

- employee openness may be desired but when someone states a different opinion to that of management then he or she may be labelled as having an attitude problem or as a 'troublemaker';
- an organisation's desire to encourage teamwork and cooperation may be discounted by a payment system and management style which 'rewards' individual success and promotes 'friendly competition';
- an organisation 'hopes' all employees will consider long-term costs and opportunities but the reward system is likely to be geared towards short-term results which are often achieved at the expense of long-term growth and profits.

(For examples, see Kerr, 1975.)

- Employees must be able to engage in 'good' performance. They must have the ability to carry out the tasks and must believe the quality of their work, and hence their reward, is directly related to and reflects the effort they put into the job. If these conditions are not there then employees will not believe that working hard etc. will lead to a reward or an increase in rewards and therefore the link between desired behaviour and desired rewards will be broken (Factor 4).
- Managers must clearly communicate their expectations and objectives, thereby ensuring employees understand which behaviours are required.
- To increase expectations that desired performance will be rewarded, managers must make sure rewards are clearly and visibly linked to performance.

Behaviour modification

Theories of behaviour modification also underpin many systems of payment which attempt to encourage new work habits. Theories suggest individuals learn that the occurrence of certain behaviours will result in reward or punishment. Designers of reward strategies must therefore take into account Thorndike's 'law of effect':

> Of several responses made to the same situation, those which are accompanied or closely followed by satisfaction (reinforcement) . . . will be more likely to recur; those which are accompanied or closely followed by discomfort (punishment) . . . will be less likely to occur.   (Thorndike, 1911: 244)

Thus behaviour modification explains motivation in terms of the external consequences of particular behaviours rather than previously discussed internal explanations such as satisfying needs (i.e. content theories) and the motivational pull of incentives (i.e. process theories). Concern here therefore is in the way organisation reward systems are administered: for example, the reinforcement/consequence (i.e. reward) should follow as soon as possible after the desired behaviour.

INFLUENCES ON PAY DETERMINATION

These include the following:

- *Beliefs about the worth of jobs.* For example the influence of the size; responsibility; skill requirements, and objectionableness of duties.

- *Individual characteristics*. For example age; experience; seniority; general qualifications; special skills; contribution; performance and potential.
- *Labour market*. The level and composition of the remuneration package will be influenced by labour supply and demand either at national level or in response to the local labour market. Companies will have to match or exceed the wages and salaries offered by their labour-market competitors in order to attract the staff they require and prevent existing employees moving to other organisations. (See also Hatchett and Pope, 1988: 38–42.)

  Organisations can use several methods to formulate a competitive pay rate, for example the use of periodic job market surveys, an exchange of information between organisations recruiting in the same labour markets or a willingness simply to 'bump up' rates when the company is having difficulty in recruiting or retaining staff (White, 1982: 268).
- *Remuneration policy and strategy of companies*.
- *Strength of bargaining groups*. For example, the strength of the two different bargaining groups will be influenced by collective bargaining arrangements, legal requirements and restrictions on either party, as well as economic factors such as unemployment levels and job security.
- *The cost of living*.
- *Government intervention*. Government may intervene in the employment relationship in terms of attempting to influence wage inflation through initiatives introduced in the public sector and by encouraging certain types of compensation such as profit sharing or share option schemes.

(For examples see Curnow (1986: 71); and Lupton and Bowey (1983: 2).)

DESIGNING A PAYMENT SYSTEM

Importance of comparability

In analysing the notion of 'fair wages', Hyman and Brough (1975) make the distinction between two types of criteria which management/workers use to calculate 'equity' in remuneration.

- *Internal* criteria are described as 'the assessment of pay of an individual or group by reference to the contribution made or capacities required in respect of such factors as effort, qualification and aptitude' (Hyman and Brough, 1975: 10). Thus equity in this respect relies on the employee–employer relationship where a 'wage–effort bargain' is implicitly agreed upon.
- *External* relativities are described as 'the assessment of pay by comparison with the incomes of other individuals or groups' (Hyman and Brough, 1975: 10). These individuals may be inside or outside of the company, in the same or different occupations, and the equity criteria not only considers pay levels but all aspects of the employment package.

These two criteria manifest themselves in many aspects of human resource management. For example, job evaluation schemes attempt to address both of these ways of quantifying equity by imposing some 'pseudo-scientific' system. The subjectivity of job evaluation schemes has been well documented by many writers elsewhere (e.g. see Wootton, 1962; Bowey, 1980; Lupton and Bowey, 1983: 5–38; Fowler, 1996) and two main arguments seem to pervade the literature: first of all the subjective selection of and weighting given to the pertinent factors thought to result in the successful accomplishment of the job; second the decoding of this factor analysis into a particular wage or salary. For example, if an analytical, factor-based scheme is used then the factors or weightings that are used can enable the organisation to emphasise specific competencies:

> when the national job evaluation scheme for a million local government workers was designed in 1987, the traditional emphasis on physical effort and working conditions was downgraded and more weight given to the skills involved in the caring for people. Consequently, the relative pay of refuse collectors and home-help workers was reversed, with the previously lower-paid home-helpers scoring 630 points against the refuse collectors' 272 points.
>
> (Fowler, 1996: 43)

Furthermore a possible conflict may develop between the introduction of a job evaluation scheme which attempts to scientifically 'discover' the fair rate for jobs, and mechanisms such as collective bargaining which traditionally attempt to protect differentials and 'customary' relativities between the incomes received by different occupations (see, for example, Wootton, 1962; Hyman and Brough, 1975: 32).

Importance of equity for employees

Employees' perceptions of how fairly they are being treated by their company is of prime importance, as we can see from Factor 5 in Figure 13.3. The dictum 'a fair day's work for a fair day's pay' is often utilised to denote a sense of equity felt by employees.

The equity theory of motivation (Adams, 1963) is based on the comparison between two variables: inputs and outcomes. Inputs are what an individual supplies to the employment relationship and outcomes illustrate which factors an individual receives in return. Examples of inputs include effort, experience, skills, training and seniority, whereas outputs include pay, recognition, fringe benefits, status symbols and promotion. Employees will formulate a ratio between their inputs and outcomes and compare it with the perceived ratios of inputs and outcomes of other people in the same or a similar situation. If these two ratios are not equal then the individual will take actions to attempt to restore a sense of equity. Adams (1963) suggests that individuals can:

- change inputs, i.e. can reduce effort, if underpaid;
- try to change their outcomes, i.e. ask for a pay rise or promotion;
- psychologically distort their own ratios or those of others by rationalising differences in inputs and outcomes;
- change the reference group to which they compare themselves in order to restore equity.

In the perception of equity the choice of comparison points and reference groups is layered with subjective notions. For example, Hyman and Brough (1975) have outlined the influence of:

- custom and tradition – occupational parochialism leading to differing frames of reference;
- differences between manual and non-manual workers;
- the pervasive concept of 'responsibility' as an assessment criteria within a job;
- the distinction between those employees with organisation-specific skills and those with transferable skills.

Blau (1994: 1253) refers to five categories of pay referent categories:

- social (e.g. family, friends, relatives);
- financial (i.e. the extent to which one's current income meet one's current financial needs);
- historical (i.e. one's current income in comparison to income received in the past);
- organisation (i.e. pay comparisons within the company);
- market (i.e. pay comparisons outside the organisation).

Deckop (1992) makes the useful distinction between organisational pay satisfaction/ dissatisfaction and career pay satisfaction/dissatisfaction with regard to employees' behavioural responses. Behaviours which are associated with organisational pay dissatisfaction include reduced effort, complaints, union activity and intra-occupational turnover, whereas career pay dissatisfaction is more likely to result in behaviours such as increased effort, retraining, or actually leaving the occupation (Blau, 1994: 1252).

Thus the assessment of equity by employees will be determined by the comparison points and rationale used. Hence it is the differentials which are important not the absolute amount.

Importance of equity for managers

A particular concern for managers for recruitment and selection purposes is whether the amount and type of remuneration offered by the company are equitable relative to those offered by competitors. Both the level of pay and the composition of the reward package must be able to attract suitable and required employees to the company, and ensure that existing employees do not feel so dissatisfied as to leave the company.

Equity has an additional meaning for managers in the sense of the 'wage–effort bargain'. Many writers have argued that labour for employers is a cost of production and will therefore attempt either to maximise the contribution of an employee relative to a level of wage or, achieving the same ends of reducing unit labour costs, minimise wage costs with respect to a level of effort (see, for example, Hyman and Brough, 1975: 14). However, the introduction of human resource management techniques portray labour as a resource to be invested in and developed. But the basic proposition remains the same: management are simply concerned with maximising the contribution of workers relative to the rewards given. Thus equity for management can be seen in terms of receiving maximum desired input from employees in terms of productivity, performance, skill, flexibility, etc. with the rewards offered.

Setting the objectives of a payment system

Simplicity and rigidity v. complexity and flexibility

There is an inherent tension between designing a differentiated payment system which reflects diversity in needs, motivation, expectations and performance of individuals and encourages career advancement, and the objective of maintaining simplicity, predictability, and control through a standardised system (White, 1981: 37–39; Child, 1984: 179).

Furthermore, as several writers have pointed out, flexibility in pay levels and the setting of 'competitive' pay rates in order to attract and retain certain categories of staff may violate the overall distribution of salaries and thus bear little resemblance to job requirements and job content. (For example, see Daniel and McIntosh, 1972: 156; Lupton and Bowey, 1983: 111.)

Many organisations have reduced complex grading structures to a simple set of wide pay bands (for example see Hofrichter, 1993; O'Neil, 1993). Pay flexibility within the bands can be based on individual performance, skill, market rates, company performance and competencies. Competencies can be 'behavioural characteristics that are necessary for the satisfactory performance of each job' or items that 'each employee acquires – whether these are of immediate use in the current job or not' (Fowler, 1996: 43). The latter would suggest the introduction of payment for potential. Furthermore in many organisations such as NHS trusts the broad bands allow for locally determined performance-related progression and pay rises and the opportunity to negotiate local top-up pay deals rather than the reliance on central pay systems based on an administrative culture.

SALARIES AND WAGES

Traditionally there has been a separation in the methods of payment for blue-collar and white-collar employees. Manual, blue-collar employees have historically been paid a weekly wage based on a rate negotiated between the employer or employer's national representatives, and the representatives of the employees. In some cases an hourly or weekly rate is unilaterally imposed by the employer. Wage earners are paid simply for the work they do and not for any personal characteristics or potential they bring to the employment relationship (Lupton and Bowey, 1983: 96).

Salary earners, however, are more likely to be paid monthly, and progress through a clearly defined career hierarchy based on factors such as age, seniority, qualifications, experience and performance.

The distinction reflects many historical assumptions. For example, Lupton and Bowey (1983: 97–99) draw out several explanations:

- Manual jobs in most cases do not constitute a basis for further career advancement. Companies traditionally have recruited graduates, technicians or professionals on a direct entry basis to provide the required skills, knowledge and attitudes to perform at high levels in the hierarchy. Furthermore: 'Family and social-class background not only inhibit educational progression, they condition expectations of advancement and a person's view of his own potential for advancement' (Lupton and Bowey, 1983: 97).
- Differences also arise due to the greater importance attached to and the difficulty in measuring factors such as discretion and judgement (believed to be involved to a greater extent in positions higher in the organisational hierarchy and/or in white-collar jobs) rather than measuring simple productivity and 'innate' physical strength (thought to be the main source of effort for manual or blue-collar workers).
- Originally it was also believed that as production decreased, direct labour would not be needed and thus had to be disposed of quickly and cheaply. However, the demand for

indirect labour would not fluctuate and hence there was a tendency to view salary earners as having greater job security, and thus greater commitment, than manual workers.

However, these assumptions seem to be changing with the development of the concept of harmonisation.

Harmonisation

'Harmonisation' has become one of the current 'in vogue' terms gaining coinage in personnel circles for a number of reasons. For example, the design of white-collar work is becoming more routine whereas blue-collar work increasingly makes use of new technology and skills. Furthermore, harmonisation is also thought to increase worker satisfaction and commitment, and to enable change and flexibility in working methods and procedures to take place without constrictions of, for example, demarcation. However, Birkett (1989: 65) points out that harmonisation describes different things in different organisations:

- *gradual elimination* of differences between blue-collar and white-collar workers' conditions of employment (e.g. separate canteens, clocking, holidays and sick pay);
- *single status* which means that all employees are treated equally in all aspects of employment – except pay;
- *extending staff status* with certain non-staff grades of employees being transferred to staff terms and conditions of employment.

Characteristics of a salary system

A salary scheme comprises progressive levels of responsibility, status and authority with corresponding pay increments, and relates effort to these rewards through a system of rules and procedures (Lupton and Bowey, 1983: 102–103). The rules and procedures define what is required to move from one level to another level in the hierarchy and how that promotion decision will be made. Organisations, however, will differ greatly in the extent to which the pay and job hierarchy is formalised and proceduralised, and the extent to which managers have discretion in pay and promotion decisions or whether progression 'takes place automatically by the application of certain fixed rules . . . ' (Lupton and Bowey, 1983: 105).

Thus Lupton and Bowey (1983: 104) summarise the characteristics of salary systems as such:

1. A hierarchy of pay levels.
2. A hierarchy of jobs.
3. A set of rules and procedures that define:
   (a) a relation between 1 and 2;
   (b) what qualities are necessary for movement from one level to another;
   (c) who makes choices, or by what process they are made, when there is competition for promotion.

Motivational issues in the design of salary systems

Lupton and Bowey (1983: 122–127) outline three motivational influences on the design of salary schemes: stick and carrot rewards, deferred gratification and prerogatives.

- *Stick and carrot* – 'those rewards which are paid when and if staff behave in a particular way' (p. 122).

This method of reward is based on the achievement of pre-determined targets or standards of performance.

- *Deferred gratification* – 'promise of high future rewards in return for present efforts and achievement' (p. 122).

This mechanism attempts to encourage commitment and loyalty to the organisation and therefore the use of initiative and discretion. It is hoped that competition for promotion encourages employees to increase their levels of effort. Indeed Flanders (1968: 74) has suggested that the prospect of promotion and future pay increases is an important part of the incentive system for managers whereas '[t]he fact that the great majority of manual workers [have] little or no career prospects in their jobs [makes] it important to supply as far as possible more immediate and direct incentives'. These schemes will be considered later in the chapter.

Problems arise, however, when the future rewards, i.e. promotion opportunities, are not forthcoming either due to a promotional blockage in the organisational hierarchy or lack of expansion. Companies may then have to consider alternative reward strategies to motivate their employees (see White, 1982: 281).

- *Prerogatives* – 'those rewards or salary increments which are paid to an employee as of right, and which do not depend upon any appraisal of his (her) work . . .'(pp. 122–123).

For example, advancement would be automatic on reaching a certain age or experience level. The intention here is to encourage a high degree of commitment and loyalty.

However, as Lupton and Bowey (1983) argue, a system based on prerogative rewards may ensure complacency and 'safe' attitudes. Thus employees may be discouraged to undertake risks, innovation and continuous improvement (p. 127).

PAYMENT BY TIME SYSTEMS

An amount of money is paid to the employee at intervals of a month, week or in some cases each day as specified in the employment contract or other agreement. Payment is determined by the number of hours in attendance at the place of work and in most cases is determined by cyclical individual or collective bargaining and agreement.

There are several reasons for using time-based schemes:

- Payment by time systems attempt to encourage cooperation among employees and recognise people's desire for a constant and predictable income (Shaw and Shaw Pirie, 1982: 300).
- Performance in many occupations cannot be measured and thus linked to pay.

- Child (1984: 192) indicates 'that with the advance of more highly mechanised and automated technologies the need for effort is being replaced by a need for reliable monitoring using cognitive and judgmental skills'.
- Conflict over pay rates is confined to certain mechanisms such as collective bargaining, and certain periods of the year.

One of the implications of installing a time-based system is the increased responsibility of supervisors/line managers for ensuring standards of performance are met (Shaw and Shaw Pirie, 1982: 305).

PAY AS AN INCENTIVE

The literature on remuneration abounds with confusing and conflicting labels and descriptions of different incentive-based payment systems. To attempt to clarify the situation the discussion below is based on the distinctions formulated by Casey *et al.* (1992). Thus incentive-based payment systems can be categorised into four broad types:

- Bonus schemes which directly reward the performance of an individual (here referred to by the generic term 'payment by results'). Examples of such systems include:
  - piecework;
  - output and target-based bonuses;
  - commission bonuses based on sales;
  - measured daywork.
- Collective bonus schemes based on output or productivity of group/section/department or the whole company.
- Collective bonus schemes based on profits generated. Examples of this method include:
  - profit sharing schemes;
  - employee share option schemes.
- An individual's pay is determined by management's assessment of his or her performance, for example performance-related pay (sometimes referred to as 'merit pay').

PAYMENT BY RESULTS

The motivational impact of linking of the rate of pay to quantity and/or quality has been recognised by management for many years. It can be argued all payment by results (PBR) systems reflect the traditions and principles of 'scientific management' when tasks which could be measured would have standards of performance. The father of scientific management, Frederick Taylor (1991), analysed and standardised work activities through the use of time-and-motion or work-study techniques. Furthermore he believed money was the *only* incentive for workers who only wanted higher wages and the opportunity to gain that extra money.

By simply paying workers a time rate there is no direct, visible relationship between effort and reward. The assumption therefore of PBR schemes is that by paying workers directly for effort, employees will work harder.

PBR schemes relate either the whole of an employee's pay or part of the income to the quantity of output produced by the individual or group to which he or she belongs; some schemes have high basic pay whereas others have low basic pay, and some schemes have symmetrical relationship between pay and work whereas other schemes have an increasing/decreasing ratio between the extra amount of work and the extra pay received. These basic principles in the design of PBR schemes are summarised in Figures 13.4 to 13.7. In Figure 13.4:

- *Line 1.* Base-rate compensation here is high and extra performance is not highly rewarded. Consequently reward and risk are low.
- *Line 2.* Here the base rate is low but increased performance is rewarded highly, therefore the amount of risk and reward is low.

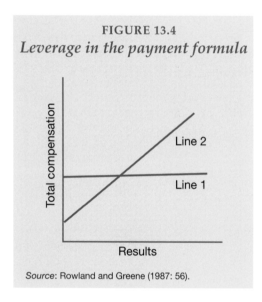

FIGURE 13.4
Leverage in the payment formula

Source: Rowland and Greene (1987: 56).

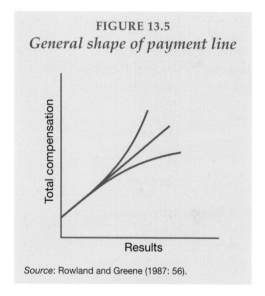

FIGURE 13.5
General shape of payment line

Source: Rowland and Greene (1987: 56).

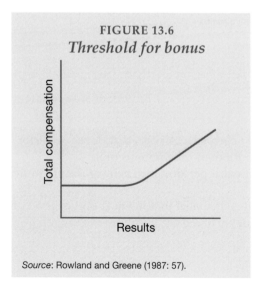

FIGURE 13.6
Threshold for bonus

Source: Rowland and Greene (1987: 57).

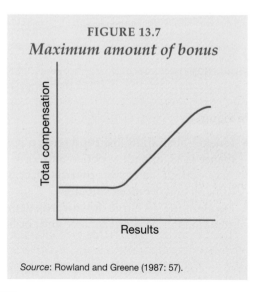

FIGURE 13.7
Maximum amount of bonus

Source: Rowland and Greene (1987: 57).

TABLE 13.1
Incentive payment systems

Broad type of system	Percentage of organisations where:	By size			Manuf. + constr.	By sector Market services	Public services
		All	<100	100+			
Merit pay	All or part of some individuals' basic pay depends on management's assessment of their performance	81	79	84	86*	83*	36*
Individual bonuses	Individual bonuses used	57	53	63	56	57	73
Collective bonuses	Group, section, or department bonuses used	20	14	25	22	16	27
	Bonuses based on output, sales or value-added of organisation used	21	14*	27*	26	18	0
Profit/share based schemes	Profit-sharing scheme operated	29	28	34	34	29	0
	Employee share plan operated	18	5*	31*	16	25	0

Note: Due to exclusion of cases where no answer was given or of cases in the public sector, the proportions for the 'all organisations' column are not always weighted averages of subsequent columns.

*Differences (between size groups or sectors) are significant at 0.05 level.

Source: PSI Payment Systems Survey, in Casey *et al*. (1992).

In Figure 13.5:

- Linear – a straight line represents a belief that each successive result/level of performance is as difficult to obtain and/or is as important as the previous unit.
- Accelerating – a curve upwards indicates that extra performance is increasingly more difficult and/or more valuable.
- Decelerating – a curve downwards demonstrates the belief that the next unit or level of attainment is easier to achieve and/or less valuable to the organisation.

TABLE 13.2

Importance of various forms of pay system for different occupational groups

Broad type of system	% of organisations employing particular categories of employee where:	Category of employee								
		1	2	3	4	5	6	7	8	9
Merit pay	Performance assessment determines all or part of their pay	73	76	65	65	37	30	67	35	32
Individual bonuses	Individual bonus schemes apply to these employees	25	17	23	15	33	7	40	40	26
Collective bonuses	Group bonus schemes apply to these employees	8	8	8	8	15	15	13	18	16
Profit/share based schemes	Profit-sharing schemes apply to these employees	29	19	20	19	12	7	21	18	12
	Employee share plans are operated for these employees	19	24	24	19	15	22	21	21	16
(Base)		(146)	(103)	(108)	(146)	(98)	(45)	(104)	(93)	(93)

Categories of employee: 1 = managers/administrators; 2 = professional; 3 = technician/lower professional; 4 = clerical/secretarial; 5 = craft; 6 = personal and protective services; 7 = sales staff; 8 = plant/machine operators; 9 = other employees.

Source: PSI Payment Systems Survey, in Casey *et al.* (1992).

Figure 13.6 outlines the decision of where to begin bonus payments, i.e. what sort of return/performance the company should expect before paying out a bonus.

Figure 13.7 represents the decision to place a limit or 'cap' on the amount of incentive which can be achieved. For example, if future opportunities are uncertain or performance is greatly influenced by external events, a company may wish to place a limit on the amount of bonuses it could have to pay out.

Table 13.1 indicates that Casey *et al.* (1992) discovered that almost three-fifths of organisations surveyed had individual bonus systems. Furthermore, from Table 13.2 it appears individual bonus schemes are most popular for semi-skilled manual workers (category 8) and sales staff who tend to be on commission schemes (category 7).

Individual bonus schemes can be further classified between schemes where:

- payment varies in relation to particular levels of output or sales (e.g. piecework, commission);
- payment of a fixed sum on the achievement of a particular level of output or sales (e.g. MDW, output or target-based bonuses).

Piecework

The first systems which attempted directly to elicit increases in effort by increases in money were piecework systems which involved individual workers directly employed on a production process, undertaking simple, routine and repetitive manual work (see, for example, Webb, 1982: 289, 290). Piecework has a strong tradition in Britain, particularly in industries such as engineering, textiles, footwear and clothing, and still remains in use in one form or another in many firms in these industries (see White, 1981: 14; Cannell and Long, 1991: 58–60; Casey *et al.*, 1992). The foundations of piecework methods lie in the techniques of work study.

There are several assumptions regarding the motivational impact and hence successful operation of PBR schemes:

- There is a direct and attestable link between individual effort and the results obtained.
- Employees have the ability and opportunity to adjust their levels of effort.
- The method of production is directly under the control of the operator (or those affected by the bonus opportunity), there are no problems with maintaining standards (e.g. quality and material usage), and there is a continuous supply of work.
- The work allows objective work standards to be set, which are attainable and can be enforced, and if the standards are achieved then workers should believe that managers will not attempt to renegotiate a lower rate of bonus payment.
- Employees are able to accept variations in their own individual earnings.
- Employees want to earn higher or extra pay. Moreover managers must believe that the 'financial motive for work is extremely important, more so than non-financial motives . . . [and] the most effective way of harnessing this motive is by the use of a system of payment by results . . . [not] simply by paying higher wages' (Behrend, 1959: 140).

(See Behrend, 1959: 140; Bowey *et al.*, 1982: 8; Webb, 1982: 289–290; Child, 1984: 192.)

Measured daywork

Measured daywork (MDW) has been defined by Shaw and Shaw Pirie (1983: 297–298) as a:

> . . . system of payment in which an additional fixed sum or bonus is paid on top of the basic rate for the job. This bonus does not vary with the amount produced. It is paid in return for maintaining a prescribed level of performance in terms of 'effort' or other composite measurement or assessment . . . The bonus is therefore a reward for maintaining a standard performance . . .

However, other writers believe that measured daywork represents a different form of payment system. For example, Flanders (1973: 377) defines MDW as 'any pay system in which workers are paid a stable wage (by the hour or week) for a measured work performance'.

Although MDW was introduced in several companies in the 1970s, particularly in the motor industry, this form of payment system has not proved to be popular in Britain (Thompson and McHugh, 1990: 33; Child, 1984: 197).

Advantages and disadvantages of PBR

Arguments for the introduction of output incentives include the following:

- *Increase in management control*. As outlined in the Porter and Lawler model of motivation, managers are able to enhance their control over pay and work performance. Indeed, the 1990 WIRS survey found that manual workers who were paid on the basis of output were less likely to clock in and out, leading the authors to suggest that '. . . individual PBR systems are used by management as an alternative to light monitoring and supervision' (Millward *et al.*, 1992: 261).
- *Less supervision and greater freedom for employees*. There is, however, a somewhat contradictory proposition that PBR schemes actually increase employees' discretion. PBR schemes emphasise output and place the responsibility for the methods and quantity of output at the feet of the workers: 'They can legitimately ask management to leave them alone to get on with their work as they see fit on the grounds that they will be the first to suffer if a high level of output is not attained' (Child, 1984: 193). Therefore the implication is that workers will take over some of the supervisory duties such as ensuring continuous and efficient production. Conversely time-based payment systems force supervisors into taking responsibility for ensuring high levels of effort and performance from workers (Child, 1984: 193). However, readers must be aware that employees' discretion is superficial for it is set within management's clearly defined parameters.
- *Opportunities to achieve high earnings*. Schemes which link performance to pay are likely to give workers the opportunity to earn as much money as they choose, i.e. workers decide for themselves how to balance the wage–effort bargain.
- *Create a joint appreciation of the necessity to increase profit so as to benefit both the company and workers*.

Many writers have described the problems and negative consequences associated with PBR schemes, and the remainder of this section provides an overview of those observations. (See Roy, 1952, 1953 and 1955; Lupton, 1972; Brown, 1973; Haraszti, 1980; Herzog, 1980; Bowey *et al.*, 1982; Cavendish, 1982: 125–135; Edwards and Scullion, 1982: 167–199; Lupton and Bowey, 1983: 153–158.)

The relationship between effort and reward is too simplistic in design and perhaps reflects the widely held assumption of the power of money to motivate. As Behrend (1959: 138) indicates: '. . . practically no valid statistical proof seems to be available to demonstrate that payment by results raises labour effort and maintains it at a high level . . .' (See, for example, Thompson (1992) for a summary of the research findings regarding incentive schemes.)

Furthermore several studies have shown there are several intervening variables in the relationship between financial reward and motivation including the importance of social relationships (Roethlisberger and Dickson, 1939) and the perception by workers of the fairness of the rules and procedures of the payment system (Roy, 1952, 1955).

The 'erosion' of management control

Often payment by results systems fail to relate performance with pay and therefore fail to motivate employees because of 'erosion'. 'Erosion' has been defined by Lupton and Bowey (1983: 153) as the '. . . progressive loss of managerial control over the relationship between pay and productivity'. The introduction by managers of control techniques based on work study and measurement may mean that workers developed routines of resistance which attempt to regain control of earnings and output.

Some of the symptoms of erosion are described below:

- One of the main problems of output incentive schemes, particularly piecework schemes, is workers' tendency to manipulate working procedures and falsify their time or output record-keeping sheets for financial gain and social rewards. In order to ensure an unfluctuating level of income, employees will bank and cross-book work (i.e. conceal work, restrict output, exaggerate 'downtime', etc.) so as to stabilise the variations caused by 'loose' and 'tight' standards.

  As a consequence management will have inaccurate control information for the purpose of human resource planning, assessing individual and group performance, scheduling decisions, and general details on the cost of labour.
- The incentive payment system may be distorted and made impotent by the propagation of special allowances to compensate workers for loss of bonuses when that loss has been a result of circumstances outside the control of the worker; for example through a breakdown of machinery or the lack of materials.
- Performance standards become 'slack' as employees receive pay for performance which is lower than originally envisaged, hence inflating unit labour costs. For example, workers may use the 'learning curve' to discover new ways of working or may deliberately overstate the methods/effort required when standards were first drawn up.
- Workers are often directly or indirectly able to assert control over the process of work allocation to install their own notion of equity (for example, in the allocation of 'loose' and 'tight' jobs) rather than directed by management's ideas of efficiency.
- Management may deliberately relax standards and make it easier for workers to obtain bonuses when, for example, there is shortage of labour. Alternatively management may be forced continually to renegotiate wage rates in order to ensure workers accept the introduction of new technology.
- Social factors may cause or augment behaviour patterns which restrict productivity thereby counteracting the incentive effect of the pay system.
- Workers may be reluctant to accept management's request for changes in working practices if their present job/task provides a high income and the change threatens their perceived ability to achieve high bonuses and receipt of other benefits.

Worker–manager conflict

A major problem, particularly in piecework, is the presence of continual negotiation and argument over the rates for particular jobs or bonus rates, and the amount of 'downtime' to be paid for dips in workers' income levels due to factors outside of their control. Perhaps one of the reasons for this dissension is the reliance on the expertise of work-study engineers and a consequent lack of involvement of shop floor workers in the initial setting of standards (Daniel and McIntosh, 1972: 159–160). This form of 'fragmented bargaining' with individuals or groups leads inevitably to a culture of conflict, and inequalities and anomalies in the pay structures.

Furthermore, piecework operates parasitically within an environment characterised by low trust, suspicion and reciprocal belief that workers will do anything to gain extra money and managers will do anything to save money. (See Flanders (1973: 384) and McGregor (1960) for a discussion of the style of motivation and leadership used in this context.)

A move away from PBR schemes

Although traditional PBR schemes do seem to be generally on the decline, their incidence is still frequent enough to make them worthy of some attention (see, for example, Cannell and Long, 1991). Moreover, the experiences of managers and subordinates as documented help greatly in the analysis of more 'modern' payment methods associated with human resource management.

Several writers, however, have suggested that PBR schemes are becoming increasingly obsolete and need to be replaced by different forms of incentive schemes such as *performance-related pay and profit sharing schemes*.

Even writing in 1970, Flanders identified this trend by suggesting that constant technological developments have meant managers cannot merely concentrate on raising levels of individual work effort as often good performance is influenced by many factors which cannot be reconciled with high effort. Indeed Grayson (1984a) points out that technology has replaced much of the manual work previously done by the shop floor worker. Individual contribution and effort will be less recognisable and hence will be unable to be systematically rewarded (Grayson, 1984a: 175).

This leads Flanders to state:

> It may be important for the pay system to reward the acquisition of knowledge and skill, or responsible behaviour in the use of discretion, or willingness to accept change, or teamwork and co-operation.   (Flanders, 1970: 78)

Furthermore the constriction of markets and decreases in production capacity have caused organisations to look towards rewarding lower costs of production rather than trying to increase the quantity of output (IRRR 332, 1984: 2).

COLLECTIVE BONUS SCHEMES

Across-the-board collective bonuses can be differentiated between schemes based on the output, sales or productivity of a group, section and department, and those schemes based on the output, sales or productivity of the entire organisation.

Group, section or department bonus schemes

Incentive schemes based on the discrete performance of a particular work group attempt to encourage flexibility and cooperation among members of the group, and to some extent provide opportunities for the employees to decide for themselves how to achieve the required results.

Armstrong (1996: 22) defines team-based rewards as:

> payments or non-financial incentives provided to members of a formally
> established team and linked to the performance of that group. The rewards
> are shared among the members according to a formula, or on an ad-hoc
> basis for exceptional achievements. Rewards for individuals may also be
> influenced by assessments of their contribution to the team.

Such schemes, however, seem to be most effective when the work groups/teams are:

- stable, mature and naturally forming;
- clearly identifiable as a performing unit and their performance can directly be measured;
- have a significant degree of autonomy;
- are composed of people whose work is interdependent;
- are made up of individuals who are flexible, multi-skilled and good team players.

(See, for example, Daniel and McIntosh, 1972: 163; Armstrong, 1996: 23.)

The introduction of team-based payment schemes may, however, lead to several problems. For example, pressures to conform and the requirement for consideration of others may lead to the reduction of effort to the lowest common denominator and the demotivation of high performers (see the classic study by Roethlisberger and Dickson, 1939). Employees may also resist transfer out of high performing teams because of the potential loss of individual earnings. Moreover, the move to a team-based reward strategy calls for a radical shift in the ways of working from an individualistic culture and a political environment, and an acceptance by individuals that their pay will not be wholly related to their own efforts.

The PSI report in Casey *et al.* (1992) revealed that about one-fifth of organisations surveyed had collective bonuses based on the output or productivity of a group, section or department, and were more prominent in larger organisations (see Table 13.2).

Collective bonuses based on company or plant output, sales or productivity

The central objective behind the introduction of plant or company-wide schemes is to encourage involvement and interest in the operation and performance of the plant, rather than offering a direct financial inducement (Daniel and McIntosh, 1972: 164).

The intention is to 'foster cooperation between all parts of the organisation so that corporate objectives may be better achieved . . . [and]. . . [t]heir motivational appeal is to the socially integrative rather than the self-assertive tendencies in human behaviour' (Wilson, Haslam and Bowey, 1982: 321).

The PSI report in Casey *et al.* (1992) also revealed that about one-fifth of organisations surveyed had collective bonuses based on the output, sales or productivity of the company, and again were more prominent in larger organisations (see Table 13.2).

The 1990 WIRS survey concluded that incentive pay schemes based on collective output either by a group or the company are less common than individual incentive schemes. Only 17% of establishments had some employees on collective incentive schemes (Millward *et al.*, 1992: 261).

COLLECTIVE BONUSES BASED ON GENERATED PROFITS

Profit sharing schemes

> Profit-related pay is defined as a part of an employee's pay formally linked to the profits of the business in which the employee works.   (IDS Study 520, 1992: 6)

Employees are usually rewarded at the end of the financial year with a cash bonus which is normally on top of their basic pay. However, as Duncan (1988: 186) suggests, the term 'profit-related pay' can indicate that '. . . the profit-linked element of pay should replace some portion of previously fixed earnings so that "normal" pay will vary with profitability'. For example, Arthur Andersen has tied the lesser of £4000 or 25% of pay to profits (IDS Study 520, 1992: 3).

The interest in profit sharing schemes was stimulated by the advent of enterprise culture and the encouragement of wider share ownership by the Conservative government during the 1980s, and was facilitated by several statutory enactments. Many observers have argued that the introduction of profit sharing should have a positive macro-economic effect on employment (for example, see Weitzman, 1984; Meade, 1986).

It has been estimated that there are in the region of 750 000 participants in around 3000 profit sharing schemes in the UK (IDS Study 520, 1992). The 1990 WIRS survey discovered there had been substantial growth in profit sharing between 1984 and 1990 when the proportion of establishments in the industrial and commercial sector with such schemes rose from 18% to 43%. In the banking, finance and insurance sector 90% of workplaces were found to be covered by some form of profit sharing arrangement (Millward *et al.*, 1992: 264). The PSI study in Casey *et al.* (1992) revealed that profit sharing schemes were employed in just under a third of organisations surveyed and a little under one-fifth of organisations had share option plans which are considered below (see Table 13.1).

The study found profit sharing was more common in larger organisations (see, for example, Table 13.1), companies with above average financial performance and increasing demand for their products and services, and in the case of WIRS, more prevalent in companies with a high proportion of non-manual workers (Casey *et al.*, 1992; Millward *et al.*, 1992).

It is perhaps surprising to discover few small companies taking advantage of profit sharing when the motivational impact of such schemes would be greater and more visible.

Growth in the adoption by companies of such schemes has been propagated/facilitated by continual tax concessions for employees in registered schemes. For example, Figure 13.8 illustrates that the increase in the number of schemes and the number of employees covered by them directly reflect successive and increasing tax concessions.

There are two types of profit sharing schemes: Method A is based on a fixed percentage of profits, and Method B is based on year-on-year increases in profits (see IDS Study 520 (1992) for a more detailed analysis of the separate schemes).

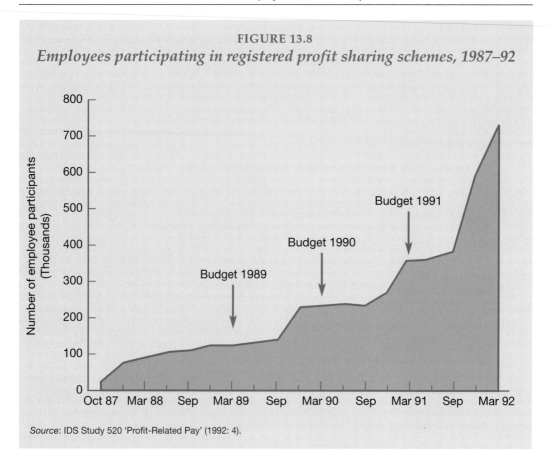

FIGURE 13.8

Employees participating in registered profit sharing schemes, 1987–92

Source: IDS Study 520 'Profit-Related Pay' (1992: 4).

Non-cash based profit sharing schemes

At the end of the 1970s the incumbent Labour government introduced a piece of legislation to encourage the distribution of company profits to all employees in the form of shares. Before 1978 most share based schemes were confined to executive employees (Smith, 1986: 380). The trend towards wider share ownership was further encouraged by the incoming Conservative government through a series of legislatory enactments and highly publicised floatations of shares in companies such as British Telecom, British Airways and British Gas.

The 1990 WIRS survey found that from 1984 to 1990 the percentage of trading sector establishments with such schemes increased from 23% to 32%. Although there was a relatively low take-up rate (approximately a quarter of those eligible to participate in share option schemes), the authors conclude:

> . . . it [is] likely that there was a substantial increase over the period 1984 to 1990 in the proportion of employees in the industrial and commercial sector of the economy who owned shares or share options in their employing company. The higher proportion of workplaces with schemes and a higher rate of participation both contributed to this.   (Millward *et al.*, 1992: 266)

A 1992 report in *The Sunday Times* indicated that almost 1000 companies, including Barclays Bank, Abbey National, TSB, GEC and Marks & Spencer, now offer their workers share options (*The Sunday Times*, 27 September 1992, p. 4.2).

Some observers, however, suggest the momentum of share option schemes has slowed due to the reduction in possible financial gain caused by the Stock Market crash in 1987 and the present recession (*The Sunday Times*, 27 September 1992, p. 4.2; *The Guardian*, 12 September 1992, p. 3).

Particular types of scheme include:

- *Approved profit sharing (APS) schemes.* The 1978 Finance Act made provisions for companies to distribute shares to employees free of charge. The company periodically pays into a trust which then uses the money to purchase shares in the company. The shares are then allocated to individual employees and are held in trust on the employees' behalf.
- *Save As You Earn (SAYE) share option schemes.* The 1980 Finance Act enables employees to have options over shares in their company. SAYE schemes give employees the opportunity to save between £10 and £250 a month for five years (average investment tends to be between £30 and £45 a month) and after this period they have the option of buying shares in the company at a special price set at the time when they started saving. The price may be set at the market rate when the option was agreed to or at a lower price. There is a safety net, however, if the market price at the end of the fixed period falls below the option price: savers have the option of taking their savings plus a tax-free cash bonus.
- *Discretionary share option schemes.* Set up under the 1984 Finance Act, these types of schemes also involve the granting of options over shares with any earnings usually exempt from income tax. However, unlike SAYE, where all employees have to be included, the company has discretion as to which employees will be granted options, therefore tending to profit managers.

There follows a summary of some of the possible objectives profit sharing and employee share ownership could hope to achieve, followed by a discussion of some of the difficulties associated with such schemes.

- As with plant or company based schemes the intention is to increase awareness and interest in the performance of the organisation, though profit sharing schemes also attempt to establish an impression of ownership of the business (Daniel and McIntosh, 1972: 166). A sense of cooperation between management and the workforce is believed to emanate, thereby eliminating the conflictual distinction between 'them and us'. Thus it is hoped employees will identify more closely with the company and the pursuit of profit, thereby acting as an incentive for greater productivity and concern for cost control, and willingness to accept changes in working practices and policies which will improve the company's profitability.
- To encourage long-term commitment and loyalty to the company.
- To ensure employees benefit from company profitability and share in the wealth they helped to create.
- Tax efficient means of reward for employees.
- Tax efficient means of reward for company.
- To help hold wage claims down and/or prevent industrial action.

- To ensure labour costs are responsive to the performance, and hence profits, of the company.
- To attract and retain employees, particularly senior executives.
- To reduce the role and therefore the need of the trade unions.

Smith in her 1986 Department of Employment survey found that the more instrumental and tangible objectives such as 'to help hold wage claims down' and 'to provide a tax efficient means of reward for the company' were to be relatively less important to management than more vague attitudinal objectives such as 'increasing commitment' or 'increasing cooperation'. (See also Ramsay, Leopold and Hyman, 1986: 24; Bougen, Ogden and Outram, 1988: 612–614.)

Although there is general support for the concept of profit sharing from both employees and managers, there is little overwhelming evidence that such schemes have any great effect on the performance, motivation or attitudes of employees. (For example, see Ramsay and Haworth, 1984: 320; Bell and Hanson, 1985: 6–8; Ramsay, Leopold and Hyman, 1986: 25–26; Poole, 1987, 1988; Duncan, 1988: 189; IDS Study 520, 1992: 7.)

Poole and Jenkins (1988: 32) succinctly sum up the difficulties in determining employees' attitudes towards profit sharing:

> . . . interpretation of widespread approval of cash based awards should be tempered with the thought that some employees felt they were being asked if they preferred a free gift (as in the case of profit-sharing and executive scheme arrangements in some of the companies studied) as against nothing.

Problems associated with collective incentive schemes include:

- Due to Inland Revenue rules on tax relief, profit sharing schemes cannot be used to reward the differential contribution of individuals in terms of effort (for example, see IDS Study 520, 1992: 7).
- The motivational impact is limited as there exists a fragile and vague relationship between individual effort and company profit either through remoteness or the intrusion of external factors which are beyond the control of either party.
- A seemingly minimal and infrequent financial reward, and the long time span between individual effort and receipt of bonus, also serves to erode any motivational force.
- The illusory concept of profit sharing schemes creating actual bona fide employee participation and decision making. Indeed even the initial decision to introduce profit sharing schemes and consequent decisions on the design of the schemes are taken in most companies by management alone without consultation with employees (see Smith, 1986: 383; Poole, 1987: 35, 1988: 24).

  Indeed, the introduction and success of profit sharing schemes appear to be a reflection and extension of a general participatory/consultative management style, thereby adding to existing employee involvement schemes rather than changing the nature of the employment relationship in these companies (see Grayson, 1984b: 177; Poole, 1987, 1988; but see Bougen, Ogden and Outram, 1988, for a differing perspective).
- Problems with accurately and fairly calculating and allocating profit.
- Problems in the setting of 'trigger points'. A balance must be set between targets which are almost impossible to achieve and those where the bonus becomes a regular and automatic lump sum payment (Wright, 1986: 48).

- The widening rather than the closing of the gap between 'them and us'. This is due to factors such as the distribution of bonuses on a pro rata basis which results in higher income groups receiving a bigger bonus and the exclusion of part-timers and new recruits.

Thus as Luther and Keating (1992: 68) conclude: 'In the circumstances . . . [profit related pay] is unlikely to succeed in promoting a community of interest in industry'. (See Duncan, 1988, and Luther and Keating, 1992, for further details and a summary of other studies.)

PERFORMANCE-RELATED PAY

The circle remains unbroken: there is continuing interest in remuneration schemes which attempt to link the assessment of individual performance to pay.

Since the early 1950s merit rating has been used by companies to evaluate the value of the individual employee. Such schemes tended to concentrate on personal qualities (e.g. commitment, cooperation, initiative and dependability) and personality traits (such as intelligence). Alternatively merit schemes simply categorised employees' performance into one of several generalisations such as 'outstanding', 'satisfactory', 'unacceptable' (Fowler, 1988: 30).

The current 'sea change' in incentive schemes is towards the assessment of performance against operating objectives rather than concentrating on the evaluation of personal qualities.

Performance-related pay (PRP) can therefore be defined as: 'a system in which an individual's increase in salary is solely or mainly dependent on his/her appraisal or merit rating' (Swabe, 1989: 17).

This rating may take into consideration not only individual output but 'other indicators of performance such as quality, flexibility, contribution to team working and ability to hit targets' (Kinnie and Lowe, 1990: 45).

Traditionally the linkage between a systematic review of performance and pay increases has been the experience solely of management. However, writers on human resource management have suggested that the emergence of integrated personnel techniques and harmonised terms and conditions has led to a trend towards some form of 'merit pay' linked to the assessment of performance against pre-determined criteria for all workers. For example, Cannell and Long in their 1991 survey discovered that 56% of companies had some secretarial and clerical grades on some form of performance-related pay. Long (1986), however, indicates that, although formal performance review procedures have been extended to non-management employees, they have not been used as a basis for the assessment of salary increases and merit awards for these employees. Indeed, the number of manual workers embraced by PRP schemes still remains rather small. For example, from Table 13.2 we can see that although two-thirds of organisations used performance assessment to determine the pay of non-manual employees, only one-third used it for manual employees (Casey *et al.*, 1992: 20; see also PABB 314). The 1990 WIRS found that individual PBR was more common than PRP for unskilled/semi-skilled workers, whereas for skilled manual workers PRP was as common. For non-manual workers PRP/merit pay was much more common than individual PBR (Millward *et al.*, 1992: 261).

From the available evidence the conclusion therefore must be that the introduction of PRP schemes to non-management and manual workers remains piecemeal and rather limited at the moment. Indeed Thompson (1992: 10) concludes from the available evidence that individual PRP is found mainly in the non-manual sector.

Managers may introduce PRP for the following reasons.

To help in recruitment and retention

For example, one of the reasons local authorities have for introducing PRP is to try to improve the attractiveness of salaries in order to improve recruitment and retention (Heery, 1992: 9). Furthermore, as Kessler and Purcell observed in their study: 'In terms of retention, PRP was viewed as sending the "right messages" in rewarding highly those the organisation wanted to keep and lowly those it was happy to lose' (1992: 20).

To facilitate change in organisational culture

The introduction of PRP can be seen as encouraging a certain 'performance oriented' awareness in the organisation by emphasising 'flexibility, dynamism, entrepreneurial spirit and careful allocation of resources' (Kessler and Purcell, 1992: 21). This has particularly been evident in the introduction of PRP in the public sector or recently privatised public companies (see Fowler, 1988).

To weaken trade union power

In assessing the impact of PRP on trade unions, one personnel director has been quoted:

> There is going to be a lot more focus on the individual; the individual's worth and the talents he or she has and the contribution they make to the business; involving them in that part of the business they work in and that really involves being far more open; involving people far more in what they do; moving people down the track to change the way in which we reward people. All this begins with cutting the power of Trade Unions in the traditional collective bargaining sense off at the knees.
>
> (Kessler and Purcell, 1992: 22)

Although PRP was not used in isolation from other management techniques, Kessler and Purcell (1992) discovered that many companies were attempting to emphasise the individual rather than the collective. Heery (1992: 4) has summarised the main possible disorganisational consequences for trade unions:

- the instrumental value of union membership may decline because pay is determined through individual performance, rather than collective bargaining;
- collective interests may be fragmented and rivalry generated among employees, thus eroding the basis for the collective discipline;
- schemes may be perceived as indicating reduced management support for collective negotiation unionism and so may indirectly discourage union membership;
- where schemes satisfy employee aspirations for recognition and reward, they may lead to the removal of grievances and a consequential collapse in support for unions.

Furthermore, if part of employees' pay is determined at management's discretion then the scope of collective bargaining may contract (Guest, 1989: 44; Heery, 1992: 3). Indeed, it could be argued that the role of trade unions will change 'from active bargaining partner to support for individual employees during appeals . . . and an overall monitoring of the pay outcomes' (Hegewisch, 1991a: 34).

However, as Heery (1992) argues, the advent of PRP is not necessarily a retrogressive move for trade unions. For example, the introduction of a PRP scheme may provide unions with a role in dealing with employee dissatisfaction within a 'low trust' environment (Heery, 1992: 4–5). Moreover, the trade unions' role may not be reduced but changed to one which emphasises a personal service to members such as legal advice (e.g. see Pickard, 1990: 43).

There, however, does not seem to be a direct attempt by managers to dismantle collective bargaining mechanisms (for example, see Batstone, 1984; Millward and Stevens, 1986; Edwards, 1987; Storey, 1987 and 1992; Marginson *et al.*, 1988; Millward *et al.*, 1992; Thompson, 1992). For as Casey *et al.* (1992: 8) discovered: '. . . flexible payment systems (including Performance Related Pay) went hand in hand with, or at least coexisted alongside, collective bargaining over wages.

Although there has been no direct attack on collective bargaining where such mechanisms exist in companies, in general collective agreements cover fewer employees and are present in fewer companies (Millward *et al.*, 1992: 352).

Thus the individualising of employee relations seems to be a secondary motive for introducing such schemes and perhaps can be seen as a by-product of other intentions.

Increased role of the line manager

Through the introduction of PRP and appraisal schemes, line managers have to pay more attention to communicating and with evaluating their subordinates. They are forced into taking 'quality time' to discuss their subordinates' performance, progress and development. Additionally supervisors (or line managers) have to clarify the role and outline the expectations of not only their subordinates but themselves (Kinnie and Lowe, 1990: 46; see also Storey, 1992).

As indicated previously, by linking reward to performance management control is increased. The subjectivity and discretion as to which people or behaviours are rewarded will give line managers more authority or power to enforce managerial prerogative. Line managers are then likely to be asked to justify their decisions and the performance of their subordinates in their own appraisal.

Greater financial control and 'value for money'

Greater financial control is thought to result from the proposition that those employees who are performing to or above standard should be the people who get pay increases, rather than rewarding those people who are not contributing to the performance of the organisation through an across-the-board pay increase.

Ability to reward and recognise good performance

PRP has often been linked with a belief that incremental salary scales are too static and inflexible to financially reward and recognise above average performance (see, for example, Grayson, 1982b: 177). Furthermore, as organisational structures become flatter, there will be less opportunities to reward exceptional performance with rapid promotion and thus highfliers will demand more pay at their existing level.

Encouragement of flexibility

Rather than simply giving a lump sum payment to employees in order for them to accept, for example, the introduction of new technology regardless of required skill level, employers are increasingly attempting to link the acceptance of flexible working practices and deployment to the payment system. Furthermore some companies are looking to reward the acquisition of skills which they require to be developed, rather than simply rewarding the use of the existing skill base (see Birkett, 1989: 65).

One production manager in Geary's study illustrated the effect of having flexibility as an assessment criterion:

> People are very much aware that it is going to cost them if they aren't flexible . . . people can see written down for the first time, if you don't do A and B, come your next review it will cost you in money terms. It's both a penaliser and a motivator.
> (Geary, 1992: 42)

Performance-related pay in practice: the link with performance appraisal

In order to be able to match pay to individual performance and/or take into consideration individual competencies, skills and team outputs, there is a clear need for the design and implementation of a sophisticated appraisal scheme.

Appraisal schemes are met by many employees with distrust, suspicion and fear. For example, one respondent in Kinnie and Lowe's study of PRP stated:

> People are very apprehensive about their appraisals. Most people working on the shopfloor have probably never come out of any formal test they have taken very well – they thus feel they have everything to fear and nothing to gain – this is at the heart of their disquiet about the whole system and why, in principle, they infinitely prefer a collective system for security. They also fear they will have the wool pulled over their eyes, and are not skilled negotiators.
> (Kinnie and Lowe, 1990: 49)

Thus there is a real need for employees to be involved completely in the appraisal process and the objective-setting process. The appraisal scheme should be set up in an atmosphere of openness with agreement between management, employees and employee representatives (Grayson, 1984b: 177).

Broadly speaking the appraisal system can be seen to have two main purposes:

- to assess performance with the intention of linking it to a pay award;
- to assess performance to highlight training and development needs.

However, in this section we shall concentrate on the first function.

The linkage between individual appraisals and performance-related pay schemes can be analysed along three dimensions (Kessler and Purcell, 1992):

- setting the performance objectives or criteria;
- the assessment of performance;
- developing the link between pay and performance.

Setting the performance objectives and criteria

A distinction can be made between *input* or *output* based criteria:

- *Input based criteria* relate to the personal characteristics, traits, competencies and skills which an employee brings to a company or job.
- *Output based criteria* are concerned with individual performance objectives or standards to be met by the employee which relate either to an overall company strategy or a specific job description.

There are several different types of assessment criteria for assessing an individual's performance (IDS Study 518, 1992), as discussed below.

Objectives

Objectives (frequently termed targets or goals) are generally jointly agreed upon by the employee and manager and used to measure and assess employee performance.

Objective setting is assumed to be an impartial process of evaluation.

Often companies use the acronym SMART to help set effective objectives:

S – Specific or Stretching
M – Measurable
A – Agreed or Achievable
R – Realistic
T – Time-bounded

There are, however, difficulties in setting objectives for certain types of jobs (e.g. R&D, medicine, teachers and lecturers – see Townley, 1990/1991) and for lower levels in the hierarchy. At low levels employees may not have the opportunity to improve their performance or demonstrate merit, and may be unable to identify and relate to organisation goals.

Competencies

Competencies are the knowledge and skills employees require to perform a job satisfactorily. Examples include factors such as commercial/customer awareness, commitment and contribution, teamwork, initiative, productivity, leadership, concern for quality, and developing and empowering others. Performance throughout the year is then judged against these competencies during the appraisal process.

Accountabilities

Accountabilities define the responsibilities of particular jobs and the results which job-holders are expected to achieve. For example, Cambridgeshire County Council assesses performance against accountabilities such as 'money (for example, maximising income), time (overcoming backlogs), effect (level of take-up of a service) and reaction (how others judge the employee)' (IDS Study 518, 1992: 4).

Skills acquisition

Employees may be assessed on their acquisition of new skills required to perform their existing or future jobs.

Output levels

Alternatively the employee's output in terms of quality, quantity and timeliness may be assessed.

Self-assessment

Self-assessment is mainly used to identify training and development requirements. But Margerison (1976) has argued that self-assessment appraisal systems are the only way to give a complete picture of the performance of the employee and to avoid a 'criticise–defend' scenario. Furthermore it can be argued that it is the appraisee who '. . . knows – or can learn – more than anyone else about his own capabilities, needs, strengths and weaknesses, and goals' (McGregor, 1957: 92).

360-degree appraisals

As the name suggests, 360-degree appraisals require a wide range of people to give feedback on an individual's performance. Combined with the traditional source of information from the direct superior and the individual themselves, 360-degree feedback schemes are designed to give a more complete and comprehensive picture of the individual's performance and contribution. For example, managers might be assessed by their employees on 'softer' people issues such as communication and training, and their peers on issues such as teamwork. Indicators of both internal and external customer satisfaction may be used, and suppliers and subcontracters may also be asked to give feedback on the individual manager's performance. (See *Human Resource Management*, 1993; Dugdill, 1994; Jacobs and Floyd, 1995; Ward, 1995).

The assessment of performance

Some methods and techniques of reviewing performance include:

Comparative methods

- *Paired comparisons*. A manager assesses the performance of pairs of individuals, until each employee has been judged relative to each other employee, or until every possible combination of individuals has been considered. A rating scale is then produced from the number of times each individual was rated as better.
- *Ranking*. Individuals are assessed with reference to a single measure of effectiveness or merit and placed in a hierarchy (i.e. from best to worst).
- *Forced distribution*. Again individuals' performances are given single ratings, but this time allocated, usually by percentage, to categories or ranked performance levels according to some pre-determined distribution.

Absolute methods

Individuals are assessed with reference to some standard(s) of performance and not to other individuals.

- *Narrative approach*. The appraiser describes in his or her own words the work performance and behaviour of the employee during a given period. The report may be in the style of an essay or a controlled written report which asks for answers to certain headings or guidelines.
- *Rating scales*. This method lists a number of factors such as job-related qualities or behaviours or certain personality traits and then the individual is rated on the extent to which they possess these factors. The rating scale can either be numerical or alphabetical, or graphically represented on a continuum, i.e. from 'very high' to 'very low'.

Critical incident techniques

The appraiser records incidents of the employee's positive and negative behaviour that have occurred during a given review period. Thus this form of appraisal is based upon specific examples not subjective assessments (see, for example, Drummond, 1993).

Behaviourally anchored rating scales (BARS)

Numerical, alphabetical and single adjectival anchors such as 'average' and 'above average' may be difficult to define and ambiguous for assessors. Thus BARS are designed to replace or, in some cases, add to these scale anchor points, with descriptions of specific examples of actual job behaviours. The first stage is to define specific activities required for successful performance in a job. Specific job behaviours which correspond to high, moderate and low performance are then identified within this dimension.

Results-oriented methods

Objectives and standards are set to assess specific results and outcomes arising from job performance and not job behaviour. The appraisal process then examines to what extent these objectives have been reached.

There are many difficulties associated with the assessment of performance:

- The inherent subjectivity of the assessment process may lead to claims of favouritism, bias and arbitrariness. For example, one of the employees studied by Geary (1992: 46) exclaimed:

> Your appraisal depends on your supervisor. If you are liked or socialise with him you're more likely to get a good review!

Appraisers may allow the evaluation of a single observed trait, characteristic, objective, competence, etc. to influence their ratings on all subsequent factors. If the appraiser judges the employee positively on one factor, he or she may give high ratings to all other areas of performance even though the appraisee's actual performance in these aspects may be weaker or unobserved. This is known as the 'halo' effect. On the other hand a negative rating in one aspect could lead to other performance factors being evaluated negatively. This is called the 'horns' effect.

Problems of subjectivity are particularly evident when non-quantifiable criteria are being used for assessment purposes.

- Appraisers may find it difficult to identify, not to mention measure, the distinct contribution of each individual (for example, see Kinnie and Lowe, 1990: 47).
- There may be many external factors beyond the control of the individual employee which affects their performance. In order to act as an incentive the rewards must be identifiable with individual performance.

    Moreover, even if an employee's performance and contribution can be evaluated, there are severe difficulties in reducing the complexity of a multi-factor appraisal into a single overall rating for pay awards (Fowler, 1988: 33).
- Line managers/supervisors may lack the required technical skills and people management skills to be able to conduct an effective appraisal.
- If there is a long time span between appraisals, managers may place greater importance on more recent performance (the recency effect) thereby possibly ignoring incidents which had occurred earlier.
- Management's resistance to appraisals may be due to a perception of being placed in the 'embarrassing' situation of having to pass judgements on and criticising their fellow workers. As McGregor states:

> Managers are uncomfortable when they are in the position of playing God.
>
> (1957: 90)

This is particularly the case when their judgements are formalised, written down and linked to some form of reward (see also Rowe, 1964: 19–20; Margerison, 1976: 30).

One of the consequences of this tension is the reluctance to rate their subordinates at the extremes of the rating scale, particularly negatively (see Carlton and Sloman 1992: 87–88; Kessler and Purcell, 1992: 25).

- A lack of time and resources may hinder line managers in providing comprehensive and effective performance reviews and objective setting. Moreover, managers may perceive the appraisal process as a bureaucratic nuisance and form filling exercise (see, for example, Long, 1986: 65). This would be particularly evident in small companies.
- There is a conflict in the nature of performance review procedures which attempt to assess performance for training and development purposes at the same time as for pay purposes. For example, Randell (1973) has argued that the reward review should be completely separate in terms of operation and documentation to performance, potential and organisation reviews.
- An appraisal outcome which labels an employee as simply 'average' or determines that he or she is not a 'highflier' may lead to demotivation. To state the general principle:

> . . . when one person begins to make a judgement on another, unless that judgement is favourable, reaction and resistance begin to set in.
>
> (Margerison, 1976: 32)

- The 'cascading' approach of progressive levels of management setting objectives for the level below and consequently being assessed themselves by the attainment of these objectives can result in the manipulation and 'fudging' of standards (see, for example, Kane and Freeman, 1987: 26–27). Furthermore, managers must be aware that the impact of the company's strategic pay policy may be reduced or diverted by lower levels of management pursuing alternative goals and objectives (Bowey and Thorpe, 1989: 17). Thus senior managers must install adequate monitoring systems and controls in order to ensure their policy or objectives are implemented as designed (see also Murlis and Wright, 1993: 33).

Developing the link between performance and pay

Difficulties in the relationship between performance and pay include the following.

- As discussed earlier the notion of there being a direct relationship between effort and reward is rather simplistic. The relationship is affected by employee expectations, perceptions and need, and social and political workplace pressures affecting both appraisee and appraiser.
- Employees will possibly concentrate on achieving the stipulated objective (for which they will be assessed and hence rewarded on) and overlook or ignore other, perhaps less tangible, aspects of their job. Furthermore, employees may be reluctant to engage in innovation or act on their own discretion in case their efforts are not acknowledged and/or their progression towards their set objectives for assessment purposes is adversely affected. For example, the prospective introduction of PRP in schools has led one teacher to exclaim:

> There will be a culture of fear. Who will be innovative, who will dare to breathe a word about child-centred education when they have to pay the mortgage at the end of the month? It will lead to the most arid and didactic teaching this century.
>
> (*The Guardian*, 22 April 1992, p. 2)

- By rewarding some individuals and not others and through the individualisation of work effort, the *esprit de corps* and cohesion of the work group, section, department or company may be undermined. To attempt to mollify the adverse effects of individualism, some companies have incorporated factors such as 'contribution to team working' in their appraisal criteria (Kinnie and Lowe, 1990: 48).
- Financial constraints, due perhaps to recessionary factors, may mean that the PRP element of a pay increase will be small or '[t]he expectations raised by positive feedback from a performance review may simply not be translated into a significant pay increase' (Kessler and Purcell, 1992: 28). For example, government restrictions on spending may reduce the impact or even prevent the introduction of PRP schemes in the public sector (*The Independent,* 1 December 1992, p. 2).

Moreover, inflation may result in cost of living increases eclipsing the performance-related increase. Thus remuneration will no longer be linked to performance and there will be little recognition of contribution.

Any incentive to increase effort will be extinguished and employees may in fact feel 'insulted by the low level of extra pay they receive' (Fletcher and Williams, 1992: 47). Furthermore, companies worried about escalating costs may enforce quotas or forced distributions to limit the number of employees who can be awarded payments (Fowler, 1988: 34). Demotivation is the inevitable consequence (for example, see Pickard, 1990: 42; Richardson and Marsden, 1992: 2, 38).

Internalisation of performance norms

Employees' behaviour can be seen to be affected by direct financial inducement and the internalisation of norms of behaviour.

The reward and appraisal system, by endorsing congruous work efforts by way of PRP increases, and by punishing objectionable, poor performance through the withholding of pay increases, can help in the internalisation of the organisation's goals or norms of behaviour among the employees of the organisation (Geary, 1992: 42). Thus, as Townley (1989) indicates, management are able to install a system of control over those aspects in the workplace which are not covered by rules and close supervision. Thereby through a pattern of 'implicit expectations' and 'shared norms of understanding' managers can control workers' increased flexibility and discretion within managerial parameters.

At the time of writing there appears to be little systematic and comprehensive evidence of the effects of PRP on employees' motivation, attitudes, performance and, particularly, productivity. (For example, see Thompson (1992: 19) for a summary of studies.) Although the discrete impact of any payment system is extremely difficult to isolate from the influence of a multitude of other factors, it is obvious further work must be carried out in this area. Indeed, very few companies have formal monitoring and evaluation procedures for their own schemes (see Keeler, 1991: 18; Thompson, 1992).

One of the few exceptions is the study of Inland Revenue staff by Richardson and Marsden (1992). Although most respondents supported the principle of PRP, the introduction of the scheme had very little impact in practice upon motivation and performance levels and in some cases had led to demotivation (Richardson and Marsden,

1992: 1). This conclusion has been supported by Heery (1992: 10) who found that while personnel managers were very enthusiastic about PRP, 'The survey of individual employee attitudes . . . provided less support for the effectiveness of PRP . . . suggesting the incentive effects of schemes are typically modest.' (See also Brindle, 1987; Kinnie and Lowe, 1990; Fletcher and Williams, 1992: 44, 47).

One of Richardson and Marsden's main observations was the importance of workers' perceptions of the rationale and mechanics of the PRP scheme. For example, many staff believed that a quota was operating, and that favouritism and unfairness was endemic within the scheme (1992: 36–38).

Performance-related pay and appraisals – some conclusions

We have seen some of the problems associated with the philosophy and mechanics of appraisal schemes, and hopefully demonstrated the importance of comprehensive and professional training for appraisers. Line managers are now becoming involved in extensive performance reviews and making judgements on individual characteristics such as 'initiative' for which psychologists have no definition. We must question whether it is possible, or desirable, to reduce the intangible to ratings and the complexity of organisational life to single dimensions. Moreover, is it possible to set objectives/measures which are wide and vague enough to cover all eventualities and encourage initiative, but tight and clearly defined enough to avoid subjectivity?

Initial surveys suggest that PRP schemes have little impact on employee performance and motivation, and in some cases the impact has been negative. It simply may be a false diagnosis that these problems are a result of faulty implementation or design of the PRP scheme and/or appraisal schemes. PRP schemes may have an inherent inability to improve the levels of motivation and hence performance of the whole workforce: do PRP schemes simply reflect indigenous individual performance differences within the company rewarding the certain few highly, rather than continuously improving the performance of all employees? (See, for example, Fowler, 1988: 34; Kinnie and Lowe, 1990; Marsden and Richardson, 1991; Institute of Personnel Management, 1992; Scott, 1994; Stewart and Walsh, 1994; Clark, 1995).

There is evidence to suggest that PRP schemes can be inflationary and suffer from erosion. This can be due to a number of reasons:

- performance-related increases may be paid in addition to existing pay increases;
- the need to attract workers;
- the lack of a corresponding increase in productivity;
- payment for acquisition of skills which are consequently not used by the company (Guest, 1992: 13–14);
- previously discussed tendency for appraisers to overrate the appraisee (see Carlton and Sloman, 1992: 87–89).

Furthermore, erosion in the motivational impact and managerial control of PRP may be beginning to surface. For example, in order to prevent PRP increments from becoming an expected 'norm', the variable element of pay needs to shrink when the company does not do well (Curnow, 1986: 75). However, evidence from the top levels of the organisation suggests this is not taking place. Gregg *et al.* (1993) discovered that the pay of directors seems to have been unrelated to their corporate performance during the 1980s and early 1990s.

Additionally, in some companies payment is beginning to be made *before* profits are actually made and recorded, and in one conglomerate middle managers have been rewarded for simply being *punctual* (*Financial Times*, 15 January 1992, p. 12). Thus we can conclude that the link between performance and reward has become in some cases very tenuous (if it were ever close), leading to the tautological conclusion that PRP may suffer the same fate as other 'incentive schemes'.

VARIABLE PAY – RESULTS FROM ACROSS NATIONS

Results from the Price Waterhouse Cranfield Study indicate that the trend towards flexibility in payment systems is not simply limited to the UK but represents a movement across Europe (see Table 13.3).

Figure 13.9 (a)–(e) shows the incidence of different incentive pay schemes such as individual and group bonuses/commissions, profit sharing and share options; and merit and performance-related pay, differentiated by staff group, among five European nations. The main observations include the popularity of profit sharing in France, where schemes are strongly encouraged by the French government, and in Germany where there is a widespread tradition of financial participation for senior managers in medium-sized owner-managed companies. The incidence of share schemes is limited to the UK where they have received considerable support from government, and the popularity of group bonuses in Sweden '. . . confirming perhaps a greater emphasis on team work and team performance in Swedish business culture' (Hegewisch, 1991b: 5).

TABLE 13.3
Variable pay across Europe

	Private sector %	Public sector %
Denmark	32	85
France	51	22
Germany	54	17
Italy	67	na
The Netherlands	29	48
Norway	40	9
Spain	60	57
Sweden	57	48
Switzerland	57	40
UK	45	56

Note: Values are percentage of organisations reporting increases in variable pay elements in the total reward package in the last three years.
Source: Hegewisch (1991a: 32).

FIGURE 13.9

Variable pay in European countries: results from the Price Waterhouse Cranfield Project

(a)

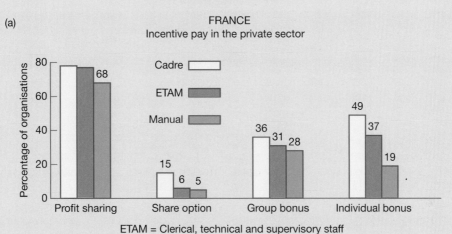

FRANCE
Incentive pay in the private sector

ETAM = Clerical, technical and supervisory staff

(b)

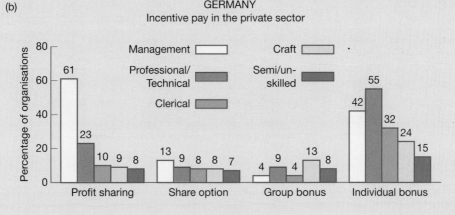

GERMANY
Incentive pay in the private sector

(c)

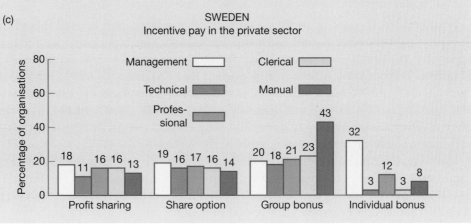

SWEDEN
Incentive pay in the private sector

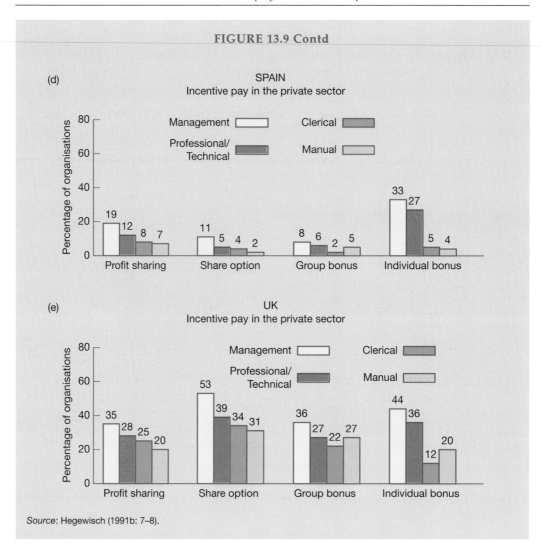

FIGURE 13.9 Contd

(d) SPAIN
Incentive pay in the private sector

(e) UK
Incentive pay in the private sector

Source: Hegewisch (1991b: 7–8).

Furthermore, the use of merit or performance-related pay is established in many European countries (see Figure 13.10 and Table 13.4). Merit/performance-related pay is especially prevalent in France, Italy, Switzerland and the UK but limited in the Scandinavian countries. Although it is evident that PRP remains more common at management and professional levels, there is evidence of schemes being extended to clerical and manual staff in France and Italy as well as the UK. Furthermore, it is clear that merit/performance-related pay does not solely exist in the private sector but has made some inroads into the public sector, particularly in the UK.

However, the rationale behind the introduction of PRP schemes in different European countries is not always to reward individual merit or performance. As Hegewisch (1991b: 6–7, 10) points out, merit pay has been used in France as a way to re-establish hierarchies and differentials and in Sweden to respond to regional labour-market difficulties.

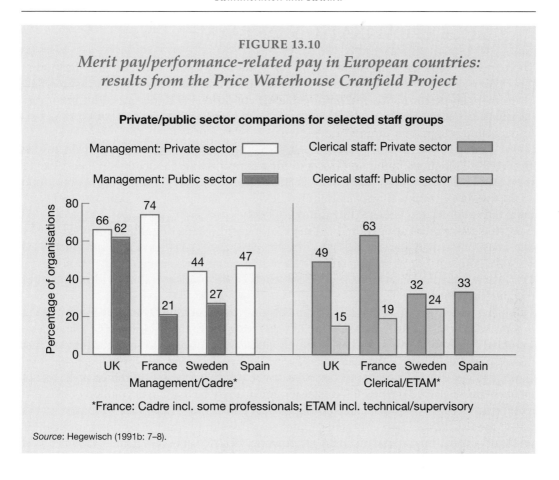

FIGURE 13.10

Merit pay/performance-related pay in European countries: results from the Price Waterhouse Cranfield Project

Private/public sector comparions for selected staff groups

Management: Private sector

Management: Public sector

Clerical staff: Private sector

Clerical staff: Public sector

*France: Cadre incl. some professionals; ETAM incl. technical/supervisory

Source: Hegewisch (1991b: 7–8).

TABLE 13.4

Merit pay/performance-related pay (percentage of organisations per staff group): results from the Price Waterhouse Cranfield Project

	CH	D	DK	E	F[a,b]	I	N	NL	S	UK
Managerial [b]	65	24	14	48	70	85	18	27	13	68
Professional	66	42	18	58		86	16	29	12	58
Technical [c]	62	41[d]							12	
Clerical	57	38	13	39	60	72	11	27	11	46
Manual [d]	56	32	19	33	41	32	15	27	32	23

[a] French figures are for 1989/90.

[b] In France, 'managerial' (*cadre*) includes some professional staff: clerical (ETAM) includes some technical and supervisory staff.

[c] In all countries apart from CH and S, 'professional/technical' are one category; in CH and S the two categories are listed separately.

[d] In D, 'manual' only refers to semi- and unskilled workers: the frequency for skilled workers (Facharbeiter) is given in the 'technical' row.

Source: Hegewisch (1991a: 33).

DECENTRALISATION OF PAYMENT SYSTEMS

There seems to be increasing academic and practitioner interest in the decentralisation of pay determination and policy-making decisions to individual sites or units so as to reflect local financial performance and labour-market conditions. The decentralisation of pay decisions can, for example, enable a company more clearly to link pay to appropriate performance measurements, targets or objectives.

For example, the 1990 WIRS study discovered that the move away from multi-employer negotiations in the unionised sector has resulted in an increase in enterprise or company-level bargaining rather than an increase in plant bargaining. In the non-union sector the survey found some, albeit limited, evidence to suggest that local managers had more discretion in pay issues (Millward *et al.*, 1992).

Furthermore there appears to be a development towards devolving individual pay decisions to line managers (Murlis and Wright, 1993) and a corresponding introduction of personal contracts for managers and certain white-collar workers (Pickard, 1990). Figure 13.11 shows diagrammatically the possible levels of devolution and individualisation of pay determination.

Initial evidence suggests that the movement towards decentralisation of decision making is somewhat limited. Hegewisch (1991a), in recounting the findings of the Price Waterhouse Cranfield Project, states: '. . . in the UK over a quarter of private sector respondents say that the establishment or site is the main locus for pay policy decisions. However, this proportion is much lower than the number of employees who say that pay is determined at establishment or site level' (p. 31). Thus the conclusion must surely be that the devolution of decision making is not shadowed by an allied delegation of power (pp. 31, 33). The shift may simply reflect the decentralisation of organisational structures to product divisions and business units and a flatter managerial hierarchy (Thompson, 1992: 33). (See also Kinnie, 1989.)

EMPLOYEE BENEFITS

Reasons for using fringe benefits

- Most fringe benefits do not attract tax and therefore can be advantageous for both employer and employee, particularly the high earner.
- Some benefits can be provided cheaply through economies of scale.
- Some benefits are needed to facilitate the execution of the job duties of the employee, for example company cars for sales representatives, and special equipment or clothing.
- Some companies may be able to offer discounts on their own products or services, for example banks and building societies, retailers, car manufacturers, etc.
- The provision of certain benefits may ensure long-term commitment to the company and 'inhibit turnover by imposing a relatively large economic cost on leavers . . . Thus, management use fringe benefits as a deterrent against quitting by making them the particular vehicle through which seniority benefits are obtained' (Green *et al.*, 1985: 263). Examples could include pension rights and several status-linked benefits such as company cars and opportunities for foreign travel.

For further details see Green *et al.* (1985: 262–263) and Woodley (1990: 45).

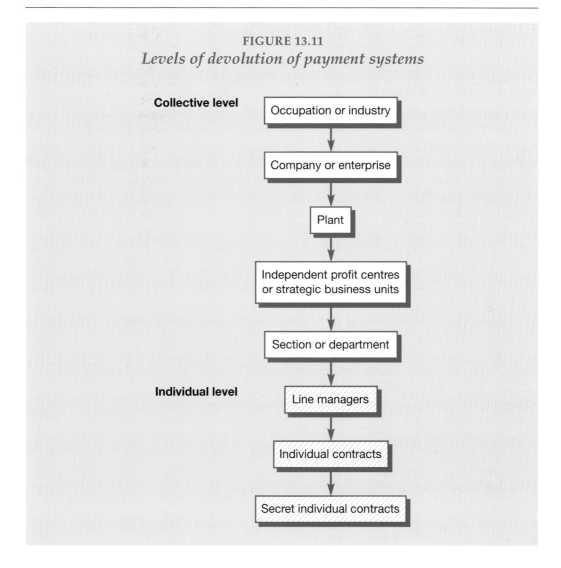

FIGURE 13.11
Levels of devolution of payment systems

Collective level

Occupation or industry

Company or enterprise

Plant

Independent profit centres or strategic business units

Section or department

Individual level

Line managers

Individual contracts

Secret individual contracts

Cafeteria benefits

There appears to be a movement towards flexible compensation schemes, more commonly known as 'cafeteria benefits'. Cafeteria benefit schemes operate by setting a 'price' for each level of the selected benefits within a menu and each employee is allocated a budget to spend on benefits, expressed as credits, points or cash amounts (see Woodley, 1990: 42; IDS Study 481, 1991). Thus employees are able to decide which benefits they prefer and how to balance the amount of cash pay to benefits.

The reasons for employers introducing flexible benefit schemes include (Woodley, 1990, 1993):

● to ensure flexibility in the compensation package to improve retention and recruitment;
● to offer employees the rewards they desire and thereby increase their motivation (see earlier);

- to maintain 'value for money' with the benefits provided;
- to create single status employment.

A recent survey, however, suggests that 'cafeteria benefits' have not been adopted on a large scale by companies. A 1991 IDS survey found that:

- In the limited number of cases where the introduction of 'cafeteria benefits' was being considered, there were only provisions to change the *level* of benefits not the *composition* of the whole benefit package.
- Employers were concerned over the burden of any possible escalation in the amount of administration, and over the increasing short-term costs as a result of the loss of economies of scale.
- Employers had worries over the tax implications and problems associated with flexible benefits.

Basic types of benefit

- Company cars – Britain seems to be unique in the provision of cars as a managerial status symbol (Hegewisch, 1991: 5) where even the specific make and specifications are crucial (Brown, 1996: 62). However, recent evidence suggests that the supply of cars is no longer so widespread in Britain. The 1992 IDS report on fringe benefits indicates that cash is being offered instead of the traditional company car (IDS Study 520, 1992: 9).
- Subsidised meals and/or the supply of canteen facilities.
- Holiday entitlements.
- Opportunities for foreign travel.
- Telephone costs.
- Discounted, or the provision of, insurance.
- Private health care, dental treatment and eye tests.
- Crèches.
- Office accommodation and facilities which may indicate a certain level of status.
- Sabbaticals.
- Sports/social facilities which can encourage identification with the company.
- Discount and company purchase plans where employees can purchase goods at a favourable price.
- Assistance with housing, i.e. company-owned houses, house-moving expenses and assistance with house purchase.
- Help with educational courses.
- Pension schemes.

Companies need to recognise what they want to achieve from the provision of each benefit and understand the motivational characteristics of each benefit for their *own* employees. For example, fringe benefits such as company cars, parking spaces and large offices will address social status motives, whereas the provision of pensions and private health care attempts to satisfy more security-based motives. From a European perspective the Price Waterhouse Cranfield survey found that the provision of certain benefits in different countries will reflect 'tradition and cultural preference'. For example, tax constraints and an inclination towards cash-based rewards limits the popularity of fringe benefits in France (Hegewisch, 1991b: 4–5).

CONTINGENCY THEORY

Some writers have argued that there is no one 'best way' to design a payment system but that effectiveness depends on a match between the scheme and the particular circumstances of the company. Managers must take into account factors such as the type of products it makes, the characteristics of the technology it uses, and the characteristics of the workforce and labour market (see White, 1981, 1985; Lupton and Bowey, 1983).

> Essentially, a contingency approach is one in which it is argued that in some industries and in some environments one kind of managerial practice will contribute to some desired objectives. But in other industries and circumstances entirely different results may occur. Therefore, in order to be sure of the outcome of a scheme the manager needs to consider the particular circumstances of his (her) firm.
>
> (Lupton and Bowey, 1983: 69)

Thus when designing a payment system Lupton and Bowey (1983: 69) suggest managers must consider the following issues:

- What are the objectives to which the payment system is intended to contribute?
- What payment systems are available?
- Which payment system(s) is most likely to contribute to the intended objectives in the particular circumstances of this firm?

It has also been suggested that the effectiveness of the payment system depends more on the *method* of selecting and implementing the system, i.e. the extent of employee participation in the process, rather than the actual *choice* of payment system (see Bowey *et al.*, 1982; Bowey, 1982: 55–62; Bowey and Thorpe, 1989; Geary, 1992: 40).

INTERNATIONAL REMUNERATION POLICIES

Many companies are beginning to respond to the globalisation of business and, more specifically, the integrated European market by designing a single international remuneration policy.

When designing a reward strategy for employees who are taking up overseas appointments many factors have to be taken into consideration:

> Knowledge of the laws, customs, environment, and employment practices of many foreign countries; familiarity with currency relationships and the effect of inflation on compensation; and an understanding of why special allowances must be supplied and which allowances are necessary in what countries – all within the context of shifting political, economic, and social conditions.
>
> (Dowling and Schuler, 1990: 116)

Indeed, consideration must also be given to the variations in the traditional method of payment in the host country. For example, salary systems in Europe and North America tend to base their salary structures on the type of work undertaken and skills required with, in some cases, some element of merit pay. However, in Japan the main determinant of pay levels has traditionally been the age and seniority of the individual employee in addition to a bonus for group or company performance (Dowling and Schuler, 1990: 134). Nevertheless some observers suggest companies in Japan are beginning to use merit pay to reward individual managerial employees (for example, see Roomkin, 1991: 220).

Design of international reward package

The main method of drawing up a compensation package is known as the 'balance sheet' approach. The balance sheet approach, illustrated in Figure 13.12, is defined by one writer as:

> A system designed to equalise the purchasing power of employees at comparable position levels living overseas and in the home country, and to provide incentives to offset qualitative differences between assignment locations.
> (Reynolds, 1986, cited in Dowling and Schuler, 1990: 118)

An example of this type of approach, with certain modifications, is provided by Willmore (1992: 22). The author describes how BT designed its expatriate remuneration policy:

> BT uses the biannual comparative cost-of-living tables, produced by consultancy Employment Conditions Abroad, and its accompanying taxation tables to calculate a net salary for each employee due to start work overseas. This is equivalent to his or her salary at home. This is later split between spendable income and a housing and savings element, the latter intended to reflect UK financial commitments and therefore not adjusted for cost-of-living differences.

The sorts of expenses incurred by expatriate families and thus the types of allowances offered in the international compensation package can be categorised as follows (Dowling and Schuler, 1990: 122–129):

- *Income taxes* incurred in both home and host country. Ensuring effective and favourable tax return administration and tax equalisation is an important but costly and complex requirement of companies.
- *Housing allowances* range from providing financial assistance so employees can maintain their home country housing standards, and company housing and/or help in the sale or leasing of an expatriate's former residence.
- *Cost-of-living allowances* help to make up the differences in prices between the home and foreign country (for example, to take account of different inflation levels).
- *Reserves* which include contributions to savings, pension schemes, investments, etc.
- *Relocation allowances* include the moving, shipping and storage of personal and household items, and temporary living expenses.
- *Education allowances* for expatriates' children are an important part of the remuneration package for medium/long-term assignments. For example, language tuition and enrolment fees in the host country or boarding school fees in the home country may be paid for by the company.
- *Medical, emergency and security cover* for expatriates are often overlooked by companies but are very important (Brewster, 1991: 74).

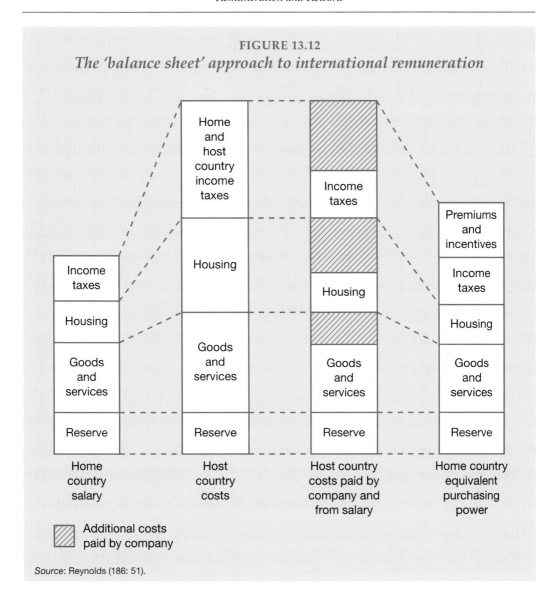

FIGURE 13.12

The 'balance sheet' approach to international remuneration

Home and host country income taxes

Income taxes

Premiums and incentives

Income taxes

Housing

Housing

Income taxes

Housing

Income taxes

Housing

Goods and services

Goods and services

Goods and services

Goods and services

Reserve

Reserve

Reserve

Reserve

Home country salary

Host country costs

Host country costs paid by company and from salary

Home country equivalent purchasing power

Additional costs paid by company

Source: Reynolds (186: 51).

In many companies the view that an overseas assignment has to be suffered by unlucky individuals is increasingly becoming obsolete as therefore is the traditional 'hardship allowance' for everyone going to work in a different country. However, some observers are unconvinced of this notion believing that 'hardship payments' are hidden in other benefits and parochial views of employees working in foreign countries still exist (for example, see Willmore, 1992: 23).

To conclude this section, it is perhaps worthwhile to err on the side of caution when we talk of less differentiated global, and especially European, markets. When formulating remuneration policies companies have to be aware that harmonisation of terms and conditions of employment, pensions, social security and taxation requirements does not exist (Willmore, 1992: 23). At the time of writing, with the advancement of the Single European

Market – and the corresponding Social Chapter – being stultified and unclear, the undifferentiated labour market remains a distant, and perhaps chimerical, possibility.

CONCLUSION: HRM AND PAYMENT SYSTEMS

In this chapter it has been suggested that the presciptive material on reward and remuneration strategy indicates a trend towards what American writers such as Schuster and Zingheim (1992) and Lawler (1995) have termed 'new pay'. The characteristics of 'new pay' are a response to the need for a flexible organisational form and a constantly changing business environment. These characteristics include the integration of the reward strategy with business strategy in order to achieve business objectives, performance-related pay schemes based on a range of different indicators, flexible benefits schemes, individualistic nature of the effort–reward bargain, and the unitary nature of employment relationship based on the principle of 'help yourself by helping the organisation' and 'partnership'. In Britain, the CBI/Hay Management Consultants 1995 survey of nearly 400 organisations in Britain discovered evidence to support the trends identified in the chapter, and there is evidence to suggest that the influence of collective bargaining over the determination of pay is declining (Milner, 1995). The trend towards 'new pay' does seem to reflect Guest's (1987) four tenants of human resource management: the encouragement of commitment, flexibility, quality and strategic integration; but we have yet to see any clear evidence of these initiatives achieving Guest's rhetorical objectives.

There is an unquestioned assumption that employees will be highly committed, and thus motivated and productive, if the philosophies and techniques of 'new pay' match the corporate and the human resource strategy and are carefully operationalised. Furthermore it is often hoped that the reward and remuneration strategy will support other management techniques such as empowerment and teamwork to blur the distinction between 'workers' and 'management'.

The belief that payment by time systems simply encourages 'minimally acceptable performance' has caused many firms to introduce payment schemes which incorporate a financial incentive to perform consistently at a high standard. Schemes such as piecework, payment by results, measured daywork, management by objectives, merit pay, team and individual bonuses, profit sharing and perfoamnce-related pay have been introduced in companies in may different guises in the belief that the main method of motivation is through direct financial incentives.

However, researchers such as Roy (1952, 1953 and 1955) and Roethlisberger and Dickson (1939) writing over forty years ago discovered the relationship between economic incentive and effort is not simple and is influenced by many factors. Indeed the problems encountered through the introduction of more 'modern' payment-by-results schemes perhaps originate from a persistent attempt by workers to regain control over work output, methods and earnings. Practitioners, academics and employees alike are questioning whether 'in vogue' payment schemes such as performance-related pay are the most effective way of increasing and harnessing the motivation of employees, and whether it is wise to ignore the lessons from history. We appear to be very reluctant to believe that most employees are not simply and solely driven by the 'cash nexus', and that most employees wish to improve their performance, learn, develop and are committed to doing a good job.

There is very litte evidence to suggest that performance-related pay schemes increase the overall performance of the organisation and indeed they may lead to dysfunctional outcomes (see, for example, Kinnie and Lowe, 1990; Marsden and Richardson, 1991; Institute of Personnel Management, 1992; Scott, 1994; Stewart and Walsh, 1994; Clark, 1995). Indeed, it can be argued that many professionals find it absurd, objectionable and maybe insulting that it is expected that they will work harder and more effectively because of an element of performance-related pay.

Performance-related pay schemes rely on discredited and simplistic notions of motivation which are based on behavioural modification techniques, and an unquestioned belief that such schemes are more equitable and thus more ethical (cf. Herriot, 1996). It can be argued, however, that motives are not simply external forces which bear down on us but exigencies only in relation to our 'stance' towards the world (Cooper, 1990: 152).

Sartre, for example, believed that the explanation of behaviour was 'hermeneutical' not causal (Cooper, 1990: 152):

> . . . we should attempt to disengage the meanings of an act by proceeding from the principle that every action, no matter how trivial, is not the simple effect of the prior psychic state and does not result from a linear determinism but rather is . . . in the totality which I am.   (Sartre 1958: 459)

Indeed, as an individual's motivation is determined by complex interaction of influences so is one's attitude towards appraisal. Fisher (1995), for example, outlines how the language used by both appraiser and appraisee suggest different ways in which they interpret and make sense of the 'theatre' of performance management and appraisal schemes. Thus, there can be no objective 'truth' of one's motivation and performance, only a reality created through language (Grint, 1994: 69) and social construction. As Leiper (1994: 204) indicates:

> There are a variety of approaches and systems which have been developed for evaluation in recent years. However, methods and materials are of less consequence than the frame of mind in which evaluation is undertaken. It requires the development of a spirit of enquiry and conditions which provide the security necessary for learning from experience, especially containing anxiety, both organizational and personal.

Literature on performance management is dominated by the consideration of the design, mechanisms and procedures of such schemes (see, for example, Fletcher, 1993) rather than critique of the principle and outcomes of performance management such as an obsession with measurement, control and rationality (Alvesson, 1984; Brunsson, 1985; Watson, 1994: 138–140). Individuals within organisations have to operate within the constraints provided by resources, processes, technology, corporate and human resource strategy, the working environment and management, and may therefore not be able to improve their actual performance to any great extent without significant changes to the work system. (For example, the 'quality' guru Deming argues that about 80% of improvement requires management effort and major change in the work system, while only 20% of improvement can be actioned by front-line employees.)

It is possible, therefore, that the role of a performance management system which is driven by evaluation and judgement will be reduced to that of a site of a political game. Authority and dependency relations are defined and reinforced (Bowles and Coates,

1993: 8) and the apportionment and avoidance of blame can very easily predominate. Leiper (1994: 201), for example, states:

> Any system of evaluation can all too easily come to feel like an accusation of inadequacy: it then comes to represent a critical 'parental' voice . . .

Predictably, employees' levels of motivation and commitment to work will be reduced (Bowles and Coates, 1993: 8) and their self-esteem will be shattered. Thus the 'images of performance', and the management of that image, become the overriding motivating factor for employees (Bowles and Coates, 1993: 5), and the appraisal process thereby becomes an end in itself rather than a means to an end (see, for example, Watson, 1994).

We may, therefore, have to accept finally both the inevitability of subjectivity in performance management systems and a pluralistic conception of organisational life. The practice and discipline of human resource management must fundamentally be based on an acceptance and consideration of different 'stakeholders' in the organisation and the contentiousness and opaqueness of concepts such as 'quality', 'efficiency', 'effectiveness', 'value for money', 'profit' and, indeed, 'performance'.

The concept of the 'psychological contract' is a useful tool in helping us understand more about the employment relationship. (For recent studies on the psychological contract see Herriot and Pemberton, 1995; Kessler and Undy, 1996.) Sims (1994: 375) defines the psychological contract as:

> . . . the set of expectations held by the individual employee that specify what the individual and the organization expect to give to the receive from each other in the course of their work relationship.

A more specific definition is provided by Spindler (1994: 326–327):

> . . . the bundle of unexpressed expectations that exist at the interfaces between humans . . . (which) are greatly influenced by the personal history and individual self-image of the parties to the relationship . . . (and) creates emotions and attitudes which form and control behavior.

Whereas a short yet perceptive view is given by Guzzo and Noonan (1994: 448):

> . . . a part of the glue that binds employees to organizations.

The interest in psychological contracts is perhaps a consequence of the uncertainty in the working environment as the 'old' employee psychological contract is seen to have been unilaterally violated by management, leaving employees feeling disorientated, weak and betrayed (see, for example, Kissler, 1994; Sims, 1994). The 'old' contract was predictable and seemed to be known to both employees and employers alike; now both sides to the bargain are searching for an understanding of the new set of employee and employer expectations.

The 'old' contract lay in individual reward being determined by hierarchical structure and a socially constructed set of rules and rituals. The bargain seemed to be based on an 'entitlement' culture where hard work and loyalty were given in exchange for job security, stable career progression, and steady and predictable rewards.

It appears that the 'new' psychological contract asks the individual employee to accept risk, ambiguity and uncertainty which has previously been borne by the organisation (Rousseau and Greller, 1994: 391). The trends outlined in the chapter with regards to reward

and remuneration have supported this displacement of risk – individually rather than collectively determined reward, pay determination based on the evaluation of the person
rather than the job, variability in pay, subjectively defined and evaluated performance
measures, and performance indicators which are influenced by factors outside of the individual's control.

The consequences of this generalised insecurity are beginning to be widely acknowledged and deliberated upon. Reports of employee insecurity (and, perhaps more
importantly, the *perception* of insecurity by employees) pervade conferences, academic
journals, media and political comment. Uncertainty created by reward and performance
management strategies add to the insecurity created by the lack of job tenure and clearly
identifiable career paths. The well-researched psychological phenomenon of the individual's need for predictability and avoidance of uncertainty can lead to poor physical and
mental health, thereby having implications for performance. Furthermore, the employee's
anxiety is also encouraged by the ominiscient and omnipotent web of performance management measures which may lead to the impression of Orwellian or Kafkaesque
technologies and practices of surveillance and control (Burrel, 1988; Barlow, 1989;
Townley, 1993a, 1993b, 1994). Thus an employee's motivation may be centred around the
need to reduce uncertainty rather than a simple equation of reward–performance based
on behaviourist theories.

In the minds of employees, the experience of development and promotion are often
intrinsically linked, but as a result of flatter organisational hierarchies this coupling can no
longer be assured (Ehrlich, 1994: 494). 'Delayering' and 'downsizing' suggest that an
organisation's reward strategy and pay structure may have to be based on encouraging
individuals to seek advancement in terms of the potential for their professional development and personal growth rather than in terms of progression up the hierarchy to higher
and higher pay grades (see, for example, Ezzamel *et al.* 1996: 69–70). Thus, if the traditional
career and promotion structure cannot be maintained by the organisation, the psychological contract has to be balanced by some other factor on the employer's side of the bargain.

In order to meet the unwritten expectations of the 'old' and 'new' psychological contracts, the more 'enlightened' company may offer as part of their reward package a 'job
for life' or an indefinite contract, and/or training and development packages which allow
the individual to have 'employability' and transferable skills.

The HR profession will have a significant role to play in the management and balancing
of the general or specific psychological contracts of employees. The HR function can act as
a focal point for helping to discovering employees' expectactions through collective channels or individual mechanisms, while seeking to provide for the meeting of employees'
expectations (see, for example, Sims, 1994). The HR professional must make sure that different facets of human resource management such as recruitment, selection, training and
reward, and different managers shape and support the psychological contracts in a consistent, integrated and balanced manner (Rousseau and Greller, 1994). Human resource
management interventions can discretely and accumulatively affect employees' psychological contracts over time, while a drastic or significant intervention or event such as
redundancy or relocation may break or significantly disrupt the psychological contract in
one go (Guzzo and Noonan, 1994; Herriot and Pemberton, 1996). If employees feel that
their psychological contract has been breached, then they may withhold or withdraw from
the relationship, consciously or unconsciously (Spindler, 1994: 326–327).

The psychological contracts of all employees are therefore an important consideration in
an organisation's reward and remuneration strategy and policy. A clearly defined, balanced

and equitable psychological contract is essential if the employment relationship is one which is to be based on mutual trust, commitment, stability and cooperation (Sims, 1994; Herriot and Pemberton, 1995). When considering concepts such as reward management, performance management and psychological contracts in the (post)modern world, the student and practitioner would be wise to note the observations of Spindler (1994: 331):

> The commitment of a free people can only be freely given. It cannot be obtained by trickery, bribery, or coercion. One can be committed only if he or she is free to withhold commitment.

The sceptic may conclude that a formal performance management system and performance-related pay schemes are ultimately a replacement for good management rather than a panacea!

SUMMARY

● Pay and motivation are central to achieving the managerial goals of increasing employee output and effort above minimally acceptable standards. Human resource management introduces the question of whether this can be achieved in a revised or reformulated manner with new forms of reward and motivation strategies.

● Individuals' needs, and the factors that are held to motivate them, are the subject of extensive analysis and debate. The work of Maslow, Herzberg, Porter and Lawler provides an introduction to the discussion of *extrinsic* and *intrinsic* rewards. A major tension in establishing adequate reward and motivation schemes is derived from such concepts as *equity*, *fairness* and *comparability* and the factors that contribute towards setting objectives in pay systems. Managements are faced with choices when designing remuneration and motivation packages as to the complexity or simplicity of the system they wish to deploy, and whether the basic system is to be based upon collective or individual factors. A further issue is raised by the appropriateness of separate pay mechanisms for manual and staff employees, in order to achieve different aspects of output and effort, or integrated into one pay and reward system for the organisation as a whole. In recent years there has been a move towards the harmonisation of manual and staff pay systems as managements have rationalised pay structures.

● The advent of human resource management approaches to the employment relationship has given rise to new forms of remuneration management with a strong tendency to locate more remuneration decisions with line managers on a decentralised basis. This has led to the introduction of pay and reward systems which may focus on individual performance in some schemes and on overall company, plant or section performance in others. Over the past decade performance-related pay and profit-related pay have come to represent the two models of reward implied in these developments. However, there may be some difficulty for management in relying on the novelty and supposedly motivational effects of these types of systems as part of an HRM model of managing employees. The general run of evidence demonstrates that, over time, all forms of motivation and reward are faced with the perennial problems of maintaining the maximum efficiency of the scheme with the maximum degree of managerial control to ensure that it does not deteriorate and lose its desired effect and that what is currently 'fashionable' may yet have to come to terms with this outcome.

Ad chief lines up £27m deal

Pauline Springett and Michael White

The chief executive of the WPP advertising group, Martin Sorrell, could receive up to £27 million in pay and bonuses in the next five years, under a remuneration package published yesterday.

Under an unusual proposal he will get a bonus of up to £14 million in shares if the company's share price hits 304p by the turn of the century. Last night's closing price was 128p.

City analysts said the company would have to perform cartwheels for him to achieve the full bonus payments.

Details of the remuneration proposals are likely to further inflame the debate over large pay packets for top company executives.

Mr Sorrell presided over the company when it nearly collapsed a few years ago. Supporters insisted yesterday he had also masterminded its return to health. He created WPP in 1987 after leaving Saatchi & Saatchi. WPP grew rapidly and is now the world's largest advertising and marketing services company.

But the rapid expansion almost brought the group to its knees in 1988 with a mountain of debt. It was saved by a financial restructuring in 1992, and a big shareholder cash call.

WPP's shareholders are to be asked to vote on Mr Sorrell's package at an extraordinary general meeting on June 26. However, it is understood that WPP has already won the approval of its major shareholders. Analysts said they did not believe shareholders would object because

Mr Sorrell would receive most of the bonus only if the company performed extraordinarily well.

The unusual element of the proposal, dubbed a capital investment plan, involves Mr Sorrell putting up £2.2 million of his own money for WPP shares.

He has been given a series of target prices for September 1999. If the price reaches the top one of 304p for 60 consecutive trading days and also out-perform the stock market average, Mr Sorrell will be awarded a maximum number of shares worth about £14 million.

Mr Sorrell's basic annual pay is £750,000, and he also gets pension contributions of £325,000. On top of that the company operates a separate bonus scheme which analysts estimate could enable him to double that to £2 million. One analyst said that it was possible, though unlikely, that this coupled with the capital investment plan could net Mr Sorrell up to £27 million.

Meanwhile, it emerged that Granville Camsey, a director and board member at National Power, yesterday took a windfall profit of more than £567,000 by selling share options.

He bought more than 200,000 shares and immediately sold them at more than double the price.

The deal brought a call from the shadow chancellor, Gordon Brown, for government action to curb boardroom pay abuses. 'It is time for the Prime Minister to act,' he said.

Source: The Guardian, 3 June 1995, p. 2.

Fat Cats and Cream

Cedric Brown, referring to his remuneration, told the Employment Select Committee: 'I'm worth every penny.' Brown's salary increased by 75% following privatisation, to £475,000. He also received £330,000 in share options. In December (1995), it emerged that he'd arranged extra pension payments worth £2m. The British Gas pensioners' Christmas party was cancelled to reduce company costs.

David Moss, chief executive of Southampton University Hospitals Trust, had his pay doubled to £100,000. The trust's 5,000 other staff received a £5 Boots voucher.

Sir Iain Vallance of BT defended his £663,000 salary: 'I'd quite like a job as a junior doctor. It might be relaxing.'

Peter Wood, chief executive of Direct Line Insurance, received £24m for the year to February 1995.

▶

'What is my husband's is also mine – what we have is shared,' said Jeanette Jefferies defending the decision of her husband, **David Jefferies**, chairman of the National Grid, to avoid tax by transferring 59,000 electricity shares into her name.

Colin Webster of Powergen realised a £250,000 share-option profit in one day.

Don Gosling and **Ron Hobson** of NCP collected a dividend of £66m each.

Dr Roger Irwin, chief executive of London Electricity, gave himself a £800,000 golden handshake before moving on to prepare the National Grid for privatisation. He stands to earn £1.7m in pay and perks.

Source: Adapted from *Guardian Weekend*, 30 December 1995.

EXERCISES

a Do you believe that senior executives are generally paid too much?
Do you believe it is ethical for executives to receive such large amounts of money?

b Research the main recommendations of the Greenbury Report on executive pay, and critically evaluate the content of the report.
Who should decide on the pay of top directors?

QUESTIONS

1 How can companies and managers help employees to satisfy the needs in Maslow's hierarchy?

2 What objectives do you believe companies hope to achieve by introducing 'employee recognition schemes'?

3 How can companies and managers prevent 'inequity' problems?

4 Identify the differences and similarities between the Porter and Lawler model, Maslow's hierarchy of needs and behavioural modification.

5 In what circumstances is pay not motivating?

6 Do you believe it is fair to reward everyone equally? Why? Do you believe it is fairer to reward employees on the basis of the evaluation of performance rather than across-the-board increases? Why?

7 Outline the circumstances in which a group incentive scheme should be used. When should an individual-based scheme be used?

8 What are the consequences and implications of 'secret' individual pay negotiations?

9 What are the advantages and disadvantages of each appraisal method?

10 How would you assess the performance of your lecturer/tutor?

11 Suggest objectives for the following types of people:
  - police officers
  - politicians
  - doctors and nurses
  - dentists
  - academics
  - social workers.

12 Are there any similarities between the problems identified in the chapter concerning appraisal and your experiences at college/university?

13 How do you think your performance at college/university should be assessed? Why?

14 Your tutor has set a group assignment. Do you believe everyone should receive the same group mark? Do you think individual group members should be rewarded on the basis of their contribution to group discussions and writing? If so, how can the tutor decide what mark to give to each group member?

How are these problems similar to those experienced in other organisations? How can they be overcome?

15 Which methods of appraisal are most suitable for linking the assessment of performance to pay increases?

16 Do you believe university lecturers should be paid on the basis of their performance? Why?

Do you believe teachers should be paid on the basis of their performance? Why? Are there any differences?

17 What are the similarities between Frederick Taylor's concepts of scientific management and human resource management techniques such as performance-related pay (PRP)?

18 How does PRP relate to Porter and Lawler's model of motivation?

19 How can the introduction of PRP and the devolution of decision making on pay issues discriminate against women and ethnic minorities?

EXERCISES

1 Imagine you are the human resources manager for a medium-sized company. Prepare a 'selling document' for the board of directors on the possible introduction of an appraisal scheme.

2 Identify and describe the possible purposes of an appraisal system other than to link performance to pay awards.

3 Read the following article on Barings Asset Management:

Can you suggest reasons for Barings Asset Management renewing its performance management system? Has the bank solved the problem?

Barings banks on skills

BARINGS ASSET Management is expanding a performance management system introduced in the wake of the merchant bank's collapse last year.

After a successful trial in the London office the competence-based system is being rolled out throughout the asset management operation.

By linking a proportion of pay to competence, the new system dilutes a traditional emphasis on achievement of specific financial objectives.

"We now have a relatively simple scoring system which is split between 70 per cent on objectives and 30 per cent on competence," said personnel director Richard Parkhouse.

▶

"On pay we track people very closely to their market value, but we use the scoring to inform the process. If they have an upper-quartile score they should be getting upper-quartile pay."

Although work on a competence framework began before the Barings collapse, Parkhouse said the events of February 1995 had heightened the sense of urgency. "It concentrated everybody's minds on performance," he said.

Barings was acquired by Dutch bank ING during 1995 and the asset management operation still employs 1,300 people worldwide.

The competence-based framework, launched in October, has become the foundation of the asset management firm's whole human resources strategy. It is a three-tier framework covering personal, managerial and task skills.

The competencies were chosen after a series of workshops, where staff identified the core skills for their jobs.

The programme is being launched at the firm's offices in Tokyo, Hong Kong, Boston, Bahrain, Bombay, Dublin and Paris. Parkhouse said the basic framework has not been altered to take into account cultural differences.

"The jobs are very similar, although the way the system is managed will depend on the culture of the place," he said.

REFERENCES AND FURTHER READING

Those texts marked with an asterisk are particularly recommended for further reading.

Adams, J.S. (1963) 'Toward an understanding of inequity', *Journal of Abnormal and Social Psychology*, Vol. 67, pp. 422–436.

Alvesson, M. (1984) 'Questioning rationality and ideology: on critical organization theory', *International Studies of Management and Organisation*, Vol. XIV, No. 1, pp. 61–79.

*Armstrong, M. (1993) *Managing Reward Systems*. Milton Keynes: Open University Press.

*Armstrong, M. (1994) *Performance Management*. London: Kogan Page.

Armstrong, M. (1996) 'How group efforts can pay dividends', *People Management*, 25 January, pp. 22–27.

*Armstrong, M. (1996) *Employee Reward*. London: IPD.

Armstrong, M. and Murlis, H. (1991) *Reward Management: A Handbook of Remuneration Strategy and Practice*, 2nd edn. London: Kogan Page.

*Armstrong, M. and Murlis, H. (1994) *Reward Management: A Handbook of Remuneration Strategy and Practice*, 3rd edn. London: Kogan Page.

Baldamus, W. (1961) *Efficiency and Effort*. London: Tavistock.

Barlow, G. (1989) 'Deficiencies and the perpetuation of power: latent functions in management appraisal', *Journal of Management Studies*, Vol. 226, No. 5, pp. 499–517.

Batstone, E. (1984) *Working Order*. Oxford: Blackwell.

Beer, M., Spector, B., Lawrence, P.R., Quinn Mills, D., Walton, R.E. (1984) *Managing Human Assets*. New York: Free Press.

Behrend, H. (1959) 'Financial incentives as a system of beliefs', *British Journal of Sociology*, Vol. 2, pp. 137–147.

Behrend, H. (1961) 'A fair day's work', *Scottish Journal of Political Economy*, Vol. 8, pp. 102–118.

Bell, D.W. and Hanson, C.G. (1985) 'Profit sharing and employee shareholding attitude survey', *Topics*, Vol. 21, March, pp. 6–8.

Birkett, K. (1989) 'Paying for change', *Personnel Management*, November, pp. 65–67.

Blau, G. (1994) 'Testing the effect of level and importance of pay referents on pay level satisfaction', *Human Relations*, Vol. 47, No. 10, pp. 1251–1268.

Bougen, P.D., Ogden, S.G. and Outram, Q. (1988) 'Profit sharing and the cycle of control', *Sociology*, Vol. 22, No. 4, pp. 607–29.

Bowey, A.M. (1980) 'Coming to terms with comparability', *Personnel Management*, February, pp. 28–33.

Bowey, A.M. and Thorpe, R. (1989) 'Payment systems and performance improvement', *Employee Relations*, Vol. 11, No. 1, pp. 17–20.

Bowey, A.M., Thorpe, R., Mitchell, F.H.M., Nicholls, G., Gosnold, D., Savery, L. and Hellier, P.K. (1982) *Effects of Incentive Payment Systems: United Kingdom 1977–80*, Research Paper No. 36. London: Department of Employment.

Bowles, M.L. and Coates, G. (1993) 'Image and substance: the management of performance as rhetoric or reality?', *Personnel Review*, Vol. 22, No. 2, pp. 3–21.

Brewster, C. (1991) *The Management of Expatriates, Issues in Human Resource Management*, Monograph 5. Cranfield School of Management, London: Kogan Page.

Brindle, D. (1987) 'Will performance pay work in Whitehall?', *Personnel Management*, August, pp. 36–39.

Brown, M. (1996) 'Britain's longest love affair', *Human Resources*, May/June, pp. 60–66.

Brown, W. (1973) *Piecework Bargaining*. London: Heinemann.

Brown, W. (1989) 'Managing remuneration in personnel management in Britain', in Sisson, K. (ed.) *Personnel Management in Britain*, 2nd edn. Oxford: Blackwell.

*Brunsson, N. (1985) *The Irrational Organization*. New York: John Wiley.

Burrell, G. (1988) 'Modernism, post modernism and organisational analysis 2: the contribution of Michel Foucault', *Organisational Studies*, Vol. 9, No. 2, pp. 221–335.

Cannell, M. and Long, P. (1991) 'What's changed about incentive pay?', *Personnel Management*, October, pp. 58–63.

Carlton, I. and Sloman, M. (1992) 'Performance appraisal in practice', *Human Resource Management Journal*, Vol. 2, No. 3, pp. 80–94.

Casey, B., Lakey, J. and White, M. (1992) *Payment Systems: A Look At Current Practice*, Research Series No. 5. Department of Employment: Policy Studies Institute.

Cavendish, R. (1982) *Women On The Line*. London: Routledge & Kegan Paul.

CBI (1995) *Trends in Pay and Benefits Systems: 1995 CBI/Hay Survey Results*. London: CBI.

Child, J. (1984) *Organisation*, 2nd edn. London: Harper & Row.

Clark, J. (1995) *Managing Innovation and Change: People, Technology and Strategy*. London: Sage.

Cooper, D.E. (1990) *Existentialism*. Oxford: Blackwell.

Curnow, B. (1986) 'The creative approach to pay', *Personnel Management*, October, pp. 70–75.

Daniel, W. and McIntosh, N. (1972) *The Right To Manage?* London: MacDonald.

Deckop, J. (1992) 'Organizational and career pay satisfaction', *Human Resource Management Review*, Vol. 2, pp. 115–129.

Dowling, P.J. and Schuler, R.S. (1990) *International Dimensions of Human Resource Management*. Boston, Mass.: PWS-Kent.

Drummond, H. (1993) 'Measuring management effectiveness', *Personnel Management*, March, pp. 38–41.

Duncan, C. (1988) 'Why profit related pay will fail', *Industrial Relations Journal*, Autumn, pp. 186–200.

Dugdill, G. (1994) 'Wide angle view', *Personnel Today*, 27 September, pp. 21–22.

Edwards, P.K. (1987) *Managing the Factory: A Survey of General Managers*. Oxford: Blackwell.

Edwards, P.K. and Scullion, H. (1982) *The Social Organisation of Industrial Conflict, Control and Resistance in the Workplace*. Oxford: Blackwell.

Ehrlich, C. (1994) 'Creating an employer–employee relationship for the future', *Human Resource Management*, Fall, Vol. 33, No. 3, pp. 491–501.

Etzioni, A. (1961) *A Comparative Analysis of Complex Organizations*. New York: Free Press.

Etzioni, A. (1964) *Modern Organizations*. Englewood Cliffs, NJ: Prentice Hall.

Eyes, P.R. (1993) 'Realignment ties pay to performance', *Personnel Journal*, January, pp. 74–77.

Ezzamel, M., Lilley, S., Wilkinson, A. and Willmott, H. (1996) 'Practices and practicalities in human resource management', *Human Resource Management Journal*, Vol. 6, No. 1, pp. 63–80.

Financial Times, 15 January 1992, p. 12.

Fisher, C. (1995) 'The differences between appraisal schemes: variation and acceptability – Part II: rhetoric and the design of schemes', *Personnel Review*, Vol. 24, No. 1, pp. 51–66.

Flanders, A. (1970) *Management and Unions: The Theory and Reform of Industrial Relations*. London: Faber, pp. 72–81.

Flanders, A. (1973) 'Measured daywork and collective bargaining', *British Journal of Industrial Relations*, November, pp. 368–392.

Fletcher, C. (1993) *Appraisal: Routes to Improved Performance*. London: IPM.

Fletcher, C. and Williams, R. (1992) 'The route to performance management', *Personnel Management*, October, pp. 42–47.

Fowler, A. (1988) 'New directions in performance pay', *Personnel Management*, November, pp. 30–34.

Fowler, A. (1996) 'How to: pick a job evaluation system', *People Management*, 8 February, pp. 42–43.

Geary, J.F. (1992) 'Pay, control and commitment: linking appraisal and reward', *Human Resource Management Journal*, Vol. 2, No. 4, pp. 36–54.

Grayson, D. (1984a) 'Payment systems for the future', *Employment Gazette*, March, pp. 121–125.

Grayson, D. (1984b) 'Shape of payment systems to come', *Employment Gazette*, April, pp. 175–181.

Green, F., Hadjimatheou, G. and Smail, R. (1985) 'Fringe benefit distribution in Britain', *British Journal of Industrial Relations*, pp. 261–280.

Gregg, P., Machin, S. and Szymanski, S. (1993) 'The disappearing relationship between directors' pay and corporate performance', *British Journal of Industrial Relations*, Vol. 31, March, pp. 1–9.

Grint, K. (1994) 'What's wrong with performance appraisals? A critique and a suggestion', *Human Resource Management Journal*, Vol. 3, No. 3, pp. 61–77.

Guardian, The, 22 April 1992, p. 3.

Guest, D. (1987) 'Human resource management and industrial relations', *Journal of Management Studies*, Vol. 24, No. 5, pp. 503–521.

Guest, D. (1989) 'Human resource management: its implications for industrial relations and trade unions', in Storey, J. (ed.) *New Perspectives on Human Resource Management*. London: Routledge, pp. 41–55.

Guest, D. (1992) *HRM: Current Trends and Future Prospects*. Paper for the London School of Economics Industrial Relations Trade Union Seminar.

Guzzo, R. and Noonan, K.A. (1994) 'Human resource practices as communications and the psychological contract', *Human Resource Management*, Fall, Vol. 33, No. 3, pp. 447–462.

Hackman, J.R. and Oldman, G.R. (1976) 'Motivation through the design of work: test of a theory', *Organisational Behaviour and Human Performance*, Vol. 16, pp. 250–279.

Hackman, J.R. and Oldman, G.R. (1980) *Work Redesign*. Reading, Mass.: Addison-Wesley.

Haraszti, M. (1980) 'Piecework and looting: Payment Systems and Productivity', in Nichols, T. (ed.) *Capital and Labour*. London: Fontana, pp. 290–301.

Hatchett, A. and Pope, C. (1988) 'Why price geography in pay determination?', *Personnel Management*, October, pp. 38–42.

Heery, E. (1992) *Divided We Fall? Trade Unions and Performance Related Pay*. Paper for LSE/TUC Trade Union Seminar, 19 March.

Hegewisch, A. (1991a) 'The decentralisation of pay bargaining: European comparisons', *Personnel Review*, Vol. 20, No. 6, pp. 28–35.

Hegewisch, A. (1991b) *European Comparisons in Rewards Policies: The Findings of the First Price Waterhouse/Cranfield Survey*, SWP 65/91. Paper presented at the 6th EIASM workshop on International HRM, St Gallen, Switzerland, March.

Hendry, C. and Pettigrew, A. (1990) 'Human resource management: an agenda for the 1990s', *International Journal of Human Resource Management*, Vol. 1, No. 1.

Herriot, P. (1996) 'Beyond equity', *Human Resources*, Mar/Apr, p. 128.

Herriot, P. and Pemberton, C. (1995) 'A new deal for middle managers', *People Management*, 15 June, pp. 32–34.

Herzog, M. (1980) *From Hand To Mouth – Women and Piecework*. Harmondsworth: Penguin.

Hilton, P. (1992) 'Using incentives to reward and motivate employees', *Personnel Management*, September, pp. 49–52.

Human Resource Management (1993) special issue, Vol. 32, Nos. 2/3, pp. 209–407.

Hyman, R. and Brough, I. (1975) *Social Values and Industrial Relations*. Oxford: Blackwell.

IDS Study 481 (1991) *DIY Benefits for the 1990s?*, March.

IDS Study 518 (1992) *Greater than the Sum of Its Parts?*, November.

IDS Study 520 (1992) *PRP Grows as Tax Relief Doubles*, December.

Independent, The, 1 December 1992, p. 2.

Industrial Relations Review and Report 319 (1984) *Merit Pay For Manual Workers*, May, pp. 2–6.

Industrial Relations Review and Report 332 (1984) *Productivity Bargaining: Profitability and Flexibility*, November, pp. 2–8.

Institute of Personnel Management (1992) *Performance Management in the UK: An Analysis of the Issues*. London: IPM.

Jacobs, R. and Floyd, M. (1995) 'A bumper crop of insights', *People Management*, 9 February, pp. 20–25.

Keeler, D. (1991) 'No more than they deserve', *Personnel Today*, 3 December, pp. 18–19.

Kennedy, C. (1986) 'Performance pay: cash on delivery', *Director*, November, pp. 34–40.

Kerr, S. (1975) 'On the folly of rewarding A, while hoping for B', *Academy of Management Journal*, Vol. 18, No. 4, pp. 769–783.

Kessler, I. and Purcell, J. (1992) 'Performance related pay: objectives and applications', *Human Resource Management Journal*, Vol. 2, No. 3, pp. 16–33.

Kessler, I. and Undy, R. (1996) *The New Employment Relationship – Examining the Psychological Contract*. London: IPD.

Kinnie, N. (1989) 'The decentralisation of industrial relations? Recent research considered', *Personnel Review*, Vol. 19, No. 3, pp. 28–34.

Kinnie, N. and Lowe, D. (1990) 'Performance related pay on the shopfloor', *Personnel Management*, November, pp. 45–49.

Kissler, G.D. (1994) 'The new employment contract', *Human Resource Management*, Fall, Vol. 33, No. 3, pp. 335–352.

Lawler, E.E. (1995) 'The new pay: a strategic approach', *Compensation and Benefits Review*, July–August, pp. 14–22.

Leiper, R. (1994) 'Evaluation: organizations learning from experience', in Obholzer, A. and Roberts, V.Z. (eds) *The Unconscious at Work: Individual and Organizational Stress in the Human Services*. London: Routledge.

Long, P. (1986) *Performance Appraisal Revisited: The Third IPM Survey*. Institute of Personnel Management.

Lupton, T. (1972) *Payment Systems*. Harmondsworth, Middx.: Penguin.

Lupton, T. and Bowey, A.M. (1983) *Wages and Salaries*. Aldershot: Gower.

Luther, R. and Keating, P. (1992) 'Ending "them and us": profit-related pay and promotion of a community of interest in industry', *Personnel Review*, Vol. 21, No. 4, pp. 57–69.

McGregor, D. (1957) 'An uneasy look at performance appraisal', *Harvard Business Review*, Vol. 35, May/June, pp. 89–94.

McGregor, D. (1960) *Human Side of the Enterprise*. New York: McGraw-Hill.

Margerison, C. (1976) 'A constructive approach to appraisal', *Personnel Management*, July, pp. 30–34.

Marginson, P., Edwards, P., Martin, R., Purcell, J. and Sisson, K. (1988) *Beyond The Workplace*. Oxford: Blackwell.

Marsden, D. and Richardson, R. (1991) *Does Performance Pay Motivate? A Study of Inland Revenue Staff Federation*. London: London School of Economics.

Meade, J.E. (1986) *Alternative Systems of Business Organisation and Workers' Remuneration*. London: Allen & Unwin.

Millward, N. and Stevens, M. (1986) *British Workplace Industrial Relations 1980–84*. Aldershot: Gower.

Millward, N., Stevens, M., Smart, D. and Hawes, W.R. (1992) *Workplace Industrial Relations in Transition: The ED/ESRC/PSI/ACAS Surveys*. Aldershot: Dartmouth.

Milner, S. (1995) 'The coverage of collective pay-setting institutions in Britain 1895–1990', *British Journal of Industrial Relations*, Vol. 33, No. 1, pp. 69–91.

Murlis, H. and Wright, V. (1993) 'Decentralising pay decisions: empowerment or abdication?', *Personnel Management*, March, pp. 28–33.

Nemeth, C.J. and Stawe, B.M. (1989) 'The trade off of social control and innovation in groups and organisations', in Berkowitz, L. (ed.) *Advances in Experimental and Social Psychology*, Vol. 12. New York: Academic Press.

O'Neil, S.L. (1993) 'Aligning pay with business strategy', *HR Magazine*, August, pp. 76–9.

Pay and Benefits Bulletin 316 (1992) *Manual Workers' Bonuses – Far From 'Dead In The Water'*, November.

Pickard, J. (1990) 'When pay gets personal', *Personnel Management*, August, pp. 41–5.

Poole, M. (1987) 'Who are the profit sharers?', *Personnel Management*, January, pp. 34–6.

Poole, M. (1988) 'Factors affecting the development of employee financial participation in contemporary Britain: evidence from a national survey', *British Journal of Industrial Relations*, Vol. 26, March, pp. 21–36.

Poole, M. (1990) 'Human resource management in an international perspective', *International Journal of Human Resource Management*, Vol. 1, No. 1.

Poole, M. and Jenkins, G. (1988) 'How employees respond to profit sharing', *Personnel Management*, July, pp. 30–34.

Porter, L.W. and Lawler, E.E. (1968) *Management Attitudes and Performance*. Homewood, Ill.: Irwin.

Ramsay, H. and Haworth, N. (1984) 'Worker capitalists? Profit-sharing, capital sharing and juridical forms of socialism', *Economic and Industrial Democracy*, Vol. 5, No. 3, pp. 295–324.

Ramsay, H., Leopold, J.W. and Hyman, J. (1986) 'Profit sharing and share ownership: an initial assessment', *Employee Relations*, Vol. 8, No. 1, pp. 23–26.

Randell, G.A. (1973) 'Performance appraisal: purposes, practices and conflicts, *Occupational Psychology*, Vol. 47, pp. 221–224.

Rawlinson, H. (1988) 'Make awards count', *Personnel Journal*, October, pp. 140–141.

Reynolds, C. (1986) 'Compensation of overseas personnel', in Famularo, J.J. (ed.) *Handbook of Human Resource Administration*, 2nd edn. New York: McGraw-Hill.

Richardson, R. and Marsden, D. (1991) *Does Performance Pay Motivate? A Study of Inland Revenue Staff*. London School of Economics.

Roethlisberger, F.G. and Dickson, W.J. (1939) *Management and the Worker*. Cambridge, Mass.: Harvard University Press.

Roomkin, M.J. (1991) 'The changing characteristics of managers and managerial employment in the 1980s', in Brewster, C. and Tyson, S. (eds) *International Comparisons in Human Resource Management*. London: Pitman, pp. 217–226.

Rousseau, D.M. and Greller, M.M. (1994) 'Human resource practices: administrative contract makers', *Human Resource Management*, Fall, Vol. 33, No. 3, pp. 385–401.

Rowe, K.H. (1964) 'An appraisal of appraisals', *Journal of Management Studies*, Vol. 1, No. 1, March, pp. 1–25.

Rowland, D.C. and Greene, B. (1987) 'Incentive pay: productivity's own reward', *Personnel Journal*, March, pp. 48–57.

Roy, D. (1952) 'Quota restriction and goldbricking in a machine shop', *American Journal of Sociology*, Vol. 57, March, pp. 427–442.

Roy, D. (1953) 'Work satisfaction and social reward in quota achievement: an analysis of piecework incentive', *American Sociological Review*, Vol. 18, pp. 507–514.

Roy, D. (1955) 'Efficiency and "the fix": informal intergroup relations in a piecework machine shop', *American Journal of Sociology*, Vol. 60, pp. 255–266.

Sartre, J.-P. (1958) *Being and Nothingness: An Essay on Phenomenological Ontology* (translated by Barnes, H.E.). London: Methuen.

Schuster, J.R. and Zingheim, P.K. (1992) *The New Pay: Linking Employee and Organizational Performance*. New York: Lexington Books.

Scott, A. (1994) *Willing Slaves? British Workers under Human Resource Management*. Cambridge: Cambridge University Press.

Shaw, A.G. and Shaw Pirie, D. (1982) 'Payment by time systems', in Bowey, A.M. (ed.) *Handbook of Salary and Wage Systems*. Aldershot: Gower, pp. 297–308.

Simons, C. (1992) 'Record mirror', *Personnel Today*, Vol. 5, May, p. 25.

Sims, R.R. (1994) 'Human resource management's role in clarifying the new psychological contract', *Human Resource Management*, Fall, Vol. 33, No. 3, pp. 373–382.

Smith, G.R. (1986) 'Profit sharing and employee share ownership in Britain', *Employment Gazette*, September, pp. 380–385.

Smith, I. (1992) 'Reward management and HRM', in Blyton, P. and Turnbull, P. (eds) *Reassessing Human Resource Management*. London: Sage, pp. 169–184.

Spindler, G. (1994) 'Psychological contracts in the workplace – a lawyer's view', *Human Resource Management*, Fall, Vol. 33, No. 3, pp. 325–333.

Stewart, J. and Walsh, K. (1994) 'Performance measurement: when performance can never be finally defined', *Public Money and Management*, April–June, pp. 45–49.

Storey, J. (1987) *Developments in the Management of Human Resources: An Interim Report*. Warwick papers in Industrial Relations No. 17, IRRU, School of Industrial and Business Studies, University of Warwick, November.

Storey, J. (1992) *Developments in the Management of Human Resources*. Oxford: Blackwell.

Swabe, A.I.R. (1989) 'Performance-related pay: a case study', *Employee Relations*, Vol. 11, No. 2, pp. 17–23.

Sunday Times, The, 27 September 1992, p. 4.2.

Taylor, F.W. (1911) *Scientific Management*. New York: Harper & Row.

*Thierry, H. (1992) 'Pay and payment systems', in Hartley, J.F. and Stephenson, G.M. (eds) *Employment Relations*. Oxford: Blackwell, pp. 136–160.

Thompson, M. (1992) 'Pay and performance: the employer experience', *IMS Report*, No. 218.

Thompson, P. and McHugh, D. (1990) *Work Organisations*. Basingstoke: Macmillan.

Thorndike, E.L. (1911) *Animal Intelligence*. Macmillan.

Townley, B. (1989) 'Selection and appraisal: reconstituting "social relations"?', in Storey, J. (ed.) *New Perspectives on Human Resource Management*. London: Routledge, pp. 92–108.

Townley, B. (1990/1991) 'The politics of appraisal: lessons of the introduction of appraisal into UK universities', *Human Resource Management Journal*, Vol. 1, No. 2, Winter.

Townley, B. (1993a) 'Performance appraisal and the emergence of management', *Journal of Management Studies*, Vol. 30, No. 2, March, pp. 221–238.

Townley, B. (1993b) 'Foucault, power/knowledge, and its relevance for human resource management', *Academy of Management Review*, Vol. 18, No. 3, pp. 518–545.

Townley, B. (1994) *Reframing Human Resource Management: Power, Ethics and the Subject at Work*. London: Sage.

Vroom, V.H. (1964) *Work and Motivation*. New York: John Wiley.

Ward, P. (1995) 'A 360-degree turn for the better', *People Management*, 9 February, pp. 20–25.

Watson, T.J. (1994) *In Search of Management: Culture, Chaos and Control in Managerial Work*. London: Routledge.

Webb, G.H. (1982) 'Payment by results systems', in Bowey, A.M. (ed.) *Handbook of Salary and Wage Systems*. Aldershot: Gower, pp. 285–296.

Weitzman, M.J. (1984) *The Share Economy*. Cambridge, Mass.: Harvard University Press.

White, M. (1981) *Payment Systems in Britain*. Aldershot: Gower.

White, M. (1982) 'Selecting a salary system', in Bowey, A.M. (ed.) *Handbook of Salary and Wage Systems*. Aldershot: Gower, pp. 265–281.

White, M. (1985) 'What's new in pay', *Personnel Management*, February, pp. 20–23.

Willmore, N. (1992) 'Is the grass always greener?', *Personnel Today*, 13 October, pp. 22–23.

Wilson, F., Haslam, S. and Bowey, A.M. (1982) 'Bonuses based on company performance', in Bowey, A.M. (ed.) *Handbook of Salary and Wage Systems*. Aldershot: Gower, pp. 321–347.

Woodley, C. (1990) 'The cafeteria route to compensation', *Personnel Management*, May, pp. 42–45.

Woodley, C. (1993) 'The benefits of flexibility', *Personnel Management*, May, pp. 36–39.

Wootton, B. (1962) *The Social Foundations of Wage Policy*. London: Allen & Unwin.

Wright, V. (1986) 'Does profit sharing improve employee performance?', *Personnel Management*, November, pp. 46–50.

EMPLOYEE INVOLVEMENT

Len Holden

OBJECTIVES

To examine the relationship of employee involvement to human resource management.

●

To explore the relationship between employee involvement and issues of control.

●

To examine various models of communication in organisations.

●

To provide a definition of employee involvement and examine its recent historical development, including cycles and waves and other discernible patterns.

●

To examine the various types of employee involvement schemes practised in organisations.

●

To investigate employee involvement practices in Sweden, Germany and Japan and other countries and make a comparative evaluation of them.

●

To examine recent employee involvement trends involving total quality management (TQM), business process re-engineering (BPR) and empowerment.

●

INTRODUCTION

Employee involvement (EI) is not a new concept and has a rich and varied history, but in recent years many managerial initiatives have mushroomed in its name. The best known of these have been quality circles, team briefing and teamworking, which are often connected with organisational culture change schemes such as total quality management, customer service initiatives and, more recently, business process re-engineering. Thus employee involvement schemes are likely to be part and parcel of an overall culture change which may involve delayering, the creation of flatter organisational structures and improvements in communication. Nevertheless, the language surrounding these initiatives has generated debates which are central to HRM. To involve employees is to gain their commitment to the organisational goals and this has often been couched in terms of empowering employees to take responsibility for their roles and function within the organisation.

This resonant rhetoric has been used freely within the more popular managerial literature, often without thought or knowledge of how it translates in day-to-day situations. Studies which have emerged in recent years have begun to examine these issues more closely. Can employee involvement only exist in unitarist frameworks, in which employee compliance is the main objective? How much responsibility can be given to employees? If one of the objectives of EI is to release employees' creative energies, what are the boundaries between creativity and responsibility? Are such schemes merely new attempts at reinforcing managerial control? What other factors impinge on the process? This chapter will attempt to answer some of these questions and at the same time outline the main EI initiatives and how they operate.

HRM AND EMPLOYEE INVOLVEMENT

Employee involvement began to flourish in the 1980s in the guise of managerial policy initiatives inspired by the new 'excellence' movement and the rise of human resource management. Management 'gurus' such as Tom Peters and Rosabeth Moss Kanter began to preach that people are the most valuable resource of an organisation and that training and developing them, adequately rewarding their performance and involving them in organisational policy making, particularly at customer interface level, could only enhance employee motivation and thus performance. In this context there was a need for management to direct employees' efforts 'in pursuit of organisational goals to ensure that tasks are performed in cost-effective and market effective ways' (Hyman and Mason, 1995: 52). Successful companies carrying out such policies were lauded as exemplars of the new managerial approach (Peters and Waterman, 1982; Kanter, 1983).

Much of this rediscovery of the intrinsic worth of the employee was driven by the relative decline in US economic performance, particularly compared to Japan. A considerable literature was generated analysing the key to Japanese success and one oft-cited element was the involvement of employees in work groups such as quality circles (Lawler, 1986).

Employee involvement was also expounded as a key instrument in the creation of HRM strategies, and the influential Harvard Business School HRM programme proposed by Beer *et al.* (1984) put 'employee influence' firmly in the centre of this approach. The Harvard HRM programme casts employees as one of the main 'stakeholders' in the organisation and therefore 'it is critical that managers design and administer various mechanisms for employee influence' (Beer *et al.*, 1984: 11). They continue: 'not only will their [the employees] interests be heard, but there will be mechanisms to help shape their company's HRM policies' (Beer *et al.*, 1984: 41).

This recognition of employees' and other stakeholders' interests raises a number of important questions for policy-makers in the organisation.

> How much responsibility, authority, and power should the organisation voluntarily delegate and to whom? If required by government legislation to bargain with the unions or consult with workers' councils, how should management enter into these institutional arrangements? Will they seek to minimise the power and influence of these legislated mechanisms? Or will they share influence and work to create greater congruence of interests between management and the employee groups represented through these mechanisms?
> (Beer *et al.*, 1984: 8)

These questions raise further concerns about the inexactitude of the language of EI in the HRM context. Terms such as 'influence', 'involvement', 'empowerment' and 'commitment' are blithely used by writers on HRM, without attempt at definition or even clarification. Of the Harvard Business School academics, Walton has had the most to say on the subject. In his view employee influence is most effective when employees have commitment to the organisation and this can only be achieved if there is congruence between the HRM and general management policies of the organisation. Walton (1984a: 4) calls this a 'high commitment' work system and he proposes that 'high commitment is the essential ingredient in the future pattern of HRM'. Walton (1984b: 36) sees the HRM conception replacing previous systems 'because the common denomination among systems being replaced is the emphasis on imposing control'. In other words, there is a move from 'control to commitment' (Walton, 1985: 36).

These arguments contain a number of non sequiturs. There is no guarantee that mutuality will 'elicit employee commitment', or that it will lead to increased economic effectiveness and human development, although there may be more likelihood of this happening in organisations with positive HRM policies than in those which have negative employee relation policies. In essence, what is happening here is what Keenoy calls a reconstruction of the employment relationship through rhetoric and metaphor (Keenoy, 1990: 371; Keenoy and Anthony, 1992: 235).

As Goss (1994: 101) states, 'the evidence suggests that commitment is a complex phenomenon that operates in different directions and at different levels. It is not something which can easily be generated or sustained, neither does it necessarily lead to improved performance'. Noon (1992: 23), in exploring these criticisms further, comments: 'employees may resent the dissonance created between commitment to the task (encouraged by the individually-based performance management mechanisms) and commitment to the company (encouraged through the rhetoric of culture and the rewards of promotion and employment security)'.

The economic downturn in the early 1990s has led some commentators to ask if HRM is 'recession proof' (Beardwell and Holden, 1994: 686). Storey (1989: 8) has identified 'hard' and 'soft' types of HRM which may sit well with different types of organisational culture and, we posit, different economic climates. Legge (1989: 33) has alluded to 'tough love' HRM in such contexts and this is readily witnessed in the experience of such 'HRM companies' as IBM with its forced redundancy programme (Noon, 1992: 24). It is pertinent to ask, therefore, how 'human resource management' changes under such circumstances, and how employee commitment and involvement are affected. Marchington (1995) proposes that EI will be considerably different in nature or may not exist at all in organisations which practise forms of 'hard' HRM, compared with those that practise 'soft' HRM. In organisations which practise 'hard' HRM:

> EI may not be seen as important by senior managers, given the emphasis on tight cost control, de-skilled jobs, and a lack of investment in training. In others, EI may be little more than one way communications channels, designed merely to convey the latest news to employees and indicate to them the merits of management's decision. In these cases, if EI is practised, it is likely to take a rather diluted and marginal form.   (Marchington, 1995: 280)

HRM can also be affected by changes in the economic climate, and Holden (1996) cites the experience of an organisation in the banking and finance sector. This company was an early convert to HRM and initiated policies which contained mechanisms to increase employee influence. In the boom economy of the late 1980s 'soft' policies were emphasised, including for example training for TQM and other EI measures. In the harsher climate of recessional Britain in the 1990s, downsizing and retrenchment became the order of the day. Survival meant a move to 'hard' HRM policies. In this climate the 'soft' mechanisms of EI tended to be overlooked and even ignored.

Control and employee involvement

One important element in the participation equation is the degree of control given to managers and non-managerial employees. For example, informational, communicational and consultational types of participation tend to come from management initiatives and are more likely to be controlled by management. However, the term 'control' itself is problematic. For example, a worker can feel in control of his or her work process, i.e. the day-to-day operations, but have little control or say in the running of the organisation in terms of influencing overall policy or strategy. Second, various issues at workplace level will allow more control and influence by the workforce than others.

These problems have long been recognised in the vast literature generated around this important subject (Edwards, 1987: 90). Drucker, for example, states that 'control is an ambiguous word. It means the ability to direct oneself and one's work. It can also mean domination of one person by another'(Drucker, 1961: 128). These positive and negative views of 'control' have spawned a parallel literature rooted in the acceptance and rejection of capitalist values, of which the latter is represented strongly by the labour process theory school inspired by the work of Braverman (1974) (see also Chapters 3, 5 and 11).

Control according to the 'labour process' school of thought postulates that technology controls the work process in its drive to help fulfil the requirements of the capitalist organisation (i.e. profits) in response to intensive competition. This obviates the necessity to control the work process in order to extract the maximum output *vis-à-vis* labour cost and the ability of labour to resist control (Salaman, 1979). According to Braverman (1974), the ability to resist control and exert greater autonomy is higher among workers whose skills are in great demand, and less among workers in unskilled or deskilled situations. Thus deskilling has considerable implications for control and the way it is applied and viewed by participants (employees, managers, employers) and hence for participation schemes, especially in institutions such as banks which have undergone intensive techno-logical change and reorganisation in the past five years.

Since Braverman's work there have been a number of refinements and challenges to his thesis, many sharing the Marxian perspective. Edwards (1979) focuses on the move away from more coercive methods rooted in new technology, with its associations with Fordist and Taylorist managerial control mechanisms, to 'bureaucratic control' systems aimed at the dual goals of dissolving class solidarity while maximising commitment to, and depen-dence on, the firm. 'Promotion, pay, security and other benefits go to employees who are good corporate citizens, who are loyal to the company, share its values and integrate them-selves and their families into the enterprise community' (Lincoln and Kalleberg, 1990: 9). Such managerial initiatives fit particularly well with HRM conceptualisations.

Friedman (1977) has divided managerial control systems into direct control and responsible autonomy. *Direct control* is associated with rules, regulation, work organisa-tion and technology which directly control the behaviour and work rate of the employee. This is strongly associated with the Fordist–Taylorist approach. *Responsible autonomy* allows the worker and the work team a degree of control over the work process and 'attempts to harness the adaptability of labour power by giving workers leeway and encouraging them to adapt to changing situations in a manner beneficial to the firm. To do this top managers give workers status, authority and responsibility. Top managers try to win their loyalty, and coopt their organisations to the firm's ideals (that is, the competi-tive struggle) ideologically' (Friedman, 1977: 78). This again has strong resonances with developments in HRM in the 1980s and 1990s, particularly in terms of participation schemes such as TQM which aim at enhancing commitment to the organisation by allow-ing a degree of autonomy to the workforce. Edwards (1992: 390) points out, however, that such HRM apologists as Walton (1985) who speak of a move from control to commitment, partly by means of employee involvement and participation policies, should perceive that commitment 'is still a form of control'.

Burawoy (1979) has also developed a dual perspective of management regimes which rely on coercion or consent. Earlier capitalist systems relied heavily on the former approach and adopted autocratic methods of workforce control, particularly in response to intensive capitalist competition. Latterly the adoption of more subtle approaches to the employment relationship has emphasised policies designed to induce commitment in the employee. This has been caused to some degree by the softening of overt autocratic sys-tems by state regulation and welfare policy. Burawoy (1983) sees such new approaches as creating a hegemonic regime under which coercive compliance is replaced by normative control, as managers make concessions in order to persuade employees to cooperate in furthering the success of the organisation. Once again we can discern echoes of HRM policy intitiatives in such hegemonic systems.

We shall return to some of these questions later in the chapter, but at this juncture it would be apposite to examine some of the mechanisms and definitions of employee involvement, beginning with a perspective from the relatively recently formed discipline of communications.

EMPLOYEE INVOLVEMENT AND COMMUNICATION

All organisations need communication systems to function, whether these are overtly recognised or subconsciously taken for granted. Over the past decade it has been increasingly recognised by many employers and managers that creating effective communication is an extremely important aspect of the efficient running of organisations. Of course, communication is a very complex series of processes operating at all levels within organisations ranging from the 'grapevine', heavily laden with rumour, to formalised systems such as joint consultative committees (JCCs) or works councils. These can operate at the localised level of the shop floor or office between supervisor and staff and the staff themselves, or at a distance by means of representatives such as union officials or messages from on high from the boardroom or the chief executive, to various branches or subsidiaries of large and complex organisations. They can be one way or two way, top down or bottom up and both top down and bottom up, as well as across the organisation.

What is being increasingly recognised is that messages to, and equally important from, the workforce have considerable significance. They are important for conveying the organisation's mission, business aims and objectives, and its general ethos or culture. They are needed to enable the thoughts and feelings of the workforce to be expressed and, of equal significance, heeded and acted upon. Such policies are being heavily influenced and underscored by HRM practices.

Communication systems also carry implicit messages about the mediation of power within organisations. Employee involvement communication systems (which are examined more closely below) are processes which enable the workforce to have a greater say in decision making to varying degrees, with the concomitant loss of managerial prerogatives; an issue which can create, as well as attempting to allay, conflict.

Communication systems are also influenced by political, social and economic trends within society which change and evolve over time and in turn influence the perceptions of those engaged in the employment relationship.

In addition, the nature of the communication channel can affect the message, as does the culture(s) existing within and outside of the organisation (Jablin *et al.*, 1987; Clampitt, 1991).

Thus even the simplest message can be misunderstood or misconstrued due to the complex influences which act on the communication process. Equally important, and potentially disastrous, is the fact that communication channels can send conflicting messages. An oft-cited case is the company which encouraged employees to take up share options which entitled them to attend the annual shareholders' meeting, where they were told how successfully the company had performed over the previous year. Many of these same employees were also in the union to which management communicated later that due to the poor performance of the company over the previous year the pay increases requested could not be met!

Models of communication

The first model of communication to emerge was conceived by Shannon and Weaver (1949) and had a mathematical basis. It was devised to help Bell Telephone Company engineers understand how to transmit electrical impulses most efficiently from one place to another. Although created for mechanistic reasons, it is applicable to organisational and other communication processes.

The message sent from the information source to the receiver travels via a channel before which the message is encoded, i.e. turned from an idea into a verbal or written message, and then decoded by the receiver either by hearing or reading the message. The problem is that the message can be distorted by noise sources or interference. In the mechanistic version of the telephone this might be interference on the telephone line, thus making the communication difficult and unclear. In the case of a manager speaking to an employee it could be more subtle. The noise source which distorts the message could be personal. For example, the employee may dislike the manager, or be unhappy with the situation in which he or she works, or have a headache or personal problems at home.

One criticism of the Shannon and Weaver model is that communication is seen as only a one-way process. Observers in the field of human behaviour have stated that this is not so, even in communications between the most seemingly compliant employee and manager. The employee may communicate dissatisfaction through body language or through another source, such as his or her work group. Later communication model builders therefore added the element of 'feedback' to the communication model (Schramm, 1954; DeFleur, 1966).

Thus whereas the Shannon and Weaver model concentrates on the channels between sender and receiver, the Osgood and Schramm model devotes discussion to the main actors in the communication process, allowing both to send and receive messages.

While these communication models have been refined and elaborated (McQuail and Windahl, 1981), they nevertheless contain the essence of the communication process as represented in most organisations.

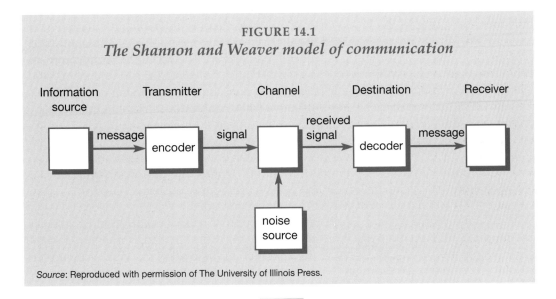

FIGURE 14.1
The Shannon and Weaver model of communication

Source: Reproduced with permission of The University of Illinois Press.

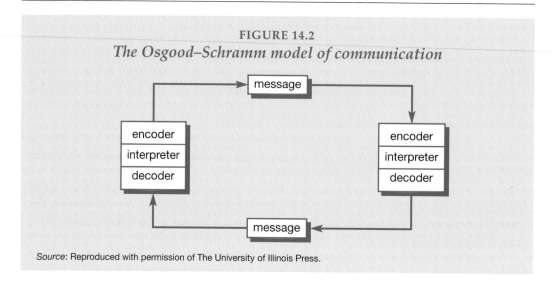

FIGURE 14.2

The Osgood–Schramm model of communication

Source: Reproduced with permission of The University of Illinois Press.

Employee involvement: history and development

One form of communication which has become popular in organisations in the past decade is employee involvement. The idea of involving the workforce may seem self-evident as employees must be involved in order to do their job. It has long been recognised, however, that doing a job does not necessarily mean being interested in it or doing it well. The school of human relations promoted by thinkers in the field such as Mayo, Vroom, Likert and Maslow, amongst others, have drawn conclusions from their various studies that positive motivational factors engendered by such methods as employee involvement may develop a more creative, interested and therefore more productive workforce.

Even though employee involvement (EI) is just one aspect of organisational communication it is, nevertheless, wide ranging and diverse in its forms. Types of EI also evolve and change with managerial vogues which are governed by political, economic and social pressures. For example, the First World War witnessed a considerable growth in worker militancy together with an increased popularity of left-wing ideologies, many of which espoused various forms of workers' control, one example being Guild Socialism (Cole, 1917). The Bolshevik revolution in Russia in 1917 also had a significant impact on work relationships, as Marxist ideology is based on an analysis of how capitalism exploits the proletariat in the workplace. These influences had, and still do have, a considerable impact on arguments surrounding work-related issues. One attempt to mollify these forces in Britain was to acknowledge legally, in the form of Whitley Councils, that employees and their representatives (trade unions) had some say in negotiations over pay and working conditions. Despite good intentions from some parties on both sides of industry, these arrangements largely fell into disuse once recession hit the British economy after 1921 and the threat of workforce militancy receded.

It was not until the Second World War that a popular revival occurred in EI schemes. The need for huge productivity increases to meet the war effort led workers to demand something in return – a greater say in the operation of the workplace. Works committees or Joint Consultative Committees (JCCs) were set up in many factories. Some continued in existence after the war, but management and unions lost interest in them in the 1950s and many fell into decline when there was a preference for direct collective bargaining via unions, employer organisations and employers. Nevertheless, there was a considerable revival in the atmosphere of industrial democracy in the 1960s and 1970s, and shop stewards were to be found filling delegational positions (Marchington *et al.*, 1992). Debates concerning the extent to which these committees existed and the real power they afforded the workforce still engage social and economic historians.

In the 1970s the Bullock Committee Report (1978) echoed an increased interest in industrial democracy. There was a growing consciousness that, while politics and society were increasingly being 'democratised', the world of work did not reflect this trend. In addition, British membership of the European Community influenced the Bullock Committee to examine forms of industrial democracy among its European partners, such as co-determination in Germany and Sweden, and some societies where more radical forms of employee involvement were being undertaken, such as worker self-management practised in Yugoslavia and at Mondragon in Spain. These practices attracted considerable interest, as did worker-director schemes and the formation of workers' cooperatives, which often happened in UK companies under threat of liquidation (Broekmeyer, 1970; Brannen *et al.*, 1976; Eccles, 1981; Thomas and Logan, 1982; there is a considerable literature on these subjects).

The political climate which had engendered industrial democracy swiftly changed under Margaret Thatcher's Conservative government, which tarred such policies with the brush of left-wing ideology.

Cycles and waves of participation

It is apparent from even this brief history that numerous influences have a bearing on the type, strength and sustainability of various participation schemes and trends. Unsurprisingly, therefore, commentators have attempted to discover patterns of EI and to place them into a theoretical framework.

For example, the relationship between the introduction of profit sharing with a high level of employment and industrial unrest down to the First World War has been indicated by Church (1971). Ramsay (1977, 1983) has argued that there are cycles of participation:

> managements have been attracted to the idea of participation when their control over labour has been perceived to be under pressure in some way. This perception has coincided with experience of a growing challenge from labour to the legitimacy of capital and its agents. In Britain these challenges have coincided with the impact and aftermath of two world wars, and with the rise of shop floor union organisation at the same time as squeezed profit margins in the 1960s and 1970s. In each case mounting pressure, including demands for 'industrial democracy' from sections of the labour movement, helped to precipitate management response.
>
> (Ramsay, 1983, quoted in Poole, 1986: 45)

Marchington *et al.* (1992) have pointed to 'waves' of employee involvement within organisations, which respond to external trends and cause the institution of new schemes and the revamping of old existing ones. For example, a quarter of organisations in their survey sample had introduced their current schemes (survey period 1989–91) between 1980 and 1984, 'and several of these were share ownership schemes which appear to have been stimulated by legislative changes from 1978 onwards' (Marchington *et al.*, 1992: 25). Other schemes such as team briefing were introduced in the early 1980s' recession to communicate 'gloom and doom' messages such as pay freezes and voluntary severance. Over half of the schemes of their survey group had been introduced within the previous five years and tended to be TQM programmes of various types. The 'wave' concept, they point out,

> is analytically more useful than cycles, in that it does not presuppose any automatic repetition of events in an historical pattern, or any all embracing theory of waxing and waning which applies in the same way across all workplaces. On the contrary waves come in different shapes and sizes and last for different lengths of time in different organisations.
>
> (Marchington *et al.*, 1992: 26)

Thus the importance of EI can only be understood if it is viewed as being central to the organisation, and not necessarily prominent. For example, a Joint Consultative Committee (JCC) may achieve a central position in an organisation over time, although the most prominent new measure may be team briefings. If the JCC becomes less important or dies out, another scheme may replace it and attain the status of centrality. Whether schemes are retained, reformed or dropped depends on multifarious influences within organisations, for example the values and beliefs of managers, which interact with other influences in complex ways.

Poole has attempted to construct a theoretical framework to explain these influences. He sees workers' participation and control as being understood as a specific manifestation of power. This is linked with 'underlying or latent power resources and a series of values which either buttress particular power distributions or facilitate their successful challenge' (Poole, 1986: 28). The relationship of power sources is illustrated in Figure 14.3.

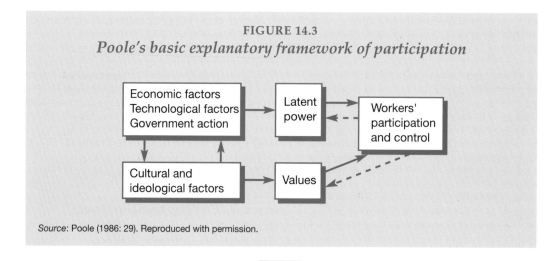

FIGURE 14.3

Poole's basic explanatory framework of participation

Source: Poole (1986: 29). Reproduced with permission.

Poole postulates that:

> *workers' participation and control are reflections of the latent power of particular industrial classes, parties or groups and the 'value' climate which may or may not be favourable to participation experiments.* These values thus mediate between certain structural factors associated with latent power and their realisation in the form of workers' participation and control. It will also be seen that the principal structural factors associated with the latent power of the main industrial classes, parties or groups are *economic factors*, such as the levels of employment, the profit margins of particular companies, the levels of competition, the degree of industrial concentration and periods of economic 'disintegration'; *technological factors*, such as the approximation of the technology of a company to a given point on the 'technical scale', the degree of complexity and education involved in any given task and the effects of the micro-electronic revolution; and finally, various forms of government *action* such as legislation on labour issues, its intervention in the workings of the economic system and so on. (Poole, 1986: 28, Poole's italics)

Finally, 'values about participation and control are shaped by the existing levels of workers' participation and control, latent power, government action and ideologies' (Poole, 1986: 29).

While this framework pinpoints the main factors influencing types and styles of employee participation and control, it cannot clearly demonstrate how these factors interact to produce such systems. Nevertheless, it is a useful model to aid understanding of these complex processes.

DEFINITIONS OF EMPLOYEE INVOLVEMENT

There is an enormous range of employee involvement schemes, varying from those which are informational mechanisms to full-blown democratic systems where employees have as much say in the decision-making processes as does management. This makes an all-encompassing definition problematic. In addition, different labels have been attached to these processes, such as employee or worker participation, industrial democracy, organisational communications, co-determination, employee influence, etc., each of which have their own definitions.

Wall and Lischerson (1977) state that there are three elements central to the concept of participation: 'influence', 'interaction' and 'information sharing'. Marchington *et al.* (1992: 6, 7) divide definitions into three categories: first, those that refer 'to employees taking part or having a say or share in decision making, with no attempt to quantify their impact on the process'; the second 'refer to participation as concerned with the extent to which employees may influence managerial actions', and the third 'link together participation and the control over decision making'.

Marchington *et al.* (1992) believe that these definitions also need to take into account:

- the *degree* of involvement (the extent to which employees influence the final decision);
- the *level* of involvement – whether at job, departmental or organisational level;
- the *forms* of involvement – direct, indirect and financial;
- the *range* of the subject matter being considered in the involvement scheme.

For example, quality circles may have a high degree of direct employee involvement and influence on decisions at workplace level, but be limited in range to matters of teamwork and job design. Works councils, on the other hand, will involve employee representatives at organisational level, and may consider a wide range of areas such as business and industrial relations strategies, in joint decision making with the management.

TABLE 14.1

Some types, levels and degrees of employee involvement

Degree	Levels of Involvement		
Control (by workers or workers and management together)	Worker self-management		Worker self-management or cooperatives
Co-determinational	Union shop steward representation		JCCs; works councils; worker directors; union–management negotiations
Consultational (two-way communication)	Quality circles; job enrichment; suggestion scheme; appraisal	Attitude survey; customer care; TQM	
Communicational	Team briefings; department or group meeting		Mass meetings
Informational (top down)	Noticeboards	Memos; briefs	Company newspaper/ magazine; bulletin
	Local (workplace level)	**Both local & distant**	**Distant** (company or organisational level)

One problem with this tabular representation is that some EI schemes may pervade many or all levels of the organisation, for example financial participation. Others may cascade through many levels, such as team briefings (Ramsay, 1991). Team briefings could also fall into both the 'informational' and 'communicational' categories. Another problem is that the degree of participation with one scheme could differ from one organisation to another. For example, JCCs could vary in power from being mere rubber-stamping operations for management decisions to forming joint consultational mechanisms covering a rich variety of organisational topics.

TYPES OF EMPLOYEE INVOLVEMENT

Marchington *et al.* (1992: 13) divide EI schemes into four categories:

- *Downwards communications* (top down), e.g. from managers to other employees. This includes forms of EI such as house journals, company newspapers, employee reports, regular briefing session, often with videos as well.
- *Upwards problem-solving forms* which are designed to tap into employees' knowledge and opinion, either at an individual level or through the mechanism of small groups; this includes practices such as suggestion schemes, attitude surveys, quality circles and total quality management and customer care programmes.
- *Financial participation* via schemes which attempt to link rewards of individuals to the performance of the unit or the enterprise as a whole. This includes schemes such as profit sharing, employee share ownership, and value-added or establishment-wide bonus arrangements.
- *Representative participation,* in which employees are involved through representatives drawn from amongst their number, often – though not always – on the basis of union membership, for example JCCs, advisory councils, works councils, co-determination, and collective bargaining.

In many organisations a combination of these forms of communication and EI schemes will exist, hopefully supporting and complementing each other.

In a book of this nature it would be impossible to examine all of these approaches, but a closer study of some of the more popular and recent schemes in each category may serve to illustrate current trends.

Downward communication

The company magazine or newspaper

One of the most common methods of downward communication which has witnessed a considerable increase over the past 20 years is the proliferation of company newspapers or magazines (CBI, 1989). Reviewing methods of communication in six surveys of organisations conducted between 1975 and 1983, Townley (1989) indicates that most put the company newspaper or house journal either as the most popular or second most popular form of communication. The problem is these can vary in quality from amateur desk top published affairs produced by employees in their 'spare' time, to lavish glossy productions which have been part of the communications systems of many large companies for a number of years.

There is also the question of editorial control which may restrict the messages conveyed to the workforce. Continual glowing reports of the company successes or anodyne and meaningless information may have negative results in the long run. Genuine expressions of employee feelings via letters pages or forthright quotes from employee represen-tatives, even of a negative nature, may show the desire of management to achieve fairness. Of course, the judgement of the editor will come into play in deciding the con-tent of the newspaper or journal, which in turn will be affected by the organisational culture and management views.

For example, during a dispute a militant shop steward called the managing director a 'fascist', which the personnel director urged the editor to expunge as being insulting. The editor defended the decision to retain the quote on the grounds that he had sought a com-ment from the shop steward and not to print it would look like corporate censorship. In addition, such a quote was so patently absurd that it would have a negative effect. In the event the quote was left to stand and the prediction of the editor proved true when the shop steward was spurned by his fellow employees and the union felt moved to apolo-gise publicly for the comment (Wilkinson, 1989). Unfortunately, many company journal editors are still unable or unwilling to follow such boldly democratic policies, and the workforce often regards publications as a conduit for managerial views. Given their pri-marily one-way nature and editorial control, this is not surprising.

Team briefings

There has been a considerable increase in team briefings in the past five years, although they have been in existence in some organisations for longer (Marchington *et al.*, 1992). They are often used to cascade information or managerial messages throughout the organisation. The teams are usually based around a common production or service area, rather than an occupation, and commonly comprise between four and fifteen people. The leader of the team is normally the manager or supervisor of the section, and should be trained in the principles and skills of how to brief. The meetings last for no more than 30 minutes, and time should be left for questions from employees. Meetings should be held at least monthly or on a regular pre-arranged basis.

Surveys often reveal considerable satisfaction with team briefings by both employers and management (e.g. CBI, 1989) as they are effective in reinforcing company aims and objectives at the personal, face-to-face level. However, Ramsay (1992a: 223) urges caution in accepting this rosy picture, because success depends on 'context to a significant extent'. For example, briefings might be postponed or cancelled at times when business is brisk, which may lessen commitment to holding them at all in the long run. If the intention is to undermine union messages, the success will very much depend on the strength of the union and the conviction of the management. A sceptical and undertrained management and supervisory force can do much to undermine the effectiveness of team briefings.

Upward, problem-solving forms of communication

These schemes can also be described as two-way communication and are most associated with 'new' managerial concepts such as HRM. They are clearly aimed at increasing employee motivation and 'influence' within the organisation, but usually at a localised level, i.e. workshop, office or service area. They also aim to improve employee morale, loyalty and commitment, with a view to increasing service and efficiency. Another facet of these types of schemes is facilitating acceptance of changes in work practices, functional flexibility and new technology, as well as engendering an atmosphere conducive to cooperation and team-building (Ramsay, 1992).

Quality circles

One of the first methods identified with the 'new' involved approach to management was the quality circle (QC). This first arrived in Britain via the USA from Japan, although the concept were implanted in Japan in the postwar years by two US consultants, W. Edwards Deming and J.M. Duran (Clutterbuck and Crainer, 1990).

QCs are made up of 6 to 10 employees with regular meetings held weekly or fortnightly during working time. Their principal aim is to 'identify problems from their own area and, using data collection methods and statistical techniques acquired during circle training, analyse these problems and devise possible solutions; the proposed solutions are then presented formally to the manager of the section who may decide to implement the circle's proposal' (Brennan, 1991).

Tremendous interest was shown in QCs by British managers in the early 1980s, but within a few years they began to decline in popularity. A number of reasons have been identified for this decline, but principal among these was the attitude of middle managers. For example, it is crucial that a manager or supervisor with the requisite qualities and training leads the circle. Technical competence alone is not enough, and studies began to highlight the necessity for interpersonal skills. Some managers also felt that their power and authority was undermined by the QC, and others lacked commitment in the initial stages which had the effect of making the circles difficult to develop effectively. There were also difficulties from overenthusiastic facilitators who deliberately gave an overtly positive but false impression of the circle's operation, possibly for career progression reasons. This made it difficult to identify problems within the circle or improve its effectiveness (Brennan, 1991). Suspicion of circles could be engendered if they were seen as a way of undermining trade union functions. Lack of consultation with the union, particularly when setting up QCs, often bred suspicion that this was another anti-union management ploy, and the initiative was, therefore, effectively undermined by non-cooperative attitudes.

Other circles failed because suggestions by the workforce were not in fact applied or even considered, thus rendering them a waste of time in the minds of the participants. Finally, many circles simply 'ran out of steam' after the initial burst of enthusiasm. The need for continual reinforcement of their function and purpose was evident (Collard and Dale, 1989; Ramsay, 1992).

Teamworking

Teamworking is one of the most recent initiatives in EI and, like QCs, originated in Japan. As yet it is not as widespread as TQM, but its influence is gradually spreading. It emphasises problem solving in a teamworking situation and, in order to function effectively, it must be bound up with policies of task flexibility and job rotation (Price, 1989). Teams vary in size from 7 to 10 people, or even more, and large elements of training are necessary to ensure that workers, team leaders, supervisors and managers have the requisite skills to enable the team to function efficiently. A large part of such training is of a managerial or interpersonal skill and communicational nature, as well as of a technical nature.

Financial participation

Financial participation differs from other forms of employee involvement in that it is less likely to involve employees in consultational or decisional processes. The general aim of such schemes is to enhance employee commitment to the organisation by linking the performance of the organisation to that of the employee. Thus, it is argued, employees are more likely to be positively motivated and involved if they have a financial stake in the company through having a share of the profits or through being a company shareholder. Although such schemes are by no means new, early profit sharing schemes were in operation in the nineteenth century (Church, 1971), their recent popularity has been partially spawned by the Conservative government's philosophy of creating a property-owning democracy in an attempt to individualise work and societal relationships, and also by the rise in human resource management initiatives (Schuller, 1989).

In addition, legislation has been introduced to bolster and lay down legal parameters for such schemes in the form of the Finance Acts 1978, 1980, 1984, 1987 and 1989. Evidence suggests that most managers' aims in introducing forms of financial participation are for positive reasons associated with employee motivation, rather than attempts to undermine trade union influence (although this is an objective in some organisations), and schemes were indeed welcomed by most employees in the organisation (Badden *et al.*, 1989; CBI, 1989; Poole and Jenkins, 1990a, 1990b; Marchington *et al.*, 1992).

Types of financial participation

Schuller (1989: 128) categorises financial participation schemes on a scale which ranges from individualism to collectivism. Towards the individual end there are personal equity plans, profit-related pay, profit sharing and employee share option schemes; at the collective end, workers' cooperatives, management buyouts, pension fund participation and wage earner funds.

Of these categories, individual forms of financial participation are the most common, especially profit-related pay and share option schemes (CBI, 1989; Marchington *et al.*, 1992). Given the controversy in recent years concerning the maladministration of pension funds, most notably that of the Maxwell organisation (although this is by no means a rare example), it would be logical to expect to see increased demands by employees for some representation on the boards which oversee these funds (for a more detailed examination of pension funds see Schuller, 1986 and 1989).

Profit-related pay and employee share options

As already noted, profit-related pay schemes have a long pedigree and were recently stimulated by the Finance Act of 1978. In essence, profit sharing or profit-related pay schemes are 'where a cash bonus or payment is made to employees based upon the share price, profits or dividend announcement at the end of the financial year' (Marchington *et al.*, 1992: 11).

Employee share options are schemes 'using part of the profits generated or earnings of employees to acquire shares for the employee in the company concerned, or discounted shares on privatisation or public quotation' (Marchington *et al.*, 1992: 11).

There are four main types of scheme (Poole and Jenkins, 1990b):

- profit sharing – with cash rewards;
- profit sharing – through shares in the company (approved deferred share trust, ADST);
- save as you earn share option schemes (SAYE);
- executive share schemes.

There is a degree of overlap in these schemes, for example ADST and SAYE both concern share options but the former is often bracketed with profit sharing, where shares are part of the reward, and the latter with employee saving schemes which lead to the purchase of shares. A considerable amount of financial legislation, and the fact that successive Chancellors of the Exchequer have made over ten concessions in successive budgets since 1978, bear testimony to the importance which the government gives to such schemes. Between 1978 and 1990 the Inland Revenue approved, for tax purposes, 6500 schemes, which are made up of 909 ADSTs, 919 SAYEs and 4521 executive share option schemes (Dunn, Richardson and Dewe, 1991: 1).

How effective are these schemes, given their apparent popularity? In general terms commentators and researchers divide into two basic camps, the optimists and the more sceptical. The optimists are backed by a plethora of positive literature emanating from consultants and the more popular business journals. The question of success, however, rests on the criteria by which they are judged and here opinion is much more mixed, but even in-depth studies differ in some of their conclusions (Badden *et al.*, 1989; Poole and Jenkins, 1990b; Dunn, Richardson and Dewe, 1991; Marchington *et al.*, 1992).

Poole and Jenkins (1991a, 1991b) represent the more optimistic view, but they still distinguish between the effect of such schemes on employee attitudes and employee behaviour. They believe employee attitudes are favourably affected in the sense that employees have increased their identity with company goals, feel more involved, and have a more positive attitude towards the company. 'Indeed, the most important impact of profit sharing is almost certainly to improve organisational identification and commitment and hence, indirectly, to enhance industrial relations performance' (Poole and Jenkins, 1991a: 96).

Ramsay *et al.* (1986) are less optimistic in their view and claim that many surveys play down the negative effects; while Dunn, Richardson and Dewe (1991: 14), using evidence from their longitudinal survey, claim that there is not even a correlation between improved employee attitudes and the introduction of such schemes. Both studies point to the fact that the 'them and us' attitude which the schemes attempt to break down may well reinforce the status quo, because executives and older workers tend to be the majority of employee shareholders as younger and less senior employees cannot afford shares.

Marchington *et al.* (1992) and Dunn, Richardson and Dewe (1991) also state that a number of internal and external factors affect employee attitudes and behaviours which is difficult to disentangle from perceptions of financial participation schemes. Marchington *et al.* (1992) state that employees viewed the scheme much more negatively in one company which was unable to pay out dividends on shares due to market pressures, than in another company which was relatively financially buoyant.

A problem with all the surveys to date is that they suffer from unrepresentativeness and a lack of comparative time-series data. Some surveys choose a qualitative in-depth approach and others a quantitative wide-survey approach; only one survey has conducted a longitudinal survey, but this was in only one company.

Representative participation

Joint consultative committees

Apart from collective bargaining, the most common form of representative participation in the UK is Joint Consultative Committees (JCCs). As already noted, these received a considerable impetus in the Second World War, declined somewhat in the 1950s and 1960s, and witnessed a revival in the 1970s which, according to various surveys, has continued. According to Badden *et al.* (1989) one-third of companies had consultation machinery, and the CBI (1989) survey puts this figure at 47%, though both stress that such mechanisms are more likely to exist in larger organisations. Shop stewards also tend to be employee representatives in unionised firms, indicating a retreat from the view held by many unionists that JCCs were mere talking shops without power, set up to dupe the employees and undermine union presence.

In examining JCCs it soon becomes evident that they operate differently in various organisations and sectors, at different levels within organisations and with different degrees of power (Marchington, 1989b). Thus in one organisation they could be rubber-stamping bodies for management initiatives, discussing at the most 'tea, toilets and trivia', and in other organisations they could be genuine conduits for the expression of employees' views with some degree of decisional power.

According to Marchington *et al.* (1992: 11) joint consultation is defined as:

> a mechanism for managers and employee representatives to meet on a regular basis, in order to exchange views, to utilise members' knowledge and expertise, and to deal with matters of common interest which are not the subject of collective bargaining.

Organisations with a strong union presence attempt to keep issues such as pay bargaining off the JCC agenda, leaving them to collective bargaining issues. This has led some commentators to the view that management in organisations which encourage employee participation may see JCCs as a less important channel of communication. This relative powerlessness may 'often leave JCCs with a marginal role in labour management relationships' (Ramsay, 1991). Marchington (1989a; Marchington *et al.*, 1992) is, however, more optimistic and sees their role as often complementing and supporting other channels of communication and EI, such as collective bargaining.

All commentators agree that, if JCCs are given only unimportant issues to deal with, then employees themselves will view them as ineffectual and they will be marginalised.

Ramsay (1992a) recommends that for the joint consultation medium to be effective it needs to be consulted in advance of decision making; to have a representative range of issues to discuss; to be adequately resourced with proper administrative back-up; to have an effective feedback mechanism to employees; for management representation to be seen to be of the requisite level (i.e. senior managers); for action on proposals to be quickly carried out; and for unions to be kept officially informed.

Other forms of consultation are types of co-determination such as works councils, often backed by government legislation as in Germany, Belgium and the Netherlands. These will be considered in the section below.

INTERNATIONAL ASPECTS OF EMPLOYEE INVOLVEMENT

In many countries in Europe and the rest of the world, trade unions still act as one of the most important communication channels, despite indications that there has been a decline in membership worldwide over the past ten years (ILO, 1993). Their importance is central in Scandinavian countries, especially Sweden, and they still carry considerable weight in Germany and Britain, though the rise in long-term unemployment and the decline in the old staple industries such as shipbuilding, coal, iron and steel and engineering, where unionism had a strong traditional base, have tended to erode their power.

Employee involvement rooted in industrial democratic processes has witnessed a surer growth over the past 20 years in legislatively supported systems such as co-determination in Germany and Sweden. The operation of these two contrasting styles of industrial democracy is also reflected by the relative union strength in each country – 85% in Sweden and 35% in Germany in 1988 (OECD, 1991).

Swedish co-determination

In many respects Sweden has the most advanced forms of participation in the world at both organisational and workplace levels (Wilczynski, 1983). The basis of industrial democracy in the country stretches back to 1948 with the setting up of the National Labour Market Board. This was composed of representatives from labour, employers and government, and participated in economic planning.

In the economic and political climate of the 1970s, demands were made for the extension of industrial democracy which led to the passage of a body of legislation, most notable of which was the Co-determination at Work Act (MBL) passed in 1977. The aim of the Act was to extend the scope of collective bargaining to areas of management policy, including organisational and technical change. It required all employers to allow consultation with employees and the participation of their representatives in decision making at both board and shop floor levels. For example, one of the central provisions of the Act requires that, when employers are contemplating making major changes in their operations or working conditions of employment, they are required to negotiate with employee representatives before the final decisions are taken and changes introduced (Edlund and Nyström, 1988).

In reality, employee representatives in the co-determination system tend to be union representatives, and it was the unions in Sweden which gave impetus for much of the drive towards industrial democracy. The union strategy was to focus on issues of health and safety and 'this created a political climate in which new laws and regulations in support of industrial democracy could be introduced . . . these laws were supplemented by financial support for training and research which to a large extent was channelled through the unions' (Hammarström, 1987). The crucial role of unions, not only in bargaining structures but in the co-determination system, meant that they would always be an important element in Swedish employee relations.

Co-determination – not a drag but a motive force

Source: Edlund and Nyström (1988).

Companies have also enhanced the reputation of Swedish employee involvement. Volvo in particular introduced job enlargement and job enrichment, 'quality of working life' techniques to its Kalmar plant in the 1970s, and became the focus of much attention worldwide as an alternative to the mass-assembly Fordist systems of production (Sell, 1988).

While these systems have been admired, they have also received criticism. The neo-liberalists have seen the corporatist state pay too heavy a price in terms of high wages and high taxes for a regulated labour market which is seen as being heavily influenced by the ability of the workforce to impede management prerogatives in policy creation. Conversely, left-wing critics have attacked the system for not addressing the real needs of the workforce, which have been emasculated by the unions in collusion with the Social Democratic Party in attempts to maintain the corporatist status quo. 'Kalmarism', as one French observer has dubbed the EI initiatives in Volvo (Lipietz, 1992), has also been attacked for being no more than a public relations exercise. Many of the EI initiatives are seen as untypical and a number have been dropped recently as being uneconomic and inappropriate.

A recent trend in Sweden has been seen to be bound up with managerial HRM initiatives which have shifted from formal to more informal models of participation and decentralised practices. Some observers suggest that these trends might eventually undermine the formal system of participation (Cressey, 1992).

What is certain is that the change in the economic climate in the 1990s as a result of recession, raising unemployment from 1.5% in 1990 to 8.5% in 1993, has had an enormous impact on the Swedish collective psyche, challenging many of the assumptions which were generally acceptable in the agreeable economic environment of the 1980s (Holden, 1996).

The balance of power between state, unions and employers continually changes with each economic phase, but there is no reason to believe that the essence of the system will not survive. Despite the fact that management prerogatives in Sweden still outweigh those of the employee, the culture of involvement is still very well developed compared with most other countries.

German co-determination

Given the embodiment of the concept of consultation and participation in the EU Social Charter and the draft European Works Council Directive, it is not surprising that the German system of co-determination and works councils has been seen by some observers to be a model for the rest of the Union.

> In contrast to other countries, the system of co-determination in Germany is very extensive, and involves the participation of employees and their representatives in nearly all decisions relating to personnel and many aspects of company policy.
> (Gaugler and Wiltz, 1992)

Co-determination is legally embodied in the work system by four key Acts: the Montan Co-determination Act of 1951, the Workplace Labour Relations Act of 1952, the Workplace Labour Relations Act of 1972 and the Co-determination law of 1976. Co-determination operates basically at company and plant levels, although there are three methods by which workers can participate: by works councils, supervisory boards and management boards. In places of work which have five or more employees the workforce elects a works council, consisting of workers' representatives only. The works council has a right to information concerning:

- health and safety;
- the organisation of work;
- the working environment and jobs;
- the hiring of executives;
- planned changes in the company which could result in considerable disadvantages to employees.

In addition, the works council has the right to make suggestions (Gaugler and Wiltz, 1992):

- during the formulation and implementation of personnel planning;
- regarding vocational training (apprenticeships, etc.);
- about other training and development measures.

The views of the works council must be considered by the employer, although there is no compulsion to accept them. In the case of larger companies (not family owned) employing more than 500 people, representatives elected by the workers sit on the supervisory board where they make up one-third to a half (depending on size) of the policy-making body. Other board members are elected by the shareholders, and a neutral chairperson is appointed. In companies over 2000 employees in size trade union representatives are guaranteed places on the board. German workers have a tendency to believe that the works councils and co-determination system generally adequately represent them and there has been a reluctance to join unions (35% as opposed to Sweden's union density of 85%), although the recession in the early 1990s has witnessed a revival of trade union militancy which may alter workers' perceptions as to the efficacy of works councils in time of mass redundancies.

The supervisory board meets four times a year and also appoints members to the management board, a full-time executive body which oversees company policy in its day-to-day operations. (For a fuller explanation of the history and detailed operation of the co-determination system, see Lawrence, 1980; Lane, 1989; Gaugler and Wiltz, 1992.)

Co-determination: an evaluation

In evaluating co-determination one must be aware of the diversity of positions from which views emanate. These are, of course, influenced by political ideology, position in the organisation (whether management or worker etc.), whether one is a shareholder and the type of organisation. Lane (1989), in her survey of research analysing the influence of co-determination in Germany, points to the diversity of findings depending on the level (whether workplace or enterprise), company size, sector and managerial style.

Not surprisingly, co-determination at enterprise level had relatively little impact on the everyday work of employees, but, it can be argued, has had the long-term positive effect of engendering a spirit of cooperation between management and labour. Labour representatives perceive more clearly the reasons for managerial policy initiatives and, conversely, the management have more understanding of the concerns of the workforce.

At workplace level there has been a wide variety of research. For example, Wilpert and Rayley (1983, quoted in Lane, 1989: 232) showed that there was a large discrepancy between formal rights and actual rights of participation. They also state that, while participation rights in Germany are high compared with most other European countries, so too is formal and actual managerial control.

Lane (1987: 232) posits the view that 'faced with a strong and control-oriented management and forced to prove themselves *vis-à-vis* their electors by concrete achievements, works councillors may decide to pursue only those issues on which they are confident to get concessions'. Thus the degree of participatory influence could also vary with each issue.

Not surprisingly, there are German employers who share the view of recent British Conservative governments that the co-determination system undermines the employer's right to manage. Survey evidence suggests, however, that works councils are supported by the overwhelming majority of employers, except in the smallest of firms (Mauritz, 1972: 80, quoted in Lane, 1989: 233).

Works councils in other European countries

Works councils bolstered by legislation also exist in Belgium, France, Italy, Luxembourg, Spain and the Netherlands, but the range of issues and decisions submitted for employee approval is smaller than in Germany. The operation of the councils is also affected by employee and management attitudes bound up with the culture of the country.

For example, the Auroux Laws 1982 extended workers' participation rights in French companies, but research reveals that the consultation process has been ignored or under-mined by management accustomed to the hierarchical and, often, autocratic ways strongly emphasised (although changing) in many French organisations (Lane, 1989: 240). In Sweden there has been much criticism of the relatively weak position of unions in the co-determinational process, particularly in time of recession (Korpi, 1981; Kjellberg, 1992). Unions often do not receive adequate information and in the recent bank crisis had much less influence than management on the restructuring and downsizing exercises (Holden, 1996).

Britain and the works council issue

As already mentioned, the British Conservative government is implacably opposed to the EU Works Council Directive 1991 and the directives on participation embodied in the Social Charter. However, the adoption of the Maastricht Treaty and with it the Social Chapter could possibly mean that works councils could be instituted in Britain through foreign-owned subsidiaries (Gold and Hall, 1992). Considerable debate has been engendered by the fact that, even if Britain does not sign the Maastricht Protocol (the part of the Maastricht Treaty which embodies the Social Chapter), large British-owned subsidiaries operating in two other EU countries will have to conform to the works council directive. Once such bodies exist it would be difficult politically to exclude British workers. Hall (1992: 563) states that 'companies covered by the Directive (on Works Councils), whether based in the UK or elsewhere, could well decide voluntarily to bring their UK employees within the ambit of their European works councils; they would certainly come under pressure from UK unions to do so'.

The current directive makes it obligatory for any company with over 1000 employees in the EU and more than 100 employees in two different countries to set up a council comprised of worker representatives. The former President of the Commission, Jacques Delors, a strong believer in works councils, believed that the bad feeling engendered by the Hoover dispute (see Part 2 Case Study) could have been avoided by directing the argument via a works council in each country (Wolf, 1993).

While the UK government claims that employee involvement is adequate at present in Britain and should be left to the discretion of each employer, a comparison of British and Dutch employee participation practices shows that this voluntary approach does not fair well when compared to countries such as the Netherlands which has legislation compelling organisations to set up EI mechanisms like works councils. Wenlock and Purcell (1991: 58) state that 'existing British practice does not go far enough in its provision of employees' rights to information, consultation and participation in the management of transfer of undertakings, whereas the Dutch jurification model exceeds even the EC legislation in its provision of employees' rights to participate in strategic management decision making'.

Nevertheless, recent evidence shows that the number of works councils (and similar bodies) is on the increase in Britain. More than half are French- and German-owned subsidiaries such as Renault, Crédit Lyonnais, Grundig and Bayer, although increasing numbers are coming from Scandinavia (e.g. Electrolux and Norsk Hydro). British companies are also creating their own works councils, most notably BP, Coats Viyella and United Biscuits (Carley, 1995). The presence of a works council does not, however, guarantee employee consultation or indeed a voice in managerial policy, as the recent experience of job losses at Coats Viyella has shown. This lack of consultation has outraged unions and employees throughout the company's British and European concerns (Littlefield, 1996).

Japanese employee involvement

Japan is often cited as an exemplar of employee participation practices, particularly giant corporations such as Komatsu, Hitachi, Nissan, Honda, Mitsubishi and Toyota. The most commonly emulated participation technique has been quality circles, which we have already noted were conceived in the USA by Deming and Juran, and were implanted in Japanese organisations in the 1950s. Since then employee involvement techniques such as QCs and teamworking have been part and parcel of the working practices of Japanese companies in the UK such as Nissan in Sunderland and Toyota in Derby. Many studies have been made of Japanese organisations in order to discover the secrets of their economic success, and teamworking techniques have received much attention as a perceived key to efficient work practices.

Pascale and Athos (1982: 125) emphasise that the work group is the basic building block of Japanese organisations: 'Owing to the central importance of group efforts in their thinking, the Japanese are extremely sensitive to and concerned about group interactions and relationships.' They liken the Japanese worker's view of the group to that of a marriage which rests on commitment, trust, sharing and loyalty, and, while power ultimately rests with management, the group leader handles the interaction within the group carefully. This 'participation assumption' is also related to a lifetime employment assumption, which ensures that the worker has a strong stake in the firm and its success. Finally, and perhaps most importantly, participation is backed up by training of both group leaders and workers in the skills of group participation (Dore and Sako, 1989). Employee involvement, like training, is thus embedded in Japanese organisations.

A number of observers (including Klaus and Bass, 1974) have pointed out that employee involvement should not be confused with decision making, particularly at the higher levels within the organisation: 'The reality is that not all employees wield real power . . . [and] when it comes to making the decision, workers feel under great pressure to agree with supervisors and unpopular decisions are simply ignored' (Naoi and Schooler, 1985, quoted in Briggs, 1991: 40). Briggs sees this paradox of employee involvement and emasculation of power as being explained by the split between opinion and behaviour. In a number of surveys Japanese workers have rated themselves low on job satisfaction and yet they work far more hours for less reward than their US and British counterparts. This cannot be explained by coercive methods alone; Briggs points to the extent of unionisation, albeit organised around large corporations, and finds this view untenable. Her explanation is based on cultural factors in that the Japanese have 'a deep felt desire to keep the realm of duty separate from the realm of personal feeling . . . duty must come first and must exist totally separate from the domain of personal feelings' (Briggs, 1991: 41).

If this is the case, it has ramifications for the export of such EI practices to other countries, most notably Britain which has received enormous amounts of Japanese investment. Wickens (1987), in his exposition of how Nissan implanted Japanese practices into its Sunderland factory, strongly believes that people are capable of change and that the institution of Japanese-style working practices was partly effected by a watering-down process to meet British attitudes, combined with a process of education and training to enable newly hired (often novice) workers in car manufacturing to be imbued with Japanese-style practices. This was reinforced by a greenfield culture with workers who had predominantly been recruited from regions where high unemployment meant an eagerness to gain and retain employment.

A number of observers have pointed out that control and the mechanisms of employee involvement in Japanese-owned British organisations still reside firmly in the hands of management. Lewis (1989), in his study of employee participation in a Japanese-owned electronics factory, found that, while a board was set up (a kind of JCC) to represent employee interests, employees were not quite sure what was meant by involvement. Most of the issues raised were not about the overall running of the operation but more parochial shop floor concerns, and the real aim in setting up the board was to introduce unitarist principles in the company such as single status terms and conditions, no-strike arrangements and flexible work practices. All were reinforced with powerful symbols of unitarism such as the brightly coloured jackets which everyone wore, replete with the owner's forename. This sent messages of egalitarianism and that the organisation was one happy family. The single status restaurants and toilets were also part of this symbolic reinforcement of unitarism. Oliver and Lowe (1991) endorse this unitarist view of Japanese-style management. In comparing styles of HRM in Japanese, US and British computer companies based in the UK, they found that the Japanese emphasised consensus and collectivism with 'a thin dividing line between the public and the private and a strong sense of mutual support and awareness'.

In essence, the implementation of EI, even in Japanese organisations which have strong commitments to such systems, is not as a decision-making instrument *per se* or even as a conduit of employee criticism, but as a mechanism which reinforces common aims and goals within the unitarist organisational context.

Ramsay (1992b) has also pointed out that few non-Japanese-owned British organisations have adopted Japanese EI measures in the long term. The use of quality circles, after an initial flurry of interest, dropped from 63% in 1980 to 10% in 1989 in British organisations, and by the late 1980s only a few companies were still experimenting with teamworking. He concludes: 'no matter what the degree of genuine autonomy or control Swedish or Japanese work group experiments, the greater constraints on the prospect for worker influence came from the institutional settings and – even more critically – the broader social and cultural contexts' (Ramsay, 1992b: 40).

Comparative aspects of employee involvement

Comparative research of a statistical and analytical nature into EI is relatively sparse, although there have been a considerable number of international surveys of institutional and legal aspects of employee involvement (Poole, 1986). Studies in the 1980s and 1990s revealed a diversity of trends influenced by a multipicity of organisational, economic, political and technical factors. The Price Waterhouse Cranfield Survey into International Strategic HRM investigated trends in employee communications in five countries (UK, Sweden, the then West Germany, Spain and France) in 1990, and ten countries in 1991 (the original five plus Netherlands, Norway, Denmark, Italy and Switzerland). Both survey years revealed a marked increase in attempts at communicating with the workforce, both via staff representative bodies, such as trade unions, and by more direct methods associated with HRM initiatives (Holden, 1990; Price Waterhouse Cranfield Project Reports, 1990 and 1991). In British organisations personnel managers reported the greatest decrease in trade union influence, at 49%, and the greatest decrease in communication through staff representative bodies, as shown in Table 14.2.

TABLE 14.2

Communication through staff representative bodies as perceived by personnel managers, 1990 (%)

	UK	*France*	*Spain*	*Sweden*	*Germany*
Increased	18	22	53	38	23
Decreased	20	12	3	7	3
Same	49	58	44	55	64

Source: Holden (1990).

This survey and the ten-country one in the following year were both conducted before the recession of the early 1990s began to bite in the UK, and the decrease in communication via staff representative bodies obviously echoes the declining influence in trade union power in Britain. Despite this decline, it would be mistaken to underestimate the still relatively strong role which trade unions play in communication. This is shown in Spain, which exhibited an enormous increase of 53% and clearly reflects the comparatively strong growth in trade unionism in the 1980s (albeit from a low base and now around 10% density), backed by legislation requiring works committees in organisations employing more than 50 people (Filella and Soler, 1992).

Parallel to overall increases via staff representative bodies in four of the five survey countries were even larger increases in verbal and written communication in all five countries (see Table 14.3). The ten-country survey revealed similar trends (Price Waterhouse Cranfield Project Report, 1991).

These increases obviously indicate a greater desire by employers to increase communication, probably inspired by HRM trends which spread in the 1980s. France and UK show particularly large increases in both verbal and written communication, which parallel the rise in team briefing and other teamwork methods, as well as increases in the more traditional written forms of communications. The survey in the following year, however, added questions to establish the main ways in which employees communicated their

TABLE 14.3

Changes in verbal and written communication as perceived by personnel managers (%)

	UK	France	Spain	Sweden	Germany
Verbal					
Increased	67	68	45	64	34
Decreased	1	2	8	1	3
Same	31	28	47	34	54
Written					
Increased	63	64	49	47	26
Decreased	1	4	3	3	3
Same	34	29	48	47	58

Source: Holden (1990).

views to management, and trade unions and/or works councils still predominated in all ten countries (Price Waterhouse Cranfield Project Report, 1991).

It would seem that communication with and from the workforce is increasing at workplace level, but the more established forms of communication and forms of EI such as unions, works councils and JCCs are still important in those organisations where they are established. The survey conducted by Marchington *et al.* (1992) in UK organisations would seem to confirm this.

Nevertheless, these surveys do not indicate the degree of participation by employees in organisations. Research by Fröhlich and Krieger (1990), Cressey and Williams (1990), Boreham (1992) and Gill (1993) have tried to address this issue in comparative contexts. Fröhlich and Krieger (1990) examined the extent of employee participation in technological change in five EC countries – UK, France, Germany, Italy and Denmark. They discovered that of the four phases of introducing new technology (planning, selection, implementation and subsequent evaluation) workers were more likely to be involved in the latter stages, and that full participation, particularly in decision making, remained relatively low for all countries and for all stages. Cressey and Williams (1990), in a similar survey but covering all of the then 12 EC countries, found comparable results and posed a 'paradox of participation'. As the scope for influence by employees over the processes of technological change decreased, so the intensity of participation increased. In other words, there was more scope for participation in the implementation stage (the latter stage) when participative influence concerning fundamental decisions was reduced, and less participation in the crucial earlier planning stages in the introduction of new technology.

Gill (1993), using the same 12-country EC data analysed by Cressey and Williams (1990), perceives differences in attitudes between Northern European and Mediterranean countries which result in a wide diversity in levels of participation. Denmark, Germany, the Netherlands and Belgium have much greater employee participation than do Portugal, Spain, Italy, Greece, France, Luxembourg and the UK. In France and the UK, however, Gill argues, 'there is a dependence by management on the skills and problem solving abilities of the labour force' (Gill, 1993: 346). Nevertheless, he claims that 'in the United Kingdom there has been a shift away from negotiation towards more consultation during the last decade and management has become increasingly paternalistic in their style' (Gill, 1993: 346). These differences are caused, he argues, by the diverse industrial relations practices in each country, shaped by historical and cultural factors.

In all three studies managers were of the view that increased participation was effective for the efficient implementation of new technology, but this may have the effect of compromising their prerogatives.

Boreham (1992) investigated the degree of employee control over labour processes in seven countries (Australia, Britain, Canada, Germany, Japan, Sweden and the USA). He was particularly interested to know whether employee control was enhanced by the introduction of new practices associated with postfordist systems such as flexible working linked to quality improvement and greater response to market conditions. The assumption here was that efficiency was improved by decentralisation and democratised decision-making practices. The findings clearly indicated that 'the nearer one approaches the core of status and power in the enterprise the more likely it is that one be allowed discretion over one's work arrangements' (Boreham, 1992: 18). He also found that there was little evidence 'to support the view that management will cede its decision making prerogatives in the interests of more rational production methods' (Boreham, 1992: 21). This pattern was generally true of Japanese and Swedish organisations which are associated with employee involvement styles of management.

These surveys clearly indicate a contradiction in managers' perceptions that employee involvement is an effective way of increasing work efficiency, but is outweighed by the challenge to their prerogatives over decision making. Thus employee involvement is very limited and is more likely to take the form of information dissemination to, and consultation with, the workforce, which is not the same as 'empowerment' to which many HRM textbooks allude.

Boreham (1992) also stresses the significance of flexible employment patterns and involvement. In a world where increases in part-time, fixed-contract and short-term working is becoming more pronounced, he shows that these employees have even less involvement in workplace decisions, and that core groups, particularly in management categories, still hold far greater sway over the organisation and control of work. Such evidence casts huge questionmarks over growing trends, for example 'zero hours contracts' alongside involvement schemes aimed at motivating workers.

What can we learn from these studies?

The findings of these pieces of research are replicated to some degree by earlier and more recent research by IDE in 1981 and 1993.

In essence, it seems that there is a contradiction in what employers and managers want from EI and what they are prepared to allow to the workforce in terms of empowerment and control. In ideological terms, the control of the organisation rests in the hands of the upper realms of the hierarchy, either the board or within the senior management teams, and there will be resistance against attempts to extend significant power to workers lower down the organisation. Thus the concept of 'industrial democracy' *per se* is perceived as a power challenge, even in societies which allow considerable autonomy to the workforce and have *in situ* sophisticated structures of co-determination, such as those which exist in Sweden and Germany. This power 'balance' will also shift with changing economic and political climates and management will allow considerably more concessions in times of labour shortage than in times of recession, when worker power is much weaker.

The ideas of 'empowerment' and 'employee influence' at workplace level have greater justification for management in HRM terms, as the rationale for the introduction of EI policies is ultimately to increase the efficiency of the organisation. The perception of management poses a dilemma in terms of how much power to extend to the workforce while harnessing their creative energies, and at the same time not undermining managerial prerogatives. This conundrum is in many ways a central one to the whole debate concerning HRM and modern organisational practices such as delayering of middle management structures, the introduction of new technology, TQM, the creation of flatter organisations, culture change and other initiatives. Perhaps the working out of these power balances is a continuing part of the managerial process, until, that is, the structure of ownership in society radically changes. Equally important is the relationship between middle management and senior management, which to some extent can be seen as similar to that between workforce and middle management, but overlaid with elements of status and role strain.

Another factor at both organisational and workplace levels is the influence of cultural values to which many commentators on EI ultimately allude. Writers such as Hofstede and Laurent have attempted to examine these influences and concede that much research still has to be completed before our understanding of these complex issues is clearer (see Chapter 16). Even then, 'culture' is in a state of permanent flux and our concept of it is ever changing, often in subtle ways. Yet observers would have us believe that British adaptations to Japanese work practices are possible despite the different cultural values of British workers. Others have stated that the practices become palatable because of the environment into which they are introduced: greenfield sites with single union deals and no-strike clauses, and a compliant workforce conscious of the lack of alternative employment in high unemployment areas.

Several factors emerge which make the proper working of EI mechanisms possible:

- a willingness by management to concede some of their prerogatives;
- the necessity to train managers in EI initiatives such as teamworking;
- to have a clear policy regarding the role and prerogatives of line managers in relation to senior management and the workforce under their supervision;
- the necessity to train workers in group skills such as presentation, leadership, assertiveness, problem solving, etc;
- the necessity of providing proper feedback mechanisms which clearly indicate that the workforce is being listened to and not purely in a lip-service fashion;
- action must be taken to implement group decisions, which reinforces the view amongst the workforce that their contributions are well received;
- conflicting views must have a place in developing initiatives.

CONTROVERSY: DOES EMPLOYEE INVOLVEMENT WORK?

The case of TQM

Whether employee involvement works or not depends on the aims and objectives of the EI scheme. In addition, there are times when certain schemes will work successfully and other times when they will be unsuccessful, and this is why EI, like many other HRM policies, goes through fashion changes. The economic, political and social context influences the type and success of the scheme which organisations adopt (Ramsay, 1992a). Further factors are the type, size and sector of the organisation. What may work in a small firm, for example, may not work so well in a large, bureaucratic organisation. What may work in a democratic organisational culture will probably be unsuccessful in a more authoritarian one (Wilkinson, 1989).

The aims and objectives of an organisation increasing the number and intensity of communication channels may be specifically 'political'. For example, in times of dispute with the union, the management may feel they need to put their side of the case more effectively to the workforce. In the past many companies found themselves at a comparative disadvantage in disputes, as the unions had a virtual monopoly of the informational channels to the workforce. This was no fault of the unions but more a reflection of the incompetence of management, who were incapable of creating effective communication channels which they suspected could be used at other times for what might be perceived as more negative purposes (Monks, 1989). In other words, management can themselves suffer from their own ideology of operating 'mushroom systems' (keeping the workforce in the dark and piling 'manure' on them) which maintains a climate of distrust and attitudes of 'us and them'. Fortunately, surveys indicate that in many organisations such ideas are becoming less popular (CBI, 1989; Marchington *et al.*, 1992).

Even schemes such as TQM which begin life for the most positive reasons, for example the enhancement of employee commitment, motivation and empowerment, may become distorted by factors, both internal and external, which turn them into something more unworkable and, from the employee point of view, into a sinister attempt to gain more commitment, work and productivity, without the concomitant reward, control or empowerment.

Total quality management (TQM) has been increasing in popularity in many organisations in recent years and is often bound up with culture changes and other HRM and managerial initiatives such as customer service programmes. TQM operates at both a local and establishment-wide level and pervades the whole organisation. It is concerned with concepts such as culture change which in turn engender attitudinal changes in the workforce. At workplace level emphasis can be placed purely on improving the quality of the product or service and, like customer service schemes, this can also be the implementation of more efficiency between internal departments (which can be seen as internal customers) and external customers themselves. Like quality circles, the idea stems from the writings of Deming, Juran, and more recently, Crosby (1979, 1984). They have also been linked to British Standard BS 5750 approaches, although many claim that this is more suitable for production oriented rather than service sector work.

Wilkinson *et al.* (1992: 5) point out clearly the differences between QCs and TQM (and their implications).

TABLE 14.4
Ideal types of quality circles and TQM

	Quality circles	TQM
Choice	voluntary	compulsory
Structure	bolt-on	integrated quality system
Direction	bottom up	top down
Scope	within departments or units	company wide
Aims	employee relations improvements	quality improvements

The compulsory nature of TQM, with its top-down overtones, suggests a system whereby worker empowerment is restricted very much within the boundaries set by management. In its operation in production companies Sewell and Wilkinson (1992) also propose that it has an air of surveillance, whereby the performance of individual workers is monitored so as to control their work to conform to the group norm – a norm set by management.

They describe how in an electronic components factory the teams, especially the team leader, which make the components 'have a great deal of discretion in the way labour resources are deployed across the cell [the unit of manufacture]' (Wilkinson and Sewell, 1992: 104). Multi-skilling is encouraged and work rotation allocated by the team and team leader. Within the team individuals are encouraged to improve personal performance and innovations should be made to improve productivity and product quality. Team meetings provide the forums where such issues are debated and information shared. Quality is controlled by a visual inspection and electronic tests, which also trace the individual responsible for the fault. This information, together with data on absenteeism, conformity to standard times and production planning targets, is prominently displayed for all the team to see. Naturally, the information forms the basis of much discussion between team members. In turn this creates a situation where the team will 'discipline' those whom they feel are not conforming to the norms. This is a form of what Friedman (1977, quoted in Sewell and Wilkinson, 1992: 106) called 'responsible autonomy', a situation where the group acts as the controller of the individual and therefore the team. Thus managers can clearly claim that the workforce is being 'empowered'. This delegation of power, however, has a dual nature which, according to Muetzfeldt (quoted in Sewell and Wilkinson, 1992: 106), 'can actually increase the power of the delegating agency, so long as it can legitimate and retain its authority, and undermine it if the obedience of the delegated agents cannot be assured' (Sewell and Wilkinson, 1992: 106).

Sewell and Wilkinson see this system of TQM as an analogy of the work of Foucault, who stressed the importance of tracing the loci of power in organisations in order to understand its importance and how it is used, like the panopticon, the hub of the surveillance system in Victorian prisons. The electronic quality-recording mechanisms in the operation of TQM in the electronics factory they dub the 'information panopticon', a device used in the control of team norms set by management.

Wilkinson *et al.* (1992), in their research into EI for the Department of Employment (see also Marchington *et al.*, 1992), visited 25 organisations of which the majority had TQM programmes in operation. In examining these practices it was evident that TQM operated in a wide variety of forms and, like HRM, was open to a variety of definitions and interpretations. In a close examination of TQM in three typical British companies in engineering, finance and marketing, the researchers discovered several problems in its implementation and operation. All of the schemes were difficult to sustain for four basic reasons.

First, the schemes were narrow in conception and 'bolted-on to rather than integrated in, key management policies' (Wilkinson *et al.*, 1992: 14). As a result some schemes looked very similar to quality circles and thus had many of their faults. Companies tended to look for immediate gains rather than look to long-term cultural changes. 'If these are not forthcoming TQM is short lived' (Wilkinson *et al.*, 1992: 15). In turn this created an obsession with 'the cost of quality and immediacy of return, concepts which are totally different from Japanese thinking' (Wilkinson *et al.*, 1992: 15).

Second, the role of middle managers became unclear and confused, and was looked upon as one group of managers imposing itself on another. This had the effect of creating conflicts. Because TQM was carried out in a highly centralised framework in most organisations, teams were reliant on the services of other departments, with which they were competing for resources, and each department was often in ignorance of how they were affected by each other. The competition thus militated against mutually cooperative solutions.

Third, industrial relations, while affecting TQM programmes, is rarely considered by employers. Thus there was usually neglect in obtaining union agreement or establishing a positive working climate before implementing TQM schemes, a situation almost guaranteed to create suspicion in either the unions or the workforce. TQM has a strong impact on such issues as job control, working practices and reward, all of which can, if not handled sensitively, create problems, as unions and workers may place obstacles in the way of the system's operation.

Fourth, employee involvement in TQM schemes can have contradictory elements. Similar to the findings of Sewell and Wilkinson, it was discovered that there was a contradiction in the language of employee involvement (empowerment of the workforce etc.) and the actuality of the work situation in which power very much rested in the hands of management.

Recent critical studies of the 'quality' movement have drawn attention to its wider implications. Wilkinson and Wilmot (1995: 13) state that it is relevant to place the quality movement 'in the wider context of pressures from shareholders upon managers to organise the work of employees in ways that are more profitable'. They continue by stating that 'quality initiatives are often imposed upon an unprepared and hesitant, if not hostile, management by the intensity of (global) competitive pressures'. They also draw attention 'to the strength and depth of the participation promoted by TQM. It is striking that participation does not extend to key decisions relating to the ownership and control of companies' (Wilkinson and Wilmot, 1995: 20). In a recent comparative study of employee involvement in the banking sector in Britain and Sweden, Holden (1996) has concluded that most participation mechanisms, particularly those related to recent HRM initiatives such as TQM, do not encourage participation by the workforce in strategic issues. Most are confined to workplace areas, and therefore tend to be restricted in their sphere of control. This is particularly surprising when much HRM literature advocates the strategic nature of HRM policy in relation to employee influence.

These studies point to a number of problems in the implementation of TQM. Ramsay (1992a) has noted, with some laconic interest, the rise and fall of fads and fashions in employee involvement and speculates about what might be next on the agenda if TQM does not succeed! What is certain is that easy solutions do not exist and the implementation of new systems have to be viewed within a long-term framework and reviewed constantly with the full consent and approval of the workforce.

Business process re-engineering

Business process re-engineering (BPR) is one of the latest 'fads' and has been hailed as the big solution to the problems facing companies and organisations in the 1990s (Peppard and Rowland, 1995). Its American advocates, such as Michael Hammer, claim that quality in production and service must now be accompanied by efficiency in process, i.e. the way that groups and departments function interactively (Hammer and Champy, 1993). BPR has enormous implications for employee involvement as its supporters advocate stripping away unnecessary layers of management and empowering the workforce to seek better process solutions in the drive towards greater efficiency.

There have been studies which relate its successful application in a number of organisations (Buchanan, 1996), but 'emphasis on the ability of re-engineering to reduce employee numbers shows how messages tend to get distorted as they are passed on. Unfortunately, the message wanted and received by most of US industry was not improvement through reorganisation, but reduced costs through staff cuts' (Mumford and Hendricks, 1996: 22). Given such experiences, it is not surprising that these schemes are viewed with an air of cynicism and fear by employees who may well become the next 'victim' in the drive towards efficiency.

Lumb (1996) has defended BPR as being 'about changing the way people think and behave. It means investing employees with the power to make decisions and encouraging them to take risks.' All laudable aims, but the *raison d'être* of companies is to operate profitably; if the confusion of message and intent is responsible for the growing cynicism which sees reduction of costs (BPR's aim) as also incorporating not only efficient processes but reduction of staff levels, then messages of trust, commitment and empowerment could be radically undermined. Nobody wants to empower themselves out of a job!

Empowerment

A more recent form of EI has been heralded under the banner of empowerment. This is a vague and all-encompassing term and describes a managerial attitude or philosophy towards the workforce which can be translated into a wide range of HRM policies. Like quality management programmes, empowerment is strongly associated with culture change initiatives, delayering and restructuring, and often involves devolving power and responsibilities to teams at workplace or customer level (Arkin, 1995). It can thus have varied meanings in differing organisational contexts. Du Gay and Salaman (1992: 625) state that the concept of empowerment is to:

> make meaning for people by encouraging them to believe that they have control over their own lives, that no matter what position they may hold within an organisation their contribution is vital, not only to the success of the company, but also to the enterprise of their own lives.

Claydon and Doyle (1996: 3) discriminate between forms of empowerment in 'soft' and 'hard' HRM systems. The 'soft' aspect can 'provide enhanced opportunities for involvement in decision making' and 'employees will gain those feelings of control, personal efficacy and self-determination which constitute the state of being empowered' (Claydon and Doyle, 1996: 3). They also point out a second but extremely important aspect of the 'soft' system, in that empowerment connects with organisational learning. 'More open communication, shared problem-solving geared to continuous improvement, and a related willingness to expose existing organisational arrangements to critical scrutiny imply more democratic, less authoritarian and bureaucratic work relations'(Claydon and Doyle, 1996: 4). Empowering employees also means that managers lose some control and must learn to accommodate a more questioning and risk-taking workforce, a problem of which many empowerment schemes fall foul (Arkin, 1995).

The 'hard' aspect of empowerment signifies the exercise of a sense of responsibility and implies elements of monitoring and accountability, and as such poses contradictions in its implementation and practice. These elements of 'responsible autonomy' are overseen by forms of surveillance via set objectives, customer reports, the policing by fellow members of autonomous work teams and other controls. 'Empowerment (like BPR) is also closely linked to organisational restructuring, job cuts and moves towards increasingly fragmented and unstable and contingent employment relationships' (Claydon and Doyle, 1996: 4).

Here we see some of the contradictions inherent in capitalist enterprise and therefore in processes such as empowerment, BPR and TQM which are related to HRM issues. Is it possible to gain commitment when employees perceive themselves as being merely disposable units of production? These and other controversial questions will continue to exercise the minds of both practitioners and academics in the continual search for congruence between the aims of companies, employees and society.

SUMMARY

● This chapter began by exploring the relationship between employee involvement and HRM, and employee involvement and control within organisations.

● Employers' increasing recognition of the significance of communications in organisations was acknowledged. Two seminal communication models were explained in order to highlight the importance of understanding the communication process.

● Over recent years employee involvement has been recognised as one important communication instrument. The history of employee involvement (EI) was traced, including forms of industrial democracy, and more recently the fashion for recognition of the centrality that employee involvement has begun to assume in HRM trends.

● Patterns of EI were investigated, ranging from theories of cycles and waves of participation, proposed by Ramsay and Marchington respectively, to an explanatory framework of participation suggested by Poole.

● Definitions of EI were summarised with an outline of the types and levels of participation within organisations. These included two broad categories of EI at macro and micro levels: macro level being types of EI at organisational or enterprise level, such as works councils or Joint Consultative Committees (JCCs), and micro level at the workplace such as quality circles and team briefings. Types of EI were examined under four basic headings: downwards communication from managers to employees, such as company journals, newspapers, videos, briefing sessions; upwards, problem-solving forms, such as quality circles, suggestion schemes, TQM and customer care programmes; financial participation, such as profit sharing and share ownership schemes; and representative participation, such as JCCs, works councils, co-determination and collective bargaining. The various strengths and weaknesses of the most popular forms of EI were analysed.

● The international ramifications of EI measures were considered, beginning with the provisions embodied in the EU Social Chapter. The difficulties of creating a homogeneous framework acceptable to all members were reviewed, as was the more difficult task of implementing such measures even under subsidiarity arrangements. A review was undertaken of the Swedish system, noted for its advanced EI practices, particularly the co-determination system and the quality of working life movement. The German co-determination and works council system was also examined in the light of suggestions that it might act as a possible European model. British practices were explored in relation to the Works Council directive of the Social Charter and the possibility that this could be implemented in Britain in the face of a hostile government via foreign-owned subsidiaries. A review of influential Japanese EI methods was undertaken, outlining the difficulties in cross-cultural transfers of work practices. The international section ended by evaluating some comparative surveys of employee involvement which highlighted similar trends as well as common problems in different countries, for example the mediation of power and control in the implementation of EI systems. Finally there was some advice as to which factors should be taken into consideration in implementing EI schemes.

In the last section an in-depth analysis of total quality management (TQM) was undertaken, based on various studies which pointed to common pitfalls in its implementation. The chapter ended with a short survey of business process re-engineering and empowerment, in which the main arguments surrounding these initiatives were explored.

ACTIVITY

The Public Relations and Human Resource Management Departments of Flexible Printing Services Ltd oversee 300 workers on 12 different sites and are conscious of the need to keep their employees aware of new developments within the company. They have therefore decided to produce a small company newsletter for this purpose. There is a relatively small but active number of union members within the company on most of the sites.

▶

EXERCISES

1 In groups, role play the members of the editorial team in the first editorial meeting to discuss the new company newsletter. Decide upon the policies and practices for the newsletter to ensure that it is a genuine communication reflective of the organisation as a whole.

2 Write a report on the meeting to the Public Relations and Human Resource Management Department describing the issues that were dealt with by the editorial committee.

QUESTIONS

1 What forms has employee involvement (EI) taken over the past 50 years? In your answer, give examples from both micro and macro levels in the organisation. What evidence is there to suggest that EI develops in waves according to economic cycles?

2 Trace the evolution of employee involvement policy in the European Union. Why has there been a considerable watering down of the 'fifth directive' and the recommendations made at the Val Duchesse meetings? How do you see EI developing in the EU in the future?

3 What evidence is there to suggest that schemes of financial participation rarely achieve their goals?

4 Why did quality circles enjoy increased popularity in the 1980s, but witness a decline in their use in Britain and the USA in the 1990s?

EXERCISES

1 As editor of a company newspaper, what policies and practices would you follow in order to make it a genuine communication reflective of the organisation as whole?

2 A prominent British bank is interested in setting up a works council. Write a report recommending the policies in terms of aims, objectives and implementation which should be considered in its foundation.

3 Divide the class into pairs. Ask one group of people to devise reasons why there should be greater participation by employees in the workplace, and ask the other group to put the case against extending participation. Each group should evaluate their reasons from the viewpoint of employers, managers and employees. Then ask the whole group to debate the question of employee participation from each side's viewpoint.

Total quality management

Precision Tool Engineering is a company producing machinery and machine tools and some other related engineering products for specialist production companies. It employs a total workforce of 400, two-thirds of which work in the production departments.

In late 1989 the company management decided to introduce a total quality management scheme to increase efficiency and quality control. Throughout the 1980s more flexible arrangements had been introduced accompanied by a breakdown of old work demarcation lines. Machines were now built by flexible teams of workers employing different skills (fitters, electricians, hydraulic engineers, etc.). In 1989 the first moves towards TQM were made with the introduction of BS 5750. Workers were asked to inspect the quality of their work, with the result that the need for specialist inspectors was greatly reduced and both time and money were saved. Agreements were negotiated with the union for extra pay as result of the increase in worker responsibility.

In early 1990 the management decided to introduce a full-blown TQM scheme on the basis of the success of the introduction of BS 5750. Problem-solving groups were formed based on work groups with voluntary participation. Group leaders, who were mainly supervisors, were trained in how to run a group and in problem-solving techniques. The aims of the groups were to:

- identify problems inside their work area;
- propose solutions;
- identify problems outside their work area;
- refer external problems to a review team.

The review team was made up mainly of managers with one representative from each group, usually the group leader. The unions were lukewarm towards the scheme and some shop stewards were directly against it.

Within the space of nine months the TQM scheme was reviewed and senior management came to the conclusion that it had not lived up to expectations, some board members calling it a failure. Some of the areas they identified were that team leaders had felt uncomfortable in their role and there had been considerable scepticism from some groups of workers.

EXERCISES

1 Why do you think the BS 5750 scheme was successful and the TQM scheme failed in Precision Engineering?

2 What suggestions would you make to a similar company who was thinking of introducing TQM in order to make it a success?

GLOSSARY

Attitude survey A survey, usually conducted by questionnaire, to elicit employees' opinions about issues to do with their work and the organisation.

BS 5750 British standard of quality, originally applied to the manufacture of products but now also being used to 'measure' quality of service. Often used in EI as a way of getting employees to self-check their quality of work against a standardised norm.

Business process re-engineering (BPR) A system which aims to improve performance by redesigning the processes through which an organisation operates, maximising their value-added content and minimising everything else (Peppard and Rowland, 1995: 20).

Cooperatives Organisations and companies either collectively owned by their customers or their employees.

EI Employee involvement, a term to describe the wide variety of schemes in which employees can be involved in their work situation.

ESOPS Employee share option scheme whereby employees are allowed to purchase company shares or are given them as part of a bonus.

JCC Joint Consultative Committee, a body made up of employee representatives and management which meets on a regular basis to discuss issues of common interest.

Job enlargement Related to job rotation, whereby a job is made bigger by the introduction of new tasks. This gives greater variety in job content and thereby helps to relieve monotony in repetitive jobs such as assembly line working.

Job enrichment Adds to a cycle of work not only a variety of tasks but increased responsibility to workers. Most associated with autonomous work groups introduced into Volvo's Kalmar plant in Sweden in the 1970s.

Job rotation Originally introduced in the 1970s whereby members of a team exchange jobs to enliven work interest, but also used recently to promote wider skills experience and flexibility among employees.

Profit sharing Schemes whereby employees are given a bonus or payment based on a company's profits.

Quality circle QCs are made up of 6 to 10 employees with regular meetings held weekly or fortnightly during working time. The principal aim is to identify problems from their own area.

Suggestion scheme (box) Arrangements whereby employees are encouraged to put forward their ideas for improving efficiency, safety or working conditions. Payment or reward is often given related to the value of the suggestion.

Team briefing Regular meetings of groups of between four and fifteen people based round a common production or service area. Meetings are usually led by a manager or supervisor and last for no more than 30 minutes, during which information is imparted, often with time left for questions from employees.

TQM Total quality management, an all-pervasive system of management-controlled EI based on the concept of quality throughout the organisation in terms of product and service, whereby groups of workers are each encouraged to perceive each other (and other departments) as internal customers. This ensures the provision of quality products and services to external customers.

Works councils Committees either made up solely of workers or joint representatives of workers, management and shareholders which meet, usually at company level, to discuss a variety of issues relating to workforce matters and sometimes general, wider-ranging organisational issues. They are usually supported by legislation which compel organisations to set them up.

REFERENCES AND FURTHER READING

Arkin, A. (1995) 'The bumpy road to devolution', *People Management*, 30 November, pp. 34–36.

Badden, L., Hunter, L., Hyman, J., Leopold, J. and Ramsay, H. (1989) *People's Capitalism: A Critical Analysis of Profit and Employee Share Ownership*. London: Routledge.

Beardwell, I. and Holden, L. (1994) *Human Resource Management: A Contemporary Perspective*. London: Pitman Publishing.

Beer, M., Spector, B., Lawrence, P., Quinn Mills, D. and Walton, R. (1984) *Managing Human Assets*. New York: Free Press.

Boreham, P. (1992) 'The myth of post-fordist management: work organisation and employee discretion in seven countries', *Employee Relations*, Vol. 14, No. 2, pp. 13–24.

Brannen, P., Batstone, E., Fatchett, D. and White, P. (1976) *The Worker Directors: A Sociology of Participation*. London: Hutchinson.

Braverman, H. (1974) *Labour and Monopoly Capital: The Degradation of Work in the 20th Century*. New York: Monthly Review Press.

Brennan, B. (1991) 'Mismanagement and quality circles: how middle managers influence direct participation', *Employee Relations*, Vol. 13, No. 5, pp. 22–32.

Brewster, C., Hegewisch, A., Holden, L. and Lockhart, T. (eds) (1992) *The European Human Resource Management Guide*. London: Academic Press.

Briggs, P. (1991) 'Organisational commitment: the key to Japanese success?', in Brewster, C. and Tyson, S. (eds) *International Comparisons in Human Resource Management*. London: Pitman.

Broekmeyer, M.J. (ed.) (1970) *Yugoslav Workers' Self-Management*. Pordrecht: Reidel.

Buchanan, D. (1996) *The Re-engineering Frame: An Assessment*, Occasional Paper Series. Leicester: Leicester Business School.

Burawoy, M. (1979) *Manufacturing Consent: Changes in the Labour Process Under Monopoly Capitalism*. Chicago: University of Chicago Press.

Burawoy, M. (1983) 'Between the labour process and the state: factory regimes under advanced capitalism', *American Sociological Review*, Vol. 48, pp. 587–605.

Carley, M. (1995) 'Talking shops or serious forums: works councils', *People Management*, 13 July, pp. 26–31.

Church, R. (1971) 'Profit sharing and labour relations in England in the nineteenth century', *International Review of Social History*, No. 14, pp. 2–16.

Clampitt, P. (1991) *Communicating for Managerial Effectiveness*. Newbury Park: Sage.

Claydon, T. and Doyle, M. (1996) 'Trusting me, trusting you? The ethics of employee empowerment', paper presented at the *Conference of Ethical Issues in Contemporary Human Resource Management*, Imperial College, London, 3 April.

Clutterbuck, D. and Crainer, S. (1990) *Makers of Management: Men and Women who Changed the Business World*. London: Macmillan.

Cole, G.D.H. (1917) *Self Government in Industry*. London: Bell and Sons; 1972 edition, London: Hutchinson.

Collard, R. and Dale, B. (1989) 'Quality circles', in Sisson, K. (ed.) *Personnel Management in Britain*. Oxford: Blackwell.

Confederation of British Industry (CBI) (1989) *Employee Involvement: Shaping the Future Business*. London: CBI.

Cressey, P. (1992) 'Worker participation: what can we learn from the Swedish experience?', *P+ European Participation Monitor*, Vol. 3, No.1, pp. 3–7.

Cressey, P. and Williams, R. (1990) *Participation in Change: New Technology and the Role of Employee Involvement.* Dublin: European Foundation for the Improvement of Living and Working Conditions.

Crosby, P. (1979) *Quality is Free.* New York: McGraw-Hill.

Crosby, P. (1984) *Quality Without Tears.* New York: McGraw-Hill.

DeFleur, M. (1966) *Theories of Mass Communication.* New York: David Mckay.

Dore, R. and Sako, M. (1989) *How the Japanese Learn to Work.* London: Routledge.

Drucker, P. (1961) *The Practice of Management.* London: Mercury.

Dunn, S., Richardson, R. and Dewe, P. (1991) 'The impact of employee share ownership on worker attitudes: a longitudinal case study', *Human Resource Management Journal,* Vol. 1, No. 3, Spring, pp. 1–17.

Du Gay, P. and Salaman, G. (1992) 'The cult[ure] of the customer', *Journal of Management Studies,* Vol. 29, No. 5, pp. 615–633.

Eccles, T. (1981) *Under New Management: The Story of Britain's Largest Cooperative.* London: Pan.

Edlund, S. and Nyström, B. (1988) *Developments in Swedish Labour Law.* Stockholm: The Swedish Institute.

Edwards, P.K. (1987) *Managing the Factory.* Oxford: Blackwell.

Edwards, P.K. (1992) 'Industrial conflict: themes and issues in research', *British Journal of Industrial Relations,* Vol. 30, No. 3, September, pp. 361–404.

Edwards, R. (1979) *Contested Terrain.* New York: Basic Books.

Filella, J. and Soler, C. (1992) 'Spain', in Brewster, C., Hegewisch, A., Holden, L. and Lockhart, T. (eds) *The European Human Resource Management Guide.* London: Academic Press.

Friedman, A. (1977) *Industry and Labour: Class Struggle at Work and Monopoly Capitalism.* London: Macmillan.

Fröhlich, D. and Krieger, H. (1990) 'Technological change and worker participation in Europe', *New Technology, Work and Employment,* Vol. 5, No. 2, Autumn, pp. 94–106.

Gaugler, E. and Wiltz, S. (1992) 'Federal Republic of Germany', in Brewster, C., Hegewisch, A., Holden, L. and Lockhart, T. (eds) *The European Human Resource Management Guide.* London: Academic Press.

Gill, C. (1993) 'Technological change and participation in work organisation: recent results from a European survey', *International Journal of Human Resource Management,* Vol. 4, No. 2, May, pp. 325–348.

Gold, M. and Hall, M. (1992) *Report on European-Level Information and Consultation in Multinational Companies – Evaluation and Practice.* Dublin: European Foundation for the Improvement of Living and Working Conditions.

Goss, D. (1994) *Principles of Human Resource Management.* London: Routledge.

Guest, D. and Peccei, R. (1992) 'Employee involvement: redundancy as a critical case', *Human Resource Management Journal,* Vol. 2, No. 3, Spring, pp. 34–59.

Hall, M. (1992) 'Behind the European Works Council Directives: the European Commission's legislative strategy', *British Journal of Industrial Relations,* Vol. 30, No. 4, December, pp. 547–566.

Hammarström, O.L. (1987) 'Swedish industrial relations', in Bamber, G. and Lansbury, R. (eds) *International and Comparative Industrial Relations.* London: Allen & Unwin.

Hammer, M. and Champy, J. (1993) *Reengineering the Corporation.* London: Nicholas Brealey.

Holden, L. (1990) 'Employee communications in Europe on the increase', *Involvement and Participation,* November, pp. 4–8.

Holden, L. (1996) 'HRM and employee involvement in Britain and Sweden: a comparative study', *International Journal of Human Resource Management*, Vol. 7, No. 1, February, pp. 59–81.

Hyman, J. and Mason, B. (1995) *Managing Employee Involvement and Participation*. London: Sage.

ILO (1993) *World Labour Report*. Geneva: International Labour Organisation.

IDE (1981) *Industrial Democracy in Europe*. International Research Group, Oxford: Clarendon Press.

IDE (1993) *Industrial Democracy in Europe Revisited*. Oxford: Oxford University Press.

Jablin, F., Putnam, L., Roberts, K. and Porter, L. (eds) (1987) *Handbook of Organisational Communication: An Interdisciplinary Perspective*. Newbury Park: Sage.

Kanter, R.M. (1983) *The Change Masters: Innovation and Entrepreneurship in the American Corporation*. New York: Simon & Schuster.

Keenoy, T. (1990) 'Human resource management: rhetoric, reality and contradiction', *International Journal of Human Resource Management*, Vol. 1, No. 2, December, pp. 363–384.

Keenoy, T. and Anthony, P. (1992) 'HRM: metaphor meaning and morality', in Blyton, P. and Turnbull, P. (eds) *Reassessing Human Resource Management*. London: Sage, pp. 233–255.

Kjellberg, A. (1992) 'Sweden: can the model survive?', in Ferner, A. and Hyman, R. (eds) *Industrial Relations in the New Europe*. Oxford: Blackwell.

Klaus, R. and Bass, B. (1974) 'Group influence on individual behaviour across cultures', *Journal of Cross Cultural Psychology*, Vol. 5, pp. 236–246 (quoted in Briggs, 1991).

Korpi, W. (1981) 'Workplace bargaining, the law and unofficial strikes: the case of Sweden', *British Journal of Industrial Relations*, Vol. 16, pp. 355–368.

Lane, C. (1989) *Management and Labour in Europe*. Aldershot: Edward Elgar.

Lawler, E. (1986) *High-Involvement Management*. San Francisco: Jossey-Bass.

Lawler, E. and Mohrman, S. (1985) 'Quality circles after the fad', *Harvard Business Review*, Vol. 63, No. 1, pp. 65–71.

Lawrence, P. (1980) *Managers and Management in West Germany*. London: Croom Helm.

Legge, K. (1989) 'Human resource management: a critical analysis', in Storey, J. (ed.) *New Perspectives on Human Resource Management*. London: Routledge, pp. 19–40.

Lewis, P. (1989) 'Employee participation in a Japanese owned British electronics factory: reality or symbolism?', *Employee Relations*, Vol. 11, No. 1, pp. 3–9.

Lincoln, J. and Kalleberg, A. (1990) *Culture, Control and Commitment*. Cambridge: Cambridge University Press.

Lipietz, A. (1992) *Towards a New Economic Order: Post Fordism, Ecology and Democracy*. Cambridge: Polity Press.

Littlefield, D. (1996) 'Works council snub infuriates employees', *People Management*, 2 May, p. 5.

Lumb, R. (1996) 'BPR: not a fad, not a failure', *People Management*, 2 May, p. 26.

Marchington, M. (1989a) 'Joint consultation in practice', in Sisson, K. (ed.) *Personnel Management in Britain*. Oxford: Blackwell.

Marchington, M. (1989b) 'Employee participation', in Towers, B. (ed.) *Handbook of Industrial Relations Practice*, 2nd edn. London: Kogan Page.

Marchington, M. (1995) 'Involvement and participation', in Storey, J. (ed.) *Human Resource Management: A Critical Text*. London: Routledge, pp. 280–305.

Marchington, M., Goodman, J., Wilkinson, A. and Ackers, P. (1992) *New Developments in Employee Involvement*. Employment Department Research Series No. 2, Manchester: Manchester School of Management.

Mauritz, W. (1972) '10 Jahre Betriebsverfassungsgesetz aus der Sicht des Eigentümer-Unternehmers', in Lezius, M. (ed.) *10 Jahre Betriebsverfassungsgesetz*. Spardorf: R.F. Wilfer (quoted in Lane, 1989: 233).

McQuail, D. and Windahl, S. (1981) *Communication Models*. Harlow: Longman.

Monks, J. (1989) 'Trade union role in communications', in Wilkinson, T. (ed.) *The Communications Challenge: Personnel and PR Perspectives*. London: IPM.

Mumford, E. and Hendricks, R. (1996) 'Business process re-engineering RIP', *People Management*, 2 May, pp. 22–29.

Naoi, A. and Schooler, C. (1985) 'Occupational conditions and psychological functioning in Japan', *American Journal of Sociology*, Vol. 90, No. 4, pp. 729–752 (quoted in Briggs, 1991).

Noon, M. (1992) 'HRM: a map, model or theory?', in Blyton, P. and Turnbull, P. (eds) *Reassessing Human Resource Management*. London: Sage, pp. 16–32.

OECD (1991) *OECD in Figures: Statistics on the Member Countries*. Paris: Organisation for Economic Cooperation and Development.

Oliver, N. and Lowe, J. (1991) 'UK computer industry: American, British and Japanese contrasts in human resource management', *Personnel Review*, Vol. 20, No. 2, pp. 18–23.

Pascale, R. and Athos, A. (1982) *The Art of Japanese Management*. London: Allen Lane.

Peppard, J. and Rowland, P. (1995) *The Essence of Business Process Re-engineering*. Hemel Hempstead: Prentice-Hall.

Peters, T. and Waterman, R. (1982) *In Search of Excellence: Lessons from America's Best Run Companies*. New York: Harper & Row.

Poole, M. (1986) *Towards A New Industrial Democracy: Workers' Participation in Industry*. London: Routledge & Kegan Paul.

Poole, M. and Jenkins, G. (1990a) *The Impact of Economic Democracy: Profit Sharing and Employee Shareholding Schemes*. London: Routledge.

Poole, M. and Jenkins, G. (1990b) 'Human resource management and profit sharing: employee attitudes and a national survey', *International Journal of Human Resource Management*, Vol. 1, No. 3, December, pp. 289–328.

Price Waterhouse Cranfield Project on International Strategic Human Resource Management (1990) *Report*. London: Price Waterhouse.

Price Waterhouse Cranfield Project on International Strategic Human Resource Management (1991) *Report*. Cranfield: Cranfield School of Management.

Price, R. (1989) 'The decline and fall of the status divide?', in Sisson, K., (ed.) *Personnel Management in Britain*. Oxford: Blackwell.

Ramsay, H. (1977) 'Cycles of control', *Sociology*, Vol. 11, pp. 481–506.

Ramsay, H. (1983) 'Evolution or cycle? Worker participation in the 1970s and 1980s', in Crouch, C. and Heller, F. (eds) *International Yearbook of Organisational Democracy*, Vol. 1, Chichester: John Wiley.

Ramsay, H. (1991) 'Reinventing the wheel? A review of the development and performance of employee involvement', *Human Resource Management Journal*, Vol. 1, No. 1, Summer, pp. 1–22.

Ramsay, H. (1992a) 'Commitment and involvement', in Towers, B. (ed.) *The Handbook of Human Resource Management*. Oxford: Blackwell.

Ramsay, H. (1992b) 'Swedish and Japanese work methods – comparisons and contrasts', *P+ European Participation Monitor*, Vol. 3, No. 1, pp. 37–40.

Ramsay, H., Leopold, J. and Hyman, J. (1986) 'Profit sharing and employee share ownership: an initial assessment', *Employee Relations*, Vol. 8, No. 1, pp. 23–26.

Salaman, G. (1979) *Work Organisations: Resistance and Control*. London: Longman.

Schramm, W. (1954) 'How communication works', in Schramm, W. (ed.) *The Process and Effects of Mass Communication*. Urbana: University of Illinois Press.

Schuller, T. (1986) *Age, Capital and Democracy: Member Participation in Pension Scheme Management*. Aldershot: Gower.

Schuller, T. (1989) 'Financial participation', in Storey, J. (ed.) *New Perspectives on Human Resource Management*. London: Routledge.

Sell, R. (1988) 'The human face of industry in Sweden', *Industrial Society Magazine*, March, pp. 30–32.

Sewell, G. and Wilkinson, B. (1992) 'Empowerment or emasculation? Shopfloor surveillance in a total quality organisation', in Blyton, P. and Turnbull, P. (eds) *Reassessing Human Resource Management*. London: Sage.

Shannon, C. and Weaver, W. (1949) *The Mathematical Theory of Communication*. Urbana: University of Illinois Press.

Storey, J. (1989) *New Perspectives on Human Resource Management*. London: Routledge.

Thomas, H. and Logan, C. (1982) *Mondragon: An Economic Analysis*. London: George Allen & Unwin.

Townley, B. (1989) 'Employee communication programmes', in Sisson, K. (ed.) *Personnel Management in Britain*. Oxford: Blackwell.

Wall, T.D. and Lischerson, J.A. (1977) *Worker Participation: A Critique of the Literature and Some Fresh Evidence*. London: McGraw-Hill.

Walton, R.E. (1984a) 'The future of human resource management: an overview', in Walton, R.E. and Lawrence, P.R. (eds) *HRM: Trends and Challenges*. Boston: Harvard Business School Press, pp. 3–11.

Walton, R.E. (1984b) 'Towards a strategy of eliciting employee commitment based on policies of mutuality', in Walton, R.E. and Lawrence, P.R. (eds) *HRM: Trends and Challenges*. Boston: Harvard Business School Press, pp. 35–65.

Walton, R.E. (1985) 'From control to commitment in the workplace', *Harvard Business Review*, March/April, pp. 76–84.

Wenlock, H. and Purcell, J. (1991) 'The management transfer of undertakings: a comparison of employee participation practices in the United Kingdom and the Netherlands', *Human Resource Management Journal*, Vol. 1, No. 2, Winter, pp. 45–59.

Wickens, P. (1987) *The Road to Nissan: Flexibility, Quality and Teamwork*. Basingstoke: Macmillan.

Wilczynski, J. (1983) *Comparative Industrial Relations*. London: Macmillan.

Wilkinson, A., Marchington, M., Ackers, P. and Goodman, J. (1992) 'Total quality management and employee involvement', *Human Resource Management Journal*, Vol. 2, No. 4, Summer, pp. 1–20.

Wilkinson, A. and Wilmot, H. (1995) *Making Quality Critical: New Perspectives on Organisational Change*. London: Routledge.

Wilkinson, T. (1989) (ed.) *The Communications Challenge: Personnel and PR Perspectives*. London: IPM.

Wilpert, B. and Rayley, J. (1983) *Anspruch und Wirklichkeit der Mitbestimmung*. Frankfurt: Campus (quoted in Lane, 1989: 232).

Wolf, J. (1993) 'Britain fights works councils plan', *Guardian*, 7 April.

MANAGING HUMAN RESOURCES IN THE PUBLIC SECTOR

Trevor Colling

OBJECTIVES

To consider the factors which have historically influenced employment policy and practice in the UK public sector.

●

To examine the creation of market relationships within the public sector and their ramifications for the employment relationship.

●

To debate whether recent changes have effectively eliminated the distinctive characteristics of management and employment practice in the public sector.

●

INTRODUCTION

Until recently, it would have been easy to identify elements of public sector employment relationships that rendered them distinctive. This is not to suggest that they were analytically separate. As elsewhere in the economy, management decisions were fundamentally driven by the contending objectives of securing employees' commitment to the goals of the organisation and maximising the value of their labour. But the frameworks and structures which conditioned the balance of those decisions differed in important respects from analogous private sector organisations. Objectives governing the management of public organisations and their workforces were subject to various forms of political control and scrutiny. In particular, public organisations were required to exemplify 'model employer' practice and employment procedures were often either explicitly prescribed or subject to informal ministerial influence.

Contemporary restructuring of the state sector has prompted changed employment and management practice. The construction of a variety of market regimes, and the perceived retreat of the state from operational decision making, have led some to question whether the day-to-day influences upon public sector managers are any longer distinguishable from their private sector counterparts. Prevailing models of industrial relations, involving centralised bargaining and collective relationships with the workforce, are increasingly vying with conceptions of human resource management grafted more or less uncritically from the private sector. Flexibility quests, innovations in communications and quality management systems are all as likely to be found in the public sector as elsewhere. Whether the management of human resources in the public sector retains any of its distinctive influences and forms is the central theme of this chapter.

The discussion begins with an examination of the historical and contemporary influences on the state sector. The policy principles underlying the so-called 'golden era', particularly the notion of 'model employer' practice, are identified and evaluated. While these undoubtedly created distinctive organisational cultures, it is argued that their influence was more variable and complex than is often appreciated. Attention then turns to recent structural changes and the emergence of new policy frameworks founded upon the apparent primacy of market forces. The implications of these changes for public sector employment relationships are then examined. The final sections assess whether these constitute a radical break from past practice. It is argued that, just as the role of 'model employer' incorporated potentially conflicting elements, recent market-driven reforms are more complex than they appear. Though they have been extensively rearticulated, policy and political influences upon the management of public sector workforces remain largely in place.

THE IMPORTANCE OF CONTEXT

Industrial relations literature has long recognised that the environment in which organisations conduct their operations critically influences the development of internal relationships. Legal frameworks established by national governments, and increasingly by supra-national bodies, regulate aspects of employment, corporate governance, and the terms on which companies engage in trade. In the private sector competition in product markets, and for investment from capital markets, may have significant implications for employment relationships. An appreciation of the context in which public sector workforces are managed is similarly critical. Changing policy frameworks have altered the incentives and assumptions which have coloured decision making within public sector organisations.

The 'Golden Era'

Much of what was until recently recognised as the public sector developed in the immediate postwar period. Between 1945 and 1950, the Labour government took into public ownership a number of basic industries including coal, steel and the railways. Together these accounted for approximately 10% of the country's total productive capacity (Dearlove and Saunders, 1984: 268). The large services which were to constitute the welfare state (e.g. health, social security) were also established under public administration and rapidly developed. By 1959, almost a quarter (23.9%) of the total working population was employed in the public sector (Fairbrother, 1982: 3). Over the next 30 years, this diverse range of enterprises, utility industries and services were gradually restructured along similar organisational principles. During this 'golden era', there was little doubt that employment practice in the public sector was different to that prevailing elsewhere in the economy, and designedly so.

There were two key contributory factors. First, distinctive management structures and cultures were developed. Their form varied between services and enterprises and, within each group, according to the history of the organisation. Yet some important elements were common across the sector. An ethos of public service, founded upon accountability, impartiality and commitment to communitarian values, was deliberately fostered and considered a primary motivating factor for employees (see Pratchett and Wingfield, 1995). In the interests of equality of treatment, uniform standards of product or service were a priority and departments would be deployed to ensure consistency across the organisation. Guaranteeing probity in the public interest required complex internal control systems and hierarchies of management and committee structures. Public sector organisations also tended to be structured according to functional expertise, with relatively rigid demarcations between professional groups. There was little, if any, requirement for general management; rather, managers would develop through the ranks of their specialism. Engineers would be managed by engineers, nurses by former nurses and so on. Such structures tended to become rather bureaucratic and introspective, reinforcing shared values between staff and their managers and sometimes eclipsing broader interests and perspectives (Stewart, 1989). Such characteristics were later to be vilified as inflexibility and the unbridled pursuit of 'producer' self-interest at the expense of the 'customer'.

Second, the public sector was assigned a particular industrial relations mission: to be a 'model' employer and implement 'a range of practices which today constitute good management' (Priestly Commission, 1955, cited in Farnham and Horton, 1995: 8). This stemmed in part from its role in broader macro-economic policy which enabled managers to offer significant job security. Though the depth of the postwar consensus is sometimes exaggerated, commitments to full employment and the welfare state structured the programmes of both of the key political parties for as long as they could be combined with economic growth (see Hills, 1990). In this context, public sector employment increased exponentially. Market notions of efficiency were generally alien to the public sector and public expenditure planning mechanisms effectively permitted public employers to pass on increasing labour costs to central government (Winchester, 1983).

'Model employer' practice also implied a range of procedures intended to set an example to organisations across the economy and many of these were stipulated by government. Given the strategic importance of public industries in particular, great emphasis was attached to the collective involvement of employees as a means of identifying and resolving grievances. The requirement on public enterprises 'to consult with organisations which appear to them to be representative' was legally specified in their respective nationalisation acts (Kelf-Cohen, cited in Pendleton and Winterton, 1993: 3). The sector came to be characterised by elaborate, formal and bureaucratic systems for negotiation and consultation, often referred to as 'Whitleyism'. Created with the brief to establish viable industrial relations systems following the end of the First World War, the Whitley Committee advocated centralised bargaining through joint industrial councils with a view to securing 'co-operation in the centre between national organisations' (Whitley Committee, cited in Clegg, 1979: 31).

There were important variations in this general picture. In the developing public services, centralisation was marked (Fogarty and Brooks, 1986). Most key employment decisions in the civil service were taken directly by national negotiators and handed down to local managers in the *Code and Guide*, 'a works handbook of monumental proportions' (Jary, 1991: 4). Elsewhere, traditions of local bargaining remained entrenched long into the 'golden era'. This is particularly true of some of the nationalised industries (e.g. coal, docks and steel), but is also the case in services with pre-established industrial relations systems such as local government (Kessler, 1991: 7). By the mid-1950s, however, trends towards centralisation were apparent even here and these conditioned a generally limited role for local management and trade union organisation.

> The principal tasks of local, traditional personnel departments were to act as monitors of policy and to maintain staffing establishments. There were few local variations in interpreting national policies and personnel management locally was essentially advisory and administrative, with line managers having a relatively passive role in managing people.
>
> (Farnham *et al.*, 1994: 4)

As in operational matters, it was the prominent influence of central government that made the management of public workforces particularly distinctive. The extent of political intervention, and the form that it took, varied between different parts of the sector. The constitutional position of local authorities, though weak by European standards, offered some protection from ministerial direction. Services with a more direct interface with government departments were much more susceptible, as Clegg noted of the National Health Service:

> The rules negotiated by the joint councils are supplemented by a great many regulations laid down by the Department [of Health] on its own authority, and on the councils themselves the unions effectively negotiate, not with their employers, but with representatives of the government.
>
> (Clegg, 1979: 106)

Government influence was often brought to bear to ensure the minimisation of conflict (see Ferner and Colling, 1993). But cost constraint, and its ramifications for the management of the public sector, were more prominent features of the 'golden era' than is acknowledged in conventional accounts, which tend to emphasise the quest for consensus. Ministerial responsibilities for containing public expenditure generated a compelling interest in the outcome of collective bargaining. As early as the 1950s, government departments intervened to veto agreements in health and public transport which potentially set precedents deemed undesirable (Crouch, 1979; Thornley, 1994). Repeated attempts to ensure that civil service pay awards were 'offset by corresponding economies' prompted shrill protests from the historically placid civil service unions:

> The National Staff Side sincerely trusts that there will be no interference in collective bargaining in the civil service. . .or any action which might bring into question the impartiality of the Civil Service arbitration tribunal or any refusal to honour awards of the tribunal.
>
> (cited in Mortimer and Ellis, 1980: 197)

It is important not to make evangelistic claims for 'model employer' principles developed during the period. In practice they were more complex and contradictory than is often acknowledged and they were not uniformly implemented. Diverse organisational histories ensured that employment practice across the public sector varied for some time. Some privileged occupational groupings came to enjoy considerable job security and improved terms and conditions. But exhortations to 'good management' did little to displace low pay and discriminatory employment procedures in large parts of the public sector (Thornley, 1994) and proclaimed aspirations to industrial harmony were pursued selectively and, increasingly, with only moderate success. Nevertheless, elaborate systems of negotiation, consultation and arbitration made the sector an exemplar, as was intended. For much of the postwar period, management structures, prescribed employment policies and procedures, and the pervasive influence of policy and political interests, combined to render public sector employment relationships distinctive.

Markets and the 'New Public Management'

When economic growth faltered, the viability of large-scale state investment came to be questioned. Attempts to control inflation through incomes policies and rein back public expenditure destabilised public sector employment relationships. Between 1969 and 1973, disputes in the public sector increased seven-fold and contributed substantially to the defeat of the Heath Conservative government in 1974 (Coates, 1989: 66). At the height of the series of public sector disputes in 1978 dubbed the 'Winter of Discontent', the Labour Prime Minister, James Callaghan, is reputed to have told senior officials from the Trades Union Congress, 'We are prostrate before you – but don't ask us to put it in writing' (cited in Taylor, 1993: 258). Out of this pervasive sense of crisis emerged a series of radical Conservative governments, committed to reducing the size and influence of the state sector and reconstituting employment relationships.

Finance was initially the principal tool of reform. Discarding the macro-economic policies which had shaped the 'golden era', governments from 1979 focused upon the control of inflation (rather than the maintenance of employment levels) and public expenditure restraint became a primary objective. Limits on capital spending, inherited from the previous Labour government, were intensified and volume planning, by which finance for existing commitments was merely increased in line with price movements, was replaced by cash limits. The discretion of local authorities to maintain spending by raising supplementary local income was progressively cut back, culminating in the wholesale revision of local authority finance and the introduction of the Community Charge and, subsequently, the Council Tax (Travers, 1989; Cochrane, 1993). This legislation removed the right of local authorities to levy rates on non-domestic/business premises and further limited the amount of revenue that could be retained from the domestic tax. As a consequence, 'the new system reduces, by about half, the level of local revenue which may be decided locally' (John, 1991: 64).

Since the signing of the Maastricht Treaty in 1992, these domestic commitments have been reinforced by convergence criteria for European Monetary Union which stipulate limits on public expenditure. In practice, reducing the aggregate level of spending has proven difficult and changes have been marginal. As a percentage of gross domestic product (GDP), public spending remained at about 43.5% between 1979 and 1994 (NIESR, 1995). The slight dip to around 39% in the late 1980s reflected growth in economic output associated with the economic boom rather than cuts in public expenditure (Grant, 1993). The implications for employment have been significant nevertheless. Large areas of the state's budget (such as health, pensions and other areas of social security provision) are more or less impervious to government intervention without the risk of severe political disruption. Labour costs, particularly increases in the wage bill, are a relatively soft area to control.

Financial stringency has increasingly been augmented by organisational restructuring to admit, or emulate, market forces. First, with the exception of the postal services, all of the major industries and utilities in public ownership in 1979 have now been privatised via flotation on the Stock Exchange or, in the case of the railways, franchising agreements. The programme started in piecemeal fashion with the sale of relatively small stockholdings in companies such as ICL, Cable & Wireless and British Aerospace. Following the successful sale of British Telecom in 1984, plans rapidly gathered pace and the large-scale privatisations of British Gas, British Airways and the water and electricity industries followed (see Colling and Ferner, 1994). Though less well publicised, elements of the public services have also been privatised via trade sales, e.g. the Property Services Agency and the Skills Training Agency (PSPRU, 1994).

Second, elements of competition have been introduced into the remaining public services. Competitive tendering was introduced into local government (1980) and the National Health Service (1983). Focused initially on ancillary services, such as cleaning, laundry and housing maintenance, competitive tendering requires public authorities to test the cost of existing provision by allowing private companies to bid for the work. Having proven successful in reducing costs (though the size of savings are a matter of dispute), such regimes have been made compulsory in local government (hence the acronym CCT for compulsory competitive tendering) and extended to cover a broader range of functions including computing, architectural and personnel services. Similar mechanisms, referred to as 'market testing', have been introduced into the civil service. In contrast to the NHS and local government, where the vast majority of work has been retained in house, the common practice of prohibiting in-house bids in the Civil Service has resulted in the simple transfer of operations to private companies (PSPRU, 1994: 9).

Finally, various forms of quasi-markets have been constructed. In education and health, service providers (i.e. schools and hospitals) have largely been released from regulation by local policy networks to compete in internal markets for status and resources. Hospitals, for example, have been vested as trusts and contract with health care purchasers (principally the health authorities) to provide services for their local area and, for some specialisms, areas further afield. The Civil Service has been restructured and operational responsibility devolved to executive agencies accountable to government departments. Though the forces of competition are more muted here, comparisons of performance across agencies and with the private sector introduce them by proxy.

These pressures have fundamentally altered the framework within which the public sector has been managed. At the extreme, managers in the former public enterprises now operate entirely in the private sector where competitors (or regulatory bodies) and shareholders provide new influences (Ferner and Colling, 1991). For this reason, they will not feature in any of the subsequent discussion which will focus upon organisations still part of the public sector. Managements here have had to accommodate a range of similar pressures and learn new skills analogous to those prevailing in the rest of the economy. To some extent this has been required by new operational environments, but private sector management practice has also been extolled repeatedly by government ministers. Various efficiency reviews have been led by prominent businessmen, such as Lord Rayner (of Marks & Spencer) and Roy Griffiths (of J Sainsbury). Bodies such as the National Audit Office and the Audit Commission have been established to promote business values of economy and efficiency in the public services. Management consultants have also played a significant role in inculcating business perspectives. One conservative estimate suggests that the public sector spent over £250 million on consultants between 1994 and 1995 alone (*Investors Chronicle*, May 1995: 17).

Out of this maelstrom, some have observed an emergent management style dubbed the 'New Public Management' (Dunleavy and Hood, 1994). One key feature is the importance attached to general management skills and the relative displacement of professional perspectives. This has been most apparent in health where, in the early waves of trusts, prominent senior positions were offered to managers with business rather than medical or public administration backgrounds. Collaborative working across and between public agencies has developed to a greater extent as previously integrated bodies have been fragmented. The requirement to source ancillary and professional services via contracts has led to a marked increase in the need for purchasing and procurement skills. Operational priorities, it is said, will often focus on cost and performance rather than equity and social impact as in the past. Finally, public service managers have been required to relinquish a perceived preoccupation with the needs of the workforce in order to focus on the priorities of their 'customers' (Harden, 1992; Heery, 1992). Though some parts of the public sector have an honourable history of developing customer service programmes independently, the requirement to do so has since been codified through the *Citizen's Charter* initiatives and the plethora of performance indicators, targets and complaints procedures they have spawned.

Thus, the assumptions underpinning public sector management practice through the 'golden era' have been eroded or systematically dismantled. Notions of affordability, flexibility and organisational efficiency have largely displaced those of consistency, probity and accountability as the guiding principles of public administration. The implications for the management of public sector workforces are examined in the following section. Whether patterns of change have effectively eliminated differences between public and private sector management practice is then discussed in the final section.

INDUSTRIAL RELATIONS TO HUMAN RESOURCING?

In the private sector, the displacement of formal and collective systems of industrial relations by human resource management practices is widely attributed to changing and intensifying competitive pressures. If similar pressures are now being experienced within the public sector, it would not be surprising to find analogous changes to employment relationships. So, what evidence exists to suggest that practices associated with HRM are developing in the public sector?

Employment: Patterns and forms

Given the high profile policy stance of rolling back the frontiers of the state, the enduring significance of public sector employment is somewhat surprising.

Official figures show 5.3 million people working in the public sector, a decline of about one-third since 1979 (see Figure 15.1). Yet the state remains a very significant employer. With one in five of the labour force working within the public sector, the state still employs one million more people than the combined manufacturing sector (Pierson, 1994; NIESR, 1995). Health and education, the two largest public services, each employed over one million people in 1992, almost exactly the same as in 1979. Central government has seen the most significant decline, principally because of the government's ability to drive through reductions in civil service employment in contrast to other areas where it is not the direct employer. Yet, as Figure 15.1 illustrates, some of the changes registered here stem from redistribution rather than absolute reductions in employment. The marked fall in central government employment since 1990 is partly explained by the transfer of NHS staff from central government payrolls to the individual trusts. Trusts are now recorded as public corporations, hence the corresponding rise in employment in this category. Transfers of staff in the education sector have been similarly interpreted. In 1989, universities, polytechnics, higher education colleges and schools opting out of local authority control were reclassified within the national accounts as private sector, non-profit-making bodies. Incomes Data Services has estimated that the total public sector headcount would be 250 000 greater were these staff to be factored back into the calculation (*Daily Telegraph*, 10 April 1995).

It is the pattern of employment and its form that are changing most significantly, trends obscured by a focus on the aggregate figures. Three important elements of change need to be noted. First, the ratio of non-manual to manual jobs is increasing as a direct consequence of marketisation. Blue-collar jobs have been subject to rationalisation following competitive tendering and market testing. The NHS was able to cut its ancillary workforce in half between 1983 and 1991 (Winchester and Bach, 1994). But cuts here have

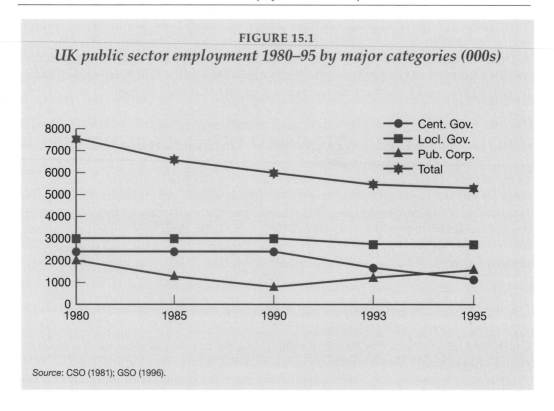

FIGURE 15.1

UK public sector employment 1980–95 by major categories (000s)

Source: CSO (1981); GSO (1996).

been offset by increased recruitment of professional, administrative and managerial posts. Employment in social services increased throughout the 1980s and new technology has generated the need for new skills across all organisations. Purchasing, accounting and contract management have been major growth areas amongst managerial groups, driven by the need to manage internal market systems.

Second, principally as a consequence of the rationalisation of traditional manual jobs, the public sector workforce is becoming increasingly feminised. As Figure 15.2 illustrates, while the male workforce declined by nearly a third, the number of women workers has remained more or less constant since 1980.

So-called 'non-standard' working arrangements have spread across organisations and professions. Part-time working has long been a feature of public sector employment and has continued to grow incrementally. Job cuts, having focused on full-time employment, have markedly affected the prevailing balance between full-time and part-time staff. Part-time workers now constitute one-third of the public sector workforce as a whole, an increase from around one-fifth (21%) in 1978 (Hogwood, 1992: 144). In health, nearly half (44%) of the workforce now work part time (Pierson, 1994; GSO, 1996). Feminisation and the trend to part-time working are strongly associated. In the NHS, 92% of part-time workers are women (GSO, 1996: 16).

Finally, increasing numbers of staff working within the public services are now employed by third parties under subcontracting arrangements. Precise numbers are almost impossible to calculate, but reference to sectoral growth beyond the public sector provides some indication. Business and miscellaneous services incorporate activities such as refuse disposal, cleaning and a variety of professional services which are commonly

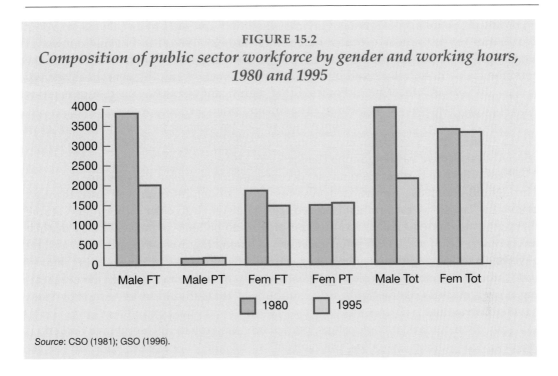

FIGURE 15.2

*Composition of public sector workforce by gender and working hours,
1980 and 1995*

Source: CSO (1981); GSO (1996).

provided through project or contract working. Though these companies will have significant customer bases in the private sector, the opening of public sector markets has been extremely significant. Between 1981 and 1991, no other sector of the economy grew as quickly. Average employment across all the services more than doubled with some, most notably refuse and other sanitary services, expanding spectacularly (Colling, 1995a: 6). Little of this growth is genuinely new employment. Rather, it is attributable to the transfer of staff, directly or indirectly, from in-house functions, particularly within the public sector, to private subcontracting companies (Dunne, 1988; Temple, 1994).

Though the size of the workforce remains more or less stable for the moment, its form and composition have changed. Commitments to job security for public servants, always more voluntaristic than other European countries, have been substantially eroded by financial and market pressures. The growth of white-collar, part-time and subcontracted work significantly challenges previous assumptions about public sector employment and the processes through which it should be managed.

Pay determination

Reform of the centralised bargaining and consultation structures, characteristic of the 'golden era', have been amongst the most tangible indicators of changing employment practice.

The growth of indexation and independent pay review mechanisms have played a significant role in reducing the scope of collective bargaining in the sector. These decide pay issues either through pre-determined formulae, in the case of indexation, or the deliberations of a panel following the submission of evidence from managers, unions and government. Some argue persuasively that the latter amounts to *de facto* negotiation. Winchester refers to them as 'quasi-bargaining forums' (1996: 10). But the removal of formal collective bargaining, and notionally thereby the threat of strike action, is the common element. Initially reserved for extremely sensitive employment areas such as judges, doctors and the Armed Forces, other significant occupational groupings now have their pay determined in this way. The fire and police services were surprisingly late additions at the end of the 1970s. Since then school teachers, nurses and midwives have been added and as a consequence one-third of public sector employees are no longer affected by collective pay bargaining (Bailey, 1996: 136).

Where collective bargaining remains, decentralisation has been the primary dynamic. Throughout the 1980s, centralised systems came under informal pressure through changes to public sector financial procedures. The switch to cash rather than volume planning (mentioned earlier) required employers to balance increases in pay against levels of service. In areas with prior traditions of bargaining independently, such as local government, these calculations began to generate calls for flexibility in the setting of local pay. Through the late 1980s, a slow but steady stream of authorities, most in the overheating labour markets of the South-east, announced their intention to withdraw from national bargaining.

The creation of market relationships, particularly the growth of competitive tendering, has provided additional impetus. Decisions about the allocations of service contracts are based primarily on price, of which labour costs are usually a substantial element. Until recently, this generated pressure on local service managers to redesign both workloads and terms and conditions of employment in the quest for savings (Colling, 1993). *Ad hoc* adjustments to employment packages have been common, irrespective of whether the work has been retained by public sector employers or whether staff have been formally covered by national agreements. Whether such undermining will now be halted by legal developments is a matter for debate. Strong court judgments under European and domestic law (the Acquired Rights Directive and its UK variant, the Transfer of Undertakings (Protection of Employment) directive, or TUPE), appear to prohibit changes to pay and conditions under such circumstances. The extent and security of such protection, however, is far from total (Napier, 1993). In the absence of meaningful directives from the UK government, discretion remains firmly at the local level and there is little doubt that national agreements have been substantially eroded.

Reform of bargaining relationships has recently become much more direct as the government has redrawn the public sector's role as 'model employer'. In 1992, a White Paper entitled *People, Jobs and Opportunity* promised to:

> encourage employers to move away from traditional, centralised collective bargaining towards methods of pay determination which reward individual skills and performance; respond to the wish of individual employees to negotiate their own terms and conditions, and take full account of business circumstances.
>
> (cited in White, 1994: 7)

A good example of the government's determination in this area is provided by the escalation of pressure on NHS trust managers. Though a prominent element of the reforms, the explicit permission offered to trusts to devise their own industrial relations policies and procedures at first received a tepid response. Aware of the considerable opposition of the unions and professional associations, local managers initially sought to innovate through job redesign and to maximise the grading flexibility offered by existing national agreements. Following the 1992 election, however, burgeoning entrepreneurial spirit was galvanised by increasingly explicit exhortations from ministers and the NHS Executive. In 1993, government evidence to the health service pay review bodies argued the case for devolved pay-setting. Though rejected on the grounds that local managers were not yet equipped, the overtures were reiterated from the floor of the House of Commons, this time with the authority of the Prime Minister, and subsequently in a letter to all trusts from the NHS chief executive. Finally, after further evidence to the pay review bodies and a protracted stand-off with the unions, the 1995 pay settlement eventually permitted some element of local bargaining for health service staff with the exception of doctors.

Following reforms in the civil service and the creation of the executive agencies, similar decentralising dynamics have been established. The Civil Service (Management Functions) Act 1992 removed responsibility for the control of pay and conditions for civil service staffs from the Treasury and 'delegated' it to the newly created agencies (*IRS Employment Trends 549*, December 1993). Over 60% of civil servants are now covered by bargaining at agency or departmental level and the government has signalled its intention to accelerate the pace of civil service reform and, in particular, to ensure the decentralisation of all pay bargaining to agency/department level.

As will be seen in the following discussion, pressures for decentralisation have been ambiguous and counteracted by other simultaneous initiatives, hence the residual importance of national bodies across the sector (see Bach and Winchester, 1994). The scope and tone of their deliberations have, nevertheless, been altered significantly. New operating environments and direct restructuring have given local actors, potentially both managements and employees, greater say in the construction of agreements and more discretion in their use.

Employee involvement and representation

Public sector employment relationships remain largely collectivised. Employment practices focused on the individual, such as personal contracts and pay awards, are limited to relatively small groups of senior managers for the moment. The vast majority of staff (78%) continue to be covered by collective agreements of some sort (Millward *et al.*, 1992). Unionism remains a potent force in the public services. Even excluding the exceptionally well-organised postal services, average union density is around 60%.

Labour force changes have taken their toll on membership figures, but public sector unions remain large and relatively well-resourced organisations. Table 15.2 highlights membership trends for the ten largest public sector unions. It does not present a complete picture because predominantly private sector unions, for example the General, Municipal and Boilermakers union (GMB) and the Manufacturing, Science and Finance union (MSF), also have significant public sector memberships. The figures here reveal that job loss has severely affected the civil service unions (Civil and Public Services Association (CPSA) and the National Union of Civil and Public Servants (NUCPS)) and those with large manual workforces affected by competitive tendering (National Union of Public

TABLE 15.1
Trade union density in the public sector, 1992

Service	Density (all employees) (%)
Postal services	81
National government	63
Local government	61
Fire, police, justice, defence and social security	53
Schools	60
Hospitals	60

Source: Bailey (1994).

Employees (NUPE)). Others have grown substantially, notably the Royal College of Nursing (RCN) and the National Association of School Masters/Union of Women Teachers (NASUWT).

Such outward signs of health notwithstanding, decentralisation of bargaining has been accompanied by a reconstitution of the relationships between employers, unions and workforces. The formal 'constitutionalism' of Whitley arrangements, which offered unions significant influence over managerial procedures and decision making, has been replaced by broader and simpler commitments. The number of 'seats' offered to trade union representatives, the frequency of meetings, and the number of subcommittees, are now specified in less detail. Unions have rarely been derecognised, except in some instances where membership in minority unions has dwindled. More important has been the selective removal of groups of staff from collective bargaining. Senior technical and professional staff in the health service and civil service have been put onto managerial grades which are not covered by collective agreements, thereby weakening the rationale for trade union membership.

A few employers have also begun to specify who may, and who may not, represent trade union members.

TABLE 15.2
Membership trends within the ten largest public sector unions, 1980–93

	1980	1985	1990	1993	% change
NALGO	782343	752131	744453	754010	−3.6
NUPE	699156	663776	578992	520123	−25.6
NUT	272902	253672	218194	232243	−14.9
UCW	202993	194244	202500	179899	−11.4
NASUWT	156167	169839	168753	206829	32.4
CPSA	216415	146537	122677	131841	−39.1
RCN	181111	251127	288924	303379	67.5
COHSE	216482	212980	203311	190798	−11.9
NCU	130976	161315	154783	122068	−6.8
NUCPS	–	–	113488	112080	–

Source: Certification Officer Annual Reports, various.

Some NHS trusts, for example, are refusing to negotiate with lay representatives not employed within the hospital (Bryson *et al.*, 1995). Where local trade union branches have been built around areas, rather than specific workplaces, organisation has been weakened as experienced representatives have not been available within the designated units. There has also been some movement towards single table bargaining. NHS trusts have widely considered moving to functional based bargaining groups, accident and emergency staff for example, rather than prevailing structures built around professional and occupational demarcations (*IRS Employment Trends 491*, 5 July 1991). The trend has been strengthened by union mergers, particularly the creation of the public service union UNISON from the Confederation of Health Service Employees (COHSE), the National Union of Public Employees (NUPE) and the National and Local Government Officers Association (NALGO). Similar objectives are being pursued in the civil service, though entrenched inter-union rivalry there offers fewer opportunities.

Managements have turned to extra-union forms of involvement, including total quality management and business process re-engineering, to establish more direct relationships with workforces and to secure ongoing organisational change (Davies and Hinton, 1993; Morgan and Murgatroyd, 1994). Their impact upon employee attitudes and union influence is difficult to gauge. Recent fieldwork in local government, conducted by the author, suggests that the implicit recognition that employees can offer important insights into the services that they provide is welcomed in some instances. The opportunity to influence change in the interests of clients can also be interpreted as a buttress to the otherwise flagging public service ethos. In the context of growing job insecurity, however, commitment is less forthcoming where schemes are associated with quests for cost savings. Some of the current interest in business process re-engineering has been stimulated by initiatives in the US health care system. According to Buchanan and Wilson, these 'appear particularly aggressive and mercenary' and 'use the language of costs, profitability and competitive advantage' (1996: 5). In any event, whether focused on quality or cost, such procedures generally obviate the traditional channels of consultation and, to that extent, undoubtedly limit the formal influence of trade unions over changes to work organisation and service delivery.

Flexibility and performance

Employers have sought to maximise the flexibility available to them in the deployment of staff. The continued growth in part-time working, discussed earlier, is one of a range of common measures to gear working time tightly to the ebbs and flows of the service. In areas affected by competitive tendering, creative interpretation of national agreements has permitted the introduction of annual hours schemes whereby staff work up to a specified number of hours spread over the year rather than a regular working week. New hybrid grades, incorporating a broad range of tasks and responsibilities from across occupational groupings, have also been introduced. NHS trusts have developed a new grade of nursing staff (referred to as a 'health care assistant') not covered by any of the existing grading structures. Elsewhere, wholesale reviews have dispensed with tightly specified grade scales in favour of broad bands. Because these are based on sets of generic skills, rather than job descriptions, they permit greater managerial discretion in job design and pay levels. The structure developed by the Inland Revenue replaced 120 grades with five broad pay bands, four of which have two or three pay spans. Forms of teamworking are also beginning to emerge, particularly in the NHS. Trusts are reported to be moving to 'patient-focused care' in which health care teams, comprised of each of the medical specialisms, become responsible for groups of patients. Such initiatives are intended to minimise the communications difficulties involved in moving patients, and their records, between departments, but are also likely to lead to the development of cross-functional skills as prevailing professional demarcations are blurred (Pinch, 1994).

Elements of 'performance management' have also become increasingly evident, often in conjunction with grading changes. Performance-related pay was introduced for senior civil servants in 1985 but agreements in 1992 permitted its increased use for all grades. Many local authorities introduced PRP schemes for staff groups in the late 1980s and NHS trusts have developed plans for managers and, more controversially, medical staff. Pay review bodies, gradually convinced by arguments from government departments, have been moving away from automatic incremental progression through pay scales and are now more willing to countenance performance-related awards. Incentive payments have been available to teachers since 1990 and the PRBs have subsequently formalised them in response to government initiatives, particularly the Citizen's Charter. Proposals have included linking pay to individual contributions to the achievement of school objectives such as positions in league tables, examination results, truancy rates and so on (Sinclair *et al.*, 1993a).

Isolating such trends in a broad discussion of this kind can be misleading. When considered in closer context, some elements of change can be mitigated by other enduring features from the past. Yet, more than any other reforms, these innovations have the potential to change fundamentally the character of public sector employment (Bailey, 1996). Individualised performance-related pay overturns the principles of equity and consistency within occupational groups which have been paramount in the past. Teamworking and changed grading structures are blurring established professional boundaries. Broad notions of public service, with their attendant processes based on consistency of treatment and formal accountability, are arguably being displaced as the defining features of state sector employment relationships. Individual contributions to 'customer service' and the achievement of measured organisational targets are now central, a reflection of the market-driven environment in which many public sector employees now work.

DISCUSSION: IS THERE A DIFFERENCE?

The increasing pervasiveness of market forces, the adoption of entrepreneurial skills and language, and evidence of moves away from traditional models of employee relations have called into question the distinctiveness of public sector management practice. Perhaps influenced by the widespread denigration of public administration in recent years, consultants and many in management education have tended to assume that public sector managers simply crave private sector skills and merit no bespoke provision. The issue of distinctiveness is inevitably complex, not least because, as other chapters in this book make clear, there is no one model of private sector employment practice with which to compare. It is possible to argue, nevertheless, that the management of human resources in the public sector retains exceptional elements. Despite widespread change, the policy and political features which have critically influenced the state sector in the past remain, even if they are now differently articulated.

Rather one-dimensional conceptions of markets and market forces are the source of much confusion in these discussions. Public policy has often been predicated on uncritical notions of market behaviour gleaned from neoclassical economics. In practice, competitive pressures, and the responses of firms and individuals subject to them, vary from one context to another (see Nolan, 1983). Noting the variety of company forms and business approaches apparent in the UK private sector, Keep (1992) suggests that public sector reforms have unconsciously incorporated random and conflicting elements of all of them. The reality of market relationships, and their wider implications for management practice in the public sector, have thereby been obscured.

Some areas do operate in recognisable market environments. The local authority manager responsible for a local swimming pool will be in competition with cinemas, health clubs and a variety of leisure facilities provided by the private sector. Since the management of leisure services is now subject to CCT, the manager will have to return at least the level of profit designated by the legislation if the operation is to remain viable. In order to attract and retain customers, managers are potentially able to use a wide range of competitive tactics, such as marketing or the provision of additional services or equipment. Even here, though, managers will not have the discretion enjoyed by their private sector competitors. Legislation pre-dating CCT restricts the ability of public bodies to engage in commercial activity for profit. Local authority organisations affected by competitive tendering are thus formally prohibited from reducing dependence upon one single customer by bidding for other work, a primary objective of most private sector subcontractors.

Elsewhere, competitive pressures are still harder to interpret and respond to. Identifying customers is the first difficulty in many instances. For example, whose needs should take priority for the contract caterer providing school meals? At one level, the school's pupils and staff are the principal consumers of the product and should therefore take precedence. On the other hand, the contract will usually be managed to a specification established by the local authority which will subsequently take considerable interest in performance and cost issues. The demands of these two 'customers' will not always be congruent and may even conflict. This raises far-reaching questions about the management of quality in public sector contexts.

> Because government agencies must serve a wide variety of customers who have widely divergent and even contradictory demands, and because the general public remains a 'hidden customer' with yet additional, often incompatible demands, government agencies often have to deliver a service or a product that reflects an uneasy compromise. In such cases, the principle of delighting or even satisfying customers begs too many questions to be a clear or useful goal.
>
> (Swiss, 1992, cited in Morgan and Murgatroyd, 1994: 54)

The need to accommodate the contending demands of internal and external customers is not unique to the public sector. The complicating factor here is that 'customer' relationships are rarely driven by purely market principles. The Citizen's Charter initiatives in the Benefits Agency, for example, have encouraged staff to treat the public as 'customers'. Yet, almost by definition, those claiming benefit are unlikely to be able to take their custom elsewhere and regulations governing entitlement to benefits make the relationship primarily one of authority. The same is true of relationships with internal customers, even where they are notionally informed by markets. Since the creation of executive agencies, civil servants will often define ministers or government departments as 'customers' in ways which some have found 'constitutionally surprising' and 'hierarchically anomalous' (Chapman, 1991: 15).

Thus, despite the growth of entrepreneurial opportunities, managerial decision making within the public sector remains intrinsically political and is still often subject to imperatives determined beyond immediate organisational boundaries. Indeed, paradoxically, political influences in some areas have increased as market mechanisms have been introduced. As Gamble notes, in the UK a free economy has required a strong state:

> Creating a 'free economy' commanded wide support in the Conservative Party when it was interpreted to mean lower taxes, lower public expenditure, less nationalisation, weaker trade unions, less government regulation and control, and more inequality. But a free economy was also understood by some to mean a state strong enough to intervene actively in all institutions of civil society to impose, nurture, and stimulate the business values, attitudes and practices necessary to relaunch Britain as a successful capitalist economy.
>
> (Gamble, 1988: 232)

The construction of markets within the public sector has been accompanied by resolute intervention of this kind. CCT, arguably the most extensive market regime in the public sector, was introduced compulsorily in 1988 after many years of exhortation failed to excite much interest in the process amongst local authority managers (Ascher, 1987). The legislation governing the award and management of contracts is extremely proscriptive and has been regularly augmented by ministerial intervention and directives. In this way, market forces have been inextricably intertwined with political imperatives.

As much of the preceding commentary should suggest, this is not to say that market mechanisms have not created areas of autonomy for public sector managers. It is important to observe, however, that these are relative and to distinguish between their different aspects. Trusts and agencies undoubtedly enjoy greater operational freedom in some areas, including increased discretion over aspects of their employment policies, but ministers continue to provide the policy framework within which those decisions are taken. Public sector managers remain bound by a proliferating array of policy constraints and centrally determined performance criteria (Carter et al., 1992; Flynn, 1992; Bach, 1994). In sensitive areas, or in times of crisis, these control mechanisms can become extremely restrictive. The appointment of Michael Howard as Home Secretary, for example, carried immediate consequences for the operational autonomy which the Prison Service had developed under his predecessors. Determined to reverse the liberal custodial policies implemented since the Strangeways riots in 1990, Home Office scrutiny of operational decision making intensified to the point where the director of the Prison Service was reportedly required to meet with the minister at least once a day (Adonis and Suzman, 1995).

Given the central policy focus of public expenditure restraint, financial autonomy is particularly tightly controlled. The introduction of market mechanisms, associated with financial freedom, have often merely reconfigured financial control mechanisms (Robinson, 1992). Devolved budget control was proclaimed as a key benefit of the local management of schools (LMS). In practice, most elements of school budgets are not subject to influence at school level and the overall funding allocation remains tightly controlled by the local education authority and the Secretary of State. The key purpose of LMS has not been to relax financial controls but to shift the primary interface away from the local education authorities. As Walsh has remarked, 'it was not so much changing the relationship between principals and agents as creating new principals and agents' (Walsh, 1995: 174).

This ebb and flow of policy and financial controls can carry direct implications for apparently devolved employment relationships. Since 1992, the entire public sector has been subject to centrally imposed pay controls which were initially expressed in terms of norms, that is centrally forecast expectations which bargainers were not permitted to exceed. While obviously aimed at bargaining behaviour, pay norms have further undermined the independence of the pay review bodies (Ferner, 1994: 58). Public sector employers were quick to highlight the contradictions between apparent decentralisation of managerial authority and bargaining and renewed central controls:

> At a stroke, the policy of 12th November 1992 – the first national pay policy for nearly twenty years – cuts across previous government statements, in particular the drive to link pay to performance and to devolve and decentralise pay decisions.
>
> (National Association of Health Authorities and Trusts, quoted in White, 1994: 8)

This tension is apparently resolved by the recent shift away from norms to a 'paybill freeze'. Percentage pay increases are no longer prescribed. Since 1994 they have been settled by bargainers themselves subject to the proviso that they do not generate increases in the overall pay bill. To the extent that this places the onus on negotiators to find 'efficiency savings' which will permit increases, the revised pay policy is more consistent with, indeed arguably strengthens, the trend towards decentralisation. The shift, however, is relative and should not obscure the real limitations on local discretion, particularly in those areas where productivity improvements are hard to define or, after several years of cost constraint, to sustain. In the first two years of the policy's operation average pay settlements were close to, or below, the level of inflation and well below agreements for comparable groups in manufacturing and the privatised utilities (Winchester, 1996: 18).

Though their form and force varies, tensions between devolution and centralisation are apparent across the public services and manifest in the relative durability of national structures for pay determination and policy making (Bach and Winchester, 1994). The civil service provides perhaps the most extreme example. While making provision for delegating specific powers to agencies (as described above), the Civil Service (Management Functions) Act 1992 ensures that the government retains significant powers of control. The Treasury can set conditions for particular initiatives and it can revoke or amend delegations at any time. These powers have been used to restrict or contain initiatives which are likely to have cost implications. Performance-related pay schemes have been subject to cost ceilings (Marsden and Richardson, 1994) and ostensibly local negotiations over job evaluation have been influenced by Treasury officials on the pretext of ensuring value for money (*IRS Employment Trends 549*, December 1993). Even the push towards local pay determination, it has been suggested, is largely cosmetic, with the Treasury setting the size of the pay bill and reserving the right to approve settlements (Bailey, 1994). As Massey concludes of agency status more generally, 'clearly it is managerial freedom on the government's terms, or perhaps more accurately, a Treasury-guided and defined managerial emancipation' (Massey, 1993: 61).

It is not only management decision making that retains distinctive elements. The size, structure and behaviour of public sector workforces also make significant contributions to the dynamics of the employment relationship. As already noted, public sector employers are far and away the largest in the economy. These workforces are still largely unionised and, relatively speaking, more inclined than many other parts of the economy to defend their interests collectively. Strike activity in the public sector accounts for over 60% of the total (TUC, 1995; Bailey, 1996). In this area, too, the political context continues to play a vital role. Public sector conflicts have always involved the government and the public in addition to employers and their workforces. Since the 'Winter of Discontent', when the use of indefinite and apparently indiscriminate strike action blackened the reputation of public sector employees, unions have become adept at utilising a broader range of tactics so as to enlist public support and, thereby, intensify pressure on employers and the government (for a detailed account of one such strategy, see Kerr and Sachdev, 1992). Various forms of 'working to grade', refusing to cover for absent colleagues or vacant posts, and selective or phased strike action have been used without alienating the public (Winchester, 1989). From the anti-privatisation campaigns, most notably in British Telecom and the water industry, public sector unions have developed additional skills in the use of market research, public relations and advertising. Distaste for such methods in some traditional quarters has now broken down to such an extent that the postal workers union, in its successful attempt to postpone privatisation in 1995, commissioned a public relations company usually retained by Conservative Central Office. More conventional, work-related grievances have also been successfully played out over advertising hoardings. Though parts of the BMA were moved to threaten action over the issue of junior doctors' working hours, the Department of Health was eventually pressed to make concessions primarily through the use of press and publicity and the public pressure that this generated. Similarly, the Department for Education was obliged to alter its proposed systems of pupil testing in 1993 following boycotts organised by education unions, but supported by head teachers, governing bodies and parents (Sinclair *et al.*, 1993b).

This is not to underestimate the impact of public sector reforms upon trade union organisation. Privatisation, contracting out and decentralisation have fundamentally destabilised public sector unions already weakened by the membership loss and legal constraints affecting all unions (Colling, 1995b). In this context, political pressure has strengthened the sinews of managers, ensuring some highly conspicuous industrial defeats, most notably the abortive mine-workers' dispute in 1984/5. It is important to recognise, however, that decentralisation and the creation of market relations do not inevitably reduce the political sensitivity of public service organisations. As the mobilisation of large-scale national disputes becomes more difficult and more expensive, organisational change potentially allows coordinated union action against isolated employers fearful of public and political exposure. Hence, perhaps, the success of the RCN, to date, in securing almost uniform pay settlements from the NHS trusts, despite the opportunity provided for local bargaining in the 1995 PRB award. As the breadth, quality and funding of public services make up an increasingly contentious terrain, managers and ministers alike have had to consider the prospect of increasingly sophisticated forms of resistance from employees and their representatives. To neglect or downplay such a political calculus is to misunderstand the nature of emerging 'market' relationships in the public sector.

Market-driven reform has reconstituted public sector employment relationships and will continue to do so. These patterns of change are now so established that they are unlikely to be reversed by a change of government. Indeed, the Shadow Chancellor has already made it apparent that the control of public expenditure, a central driving force behind many of the recent changes, will continue to be a primary objective:

> We will not build the new Jerusalem on a mountain of debt. So with a Labour Government there will be no stop–go, no inflationary booms, no massaging the figures, no quick fixes, no blank cheques, no short cuts, and no pay explosions.

(Brown, 1995: 5)

Yet, just as the role of the 'model employer' was more complex and contradictory than conventional accounts suggest, so the influence of market forces continues to be intertwined with more traditional political pressures. Current management practice consequently exhibits continuities from the past as well as innovation and, to this extent, should still be considered distinctive.

SUMMARY

Evaluating the changing nature of public sector employment relationships has been the central task of this chapter. Contextual change, particularly the shift to market-based forms of organisation and service delivery, has prompted far-reaching reforms of employment practice. HRM techniques are now as likely to be found in the public sector as elsewhere in the economy. It is argued here, however, that employment relationships retain elements which distinguish them from those apparent in the private sector.

The context in which public sector employee relations have developed, and the distinctive features this has conditioned historically, is considered in the first section. Though there was more variation across the sector than is often appreciated, objectives governing the management of public organisations and their workforces were generally subject to public policy imperatives and political scrutiny. Management structures and cultures consequently prioritised accountability, probity and due process, principles which influenced employment practice to some extent. Requirements to be 'model' employers generated specific policies and procedures in areas such as job security, collective bargaining and dispute resolution.

Recent restructuring within the sector was then examined. Financial pressure has been augmented by organisational change and the admittance of market or quasi-market forces. These new pressures have altered fudamentally the frameworks within which

ACTIVITY

Form a group of up to five with your colleagues. Imagine that you are a working group convened to examine ways of introducing total quality management in part of a local authority social work department. The teams for which you are responsible are concerned with child protection, that is investigating apparent cases of child abuse, assessing the risk of further abuse, and arranging social work and legal intervention to prevent it when necessary. Cases are handled by professionally qualified social workers usually working in collaboration with colleagues in other social services (e.g. residential childcare and fostering) and agencies (e.g. the police and the courts, medical and psychiatric specialists). Your central tasks are to identify targets for quality improvements and recommend how these might be operationalised.

EXERCISES

1 *Define service quality and identify targets for improvements*. What constitutes quality of service in such a setting? How might you go about improving the quality of service as experienced by your customers? Can you think of analogous services in the private sector from which you may want to draw examples of good practice? If not, why do you think this is? In what ways will your employees and their work tasks differ from those in private sector services? To what extent can they, or should they, expand their 'business'? Who are their customers? Should measures of customer satisfaction be used when assessing improvements in service delivery? If not, what alternative indicators are available?

2 *Recommend how performance targets might be operationalised*. Would you wish to link them to the terms and conditions of employees, through individualised performance-related pay for example? Would this generate any difficulties in a social work setting? Consider the extent to which performance targets are attainable by employees acting individually.

3 *Reflect on your discussions*. It is likely that you will have found some of these questions difficult. What implications do they have for the development of total quality management, and HRM techniques more generally, in the public sector? Is social work a unique case?

public organisations are managed. Notions of affordability, flexibility and organisational efficiency are now to the fore in what has been dubbed the 'new public management'.

The second section traces the implications of this contextual change for contemporary public employment relationships. Though public organisations remain substantial employers, the characteristics of their workforces have changed considerably. Public sector work is now increasingly white-collar, part-time and carried out under some form of subcontracting or franchising arrangement. Pay bargaining has been altered with the introduction of pay review bodies and decentralised negotiating forums. The majority of employees are still represented collectively by trade unions. Their influence and resources, however, have declined and the nature of union–management relationships is changing rapidly.

Experimentation with various forms of quality management systems, performance-related pay, and business process re-engineering is now widely evident.

The extent to which the growth in HRM-type approaches has removed the traditionally distinctive features of public sector employment is discussed in the final section. The template provided by notions of the 'model employer' has been discarded. Increased operational autonomy has permitted a greater degree of diversity across the sector. Yet, it is argued, the appearance of market freedom is deceptive. Decision making in the public sector remains intrinsically political in that government departments continue to be involved and the actions of managers, employees and unions have public policy ramifications. In such circumstances, employment relationships retain distinctive dynamics even if they are now differently configured.

Acknowledgements

I am indebted to Dr Rob Baggot (Leicester Business School) and Colin Meech (Public Services Privatisation Research Unit) who provided valuable advice and information during the writing of this chapter.

QUESTIONS

1 Identify the traditional characteristics of public sector employment relationships in the United Kingdom.

2 What have been the main consequences of the shift to market-based organisations and policy for employee relations?

3 To what extent has trade union influence in the public sector been weakened by restructuring and changing employment practice?

EXERCISES

1 Using figures from the *IRS Employment Review* and *Incomes Data Services Reports* (usually available in university libraries), establish and examine the pattern of public sector pay settlements over the past three years. Do you detect any variation between the different services and occupational groupings? Explain your findings, paying particular attention to current public sector pay policy, methods of pay determination, and the 'bargaining power' of the employees involved.

2 Write a brief options review paper for a large NHS general hospital trust outlining the principal benefits and difficulties likely to accrue from the transition to local bargaining. Pay particular attention to the discretion available for innovations in pay structures (new grades? performance-related pay?) and possible responses of employees and their trade unions. You may wish to refer to Bach and Winchester (1994) and Brown and Rowthorn (1990) for this exercise.

3 Form a group with your colleagues and debate the proposition that, 'The strike weapon has no place in a modern public service and should be outlawed'. You may wish to refer to Kerr and Sachdev (1992) and Nichol (1992) for background information.

GLOSSARY OF ABBREVIATIONS

BMA   British Medical Association

CCT   Compulsory Competitive Tendering

COHSE   Confederation of Health Service Employees

CPSA   Civil and Public Servants Association

GDP   Gross Domestic Product

LMS   Local Management of Schools

NALGO   National and Local Government Officers Association

NASUWT   National Association of School Masters/Union of Women Teachers

NCU   National Communications Union

NHS   National Health Service

NUCPS   National Union of Civil and Public Servants

NUPE   National Union of Public Employees

NUT   National Union of Teachers

PRB   Pay Review Body

RCN   Royal College of Nursing

TUPE   Transfer of Undertakings (Protection of Employment) Regulations

UNISON   Public service union formed following merger of COHSE, NALGO and NUPE.

REFERENCES AND FURTHER READING

Adonis, A. and Suzman, M. (1995) 'Breaking free from policy: lessons for the public sector from the UK's prison service crisis', *Financial Times*, 23 October.

Ascher, K. (1987) *The Politics of Privatisation: Contracting Out Public Services*. London: Macmillan.

Bach, S. (1994) 'Restructuring the personnel function: the case of NHS trusts', *Human Resource Management Journal,* Vol. 5. No. 2, pp. 99–115.

Bach, S. and Winchester, D. (1994) 'Opting out of pay devolution? Prospects for local pay bargaining in the UK public services', *British Journal of Industrial Relations*, Vol. 32, No. 2, pp. 263–284.

Bailey, R. (1994) 'Annual review article – 1993', *British Journal of Industrial Relations*, Vol. 32, No. 1, pp. 113–136.

Bailey, R. (1996) 'Public sector industrial relations', in Beardwell, I.J. (ed.) *Contemporary Industrial Relations: A Critical Analysis*. Oxford: Oxford University Press.

Brown, G. (1995) *Speech to Labour Party Conference 1995*. Text issued by Labour Party Conference Media Office, Brighton, October.

Brown, W. and Rowthorn, B. (1990) *A Public Service Pay Policy*. Fabian Pamphlet 542. London: Fabian Society.

Bryson, C., Jackson, M. and Leopold, J. (1995) 'The impact of self-governing trusts on trade unions and staff associations in the NHS', *Industrial Relations Journal*, Vol. 26, No. 2, June, pp. 120–133.

Buchanan, D. and Wilson, B. (1996) *Re-engineering Operating Theatres: The Perspective Assessed*. Occasional Paper 34. Leicester: Leicester Business School.

Carter, N., Klein, R. and Day, P. (1992) *How Organisations Measure Performance: The Use of Performance Indicators in Government.* London: Routledge.

Central Statistical Office (CSO) (1981) *Economic Trends.* No. 338, December. London: HMSO.

Chapman, R. (1991) 'Concepts and issues in public sector reform: the experience of the United Kingdom in the 1980s', *Public Policy and Administration*, Vol. 6, No. 2, Summer, pp. 1–19.

Clegg, H. (1979) *The Changing System of Industrial Relations in Great Britain.* Oxford: Blackwell.

Coates, D. (1989) *The Crisis of Labour: Industrial Relations and the State in Contemporary Britain.* Oxford: Philip Allan.

Cochrane, A. (1993) *Whatever Happened to Local Government?* Buckingham: Open University Press.

Colling, T. (1993) 'Contracting public services: the management of CCT in two county councils', *Human Resource Management Journal*, Vol. 3, No. 4, pp. 1–15.

Colling T. (1995a) *From Hierarchy to Contract? Subcontracting and Employment in the Service Economy.* Warwick Papers in Industrial Relations, No. 52, Spring. Coventry: Industrial Relations Research Unit.

Colling, T. (1995b) 'Renewal or rigor mortis: union responses to contracting in local government', *Industrial Relations Journal*, Vol. 26, No. 2, June, pp. 18–32.

Colling, T. and Ferner, A. (1994) 'Privatisation and marketisation', in Edwards, P.K.E. (ed.) *Industrial Relations: Theory and Practice in Britain.* Oxford: Blackwell.

Corby, S. (1993) 'How big a step is Next Steps? Industrial relations developments in civil service executive agencies', *Human Resource Management Journal*, Vol. 4, No. 2, pp. 52–69.

Crouch, C. (1979) *The Politics of Industrial Relations.* London: Fontana.

Crouch, C. and Marquand, D. (1989) *The New Centralism: Britain Out of Step in Europe?* Oxford: Blackwell.

Davies, K. and Hinton, P. (1993) 'Managing quality in local government and the health service', *Public Money and Management*, Vol. 13, No. 1, January–March, pp. 51–55.

Dearlove, J. and Saunders, P. (1984) *Introduction to British Politics.* Cambridge: Polity Press.

Dunleavy, P. and Hood, C. (1994) 'From old public administration to new public management', *Public Money and Management*, Vol. 14, No. 3, July–September, pp. 34–43.

Dunne, J. (1988) 'The structure of service employment in the UK', in Barker, T.S. and Dunne, J. (eds) *The British Economy after Oil: Manufacturing or Services?* London: Croom Helm.

Fairbrother, P. (1982) *Working for the State.* Studies for Trade Unionists, 8.29. London: Workers Educational Association.

Farnham, D. and Horton, S. (1992) 'Human resources in the new public sector: leading or following private employer practice?', *Public Policy and Administration*, Vol. 7, No. 3, Winter, pp. 42–55.

Farnham, D. and Horton, S. (1995) 'The New People Management in the UK's public services: a silent revolution?' Paper presented to the International Colloquium on *Contemporary Development in HRM*, École Supérieure de Commerce, Montpellier, France, October.

Farnham, D., Horton, S. and Giles, L. (1994) 'Human resource management and industrial relations in the public sector: from model employer to a hybrid model'.

Paper to Employment Research Unit Annual Conference, *The Contract State: The Future of Public Management*, September.

Ferner, A. (1994) 'The state as employer', in Hyman, R. and Ferner, A. (eds) *New Frontiers in Industrial Relations.* Oxford: Blackwell.

Ferner, A. and Colling, T. (1991) 'Privatisation, regulation and industrial relations', *British Journal of Industrial Relations*, Vol. 29, No. 3, pp. 391–409.

Ferner, A. and Colling, T. (1993) 'Electricity supply', in Pendleton, A. and Winterton, J. (eds) *Public Enterprise in Transition.* London: Routledge.

Flynn, N. (1993) *Public Sector Management*. Hemel Hempstead: Harvester-Wheatsheaf.

Flynn, R. (1992) *Structures of Control in Health Management*. London: Routledge.

Fogarty, M. and Brooks, D. (1986) *Trade Unions and British Industrial Development*. London: Policy Studies Institute.

Gamble, A. (1988) *The Free Economy and the Strong State: The Politics of Thatcherism*. London: Macmillan.

Government Statistical Office (GSO) (1996) *Economic Trends*, No. 508, February. London: HMSO.

Grant, W. (1993) *The Politics of Economic Policy*. Hemel Hempstead: Harvester-Wheatsheaf.

Harden, I. (1992) *The Contracting State*. Buckingham: Open University Press.

Heery, E. (1992) 'Industrial relations and the customer'. Paper presented to the British Universities Industrial Relations Association (BUIRA) Annual Conference, July.

Hills, J. (1990) *The State of Welfare: The Welfare State in Britain since 1974*. Oxford: Clarendon Press.

Hogwood, B. (1992) *Trends in British Public Policy*. Buckingham: Open University Press.

Jary, S. (1991) 'Decentralisation in the civil service: the implications for industrial relations'. Paper presented to symposium on *Public Sector Employee Relations in the 1990s: Continuity and Change*, University of Greenwich, November.

Jenkins, S. (1995) *Accountable to None: The Tory Nationalisation of Britain*. London: Hamish Hamilton.

John, P. (1991) 'The restructuring of local government in England and Wales', in Batley, R. and Stoker, G. (eds) *Local Government in Europe*. London: Macmillan.

Keep, E. (1992) 'Schools in the marketplace? Some problems with private sector models', in Wallace, G. (ed.) *Local Management of Schools: Research and Experience*. BERA Dialogue Series, No. 6. Clevedon: Multilingual.

Kerr, A. and Sachdev, S. (1992) 'Third among equals: an analysis of the 1989 ambulance dispute', *British Journal of Industrial Relations*, Vol. 30, No. 1, pp. 127–143.

Kessler, I. (1990) 'Personnel management in local government: the new agenda', *Personnel Management*, November, pp. 40–44.

Kessler, I. (1991) 'Workplace industrial relations in local government', *Employee Relations*, special issue, Vol. 13, No. 2, complete issue.

Lloyd, C. and Seifert, R. (1993) 'Restructuring in the NHS: labour utilisation and intensification in four hospitals'. Paper to the XI Labour Process Conference.

Mackintosh, M., Heery, E. and Jarvis, R. (1994) 'On managing hybrids: financial and human dilemmas', *Management Research in the Public Sector*, Vol. 1, No. 1, pp. 61–89.

Marsden, D. and Richardson, R. (1994) 'Performing for pay? The effects of merit pay on motivation in a public service', *British Journal of Industrial Relations*, Vol. 32, No. 2, pp. 243–261.

Massey, A. (1993) *Managing the Public Sector: A Comparative Analysis of the United Kingdom and the United States*. Aldershot: Edward Elgar.

Millward, N., Stevens, M., Smart, D. and Hawes, W. (1992) *Workplace Industrial Relations in Transition*. Aldershot: Dartmouth.

Morgan, C. and Murgatroyd, S. (1994) *Total Quality Management in the Public Sector*. Buckingham: Open University Press.

Mortimer, J. and Ellis, V. (1980) *A Professional Union: The Evolution of the Institution of Professional Civil Servants*. London: Allen & Unwin.

Napier, B. (1993) *CCT, Market Testing and Employment Rights: The Effects of TUPE and the Acquired Rights Directive*. London: Institute of Employment Rights.

National Institute of Economic and Social Research (NIESR) (1995) *The UK Economy*. London: Heinemann.

Nichol, D. (1992) Unnecessary conflict: NHS management's view of the 1989–90 ambulance dispute', *British Journal of Industrial Relations*, Vol. 30, No. 1, pp. 145–154.

Nolan, P. (1983) 'The firm and labour market behaviour', in Bain, G.S. (ed.) *Industrial Relations in Britain*. Oxford: Blackwell.

Pendleton, A. and Winterton, J. (1993) 'Public enterprise industrial relations in context', in Pendleton, A. and Winterton, J. (eds) *Public Enterprise in Transition*. London: Routledge.

Pierson, C. (1994) 'Continuity and discontinuity in the emergence of the 'post-Fordist' welfare state', in Burrows, R. and Loader, B. (eds) *Towards the Post-Fordist Welfare State?* London: Routledge.

Pinch, S. (1994) 'Labour flexibility and the changing welfare state: is there a post-Fordist model?', in Burrows, R. and Loader, B. (eds) *Towards the Post Fordist Welfare State?* London. Routledge.

Pollert, A. (1991) 'The orthodoxy of flexibility', in Pollert, A. (ed.) *Farewell to Flexibility*. Oxford: Blackwell.

Pratchett, L. and Wingfield, M. (1995) *Reforming the Public Service Ethos in Local Government: A New Institutional Perspective*. Leicester Business School Occasional Paper 27. Leicester: De Montfort University.

Public Services Privatisation Research Unit (PSPRU) (1994) *Private Corruption of Public Services*. London: PSPRU.

Robinson, R. (1992) 'Health policy in 1991', in Terry, F. and Jackson, P. (eds) *Public Domain – The Public Services Yearbook 1992*. London: Chapman & Hall.

Sinclair, J., Ironside, M. and Seifert, R. (1993a) 'Classroom struggle? Market oriented education reforms and their impact on teachers' professional autonomy'. Paper to the XI Labour Process Conference.

Sinclair, J., Ironside, M. and Seifert, R. (1993b) 'The road to market: management and trade union initiatives in the transition to school level bargaining under local management of schools'. Paper to the British Universities Industrial Relations Association Annual Conference, University of York.

Stewart, J. (1989) 'The changing organisation and management of local authorities', in Stewart, J. and Stoker, G. (eds) *The Future of Local Government*. Basingstoke: Macmillan.

Taylor, R. (1993) *The Trade Union Question in British Politics*. Oxford: Blackwell.

Temple, P. (1994) 'The agents of change – notes on the developing division of labour', in Buxton, T., Chapman, P. and Temple, P. (eds), *Britain's Economic Performance*. London: Routledge.

Thornley, C. (1994) 'Nursing pay policy: chaos in context'. Paper presented to Employment Research Unit Annual Conference, Cardiff Business School, September.

Trades Union Congress (TUC) (1995) *Trends in Trade Unions: Industrial Action*. London: TUC.

Travers, T. (1989) 'The threat to the autonomy of elected local government', in Crouch, C. and Marquand, D. (eds) *The New Centalism: Britain Out of Step in Europe?* Oxford: Blackwell.

Walsh, K. (1995) *Public Services and Market Mechanisms: Competition, Contracting and the New Public Management*. London: Macmillan.

White, G. (1994) 'Public sector pay: decentralisation versus control'. Paper to Employment Research Unit Annual Conference, *The Contract State: The Future of Public Management*, September.

Winchester, D. (1983) 'The public sector', in Bain, G.S. (ed.) *Industrial Relations in Britain*. Oxford: Blackwell.

Winchester, D. (1989) 'Pay, conflict and efficiency in the UK public sector'. Paper to the Italian Association of Labour Economists Conference, *Pay and Productivity in the Public Sector*, Cagliari.

Winchester, D. (1996) 'The regulation of public services pay in the united Kingdom'. Paper to the Industrial Relations in the European Community (IREC) Network Annual Conference, *Industrial Relations in Europe: Convergence or Diversification?* University of Copenhagen: FAOS.

Winchester, D. and Bach, S. (1994) 'The state: the public sector', in Edwards, P.K.E. (ed.) *Industrial Relations: Theory and Practice in Great Britain*. Oxford: Blackwell.

PART 4 CASE STUDY

Whitewater Engineering Ltd

A large engineering firm specialising in the manufacture of marine engines and casings has developed to separate business units operating as individual profit centres. At plant 1, a new HRM director has been appointed with the mandate to review the existing employment relationship. The firm has the following characteristics.

- a multi-union site with the AEEU representing the majority of the employees who are skilled workers, although the TGWU and MSU are also present on site;

- the site has a reputation for 'good' industrial relations with a professional personnel department in place – there is a well-established system of collective bargaining which encompasses both integrative and distributive issues;

- in recent years the company as a whole has experienced falling profitability and a declining market share. The response to date has been to negotiate voluntary redundancies through the corporate structure and to establish local profit centres, but it is now felt that further measures must be taken. The workforce is aware that the company is experiencing recessionary pressures and will need to consider alternative strategies to ensure long-term survival.

As HRM director, your mandate is to outline a series of initiatives aimed at the labour process which you believe will improve the efficient operation of your site. In your report you must recognise the implications for the collective bargaining process of your plans, identify possible areas of conflict and suggest ways to bypass potential problems.

INTRODUCTION

This section deals with a subject very much in its infancy, the parameters of which are still being set, and the debate about approaches to it is still being drawn together. The problem with examining HRM in a global context raises far-reaching and complex questions, but the present state of research and theorising is, as yet, a long way from producing satisfactory explanations of the dynamics of HRM in a comparative context.

The interest in the subject has arisen with the increasing intensification of globalisation in industry, commerce and trade, creating increased competition which in turn is producing a more volatile and uncertain world (Schuler *et al.*, 1993). It has become imperative to understand these developments in a world of increasing competition, not only between companies but also between nations and regions with their own ideologies and socio-political systems.

These economic trends have taken place against a backcloth of social and political turbulence in the twentieth century, which has been hallmarked by two World Wars, the decline of empire, the rise and decline of systems rooted in totalitarian ideologies, and the rise and decline of the 'cold war' with its omnipresent nuclear threat to survival. There has been a huge and continuing growth in the world's population, which has intensified the problems of poverty for many poor nations. Pollution has raised green issues to the forefront of consciousness of many political and business policy-makers. We are also witnessing a challenge to Western economic supremacy with the rapid growth of Asia Pacific states led by the 'Tigers', Japan, China, South Korea, Taiwan and Hong Kong, to which can be added Singapore and Malaysia.

The chapters in this section cannot do justice to these massive changes within the narrow context of HRM, so they will merely serve, therefore, to give the reader a flavour of some of the developments in the field and some of the main debates now emerging.

The section begins with an examination of some definitions of international HRM and some of the major debates emerging, influenced by parallel disciplines using comparative analyses. This is followed by a chapter reviewing some of the developments of HRM in a European context, including both the European Union and recent developments in Eastern Europe.

The last two chapters examine in detail two countries, USA and Japan, whose industrial and management systems have been much admired and emulated by many nations in the world, and which have had an enormous impact on the theory and practice of management and human resource management.

REFERENCE

Schuler, R. Dowling, P. and Jackson, S. (1993) 'An integrature framework of strategic international human resource management', *International Journal of Human Resource Management* , Vol. 4, No. 4, December, pp. 717–764.

INTERNATIONAL HUMAN
RESOURCE MANAGEMENT

Len Holden

OBJECTIVES

To define and distinguish between international HRM
and comparative HRM.

●

To examine comparative HRM and approaches to its study.

●

To examine international HRM and approaches to its study.

●

To examine some models of comparative HRM and
international HRM.

●

To explore expatriation issues.

●

To review some international and comparative surveys.

●

INTRODUCTION

There is increasing recognition of the importance of human resources in international competition. Porter (1990) states that the most important factors which influence national competitiveness are skilled human resources and the scientific base. He asks why a nation achieves international success in a particular industry. Switzerland, for example, is a landlocked nation with high cost labour, strict environmental law and few natural resources – least of all cocoa. Yet it is a world leader in chocolate, not to mention pharmaceuticals, banking and specialised machinery. Similarly, Japan has few natural resources and yet from a shattered postwar position has built itself up into one of the most formidable economies in the world, rivalling, and in some industries superseding, the United States. What both Switzerland and Japan lacked in natural resources they strongly compensated for in human resources, nurturing the education, skills and abilities of their populations. Porter (1990) claims that understanding these lessons is vital for nations wishing to achieve competitive advantage.

INTERNATIONAL HRM: SOME ATTEMPTS AT DEFINITION

The recognition of the significance of human resources to organisational and national productivity has led to a surge of interest in international human resource management (IHRM), but there is still some confusion as to what it means. The growth in popularity of international business has led to an increase in the number of publications pertaining to international management, which itself can be observed in a national and organisational context (Bartlett and Ghoshal, 1989; Hodgetts and Luthans, 1991; Pucik *et al.*, 1992; Deresky, 1994; Ghauri and Prasad, 1995; Fatehi, 1996). Much of this literature deals directly with many issues which would appear in HRM texts, as well as with expatriation issues. Other works concerning international human resource management deal with comparative issues in a purely intra-national context (Brewster and Tyson, 1991; Hegewisch and Brewster, 1993; Brewster and Hegewisch, 1994; Kirkbride, 1994; Calori and De Woot, 1994; Hendry, 1994; Sparrow and Hiltrop, 1994; Shenkar, 1995; Hollinshead and Leat, 1995; Harzing and Van Ruysseveldt, 1995), and yet others deal with comparative employment and industrial relations issues (Baglioni and Crouch, 1990; Ferner and Hyman, 1992; Bamber and Lansbury, 1993; Hyman and Ferner, 1994; Bean, 1994; Van Ruysseveldt *et al.*, 1995). A further group deals with purely organisational issues locating IHRM in multinational corporations (MNCs) and explore global HRM strategies of the organisation relating to issues of succession, expatriation, recruitment, selection, appraisal, reward and training and development (Brewster, 1991; Tyson *et al.*, 1993; Dowling *et al.*, 1994; Torrington, 1994; Briscoe, 1995).

A further group, though not often labelled IHRM, strongly encroaches upon the subject area and deals with issues of culture and acculturation often in relation to MNC management policy such as expatriation (Hofstede, 1980, 1991; Laurent, 1983; Trompenaars, 1993; Ferraro, 1994; Jackson, 1995; Gatley *et al.*, 1996; Tayeb, 1996).

We can thus see that IHRM can be studied in an organisational and a comparative (both organisational and intra-national) context. Definitions would therefore need to recognise the locations of, and the approaches to, IHRM. Boxall (1995: 5) arrives at similar conclusions and defines international human resource management as being 'concerned with the human resource problems of multinational firms in foreign subsidiaries (such as expatriate management) or, more broadly, with the unfolding HR issues that are associated with the various stages of the internationalisation process'. This accords with Dowling *et al.* (1994: 2), Torrington (1994: 6) and Briscoe (1995: 9), who sees IHRM as 'simply HRM on a larger scale'.

Comparative HRM, on the other hand, has much wider significance both in terms of the HRM role which Boxall (1995: 6) states 'should be interpreted as the comparative study of labour in its broadest sense' and in the national contexts in which it exists. He points out that HRM as such was initially perceived in mainly Anglo-American terms, but the comparative label would suggest a move beyond this 'into an intellectual and cultural terrain where there may well be diverse notions of management itself and of labour management institutions and practices' (Boxall, 1995: 6).

Here he suggests an examination of the richer vein of comparative industrial relations and comparative labour market theory, incorporating the historical development of management labour systems as, for example, in the work of Gospel (1992), which attempts to offer explanations of poor British productivity throughout the preceding century by an examination of internal and external labour markets.

Boxall also notes the lack of rigour in the theoretical development of the subject and comparative studies which have been conducted to date tend to lack depth of analysis as a result. Other commentators have suggested that perhaps a move towards the comparative case study approach may prove more fruitful. We shall examine this later in the chapter when we consider some analytical frameworks of IHRM.

APPROACHES TO THE STUDY OF COMPARATIVE HRM

The discussion of definitions of comparative HRM leads us to approaches to its study. Writers in this wide arena have borrowed freely from theories of various philosophies and academic disciplines, and these approaches can be categorised into four main areas: convergence theory, marxist theory, the cultural approach and the institutionalist perspective. (These categories follow closely those of Lane, 1989.) Each approach attempts to examine the relationship between social settings and organisational forms and the similarities and differences which would point to convergence or divergence.

Convergence theory

This theory came from the writings of Kerr *et al.* (1960). They posited the view that technological change ultimately creates similar industrial systems. These systems are rooted in the industrial organisation where technology imposes the need for similar structures and work forms. This growth in similarity of organisational structures over time Kerr *et al.* called convergence theory.

An argument of the convergence school claims that, when organisations reach a certain scale, defined by the numbers of employees, it becomes necessary to introduce functional specialisation. Coordinating and controlling these functions results in a more formalised system of organisation, with rules, regulations and hierarchies. More staff are thus needed to perform these roles, with parallel development of more centrally controlled systems.

In other words, ways of working in countries throughout the world become similar when influenced by the same technologies and organisation size. For example, car plants, whether in Brazil, South Africa, Britain or the United States, will have similar production lines, which in turn influence the kind of human resource and work policies each nation will tend to follow, for example speed of the line, control over the work process and payment systems, etc.

Later Kerr *et al.* (1971) revised their views on convergence theory and claimed that they had been far too simplistic in explaining how technology influences organisational structure and behaviour. Other critics claimed that the convergence approach only considers the formal structures and remains insensitive to informal structures within organisations. Cultural theorists have also taken convergence theory to task. Nevertheless, it has enjoyed some revival in a revised form in recent years. Mueller and Purcell (1992: 15), for example, claim that in the automobile industry 'convergent forces in the shape of globalisation of markets, European legislation and common product standards, as well as the easing of cross border shipments of components or half finished products, have led to the emergence of remarkably similar operational requirements in management policies in various countries'.

Marxist theory

This approach emanates from the ideas of Karl Marx and his view of the development of capitalism. Like convergence theory, this view ignores cultural and other informal influences on organisational development.

Essentially, this view sees capitalism as a mode of production in which private ownership of capital and competition between capitalist enterprises are the primary features. The need for profit drives the system which is achieved by appropriation of surplus value from labour, i.e. paying a wage which is lower than the value of the goods. Therefore in order to be competitive there is a need to exploit labour for higher and higher productivity for comparatively less return.

A relatively recent reinterpretation of the Marxist view of capitalism was developed by Braverman (1974). The Marxists, unlike the convergence theorists, shift the emphasis from the structure of the organisation to the relationship between management and labour. In other words, there is a focus on the actors in relation to the processes of production. Braverman and his followers emphasise the importance of managerial control over the workforce, deskilling and the cheapening of labour. They emphasise the importance to management and owners of the necessity of breaking down skill processes by the use of new technologies and the implementation of flexible work practices.

According to this approach, the variety of management–labour relations throughout the world merely reflects the various stages of capitalism through which economies are passing.

The cultural approach

Other writers stress the importance of cultural differences. Geert Hofstede, for example, believes 'that there is no evidence that the cultures of present-day generations from different countries are converging' (Hofstede, 1991: 17). Cultural theorists like Hofstede believe that cultural influences play an enormous part in the way employees behave in organisations and that the introduction of technology produces only superficial similarities.

Culture is in itself notoriously difficult to define, and can mean many things, ranging from expression through the arts and other creative media to societal perceptions of history and spirituality. The most commonly accepted definition is the one put forward by Kroeber and Kluckhohn:

> Culture consists of patterns, explicit and implicit of and for behaviour acquired and transmitted by symbols, constituting the distinctive achievement of human groups, including their embodiment in artifacts; the essential core of culture consists of traditional (i.e. historically derived and selected) ideas and especially their attached values; culture systems may, on the one hand, be considered as products of action, on the other as conditioning elements of future action.
>
> (Kroeber and Kluckhohn, 1952)

Even with this definition, the multiplicity of meaning makes social investigation using empirical tools very difficult. Attempts at measuring attitudes in human beings are difficult enough (as the wealth of research work in the social sciences testifies), but the application of numerous cultural values to the equation makes the work of disentangling one value from another extremely problematic, if not impossible. The cultural values of the researcher must be considered and how much they are embodied in the research, from its conception to the analysis of the findings.

The work of Hofstede

Hofstede's research in IBM using the responses of managers from 66 different countries produced some interesting if controversial evidence on cultural differences. He found that managers and employees vary on four primary dimensions, which he called power distance (PDI), uncertainty avoidance (UAI), individuality (INV) and masculinity (MASC) (Hofstede, 1980).

Power distance

By power distance (PDI) Hofstede means the extent to which members of a society accept that power in institutions and organisations is and should be distributed equally. For example, in democratic societies the distance between the government and the governed is narrower than in dictatorships. In other words, a worker in the Philippines will have far less chance of influencing the decisions of the government than would a worker in Sweden, and the same applies in the workplace; there is a high PDI in the Philippines and a low PDI in Sweden. Hofstede believes that such work attitudes are culturally determined and are liable to be accepted as much by the workforce as by the managers.

A Swedish company set up a subsidiary in Malaysia and employed Malaysian workers and middle managers. The Swedish senior managers attempted to run the subsidiary as it had done in Sweden, i.e. by involving the Malaysian workers and managers in democratic decision making. When there was a problem to be solved the Swedish managers would gather the Malaysian workforce and managers into groups for joint problem-solving exercises. After a couple of months of this practice, the Malaysian middle managers approached the Swedish senior managers and stated that they and the workers felt uncomfortable with this style of working and found much easier a style in which the boss acted more like a 'boss' and gave orders to be carried out with minimum responsibilities.

What the Swedes had discovered was that, although the company set-up was similar in Malaysia to that of Sweden, cultural differences produced differing expectations of ways of working. Swedes prefer a more democratic style of management, Malaysians a more autocratic style, for both managers and workers.

Uncertainty avoidance (UAI)

The definition of uncertainty avoidance involves, *inter alia*, the creation of rules and structures to eliminate ambiguity in organisations and support beliefs promising certainty and protecting conformity. In simple terms, this means that human beings try in various ways to avoid uncertainty in their lives by controlling their environment through predictable ways of working. For example, France and Germany have a much higher UAI than do Britain and Sweden. In other words, the Germans and French feel a much greater need for rules and regulations than do the Swedes and British.

In France and Germany there are penalties for jay walking and in those countries most pedestrians in towns and cities will only cross the road at pedestrian lights and when the 'walking green' light is showing. In Britain, while such controlled crossings exist, people are more inclined to ignore them. The attitude prevails there that 'rules are made to be broken' when it is perceived as not being important. This attitude is much frowned on in high PDI countries such as Germany.

The following story was told to the authors by a German colleague. In Bonn a man had a heart attack on the steps of the Bundestag (the then German Parliament). Another man who had observed this rushed to the doorman of the Bundestag and hurriedly suggested that an announcement be made over the public address system that a doctor was urgently required. Like many Parliaments there are some deputies (MPs) who are medical doctors. The doorman, after consulting his rule book, refused to do this, stating that once the Bundestag was in session it must not be disturbed. The man then called for an ambulance, but by the time it arrived the heart attack victim had died.

The story did not end there. The relatives of the man who had died proceeded to sue the doorman of the Bundestag for negligence. Unable to comprehend why he was being 'punished', the doorman had a nervous breakdown. After all, he had only been doing his duty in strictly adhering to the rules of the Bundestag!

This explains why in French and German organisations personnel managers are more likely to have large rule books which are observed in everyday practice than would be the case in British or Swedish organisations.

Individualism (INV)

Individualism, as described by Hofstede, is the degree of preference of individuals for loosely knit frameworks in which individuals are supposed to take care of themselves and their immediate families. In simple terms, this means the preference for living and working in collectivist or individual ways. Not surprisingly, USA and Britain score high on the individual index and South American and Asian countries score low. In the latter there is much more reliance on the extended family and the subsuming of the individual identity within the group, whereas in countries, with high individual indexes, like USA and Northern European countries, there is a tendency for individual achievement to be emphasised.

Ivan, a middle manager in an Eastern European company, attended a managerial course on Western management techniques. He attended dutifully and learned his lessons well. When he returned to his organisation he attempted to carry out some of these reforms, but after some futile months he gave up and carried on much as before. Ivan realised that he could not change the values of his workers and fellow managers overnight.

Under the old communist regimes in Eastern Europe collectivism rather than individualism was the predominant value. Thus, when many Eastern European countries began to import US and Western-style managerial education packages, it was found that they often did not have the desired effect. One of the chief reasons for this was that in Eastern European communist societies, particularly those with less developed industry and commerce (i.e. predominantly peasant cultures), collectivist patterns of working permeated the hierarchical structures of organisations. In addition, collectivism had developed into a form of corruption which became the norm. In order for Ivan to do well, therefore, it was not *what* he knew as an individual but *whom* he knew which would make a success of his job.

Masculinity

Hofstede's last and perhaps most controversial index of culture is masculinity (MAS). This pertains to societies in which social gender roles are clearly distinct, i.e. men are supposed to be assertive, tough and focused on material success. Femininity pertains to societies in which women are supposed to be more modest, tender and concerned with the quality of life (Hofstede, 1991: 82). In his index masculine and feminine values can apply to both men and women. Thus we find that in Sweden, the least masculine country in the index, feminine values apply also to men. However, in the most masculine country, Japan, women seem to retain their feminine values.

Some commentators have pinpointed feminine values as being those most required in management practices in the organisation of the future. If that is the case, then some cultures will have considerable problems in adapting to those values, if we are to believe Hofstede's masculinity index.

The Netherlands comes very low on the masculinity index (MAS score 14) and the USA quite high (MAS score 62). Naturally, managerial practices could pose cultural misunderstandings between managers and workforces from the two countries. Hofstede (1991: 92) gives the following example.

Three managers of a Dutch manufacturing plant of a major US corporation had been lost to the parent company. The Dutch managers had been seen as 'softees' by the American managers. They hesitated to implement unpopular measures and seemed to pay too much heed to the works council – a body elected by the workers and required by Dutch law but disliked by the American vice-president.

The vice-president decided to appoint the fourth manager himself and, much against the Dutch personnel manager's wishes, chose a man whom he considered had the right 'tough' qualities for the job. He had come to this conclusion because of the forthright views which the man had expressed in his reports back to senior management, advocating drastic action and disregarding its unpopularity. The vice-president felt that this man had the right approach and would not be sidetracked by this works council nonsense.

Unsurprisingly to the Dutch, the new plant manager proved disastrous. Within six months he was on sick leave and the plant was in a state of chaos.

The Dutch had known the plant manager as a weak but congenial personality, who had compensated for his insecurity by using powerful language in his reports to his American bosses. This assertiveness which had impressed the vice-president was regarded by his Dutch fellow employees as bragging. As a manager he had received cooperation from no one. He had tried to do everything himself, and suffered a nervous breakdown in a very short time. The masculine values which had superficially impressed the American vice-president had created a cultural blind which obscured the real issue – was he the right person for the job?

Confucian dynamism

Hofstede began to realise that the values he had chosen to describe managerial difference were Western oriented when he attempted to correlate economic performance of countries to cultural dimensions. Three of his previous dimensions, power distance, individualism and masculinity, were found to coincide with Chinese values; however, no dimension corresponded to that of uncertainty avoidance. Instead, he and Michael Bond substituted 'Confucian dynamism', a dimension which ranged from a future-oriented mentality to one which has more static and is tradition oriented (Bond and Hofstede, 1990).

Uncertainty avoidance is associated with a human being's search for 'truth'. This does not mean that the Chinese are dishonest, but that questions related to absolute truth, and its opposite – falsehood – are not relevant. What is more relevant is a search for 'virtue'. In Chinese thought, fundamentalism is less likely to exist because if things are of the earth then everything contains 'virtue'. As Hofstede states, 'the Western concern with Truth is supported by an axiom in Western logic that a statement excludes its opposite: if A is true, B, which is the opposite of A must be false. Eastern logic does not have such an axiom. If A is true, its opposite, B, may also be true and together they produce a wisdom which is superior to either A or B. . . Human truth in this philosophical approach is always partial' (Hofstede, 1991: 171).

Confucian dynamism was composed of the following values (Holstede, 1991: 165, 166):

'Long-term orientation':

- persistence (perseverence);
- ordering relationships by status and observing this order;
- thrift;
- having a sense of shame.

On the opposite pole 'short-term orientation':

- personal steadiness and stability;
- protecting your face;
- respect for tradition;
- reciprocation of greetings, favours or gifts.

Controversially, Bond and Hofstede have correlated some of these values with economic performance, particularly 'thrift' and 'perseverence', and long-term and short-term orientations. Not surprisingly, China and Japan score highly on long-term orientations and USA and Britain low (Hofstede, 1991: 166).

The work of André Laurent

André Laurent of INSEAD in France has also achieved considerable recognition through his research on work-related values.

He studied the attitudes of managers in Western European countries, the United States and two Asian countries, Indonesia and Japan. He asked managers from these countries to describe their approaches to over 60 normal work situations. He discovered clear groupings of attitudes for managers in each country.

For example, when he posed the statement, 'The main reason for hierarchical structure is so that everybody knows who has authority over whom', there was a variety of responses. Americans tended to disagree with the statement, believing the purpose of hierarchy is to organise tasks to assist in problem solving. The Americans tended to appreciate an organisation with as few levels of bureaucracy or hierarchy as possible. By contrast, many Southern European and most Asian managers strongly agreed with Laurent's statement. These managers regard hierarchy as important in making sense of work structures and thus work itself. The structure being distinct enables them to know more clearly where they fit in and what their role is in the work process.

TABLE 16.1
'The main reason for hierarchical structure is so that everybody knows who has authority over whom'

	Agreement rate across the countries (%)
Indonesia	86
Japan	52
Italy	50
France	45
Netherlands	38
Great Britain	38
Germany	24
United States	18

Source: Laurent (1983). Reprinted by permission from M. E. Sharpe, Inc., Armonk, NY 10504.

In response to the statement 'In order to have efficient work relationships, it is often necessary to bypass the hierarchical line', cultural differences were also revealed (Table 16.2).

TABLE 16.2

'In order to have efficient work relationships, it is often necessary to bypass the hierarchical line'

	Disagreement across countries (%)
Italy	75
Germany	46
France	42
Netherlands	39
United States	32
Great Britain	31
Sweden	22

Source: Laurent (1983). Reprinted by permission from M. E. Sharpe, Inc., Armonk, NY 10504.

On this index the Swedes scored the lowest, which is consistent with the Swedish style of working in which employee involvement is emphasised and many responsibilities are given to the workforce by comparison to other countries. However, cultural theorists would regard it as being simplistic and unjustified to place a value judgement on these attitudes as they are rooted very much in the values of a society. In Italy, for example, it would be considered disrespectful and even challenging to bypass the boss, even to solve a problem advantageous to the organisation. This would be regarded as a challenge to the boss's authority.

In other words, while employees in different countries outwardly appear to be carrying out the same type of work processes, the cultural values which each individual carries shape their perception and understanding of the workplace and their preferences for certain styles of working.

The research of Trompenaars

Trompenaars has also examined cultural differences in a world context. He uses seven dimensions of culture, each of which has within it a tension as exemplified by two opposite or polarised values. These measures are:

1. *Universalism–particularism* in which individuals from a 'universalist' culture would focus on rules, and from a 'particularist' culture on relationships (Trompenaars, 1993: 29). For example, he asked respondents to state whether they would tell the truth to the authorities if they were accompanying a friend who, driving at 35 mph in a 20 mph speed-restricted zone, knocked down a pedestrian. In universalist cultures the respondents would feel a greater obligation to state that the friend had been travelling at 35 mph, but in a particularist culture respondents felt a greater obligation to the relationship by protecting the friend from a possible serious conviction.

2. The *analysing–integrating* dimension examines the tension between the tendency to 'analyse phenomena into parts i.e. facts, items, tasks, numbers, units, points, specifics, or. . . to integrate and configure such details into whole patterns, relationships, and wider context' (Hampden-Turner and Trompenaars, 1994: 11).

3. *Individualism-collectivism* is the 'conflict between what each of us wants as an individual, and the interests of the group we belong to' (Trompenaars, 1993: 47).

4. The *inner directed–outer directed* scale ranges from individuals who are influenced to action by 'inner directed judgements, decisions and commitments, or signals, demands and trends in the outside world to which we must adjust' (Hampden-Turner and Trompenaars, 1994: 11).

5. *Time as sequence–time as synchronisation* is the preference for doing 'things fast, in the shortest possible sequence of passing time, or to synchronise efforts so that completion is coordinated' (Hampden-Turner and Trompenaars, 1994: 11).

6. *Achieved status–ascribed status* examines the view that 'the status of employees depends on what they have achieved and how they have performed, or on some characteristic important to the corporation, i.e. age, seniority, gender, education, potential, strategic role' (Hampden-Turner and Trompenaars, 1994: 11).

7. *Equality–hierarchy* asks the question, 'is it more important that we treat employees as equals so as to elicit from them the best they have to give, or to emphasise the judgment and authority of the hierarchy that is coaching and evaluating them?' (Hampden-Turner and Trompenaars, 1994: 11). This dimension has similarities to Hofstede's power distance index. Table 16.3 indicates where some major industrial powers would be located on Trompenaars' scale of cultural measures.

High and low context cultures

Hall (1976; Hall and Hall, 1990) has made a comparative study of national attributes in the setting of 'high context' and 'low context' cultures.

> Low context people appreciate explicit, clear written forms of communication, as provided by computers books and letters. In contrast high context peoples, such as the Japanese, Arabs and Southern Europeans divulge less information officially in written forms, but tend to be better informed than low context people, since they tend to develop extensive informal networks for exchanging information verbally face to face or by telephone. High context people are also more adept in interpreting non-verbal aspects of communication, and seeing the significance of what is implicit or not said, pauses, silence, tone, and other subtle signals.
> (Leeds *et al.*, 1994: 12)

TABLE 16.3

The position of some major industrial countries on Trompenaars'
cultural dimensions

Universalism Britain, Sweden, USA, Germany	**Particularism** France, Japan
Analysis Britain, Sweden, USA, Netherlands	**Integration** France, Germany, Japan
Individualism Britain, Sweden, USA, Netherlands	**Collectivism** Germany, France, Japan
Inner direction Britain, USA, Germany	**Outer direction** Sweden, Netherlands, France, Japan
Time as sequence Britain, Sweden, USA, Germany, Netherlands	**Synchronised view of time** France, Japan
Status by achievement Britain, Sweden, USA, Germany, Netherlands, Japan	**Status by ascription** France
Equality Britain, Sweden, USA, Germany, Netherlands	**Hierarchy** France, Japan

Source: Hampden-Turner and Trompenaars (1994: 301). Reprinted from *The Seven Cultures of Capitalism* by permission of Piatkus Books.

One could say that the British 'old boy network' falls very much into this high context category as does the felt need for exclusive clubs and societies, providing an entrée into various influential networks which pervades British society. It is no accident that the freemasons, for example, originated in England.

In a study by Brewster *et al.* (1993), expatriate Swedish managers working in the UK gave several incidents of the difficulties coming from a low context culture to a relatively high context one. For example, one Swedish manager who had worked in England stated:

> people sometimes said 'I had a big problem'. I often learned that this was not the case. The reason that I took it that way is because the Swedes take the words in. The words themselves are more important to a Swede. The drama is quite important in England and the debate around it and how can you solve it etc. I think the biggest problem when you go to another country is to find out what people are actually saying, and get rid of all other noise.

> (Brewster *et al.*, 1993: 17)

The cultural approach to HRM has received considerable criticism from academics working in other HRM-related fields. Research such as that of Hofstede, Trompenaars and Laurent which uses a positive approach has been attacked for being too narrow in focus, and that using ethnographic approaches as often being too nebulous (Hollinshead and Leat, 1995: 3). Altman (1992: 36) sums up the dilemma of the positive approach:

> Hofstede's strength lies in a finely tuned and rigorously applied research design. This is also his limitation. His approach can be likened to a powerful torch – sending a concentrated and bright, extremely sharp, ray of light, but, necessarily, leaving much in the dark.

TABLE 16.4
Locating low and high context cultures

Country	High context	Low context
Western Germany		XXXX
German Swiss		XXXX
Scandinavian		XXX
North American		XXX
Belgium, Netherlands, Denmark		X
France	X	
Britain	XX	
Southern Europe	XXX	
Middle East	XXX	
Asia, Africa, Latin America	XXX	
Japan	XXXX	

Source: Leeds *et al.* (1994: 13).

The use of qualitative and anecdotal evidence has been acknowledged by most researchers in the cultural field as helping them towards a greater understanding of their subject, but the limitations of this study have caused us to leave out much that is illuminating in literature, the arts in general and observations by travellers and expatriate workers.

The institutional perspective

The institutional view essentially sees the business environment as socially constituted. In other words, the influence of national and regional institutions and the historical traditions from which they have emerged is important in understanding why institutions differ throughout the world.

Such influential factors as education and training, for example, have evolved in diverse ways in different countries which in turn affect the way in which organisations develop. In Germany there is strong structural support for training by government, although the costs are mainly borne by employers. By contrast in the UK, structural supports, while existing, have emerged from different sociopolitical traditions and emphasis at present is on a voluntarist approach which relies on organisations being willing to participate in government-inspired schemes such as TECs (see Chapter 8).

Supporters of the institutional perspective claim that it avoids the controversial issues associated with cultural theory which can be heavily laden with culturally based value judgements.

However, significant work using an institutional perspective does rely to some extent on the interpretation of culture. Dore's work comparing a British and a Japanese corporation shows how the Japanese employment system is 'partly an adaption of earlier pre-industrial patterns, partly a conscious attempt to create new arrangements consonant with dominant cultural values, and partly the result of borrowing elements from industrialised nations' (Dore, 1973, quoted in Lane, 1989: 32). He finds, for example:

- adaption of earlier pre-industrial patterns, i.e. European and US;
- adaption of Japanese values, 'Bushido spirit', loyalty, group work, respect, duty;
- elements borrowed from other industrialised nations, e.g. Deming's ideas on TQM.

Whatever comparative method or combinations of methods we choose to use, uncertainty and inexactitude will remain important weaknesses. With so many influential factors playing on the employment relationship and the relationship of organisations to governments, considerable room for debate and controversy will remain.

A synthesis of approaches

A synthesis of the main ideas and approaches which have influenced the scope, direction and ideological interpretation of comparative HRM may prove a useful way forward. Each of the above four approaches has its weaknesses and limitations, which adherents as well as critics usually acknowledge. We have seen how the weakness in convergence theory has been critiqued by those who view the workplace experience through a cultural paradigm, and that cultural theorists themselves acknowledge the limitations of their own forms of enquiry. Since the 1920s, inspired by those associated with the Frankfurt School, many marxists have begun to examine the limitations of the basis of dialectical materialism rooted purely in an economic determinist and positive tradition (Kolakowski, 1978; Bronner, 1994). Some marxists have turned towards an examination of the role of culture in influencing attitudes and behaviour in the work context (Wuthnow *et al.*, 1984; Halperin, 1988; Nelson and Grossberg, 1988) most notably Habermas (1983, 1987). The institutional perspective, while valid, fails to take account of a number of important dimensions (e.g. the cultural perspective) and as a result can only offer a unidimensional view of the employment relationship.

Essentially, then, the four approaches to the employment relationship in a comparative context can be placed in convergent and divergent categories as illustrated in Table 16.5.

TABLE 16.5
A synthesis of theoretical approaches to comparative employee relations

Convergent

Convergence or contingency theory – Kerr *et al.*, Purcell and Mueller, McLuhan

Marxist theory – Braverman, Friedman, Edwards, Burawoy

Divergent

Cultural theorists – Hofstede, Laurent, Trompenaars, Hall

Institutional perspective – Aix School (Maurice *et al.*), Sorge and Warner, Dore, Gallie.

An application of convergence–divergence bi-polarity

The author has recently attempted to use these approaches in examining one aspect of HRM in a comparative context (Holden, 1996). In investigating employee participation practices in Swedish and British banks over a period of rapid change, it was possible to observe the dynamics of its operation. This analysis was rooted in the adaptation of the framework of employee involvement created by Poole (1986b) (see Chapter 14, Employee Involvement).

By relating the research to convergent factors such as economic trends and government action, i.e. the move towards neo-liberalist policies, the influence of recession and the banking crisis in the early 1990s, and the convergence of technologies such as computerisation, it could be observed how convergent pressures created similar responses in different national settings. However, the divergent factors (cultural values, ideology and the actual interpretations of government policy) in these contexts ensured that the HRM outcomes would never be exactly the same.

We found that employee participation was greater in the consensual, more involving culture of Sweden than in the comparatively individualistic and autocratic culture of Britain, particularly at workplace (micro) level. However, when pressures such as economic recession and a banking crisis affected both British and Swedish banks, there was a remarkable similarity of response by British and Swedish managements at board level (macro), despite the existence of co-determinational laws in Sweden. Employees' representative bodies had little say in the strategic policies created and implemented in response to the crisis. Although consultation did take place it was within minimum legal requirements in Sweden, and in the UK the situation was kept more or less at an informational level.

FIGURE 16.1
Adaptation of Poole's basic explanatory framework of participation

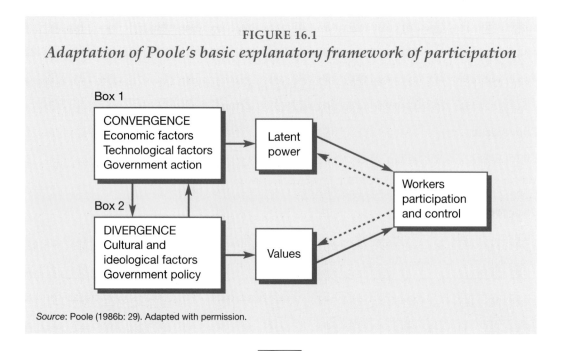

Source: Poole (1986b: 29). Adapted with permission.

It would seem that the nature of the capitalist organisation still creates contradictions between its avowed HRM aims of empowerment and commitment of the workforce and the difficulties of dealing with an organisation in crisis. Here it is obvious, as any economic determinist may well observe, that the exploitative nature of the capitalist system reverts to overt forms of control when under sufficient pressure to survive. However, the research reveals that the cultural and ideological influences have a greater effect at micro level where the workforce is estranged from strategic decision making. Thus it would appear that involving forms of HRM are more likely to be vigorously implemented at workplace (micro) level than at the strategic (macro) level of organisations. HRM is thus, consciously or subconsciously, seen by management as a means of gaining the commitment of employees without losing overall strategic control (Holden, 1996).

A model of comparative HRM

The Brewster and Bournois model

Brewster and Bournois, while acknowledging the difficulties of producing a comparative model of HRM, feel that it is possible to present a model for scrutiny, although they modestly call it a 'perspective'. This emerged out of the Price Waterhouse Cranfield Survey on international strategic HRM. As the work was European based they state that they initially present a model from a European viewpoint (Brewster and Bournois, 1991: 4).

They identify a major weakness of the Matching and Harvard models as being imbued with an American view of the employment relationship and question whether they can be applied to Europe with its different employment laws and practices. They refer to Guest's view that these notions of HRM are very much bound up with values encapsulated in the 'American dream' (Guest, 1990).

They claim that their 'tentative' model is rooted in the views of Kochan *et al.* (1986), who argue that government, market and labour–management relations are interwoven, but that the argument 'would have been all the stronger if they had drawn international comparisons' (Brewster and Bournois, 1991: 11). They then propose 'an outline. . .as a first step towards a European model of HRM. This places the process of human resource management firmly at the centre of concentric circles of influence and constraint' (1991: 12).

Three circles of constraint act on the HRM process: the organisation (size, structure and culture), sector, and national culture (including laws, labour markets, etc.). While the outcomes of HR strategy, in terms of cost-effective deployment of human resources, will take place at the organisational level, there is a considerable degree of influence from the outlying dimensions. In a sense the organisational strategic trajectories are shaped by the orbital pull of national and regional factors.

In recent work by Clark and Mallory (1996) the Brewster–Bournois model has been seen to have four main problems. First, can there possibly be a European model of HRM given the diversity of European cultures which commentators have placed within different cultural groupings, e.g. Scandinavian, Latin, Anglo, which have differing characteristics? Second, they argue that the amount of autonomy afforded to American organisations in terms of HRM policies may have been exaggerated in comparison to their European counterparts (Clark and Mallory, 1996: 20, 21). However, it can be equally

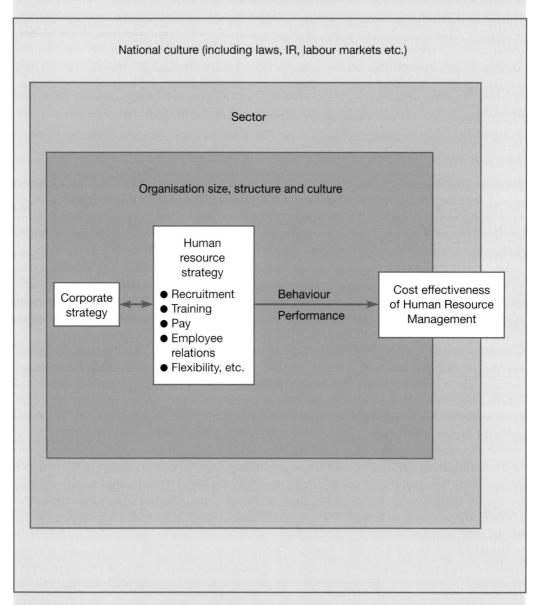

FIGURE 16.2
Brewster and Bournois' model for investigating human resource strategy

National culture (including laws, IR, labour markets etc.)

Sector

Organisation size, structure and culture

Human resource strategy

- Recruitment
- Training
- Pay
- Employee relations
- Flexibility, etc.

Corporate strategy

Behaviour

Performance

Cost effectiveness of Human Resource Management

Source: Brewster and Bournois (1991). Reprinted with permission of MCB University Press.

argued that national bargaining practices in many European countries place strong restraints on the HRM function compared with the USA. Third, they accuse Brewster and Bournois of being Anglo-American in that they take the parameters of the HRM debate purely from the literature of the UK and the USA without due regard to writings in related areas in European organisations. Again this is an argument which conveniently forgets that the origins of the HRM debate emanated from the USA and thence to the UK and Anglocentric countries such as Australia, New Zealand and Canada. Naturally, the starting point in building a framework would be in the arguments emanating from these countries, many of which are clearly being adopted in varying forms across Europe. Their fourth point is that the Brewster–Bournois model suffers from ethnocentrism. 'In conducting ethnocentric studies researchers such as Brewster genuinely fail to adequately specify the nature of national culture and its relevance to the phenomena under investigation. This arises since the central aim of ethnocentric research is replication' (Clark and Mallory, 1996: 23). Undoubtedly, the debate concerning models and frameworks of comparative HRM will continue.

INTERNATIONAL HRM

At the beginning of this chapter we made a distinction between comparative HRM and international HRM, in that the latter exists primarily in multinational corporations (MNCs) and the former has a wider contextual setting. This section will explore developments in international HRM.

MNCs are now recognising that internationally minded management teams with international skills and experience are becoming a significant competitive advantage. Increasingly, multinational corporations are expecting their senior executives to have had international experience. The implications for management training and development are enormous, a fact which nations and companies ignore at their peril (Pucik, 1984: 404).

In addition national, regional and global strategies on fundamental business issues, including human resourcing, mean that a global awareness of how changes in the world can affect business policy is becoming increasingly essential.

This includes awareness not only of macro-economic concerns and technological change, but of political changes and cultural issues. These influences bear strongly on human resource matters.

Multinational corporations (MNCs) have been increasingly aware of the growing necessity to have not only international business strategies but also international human resource strategies (Pucik, 1984). Such issues as global management succession planning, recruitment, selection and training for the expatriation process, recruitment from the indigenous population, awareness of labour and human resource practices in different countries and regions have focused attention on issues related to HRM.

Organisational approaches to international HRM

As we noted in the introduction to this chapter, there is a burgeoning literature on HRM in the multinational corporation (MNC). Much of this is concerned with HRM as perceived in a domestic context, with added international factors such as expatriation issues, and the relationship between the host country, the host country subsidiary and the parent company. Issues of control between the parent and host subsidiary companies become important, as well as concerns about management and human resource issues (Brewster, 1991). These issues thus become attached to the normal HRM concerns of recruitment, selection, reward, appraisal, training and development.

Four approaches have been identified to describe the way in which MNCs conduct their international HRM policies: ethnocentrism, polycentrism, geocentrism and regiocentrism (Dowling *et al.*, 1994).

The ethnocentric approach

This approach has all key positions in the host country subsidiary filled by parent company nationals. It therefore offers the most direct control by the parent company over the host country subsidiary, when there is a felt need to maintain good communication between the subsidiary and the MNC HQ. This is common in the early stages of internationalisation when the MNC is establishing a new business process or product in another country. It may also be used because there is a lack of qualified host country nationals.

The polycentric approach

This is directly opposite in approach to ethnocentricity and host country nationals are recruited to manage the subsidiary in their own country. This allows the MNC to take a lower profile in sensitive economic and political situations, and to avoid intercultural management difficulties.

The geocentric approach

This approach utilises the best people for the key jobs throughout the organisation, drawing on all parts of the world MNC operation. This enables the development of an international executive team.

The regiocentric approach

This is when an MNC divides its operations into geographic regions and moves staff within these regions, e.g. Europe, America, Asia Pacific rim. Some see such regionalisation as an effective way of developing management succession programmes.

An MNC may pass through several of these stages depending on its familiarity with the host country setting, the calibre and quality of its host country national staff, and the degree of direct control which it is felt necessary to impose on the subsidiary. These decisions are all bound up with wider economic, political and social concerns.

Expatriation

Three of the above approaches rely heavily on the use of expatriate managers. Research by Scullion (1992: 59) shows that the majority of the British and Irish MNCs in his study used expatriate managers, and the shortage of such managers was of considerable concern to them. These findings are similar to research into American MNCs (Dowling *et al.*, 1994).

A large part of the literature on expatriation is concerned with the failure of assignments and devising methods to prevent this. Much of this is focused on the difficulties of acculturation in terms of a 'culture clash' between expatriate managers, the host country environment and the host country employees (Torbiörn, 1982). A growing subsidiary, but nevertheless equally important, concern is the high failure rate of assignments associated with the unhappiness of the spouse and the family (Black and Stephens, 1989).

Considerable attention has therefore been given to recruitment, selection and training of potential expatriate managers and acculturation and acclimatisation issues (Dowling *et al.*, 1994). There is also a growing body of research on repatriation issues, particularly the re-acculturation of expatriates who have spent considerable time abroad (as much as 10 or 20 years) and the problems of 're-entry', not only into their home country culture, but into their HQ organisational culture (Black and Gregersen, 1991; Forster, 1994). Another area of growing interest is the experience of the international woman manager (Adler and Izraeli, 1994).

Other areas of international HRM are related to issues concerning the management and motivation of host country staff by expatriate managers, and issues of compensation and staff promotion. For example, a performance-related pay scheme which works in the USA (a highly individualistic culture) may well prove disastrous in Indonesia (a highly collectivist culture). Thus the way HRM policies are transferred and translated into subsidiary host country contexts can prove crucial to their success.

There is also a considerable interest in the HRM problems of joint ventures and a high failure rate has often been associated with ignorance of the national custom and culture of the companies involved, as well as failure to understand working practices and laws (Lorange, 1986).

International HRM models and frameworks

The growth of interest in international HRM issues has led observers to attempt to systematise its processes and influences in the organisational context. The first attempts to create a coherent framework were extensions of existing models rooted in Anglo-American experience. Thus Poole (1990), in the first edition of the *International Journal of Human Resource Management,* begins the process by examining the Harvard model for its suitability for international application. The Harvard model of Beer *et al.* (1984), as we have noted in Chapter 1, is rooted in the organisational view of HRM and is very much reflective of its North American origins. Nevertheless, Poole argues that the Harvard model lends itself readily to international HRM because of its pluralist nature, in that it accepts differing approaches and attitudes to the employment relationship (Poole, 1990).

We have already noted the difficulties of attempting to create a model of HRM even within the cultural context of one country, the United States, and the further complexities of attempting to apply such models to other national settings (see Chapter 1). This is also compounded by the variety of organisational and managerial styles which abound within different organisations in different sectors, depending on the products they make and the services which they perform, within the diversity of national and regional cultures. Not surprisingly, 'underlying theory which describes and explains variations in comparative human resource systems has been slow to develop' (Begin, 1992).

Poole's adaption of the Harvard model

Due to the fact that some of the key features of the Harvard model reflect its North American origin, Poole believes that three key modifications are necessary for it to be accommodated into a new framework of international HRM:

- the global development of business;
- the power of different stakeholders;
- the more specific links between corporate and human resource strategies (Poole, 1990: 3).

Taking his cue from writers on other aspects of the international employment relationship, including his own work on comparative industrial relations (Poole, 1986b), Poole emphasises the notion of strategic choice in international HRM. He sees the main areas of strategic human resource choice as:

- employee influence;
- human resource flow;
- reward systems;
- work systems.

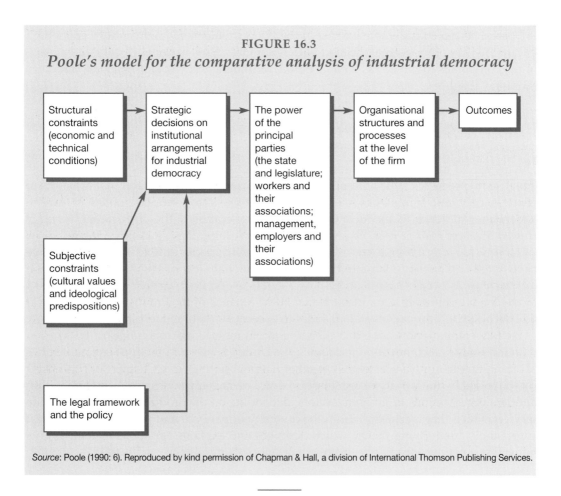

FIGURE 16.3
Poole's model for the comparative analysis of industrial democracy

Source: Poole (1990: 6). Reproduced by kind permission of Chapman & Hall, a division of International Thomson Publishing Services.

Employee influence

Long recognised as important in employee relations is the concept of empowerment of the workforce, and this has taken many forms in national and organisational cultures: for example quality circles, job enrichment, union representation, works councils, co-determination, producer cooperatives, self-management and many other forms. Not all of these forms of participation will fit into HRM frameworks, but 'most are (a) relevant and (b) are the subject of vibrant comparative research' (Poole, 1990: 5).

Human resource flow

This is divided into *inflow* (recruitment, assessment and selection, orientation and socialisation), *internal flow* (evaluation of performance and potential, internal placement, promotion and demotion, education and training) and *outflow* (termination, outplacement and retirement). Each of these policy levers is governed by the government legislation, educational institutions, unions, societal values and public policy of each national and regional context.

Reward systems

These would not only include in the framework the traditional methods of rewards such as pay, but intrinsic rewards such as employee satisfaction and motivation to work.

Work systems

The aim of all organisations is to gain high commitment from employees and the various ways of achieving this reflect work-related value systems which need to be recognised and integrated.

Apart from these additions and adaptations to the Harvard model, Poole emphasises the necessity of recognising the role of globalisation, power and strategy in the evolution of international HRM.

The transcendence of national boundaries by MNCs and their relation to supranational bodies such as the European Union are becoming crucially important in the HRM process. Intertwined are the power structures of such bodies which may conflict strategically and politically at company, country or regional level. The creation of strategies to take account of these possibilities becomes crucial in shaping the strategy of human resources. New technologies, the economies of large markets and market competition are other important factors to add to this strategic melting pot.

Poole sums up this process by quoting Adler and Ghadar (1989): 'The central issue of MNEs is not to identify the best international HRM policy per se, but rather to find the *best fit* between the firm's external environment, its overall strategy, and its HRM policy and implementation.'

Strategic international human resource management

Schuler *et al.* (1993: 717) have taken the process a step further by linking human resource management with organisational strategy into a framework of strategic international human resource management, which they hope will be useful to both academics and practitioners alike. They claim that a considerable amount of the research literature has concentrated on the problems of expatriation and that the 'next task for researchers is to examine the influence of exogenous and endogenous factors on strategic international HRM and to consider the consequences of these influences and interrelationships' (Schuler *et al.*, 1993: 753). By exogenous factors they mean those external to the MNC, e.g. industry characteristics and country/regional characteristics. By endogenous factors they mean those internal to the MNC, e.g. structure of international operations, headquarters international orientation, competitive strategy and the experience of managing international operations.

These two factors influence the MNC's strategic IHRM function's policies and practices, which in turn influence the MNC's competitiveness, efficiency, local responsiveness, flexibility and transfer of knowledge and skill. The model is highly complex and space dictates that we cannot do justice to it here, but it points a way forward to further refinements to future models and theorisation.

The impossibility of an international HRM model?

Pieper (1990) holds the view that no universal model of HRM is possible. He states three reasons for this view.

'First of all, HRM seems to be more a theoretical construct than an applied reality' (Pieper, 1990: 18). He supports this argument by quoting Gaugler, who claims that 'what companies generally practise is personnel management instead of HRM' (Pieper, 1990: 18). Gaugler claims that 'no company can do without personnel' (1988: 24) and that as a result they choose to ignore cultural or general environmental differences in pursuing their international human resource policies. This can only mean the practice of personnel, not HRM policies *per se*.

Second, Pieper states that 'both practical and theoretical concepts in the various nations vary widely' and that one of the main factors in these variances is the degree of state interference. In Western European countries state interference is very high in comparison to Japan and USA. In countries where state interference is high, personnel policies such as recruitment, pay, training and other aspects of the employment relationship are shaped by national legislation rather than the freedom of individual companies to act.

There are also differences in working practices in terms of collectivism and individualism. While Japan has less state interference than Western European nations, it has greater group identity in the work situation than does the United States, for example.

Third, culture has been exaggerated in its influence on HRM practices. Pieper concludes that what is most lacking is a clear theoretical framework with which to compare differing forms of human resource practices. This lack of adequate theory in turn prevents a proper methodology being developed with which to test the theory (Pieper, 1990: 20).

Problems of international research

The problems highlighted by Pieper concerning the lack of an adequate theory of HRM are made more complex when current 'evidence' is presented for examination. For one thing there is comparatively little research, and that which exists poses problems of interpretation. These include:

1 *Lack of data.* It is only relatively recently that many countries have begun to keep detailed records of their economic performance, e.g. GNP, growth rate, unemployment, trade balances, workforce statistics, etc.
2 Even though advanced industrial nations have been keeping such statistics for many years, there is still a *lack of comparative data,* e.g. trade union statistics, the measurement of GNP, unemployment, etc. can all be measured quite differently in different countries.
3 Statistics and similar data are highly political and open to *manipulation and bias,* in the way they are collected and the way they are presented for public consumption.
4 Another difficulty is to find a series of figures which do not have a *break of consistency.* For example, is it possible to compare unemployment statistics of the 1930s meaningfully with those of the 1980s?
5 International statistics are also noted for having *time lags* where one economy is behind in furnishing statistics. Thus one country may be giving data pertaining to a period as much as one year behind another country's data on the same subject.
6 *Language and meaning can be diverse.* Even though the same words are often used, these can cause confusion. Job titles vary widely from country to country. For example, the equivalent term for 'management' in France is *cadre,* although the meanings are not the same. In consequence, the English term 'manager' is increasingly being used in French organisations. Japanese corporations have no concept of management development and prefer what can only be described as 'capability development' and this includes all employees.
7 Some national economies emphasise *some aspects of economic performance* than others because these are the areas in which they are strong, e.g. agriculture, new technology, engineering, and this can skew comparisons.
8 *Cultural differences* can result in quite differing approaches to the same data. This can affect interpretation and meaning. This is explored in detail below.
9 *Generalisation is necessary but leads to dilution* to the point where the interpretation of the data can become meaningless. For example, regional differences could be ignored because they do not closely fit the national pattern.

Thus the area of comparative study is fraught with many pitfalls and dangers.

Surveys in international HRM

Comparative studies into international aspects of the employment relationship have been carried out for a number of years, but from an industrial relations or labour market perspective, and do not lend themselves easily to an HRM re-interpretation (Wilczynski, 1983; Bean, 1985; Poole, 1986; Bamber and Lansbury, 1987; Lane, 1989; Baglioni and Crouch, 1990).

There is a growing body of literature concerned with transnational and expatriate managers, as these are the people most likely to experience a variety of international settings, and greater attention has been given to their selection, training, development and career succession by a number of multinational companies (Brewster, 1991). Torbiörn (1982) has made a close examination of the adjustment process which expatriate managers experience in postings abroad and, as we have already noted, Hofstede (1980) and Laurent (1983) have examined managers' cultural differences. Kakabadse (1991) has made a wide quantitative and qualitative international survey of managerial top teams, which is continuing. But the concerns of these managers constitute a limited, though important, part of HRM-related subject areas.

Studies of comparative and contrasting aspects of personnel management, management, management styles, international business and organisational behaviour have been undertaken, but these, in many ways, serve to illustrate the hybrid nature of the relatively new discipline of HRM. There have been a number of single national surveys of aspects of HRM (Brewster and Tyson, 1991; Tyson *et al.*, 1993), and various dual or multiple country qualitative studies and case studies, but there have been few internationally comparative quantitative surveys.

One such survey is the Price Waterhouse Cranfield Survey on strategic human resource management. This undertook to examine HRM practices in five countries (France, Germany, Spain, Sweden and the UK) in 1989–90 and ten countries (the original five plus Denmark, Italy, the Netherlands, Norway and Switzerland) in 1990–91. The methodology of the survey confronted the research team with many problems and as such the results have to be handled with care. For example, creating a questionnaire which would be completely compatible in all national employment settings posed enormous difficulties. Meanings of words change in context and in translation. For example, in France three general staff categories are used:

> Cadres, referring to managers and some professional employees, ETAM who are administrative, technical and advisory staff and ouvriers or operatives. These are not only the customary definitions but are also defined in law. There is little point therefore in trying to force French personnel managers into the customary British fourfold division of: 'management'; 'professional/ technical'; 'clerical', and 'manual'. (Brewster *et al.*, 1991)

Meanings of work typologies alluded to earlier in this chapter also presented problems of interpretation. Another restricting factor was that the survey only dealt with organisations in European countries, although a number were owned by American, Japanese and other non-European based companies.

The survey questionnaire was also directed at personnel managers, and therefore responses could well be flavoured with their interests and biases. Despite these and other methodological problems, observable trends were in evidence. Strategic HRM, as we have noted in Chapter 1, is concerned with the view that the creation of HRM policy is aligned to, and is an important part of, the business strategy. In companies employing over 200 people the survey revealed that it would seem that the HRM function is becoming a more important part of organisations, indicated by the high perecentages of HRM managers or their equivalents having places on the board of directors.

TABLE 16.6
Head of human resource function on main board of directors
or equivalent (% of organisations)

CH	D	DK	E	F	I	N	NL	S	UK
58	18*	53	80	83	18	67	44	87	47

Note: CH=Switzerland; D=Germany; DK=Denmark; E=Spain; F=France; I=Italy; N=Norway; S=Sweden; UK=United Kingdom.

Source: Brewster and Bournois (1991). Reprinted with permission of MCB University Press.

Of course, having a place on the board does not mean that HRM managers necessarily have an influence on the business strategy, and it is well accepted that cabals of powerful managers often create influential policy outside the board, and the board becomes a rubber-stamping body for such preconceived policies. There is also limited evidence that strong connections between HRM and business strategy exist on a widespread basis. In order to try to ascertain the extent of influence of HRM managers, they were also asked how much involvement they had in developing corporate strategy.

TABLE 16.7
HR involvement in the development of corporate
strategy (% of organisations)

	CH	D	DK	E	F	I	N	NL	S	UK
From the outset	48	55	42	46	50	32	54	48	59	43
Consultative	20	19	30	21	22	23	24	31	28	27
Implementation	6	6	9	8	12	17	6	8	4	8
Not consulted	14	8	4	2	2	3	4	3	5	7
Don't know/missing	12	13	15	13	13	25	11	12	6	15

Note: CH=Switzerland; D=Germany; DK=Denmark; E=Spain; F=France; I=Italy; N=Norway; S=Sweden; UK=United Kingdom.

Source: Brewster and Bournois (1991). Reprinted with permission of MCB University Press.

We can see a drop, significant in some cases, in the figures between Table 16.6 and the first line of Table 16.7, which indicates varying degrees of involvement of HRM managers in the creation of corporate strategy. Nevertheless, involvement from the outset for one-third to one-half of all organisations in the survey would seem to be impressive, particularly Sweden, Norway and Germany. Once again, these figures are only indicators and do not reveal how such policy formulation happens, or the degree of influence of HRM managers in this process.

The survey also revealed that the Scandinavian countries (Denmark, Norway, Sweden) had the highest percentage of organisations (over 60%) which had written personnel or HR strategies, and Netherlands and Switzerland had over 50%, while the rest, including the UK, had less than 50%. Of those which had a personnel/HR strategy, only half to three-quarters translated these into work programmes and 'this raises a substantial question mark over the extent of strategic human resource management in Europe' (Price Waterhouse Cranfield Project, 1991: 8).

The survey, however, confirmed a number of trends, including the continuing devolution of some aspects of HRM to line managers, particularly in recruitment and selection. Training is also tending to be devolved much more, albeit with consultation from the HR function. Industrial relations, however, remains typically within the personnel department's purview, which clearly indicates some of the differences between US organisational autonomy and the more centralised and coordinated European systems of collective bargaining. This, of course, is reflected in pay bargaining, which, while indicating a drop at national level in Britain and France, still remains relatively stong in these countries, and very strong in the rest of the survey countries, particularly Scandinavia (Brewster and Bournois, 1991; Price Waterhouse Cranfield Survey Report, 1991). Trade union strength, while showing a relative decline in some countries, still retains a strong influence, and even low density figures in France and Spain belie the considerable political power which the trade union movement can exert in these countries (Estevill and de la Hoz, 1990; Segrestin, 1990).

As we have noted in Chapter 14, employee communication is one of the central tenets of HRM and the survey indicates a significant increase in its use; but in many European countries it is supported by legal requirements (and EC directives) to consult and inform the workforce, another element which does sit well with US views of HRM (Brewster and Bournois, 1991: 9).

Atypical working patterns have seen increases in recent years, and have significance for organisations which practise 'soft' HRM, associated with unitarist concepts aligned to internal labour markets, and 'hard' HRM associated with the core–peripheral external labour-market model. Evidence from the survey shows a distinct increase in part-time working, and to a lesser degree fixed-term contracts. 'There is some evidence from the survey that Germany approximates more to the internal labour market model and Britain to the external' (Brewster and Bournois, 1991: 10). Aligned to these trends are the legal requirements of the Social Chapter, particularly for part-time workers; the present British government opposes these, underscoring the UK evidence on atypical working. 'Currently, however, there are indications here that support the view that European organisations are looking to create a more controlled external labour market for themselves' (Brewster and Bournois, 1991: 11).

The survey gives credence to the views of Guest, Poole and others that HRM trends in Europe must be contextualised against many different working practices (both internal and external to organisations), resting on different legal requirements and national assumptions, which contrast strongly with American HRM. Only further research will enable the development and refinement of both an international model and a European model, which begs the question whether HRM models can be universally applied in all contexts.

Another survey conducted by Towers Perrin and analysed by Sparrow *et al.* (1994) looked at 12 countries worldwide. They asked the question, do firms in different parts of the world practise HRM for competitive advantage differently? Data gathered from a questionnaire postal survey of chief executive officers and human resource managers revealed after analysis that there was convergence in the use of HRM for competitive advantage. The results included:

- changes in organisational culture to create greater empowerment and equality of employees and greater diversity in their roles;
- organisational restructuring to reduce the number of vertical layers (delayering) and increase employee flexibility;
- an increase in the number and variety of performance management policies;
- improvements in resourcing – acquiring personnel and training functions and developing them;
- improvements in communication and corporate responsibility.

There were divergences in the way that specific aspects such as culture, work structuring, performance management and resourcing were utilised, but these, they claimed, differed more in degree than in kind (Sparrow *et al.*, 1994: 295).

It would seem that the influence of HRM and management trends is beginning to have a global impact on organisations and that there is a degree of convergence of practices and approaches. Easterby-Smith *et al.* (1995), using a case study approach in conducting a comparative piece of research between Chinese and UK companies, also found a convergence of approaches. However, they associated this convergence with 'hard' HRM policies such as manpower planning, and they noted divergence in 'soft', culture-sensitive areas, bound up with motivational issues such as remuneration and reward.

The research findings in the above surveys would seem to suggest that the impact of managerial education, through international management programmes such as the MBA, and the increase in the worldwide popularity of management issues with an ever-increasing high profile in the media, is influencing a convergence of policy and practice in HRM. Equally, however, we must not be fooled into thinking that these practices are carried out in the same way in each country and organisational context. An awareness of the factors which influence our cultural perceptions of the employment relationship is equally important, and international managers ignore them at their peril.

SUMMARY

- This chapter examined the increasing importance of human resource management in an ever-changing competitive international environment and the growth of multinational corporations. An examination was undertaken of the distinctions between comparative HRM and international HRM, which saw international HRM located in multinational organisations, and comparative HRM being concerned about a much wider context of HRM.

- A number of major theories related to comparative HRM were explained. These included convergence theory, which poses the view that technological developments create homogeneous global work practices; Marxist theory, with its class-based view of the processes of work in capitalist organisations; cultural theory, which emphasises the differences in work practices influenced by cultural values; and the view of how work practices in different national settings are influenced by institutional aspects such as legal and political structures, which are in turn affected by social factors. An attempted synthesis was made of these convergent and divergent approaches to comparative HRM.

● Comparative and international HRM models by Poole, Brewster and Bournois, and Schuler *et al.* were outlined. Pieper, it was noted, views such attempts as futile, because he sees HRM as more of a theoretical construct and not rooted in reality and considers that practices vary too widely between nations to construct a credible international (and indeed comparative) HRM model.

● Problems of international research were outlined which often hinge on differing practices in collecting data and varying interpretations based on cultural and linguistic influences.

● A review of the quantitative survey conducted under the banner of the Price Waterhouse Cranfield Project revealed the similarity in a number of trends across Europe, such as moves towards atypical working; decentralisation and devolvement of HRM practices, particularly to line managers; increases in direct communication channels to the workforce; the decline in influence of trade unions; and the increasing decentralisation of pay bargaining. The survey researchers warn, however, that practices vary widely and are still heavily influenced by national employee relations laws and practices.

● The Towers Perrin Survey, analysed by Sparrow *et al.*, concluded that there was a convergence in the use of HRM for competitive advantage.

ACTIVITY

Divide the class into groups of two. Ask one group to draw up a list of US characteristics or cultural traits. Ask the other group to draw up a list of British characteristics or cultural traits. On a flipchart or board write a comparative list of US and British traits from the feedback from the groups.

EXERCISES

1 Pinpoint the traits which are similar and those which are different.

2 Choose three traits which are essentially British and three which are essentially US.

3 How could these traits affect styles of recruitment, selection, reward, and communication in organisations?

QUESTIONS

1 What kind of training programme would you devise to send an employee on an overseas assignment?

2 How can HRM help organisations compete on a national and a global scale?

3 What is the relationship of HRM to governmental and regional policy? Illustrate your answer with two contrasting countries, e.g. Britain and Sweden, or USA and Germany.

4 How could national traits and characteristics affect methods of recruitment, selection, reward and communication in organisations in different countries?

5 What evidence is there that HRM practice and policy are converging in the global context?

6 Answer the following questions about work-related values in Germany, France and Italy. At the end of these questions is a series of values which may help you.

GERMANY

a Germans prefer to keep to regulations at all costs even when it is practical to ignore them.

   True ☐   False ☐

b German employees look for strong decisive leadership in their bosses.

   True ☐   False ☐

c German organisations are very 'change' oriented.

   True ☐   False ☐

d Technical competence is more highly respected in a boss than is a forceful personality.

   True ☐   False ☐

e In meetings in a German organisation debate and criticism from junior employees are encouraged.

   True ☐   False ☐

f When speaking at a German business conference it is acceptable to make jokes and introduce humorous stories.

   True ☐   False ☐

FRANCE

a French political and organisational systems tend to be:

   ● regional   ☐
   ● decentralised   ☐
   ● centralised   ☐

b The French director of a company (PDG) is expected to:

   ● consult all employees at all levels in the organisation   ☐
   ● take only the views of senior management into account   ☐
   ● have at his/her fingertips precise answers to all questions   ☐

c A French boss will always share problems with subordinates:

   True ☐   False ☐

d French employees respect a leader who has:

- a strong personality ☐
- is competent at his/her job ☐

e French employees prefer:

- to wait for the group concensus before taking action ☐
- take a personal initiative in a spirit of competition ☐

f It is more important to demonstrate practicality than logic in a French organisation:

True ☐   False ☐

ITALY

a It is more important to have the right qualities for the job than to have good personal connections in employee selection in Italy:

True ☐   False ☐

b Directors favour technical competence in their managers more than personal qualities:

True ☐   False ☐

c Italian management style is:

- democratic ☐
- friendly and open but hierarchical ☐
- authoritarian ☐

d Employees only obey their boss if:

- they feel a personal commitment to him/her ☐
- if they are told authoritatively to carry out orders ☐
- if they are given precise instructions ☐

e Decisions taken at formal meetings:

- are carried out with speed and efficiency ☐
- are carried out after some delay ☐
- may never be carried out at all ☐

f Italians have a high tolerance of inefficiency and genuine mistakes, but a low tolerance of arrogance and rudeness:

True ☐   False ☐

GERMAN WORK-RELATED VALUES

- Rules and regulations oriented.
- Strong decisive leadership.
- Conservative towards organisational change.
- Systematically pragmatic.
- Formal in work relationships.

FRENCH WORK-RELATED VALUES

- Centralised.
- Autocratic.
- Critical.
- Competitive.
- Intellectual – abstract theory, logical analysis.
- Competent, knowledgeable.

ITALIAN WORK-RELATED VALUES

- Personal ties, family (and patronage) important.
- Personal relations very important in business/management.
- Authoritarian – but informal based on personal relations.
- Employer–employee relationships based on personal criteria.
- Meetings are sounding boards to gain consensus, rather than decision-making bodies.

REFERENCES AND FURTHER READING

Adler, N. (1986) *International Dimensions of Organisational Behaviour.* Boston, Mass.: Kent Publishing.

Adler, N.J. and Ghadar, F. (1989) 'International business research for the twenty first century: Canada's new research agenda', in Rugman, A. (ed.) *Research in Global Strategic Management: A Canadian Perspective,* Vol. 1. Greenwich, Conn.: JAI Press.

Adler, N. and Izraeli, D. (1994) *Competitive Frontiers: Women Managers in a Global Economy.* Cambridge, Mass.: Blackwell.

Altman, Y. (1992) 'Towards a cultural typology of European work values and work organisation', *Innovation in Social Science Research*, Vol. 5, No. 1, pp. 35–44.

Baglioni, G. and Crouch, C. (1990) *European Industrial Relations.* London: Sage.

Bamber, G. and Lansbury, R. (1993) *International and Comparative Industrial Relations: A Study of Developed Markets.* Sydney: Allen & Unwin.

Bartlett, C. and Ghoshal, S. (1989) *Managing Across Borders: The Transnational Solution.* London: Hutchinson.

Bean, R. (1994) *Comparative Industrial Relations: An Introduction to Cross-National Perspectives.* London: Routledge.

Beer, M., Spector, B., Lawrence P.R., Quinn Mills, D. and Walton, R.E. (1984) *Managing Human Assets.* New York: Free Press.

Begin, J. (1992) 'Comparative human resource management: a systems perspective', *International Journal of Human Resource Management*, Vol. 3, No. 3, December.

Black, J. and Stephens, G. (1989) 'The influence of the spouse on American expatriate adjustment and intent to stay in Pacific rim overseas assignments', *Journal of Management*, Vol. 15, No. 4, pp. 529–544.

Black, S. and Gregersen, H. (1991) 'When Yankee goes home: factors related to expatriate and spouse repatriation adjustment', *Journal of International Business Studies,* Vol. 22, No. 4, pp. 671–694.

Bond, M. and Hofstede, G. (1990) 'The cash value of Confucian values', in Clegg, S. and Gordon Redding, S. (eds) *Capitalism in Contrasting Cultures.* Berlin: Walter de Gruyter.

Boxall, P. (1995) 'Building the theory of comparative HRM', *Human Resource Management Journal*, Vol. 5, No. 5, Autumn, pp. 5–17.

Braverman, H. (1974) *Labour and Monopoly Capitalism*. New York: Monthly Review Press.

Brewster, C. (1991) *The Management of Expatriates*. London: Kogan Page.

Brewster, C. and Bournois, F. (1991) 'Human resource management: a European perspective', *Personnel Review*, Vol. 20, No. 6, pp. 4–13.

Brewster, C. and Hegewisch, A. (eds) (1994) *Policy and Practice in European Human Resource Management: The Price Waterhouse Cranfield Survey*. London: Routledge.

Brewster, C. and Tyson, S. (eds) (1991) *International Comparisons in Human Resource Management*. London: Pitman.

Brewster, C., Hegewisch, A. and Lockhart, T. (1991) 'Researching human resource management: methodology of the Price Waterhouse Cranfield Project on European trends', *Personnel Review*, Vol. 20, No. 6, pp. 36–40.

Brewster, C., Lundmark, A. and Holden, L. (1993) *A Different Tack: An Analysis of British and Swedish Management Styles*. Lund: Studentlitteratur.

Briscoe, D. (1995) *International Human Resource Management*. Englewood Cliffs, NJ: Prentice Hall.

Bronner, S. (1994) *Of Critical Theory and its Theorists*. Oxford: Blackwell.

Calori, R. and De Woot, P. (1994) *A European Management Model: Beyond Diversity*. Hemel Hempstead: Prentice Hall.

Clark, T. and Mallory, G. (1996) 'The cultural relativity of human resourse management: Is there a universal model?', in Clark, T. (ed) *European Human Resource Management*. Oxford: Blackwell.

Deresky, H. (1994) *International Management: Managing Across Borders and Cultures*. New York: HarperCollins.

Dore, R. (1973) *British Factory – Japanese Factory. The Origins of National Diversity in Industrial Relations*. London: Allen & Unwin (quoted in Lane, 1989: 32).

Dowling, P., Schuler, R. and Welch, D. (1994) *International Dimensions of Human Resource Management*. Belmont: Wadsworth.

Easterby-Smith, M., Malina, D. and Yuan, L. (1995) 'How culture sensitive is HRM? A comparative analysis of practice in Chinese and UK companies', *International Journal of Human Resource Management*, Vol. 6, No. 1, February, pp. 31–59.

Estevill, J. and de la Hoz, J. (1990) 'Transition and crisis: the complexity of Spanish industrial relations', in Baglioni, G. and Crouch, C. (eds) *European Industrial Relations*. London: Sage.

Fatehi, K. (1996) *International Management: A Cross Cultural Approach*. Englewood Cliffs, NJ: Prentice Hall.

Ferner, A. and Hyman, R (eds) (1992) *Industrial Relations in the New Europe*. Oxford: Blackwell.

Ferraro, G. (1994) *The Cultural Dimensions of International Business*. Englewood Cliffs, NJ: Prentice-Hall.

Forster, N. (1994) 'The forgotton employees? The experience of expatriate staff returning to the UK', *International Journal of Human Resource Management*, Vol. 5, No. 2, May, pp. 405–426.

Gatley, S., Lessem, R. and Altman, Y. (1996) *Comparative Management: A Transcultural Odyssey*. London: McGraw-Hill.

Gaugler, E. (1988) 'HR management: an international comparison', *Personnel*, August, pp. 24–30.

Ghauri, P. and Prasad, S. (eds) (1995) *International Management: A Reader*. London: Dryden Press.

Gospel, H. (1992) *Markets, Firms and the Management of Labour in Modern Britain.* Cambridge: Cambridge University Press.

Guest, D. (1990) 'Human resource management and the American dream', *Journal of Management Studies*, Vol. 27, No. 4, pp. 377–397.

Habermas, J. (1983) *The Theory of Communicative Action,* 2 Vols. Boston: Beacon.

Habermas, J. (1987) *The Philosophical Discourse of Modernity.* Cambridge: Polity Press.

Hall, E. (1976) *Beyond Culture.* New York: Anchor Press/Doubleday.

Hall, E. and Hall, M. (1990) *Understanding Cultural Differences.* Yarmouth: Intercultural Press.

Halperin, R. (1988) *Economies Across Cultures: Towards a Comparative Science of Economy.* Basingstoke: Macmillan.

Hampden-Turner, C. and Trompenaars, F. (1994) *The Seven Cultures of Capitalism.* London: Piatkus.

Harzing, A.-W. and Van Ruysseveldt, J. (eds) (1995) *International Human Resource Management.* London: Sage.

Hegewisch, A. and Brewster, C. (eds) (1993) *European Developments in Human Resource Management.* London: Kogan Page.

Hendry, C. (1994) *Human Resource Strategies for International Growth.* London: Routledge.

Hodgetts, R. and Luthans, F. (1991) *International Management.* New York: McGraw-Hill.

Hofstede, G. (1980) *Culture's Consequences: International Differences in Work Related Values.* Beverly Hills, CA: Sage.

Hofstede, G. (1991) *Cultures and Organisations: Software of the Mind.* London: McGraw-Hill.

Holden, L. (1996) 'HRM and employee involvement in Britain and Sweden: a comparative study', *International Journal of Human Resource Management*, Vol. 7, No. 1, February, pp. 59–81.

Hollinshead, G. and Leat, M. (1995) *Human Resource Management: An International and Comparative Perspective.* London: Pitman.

Hyman, R. and Ferner, A. (eds) (1994) *New Frontiers in European Industrial Relations.* Oxford: Blackwell.

Jackson, T. (1995) *Cross-Cultural Management.* Oxford: Butterworth-Heinemann.

Kakabadse, A. (1991) *The Wealth Creators.* London: Kogan Page.

Kerr, C., Dunlop, J.T., Harbison, F. and Myers, C.A. (1960) *Industrialism and Industrial Man.* Cambridge, Mass.: Harvard University Press.

Kerr, C., Dunlop, J.T., Harbison, F. and Myers, C.A. (1971) 'Postscript to industrialism and industrial man', *International Labour Review*, Vol. 103.

Kirkbride, P. (ed.) (1994) *Human Resource Management in Europe: Perspectives for the 1990s.* London: Routledge.

Kochan, T., Katz, H. and McKersie, R. (1986) *The Transformation of American Industrial Relations.* Cambridge, Mass.: Harvard Business School Press.

Kolakowski, L. (1978) *Main Currents of Marxism: Volume 3 – The Breakdown.* Oxford: Oxford University Press.

Kroeber, A.L. and Kluckhohn, C. (1952) 'Culture: a critical review of concepts and definitions', *Peabody Museum Papers*, Vol. 47, No. 1 (Cambridge, Mass.: Harvard University).

Lane, C. (1989) *Management and Labour in Europe.* Aldershot: Edward Elgar.

Laurent, A. (1983) 'The cultural diversity of Western conceptions of management', *International Studies of Management and Organisation*, Vol. XIII, No. 1–2, Spring–Summer, pp. 75–96.

Leeds, C., Kirkbride, P. and Durcan, J. (1994) 'The cultural context of Europe: a tentative mapping', in Kirkbride, P. (ed.) *Human Resource Management in Europe: Perspectives for the 1990s.* London: Routledge, pp. 11–27.

Lorange, P. (1986) 'Human resource management in multinational cooperative ventures', *Human Resource Management.* Vol. 25, No. 1.

Mueller, F. and Purcell, J. (1992) 'The Europeanisation of manufacturing and the decentralisation of bargaining: multinational management strategies in the European automobile industry', *International Journal of Human Resource Management,* Vol. 3, No. 1, May, pp. 15–34.

Nelson, C. and Grossberg, L. (1988) *Marxism and the Interpretation of Culture.* Basingstoke: Macmillan.

Pieper, R. (ed.) (1990) *Human Resource Management: An International Comparison.* New York: Walter de Gruyter.

Poole, M. (1986a) *Industrial Relations: Origins and Patterns of National Diversity.* London: Routledge & Kegan Paul.

Poole, M. (1986b) *Towards a New Industrial Democracy: Workers' Participation in Industry.* London: Routledge & Kegan Paul.

Poole, M. (1990) 'Editorial: human resource management in an international perspective', *International Journal of Human Resource Management,* Vol. 1, No. 1, June, pp. 1–15.

Porter, M. (1990) *The Competitive Advantage of Nations.* London: Macmillan.

Price Waterhouse Cranfield Project (1991) *Report on International Strategic Human Resource Management.* Cranfield: Cranfield School of Management.

Pucik, V. (1984) 'The international management of human resources', in Fombrun, C.J., Tichy, N.M. and Devanna, M.A. (eds) *Strategic Human Resource Management.* New York: John Wiley.

Pucik, V., Tichy, N. and Barnett, C. (eds) (1992) *Globalising Management: Creating and Leading the Competitive Organisation.* New York: John Wiley.

Schuler, R., Dowling, P. and De Cieri, H. (1993) 'An integrative framework of strategic international human resource management', *International Journal of Human Resource Management,* Vol. 4, No. 4, December, pp. 717–764.

Scullion, H. (1992) 'Strategic recruitment and development of the "international manager": some European considerations', *Human Resource Management Journal,* Vol. 3, No. 1, Autumn, pp. 57–69.

Segrestin, D. (1990) 'Recent changes in France', in Baglioni, G. and Crouch, C. (eds) *European Industrial Relations.* London: Sage.

Shenkar, O. (ed.) (1995) *Global Perspectives of Human Resource Management.* Englewood Cliffs, NJ: Prentice Hall.

Sparrow, P. and Hiltrop, J.-M. (1994) *European Human Resource Management in Transition.* Hemel Hempstead: Prentice Hall.

Sparrow, P., Schuler, R. and Jackson, S. (1994) 'Convergence or divergence: human resource practices and policies for competitive advantage worldwide', *International Journal of Human Resource Management,* Vol. 5, No. 2, May, pp. 267–299.

Tayeb, M. (1996) *The Management of a Multicultural Workforce.* Chichester: John Wiley.

Torbiörn, I. (1982) *Living Abroad: Personal Adjustment and Personal Policy in the Overseas Setting.* Chichester: John Wiley.

Torrington, D. (1994) *International Human Resource Management: Think Globally, Act Locally.* Hemel Hempstead: Prentice Hall.

Trompenaars, F. (1993) *Riding the Waves of Culture.* London: Nicholas Brealey.

Tyson, S., Lawrence, P., Poirson, P., Manzolini, L. and Soler, C. (1993) *Human Resource Management in Europe: Strategic Issues and Cases.* London: Kogan Page.

Van Ruysseveldt, J., Huiskamp, R and Van Hoof, J. (eds) (1995) *Comparative Industrial and Employment Relations.* London: Sage.

Wilczynski, J. (1983) *Comparative Industrial Relations.* London: Macmillan.

Wuthnow, R., Davison Hunter, J., Bergeson, A. and Kurzweil, E. (1984) *Cultural Analysis: The work of Peter L. Berger, Mary Douglas, Michel Foucault and Jurgen Habermas.* London: Routledge & Kegan Paul.

HUMAN RESOURCE
MANAGEMENT AND EUROPE

Len Holden

BACKGROUND TO EUROPE

The concept of a unified Europe is not a new one. It stretches back to the Roman Empire, the Holy Roman Empire which emerged from its collapse and the attempts by Napoleon and Hitler to impose a unified authority by force. Until the Reformation in the sixteenth century the single most powerful agent of unity was the Catholic church, using its doctrines, Latin, its language of communication, and a vast bureaucracy to impose its authority. Even then there were many concepts of Europe and 'Christendom', as Europe was known until relatively recent times, was divided between the Eastern Orthodox churches based in the Balkans and Russia, and the Catholic and Protestant churches represented in what might loosely be termed the 'West'.

Most of the nation states of Europe, as we know them, have emerged over the past 150 years and many of them have experienced considerable changes in borders and ethnic composition since then. This process has continued recently with the break-up of the former Soviet Union and its satellite states, and of the former Yugoslavia.

Thus the concept of a unified Europe begs many questions, which must fundamentally include an answer to 'What is Europe? and 'How unified can it be?'. The latter question has already caused considerable controversy concerning the ratification of the Maastricht Treaty, and the former over whether Eastern European states, as well as Turkey, should be included in the European Union. Answers to these basic but essential questions have a fundamental influence on economic, political and social policy.

The European Union: origins and development

It is neither possible nor appropriate to cover the historical origins of the EU in detail in this book, but a brief outline of these events would be of value to students new to the subject in helping them contextualise some of the factors which influence European human resource issues.

The European Union arose out of the wreckage of the Second World War. There was a consensus amongst most politicians that the devastation wreaked upon Europe should never be repeated, and that cooperation between nations was one important way of preventing conflict. Partly towards this end and to help war-torn economies revive, the European Coal and Steel Community (ECSC) was set up between France, West Germany, Belgium, the Netherlands, Italy and Luxembourg in 1952. The general aim was to dismantle tariff barriers between these nations, affording a single market for iron, steel and coal. Robert Schuman, one of its prime architects, anticipated that one day the ECSC would broaden into a movement towards economic and even political unity.

Cooperation among Western European states was also rooted in the desire to create a bulwark against the Soviet Union, a perceived threat heightened by the Cold War. From this arose NATO and the European Defence Community (EDC), which incorporated West Germany.

The success of these early attempts at cooperation naturally led to the desire to forge stronger links, and after a number of preliminary reports and meetings the six ECSC countries formed the European Economic Community (EEC) under the Treaty of Rome,

1957. The aim of the Treaty of Rome was to create a 'common market' amongst its members, although it was accepted at this time that political union was a long way off. The Treaty of Rome also established the European Atomic Energy Community (EURATOM), which still influences many aspects of EU legislation.

Britain at first refused to join the EEC, having to come to terms with its role as an ex-colonial power which still had strong ties within the British Commonwealth. The success of the EEC and the relative economic and political decline of Britain in the 1960s and 1970s led to a re-examination of the country's future role within Europe. Following two vetoes from President de Gaulle of France, Britain finally became a member of the European Community (EC) in 1973 along with Denmark and the Republic of Ireland. In 1981 Greece joined and in 1986 Spain and Portugal. In 1995 Sweden, Austria and Finland were granted membership of what by then had become the European Union, although after a referendum Norway decided to stay out of the Union. At present six more countries have applied for membership, including Turkey, Cyprus, Malta, Switzerland, Poland and Hungary. Such an expansion will constitute a much more representative bloc of European states.

A chronology of the EU

1952   European Coal and Steel Community founded (Belgium, France, Italy, Luxembourg, the Netherlands and West Germany)

1957   Treaty of Rome sets up the European Economic Community (EEC) or the 'Common Market' (Belgium, France, Italy, Luxembourg, the Netherlands and West Germany)

1957   Treaty of Paris set up European Atomic Energy Community (EURATOM) (Belgium, France, Italy, Luxembourg, the Netherlands and West Germany)

1958   EEC and EURATOM come into being

1972   Paris Summit gives commitment to action in social field

1973   UK, Denmark and Republic of Ireland join EC

1974   Commission's 'Action Programme' comes into being

1981   Greece joins the EC

1986   Spain and Portugal join the EC

1987   The Single European Act passed

1989   The Social Charter ratified by 11 states except the UK

1991   Austria, Norway and Sweden apply to join the EC

1992   Hungary, Poland and the former Czechoslovakia express a desire to join

1992   Maastricht Treaty signed but UK insists on separate protocol for the Social Charter/Chapter, and the European Community is renamed the European Union (EU)

1995   Austria, Finland and Sweden join the EU

The institutions of the EU

There are five main institutions which govern the European Union:

- the European Council
- the Council of Ministers (based in Brussels)
- the Commission (based in Brussels)
- the Court of Justice (sits in Luxembourg)
- the Parliament (based in Strasbourg).

The European Council

The European Council consists of the heads of each member state, who usually meet twice a year to give overall direction to the EU's programme.

The Council of Ministers

The Council of Ministers is made up of one representative, usually a government minister or highly placed politician, from each member state and is presided over in turn by each state for a six-month period. Thus, for example, from July to December 1995 it was Spain, from January to June 1996 Italy and from July to December 1996 Ireland.

The Council is the EU's main decision-making body and acts on proposals by the Commission. Decisions are taken on a unanimous vote, although majority voting was introduced via the Single European Act for some issues.

The Commission

The Commission is composed of 20 members or commissioners and is made up of two representatives from the larger countries (France, Germany, Italy, Spain, the UK) and one from the rest. Commissioners are appointed for four years and act only in the interest of the Union. The current Commission President is Jacques Santer, who took over in 1995 from Jacques Delors who had held the position since 1985. The President serves for a four-year period on a renewable basis.

The Commission proposes and executes EU policies and acts as a mediator between the 15 governments of the Union. It also has the power to bring legal action via the Court of Justice against member states which it deems have violated EU laws. It is ultimately subservient to the Council of Ministers.

The European Court of Justice

The European Court of Justice comprises one judge from each member state assisted by advocates-general, who rule on questions of community law. Judgements are by majority vote and directly binding on all parties. This is the final court of appeal for member states, and is often used by individuals, groups and organisations to challenge national laws or rulings which are perceived as being in contravention of EU law.

The European Parliament

The European Parliament has 626 members, 99 from Germany, 87 each from France, Italy and the UK, 64 from Spain, 31 from the Netherlands, 25 each from Belgium, Greece and Portugal, 22 from Sweden, 21 from Austria, 16 each from Denmark and Finland, 15 from Ireland and 6 from Luxembourg.

Members of the European Parliament (MEPs) are directly elected by citizens of their countries for a five-year term. The last election took place in 1994 and the next will be June 1999.

The European Parliament does not have the same power as the Council of Ministers or a national Parliament, but very few texts can be adopted without its opinion being sought. It also has the power to dismiss the Commission on a two-thirds majority vote.

Other institutions concerned with human resource issues

Economic and Social Committee

This is an advisory body which is consulted by the Commission and Council. It is made up of representatives of employers, trade unions, and other interests including consumers, small firms and professions. It provides detailed information and advice in the following areas:

- agriculture
- transport and communications
- energy and nuclear questions
- economic and financial questions
- industry
- commerce, crafts and services
- social questions
- external relations
- regional development
- protection of the environment, public health and consumer affairs

Val Duchesse meetings

This is the name given to a series of meetings initiated in 1985 at the Val Duchesse Château in Belgium. The meetings were between the European Trade Union Confederation (ETUC), the European Centre for Public Enterprise (CEEP) and the Union of Industrial and Employers Confederations of Europe (UNICE). These talks between employer and employee representatives of member countries concentrated on examining macro-economic policy and employment, and new technology and work. From these talks two committees were formed which dealt with training and labour-market issues. In recent years there has been concentration on examining flexibility and adaptability of the workforce.

These meetings also led to the creation of the 'European Framework Agreement' which proposed that the Commission would consult the social partners at European level before putting proposals forward. This could have important ramifications in creating controversy between those states which have relied on negotiations at the workplace (Denmark, Ireland and the UK) and those that rely on centralised regulation in their industrial relations systems (Lockhart and Brewster, 1992).

European Foundation for the Improvement of Living and Working Conditions

This is a body set up primarily for investigating and disseminating information on living and working conditions in the EU, including health and safety, environmental protection, industrial relations, restructuring working life and assessing new technologies and the future of work. It is based in Dublin.

The Legislative process

In simplistic terms, legal proposals emanate from the Commission and are sent for consideration to the Council, which seeks approval from the Parliament and advice and information from the Economic and Social Committee. The Commission then has the right to amend the proposal in the light of these opinions and return it to the Council for acceptance or rejection.

There are four types of EU legislation:

- *Regulations* are binding on all member states without any further process of confirmation by national Parliaments.
- *Directives* are binding on all member states but leave to national discretion how these laws are to be complied with. Target dates are also set for implementation.
- *Decisions* are binding on those to whom they are addressed (member states, enterprises, individuals).
- *Recommendations and opinions*, which are not binding. These are not laws as such but may help encourage particular responses. 'The Commission places emphasis on using such Recommendations to achieve 'convergence', i.e. to move towards harmonisation of policy and practice' (Hughes, 1991).

Regulations are generally used when an identical law is required across the Union, often where none has existed in member states previously. Directives are more appropriate as a mechanism where the method of implementation may vary at national level and has to be related to existing laws. This incorporates the principle of 'subsidiarity', i.e. that legislation should be passed by the lowest level of government competent to enact it.

THE SOCIAL CHARTER

In terms of human resource management the Social Charter is the key indicator of EU legislation, as its proposals will have considerable impact on employee relations at international, national and local levels.

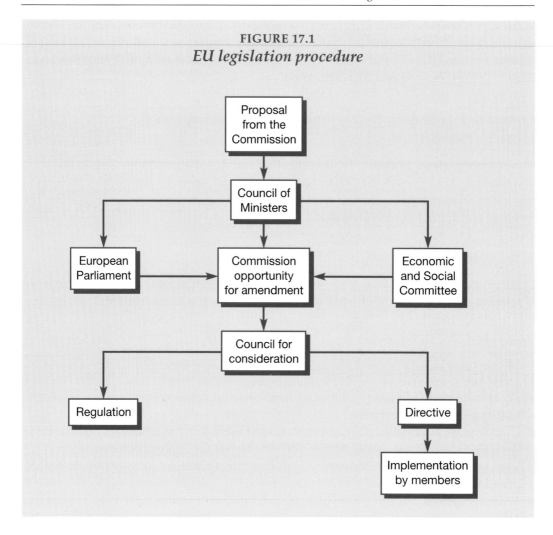

FIGURE 17.1

EU legislation procedure

Origins and development

Much of the Social Charter is an amalgam and extension of the articles embodied in the various treaties which jointly created the EU, i.e. the Treaty of Paris which set up the ECSC in 1952 and the Treaties of Rome and Paris which created the EEC and EURATOM respectively in 1957.

At the Paris summit in 1972 it was agreed that as much importance should be attached to the reduction in disparities of living conditions and improving the quality of life within the Union as to issues of economic and monetary union. This resulted in the creation of an 'Action Programme' in 1974 which became committed to the promotion of employment, upward harmonisation of living conditions, and the increased involvement of management and labour in the decision-making processes of organisations. This was to be achieved by coordinating provisions in the treaties with new initiatives. A number of economic problems were besetting the community and the reaction by member states at the time was, at best, mixed. In this period of 'Eurosclerosis' and 'Europessimism', however, it can be argued that incremental agreements, particularly in areas such as equal opportunities, witnessed the foundation of what is still the most effective part of legislation embodied in the Social Charter (Lockhart and Brewster, 1992).

A revival of interest in the 'social dimension' occurred in the 1980s as a result of the debate over, and the subsequent agreement to, the creation of a Single European Market (SEM) under the Single European Act, 1987. The creation of a unified market across 12 European states would have deep implications for the labour market and employment relationships, and therefore under the influence of Jacques Delors, the President of the Commission (1985–95), it was proposed that policies which addressed employment relations issues should be created. In December 1989 the Social Charter was finally adopted by the Council of Ministers (with the exception of the UK) and a Social Action Programme set up to implement it.

The Social Charter provisions

The Social Charter states that:

> the completion of the internal market must offer improvements in the social field for workers of the European Community, especially in terms of freedom of movement, living and working conditions, health and safety at work, social protection education and training.
>
> Whereas, in order to ensure equal treatment, it is important to combat every form of discrimination, including discrimination on grounds of sex, colour, race, opinions and beliefs, and whereas in a spirit of solidarity it is important to combat social exclusion.

The main 12 provisions are:

- *Free movement*: The right for all workers to free movement within the Union.
- *Employment and remuneration*: All employment should be fairly remunerated. Workers should have an equitable wage, i.e. a wage sufficient to enable them to have a decent standard of living (often interpreted as a minimum wage). Workers subject to atypical terms of employment (e.g. part-time work) should benefit from an equitable reference wage, i.e. a wage in line with full-time employee remuneration.
- *Improvement of living and working conditions*: The process must result from an approximation of conditions, as regards, in particular, the duration and organisation of working time and forms of employment; the procedure must cover such aspects of employment as collective redundancies and bankruptcies; every worker must have a weekly rest period and annual paid leave and a contract of employment.
- *Social protection*: Every worker in the Union shall have a right to adequate social protection and shall, regardless of status, enjoy an adequate level of social security benefits. Persons outside the labour market (those unable to work, e.g. retired, ill) must receive sufficient resources and social assistance in keeping with their particular situation.
- *Freedom of association and collective bargaining*: Employers and employees have the right of association (i.e. employers' associations and trade unions) to protect their social and economic interests. There is also the right *not* to join.

There shall be the right to negotiate and conclude collective agreements, and the right to collective action (e.g. strikes and lock-outs), subject to national legislation.

- *Vocational training*: Every worker must have access to and receive vocational training, with no discrimination on grounds of nationality.
- *Equal treatment for men and women*, in particular as regards access to employment, remuneration, working conditions, social protection, educational training and career development.
- *Information, consultation and participation of workers* must be developed along appropriate lines, taking account of the practices in force in the various member states. This shall apply especially in companies or groups of companies having establishments in several member states.

    These processes must be implemented when technological change takes place having major implications for the workforce; in connection with restructuring operations or mergers; in cases of collective redundancy; when trans-frontier workers in particular are affected by employment policies by the undertaking where they are employed.

- *Health protection and safety in the workplace*: Every worker must enjoy satisfactory health and safety conditions in the workplace. Appropriate measures must be taken to achieve further harmonisation of conditions in this area.
- *Protection of children and adolescents in employment*: The minimum employment age must not be lower than school-leaving age, neither of which must be lower than 15 years of age. The duration of work must be limited, and night work prohibited under 18 years of age. After compulsory education young people must be entitled to receive initial vocational training of reasonable duration.
- *Elderly persons*: Every worker must, at the time of retirement, be able to enjoy resources affording him or her a decent standard of living, and those not entitled to a pension must be provided for.
- *Disabled persons*: All disabled people must be entitled to additional concrete measures aimed at improving their social and professional integration. These measures must concern vocational training, ergonomics, accessibility, mobility, means of transport and housing.

Difficulties of implementation and interpretation

The implementation of the Social Charter has proved to be more controversial than the debate over what it should contain, although these processes are inextricably intertwined (Hughes, 1991). Implementation hinges on the influence and interpretations of:

- political parties and groupings;
- national governments;
- employers and employee bodies;
- multinational corporations;
- the economic and political climate;
- the ambiguities and imprecisions of Charter policies.

Deciding on the provisions of the Social Charter was, and still is, a difficult process given the varied opinions within the EU in terms of political and economic ideology.

Margaret Thatcher's Conservative government was the most prominent and vocal opponent. Given her neo-liberalist position she was never happy with the Social Charter *per se* and raised many objections to proposals, and ultimately refused to ratify it in 1989 – the UK being the only government of the 12 member states to do so. John Major, her successor, has continued this policy and demanded that the Maastricht Treaty should have a separate protocol for the Social Chapter, as the Social Charter is also called, upon which member states vote separately. This involves minimalist legislation agreed by all 12 governments with more ambitious social standards set by the other eleven alone (Palmer, 1993).

The process of amendment and change is still continuing and past and present efforts to please Margaret Thatcher and other critics have meant that the original proposals from the mid-1980s have been watered down, some considerably. The implementation of the Charter under the Social Action Programme has also been significantly revised and the biting recession of the early 1990s has had another slowing effect on its implementation. Thus Jacques Delors, and other parties of the opinion that a strong social dimension is an important part of the Single European Market, have had to revise their views on the timetable for implementation. It is now agreed, even by its strongest advocates, that the full Charter will take a very long time to complete, if at all! (See Piachaud, 1991; Goodhart, 1992; Milne, S., 1992.)

At the end of 1992 about 60% of the Social Action Programme had been passed, some legislation was to be accepted in the near future in a watered-down form and some had been blocked entirely.

Position of Social Charter directives

Passed

- Six health and safety directives.
- Written proof of employment directive requiring contracts of employment.
- Collective redundancies (revised) directive requiring consultations on job cuts.
- Maternity leave directive – diluted version of original proposal giving women minimum pay and time off. European works council directive – requiring companies operating in more than two EU countries to set up employee consultation committees.
- Protection of young workers directive – diluted version of curbs on child labour.

Probable

- Working time directive – diluted version of proposal limiting the working week.

Blocked

- Atypical workers directive – providing protection for part-time workers.
- Subcontracting directive – to prevent employers taking workers from another EU country and paying them below national rates.

Even if the Social Charter had been accepted in principle by all member states, interpretation of the directives is problematic. Directives rather than regulations were deliberately used in framing the Charter in order to allow for national differences and the accommodation of existing laws. As one commentator accurately notes, 'responsibilities for such implementation often rests with national governments who have a reputation for giving variable priority both to implementation and enforcement' (Butt Philips, 1988).

In addition, some of the directives are so vague that they are open to a variety of interpretation. The provision for 'information, consultation and participation of the workforce' has many varied interpretations, ranging from works councils in Germany, Belgium and the Netherlands to multifarious practices in the UK, covering schemes as representative as works councils to organisations which barely give the workforce minimum information. Yet the CBI claimed that British organisations already adequately conform to the provisions of this directive.

The Transfer of Undertakings (Protection of Employment) directive

Another directive, the Transfer of Undertakings (Protection of Employment), has caused considerable controversy over interpretation in the UK. This directive (77/187) protects employees' pay and conditions when an undertaking is transferred as, for example, when privatisation of government and local government services take place. 'If the directive applies a successful bidder must take over staff on their existing terms and conditions which will reduce scope for saving through lower pay or staff cuts' (Willman, 1993). This would in effect:

> put an end to private contractors depressing their pay and conditions to lower bid costs when competing for contracts against the public sector. Contractors are increasingly jittery about the lack of clarity and are reluctant to bid for contracts without knowing the extent of their liabilities.
>
> (Weston, 1993)

In addition, the government could face a huge number of retrospective compensation cases by thousands of local authority workers, such as cleaners and school dinner staff, whose wages and conditions were worsened under competitive tendering when they transferred from council to private employers. It has also cast a cloud of uncertainty over plans to put over £1.5 billion's worth of civil service work out to tender.

Arrayed on one side are the government and private company tenderers, and on the other opposition parties, unions and employees adversely affected by changes in their employment conditions. In the middle are local authorities and government departments, which have the unenviable task of attempting some interpretation of the directive. In an attempt to resolve the dispute the Association of Metropolitan Councils travelled to Brussels for talks with the EU Social Affairs Commissioner about the difficulties caused by differing interpretations.

UK government ministers have argued that the directive does not apply to contracting out, but the EU has forced the government to amend the existing law which covers this situation, the new wording of which, trade unions believe, extends protection to cover many public sector and former public sector activities. The government has played for time by avoiding cases which might set a legal precedent, particularly if the decision went against them. However, COHSE, the then health service union, won a case brought against South Glamorgan Health Authority in March 1993 which challenged its claim that canteen services put out to competitive tendering did not come under the aegis of the directive. Despite UK government pleas, Padraig Flynn, the conservative Irish EU Commissioner of Social Affairs, has stated that there should be no retrospective amendment to accommodate the British government's difficult situation.

Enforcement

There is also the problem of enforcement. The EU has no inspectorate and relies heavily on member states to enforce directives, which, as we have already noted, could vary widely. The most common way is through legal action by individuals or groups via the Commission. These actions take time to investigate, prepare and process through the Court of Justice. Leaving the enforcement to individuals or groups often means that such contraventions of directives depend on the strength of mind of individuals and groups in bringing the action, who may be subject to pressures not to protest, particularly if it is against their employer.

Controversy: 'Eurosclerosis' or 'social dumping'

A wider debate also emerged in the 1980s rooted in the differing ideological viewpoints concerning the effects of the Social Charter on the European labour market. Essentially, three main groups of opinion have emerged.

The minimalist or deregulatory school is supported by Margaret Thatcher, John Major, employers and conservatives, who believe that legislative interference prevents the efficient operation of the labour market.

The maximalists or regulatory school is supported by Jacques Delors and Commissioner Vasso Papandreou (Greek socialist), socialists and trade unions, who believe in a 'level playing field' based on labour market regulation.

The third group, the centrists, resides somewhere between the other two and believes that, while the intent of the Social Charter is good, it must be realistic in its provisions and non-obstructive in scope; in other words, not rooted in ideology but in pragmatism. This third group has supporters in centre parties as well as both socialist and conservative groups, with the support of some employers and trade unionists.

Dividing the varied opinions over the social dimension into three groups can be viewed as a gross simplification, as there are prominent trade unionists who view some of the provisions as undermining collective bargaining by a greater emphasis on individual rights and consultative arrangements (Gospel, 1992), and some employers who believe that the full Social Charter should be adopted as it will bring order and the advantage of homogeneity to a European-wide market. Nevertheless, the argument to date has been based on the regulatory and deregulatory schools and median positions.

The minimalist or neo-liberal school

In political terms the minimalists see the Social Charter as a 'socialists' charter' and Delors, its past champion, an 'old-fashioned bureaucratic socialist'. Deregulationists believe that 'prosperity, progress and liberty presuppose economic freedom' (Marsland, 1991). Economic freedom means freedom from any regulatory influences which might hinder the industrial and commercial competitive process and therefore the operation of the market.

In economic terms, the neo-liberals see the provisions of the Charter as creating the conditions for 'Eurosclerosis', a hardening of the free flow of labour-market arteries. The Eurosclerosis view emanated from the 1970s and 1980s when the EU states were perceived as doing less well economically than the United States. 'Reaganomics' (the policies of Ronald Reagan, US Republican President 1980–88) argued that abolishing or moderating regulatory restrictions had freed up the labour market and had lowered unemployment by enabling the creation of more jobs. 'Thatcherism' (the policies of British Conservative Prime Minister Margaret Thatcher, 1979–91) had attempted similar deregulatory measures in the UK with comparable success in the 1980s, or so claimed her supporters. Such Social Charter proposals as a minimum wage would create a rigid high-wage economy with small differentials where workers would be priced out of a job. 'Furthermore, legally based labour rights and employment protection schemes have gone too far, leading to high labour costs which in turn cause redundancies and discourage hiring'(Teague, 1991).

The cost to employers of implementing this and other provisions would have the effect of decreasing jobs and slowing the labour market. For example, the UK Conservative government claimed that 100 000 jobs would be lost in Britain in implementing maternity rights for women and safeguards for working hours and part-time working contained in the Charter.

Other critics believe that imposition of a European-wide Social Charter would not benefit those for whom it was intended, i.e. poorer workers (Addison and Stanley Siebert, 1991, 1992). They argue that 'it will not succeed in making the desired transfer to disadvantaged groups. Since mandated benefits work at the level of the firm, rather than at the level of the tax transfer system, firms will tend to make countervailing moves which frustrate the redistributive aims of the policy' (Addison and Stanley Siebert, 1992). They also claim that the unskilled will lose out as a result of better safety protection because 'they were the ones doing the unsafe jobs for high pay; now the unsafe jobs have been removed, wages have been reduced but the skill gap remains' (Addison and Stanley Siebert, 1992: 511). In addition, the attempts to impose uniformity on nations with diverse systems of social legislation will impede competition (Addison and Stanley Siebert, 1992: 495).

Most minimalists do support some of the measures in the Social Charter to varying degrees, namely:

- freedom of movement of workers;
- provision of training;
- harmonisation of qualifications;
- pensions to become portable;
- help to the less favoured regions through the Social Fund;
- schemes to help the long-term unemployed.

They remain, however, strictly against measures to regulate the labour market, which they believe should be made freer by clipping the power of trade unions, reducing the government role in industrial relations and increasing functional and numerical flexibility.

The maximalists or regulatory school

The supporters of the maximalist position are generally those that advocate the view that, if the Single European Market is to create a free market in terms of a competitive 'level playing field' for goods, industry and services, then the same principle should apply to the social dimension to prevent 'social dumping'. The term 'social dumping' is an imprecise one but has come generally to mean 'the potentially adverse and retrogressive effects of a deregulated and decentralised European Labour market' (Teague, 1989). Unregulated markets would lead to poorer countries and employers holding down 'wages and social benefits to limit imports from richer member states and at the same increase their exports to those countries. Such a strategy would amount to exporting domestic unemployment . . . Such action would inevitably force richer countries to check real wage growth and streamline existing labour market regulations triggering a price and cost reducing war inside the community' (Teague, 1991). From this would ensue redundancies and high unemployment.

A second and concomitant view of 'social dumping' envisages:

> a sizable shift in production from Northern to Southern Europe as companies chase after low wage investment sites. It is feared the combination of these two processes would de-stabilise European economies by shifting the concern of governments and managers away from product and process innovations, towards cost reducing strategies. In this scenario of social dumping the main casualties of the competitive regime would be workers and their families who would experience a lowering of their incomes.
>
> (Teague, 1991)

A recent example to illustrate this is the exposure by a television documentary of the high incidence of illegal child labour in Portugal, which had the effect of removing manufacturing jobs from the UK shoe industry as labour costs were so much cheaper in Portugal. Consequently, many British companies choose to manufacture there rather than in the UK (Twenty Twenty Television, 1993).

Another recent example seized on by the maximalists to illustrate their argument was the decision by the Hoover Company to transfer its production facilities from Dijon, France to Cambuslang, near Glasgow, Scotland. Hoover president, William Foust, claimed that the prime motive for moving the company's whole production facilities was that non-wage labour costs were only 10% in Scotland as opposed to 45% in France (Goodhart, 1993). Other examples have been Bowater, the UK-based packaging group, which recently shifted production of some of its cosmetic packaging to the UK from Italy and France. 'The company has calculated national ratios for average employment costs at its plants, from managing director down to apprentice. If the UK is 100', says Michael Hartnell, Bowater's Finance Director, 'Italy is 130, France 140 and Germany 170' (Jackson, 1993).

The maximalists claim that such practices play off one national workforce against another in an attempt to bid down labour costs. The minimalists point out that companies will be attracted by cheap labour costs because they reflect maximum efficiency in terms of productivity.

The centrists

The centrists are in many ways an uncohesive group and represent many median positions. What they do accept, however, is that the claims by the maximalists and the minimalists are exaggerated and rooted more in ideology than reality. They see that the effects of the Single European Market will be diverse and will differ according to time, place and economic circumstances.

The centrists believe that the Social Charter should provide certain inalienable rights for the protection of all employees. Much of the detail should be worked out by the social partners (employers and employee organisations and various economic and social groups) and, rather than passing or failing, directives bring in 'desirable' social policy by piecemeal measures. Therefore, instead of basing all EU legal requirements in the form of directives, it might be more effective to put some proposals in the form of recommendations. Centrists place considerable emphasis on the efficacy of subsidiarity, whereby responsibility legislation is passed down to the lowest levels competent to deal with it. They also recognise that acceptance of Social Charter proposals rest very much on how officials at these levels interpret them, but their main concern is that legislation is at least accepted in principle. Forcing governments to accept legislation against their wishes is viewed as counter-productive. This median approach will go a long way to breaking the deadlock which could, and has, taken place between the ideologues of right and left, it is argued.

The regime approach

Teague has argued convincingly, however, that the polarised views of the regulatory and deregulatory schools are in many ways irrelevant in creating an appropriate model for EU labour market policy. He calls this 'third way' the 'regime' approach, and he emphasises the importance of the adoption of the Social Charter 'since it represents the first step towards a new institutional tier being drafted onto national industrial relations systems in Europe' (Teague, 1991).

> Rather than attempting to obtain labour market harmonisation or centralisation, the regime approach is about obtaining policy convergence across the community in the context of diverse national industrial relations systems.
>
> (Teague, 1991)

In other words, it is an acceptance of the reality of the considerable differences which exist in national labour relations systems throughout the European Union, and the difficulties of imposing a centralised system on national structures.

Grahl and Teague (1992) further argue that the ways in which political scientists and economists view the integration of labour markets and employment relations are fundamentally different. But each has influenced how the social dimension is perceived. However, because political science views the process as dynamic rather than static, it has 'a more concrete grasp of the ambivalent stages of the integration process where both old and new structures and practices co-exist' (Grahl and Teague, 1992: 516).

> Thus, institutional interventions and other co-ordination mechanisms are required to promote economic adaptability. Viewed from this standpoint, the Social Charter and related initiatives can be seen as promoting orderly integration of the Community's labour market.   (Teague and Grahl, 1992: 515)

HUMAN RESOURCE MANAGEMENT AND THE SINGLE EUROPEAN MARKET

While speculation on the influence of the Social Charter on labour markets has fuelled a major debate, little research has taken place as to its actual influence on organisations. Research carried out by Wood and Peccei (1990) on the preparation of personnel strategies for the Single European Market (SEM) in British organisations showed that most firms did not perceive this as a critical issue. The minority of companies that did have some sort of human resource strategy were those already involved in EU trading with more awareness of the need for policies for the SEM. However, many of these HR initiatives were business led, and 'more often than not are developed downstream from corporate strategy and are treated as "third order" within the strategic planning process' (Wood and Peccei, 1990).

The Price Waterhouse Cranfield Project (1991) surveyed human resource initiatives in organisations across 10 countries in Europe. While concern was expressed about the effects of the SEM, few organisations had developed a conscious strategy for the SEM and even fewer had a human resource strategy for this purpose. Most had positive policies on the Social Charter directives associated with equal opportunities and health and safety, but many of these policies had been established long before by national legislation. It would seem from these studies that most organisations will only respond to the influences of the Social Charter and the SEM when it is necessary to do so. Many HRM policies are still influenced by the attitudes of national governments towards enforcement of directives, which in turn rest on varying interpretations of the subsidiarity process.

However, despite a picture of relative parochialism in terms of organisational responses to the Social Charter and the SEM, the Price Waterhouse Cranfield survey revealed many similar human resource trends taking place across Europe, despite the varying employee relations systems at both macro and micro levels. There are strong trends towards the decentralisation of human resource functions in terms of the devolvement to line management of recruitment and selection, training and development and other functions. However, in such areas as pay bargaining and industrial relations responsibility still resides very much in the personnel function and is strongly influenced by national bargaining structures, particularly in Germany and Sweden. Nevertheless, 'decentralisation in the level of decisions within the organisation and devolution to line management continues apace. Line management responsibility is increasing in all countries and for all subjects with the single exception of Italian industrial relations' (Price Waterhouse Cranfield Project Report, 1991: 8).

This would seem to suggest that it is premature for EU initiatives to have had an influence on personnel and HR policies in organisations. The reality seems to be that organisations are still more influenced by their own particular markets and global trends in HRM rather than by regional initiatives. Thus local, national and international organisations have been influenced by many trends in HRM emanating from, in particular, the USA and Japan, but the extent and the ways in which these strategies are adopted depend on the size, sector, geographical distribution of the market, industrial relations and bargaining systems in which organisations are placed.

EASTERN EUROPE

The system of human resource management and industrial relations in Eastern Europe has been undergoing enormous change since 1989 and will continue to do so for some time to come. The fundamental problem is the transition from a unitarist system, very tightly controlled by communist governments which influenced every corner of the economy, to a more pluralist system operating in some type of free market. It is obvious to most observers that some form of pluralistic balance needs to be achieved to contain unbridled free market forces. At present most Eastern European countries are wedged in the transitional phase between these two states. This section will, first, examine the role of labour under the previous communist regimes; second, review the transitional phase now occurring; and third, examine the various prognoses for the future of labour in Eastern European states.

Labour under communist governments

The view projected to the outside world by communist governments, if somewhat crudely, was that in a workers' state, such as the Soviet Union and its Eastern European satellites, the interests of the workers were as one with the government, because the government was controlled by a dictatorship of the proletariat. From the 1950s and 1960s this view was increasingly challenged, not only by anti-communist groups but also socialists, Marxists and some communists themselves.

For example, in the former communist regimes the function of trade unions was very much that of an arm of the state. Lenin viewed them 'as a school of administration, a school of economic management and a link between the vanguard [the Communist Party] and the masses' (Lenin, 1964). As they have evolved within the communist system, the role of defender of workers' rights was limited because logic dictated that if the workforce lived in a workers' state then there was no need for a separate entity to uphold the rights and freedoms of the workforce. Thus striking was 'virtually a taboo on ideological, political and economic grounds' (Wilczynski, 1983).

The problem with such a unitarist system is that it allows for little realistic criticism which might afford changes and reforms to meet real challenges. In theory trade unions were a separate entity from the Communist Party, but in reality they were often controlled by Party members. As striking Soviet miners in Western Siberia, Donetz and Kazakhstan explained during the strike of 1988:

> Trade unions in many areas are simply not defending their members . . . In fact, trade union committees have up to now been controlled by and responsible to the local Communist Party organisations . . . and are often laid open to accusations of favouritism or injustices . . . [unions] should be independent of the Communist Party and the Government. (*Morning Star*, 1988)

Another major problem for critics both inside and outside these regimes was the lack of accurate information, and Soviet bureaucrats and managers had become extremely adept at massaging statistics to the point where data on the economy had become meaningless. These figures were often false, and if not false often achieved at enormous human cost. The immense power wielded by their political masters ensured that Soviet managers became proficient at covering up inefficiencies, mistakes and blunders, by systems of ingenious creative accounting and statistical manipulation (Holden and Peck, 1990). However, this was not a benign system which operated in the workers' favour. All enterprises had their 'norms' departments staffed with specialists, who set targets for each work group and individual. Basic wages were set at a low level so that the worker had to strain to fulfil the norm. 'But the norm was not something permanent: as soon as it was overfulfilled by ten per cent, that was the signal to raise it' (Markov, 1983). Such working practices led to exhaustion, deterioration of health and even the inability to work for many workers (Haraszti, 1977).

Management style in the Soviet system

The qualities which were required by managers of Soviet enterprises were the ability to bargain, the possession of a network of suppliers and purchasers, and the ability to manipulate production and financial data (Altman, 1989). This style of management was driven by the response to the allocation of resources by a centralised bureaucracy in which rivalry between enterprises for resources led to unnecessary hoarding of materials. The surplus material was then used by managers to bargain with other enterprises. The long-term result was the creation of shortages (Stark, 1992). In this way there was collusion between the state bureaucracy, management of state enterprises and the trade unions to exploit the workforce in the name of socialism (Burawoy, 1992).

The increasingly moribund Soviet system

By the 1980s the Eastern European economies were undergoing economic crisis and even the heavy hand of the communist state could not hide this. Changes were attempted, but the system had become a self-perpetuating oligarchy in which only far-reaching reforms would have any effect, and such measures would threaten those with a vested interest in the system. Attempts at reform, for example in Bulgaria by the introduction of the Brigade system, in theory seemed a bold attempt to bring an element of initiative to the labour force by the introduction of 'planning from below' (Thirkell, 1985; Wallimann and Stojanov, 1988). By the mid-1980s the system was widespread in Bulgaria but the reforms were overtaken by the 1989 revolution. Similar reforms were attempted without success in the former Czechoslovakia and Hungary.

The need for change was only recognised when the possibility of the implosion of the Soviet economic system was acknowledged by the more forward-looking members of the *nomenklatura* (bureaucratic caste), such as Gorbachev. The policies of *glasnost* and *perestroika* were the direct result of these concerns, ultimately leading to the collapse of the communist regimes in the Soviet Union and the Eastern European satellites from 1989.

The transitional phase

The cause of the collapse of the political regimes sprang from reforms initially intended to re-energise the economic sector. Economic reform was only made possible by freeing up the processes which would enable a mixed economy to operate, i.e. greater freedom from state interference.

Many embraced the view that free market capitalism would bring the benefits so transparently obvious in the West – consumer products, full shops, a higher standard of living, and economic and political freedom. This was reinforced by a parade of business people, consultants and politicians bringing the word of 'free market' forces to an eager audience. Once again a credibility gap opened up between reality and ideology. Unemployment rose considerably in all Eastern European states. This was accompanied by inflation and the undermining of currencies. The immediate result in the following three years was a fall in standards of living for many people and the emergence of poverty. Thousands of enterprises went into liquidation, unable to compete in open markets after being confronted with their inefficiencies (Blanchard *et al.*, 1991).

Responses to these changes have varied considerably throughout Eastern Europe and within the former Soviet Union, influenced by cultural and historical factors. The former Czechoslovakia and Hungary, which had developed industries before the advent of communism, have been able to use these pre-communist memories and experiences in the process of adaption and change. Bulgaria, Romania, Albania and the newly constituted states of Yugoslavia, coming from peasant pre-communist conditions, will have greater difficulties in constructing a modern economy (Smith and Thompson, 1992; Holden, 1993).

Channon and Dakin (1995) believe that the former Soviet states can now be divided into three regions according to geography, responses to and experiences of the post-communist world:

- Central Europe – the Czech Republic, Poland, Slovakia, Hungary and Slovenia, the Baltic States (Latvia, Lithuania and Estonia);
- Russia and the former Soviet Union;
- South-central region (the Balkans) – Romania, Bulgaria, Albania and the former Yugoslavia.

The Central European states have fared the best, partly because they have proved most attractive to foreign capital investment. This is due to the presence of industry and commerce before the ascendancy of communism, and partly because of the less hardline version of communism in these states between the late 1940s and 1989. The people are also viewed as being more positive about changes towards market forces. The South-central region has been less attractive to capital investors because of the rise of nationalist turbulence there, and its relatively underdeveloped nature of its economies. There had also been particularly hardline regimes in Albania, Bulgaria and Romania, which cause difficulties in effecting the attitudinal changes in the population necessary for working in and running capitalist enterprises.

Russia and the former Soviet Union have in many ways proved the most difficult to deal with for foreign companies, because of the deep-rooted nature of the old communist system and its greater historical isolation from Western Europe.

> There was autocratic government and a peasant culture, with a strong tra-
> dition of collectivism and mutual support or patronage mechanisms in the
> face of a harsh external climate. This is a far more difficult culture in which
> to establish an operation, because there are no deep seated traditions of pri-
> vate enterprise or private property.   (Channon and Dakin, 1995: 26)

Management and personnel management in Eastern Europe

One of the main problems facing both economies and organisations is the change not
only in organisational structures, but in management attitudes which remain inured in
old bureaucratic ways in many organisations (Holden and Peck, 1990; Watts, 1991).

Attempts at reform in management practices were already underway in many Eastern
European states before 1989, with patchy results. Management in post-communist society
was seen as gaining the right to manage unfettered by the shackles of the Communist
Party, state and trade unions, creating an efficient human resource capable of competing
with Western countries (Landa, 1990). Not surprisingly, there has been a considerable
emphasis on management development, with many Eastern European managers and academics forging links with Western business schools, universities, companies and
organisations to set up business management courses of various kinds. There have been
considerable problems, largely because of differences in attitudes and perceptions.
Though many senior managers lost their positions after 1989 because of their associations
with the communist system, others have thrived in the new atmosphere, holding on to
their positions and making full use of their connections and networks built up under the
old regimes (Meyer, 1990; Pieper, 1990; Randlesome, 1991). This has posed considerable
problems; the author attests to attempts to create a management programme between a
well-known British business school and a newly formed Eastern European management
school which was unsuccessful due to the fact that too many of the students were senior
managers lacking sufficient language capability and flexibility of attitude in new
approaches to management. This suggests that neither side is 'wrong', but that the credibility gap of perceptions, aims and objectives between East and West still has a long way
to go before it can be bridged. As one Western academic stated, 'it is very difficult to say
to a Russian manager that Western management techniques are correct when the abilities
he or she needs to operate effectively in Moscow are still based on personal contacts and
the ability to wheel and deal'.

Suffice to say, personnel management and its new offspring human resource management still have a long way to go before they reach anything like the basic operational
level in many Western organisations. The evolution will be one from bureaucratised institutional functions, involving administrative operations strongly controlled by the
nomenklatura, to one responding to market operations. Such a change will take some time
to bring about. In the first instance, personnel and HRM had a low priority in most
Eastern European organisations, with many training and recruitment functions still
inured in practices associated with the former regimes, although attempts to bring in payment systems linked to performance have been more successful (Landa, 1990).

Recently companies have given much more emphasis to HRM issues since having initially had their 'fingers burnt' by underestimating personnel problems. A survey

conducted by the School of Slavonic Studies at London University and a corporate language training company, Communicaid, found that 'almost all HR directors and managers of 30 British companies questioned agreed that western companies had generally underestimated cultural differences and their impact on the establishment of operations and the nature of the local workforce' (Channon and Dakin, 1995: 24). As a result, a number of recommendations are beginning to emerge as important for companies setting up and operating in Eastern Europe. Training of staff has become a high priority, and this includes not only training in work skills but also attitudinal training. Another problem is poaching: as some companies train, other companies will attract away workers with desirable skills by offering larger wages and salaries. This means that the compensation package also becomes important in retaining staff.

Another consideration is succession planning and the take-over of operations by host country staff from expatriate staff. Considerations of when and how this should take place are also important. The necessity of having 'connections' (being someone who can 'fix' things and who has contacts to smooth operations) is very important, especially in Russia and the South-central region (the Balkans). The system of patronage can also cause difficulties in removing staff who may appear to no longer fit the job. In this respect recruitment and selection will prove crucial, but the criteria used in Western companies may not always be appropriate.

Trade unions in the 'new' economies

The creation of a trade union movement has also been hampered by the fact that many of the existing unions had close associations with the old Communist Parties. Hence as Communist Parties decline, so too do the unions (Mickler, 1992). But the experience of trade unions has been mixed. With the backlash against the hardships wrought by free market policies, by 1992 the old 'official' unions had fared the best, 'partly because of organisation, habit and resources, partly because they are the more consistent opponents of the new power' (Milne, A., 1992). In the former Czechoslovakia unions have adapted to the changes comparatively well and, although membership fell immediately after the 'Velvet Revolution', it increased once again due to the fear of redundancies (Brewster, 1992). Subsequent rises in unemployment have, however, caused membership to fall, although not to previous levels, but the efficacy of the unions has not been aided by the attitude of the government, which is perceived by union officials to be hostile to the point of wishing them to be non-existent (Brewster, 1992).

In Poland, OPZZ, the old 'official' union organisation, while experiencing some decline, has been relatively successful in the long term compared with Solidarnost, which has witnessed a fall in membership from 10 to below 2 million (Milne, 1992). In Hungary the main union organisation, MSZOSZ, has fared less well 'and is now less than half of its [communist government-controlled] predecessor SZOT' (Gill, 1990; Brewster, 1992). In Bulgaria a large independent trade union, Podkrepa, was created in the aftermath of the fall of the communist regime. Initially born out of the desire to defend workers' rights against communist abuse, it joined forces with a united front of anti-communist groups under the banner of the Union of Democratic Forces (UDF), but in the post-communist Bulgarian state has threatened and initiated strikes in protest at the undermining of its members' living standards (Holden, 1991).

In Russia the old unions remain the most important organisation representative of the workers. The Soviet All Union Council of Trade Unions (AUCTU) had 142 million members in 32 branch unions in 1990, although since then its membership has witnessed some decline (Lloyd, 1990). As one Moscow worker stated, 'most of us belong to the official trade unions, because there is no serious alternative' (Weir, 1992). As with many of the new non-communist governments in Eastern Europe, trade unions are not encouraged. In the initial desire to copy Western government practices, particularly the Conservative government in Britain, many anti-union laws have been passed. For example, the draft law on collective agreements states that groups other than trade unions can participate in collective bargaining. As one Russian trade unionist states, 'Of course it undermines the position of the union. At any workplace or enterprise, the manager can say to the workers "why do you need to join the union in order to have a collective agreement?"'(Cathcart, 1992).

Nevertheless, the unions have expressed dissatisfaction with government and organisational policies and strikes have occurred in Russia, Poland, Bulgaria and the former East Germany. Government responses have not been encouraging and the argument is regularly stated that industrial unrest will have the effect of discouraging foreign investment.

The future for trade unionism is not particularly optimistic although responses in the former communist satellite states and Russia will vary. Increased privatisation will help undermine union membership and evolving industrial relations legislation by many governments looks set to curb many powers, even those enjoyed by unions in the West (Lloyd, 1990; Blanchard *et. al.*, 1991; Brewster, 1992; Cathcart, 1992; Milne, 1992; Smith and Thompson, 1992; Weir, 1992).

The future: a prognosis

In predicting future developments in Eastern European economies there is considerable room for error, but the pundits, politicos and futurologists have not been averse to attempting to read the crystal ball. After all, who could have predicted the fall of the Berlin Wall before 1989? Since then events have moved through a series of phases. Initial euphoria gave way to cynicism and finally to an air of resigned realism. But just as there are optimists and pessimists in the West, so there are too in the East. Much depends on one's own position in the economy.

The optimists admit that their hopes of a swift move to free market forces, bringing considerable benefits, have been not been immediately realised; but there is still an air of hope that the future (if only perhaps the long-term future) is one where a Western-style system will ultimately prevail.

The pessimists, notably those on the left, take the view that many Eastern European economies, particularly those of the Balkan states, will be driven into a 'third world' status, ultimately providing cheap labour to an increasingly ageing and labour-starved Western Europe.

Of course, the reality will probably be somewhere between the two extremes. Some Eastern European states will ultimately benefit from the changes, particularly those which had an established industrial and commercial base before the arrival of communism; for example Hungary, the former Czechoslovakia, Poland and European Russia. Other states with peasant-based pre-communist systems, such as Bulgaria, Romania,

Albania and the former Yugoslavia, will have considerably more problems in readjusting. Such outcomes depend on the collective will of their populations influenced by many cultural factors.

SUMMARY

● Human resource management is a concept which is slowly becoming absorbed into the language of European models of personnel management, but a very different circumstances from that which obtain in the UK, the US or Japan. Within many Western European countries there is a strong tradition of employee rights incorporated into State provision and the nature of the employment relationship. This helps to explain the move towards the Social Charter which has dominated the European Community's agenda in the early 1990s. The advent of the Single European Market stimulated a debate about the proper role of a 'social dimension' in the operation of EC and the Maastricht Treaty, committing the EC to 'ever closer monetary and political union', was eventually amended to permit Britain to 'opt out' of the social provisions of the Charter in order to overcome British objections to what were seen as measures likely to weaken the competitive labour markets which UK governments had pursued since 1979. Despite the importance of the Social Charter debate, it has had little explicit connection with the question of HRM in a European context. Nevertheless there is evidence that some common HRM developments are occurring across Europe within EC members as well as those economies which are not yet EC members; among the more notable HRM shifts are those connected with the decentralisation of decision taking and the devolution to line managers of decisions relating to the management of employees.

● In Eastern Europe the agenda for change has been sudden and large; the replacement of highly centralised state run economies with the 'shock treatment' of market forces has led to vast upheaval in terms of unemployment. Traditional groups, such as the trade unions, have been discredited by their association with former regimes but, in some cases, have been able to rebuild membership as a result of the hardships of post-liberalisation. The structures and attitudes of management in former communist countries have equally felt the stress of reform and the difficulty of transition to more market-oriented and less bureaucratic modes of operation. In these circumstances the very nature of HRM is a concept that has little currency. At the present time the approach to personnel management owes more to the administrative systems of the past forty years than to the market-led models of the Western European employment relationship.

ACTIVITY

Kotel is a British-based hotel group which has recently acquired a group of five hotels in Poland. The board of the company is divided as to which human resource strategy it should pursue. One board group, represented by the finance director and marketing director, wants to go for a policy whereby labour is recruited from other hotels at the cheapest possible price. The other group, represented by the human resource director and operations manager, desires a full HRM strategy based on careful recruitment and selection, with full training and development policies, and remuneration policies based on performance and quality of service.

EXERCISES

1 Divide into three groups, two of these representing each of the two strategies proposed for the Kotel Group. Role play a board meeting with each group putting forward their views, backed by rational argument as to why their strategy should be adopted. A person should be selected to act as managing director to chair the meeting. The third group will act as neutral observers, with the power to question members of each group as to their views. At the end of the meeting the third group will decide by vote which is the most convincing strategy to adopt.

2 Draw up a list of problems, particularly related to human resource and employment relationship issues, which would face the Kotel Group setting up its company in Poland.

QUESTIONS

1 What difficulties might there be in the operation of the principle of subsidiarity in enforcing the provisions of the Social Charter?

2 Will the effects of the Social Charter's provisions on the operation of the EU labour market lead to 'Eurosclerosis' or 'social dumping'?

3 What problems face the workforce in ex-communist Eastern European states in the transition to a market economy?

EXERCISES

1 Divide the group into three and ask each subgroup to put forward one of the following arguments surrounding the Social Charter:

- the maximalist view
- the minimalist view
- the centrist view

Each group shall make a small presentation of their view with the assistance of visual aids.

2 Divide the group into pairs. Ask each pair to take one provision of the Social Charter and evaluate it, putting the points for and against and commenting on the difficulties of implementing it. When this has been done, a feedback session should take place in which each pair communicates its evaluation to the rest of the group.

743

CASE STUDY

A human resource strategy for Europump Ltd

Background

Europump is a UK-based engineering company specialising in hydraulic and pumping equipment. It was founded as a partnership by John Wall, an engineer who has responsibility for research and development and the production side of the company; Bill Hodges, an accountant with managerial experience; and Paul Marceau, a manager experienced in the engineering business. The company was founded in 1976, saw considerable growth in the earlier years and, though experiencing some difficulties in the 1980s' recession, survived to prosper in the late 1980s.

The board members have cultivated a profile of looking to the future and, with the imminence of the European Single Market in 1992, decided on expansion into continental Europe. A small subsidiary was set up in Lyons, France in 1987, the founding of which was greatly facilitated by Paul Marceau, who speaks fluent French as a result of having a French father. The company quickly expanded and, influenced by this success, the UK board decided to set up another subsidiary in the Netherlands. Because of the specialised nature and excellent marketing of its products it was able to establish a successful medium-sized company in Groningen which, while not enjoying the same degree of success as the UK and French companies, has managed to establish a market niche.

Structure of the company

The UK-based Northampton operation is situated on a greenfield site in a business park on the edge of the town and employs 340 people, 35% of whom are in unions. Pay is in line with national trends in the engineering and related industries. There is a personnel department with three full-time and two part-time staff. The production department employs 295 people, making up the majority of the workforce.

The research and development department (R&D) employs 5 people, and the finance and marketing department 35 people. Some extra services in these areas are purchased on an agency or consultancy basis.

The French operation in Lyons, Europump (France), employs 200 people with a composition in a similar ratio to that of the UK company in regard to departmental size and functions, although there is no R&D department. It has a French director who is ultimately responsible to the UK board. Only 10% of the workforce is unionised, but pay reflects national standards. There is, however, a works council which conforms to French law.

The Dutch operation (Europump AB) employs 175 people with a similar composition to the French organisation in terms of size and function; 25% of the workforce is unionised and there is a works council in operation.

Developments in the 1990s

While Europump Ltd as a whole enjoyed considerable success in the 1990s, the recession has affected sales in the UK. It has not been able to pay the workforce the rises demanded by their unions and it may have to make redundant part of the workforce if it is to meet the union demands even half way.

The recession is also affecting the French and Dutch companies and the possibility of redundancies may be in the offing in both subsidiaries if the market does not improve.

The UK board has decided to invite the directors and personnel managers to an international board meeting in a London hotel to hammer out an HRM policy for the organisation as a whole.

While all the Board are 'good' Europeans and believe wholeheartedly in the SEM, John and Bill hold the view that the provisions of the Social Charter can be detrimental to the company's future. Paul, however, believes that the Social Charter is correct and should pave the way for more harmonised and harmonious working conditions within the company. An additional proposal has been made by Jane Lawson, the UK personnel manager, for the introduction of more flexible working practices in the form of part-time working, restricted contracts, the expansion of agency contract workers and greater functional flexibility options.

Bill, on the other hand, has felt that it might be a good policy to open up a subsidiary near Barcelona in Spain. In a recent trip there he found a suitable site from which they could manufacture their products for European markets. Advantages would be in having a labour force which could be paid lower than British, French and Dutch workers with the ability to hire them on more flexible terms and conditions. Disadvantages would be a less skilled workforce which may well require a considerable investment in training and development.

QUESTIONS

1 Create a European-wide human resource policy for Europump Ltd, bearing in mind the possible responses from the unions and works councils in UK, France and the Netherlands.

2 Outline the difficulties and advantages of possible policy options and give reasons for the one on which you finally decide.

These HRM strategies should take into account:

- the possibility of a prolonged recession;
- the possibility of an end to recession in the near future.

GLOSSARY

CEEP European Centre of Public Enterprises.

EC European Community. The term superseded the EEC after the SEM, as describing more than purely economic union. Since 1992 has been renamed European Union (see below).

ECSC European Coal and Steel Community, founded in 1952.

EEC European Economic Community. A term used to describe the Common Market after the Treaty of Rome, 1957.

EMU Economic and monetary union.

EPU European political union.

ETUC   European Trade Union Confederation.

EU   European Union, so named in 1992 (formerly EC).

EURATOM   European Atomic Energy Community.

Maastricht Protocol   Part of the Maastricht Treaty dealing with the Social Chapter (Social Charter), allowing Britain to sign the treaty without signing the Maastricht Protocol or Social Chapter.

Maastricht Treaty   The content was agreed at a meeting at Maastricht in the Netherlands and signed in a watered-down form in Edinburgh in 1992. It was rejected then and accepted by the voters of Denmark in two referendums. It concerns extending aspects of European political union (EPU) and economic and monetary union (EMU), but some of its proposals have run into opposition in the UK (particularly the Social Chapter and EMU).

SEA   Single European Act, 1987. Proposed the creation of a Single European Market for trade on 31 December 1992.

SEM   Single European Market, also known as '1992' due to the date it was set up. See SEA.

Social Chapter   Another name for the Social Charter which emerged from the Maastricht Meeting in 1989.

Social Charter   A programme to implement the 'social dimension' of the single market, affording rights and protection to employees.

UNICE   Union of Industrial and Employers Confederations of Europe.

REFERENCES AND FURTHER READING

Addison, J.T. and Stanley Siebert, W. (1991) 'The Social Charter of the European Community: evolution and controversies', *Industrial and Labor Relations Review*, Vol. 44, No. 4, July, pp. 597–625.

Addison, J.T. and Stanley Siebert, W. (1992) 'The Social Charter: whatever next?', *British Journal of Industrial Relations*, Vol. 30, No. 4, December, pp. 495–513.

Altman, Y. (1989) 'Second economy activities in the USSR: insights from the southern republics', in Ward, P. (ed.) *Corruption, Development and Inequality*. London: Routledge.

Blanchard, O., Dornbusch, R., Krugman, P., Layard, R. and Summers, L. (1991) *Reform in Eastern Europe*. Cambridge, Mass.: MIT Press.

Brewster, C. (1992) 'Starting again: industrial relations in Czechoslovakia', *International Journal of Human Resource Management*, Vol. 3, No. 3, December, pp. 555–574.

Burawoy, M. (1992) 'A view from production: the Hungarian transition from socialism to capitalism', in Smith, C. and Thompson, P. (eds) *Labour in Transition: The Labour Process in Eastern Europe and China*. London: Routledge.

Butt Philips, A. (1988) 'Management and 1992 – illusions and reality', *European Management Journal*, Vol. 6, No. 4, pp. 345–350.

Cathcart, R. (1992) 'Struggling to survive in the "free" market', *Morning Star*, 16 May.

Channon, J. and Dakin, A. (1995) 'Coming to terms with local people', *People Management*, 15 June, pp. 24–29.

Gill, C. (1990) 'The new independent trade unionism in Hungary', *Industrial Relations Journal*, Vol. 21, No. 3, pp. 14–25.

Goodhart, D. (1992) 'Community's social action plans succumb to sabotage and recession', *Financial Times*, 19 November.

Goodhart, D. (1993) 'Social dumping: hardly an open and shut case', *Financial Times*, 4 February.

Gospel, H. (1992) 'The Single European Market and industrial relations', *British Journal of Industrial Relations*, Vol. 30, No. 4, December, pp. 483–494.

Grahl, J. and Teague, P. (1992) 'Integration theory and European labour markets', *British Journal of Industrial Relations*, Vol. 30, No. 4, December, pp. 515–545.

Haraszti, M. (1977) *A Worker in a Worker's State.* Harmondsworth: Penguin.

Holden, L. (1991) *Bulgaria, Perestroika, Glasnost and Management.* Cranfield School of Management Working Paper SWP 14/91.

Holden, L. (1993) 'Bulgaria: economic and political change', *Critique: Journal of Socialist Theory*, No. 25, pp. 133–143.

Holden, L. and Peck, H. (1990) 'Perestroika, glasnost, management and trade', *European Business Review*, Vol. 90, No. 2, pp. 26–31.

Hughes, J. (1991) *The Social Charter and the Single European Market.* Nottingham: Spokesman.

Jackson, T. (1993) 'Footloose across Europe's frontiers', *Financial Times,* 9 March.

Landa, O. (1990) 'Human resource management in Czechoslovakia – management development as the key issue', in Pieper, R. (ed.) *Human Resource Management: An International Comparison.* New York: Walter de Gruyter.

Lenin, V.I. (1964) *Collected Works*, Vol. 32. Moscow: Progress Publishers, pp. 20–21.

Lloyd, J. (1990) 'Trade unions: A tough transition', *Financial Times*, Soviet Union Supplement, 12 March.

Lockhart, T. and Brewster, C. (1992) 'Human resource management in the European Community', in Brewster, C., Hegewisch, A., Holden, L. and Lockhart T. (eds) *The European Human Resource Management Guide.* London: Academic Press.

Markov, G. (1983) *The Truth That Killed.* London: Weidenfeld & Nicolson.

Marsland, D. (1991) 'The Social Charter: rights and wrongs', *The Salisbury Review*, June, pp. 16–18.

Meyer, H. (1990) 'Human resource management in the German Democratic Republic: problems of availability and the use of manpower potential in the sphere of the high qualification spectrum in a retrospective view', in Pieper, R. (ed.) *Human Resource Management: An International Comparison.* New York: Walter de Gruyter.

Mickler, O. (1992) 'Innovation and division of labour in state socialist and capitalist enterprises', in Smith, C. and Thompson, P. (eds) *Labour in Transition: The Labour Process in Eastern Europe and China.* London: Routledge.

Milne, A. (1992) 'The past with a punch', *Guardian*, 13 March.

Milne, S. (1992) 'Delors' social Europe is workers' paradise lost', *Guardian*, 14 November.

Morning Star (1988) 19 January.

Ouazan, J. -M. and Maury, J.-M. (1989) *1992, The Social Dimension.* Paris: EURO2C 82.

Palmer, J. (1993) 'Win or lose, Major on a sticky wicket', *Guardian*, 13 February.

Pieper, R. (1990) 'The history of business administration and management education in the two Germanies – a comparative approach', *International Journal of Human Resource Management*, Vol. 1, No. 2, September, pp. 211–229.

Piachaud, D. (1991) 'A Euro-Charter for confusion', *Guardian*, 13 November.

Price Waterhouse Cranfield Project (1991) *Report on International Strategic Human Resource Management*. Cranfield: Cranfield School of Management.

Randlesome, C. (1991) *East German managers: from Karl Marx to Adam Smith?*. Cranfield School of Management Working Paper SWP 14/91.

Smith, C. and Thompson, P. (1992) *Labour in Transition: The Labour Process in Eastern Europe and China*. London: Routledge.

Stark, D. (1992) 'Bending the bars of the iron cage: bureaucratization and formalization in capitalism and socialism', in Smith, C. and Thompson, P. (eds) *Labour in Transition: The Labour Process in Eastern Europe and China*. London: Routledge.

Teague, P. (1989) *The European Community: The Social Dimension*. London: Kogan Page.

Teague, P. (1991) 'Human resource management, labour market institutions and European integration', *Human Resource Management Journal*, Vol. 2, No. 1, Autumn, pp. 1–21.

Thirkell, J. (1985) 'Brigade organisation and industrial relations strategy in Bulgaria 1978–83', *Industrial Relations Journal*, Vol. 16, No. 1, Spring, pp. 33–43.

Twenty Twenty Television (1993) 'The secret children', in the *Storyline Series* for Carlton Television.

Wallimann, I. and Stojanov, C. (1988) 'Workplace democracy in Bulgaria: from subordination to partnership in industrial relations', *Industrial Relations Journal*, Vol. 19, No. 4, Winter, pp. 310–321.

Wallimann, I. and Stojanov, C. (1989) 'Social and economic reform in Bulgaria: economic democracy and problems of change in industrial relations', *Economic and Industrial Democracy*, Vol. 10, No. 3, pp. 226–234.

Watts, S. (1991) 'Clasping the competitive nettle', *Times*, 1 August.

Weir, F. (1992) 'When thunder roars', *Morning Star*, 9 May.

Weston, C. (1992) 'Court puts new price on privatised jobs', *Guardian*, 10 November.

Weston, C. (1993) 'Whitehall farce over EC job directive row', *Guardian*, 23 March.

Wilczynski, J. (1983) *Comparative Industrial Relations*. London: Macmillan.

Willman, J. (1993) 'EC laws "will not delay tendering"', *Financial Times*, 12 March.

Wood, S. and Peccei, R. (1990) 'Preparing for 1992? Business-led versus strategic human resource management', *Human Resource Management Journal*, Vol. 1, No. 1, Autumn, pp. 63–89.

HUMAN RESOURCE

MANAGEMENT

AND THE USA

Tim Claydon

OBJECTIVES

To explore recent developments in HRM and labour relations in
the USA.

●

To examine the background to the growth of US interest in HRM
and the extent of HRM practice among US employers.

●

To survey the history of US labour management policies since
the 1960s.

●

INTRODUCTION

Human resource management was born in the USA. While much of the practice of HRM as we have come to conceive of it is commonly associated with large Japanese enterprises, the theories which underlie HRM and the prescriptions for managing organisations which make up so much of the HRM literature have their main origins in the USA. HRM theory was articulated first and most fully at Harvard Business School, where innovations in the organisation of work and management of workers were reported and analysed in the *Harvard Business Review* (Walton, 1972, 1974, 1979) and where human resource management was developed as a distinctive subject of study for students of business administration. We shall not discuss the content of these theories and prescriptions in detail here since they have been covered in the opening chapter of this book. This chapter is concerned with the main features of HRM as defined in the US literature and the practice of HRM-oriented organisations; and the background to the growth of US interest in HRM and the growth of HRM influence on management.

The US approach to HRM

Within the US literature HRM can be seen as having four main dimensions:

- An emphasis on the importance of strategy in the management of organisations and the desirability of linking external strategies for competing in the product market to internal strategies for the management of organisational resources (Fombrun *et al.*, 1984; Beer *et al.*, 1985).
- An insistence that basic conflicts of interest are not an inevitable feature of the employment relationship, and that effective management can 'integrate the goals of employees with those of the firm' (Kochan *et al.*, 1986: 95). In this HRM has not incorporated the explicitly pluralist focus on management's role in 'balancing and rebalancing the multiple interests served by the company' (Beer *et al.*, 1985: 22) which was a feature of some of the writing of the Harvard school.
- A focus on developing individual workers' commitment to the organisation, i.e. loyalty and willingness to remain with the organisation, and strong motivation to deliver high levels of performance (Walton, 1985).
- The importance of developing a strong organisational culture which is supportive of HRM policies aimed at developing employee commitment. The values of the founders of companies have been seen as one of the most important factors in developing such cultures (Foulkes, 1980; Beer *et al.*, 1985).

The roots of US HRM

The concerns of HRM outlined above can be seen to have their antecedents in earlier strands of management and social scientific thought (Springer and Springer, 1990). The first of these is, paradoxically perhaps, scientific management.

Scientific management

In general, HRM is seen as marking a break with scientific management in that it rejects the idea that money is the sole or main motivator at work. It also advocates moving away from tightly specified, closely controlled tasks as the basis for the organisation of work within the classic scientific management model. Instead, there is a strong emphasis on giving workers scope for self-expression and development through varied and challenging work and by providing opportunities for job progression through training and the acquisition of skills.

At the same time, however, HRM has carried over from scientific management

> the belief that the selection and motivation of a workforce is . . . amenable to objective, rational and testable criteria. (Springer and Springer, 1990: 42)

This may be debatable in the light of the growth of interest in intangible, 'anti-rational' qualities such as myth and symbolism in the development of the cultures of HRM-style organisations (Kanter and Mirvis, 1989). Nevertheless, there is a clearly defined 'scientific' strand within HRM represented by the advocacy of rational, valid approaches to the efficient selection, deployment and management of employees, which stems from HRM's concern with strategy and the need for 'fit' between human resource strategy and policies and business strategy.

Behavioural and humanistic psychology

The 'scientific' strand of HRM above also stems from behavioural psychology and the development of methods for testing and evaluating individuals which is associated with it. In a rather different vein, humanistic psychology – specifically the work of Maslow, McGregor and Herzberg – has been used to underpin prescriptions for management which stress the importance of the content and organisation of work and the quality of relationships between managers and managed to the successful motivation of employees. Thus Maslow and Herzberg pointed to the need to provide workers with opportunities for self-expression and self-development through responsible, challenging and creative work. McGregor's distinction between Theory X and Theory Y approaches to management defined a management style based on providing workers with a degree of autonomy stemming from mutual trust between managers and managed. There is a direct line from humanistic psychology to HRM's concern for job enrichment and enlargement, provision of opportunities for training and development, the design of work around autonomous or semi-autonomous work groups, and open, direct communication between managers and workers.

Organic theories of management

A third source for HRM, noted by Beaumont (1992), is the concept of the organic as opposed to the mechanistic organisation. This distinction was developed by Burns and Stalker (1961). Mechanistic organisations are classic bureaucracies. There is a precise division of labour within which workers perform well-defined, relatively narrow tasks.

They are coordinated by a management hierarchy which processes information passed up the hierarchy in order to reach decisions which are passed back down. Organic organisations, by comparison, have a less clearly defined division of labour and individuals' responsibilities are to help achieve the goals of the organisation as a whole rather than fulfilling a pre-defined specialist task. There is an emphasis on communication at all levels with a greater degree of consultation and shared responsibility for decisions.

Whereas mechanistic organisations may be suited to stable environments, it is argued that they are incapable of responding effectively to rapid change. Organic organisations are more flexible and adaptable because they have less rigid delineations of functions and tasks and, being more open and participative, are better geared to problem solving and innovation. There are clear links here with HRM's emphasis on the management of change and the need for organisational flexibility in face of volatile product markets or rapidly changing and uncertain political environments.

The appeal of HRM in the USA

The 1980s saw an apparent upsurge of interest in HRM on the part of managers. At the most superficial level this was shown by a noticeable move to rename personnel departments 'human resource departments'. This was often associated with an increase in status for the head of the department, rising from manager to director or director to vice-president. More substantively, surveys conducted for the American Management Association and the Bureau of National Affairs during the mid-1980s found evidence of the growing use of techniques associated with HRM such as quality circles, new training and development programmes, and autonomous and semi-autonomous work groups (Guest, 1990). Beer *et al.* (1985) argued that not only were HRM issues coming more to the forefront, they were becoming the concern of general managers as well as personnel specialists.

However, it has been argued that HRM began to emerge considerably earlier than this, during the 1960s and 1970s (Kochan and Capelli, 1984; Kochan *et al.*, 1986). This emergence was closely linked to the decline of trade union organisation and the growing rejection by managers of established patterns of unionised industrial relations.

Beer *et al.* (1985) offered the following reasons for the spread of HRM ideas and techniques:

- *Increased international competition* and the weakened competitiveness of key industrial sectors in the USA, e.g. steel and automobiles.
- Relatedly, the *competitive success of Japan* and the apparent link between this success and the way Japanese companies managed their workforces.
- *Concern at the growth of bureaucracy* as organisations became larger and more complex. High degrees of bureaucracy came to be seen as costly, and also as creating a barrier between the individual and the organisation and reducing individuals' awareness of the competitive pressures on the organisation.
- *Slower growth of the economy* and of organisations meant that existing methods of retaining and motivating valued employees such as promotion channels and employment security became more difficult to operate.
- *Changes in the nature of the labour force,* such as rising education standards and more questioning attitudes towards authority, encouraged employers to re-examine their

assumptions and policies with respect to the amount of responsibility which employees could be expected to exercise and what level of involvement in decision making might be appropriate.

- *Government legislation*, particularly relating to fair employment practices, increased the significance of personnel/HRM issues in the eyes of general managers anxious to avoid costly and damaging lawsuits.

We can add to these the factors identified by Kochan and his colleagues in explaining the longer-term growth of non-unionism:

- *The decline of trade union organisation from the mid-1960s.* The proportion of non-agricultural workers who were union members rose from 10% in 1932 to 35% in 1955. This percentage then remained constant until 1965, when it began to decline. By 1988 it was 17% and today it is less than 16% (Kochan and Weaver, 1991; *Financial Times*, 15 February 1993, p. 15). Much of this decline has been due to structural changes in the labour force, with employment shifting from manual to non-manual, from North to South, and from manufacturing to service industries. It also, however, stemmed from employers' policies which reflected the following point.

- *Deep-seated anti-union values among management.* Unions were opposed by a variety of means during the nineteenth and twentieth centuries. Some employers used force, as did, for example, the Ford Motor Company against union organisers at its River Rouge plant in Detroit in 1937. Two union organisers were badly beaten by men employed in Ford's notorious 'Service Department', a department set up to spy on workers and intimidate and expel trade unionists. The use of 'union busters' to break up strikes by force and run union organisers out of town was common practice. Indeed, violent confrontations during disputes have remained a feature of American industrial relations. In the state of Virginia during 1989 the management of the Pittston Company hired so-called 'asset protection teams' and 350 state troopers were deployed to break a strike of coal-miners. The use of violence and intimidation against trade union organisers is still alleged to be widespread in the Southern states of the USA.

  A long-established alternative to the use of force to resist unionisation is 'welfare capitalism'. Welfare capitalism was adopted by a number of large corporations during the 1920s in order to forestall demands for union representation. Typically welfare capitalism involved favourable rates of pay, fringe benefits such as canteens and social facilities, and even employee stock ownership schemes. Welfare capitalism largely collapsed during the great depression of 1929–33, but did not disappear entirely. Firms such as IBM, Motorola, Delta Airlines and Burlington Mills continued successfully to operate welfare capitalism and avoided unionisation during the upsurge of union membership and recognition that occurred during 1935–55. Kochan *et al.* argue that these firms came to serve as a model for others during the 1960s and 1970s (Kochan *et al.*, 1986: 58).

- *Developments in federal and state government policy* provided a climate in which employers are free to oppose unionisation of their workforces. For example, during the 1950s and 1960s a number of states, mainly in the South, passed 'right to work' laws which outlawed union 'closed shops', i.e. agreements between unions and employers which made union membership or the payment of union dues a condition of employment (Cullen, 1986). There have also been changes in federal legislation which allow companies to relocate plant during the lifetime of a collective agreement, allow employers to hire 'temporary replacements' during a lock-out (where the employer excludes workers from the workplace in the course of a dispute), and prohibiting unions from fining members who break union rules by working during a strike (Rosenberg, 1989).

● *The economic incentive to avoid unions* rose during the 1970s. This was because the union – non-union wage differential widened during the 1970s from between 10 and 15% to between 20 and 30%. This encouraged companies to open new non-union plants rather than expand existing unionised sites. This process accelerated during the 1980s as recession and intensifying competition increased pressures to reduce costs (Kochan *et al.*, 1986).

In accounting for the growth of interest in HRM in the United States, it is therefore important to recognise that trade unions and collective bargaining have had a precarious existence for most of America's industrial history. The period between 1935 and 1965, when an industrial relations system based on unions and collective bargaining developed, can be seen from the perspective of the 1990s as marking an exception in the longer anti-union history of US industrial relations. The survival and spread of non-unionism during the 1960s and 1970s meant that for a growing number of organisations union avoidance was a clear aim of personnel and industrial relations policy. There was therefore a predisposition to adopt approaches to the management of labour which drew their inspiration from theories which stressed individualism and the possibility of common interest between workers and management.

THE PRACTICE OF HRM IN US ORGANISATIONS

Defining HRM practice

HRM has been closely associated with large, non-union companies which have pursued a distinctive combination of personnel management policies. It is these policies which in combination have been seen as defining HRM in practical terms. Thus Guest (1990) describes HRM in the USA as a distinctive style of management which he labels 'unitarist/innovative'. This approach seeks to generate individual commitment to the organisation and foster employee identification with managerial goals and priorities. HRM is, in addition, 'based on values and policies designed to make full use of the talents of all the people in the organisation'. What this means precisely is not spelled out, but it can be taken to include provision for the enlargement of workers' skills through training and promotion, and designing jobs and organising work in such a way as to utilise fully and develop workers' skills, abilities and responsibilities. This distinguishes HRM from another unitarist/innovative approach to management which he terms 'behavioural Taylorism'. This involves routine, deskilled jobs combined with an emphasis on motivational techniques to obtain desired levels of performance. The McDonald's fast-food chain is offered as an example of this latter approach.

There is a tendency, therefore, to see HRM in terms of an integrated package of personnel policies geared to improving employee performance and hence business performance. The main components of this package have been identified as follows (Beaumont, 1987):

- employee involvement through joint health and safety committees, briefing groups, quality circles and other forms of direct communication between managers and employees. This is linked to
- a high ratio of managers to managed employees;
- attention to work design to meet employees' needs for interesting, satisfying work in a non-alienating work environment;
- strong training provision and employment security linked to training and the acquisition of new skills, together with
- career opportunities through internal promotion;
- an independent wages policy, with pay levels and pay structures designed to support the internal labour market rather than reflecting external labour-market pressures. In addition to wages in the top quartile of the industry, further benefits such as profit-sharing schemes and employee share ownership schemes could add up to 50% to the value of rewards;
- minimisation of artificial status distinctions between managers and different grades of employee, e.g. salaried status for all staff.

The companies which exemplified this approach to employee relations most clearly in the 1970s and early 1980s were a small group of 'household name' firms operating internationally, e.g. IBM, Gillette, Hewlett-Packard. However, the impact of HRM was wider than this. A number of firms, while not pursuing fully developed and integrated HRM strategies, drew on elements of HRM theory and practice in an attempt to free themselves from what were seen as the unacceptable constraints of unionised industrial relations.

The broader impact of HRM

Union avoidance

The first type of impact is one we have already noted, i.e. to encourage further moves towards non-unionism in hitherto unionised companies. Thus Kochan and Cappelli argued that 'The possibility of maintaining non-union operations combined with the rise of psychology-based, individual-oriented personnel policies gave management a new method for avoiding unions, an alternative to the labor relations approach' (Kochan and Cappelli, 1984).

The evolution of union avoidance strategy has been outlined as follows. During the early twentieth century the top management of some firms decided that trade unions were unacceptable and developed welfare capitalist policies of union avoidance. However, during the late 1930s and 1940s union organising campaigns, backed by federal legislation establishing unions' rights to organise, forced union recognition.

The next phase came during the late 1940s to 1960s, when firms set up their first non-union plants following industrial disputes. In setting up the new plant senior line managers were selected who were 'human relations oriented', a strong personnel department was established to represent worker interests and a non-union grievance procedure put in place. Local standards of pay and conditions were matched and a wide range of social and recreational facilities was provided. Care was also taken to avoid hiring union members or activists. During the 1970s and 1980s any new plants were opened on a non-union basis and managers were 'encouraged to follow innovative work designs' (Kochan *et al.*, 1986: 59). This meant designing work so as to provide a greater variety of tasks, opportunity to acquire skills and a degree of task autonomy. Teamworking was and continues to be a feature of innovative work design.

Some other firms not only set up new plants on a non-union basis but also concentrated cutbacks in capacity and plant closures on unionised sites, effectively transferring their investment from unionised plants to non-union ones. Others also transferred existing production from union to non-union plants. This process of 'rapid disinvestment' in union plants accelerated and became more widespread during the 1980s (Kochan *et al.*, 1986: 66–80).

Transforming unionised industrial relations

In some cases union organisation has proved too strong for employers to be able to adopt strategies of union avoidance. An example is General Motors, which tried unsuccessfully to set up new plants on a non-union basis in the Southern states of Georgia and Mississippi. Where this has been the case, managements have sought to involve the union in a limited partnership aimed at achieving cooperation in raising productivity and quality of output. The main features of this approach are as follows:

- To move away from union job control based on formal rules regarding job descriptions and demarcation agreed between management and unions. Such arrangements are replaced by simpler, less formal work rules which give management greater freedom or 'flexibility' in deploying workers within the plant.

- To increase the participation of individual workers and work groups in decision making. This has involved a variety of means, generally labelled as quality of working life (QWL) programmes.

By adopting such an approach managements are attempting to break away from older patterns of adversarial industrial relations based on assumptions of underlying conflicts of interest at work. Fairris (1991) provides a useful discussion of the background to this development.

QWL clearly exhibits features which have also been associated with HRM. However, QWL programmes vary in their scope, and hence in the extent to which they represent a strategic approach to the organisation of work and the management of the employment relationship. Three types of innovative work arrangements were identified by Kochan *et al.* The first approach confines QWL initiatives to narrow task-based issues and improved management–worker communications. Typical of such programmes are quality circles, briefing groups and worker attitude surveys.

The second approach includes the elements of the first, but also involves teamworking, work restructuring, payment systems based on knowledge and skills acquired, and business information being supplied to workers and unions. This means that QWL becomes linked to collective bargaining issues and provides for fuller union involvement in QWL.

The third approach includes the elements of the first two but also extends to 'strategic' issues such as employment security provisions, the sharing of gains from productivity improvements, union representation on management planning committees, and union involvement in decisions relating to the size and structure of the workforce and to training. In some organisations QWL programmes have evolved from the first to the second or third approaches in order to 'more fully address competitive pressures and employment-security interests of workers and their unions' (Kochan *et al.,* 1986: 148–149).

QWL initiatives have been closely associated with the motor industry in the USA. Here the history of adversarial industrial relations came to be seen as a major threat to firms' ability to cope with increased competition and the production requirements of new technology. A celebrated example of new approaches to work organisation is that of the NUMMI automobile plant in Fremont, California, a joint venture between General Motors and Toyota. Production is team based and union representatives are informed of and often involved in informal discussions about 'equipment use, hiring policy, scheduling, and work standards' (Turner, 1991: 59).

In many cases, however, QWL initiatives have met with considerable opposition from workers and unions, and from management. The former often view QWL as a means of marginalising the union role, since its emphasis is upon individual motivation, problem solving and building informal systems of participation. This is in contrast to the traditional focus of industrial relations on the management of the effort–reward bargain through formal rules to provide equity of treatment through 'due process' arrangements and the regulation of conflict. The latter have often seen it as undermining their authority on the shop floor. These responses may help to explain why QWL initiatives have had mixed success in terms of their impact on the quality of management–worker relations and on performance. Some managements have used techniques such as employee involvement and work reorganisation in a piecemeal way rather than as part of a wider human resource strategy. Turner (1991), in explaining why QWL initiatives had been less successful at some other General Motors plants than at NUMMI, concluded that:

> the critical difference . . . is the presence at NUMMI of a new management approach, strategic orientation, and focus on human relations.

In other words, many managements have tried to use HRM techniques to raise productivity without re-examining the place of human resources in strategic decision making and without giving up the traditional approach to 'management's right to manage'.

However, there is also disagreement about how QWL impacts on workers even where it appears to have been successful in raising performance. This is illustrated by these very different perspectives on work at the NUMMI plant:

> The workers' revolution has finally come to the shop floor. The people who work on the assembly line have taken charge and have the power to make management do their jobs right . . . It is due to . . . team production . . . run by the workers themselves.
>
> (Regional Director, United Automobile Workers, *New York Times,*
> 25 December 1988, quoted in Turner, 1991: 53–54)

> In fact, NUMMI has achieved its gains through far greater regimentation of the workforce than exists in traditional American auto plants. Tight specifications and monitoring of how jobs are to be done, a barebones workforce with no replacements for absentees and a systematic and continuing speedup are the methods used.

> We use the term 'management by stress' to describe this system, which
> often goes by the names 'team concept' or 'synchronous manufacturing'.
>
> (M. Parker and J. Slaughter, *New York Times*, 4 December 1988, quoted in Turner, 1991: 53)

The tensions revealed here between what might be seen as the benefits of greater responsibility and influence over production decisions on the one hand, and the costs of work intensification and stress on the other, are replicated more widely within the practice of HRM, as we shall see in the next section.

RECENT DEVELOPMENTS IN HRM PRACTICE

From what we have seen of experiments with QWL, it seems that, although HRM became fashionable as a management discourse during the 1970s and 1980s, its take-up in practice was limited and, where firms formally espoused HRM, there were considerable gaps between management rhetoric and actual practice. This appears to be borne out by wider investigations. One indication of the limits to the spread of HRM in practice was provided by a Conference Board survey of partially unionised firms. It found that 33% of respondents operated salaried status for all workers and profit sharing schemes in their non-union plants. Between 20 and 30% 'encouraged use' of autonomous work groups and flexible work schedules. In citing these results Kochan *et al.* (1986) concluded that HRM had not yet bitten hard into the organisation of work. Participative HRM styles of management applied to a minority of employers and 'aggressive resistance to unions and harsh personnel policies are also part of the story' (p. 452). In similar vein, Guest (1990) argued that in most cases where employers had experimented with HRM, individual techniques had been implemented in a piecemeal fashion with little attempt to integrate them strategically. He concluded that in view of this, they were 'unlikely to have any positive impact on organisational performance' (p. 515).

We need to bear in mind, however, that these judgements were based on developments up to the mid-1980s. Therefore it is worth asking how far they have been validated by subsequent developments. Are there any signs that HRM practices have become more widespread since the late 1980s? Recent research suggests that there has been a number of significant developments, although what they imply for the current status of HRM and its future is rather uncertain. They are:

- an increased take-up of employee involvement schemes, which, in the case of manufacturing, has been linked to
- innovations in work organisation linked to the concept of 'lean production';
- signs of a weakening of internal labour-market arrangements.

Employee involvement

According to Freeman (1995), the 1990s have seen the spread of management-initiated schemes of employee involvement (EI) such as teamworking, quality circles, problem-solving groups and total quality management systems. Over half of the respondents to a survey of over 2400 workers in private sector establishments with more than 25 employees reported such initiatives in their place of work. How is this growth to be explained? From a radical perspective, it might be argued that EI is aimed at substituting managerially controlled channels of communication for trade union representation. However, according to Freeman it is unlikely that anti-unionism has inspired the recent growth of interest in EI because unionisation is now so low among private sector employees in the USA; the proportion of union members among private sector workers was just 11% in 1993. In other words, most private sector employers are not unionised and are not 'threatened' by the prospect of becoming unionised. Thus, while it is possible that some unionised firms might welcome any tendency of EI to marginalise trade union influence in the workplace, this cannot be the main explanation for management's interest. Accordingly, Freeman argues that management sees EI as delivering benefits in terms of improving the quality of employee relations and generating greater productive efficiency by improving communication between management and employees and encouraging shared job knowledge, problem solving and increased flexibility of labour, in ways suggested in Chapter 3, page 98.

Teamworking and 'lean production'

In the previous section we noted the limited impact of HRM thinking on the organisation of work by the mid-1980s. However, there is strong evidence that since then the pace of change has accelerated. Surveys of the *Fortune* 1000 companies conducted in 1987 and 1990 indicated an increase in the rate of adoption of new approaches to work organisation; the proportion of companies operating self-managed work teams (SMWTs) increased from 28% in 1987 to 47% in 1990. Subsequent investigations by other researchers suggest that this has continued into the 1990s (Cappelli, 1995). SMWTs, sometimes also referred to as 'empowered' work teams, are given delegated responsibility for decisions relating to a range of task- and shop floor-related issues. The general features of team-based production in the USA have been outlined by Fairris (1991: 46) as follows:

- fewer separate job classifications;
- workers skilled over a wider range of activities;
- regular meetings of work teams to discuss production issues;
- team leaders – usually a union member in unionised plants;
- group leaders (not union members) to coordinate the activities of teams;
- pay-for-knowledge payments systems;
- a requirement that workers and supervisors use the team structure to ensure speedy resolution of shop floor disputes.

On the face of things, team-based work organisation can be seen as an innovation in the human relations tradition, extending workers' autonomy and control over their work and providing a basis for greater employee commitment and more harmonious, cooperative industrial relations. Thus, commenting on SMWTs at Otis Engineering, Yeatts *et al.* (1994: 14) stated that team members had 'gained a sense of individual leadership. They have broadened their horizons and become more knowledgeable about all that is involved in getting the product out of the door.'

On the other hand, Cappelli and Rogovsky (1994) argue that recent developments in team-based production have been guided less by human relations, with its emphasis on the needs of employees for autonomy, and more by considerations of productive efficiency and moves towards 'lean production' and 'continuous improvement'. Lean production is an approach to the organisation of the production process which seeks to eliminate non-productive labour as far as possible by transferring responsibilities to the shop floor, thereby reducing the number of indirect workers such as managers and supervisors. It is also associated with 'just-in-time' production (JIT). JIT minimises the amount of firms' capital tied up in stocks of raw materials, parts and work in progress by arranging for them to enter the production flow as and when they are needed. 'Continuous improvement' is a management approach which 'requires the performance of individual tasks to be completely routinised, so that work teams can discover whether minute changes in tasks lead to an improvement in performance' (Cappelli and Rogovsky, 1994: 207). Any change resulting in improvement then becomes the new, standardised routine. Thus Cappelli and Rogovsky argue that lean production linked to continuous improvement provides workers with little individual autonomy, although it might represent a modest improvement over classic Taylorism. Moreover, Fairris (1991) argues that under such regimes, team production is a way of getting workers to take over responsibility for policing the activities of their fellow team members. In the light of these findings, it seems that the coercive features of teamworking observed in QWL initiatives during the 1980s have remained.

Weakening internal labour markets

We saw above that a feature of HRM in 'household name' US firms was a high degree of employment security coupled with pay and benefits which tended to be above the market rate. This reflected the link between HRM and the operation of internal labour markets within large organisations, as explained in Chapter 3. Employment security and internalised pay and benefits systems can be seen as an element of employer policies aimed at generating employee commitment and cooperation in production. However, according to Cappelli (1995), there is considerable evidence that internal labour markets are weakening in the USA.

Cappelli cites survey evidence which suggests that not only has a large proportion of firms shed workers during the first half of the 1990s, the proportion planning workforce reductions rose during the mid-1990s. Furthermore, the decision to cut workforces is increasingly the result of strategic business decisions rather than responses to short-term fluctuations in the economy. Such 'strategic' job cuts, often unaccompanied by any reduction in output, are known as 'downsizing'. It is also the case that job losses are no longer largely confined to workers who have always been most vulnerable to layoff. Groups who have previously been relatively well insulated from job cuts – managers, white-collar workers and older, skilled workers – are increasingly likely to be laid off. Moreover, the likelihood of workers being recalled by their employer after having been laid off for a period has declined. Now layoffs are more likely to be permanent.

At the same time, the use of outside contractors and contingent workers – part-time and temporary employees – has increased since the mid-1980s (Cappelli, 1995). The firms making most use of temporary workers are those with over 1000 employees, in other words those most likely to have internal labour markets. Cappelli suggests that the motive is to avoid the higher fixed costs of employing permanent workers. There are grounds for thinking that workers employed by temporary help agencies or contracting firms in the USA are denied the benefits of employment security, job progression and benefits such as pensions that go with internal labour markets.

Finally, it seems that internalised wage structures may be weakening and employees are becoming more exposed to external labour-market forces as a key influence on their pay. Cappelli cites a number of studies which show that wages have become more sensitive to local labour-market conditions and that this is changing established internal pay differentials within firms. This has also meant that the link between pay and length of time in the job (seniority) has weakened, and there are signs too that firms have begun to place increasing emphasis on individual performance in determining employees' pay. This development is being accompanied by changes in companies' pension provision for employees, which limit employers' financial obligations to the employee and transfer much of the risk and responsibility for maintaining the value of pension benefits to the worker (Cappelli, 1995).

Implications for HRM

The developments that we have just examined appear to represent a retreat from the focus on the need to generate employee commitment which was influential in HRM thinking during the 1970s and early 1980s (see pp. 751, 754–755). The extent to which internal labour markets are in decline may be debatable, however. The devolution of responsibility for production to the shop floor and the training investments necessary to equip workers for more functionally flexible roles may mean that issues of employee commitment and the retention of employees by firms will continue to be important influences on the management of employee relations (Benson, 1995).

On the other hand, there is evidence that employees themselves are losing faith in their employers and are responding with reduced commitment and low morale. Cappelli cites survey evidence that shows a sharp decline in commitment to their employers among both managerial and non-managerial employees. However, employers do not seem to be greatly concerned about the effects of this on employee performance, since heightened employment insecurity and a weak labour market mean that disaffected workers have limited opportunities to leave their existing employer, and the weakening of trade union power over the years has deprived them of the ability to mount collective pressure in defence of their interests (Cappelli, 1995). It may also be the case that workers, and particularly new entrants to the labour market, are developing lower expectations concerning the effort–reward bargain, expecting to have to deliver more and receive less.

In the light of these developments it seems that commitment-based HRM has not established itself securely in the USA and might be giving way to more coercive ways of extracting effort from workers, based on variable pay and new forms of surveillance and measurement of individual performance. Within the discourse of HRM, specific policies such as employee involvement and teamworking are possibly being redefined in much 'harder' terms than those envisaged by Harvard academics in the 1970s and early 1980s. Rather than proceeding from the 'liberating' agenda of the human relations school, which emphasised the mutual gains to be had from meeting employees' needs for autonomy, variety and a degree of security, these initiatives may be being recast so as to enable senior managers to exert more effective domination over employees. In so far as decisions to 'downsize', increase the proportion of contingent workers, introduce more variable, individualised pay and use work redesign to enhance managerial surveillance and control, rather than increase the willing commitment of workers, are strategically linked to business goals, then they can be presented as strategic HRM. However, this marks a definite departure from the progressive managerial agenda based on integrating the interests of organisational 'stakeholders' which was the intellectual source of HRM in the USA.

CONCLUSION

HRM in the USA has its roots in earlier strands of managerial thought, particularly the human relations school and socio-technical systems thinking. This provided the theoretical basis for the focus on employee commitment within HRM. It also came to be influenced by the thinking on strategic management that developed during the 1980s, emphasising the need for internal strategies for the management of the organisation's resources to be linked to product market strategies. However, it has been shown that a strategic approach to HRM which sees human resource strategy as supporting product market strategy need not necessarily imply a commitment-based approach to HRM, and that policies towards employees may vary according to the nature of the product market. In some circumstances a strategic approach to human resources could involve routinised work, close supervision or surveillance, and relatively unfavourable terms and conditions of employment (Hendry and Pettigrew, 1986). Thus at a strategic level there has always been an ambiguity in HRM thinking, which may help to explain the variety of employment practice in US firms and the piecemeal take-up of HRM techniques.

At the same time, it is also probably true that employers in the USA, like those in the UK, have been unable or unwilling to adopt a strategic approach to human resources which is integrated with wider business strategy. In such circumstances, human resource issues are seen as downstream from wider strategic decisions and human resource initiatives are conceived in narrow terms. Turner (1991) addressed this issue when investigating why QWL initiatives had been less successful at some other GM plants than at NUMMI.

The history of the 1970s and 1980s suggests that defence or reassertion of managerial prerogative has been a powerful influence on the US practice of HRM. The main appeal of HRM for many managements was that it offered a set of techniques for de-unionisation, and for others a way of reducing union power on the shop floor. Certainly, according to Kochan *et al.* (1986) the most significant impact of HRM thinking in the USA has been on unionised industrial relations. This point has also been taken up by Guest, who has suggested that the main effect of HRM during the 1970s and 1980s was 'to provide a smokescreen behind which management can introduce non-unionism or obtain significant concessions from trade unions' (Guest 1990: 515).

The more recent spread of HRM initiatives, however, cannot be explained convincingly in terms of union avoidance now that union membership is so low, especially in the private sector. As Freeman (1995) suggests, it seems likely that now employers are motivated by a search for higher productivity, better quality and lower costs when they adopt HRM techniques. At the same time, recent developments indicate that managements have not been widely imbued with the 'progressive' elements of HRM philosophy. Their emphasis still seems to be on using HRM techniques as ways of exerting control and domination over employees. Furthermore, organisational commitment to employees looks to be in retreat as employers withdraw employment and income security from workers. As HRM comes to be redefined in ways which expose employees much more directly to external market forces, two questions arise which may become important foci for future debate: first, is HRM dead? Second, what are the possible longer-term effects of current developments on America's economic performance?

SUMMARY

● Human resource management owes its origins to the United States where it was first articulated and developed as a series of managerial prescriptions. The US model of HRM stresses four main dimensions: strategy and the linkage of product market goals to the internal management of resources; an insistence that the employment relationship does not inevitably rest on conflicts of interest; a focus on the individual's commitment to the organisation; the importance of developing a strong organisational culture to support HRM.

● Among the more important factors which help to account for the emergence and popularity of HRM in the USA in the 1970s and 1980s are those which stress the decline of unionisation amongst employees and the desire on the part of managements to rectify the declining competitiveness of many sectors of the US economy (automobiles and steel among them). Two very important cultural influences in the US labour market which have supported the spread of HRM have been a historical aversion by many US employers to unionisation, and the acceptance of 'welfare capitalism' on the part of a number of major employers who, though limited in number, served as models for others.

● A difficulty arises in assessing how far the well-known examples of HRM philosophy represent its wider adoption, and whether the practice of HRM has become more widespread. In the US context it is probably the case that HRM has encouraged a stronger anti-union stance on the part of employers, and encouraged employers to adopt more managerially derived employment agendas as a consequence – even in unionised plants. Managements have been concerned to respond to the threat posed by Japanese companies in their traditional domestic markets, and have therefore seen HRM as a means to restructure work to counter this challenge to their formerly secure industrial and commercial supremacy. In this process it is difficult to disentangle HRM from the older and stronger tradition of hostility to unions.

● More recent developments in HRM probably owe less to union avoidance and more to the search for productivity and cost improvements. However, there are signs that they represent a movement away from the 'commitment-centred' philosophy of HRM derived from humanistic psychology, socio-technical systems theory and the early practice of welfare capitalism. It is possible that HRM is being recast in a way which exposes employees much more directly to external market forces.

A US company which manufactures electronic equipment for the aerospace industry has set up a plant in Southern England in order to break into the European market. In the USA it is well known for its anti-union stance and has fought off many attempts by unions to obtain recognition in the past. However, in recent years it has found that the union pressure in the USA has abated and part of its decision to locate to the UK is the belief that unionisation has dropped there too and so the company will find similar conditions for its new plant. The plant will be 'greenfield' and all the employees will be newly recruited, with the exception of some very senior US managers for production, finance and marketing. The US managing director has decided to appoint a British HRM manager in order to set up the personnel function.

EXERCISES

1 Assume that you have been appointed to the HRM post. The MD has asked you to adopt US styles of labour relations in creating the new personnel function. What factors would you decide to consider in your task of adapting the US model to the UK situation?

2 The MD believes that the new plant should be a model of contemporary HRM practice. From your own experience you are not convinced that there is a single style of HRM that can be easily adopted and introduced into the plant. Outline the arguments you would use to convince the MD that traditional personnel management still has a role to play alongside his conception of 'all-American HRM'.

QUESTIONS

1 What have been the main influences on the development of HRM in the United States?

2 Can HRM in the USA be equated with non-unionism?

3 What effects has the spread of HRM had on unionised industrial relations in the USA?

4 Examine the pros and cons of the QWL programme introduced at the NUMMI plant.

5 What problems for organisations might arise from a move to a more market-oriented approach to HRM?

REFERENCES AND FURTHER READING

Beaumont, P.B. (1987) *The Decline of Trade Union Organisation*. London: Croom Helm.

Beaumont, P.B. (1992) 'The US human resource management literature: a review', in Salaman, G. (ed.) *Human Resource Strategies*. London: Sage, pp. 20–37.

Beer, M., Spector, B., Lawrence, P.R., Quinn Mills, D. and Walton, R.E. (1985) *Human Resource Management: A General Manager's Perspective*. New York: Free Press.

Benson, J. (1995) 'Future employment and the internal labour market', *British Journal of Industrial Relations*, Vol. 33, No. 4, pp. 603-608.

Burns, T. and Stalker, G.M. (1961) *The Management of Innovation*. London: Tavistock.

Cappelli, P. (1995) 'Rethinking employment', *British Journal of Industrial Relations*, Vol. 33, No. 4, pp. 563–602.

Cappelli, P. and Rogovsky, N. (1994) 'New work systems and skill requirements', *International Labor Review*, Vol. 133, No. 2, pp. 205–220.

Cullen, D.E. (1986) 'Where have all the unions gone?', *University of Tennessee Survey of Business*, Vol. 21, No. 4, pp. 13–22.

Fairris, D. (1991) 'The crisis in US shopfloor relations', *International Contributions to Labour Studies*, Vol. 1, pp. 133–156.

Fombrun, C., Tichy, N.M. and Devanna, M.A. (1984) *Strategic Human Resource Management*. New York: John Wiley.

Foulkes, F.K. (1980) *Personnel Policies in Large Nonunion Companies*. Englewood Cliffs, NJ: Prentice Hall.

Freeman, R.B. (1995) 'The future for unions in decentralised collective bargaining systems: US and UK unionism in an era of crisis', *British Journal of Industrial Relations*, Vol. 33, No. 4, pp. 519–556.

Guest, D. (1990) 'Human resource management and the American dream', *Journal of Management Studies*, Vol. 27, pp. 503–523.

Hendry, C. and Pettigrew, A. (1986) 'The practice of strategic human resource management', *Personnel Review*, Vol. 15, No. 5, pp. 3–8.

Kanter, D. and Mirvis, P. (1989) *The Cynical Americans*. San Francisco: Jossey-Bass.

Kochan, T.A. and Capelli, P. (1984) 'The transformation of the industrial relations and personnel function', in Osterman, P. (ed.) *Internal Labor Markets*. Cambridge, Mass.: MIT Press, pp. 133–161.

Kochan, T.A. and Weaver, K.R. (1991) 'The United States of America', in Niland, J. and Clarke, O. (eds) *Agenda for Change: An International Analysis of Industrial Relations in Transition*. London: Allen & Unwin, pp. 19–52.

Kochan, T.A., Katz, H.C. and McKersie, R.B. (1986) *The Transformation of American Industrial Relations*. New York: Basic Books.

Lengnick-Hall, C. and Lengnick-Hall, M. (1988) 'Strategic human resource management: a review of the literature and a proposed typology', *Academy of American Management Review*, Vol. 13, pp. 454–470.

Lincoln, J.R. and Kalleberg, A.L. (1990) *Culture, Control and Commitment: A Study of Work Organization and Attitudes in the United States and Japan*. Cambridge: Cambridge University Press.

Rosenberg, S. (1989) 'The restructuring of the labor market, the labor force, and the nature of employment relations in the United States in the 1980s', in Rosenberg, S. (ed.) *The State and the Labor Market*. New York: Plenum, pp. 63–85.

Springer, B. and Springer, S. (1990) 'Human resource management in the US – celebration of its centenary', in Pieper, R. (ed.) *Human Resource Management: An International Comparison*. Walter de Gruyter: Berlin, pp. 41–60.

Turner, L. (1991) *Democracy at Work: Changing World Markets and the Future of Labor Unions*. Ithaca: Cornell University Press.

Walton, R.E. (1972) 'How to counter alienation in the plant', *Harvard Business Review*, November–December, pp. 70–81.

Walton, R.E. (1974) 'Improving the quality of working life', *Harvard Business Review*, May–June, p. 12.

Walton, R.E. (1979) 'Work innovations in the United States', *Harvard Business Review*, July–August, pp. 88–98.

Walton, R.E. (1985) 'From control to commitment in the workplace', *Harvard Business Review*, March–April, pp. 77–84.

Yeatts, D.E., Hipskind, M. and Barnes, D. (1994) 'Lessons learned from self-managed work teams', *Business Horizons*, July/August, pp. 11–18.

HUMAN RESOURCE

MANAGEMENT AND JAPAN

Ian Beardwell

OBJECTIVES

To explore recent developments in HRM and labour
relations in Japan.

●

To outline some innovative Japanese management techniques
such as just-in-time theory, quality circles and Kanban.

●

To explore the influence of Japanese management practices on
Western employment practices.

●

INTRODUCTION

The emergence and effect of Japan as a major industrialised economy in the postwar period has given rise to persistent Western-oriented attempts to explain, rationalise and categorise this phenomenon. Variously viewed as a cultural stereotype, threat or exemplar, the Japanese economy in general, and its employment practices in particular, have provided rich grounds for analytical and prescriptive work. As the debate over the emergence of human resource management in Western economies became broader and more encompassing throughout the 1980s, so the question of the influence of Japanese management and employment practices has come to be associated with certain aspects of that discussion. Whether it is correct to link the Western concern with HRM to the longer-term issues underpinning Japanese socio-economic organisation is the subject of this chapter.

KEY ELEMENTS OF JAPANESE EMPLOYEE MANAGEMENT

Western interest in Japanese management processes has tended to focus on those elements which are readily identifiable and held to be the 'core' of this system of employee relations: lifetime employment, wage and promotion systems based on seniority, and work organisation systems based on quality and flexibility. Taken together these have often been seen as the principal components of a sophisticated and integrated managerial philosophy which has much to offer (see Wickens, 1987). An important part of the discussion surrounding the effect of 'Japanisation' is the extent to which these elements come together to form a systematic Japanese approach to dealing with employment policies that have often posed considerable problems in Western market economies. In addition, there are the questions of whether these approaches can be seen as, in any sense, a form of human resource management that can be adopted and adapted in the West, or whether the American-derived models of HRM are themselves a genuine alternative to Japanese management.

Lifetime employment

The concept of lifetime employment is a good starting point. One of the core elements in the Japanese model of employee relations is the system which provides certain categories of staff with employment that lasts throughout their working life. Once employed by one of the great Zaibatsu (formerly a conglomerate trading company, many of which contributed to the economic development of Japan before the Second World War, and now known as Keiretsu), an employee might expect to work uninterruptedly until retirement age in the knowledge and expectation that work, training and, quite often, housing and education for dependants would be provided. The sources of this relationship are complex and not easily translated into a Western economy, but they draw upon the concept of a relationship that has historical feudal roots which were adapted by the Zaibatsu for modern economic conditions. The effect of this system, it is claimed, is to inculcate a stronger sense of identification with the organisation on the part of the workforce than is customarily experienced in the West. Thus Dore (1973) points to significantly different patterns of recruitment, labour turnover, and wider labour-market experience on the part of Japanese and British employees in his study, with the former displaying fewer job changes and longer work experience with their respective employers than the latter. This relationship has also been described by Ouchi (1981) as a 'holistic relationship'. Saha (1990) suggests that it is akin to adoption.

It is now more widely appreciated in the West that this system of employment is perhaps better understood as a lifetime 'commitment' rather than as 'employment', in the important sense that employees may well remain on the payroll of the company but may not necessarily remain in a particular job or even a particular plant for the totality of their working life. It would not be unusual for such an employee to have to transfer (tenseki) or be lent (shukkuo), to another associated firm in order to remain within the 'commitment' system. It is estimated by Takahashi (in Pieper, 1990), from Japanese Ministry of Labour data for 1987, that over 30% of employees over 45 years of age were 'lent' (shukkuo) to other plants or even subcontracting firms.

Life outside such an employment structure can be difficult. The minority of Japanese workers rely on this system: around it has grown a much larger 'unregulated' labour market made up of satellite suppliers and subcontractors to the Zaibatsu, and the generality of medium-to-small firms in which the majority of Japanese industrial workers find employment. In this large part of the labour market there is no equivalent to lifetime commitment. Even within the Zaibatsu it is only the 'core' workforce which enjoys this right; there are many other grades of worker who do not qualify for such security. Kamata (1983) described life as an unsecured temporary worker on the Toyota production line, and highlighted the considerable degree to which such employment is precarious and short term. Even within the 'core' workforce the lifetime commitment system has its drawbacks: usually such workers retire at 55 and pensions are either short term or non-existent (Dore, 1973). This reflects the lower life expectancy once found in Japan, but Japanese life expectancy has now risen to match Western levels and so many workers face perhaps a further 20 years without formal labour-market or social support. For these employees the choice is either to take on a lower paid subsidiary job with their existing employer (but outside the core workforce), or to work in the unregulated labour market – perhaps in a supplier or subcontractor to their original firm, or in a smaller independent firm. Thus the lifetime system is not the all-embracing model of employment that has sometimes been assumed.

For many Western industrial and commercial organisations the notion that employees might be accorded a secure pattern of employment for the whole of their working life was and, particularly in the 1990s, is an impractical proposition. Even where some form of lifetime commitment was practised, most notably in government service and some commercial institutions such as banks, this has tended to be modified as newer forms of flexible working have been introduced. The more usual approach to employment has been by means of a reliance on market and contractual arrangements, described earlier in this book in Chapters 3 and 12.

The seniority wage system

The second key component of the regulation and development of Japanese labour lies in the seniority system deployed in the Zaibatsu. This approach links reward with service (nenko joretsu) rather than with innate skill or individual characteristics. Dore noted the subtlety and complexity of this system:

> It is scale of 'person-related' payments – as opposed to 'job-related payments' . . . It is an intricate set of rules, based on the exponential principle that the higher you go the faster you rise, designed to give recognition to both seniority and merit. The seniority principle requires that everybody goes up a notch every year of some minimal proportions. (Dore, 1973: 99)

The longevity and robustness of this pattern of pay is demonstrated by the evidence of Sano (1993), writing fully twenty years after Dore, who was still able to conclude that the Japanese system was typified by wage rigidity:

> In Japan it is especially difficult to define jobs or occupations which are assumed to be an essential category of work-force skill in the labour market . . . Workers are expected to stay at a firm a long time, and they actually stay long within some framework of payment system. The majority are on a time payment. (Sano, 1993: 15)

This pattern of pay poses considerable difficulties for many Western market economies. It has grown in Japan as part of the 'commitment' system, based on the constant evaluation of the employee in terms of length of service, skill attainment, and status, and expressed as 'older = more experienced = better worker' (Dore, 1973: 107). By far the most important methods of determining pay in the West are reliant on output or skill/occupationally related factors for a great deal of manufacturing work, where the pay of the individual is tied to certain production criteria, usually assessed by means of work study or other variants derived from scientific management principles of job fragmentation. This Western emphasis on the components of the job, and their measurement, tends to run against the integrated view of the job and its performance in the Japanese model.

The emergence of HRM in Western economies tends to make comparisons with this particular aspect of the Japanese system more complicated, rather than simplified. One good example of this problem is that provided by performance-related pay. In the Japanese system the individual's performance is certainly assessed, and there can be quite marked differentials between employees in the same jobs as a result of the seniority and status process of pay settlement. However, this takes place in the context of the complex Japanese relationship between the individual, the job and the organisation. The Western HRM model of performance-related pay, although supposedly relating some of these factors in the same way, is much more driven by the individualistic model of performance which is found in the more traditional payment systems. In addition, it is unlikely that many Western organisations would be willing to tolerate, or even accommodate, the consequences of the Japanese pay system which permitted an employee to perform far ahead of their peers on the basis of their seniority.

Quality and flexibility

The third area that is central to the Japanese system is work organisation and the judgement of its quality. In many respects it is this group of issues that has been the focus of concentrated Western attention throughout the 1980s and into the 1990s and where the relationship between Japanese systems and HRM is sought most actively.

If lifetime commitment and seniority systems have proved difficult for Western organisations to absorb, then quality and flexibility have been taken up as the processes which have demonstrated the greatest transferability from Japan. This is particularly the case where Japanese transplant companies in the West have not only set up their own procedures but have encouraged or required Western suppliers and subcontractors to follow suit. Perhaps the most significant work organisation innovations that have been adopted in the West are the group of operations which are variously known as JIT (just-in-time) and Kanban. Each of these is different, and represents a variation on tighter and more controlled supply and manufacturing systems.

JIT refers to the delivery and use of components and supplies for manufacturing so that stocks are held to a critical minimum level, reducing stockholding space, time and finance; Kanban refers to an internal management control system, developed at Toyota, for initiating production of components to link closely with production requirements: if no request card (Kanban) is generated, no components are produced for that element of production. Thus Kanban may be seen as a refinement of the general JIT approach (Oliver and Wilkinson, 1992). These approaches have posed a radical alternative to many Western manufacturing systems which have traditionally relied on a pattern of lengthy supply lines from a variety of suppliers, and a dependence on stockholding within the firm of several months' supplies. Throughout the 1980s Western manufacturers have sought to emulate JIT by drastically cutting their supply times and reducing the number and range of suppliers so that they can deal with a limited number of firms on a suitable JIT basis.

Within the manufacturing process there is now a greater emphasis on the flexibility of the workforce in order to capitalise on these intensified processes. Thus JIT has spawned a greater awareness of Japanese labour deployment in manufacturing and a pressure for Western firms to adapt and introduce similar labour processes in their own operations. The whole area of flexibility is a large and complicated issue involving, on the one hand, the detailed consideration of functional, numerical and task flexibility amongst employees and, on the other, a fundamental debate about the role and nature of flexibility within labour markets and the implications for individuals of skill acquisition, retention and development (Atkinson, 1984, and Pollert, 1988). The concerns of large manufacturing organisations have tended to push to the fore the issues of labour utilisation and the widespread adoption of work systems which require a wider range of functional skills on the part of individual employees coupled with a reduction in the total manufacturing workforce. In this process the concept of quality has assumed an important role, often presented in the format of total quality management (TQM).

In the Japanese system quality is expressed in relation to 'continuous improvement' (kaizen). Thus manufacturing systems as a whole are focused on the concept of 'the idea of linear progress, without any limit to possible improvement' (Oliver and Wilkinson, 1992: 35). It is this view of work organisation as offering almost limitless possibilities for improvement that defines this approach to quality. Individuals and groups are encouraged to play their part in this by means of quality circles, which have been widely adopted in the West. In a study of the quality circle issue, Bradley and Hill (1983) suggested that they offered a viable way of integrating employees into the quality process as long as management had a philosophy which accepted a high trust relationship with staff and inculcated a belief that quality was a part of the production process, not simply a later addition. Less than that and the quality circle process would collapse.

A difficulty in translating the concept of 'continuous improvement' into a Western context is that, culturally at least, there is an expectation in the West that there is a definable point at which quality is achieved by the 'best' having been attained or there being no further capacity for improvement. A major problem with the interrelationship between flexibility and quality as major issues in their own right is that of the overloading of these concepts with unrealistic expectations. This is exacerbated by the addition of the human resource management debate, which has seen the inclusion of many of the Japanese concepts outlined above as constituents in that discussion. Whatever the reservations expressed about the merits of the Japanese labour management process (Garrahan and Stewart, 1992), within its own terms it has posed difficult questions for Western organisations and commentators to answer satisfactorily. Bradley and Hill, in pointing to the tendency for Western firms to view quality circles in the context of short-term exercises to cure particular problems, are highlighting a wider Western preoccupation to take piecemeal approaches to the complex process of managing with the active consent of workforces in market economies. In order to understand why the Japanese model has been so influential it is necessary to examine some of the reasons for its ready adoption by Western organisations and its relationship to the styles of human resource management that emerged in the 1980s in the US and Britain.

THE ABSORPTION OF JAPANESE MANAGEMENT CULTURE

A particular difficulty in dealing with some of the key aspects of Japanese employee management is that Western, and often specifically British, concerns have overtaken the more general examination of Japanese industrial organisation because of the acute nature of domestic economic problems that push themselves forward for examination and comparison. In the period between the mid-1960s, when systematic work on Japan first became more widely available in Western academic circles, and the first third of the 1990s, with its flood of 'Japanisation' material, the concerns of Western economies have imposed a framework on how the Japanese experience is analysed and presented. In the case of Britain the domestic concerns which have formed the 'lens' through which the Japanese experience has been viewed range from analysis of the British 'strike problem' to the restructuring of manufacturing work patterns; along the way is a variety of specific issues such as employee commitment and attachment, quality management and teamworking. In the United States the same period has seen the move from the panic reactions over import penetration in key areas of the US economy (graphically demonstrated by outbreaks of organised wrecking of Japanese cars by US auto workers) to the fight back by Ford and General Motors, in particular, to achieve Japanese levels of quality and efficiency.

The thirty-year period since Japan began to make a large impact on the world economy has seen an important shift in analysis of its work and managerial organisation; the focus of the 1960s largely reflected a desire to discover and explain the processes of Japanese organisation from within that culture, with very little expectation that this was an exportable paradigm. The highly influential *British Journal of Industrial Relations* Special Edition of 1965, while containing an important set of articles which set out the sophistication and complexity of such vital large-company practices as 'lifetime employment' and the nature of Japanese trade unionism, did not hint at either the importation of these concepts by Western firms or, indeed, their transplantation by outward-investing Japanese firms. The question of whether European or American firms could emulate the Japanese by copying the observable manifestations of such managerial processes within their own Western organisations was to come later, and the impact of the Japanese using such policies with Western employees in Japanese-owned firms in Western economies was to come later still. Thus it is possible to trace a three-stage development in the widening impact of Japanese management culture and policies: first, the interest in the *internal* Japanese labour market; second, the emulation of some, usually highly selected, of those aspects of the Japanese experience that firms thought would 'fix' particular problems of production, flexibility or compliance, for example; third, the export of Japanese processes through the conduit of the Japanese firm, using Western workforces and Western managers to achieve that which had originally been seen as an indigenous Japanese phenomenon thirty years ago. A reading of the *BJIR* of 1965 in conjunction with the work of Peter Wickens of 1987 demonstrates the point neatly.

Perhaps a turning point in the British debate over the significance of a Japanese paradigm for labour organisation and management coincided with the publication in 1973 of Dore's *British Factory – Japanese Factory*. By the time of the book's publication there was a deep and anxious appreciation in the UK that the British economy was structurally very weak; the possibility that there might be new and successful variants on the traditional (often with the connotation of 'failed') patterns of indigenous management became one of the management panaceas of the mid-1970s and early 1980s. Britain became peculiarly susceptible not only to the inward flow of Japanese investment, but to the attendant ideologies and prescriptions that came with it. It was therefore possible for government and business representatives to argue that both the physical and attitudinal investments that were occurring in Britain were, in some way, absorbable and could be regarded as 'indigenous'. This might have been true to some extent with the adoption by British organisations of externally derived Japanese practices, but became less convincing once Japanese firms themselves had relocated and were applying their own labour management policies in transplanted plants. The well-publicised explanation of this 'indigenous' philosophy provided by Peter Wickens of Nissan (Wickens, 1987) is an exemplar of this strand of the argument.

The British and American stances on the 'Japanese question' derive from different bases: in the UK there has been a greater willingness to absorb and digest new forms of management, but principally because of an impatience with, and rejection of, the discredited forms of British management training and development identified by both Constable and Handy. In this sense there has been a failure in the British management culture which thus provided a ready location for an attractive and compelling model of management to redress the ills of at least the past twenty years, albeit in a somewhat promiscuous manner. By contrast, US management has been more antagonistic toward Japanese influence, arguing either for import controls to stem the physical inflow of goods, or looking towards the long US traditions in business and organisational theory to provide answers. In this situation the emergence of HRM in the US can be seen as not only a product of the wider American culture – the 'American Dream' discussed by Guest (1990) – but as a signal of failure in the American managerial culture at least as deep as that experienced in Britain and thus as equally susceptible to admitting and incorporating new theories of employee management in order to redress the inefficiencies of the old. The emergence of HRM was a by-product of that search for the new. In this context HRM heading East and Japanisation heading West collided in an unholy tangle as the 1980s unfolded, with the result that widely varying styles and approaches to employee management emerged, particularly in Britain, which owed large debts to each yet could not be described as either wholly HRM or wholly Japanese. As in so much of its industrial and economic development, the British absorption of these two influences was opportunistic, unsystematic and driven by short-term concerns to address pressing problems with manufacturing deficiencies.

The paradox facing both Western and Japanese organisations is that the full impact of the adoption of Japanese techniques has been absorbed, at least among many product and sector leaders in the West, whereas many Japanese firms are seeking to reduce their hitherto influential systems in favour of more flexibility. There is a growing realisation in Japan that it is a mature economy in which endogenous growth has been slowing over the past decade. In order to maintain market leadership many Japanese organisations have become major inward investors in the USA and the European Union – particularly the UK. The attractions of 'flexibility' appear to offer a new route to higher productivity. It would be ironical indeed if Japanese managerial practice were to adopt the low-cost lean methods of the West, just at the time when Japanese commitment and quality were becoming benchmarks in the UK economy.

SUMMARY

● The search in a number of Western economies to achieve improved labour market performance has led to intense interest in the success of the Japanese economy in the postwar period. This has been most noticeable in Britain and America, where the associated development of human resource management has been most keenly pursued and debated.

● An important part of the desire to identify new methods of managing employees to achieve greater economic success has been the portrayal of indigenous British managerial styles and strategies as displaying fundamentally flawed characteristics. In their place has come a belief that some of the inherent strengths of the Japanese system can be translated across to the British context, and that the 'Japanisation' of the employment relationship has a great deal to do with the emergence of human resource management in the 1980s.

● A considerable gap exists between the Western conception of the employment relationship and that which has formed the basis, at least by tradition, of its equivalent in Japan. Amongst the large Zaibatsu there has been a history of lifetime employment, although this might well be in the form of being transferred or lent to dependent plants or subcontractors; this is associated with a seniority wage system that rewards incrementally for age and long service. Against this there are demanding work schedules for quality and flexibility inherent in the JIT system with the concept of 'continuous improvement'.

● Against this background it is difficult to see HRM as being closely or even logically connected to moves to adopt Japanese management practices. Earlier chapters have pointed to the strong individual orientation of many HRM prescriptions, with an emphasis on individual effort, output and reward, which does not sit well with much of the collectivist ethic inherent in the Japanese approach. In the British context, in particular, it would appear that both HRM and 'Japanisation' are attempts to reform and overhaul deficient managerial patterns which have occurred by chance at a similar time but are not necessarily synonymous and interchangeable.

ACTIVITY

A British company has recently sent some of its senior executives to a seminar on Japanese employee management practices, as a result of which they have become enthusiastic about the prospects of introducing some aspects of these approaches into the firm. The company makes gearbox components for the vehicle industry and the managers feel that a great deal of the work, which is largely repetitive, lends itself to 'Japanisation' in terms of organisation, motivation and quality. They also see the potential for attracting orders from a recently opened Japanese car plant in the region.

In the past the company has been heavily unionised and has used traditional work organisation and piecework pay systems for its workforce. More recently unionisation has fallen to less than 30% of the workforce as a result of redundancies throughout the 1980s and a lack of interest amongst the remaining employees.

EXERCISES

1 Assuming that you are one of the managers who went on the course, discuss the key elements of the Japanese approach to employee management with your colleagues and suggest ways in which they could be introduced into your firm. Prepare a brief for the board from your discussions.

2 The board wish to take advice on this step. They hire you as an expert in Japanese employment systems to prepare a report which examines the strengths and weaknesses of this brief. Outline the case you would make to the board.

QUESTIONS

1 How far can the UK be said to have provided a fertile home for Japanese labour relations practices? What features of Japanese employee management appear to you to be the most attractive to UK employers?

2 To what extent does the adoption of particular activities (such as 'just-in-time' management) really provide a systematic basis for constructing a new UK approach to employee management?

3 Is human resource management a European variant of Japanese management, or are the two concepts quite distinct and not to be confused with each other?

1 If you were asked to devise an HR strategy for a UK company based on Japanese best practice, debate in groups which aspects would transfer most easily to a UK context.

2 If the Japanese manage so well and their companies are so profitable, explore the reasons why it has not been so easy to transfer their HRM practices wholesale to the UK.

3 Using library resources, find examples of UK companies that have adopted Japanese HR practices.

4 Choosing two examples of Japanese management techniques, critically appraise these methods.

REFERENCES AND FURTHER READING

Atkinson, J. (1984) 'Manpower strategies for flexible organisations', *Personnel Management*, August, pp. 28–31.

Bradley, K. and Hill, S. (1983) 'After Japan: the quality circle transplant and productive efficiency', *British Journal of Industrial Relations*, Vol. 21, No. 3, pp. 291–311.

British Journal of Industrial Relations (1965) Special Japanese Edition, Vol. 3, No. 1.

Dore, R. (1973) *British Factory – Japanese Factory*. London: Allen & Unwin.

Garrahan, P. and Stewart, P. (1992) *The Nissan Enigma*. London: Mansell.

Guest, D. (1990) 'HRM and the American Dream', *Journal of Management Studies*, Vol. 27, No. 4, pp. 377–397.

Kamata, S. (1983) *Japan in the Passing Lane*. London: Counterpoint.

Oliver, N. and Wilkinson, B. (1992) *The Japanisation of British Industry*. Oxford: Blackwell.

Ouchi, W. (1981) *Theory Z: How American Business Can Meet the Japanese Challenge*. Reading, Mass.: Addison-Wesley.

Pieper, R. (ed.) (1990) *Human Resource Management: An International Comparison*. Berlin: Walter de Gruyter.

Pollert, A. (1988) *Farewell to Flexibility?* Oxford: Blackwell.

Saha, A. (1990) 'Basic human nature and management – Japan', *Journal of Managerial Psychology*, Vol. 5, No. 3, pp. 3–12.

Sano, Y. (1993) 'Changes and continued stability in Japanese HRM systems', *International Human Resource Management Journal*, Vol. 4, No. 1.

Takahashi, Y. (1990) 'Human resource management in Japan', in Pieper, P. (ed.) *Human Resource Management: An International Comparison*. Berlin: Walter de Gruyter.

Wickens, P. (1987) *The Road to Nissan*. Basingstoke: Macmillan.

Resetting the clock

Asea Brown Boveri is transforming its factories by
slashing lead times, reports **Robert Taylor**

Asea Brown Boveri, the Swedish-Swiss engineering giant, is going through what it calls "a new industrial revolution" in its plants around the world.

Known as the T50 strategy in Sweden, where it is most advanced, it has a firm objective: to halve all lead times in the company's activities by the end of this year. This is being done by decentralising work responsibilities and widening individual worker skills within teams.

"We have made work cycle times the instrument for reform," declares Bert-Olof Svanholm, ABB's Swedish president, the inspiration behind T50. "Time at work is a concept everybody can understand."

The company can point to some early successes for the strategy. In its power systems production it has cut the time for making high-voltage direct current transmission equipment from three to two years. The time for supplying customers with standard switch gear has fallen from three to five weeks to three to five days from receipt of the order to delivery. Cycle times in ABB's components division have been reduced from 86 to 35 days.

ABB started to introduce T50 into its Swedish plants in June 1990. In the company's words it is "a programme with a beginning but no end". An estimated half of the company's 32,000 Swedish workers are now involved actively in the strategy with most of the rest in the initial stages. So far the company claims that, on average, cycle times have been slashed by 21 per cent and more than 300 high-performance teams have been created.

Until now, ABB argues, most companies have given the highest priority to reforming direct production methods. "For too long the direct production area alone has been the *autostrada* of manufacturing and little attention was being given to what happened before and after it," explains Svanholm.

He draws inspiration for the strategy from the practice of lean management so widespread in Japan's auto industry. "We are trying to blend Japanese methods with the Swedish work culture," he explains.

The drive behind T50 has come from the top of ABB under the direction of Percy Barnevik, the company's charismatic chief executive. He made his senior managers read and digest the influential management study from the Boston Consultancy group – Competing Against Time – when it was published three years ago.

The company is perhaps better suited than most Swedish enterprises to introduce the time-based concept into its operations. "We have become a very decentralised organisation over the past 10 years," explains Svanholm. "If we had tried this in the old days of stratified management hierarchies there would have been so much resistance and it would have been abandoned within a fortnight."

It was the structural change pushed through by Barnevik in Asea during the early 1980s that paved the way. The T50 concept was a logical evolution from the existing organisation, not a radical break with past practice.

T50's most important result has been to place the much-hyped, but seldom-practised, principle of customer satisfaction at the centre of ABB's priorities. "The customers are our focus. We must respond to their demands for the delivery of orders on time," says Svanholm.

It is the close alliance forged between the company and the trade unions that smoothed the way for T50. Indeed, says Svanholm, the trade unions at ABB are as enthusiastic as the company in transforming the work process. "They were in on the strategy from the start," he points out.

According to Klaus Eklund, who headed a government-commissioned inquiry into

Sweden's productivity problems, ABB has gone much further than other companies in creating "a coalition between progressive management and blue-collar unions in boosting productivity".

The unions, moreover, have established their own committees to monitor T50 and make sure it works with the full involvement of their members. Without such co-operation it is hard to see how T50 could make any headway in ABB's Swedish plants, where the unions remain powerful.

In part, the strategy has developed in response to the expressed views of the company's own employees. Three years ago ABB commissioned an independent opinion survey of the shopfloor mood. It found that while manual as well as white-collar workers were loyal and committed to the company they felt they did not enjoy enough influence over their own working conditions, their work was not being managed effectively enough and there was a lack of team spirit.

Such findings strengthened Svanholm's conviction that the company needed to reappraise its attitude to its own employees. "We want to create a new kind of independent-minded, all-round worker," he explains. "There is a lot of bullshit in management theory about treating people as a human resource. But too often that has meant very little in practice. We really do believe workers should become adaptable and independent and as a result gain more control over their own work."

For ABB T50 means the prospect of bigger profits, better productivity and higher-quality products as well as lower absenteeism and labour turnover. For the employees it means a better working environment, greater job interest with constant skill upgrading, and eventually a better wage rate linked more closely to individual effort.

The creation of what ABB calls Target Oriented High Performance work teams made up of 10 to 15 workers is crucial to the T50 strategy. "The old system handed down orders from above through different, fragmented departments and it was very time-consuming," explains Kenneth Synnersten, ABB's executive vice-president in charge of T50 in Sweden. "Now we organise around the flow of production through the team approach."

The traditional system involved specialised demarcation of responsibilities for sales, inventories, production and distribution with an inevitably high level of bureaucratic managerial control and top-heavy administration. By creating smaller, flexible work teams with wider responsibilities the frontiers between administration and production have been abolished.

The new strategy has also brought the collapse of the barriers separating white- from blue-collar workers. Now all ABB employees are called "associates" and under new agreements will have the same pay rates, working hours, holidays and travel allowances, although this has brought some difficulty with some white-collar workers who fear a threat to their status.

T50 has also introduced what Svanholm calls a "flat organisation with fewer bosses and more workers taking on responsibilities". As a result the functions of ABB's line managers have been transformed.

"They have many more demanding job tasks to do now," says Svanholm. "Before they were a combination of policeman and errand boy. Now they act as a support for workers." The foremen and the production engineer are being turned into "coaches" who move between the work teams to assist when needed.

The company puts a strong emphasis on training and education. The need to upgrade worker skills lies at the heart of the T50 strategy. What ABB wants is to heighten the competence of each worker within the team.

The strategy, however, is not trouble-free. It is being introduced at ABB in the middle of recession. "So far this has not affected the programme," insists Synnersten. But the strategy means a leaner workforce. Without any growth in production up to a quarter of ABB's jobs may disappear as a result.

"Yes, T50 will mean fewer jobs," admits Anders Vallius from the Metalworkers union. "But if we can increase sales in the longer term then employment opportunities will go up as well. We know ABB must stay ahead of its competitors."

Source: The *Financial Times*, 10 February 1993.

The Asea Brown Boveri (ABB) Case Study raises a number of important issues for HRM in an international perspective. The following questions indicate some of the principal concerns of establishing whether international HRM can be viable.

1 How far do the circumstances outlined in the case support the Chief Executive's view that 'We are trying to blend Japanese methods with Swedish work culture'? Using Chapter 18 compare the Japanese labour management process discussed there with ABB's strategy.

2 To what extent might the European Community issues in employment policy, outlined in Chapter 16, be compatible with ABB's plan? Is the Social Charter likely to be a help or a hindrance in circumstances like these?

3 Compare ABB's strategy with the American experience discussed in Chapter 17. Is the Company's approach to managing labour compatible with the American concepts of HRM?

4 How far is ABB's approach comparable with the wider issues of Human Resource Management raised throughout this book?

5 Is it realistic to expect that 'a coalition between progressive management and blue-collar unions in boosting productivity' can be achieved?

6 Is 'international HRM' a feasible proposition? Could ABB's example be applied by *other* companies, or do you think it can only work with one culture and one company?

INDEX